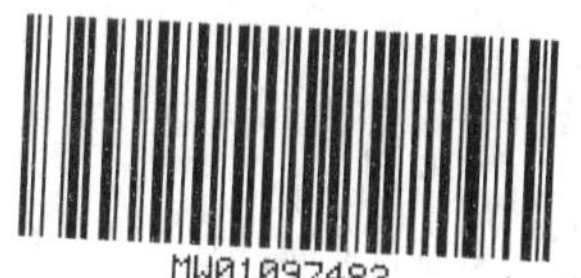

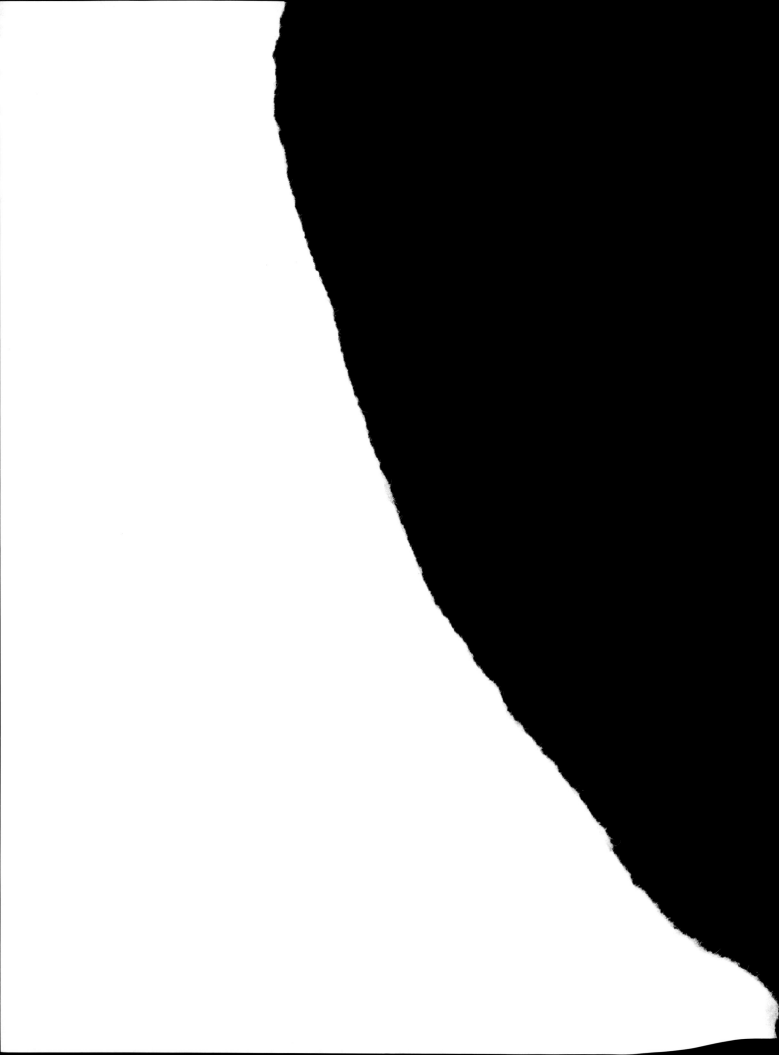

Handbook of Oncology Social Work

Psychosocial Care for People with Cancer

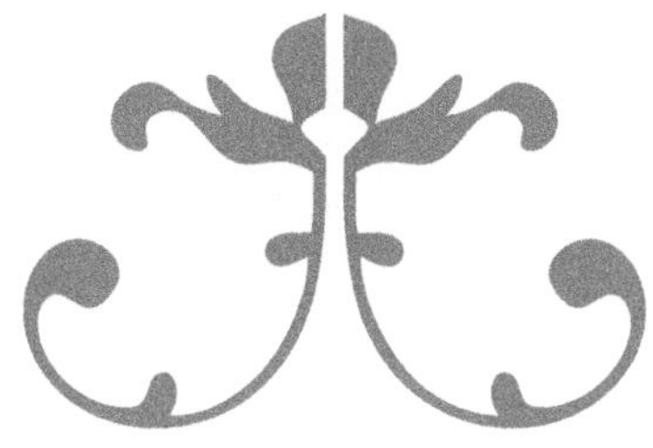

EDITED BY

Grace Christ, DSW/PhD
Professor Emerita, Research Scientist
Columbia University School of Social Work
Board Chair, Social Work Hospice and Palliative Care Network

Carolyn Messner, DSW, ACSW, BCD, LCSW-R, OSW-C
Director of Education and Training
CancerCare
Adjunct Lecturer
Silberman School of Social Work at Hunter College

Lynn Behar, PhD, ACSW, LICSW, OSW-C
Founder, Carol LaMare Initiative
University of Washington School of Social Work
Co-Chair, Advisory Board
Cancer Lifeline

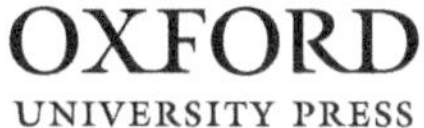

OXFORD
UNIVERSITY PRESS

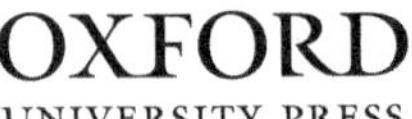

Oxford University Press is a department of the University of Oxford. It furthers the University's objective of excellence in research, scholarship, and education by publishing worldwide.

Oxford New York
Auckland Cape Town Dar es Salaam Hong Kong Karachi
Kuala Lumpur Madrid Melbourne Mexico City Nairobi
New Delhi Shanghai Taipei Toronto

With offices in
Argentina Austria Brazil Chile Czech Republic France Greece
Guatemala Hungary Italy Japan Poland Portugal Singapore
South Korea Switzerland Thailand Turkey Ukraine Vietnam

Oxford is a registered trademark of Oxford University Press in the UK and certain other countries.

Published in the United States of America by
Oxford University Press
198 Madison Avenue, New York, NY 10016

Library of Congress Cataloging-in-Publication Data
Handbook of Oncology Social Work : Psychosocial Care for People with Cancer / edited by Grace Christ, Carolyn Messner, Lynn Behar.
pages cm
Includes index.
ISBN 978-0-19-994192-6 (hardcover : alk. paper)
1. Medical social work. 2. Cancer—Patients—Services for. I. Christ, Grace Hyslop. II. Messner, Carolyn. III. Behar, Lynn C.
HV687.H26 2015
362.19699′44053—dc23
2014037065

9 8 7 6 5 4 3 2 1
Printed in the United States of America
on acid-free paper

Advance Praise for the *Handbook of Oncology Social Work*

For decades, the Institute of Medicine has released one report after another lamenting the gap between the recognition that cancer affects the whole person, and our ability to address the human needs of the growing population of cancer survivors and their loved ones. With the inaugural publication of the *Handbook of Oncology Social Work*, help is at hand. This long-awaited volume, written by pioneers in the field of oncology social work, provides a wealth of evidence-based information on how to deliver cancer care for the whole person—care that encompasses individuals' emotional, cognitive, social, economic and existential well-being—in a rapidly evolving health care delivery system. It is clear that the key to our success in enabling individuals to live fully with, through and beyond cancer, will be the extent to which we actively incorporate and build upon the unique contributions of oncology social workers to high quality oncology care. Kudos to the editors of and many contributors to this outstanding volume, a must read for anyone practicing in oncology.

Julia H. Rowland, PhD, Director, Office of Cancer Survivorship, National Cancer Institute, NIH/DHHS

We welcome with great anticipation this comprehensive new *Handbook of Oncology Social Work*, edited by Christ, Messner and Behar. The *Handbook* addresses those issues frequently associated with the social needs of patients including psychological and bereavement issues. Uniquely, it also includes in-depth chapters on current topics such as identifying distress earlier, approaches to diversity issues so frequent in our patient populations, and concepts brought about by longer survivorship. Never before has excellence in care for patients with cancer required as strong a multidisciplinary team as now: this new resource will contribute not only to social workers, but also to all involved with patients and families in the cancer setting. The breadth of experience of the editors and authors is clear throughout the book and enhances its value for all health care professionals in oncology.

Richard J. Gralla, MD, FACP, Professor of Medicine, Albert Einstein College of Medicine, Jacobi Medical Center

While there have been significant medical advances and increasing numbers of cancer survivors, the human adaptive challenges to this disease have in fact become more complex and long term. Social workers are at the forefront of developing, implementing, and evaluating a broad range of psychosocial services for this population. The *Handbook of Oncology Social Work* offers educators as well as new and seasoned professionals a wealth of evidence-based information, practice wisdom, and the lived experiences of patients and families to undergird their teaching and provision of care. It is an indispensable text and resource for all educators and practitioners in health care.

Jeanette C. Takamura, MSW, PhD, Dean and Professor, Columbia University School of Social Work

The *Handbook of Oncology Social Work* is an exceptional, state-of-the-art book that clearly addresses the key issues confronting oncology social workers today. The book emphasizes social work's strong values for sharing decision-making, helping the most vulnerable and distressed, and reducing health disparity. It is an essential resource for social workers and other professionals who want to provide high quality, evidenced-based care to people with cancer and their family members.

Laurel Northouse PhD, RN, FAAN, Professor Emerita, University of Michigan

The inaugural *Handbook of Oncology Social Work* is truly a social work masterpiece. The editors have gathered the experts in the field to compile the most recent evidence-based data in terms of screening, assessment, and interventions that can provide the greatest benefit to cancer patients and their families.

James Zabora, ScD, MSW, Director, Research & Professional Development, Life with Cancer©, Inova Health System; Assistant Professor of Oncology, The Johns Hopkins University School of Medicine President-Elect, APOS

The field of oncology has seen exciting changes in the past decade offering patients improved treatment options and extended survival, while simultaneously resulting in substantially more complex care delivery. Optimal support for cancer patients and their caregivers requires multidisciplinary teamwork, with an oncology social worker being an essential partner. The *Handbook of Oncology Social Work* is a comprehensive manual addressing the multiple roles and evolving practice of this specialty. By providing psychosocial support beginning at diagnosis and palliative care through the end of life, navigating financial issues and ongoing changes in the health care system, and helping simplify the complexity of the new era of genomic profiling and targeted therapies, the oncology social worker plays a critical role in enabling patients to optimize quality of life while dealing with the emotional, social, physical and financial burdens of cancer. This handbook is an invaluable resource for the entire cancer community.

Julie R. Gralow, MD, Professor and Director, Breast Medical Oncology, Jill Bennett Endowed Professorship in Breast Cancer, University of Washington School of Medicine; Seattle Cancer Care Alliance; Fred Hutchinson Cancer Research Center

It is extremely rare for there to be a textbook that is simultaneously so comprehensive, well-researched and clinically practical. The *Handbook of Oncology Social Work* is clearly the new gold standard for oncology social work. But to say that this textbook is limited to social workers or cancer alone grossly misses the point. The clinical, educational and research implications of this monumental accomplishment are relevant for other health care professionals and chronic illnesses. The editors and authors represent the encyclopedic wisdom and diversity of thinking of many of the foundational leaders in the field and across disciplines. Significantly, there are also provocative contributions by many evolving leaders in psychosocial oncology that deeply enriches this "must own" treasure trove of compassionate expertise.

Matthew Loscalzo, MSW, BA, LCSW, Liliane Elkins Professor in Supportive Care Programs, Professor, Department of Population Sciences; Administrative Director, Sheri & Les Biller Patient and Family Resource Center; and Executive Director, Department of Supportive Care Medicine, City of Hope National Medical Center

Persons with cancers are confronted with a deluge of information and decisions about their illnesses and the impact on their lives. Oncology social workers play a crucial role in helping patients and caregivers navigate this sea of choices. The *Handbook of Oncology Social Work* encompasses the breadth and depth of expertise and compassion that oncology social workers bring to individuals and families living with cancers.

Mark G. Kris, MD, Attending Physician, Thoracic Oncology Service; The William and Joy Ruane Chair in Thoracic Oncology, Memorial Sloan Kettering Cancer Center; Professor of Medicine, Weill Cornell Medical College

The *Handbook of Oncology Social Work* comes at a perfect time. Since beginning my career 23 years ago, I have seen the challenges of serving oncology patients and their families become exceedingly complex, with rising incidents of cancer, many more individuals living with cancer, and increasing numbers of survivors, many of whom, however, experience a reduced quality of life linked to treatment side effects. The breadth and depth of the learnings covered in the *Handbook* is a brilliant blending of the history, knowledge, wisdom, and experiences of the nation's oncology social workers integrated with the stories and voices of patients and families. The *Handbook* is the manual that every oncology health care team should read.

Moreen Shannon-Dudley, MBA, MSW, LICSW, Director, Supportive Care, Radiation Therapy and Specialty Clinics, Seattle Cancer Care Alliance

The scope of practice covered in this handbook is essential for any oncology social worker, whether they are new to the field or an experienced practitioner. The handbook will be required reading for all social work interns and fellows. The sheer number of topics and authors reflects the great advances we have made in providing psychosocial care for people living with cancer and their families over the last three decades. It is written in language that is easily transferrable to practice, which will be helpful to social work practitioners and others across the continuum of care in oncology. The authorship of this book is astounding! Congratulations to the many contributors and editors of this wonderful handbook.

Christina Austin-Valere, PhD, LCSW, Clinical Oncology Social Worker, Bienes Comprehensive Cancer Center, Holy Cross Hospital

Oncology social workers have played a central role in developing the science and art of psychosocial care for people affected by cancer. The size and scope of this inaugural edition of the *Handbook of Oncology Social Work* is a testament to the numerous important contributions oncology social work has made to the field of psychosocial oncology in the areas of clinical care, education, research, program development, and health policy. Although the focus is on oncology social work, I am certain that professionals in all other fields of oncology that involve patient and family care will find it to be an invaluable resource.

Paul Jacobsen, PhD, Associate Center Director, Division of Population Science, Moffitt Cancer Center

This inaugural *Handbook of Oncology Social Work* codifies in exemplary fashion the wisdom, clinical practice, and art of the oncology social work profession. This outstanding publication highlights the variety of challenges experienced by people living with and undergoing treatment of cancer, cancer survivors, their caregivers, and the bereaved. It provides an overview of multiple topics and excellent clinical practice guidelines for all oncology disciplines. I congratulate the editors and authors for their vision in creating this exceptional book, which is an invaluable resource in psychosocial oncology and for all health care professionals.

Edith P. Mitchell, MD, FACP, Clinical Professor of Medicine and Medical Oncology, Program Leader, Gastrointestinal Oncology, Department of Medical Oncology; Director, Center to Eliminate Cancer Disparities; Associate Director, Diversity Affairs, Kimmel Cancer Center at Jefferson

In this rapidly changing health care environment, the comprehensive *Handbook of Oncology Social Work* is a valuable resource for social workers and members of the health care team who are working to meet the complex needs of people with cancer and their loved ones. Recognition of psychosocial needs and their impact on outcome has led to mandates requiring assessment of social, emotional, and financial concerns and protocols for addressing these needs. Social workers are on the front lines in implementing these new quality measures and in developing programs to assist a growing population. The *Handbook* defines and describes the range of interventions used by social workers to meet 21st-century needs and will become the cornerstone of oncology social work practice.

Diane Blum, LMSW, Former Executive Director, Cancer*Care*; Former Editor-in-Chief, Cancer.Net; American Society of Clinical Oncology (ASCO)

This comprehensive handbook written for oncology social workers is an important resource for anyone who works with people with cancer. It is practical, informative and organized in a manner that makes it easy to use. The nonmedical needs of a person with cancer are vast and always changing, and this handbook strives to address them all. As an attorney in this field, this handbook will further my understanding of the psychosocial and practical needs of my clients.

Randye Retkin, Esq, Director LegalHealth, New York Legal Assistance Group

The *Handbook of Oncology Social Work* is truly historic. It is the first book that provides both a comprehensive and deep sense of the myriad roles and values of social work in addressing the complex issues associated with the number two cause of death in the United States. Whether seasoned or new to the field, social workers will find this volume a constant companion to increase their knowledge, skill, and influence on the health care system. Its framework is essential social work—addressing the biopsychosocial and environmental factors affecting cancer patients, their families, and the settings in which they receive services and benefits. Beyond social workers, its interdisciplinary focus should speak to physicians, nurses, and other health care providers, as well as family and professional advocates across the continuum of care.

Terry Mizrahi, PhD, MSW, Professor, Silberman School of Social Work at Hunter College; Co-Chair, Community Organizing, Planning & Development; Director, Education Center for Community Organizing

CONTENTS

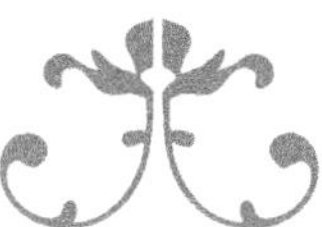

FOREWORD BY EDWINA SATSUKI UEHARA

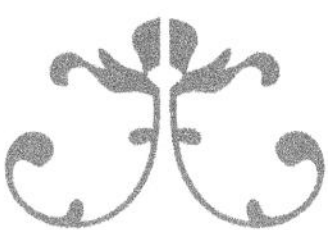

The Handbook of Oncology Social Work: Psychosocial Care for People with Cancer is the most comprehensive volume on the science and art of oncology social work ever published. This remarkable book, edited with great skill by Grace Christ, Carolyn Messner, and Lynn Behar, brings together 160 authors—oncology social work practitioners, educators, researchers and administrators—whose collective expertise covers the complex, expansive terrain of contemporary psychosocial care of people with cancer and their families.

The publication of the *Handbook* is especially timely. The field of oncology social work has experienced dramatic growth and evolution over the past thirty years. This growth is in part attributable to advances in the science of cancer treatment, which have led to both success in prolonging life through more effective treatment *and* greater complexity in oncology diagnostic and treatment processes. As a result, those who are coping with cancer now comprise a diverse and growing population with a wide spectrum of needs and psychosocial care requirements. We have long been in need of a publication that describes advances in oncology social work practice and science and delineates key questions and issues facing the field. The *Handbook of Oncology Social Work* masterfully meets these needs. The *Handbook*'s 109 chapters are far-reaching, addressing such topics as screening, assessment, and interventions across the life span and continuum of care; coping with pain, loss, grief, and bereavement; sociocultural and economic diversity implications for psychosocial care; strengthening professional development, education, interprofessional practice and practice settings; and key issues for research, policy, and advocacy. In short, the authors of the *Handbook* create a rich reservoir of knowledge for anyone interested in this large and increasingly important arena of social work practice and science.

Perhaps just as important, the authors of the *Handbook of Oncology Social Work* also succeed in bringing to life the leadership of social workers in the evolution of humane and effective oncology care. Since the inception of oncology social work practice three decades ago, social workers have been at the forefront of efforts to identify and meet the psychosocial needs of cancer patients and their families. Throughout this remarkable book, the authors document the success of oncology social workers in advocating for the integration of psychosocial care into the cancer treatment system, promoting patient empowerment, patient- and family-centered care, expanding the reliance on research findings to inform psychosocial care, and generating new knowledge through practice-based research. As the *Handbook* editors observe, oncology social workers "have become effective leaders and innovators in ways not previously imagined."

The *Handbook*'s editors view this inaugural volume as "an opportunity to create a repository of state-of-the-art information about this specialty, to consider what has been achieved, and to explore directions for the future." They have made the most of the opportunity and in the process succeeded at much more. The *Handbook* is a definitive publication that will guide and inform oncology social workers for generations to come. It is also a source of inspiration for *all oncology health care professionals* who aspire to improve the efficacy, dignity and quality of care for those who must cope with the complexity and uncertainty of living with cancer and chronic illness.

Edwina Satsuki Uehara, MSW, PhD
Professor and Ballmer Endowed Dean in Social Work
School of Social Work, University of Washington
Seattle, Washington

FOREWORD BY LIDIA SCHAPIRA

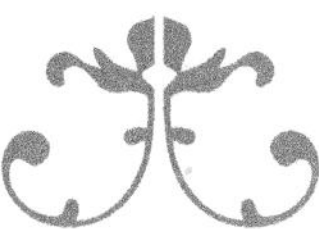

The care of patients with cancer has evolved swiftly over the past twenty years as a consequence of tremendous strides made in basic and translational sciences. We have identified molecular targets within cancers and developed specific and tailored treatments that are both more effective and less toxic than those that came before. Oncologists are proud of the emerging array of tailored or personalized therapies that have transformed the landscape of clinical care giving hope to thousands of patients with diseases previously thought incurable or refractory to treatment. But the term *personalized care* has a different meaning to patients and their loved ones. It means being known and cared for by professionals trained to identify and address their unique concerns, to allay their fears, and to help them navigate the complex system of healthcare services. It takes a multidisciplinary team of highly specialized professionals to care for a single patient with cancer. Social workers are requisite partners in this enterprise. Their distinct perspective, knowledge, skills, and commitment to social justice have shaped our models of clinical care and impacted policies and clinical guidelines. A patient of mine said she felt buoyed by the connection to her professional team. She compared her illness to a roller coaster, adding that her professional caregivers formed a pillar that kept the roller coaster from crashing. Oncology social workers are witnesses to the most fundamentally human aspect of cancer. They are champions and advocates for the most vulnerable and repositories of stories of courage and resilience in the face of adversity and disability. They are often informal therapists and teachers for overworked nurses and doctors who turn to them when they are frazzled by demands from patients they find unreasonable or difficult, or when they are simply exhausted from constant exposure to suffering and loss.

The *Handbook of Oncology Social Work: Psychosocial Care for People with Cancer* is a comprehensive volume whose contributors address both the science of caring and the art of social work practice. The chapters provide instruction and inspiration and showcase the specialization of oncology social workers, the complexity of the challenges facing patients and families, and the scope of interventions vetted by research. Social workers constitute the largest segment of mental health professionals in the cancer workforce, and the demands for their services are expected to grow with the aging of the population and the increased numbers of cancer survivors. Social work has expanded beyond practice to leadership roles in cancer centers, academic institutions, and governmental agencies. The legacy and success of social workers is evident in the widespread implementation of patient- and family-centered care and psychosocial screening.

When confronted with patients who are suffering, medical professionals turn to social workers to provide counsel, solace, and guidance. Oncology social workers debrief with patients after complex consultations with clinical specialists, help them think about trade-offs inherent in treatment choices, and empower them to articulate their needs and wishes for end-of-life care. Social workers help patients speak sooner, voice their concerns, imagine an uncertain future, and find ways of reconstructing normalcy after the major disruptions a life-altering illness causes. This inaugural *Handbook* celebrates the accomplishments and expertise of oncology social workers and identifies opportunities and challenges for years to come.

Lidia Schapira, M.D.
Associate Professor of Medicine
Harvard Medical School
Associate Physician
Massachusetts General Hospital Cancer Center
Boston, MA

FOREWORD BY BARBARA A. GIVEN

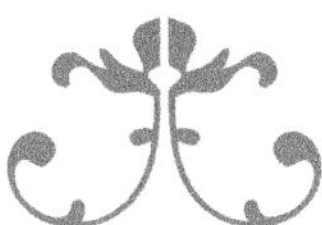

At a time when major advances in cancer treatment result in enhanced survivorship, concern for psychosocial care becomes ever more essential. With increased longevity are new psychosocial challenges. This *Handbook* reflects these important changes and articulates the important role of the oncology social worker in caring for patients and their families in our evolving health care system.

The Sections and chapters in the *Handbook* will be invaluable to oncology social workers and other psychosocial specialists. The content portrays a greater appreciation of the cancer experience and provides clear guidance on psychosocial assessments and interventions. The breadth, scope, and variation in clinical practice are evident in this book, and document the value and extensive contributions of oncology social work to patients and the interprofessional health care team.

The *Handbook* provides wonderful examples of the complexity of psychosocial care offered by oncology social workers and illustrates the necessity of increased specialization. Vitally important to helping people deal with cancer as a chronic illness, social work requires knowledge, skill, evidence based practice, and compassion. Content on the continuum of care across the lifespan, survivorship, distress screening, quality of life, adherence, genetics and sociocultural and economic diversity provides a wealth of knowledge in psychosocial oncology. Having all of this information gathered in the *Handbook* means that social workers need not look any further for an excellent guide to oncology social work practice, education, research, and policy.

Oncology social workers have much to contribute to the psychosocial well-being of our patients and their caregivers. As the aging population expands, more social workers will be needed to meet their needs. Social workers are critical to patients' access to quality health care in our current and future health systems. Oncology social workers ensure that psychosocial care is integrated into patient care.

Social workers will benefit from the outstanding repository of scholarship in the *Handbook*. It will facilitate social workers' continued ability to make significant differences in the quality of cancer patients' and their caregivers' lives, enhancing their access to care.

What a rare opportunity to have such a state-of-the-art *Handbook* to provide existing evidence based practice models of care in psychosocial oncology. Not only is it important to summarize where we have been and where we are but we must also look to the future. This book fulfills all three of these goals. Its editors and contributors reflect the change in care to ambulatory and community settings away from hospital settings. They illustrate the many contributions that oncology social workers make to this system of care where so much more is expected of patients, their families and their health care teams.

This book gathers the contributions of some of the best experts in the field and could not be more timely. Using wisdom from this much-needed and outstanding comprehensive *Handbook*, oncology social workers and other oncology disciplines will be better equipped to meet the challenges ahead in providing psychosocial care to people with cancer.

Barbara A. Given, PhD, RN, FAAN
University Distinguished Professor
Director of the PhD Program
College of Nursing
Michigan State University

PREFACE

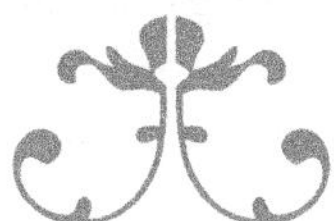

Grace Christ, DSW/PhD
Professor Emerita, Research Scientist
Columbia University School of Social Work
Board Chair, Social Work Hospice and Palliative Care Network

Carolyn Messner, DSW, ACSW, BCD, LCSW-R, OSW-C
Director of Education and Training
CancerCare
Adjunct Lecturer
Silberman School of Social Work at Hunter College

Lynn Behar, PhD, ACSW, LICSW, OSW-C
Founder, Carol LaMare Initiative
University of Washington School of Social Work
Co-Chair, Advisory Board
Cancer Lifeline

We are honored to write this preface for the inaugural *Handbook of Oncology Social Work: Psychosocial Care for People with Cancer*. This *Handbook* provides a repository of the breadth and scope of oncology social workers' clinical practice, education, research, policy, and program leadership in the psychosocial care of people with cancer and their families. It focuses on the unique synergy of social work perspectives, values, knowledge, and skills with the psychosocial needs of cancer patients, their families, and the health care systems in which they are treated. At the same time, we recognize and respect the vital importance of interdisciplinary competence and sharing that are fundamental to providing the best possible oncology care.

Expansion of the Oncology Social Work Role: "Trail Angels" and "Trail Magic"

The remarkable expansion and evolution of oncology social work practice over more than 60 years can be attributed in part to the dramatic growth in the number of adults living with cancer due to technological advances in the treatment of cancer in combination with an aging population. For many people, cancer has become a chronic illness, and coping with it during all of its phases is more of a marathon than a sprint, with many ups and downs, challenges and opportunities, joys and sorrows. All of this requires greater knowledge and skill for oncology social workers, but also enormous courage, sensitivity, compassion, thoughtfulness, creativity, and inventiveness in problem solving.

The metaphor of "trail angels," first identified on the 2,000-mile-long Appalachian Trail, has relevance to the role oncology social workers play and to their experience of this work. Trail angels are individuals who position themselves at key points (transitions) along the trail to provide help, housing, transportation, and all manner of sustenance (care coordination) to the hikers on their journey (Baker, 2012). The trail angel's first question to hikers is "What can I get you right now?" (starting where the patient is). Trail angels dispense "trail magic" (evidence-based therapeutic support) when it is most needed, when hikers are beat, downtrodden, lonely, and hungry and when the weight of their pack and the miles ahead are crushing their will. The trail angel's goal is to do whatever he or she can to help hikers get where they want to go. Veterans sometimes say they are using the trail to walk off the war. Listening to the hiker's story is also important (nonjudgmental acceptance). "The hikers cry, they spill, and they leave. Your job is to listen. This is their cathartic moment where they verbalize the work they've done in their head on the trail" (Baker, 2012; sense and meaning making). And you are left as the trail angel (oncology social worker) to process what you have just experienced, conceptualize your work, teach it to others, research the interventions found to be most helpful, and find strength (resilience) to continue this work and build your career.

Purpose and Structure of the *Handbook*

The *Handbook of Oncology Social Work* addresses both the science and art of psychosocial care. The chapters within also identify the increasing specialization of oncology social work related to its unique knowledge, skill base, and role and the progressive complexity of psychosocial challenges for patients with cancer. Areas are covered here that are not addressed in similar depth in other oncology publications.

The *Handbook* is built on the shoulders of founding members of the profession whose work has been described in two seminal oncology social work texts published by the American Cancer Society, the last one over a decade ago (Lauria, Clark, Hermann, & Stearns, 2001; Stearns, Lauria, Hermann, & Fogelberg, 1993). Much of the content about the oncology social work role of these and other earlier publications remains sound and relevant to practice today.

To reflect contemporary oncology social work practice, the *Handbook* is divided into 19 sections, each with three to 10 thematically connected chapters that address different aspects of a particular area of practice, education, research, and/or policy. Each section is introduced by an expert in the field. Each chapter begins with key concepts and ends with pearls of wisdom and pitfalls. Case vignettes are included wherever possible to ensure the integration of patients' voices and experiences, which are central to oncology social work practice, as well as references and websites for further learning.

Major topical areas the *Handbook* addresses are an overview of oncology social work; cancer across the continuum of care; survivorship; site-specific cancers; distress screening; research; quality of life; genetics, sociocultural and economic diversity; assessment and interventions with adults living with cancer, their families, and caregivers; parental cancer; children and adolescents; pediatrics; adult life span issues; loss, grief, and bereavement; patient- and family-centered care; legal and ethical issues; care coordination; technology-integrated interventions; oncology social work practice settings; professional development and education; and building resilience in interprofessional settings.

Using the Table of Contents

Our Table of Contents (TOC) was intentionally designed as a guide to what each section contains. The TOC reflects the topics mentioned previously with greater detail. We encourage you to use the TOC to find what you are looking for and to discover areas that are new to you or that you hope to learn more about.

The *Handbook* reflects the wealth of knowledge in psychosocial oncology now. It is the first time these topics are all housed in one place. It can be used as a reference for difficult patient assessments and interventions, a new support group or program, conducting research, writing a grant proposal, incorporating distress screening in the practice setting, ethical or legal dilemmas, career paths and resilience, and professional growth and support. We hope this book will serve many purposes for each of you at different points in your own career trajectory—we want it to be a trail angel for you as you encounter the different challenges and needs that being a provider of psychosocial services in oncology can create.

How Many of Us Are There?

Social workers make up the largest number of mental health providers in the nation in both hospice and palliative care. Furthermore, it is projected that social workers in health care settings will experience a growth of 27% over the next decade, an increase attributed to the aging of our population (Bent-Goodley, 2014; U.S. Department of Labor, Bureau of Labor Statistics, 2014). Historically, their provision of supportive counseling specifically for cancer patients was documented in a 1995 national survey that found that 75% of counseling for all cancer patients at National Cancer Institute (NCI)–designated cancer centers was provided by social workers (Coluzzi et al., 1995). Finally, in a recent worldwide survey of over 700 professionals working in pediatric oncology (Wiener et al., 2012), social work was reported to be the discipline that most frequently provided services to parents and children in oncology settings.

Development of the Specialty

In 1984, when the Association of Oncology Social Work (AOSW) was formed, social work was formally organized as a specialty within oncology. This was preceded by the formation of the Association of Pediatric Oncology (Fobair et al., 2009). Many authors in this book are also members of the more recently formed Social Work Hospice and Palliative Care Network (SWHPN), an organization that focuses on the biopsychosocial care of individuals with advanced cancer and other end-of-life conditions (Blacker & Christ, 2011). Currently, all three organizations are thriving with over 3,000 members, national and international conferences, certifications, national networks of education and training programs, active listservs, and two membership journals, the *Journal of Psychosocial Oncology* and the *Journal of Social Work in Hospice and Palliative Care*.

Mandates for Integration of Psychosocial Science Into the Medical System

The psychosocial challenges for patients and families have become progressively more complex in ways that are addressed throughout the *Handbook*. At the same time, multiple government reports have clarified the limited integration of advances in psychosocial science within the medical care system. Improving this integration was proposed as a critical way to address the growing complexity of patients' needs. As a consequence, patient- and family-centered care and psychosocial screening, two initiatives long advocated by oncology social workers, have become regulatory mandates (ACOS, 2014; IOM, 2006, 2007a, 2007b; Joint Commission, 2010). Both initiatives make up sections with multiple chapters in this *Handbook*. Policy and regulatory agencies are increasingly recognizing the uniqueness of the social work role—its strengths-based and multisystem approaches—as critical to improving the quality of care and the integration of psychosocial care within the medical care system.

Contributions of Social Work to Oncology

The sections in this *Handbook* reflect unique aspects of the oncology social work role. Social work plays a critical role in oncology because of its distinctive perspective, knowledge, and skills, including (1) expertise in navigating medical and social systems; (2) a knowledge and skill base in support, education, and psychosocial interventions with patients, families, and interdisciplinary teams; (3) commitment to social justice for the most vulnerable, oppressed, and distressed members of society, including alleviation of health disparities; and (4) creation of multisystem and strengths-based approaches. Multisystem interventions address the patient's complex challenges at a biopsychosocial, family, community, educational, health care system, and practical level. Increasingly, these approaches are recognized as most effective in reducing patient distress and improving the quality of care (Lo et al., 2014).

This *Handbook* details the leadership role played by oncology social workers in cancer centers, community cancer programs, major cancer education initiatives, private and consultative practices, academic institutions, corporate and medical institutions, governmental research, and policy organizations. The oncology social work role encompasses direct practice with patients and families; local and national education for patients, families, communities, and other disciplines; advocacy for patients; and increased involvement in psychosocial research and institutional and policy issues.

REFERENCES

American College of Surgeons (ACOS). (2014, January 21). *Cancer program standards 2012: Ensuring patient-centered care*. Retrieved from http://www.facs.org/cancer/coc/programstandards2012.html

Baker, B. (2012, September 16). A town that steps up on the Appalachian Trail: Monson's "angels" are a sight for sore hikers. *Boston Globe*. Retrieved from http://www.bostonglobe.com/metro/2012/09/15/trail-angels-lighten-load-for-appalachian-trail-hikers/CQbzptXzdpUk2w8FCqHoOM/story.html

Bent-Goodley, T. B. (2014). Social work: A profession of power, passion, and purpose. *Social Work, 59*(3), 197–199.

Blacker, S., & Christ, G. (2011). Defining social work's role and leadership. In T. Altilio & S. Otis-Green (Eds.), *Oxford textbook of palliative social work* (pp. 21–30). New York, NY: Oxford University Press.

Coluzzi, P. H., Grant, M., Doroshow, J. H., Rhiner, M., Ferrell, B., & River, L. (1995). Survey of the provision of supportive care services at National Cancer Institute-designated cancer centers. *Journal of Clinical Oncology, 13*, 756–764.

Fobair, P., Stearns, N. N., Christ, G., Dozier-Hall, D., Newman, N. W., Zabora, J., . . . Desonier, M. J. (2009). Historical threads in the development of oncology social work. *Journal of Psychosocial Oncology, 27*(2), 155–215. doi:10.1080/07347330902775301

Institute of Medicine (IOM). (2006). *From cancer patient to cancer survivor: Lost in transition*. Washington, DC: National Academies Press.

Institute of Medicine (IOM). (2007a). *Cancer care for the whole patient: Meeting psychosocial health needs*. Washington, DC: National Academies Press.

Institute of Medicine (IOM). (2007b). *NCCN clinical practice guidelines in oncology: Distress management*. Fort Washington, PA: NCCN Clinical Practice Guidelines.

The Joint Commission. (2010). *The Joint Commission: Advancing effective communication, cultural competence, and patient- and family-centered care: A roadmap for hospitals*. Oakbrook Terrace, IL: Author.

Lauria, M., Clark, E., Hermann, J. F., & Stearns, N. (Eds.). (2001). *Social work in oncology: Supporting survivors, families, and caregivers*. Atlanta, GA: American Cancer Society.

Lo, C., Hales, S., Jung, J., Chiu, A., Panday, T., Rydall, A., . . . Rodin, G. (2014). Managing Cancer and Living Meaningfully (CALM): Phase 2 trial of a brief individual psychotherapy for patients with advanced cancer. *Palliative Medicine*, *28*(3), 234–242.

Stearns, N. M., Lauria, M. M., Hermann, J. F., & Fogelberg, P. R. (Eds.). (1993). *Oncology social work: A clinician's guide.* Atlanta, GA: American Cancer Society.

U.S. Department of Labor, Bureau of Labor Statistics. (2014, January 8). Social workers: Job outlook. In *Occupational outlook handbook*. Retrieved from http://www.bls.gov/ooh/community-and-aosicla-service/social-workers.htm#tab-6

Wiener, L., Oppenheim, D., Breyer, J., Battles, H., Zadeh, S., & Farkas-Patenaude, A. (2012). A worldview of the professional experiences and training needs of pediatric psycho-oncologists. *Psycho-Oncology*, *21*(9), 944–953.

ACKNOWLEDGMENTS

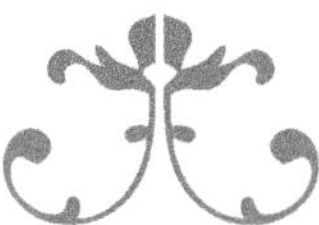

We could not have edited this inaugural *Handbook of Oncology Social Work* without all our section heads and authors. We are very grateful to each of them for their tireless work and wonderful energy and enthusiasm that made this book possible. We especially wish to thank our colleague, Stewart Fleishman, MD, for his invaluable assistance and support to us. We also thank Heather Lee Miller, PhD, and Mark Berens of Miller Berens Group for their copy editing assistance. We are indebted to our Oxford team for their unwavering encouragement and support of our inaugural book.

Dedication to People Living With Cancer

This *Handbook* has been written to capture the voices of oncology social workers and of people living with cancer, their caregivers, cancer survivors, and the bereaved with whom we have the great privilege to work. Their experiences have informed this book immensely. Oncology social workers share a common bond to make a difference in the lives of people with cancer. And it is people living with cancer to whom this book is dedicated. As you read the chapters contained herein, listen for their voices.

This inaugural *Handbook of Oncology Social Work: Psychosocial Care for People with Cancer* is a repository of the work of our era and written as a reference for each of you. These are not easy times for our profession, with growing global conflicts, poverty, climate changes, and so many people without safe harbor. As the scientific breakthroughs in cancer treatment grow, there are many patients who lack access to oncology care. As oncology social workers, we are often referred to those patients for whose needs there are no easy solutions. We hope that in this book you will find solace, novel approaches to your work, and reflective time to discover innovative solutions to the challenges that lie ahead for all of us.

CONTRIBUTORS

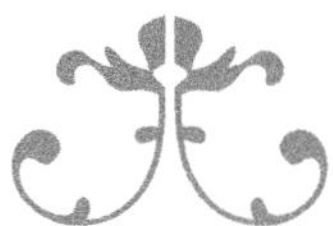

Jeasmine E. Aizvera, MSSW, LCSW-C, BCD, Assistant Chief for Performance Improvement CAPT, United States Public Health Service Commissioned Corps, Social Work Department, National Institutes of Health Clinical Center, Bethesda, MD

Hannah Allison, MSW, LCSWA, Graduate Research Assistant, North Carolina State University, Department of Social Work, Raleigh, NC

Gunnar Almgren, BA, MA, MSW, PhD, Associate Professor of Social Work and Social Welfare, University of Washington, School of Social Work, Seattle, WA

Terry Altilio, LCSW, ACSW, Social Work Coordinator, Department of Pain Medicine and Palliative Care, Beth Israel Medical Center, New York, NY

Amanda Amodio, BS, MSW, LCSW, Clinical Social Worker, Memorial Sloan Kettering Cancer Center, and Consultant, Refugee Immigrant Fund (RIF), New York, NY

Mark E. Anderson, JD, MSSW, LMSW, Social Work Counselor, The University of Texas MD Anderson Cancer Center, Houston, TX

Christopher Anrig, LCSW-R, BA, MSSW, Clinical Social Worker, Department of Social Work, Memorial Sloan Kettering Cancer Center, New York, NY; and Lecturer of Social Work in Psychiatry, Cornell Medical College Faculty, Ithaca, NY

Lynn Behar, PhD, LICSW, ACSW, OSW-C, Founder, Carol LaMare Initiative, University of Washington School of Social Work; and Co-Chair, Advisory Board, Cancer Lifeline, Seattle, WA

Ramona E. Beltrán, PhD, MSW, Assistant Professor, Graduate School of Social Work, University of Denver

Rebecca G. Block, PhD, MSW, LCSW, Assistant Professor of Medicine/Adolescent and Young Adult, Oncology Psychosocial Research Leader, Oregon Health Sciences University, Knight Cancer Institute, Portland, OR

Amy Z. Boelk, MSSW, PhD, Professor, University of Wisconsin–Stevens Point Department of Sociology & Social Work, Stevens Point, WI

Sage Bolte, PhD, MSW, LCSW, OSW-C, Director, Life With Cancer, Inova Cancer Services, Inova Heath System, Fairfax, VA

Jane Bowling, BA, MS, MSW, DSW, Retired Director of Social Work, Memorial Sloan Kettering Cancer Center, New York, NY

Karen Bullock, PhD, MSW, BSW, Professor, North Carolina State University, Department of Social Work, Raleigh, NC

Barry D. Bultz, PhD, Professor and Head, Division of Psychosocial Oncology, Faculty of Medicine, University of Calgary and Tom Baker Cancer Centre, Calgary, AB, Canada

Mary Ann Burg, MSW, PhD, Professor, School of Social Work, University of Central Florida, Orlando, FL

Christa G. Burke, MSW, LCSW, Social Worker, Palliative Care Team, Barnes-Jewish Hospital, St. Louis, MO

John G. Cagle, PhD, MSW, Assistant Professor, School of Social Work, University of Maryland - Baltimore

Heather Campbell-Enns, PhD, MSc, BEd; PhD Candidate, Interdisciplinary Cancer Control, University of Manitoba; and Research Studies Coordinator, Cancer*Care* Manitoba, Winnipeg, MB, Canada

Rosalie Canosa, MSW, MPA, LCSW, Executive Director, Cancer Support Team, Purchase, NY

Deborah Carr, PhD, Professor, Sociology, Rutgers University, New Brunswick, NJ

Cecilia L. W. Chan, PhD, Head of Department of Social Work and Social Administration, University of Hong Kong, Centre of Behavioral Health, Pokfulam, Hong Kong

Maria Chi, MS, LCSW, Clinical Supervisor, Intern Program Coordinator, Cancer*Care*, New York, NY

Amy Yin Man Chow, BSoSc, MSocSc, PhD, Associate Professor, Department of Social Work & Social Administration, University of Hong Kong, Pokfulam, Hong Kong

Grace Christ, PhD/DSW, Professor Emerita and Research Scientist, Columbia University School of Social Work, Seattle, WA

Nancy F. Cincotta, MSW, MPhil, Psychosocial Director, Camp Sunshine at Sebago Lake, Casco, ME; and Adjunct Faculty, Icahn School of Medicine, Department of Behavioral Medicine, New York, NY

Elizabeth J. Clark, PhD, MSW, MPH, Past Chief Executive Officer, National Association of Social Workers, Washington, DC

Karen Clark, MS, Program Manager, City of Hope, Department of Supportive Care Medicine, Duarte, CA

Paul G. Clark, PhD, MSW, Assistant Professor, Department of Sociology, Anthropology & Social Work, University of North Florida, Jacksonville, FL

Stacy Collins, MSW, Senior Practice Associate, National Association of Social Workers, Washington, DC

Yvette Colón, PhD, ACSW, BCD, Assistant Professor, School of Social Work, Eastern Michigan University, Ypsilanti, MI

Erin Columbus, MSW, LCSW, Clinical Supervisor/ Program Director of Online Services, Cancer*Care*, New York, NY

Constance Connor, BA, MSW, LCSW, Pediatric Oncology Social Worker, Life With Cancer, Inova Heath System, Fairfax, VA

Nancy Contro, MSW, LCSW, Director, Bereavement and Family Guidance Program and the Family Partners Program, Lucile Packard Children's Hospital at Stanford, Palo Alto, CA

Catherine Credeur, MSW, LMSW, OSW-C, Social Worker, Harold C. Simmons Cancer Center, UT Southwestern, Dallas, TX

Penny Damaskos, PhD, LCSW, OSW-C, Director, Department of Social Work, Memorial Sloan Kettering Cancer Center, New York, NY

Sheila Damore-Petingola, BSW, MSW, RSW, Faculty Appointment—Lecturer, Division of Human Sciences, Northern Ontario School of Medicine, Laurentian University, Lakehead University; and Coordinator, Supportive Care Oncology Network—NE Region, Health Sciences North/Horizon Sante-Nord, Northeast Cancer Centre, Sudbury, ON, Canada

Louisa Daratsos, PhD, LCSW, Psychosocial Coordinator for Oncology/Palliative Care, VA New York Harbor Healthcare System, Brooklyn, NY

Cindy Davis, PhD, Professor, University of Tennessee, College of Social Work, Nashville, TN

Kim Day, MSSA, LISW-S, OSW-C, ACHP-SW, Clinical Oncology Social Worker, University Hospitals Seidman Cancer Center, Cleveland, OH

Richard R. Dickens, MS, LCSW-R, DPNAP, Clinical Supervisor, Mind-Body Project Coordinator, Cancer*Care*; and Mentor, Leadership Fellowship, Zelda Foster Studies Program in Palliative and End-of-Life Care, NYU Silver School of Social Work, New York, NY

Jessica H. L. Elm, MSW, PhD Student, Research Assistant, University of Washington School of Social Work

Lorena Estrada-Martinez, PhD, MPH, Assistant Professor, College of Public and Community Service, University of Massachusetts, Boston, MA

Wendy J. Evans, MSW, MBA, LCSW, Assistant Vice President, Clinical Services, Cenikor Foundation, Houston, TX

Teresa Evans-Campbell, PhD, MSW, Associate Professor, University of Washington School of Social Work, Seattle, WA

Elizabeth Ezra, LCSW, OSW-C, Pancreatic Cancer Program Coordinator, Cancer*Care*, New York, NY

Ann Fairchild, LCSW, Former President, Association of Oncology Social Work, Deerfield, IL

Anna Faul, BSc, MSSW, PhD, Professor and Associate Dean, Academic Affairs, Kent School of Social Work, University of Louisville, Louisville, KY

Stacy Stickney Ferguson, MSW, LICSW, President, Board of Directors, Association of Pediatric Oncology Social Workers; and Manager, Education and Outreach, Patient and Health Professional Services, National Marrow Donor Program, Be the Match, Minneapolis, MN

Iris Cohen Fineberg, PhD, MSW, ACSW, OSW-C, Associate Professor and Associate Dean for Academic Affairs, School of Social Welfare, Stony Brook University, Stony Brook, NY

Stewart B. Fleishman, MD, BS, Founding Director, Cancer Supportive Services, Continuum Cancer Centers of New York and Accreditation Surveyor American College of Surgeons Commission on Cancer Chicago, IL

Les Gallo-Silver, LCSW-R, Associate Professor of Health Services, Health Sciences Department, LaGuardia Community College/City University of New York, New York, NY

Patrick Garbe, BA, Electronic Discovery Specialist, New York Law Firm, New York, NY

Daniel S. Gardner, PhD, LCSW, Associate Professor, Silberman School of Social Work at Hunter College, City University of New York, New York, NY

Sarah Gehlert, MA, MSW, PhD, E. Desmond Lee Professor of Racial & Ethnic Diversity, and Professor, Department of Surgery, School of Medicine, George Warren Brown School of Social Work, Washington University, St. Louis, MO

Brian Giddens, LICSW, ACSW, Director, Social Work and Care Coordination, University of Washington Medical Center; and Clinical Professor University of Washington School of Social Work, Seattle, WA

Susan Glaser, LCSW, Senior Clinical Social Worker, Memorial Sloan Kettering Cancer Center, New York, NY

William Goeren, LCSW, ACSW, Director of Clinical Program, Coordinator of LGBT Program, Cancer*Care* National Office, New York, NY

Karen Gold, BEd, MSW, Social Worker/Interprofessional Education Coordinator, Women's College Hospital; and Adjunct Lecturer, Faculty of Social Work, University of Toronto, Toronto, ON, Canada

Greta Greer, MSW, LCSW, BA, Director of Survivor Programs, American Cancer Society, Atlanta, GA

Shannon Groff, MSc, BSc, Provincial Screening for Distress Coordinator, Community Oncology, Alberta Health Services—Cancer*Care*, Holy Cross Site, University of Calgary, Calgary, AB, Canada

Sheila L. Hammer, MSW, LCSW, Clinical Program Director, Cancer Support Community Santa Monica, Los Angeles, CA

Richard T. Hara, PhD, MSSW, Assistant Director of Field Education, Adjunct Assistant Professor, Columbia University School of Social Work, New York, NY

Lou Harms, BA, BSW, MSW, PhD, Associate Professor and Deputy Head, Department of Social Work, The University of Melbourne, Melbourne, Australia

Karen Kell Hartman, LCSW, MSW, OSW-C, Senior Clinical Social Worker, Memorial Sloan Kettering Cancer Center, Commack, NY

Barbara Head, PhD, RN, CHPN, ACSW, FPCN, Associate Professor, University of Louisville School of Medicine, Kent School of Social Work, Louisville, KY

Christine Healy, MSW, LCSW, Clinical Social Worker, H. Lee Moffitt Cancer Center, Tampa, FL

Susan Hedlund, BS, MSW, LCSW, OSW-C, Faculty, Portland State University, Graduate School of Social Work, School of Medicine-Oregon Health & Sciences University; and Manager, Patient/Family Support Services, Knight Cancer Institute, Portland, OR

Julie Keany Hodorowski, RN, MA, Clinical Chemotherapy Coordinator, Memorial Sloan Kettering Cancer Center, New York, NY

Darrell Hudson, PhD, MPH, Assistant Professor, Brown School of Social Work, Washington University in St. Louis, St. Louis, MO

Kerry Irish, BS, MSW, Clinical Social Worker, The Patrick Dempsey Center for Cancer Hope & Healing, Lewiston, ME

Terry L. Irish, BA, MDiv, DMin, BCC, Chaplain, City of Hope National Medical Center, Duarte, CA

Barbara L. Jones, PhD, MSW, Associate Professor, Assistant Dean for Health Affairs, The University of Texas at Austin School of Social Work, The Institute for Grief, Loss and Family Survival, Austin, TX

Annamma Abraham Kaba, LCSW-R, MSW, Clinical Supervisor and Program Coordinator, Memorial Sloan Kettering Cancer Center, New York, NY

Karen Kayser, PhD, MSW, Professor, Renato LaRocca Chair, Oncology Social Work, University of Louisville Kent School of Social Work, Louisville, KY

Victoria Kennedy, MSW, LCSW, Vice President, Program Development & Delivery, Cancer Support Community, Washington, DC

Jeanne Kerwin, D.MH, Ethics & Palliative Care Program Manager, Overlook Medical Center, Atlantic Health System, Atlanta, GA

Roz Kleban, LCSW, Clinical Supervisor/Program Coordinator, Breast and Imaging Center, Memorial Sloan Kettering Cancer Center, New York, NY

Louise Knight, MSW, LCSW-C, OSW-C, Director, Harry J. Duffey Family Patient and Family Services Program, Johns Hopkins Hospital, Sidney Kimmel Comprehensive Cancer Center, Baltimore, MD

Caroline Kornhauser, MPH, Education Outreach Coordinator, Cancer*Care*, New York, NY

Betty J. Kramer, PhD, MSSW, Professor, School of Social Work, University of Wisconsin-Madison, Madison, WI

Virginia Krawiec, MPA, Program Director, Health Professional Training in Cancer Control, American Cancer Society, Atlanta, GA

Carrie Lethborg, PhD, MSW, BSW, Clinical Leader, Cancer Social Work Coordinator, Psychosocial Cancer Research, St. Vincent's Hospital, Fitzroy; Research Fellow, Monash University, Clayton; and Research Fellow (Hon.), Peter MacCallum Cancer Centre, Melbourne, Australia

Pamela Pui-Yu Leung, PhD, BSW, Director of Rehabilitation, Hong Kong Society for Rehabilitation; and Honorary Assistant Professor and Honorary Research Fellow, University of Hong Kong, Pokfulam, Hong Kong

Jane Levy, MS, LCSW-R, Director of Patient Assistance Programs, Cancer*Care*, New York, NY

Frances Marcus Lewis, PhD, MN, MA, BSN, Professor & Affiliate, Fred Hutchinson Cancer Research Center; and Endowed Professorship, University of Washington Professor of Nursing Leadership, University of Washington & Fred Hutchinson Cancer Research Center, School of Nursing, Seattle, WA

Taryn Lindhorst, PhD, MSW, BA, Carol LaMare Associate Professor of Social Work, School of Social Work, University of Washington, Seattle, WA

Matthew Loscalzo, MSW, BA, LCSW, Liliane Elkins Professor in Supportive Care Programs, Professor, Department of Population Sciences; Administrative Director, Sheri & Les Biller Patient and Family Resource Center; and Executive Director, Department of Supportive Care Medicine, City of Hope National Medical Center, Duarte, CA

Mandy Lowe, BSc, (OT), MSc, OT Reg (Ont), Director, Education and Professional Development, University Health Network; Co-Director, UHN International Centre for Education, University of Toronto; Associate Director, Centre for Interprofessional Education; and Associate Professor, Rehab Medicine, University of Toronto, Toronto, ON, Canada

Carol P. Marcusen, MSW, LCSW, BCD, Director of Social Services, Patient Education, and Spiritual Care, Keck Medical Center of USC, USC Norris Cancer Hospital, Los Angeles, CA

Debra Mattison, MSW, LMSW, OSW-C, BCD, Adjunct Lecturer, School of Social Work, University of Michigan; and Oncology Social Worker, St. Joseph Mercy Cancer Care Center, Ann Arbor, MI

Carole Mayer, PhD, RSW, Director of Research and Regional Clinical Lead for the Supportive Care Oncology Program, Northeast Cancer Centre, Health Sciences North/Horizon Sante Nord, Sudbury, ON, Canada

Angela McCabe, MSW, LCSW, OSW-C, Director of Psychosocial Support Services and Community Outreach, Saint Barnabas Medical Center Cancer Program, Livingston, NJ

Paula G. McCarthy, MSW, BA, ACSW, LCSW, Medical Social Work, St. Jude Children's Research Hospital, Memphis, TN

Michele McCourt, Director, Cancer*Care* Co-Payment Assistance Foundation, New York, NY

Patricia McGillicuddy, BA, BSW, MSW, Director of Professional Practice, Collaborative Academic Practice, University Health Network; and Lecturer, Faculty of Social Work, School of Social Work, University of Toronto, ON, Canada

Cynthia Medeiros, MSW, LICSW, Psychotherapist, Atlantic Counseling, Weymouth, MA

Carolyn Messner, DSW, ACSW, BCD, LCSW-R, OSW-C, Director of Education and Training, Cancer*Care*; and Adjunct Lecturer, Silberman School of Social Work at Hunter College, New York, NY

Margaret Weld Meyer, BSW, MSW, MBA, LCSW, OSW-C, Director, Social Work, The University of Texas MD Anderson Cancer Center, Houston, TX

Jennifer Mills, PhD, MSW, MPH, Advocacy Relations, Genentech, a Member of the Roche Group, South San Francisco, CA

Mary Beth Morrissey, PhD, MPH, JD, Research Fellow; Program Director, Post-Master's Healthcare Management Certificate Program, Fordham University Schools of Business, West Harrison, NY

Margrett R. Myhre, MSSW, LCSW, Social Work Counselor, The University of Texas, MD Anderson Cancer Center, Houston, TX

Krista Nelson, MSW, LCSW, OSW-C, Program Manager, Quality and Research, Cancer Support Services, Providence Cancer Center, Portland, OR

Nancy W. Newman, BA, MSW, Director, Patient Support and Advocacy, Moffitt Cancer Center, Tampa, FL

Lisa O'Brien, LCSW, OSW-C, Social Work Coordinator, Clinic Cancer Care; and Association of Oncology Social Work Director at Large, Western Region, Association of Oncology Social Work, Great Falls, MT

Rachel Odo, LCSW, Clinical Social Worker, Cancer*Care*, New York, NY

Julianne S. Oktay, MSW, PhD, Professor Emeritus, University of Maryland School of Social Work, Baltimore, MD

Shirley Otis-Green, MSW, ACSW, OSW-C, Founder and Consultant, Collaboratie Caring, Toluca Lake, CA, and Consultant and Faculty, Kent School of Social Work, University of Louisville, Louisville, KY

Lynne E. Padgett, PhD, Program Director, Basic Biobehavioral and Psychological Sciences Branch, Behavioral Research Program, Basic Biobehavioral and Psychological Sciences, DHHS/NCI/DCCPS, Behavioral Research Program, Rockville, MD

Guadalupe R. Palos, LMSW, RN, Manager, Clinical Protocol Administration, Cancer Survivorship, Office of Cancer Survivorship, Division of Medical Affairs, The University of Texas MD Anderson Cancer Center, Houston, TX

Carly Parry, PhD, MSW, MA, Program Director, Behavioral Research Program/Process of Care Research Branch, National Cancer Institute, Rockville, MD

Lissa Parsonnet, PhD, LCSW, Psychotherapist, Clinical Supervisor, Consultant, Private Practice, Montclair, NJ

Kate Pederson, MSW, LICSW, Patient and Health Professional Services, Be the Match, National Marrow Donor Program, Minneapolis, MN

Shlomit Perry, MSW, PhD, Head of the Psychosocial Oncology Service, Davidoff Cancer Center, Beilinson Hospital, Petach Tikva, Israel

Jayne Phillips, BASW, MS, ANP-C, Nurse Practitioner, Pain and Palliative Care Consult Service, National Institutes of Health, Bethesda, MD

G. Stephane Philogene, MSc, PhD, Deputy Director, Office of Behavioral and Social Sciences Research, National Institutes of Health, Bethesda, MD

Stacy S. Remke, LICSW, Faculty, School of Social Work, University of Minnesota

Rian Rodriguez, MPH, Director, Patient Navigator Program, American Cancer Society, New York, NY

Elizabeth A. Rohan, PhD, MSW, Health Scientist, Centers for Disease Control and Prevention, Division of Cancer Prevention and Control, Chamblee, GA

Max Rorty, LCSW, Case Manager and Consultant, Cottage Rehabilitation Hospital, Santa Barbara, CA

Upal Bau Roy, MS, PhD, MPH, Assistant Research Scientist, NYU School of Medicine, New York, NY

Connie Rust, BS Pharmacy, MSSW, PhD, Assistant Professor, South College School of Pharmacy, Knoxville, TN

Alison Mayer Sachs, MSW, CSW, OSW-C, Director Community Outreach, Patient Support Services, Eisenhower Lucy Curci Cancer Center; and Instructor, Graduate Medical Program, Eisenhower Medical Center, Family Practice & Internal Medicine, Residency Program, Rancho Mirage, CA

Ursula M. Sansom-Daly, Bachelors of Psychology (Hons I), PhD/Masters of Clinical Psychology, Postdoctoral Research Officer, Kids Cancer Centre, Sydney Children's Hospital; and Clinical Psychologist, Sydney Youth Cancer Service, Sydney Children's and Prince of Wales Hospitals, Randwick, NSW, Australia

Tara Schapmire, PhD, MSSW, CSW, CCM, OSW-C, Assistant Professor, School of Medicine and Affiliated Assistant Professor, Kent School of Social Work, University of Louisville, Louisville, KY

Hester Hill Schnipper, BA, MSW, LICSW, OSW-C, Program Manager, Oncology Social Work, Beth Israel Deaconess Medical Center, Boston, MA

Johanna Schutte, BA, MSW, LCSW, OSW-C, Oncology Social Worker, Ochsner Medical Center/Cancer Institute, New Orleans, LA

Jennifer L. Scott, PhD, MCP (Master in Clinical Psychology), Grad Dip (Psych), BA, Professor of Clinical Psychology, Associate Head (Psychology), School of Medicine, and Faculty of Health, University of Tasmania, Hobart, Tasmania, Australia

Carole F. Seddon, LCSW-C, BCD, OSW-C, AM, Director, Cancer Counseling Center, The Johns Hopkins University, School of Medicine, Department of Oncology, Harry J. Duffey Family Patient and Family Services Program, Cancer Counseling Center, Baltimore, MD

Kate Shafer, MSW, Social Worker, Children's National Health System, Center for Cancer and Blood Disorders and George Washington University Medical Faculty Associates, Thriving After Cancer Program, Washington, DC

Katie Schultz, BA, MSW, PhD Student, School of Social Work, University of Washington, Seattle, WA

Kathryn M. Smolinski, MSW, JD, Director, Legal Advocacy for People with Cancer & Adjunct Assistant Professor, Wayne State University Law School, Detroit, MI

Mary Sormanti, MS, PhD, MSW, Professor of Professional Practice, Columbia University School of Social Work, New York, NY

Gary L. Stein, JD, MSW, Professor, Wurzweiler School of Social Work—Yeshiva University, New York, NY

Melissa Sileo Stewart, MSW, LCSW, Director, Navigation Services, LIVESTRONG Foundation, Austin, TX

Donna Suckow, BA, MSW, MBA, LCSW, Associate Director, UT MD Anderson Cancer Center—Department of Social Work, Houston, TX

Bridget Sumser, BA, MSW, Director of Palliative Social Work, Division of Palliative Medicine and Bioethics, Winthrop University Hospital, Mineola, NY

Stephen Taplin, MD, MPH, Chief, Process of Care Research Branch, Behavioral Research Program, Division of Cancer Control and Population Sciences, National Cancer Institute, Rockville, MD

Jill Taylor-Brown, MSW, RSW, Adjunct Professor, Faculty of Social Work, University of Manitoba; and Director of Patient and Family Support Services, Cancer*Care* Manitoba, Winnipeg, MB, Canada

Brian Tomlinson, MPA, BSW, Chief Program and Communications Officer, Cancer*Care*, New York, NY

Matthew A. Town, MPH, BS, PhD Candidate, Department of Sociology, Portland State University, Portland, OR

Laurel Eskra Tropeano, BA, MSW, Palliative Care Social Worker for Kaiser Special Services, The Denver Hospice, Denver, CO

Analisa Trott, LCSW, Pediatric Oncology and Neuro-Oncology Social Work Clinician, Lucile Packard Children's Hospital at Stanford, Palo Alto, CA

Virginia Vaitones, MSW, OSW-C, Oncology Social Worker, Penbay Medical Center, Rockport, ME

Ashley Varner, MSW, MBA, LCSW-C, OSW-C, Manager, Psychosocial Oncology Support Program, DeCesaris Cancer Institute at Anne Arundel Medical Center; and PhD Candidate, The Catholic University of America, Annapolis, MD

Kate Wakelin, BS (Nursing), Grad. Dip. (Psycho-Oncology), Honorary Associate (Research), Program Manager, Telephone and Internet Support Groups, Cancer Information and Support Service, Cancer Council Victoria, Carlton, Victoria, Australia

Deborah Waldrop, MSW, PhD, Professor & Associate Dean for Faculty Development, School of Social Work, University of Buffalo, Buffalo, NY

Katherine Walsh, PhD, MSW, LICSW, Professor, Westfield State University, Westfield, MA

Karina L. Walters, PhD, MSW, Professor and Associate Dean of Research, University of Washington School of Social Work, Seattle, WA

Sherri Weisenfluh, LCSW, ACHP-SW, Retired Clinical Officer, Counseling, Hospice of the Bluegrass, Lexington, KY

Anjanette Wells, PhD, MSW, LCSW, Assistant Professor, School of Social Work/Public Health, Affiliated Faculty, Interdisciplinary Program in Urban Studies & Center on Urban Research & Public Policy, Faculty of Arts & Sciences, Washington University in St. Louis, St. Louis, MO

Allison Werner-Lin, PhD, LCSW, Assistant Professor, Social Policy and Practice, University of Pennsylvania, Philadelphia, PA

Lori Wiener, PhD, DCSW, Co-Director, Behavioral Science Core, Head, Psychosocial Support and Research Program, National Cancer Institute, National Institutes of Health, Pediatric Oncology Branch, Bethesda, MD

Debra Wolf, BS, JD, Supervising Attorney, LegalHealth, New York Legal Assistance Group; and Adjunct Professor of Law, Fordham University School of Law, New York, NY

Margaret S. Wool, PhD, LICSW, BCD, MSW, Clinical Associate Professor, Brown University, Warren Alpert Medical School Department of Family Medicine, Department of Psychiatry & Human Behavior, Brown University School of Public Health, Department of Behavioral & Social Sciences; and Clinical Consultant, NorthMain Radiation Oncology, Providence, RI

James R. Zabora, ScD, MSW, Director, Research & Professional Development, Life with Cancer, Inova Health System; Assistant Professor of Oncology, The Johns Hopkins University School of Medicine, Baltimore, MD; President-Elect, APOS

Sima Zadeh, PsyD, Pediatric Psychology Fellow, National Institutes of Health, National Cancer Institute, Bethesda, MD

Brad Zebrack, PhD, MSW, MPH, Associate Professor, School of Social Work, University of Michigan, Ann Arbor, MI

I

Overview of Oncology Social Work

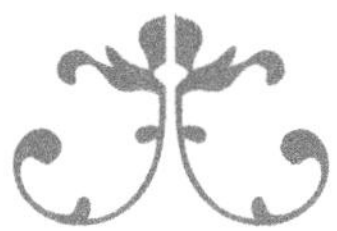

Carolyn Messner

The recognition that social workers could contribute to the care of the medically ill occurred in the early 20th century. Thirty-five years ago, oncology social work emerged as a subspecialty of medical social work, exclusively for the provision of professional social work services to cancer patients and their caregivers. This section of the *Handbook of Oncology Social Work: Psychosocial Care of People With Cancer* offers a comprehensive introduction to oncology social work.

In "Cancer in Contemporary Society: Grounding in the Science of Oncology and Psychosocial Care," Stewart B. Fleishman and Carolyn Messner highlight that oncology social work is the convergence of two distinct bodies of knowledge: social work theory and practice and the science and treatment of cancer. They encourage an ongoing understanding of innovations in both arenas to maximize the efficacy of psychosocial care to people living with cancer.

In "Oncology Social Work: Past, Present, and Future," Susan Hedlund describes oncology social work's rich and evolving history over the past 30 years. She characterizes the future as holding great promise for oncology social workers to develop new models of coordinated and collaborative care, to initiate creative programs, and to be "at the table" in cancer committees as well as regional and national initiatives.

In "Integrating Research and Evidence-Based Practice With Clinical Knowledge," Julianne S. Oktay proposes that evidence-based practice is a process that the oncology social worker goes through to integrate research results with practice knowledge. Using a four-step model for conducting evidence-based practice with illustrative case vignettes, she creates a structure to incorporate evidence-based practice into social work more generally.

In "Oncology and Health Care Disparities," Anjanette Wells, Darrell Hudson, Lorena Estrada-Martinez, and Sarah Gehlert remind us that problems that come from a cancer diagnosis occur in a sociocultural context, with racial/ethnic minorities and persons of lower socioeconomic status bearing a disproportionate burden. They conclude with a number of recommendations, including establishing long-lasting relationships with community stakeholders to enhance care to vulnerable communities.

In "Meeting Psychosocial Health Needs: An Institute of Medicine Report Comes to Life," Kim Day discusses the impact on oncology social work of the Institute of Medicine report *Cancer Care for the Whole Patient: Meeting Psychosocial Health Needs* as all cancer centers and institutions are moving forward to carry out the mandate of this report and previous related reports on patient- and family-centered care. She identifies the recommendations of *Cancer Care for the Whole Patient* to integrate psychosocial care with biomedical care to achieve a new standard of care. She weaves in specific examples of how to implement the report's comprehensive recommendations.

Each of these topics describes critical areas of history, science, knowledge, skills, and values that provide the foundational pillars for the practice of oncology social work. The influence of these perspectives is seen throughout this handbook in describing current standards of biopsychosocial care in oncology.

1

Stewart B. Fleishman and Carolyn Messner

Cancer in Contemporary Society: Grounding in Oncology and Psychosocial Care

Key Concepts

- *Cancer treatments reflect our evolving understanding of cancer and innovations in cancer care.*
- *Because cancer is a complex disease, oncology social workers, in addition to their social work education, training, and experience, require knowledge of the science of cancer and its treatment and management.*
- *The domain of oncology social work includes the psychosocial component of coping with cancer.*
- *Oncology social workers attend to the whole patient in collaboration with the multidisciplinary health care team.*

Oncology social work is the convergence between two distinct bodies of knowledge: (1) social work theory and practice and (2) the science and treatment of cancer. Essential to the effective practice and delivery of oncology social work services is knowledge of the art and science of each. Because oncology social workers are well versed in the psychosocial issues that confront people living with cancer, as well as the impact of cancer treatments on psychosocial functioning, they are able to evaluate problems that confront people living with cancer from a biopsychosocial perspective (Rehr & Rosenberg, 2006). For example, when Marty described extreme fatigue to his social worker, the social worker began by working with the patient, family, and health care team to assess whether there was a biologic cause to this presenting symptom. Understanding the science of cancer is critical to the efficacy of the oncology social worker's interventions with patients, their families, and the health care team.

This chapter focuses on a framework to understand the complex science of cancer. It includes information that enhances oncology social workers' knowledge of cancer and its treatment and highlights the biopsychosocial underpinning unique to the field of oncology social work.

The face of cancer and cancer treatment has changed dramatically since World War II, when scientific and societal advances harnessed the growing collective power of chemotherapy, radiation therapy, and surgery. Advances in cancer prevention, early detection, and treatment have also fostered patients' hope for a cure or to control what was formerly considered a uniformly fatal disease. In just 75 years, such technical advances have brought us increased survival and improved quality of life but also the new and different challenges that more rigorous treatments create (Mukherjee, 2010).

Cancer: Uncoordinated Local Cell Growth Is a Systemic Problem

Cancer is a general term for bodily cell growth gone awry, with too many cells in too small a space whose genetic programming or microenvironment allows the cells to, metabolically speaking, misbehave. Growing cancer cells steal valuable energy from the rest of the body, causing fatigue and full organ systems to shut down or malfunction. Cancer in a bone or pressing on end-receptors causes pain syndromes; most are manageable, but some are intractable. We have learned that cancer, once thought to be a local phenomenon limited to a small area surrounding a visible or palpable tumor, exerts its influence throughout the system in other ways as it grows. As the cells in the tumor duplicate, they deplete oxygen and nutrients from the bloodstream while releasing their own waste products. The high pressure of the vascular system draws cells into its torrent, circulating cancer cells to areas of the body far from the original locus. Simultaneously, the natural waste collection system in the lymph nodes traps cancer cells in its closed system, and this environment encourages cancer to implant and grow (Talmadge & Fidler, 2010).

It is commonly accepted that cancer grows in the same area where it starts (local growth), spreads through the body in the bloodstream (hematogenous spread), and enters the lymphatic system, a closed filtration loop apart from the blood supply. Surgery and radiation therapy help control the cancer growth locally, and antimetabolic medicines—chemotherapy—move to far-reaching parts of the body to destroy errant deposits transported in the bloodstream. Cancer spread through lymph glands may be controlled with surgical removal or chemotherapy. Today, we know that proteins released through the bloodstream as the cancer grows (cytokines: from Greek origin *cyto* [cell] and *kinos* [movement]) travel throughout the system and likely account, at least in part, for the most distressing symptoms: weight loss, fatigue, cognitive impairment, and worsening pain and nausea (Dranoff, 2004; Fleishman, 2011).

A Matrix of Disorders

With all of these advances, we have begun to appreciate that cancer is not one disease but an umbrella of many diseases. We also better understand that not all cancers are created equally. The rapidity of progression for some lung or gastrointestinal cancers is counterbalanced by the slow pace of multiple myeloma or chronic lymphocytic leukemia. The myth of the unidimensional cancer virus has led us to appreciate the "spectrum" of cancer diseases.

Cancer Treatment

With its physiological mechanisms in mind, cancer treatment focuses on reducing the tumor burden on the body as a whole by removing the original cancer, "sterilizing" neighboring tissues if residual cells too small to be seen do remain, and reaching throughout the body to discourage new tumors from growing. Although seemingly random, many predictable patterns have been established through years of experience to anticipate where a particular type of cancer is likely to grow. A diagnostic workup establishes that a particular growth is indeed malignant by its appearance or chemical thumbprint in a biopsy. By searching other organ systems, an extent-of-disease or staging workup (NCI, 2014a) qualifies cancer's presence at its likely destinations of spread via imaging studies.

Until recently, surgery came first, guided by the principle of reduced tumor burden. The current emphasis on organ-sparing surgery has altered the sequence of treatments, featuring chemotherapy and/or radiation therapy first, to physiologically deactivate the initial tumor, reduce its size, and discourage growth in the surrounding tissues.

Chemotherapy

Chemotherapy has come a long way since mustard gas was employed as a means to slow cancerous growths after World War II (DeVita & Chu, 2008). Chemotherapy drugs work to stop cancer's metabolic products in their tracks; destroy cell walls, evicting the faulty genetic information from its cellular home in the nucleus; and stop cancer genes from being passed to future generations of cells. Chemotherapy inactivates cancer cells at the original tumor site and other parts of the body where the cancer has spread to far-reaching *metastatic* locations.

Targeted and Personalized Treatments

Newer and more specific chemotherapy drugs block the epidermal growth receptors, targeting proteins on the surface of the cancer cells to discourage future growth. Traditional chemotherapies affect the growth of both cancer and noncancer cells but damage those cells that replicate rapidly: cancer cells, linings of the mouth and esophagus, hair, skin, and nail-bed tissues. The advantage of today's *targeted* treatments is that they point the cell-destroying action to the cancer cells only, sparing the noncancer cells to minimize side effects. Targeted therapies can be even more specific when their use is guided by other cancer cell characteristics, such as proteins that are released as cancer grows, creating certain *biomarkers* that are present in subgroups of patients with a particular kind of cancer. Recently introduced chemotherapies block cell growth by choking the blood supply to growing cancer, which cannot thrive without oxygen or nutrients (NCI, 2014b).

These new technologies help direct the optimal treatment based on specific anatomic, physiological, or genetic profiles of a particular patient's cancer. We hope this trend will continue to revolutionize cancer treatment as we know it today.

Radiation Therapy

Technology has revolutionized radiation medicine. Optimized computer-driven radiation can be given over a shorter and more focused course, improving quality of life by reducing the burdens of travel to the radiation treatment center. Surgically implanted radiation seeds—brachytherapy—radiate from the cancer to the outside, supplanting traditional external beam radiation and further sparing healthy tissues.

Surgery

Surgical advances similarly abound in their marriage to technology. Robotics using computer-assisted instruments with modern optics allows tissue-sparing surgery to be performed in its smallest effective field, further protecting healthy surroundings. Finely directed surgeries that avoid nerve damage better preserve functioning and quality of life. Adding heat and cold leverages surgical effectiveness even further to remove cancerous tissues and leave the surrounding healthy tissue in place to continue its natural functions. Unthinkable in previous generations, surgical removal of metastases to the lung, brain, and liver in selected situations further minimizes cancer's effects on the rest of the body. Similarly, advances in anesthesiology help make surgical procedures safer and shorten the recovery period, which affects survival rates and quality of life.

All Treatments Have Side Effects

Along with the growing complexities of today's cancer therapies, patients' and families' needs have grown in tandem. What was routinely accepted—that disabling side effects are the price one pays for having cancer and getting treatment—has become a less acceptable option.

Until recently, an individual's tolerance for the range of cancer therapies was limited by its effects on organ functions, commonly called *side effects* or *toxicities*. Pain; severe nausea and vomiting, which create fluid and salt imbalances; infections; anemia; or blood clots could quickly cascade into life-threatening emergencies or impinge on quality of life. Fatigue and weight loss, once thought to be expectable states to endure with treatment, have been found to be life altering and even dangerous.

Modern technological advances in medicine have made such toxicities tolerable or even avoidable, saving countless lives and minimizing emergency hospitalizations. Pain can be treated with more purified versions of narcotic analgesics via skin patch or oral preparations taken as infrequently as once a day or through small pumps. Newer classes of anti-nausea drugs provide full relief for some, avoiding hospitalizations for intravenous fluids and interruptions to work or school while receiving outpatient care. Medications that prevent anemia and blood transfusions preserve functioning. A more detailed understanding of the mechanisms that cause fatigue or weight loss (or gain) has led to the incorporation of improved diet, exercise, and energy management to maintain quality of life and avoid unnecessary hospitalizations or deaths.

As cancer treatment affects healthy as well as malignant tissues, survivors often struggle with subtle or obvious lingering effects. Nerve damage and compromised heart, lung, or gastrointestinal systems can serve as constant reminders of one's life as a cancer survivor. Deciding how much of an incursion on daily life such symptoms hold is a deeply personal judgment. That chemotherapy may affect thinking or memory long after it has been completed has led to the concept of *chemobrain* (Clegg, 2008), with clinical and laboratory investigation under way to learn more about this newly recognized phenomenon. Cancer survivors explain that "life is never the same" after treatment when lingering effects become superimposed on the uncertainties of survivorship.

Clinical Trials

The great strides made over the past half century in cancer medicine are directly the result of the development and refinement of the *clinical trial*. Much misunderstood by the public, clinical investigations do not render vulnerable patients "guinea pigs." Rather, clinical trials test the safety and effectiveness of a certain treatment (drug, type of radiation, device, or surgical technique or process) in a logical step-by-step approach. Apart from the altruistic desire to help others, clinical trials allow individual patients to access innovative or expensive treatments before they are released to the general public. Clinical research centers follow strict ethical guidelines to safeguard the public. Being part of a trial translates into greater attention to monitoring both the cancer and the effects of the element in question.

Symptom Management: Current and Emerging Models of Care

Through the advances in cancer treatment described earlier, society and cancer professionals alike have begun to accept that cancer treatment is more than definitive surgery, a cocktail of drugs, and ionizing radiation. Once a cancer diagnosis is confirmed and a treatment plan is set, the body of knowledge and experience members of the multidisciplinary treatment team share can provide both great meaning and challenges to the oncology social worker's role. Whether the tasks are practical, emotional, or spiritual or address specific physical symptoms, they call upon the skills of professionals within a variety of disciplines sharing an understanding of the process of cancer growth and the experience of living with cancer. Counseling and educational interventions are rarely, if ever, limited to anxiety or depression but center on the particular and unique needs of a patient and family having cancer and receiving treatment, then proceeding to long-term survivorship or end-of-life care. With techniques borrowed from end-of-life care, symptom management follows the literal context of *palliative care* for patients who have a serious illness but are not at the end of life.

Symptom management has traditionally been more *reactive* in nature, responding to the symptoms patients and families endure during cancer treatment with specialized interventions. With more experience, we can now be more *proactive*, advising in advance about how to prevent or blunt these symptoms. When such knowledge is put into practice, patients' feelings of worry, isolation, or fear can be blunted because symptoms are anticipated and preventive plans are part of routine care.

Cancer Treatment of the Present and the Future

Treatment approaches for cancer have changed vastly over the last few years and portend a move closer to better control of cancer, though still short of the expectations raised during the 1970s' "war on cancer" (NCI, 2014a). New cellular technologies recognize that no two cancers are identical; just as fingerprints or facial expressions differ between people, so do cancer cells. Cell markers on the surface and patterns of genetic material in the cell's nucleus likewise differ, so the treatments to stop their cell production can now be better individualized. Such a movement under the umbrella of *personalized medicine* takes these differences into account. Combined with treatment planning that reflects the expected speed at which cancer cells multiply or spread, management of some cancers (certain lymphomas, leukemias, multiple myeloma, prostate cancers) is thought to be better after they progress, as the side effects to be endured when treatment starts too soon can be more hazardous than the cancer itself. These advances underscore the necessities of getting second opinions about treatment when possible, from subspecialty oncologists who are intimately familiar with the advances in key areas. The very newest *targeted therapies* that work by interfering with cell growth may be available by clinical trial or reimbursed only after older treatments have been exhausted.

Quality-of-Life Concerns

A term that is often used in cancer treatment is *quality of life*, which can be taken literally as the foil to *survival* or length of life. There are many dimensions to the concept of quality of life that are different for each person, vary at different points in time, and are affected by socioeconomic, cultural, and educational variables as well as enduring lifelong values. As cancer treatments become more burdensome, quality-of-life concerns grow. A consensus compendium of the core components of *quality of life* can be found in the "Problem List" in the original form of the Distress Screening tool of the National Comprehensive Cancer Network (2013) guidelines (see Section 4).

Provider–Patient/Family Communication

Communication is the cornerstone of every good medical encounter, and within the framework of cancer treatment, it is essential. The best care occurs when the matrix of communication is fortified between providers themselves. The advent of the uniform, shared electronic medical record may improve such interchange and may be open to patients and families via electronic portals. The essence, however, of good communication extends beyond the exchange of information to an ongoing dialogue with context and nuance. Human relatedness to the patient's experience is vital when discussing potentially life-threatening illness. Setting realistic goals and explaining the expected outcomes of treatment in words that are understandable and exacting remain formidable challenges.

Addressing the Biopsychosocial Impact of Cancer

The recognition that social workers could contribute to the care of the medically ill occurred in the early 20th century. These medical social workers usually practiced in hospital settings with the goal of helping patients and families adjust to illness, assisting with practical issues, planning for post-hospital care, and advocating for patients' specific needs. In the mid-1970s, oncology social work emerged as a subspecialty of medical social work, exclusively for the provision of professional social work services to cancer patients (Lauria, Clark, Hermann, & Stearns, 2001).

Oncology social workers provide emotional, practical, and social support with problems encountered by people affected by cancer. These problems include coping with a cancer diagnosis; crisis points in dealing with cancer; the role of hope in coping with cancer; disclosure to family, partners, children, friends, and the workplace; access to health coverage; existential dilemmas of living with a potentially life-threatening illness; practical daily issues; and grief, loss, and bereavement (Messner, 2013). Oncology social workers help patients and their loved ones problem solve and cope with the "new normal" of living with illness (Zammett, 2005).

Oncology social work specialists also support other members of the health care team, developing interdisciplinary education and support programs, as well as providing individual staff assistance (see Section 18). Patients, families, and colleagues value the oncology social worker's relationship, interpersonal sensitivity, care, and compassion, as well as specific psychosocial knowledge and skills. Many oncology social workers also conduct psychosocial research, advocate with policymakers, administer psychosocial oncology and social work departments, supervise and train oncology social workers, and work in academic settings as described throughout this handbook.

Pearls

- Interdisciplinary collaboration is a vital cornerstone of cancer care.
- Cancer is not one illness, but a spectrum of diseases whose presentation and treatment follow basic patterns while carrying a hefty dose of uncertainty.
- Psychosocial distress and states of being must be evaluated in the context of the physiological backdrop of cancer affecting the brain, mind, and spirit.

Pitfalls

- Believing that cancer is the result of a *moral failure* or *poor emotional reserve.*
- Assuming that every tear is a sign of major depression and every headache is a brain tumor.
- Believing that untested interventions that overpromise a response or offer false hope are beneficial.

More than ever, cancer is understood as an illness that affects the body, mind, and spirit. With so much of today's workup and treatment of cancer done in the ambulatory setting, the family, caregivers, friends, partners, and our extended communities have taken on burdens once shouldered solely by hospitals and their staff. Metaphorically, we use the term *cancer* as the epitome of things gone wrong or whose functions are too chaotic or too broken to be fixed, requiring a full mobilization to attack.

Cancer, with its personal and professional challenges, continues to challenge us. Virtually all people have been touched by cancer in their families, themselves, or their social circle. We remain awed, humbled, and hopeful at the same time. The solid voice of oncology social work helps maintain our focus on the personal side of cancer. No matter what we learn about the science of cancer or what unknowns we expose in the future, the psychosocial dimension of cancer should not and cannot be lost.

ADDITIONAL RESOURCES

American Cancer Society: http://www.cancer.org
American Society of Clinical Oncology: http://www.cancer.net
National Cancer Institute: http://www.cancer.gov
National Comprehensive Cancer Network: http://www.nccn.org

REFERENCES

Clegg, E. (2008). *ChemoBrain: How cancer therapies can affect your mind.* New York, NY: Prometheus.

DeVita, V. T., Jr., & Chu, E. (2008). A history of cancer chemotherapy. *Cancer Research, 68,* 8643. doi:10.1158/0008-5472.CAN-07-6611

Dranoff, G. (2004). Cytokines in cancer pathogenesis and cancer therapy. *Nature Reviews Cancer, 4,* 11–22.

Fleishman, S. B. (2011). *Manual of cancer treatment recovery: What the provider needs to know and do.* New York, NY: Demos Medical.

Lauria, M., Clark, B., Hermann, J., & Stearns, N. (2001). *Social work in oncology.* Atlanta, GA: American Cancer Society.

Messner, C. (2013). Resources for cancer patients. In J. Steel & B. Carr (Eds.), *Psychological aspects of cancer.* New York, NY: Springer Press.

Mukherjee, S. (2010). *The emperor of all maladies.* New York, NY: Scribner.

National Cancer Institute (NCI). (2014a). SEER training modules. Retrieved from http://training.seer.cancer.gov/

National Cancer Institute (NCI). (2014b). Targeted therapies fact sheet. Retrieved from http://www.cancer.gov/cancertopics/factsheet/Therapy/targeted

National Comprehensive Cancer Network. (2013). NCCN distress thermometer for patients. Retrieved from http://www.nccn.org/patients/resources/life_with_cancer/pdf/nccn_distress_thermometer.pdf

Rehr, H., & Rosenberg, G. (2006). *The social work-medicine relationship.* New York, NY: Haworth Press.

Talmadge, J. E., & Fidler, I. J. (2010). AACR centennial series: The biology of cancer metastasis: Historical perspective. *Cancer Research, 70*(14), 5649–5669.

Zammett, E. (2005). *My (so-called) normal life.* London, England: Duckworth Publishers.

2

Susan Hedlund

Oncology Social Work: Past, Present, and Future

Key Concepts

- *Oncology social work has enjoyed a rich and evolving history over the past 30 years.*
- *Psychosocial care is an essential component of caring for the "whole person."*
- *Oncology social workers have the unique skills to provide leadership in psychosocial care.*
- *Oncology social workers are core members of the caregiving team for cancer patients and their loved ones.*

Oncology social work has enjoyed a rich and evolving history over the past 40 years. Some of our practice has remained the same—such as the need to engage and support patients and caregivers to provide a range of psychosocial services—but over time, services have become more sophisticated, diverse, and multisystemic. However, starting where the patient is, thoughtfully assessing in the context of the disease and treatment, and tailoring interventions to meet patients' most urgently felt needs remain the core tenets of social work practice.

At a retreat for breast cancer patients finishing treatment, an ice storm kept our group at the retreat center longer than planned. After spending the weekend discussing all that had changed in their lives as a result of their cancer experience, one participant commented: "This is the perfect metaphor for the cancer experience. We are isolated, trying to stay safe, and yet no one can really reach us." Again, while much has changed over the years in the cancer experience, trying to stay safe, feeling isolated, and experiencing distance, even from loved ones, remain constants.

The Beginnings

In the past 40 years, social work practice in oncology has changed remarkably related to changes in treatment, increases in survival, and public attitudes toward the disease. Earlier treatment options included surgery, high-dose radiation treatments, and the beginning of chemotherapy. Side effects, including protracted nausea and vomiting and pain, were difficult to control. The first writings about social work practice in oncology were by Ruth Abrams in her work *Not Alone With Cancer* (1974), in which she described the experience of patients with cancer and her attempts to alleviate their suffering. As Abrams wrote, "The fears and anxieties generated by this disease erect a wall of silence around the patient and those who are involved, frequently presenting barriers to management, adjustment, and rehabilitation" (p. xviii). Because little was known then about cancer or its etiology, widespread fear of contagion resulted in stigmatization and isolation of the patient (Sontag, 2001). Rehabilitation (e.g., even construction of prostheses for patients receiving amputations) was thought unnecessary since the patient's chances of survival were viewed as limited.

The "Big C" was code for a cancer diagnosis. In 1979, in *Coping With Cancer*, Avery Weisman wrote about the experiences of people with cancer and the stages of adjustment that patients experienced: "In the early stages they were optimistic, but quite often in the advanced stages, after all efforts to cure or arrest the disease had failed, the medical staff and even the family turned away from the patient. For the sake of continued care, the patient repressed his feelings of abandonment and fear. His plight, as well as that of his family, was obvious and tragic." Greater awareness began to occur about the human side of cancer, including the need for support, the ability to cope, and the impact of cancer on families. Weisman continued that the "diagnosis of cancer is not the same as being a cancer patient" (Weisman, 1979, p. xvi). He also acknowledged that "psychosocial cancerology was barely in its infancy," and wrote that "cancer is not just another chronic disease. It evokes many of the deepest fears of mankind. Despite assiduous, skillful, and intelligent treatment, it can spread throughout the body. It can also spread into social and emotional domains, drastically disrupting families and challenging the very values that make life worth living" (Weisman, 1979, p. 1).

In earlier years, fear and denial surrounded a cancer diagnosis, which in the minds of many amounted to a certain death sentence. Physicians sometimes did not tell their patients they had cancer, and patients often did not tell their families and friends they had been diagnosed. It was only in the 1970s that the stigma had begun to diminish to the extent that patients were regularly told their diagnosis, thus making it possible to openly study psychosocial issues. A second factor contributing to the field's late development was the stigma attached to mental illness and psychological problems, even in the context of a foreboding medical illness such as cancer.

Over the next 10 to 20 years, treatment options for people with cancer continued to expand and improve: Childhood cancers were more successfully treated and cured; treatment for breast cancer, colon cancer, lymphomas, and other cancers continued to progress; and the management of side effects drastically improved. Awareness of the psychological impact of cancer also increased, spurring a dramatic rise in the availability of support groups, education, advocacy, and community resources (e.g., American Cancer Society, Leukemia and Lymphoma Society) that provided education and support services to patients and families, reducing both the isolation and stigma they felt. No longer seen as an automatic death sentence, cancer began to be seen as a more treatable, sometimes curable, cluster of diseases.

By the 1990s, the awareness and treatment of cancer had changed, and patients took on more active roles in dealing with their disease. Cancer patients were inspired in part by the activism of patients diagnosed with AIDS, often treated in cancer centers, who were able to influence the direction of research and treatment, as well as receiving psychosocial services during the 1980s. The National Coalition for Cancer Survivorship was formed in 1986. This organization, empowered by the real increase in numbers of patients who were living longer with cancer, began to demand recognition and help with their long-term recovery process and greater attention to their quality-of-life concerns, as well as influencing policy and research directions.

The Present

As a result of progress in understanding and treating cancer, in the 1990s, thinking began to shift from seeing cancer as an acute, life-threatening disease to seeing it as a chronic disease, with greater emphasis on quality of life and living with chronic illness. Cancer treatments were modified to be just as effective in curing the disease but with fewer side effects—surgery, for example, became less disfiguring and chemotherapy less disabling. Cancer is an incredibly complex "number of diseases," and although progress in cancer molecular biology is encouraging, there is a long way to go.

Psychosocial Care

During the past 40 years, the subspecialty devoted to cancer-related psychosocial care has become firmly established, with its own journals, scientific meetings, and professional societies (Christ & Carroff, 1984; Fobair, 2009; Holland, 2002). Support groups began to emerge as a resource for information and support and to share the experiences of others. They were not always well received, particularly by physicians, who were sometimes skeptical about the information and content shared in these meetings. A landmark study published by Spiegel, Bloom, Kraemer, and Gottheil (1989) suggested that women with metastatic breast cancer had less depression and better quality of life if they attended a psychoeducational support group in addition to their medical treatment. This study also suggested that group support may increase the longevity of these patients, and although this finding was not replicated in clinical trials, it increased the requests for, and popularity of, support groups. Groups and other psychosocial services were most often provided by social workers (Coluzzi et al., 1995); therefore, such findings increased professional and patient and family confidence in the therapeutic value of psychosocial support and strengthened the social work role.

Current Trends in Psychosocial Care

Psychosocial needs have become increasingly complex as treatment has shifted to the outpatient setting, patients are being presented with more treatment choices, and the patient and family bear increasing responsibility for managing care. Patients and families spend less time with health care providers than in the past and are expected to manage complex treatment regimens on their own. With improvements in symptom management, many patients continue to work. While these changes have lessened the debilitating aspects of cancer during treatment and afterward, they have created new challenges and burdens for both the patient and family: 32% of cancer survivors report a lack in advancement opportunities at work, 34% feel trapped because of health insurance concerns, and 81% do not make career changes (Wolff et al., 2005).

Cancer has always been expensive. An explosion of outpatient drugs has increased treatment options. However, many are not reimbursable under insurance plans and the financial burden is shifted to the patient and family (see Chapter 89). For patients receiving long-term care, navigating insurance and financial issues can become very complex, requiring patients to become strong advocates for their needs. Among patients surveyed, 25% reported having used up all or most of their savings, 13% borrowed money from relatives, 13% were contacted by collection agencies, 11% sought the aid of a charity or public assistance, and 11% borrowed money or obtained a loan (*USA Today*, Kaiser Family Foundation, & Harvard School of Public Health, 2006) to pay for their cancer treatments and related medical and psychosocial services.

The impact of cancer on families is great, with 32% saying that cancer caused someone in the family to have psychological problems, 25% noting that cancer caused severe strains with other family members, 22% indicating that cancer caused someone in the family to have lower income, and 19% reporting that someone lost or changed jobs due to cancer (*USA Today* et al., 2006).

Fortunately, psychosocial support has become increasingly available, particularly in major U.S. cancer centers, which offer psychoeducational programs, support groups, counseling, and a range of support services to patients and their families. Research on the psychosocial issues of patients with cancer has emerged (Jacobsen & Wagner, 2012) and influenced program development for cancer centers.

Implementation of psychosocial care services in oncology received increased attention after the 2008 publication of an Institute of Medicine report entitled *Cancer Care for the Whole Patient: Meeting Psychosocial Health Needs*. The report reflects the work of a multidisciplinary panel that sought to evaluate how best to translate research findings about psychosocial care into practical applications to improve the quality of cancer care. The panel found evidence for the effectiveness of an array of psychosocial services, including counseling and psychotherapy, pharmacological management of psychological symptoms, self-management and self-care programs, family and caregiver education, and health promotion interventions. They also reported that despite this evidence, many individuals who could benefit from these services do not receive them.

The National Comprehensive Cancer Network (NCCN) was among the first organizations to propose interdisciplinary guidelines related to psychosocial care. The guidelines, first issued in 1999, focus on the recognition and management of distress in patients with cancer. The rationale for focusing on distress, even though it is not a precise clinical term, is that it is easily understood by the layperson and does not carry the stigma that is often associated with more formal psychiatric terminology (NCCN, 2010).

In 2012, the College of Surgeons initiated new standards for all accredited cancer programs that affect the role of psychosocial support services. By 2015, all accredited cancer centers must implement three components of psychosocial care: (1) patient navigation, which attempts to assess, identify, and eliminate barriers to access for cancer treatment; (2) implementation of distress risk screening for all newly diagnosed cancer patients being treated at the cancer center; and (3) implementation of survivorship care planning (ACOS COC, 2012). Based on the Institute of Medicine's report *From Cancer Patient to Cancer Survivor: Lost in Transition* (2005), many cancer patients reported feeling "lost," confused about follow-up recommendations, and generally abandoned at the end of treatment. The new College of Surgeons' standards attempt to address this and have implications for social workers practicing in these settings.

As the field of psychosocial oncology has evolved, so have different models concerning the clinical skills and services social workers offer. In smaller, community-based health care systems, oncology social workers in hospitals may assist patients with discharge planning, coordinate with such community agencies as the American Cancer Society or the Leukemia and Lymphoma Society, and/or facilitate cancer support groups and education programs. Social workers practicing in large urban cancer centers may provide psychosocial screening, assessment of at-risk patients, crisis intervention and problem solving, short- and long-term counseling, advocacy, facilitation of support groups, and program development. All oncology social workers, however, help patients and families to better understand treatments and services; cope with emotions surrounding cancer and its treatment; manage treatment side effects; make behavioral changes to minimize disease impact; manage disruptions in work, school, and family life; and locate and secure financial assistance.

Psychosocial Screening and Assessment

As greater understanding emerges about the psychosocial impact of a cancer diagnosis and its treatment, the development and application of screening and assessment tools are critical to clearly delineating how patients are responding to cancer and how best to help them. Given the variations that exist in each patient's and family's attempts to adapt and manage a life-threatening diagnosis, models are required that apply brief and effective methods of psychosocial screening followed by assessments and evidence-based interventions for the problems screening identifies (Kilbourn et al., 2011) (see Section 4).

Evidence indicates that most newly diagnosed cancer patients and patients with recurrent disease—and even those with a terminal diagnosis—gradually adapt to these crises (Zabora et al., 2001). Adaptation begins as patients comprehend and integrate the diagnosis into their daily lives and are able to effectively address problems or concerns created by their changed health status and the treatment process (see Chapters 16 and 45). Approximately 75% of patients report the ability to cope with the diagnosis and treatment with some or little support (Zabora et al., 2001).

As more information about patient experiences is gained through distress screening, social workers are increasingly tasked to identify interventions that most adequately address patient concerns and problems. All patients experience some level of distress as they attempt to normalize their early reactions to a cancer diagnosis, a recurrence, or the anticipation of death. The most powerful predictors of distress are poorer quality of life, disability, and ongoing unmet needs. Studies have also shown correlations with distress and lower social support, family functioning, problem-solving skills, and performance status (Kissane, Maj, & Sartorius, 2011; Williams et al., 2009). These are all areas that have been the focus of oncology social work assessments and interventions since its inception and documented in current oncology social work standards (AOSW, 2012; see Chapter 101).

According to distress screening guidelines, all patients should undergo brief psychosocial screening, and those patients found to have moderate to severe distress should be referred to psychosocial care professionals (see Chapter 17 on distress screening). These guidelines offer important opportunities for oncology social workers to take leadership in responding to and treating distress and developing programs of intervention to address identified problems at many points along the treatment continuum and with different populations of cancer patients and their families.

Survivorship Issues

The Centers for Disease Control and Prevention and the National Cancer Institute (NCI) estimated that as of 2007, there were 11.7 million cancer survivors in the United States, and this number is expected to grow with continued advances and the aging of the population (Smith, Smith, Hurria, Hortobagyi, & Buchholz, 2009). As noted, the 2005 Institute of Medicine report *From Cancer Patient to Cancer Survivor: Lost in Transition* highlighted patients' special needs that arise from late-occurring health problems from cancer and its treatment, as well as financial, legal, logistical, and psychological challenges. The Institute of Medicine recommended the use of survivorship care plans, and the implementation of such is mandated by the College of Surgeons for accredited cancer centers by 2015. These care plans, generated at the end of active treatment and created by the primary oncologist or nurse practitioner, are personalized documents that summarize the patient's diagnosis and treatment, possible late effects, and other challenges that survivors commonly face, and they recommend ongoing care and offer resources to support patients in the survivorship transition. For oncology social workers, opportunities exist to assist patients through individual and group psychoeducation that acknowledges the psychosocial challenges that occur at this transition, in addition to providing practical information about insurance, workplace concerns, and financial and legal issues. Specifically, survivors need resources to help with relationship issues such as communication, intimacy, and sexuality. Wellness programs such as yoga, mindfulness-based stress reduction, exercise, nutrition, and rehabilitation should also be recommended and are often coordinated by oncology social workers (see Chapter 53).

Patients often struggle with issues at the end of treatment. They include the following: How can I stay well? Who am I now? How do I integrate this experience and re-enter "normal" life? How do I balance my fear of recurrence with living life? Retreats can be an opportunity for cancer survivors to "step apart" from daily life to meet others considering similar issues, to begin to integrate the cancer experience, and to move forward with new tools and hope. Oncology social workers are the ideal professionals to facilitate these retreats. At a retreat, one participant said, "I am going home with new hope about my future and with a group of new friends who really get it."

Leadership in Oncology Social Work

Oncology social work practice offers numerous opportunities to not only impact the patient and family experience on an individual level but also to develop programs, community outreach, and policies that affect the broad range of services and resources available to patients and families. For example, the skilled oncology social worker advocates for whole-person and -family care on hospital committees, such as the cancer committee, and on boards of community agencies; facilitates liaisons with community services; and influences legislation and public policy. At the national level, the Association of Oncology Social Work and the Association of Pediatric Oncology Social Workers are often invited to participate in professional liaisons with other oncology professional societies, as well as serve in leadership capacities at the national offices of the American Cancer Society, Leukemia and Lymphoma Society, National Cancer Institute, and College of Surgeons. By participating in research and teaching, social workers can contribute to the understanding of the psychosocial impact of cancer, create new models of care, and offer more effective interventions. The social worker continues to be recognized as a core member of the interdisciplinary oncology team, often the sole voice advocating for recognition of psychosocial care needs and often the largest provider of mental health services on the oncology team (Coluzzi et al., 1995).

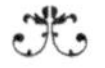

Pearls

- Cancer care must attend to the psychological and social needs of the patient and his or her loved ones.
- Oncology social workers possess the skills necessary to support the whole person.
- Psychosocial care should extend along a continuum from diagnosis through survivorship, advanced illness, and end-of-life care.

Pitfalls

- Social workers will need to continue to advocate for their role in comprehensive cancer care.
- Patients' needs will continue to be greater than social workers' capacity to attend to all of them.
- Oncology social work can be personally challenging, and attention to self-care is essential (see Section 19).

The Future

The future holds great promise for oncology social workers striving to support the "whole patient," to represent the patient and family voice in treatment settings, to develop new models of coordinated and collaborative care, to attend to care transitions and gaps in services, and to develop and provide a broad range of psychosocial services that more adequately support patients and families across the continuum of care. Clinically, we can use our expertise to be creative in program development that may offer less traditional models, such as retreats, creative arts, and integrative approaches (e.g., yoga, meditation, stress management, acupuncture, meditation), which attend to a broad array of patient needs while also keeping the work "new" for the oncology social worker. We can ensure that the patient's and family's voice is represented by being "at the table" in cancer committees, cancer program development, and other community, state, and national initiatives.

REFERENCES

Abrams, R. (1974). *Not alone with cancer: A guide for those who care—what to expect, what to do*. Springfield, IL: Charles C. Thomas Publisher.

American College of Surgeons' Commission on Cancer (ACOS COC). (2012). *Cancer program standards 2012: Ensuring patient-centered care* (Vol. 2). Retrieved from http://www.facs.org/cancer/coc/cocprogramstandards2012.pdf

Association of Oncology Social Work (AOSW). (2012). AOSW standards of practice in oncology social work. Retrieved from http://www.aosw.org/html/prof-standards.php

Christ, G., & Carroff, P. (1984). Summary of oncology social work survey, American Cancer Society. Unpublished summary of survey. In possession of author.

Coluzzi, P. H., Grant, M., Doroshow, J. H., Rhiner, M., Ferrell, B., & Rivera, L. (1995). Survey of the provision of supportive care services at National Cancer Institute—Designated cancer centers. *Journal of Clinical Oncology, 13*(3), 756–764.

Fobair, P. (2009). Historical threads in the development of oncology social work. *Journal of Psychosocial Oncology, 27*(2), 155–215.

Holland, J. C. (2002). History of psycho-oncology: Overcoming attitudinal and conceptual barriers. *Psychosomatic Medicine, 64*(2), 206–221.

Institute of Medicine. (2005). *From cancer patient to cancer survivor: Lost in transition*. Washington, DC: National Academies Press.

Institute of Medicine. (2008). *Cancer care for the whole patient: Meeting the psychosocial health needs*. Washington, DC: National Academies Press.

Jacobsen, P., & Wagner, L. (2012). A new quality standard: The integration of psychosocial care into routine cancer care. *Journal of Clinical Oncology, 30*(11), 1154–1159.

Kilbourn, K. M., Bargai, N., Durning, P. E., Deroche, K., Madore, S., & Zabora, J. (2011). Validity of the psychooncology screening tool (POST). *Journal of Psychosocial Oncology, 29*, 475–498.

Kissane, D. W., Maj, M., & Sartorius, N. (Eds.). (2011). *Depression and cancer*. Chichester, England: Wiley-Blackwell, 2011.

National Comprehensive Cancer Network (NCCN). (2010). NCCN guidelines. Retrieved from http://www.nccn.org/professionals/physician_gls/f_guidelines.asp

Smith, B. D., Smith, G. L., Hurria, A., Hortobagyi, G., & Buchholz, T. A. (2009). Future of cancer incidence in the United States: Burdens upon an aging, changing nation. *Journal of Clinical Oncology, 27*(17), 2758–2765.

Sontag, S. (2001). *Illness as metaphor and AIDS and its metaphors*. New York, NY: Picador.

Spiegel, D., Bloom, J. R., Kraemer, H. C., & Gottheil, E. (1989). Effect of psychosocial treatment on survival of patients with metastatic breast cancer. *Lancet, 2*(8668), 888–891.

USA Today, Kaiser Family Foundation, & Harvard School of Public Health. (2006, Nov. 1). National survey of households affected by cancer. Retrieved from http://kaiserfamilyfoundation.files.wordpress.com/2013/01/7591.pdf

Weisman, A. D. (1979). *Coping with cancer*. New York, NY: McGraw-Hill.

Williams, J. B., Pang, D., Delgado, B., Kocherginsky, M., Tretiakova, M., Krausz, T., ... Conzen, S. D. (2009). A model of gene environment interaction reveals altered mammary gland gene expression and increased tumor growth following social isolation. *Cancer Prevention Research, 2*(10), 850–861.

Wolff, S. N., Nichols, C., Ulman, D., Miller, A., Kho, S., & Armstrong, L. (2005). Survivorship: An unmet need of the patient with cancer implications of a survey of the Lance Armstrong Foundation (Abstract No: 6032). *Journal of Clinical Oncology, 23*(16S), 6032.

Zabora, J., BrintzenhofeSzoc, K., Curbow, B., Piantadosi, S., Hooker, C., & Piantadosi, S. (2001). The prevalence of psychosocial distress by cancer site. *Psycho-Oncology, 10*, 19–28.

3 Integrating Research and Evidence-Based Practice With Clinical Knowledge

Julianne S. Oktay

Key Concepts

- *Evidence-based practice can be a valuable resource for oncology social workers.*
- *Evidence-based practice provides a structure to integrate research findings into oncology social work practice.*
- *Evidence-based practice is a process that the oncology social worker goes through to integrate research results with practice knowledge.*
- *Evidence-based practice does not mean that some practices are "evidence based" and others are not, because evidence-based practice requires the social worker to evaluate a practice in light of his or her practice setting and population.*

The *Standards of Practice in Oncology Social Work* states that oncology social workers should "engage in Evidence Based Practice" (AOSW, 2012). Evidence-based practice (EBP) has become the standard used to determine quality in the health professions, initially in medicine, then in nursing, and now in social work. All social workers are ethically bound to provide interventions that are effective. Using EBP has the potential to enhance our status with colleagues, the health team, patients, and those who fund our services. What is meant by evidence-based practice and to what extent it can be effectively integrated into oncology social work practice is not always clear. EBP was developed in the medical profession, where, in the traditional model, the physician makes the decision as to which treatment to recommend to the patient, the patient is not actively involved until after the physician selects the intervention, and if the patient does not agree, he or she is considered "noncompliant." In contrast, social work uses a more egalitarian model, where intervention is based on "client self-determination" and client empowerment is an important goal. Can EBP be used in social work in a way that does not diminish the essential contribution of social work and the value of client self-determination? Will it actually enhance the effectiveness of oncology social work services? The aim of this chapter is to provide an introduction to EBP and to discuss its potential and problems in the context of oncology social work.

What Is Evidence-Based Practice?

EBP is a process wherein a practitioner (oncology social worker) combines his or her expertise (often called "practice wisdom") with the best available evidence (research) while taking into consideration the values and expectations of his or her work settings and patients or clients (APA, 2005; Gambrill, 1999; Sackett, Straus, Richardson, Rosenberg, & Haynes, 1997). Although the acronym EBP is sometimes used as if it were a characteristic of a specific technique or intervention (i.e., as if some interventions were evidence based and others were not), it actually describes a process that an oncology social worker uses to explore and assess various treatment options. It is sometimes called evidence-informed practice, emphasizing the process of decision making. In this chapter, I focus on the first four steps of this process (Mullen, Bellamy, & Bledsoe, 2008): (1) articulating information needs, (2) finding the best evidence to meet those needs, (3) critically assessing the evidence for applicability of the findings for the identified problem area, and (4) drawing on clinical expertise and client circumstances to appraise evidence (for more information, see Section 5). In addition to describing and illustrating each of the steps, I will identify some problems that might come up when an oncology social worker tries to integrate EBP into his or her practice.

First Four Steps of Evidence-Based Practice

1. *Articulating information needs.*
2. *Finding the best evidence to meet those needs.*
3. *Critically assessing the evidence for applicability of the findings for the identified problem area.*
4. *Drawing on clinical expertise and client circumstances to appraise evidence.*

Step 1: Articulating Information Needs

EBP begins when the oncology social worker formulates a question that he or she wants to answer. This question focuses on what the oncology social worker aims to achieve (outcome) with an intervention: for example, What intervention(s) are effective in achieving a desirable outcome? The desirable outcome should be based on the oncology social worker's knowledge of the patient population and the problems they experience. For example, if your patients often experience depression, you may want to know what interventions are effective in reducing depression. Other outcomes appropriate to oncology social work might be to reduce distress, anxiety, and cost; to improve quality of life; to reduce a specific symptom (e.g., fatigue); to prolong life; and/or to improve communication with providers, partners, and family. Sometimes the question focuses on a specific intervention: for example, Are support groups effective in achieving the outcome in this population? You may want to limit your search to interventions known to reduce depression in cancer patients. Once the outcome is clear, you are ready to search for evidence on which interventions have been found to be effective in achieving this outcome (Step 2).

Step 2: Finding the Best Evidence

Once the desired outcome has been identified, you are ready to explore which interventions effectively achieve it. Although psychosocial oncology is a relatively new field, a fairly substantial body of literature is available on interventions for cancer patients and, to a lesser extent, their families. Although this is good and necessary for EBP, the task of critically examining the evidence can be overwhelming for practitioners, who lack the time to sort out myriad complex findings and how they apply in a given practice situation. For this reason, I recommend beginning Step 2 by searching for existing research syntheses or summaries. If you are fortunate, the question you have identified has already been examined in research studies and you may find a meta-analysis that synthesizes these studies. In the meta-analysis, a researcher combines the data from different studies and analyzes the results. A meta-analysis provides more certainty that the results form a pattern than do the results of any single study alone.

Less sophisticated but nonetheless highly valuable is the "review" article, which identifies the best studies in a specified field and then compares the studies' characteristics and results. Generally, a table is provided where you can easily compare the populations studied, the interventions provided, the outcome measures used, and the results. One way to find these articles is to add "meta-analysis" and "review articles" as search terms or filters.

Meta-Analyses and Review Articles in Psychosocial Oncology (Selected Examples)

- *Meta-analysis of clinical trials on family interventions (Northouse, Katapodi, Song, Zhang, & Mood, 2010).*
- *Review of the effectiveness of professionally led groups in cancer care (Gottlieb & Wachala, 2007).*
- *Review of interventions for couples (Baik & Adams, 2011).*

Other resources that facilitate the exploration of research evidence in a specific field include organizations that maintain websites and publications that provide overviews of the research literature and synthesize its conclusions. Books are an excellent resource for oncology social workers; however, because they take more time to become published, you need to also reference peer-reviewed journal studies. If you cannot find review articles in your area of interest, you will need to explore the original research literature itself. A wide variety of journals publish research on interventions.

Organizations That Maintain Websites and Publications That Provide Overviews of the Research Literature and Synthesize Its Conclusions

- Federal government (e.g., National Cancer Institute, http://www.cancer.gov)
- Private organizations (e.g., American Cancer Society, http://www.cancer.org)
- Major cancer centers (e.g., University of Pennsylvania, http://www.oncolink.org)
- Professional organizations (e.g., Association of Oncology Social Work, http://www.oncolink.org www.aosw.org)
- Collaboratives (e.g., The Cochrane Collaboration, http://www.cochrane.org)
- Universities (e.g., University of Leicester, http://www.psycho-oncology.info/evidence.htm)

Journals That Publish Research on Interventions Relevant to Oncology Social Work (Selected Examples)

- *Journal of Psychosocial Oncology*
- *Journal of Psycho-Oncology*
- *Cancer: Journal of the American Cancer Society*
- *Journal of Cancer Survivorship*

In addition to journals, the Internet is becoming increasingly important as a resource for information on research on interventions in psychosocial oncology. Because Internet sites are not subject to peer review, only sites from reputable organizations should be used. Google Scholar is one commonly used and easily accessible for literature search.

Once you have found the "best evidence" in your field, it is possible to identify which interventions have been found effective in achieving your desired outcome (goal) in your field. When you have successfully identified one or more effective interventions, you are ready to move to Step 3.

Step 3: Critically Assessing the Evidence for Applicability of the Findings for the Identified Problem Area

Once an effective intervention has been identified through Steps 1 and 2, the oncology social worker is ready for Step 3. Assessment of the available evidence means looking carefully at the populations that have been studied in the intervention research and comparing them to your own. Interventions (e.g., supportive expressive group therapy) that have been successful with female breast cancer patients may not be effective with male prostate cancer patients. The fact that an intervention has proved successful in a population at the end of life does not mean that it will be effective with newly diagnosed patients. Also, population characteristics, such as socioeconomic status and ethnicity, are extremely important. An intervention that has been shown to be effective in a middle-class, well-educated population may not be as effective (or even acceptable) in the population that you serve.

Another important consideration in this assessment is the type of setting available to the oncology social worker. A treatment may be known to be effective in reducing depression (e.g., cognitive behavioral therapy), but there may be no evidence of its having been tested in an oncology setting, in the patient's home, or by telephone. Critical components of your assessment are the type of cancer and the stage. An intervention that has been effective in an urban setting may be impossible to implement in a rural area where transportation is not available. A community-based program may be able to initiate a program fairly easily. However, an oncology social worker working in a tertiary level cancer center might have to get approval from multiple levels of authority, have difficulty finding space to conduct the program, and have a hard time making the program known to doctors, nurses, interns, and other mental health professionals who are needed to recruit patients.

After the literature has been examined for similarity of population, cancer type and stage, and setting, you are ready to move on to Step 4, combining the results of the literature review with your clinical expertise.

Step 4: Drawing on Clinical Expertise and Client Circumstances to Appraise the Evidence

To complete the first four steps of the EBP process, you need to combine the knowledge gained from reviewing the research evidence with your own practice wisdom. This is also the point where the perspective of the patient must be incorporated. The strength of the social work field is that the context of practice is critically important. Social workers recognize that a lack of attention to the broader cultural, organizational, and systemic factors often leads to a lack of successful implementation of interventions.

In Step 4 (and to some extent Step 3 as well), patient circumstances and culture are considered. Here, the "appraisal" of the evidence reflects collaboration between the oncology social worker and the client. Just because an intervention has been extensively researched does not mean it is necessarily a better choice than the one the clinician thinks will be acceptable to the population and feasible in the setting.

The social work perspective, where patients are involved in the treatment choices, is most helpful in this step. Here, too, is where the "person in environment" perspective is most valuable. Even when effective interventions that fit the patient population and setting have been found in the literature, the social worker needs to consider whether the intervention will be appropriate for his or her setting and patients. This is where client consultation and joint decision making come into the model.

Sometimes an intervention, even though known to be effective, is not acceptable to the other professionals in the setting. It may be considered too costly or require other resources that are not available (e.g., space). It may not fit well with the organizational mission or the culture of the patient population. For example, an effective intervention based on consultation with the social worker for couples counseling may be unacceptable to a population where mental health services are highly stigmatized.

It may be possible for the oncology social worker to adapt an effective intervention to a specific population. For example, using language that is culturally appropriate may make the difference between a successful and an unsuccessful intervention. In a culture where mental illness is highly stigmatized, focusing on the physical manifestations of distress including fatigue, difficulty sleeping, and poor appetite may make the intervention more acceptable. If there is a well-understood cultural symptom, this language can be used in place of American diagnostic terms. In a very family-oriented culture, a family intervention may be more acceptable than an individual one. Sometimes qualitative studies can be used to provide a better understanding of the patient culture. For example, qualitative studies of African American breast cancer patients (Masi & Gehlert, 2009) may alert the oncology social worker to the importance of spirituality in this population and to a lack of trust in the medical facility. This may suggest that providing the intervention in a community church may make it more attractive than if it were provided in the hospital.

Peer consultation is an important resource for oncology social workers in Step 4 appraisal. Colleagues who work with similar populations in similar settings are usually glad to share their experiences with interventions so that the oncology social worker does not have to "reinvent the wheel." National associations, such as the Association of Oncology Social Work (AOSW) and the Association of Pediatric Oncology Social Workers (APOSW), provide excellent opportunities to consult with colleagues. The AOSW provides an Internet-based discussion board (the Social Work Oncology Network [SWON]) where oncology social workers consult with others about specific interventions. This discussion board is indexed in the archives and accessible to all AOSW members.

Case Example of Integration of Evidence-Based Practice in Oncology Social Work

Sarah is an oncology social worker working in a survivorship program. Most of her patients are breast cancer survivors, many of whom suffer from severe fatigue, sometimes for years after their treatment is complete. Sarah uses the EBP process to identify an effective intervention to reduce fatigue in her patients. In Step 1, she formulates her question: What interventions are effective in reducing fatigue in breast cancer survivors? Searching the literature using the search terms fatigue, review, and cancer, she locates two reviews of psychosocial interventions designed to reduce fatigue during cancer treatment (Goedendorp, Gielissen, Verhagen, & Bleijenberg, 2009; McNeely, Campbell, Rowe, Klassen, & Courneya, 2006). The first paper concludes that interventions that provide education about fatigue, self-care, coping techniques, and skills for managing activity are promising. The second looks at the impact of exercise on a variety of outcomes, including fatigue. Next, she critically assesses the evidence for applicability of the findings for the identified problem area (Step 3). Although neither of the review articles is a perfect fit with Sarah's population and setting, she nonetheless is encouraged that a variety of interventions have proved successful in reducing fatigue in cancer patients. Sarah collaborates with her medical colleagues to develop a multicomponent intervention that includes exercise, nutrition, education about fatigue, relaxation, and cognitive behavioral therapy (Step 4). She feels that a program focusing on exercise would not appeal to her patient population. However, a supportive group program, focused on education and healthy lifestyle, might be well received, and elements that are known to be effective, such as exercise, would be accepted if sandwiched between other more popular elements. Sarah and her colleagues hold several focus groups to get patient input as they formulate the intervention. As they gain experience with the intervention, they adapt the format to the needs of different patient populations. Sarah and her team evaluate the effectiveness of their intervention (Step 5). Their results show dramatic reduction of fatigue in the women who attended the group sessions (Appling, Scarvalone, Ryan, McBeth, & Helzlsouer, 2012). In publishing their results, the group contributed to the knowledge base of the profession (Step 6).

Pearls

- Using EBP has the potential to enhance our status with the health team, with our patients, and with those who fund our services.
- Oncology social workers need to be better trained in the EBP steps and when it is (and is not) likely to be helpful as a strategy to improve practice.
- Professional organizations (e.g., AOSW, APOSW) can play an important role in providing their members with needed training through workshops and seminars.
- Funding is needed to facilitate the integration of EBP into oncology social work and to support increased research in those areas where there is no (or not enough) research to allow the EBP process.

Pitfalls

- In oncology social work, it is not always possible to identify a specific narrowly defined "intervention" or a single desired outcome.
- It is not always possible to find interventions that have been rigorously tested and found to be effective in the populations or settings most relevant to oncology social work.
- When you have identified relevant studies, you may find that the results are difficult to interpret, especially in the absence of review articles.
- Considering the workload of the average oncology social worker, most will simply not have the time needed to search and integrate the existing literature in a given practice situation.

REFERENCES

American Psychological Association (APA). (2005). *Policy statement on evidence-based practice in psychology.* Washington, DC: Author.

Association of Oncology Social Work (AOSW). (2012). AOSW standards of practice in oncology social work. Retrieved from http://www.aosw.org/html/prof-standards.php

Appling, S. E., Scarvalone, S., McDonald, R., McBeth, M., & Helzlsouer, K. J. (2012). Fatigue in breast cancer survivors: The impact of a mind-body intervention. *Oncology Nursing Forum, 29*(3), 278–286. doi:10.1188/12.ONF.278-286

Baik, O. M., & Adams, K. B. (2011). Improving the well-being of couples facing cancer: A review of couples-based psychosocial interventions. *Journal of Marital and Family Therapy, 37*, 250–266. doi:10.1111/j.1752-0606.2010.00217.x

Gambrill, E. (1999). Evidence-based practice: An alternative to authority-based practice. *Families in Society: The Journal of Contemporary Human Services, 80*(4), 341–350.

Goedendorp, M. M., Gielissen, M. F. M., Verhagen, C. A., & Bleijenberg, G. (2009). Psychosocial interventions for reducing fatigue during cancer treatment in adults. *Cochrane Database of Systematic Reviews*, 1. doi:10.1002/14651858.CD006953.pub2

Gottleib, B. H., & Wachala, E. D. (2007). Cancer support groups: A critical review of empirical studies. *Psycho-Oncology, 16*, 379–400. doi:10.1002/pon.1078

Masi, C. M., & Gehlert, S. (2009). Perceptions of breast cancer treatment among African American women and men: Implications for interventions. *Journal of General Internal Medicine, 24*(3), 408–414.

McNeely, M. L., Campbell, K. L., Rowe, B. H., Klassen, T. P., & Courneya, K. S. (2006). Effects of exercise on breast cancer patients and survivors: A systematic review and meta-analysis. *Canadian Medical Association Journal, 175*(1), 34–41. doi:10.1503/cmaj.051073

Mullen, E. J., Bellamy, J., & Bledsoe, S. E. (2008). Evidence-based practice. In R. Grinnel & Y. A. Unrau (Eds.), *Social work research, evaluation: Quantitative, qualitative approaches* (8th ed.). New York, NY: Oxford University Press.

Northouse, L. L., Katapodi, M. C., Song, L., Zhang, L., & Mood, D. W. (2010). Interventions with family caregivers of cancer patients: Meta-analysis of randomized trials. *CA: A Cancer Journal for Clinicians, 60*, 317–339.

Sackett, D. L., Straus, S. E., Richardson, W. S., Rosenberg, W., & Haynes, R. B. (1997). *Evidence-based medicine: How to practice and teach EBM* (2nd ed.). Edinburgh, Scotland: Churchill-Livingstone.

4

Anjanette Wells, Darrell Hudson, Lorena Estrada-Martinez, and Sarah Gehlert

Oncology and Health Care Disparities

Key Concepts

- *The problems that come from a cancer diagnosis occur in a sociocultural context.*
- *Racial and ethnic minority group members and persons of lower socioeconomic status have a higher mortality rate from cancer.*
- *Racial and ethnic minority group members and persons of lower socioeconomic status are less able to afford cancer treatment and care.*

Cancer is currently the second leading cause of death in the United States. Although President Richard M. Nixon declared war on cancer in his 1971 State of the Union address, little progress has been made toward a cure, and the incidence of some cancers has increased. Perhaps even more troubling is the growing disparity in cancer incidence and mortality between U.S. racial and ethnic minority groups. Disparities exist in cancer screening, diagnosis, treatment, and mortality across racial/ethnic groups and socioeconomic status.

Improving the health of all Americans requires eliminating disparities in cancer screening, diagnosis, treatment, and mortality (Gehlert & Colditz, 2011). Racial/ethnic minorities, persons of lower socioeconomic status, and those living in inner-city or rural areas have poorer health outcomes (Murray et al., 2005). Explanations for these disparities include advanced disease at the time of diagnosis, decreased access to and lower quality of treatment, and discrimination.

Understanding the determinants of cancer disparities is important for preventing them and treating those affected by the disease. In this chapter, we provide an overview of cancer disparities by race/ethnicity and socioeconomic status and focus specifically on the complex social determinants of cancer disparities and how they affect cancer through multiple pathways, both directly and synergistically. We close our chapter by describing how oncology social workers might incorporate this information into their practices.

Race/Ethnicity and Cancer Disparities

Although referring explicitly to differences in the cancer experience for people of different races and ethnicities in cancer and other diseases is not without controversy (Gehlert & Colditz, 2011), racial/ethnic disparities in the United States certainly exist. Most research and intervention efforts to date have focused on race/ethnicity over other sources of disparity. As a whole, Black Americans have the highest mortality from cancer of all racial/ethnic groups. Although the cause of this disparity has been debated (Huo et al., 2009), Black and Latina women are more likely to be diagnosed at later stages of breast cancer, and minority women are less likely to receive recommended treatments than White women (Li, Malone, & Daling, 2003).

Gehlert and Colditz (2011) have cautioned that race is a social rather than a biological phenomenon that speaks to the United States' history of racial stratification. Self-reports of race often do not match ancestry informative markers, and thus reliance on race/ethnicity can mask underlying social determinants of disparities. However, race/ethnicity holds strong associations with cancer at multiple levels.

Racial discrimination is widely considered a major stressor that is independently linked to multiple adverse health outcomes (Williams & Mohammed, 2009). Clinician bias may result in differential treatment and misdiagnosis, which are critical issues during cancer screening (Institute of Medicine, 2003). Results from numerous studies and reports indicate that Black patients are less likely than White patients to receive timely treatment (Van Houtven et al., 2005). Patient and provider communication gaps may also result in lower quality treatment if racial/ethnic minority clients feel disrespected by and mistrust the medical provider. At a broader level, stressors such as the cumulative impact of material hardships and frustration with structural-level inequalities could impact racial/ethnic cancer disparities (Geronimus, Hicken, Keene, & Bound, 2006).

Socioeconomic Status and Cancer Disparities

Socioeconomic status continues to be the strongest predictor of cancer burden across and within racial/ethnic groups. Insurance status, education, and income have all been linked to cancer mortality. The United States has a primarily employer-driven health care system, and racial/ethnic minority populations are more likely to be employed in positions that don't offer health care benefits. This contributes to disparities, because privately insured adults are twice as likely to receive timely screening as Medicaid recipients or the uninsured (Halpern, Bian, Ward, Schrag, & Chen, 2007) and have better survival rates regardless of stage of diagnosis (Bradley, Gardiner, Given, & Roberts, 2005). This is true for privately insured racial/ethnic minorities as well (Harlan et al., 2005). Poor White women receive later stage breast cancer diagnoses than higher socioeconomic status White women (Gordon, 1995).

Lack of health care coverage may prevent minority clients from seeking cancer screening or prescribed treatment and follow-up. Black women in particular are often employed in occupations without fringe benefits such as paid sick leave or ones that do not allow them to take time off from their workdays without penalty (Montez, Angel, & Angel, 2009).

Place and Cancer Disparities

A person's region, country, and city of residence are also markers for disparities in cancer risk through their influence on factors like environmental exposures and access to treatment. The quality and content of the built environment, defined as "the human made space in which people live, work, and recreate on a day-to-day basis" (Roof & Oleru, 2008), have a profound effect on health. Race/ethnicity and socioeconomic status are strongly associated with the built environment in the United States, largely due to racial residential segregation. Neighborhoods influence health and are linked to multiple risk factors and diseases; thus, racial residential segregation must also be considered a determinant of disease. Racial and regional differences exist in cancer incidence and mortality (Underwood et al., 2012).

Prominent access issues related to place and cancer screening include accessibility to and the location of medical facilities and their quality. The ability of some inner-city and rural women to receive breast cancer screening may depend on their distance from clinics (Tarlov, Zenk, Campbell, Warnecke, & Block, 2009). Local public health policies may also shape cancer disparities. The persistent mortality ratio disparity suggests that although screening rates have increased, Black women may receive later and lower quality treatment than White women.

Evidence-Based Approaches to Cancer Disparities

Developing interventions that address multiple determinants of disparities is essential to their elimination. This is congruent with social workers' holistic approach and their dual aims of alleviating suffering and conducting research to improve the social conditions that produce suffering. Multilevel approaches are needed to address the barriers that reduce access to evidence-based oncology care.

Individual-Level Approaches

Cancer patients face myriad psychological problems (Gardner & Werner-Lin, 2011). Individual-level psychotherapeutic approaches improve well-being (Chow, Tsao, & Harth, 2004), decrease feelings of depression and anxiety (Andrykowski & Manne, 2006), and improve quality of life (Bloom, 2008). Cognitive behavioral therapy (CBT) is commonly used as a psychosocial intervention (Tatrow & Montgomery, 2006). CBT may be combined with other interventions to improve emotional adjustment and ease symptoms (Drageset, Lindstrom, and Underlid, 2010; Tremblay, Savard, & Ivers, 2009).

Although CBT often is effective, it may be less so for individuals living in marginal environments. For them, cognitive distortions may be less salient in coping with cancer than environmental obstacles, and asking them to increase their ability to cope may produce additional stress (Berlin, 2002; Gehlert, 2012). Gehlert and colleagues found that lower socioeconomic status Black women with poorer outcomes often did not include breast cancer among the worst things to happen to them (Gehlert, Mininger, & Cipriano-Steffens, 2011).

Interpersonal-Level Approaches

Patient navigation is designed to help patients negotiate complex health care systems (Parker, Davison, Tishelman, & Brundage, 2005). It has been linked to higher screening rates among lower socioeconomic status and racial/ethnic minority populations (Ferrante, Chen, & Kim, 2007) and to improved treatment adherence (Hendren et al., 2010).

Participation in social support groups and networks has been linked to improved outcomes (Grande, Myers, & Sutton, 2006). Support groups decrease social isolation, but although support and self-help groups have demonstrated effectiveness (Fogel, Albert, Schnabel, Ditkoff, & Neugut, 2002), they are usually not located in high-poverty neighborhoods (Gehlert, 2012).

Community-Level Approaches

Healthy People 2020 recognizes the importance of health communication strategies and information technology to improve health outcomes and achieve health equity (U.S. Department of Health and Human Services, 2010). It emphasizes *health literacy* as a tool for decreasing disparities (Riley, Dodd, Muller, Guo, & Logan, 2012). People with limited health literacy generally have lower medication and treatment adherence rates, higher hospitalization rates, and poorer health outcomes (Karten, 2007). Although websites have become important sources of health care information, low health literacy may impede their full use (Donelle & Hoffman-Goetz, 2009). Narrative forms of communication—including entertainment and storytelling—are also emerging as tools for cancer communication. Communication-based interventions improve patients' understanding of information during medical visits, resulting in improved treatment adherence (Parker et al., 2005).

Community-engaged interventions are promising tools for increasing trust among minority populations. Community-based participatory research (CBPR), defined by the Agency for Healthcare Research and Quality (2010) as "a collaborative process involving researchers and community representatives" (p. 1), integrates practice and research. In a CBPR framework, community members can be invested in the dissemination and implementation of research findings that could improve cancer outcomes (Gehlert, 2012). Strategies to enhance cancer outreach, education, screening, and treatment should be based on suggestions from underserved groups that may be perceived as "nonadherent" (Braun et al., 2002). Community members who are allowed to voice their needs and shape solutions are more likely to participate in cancer diagnosis and treatment (Braun et al., 2002; Gehlert & Coleman, 2010). Community-engaged interventions that provide combined education and patient navigation, for example, have proved effective in overcoming the linguistic and access barriers to screening faced by Chinese American women (Wang, Fang, Tan, Liu, & Ma, 2010).

Pearls

- The psychosocial problems that come with a cancer diagnosis are embedded within a nexus of social environmental barriers.
- Racial/ethnic minorities and persons of lower socioeconomic status are less likely to be able to afford preventive, palliative, and other treatments.
- Clinical social workers can participate in practice-based treatment networks that pool clinical samples to allow promising new interventions to be tested that address the needs of minority populations.

Pitfalls

- Most psychotherapeutic interventions were developed for and evaluated among middle-class White populations and may be ineffective with racial/ethnic and lower socioeconomic status populations.
- Culturally sensitive adaptations of existing treatment models for lower socioeconomic status and racial/ethnic minority groups are lacking.

In this chapter, we have detailed higher rates of cancer incidence and mortality among racial/ethnic minority and lower socioeconomic status groups and those living in certain locations in the United States. Although numerous challenges are shared by everyone who develops cancer, racial/ethnic minorities and persons of lower socioeconomic status bear a disproportionate burden. Not only are they less likely to be able to afford preventive, palliative, and other treatments, but most treatment research has also omitted them from study. Yet the psychosocial problems that come with a cancer diagnosis are embedded within a nexus of social environmental barriers.

Social workers are trained to consider social context in assessing problems and devising solutions. Taking a multilevel approach to disparities allows them to draw from a menu of interventions from the individual to community levels. These interventions can be used separately or together to tailor treatment approaches to the needs of individuals.

For many years, health social workers focused on the individual-level intrapersonal treatment modalities aimed at coping with disease, to the exclusion of group-, neighborhood-, or community-level interventions. They have begun to participate in intervention research and advocacy for policy change, including policies to shift public funding from cancer treatment to cancer prevention.

Social workers also have a role in developing and implementing interventions. Most psychotherapeutic interventions were primarily developed for and evaluated among middle-class White populations (Alvidrez, Azocar, & Miranda, 1996). Culturally sensitive, respectful, and accessible adaptations of existing treatment models for low-income and ethnic minority groups are needed. Effectiveness may vary by persons and settings, and interventions can be tailored to specific settings and situations (Maliski et al., 2004).

Although not all social workers are in positions to develop and test new treatment modalities, they can work together to pool resources. Clinical social workers can, for example, participate in practice-based treatment networks that pool clinical samples to allow the sample sizes needed to fully test promising interventions. Even if unable to participate in these efforts, social workers should locate information on current evidence-based prevention and treatment approaches for use with racial/ethnic minority and lower socioeconomic status populations.

Social workers can also draw on the knowledge and resources of vulnerable communities to choose interventions that best match the experiences of those community members, which demonstrates respect and will lead to greater trust in medical providers and improve treatment adherence. The key is to establish long-lasting relationships with community stakeholders, a natural enterprise for social workers. The payoff is prevention and treatment approaches that have greater chances of improving the lives of individuals with cancer, their social networks, and their communities.

REFERENCES

Agency for Healthcare Research and Quality. (2010). *Community-based participatory research*. Retrieved from http://archive.ahrq.gov/downloads/pub/evidence/pdf/cbpr/cbpr.pdf

Alvidrez, J., Azocar, F., & Miranda, J. (1996). Demystifying the concept of ethnicity for psychotherapy researchers. *Journal of Consulting and Clinical Psychology, 64*(5), 903–908.

Andrykowski, M. A., & Manne, S. L. (2006). Are psychological interventions effective and accepted by cancer patients? I. Standards and levels of evidence. *Annals of Behavioral Medicine, 32*(2), 93–97.

Berlin, S. B. (2002). *Clinical social work practice: A cognitive integrative perspective*. New York, NY: Oxford University Press.

Bloom, J. R. (2008). Improving the health and well-being of cancer survivors: Past as prologue. *Psycho-Oncology, 17*, 525–532.

Bradley, C. J., Gardiner, J., Given, C. W., & Roberts, C. (2005). Cancer, Medicaid enrollment, and survival disparities. *Cancer, 103*(8), 1712–1718.

Braun, K. L., Mokuau, N., Hunt, G. H., Kaanoi, M., Gotay, C. C., & Sanchez, W. (2002). Supports and obstacles to cancer survival for Hawaii's native people. *Cancer Practice, 10*(4), 192–200.

Chow, E., Tsao, M. N., & Harth, T. (2004). Does psychosocial intervention improve survival in cancer? A meta-analysis. *Palliative Medicine, 18*, 25–31.

Donelle, L., & Hoffman-Goetz, L. (2009). Functional health literacy and cancer care conversations in online forums for retired persons. *Informatics for Health and Social Care, 34*(1), 59–72.

Drageset, S., Lindstrom, T. C., & Underlid, K. (2010). Coping with breast cancer: Between diagnosis and surgery. *Journal of Advanced Nursing, 66*, 149–158.

Ferrante, J. M., Chen, P., & Kim, S. (2007). The effect of patient navigation on time to diagnosis, anxiety, and satisfaction in urban minority women with abnormal mammograms: A randomized controlled trial. *Journal of Urban Health: Bulletin of the New York Academy of Medicine, 85*(1), 114–124.

Fogel, J., Albert, S., Schnabel, F., Ditkoff, B. A., & Neugut, A. I. (2002). Internet use and social support in women with breast cancer. *Health Psychology, 21*(4), 398–404.

Gardner, D., & Werner-Lin, A. (2011). Oncology social work. In S. Gehlert & T. Browne (Eds.), *Handbook of health social work* (pp. 498–525). Hoboken, NJ: Wiley.

Gehlert, S. (2012).The relationship of practice, policy, and research in breast cancer disparities. In B. Clarke (Ed.), *Social work matters: The power of linking policy and practice* (pp. 245–250). Washington, DC: NASW Press.

Gehlert, S., & Colditz, G. A. (2011). Cancer disparities: Unmet challenges in the elimination of disparities. *Cancer Epidemiology, Biomarkers, and Prevention, 20*(9), 1809–1814.

Gehlert, S., & Coleman, R. (2010). Using community-based participatory research to ameliorate cancer. *Health & Social Work, 35*(4), 302–309.

Gehlert, S., Mininger, C., & Cipriano-Steffens, C. M. (2010). Placing biology in breast cancer research. In L. M. Burton, S. A. D. Matthews, S. Kemp, & D. Takeuchi (Eds.), *Communities, neighborhoods, and health: Expanding the boundaries of place* (pp. 57–72). New York, NY: Springer.

Geronimus, A. T., Hicken, M., Keene, D., & Bound, J. (2006). "Weathering" and age patterns of allostatic load scores among blacks and whites in the United States. *American Journal of Public Health, 95*(5), 826–833.

Gordon, N. H. (1995). Association of education and income with estrogen receptor status in primary breast cancer. *American Journal of Epidemiology, 142*(8), 796–803.

Grande, G. E., Myers, L. B., & Sutton, S. R. (2006). How do patients who participate in cancer support groups differ from those who do not? *Psycho-Oncology, 15*, 321–334.

Halpern, M. T., Bian, J., Ward, E. M., Schrag, N. M., & Chen, A. Y. (2007). Insurance status and stage of cancer diagnosis among women with breast cancer. *Cancer, 110*(2), 403–411.

Harlan, L. C., Greene, A. L., Clegg, L. X., Mooney, M., Stevens, J. L., & Brown, M. L. (2005). Insurance status and the use of guideline therapy in the treatment of selected cancers. *Journal of Clinical Oncology, 23*(36), 9079–9088.

Hendren, S., Griggs, J. J., Epstein, R. M., Humiston, S., Rousseau, S., Jean-Pierre, P., & Fiscella, K. (2010). Study protocol: A randomized controlled trial of patient navigation-activation to reduce cancer health disparities. *BMC Cancer, 10*(551), 1–11.

Huo, D., Ikpatt, F., Khramtsov, A., Dangou, J.-M., Nanda, R., Digman, J., … Olopade, O. (2009). Population differences in breast cancer: Survey in indigenous African women reveals overrepresentation of triple-negative breast cancer. *Journal of Clinical Oncology, 27*(27), 4515–4521.

Institute of Medicine. (2003). *Unequal treatment: Confronting racial and ethnic disparities in health care.* Washington, DC: National Academies Press.

Karten, C. (2007). Easy to write? Creating easy-to-read patient education materials. *Clinical Journal of Oncology Nursing, 11*(4), 506–510.

Li, C. I., Malone, K. E., & Daling, J. R. (2003). Differences in breast cancer stage, treatment, and survival by race and ethnicity. *Archives of Internal Medicine, 163*(1), 49–56.

Maliski, S. L., Kwan, L., Krupski, T., Fink, A., Orecklin, J. R., & Litwin, M. S. (2004). Confidence in the ability to communicate with physicians among low-income patients with prostate cancer. *Urology, 64*, 329–334.

Montez, J. K., Angel, J. L., & Angel, R. J. (2009). Employment, marriage, and inequality in health insurance for Mexican-origin women. *Journal of Health and Social Behavior, 50*(2), 132–148.

Murray, C. J. L., Kulkarni, S. C., Michaud, C., Tomijima, N., Bulzacchelli, M. T., Iondiorio, T. J., & Ezzati, M. (2005). The eight Americas: Investigating mortality disparities across races, counties, and race-counties across the United States. *PLoS Medicine, 29*(5S1), 4–10.

Parker, P. A., Davison, B. J., Tishelman, C., & Brundage, M. D. (2005). What do we know about facilitating patient communication in the cancer care setting. *Psycho-Oncology, 14*, 848–858.

Riley J. L. III, Dodd, V. J., Muller, K. E., Guo, Y., & Logan, H. L. (2012). Psychosocial factors associated with mouth and throat cancer examinations in rural Florida. *American Journal of Public Health, 102*(2), e7–e14.

Roof, K., & Oleru, N. (2008). Public health: Seattle and King County's push for the built environment. *Journal of Environmental Health, 71*, 24–27.

Tarlov, E., Zenk, S. N., Campbell, R. T., Warnecke, R. B., & Block, R. (2009). Characteristics of mammography facility locations and stage of breast cancer diagnosis in Chicago. *Journal of Urban Health, 86*(2), 196–213.

Tatrow, K., & Montgomery, G. H. (2006). Cognitive behavioral therapy techniques for distress and pain in breast cancer patients: A meta-analysis. *Journal of Behavioral Medicine, 29*(1), 17–27.

Tremblay, V., Savard, J., & Ivers, H. (2009). Predictors of the effect of cognitive behavioral therapy for chronic insomnia comorbid with breast cancer. *Journal of Consulting and Clinical Psychology, 77*(4), 742–750.

Underwood, J. M., Townsend, J. S., Tai, E., Davis, S. P., Stewart, S. L., White, A., … Fairley, T. (2012). Racial and regional disparities in lung cancer incidence. *Cancer, 118*, 1910–1918.

U.S. Department of Health and Human Services. (2010). Office of Disease Prevention and Health Promotion. Healthy people 2020. Retrieved from http://www.healthypeople.gov/2020/default.aspx

Van Houtven, C., Voils, C., Oddone, E., Weinfurt, K., Friedman, J., Schulman, K., & Bosworth, H. B. (2005). Perceived discrimination and reported delay of pharmacy prescriptions and medical tests. *Journal of General Internal Medicine, 20*(7), 578–583.

Wang, X., Fang, C., Tan, Y., Liu, A., & Ma, G. X. (2010). Evidence-based intervention to reduce access barriers to cervical cancer screening among underserved Chinese American women. *Journal of Women's Health, 19*(3), 463–469.

Williams, D., & Mohammed, S. (2009). Discrimination and racial disparities in health: Evidence and needed research. *Journal of Behavioral Medicine, 32*(1), 20–47.

5

Kim Day

Meeting Psychosocial Health Needs: An Institute of Medicine Report Comes to Life

Key Concepts

- *The Institute of Medicine, adviser to the federal government on matters related to health, publishes in-depth analyses on current issues in health care.*
- *The Institute of Medicine reports on cancer have synergy and build upon one an other.*
- *Among several social work–specific recommendations, the Institute of Medicine committee concluded that a sound evidence base exists to recommend supportive psychotherapy, psychoeducation, and resource provision as valid therapeutic interventions.*
- *Cancer Care for the Whole Patient: Meeting Psychosocial Health Needs has generated numerous initiatives as stakeholders have coalesced to implement its recommendations.*
- *Oncology social workers who are on the front lines of delivering psychosocial care played an important role in the development of this report and the ongoing implementation of its recommendations.*

One should never underestimate the power that one voice can have. At a leading cancer center, an oncology social worker grasped the significance of *Cancer Care for the Whole Patient: Meeting Psychosocial Health Needs* (Adler, 2008) and made certain that senior leadership read the report. The report was released at a time when the institution was poised for change. Although there were excellent values and programs in place, the report, with its emphasis on the importance of psychosocial care, led to further initiatives. The message to oncology social workers, the primary providers of psychosocial services, was the importance of working together with other concerned professionals, patients, and families to move the agenda forward and lead the way in advancing psychosocial care.

The Institute of Medicine (IOM) issues annual reports on health-related matters, and numerous editions devoted to oncology have propelled the delivery of cancer care forward. *Cancer Care for the Whole Patient* resonates especially with social workers due to its focus on the emotional and practical challenges of the illness, with the role oncology social workers play in helping patients meet challenges figuring prominently throughout. The need to identify problems and formulate interventions is a major theme and is embodied in the Standard of Care formulated by the committee. The IOM committee concluded that a sound evidence base exists to recommend supportive psychotherapy, psychoeducation, and resource provision as valid therapeutic interventions, which are specifically relevant to social work practice.

This chapter of the *Handbook of Oncology Social Work* places the report in historical context and focuses on the initiatives that ensued following its release. The actions and policies that came into being in the wake of the IOM publication brought the report to life. The report highlights the importance of psychosocial care and the key role oncology social workers play in providing that care to patients and their families.

In the fast-paced world of health care, with information and research being generated at a mind-numbing pace, it is noteworthy that *Cancer Care for the Whole Patient* is still in the limelight with congressional hearings, meetings, training, research articles, and action plans related to its recommendations. The report focuses on the emotional, practical, and psychosocial needs of people living with cancer. It reverberates with the medical community, public policy makers, grassroots organizations, accrediting bodies, and health care providers around the country. The degree to which psychosocial concerns are at the forefront of this report was gratifying to those who have long been aware of the psychosocial challenges of coping with cancer. The IOM's perspective, not only on problems, but also on potential solutions, is invaluable.

Historical Context

It is useful to understand the background of the National Academy of Sciences (NAS) and the IOM. Congress established the NAS during Abraham Lincoln's term with the purpose of advising the federal government on matters related to science and technology. The IOM was established in 1970 under the auspices of the NAS with the purpose of advising the federal government on issues related to medical care, research, and education. The IOM provides independent analyses of heath care using evidence-based information and research. Its in-depth reports address health, mental health, nutrition, aging, prevention, public health policy, specific diseases, and global health. Every report undergoes extensive review to ensure it is objective, accurate, and evidence based. These reports are useful to decision makers in the public and private sector who rely on them to inform policy decisions (IOM, 2014).

Each year, 65 members are elected to the NAS based on their professional expertise and experience. The scientists that are members of the IOM and NAS are leading experts in their fields. Social scientists and oncology social workers were on the IOM committee that wrote and reviewed *Cancer Care for the Whole Patient*. Throughout the report, oncology social work played a key role in providing expert opinion, focus, and information.

Other Institute of Medicine Reports

Before the release of *Cancer Care for the Whole Patient*, the IOM published other studies that made important contributions to improving the quality of care provided to cancer patients. *Ensuring Quality Cancer Care* (Howley & Simone, 1999) explored the assertion that quality cancer care is not provided consistently across the United States due to the complexity and organizational challenges of the health care delivery system. Within 18 months of this report, health care organizations began working together to implement its recommendations (Finn, 2000). The American Cancer Society, the National Cancer Institute, and the American Society of Clinical Oncology all initiated studies looking at the quality of cancer care. The National Dialogue on Cancer, now C-Change, was formed as a group of 125 individuals and organizations whose mission is to improve the quality of cancer care.

Another IOM report, *From Cancer Patient to Cancer Survivor: Lost in Transition* (Hewitt, Greenfield, & Stovall, 2006), focused on improving palliative care, prevention, early detection, and survivorship. This report asserted that the period following active treatment was a distinct phase of the cancer experience and warranted attention. It unleashed a flurry of activity as cancer centers around the country began developing survivor clinics, treatment summaries for survivors, and action plans for ongoing care (Houlihan, 2009). Oncology social workers were often leaders in the development of survivorship clinics and programs as they understood the psychosocial implications of survivorship.

The IOM published *Delivering High-Quality Cancer Care: Charting a New Course for a System in Crisis* (Ganz, 2013). This report has implications for oncology social work with its focus on an imperative for change in the delivery of care to cancer patients and emphasis on quantity and quality of the workforce, communication, patient- and family-centered care, shared decision making, palliative care, reducing disparities in accessing care, patient navigation, and improved affordability. These are issues that oncology social workers are uniquely positioned to address.

Defining the Standard of Psychosocial Care in Oncology

Cancer Care for the Whole Patient built on initiatives brought to light by prior reports. The value of this report lies in its affirmation of the importance of considering psychosocial factors when caring for patients with cancer. No longer can the emotional toll of cancer be ignored. This report resonated with a moral imperative to look at the whole patient, a value long held by the oncology social work community and now one being embraced by a broader coalition (Jacobsen & Wagner, 2012).

The basic premise of the report is that although we have state-of-the-art medical care in the United States, the system fails to adequately address the psychological and psychosocial sequelae of cancer. "Failure to address these problems results in needless suffering of the patient and their family, obstructs quality health care, and can potentially affect the course of the disease" (Adler, 2008, p. 51). Depression, anxiety, and other behavioral health problems, coupled with a lack of social support and practical resources, adversely affect a patient's ability to manage illness. Lower socioeconomic status and inadequate social supports are associated with increased morbidity and mortality.

The report explores models of care and tools for screening for psychosocial needs, examines evidence-based interventions, and provides an extensive list of resources. It identifies key elements that should be part of comprehensive cancer care. These became the major recommendations in the Standard of Care, which states the following:

> *All cancer care should ensure the provision of appropriate psychosocial health services by facilitating effective communication between patients and care providers; identifying each patient's psychosocial health needs; designing and implementing a plan that links patients with needed psychosocial services, coordinates biomedical and psychosocial care, engages and supports patients in managing their illness and health; and systematically following up on, reevaluating, and adjusting plans.*
>
> *(Adler, 2008, p. 9)*

Comprehensive in scope, *Cancer Care for the Whole Patient* suggests additional actions that should be taken to respond to the needs of oncology patients, including the following:

- Research aimed at developing tools to enhance patient–provider communication and screen reliably for distress.
- Directories of psychosocial services available to patients.
- Information that facilitates problem solving and decision making.
- Demonstration projects aimed at evaluating different approaches to the delivery of psychosocial health care.
- Insurance plans to support evidence-based interventions.
- Oversight mechanisms to measure quality care.

These recommendations suggest a plan that health care providers, consumer advocates, governing and accrediting bodies, payers, researchers, and policy makers can follow to bring psychosocial care on par with the excellent standard already achieved by biomedical care (Adler, 2008, pp. 9–16).

The Standard of Care, which stresses the importance of identifying psychosocial needs and the importance of linking patients with needed services, spawned a wave of activity across the nation as accrediting bodies incorporated this into regulations governing health care providers. Agencies and organizations coalesced to see that the Standard of Care, as well as the other recommendations, was implemented (Alter, 2009).

Synergy of Effort

The National Comprehensive Cancer Network (NCCN) had already been active in addressing the need to improve quality of care through screening and assessment of patients' psychosocial and spiritual needs (NCCN, 2014b). In 1997, the NCCN assembled a representative panel of experts from the major disciplines providing clinical care that was tasked with developing practice guidelines for psychosocial care. The panel stated clearly that emotional distress needed to be identified and treated as part of routine care. The NCCN panel developed guidelines and an algorithm to facilitate management of distress (NCCN, 2014a). This initiative predated *Cancer Care for the Whole Patient*; however, the impact of the NCCN guidelines became more important following the release of this report due to the subsequent increase in the United States in efforts to address psychosocial concerns. Institutions referred to the NCCN guidelines as they implemented distress screening. The American College of Surgeons' Commission on Cancer (ACOS COC) now mandates that cancer patients be screened for distress and that plans be formulated to deal with the problems identified through the screening process (ACOS COC, 2012).

The 2007 IOM report touched a nerve with its examination of where the field is falling short in meeting patient needs. The Alliance for Quality Psychosocial Cancer Care (Alter, 2009; Rose, Stovall, Ganz, Desch, & Hewitt, 2008) was formed with the goal of establishing a coalition of interested parties to implement the report's recommendations to ensure that psychosocial health needs were met. The alliance made a commitment to see that the report was not left on an academic shelf but instead had actionable items. The alliance's other goals include advocating for policies that ensure patients are screened for distress and have access to quality psychosocial health care, and advancing translational research and standards of care in psychosocial oncology. The alliance is composed of 32 key organizations working together to promote the shared vision that psychosocial care must be integrated into biomedical care for all (CFAH, 2014).

ExCEL, Excellence in Cancer Education and Leadership, is another example of an initiative developed in direct response to the IOM report. Funded through a 5-year grant from the National Cancer Institute, ExCEL had as its goal improvement of the delivery of quality psychosocial health care to oncology patients through education of oncology social workers in the following six key competencies discussed in the IOM report: communication, screening, needs assessment, care planning and coordination, illness management, and collaboration across disciplines. Social workers provide the majority of mental health services in the United States and are well versed in these competencies. The goal of the ExCEL training was to enhance the skills and leadership capabilities of oncology social workers so that key concepts of the IOM report would be successfully implemented in oncology practices and health care settings. To maximize the ability to reach oncology social workers, the City of Hope, under the leadership of principal investigator Shirley Otis-Green, partnered with the Association of Oncology Social Work (AOSW) and the Association of Pediatric Oncology Social Workers (APOSW) to provide training as a preconference program tied to the respective organizations' annual conferences. The projected goal was that 400 social workers would receive this training and facilitate implementation of the IOM recommendations. This grant is a model for future initiatives to train large cohorts of oncology social workers on these key issues (City of Hope, 2014).

The ACOS COC is a consortium of professional health care organizations that sets standards, accredits cancer programs, collects data, and monitors compliance. The original focus was surgical but has evolved to encompass all aspects of cancer care. In the mid-1960s, the ACOS added Commission on Cancer to its name to reflect this broader focus (ACOS COC, 2012). The COC paid close attention to incorporating recommendations from the IOM report *Ensuring Quality Cancer Care* and continues to draw on subsequent IOM reports, such as *Cancer Care for the Whole Patient,* as standards are developed, reviewed, and refined to ensure that the highest quality of cancer care is achieved.

The COC program standards are ensuring patient-centered care is a priority, with guidelines being phased in over several years that relate to screening for psychosocial distress; providing cancer survivors with increased support; ensuring palliative care services are available; and encouraging the use of patient navigators to guide patients through complicated procedures and systems.

The AOSW has supported the aims of the IOM report in specific ways by becoming a member of the Alliance for Quality Psychosocial Cancer Care, by having the AOSW represented as an important member of the ACOS COC, and by partnering with City of Hope to host the ExCEL program. The November 2012 edition of the *Journal of Psychosocial Oncology,* the official journal of the AOSW, is devoted entirely to scholarly articles related to distress screening (Zabora, 2012).

The American Psychosocial Oncology Society (APOS) has been active in promoting implementation of the recommendations of the IOM report. Members of APOS were key in bringing the *Alliance for Quality Cancer Care* into being. APOS published a special edition of the *Journal of Clinical Oncology* devoted to the science of psychosocial care (APOS, 2012). The special journal editions, the webinars, and ExCEL are but a few of the many examples of publications and trainings that have been a direct result of the publication of this report and a response to the challenge to improve psychosocial care for the whole patient.

Finally, the American Society of Clinical Oncology (ASCO) developed a Quality Oncology Practice Initiative that began as a pilot project and has grown steadily over the years. In the beginning, the quality indicators looked at issues related to staging disease, chemotherapy administration, pain management, and smoking cessation. In 2008, ASCO, in conjunction with APOS, integrated new psychosocial indicators related to emotional well-being. They recognized the value of paying attention to the emotional and psychosocial impact of illness and felt this needed to be monitored (Jacobsen & Wagner, 2012). ASCO and the Oncology Nursing Society (ONS), in a joint consensus project, developed Standards for Safe Chemotherapy Administration (ASCO-ONS, 2011) for the ambulatory setting. These standards now include a recommendation that oncology practices and institutions assess for psychosocial concerns and maintain referral resources for psychosocial and other supportive care services. Chemotherapy guidelines now include mention of the psychosocial needs of patients and draw attention to the fact that the whole patient must be the focus of attention.

Although each IOM report is important in its own right, *Cancer Care for the Whole Patient,* with its in-depth examination of psychosocial concerns and the value the report placed on screening, assessment, and intervention, is especially important to the social work profession. Having experts from multiple fields do a thorough examination of the issues validates what oncology social workers know to be true.

Focusing on the whole patient is an imperative, not an option. Relieving suffering and overcoming barriers where we can is morally and ethically appropriate. Excellent and complete cancer care of the highest quality will be achieved when we combine the best in psychosocial care with the best in biomedical care. Social workers can continue to lead the way.

Pearls

- *Cancer Care for the Whole Patient* strongly advocates the long-standing value and practice standard of oncology social work that psychosocial care needs to be on par and integrated with medical care.
- Developing stronger synergy between oncology institutions and oncology social work departments can propel greater change.

Pitfalls

- Failure to address psychosocial problems results in needless suffering and obstructs quality care.
- Not all practice settings have the infrastructure to implement change.

ADDITIONAL RESOURCES

American College of Surgeons' Commission on Cancer: http://www.facs.org/cancer/
American Psychosocial Oncology Society: http://www.apos-society.org
American Society of Clinical Oncology: http://www.cancer.net
Association of Oncology Social Work: http://www.aosw.org
C-Change, Collaborating to Conquer Cancer: http://c-changetogether.org

ExCEL Training: http://www.cityofhope.org/excel-curriculum
National Comprehensive Cancer Network: http://www.nccn.org/about/

REFERENCES

Adler, N. (Ed.). (2008). *Cancer care for the whole patient: Meeting psychosocial health needs.* Washington, DC: National Academies Press.

Alter, C. (2009). Predictors of referral for psychosocial services: Recommendations from the IOM report; Cancer Care for the Whole Patient. *Journal of Clinical Oncology, 27*(5), 659–660.

American College of Surgeons' Commission on Cancer (ACOS COC). (2012). *Cancer program standards 2012: Ensuring patient-centered care.* Chicago, IL: ACOS.

American Psychosocial Oncology Society (APOS). (2012). [Special issue]. *Journal of Clinical Oncology, 30*(11).

American Society for Clinical Oncology and Oncology Nursing Society (ACSO-ONS). (2011). Standards for safe chemotherapy administration 2011. Retrieved from http://www.asco.org/quality-guidelines/asco-ons-standards-safe-chemotherapy-administration

Center for Advancing Health (CFAH). (2014). Alliance for Quality Psychosocial Cancer Care. Retrieved from http://www.cfah.org/about/alliance-for-quality-psychosocial-cancer-care

City of Hope. (2014). ExCEL in social work curriculum. Retrieved from http://www.cityofhope.org/excel-curriculum

Finn, R. (2000). Flurry of activity follows report on quality cancer care. *Journal of the National Cancer Institute, 92*(23), 1871–1873.

Ganz, P. (2013). *Delivering high-quality cancer care: Charting a new course for a system in crisis.* Washington, DC: National Academies Press.

Hewitt, M., Greenfield, S., & Stovall, E. (Eds.). (2006). *From cancer patient to cancer survivor: Lost in transition.* Washington, DC: National Academies Press.

Houlihan, N. (2009). Transitioning to cancer survivorship: Plans of care. Retrieved from http://www.cancernetwork.com/nurses/content/article/10165/1434523

Howley, P., & Simone, J. (Eds.). (1999). *Ensuring quality cancer care.* Washington, DC: National Academies Press.

Institute of Medicine (IOM). (2014). About the IOM. Retrieved http://www.iom.edu/About-IOM.aspx

Jacobsen, P., & Wagner, L. (2012). A new quality standard: The integration of psychosocial care into routine cancer care. *Journal of Clinical Oncology, 30*(11), 1154–1159.

National Comprehensive Cancer Network (NCCN). (2014a). Clinical practice guidelines in oncology practice for distress management. Retrieved https://www5.medicine.wisc.edu/~williams/distress.pdf

National Comprehensive Cancer Network (NCCN). (2014b). NCCN history. Retrieved http://www.nccn.org/about/history.aspx

Rose, C., Stovall, E., Ganz, P., Desch, C., & Hewitt, M. (2008). Cancer Quality Alliance: Blueprint for a better cancer care system. *CA: Cancer Journal for Clinicians, 58,* 266–292.

Zabora, J. (Ed.). (2012). Distress screening: Approaches and recommendations for oncology social workers. *Journal of Psychosocial Oncology, 30*(6), 694–714.

II

Cancer Across a Continuum of Care: Clinical Practice, Opportunities, and Challenges

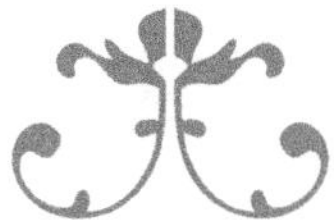

Brad Zebrack

From the moment of diagnosis, people are living with cancer. They may have been living with cancer-related pain, discomfort, or consternation before their diagnosis, suggesting that cancer patients bring a medical history, as well as a psychosocial history, into their encounters with oncology care providers.

In "Oncology Social Work Interventions Throughout the Continuum of Cancer Care," Brad Zebrack, Barbara L. Jones, and Kathryn M. Smolinski emphasize that cancer is not simply a biological or physiological condition but also a process of living that encompasses a broad range of psychosocial, spiritual, and cultural issues. They describe how oncology social workers attend to the impact of cancer in these multiple and varied life domains throughout a continuum of care that initiates at diagnosis and continues through phases of treatment and subsequent transitions to off-treatment survivorship or the end of life.

Subsequent chapters in this section detail the specific challenges faced by cancer patients throughout a continuum of care and the processes of resilience they employ. In "Diagnosis and Initiation of Cancer Treatment," Karen Kell Hartman identifies key psychosocial issues that arise for patients as they react to their diagnosis, engage in initial testing and staging procedures, gather and attempt to make sense of information, confront important decisions, and engage in an initial treatment process.

Following diagnosis and the initiation of treatment, patients are challenged to adapt to the disruptions that cancer and its treatment will have on their lives. Paul G. Clark and Sage Bolte discuss these challenges in "Sense Making in Living With Cancer as a Chronic Illness." They describe how patients try to comprehend what is happening to them and the role that oncology social workers can play in guiding patients in this coping process.

When active treatment ends, the posttreatment phase of survivorship begins for increasing numbers of people whose cancers have been resected, "cured," or put into remission for some uncertain length of time. In "Cancer Survivorship: Concepts, Interventions, and Research," Penny Damaskos and Carly Parry examine various conceptualizations of cancer survivorship and what it means to people to be (or not be) a cancer "survivor." They offer a review of psychosocial care options for patients and families as they transition into this phase of the cancer care continuum.

For all cancer patients, there is an end to therapy. This end may signify a transition to disease-free survival or a need to manage recurring malignancies or chronic health conditions related to cancer or its treatment. For some, the end of therapy signifies the end of life. In "Transition to End-of-Life Care in Oncology," Deborah Waldrop and Sherri Weisenfluh describe the emotional, psychological, social, and spiritual conditions that accompany this transition and the need for support that oncology social workers can and do provide.

6

Brad Zebrack, Barbara L. Jones, and Kathryn M. Smolinski

Oncology Social Work Interventions Throughout the Continuum of Cancer Care

Key Concepts

- *Oncology social work services are provided throughout a continuum of care that begins at diagnosis, continues through phases of treatment, and transitions to off-treatment survival or advanced illness.*
- *Patient-centered care may be best understood as a theoretical conceptualization of survivorship that goes beyond an exclusive focus on the trajectory of the disease and treatment process to encompass a broad range of psychosocial, spiritual, and cultural issues.*
- *Achieving quality cancer care in the 21st century requires oncology social workers to deliver care and services that will vary depending on where patients and families are on the continuum of care.*

Cancer is not a single event with a certain end. It is an enduring condition characterized by ongoing uncertainty, potentially delayed or late effects of the disease or treatment, and concurrent psychosocial and contextual issues. Cancer is not just "a disease process with associated medical treatment, but also a succession of social interactions and psychological conditions that accompany and sometimes affect the etiology, timing, and course of the disease" (Riley, 1983, p. 26). Understanding cancer as an experience of illness, and not simply as a physiologic or biologic state of disease, is imperative for delivering high-quality, patient-centered care.

Patient-centered care is a goal for oncology care (Rose, Stovall, Ganz, Desch, & Hewitt, 2008), as well as a fundamental principle guiding the practice of social work. This focus emphasizes the importance of the patient's and family's voices in decision making, medical planning, and care. It requires those caring for cancer patients and their families to be attuned to patient values and concerns, such as pain and symptom management, psychological and emotional distress, future orientation, and attainment of goals and achievements (even short-term ones). Patient-centered care also considers the impact of cancer on family members and loved ones, relationship and identity issues, re-entry into school or work, adequate health insurance coverage, financial stability, and even end-of-life decision making and grief. Oncology social workers recognize that providing the best possible services across a continuum of care requires an understanding of how cancer impacts the multiple and varied dimensions of people's lives.

The concept of cancer survivorship provides a framework for understanding how cancer impacts people's lives from the time of diagnosis through treatment and transitions into posttreatment survival or the end of life (Clark & Stovall, 1996). *Cancer survivorship* is a term that has come to represent a state or process of living following a cancer diagnosis, regardless of how long a person lives. Many health care professionals, researchers, and cancer patients use this concept to understand not only the physical but also the social, psychological, and spiritual/existential qualities of one's life. When viewed as a continual, dynamic, and ever-changing process that begins at the moment of diagnosis and may continue for the remainder of life, cancer

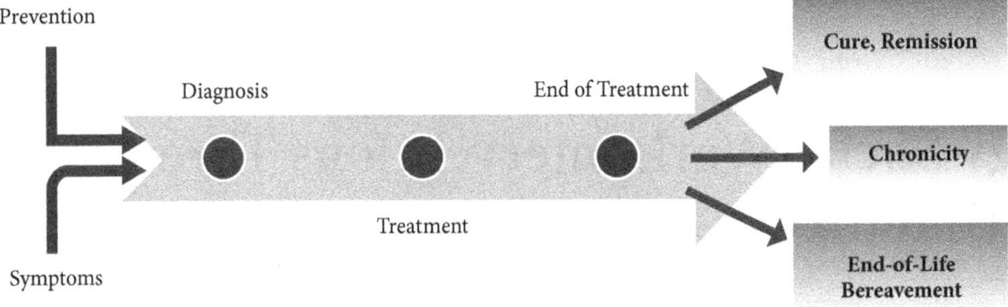

Figure 6.1. Cancer Survivorship Continuum of Care

survivorship can be defined as the experience of "living with, through, or beyond cancer" (Leigh, 1992).

Cancer survivorship is *not* the same as surviving a cancer diagnosis, nor is it a distinct event or even a series of distinct events bounded by time. This constantly shifting landscape is limited neither to people who are cancer free nor to people who have completed cancer treatment, and it involves others beyond the person who has had a cancer diagnosis. A dominant biomedical perspective on survivorship suggests that it is a spectrum of medical and nonmedical issues, including short- and long-term treatment-related side effects, development of second cancers, and psychological and psychosocial perturbations associated with a post-treatment phase (Wolff, 2007). However, the biomedical conceptualization of survivorship has limited application to clinical practice because it does not mesh with how patients and families view themselves and their experiences. For example, some patients who have completed treatment and are disease free do not consider themselves "survivors," whereas others in active treatment may consider themselves "survivors" by virtue of being alive and enduring therapy. The true nature of cancer often involves moving back and forth, in and out, through phases of diagnosis, treatment, remission, recurrence, more treatment, "cure," and, in some cases, end of life.

This chapter describes the continuum-of-care perspective, the psychosocial impact of cancer, and strategies for improving quality in cancer care in the 21st century. We also discuss the role of research in advancing social work practice and future opportunities and challenges in oncology social work with both children and adults.

Continuum of Care

Cancer survivorship provides an excellent framework for guiding oncology social work practice. Conceptualizing survivorship as a process of living that is initiated at diagnosis and continues throughout the phases of treatment and transition to off-treatment survival and, for some, the end of life gives a context for understanding and addressing patient and family needs and issues as they occur and reoccur throughout a continuum of care (see Figure 6.1). A continuum of care suggests that oncology care providers need to assess and address patient and family risks and needs over time. Furthermore, these risks and experiences vary depending on such factors as age at diagnosis, race, ethnic and cultural background, socioeconomic status, and the extent and quality of a person's relationships and support networks.

Psychosocial Impact of Cancer

A patient-centered approach to care involves assisting individuals and their families to retain or return to quality functioning in social roles, such as spouse/partner, parent, worker, or friend. Successful interventions enable individuals and families to overcome the detrimental impact of a crisis and strengthen the environmental and intrapersonal resources available to them to cope with that crisis. Stress-coping theories, theories of human development and the life span, and ecological systems theories are useful for enhancing our understanding of how cancer affects people's lives and how oncology social workers may intervene to prevent or mitigate negative psychosocial outcomes and also promote positive adaptation and coping.

Stress-Coping Models

Psychosocial care is grounded in a stress-coping paradigm that emphasizes biological and environmental, as well as psychosocial and behavioral, risk factors that influence the impact of cancer on patients and their families. Since cancer is not a single stressor but a collection of diverse stressful situations and challenges that occur from the time of diagnosis throughout the remainder of one's life, it makes sense to identify issues likely to disrupt patients' lives that may have lifelong implications.

Stress-coping models are informative for understanding how stressful experiences like cancer challenge people in various domains of their life experience, requiring coping strategies. Stress emerges from having to seek and understand medical information; from having to deal with practical/instrumental activities of daily living and emotional responses to cancer, as well as the emotional responses of others and changes and challenges in interpersonal relationships; and finally, from existential challenges. These challenges occur throughout the cancer survivorship continuum, and they may wax and wane depending on where individuals fall along the continuum.

In a review of studies on coping and adjustment, Rowland (1989) categorized a universal set of cancer-related disruptions that occur across social roles and throughout the survivorship trajectory. These disruptions involve (1) altered interpersonal relationships, (2) struggles with dependence and independence, (3) goals and achievements, (4) concerns about body and sexual image, and (5) existential issues, including fears of mortality. As a result of these stressors, patients and families draw upon intrapersonal, interpersonal, social, and environmental resources to help them cope. Merluzzi, Nairn, Hegde, Sanchez, and Dunn (2001) suggest that adequate coping with cancer requires that patients successfully seek and understand medical information, manage side effects/late effects of therapy, manage stresses of everyday life, respond to emotional reactions (their own and those of others), maintain social and physical activity to the extent possible, locate peer support, and achieve acceptance.

Developmental Perspectives

A life-course perspective on cancer suggests that individuals at different life stages experience a common set of disruptions but experience them differently. They focus on issues most relevant to their stage and attach varying levels of importance to aspects of their experience. In their qualitative study of women with breast cancer, Oktay and Walter (1991) found that regardless of age, "each woman must manage the psychological reactions . . . , learn to preserve and satisfy body image, maintain satisfactory sexual relationships, adjust to role shifts, and deal with an uncertain future. In different life stages, however, different tasks come into sharper focus and seem to occupy more of the attention of the women at this stage" (p. 192). For example, "achieving independence," "developing intimate relationships," and "finding a place in the adult world" were key issues young adult women in their 20s emphasized, whereas women in middle adulthood (40s and 50s) were more concerned with issues involving their relationships with mothers, spouses, and adolescent children. In this case, an individual's life stage determined relevant life tasks, and the cancer experience was tied to the achievement of those tasks. Given the potential for long-term and late effects of cancer and its treatment, cancer-related life disruptions are not limited to the periods of diagnosis and active treatment (or watchful waiting) but may occur throughout the remainder of one's life. Cultural values and beliefs further influence how these disruptions are experienced and expressed to others.

Socioecological Systems Perspective

A socioecological model is an effective way to identify the multilevel psychosocial barriers that may contribute to disparities in cancer patient outcomes and benefits from health care services (Green, Richard, & Potvin, 1996; Wells & Zebrack, 2008). It enables us to examine how micro-, meso-, and macro-level factors influence patients' and families' experiences of cancer. An assumption of a socioecological perspective is that varying levels of influence operate simultaneously within and between levels and subsequently impact individual behavior. The model thus guides social workers to think about multilevel interventions and about how attention to, and changes within, communities, institutions, and/or society at large may be required to achieve enhanced patient and family outcomes.

Quality Cancer Care in the 21st Century

Given cancer's universal disruptions and their variation by age-graded life stages, "adjustment" becomes the extent to which individuals are able to overcome the effects of these disruptions in the performance of salient social roles and everyday lives. Furthermore, the extent to which individuals appraise these disruptions as meaningful or necessitating a response depends on the developmental, sociocultural, biomedical, and psychological contexts in which they are experienced. For instance, the experience and meaning of intimacy, an important factor affecting well-being, will be different for a young, unmarried, off-treatment survivor trying to figure out if and when to disclose the effects of cancer treatment to a potential partner than it will be for an older adult in an established relationship. Add in ways in which culturally influenced beliefs, attitudes, and values about religion, illness, medical treatment, and social relationships contribute to behavior and experience, and the result is great variation both within and across different survivorship trajectories.

Therefore, culturally appropriate and relevant social work involves adequate assessment of the multiple and varied ways in which patients understand and experience their disease. Psychosocial assessments must account for the extent to which the physical, social, emotional, spiritual, or financial concomitants of illness affect patient and family well-being.

Each year, approximately 1.4 million people in the United States are diagnosed with cancer (Jemal et al., 2005). Only 11% of adult patients obtain care at a hospital or comprehensive cancer center; most (80%) will receive care through a community-based physician's office or group practice (Institute of Medicine, 2008). For children diagnosed with cancer, over 90% will receive their care in one of the nearly 250 children's hospitals in the United States. By 2050, the absolute number of people aged 65 and older diagnosed with cancer is expected to double, thereby putting greater demand on service providers and systems of care (Edwards et al., 2002). With mortality and survival rates having improved over the past 35 years in the United States, we can anticipate greater numbers of people living with, through, and beyond cancer. However, these improvements have not been experienced equally by individuals who are poor or of racial/ethnic minority status (Jemal et al., 2005).

Oncology Social Work in the United States

Oncology social workers have a long tradition of working on the front lines of cancer care, helping cancer patients access needed health care services and overcome barriers to care. Today, oncology social workers are the primary providers of psychosocial services in major oncology treatment centers and community health care settings throughout the world. Oncology social workers serve on multidisciplinary teams in cancer centers, children's hospitals, and community hospitals, and sometimes in oncology group practices. Some devote all their time to oncology services; others rotate through oncology as one among several service units.

In most ambulatory fee-for-service or managed-care institutional settings, oncology social workers receive a set salary, and their work is included as part of a cost-center reimbursement formula. Except for some who maintain private practices, few oncology social workers charge a fee for services rendered. For those in private practice who provide psychotherapy, reimbursement rates vary by insurer.

Oncology social workers are uniquely positioned to build networks for their patients and families involving health care clinical settings, community agencies, and cancer advocacy groups. This is a pivotal task designed to secure a continuum of services throughout treatment and survivorship for cancer patients and their caregivers. Numerous community agencies and national cancer organizations employ social workers to provide direct services. In fact, the Institute of Medicine (2008) report *Cancer Care for the Whole Patient: Meeting Psychosocial Health Needs* identifies over 50 national organizations that provide psychosocial health services in the form of information and/or support for cancer patients. They include, but are not limited to, the American Cancer Society, Wellness Community, Cancer*Care*, Leukemia and Lymphoma Society, Children's Brain Tumor Foundation, and the LIVE**STRONG** Foundation. Social workers employed by these organizations provide crucial support, education, and advocacy, as well as opportunities for mutual support and connection among patients and survivors.

Smith, Walsh-Burke, and Cruzan (1998, p. 1061) noted that "the complexity and variability of psychosocial issues associated with cancer has created the demand for highly skilled practitioners who are trained to provide multilevel assessment and intervention throughout the [continuum of care]." The direct service tasks oncology social workers carry out include (1) screening and psychosocial assessment; (2) facilitating adjustment to illness; (3) provision of emotional support, counseling, and psychotherapy for individuals, families, and groups; (4) discharge planning; (5) referral; and (6) advocacy. Walsh (2005) identifies points along a continuum of care—from diagnosis through treatment through off-treatment survivorship or end of life—at which these tasks are required. Both the Association of Oncology Social Work (AOSW, http://www.aosw.org) and the Association of Pediatric Oncology Social Workers (APOSW, http://www.aposw.org) have documents detailing the goals, scopes, and standards of practice for oncology social workers.

Pediatric Oncology

Pediatric oncology social work is a specialty discipline committed to enhancing the emotional and physical well-being of children with cancer and their families. Pediatric oncology social work has many similarities to that for adults, yet some areas of focus are distinctive. Care for children with cancer differs from that for adults in part because children cannot consent to and sometimes do not understand their treatment regimens. Pediatric oncology social work must incorporate a unique understanding of developmentally appropriate interventions and communication, the role of parents as surrogate decision makers, and the needs of siblings and other children. Pediatric oncology social workers focus on empowering children to be involved in their own decision making along with their families and treatment teams. Practice is based on knowledge and expertise in the areas of child and adolescent development and family systems. Pediatric oncology social workers also work in community-based agencies, hospices, camps, and advocacy organizations. In children's hospitals, pediatric oncology social workers provide assessment, counseling and support, advocacy, resources, and medical education.

Pediatric oncology social workers offer supportive counseling and developmentally appropriate interventions with children. The social worker often plays an essential supportive role in helping the family during transitions from curative to palliative or survivorship care (Jones, 2005). Interventions include but are not limited to biofeedback, hypnosis, meditation, psychoeducational and therapeutic support groups, implementation of neurological testing, cognitive behavioral interventions, art therapy, school re-entry, and exercise promotion. Pediatric oncology social workers also provide palliative care to mitigate symptoms and support children and families when cure may no longer be possible.

Culturally Appropriate Care

Understanding patient and family needs, risks, lifestyles, and potentials for positive adaptation to a life-threatening illness necessitates an awareness of the strong, often covert influences of culture, race/ethnicity, and socioeconomic status in shaping family reactions and responses to health problems (McCubbin, Thompson, Thompson, McCubbin, & Kaston, 1993). Results from a survey of oncology social work professionals (Zebrack, Walsh, Burg, Maramaldi, & Lim, 2008) suggest that too few oncology social workers are prepared to meet the needs of multiethnic groups of cancer patients. For example, half of the sample reported little to no competence in working with non-English-speaking populations. Thus, educating and training social workers who themselves have diverse backgrounds and languages is an important, growing need in all fields of social work, including oncology. To meet the needs of an increasingly diverse patient population, the social work profession should develop innovative methods for recruiting new social workers from various ethnic and language groups and at the same time prepare new and seasoned social workers to conduct psychosocial assessments and implement supportive interventions within patients' own cultural context and language.

Observations and studies of accumulative stress and temporal clustering of stressful life events among minority populations suggest a higher prevalence of psychological and physical health morbidity in low socioeconomic status and racial/ethnic minority populations (Williams & Jackson, 2000). These are the undeniable effects of the everyday realities of racism, sexism, and other forms of interpersonal and institutionalized discrimination. Their existence reinforces the need for clinicians to be cognizant of stressful, nonmedical events (e.g., inadequate funds for transportation to clinics or job loss for a parent who missed work to be with an ill child), as well as the context of cultural and socioeconomic inequality and discrimination in which these events take place and the culturally derived meanings persons of diverse backgrounds attribute to these events.

Oncology Social Work Research and Future Prospects

Oncology social workers are ethically obligated to provide services informed by evidence (National Association of Social Workers' Code of Ethics). Indeed, the psychological and social problems created or exacerbated by cancer can be effectively addressed by psychosocial interventions that are often delivered or facilitated by social workers (Cwikel, Behar, & Rabson-Hare, 2000; Faller et al., 2013; Gottlieb & Wachala, 2007; Graves, 2003; Holland et al., 2010; Jacobsen & Jim, 2008; Meyer & Mark, 1995). Yet many empirical and practical questions remain regarding the value and efficacy of new and emerging psychosocial assessment strategies and interventions such as distress screening, survivorship care planning, and the use of technology to address the supportive care needs of patients, survivors, and their families. Further research is needed to bolster an evidence base regarding best practices, processes, and measurement approaches as they relate to these social work practices. Continuous evaluation efforts also are needed within institutions, clinics, and agencies to monitor the uptake, efficiency, and effectiveness of psychosocial support strategies for performance measurement and quality improvement purposes (Parry, Padgett, & Zebrack, 2012).

In support of the delivery of quality and equitable cancer care, it is incumbent upon the oncology social work profession to promote the dissemination and diffusion of evidence-based practice as informed by an adequate knowledge base, practice wisdom, and common sense (Gilgun, 2005). Oncology social workers must play a role in enhancing the social work knowledge base, thereby enhancing a foundation from which strengths-based interventions and other information of relevance promote the practice of social work in clinical and community settings. Moreover, organizations should increase efforts to work collaboratively to advance the preparation and ability of oncology social workers to take part in the research enterprise.

The Future of Oncology Social Work

Current social trends toward self-care, empowerment, consumer activism, improved access to information, and growth in mutual aid networks are challenging. They will continue to challenge medical social workers to shift from an emphasis on delivering inpatient direct services to providing some outpatient direct services and to collaborate more extensively with family caregivers, community-based agencies, and other key supporters involved in providing ongoing care for patients and families (Blum et al., 2006).

Community-focused interventions offer new and fertile ground for proactive social work involvement. Social work at the community level requires establishing relationships with community leaders, assessing gaps in community service, and facilitating establishment of new services. As clinicians, social workers serve as direct advocates, a role assumed when addressing the psychosocial needs of groups of patients and families. Yet, the work need not stop at the level of interpersonal practice:

> *As advocates for the consumers of health care services, clinical social workers can design programs and develop or promote policies that include opportunities for patients and family members to offer their perspectives on health care delivery. Parents and patients may be invited to offer suggestions to committees that set policies for clinic*

> *and hospital operations or may serve as representatives to these committees. Social workers can effectively serve families by assuming this kind of advocacy stance when participating in activities sponsored by voluntary health organizations or governmental agencies.*
>
> *(Stovall, 1993, p. 252)*

Underserved Populations

The barriers faced in accessing quality cancer care by underserved and vulnerable individuals within subgroups of the population require novel approaches to meet patients' needs. Using patient navigators for vulnerable cancer patients is one such method (Steinberg et al., 2006). The National Cancer Institute and many community-based organizations together are sponsoring the development and evaluation of patient navigation programs in oncology settings to reduce disparities in cancer detection, treatment, and outcomes among racial and ethnic minorities and vulnerable patients. Patient navigation "refers to individualized assistance offered to patients, families, and caregivers to help overcome health care system barriers and facilitate timely access to quality medical and psychosocial care from pre-diagnosis through all phases of the cancer experience" (C-Change, 2005). Some navigation models use volunteer navigators who require oversight and supervision, whereas others use paid staff, including social workers and nurses. Oncology social workers are trained to implement and promote patient navigation programs within their institution and out in the community. In some instances, social workers take on the role of the navigator, depending on how it is structured, or else direct the navigator program itself, including supervision and training of volunteers in areas of communication skills and interpersonal relations.

Patient navigation programs, which often provide case management and advocacy, are based on social work principles and reflect the functions of oncology social workers. In fact, oncology social workers were instrumental in shaping one of the first navigation systems for cancer patients and their caregivers, the *Cancer Survival Toolbox* (National Coalition for Cancer Survivorship, 2004). This 10-module audio program was designed to help individuals develop skills to better meet and understand the challenges of cancer, including communicating with the care team, finding and integrating essential information about cancer, and paying for their care costs. It was produced through a collaboration of the National Coalition for Cancer Survivorship, the Oncology Nursing Society, and the AOSW. Today, many oncology social workers are leading navigation services in medical settings (Lauria & Walsh, 2005).

Professional Associations

The need for networking, resource sharing, and evidence-based research is inherent in a helping profession such as social work, especially in the oncology setting where limited resources are tapped daily and science dominates the selection of treatment approaches. Professional associations such as the AOSW, the APOSW, and the American Psychosocial Oncology Society specialize in training and education, research, networking, and advocacy to enhance clinical practice for both their members and oncology professionals at large. Many oncology social workers belong to at least one of these organizations. Both the AOSW and APOSW focus primarily on the continuing educational and professional needs of social workers along with advocacy, education, and research efforts to improve care for cancer patients and their families.

Pearls

- Assess and provide support throughout a continuum of survivorship, which may encompass many phases of diagnosis, treatment, remission, recurrence, more treatment, "cure," and, for some, end-of-life care, and work with patients who are dying.
- Providing culturally appropriate and beneficial services requires that social workers understand how individuals' life experiences and socioecological contexts influence their experience with cancer. Social workers function as advocates for this perspective within the interdisciplinary team.

Pitfalls

- Confusing cancer survivorship with survival or conceptualizing survival as that phase of life that occurs after completion of therapy.
- Insufficient understanding of strategies for working with racially, ethnically, and culturally diverse groups of patients.

Today, oncology social workers must be knowledgeable about myriad factors that influence the delivery and receipt of cancer care in the United States and around the world. They also must intervene to address psychosocial needs where they are most acute and be proactive in the innovation, creation, and delivery of relevant and appropriate services to socioeconomically, culturally, and ethnically diverse populations. This often requires not only the development of programs and treatment models but also simultaneous implementation and evaluation studies to determine which programs and interventions are most effective for which clients and client populations.

The societal benefits of social work interventions with cancer patients will be expansive if evidence-informed interventions are accessible to all survivors, from the start of treatment on, and to their caregivers. To remain viable, the profession must provide basic training and continuous professional development opportunities that prepare workers to effectively deliver quality care in the 21st century. Much of this effort needs to be provided in the context of community-based care as the health care continuum continues to shift from acute-care settings to outpatient settings, including people's own homes. As geographic communities increasingly become the settings for provision of services, social workers must be prepared to work effectively and appropriately with persons and families of varied race and ethnic groups, ages, socioeconomic levels, languages, and sexual orientations. The oncology social work profession is contributing to the development of this body of knowledge and skills. The challenge now is to translate and expand this knowledge base so as to impact a wider population of survivors over the entire continuum of care.

REFERENCES

Blum, D., Clark, E. J., Jacobsen, P. B., Holland, J., Monahan, M. J., & Duquette, P. D. (2006). Building community-based short-term psychosocial counseling capacity for cancer patients and their families: The Individual Cancer Assistance Network (ICAN) model. *Social Work in Health Care, 43*(4), 71–83.

C-Change. (2005). Cancer patient navigation: Care for your community. Retrieved from http://www.cancerpatientnavigation.org/resources.html

Clark, E. J., & Stovall, E. L. (1996). Advocacy: The cornerstone of cancer survivorship. *Cancer Practice, 4*(5), 239–244.

Cwikel, J., Behar, L., & Rabson-Hare, J. (2000). A comparison of a vote count and meta-analysis review of intervention research with adult cancer patients. *Research on Social Work Practice, 10*(1), 139–158.

Edwards, B. K., Howe, H. L., Ries, L. A. G., Thun, M., Rosenberg, H. M., Yancik, R., ... Feigal, E. G. (2002). Annual report to the nation on the status of cancer, 1973–1999, featuring implications of age and aging on the US cancer burden. *Cancer, 94*(10), 2766–2792.

Faller, H., Schuler, M., Richard, M., Heckl, U., Weis, J., & Kuffner, R. (2013). Effects of psycho-oncologic interventions on emotional distress and quality of life in adult patients with cancer: Systematic review and meta-analysis. *Journal of Clinical Oncology, 31*(6), 782–793.

Gilgun, J. F. (2005). The four cornerstones of evidence-based practice in social work. *Research on Social Work Practice, 15*(1), 52–61.

Gottlieb, B. H., & Wachala, E. D. (2007). Cancer support groups: A critical review of empirical studies. *Psycho-Oncology, 16*, 379–400.

Graves, K. D. (2003). Social cognitive theory and cancer patients' quality of life: A meta-analysis of psychosocial intervention components. *Health Psychology, 22*(2), 210–219.

Green, L. W., Richard, L., & Potvin, L. (1996). Ecological foundations of health promotion. *American Journal of Health Promotion, 10*(4), 270–281.

Holland, J., Andersen, B., Breitbart, W. S., Compas, B., management. *Journal of the National Comprehensive Cancer Network, 8*, 448–485.

Institute of Medicine. (2008). *Cancer care for the whole patient: Meeting psychosocial health needs*. Washington, DC: National Academies Press.

Jacobsen, P. B., & Jim, H. S. (2008). Psychosocial interventions for anxiety and depression in adult cancer patients: Achievements and challenges. *CA: A Cancer Journal for Clinicians, 58*, 214–230.

Jemal, A., Murray, T., Ward, E., Samuels, A., Tiwari, R. C., Ghafoor, A., ... Thun, M. J. (2005). Cancer statistics, 2005. *CA: A Cancer Journal for Clinicians, 55*(1), 10–30.

Jones, B. (2005). Pediatric palliative and end-of-life care: The role of social work in pediatric oncology. *Journal of Social Work in End-of-Life and Palliative Care, 1*(4), 35–62.

Lauria, M., & Walsh, K. (2005, May). *Patient navigation: Helping survivors and families through the cancer care maze*. Paper presented at the Association of Oncology Social Workers, Austin, TX.

Leigh, S. (1992). Myths, monsters, and magic: Personal perspectives and professional challenges of survival. *Oncology Nursing Forum, 19*, 1475–1480.

McCubbin, H. I., Thompson, E. A., Thompson, A. I., McCubbin, M. A., & Kaston, A. J. (1993). Culture, ethnicity, and the family: Critical factors in childhood chronic illnesses and disabilities. *Pediatrics, 91*(5), 1063–1070.

Merluzzi, T. V., Nairn, R. C., Hegde, K., Sanchez, M. A. M., & Dunn, L. (2001). Self-efficacy for coping with cancer: Revision of the Cancer Behavior Inventory (Version 2.0). *Psycho-Oncology, 10*, 206–217.

Meyer, T. J., & Mark, M. M. (1995). Effects of psychosocial interventions with adult cancer patients: A meta-analysis of randomized experiments. *Health Psychology, 14*(2), 101–108.

National Coalition for Cancer Survivorship. (2004). *Cancer survival toolbox*. Silver Spring, MD: Author.

Oktay, J. S., & Walter, C. A. (1991). *Breast cancer in the life course* (Vol. 20). New York, NY: Springer Publishing Company.

Parry, C., Padgett, L. S., & Zebrack, B. (2012). Now what? Toward an integrated research and practice agenda in distress screening. *Journal of Psychosocial Oncology, 30*, 715–727.

Riley, M. W. (1983). Cancer and the life course. In R. Yancik (Ed.), *Perspectives on prevention and treatment of cancer in the elderly* (pp. 25–32). New York, NY: Raven Press.

Rose, C., Stovall, E. L., Ganz, P. A., Desch, C., & Hewitt, M. (2008). Cancer quality alliance: Blueprint for a better cancer care system. *CA: A Cancer Journal for Clinicians, 58*(5), 266–292.

Rowland, J. H. (1989). Developmental stage and adaptation: Adult model. In J. C. Holland & J. H. Rowland (Eds.), *Handbook of psychooncology* (pp. 25–43). New York, NY: Oxford University Press.

Smith, E., Walsh-Burke, K., & Cruzan, C. (1998). Principles of training social workers in oncology. In J. Holland (Ed.), *Psycho-oncology* (pp. 1061–1068). New York, NY: Oxford University Press.

Steinberg, M. L., Fremont, A., Khan, D. C., Huang, D., Knapp, H., Karaman, D., ... Streeter, O. E. (2006). Lay patient navigator program implementation for equal access to cancer care and clinical trials: Essential steps and initial challenges. *Cancer, 107*(11), 2669–2677.

Stovall, A. (1993). Social work services for the child and family. In

(Eds.), *Oncology social work: A clinician's guide* (pp. 237–255). Atlanta, GA: American Cancer Society.

Walsh, K. (2005). *Oncology social work roles and functions across the continuum of care.* Washington, DC: National Patient Advocate Foundation.

Wells, A. A., & Zebrack, B. J. (2008). Psychosocial barriers contributing to the underrepresentation of racial/ethnic minorities in cancer clinical trials. *Social Work in Health Care, 46*(2), 1–14.

Williams, D. R., & Jackson, J. S. (2000). Race/ethnicity and the 2000 census: Recommendations for African American and other black populations in the United States. *American Journal of Public Health, 90*(11), 1728–1730.

Wolff, S. N. (2007). The burden of cancer survivorship: A pandemic of treatment success. In M. Feuerstein (Ed.), *Handbook of cancer survivorship* (pp. 7–18). New York, NY: Springer.

Zebrack, B., Walsh, K., Burg, M., Maramaldi, P., & Lim, J. (2008). Oncology social worker competencies and implications for education and training. *Social Work in Health Care, 47*(4), 355–375.

7 Diagnosis and Initiation of Cancer Treatment

Karen Kell Hartman

Key Concepts

- *The use of targeted cancer therapies requires genetic testing and other studies, which may lengthen the diagnosis timeline.*
- *High stress levels reported by patients and families at diagnosis and initiation of treatment create an opportune time for distress screening, assessment, problem solving, and psychosocial preventive intervention.*
- *Oncology social work interventions focus on helping the patient with managing the flow of information, decision making, and problem solving urgent needs.*
- *Interventions also focus on optimizing communication with the medical team, work, family, and friends.*
- *Beginning treatment, including "watchful waiting," is welcomed but creates additional stress.*
- *Assisting with language and cultural differences can reduce stress for patients who may otherwise become marginalized.*
- *Financial and other practical problems can also become acute during this period.*

"You have cancer." The power of this statement to shock and devastate patients and families is well known. For patients, the physician's often brief announcement is followed by weeks or even months of heightened anxiety (Fang et al., 2012). Although there are other crisis points along the disease trajectory, the period immediately following diagnosis, up to and including initiation of treatment, often evokes acute stress reactions as patients struggle to comprehend the diagnosis, treatment options, prognosis, and probable effect on their lives.

Oncology social workers' knowledge and skills prepare them to appreciate the patient's intense anxiety and disorientation and then to validate and normalize these reactions. This chapter reviews the psychosocial issues that patients confront during this period and discusses specific ways the oncology social worker can help them make sense of their intense emotional reactions, comprehend complex medical information, make decisions, and solve problems.

First Reactions

People universally and reasonably fear cancer. As a consequence, the mere fact of a cancer diagnosis creates a state of mental ill-being that is sometimes more punishing than the disease's biologic presence (Mullan, 1985).

Despite considerable advances in treatment and survival since Mullan first wrote about his own personal experience, his description of the emotional impact of a cancer diagnosis still applies. Patients use a variety of terms to describe their initial feelings upon hearing that they have cancer; most include expressions of shock and fear for their survival. The setting and tone of the doctor's voice during this initial conversation carries great significance, whether the doctor conveyed the news over the telephone or in person, or whether the patient was alone or with a family member. All of these factors contribute to the usually indelible memory of the life-changing event that is a cancer diagnosis.

Whether the social worker is asked to provide emotional support, practical services, or community resources, a conversation with a newly diagnosed patient provides an opportunity to normalize stress responses and emphasize that time is required to manage such reactions. Social workers validate concerns, provide information, and identify personal strengths that a patient may draw upon to cope with the challenges ahead. Even if a full psychosocial assessment is not possible, the social worker can begin to problem solve by suggesting the availability of social supports and coping capabilities.

> *Mrs. B, a 63-year-old homemaker who cared 3 days per week for her autistic grandchildren, presented to the social worker as anxious and reluctant to agree to the adjuvant radiation therapy that both her breast surgeon and oncologist were recommending. "I have a life! How do they expect me to ask my husband to drive me there every day!? He works! Don't they know that I have responsibilities!?" The patient admitted that treatment was important but felt overwhelmed at the prospect of managing logistics, coping with side effects, and providing care for her grandchildren. Mrs. B was referred to social work for assistance with transportation to treatment. The social worker normalized Mrs. B's initial anxiety, discussed self-care, and explored ways she might obtain additional help with her grandchildren. This discussion helped the patient to gain perspective on the temporary but necessary disruption required by the radiation treatment schedule. Ultimately, the patient's transportation issues proved to be less of an obstacle than her intense anxiety about the impact of diagnosis and treatment on her life, which the intervention helped her to address.*

Initial Testing and Staging

The time between the first hint of cancer and the beginning of treatment is increasing as the use of more targeted therapies may require genetic testing or other studies. The process of refining a cancer diagnosis and determining staging can lead to extraordinary distress for patients as they feel urgency to get started on some form of treatment and stop the cancer's growth. Because patients sometimes perceive cancer as a foreign substance in the body, they may feel an urgency to "get it out" (surgically). Test analyses provide the patient with more effective medical treatment options, and this period also offers an important opportunity to provide education, information, debriefing, and stress reduction techniques that support patients experiencing acute stress reactions.

The oncology social worker reinforces the information provided by other members of the interdisciplinary team while validating for patients that it can be difficult to wait. Reviewing with them what they understand the doctors to be saying about diagnostic and treatment options and how they are interpreting and processing that information can help reduce patients' anxiety, which can be exacerbated by misinterpretation or misunderstanding

Information Gathering and Decision Making

One of the many challenges during the early days of a new diagnosis is making decisions about treatment. Barry and Edgman-Levitan wrote, "The most important attribute of patient-centered care is the active engagement of patients when *fateful* health care decisions must be made" (2012, p. 780, emphasis added). For the newly diagnosed cancer patient, it can be overwhelming simply to absorb the reality. In addition, collecting sufficient information about one's treatment options often seems impossibly difficult. Friends and family members may step in to help with research, which can be simultaneously helpful and distressing if this "help" generates confusion and differences of opinion about potential treatment choices.

Using the Internet

Although the Internet has made research easier and more available, the seemingly infinite number of resources online can be challenging to navigate. As Davis, Williams, Marin, Parker, and Glass noted, "searching the Internet for cancer information is a high order literacy skill" (2002, p. 143). Entering "breast cancer" into a search engine turned up 119 million hits; "lung cancer" resulted in 64 million. Clearly, patients need help distinguishing valid, reliable, and reputable information.

Health Literacy

An association has been shown between limited health literacy and poorer health outcomes (Simon, Dong, Nonzee, & Bennett, 2009). The premorbid health literacy of the patient may influence the methods of information gathering. Many patients enter the world of oncology with only a cursory understanding of the complexities of the disease. A critical role for the oncology social worker can be supporting patients in their learning and normalizing the learning curve. "What have you found online?" and "Where are you searching?" can start a helpful conversation.

The social worker can be particularly helpful in directing patients to appropriate resources (e.g., the National Cancer Institute or American Cancer Society) and in providing general information about a diagnosis. Although some physicians caution patients against using the Internet at all, there is usually someone in a family, if not patients themselves, who checks regularly to see what research, treatments, and facility options may be available. The social worker's awareness of the patient's use of online and other sources can be very useful in understanding potential concerns and misconceptions, as well as how language and cultural differences may affect cancer literacy. In a study of Latina breast cancer patients, lower levels of health literacy were independently associated with poor decision outcomes, suggesting that language and cultural differences may contribute to poor decision making (Hawley et al., 2008, p. 368).

Decision Aids

The use of decision aids (e.g., educational audio and video tapes, computer programs, brochures, pamphlets, etc.) can help by giving patients treatment information in a variety of formats and presentations. Most patients employ some sort of decision aid in their information gathering and may choose the format best suited to their learning style. In their review of the impact of decision aids on surgical choices of breast cancer patients, Waljee, Rogers, and Alderman found that they "reduced decisional conflict and increased patients' satisfaction with their decisions" (2007, p. 1070). In a randomized control trial looking at possible cognitive bias involved in decisions regarding taking tamoxifen among women at high risk for breast cancer, Ubel and colleagues cautioned that "research on judgment and decision making has demonstrated that knowledge alone is not sufficient for optimal decision making" (2010, p. 158). They found that even the order in which patients hear details of risks and benefits affected their perceptions and understanding. And despite the variety of decision aids available, the efficacy of such tools depended on the patient's health literacy. The oncology social worker can assist patients in locating aids that are suited to both their literacy levels and learning preferences.

Variations in Information Gathering

Although "patient-centered care" assumes active engagement in decision-making processes, for some patients it is too stressful to manage. Looking at the research to help understand a diagnosis and treatment options can be a way for patients to feel some control over their illness (Poe, Hayslip, & Studts, 2012). However, the patient who explores his or her diagnosis and treatment options in great depth can also be a challenge for the treatment team. Some patients take a passive approach to controlling information by allowing others to do the information seeking for them. In this way, patients control their anxiety by having others worry and decide (Dickerson, Alqaissi, Underhill, & Lally, 2011). The social worker can be instrumental in facilitating communication with patients, validating their learning styles while assessing how much information they can take in and whom they may prefer to be the gatherers of information or decision makers on their behalf.

> *Mr. B is a 70-year-old man with an early-stage blood cancer who regularly prints his blood test results to share at his monthly support group. He directs pointed questions at group members about their blood levels and frequently tells them that they "must" become familiar with all of their numbers. The social work facilitator is aware that Mr. B manages his own anxiety in this way but must allow group members their own comfort levels with information.*

An appropriate role for the oncology social worker is to explore their use of facts and figures to cope with possible do those articles tell you about your diagnosis?" or "How have you managed to gather so much data?" may open a dialogue. For most patients, a cancer diagnosis brings with it an unsettling loss of control. The social worker can intervene with patients by normalizing such efforts to regain a sense of control.

Communication With Work, Family, Friends, and Medical Team

The ways in which doctors inform patients about their cancer diagnosis often take on major significance in the patients' retelling of their experience with cancer. During this initial conversation, "as is so common, the patient may not have heard what was said, concentrating instead on the word 'cancer'" (Cassileth & Ackerman, 2000, p. 229). In addition to communicating with the team, patients must navigate whom they communicate with in their social networks, workplace, and family to maintain these supportive relationships.

As part of the psychosocial assessment, the social worker asks specifically about the issue of communication. "Who knows about your cancer?" and "What do your children/family/boss know?" are key questions that can elicit patients' concerns about the effect of their diagnoses on loved ones and their larger network. Social workers can offer language to use and role-play hypothetical conversations. This is a particularly helpful intervention in relation to communication with children as parents often wish to protect their young (and sometimes not-so-young) children from the realities of a cancer diagnosis (see Chapter 59).

Communication With Work, Friends, and Family

"What do I say to my boss?" is another challenge for newly diagnosed patients. The social worker can be helpful by offering role-plays and appropriate language, as well as providing specifics about the Family Medical Leave Act and the Americans with Disabilities Act, disability issues, and other areas of practical concern. The oncology social worker's knowledge of resources both online and in the community will be important to the patient's initial adjustment to the diagnosis.

Communication With the Medical Team

Despite the advances in cancer treatments and improved survival statistics, it is clear that cancer is still viewed with fear and anxiety. Patients' conversations with their oncologists are primary sources of both hope and concern. "Maximizing

can contribute to psychological adjustment early in the treatment process" (Sardell & Trierweiler, 1993, p. 3356). The social worker helps the patient identify important issues regarding treatment goals and prognosis. These two critical areas may be unclear, as Gabriel and colleagues noted: "Little is known about what constitutes adequate and satisfying exchanges within this challenging context [of disclosure of diagnosis]" (2008, p. 297). The social worker offers patients the opportunity to put into their own words what they heard from the oncologist. Asking, "What did you understand Dr. Smith to say about the goals of treatment?" can give a patient the opening to express either understanding or uncertainty about the treatment that he or she is facing.

Social workers can identify gaps in patients' understanding that patients themselves may not recognize and support them in developing questions for the next meeting with the team (e.g., an older patient who witnessed her own mother's cancer treatment that was more arduous and ineffective than contemporary treatments or where family members are challenging the efficacy of recommended treatments). Delving into the patient's personal story may also reveal personal strengths that aid in managing emotional adjustment to the diagnosis. As an integral member of a multidisciplinary team, the social worker is also positioned to be able to convey information to the team when warranted.

Communication With Children

For patients that are parents of young children, sharing information about their diagnoses is often particularly difficult. As Harpham (1997, p. 15) wrote, "Your first duty to your children is the formidable one of telling them the news. There is no easy way to tell your children that you have cancer." The parental instinct to protect children from pain and sadness sometimes overrides the conflicting instinct to prepare children for life's realities. While managing the tumult of emotions, patients can benefit from conversations with the oncology social worker about communication with their children. "What do your children know about your diagnosis?" is an appropriate opening for the social worker to explore parents' needs and concerns. Providing parents with age-appropriate language (role-playing the conversation is especially helpful) to use in their conversations with children is an important intervention, arming the patient with tools to manage this emotionally fraught communication. There are many useful books both for children coping with cancer in their families and for their parents. The oncology social worker provides either the literature itself or a bibliography to direct anxious parents to reliable and helpful sources.

Although it may be best for most children to know about their parent's cancer, the oncology social worker may need to guard against pressing this issue with reluctant newly diagnosed parents. There are many reasons for parents to defer telling their children, including the parent's own need to absorb the shock of the diagnosis. The social worker's role may be helping patients to process the reality of the diagnosis to prepare themselves to speak about it with their children in a constructive way (see Chapters 59 and 61).

Caregivers

The social worker has an important role with partners and other primary caregivers both in acknowledging the impact on the family unit and in providing resources for them. Their needs may be lost amid the often more urgent emotional and practical needs of newly diagnosed patients. Social work interventions with these critically important people can be beneficial indirectly to patients as well. According to Zahlis and Lewis, "spouses are not background or context but are themselves directly and deleteriously affected by her illness" (2010, p. 95). By validating the experiences of those who are not themselves facing a diagnosis, the oncology social worker may give a voice to the reality of cancer as a family disease.

Language and Cultural Differences

Language

At a time of heightened stress and fear, the basic need to communicate in one's native or most familiar language is essential. Many health care systems employ interpreters, either on staff or via telephone translation services, to ease this challenge. The oncology social worker needs to be attuned to both the patients' needs and the available tools including medically qualified interpreters (Guidry, Torrence, & Herbelin, 2005, p. 2578).

In addition to the obvious issue of language, there may be cultural and ethnic factors that affect a patient's or family's adjustment to a new diagnosis of cancer. As McGoldrick, Giordano, and Pearce have argued, "a group whose characteristic response to illness is different from the dominant culture may be labeled 'abnormal'" (1996, p. 9).

Mrs. G was a 71-year-old widow from the Dominican Republic who came to New York to be with her adult children when she was diagnosed with breast cancer. Mrs. G spoke no English. She was referred to the oncology social worker and dietician for support as the oncologist thought she had lost a good deal of weight and was severely depressed. Although the team always used a telephone translation service during consults, Mrs. G did not participate actively in those discussions. In the absence of a Spanish-speaking oncology social worker, the social worker also used the telephone translation service for each counseling session. During the session, Mrs. G responded to a few key questions, including "What has it been like for you to be away from your home at this time?" and

"Whom do you talk to about the loss of your breast?" The patient expressed her fear and sadness at the diagnosis and the side effects of treatment. She began to respond eagerly to this opportunity to explore her emotional concerns freely and asked to see the social worker weekly. The patient said that she revealed feelings in session that she had not shared with anyone (see Section 7 for more discussion on the impact of diversity and culture).

Initiation of Treatment

Although patients are often anxious to start treatment, the anticipation of surgery, radiation, or chemotherapy may bring on a new wave of anxiety. Having met with the oncologist and discussed treatment options, the patient has also learned a great deal about potential side effects. Many patients approach their first treatments with considerable trepidation. A simple intervention, such as meeting with the patient in the treatment room on the first day, can underscore both the social work role and the availability of professional support.

Given the wide variety of treatment modalities available, patients may experience this event in many ways. "It" may not even be an event at all. For patients whose recommended course is "watch and wait" or "expectant observation," the perceived lack of treatment exacerbates anxiety: "A 'watch and wait' approach, [is] commonly interpreted by patients as 'wait and worry'" (Aragon-Ching, 2010, p. e265). In a study of early-stage prostate cancer patients, Dall'Era and colleagues found "the need for psychosocial intervention to support men's emotional responses to active surveillance" (2008, p. 1656).

Uncertainty, whether about side effects or outcome, is frequently a key component of patients' anticipatory anxiety around starting treatment, and "fear of recurrence and anxieties are prominent in the immediate postoperative period" (Stephens, Osowski, Fidale, & Spagnoli, 2008, p. 257). For those patients who will undergo radiation or chemotherapy, the oncology social worker again normalizes concerns and provides strategies for managing the uncertainty that will confront the patient throughout his or her disease trajectory. Exploring specific strategies for the night or weekend before starting treatment can be especially helpful: for example, "What are your plans for tonight?" or "How are you spending the weekend?" A simple way to reduce uncertainty is to allow the patient to see the treatment area, if this is practical. Telling a patient that he or she may have a snack during chemo can bring relief: In the words of one patient, "How bad can it be if I'm eating a sandwich?"

Financial, Home Care, and Caregiver Support

The oncology social worker also has a critical role in pro-

treatment initiates. At a time when patients may be overwhelmed by the need to make treatment decisions, they are often confronted with worry about paying for it all. Since most health insurance in the United States is employment based, patients may have concerns about continuing to work during treatment to maintain their benefits. Social workers provide information regarding legal protections including the Family Medical Leave Act and the Americans with Disabilities Act, with due caution about the limitations of these laws. Many patients are unaware of their own benefits until they have a diagnosis.

The economic burden of cancer can be compounded by high out-of-pocket expenses for prescription drugs and medical devices and supplies, as well as expenses related to coinsurance and co-payments. Employment, insurance, and economic issues are not necessarily limited to the cancer survivor—they may extend to family members, limiting access to insurance and posing a financial burden (Hewitt, Greenfield, & Stovall, 2006, p. 363).

The financial impact of a new cancer diagnosis can be staggering even for those with very good medical coverage. Patients usually look to the oncology social worker to offer guidance and referral to financial assistance resources for ancillary expenses including transportation and child care. The social worker maintains a current roster of appropriate resources, local and national, that can offer some relief to financially stressed patients and families. Even relatively small grants offered by cancer organizations can make a difference at this time. The oncology social worker may urge a patient to avail him- or herself of these resources despite initial reluctance. One often hears, "I don't want to take that if someone else really needs it." Organizations such as Cancer*Care* have a mission to assist people with cancer; the oncology social worker may need to "sell" those services as small but effective resources intended to soften the financial impact of a new diagnosis.

Since cancer treatment is primarily performed on an outpatient basis, at-home management of side effects and treatment needs becomes largely the responsibility of patients and their families. Social workers will be called upon to facilitate the transition from the cancer center to the home both concretely (as with home care arrangements) and supportively as families often struggle with the unaccustomed role of medical care provider. As the spouse of a patient diagnosed with head and neck cancer asked, "How do they expect me to take care of his feeding tube? And they tell me that I have to be sure that he eats and drinks enough—I'm not a nurse!" Interventions that can reduce caregiver stress include education and supportive expressive counseling. In their study of program preferences of caregivers for brain tumor patients, Swartz and Keir found that caregivers "want information to reduce stress and believe that stress-reduction programs and interventions can help" (2007, p. 726). Northouse, Williams, Given, and McCorkle (2012) proposed guidelines for supporting cancer caregivers that include assessment, education, support, and referral to resources. As with other stressors that patients and families face, acknowledging and validating caregivers' reactions to their new roles can be helpful interventions.

Pearls

- Because of the almost universal experience of acute stress reactions at the time of diagnosis and beginning treatment, this phase provides an opportunity for distress screening, assessment of high risk, and preventive interventions.
- The longer diagnostic process and the treatment of "watchful waiting" increase anxiety.
- Facilitating communication with the patient's work, family, friends, and medical team is a critical social work role.
- Helping patients with information gathering and decision making is challenged by health literacy, patient and family communication styles, ethnicity, and the huge amount of information easily accessible online.

Pitfalls

- Failing to recognize that the patient's intense anxiety at diagnosis is an acute stress reaction to the diagnosis of and beginning treatment for cancer.
- Inadequate provision of resources to overcome language and literacy barriers.

Key issues identified in this chapter for work with newly diagnosed patients include the almost universal crisis that patients experience with a new diagnosis of cancer, patients' sense of urgency to start treatment (and frequently corresponding frustration with medical investigations that usually precede any treatment plan), their varying degrees of tolerance for information, the impact of a cancer diagnosis on family members, and the importance of exploring information-processing and communication styles and needs. Bridging communication between the patient and the interdisciplinary team during this initial stressful period can alleviate some patient concerns. Problems can arise with respect to treatment adherence and patients' emotional reactions or information needs not being acknowledged or supported by the team. As an important member of the interdisciplinary team, the oncology social worker's interventions can enhance coping skills and reduce stress to help patients adjust to their diagnoses and make important decisions.

ADDITIONAL RESOURCES

Adler, N. E., & Page, A. E. K. (Eds.). (2008). *Cancer care for the whole patient: Meeting psychosocial health needs.* Washington DC, National Academies Press.

American Cancer Society: http://www.cancer.org/Treatment/UnderstandingYourDiagnosis/index?ssSourceSiteId=null

Cancer*Care*: http://www.cancercare.org/

Diviani, N., & Schultz, P. (2011). What should laypersons know about cancer? Towards an operational definition of cancer literacy. *Patient Education and Counseling, 85*, 487–492.

National Cancer Institute: http://www.cancer.gov/cancertopics/pdq/supportivecare/adjustment/HealthProfessional/page1

REFERENCES

Aragon-Ching, J. (2010). Active surveillance for prostate cancer: Has the time finally come? *Journal of Clinical Oncology, 28*(16), e265–e266.

Barry, M., & Edgman-Levitan, S. (2012). Shared decision making—the pinnacle of patient-centered care. *New England Journal of Medicine, 366*(9), 780–781.

Cassileth, B., & Ackerman, B. (2000). Listen to the patient. *Cancer, 89*, 229–231.

Dall'Era, M., Cooperberg, M., Chan, J., Davies, B., Albertsen, P., Klotz, L., ... Carroll, P. (2008). Active surveillance for early-stage prostate cancer. *Cancer, 112*(8), 1650–1659.

Davis, T., Williams, M., Marin, E., Parker, R., & Glass, J. (2002). Health literacy and cancer communication. *Cancer Journal for Clinicians, 52*(3), 134–149.

Dickerson, S., Alqaissi, N., Underhill, M., & Lally, R., (2011). Surviving the wait: Defining support while awaiting breast cancer surgery. *Journal of Advanced Nursing, 67*(7), 1468–1479.

Fang, F., Fall, K., Mittleman, M., Sparen, P., Weimin, Y., Adami, H., & Valdismarsdottir, U. (2012). Suicide and cardiovascular death after a cancer diagnosis. *New England Journal of Medicine, 366*(14), 1310–1318.

Gabriel, S., Grize, L., Helfenstein, E., Brutsche, M., Grossman, P., Tamm, M., & Kiss, A. (2008). Receiving the diagnosis of lung cancer: Patient recall of information and satisfaction with physician communication. *Journal of Clinical Oncology, 26*(2), 297–302.

Guidry, J., Torrence, W., & Herbelin, S. (2005). Closing the divide: Diverse populations and cancer survivorship. *Cancer, 104*(11), 2577–2583.

Harpham, W. (1997). *When a parent has cancer.* New York, NY: Harper Collins.

Hawley, S., Janz, N., Hamilton, A., Griggs, J., Alderman, A., Mujahid, M., & Katz, S. (2008). Latina patient perspectives about informed treatment decision making for breast cancer. *Patient Education and Counseling, 73*, 363–370.

Hewitt, M., Greenfield, S., & Stovall, E. (Eds.). (2006). *From cancer patient to cancer survivor: Lost in transition.* Washington, DC: National Academies Press.

McGoldrick, M., Giordano, J., & Pearce, J. (Eds.). (1996). *Ethnicity and family therapy.* New York, NY: Guilford Press.

Mullan, F. (1985). Seasons of survival: Reflections of a physician with cancer. *New England Journal of Medicine, 313*, 270–273.

Northouse, L., Williams, A., Given, B., & McCorkle, R. (2012). Psychosocial care for family caregivers of patients with cancer. *Journal of Clinical Oncology, 30*(11), 1227–1234.

Poe, J., Hayslip, J., & Studts, J. (2012). Decision making and distress among individuals diagnosed with follicular lymphoma. *Journal of Psychosocial Oncology, 30*, 426–445.

Sardell, A., & Trierweiler, S. (1993). Disclosing the cancer diagnosis: Procedures that influence patient hopefulness. *Cancer, 72*(11), 3355–3365.

Simon, M., Dong, X., Nonzee, N., & Bennett, C. (2009). Heeding our words: Complexities of research among low-literacy populations. *Journal of Clinical Oncology, 27*(12), 1938–1940.

Stephens, P., Osowski, M., Fidale, M., & Spagnoli, C. (2008). Identifying the educational needs and concerns of newly diagnosed patients with breast cancer after surgery. *Clinical Journal of Oncology Nursing, 12*(2), 253–258.

Swartz, J., & Keir, S. (2007). Program preferences to reduce stress in caregivers of patients with brain tumors. *Clinical Journal of Oncology Nursing, 11*(5), 723–727.

Ubel, P., Smith, D., Zikmund-Fisher, B., Derry, H., McClure, J., Stark, A., ... Fagerlin, A. (2010). Testing whether decision aids introduce cognitive biases: Results of a randomized trial. *Patient Education and Counseling, 80*, 158–163.

Waljee, J., Rogers, M., & Alderman, A. (2007). Decision aids and breast cancer: Do they influence choice for surgery and knowledge of treatment options? *Journal of Clinical Oncology, 25*(9), 1067–1073.

Zahlis, E., & Lewis, F. (2010). Coming to grips with breast cancer: The spouse's experience with his wife's first six months. *Journal of Psychosocial Oncology, 28*(10), 79–97.

8 Sense Making in Living With Cancer as a Chronic Illness

Paul G. Clark and Sage Bolte

Key Concepts

- *A sense-making framework can be applied to psychosocial issues to help patients comprehend and cope with their diagnosis and treatment experiences.*
- *Identifying changes in survivorship needs and maintaining continuity of care through the lens of sense making is important in oncology social work.*
- *The social worker can engage in sense-making activities with patients.*

Extending well beyond the biomedical aspects of cancer and its treatment, the *sense-making perspective* addresses individuals' own experiences and attributions of what cancer means to them. Furthermore, it explores this meaning within the context of their everyday lives.

In this chapter, we use a general sense-making framework for understanding how cancer patients experience their disease within the contexts of communication and interaction with (1) health care providers; (2) family members, friends, and community members with whom patients have a caring bond; (3) members of their work and social networks; and (4) systems that provide resources, support, and assistance. Additionally, we explore the key role oncology social workers play in helping cancer patients make sense of their experiences, thus facilitating their ability to cope with, and successfully adapt to, cancer's daily impingement on their lives.

Sense Making as a Framework for Oncology Social Work

At its most basic, sense making is defined as seeking comprehensibility (Dransart, 2013), a process through which we make sense of our lives by reconciling our personal histories, sense of self, behaviors, and social context with external messages and information (Andsager & Powers, 2001). For example, in oncology settings, it is not uncommon for a gap to exist between what is "real" to newly diagnosed cancer patients—their very personal fears, uncertainties, expectations, and emergent concerns—and the biomedical and technology-informed "realities" of physicians and other members of the health care team. For instance, at the time of diagnosis, a well-meaning physician may follow the word *cancer* with a discussion of conventional therapies and next steps. Simultaneously, the patient may not hear the physician's words as he or she spirals into shock, fear, and confusion after hearing the word *cancer.* In that moment, a gap may occur between the physician, who is working valiantly to provide accurate diagnostic information while proposing scientifically grounded next steps, and the patient, who is focused on his or her fear-filled reality.

In the sense-making process, bridging such gaps requires continual engagement, where external realities are negotiated and ultimately reconciled with patients' own attributions of meaning. People engage in sense making when they face new situations or situations that produce uncertainty and they attempt to resolve these situations by creating frameworks through which they can increase understanding (Dervin, 1998; M. Stein, 2004). These frameworks reflect individuals' own histories, socialization, contexts, and prior experiences with life stressors. For example, an internal narrative characterized by thoughts such as "It can't be cancer. I'm a healthy person. I just finished biking across Europe" might reflect the patient's reality at the time of diagnosis. However, through the sense-making process, the personal narrative can be transformed into one characterized by thoughts like "Cancer can happen to anyone. I'll continue to focus on maintaining my healthy diet and exercise routines as much as I can to get through this."

Sense making is a cognitive and emotional process central to the creation of the ubiquitous *new normal* perspective that blends medical science and personal meaning. Engagement in this process occurs in ways both solitary and social. Through the sense-making process, people living with cancer reconcile the unforeseen challenges that cancer brings to their previously held expectations about the course their lives would take.

Promoting Sense Making: The Role of the Oncology Social Worker

Assessment, intervention, and evaluation of outcomes are processes that oncology social workers perform throughout the patient's cancer continuum. During assessment, in particular, it is important to aggregate, evaluate, and integrate patient information while concurrently assessing and incorporating the patient's sense-making process into interventions. To follow, we describe assessment using a sense-making perspective at diagnosis and treatment, at the conclusion of treatment, and during off-treatment survival.

Assessment

During initial assessment, it is important to identify and document biopsychosocial risks that require immediate intervention, including incapacitating treatment side effects, levels of depression and anxiety, current and past mental health challenges, economic difficulties, and familial and interpersonal issues. Once addressed and stabilized, assessment using a sense-making perspective can proceed.

Understanding Gaps in Communication

Assessment of sense-making issues involves the identification and exploration of communication, knowledge, and understanding of gaps between patients and their care team members, significant others, and work and social environments. By knowing more about the gaps between a patient's personal and external experiences, oncology social workers can find ways to help patients bridge or negotiate these gaps to better comprehend their situation. Ultimately, oncology social workers create a shared context or narrative with patients that facilitates exploration, discussion, and problem solving (Dervin, 1998) by becoming familiar with a patient's experience of a situation through his or her personal language. Oncology social workers explore how patients' conceptualizations, understandings, emotions, questions, struggles, anxieties, intuitions, visions, and aspirations combine to inform their comprehension of their experience across the cancer continuum. Consider asking the following questions, adapted from Dervin (1998), to identify gaps with which patients or family members may be struggling:

Related to the Medical Team

- What happened when you were at the doctor? At the lab? At the . . . ?
- What did you feel like at the doctor? At the lab? At the . . . ?
- What helped or made things worse?
- If you could magically have me fix this, what would I be doing for you?
- Tell me what you've learned about your cancer and its treatment.
- Based on what you've learned, do you believe you are able to ask your doctors and other health professionals about: What treatments are available? How the treatments will affect you?
- What are your concerns or worries about managing the cancer and its treatment?

Related to Family/Significant Others

- How are your family members handling things since your diagnosis? Surgery? Radiation? Chemotherapy?
- What are your concerns about managing things at home?
- Since your diagnosis, are you feeling confused about your relationships with anyone at home?

Related to the Social Network

- How did friends and acquaintances react when they learned about your cancer?
- Did you get the response you expected?

- What was it like telling them? Did anything get in the way of telling them? How did you feel? What sorts of emotions did you experience?
- Were friends able to give you the help you wanted?

Related to Work and Resources

- Have you told others at work/at your church/in your community about your cancer?
- How have coworkers and supervisors/church members/community members responded?
- What challenges are you facing with being at work/at church/in the community?
- Will treatment/side effects change things for you at work/at church/in the community?

By asking these questions, oncology social workers identify and explore gaps that occur between what patients know and what they want or need to know to understand or make sense of what they have encountered. The goal is to support patients and their significant others in bridging those gaps, evaluating the outcomes, and proceeding on to incorporate continuing challenges into their evolving narrative (Dervin, 1998).

Diagnosis and Treatment

Many challenges, not least of which are emotional, accompany the receipt of a life-threatening diagnosis (Chantler, Podbilewicz-Schuller, & Mortimer, 2006; Grimsbø, Finset, & Ruland, 2011; Hill, Amir, Muers, Connolly, & Round, 2003; Sutherland, Hill, Morand, Pruden, & Mclachlan, 2009). Although less radical over the past four decades, cancer treatments continue to present ongoing physical demands including fatigue, insomnia, pain, and sexual dysfunction, as well as spiritual and existential concerns (Manne & Badr, 2008).

A cancer diagnosis can challenge sense-making capacity as it threatens one's previously conceived life course and alters future expectations. Indeed, among some populations, increased rates of suicide have been noted at early stages in the continuum of care (Llorente et al., 2005; Nasseri, Mills, Mirshahidi, & Moulton, 2012). A primary focus of the oncology social worker during the diagnostic process is to help the patient comprehend what can be a cascade of medical information from which important decisions must be made. Sense-making activities for the patient during diagnosis and treatment are likely to involve information gathering about the interpretation of scans and lab tests, as well as explanations of treatment options and their possible benefits and burdens (Chantler et al., 2006; Hesse, Arora, Burke Beckjord, & Finney Rutten, 2008; Sutherland et al., 2009). The oncology social worker supports the patient's translation of this information into schemas, plans, or strategies for making treatment decisions and managing the concomitant biopsychosocial and spiritual issues.

Although much of the sense-making activity early in the cancer continuum concerns the patient and medical team, a cancer diagnosis also has repercussions on the patient's spouse, partner, and family members, who worry about the illness and its treatment and fear managing the challenges and demands related to care, not to mention losing a loved one (Skerrett, 1998). Additional concerns can include the renegotiation of family roles necessary to provide for child care and home maintenance (Manne & Badr, 2008). It is not uncommon for family members to sense a loss of order as routines become more difficult to follow, and the previously developed capacity for thinking challenges through or talking them out together is altered (M. Stein, 2004).

When presented with these and other challenges, oncology social workers can aid in the sense-making processes for family members by recognizing their information-gathering preferences related to cancer and cancer treatment, as they did for the patient. Patient and family preferences for information gathering and decision making can vary and lead to difficulties not only with communication but also with the collaborative processes that underlie the creation of the new normal. The oncology social worker can facilitate communication by identifying differences and helping all stakeholders understand them. For instance, a family member may ask *how* and *what* questions, expressing a need for specific details and facts that are presented in a sequential fashion, whereas the patient's information preferences may emphasize generalities and possibilities. The oncology social worker identifies and helps reconcile these differences in information gathering.

Making sense of relationships with friends and acquaintances may also present challenges for newly diagnosed patients. This can be especially true when patients must reconceptualize relationships with others to include receiving support, perhaps for the first time in their lives. Through the sense-making process, patients can be more directive when responding to inquiries about their health status or to offers of assistance by others outside their families.

Scott is a 34-year-old man who began treatment for Hodgkin lymphoma a month ago. He is married and has two small children under age 5. The oncology social worker began seeing Scott after he was first diagnosed and had a high score on the psychological distress screening instrument. Over the course of four weekly meetings with Scott, the social worker assessed his psychological distress and found that Scott was experiencing anger, emotional withdrawal, symptom checking, and "scanxiety," as well as feeling overwhelmed. His feelings were related to gaps that both presented sense-making challenges and produced strong emotional responses. He reported, "Everyone is always telling me I am going to be fine, and I am so strong. But all I can think about is what if I don't make it. What if the next blood test shows something is wrong, or the next scan shows that the cancer hasn't responded? My mom barely lets me breathe when I give updates on my treatments or appointments. She just asks way too many questions." He also reported that he is "too scared" to tell his wife or his friends about his fears because "I don't want them to think I am negative or not fighting hard" and "I don't want them to be more scared than they already might be."

Supporting Scott's sense-making process and development of a new normal included active listening and normalizing many of his fears and feelings. In addition, the oncology social worker educated him about the various ways anxiety can appear, such as sleep interruption, restlessness, negative intrusive thoughts, anger, or increased frustration. The social worker made use of cognitive and behavioral techniques and discussed the benefit of wellness approaches for the management of anxiety and other strong emotions. During the second and third sessions, two techniques were taught to Scott to help him begin to manage the negative effects of anxiety. The first included deep breathing and progressive muscle relaxation to help dissipate the physical sensations of anxiety, along with a resource list of guided imagery CDs. The second was the use of thought stopping and reframing techniques to help manage negative and intrusive thoughts and provide an increased sense of control of thought processes. Additionally, the social worker supported the bridging of gaps with friends and family by suggesting communication strategies that helped Scott describe his feelings and experiences while also providing alternative ways for family members to respond. For example, with respect to his concerns about his mother, Scott learned to say: "It's not helpful when you ask me a lot of questions about my appointments, treatments, or scans. When I get new information I promise I will let you know and will keep you informed of any changes. I am glad you are concerned about me, but talking about it too much just creates more anxiety and doesn't help." During the fourth session, Scott reported that he had noticed that his anxiety did seem to be less overwhelming. He had a better understanding of anxiety triggers and recognized intrusive thoughts. Implementing relaxation techniques also reduced anxiety. His improvement was supported by the distress screening on the fourth visit that demonstrated a lower rate of distress.

Conclusion of Treatment

Following the end of treatment, as patients enter the active surveillance phase, contacts with members of the health care team are diminished, leaving fewer opportunities to obtain and exchange information and receive support. This represents a change in the continuity of care that can create a sense of disequilibrium as patients enter a state of unknowing about health status and of feeling they have to manage their cancer alone. Some have described this experience as feeling like "hanging in the air" or "being 'left in a void'" (Grimsbø et al., 2011, p. 112). Sense-making activities during this stage center on the negotiation of the new normal or spanning the gap between posttreatment life and life before diagnosis and treatment. This may involve finding a new cadence or pace, especially if continuing to manage pain, fatigue, or other treatment-related side effects. Questions about which pre-cancer lifestyle choices can be returned to and which must be eliminated can be posed to aid the sense-making process. Sense making here is about supporting the development of patients' capacity to self-confirm and define their choices in ways they can accept.

Sense making as treatment ends can involve recovering and revising life plans, re-developing relationships, and handling the ever-present fears about disease recurrence. Fear of recurrence or worsening of health status can be heightened by continual awareness of physical changes as a result of treatment and may continue to interfere with daily activities. Between 4% and 22% of cancer patients have a risk of developing posttraumatic stress disorder (PTSD) at some point in their lifetime, and for some, a scan may actually trigger symptoms of PTSD (Andrykowski & Kangas, 2010). Certainly, it is essential for oncology social workers to be mindful of the very powerful experience a cancer recurrence can have. *Scanxiety*, a word used to describe the experience of heightened anxiety and distress both immediately before and after a scheduled scan, is a significant experience for many throughout the survivorship experience. Cognitive behavioral approaches can be directed toward the reasonable monitoring of bodily changes and keeping "abnormal" lab results in context. The use of thought-stopping techniques or cognitive reframing can be helpful; for example, when a patient notices a heightened sense of anxiety about his or her scan or feels "out of control," the oncology social worker might offer: "You are taking steps toward managing your care." Additionally, providing resources on relaxation techniques to help manage anxiety can be helpful.

Reintegration of family, work, and social activities the patient was involved in before diagnosis and treatment can also present challenges. In much the same way that powerful and sometimes toxic treatments produce ongoing effects in the quality of patients' lives, the quality of life within families can also be profoundly affected (Steinglass, Ostroff, & Steinglass, 2011). Moving forward creates a gap for patients and their families as they attempt to make sense of their pre- and posttreatment lives. At this juncture on the cancer continuum, sense-making efforts can be directed toward supporting families as they learn the new landscape of life following cancer treatment. These efforts can include directing patients and their families to psychoeducational support groups. When relationship or individual functioning is severely stressed, referring patients and families to individual, couples, group, or family counseling can be of help. Intervention strategies that are grounded in cognitive behavioral, communication, stress management, or problem-solving approaches have been found especially effective (Andersen, 2002; Andersen et al., 2004; Meyer & Mark, 1995; Waldron, Jahnke, Bechtel, Ramirez, & Cohen, 2013).

Returning to work and social activities following treatment also presents sense-making challenges as patients reconcile gaps between pre-diagnosis, treatment performance, and other expectations with posttreatment realities. For some, a return to work can mean that life has been fully recovered. However, for others, not being able to resume work or maintain a full-time schedule represents a less-than-full recovery. The aim of assessment and intervention regarding work issues is to develop clarity with patients about the degree to which their current capacity for work activity fits with their pre-diagnosis and treatment status. The oncology social worker suggests a diverse array of situational alternatives for moving forward.

Social support has the potential for improving adjustment to cancer (Paredes, Canavarro, & Simões, 2012). Patients can experience shifts in social relationships as members of their social network react positively and supportively by providing emotional and tangible forms of support. Conversely, patients may experience avoidance or abandonment by members of their support networks who may be fearful of the disease and its potential outcome. Re-establishing social relationships can be further complicated when patients experience difficulties with their own perceptions about how the profound effect of the diagnosis or treatment has changed the ways in which others view them. For instance, patients may believe that other people can "see" that they have had cancer after the texture of their hair changes when it re-emerges following cessation of chemo. They may believe that some other treatment-related characteristic is as visible to others as a scarlet letter. Professionally facilitated support groups are another option that some patients find helpful in making meaning of cancer and reducing anxiety. A support group can offer patients (and loved ones) an opportunity to experience normalcy and acceptance while expressing their fears, sadness, disruptions to life, and re-evaluations of life. Providing resources for online support groups, chat forums, or other social media outlets might also be a helpful source of connection to people.

Off-Treatment Survival

Gaps in comprehension can occur for long-term patients as they yearn to return to a life resembling their pre-cancer life while having to adjust to a phantom sense of the future and uncertainties about their forever-changed bodies (Grimsbø et al., 2011). Patients can also experience a conflict between wanting continued support from others while also wanting to be treated as normal (Chantler et al., 2006).

Late effects of cancer treatment can have profound and lasting effects on physical and emotional aspects of quality of life. Some of these effects emerge during treatment; others may not emerge until well after treatment has concluded and perhaps even years later. Ongoing physical issues include fatigue, insomnia, difficulties with sexual functioning, and musculoskeletal problems. Although it is difficult to identify anxiety, depression, body image, or other emotional difficul-

treatment, evidence supports slightly higher rates of depression and PTSD in long-term patients (K. D. Stein, Syrjala, & Andrykowski, 2008). Sense-making efforts regarding health issues throughout survivorship can be directed toward maintenance of continuity of care and establishing and maintaining positive health behaviors, as well as continued participation in prevention and screening activities.

Support groups and survivorship activities can continue to be a source of support as patients move from sense making to meaning making "after cancer." As individuals develop a more coherent meaning of their illness experience over time, they may seek out different types of activities varying from professional-led to peer-led groups, individual therapy to explore new directions, and creative outlets consistent with their enhanced appreciation of life; participation in cancer awareness, prevention, and fund-raising activities; or distancing themselves from cancer reminders. Again, connections to others who can provide support and normalize many of the issues that people face after the cancer treatment is finished can be a powerful healer.

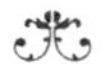

Pearls

- The sense-making process requires that the oncology social worker help patients comprehend their diagnoses and treatments by listening carefully for what is confusing, unclear, or missing from their understandings and what most troubles them.
- At the heart of the sense-making process is a willingness on the part of oncology social workers to be open to patients' unique experiences of distress and to help them problem solve.

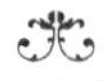

Pitfalls

- When a patient's distress is extreme, it is unlikely that the sense-making process can proceed until the distress is alleviated.
- If patients are in a great deal of denial, they will have a diminished awareness of the dangerousness of the situation that may make sense making more difficult.
- Stoicism can reflect the patients' desire to do what they believe is socially expected. A person may devote a great deal of energy toward being perceived as the "good patient" and, with family members, as the "strong one." Fatalism and resignation may be in some situations a strategy for saving face or protecting others from experiencing the potentially overwhelming nature of the diagnosis or treatment.

As cancer treatment has evolved and continues to show promise, oncology social workers have garnered a central role in providing psychosocial oncology services at many junctures along the cancer continuum, often at times of change in the disease and treatment process or when patients experience changes within their family and personal network. Oncology social workers understand survivorship as a complex and layered experience that reflects historical influences, as well as the personal, familial, ethnic, cultural, and socioeconomic contexts of individual patients.

Sense making focuses on helping patients and their families comprehend what is happening to them in ways that enhance their ability to make decisions, manage their emotions, and maintain an acceptable quality of life as they progress along the cancer continuum. Oncology social workers bridge gaps with patients between what is familiar or known and circumstances that are obscure, unknown, or alien.

REFERENCES

Andersen, B. L. (2002). Biobehavioral outcomes following psychological interventions for cancer patients. *Journal of Consulting and Clinical Psychology, 70*(3), 590–610. doi:10.1037/0022-006X.70.3.590

Andersen, B. L., Farrar, W. B., Golden-Kreutz, D. M., Glaser, R., Emery, C. F., Crespin, T. R., ... Carson, W. E. (2004). Psychological, behavioral, and immune changes after a psychological intervention: A clinical trial. *Journal of Clinical Oncology, 22*(17), 3570–3580. doi:10.1200/JCO.2004.06.030

Andrykowski, M. A., & Kangas, M. (2010). Posttraumatic stress disorder associated with cancer diagnosis and treatment. In J. C. Holland, W. S. Breitbard, P. B. Jacobsen, M. S. Lederneg, M. J. Loscalzo, & R. McCorkle (Eds.), *Psycho-Oncology* (2nd ed., pp. 348–357). New York, NY: Oxford University.

Andsager, J. L., & Powers, A. (2001). Framing women's health with a sense-making approach: Magazine coverage of breast cancer and implants. *Health Communication, 13*(2), 163–186. doi:10.1207/S15327027HC1302_3

Chantler, M., Podbilewicz-Schuller, Y., & Mortimer, J. (2006). Change in need for psychosocial support for women with early stage breast cancer. *Journal of Psychosocial Oncology, 23*(2–3), 65–77. doi:10.1300/J077v23n02_05

Dervin, B. (1998). Sense-making theory and practice: An overview of user interests in knowledge seeking and use. *Journal of Knowledge Management, 2*(2), 36–46. doi:10.1108/13673279810249369

Dransart, D (2013). From sense-making to meaning-making: Understanding and supporting survivors of suicide. *British Journal of Social Work, 43*, 317–335.

Grimsbø, G. H., Finset, A., & Ruland, C. M. (2011). Left hanging in the air: Experiences of living with cancer as expressed through e-mail communications with oncology nurses. *Cancer Nursing, 34*(2), 107–116. doi:10.1097/NCC.0b013e3181eff008

Hesse, B. W., Arora, N. K., Burke Beckjord, E., & Finney Rutten, L. J. (2008). Information support for cancer survivors. *Cancer, 112*(S11), 2529–2540. doi:10.1002/cncr.23445

Hill, K. M., Amir, Z., Muers, M. F., Connolly, C. K., & Round, C. E. (2003). Do newly diagnosed lung cancer patients feel their concerns are being met? *European Journal of Cancer Care, 12*(1), 35–45. doi:10.1046/j.1365-2354.2003.00324.x

Llorente, M. D., Burke, M., Gregory, G. R., Bosworth, H. B., Grambow, S. C., Homer, R. D., ... Olsen, E. J. (2005). Prostate cancer: A significant risk factor for late-life suicide. *American Journal of Geriatric Psychiatry, 13*(3), 195–201. doi:10.1176/appi.ajgp.13.3.195

Manne, S., & Badr, H. (2008). Intimacy and relationship processes in couples' psychosocial adaptation to cancer. *Cancer, 112*(S11), 2541–2555. doi:10.1002/cncr.23450

Meyer, T. J., & Mark, M. M. (1995). Effects of psychosocial interventions with adult cancer patients: A meta-analysis of randomized experiments. *Health Psychology, 14*(2), 101–108. doi:10.1037/0278-6133.14.2.101

Nasseri, K., Mills, P. K., Mirshahidi, H. R., & Moulton, L. H. (2012). Suicide in cancer patients in California, 1997–2006. *Archives of Suicide Research, 16*(4), 324–333. doi:10.1080/13811118.2013.722056

Paredes, T. F., Canavarro, M. C., & Simões, M. R. (2012). Social support and adjustment in patients with sarcoma: The moderator effect of the disease phase. *Journal of Psychosocial Oncology, 30*(4), 402–425. doi:10.1080/07347332.2012.684852

Skerrett, K. (1998). Couple adjustment to the experience of breast cancer. *Families, Systems, & Health, 16*(3), 281–298. doi:10.1037/h0089855

Stein, K. D., Syrjala, K. L., & Andrykowski, M. A. (2008). Physical and psychological long-term and late effects of cancer. *Cancer, 112*(Suppl. 11), 2577–2592. doi:10.1002/cncr.23448

Stein, M. (2004). The critical period of disasters: Insights from sense-making and psychoanalytic theory. *Human Relations, 57*(10), 1243–1261. doi:10.1177/0018726704048354

Steinglass, P., Ostroff, J. S., & Steinglass, A. S. (2011). Multiple family groups for adult cancer survivors and their families: A 1-day workshop model. *Family Process, 50*(3), 393–409. doi:10.1111/j.1545-5300.2011.01359.x

Sutherland, G., Hill, D., Morand, M., Pruden, M., & Mclachlan, S.-A. (2009). Assessing the unmet supportive care needs of newly diagnosed patients with cancer. *European Journal of Cancer Care, 18*(6), 577–584. doi:10.1111/j.1365-2354.2008.00932.x

Waldron, E. A., Jahnke, E. A., Bechtel, C. F., Ramirez, M., & Cohen, A. (2013). A systematic review of psychosocial interventions to improve cancer caregiver quality of life. *Psycho-Oncology, 22*(6), 1200–1207. doi:10.1002/pon.3118

9

Penny Damaskos and Carly Parry

Cancer Survivorship: Concepts, Interventions, and Research

Key Concepts

- *This chapter provides an overview of the history of cancer survivorship and the evolution of survivorship care plans.*
- *A review of psychosocial adjustment in survivorship and clinical interventions after cancer treatment is provided.*

The number of cancer survivors living in the United States today is estimated to be nearly 12 million, a number continuing to grow due to the combined effects of improved survival rates and of an aging population (Parry, Kent, Mariotto, Alfano, & Rowland, 2011). This prevalence has been accompanied by increased attention to cancer survivorship in research and policy realms (Rowland, 2008). Between 2003 and 2008, the Institute of Medicine (IOM) produced several key publications addressing the medical and psychosocial issues associated with cancer survivorship, including reports dedicated to whole-patient care and follow-up care delivery for cancer survivors (Adler & Page, 2008; Hewitt, Greenfield, & Stovall, 2006). In 2004, the Centers for Disease Control and Prevention partnered with the Lance Armstrong Foundation to develop a National Action Plan for Cancer Survivorship to Advance Public Health Strategies, and the President's Cancer Panel provided recommendations for the standardization of follow-up care for cancer survivors (Rowland, 2008). Together, this body of reports demonstrated increased pressure on the political, medical, and scientific communities to devote resources to cancer survivorship (Rowland & Stefanek, 2008).

Concurrently, the topic of cancer survivorship experienced heightened visibility in popular culture and media outlets, with the increased awareness and social discourse representing a major shift in our collective understanding of how cancer affects individual lives and families. This new understanding has emerged from a multidecade dialogue between coalitions of leaders and advocates in national and grassroots cancer organizations, as well as research entities (Rowland, 2008). Today, we see images of cancer survivors that underscore the possibility of a satisfying "new normal" life after cancer. The efforts of such coalitions have also contributed to increased understanding of the challenges to cancer survivors' quality of life following treatment, the needs for coordinated follow-up care for this rapidly growing population, and the continued evolution of agendas for research and practice in cancer survivorship (Parry, Kent, et al., 2011).

History of the Cancer Survivorship Movement

For over 30 years, the cancer survivorship movement has represented collaboration between grassroots advocates, governmental and nongovernmental organizations, and the medical community. The concept of cancer advocacy was first developed through peer-led support groups, which were eventually absorbed into professionally led programs and subsequently standardized to meet the needs of a broad range of cancer survivors (Hoffman & Stovall, 2006). Early cancer survivorship advocacy efforts were aligned with established organizations such as the American Cancer Society, which in 1977 promoted the I Can Cope program to help patients with advocacy and emotional support. In 1982, the Susan G. Komen Foundation was established and became a predominant national cancer advocacy group and granting source (Hoffman & Stovall, 2006). In 1986, the National Coalition for Cancer Survivorship (NCCS) was formed by 20 patient advocacy organizations whose representatives organized around the issue of limited resources for cancer survivors, advocated for a national network to coordinate survivorship activities, and pressed for policy changes in an underaddressed area: long-standing treatment side effects (Miller, Merry, & Miller, 2008). The NCCS also defined cancer survivorship to include individuals with cancer *from the point of diagnosis onward* and family members, in recognition of the effects cancer has on the families and friends of those with cancer (Hewitt et al., 2006; Hoffman & Stovall, 2006; Miller et al., 2008). In 1991, the National Breast Cancer Coalition was created as a lobbying group for breast cancer research, and in 1996, the Lance Armstrong Foundation (aka LIVE**STRONG**) was established and became a leader in advocacy, lobbying, and funding for survivors of all types of cancer (Hoffman & Stovall, 2006).

In 1996, through the NCCS's advocacy efforts, the National Cancer Institute's Office of Cancer Survivorship (OCS) was established and adopted the NCCS definition of survivorship. It was through the OCS that funding for cancer survivorship was centralized and tracked in an organized way, symbolizing a solidification of support by the government for cancer survivorship. The OCS was created in response to demand from the cancer advocacy community for a better understanding of the physical, psychosocial, and practical needs of cancer survivors and their communities. The OCS is dedicated to developing a body of evidence-based research delineating the impact of treatment-related outcomes on individuals, including the late and long-term effects of cancer and its treatment, with the aim of improving survivors' quality of life (Rowland & Bellizzi, 2008).

Conceptualizing Survivorship: The Evolving Nomenclature

We now recognize that the time period following primary treatment for cancer is a discrete phase in the cancer continuum, often described as a time when individuals make a transition from "patient" to "survivor" (Miller et al., 2008; Rowland, 2008). The NCCS definition states that an individual is considered a survivor from the time of diagnosis onward (as opposed to the traditional 5-year mark) and that the term *survivor* includes the individual's community of friends and family (Hoffman & Stovall, 2006; Miller et al., 2008). Health care providers have used the word *survivor* to distinguish different phases of the cancer experience. However, as a term, *survivor* has not uniformly been embraced by individuals with a cancer experience, with some rejecting it outright in preference of other terms, such as *thriver.* In this chapter, we use the term *survivor* not as an endorsement of the term but because it is most readily understood by the cancer community at large. Survivorship refers to distinct phases in treatment, but it also reflects an approach to care that is inclusive of specific treatment plans that address every aspect of quality of life for the survivor.

While the NCCS-endorsed definition of survivor includes a range of experiences "from the point of diagnosis to the balance of his or her life," survivorship is neither a broad nor a uniform experience (Hewitt et al., 2006, p. 29). The continuum of cancer survivorship may be divided into distinct and clinically unique phases, in which survivors' experiences, needs, and concerns vary. Survivors who have been recently diagnosed or who are in active treatment may be concerned with managing the impact of treatment; survivors who have completed primary treatment may be coping with adjustment to life after cancer (return to work, physical aftereffects, etc.); and survivors facing end-of-life issues may be more focused on symptom management.

Shifting Understandings of "Posttreatment" Survivorship

When active treatment ends, the posttreatment phase begins and may be characterized by unexpected anxiety, generalized fear, and management of late and long-term effects resulting from treatment (Ganz, 2006; Rowland & Bellizzi, 2008). Researchers have demonstrated that survivors may experience long-term consequences of cancer and that these aftereffects could have a negative impact on quality of life and on physical, cognitive, social, and emotional functioning (Rowland & Bellizzi, 2008; Schnoll, Knowles, & Harlow, 2002). Survivorship research findings have indicated that the posttreatment experience involves a series of adjustments occurring in three primary domains of quality of life: physical (changes in body and hair and lingering side effects), practical (financial losses, insurance concerns), and emotional (fear of recurrence, issues of mortality, and search for existential meaning; Rowland, 2008; Rowland & Bellizzi, 2008). Adjustment to life after treatment requires acceptance and integration of changes in these domains as survivors adapt to their altered ("new normal") lives—lives that are both deeply familiar and profoundly changed.

Posttreatment survivorship has been conceptualized as having "seasons," or distinct phases: *acute survival* refers to the diagnosis and treatment phase; *extended survival* is the time period immediately after treatment, characterized by hypervigilance and watchful waiting; and *permanent survival* refers to the phase in which survivors are disease free and have returned to their lives fully functioning (Miller et al., 2008; Mullan, 1985). This last phase can be marked by complications with employment and long-standing side effects, but it also tends to include a decrease in the anxiety and hypervigilance regarding health issues that marked the previous phases (Miller et al., 2008). Miller, Ben-Aharon, and Haines (2011) proposed a revised paradigm that includes additional phases of survivorship to reflect a new understanding of the complexity and multiplicity of pathways inherent in cancer survivorship. This model includes acknowledgment of survivors living with chronic disease (*chronic survivorship*) and those facing end of life (*end of life*).

In the last decade, researchers and practitioners have begun to explore the applicability of chronic illness models to cancer care. Such models may have relevance to the management of late- and long-term effects of cancer in survivors who are disease free, but they may also be useful in addressing the needs of survivors with chronic, recurrent, or metastatic illness. With the successes of newer targeted therapies, an increased number of cancer survivors are living for many years with cancer as a chronic illness. For this subset of cancer survivors, adjustment tasks center on learning to manage the progression of disease that is controlled by additional treatment or that is indolent, is slow growing, and requires a "watchful waiting" approach to care. The psychosocial tasks for this population include learning to live in the present and learning to sustain a balance between living life and negotiating an uncertain future (Breitbart, 2005). Survivors living with chronic or metastatic disease may find that their experiences and needs do not mesh neatly with those of individuals requiring end-of-life care or those whose disease is in remission. Mixing of survivors in different disease stages could have a negative impact on coping and adjustment (Cella, Sarafian, Snider, Yellen, & Winicours, 1993; Vilhauer, 2011). Consequently, from a clinical perspective, creating support services tailored to the needs of survivors at each phase of the survivorship continuum is vital (Vilhauer, 2011).

Predominant Issues Associated With Survivorship

Physical difficulties. *More than 40% of survivors struggle with long-standing side effects from treatment (Schnoll et al., 2002). For example, medical aftereffects, such as cardiac toxicities and secondary cancers, can be present with survivorship (Dow, 2003). Survivors who underwent intensive chemotherapy regimens can experience common side effects, such as neuropathy, persistent fatigue, and changes in cognitive functioning (Dow, 2003; Schnoll et al., 2002; Stanton, 2012). Other aftereffects, such as decreased sexual functioning, infertility, reduced ability to function in interpersonal relationships, depression, or posttraumatic stress disorder (PTSD), can negatively affect survivors' quality of life (Dow, 2003; Schnoll et al., 2002; Stanton, 2012).*

Practical difficulties. *Survivors may experience functional limitations or psychosocial difficulties that adversely affect their ability to work or to do so at their precancer level. A cancer diagnosis and treatment can lead to financial debt, complications with health insurance, and disruption of one's educational trajectory (Farley Short, Vasey, & Tunceli, 2005; Main, Nowels, Cavender, Etschmaier, & Steiner, 2005; Rechis, Reynolds, Beckjord, & Nutt, 2011). Many survivors report problems related to employment: for example, a sense of "job lock" (feeling stuck in one's current job), reticence about explaining gaps in their resumé, or subtle discrimination in the workplace (Rechis et al., 2011; Stanton, 2012).*

Emotional difficulties. *Survivors' reactions to the end of active treatment can be complicated: For example, relief may be mixed with anxiety because of reduced scrutiny by the health care team (Ganz, 2006; Parry, Morningstar, Kendall, & Coleman, 2011; Rowland, 2008; Rowland & Bellizzi, 2008; Stanton, 2006). Some survivors may feel "out of sync" with family and friends, who are confused by the survivor's mixed responses to the end of treatment (Rowland, 2008; Stanton, 2006). Survivors may have an increased sense of vulnerability caused by a heightened awareness of their own mortality, reduced sense of future, and hypervigilance about a possible recurrence (Rowland, 2008). Fear of mortality can be exacerbated by reduced medical follow-up visits (Deimling, Bowman, Sterns, Wagner, & Boaz, 2006; Stanton, 2012). Up to 32% of survivors experience symptoms of PTSD, and up to 58% experience clinical depression—a rate three times that in the general population (Andrykowski, Lykins, & Floyd, 2008; Li, Fitzgerald, & Rodin, 2012). Depression can range from a relatively brief period of depressed mood to more serious and prolonged conditions such as dysthymia (Li et al., 2012).*

Finally, survivors of a life-threatening illness often re-examine their identity and self-concept, which includes existential reflection and personal growth and has the potential to initiate profound life changes (Andrykowski et al., 2008). Periods of positive change and deeper understandings of self can develop concurrently with periods of grief and depression, all of which makes the posttreatment period one that is often marked by emotional growth.

Clinical Delivery Options in Psychosocial Care for Cancer Survivors

Comprehensive psychosocial care involves both broad informational programs and more targeted support such as individual and couples counseling, supportive expressive groups, or relationship-building adventure programs. An individual's personal history, interests, and learning preferences may influence which modality he or she will choose for support after cancer. The clinical goals of informational programs and targeted support allow survivors to strengthen coping skills, adjust to long-standing side effects, and learn to manage fear of recurrence. Research on the efficacy of supportive interventions for cancer survivors has shown that cognitive behavioral therapeutic (CBT) approaches have the most success in promoting better coping skills for survivors (Traeger, Greer, Fernandez-Robles, Temeland, & Pirl, 2012). CBT-based interventions that help survivors monitor their cancer-related thoughts or thoughts about fear of recurrence and changes to their body and self-image have the longest-lasting impact on optimal adjustment after treatment (Traeger et al., 2012). In addition, relaxation skills, problem solving, and development of new coping skills and patterns have been shown to be effective in helping survivors transition to a cancer-free future (Stanton, 2012).

Individual, Couples, and Family Counseling

Individual counseling can provide one-to-one focused support for integrating changes resulting from cancer treatment in the physical, practical, and emotional domains. Individual counseling is usually time limited (six to eight sessions) and focused on survivorship issues. Grief related to losses associated with the diagnosis and difficulties in determining how to disclose one's cancer history to employers or potential romantic partners are examples of typical issues. The therapist and survivor develop therapeutic goals for discussion and use a combination of CBT and psychotherapeutic interventions to address pressing issues and develop coping skills to resolve complex issues (Traeger et al., 2012). Once targeted issues are addressed, the survivor will either follow up as needed or perhaps benefit from a supportive expressive group model with peers to gain a sense of community connection with other survivors.

The impact of the cancer diagnosis can cause aftereffects that ripple into couple or family support systems. Survivors often report that family members act as if everything is "normal" after treatment in an effort to move forward and protect their loved one and to return to a pre-cancer homeostasis. Common issues such as fear of mortality, changes in sexual functioning, and identity shifts can be difficult topics to discuss with family members. Silence around these topics causes stress and deep misunderstandings within relationships and, in these instances, couples and family counseling can provide a forum for articulation of feelings and renegotiation of roles and relationships disrupted by the cancer experience (Manne & Badr, 2008).

Group Approaches in Survivorship Counseling and Support

Despite research gaps on the use of group therapies in the posttreatment survivor population, survivors who attend psychoeducational support groups have reported fewer symptoms and better coping strategies than have those who did not attend such groups (Goodwin et al., 2001; Kissane et al., 2004; Spiegel, Kraemer, Bloom, & Gottheil, 1989). Existing research points to the utility of problem-solving strategies to facilitate adaptation among survivors in changing health behaviors, fostering acceptance, finding meaning, expanding and building social support, and encouraging adaptive coping mechanisms (Kissane et al., 2004; Schnoll et al., 2002).

An awareness of basic group counseling principles is necessary when designing a survivorship-oriented group: instill hope, promote universality, impart information, create group cohesiveness to reduce isolation, address existential issues, and promote greater openness and emotional expressiveness within and outside the group (Maldonado et al., 1996). The goals of survivorship groups are to facilitate mutual support among group members, reduce isolation, and create commonality. Professionally led support groups can decrease feelings of loneliness and guilt and provide a venue wherein group members may discuss issues with other survivors that

Martin, a 27-year-old single man, was diagnosed with Burkitt's lymphoma in 2005. The diagnosis came as a shock because Martin was an avid athlete who had maintained a healthy diet for as long as he could remember. Martin had always assumed that if he kept up his "exceptionally healthy lifestyle," he would avoid any major illnesses. He was treated with chemotherapy as an inpatient and was hospitalized for approximately a month.

A year after treatment ended, Martin found himself grappling with a pervasive feeling of sadness, isolation, and depression. Although he accepted social invitations, he did not feel as though he had anything to contribute to conversations and wondered whether he could ever feel connected to his friends again. His oncologist referred him for counseling and Martin attended six individual sessions with an oncology social worker on staff. The focus of the sessions was Martin's deep feelings of loneliness—the sense that he had "used up" all his friends when he was sick and his reluctance to lean too hard on them anymore. He remarked that compared with the treatment period, the posttreatment phase felt "much more difficult. I can't seem to transition back to my old life the way I thought I'd be able to." The oncology social worker encouraged Martin to attend a time-limited support group for men to reduce his feelings of isolation and to give him the opportunity to vent about some of the difficult feelings he was experiencing.

In the group, Martin found that he was able to speak freely about his anxieties and concerns without worrying that he would alienate the other men. He also benefited greatly by listening to how the other group members coped with some of the difficulties he faced. He felt a sense of connectedness he had not known for many, many months. He had always felt close to his family members and friends, but he had never shared such deeply personal aspects of himself with other men before and felt surprised and grateful for the experience.

they are unable to discuss with family members (Kissane et al., 2004). This opportunity to articulate unspoken feelings among peers allows for a better understanding of these feelings and can result in improved social and family support. Because issues of death and mortality are common concerns in survivorship, support groups can serve to detoxify feelings around death and dying and consequently enhance quality of life (Maldonado et al., 1996; Yalom, 2005). Group cohesion can also be enhanced by designing survivorship groups for specific populations, such as young adults, men, women, older adults, and lesbian, gay, bisexual, or transgender (LGBT) survivors (Hermann, 2005).

Care Coordination and Delivery Across the Cancer Continuum

As cancer survivors move across the continuum of care, they face many transitions (from screening to diagnosis, from active treatment to being off treatment, and from curative to palliative care and to end of life. For example, for many cancer patients, the end of primary treatment delineates a major transition in care from oncology to primary care providers or, in the case of patients with complex or multiple conditions, to a host of providers (Grunfeld & Earle, 2010; Taplin & Rodgers, 2010). If care is not planned and coordinated and a posttreatment care plan not communicated to survivors, they may lack the knowledge and resources to acquire recommended follow-up care and surveillance, with the potential for negative impact to their long-term health and well-being (Hewitt et al., 2006).

Transitional Care Models

The literature on chronic illness care suggests potentially beneficial models, instruments, and approaches to delivering patient-centered transitional care in primary and specialty care settings (Coleman, Parry, Chalmers, & Min, 2006; Naylor, Brooten, Campbell, & Maislin, 2004). Transitional care is defined as "a set of actions designed to ensure the coordination and continuity of health care as patients transfer between different locations or different levels of care within the same location" (Coleman & Boult, 2003). Transitional care models hold promise as a means for patients to manage late- and long-term effects and to navigate transitions of care across the survivorship continuum. The limitation is that these models have not yet been rigorously tested in the context of cancer. Likewise, interdisciplinary team models offer an approach to leveraging the resources and expertise necessary to meet survivors' ongoing needs. However, questions remain as to what constellation of providers is best equipped and prepared to provide care across the continuum; how best to promote teamwork, coordination, and communication among providers; and the most useful strategies and instruments to assess the effects of team approaches to care (Parry, Kent, et al., 2011).

Approaches to Care Delivery

The 2006 report *From Cancer Patient to Cancer Survivor: Lost in Transition* listed five barriers to the delivery of quality survivorship care: (1) fragmentation of the delivery system, (2) lack of targeted education and training on survivorship care among providers, (3) lack of evidence-based standards of survivorship care, (4) communication difficulties, and (5) lack of clarity about responsibility for care (Hewitt et al., 2006, p. 201). In the intervening years since the release of the report, multiple models have been elaborated and proposed, including patient-centered primary care or specialist-led models, consultative clinic models, multidisciplinary team models, and the patient-centered medical home model (Agency for Healthcare Research and Quality, 2012; Howell et al., 2012; Oeffinger & McCabe, 2006). However, to date, research exploring the application, efficacy, and cost-effectiveness of these models in cancer care has been limited and lacks a high-quality evidence base (McCabe & Jacobs, 2012). Additional strategies to enhance the quality and continuity of transitional and follow-up care for cancer survivors include attending to *processes* of care delivery between settings, types, and providers of care; adoption of risk-based models of care; meaningful use of electronic medical records as a vehicle to promote communication and coordination of care; and the use of survivorship care plans and care planning interventions to improve the transitional and follow-up care experience for survivors (Oeffinger & McCabe, 2006; Parry, Kent, et al., 2011; Taplin & Rodgers, 2010). Two approaches that have received support from accreditation organizations to enhance the quality of cancer care include the use of treatment summaries/care plans and the implementation of distress screening.

Survivorship Care Planning

In its landmark 2006 report, the IOM recommended survivorship care plans as a means of promoting communication among providers and coordination of care. The IOM suggested that every patient completing primary treatment receive a written treatment summary and care plan in conjunction with a consultative visit. Subsequently, the American Society of Clinical Oncology recommended provision of treatment summaries and the American College of Surgeons' Commission on Cancer (ACOS COC, 2012) recommended provision of a written treatment summary and care plan as standard practice for quality oncology care. Preliminary evidence suggests that survivorship care planning may be associated with improved compliance with surveillance recommendations, reductions in duplicative service use, and improved patient preparation for follow-up care. Evidence to date suggests the need for further exploration of the relative and combined contributions of treatment summaries/care plans, the consultative visit, and strategies for coordinating transitional and follow-up care between primary care providers, oncologists, and other members of a patient's health care team. Moreover, research is needed to establish best practices for implementation of patient-centered survivorship care planning that is delivered in accordance with the IOM recommendations and to explore the staff time, costs, and reimbursement mechanisms associated with the delivery of care planning (Earle, 2007; Stricker et al., 2011).

Distress Screening and Management

A second innovation proposed to enhance the quality of care across the survivorship continuum is distress screening. Championed by the NCCN and underscored by the IOM's goal of whole-patient care, distress screening is intended to identify patients with high levels of psychosocial morbidity, for subsequent treatment and management (Adler & Page, 2008; Holland et al., 2010). Guidelines released by the ACOS COC (2012) call for incorporation of distress screening into oncology care, with phased-in implementation through January 2015. As discussed in the distress screening section of this book (Section 4), an integrated practice and research agenda in psychosocial care is needed to assess the best constructs and measures to evaluate distress; to determine appropriate intervals for assessment; to assess the impact of distress management on patient, provider, and system-level outcomes in cancer care; and to determine the best means of achieving integrated psychosocial care across the survivorship continuum (Parry, Padgett, & Zebrack, 2012).

Implications of Policy Changes for Cancer Survivorship: The Affordable Care Act

Survivorship care may be influenced by policy changes spurred by the Affordable Care Act (ACA), as outlined comprehensively elsewhere in this volume. As it is implemented, the ACA will have implications for the care of cancer survivors. First, ACA stipulations remove annual and lifetime limits on care coverage, which will support continuity and access to care for cancer survivors who might otherwise face financial barriers to treatment and follow-up care. Second, the ACA Guaranteed Issue clause prevents denial of insurance provision because of preexisting conditions, such as cancer. Guaranteed Issue has the potential to affect the insurability of all cancer survivors, but especially the unemployed and those under age 65. Finally, the ACA allows inclusion of children on parents' insurance plans until age 26 (of import to young adult cancer survivors) and a "no cost sharing" model for screening and preventive care, including cancer screening, both of which may improve access to care across the survivorship continuum.

This chapter has provided a brief history of the cancer survivorship movement and its evolution to a present-day reality in which "survivorship" is a widely recognized phenomenon, bolstered by policy and research. However, as the population of cancer survivors continues to grow and our understanding of survivors' complex needs deepens, many important questions remain for researchers and clinicians.

Directions for Future Research

- *Which survivors are at greatest risk for physical or psychosocial morbidity?*
- *What is the best method of assessing such risks?*
- *How can risk assessment be integrated into care delivery models and decision-making processes?*
- *What models (e.g., interdisciplinary teams, shared care) will be most effective for coordinating care between providers in which settings (community centers vs. academic medical centers)?*
- *Which tools can facilitate delivery of care (e.g., care plans; distress detection instruments, processes, or both; electronic medical records)?*
- *What strategies for using these tools will prove meaningful to patients and providers?*
- *What kind of prospective longitudinal studies are needed to understand the late- and long-term effects of cancer and its treatment?*
- *How do these effects intersect with the development, progression, and management of comorbid conditions and age-related decline?*
- *What approaches, models, and tools would be most effective for delivering high-quality transitional and follow-up care to a diverse and aging population of cancer survivors?*

The past decades have borne witness to an evolving understanding of cancer survivorship, informed by an iterative dialogue among researchers, clinicians, advocates, and policymakers. As we move into the future, our conception of cancer survivorship is being shaped by changing demographic trends, a shifting health care environment, and technological advances. This context provides the field of social work with opportunities to map new territory in models and processes of care that may improve the experience of cancer survivors and ultimately reduce the burden of cancer.

Pearls

- Posttreatment is a distinct phase in survivorship with unique physical, practical, and emotional issues.

- Care coordination and treatment plans are integral to successfully addressing the long-standing and complex issues that continue in the posttreatment phase.
- The posttreatment survivorship phase comprises "seasons" of adjustments, including emotional, physical, and practical domains.

Pitfalls

- Most of the resources for psychosocial support continue to be dedicated to the crisis of treatment neglecting the impact of long-standing side effects on multiple domains.
- Coordination of posttreatment care plans can be complicated by disrupted communication between treatment centers and the medical team conducting follow-up.
- Our conception of cancer survivorship will be shaped by changing demographic trends, a shifting health care environment, and technological advances, making the need for clear care plans and communication all the more important.

REFERENCES

Adler, N. E., & Page, A. E. K. (2008). National Institute of Medicine Committee on Psychosocial Services to Cancer Patients/Families in a Community Setting. In *Cancer care for the whole patient: Meeting psychosocial health needs*. Washington, DC: National Academies Press.

Agency for Healthcare Research and Quality. (2012). Patient Centered Medical Home resource center. Retrieved from http://www.pcmh.ahrq.gov/portal/server.pt/community/pcmh__home/1483

American College of Surgeons' Commission on Cancer. (2012). *Cancer program standards 2012: Ensuring patient-centered care* (Vol. 2, pp. 76–77). Retrieved from https://www.facs.org/~/media/files/quality%20programs/cancer/coc/programstandards2012.ashx

Andrykowski, M. A., Lykins, E., & Floyd, A. (2008). Psychological health in cancer survivors. *Seminars in Oncology Nursing, 24*(3), 193–201.

Breitbart, W. (2005). Spirituality and meaning in cancer. *Revue Francophone de Psycho-Oncologie, 4*, 237–240.

Cella, D. F., Sarafian, B., Snider, P. R., Yellen, S. B., & Winicours, P. (1993). Evaluation of a community-based cancer support group. *Psycho-Oncology, 2*, 123–132.

Coleman, E. A., & Boult, C. E. (2003). Improving the quality of transitional care for persons with complex care needs. *Journal of the American Geriatrics Society, 51*(4), 556–557.

Coleman, E. A., Parry, C., Chalmers, S., & Min, S. (2006). The care transitions intervention: Results of a randomized controlled trial. *Archives of Internal Medicine, 166*, 1822–1828.

Dow, K. H. (2003). Challenges and opportunities in cancer survivorship research. *Oncology Nursing Forum, 30*(3), 455–469.

Earle, C. C. (2007). Long-term care planning for cancer survivors: A health services research agenda. *Journal of Cancer*

Farley Short, P., Vasey, J. J., & Tunceli, K. (2005). Employment pathways in a large cohort of adult cancer survivors. *Cancer, 103*(6), 1292–1301.

Ganz, P. A. (2006). Monitoring the physical health of cancer survivors: A survivorship-focused medical history. *Journal of Clinical Oncology, 24*(32), 5105–5111.

Goodwin, P. J., Leszcz, M., Ennis, M., Koopmans, J., Vincent, L., Guther, H., . . . Hunter, J. (2001). The effect of group psychosocial support on survival in metastatic breast cancer. *New England Journal of Medicine, 345*, 1719–1726.

Grunfeld, E., & Earle, C. (2010). The interface between primary and oncology specialty care: Treatment through survivorship. *Journal of the National Cancer Institute Monograph, 40*, 18–24.

Hermann, J. (2005). *Cancer support groups: A guide for facilitators*. New York, NY: American Cancer Society.

Hewitt, M., Greenfield, S., & Stovall, E. (Eds.). (2006). *From cancer patient to cancer survivor: Lost in transition*. Washington, DC: National Academies Press.

Hoffman, B., & Stovall, E. (2006). Survivorship perspectives and advocacy. *Journal of Clinical Oncology, 24*(32), 5154–5159.

Holland, J., Andersen, B., Breitart, W., Compas, B., Dudley, M., Fleishman, S., . . . Zevon, M. (2010). The NCCN distress management clinical practice guidelines in oncology. *Journal of the National Comprehensive Cancer Network, 8*(4), 448–485.

Howell, D., Hack, T. F., Oliver, T. K., Chulak, T., Mayo, S., Aubin, M., . . . Sinclair, S. (2012). Models of care for post-treatment follow-up of adult cancer survivors: A systematic review and quality appraisal of the evidence. *Journal of Cancer Survivorship, 6*(4), 359–371.

Kissane, D. W., Grabasch, B., Clarke, D. M., Christie, G., Clifton, D., Gold, S., . . . Smith, G. C. (2004). Supportive-expressive group therapy: The transformation of existential ambivalence into creative living while enhancing adherence to anti-cancer therapies. *Psycho-Oncology, 11*, 755–768.

Li, M., Fitzgerald, P., & Rodin, G. (2012). Evidence-based treatment of depression in patients with cancer. *Journal of Clinical Oncology, 30*(11), 1187–1196.

Main, D. S., Nowels, C. T., Cavender, T. A., Etschmaier, M., & Steiner, J. F. (2005). A qualitative study of work and work return in cancer survivors. *Psycho-Oncology, 14*(11), 992–1004.

Maldonado, J., Gore-Felton, C., Duran, R., Diamond, S., Koopman, C., & Spiegel, D. (1996). *Supportive-expressive group therapy for people with HIV infection: A primer*. Palo Alto, CA: Psychosocial Treatment Laboratory, Stanford University School of Medicine. Retrieved from http://stresshealthcenter.stanford.edu/research/documents/GroupLeaderPrimerforHIVGroupTherapyStudy.pdf

Manne, S., & Badr, H. (2008). Intimacy and relationship processes in couples' psychosocial adaptation to cancer. *Cancer; Supplement: Cancer Survivorship Embracing the Future, 112*(11), 2541–2555.

McCabe, M. S., & Jacobs, L. A. (2012). Clinical update: Survivorship care—models and programs. *Oncology Nursing, 28*(3), e1–e8.

Miller, K., Ben-Aharon, I., & Haines, L. (2011). Seasons of survival: Redefining the paradigm of cancer survivorship for 2011. *Oncology Practice Management*. Retrieved from http://issuu.com/aonn/docs/jons_sept2011

Miller, K., Merry, B., & Miller, J. (2008). Seasons of survivorship revisited. *Cancer Journal, 14*(6), 369–374.

Mullan, F. (1985). Seasons of survival: Reflections of a physician with cancer. *New England Journal of Medicine*, *313*, 270–273.

Naylor, M. D., Brooten, D. A., Campbell, R. L., & Maislin, G. (2004). Transitional care of older adults hospitalized with heart failure: A randomized, controlled trial. *Journal of the American Geriatric Society*, 52, 675–684.

Oeffinger, K. C., & McCabe, M. S. (2006). Models for delivering survivorship care. *Journal of Clinical Oncology*, *32*(10), 5117–5124.

Parry, C., Kent, E., Mariotto, A., Alfano, C., & Rowland, J. (2011). Cancer survivors: A booming population. *Community Epidemiology, Biomarkers and Prevention*, *20*(10), 1996–2005.

Parry, C., Morningstar, E., Kendall, J., & Coleman, E. (2011). Working without a net: Leukemia and lymphoma survivors' perspectives on care delivery at end of treatment and beyond. *Journal of Psychosocial Oncology*, *29*(2), 175–198.

Parry, C., Padgett, L., & Zebrack, B. (2012). Now what? Toward an integrated research and practice agenda in distress screening. *Journal of Psychosocial Oncology*, *30*(6), 715–727.

Rechis, R., Reynolds, K. A., Beckjord, E. B., & Nutt, S. (2011). "I learned to live with it" is not enough: Challenges reported by post-treatment cancer survivors in the LIVESTRONG surveys. LIVESTRONG reports. Retrieved from http://livestrong.org/pdfs/3-0/LSSurvivorSurveyReport_final

Rowland, J. H. (2008). What are cancer survivors telling us? *Cancer Journal*, *14*(6), 361–368.

Rowland, J., & Bellizzi, K. M. (2008). Cancer survivors and survivorship research: A reflection on today's successes and tomorrow's challenges. *Hematology Oncology Clinics of North America*, 22, 181–200.

Rowland, J. H., & Stefanek, M. (2008). Introduction: Partnering to embrace the future of cancer survivorship research and care. *Cancer Supplement*, *112*(11), 2523–2528.

Schnoll, R. A., Knowles, J. C., & Harlow, L. (2002). Correlates of adjustment among cancer survivors. *Journal of Psychosocial Oncology*, *20*(1), 37–59.

Spiegel, D., Kraemer, H. C., Bloom, J. R., & Gottheil, E. (1989). Effects of psychosocial treatment on survival of patients with metastatic breast cancer. *Lancet*, *334*(8668), 888–891.

Stanton, A. L. (2006). Psychosocial concerns and interventions for cancer survivors. *Journal of Clinical Oncology*, *24*, 5132–5137.

Stanton, A. L. (2012). What happens now? Psychosocial care for cancer survivors after medical treatment completion. *Journal of Clinical Oncology*, *30*(11), 1215–1220.

Stricker, C. T., Jacobs, L. A., Risendal, B., Jones, A., Panzer, S., Ganz, P., … Palmer, S. C. (2011). Survivorship care planning after the Institute of Medicine recommendations: How are we faring? *Journal of Cancer Survivorship*, *5*(4), 358–370.

Taplin, S. H., & Rodgers, A. B. (2010). Toward improving the quality of cancer care: Addressing the interfaces of primary and oncology-related subspecialty care. *Journal of the National Cancer Institute Monograph*, *40*, 3–10.

Traeger, L., Greer, J. A., Fernandez-Robles, C., Temeland, J. S., & Pirl, W. F. (2012). Evidence-based treatment of anxiety in patients with cancer. *Journal of Clinical Oncology*, *30*(11), 1197–1205.

Vilhauer, R. P. (2011). "Them" and "us": The experiences of women with metastatic disease in mixed-stage versus stage-specific breast cancer support groups. *Psychology and Health*, *26*(6), 781–797.

Yalom, I. D. (2005). *The theory and practice of group psychotherapy* (5th ed.). New York, NY: Basic Books.

10

Deborah Waldrop and Sherri Weisenfluh

Transition to End-of-Life Care in Oncology

Key Concepts

- *Distress management involves attention to the emotional, psychological, and spiritual responses that accompany challenges of people with cancer and their loved ones across the illness trajectory.*
- *Palliative care is holistic, interdisciplinary, and focused on the person with cancer and his or her family as a unit of care.*
- *End-of-life care can be delivered in many settings: at home, in long-term care, in freestanding inpatient units, and in hospitals.*
- *Psychosocial concerns include changing roles, communication about disease progression, fear of what is ahead, health care decision making, financial issues, and the need for social support, and they affect the well-being of all people in the family.*

For patients and their family members, the transition between living with and dying from cancer can bring distress along a continuum, from normal feelings of vulnerability, sadness, and fear to potentially disabling problems of depression, anxiety, panic, social isolation, and existential or spiritual crises (National Comprehensive Cancer Network, n.d.). Distress also intensifies as the patient declines; it should be evaluated across the cancer trajectory and at the end of life. Understanding distress is critical for awareness of the challenges facing people who are terminally ill and their families (Chochinov et al., 2009).

Each year 6 million people die from cancer, but with projections indicating an increase to 15 million by 2020 (Ferris et al., 2009), the need to integrate palliative care into cancer treatment is greater than ever. Palliative care focuses on relieving suffering and achieving the best possible quality of life for the seriously ill and their family caregivers (Abrahm, 2011) while alleviating physical, psychological, social, and spiritual pain and suffering, whether or not cure is an option (World Health Organization, 2002). Cancer patients nearing life's end *and* their families are in particular need of palliative care, which involves treating all as a unit of care, optimizing function, helping with decision making, and providing opportunities for personal growth. This chapter provides a literature review of the state of cancer palliation and describes settings for end-of-life care, transitional issues, interventions, and preparation for bereavement.

The State of the Art and Science of Palliative Cancer Care

Historically, the term *hospice* referred to a place of shelter and rest for weary or ill travelers. Dame Cicely Saunders, however, applied the concept to the process of dying and opened the first hospice in London (St. Christopher's) before introducing the idea to the United States in 1963, where it gained momentum during the 1970s and became a Medicare benefit in 1982 (NHPCO, 2008). By 2006, *palliative care* became an officially recognized subspecialty of internal medicine as a means for achieving the goal of improved quality of life in hospice care (AAHPM, 2008).

The Center for the Advancement of Palliative Care (CAPC) contributed to the rapid growth and sustainability of palliative care programs in the United States, and by 2008, the CAPC had trained thousands of U.S. administrators and clinicians (Weissman, Meier, & Spragens, 2008). Simultaneously, major educational efforts undertaken by the American Society for Clinical Oncology (ASCO) increased attention to psychosocial issues in cancer care (Adler & Page, 2008). ASCO issued a provisional opinion that palliative care, when combined with standard cancer care, leads to better patient and caregiver outcomes and should be considered early the illness for any person with metastatic cancer and/or high symptom burden (Smith et al., 2012). As a result, social work in oncology, hospice, and palliative care settings has developed in concert with this interdisciplinary movement.

Social workers are core members of oncology, hospice, and palliative care teams. Zebrack, Walsh, Burg, Maramaldi, and Lim (2008) surveyed oncology social workers and found that the majority felt competent in dealing with end-of-life issues and advanced directives, as well as grief and bereavement in adult patients and families (Zebrack et al., 2008). AOSW and the Oncology Nursing Society (ONS) developed a joint position statement that addresses patient and family rights; palliative care, interdisciplinary teams, and integrated care systems; and public advocacy (ONS & AOSW, 2012). Social workers need to play pivotal roles in helping families navigate the complex health care system and transitions between settings for care.

Settings for End-of-Life Care

When asked, most people express the wish to die at home; yet, despite increased support for home-based cancer care, most die in a hospital (Bell, Somogyi-Zalud, & Masaki, 2010; Burge, Lawson, & Johnston, 2003). Improving congruence between the actual and preferred place of death requires physician involvement, hospice enrollment, and family support (Bell et al., 2010). Likewise, social workers should engage in active planning with their patients and patients' families to address increasing needs, support family caregivers, and uphold end-of-life wishes so patients can die where they wish.

Hospitals

Cancer patients who die in a hospital experience poorer quality of life than those who die at home, and their caregivers are at increased risk for bereavement difficulties (Wright et al., 2010). Because acute medical problems can accompany cancer treatment (e.g., chemotherapy, surgery, radiation), many patients visit emergency rooms or require intensive care unit (ICU) admission. Because most ICU deaths occur after limiting or withdrawing life support, provider–family meetings are particularly important (Gaeta & Price, 2010), where consideration of the elements of a "good death," directed by the patient/family, consistent with their values and beliefs, and occurring in the setting of choice, can contribute to quality care for cancer patients who die in an ICU.

Home Care

Moving cancer care from an inpatient to a home setting requires increased family involvement and hands-on care, which can result in intense physical, emotional, psychological, and financial distress (Townsend, Ishler, Shapiro, Pitorak, & Matthews, 2010). Cancer patients have multifaceted needs, including disease and treatment monitoring, symptom management, medication administration, emotional support, and assistance with personal care. Although in-home nursing care, housekeeping, and religious support have been identified as important support services (Brazil et al., 2005), family members may be ill prepared to assume these tasks and require instruction in technical care (Dubus, 2010). Social workers can help identify and access services and normalize family caregivers' emotional responses to the patient's diagnosis and prognosis that can become more intense in end-stage care.

Hospice

Many barriers and misconceptions related to the transition to hospice and palliative care can impede discussions, preventing timely referrals. Often fraught with emotion and uncertainty, hospice enrollment is a major transition on the cancer trajectory (Wittenberg-Lyles & Thompson, 2006). Although the use of end-of-life hospice and palliative care services has increased, many patients still enroll in hospice only days to weeks before death, limiting its benefits and caregivers' adaptation to bereavement (Bradley et al., 2004; NHPCO, 2012)

"I told her she wouldn't have to go to a nursing home," Janet wept as she explained this conversation that occurred two years ago. Now Janet finds herself caring for both her 82-year-old mother and her 85-year-old father. Janet's mother was diagnosed with lung cancer 2 years ago and was recently admitted to hospice. Janet's father, also admitted to hospice, was diagnosed with pancreatic cancer a month ago. "I am exhausted and don't know how much longer I can do it," she explained. "With both of them needing so much, I find myself thinking I might have to put mom in a home. How much longer do you think it will be? What do you think I should do?"

The social work role would first involve helping Janet express her feelings and validating the emotional and physical exhaustion that accompanies caregiving. It would also be important to help Janet identify options for additional assistance, respite, and possible placement and to help her think about how to approach caring for her parents with alternate plans.

Nursing Home

Nursing home residents who have cancer have been found to have more pain, shortness of breath, vomiting, weight loss, and diarrhea, and symptom control has been found to need improvement (Duncan, Bott, Thompson, & Gajewski, 2009). Despite the fact that many are likely to experience cancer-specific symptoms and marked physical decline before death, very few cancer-related services are provided to nursing home patients (Bradley, Clement, & Lin, 2008).

Issues in the Transition from Cure-Focused to Palliative Care

Nonstandard Definitions

A lack of definitional clarity has led to confusion and uncertainty about the nature of care in the end-stage of life. Hui and colleagues (2012) systematically reviewed the number of occurrences of the terms *palliative care, end of life*, and *terminally ill* in palliative care journals, finding that they appeared more frequently, whereas the terms *supportive care* and *best supportive care* were used often in oncology journals. Although much has been done to inform the public about differences between hospice, palliative care, and supportive care, standardizing definitions will improve care and access across settings.

Avoidance of Prognosis Discussions

Communication is essential to quality care at life's end, yet discussing prognoses and end-of-life wishes during aggressive treatments is often avoided, leading to poor health outcomes (Cohen & Nirenberg, 2011). There seems to be an underlying fear of harming people by discussing end-of-life wishes; however, evidence demonstrates that these discussions create no psychological harm (Detering, Hancock, Reade, & Silvester, 2010), and social workers are well poised to facilitate the goals of care discussions in all health care settings.

Race and Culture

Along with the difficulty of presenting hospice and palliative care options to a patient and family reluctant to discuss a terminal prognosis, racial and cultural preferences also influence the transition to end-stage care. Among patients with advanced cancer, Whites have been found to be more likely than Blacks to receive their preferred form of care at life's end. Loggers and colleagues (2009) found that discussions about end-of-life care "do not resuscitate" orders occur less often with Black patients, and as a result, they receive more life-prolonging care. For Latinos, denial, secrecy about prognosis, and a collective, family-centered system influence hospice decisions and the hospice experience (Kreling, Selsky, Perret-Gentil, Huerta, & Mandelblatt, 2010).

Lack of Caregiver Experience

Caregiving intensifies during the transition to end-of-life care, and caregivers often assume the role under sudden and extreme circumstances with minimal preparation and uneven provider guidance. As such, identifying family caregivers at risk for difficulty in bereavement is key to improving end-of-life care (Townsend et al., 2010).

Influencing the end-of-life caregiving experience includes recognizing the unique characteristics of the family caregiver and patient, symptoms of the patient's illness and functional status, relational context, and level of social and professional support (Dumont, Dumont, & Mongeau, 2008). The process of transition to end-of-life care is enhanced by assessment of differential needs, preparation for the final stage, and information on disease progress, food and nutrition, body positioning, and body mechanics (Ronaldson & Devery, 2001), and the use of specific protocols reduces fragmentation of care (see Table 10.1) (Gaeta & Price, 2010).

Loss of Care Continuity

A sense of abandonment can occur if an oncologist shifts care to a palliative medicine specialist (Storey, Fallon, & Smyth, 2011), which breaks the continuity between the patient and physician and the sense of closure for patients and their loved ones (Back et al., 2009). Social workers can ease the transition from cure to palliative or hospice care by providing emotional and informational support.

Interventions

Patient navigation is an intervention that helps patients address care disparities and barriers (Commission on Cancer, 2014). The Commission on Cancer standards require that cancer centers and other health care organizations use patient navigation to improve care for those facing barriers to access or quality of care (Fashoyin-Aje, Martinez, & Dy, 2012). As such, social workers need to be knowledgeable about resources, health care policy, and insurance eligibility requirements while also facilitating timely discussion about the changing goals of care and the patient's wishes at life's end.

Advance Care Planning

Advance care planning (ACP) is a process by which patients'

Table 10.1.
Selected Assessment Tools

Assessment Tool	Focus	Reference
Screen for Palliative and End-of-Life care needs in the Emergency Department (SPEED)	Assessment of end-of-life needs	Richards et al. (2011)
Social Work Assessment Tool (SWAT)	Assessment of patient/family psychosocial well-being	NHPCO (n.d.)
Caregiver Pain Medicine Questionnaire	Assessment of caregivers' understanding of pain medication	Oliver et al. (2008)
Cancer Communication Assessment Tool for Patients and Families (CCAT-PF)	Assessment of patient/family congruence in communication	Siminoff, Zyanski, Rose, & Zhang (2008)
Quality of Care Through the Patients' Eyes (QUOTE)	Assessment of unmet needs of people who are experiencing chemotherapy	Van Weert et al. (2009)
The Caregiver Reaction Assessment	Assessment of negative and positive aspects of caregiving	Bachner, O'Rourke, & Carmel (2007)
Quality Care Questionnaire–End-of-Life Care	Assessment of unmet needs: financial assistance, symptom management, psychosocial support	Park et al. (2010)

clarified, allowing for expression of their wishes for end-of-life care (Fried, Bullock, Iannone, & O'Leary, 2009). ACP should begin at the time of diagnosis and include listening to the patient's and family's beliefs and values while encouraging the patient to designate a critical surrogate decision maker.

Advance directives are written documents that express patients' wishes about specific medical interventions. Because predicting and outlining guidance for all scenarios is difficult, advance directives rarely dictate patient preferences in specific situations as a disease progresses. Although written documents are important, social workers should recognize the benefit to families of speaking with the surrogate decision maker and other relevant family members about end-of-life choices early in the disease trajectory.

Physician or Medical Orders for Life-Sustaining Treatment

Physician or medical orders for life-sustaining treatment (POLST or MOLST) forms are doctors' orders that provide explicit directions about wanted or unwanted resuscitation status and interventions (Bomba & Vermilyea, 2006). Because they travel with the patient across health care settings, POLST and MOLST forms are also helpful in providing care continuity. Social workers play integral roles in helping people with cancer and their families to consider and document their wishes.

Therapeutic Interventions

Traditionally used by social workers to facilitate a sense of meaning, importance, and dignity to patients and their families, therapeutic interventions can ease the distress of dying people and their families. A *life review* can emphasize a patient's value, contribution, and legacy. *Dignity therapy* is a short-term psychotherapy developed for people facing a life-threatening illness that has been found to mitigate distress (Chochinov et al., 2011; Csikai &Weisenfluh, 2012). *Family-focused grief therapy* helps families prepare for an approaching death and loss (Kissane et al., 2006). Supportive, therapeutic attention to intense emotions can facilitate preparation for bereavement.

Children Coping With Cancer: A Programmatic Example

Hospice of the Bluegrass (HOB) in Lexington, Kentucky, serves over 900 patients per day, approximately 40% of whom have been diagnosed with cancer. The staff identified the special needs of children living with a parent or sibling with a cancer diagnosis and the need for a camp to help children living in families dealing with cancer. A planning committee (administrative, bereavement, and social work staff) developed the mission to create an opportunity for children to come together and meet others coping with cancer. The goals were to help children:

- *Feel less alone.*
- *Express emotions without having to "protect" the feelings of other family members.*

- *Have fun in a safe environment.*

Children ages 6 to 12 who had family members with cancer who were enrolled in hospice were invited to attend Triple C (Children Coping With Cancer). Triple C was held at Camp Horsin' Around, a rural facility built to serve children dealing with life-limiting illness. Art therapy and recreational activities were coordinated to ensure that children had fun. Volunteer and staff ratios were approximately one adult to one child. A pet therapy dog and handler were part of the program. The social work role was to foster expression of emotions, encourage socialization, decrease isolation, and normalize the experiences of children dealing with cancer.

Preparation for Bereavement

The end-stage of cancer can trigger family conflict, and other factors, such as the existence of prior family conflict, race, communication constraints, and overly assertive family members, can be indicators of potential conflict at life's end (Kramer, Kavanaugh, Trentham-Dietz, Walsh, & Yonker, 2010b). Family members experience a sense of isolation and powerlessness often unrecognized by health care professionals; social work interventions that help family members meet their needs and prepare for the end of life can ease this bereavement (Clark, Brethwaite, & Gnesdiloff, 2011).

Bereaved family members are at high risk for distress, depression, and sleeplessness related to a range of variables such as age, gender, social support, and their experiences during caregiving (Holtslander, 2008). As such, assessing caregivers' receptivity to bereavement services is important for making timely referrals (Cherlin et al., 2007).

Psychological distress detected during caregiving continues into bereavement (Kapari, Addington-Hall, & Hotopf, 2010). Complicated grief symptoms were found to be higher in caregivers with less education, families with lower prior conflict but higher conflict at the end of life, family members who had difficulty accepting the illness, and those caring for patients with a greater fear of death. Family conflict, intrapsychic strain, and hospice utilization may help explain the variability among bereaved caregivers. Assessment of grief responses and preventative interventions are important across the continuum of cancer care (Kramer, Kavanaugh, Trentham-Dietz, Walsh, & Yonker, 2010a).

Pearls

- Family caregivers' distress intensifies as the patient declines and personal caregiving tasks increase in the home.
- The transition from cure-focused to end-stage care offers important opportunities for social workers to help families make difficult choices, talk openly about an approaching death, resolve conflicts, realize opportunities for growth, and complete relationships.
- Meaningful communication and interventions can improve the quality of care and prepare families for bereavement.

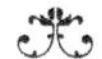

Pitfalls

- Prognostication about an approaching death can be difficult and create barriers to timely and appropriate transitions to palliative cancer care.
- The perception of medical abandonment can prompt the need for social work intervention to address the emotional responses to the transition to end-stage care.

Social work practice on oncology, hospice, and palliative care teams has "come of age." Recognition of the important psychosocial issues that occur in the late stages of cancer and with the transition to end-of-life care has underscored the development of astute assessment tools and effective interventions and has been a catalyst to professional commitment to interdisciplinary person-centered, family-focused care for people who are dying and their family members.

ADDITIONAL RESOURCES

Oncology

Cancer Control: Knowledge Into Action: Guidelines for Successful Programmes: http://www.who.int/cancer/publications/cancer_control_palliative/en/

National Quality Forum: National Voluntary Consensus Standards for Cancer Care: http://www.qualityforum.org/Publications/2009/05/National_Voluntary_Consensus_Standards_for_Quality_of_Cancer_Care.aspx

National Quality Forum: Project on Palliative Care and End-of-Life Care: http://www.qualityforum.org/Projects/Palliative_Care_and_End-of-Life_Care.aspx

NCCN Guidelines for Supportive Care Distress Management and Palliative Care: http://www.nccn.org

Patient Navigation in Cancer Care: http://www.patientnavigation.com/

Patient Navigation Research Program: http://crchd.cancer.gov/pnp/pnrp-index.html

END-OF-LIFE AND PALLIATIVE CARE

Center for the Advancement of Palliative Care: http://www.capc.org/

National Consensus Project for Quality Palliative Care: http://www.nationalconsensusproject.org/
National Hospice and Palliative Care Organization: http://www.nhpco.org
World Health Organization: http://www.who.int/cancer/palliative/en/

SOCIAL WORK

NASW Standards for Social Work Practice in Palliative and End of Life Care: http://www.naswdc.org/practice/bereavement/standards/standards0504New.pdf
NHPCO Social Work Guidelines: http://www.nhpco.org
Social Work Hospice and Palliative Care Network: http://www.swhpn.org/resourcelibrary/
Weisenfluh, S. (2007). Guidelines for social workers. National Hospice and Palliative Care Organization. NHPCO Marketplace. Retrieved from http://www.nhpco.org/search/node/Guidelines%20for%20Social%20Workers

REFERENCES

Abrahm, J. L. (2011). Advances in palliative medicine and end-of-life care. *Annual Review of Medicine*, *62*, 187–199.

Adler, N. E., & Page, A. E. K. (Eds.). (2008). *Cancer care for the whole patient: Meeting psychosocial health needs*. Washington, DC: National Academy of Medicine.

American Academy of Hospice and Palliative Medicine (AAHPM). (2013). Palliative care. Retrieved from http://www.aahpm.org/

Bachner, Y. G., O'Rourke, N., & Carmel, S. (2007). Psychometric properties of a modified version of the Caregiver Reaction Assessment Scale measuring caregiving and post-caregiving reactions of caregivers of cancer patients. *Journal of Palliative Care*, *23*(2), 80–86.

Back, A. L., Young, J. P., McCown, E., Engelberg, R. A., Vig, E. K., Reinke, L. F., & Curtis, J. R. (2009). Abandonment at the end of life from patient, caregiver, nurse, and physician perspectives: Loss of continuity and lack of closure. *Archives of Internal Medicine*, *169*(5), 474–479.

Bell, C. L., Somogyi-Zalud, E., & Masaki, K. H. (2010). Factors associated with congruence between preferred and actual place of death. *Journal of Pain and Symptom Management*, *39*(3), 591–604.

Bomba, P. A., & Vermilyea, D. (2006). Integrating POLST into palliative care guidelines: A paradigm shift in advance care planning in oncology. *Journal of the National Comprehensive Cancer Network*, *4*(8), 819–829.

Bradley, C. J., Clement, J. P., & Lin, C. (2008). Absence of cancer diagnosis and treatment in elderly Medicaid-insured nursing home residents. *Journal of the National Cancer Institute*, *100*(1), 21–31.

Bradley, E. H., Prigerson, H., Carlson, M. D. A., Cherlin, E., Johnson-Hurzeler, R., & Kasl, S. V. (2004). Depression among surviving caregivers: Does length of hospice enrollment matter? *American Journal of Psychiatry*, *161*(12), 2257–2262.

Brazil, K., Bedard, M., Krueger, P., Abernathy, T., Lohfeld, L., & Willison, K. (2005). Service preferences among family caregivers of the terminally ill. *Journal of Palliative Medicine*, *8*(1), 69–78.

Burge, F., Lawson, B., & Johnston, G. (2003). Trends in the place of death of cancer patients, 1992–1997. *Canadian Medical Association Journal*, *168*(3), 265–270.

Cherlin, E. J., Barry, C. L., Prigerson, H. G., Green, D. S., Johnson-Hurzeler, R., Kasl, S. V., & Bradley, E. H. (2007). Bereavement services for family caregivers: How often used, why, and why not. *Journal of Palliative Medicine*, *10*(1), 148–158.

Chochinov, H. M., Hassard, T., McClement, S., Hack, T., Kristjanson, L. J., Harlos, M., & Murray, A. (2009). The landscape of distress in the terminally ill. *Journal of Pain and Symptom Management*, *38*(5), 641–649.

Chochinov, H. M., Kristjanson, L. J., Breitbart, W., McClement, S., Hack, T. F., Hassard, T., & Harlos, M. (2011). Effect of dignity therapy on distress and end-of-life experience in terminally ill patients: A randomised controlled trial. *Lancet Oncology*, *12*(8), 753–762.

Clark, P. G., Brethwaite, D. S., & Gnesdiloff, S. (2011). Providing support at time of death from cancer: Results of a 5-year post-bereavement group study. *Journal of Social Work in End-of-Life and Palliative Care*, *7*(2–3), 195–215.

Commission on Cancer. (2014). Cancer Program Standards 2012. Revised January 21, 2014. https://www.facs.org/quality%20programs/cancer/coc/standards

Csikai, E., & Weisenfluh, S. (2012). Hospice and palliative social workers' engagement in life review interventions. *American Journal of Hospice and Palliative Medicine*, *30*(3), 257–263.

Cohen, A., & Nirenberg, A. (2011). Current practices in advance care planning: Implications for oncology nurses. *Clinical Journal of Oncology Nursing*, *15*(5), 547–553.

Detering, K. M., Hancock, A. D., Reade, M. C., & Silvester, W. (2010). The impact of advance care planning on end of life care in elderly patients: Randomised controlled trial. *British Medical Journal*, *340*, c1345.

Dubus, N. (2010). Who cares for the caregivers? Why medical social workers belong on end-of-life care teams. *Social Work in Health Care*, *49*(7), 603–617.

Dumont, I., Dumont, S., & Mongeau, S. (2008). End-of-life care and the grieving process: Family caregivers who have experienced the loss of a terminal-phase cancer patient. *Qualitative Health Research*, *18*(8), 1049–1061.

Duncan, J. G., Bott, M. J., Thompson, S. A., & Gajewski, B. J. (2009). Symptom occurrence and associated clinical factors in nursing home residents with cancer. *Research in Nursing and Health*, *32*(4), 453–464.

Fashoyin-Aje, L. A., Martinez, K. A., & Dy, S. M. (2012). New patient-centered care standards from the commission on cancer: Opportunities and challenges. *Journal of Supportive Oncology*, *10*(3), 107–111.

Ferris, F. D., Bruera, E., Cherny, N., Cummings, C., Currow, D., Dudgeon, D., & Von Roenn, J. H. (2009). Palliative cancer care a decade later: Accomplishments, the need, next steps—from the American Society of Clinical Oncology. *Journal of Clinical Oncology*, *27*(18), 3052–3058.

Fried, T. R., Bullock, K., Iannone, L., & O'Leary, J. R. (2009). Understanding advance care planning as a process of health behavior change. *Journal of the American Geriatrics Society*, *57*(9), 1547–1555.

Gaeta, S., & Price, K. J. (2010). End-of-life issues in critically ill cancer patients. *Critical Care Clinics, 26*(1), 219–227.
Holtslander, L. F. (2008). Caring for bereaved family caregivers: Analyzing the context of care. *Clinical Journal of Oncology Nursing, 12*(3), 501–506.
Hui, D., Mori, M., Parsons, H. A., Kim, S. H., Li, Z., Damani, S., & Bruera, E. (2012). The lack of standard definitions in the supportive and palliative oncology literature. *Journal of Pain and Symptom Management, 43*(3), 582–592.
Kapari, M., Addington-Hall, J., & Hotopf, M. (2010). Risk factors for common mental disorder in caregiving and bereavement. *Journal of Pain and Symptom Management, 40*(6), 844–856.
Kissane, D. W., McKenzie, M., Bloch, S., Moskowitz, C., McKenzie, D. P., & O'Neill, I. (2006). Family focused grief therapy: A randomized, controlled trial in palliative care and bereavement. *American Journal of Psychiatry, 163*(7), 1208–1218.
Kramer, B. J., Kavanaugh, M., Trentham-Dietz, A., Walsh, M., & Yonker, J. A. (2010a). Complicated grief symptoms in caregivers of persons with lung cancer: The role of family conflict, intrapsychic strains, and hospice utilization. *Omega: Journal of Death and Dying, 62*(3), 201–220.
Kramer, B. J., Kavanaugh, M., Trentham-Dietz, A., Walsh, M., & Yonker, J. A. (2010b). Predictors of family conflict at the end of life: The experience of spouses and adult children of persons with lung cancer. *Gerontologist, 50*(2), 215–225.
Kreling, B., Selsky, C., Perret-Gentil, M., Huerta, E. E., & Mandelblatt, J. S. (2010). "The worst thing about hospice is that they talk about death": Contrasting hospice decisions and experience among immigrant Central and South American Latinos with US-born white, non-Latino cancer caregivers. *Palliative Medicine, 24*(4), 427–434.
Loggers, E. T., Maciejewski, P. K., Paulk, E., DeSanto-Madeya, S., Nilsson, M., Viswanath, K., & Prigerson, H. G. (2009). Racial differences in predictors of intensive end-of-life care in patients with advanced cancer. *Journal of Clinical Oncology, 27*(33), 5559–5564.
National Comprehensive Cancer Network. (n.d.). Guidelines for supportive care distress management and palliative care guidelines version 1.2013; distress management. Retrieved from http://www.nccn.org
National Hospice and Palliative Care Organization. (n.d.). Social Work Assessment Tool (SWAT): Guidelines for use and completion. Retrieved from http://www.nhpco.org/sites/default/files/public/nchpp/SWAT_Information_Booklet.pdf
National Hospice and Palliative Care Organization (NHPCO). (2008). History of hospice care. Retrieved from http://www.nhpco.org/i4a/pages/index.cfm?pageid=3285.
National Hospice and Palliative Care Organization (NHPCO). (2012). NHPCO facts and figures: Hospice care in America. Retrieved from http://www.nhpco.org/sites/default/files/public/Statistics_Research/2012_Facts_Figures.pdf
Oliver, D. P., Wittenburg-Lyles, E., Demiris, G., Washington, K., Porock, D., & Day, M. (2008). Barriers to pain management: Caregiver perceptions and pain talk by hospice interdisciplinary teams. *Journal of Pain and Symptom Management, 36*(4), 374–382.
Oncology Nursing Society (ONS) & Association of Oncology Social Work (AOSW). (2012). Joint position on palliative and end-of-life care. http://www.aosw.org/imis201/AOSWMain/pdfs/aosw-public-docs/PaperPalliativeEndOfLife.pdf
Park, S. M., Kim, Y. J., Kim, S., Choi, J. S., Lim, H. Y., Choi, Y. S., ... Yun, Y. H. (2010). Impact of caregivers' unmet needs for supportive care on quality of terminal cancer care delivered and caregiver's work performance. *Supportive Care in Cancer, 18*(6), 699–706.
Richards, C. T., Gisondi, M. A., Chang, C. H., Courtney, D. M., Engel, K. G., Emanuel, L., & Quest, T. (2011). Palliative care symptom assessment for patients with cancer in the emergency department. Validation of the Screen for Palliative and End-of-life care needs in the Emergency Department instrument. *Journal of Palliative Medicine, 14*(6), 757–764.
Ronaldson, S., & Devery, K. (2001). The experience of transition to palliative care services: Perspectives of patients and nurses. *International Journal of Palliative Nursing, 7*(4), 171–177.
Siminoff, L. A., Zyanski, S. J., Rose, J. H., & Zhang, A. Y. (2008). The Cancer Communication Assessment Tool for Patients and Families (CCAT-PF): A new measure. *Psycho-Oncology, 17*(12), 1216–1224.
Smith, T. J., Temin, S., Alesi, E. R., Abernethy, A. P., Balboni, T. A., Basch, E. M., & Von Roenn, J. H. (2012). American Society of Clinical Oncology provisional clinical opinion: The integration of palliative care into standard oncology care. *Journal of Clinical Oncology, 30*(8), 880–887.
Storey, D. J., Fallon, M. T., & Smyth, J. F. (2011). The interface between medical oncology and supportive and palliative cancer care. *Seminars in Oncology, 38*(3), 337–342.
Townsend, A. L., Ishler, K. J., Shapiro, B. M., Pitorak, E. F., & Matthews, C. R. (2010). Levels, types, and predictors of family caregiver strain during hospice home care for an older adult. *Journal of Social Work in End-of-Life and Palliative Care, 6*(1–2), 51–72.
Van Weert, J. C. M., Jansen, J., de Bruijn, G. J., Noordman, J., van Dulmen, S., & Bensing, J. M. (2009). QUOTEchemo: A patient-centered instrument to measure quality of communication preceding chemotherapy treatment through the patient's eyes. *European Journal of Cancer, 45*(17), 2967–2976
Weissman, D. E., Meier, D. E., & Spragens, L. H. (2008). Center to Advance Palliative Care palliative care consultation service metrics: Consensus recommendations. *Journal of Palliative Medicine, 11*(10), 1294–1298.
Wittenberg-Lyles, E. M., & Thompson, S. (2006). Understanding enrollment conversations: The role of the hospice admissions representative. *American Journal of Hospice and Palliative Medicine, 23*(4), 317–322.
World Health Organization. (2013). Palliative care. Retrieved from http://www.who.int/cancer/palliative/en/
Wright, A. A., Keating, N. L., Balboni, T. A., Matulonis, U. A., Block, S. D., & Prigerson, H. G. (2010). Place of death: Correlations with quality of life of patients with cancer and predictors of bereaved caregivers' mental health. *Journal of Clinical Oncology, 28*(29), 4457–4464.
Zebrack, B., Walsh, K., Burg, M. A., Maramaldi, P., & Lim, J. W. (2008). Oncology social worker competencies and implications for education and training. *Social Work in Health Care, 47*(4), 355–375.

III

Psychosocial Challenges of Site-Specific Cancers

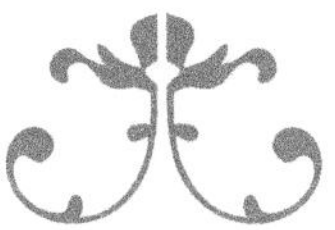

Carolyn Messner

People living with cancer have both visible and invisible scars. The site of the cancer may trigger intrinsic responses to one's identity of wholeness and integrity, and patients may feel damaged as a result. This sense of impairment may have a negative impact on self-esteem, social relationships, and sexuality. This section of the *Handbook of Oncology Social Work* presents six chapters that focus on particular cancer sites, their effects on patients and their loved ones, and suggested models for psychosocial intervention.

In "The Biopsychosocial Implications of the Site of the Cancer," Carolyn Messner, Caroline Kornhauser, and Rosalie Canosa emphasize that the site of the cancer, whether internal or external, is an important factor in considering its biopsychosocial sequelae for patients. They describe how the site factors into the distinct physical and psychosocial challenges that cancer patients and survivors confront. Using a strengths-based approach, they offer tailored interventions to facilitate a patient's coping with disruptions in his or her appearance and physical and cognitive functioning to achieve a new normal.

In "Living With a Rare Cancer Diagnosis: A Survivor's Perspective," Patrick Garbe offers his personal reflections on how oncology social workers helped guide him on a path of self-discovery by winning his trust and respect. He credits their sensitivity with enabling him to cope with his fears and anxieties; reach out to family, friends, and coworkers; practice yoga and mindful meditation; explore the genetic testing landscape with his family; and embrace spirituality as a cornerstone to shaping his life.

In "Working With Men Challenged by Prostate Cancer," Les Gallo-Silver identifies specific treatment side effects, including changes in sexual functioning, erectile dysfunction, and related emotional issues challenging men living with prostate cancer. He describes the importance of sexual rehabilitation and offers a comprehensive framework of interventions using case vignettes to illustrate how an oncology social worker can sensitively and knowledgeably explore concerns about masculinity, virility, and sexuality with these men and their partners.

In "The Many Dimensions of Breast Cancer: Determining the Scope of Needed Services," Roz Kleban and Susan Glaser describe common issues that people with breast cancer experience across the continuum of care and their changing emotions over time. They identify interventions that are organized to help patients cope at different stages in the disease trajectory and treatment process. They highlight two interventions, group work and the patient-to-patient connection, that they have found most helpful for this population. They advise practitioners to continually update their knowledge on progress in the treatment of breast cancer to understand and address the concerns of their patients.

In "Hematologic Cancers: Patients' Needs for Specialized Care," Kate Pederson, Brian Tomlinson, and Lisa O'Brien describe the treatment of hematologic cancers, including leukemia, lymphoma, multiple myeloma, and myelodysplasia, as very specialized and based on subtype. Optimal management of hematologic malignancies requires cancer treatment team members with specialized experience, including oncology social work. They remind us that treatments vary widely, from watchful waiting to bone marrow transplantation. They conclude with the psychosocial challenges these patients and their caregivers face and specialized opportunities for oncology social work interventions.

In "When the Other Shoe Drops: Unique Fears and Challenges of Recurrent Disease," Elizabeth Ezra and Maria Chi emphasize that a recurrence or relapse of cancer is a vulnerable time for patients. They describe the depth of psychological injury, renewed crisis, and fear of dying that these patients face. Using a strengths-based approach, they provide clear examples of a step-by-step approach for helping patients identify new meanings of hope. With eloquence, they conclude that "oncology social workers help these clients put one foot in front of the other, living in smaller steps on a shorter road, but with an eye toward the horizon."

The site of the cancer, its type, the trajectory of the disease, and its treatments have a profound effect on patients' initial responses to their condition. Addressing the challenges created by cancer-related factors is critical to effective oncology social work interventions.

11

Carolyn Messner, Caroline Kornhauser, and Rosalie Canosa

The Biopsychosocial Implications of the Site of the Cancer

Key Concepts

- *The site of the cancer, whether or not it is visible, is an important factor in considering the biopsychosocial sequelae for patients.*
- *The site of the cancer factors into distinct physical and psychosocial challenges that cancer patients and survivors must confront.*
- *Oncology social workers use a strengths-based approach to develop tailored interventions that facilitate patients' coping with disruptions in appearance and physical and cognitive functioning to achieve a new normal.*

People living with cancer are not immune to the dread that society associates with the disease (Mukherjee, 2010). A cancer diagnosis is a traumatic life event that may threaten one's physical, emotional, and social existence (Holland & Lewis, 2000). For many people, the hallmarks of the cancer experience include feelings of vulnerability coupled with fears of recurrent disease, suffering, and death (Fleishman, 2011). The perception that all people living with cancer have the same experience diminishes each patient's metamorphosis. Each diagnosis has a unique footprint with biopsychosocial sequelae that are based on location, disruption of physical and cognitive functioning, and the value or importance of the cancer site to the patient (Fingeret, Teo, & Epner, 2014).

Biopsychosocial oncology refers to the dynamic interaction among the physical, emotional, social, and cultural factors that come into play during the cancer trajectory. Every individual experiences cancer differently—for example, altered relationships, dependency issues, achievement disruptions, and changed sense of self and body image. The cancer site often contributes to how people tackle these life disruptions (Zebrack, Yi, Petersen, & Ganz, 2008). Cancers that require the surgical removal of parts of the body may cause increased body image complications. It is essential to understand the importance of the cancer site because it factors greatly into the distinct challenges confronted by cancer patients and survivors.

This chapter discusses how the site of the cancer may cause specific functional disruptions that require restorative interventions by oncology social workers, often in collaboration with other disciplines. It addresses disruptions in self-perception, social relationships, appearance, physical ability, and cognition. These disruptions have the potential to precipitate body image concerns, which in turn lead to decreased social interaction, less confidence, and increased social isolation (Fingeret et al., 2014). Choosing an intervention to improve a patient's quality of life requires an understanding of the impact that the cancer location can have on a person's physical, emotional, and social well-being. Clinical vignettes are used to exemplify the role of oncology social work interventions in revitalizing a patient's hope and sense of self. These examples illustrate the role of the cancer site in the isolation, stigmatization, and loss of autonomy experienced by people living with cancer. Each vignette showcases

Janet is a 60-year-old widow who lives in a small town. She lives alone in a modest home and has family nearby. She had an uncomfortable cough for a few weeks after having a cold and coughed up blood one morning. Janet was able to see a doctor in the clinic that same day, as well as other specialists. She was diagnosed with lung cancer and did not keep her follow-up appointments with the oncology team. William, the oncology social worker, called Janet to schedule a home visit; his goal was to assess why Janet was not keeping her appointments.

They began to talk, and Janet offered William a cup of tea, which he readily accepted. She brought out a tea set and cups. They both sipped tea as they talked about Janet's life and her cancer diagnosis. As the visit was ending, Janet blurted out to William, "Ever since my cancer diagnosis, no one who comes to my house uses my plates or cups! They insist on using paper cups and plates. My children and grandkids too! No more hugs or kisses! You are the first person who drank tea with me using my tea cups since my lung cancer. I will come to the clinic if I can see you too." These words speak volumes about her feeling socially stigmatized, alone, and isolated. Janet experienced what Alice Trillin (1981) so eloquently expressed: "What changed was other people's perception of me. Everyone regarded me as someone who had been altered irrevocably." William's behavior modeled acceptance to Janet, who was able to use her connection to William as a bridge to follow up with other clinic staff. The halo effect of her positive relationship with her social worker extended to the rest of the health care team.

Janet responded to acceptance, a core social work intervention and the essential backdrop to everything social workers do. It was transformative in reaching out to a patient who did not feel accepted by her children, grandchildren, and friends. She believed that her family members were afraid they might catch cancer from her dishes or from touching and hugging her, which in turn made her feel rejected and alienated from those she loved most.

William had his work cut out for him. He was able to appeal to the family's curiosity about lung cancer by introducing the patient and others to educational materials and workshops. This tactic enabled them to learn that lung cancer is not contagious. He provided Janet with booklets for adults and children, websites, and webinars. With permission from Janet and her family, he met some of her friends in the clinic and others in Janet's home to role model being with Janet and drinking tea from her tea cups.

Janet now keeps her appointments and adheres to her treatment protocol. She participates in a lung cancer support group. William's supportive, nonjudgmental presence and acceptance enabled Janet and her family to weather their cancer experience. As part of the process, they learned to accept Janet's diagnosis and reach out to others for information and help. Janet's coughing and spitting up blood frightened her family and attacked the core of its safety. The oncology social worker enabled them to overcome their fears of catching Janet's cancer. Once those fears were addressed, Janet and her family were able to resume their close social interaction. Janet was no longer alone and isolated; she had her family's hugs and support.

the patient's mode of adapting to a disease that attempts to disrupt the most valued aspects of life.

Strengths-Based Approach

William's work with Janet and her family utilized a strengths-based approach to help them regain mastery and control after the cancer diagnosis. Strengths-based techniques allow oncology social workers to collaborate with patients, encouraging them to use their own resourcefulness and courage to solve problems and surmount obstacles. This approach focuses on the patient's personal strengths to rebuild self-esteem and confidence and create new possibilities (Graybeal, 2001).

Strengths-based techniques are applied most effectively on a case-by-case basis and are often dependent on the location of the cancer. Oncology social workers must understand the significance of the site of the cancer because it is important in choosing the appropriate psychosocial interventions. The location of the cancer has a tremendous impact on a patient's identity, personal confidence, and quality of life, as exemplified in the earliest writings by Weisman (1979) regarding "self-appraisal concerns." This theme continues to appear in contemporary writing as well (cf. Fingeret et al., 2014, on "body image difficulties").

Restorative Intervention: Reconstructive Cosmetic Consultation

Some people living with cancer may experience physical alterations in their appearance. These visual reminders may trigger hypervigilance about one's physical appearance, which leads to an impaired self-image and increased self-consciousness. When assessing the biopsychosocial impact, it is important to consider whether the cancer is external and visible—for example, skin cancer on the face (Trask & Butow, 2010).

Lisa is an attractive fashion model for a clothing designer. Her face was scarred as a result of surgery for skin cancer. Although her surgery was considered curative, she was devastated by her "perceived disfigurement" and silently feared its resulting consequences on her career. She sought counseling with an oncology social worker for her anxiety about her changed appearance and the "loss of symmetry in her face," a key requirement in modeling. Through therapy, she was able to acknowledge that she never possessed "perfect features" but that the exotic composite of her face and body contributed to her successful career. She became an expert in the cosmetic use of makeup to highlight and camouflage her features and was very receptive to reconstructive cosmetic consultation. She redesigned her use of cosmetics and hair style to create her "new normal," thereby re-establishing her confidence in herself, her work, and her personal life (Zammett, 2005). Lisa was able to regain "symmetry" by creatively using what she had learned from a team of pro bono reconstructive cosmetic consultants (Ovitz & Kabak, 2004). She worked with her oncology social worker on strengths-based techniques and learned that there was more to her than just her external appearance. She found that many of the skills she had learned as a model could be applied in coping with the scar on her face. She was able to redefine her self-image to include her appearance, people skills, and intellect. She used her cadre of skill sets to find creative ways to cope with cancer. Small imperfections can result in loss of work in the competitive world of modeling. Although the skin cancer diagnosis was particularly devastating for Lisa, working with a supportive team, including her oncology social worker, allowed her to recognize and build upon her personal skill sets to advance her career.

Bone metastases to the spine and pelvis made it impossible for Robert to play his trumpet as a jazz musician. His sadness was palpable to all who knew him. His grief was further compounded by fears of loss of independence and autonomy in walking and standing. He worried that he would have to increasingly rely on his wife and friends to perform everyday tasks. Adjusting to an increased lifestyle of dependency was a difficult transition for a man accustomed to organizing and planning his own jazz productions.

Robert vividly described his current needs and goals of care to an oncology social worker recommended by a friend, and together they came up with an agreeable plan. He wished to access state-of-the-art oncology care to treat his pain and metastatic disease. He accepted a referral from his social worker to an oncology team skilled in treating his specific cancer and pain. The care he received made it possible for him to resume playing his trumpet, which acted as an antidote to his despair and restored joy and friendship to his life. As he became stronger, he organized a concert for patients so that they could hear his story and benefit from his experience. The concert was an affirmation of his life, as well as his way of expressing gratitude for the help he had received. While bone metastases to the spine threatened to end Robert's career and destroy his sense of self, working with an oncology social worker helped him regain his sense of control. What began as a devastating diagnosis evolved into a learning opportunity for Robert and his friends and colleagues.

Treatment Side Effects and Their Impact on Identity

The physical changes that arise from cancer or its treatment are most noticeable to patients and their significant others. Common chemotherapy side effects include hair loss, fatigue, and weight changes. These symptoms cause suffering for patients and may signal the transition from health to illness (Ferrell & Coyle, 2008). The need to adapt to hair loss, cognitive issues, and fluctuations in weight may have unexpected consequences on body image and self-perception. Fingeret et al. (2014, p. 637) advise that "it would be ideal to discuss body image with every patient during each encounter but given the infeasibility of this goal, it is important to focus on patients whose disease or treatment causes significant self-perceived changes in physical appearance or function."

Cognitive Impairments

In addition to its physical implications, cancer affects one's cognitive ability: thinking, memory, word retrieval, problem solving, executive function, and multitasking. Some cancer treatments impact cognitive functioning—for example, thinking, learning, processing, or remembering information. These changes, often called "chemo brain," can severely impact many aspects of daily life and are considered the most frequent quality-of-life complications faced by long-term cancer survivors (Clegg, 2008). Cognition may also be affected by some types of systemic chemotherapy.

Specific cancers, such as tumors located in the brain and spinal cord, have been shown to directly lead to decreased cognitive functioning. For example, people living with glioblastoma, a brain tumor, have well-documented neurocognitive impairments, which lead to behavioral, emotional, and intellectual difficulties (Calabrese & Schlegel, 2009). This decrease in functioning is often related to the nature of the tumor itself. Cognitive functioning is an important measure of overall quality of life. The overall prognosis for glioblastoma makes quality of life especially important for people living with it (Henriksson, Asklund, & Poulsen, 2011). The effect on cognitive functioning may oscillate with each cancer type and its particular treatments.

Site-Specific Loss of Independence and Autonomy

A cancer diagnosis commonly results in a loss of independence and autonomy, as physical functioning may decrease over time and cancer impacts every aspect of daily life. Many people living with cancer rely on family, friends, and health care professionals to maintain a sense of normalcy and perform everyday tasks. Many head and neck cancer patients have decreased quality of life at diagnosis, and it may further decline during and after treatment. Approximately 75% of patients undergoing surgery for head and neck cancer report feelings of concern or embarrassment due to changes in body image (Fingeret et al., 2014).

Joseph had a radical neck dissection to treat metastatic thyroid cancer. He was a successful engineer who stopped working due to increasing weakness. He was referred for counseling by his oncologist, who was concerned about depression in this vibrant person. Joseph met with his oncology social worker Susan weekly and they talked about his life. During one of their sessions, Susan commented that many people have underlying feelings of anger as a result of a cancer diagnosis. Joseph responded instantly by saying that he could never be angry about his diagnosis. He explained that he is a Holocaust survivor. At age 12, when he was in Auschwitz concentration camp, his job was to dig graves for those who had been shot. At that time, he made a "pact" with God. "I asked to be freed from this camp, to go live in the United States and get a college degree. I promised I would never be angry or question what God does. And all of my requests were granted. I am not angry with God." After telling his story, he realized he was at peace with his cancer. Revealing his past enabled Joseph to move forward, releasing a heavy burden and permitting him to join a support group, where he became a valued and gregarious member.

Joseph's story exemplifies the notion that no two people are alike. Before meeting Joseph, Susan understood that his type of cancer often has a profound impact on quality of life and body image. Susan made the assumption that Joseph must be angry because his radical neck dissection caused noticeable disfigurement. She soon understood that this was not the case. It is vital for oncology social workers to release any preconceived notions about all patients responding to their cancer site in the same way. Psychosocial interventions can only be tailored for each individual after the meaning of the person's cancer has been determined.

Pearls

- Assess the meaning of the cancer site for each patient.
- Tailor psychosocial interventions to the degree of functional disruption or body image concerns caused by the cancer site.
- Working with a multidisciplinary team will provide optimal restorative interventions for patients.

Pitfalls

- Do not assume that all cancer patients will respond to the cancer site in the same way.
- Do not assume that a curable cancer does not disrupt a patient's functioning.
- The oncology social worker is uncomfortable exploring body image concerns as these may be embarrassing for the social worker and the patient.

Oncology social workers are tasked with knowing, identifying, and applying myriad strategies to help build the client's self-esteem and strength throughout the cancer journey (Devins, Otto, Irish, & Rodin, 2010). This task is made even more difficult by the complex physical and psychological changes experienced by a person living with cancer, many of which are attributed to the site or location of the cancer. Oncology social workers need to stay abreast of the plethora of possible outcomes patients may confront, as well as needed resources (Messner, 2013). Cancers that leave scarring are easy to detect; cancers that leave internal and severe emotional scarring require in-depth exploration. Cancer and its treatment are known to cause changes in cognitive ability, self-perception, and body image. The oncology social worker must learn to detect these changes to appropriately guide and counsel the client. The need to identify high-risk patients through psychosocial screening to provide early intervention has never been more critical (Zabora, 2009). The world of oncology is constantly evolving. Recognizing the biopsychosocial implications of the cancer site enables oncology social workers to identify and reach out to high-risk patients and their caregivers. The following chapters in this section address living with a rare cancer diagnosis, working with men challenged by prostate cancer, the many dimensions of breast cancer, hematologic cancers, and the unique fears and challenges of recurrent disease.

ADDITIONAL RESOURCES

Body Image Information

Changing Faces: https://www.changingfaces.org.uk/Home
LIVESTRONG Body Image: http://www.livestrong.org/we-can-help/emotional-and-physical-effects-of-treatment/body-image/
MD Anderson Cancer Center Body Image Therapy Service: http://www2.mdanderson.org/cancerwise/2011/05/qa-body-image-therapy-service.html
Support for People with Oral and Head and Neck Cancer: http://www.spohnc.org

General Cancer Information

American Cancer Society: http://www.cancer.org
American Psychosocial Oncology Society: http://www.apos-society.org
American Society of Clinical Oncology: http://www.cancer.net
Cancer*Care*: http://www.cancercare.org
Cancer Support Community: http://www.cancersupportcommunity.org
National Coalition for Cancer Survivorship: http://www.canceradvocacy.org
National Comprehensive Cancer Network: http://www.nccn.org

REFERENCES

Calabrese, P., & Schlegel, U. (2009). Neurotoxicity of treatment. *Gliomas, 171*, 165–174.

Clegg, E. (2008). *ChemoBrain: How cancer therapies can affect your mind*. New York, NY: Prometheus.

Devins, G., Otto, K., Irish, J., & Rodin, G. (2010). Head and neck cancer. In J. C. Holland, W. S. Breitbart, P. B. Jacobsen, M. S. Lederberg, M. J. Loscalzo, & R. McCorkle (Eds.), *Psycho-oncology* (2nd ed., pp. 135–139). New York, NY: Oxford University Press.

Ferrell, B. R., & Coyle, N. (2008). *The nature of suffering and the goals of nursing*. New York, NY: Oxford University Press.

Fingeret, M. C., Teo, I., & Epner, D. E. (2014). Managing body image difficulties of adult patients: Lessons from available research. *Cancer, 120*(5), 633–641.

Fleishman, S. B. (2011). *Learn to live through cancer: What you need to know*. New York, NY: Demos Medical Publishing.

Graybeal, C. (2001). Strength-based social work assessment: Transforming the dominant paradigm. *Families in Society: The Journal of Contemporary Human Services, 82*(3), 233–242.

Henriksson, R., Asklund, T., & Poulsen, H. S. (2011). Impact of therapy on quality of life, neurocognitive function and their correlates in glioblastoma multiforme: A review. *Journal of Neuro-Oncology, 104*(3), 639–646.

Holland, J., & Lewis, S. (2000). *The human side of cancer*. New York, NY: Harper Collins Publishers.

Messner, C. (2013). Resources for cancer patients. In J. Steel & B. Carr (Eds.), *Psychological aspects of cancer*. New York, NY: Springer Press.

Mukherjee, S. (2010). *The emperor of all maladies*. New York, NY: Scribner.

Ovitz, L., & Kabak, J. (2004). *Facing the mirror with cancer: A guide to using makeup to make a difference*. Chicago, IL: Belle Press.

Trask, P. C., & Butow, P. (2010). Skin neoplasms and malignant melanoma. In J. C. Holland, W. S. Breitbart, P. B. Jacobsen, M. S. Lederberg, M. B. Loscalzo, & R. McCorkle (Eds.), *Handbook of psycho-oncology* (pp. 172–176). New York, NY: Oxford University Press.

Trillin, A. S. (1981). Of dragons and garden peas: A cancer patient talks to doctors. *New England Journal of Medicine, 304*(12), 699–701.

Weisman, A. D. (1979). *Coping with cancer*. New York, NY: McGraw Hill Book Company.

Zabora, J. (2009). The oncology social worker in the medical setting: Traditional versus innovative roles. In A. R. Roberts (Ed.), *Social workers' desk reference*. New York, NY: Oxford University Press.

Zammett, E. (2005). *My (so-called) normal life*. London, England: Duckworth Publishers.

Zebrack, B. J., Yi, J., Petersen, L., & Ganz, P. A. (2008). The impact of cancer and quality of life for long-term survivors. *Psycho-Oncology, 17*, 891–900.

12

Patrick Garbe

Living With a Rare Cancer Diagnosis: A Survivor's Perspective

Key Concepts

- *Oncology social workers strive to help patients and caregivers understand that one's emotional stability and stress management are key components in a person's overall well-being.*
- *A client's fears and anxiety cannot go unchecked and are best addressed through an oncology social worker's skill at winning the client's trust and respect.*
- *Scientific advances, especially in the area of genetics, will require oncology social workers to remain up to date on the evolution of technology and medicine to provide clients with relevant advice.*

Life-Changing Events

In spring 1991, a recurrence of paraganglioma left me an emotional wreck. It had been almost 10 years since paraganglioma was first resected from around my carotid artery, but this recurrence separate from my head and neck made me afraid of what might happen next. I was told that the recurrence of paraganglioma was rare, but what surprised me most was the heightened level of care and concern that arose from my medical team. My oncology surgeons explained that paragangliomas are mostly benign, slow-growing, carotid body tumors and once the tumor is resected, the chance of recurrence is considered low, with treatment generally not being necessary. Although concerned about the risks associated with head and neck surgeries, I grew more worried when the conversations escalated to possible metastasis and treatments.

At this time, another important event directly impacted my thoughts about managing cancer and survivorship. In May 1991, Cancer*Care*, a nonprofit organization providing professional cancer support services, sponsored "Living With Cancer, Confronting the Challenge"—and the event changed my life. At the conference, I was surprised to learn that although many oncology teams at major cancer centers provided medical support, they rarely address the associated *emotional* distress. Knowing that "toughing it out" was no longer an option, I accepted the conference message that education and assistance from trained oncology social workers can help you confront the challenges. While the message was uplifting, I felt envious, and maybe somewhat jealous, hearing the survivors' stories and knowing I had a tough road ahead. A 10-year cancer survivor delivered the keynote address, and through her frank discussion, I realized that there was much to learn.

An Introduction to Oncology Social Workers

At the conference, I attended a session about oncology social work and what it provides to patients, families, and friends affected by cancer. For some, including myself, seeking professional help for emotional issues is often perceived as unnecessary or a weakness, but after meeting with a social worker to discuss my background and learn about the counseling process, I got on board. My first counseling experience was a weekly "men's group." I quickly realized that I was uncomfortable with the format of sharing one's problems and emotions. Two men who were seasoned Alcoholics Anonymous veterans simply asked, "So, what's wrong with you?" While evading these questions felt natural, it wasn't an option in this setting. What I learned over the ensuing months were, and continue to be, two key strategies for addressing emotional stress: first, that ignoring emotions will eventually catch up with me, and second, that it's important to find a level of emotional comfort to feel confident enough to discuss my own stress levels with family and friends, who are likely to also be suffering in their own way.

Winning a Client's Trust

Seeing that I was a novice, my social workers guided me on a path of self-discovery, creating a trusting and caring atmosphere devoid of apathy or tired routines. Furthermore, they provided a balance between factually reliable resources and probing questions that cracked my thoughts, fears, and concerns. Last, they subtly addressed the issue of dying on more than one occasion; their sensitivity to the issue remains with me today, especially following the deaths of a few members of the support groups. However, perhaps their most important traits were deep caring and genuine compassion. Through their skillful counseling, I learned to express myself in ways that felt new and liberating.

Over the years, I've learned that a counselor's success seems to rest on a fine edge—finding and balancing the appropriate techniques, managing various personalities, and achieving their own professional goals. As with any "customer service" role, solid people-reading instincts help deliver common-sense advice that appropriately suits the client's situation. Since 1991, I've attended several of the "Living With Cancer, Confronting the Challenge" conferences, humbly and happily delivering the keynote address a few times as well. Through volunteering and attending conferences and educational events, I remain aware of cancer research progress, which restores my focus on many of the typical concerns associated with recurrence and survivorship.

Some Background Information

As noted earlier, paragangliomas are generally benign, slow-growing, carotid body tumors that originate from the ganglia of the sympathetic nervous system. They are typically resected, and then the patient is monitored annually for signs of recurrent growth, though the odds of recurrence are low. Patients are often asked to "wait and see" before opting for tumor resection, largely because of risk factors associated with head and neck surgeries. These were the instructions that I received in the early 1980s, and although I was certainly very concerned, I truly believed I would be fine based on the diagnosis and the statistical information available at the time. Things, however, did not work out as I had hoped.

The original tumor site was biopsied, and after a period of "wait and see," the tumor was resected. The resection caused Horner's syndrome, resulting in my right eyelid drooping slightly, constricting the pupil, and compromising the sweat glands on the right side of my face. Overall, however, I felt fine, and after discussions with my medical team, a decision was made against the use of radiation or chemotherapy treatments.

Several years later, however, severe pain developed in my neck, and imaging confirmed that I had a recurrence in the cervical vertebrae. A complicated resection and bone graph followed and pathology confirmed that it was paraganglioma. Before radiation treatments, scans revealed an additional tumor, which a biopsy confirmed was paraganglioma in the right hip. Again, a resection and bone graph were performed and radiation treatments to the cervical spine and pelvis were administered.

Some months later, even more tumors were located in other areas of the spine. The recurrences prompted my participation in an early clinical trial focusing on monoclonal antibodies, an area of medicine that has led to important developments but that, for me, ended when the grant funding ran out. After a couple of months discussing the efficacy of radiation treatments and the potential benefits of other treatments, including certain chemotherapy protocols, we opted for another round of radiation.

I recall having very mixed feelings about the process and the decision not to use chemotherapy. Some doctors believed that a protocol should be selected, perhaps believing in its effectiveness or perhaps because they wanted more data from a prime candidate; it was hard to know. However, because a paper was being written on the use of radiation for paraganglioma, I was a "person of interest." Nonetheless, it was an intensely emotional process fueled by the physical impacts from the tumors and treatments and the vagaries surrounding my particular circumstances.

Emotional Toll of Recurrence

The nature of this tumor type and the physical location of the primary tumor initially deflected some of my concern about recurrence, and it was only gradually that I realized the impact of the recurrences over a period of several years.

When paraganglioma recurred in areas remote to the original tumor site, resulting in more complicated resections, bone graphs, and treatments, my internalized fears hit me hard. Adding to my stress during this time was a relocation from California to New Jersey, starting a new job in Manhattan, the birth of my third child, deaths of family members, and complications associated with my health care coverage and the related financial burdens.

Trying to casually address these emotional highs and lows was not enough, and I knew that it was time to up my game and seek professional help. It was at this stage—some 11 years removed from my first biopsy—that I started to receive free, no-cost assistance from oncology social workers.

Lessons Learned

Thirty years ago, there was a limited body of research about paraganglioma; during that time, I was one of just two active patients diagnosed and being treated for it at a major cancer center whose medical team was deemed to be better than most, but still uncertain about the effectiveness of radiation, chemotherapy, or both. When rare tumors act in unusual ways, such as in my situation, the research and actual hands-on knowledge appear limited to only specialized individuals. This all weighed heavily on my mind while I tried to make the right decisions regarding surgical procedures, treatments, imaging, and diagnostic testing.

By nature, I was eager for information, meeting regularly with social workers who guided me through the exploration of my key stressors and skillfully maneuvered our conversations. They helped me explore and better understand my emotions by (1) moderating question-and-answer dialogues in a relaxed, welcoming manner; (2) encouraging me to take a more in-depth approach to journal writing and sharing the experience if I chose to; and (3) suggesting ways in which I could extend the conversation to family, friends, and coworkers. Also, understanding that I was a reasonably fit young person active in sports, the counselors recommended that I attend various classes on yoga and mindful meditation (any type of impact sport was forbidden for some time). Gradually, I learned ways to recognize and process the stress, including simply allowing myself to be overwhelmed sometimes until I found a way to accept it.

Through one-on-one sessions with a social worker, I learned to feel more comfortable with the unwanted attention from everyone who wished me well. I certainly didn't want to come across as ungrateful, but I wasn't comfortable when others had a newfound interest in my health. I had heart-to-heart conversations with family and friends and listened more intently to their concerns. Although normally one might welcome such concern, it took me some time before I learned how to respond honestly and how to accept their offers when I or my family needed help. As strange as it was to hear my name on the prayer list while attending mass, I got used to that, too.

Workplace Issues and Health Insurance

Living with cancer and managing a career also raises many challenges. When recurrence struck in the early 1990s, I had been employed at a law firm for only 5 months. I chose to disclose my situation, partly because it fits with my personality and partly because I was confident that I would find solutions through a revised work schedule and adjusting my responsibilities. I considered sharing the information with only those who needed to know, but in reality, you can't control the dialogue—once the news is out that you have cancer, the story takes on a life of its own.

I was fortunate that my coworkers were understanding. Over a 2-year period, I had two 25-day sessions of radiation therapy, and by working closely with office management, I was able to adjust my schedule and responsibilities to accommodate leaving the office during the day for treatments and then returning afterward to complete the day. When the treatments ended, I settled into an intense routine, working long hours, eager for both the paycheck and a stable work environment.

Having health care coverage through my employer was, of course, an important benefit. I did learn, however, some hard lessons along the way, especially while trying to obtain out-of-network coverage. In the early 1990s, out-of-network HMO plans were not well established; the provider paid a reasonable amount if it approved the patient's case and the patient was responsible for negotiating the balance with the hospital. Health care management became a project for me unto itself.

Managing your career during and after cancer can be complicated, and it's perhaps best to listen to your instincts. I've known cancer patients who determined that they did not have the option to freely discuss their health because of the likelihood that their clients would drop them to find a more stable arrangement. Despite many laws protecting employees and their families who are confronting medical issues, there can be a lack of confidence in the laws, especially when you're feeling vulnerable. The reality is that job status changes do occur and should be considered while you are confronting major medical issues. I was very fortunate and, in the end, incredibly thankful for the ways things were managed.

Wonders of Science and Technology

I was fortunate that my tumors were detected, resected, and treated using the current technology, with magnetic resonance imaging proving to be an effective diagnostic tool for monitoring my health. Today, however, testing for genetic markers for paraganglioma is an option. Although I find genetic testing to be an exciting new development, it does require some emotional soul-searching. I'm seeing new demands for genetic counselors and social workers to provide patients and families with the tools to navigate this process.

I regularly use the Internet for obtaining and sharing medical information about the genetic markers for paraganglioma. Although one needs to be cautious when conducting research without proper medical training, social networking specific to paraganglioma has expanded the dialogue about this rare tumor type in ways that seemed inconceivable just a few years ago.

As a family, we currently are exploring the genetic testing landscape. A younger relative recently underwent a resection of paraganglioma. Afterward, she met with a counselor who recommended genetic testing. A blood test led to the identification of a known genetic mutation for paraganglioma, and subsequently, other family members have tested positive for this genetic change.

This event, however, poses challenges to other family members and raises issues that might best be addressed through counseling. What do we do with this information? As logical as it is to be proactive, it's often human nature to delay these types of decisions. I've opted to dive into the genetic research for two reasons: first, for my own health and well-being, and second, to add to a growing body of data about this tumor for which, historically, there was little information. I'm excited, yet nervous about what might be ahead.

Spirituality and Survivorship

Faith and spirituality are cornerstones that have shaped my life. When I raised my beliefs with the social workers or group members, it didn't matter that we had differing opinions about religion. Although we had some lively discussions, the people I met were fortunately very respectful of each other. After a group or one-on-one session, I would often go to the Lady Chapel in St. Patrick's Cathedral on 5th Avenue to sit and think before heading back to the office a couple blocks away or heading home on my long commute.

On reflection, I believe that spirituality helped open my mind to learning from others, to listening compassionately to others in need, and to facing my internal fears by also listening to myself while trying to keep things in perspective. When confronting adversity, regardless of its nature, we are tested to overcome all kinds of worrisome problems. For me, I probably think too much about a million little things that don't matter. On one hand, it's my nature, but on the other hand, I've been facing this challenge for many years and my concerns and worries have become enmeshed in the fabric of my life.

Pearls

- Gain the client's trust by earnestly and compassionately engaging in conversations. Create a trusting and caring atmosphere that is devoid of apathy or tired routines.
- Seeking professional help for emotional issues is often perceived as unnecessary or even a weakness for some people. Whether or not one must pay for counseling can further impact these concerns. Listen carefully when clients explain their motivation for attending counseling. An explanation about the counseling process may help put the person at ease.
- Integrating a cancer diagnosis into life's complexities can exacerbate preexisting emotional issues. Skillfully maneuver the conversations in individual or group sessions to identify those things that are creating anxiety and stress. Some issues may have been rooted long before the diagnosis.

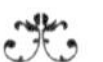

Pitfalls

- Although information can be powerful, the Internet can be both a blessing and a curse. With no medical training, reading "relevant" medical stories involves a lot of additional research just to get even a basic understanding. Consider providing clients with Internet use guidelines. Determine if the client is concerned about actual medical issues or whether those concerns were fueled by playing Internet doctor.
- Be tactful when putting an end to discussions about extraneous topics to keep the conversation on track. Conveying that session time is limited and encouraging the best use of the time might help. However, counseling is a process—you won't solve all of the problems in one session.
- Managing a career and workplace issues can be complicated after a cancer diagnosis. Whether and how the patient shares this information with friends and colleagues is a very personal decision. Despite legal protections, people can feel vulnerable under the stressful circumstances.

I have been fortunate to have a strong network supporting me: excellent medical teams; a cousin who's also an oncologist; incredible social workers who helped me, my family, and my friends deal with the emotional distress; and steady employment and essential insurance coverage throughout the ordeal. I'm truly thankful for these many things.

Cancer survivorship has taught me that it is in many ways similar to surviving any number of life's challenges. When events send us off our intended paths, instincts generally tell us to find a way back. Sometimes, however, important pieces of our lives are missing, making it hard to get back on track. Often we struggle to reclaim those dreams and forget to make new ones. Before moving forward after recurrence, I went through a period of grief not unlike the grieving process one goes through after any of a number of heartbreaks that are a part of life. Cancer at a young age was certainly not in the picture, and a recurrence of cancer at any age remains a concern.

Yet, not too surprisingly, I feel rewarded by the experience. I firmly believe that life is about the journey. The experience and knowledge gained along the way doesn't ease those fears and, indeed, even fuels the anxiety when not kept in check. I'm encouraged that medical advances continue to provide hope for a cure. I take solace in living a life of faith, and I'm comforted in knowing that I am not alone on the journey.

13 Working With Men Challenged by Prostate Cancer

Les Gallo-Silver

Key Concepts

- *Changes in sexual functioning and/or alterations in genital appearance can cause depression, especially in men with histories of prior trauma.*
- *Emotional difficulties often affect relationships with partners, as well as adherence with treatment follow-up and personal hygiene.*
- *Sexual rehabilitation is often needed to help men cope with and problem solve issues of erectile dysfunction, lack of ejaculate, diminished orgasmic intensity, and urinary stress incontinence during sexual activities.*

The 2012 American Cancer Society statistics report approximately 240,000 new diagnoses and 370,000 deaths from prostate cancer in the United States. When confronted with a new prostate cancer diagnosis, men embark on a perplexing quest to determine the best treatment. A treatment's impact on sexual functioning can be as important a factor in medical decision making as the effectiveness of the treatment (Gallo-Silver & Bimbi, 2012; Walsh & Worthington, 2012).

This chapter focuses on the specific treatment side effects and the related emotional issues challenging men with prostate cancer. Primary oncology social work interventions for men focus on penile functioning, sexual intimacy, and the injury to their sense of masculinity. The oncology social worker helps men negotiate the change in their sexual functioning, related self-esteem, and overall self-definition through use of psychoeducation and cognitive behavioral techniques. To be effective, the oncology social worker needs to be comfortable with issues of male sexuality, respectful of traditional male self-definitions, and creative in helping men redefine virility, sexual performance, and emotionality.

Self-Concept and Body Image

Issues of self-concept entwine with issues of masculinity and virility for men with prostate cancer (Wall & Kristjanson, 2005). Definitions of masculinity are static and fluid at the same time, with factors of culture, ethnicity, generation, education, and socioeconomic status further embellishing them (Halbert et al., 2010; Wittmann, Foley, & Balon, 2011).

Angel, a computer graphic artist originally from El Salvador, was 55 when diagnosed with prostate cancer. He is married with two daughters in college. Angel's new onset of erectile problems activated his historical concerns about his masculinity and sexual identity. Angel's history of childhood sexual abuse by his older half-brother resulted in a major depressive episode following his prostate biopsy (an invasive procedure using a rectal approach reminded him of anal penetration). For male survivors of childhood sexual abuse, a new trauma, such as a cancer diagnosis, can reignite and release memories and feelings of the earlier trauma of abuse. Angel was unable to focus on treatment until stabilized on psychotropic medication. His oncology social worker helped him sort through his present medical issues while acknowledging the impact of his traumatic history. The oncology social worker focused on helping him and his wife gather information, develop questions for his urologist, investigate prostate support group programs, and rehearse how and what to tell their two young adult daughters. This psychoeducational therapeutic approach enabled Angel and his wife to make necessary treatment decisions (Gallo-Silver & Weiner, 2006).

Fears of Feminization

For some men, the vicissitudes of prostate cancer treatments cause body changes that may activate fears of physical feminization (O'Brien, Hunt, & Hart, 2005). In addition, preexisting fears concerning gender identity, prior sexual trauma, and history of depression can intensify fears of feminization (Mehnert, Lehmann, Graefen, Huland, & Koch, 2010). Loss of penile length, girth, or functioning causes feelings of dread. For example, men may experience retraction of the penile shaft (shortening of the penis) as a side effect of surgery, causing feelings of inadequacy and lowered self-esteem (Haliloglu, Baltaci, & Yaman, 2007; Savoie, Kim, & Soloway, 2003).

Penile Shortening

The surgical removal or irradiation of the prostate may result in penile shortening. Research indicates that measured shortening of the penis following treatment is slight. Nonetheless, it is noticeable to the affected men. The penis needs to experience periodic engorgement with blood and can atrophy if denied engorgement over time. Atrophy can diminish the length and girth of the flaccid and erect penis.

- Many urologists prescribe the use of an oral erectile dysfunction (ED) medicine before bedtime once the urinary catheter is removed after surgery.
- The use of a bedtime dose of an oral ED medication is thought to potentiate the penis's engorgement with blood during the dream (REM) cycle of sleep.
- The use of a vacuum pump can draw blood into the penis, nourishing the erectile tissues and gradually stretching the skin of the penile shaft (though this does not alter overall length).
- Use of penile suppository or injected medications can produce firm erections, further preserving the penis.
- In addition to or in lieu of partner availability, weekly masturbation with or without a full erection is helpful to overall penile health.
- Penile shortening in circumcised men may result in the head of the penis retreating beneath the loose skin of the flaccid penile shaft, requiring the man to retract the skin to stimulate the penis.

Gynecomastia, the development of fat deposits over the pectoral muscles, can be a side effect of hormonal treatments (Autorino et al., 2006). In addition, hormonal treatments can cause weight gain, loss of desire for sex (libido), and shrinkage of the testes (Costanzo, Ryff, & Singer, 2009). Gary, a 58-year-old high school science teacher treated for prostate cancer with hormonal treatments, complained about episodes of crying while driving. He shared his distress with his oncology social worker about having increasingly sensitive nipples and weight gain, as well as his perceived change in the appearance of his scrotum. He was ashamed of his changed appearance and hid from his wife while undressing. The oncology social worker suggested he consult with a psychiatrist to determine if he could get relief from medication and to ask questions about the sexual side effects of psychotropic medications so that he did not prolong his loss of libido. The oncology social worker used a client-centered nondirective approach with Gary to help him proactively address concerns with his wife and urologist.

Urinary Stress Incontinence

Urinary incontinence can have an impact on a man's personal hygiene regimen. Urinary stress incontinence can be short term or long term depending on the impact of prostate cancer treatment on the urinary bladder's neck or sphincter that potentiates continence (Song et al., 2011). Men with urinary stress incontinence may not be able to prevent leakage when coughing, laughing, or passing flatulence (gas); during physical/sexual activity; or when changing body position (sitting, standing). Men risk developing "diaper rash" or other skin issues due to overexposure to urine. Poor personal hygiene can be a symptom of depression (Roberts, Lepore, & Hanlon, 2010). The oncology social worker needs to address any gaps in the patient's information or problem-solving abilities.

Hygiene

Men with urinary stress incontinence, whether acute and short term or chronic and long term, need specific instructions on maintaining good personal hygiene. Kegel exercises can improve continence but may not eliminate the problem.

- In order to use incontinence pads effectively, men need to wear 100% cotton boxer briefs instead of boxer shorts.
- Restricting fluid intake causes dehydration and more-concentrated, foul-smelling urine.
- Caffeinated and alcoholic beverages and some foods (e.g., asparagus) can result in foul-smelling urine.
- Men should always carry a change of underwear and extra incontinence pads.

- Men should use bathroom wet wipes to clean their genitals following urination and/or following a change of incontinence pad.
- It is best to change incontinence pads before they become soaked with urine.
- Men should wear dark-colored pants to hide urine mishaps and use a fabric deodorizer to freshen up pants with minimal urine mishaps.
- Injected erectile medications can produce an erection firm enough to diminish urinary stress incontinence during sexual activity.

Emotional Intimacy and Communication

The crisis of prostate cancer can cause a man to lean heavily on older methods of coping, whether they are adaptive or maladaptive to the crisis. Reluctance to verbalize his feelings, concerns, fears, or thoughts can be part of traditional defense strategies of "toughing it out," "acting like a man," and "being brave." These defense strategies can be maladaptive if the result is an uncharacteristic silent social withdrawal and increased irritability (Cockle-Hearne & Faithful, 2010; Gallo-Silver & Dillon, 2011).

Men with prostate cancer often seek a community of men similar to a club or a team (Queenan, Feldman-Stewart, Brundage, & Groome, 2010). A sense of male community can create and reinforce a shared definition of masculinity, enables reality testing about self-doubts related to body image changes, and becomes a safe environment for formal and informal sharing and information gathering (Oliffe, Gerbrandt, Bottorff, & Hislop, 2010).

Reggie, a 51-year-old widower and a bank manager originally from the Bahamas, joined a prostate cancer support group. Erectile problems became an increasing source of sadness for him as time passed after his prostate surgery. He tried oral erectile dysfunction medications that made his penis more sensitive to being stimulated, but he did not achieve an erection. A urologist specializing in erectile dysfunction addressed Reggie's support group. Having met the urologist in a safe setting, Reggie was willing to go to the urologist's office (Winterrich et al., 2009). He told his support group that without their support, he would "never consider having another man inject my penis and check on the hardness of my erection." This is reflective of a support group's role in normalizing the atypical situations related to prostate cancer through frank discussions, exchanges of information, and humor (Oliffe, Ogrodniczuk, Bottorff, Hislop, & Halpin, 2009). The oncology social worker helped him strategize when and how to share information with potential partners and use coping statements to counter his negative thoughts about his sexual "performance." A year later, Reggie married a woman he met at his church who was a nurse and who "happily" injected him.

Gay Men

Some prostate cancer support groups are exclusively for gay men, although gay men also often opt to attend general-membership prostate support groups open to all men. Given the nonbinary nature of human sexuality, all prostate support groups have members of a variety of sexual interests. It is the responsibility of the support group leaders to set the tone of mutual respect and acceptance of all group members and establish a safe environment. Issues of prejudice and homophobia can result in gay men remaining silent about partner and sexual-functioning issues in general membership prostate support groups. No sexual orientation owns any specific sexual activity or practice. Erectile dysfunction impedes many forms of sexual pleasure (Blank, 2005). Gay partners of a man with prostate cancer have the same concerns about loss, separation, communication, and physical/sexual changes as a female partner (Ezer, Chachamovich, & Chachamovich, 2011). Just as with any other couple, gay sexual practices do not always require a firm erection but do require mutual sexual satisfaction.

Transgender Women

A transgender woman is a person who was born biologically male and identifies as a woman. To help feminize the individual, hormonal manipulation is introduced many years after male puberty or sexual reassignment surgery. Because the prostate is not removed, a transgender woman remains at risk of prostate cancer (Hembree et al., 2009). The transgender woman with prostate cancer needs to have her womanhood preserved even though she has a male cancer. In this way, she is not unlike a biological man with breast cancer. Further, because transgender women refer to themselves using female pronouns and expect others to do the same (Gallo-Silver & Bimbi, 2012), the issue of developing a male cancer within the context of being a woman is highly isolating and psychologically complex (Gooren, Giltay, & Bunck, 2008). Returning to the psychotherapist who assisted the woman while she transitioned is a helpful step in addressing the social isolation caused by prostate cancer in this population. Loss of libido and diminished sexual response are concerns for sexually reassigned and nonreassigned transgender women.

Couples Communication

Partners participating in facetious conversations to avoid actual communication about prostate cancer are practicing mutual protection. In this way, partners do not address issues of loss, separation, diminished emotional intimacy, absence of physical affection, and suspension of physical intimacy (Hubiak, 2011). Without discussions about these issues, mutual protection easily turns into mutual isolation that can only diminish a couple's coping abilities (Garos, Kluck, & Arnoff, 2007). Of particular frustration to partners is facetious communication between the man with prostate cancer and his treating physicians. Partners may witness or suspect the denying of, minimizing of, or lying about symptoms and side effects. Partners can often benefit from couples counseling that focuses primarily on the clarification of communication, roles, and responsibilities within the relationship.

Tom, a 60-year-old bus driver, completed full pelvic radiation. He and his wife, Lilly, are third-generation Chinese Americans. Lilly was concerned because Tom had bloody stools 5 months after he completed full pelvic radiation. She accompanied him to his doctor visits and he never mentioned this problem. Lilly was furious until a colonoscopy discovered damage to the lining of Tom's large intestine called radiation proctitis (Do, Nagle, & Poylin, 2011). Lilly believed Tom did not trust her and had given up on getting better. She insisted they try couples counseling. The oncology social worker engaged them as a couple and did not meet with them individually, using the premise that the marriage was the identified patient and not the individual participants in the marriage. The oncology social worker was able to prevent splitting and assumptions of favoritism. Tom wanted his privacy respected and not questioned by Lilly. Lilly wanted Tom to trust her to be of help to him. The oncology social worker helped the couple to reminisce with the assistance of photographs, keepsakes, and mementos of their courtship, marriage, and milestones (births, graduations, and weddings of children/grandchildren). This gave Tom and Lilly the opportunity to discuss their expectations of marriage and the development of roles in the marriage over time (Gallo-Silver, 2011). Gradually, their communication gained greater clarity as both relearned how to listen to each other.

Sexual Functioning and Sexual Pleasure

The sexual functioning of male genitalia changes over time due to the natural aging process. These changes are sensitive to the addition of oral ED medications that improve functioning by potentiating the flow of blood into the penis (McCarthy & McCarthy, 2012). The vicissitudes of prostate cancer treatments can increase the impact of changes resulting from the natural aging process. Treatments may cause diminished blood supply to the penis, weakening or severing of nerve connections to the penis, lowering of testosterone levels, and cessation of emission of ejaculate (Mulhall, 2008). Men may have withdrawn from sexual activity before treatment for prostate cancer because of their undiagnosed symptoms and/or other health problems (Gallo-Silver & Bimbi, 2012).

Men who were sexually active before prostate cancer treatment may have difficulty resuming sexual activity or disappointment/dissatisfaction with their sexual recovery. Recovery of functioning often requires medical intervention by a urologist that specializes in erectile dysfunction. Incorporating medical interventions such as oral, suppository, and injected erectile medications into a couple's lovemaking routine and sustaining these changes is an area that can require social work intervention (Gallo-Silver & Dillon, 2011).

Sixty-year-old Patrick had nerve-sparing robotic surgery to address his prostate cancer. His urologist prescribed an oral erectile dysfunction medication for 3 nights a week after the removal of his Foley catheter. Two months after the surgery, Patrick was able to achieve only a partial erection and was not satisfied with his sexual recovery. He did not feel "like a true man" because he was unable to have vaginal intercourse with his wife, Gloria. Injected medications gave Patrick a firm erection and he and Gloria resumed making love. Still, though, Patrick felt a loss of sensation in his penis, missed ejaculating, and felt his orgasms were weak. The oncology social worker explored with Patrick the differences in his perceived sensations using the oral ED medication versus the injected ED medication. Patrick believed that his penis was more sensitive with the oral medication but that the injected medication provided him with a firm erection. Gloria was concerned that she might feel discomfort if Patrick had a firmer erection. This indicated the need for the couple to try various vaginal lubricants and for Patrick to be open to trying sexual positions that promote gentler thrusting. The oncology social worker suggested he discuss with his urologist the possibility of combining the two approaches. Following the physician's approval of combining the medications, adding a lubricant, and changing intercourse positions, Patrick and Gloria reported that sexual intercourse was more satisfying.

Pearls

- The man with prostate cancer needs an oncology social worker who can sensitively and knowledgably explore his concerns about masculinity, virility, and sexuality.
- Recognize that masturbation may be the preferred form of sexual activity and value this as much as partner sexual activity.
- Hypothesizing that a man with prostate cancer remains a sexual being in need of education, comfort, and problem solving supports his quality of life.

Pitfalls

- The oncology social worker's concerns about discussing sexual issues as somehow inappropriate, voyeuristic, or seductive reflects the rationalization of countertransference.
- Waiting for the patient to ask about sexual issues is avoiding professional responsibilities.

- The gender of the oncology social worker is not an essential issue, because openness, acceptance, and a nonjudgmental attitude are factors that are more important.

ADDITIONAL RESOURCES

Sources for Further Learning

Albaugh, J. (2012). *Reclaiming sex and intimacy after prostate cancer.* Pittman, NJ: Jannetti Publications.

American Association of Sexuality Educators, Counselors, and Therapists: a professional organization that sponsors and certifies training programs on sexuality and provides a bank of certified professionals throughout the United States: http://www.aasect.org

American Cancer Society. (2014). How pelvic radiation therapy can affect erections. http://www.cancer.org/treatment/treatmentsandsideeffects/physicalsideeffects/sexualsideeffectsinmen/sexualityfortheman/sexuality-for-men-with-cancer-erections-and-pelvic-radiation

American Cancer Society. (2014). Sexuality for the man with cancer. http://www.cancer.org/ssLINK/sexuality-for-the-man-with-cancer-toc

American Cancer Society. (2014). Treatment and side effects. http://www.cancer.org/treatment/treatmentsandsideeffects/index

Hill, R. (2010). *Dead men don't have sex.* North Charleston, SC: Createspace Publishers.

Websites Helpful for Locating Support Groups

American Cancer Society: http://www.cancer.org

Malecare Prostate Cancer Support Programs: http://www.Malecare.org

US TOO International Prostate Cancer Education and Support: http://www.ustoo.org/

REFERENCES

American Cancer Society. (2012). *Cancer facts & figures 2012.* Atlanta, GA: Author. Retrieved from http://www.cancer.org

Autorino, R., Perdona, S., D'Armiento, M., De Sio, M., Damiano, R., Cosentino, L., & Di Lorenzo, G. (2006). Gynecomastia in patients with prostate cancer: Update on treatment options. *Prostate Cancer and Prostatic Diseases, 9,* 109–114. doi:10.1038/sj.pcan.4500859

Blank, T. O. (2005, April 20). Gay men and prostate cancer: Invisible diversity. *Journal of Clinical Oncology, 23*(12), 2593–2596. doi:10.1200/JCO.2005.00.968

Cockle-Hearne, J., & Faithful, S. (2010). Self-management for men surviving prostate cancer: A review of behavioral and psychosocial interventions to understand what strategies can work, for whom and in what circumstances. *Pyscho-Oncology, 19,* 909–922. doi:10.1002/pon.1657

Costanzo, E. S., Ryff, C. D., & Singer, B. H. (2009). Psychosocial adjustment among cancer survivors: Findings from a national survey of health and well-being. *Health Psychology, 28*(2),

Do, N. L., Nagle, D., & Poylin, V. Y. (2011). Radiation proctitis: Current strategies in management. *Gastroenterology Research and Practice,* 2011, Article ID 917941, 1–9. doi:10.1155/2011/917941

Ezer, H., Chachamovich, J. L. R., & Chachamovich, E. (2011). Do men and their wives see it the same way? Congruence within couples during the first year of prostate cancer. *Psycho-Oncology, 20,* 155–164. doi:10.1002/pon.1724

Gallo-Silver, L. (2011). Sexuality, sensuality, and intimacy in palliative care. In T. Altilio & S. Otis-Green (Eds.), *Oxford textbook of palliative social work* (pp. 261–270). New York, NY: Oxford University Press.

Gallo-Silver, L., & Bimbi, D. S. (2012). Human sexual health. In S. Gehlert & T. A. Browne (Eds.), *Handbook of health social work* (2nd ed., pp. 343–370). Hoboken, NJ: John Wiley & Sons.

Gallo-Silver, L., & Dillon, P. (2011). Sexuality and reproductive issues. In J. L. Lester & P. Schmitt (Eds.), *Cancer rehabilitation and survivorship: Transdisciplinary approaches to personalized care* (pp. 123–132). Pittsburgh, PA: Oncology Nursing Society Publications.

Gallo-Silver, L., & Weiner, M. (2006). Survivors of childhood sexual abuse with cancer: Managing the impact of early trauma on cancer treatment. *Journal of Psychosocial Oncology, 24*(1), 107–134.

Garos, S., Kluck, A., & Arnoff, D. (2007). Prostate cancer patients and their partners: Differences in satisfaction indices and psychosocial variables. *Journal of Sexual Medicine, 4,* 1394–1403. doi:10.111/j.1743-6109.2007.00545.x

Gooren, L. J., Giltay, E. J., & Bunck, M. C. (2008, January). Long-term treatment of transsexuals with cross-sex hormones: Personal experience. *Journal of Clinical Endocrinology and Metabolism, 93*(1), 19–25. doi:10.1210/jc.2007-1809

Halbert, C. H., Wrenn, G., Weathers, B., Delmoor, E., Have, T. T., & Coyne, J. (2010). Sociocultural determinants of men's reactions to prostate cancer diagnosis. *Psycho-Oncology, 19*(5), 553–560. doi:10.1002/pon./1574

Haliloglu, A., Baltaci, S., & Yaman, O. (2007). Penile length changes in men treated with androgen suppression plus radiation therapy for locally advanced prostate cancer. *Journal of Urology, 177*(1), 128–130. doi:10.1016/j.juro.2006.08.113

Hembree, W. C., Cohen-Kettenis, P., Delmarre-van de Waal, H., Gooren, L. J., Meyer III, W. J., Spack, N. P., ... Montori, V. M. (2009, September). Endocrine treatment of transsexual persons: An Endocrine Society clinical practice guideline. *Journal of Clinical Endocrinology and Metabolism, 94*(9), 3132–3154. doi:10.1210/jc.2009-0345

Hubiak, C. (2011). *A woman's guide to thriving after prostate cancer: You've helped him through—now what about you?* Scottsdale, AZ: Allied Synergistics International.

McCarthy, B., & McCarthy, E. (2012). *Sexual awareness: Your guide to healthy couple sexuality* (5th ed.). New York, NY: Taylor & Francis Group.

Mehnert, A., Lehmann, C., Graefen, M., Huland, H., & Koch, U. (2010). Depression, anxiety, post-traumatic stress disorder and health-related quality of life and its association with social support in ambulatory prostate cancer patients. *European Journal of Cancer Care, 19,* 736–745. doi:10.1111/j.1365-2354.2009.01117.x

Mulhall, J. P. (2008). *Saving your sex life: A guide for men with prostate cancer.* Chicago, IL: Hilton Publishing Company.

O'Brien, R., Hunt, K., & Hart, G. (2005). "It's caveman stuff, but

of masculinity and help seeking. *Journal of Social Science and Medicine*, *61*, 503–516. doi:10.1016/j.socscimed.2004.12.008

Oliffe, J. L., Gerbrandt, J. S., Bottorff, J. L., & Hislop, T. G. (2010). Health promotion and illness demotion at prostate cancer support groups. *Health Promotion Practice*, *11*(4), 562–571. doi:10.1177/1524839908328990

Oliffe, J. L., Ogrodniczuk, J., Bottorff, J. L., Hislop, T. G., & Halpin, M. (2009). Connecting humor, health, and masculinities at prostate cancer support groups. *Psycho-Oncology*, *18*, 916–926. doi:10.1002/pon.1415

Queenan, J. A., Feldman-Stewart, D., Brundage, M., & Groome, P. A. (2010). Social support and quality of life of prostate cancer patients after radiotherapy treatment. *European Journal of Cancer Care*, *19*, 251–259. doi:10.1111/j.1365-2354.2008.01029.x

Roberts, K. J., Lepore, S. J., & Hanlon, A. I. (2010). Genitourinary functioning and depressive symptoms over time in younger versus older men treated for prostate cancer. *Annals of Behavioral Medicine*, *40*, 275–283. doi:10.1007/s12160-010-9214-4

Savoie, M., Kim, S. S., & Soloway, M. S. (2003). A prospective study measuring penile length in men treated with radical prostatectomy for prostate cancer. *Journal of Urology*, *169*(4), 1462–1464. doi:10.1097/01.ju.0000053720.93303.33

Song, L., Northouse, L. L., Braun, T. M., Zhang, L., Cimprich, B., Ronis, D. L., & Mood, D. W. (2011). Assessing longitudinal quality of life in prostate cancer patients and their spouses: A multilevel modeling approach. *Quality of Life Research*, *20*, 371–381. doi:10.1007/s11136-101-9753-y

Wall, D., & Kristjanson, L. (2005). Men, culture, and hegemonic masculinity: Understanding the experience of prostate cancer. *Nursing Inquiry*, *12*, 87–97.

Walsh, P. C., & Worthington, J. F. (2012). *Dr. Patrick Walsh's guide to surviving prostate cancer* (3rd ed.). New York, NY: Grand Central Life & Style, Hachette Book Group.

Winterrich, J. A., Quandt, S. A., Grzywacz, J. G., Clark, P. E., Miller, D. P., Acuna, J., & Arcury, T. A. (2009, December). Masculinity and the body: How African-American and white men experience cancer screening exams involving the rectum. *American Journal of Men's Health*, *3*(4), 300–309. doi:10.1177/1557988308321675

Wittmann, D., Foley, S., & Balon, R. (2011). A biopsychosocial approach to sexual recovery after prostate cancer surgery: The role of grief and mourning. *Journal of Sex & Marital Therapy*, *37*, 130–144. doi:10.1080/0092623X.2011.560538

14 Roz Kleban and Susan Glaser

The Many Dimensions of Breast Cancer: Determining the Scope of Needed Services

Key Concepts

- *All people with breast cancer face similar challenges along the continuum of care.*
- *Common issues addressed throughout the continuum of care include fear of mortality, vulnerability, loss of control, alteration in body image and integrity, the illness's impact on relationships, multiple losses, and the need to reprioritize.*
- *Emotions experienced at the time of diagnosis change during treatment and after treatment and are different for those diagnosed with advanced disease.*
- *Interventions are organized to help patients cope with these issues at different stages in the disease and treatment process.*

Breast cancer is second only to nonmelanoma skin cancer as the most commonly diagnosed cancer among U.S. women. It represents a significant health concern. Research indicates that one in eight women will develop invasive breast cancer over her lifetime (American Cancer Society, 2012); in addition, most people know someone who has been diagnosed with the disease. Psychosocial stress and higher levels of distress are expected during the diagnostic and treatment process.

This chapter reflects a perspective developed by working with women and men with breast cancer over the past 25 years. Services are provided for patients across the continuum of care, often related to stages in the disease and treatment trajectory. We have observed that people face similar psychosocial issues and adaptive challenges during this process; the emotional state and intensity of responses change over time and at different stages of treatment. This chapter describes the psychosocial, emotional, and existential issues confronted throughout the experience with breast cancer and interventions utilized along the disease trajectory. Two particularly effective programs for this population are highlighted.

Oncology social work begins with those who are newly diagnosed with an early-stage breast cancer as they approach surgery and adjuvant treatment (chemotherapy and/or radiation therapy). Interventions are continued during the posttreatment period and with those diagnosed with advanced disease. We have developed our own perspectives on the adaptive challenges faced by this population and how to best help patients.

Common Issues Across the Continuum of Care

Concretization of Mortality

Threat of mortality is the immediate issue that arises when a person receives a diagnosis of breast cancer (Spiegel, 1997; Zabora et al., 1997). The patient's first thoughts are often of dying, even when the prognosis is not grave. Reassurances about the early stage of diagnosis are often overshadowed by fears that normal aches and pains signify the disease is spreading and that the patient will die from the disease. For some patients, anesthesia represents a loss of control, and cancer fears are displaced onto the surgical intervention—that is, they are convinced they will not awaken after surgery. Fear of death can last for months or years. People diagnosed with metastatic disease have more realistic concerns about mortality and death (Block, 2001; Breitbart & Heller, 2003; Breitbart et al., 2010; Christ & Sormanti, 2000). Even though facing one's mortality means different things to different people, the uncertainty of the disease trajectory causes great distress. Ready access to media information fuels fears of mortality. Frequently, anticipation of pain, suffering, and becoming dependent on others just before death creates as much anxiety as the fear of death.

Increased Sense of Vulnerability

A breast cancer diagnosis is also accompanied by an increased sense of vulnerability, which some patients believe is the most terrible thing imaginable. They fear that life's safeguards are no longer effective. Some use pessimism as a coping mechanism to ward off fears of impending disaster. Vulnerability is heightened during the posttreatment period when many people may feel alone and abandoned by friends, family, and the medical team. The sense of vulnerability in people with advanced disease is validated by treatment effects, as well as the constant wait for test results, which they often believe will tell them when, not if, they will die.

Loss of a Sense of Control

Loss of a sense of control is another issue people face throughout the disease continuum. The diagnosis itself can undermine the person's sense of knowing and connecting to his or her body. The sense of control is further undermined by the need to negotiate health care bureaucracies, keep up with medical appointments and treatment, and wait for return calls or test results. Once treatment begins, side effects can cause the body to behave in unfamiliar and unwanted ways. It is difficult to deal with the fact that weakness may create a sense of being out of control and dependent on others.

Alterations in Body Image and Integrity

Alterations in body image and integrity affect people at every stage of breast cancer. Because breasts are symbols of femininity, motherhood, and sexuality across cultures, the diagnosis can threaten a woman's sense of self and her connection to her body. Advances in surgical and reconstructive procedures, however, offer women more options for surgical treatment. Lumpectomies or limited resections may be less physically marring than mastectomies, but there are still scars and breast shape may change. Some women choose to have bilateral mastectomies to reduce the emotional stress caused by fears of a second breast cancer or in response to a family history of the disease. Although many women with breast cancer are able to look beyond the scars and breast changes, the assault to the body's integrity cannot be underestimated. Surgical interventions can also cause a loss of breast sensation, which can affect sexuality and intimacy. Other cancer treatments, such as chemotherapy and radiation therapy, can lead to additional physical alterations that threaten a woman's connection to and comfort with her body, including hair loss, weight fluctuation, skin discoloration, and hot flashes (Fobair & Spiegel, 2009; Schover, 1997). People with advanced disease may suffer from many long-lasting side effects as they move from one treatment to the next. The emotional and physical effects of treatment influence each person uniquely throughout the disease continuum.

Concerns About Relationships

Concerns about relationships affect people with breast cancer, particularly with respect to disclosure of the diagnosis. Varied responses to the diagnosis by family, friends, and coworkers have profound effects. For example, a loved one may disappoint the patient, whereas another person may surprise him or her with an act of kindness and support. The time demands of appointments, the stresses of treatment decisions, and the burden of managing financial issues combine with the stress of treatment to challenge relationships and lead to changing roles and responsibilities for individuals and families. Everyday tasks may need to be delegated to someone else or put off until a future time.

Breast cancer treatment can drastically affect one's emotional or physical ability to work. Though many are eager to continue to work to maintain a sense of normalcy, treatment may require reduced time on the job (Messner & Patterson, 2001). At times, necessary role changes may be more stressful than the diagnosis. Asking for help can be extremely difficult for someone who has been the family caregiver. Children may become saddened when a parent is unable to play with them, or a partner may resent doing chores that were once shared. Some family, friends, or coworkers may have difficulty relating to a person with a life-threatening disease. They may withdraw because they don't know how to handle their emotions or communicate in a manner they think will be helpful. The fact that public figures are very open about their own experiences with the illness may make it easier for early-stage, newly diagnosed patients to discuss the illness with family, friends, and colleagues. There is less openness among people with advanced disease. This is still a diagnosis that elicits fear, sometimes ostracism, and feelings of isolation (Holland, 2002).

Mourning and Accepting Losses

The diagnosis and treatment of breast cancer includes a "roller-coaster ride" of emotions and coping with a series of losses. For some, it is the loss of a body part; for others, it is the loss of a sense of being attractive. Although they may appear unchanged to the outside world, people with breast cancer may believe that they are altered and that everyone can see the damage. Lymphedema patients may feel unattractive because of the intermittent swelling of a hand or arm and the occasional need to wrap it for treatment. Younger women may be devastated by the possible loss of a lifelong dream to bear children (Senkus et al., 2014). A life-threatening disease challenges one's confidence in one's body and the immediate world. Questions are often raised about nutrition, coping styles, behavior, and spirituality in an effort to understand why this happened and what can be done to prevent it from happening again. The process of coping with advanced disease is often characterized by a diminished ability to participate in usual life. People may give up careers, rely on family and friends to do household chores, and relinquish once-cherished child-care activities (Mayer, 2010). Early or metastatic breast cancer patients may experience the disease as a series of losses.

Need to Reprioritize

Those who have lived through an overwhelming, life-threatening, and all-encompassing experience such as breast cancer often respond by feeling a need to reprioritize. As a result, people question their values, behaviors, and the meaning in their lives. These life assessments commonly go on for a few years after treatment has been completed. The process will often slow down and life will seemingly return to normal, but lifelong alterations can sometimes occur. People in unhappy relationships or unsatisfying careers may use this opportunity to review their lives and make changes. The need to reprioritize is an imperative for those coping with metastatic disease, due to their changing physical abilities and the increased attention paid to time.

The preceding seven psychosocial issues occur throughout the disease. We have also observed that the patient's emotional state can change at any given time.

Issues Specific to the Disease and Treatment Phases

At Diagnosis

Shock

Most people experience shock at the time of diagnosis. We are reminded of Kendra, a woman in her 30s who was followed in a breast cancer surveillance clinic because of the prevalence of breast cancer in her family. She felt calm and in total control over her future. She often spoke about knowing that she would get breast cancer at some point in her life; it was just unclear when the diagnosis would be made. She was so overwhelmed when she received her diagnosis that she locked herself in her bedroom for days and would not talk to family or friends. Kendra's cancer was surprising to her despite her family history and the fact that she was being monitored in a specialty clinic. People often respond to a cancer diagnosis with shock, even though they have advance knowledge of its probability.

Denial

Denial is another common reaction to the diagnosis of breast cancer. Though some people deny the illness itself, others may deny its emotional consequences. Denial allows the person to seek medical advice and endure follow-up tests and procedures but simultaneously believe that they are "fine." Anger and guilt appear to be related emotional reactions on different sides of the same coin. People who experience anger might blame some outside source for their illness, such as the food industry or the environment. Those who turn this blame inward experience guilt by asking, "What did I do?" These people often see breast cancer as a form of "payback" for a misdeed, such as a poor diet. One patient even thought she was being punished for putting her elderly mother in a nursing facility.

Anxiety

Anxiety is often free floating and can be experienced for periods at a time. The reasons for this anxiety are often unclear to the person. When Ana was seen as a postsurgical inpatient, she shared that she was feeling anxious and was perplexed as to the reason. Ana was surprised when she was asked whether she might be anxious because she had just undergone surgery for cancer.

Depersonalization

Depersonalization is also a common experience for newly diagnosed patients and is evidenced by a sense of observing oneself from outside one's own body. Patients' lives are pervaded by a surreal feeling and a sense that they do not feel like themselves. Patients often say, "I feel like I am watching myself in a movie."

"Chemobrain"

Intellectual and cognitive functioning are often taxed when energy is focused on coping with the stress of a cancer diagnosis. The phenomenon of "chemobrain" has been studied. Even before people receive treatment, they can experience a decline in intellectual and cognitive functioning secondary to the emotional distress caused by the diagnosis (Wefel et al., 2004).

During Treatment

Emotions shift during treatment. Many people will say, "I can beat this," and focus on maintaining a positive attitude. Although intellectualization and rationalization may help them feel empowered and focused, denying their fears may result in a continued feeling of free-floating anxiety. People use a variety of coping strategies to deal with their anxiety and fears while undergoing treatment. For example, they may present information to their health care team about a treatment found on the Internet or in a journal that is touted as preventing a breast cancer recurrence. Women who have been the primary family caregivers may sometimes have a greater investment in focusing on their own treatment needs. Some women need to announce to everyone that this is the time for them to take care of themselves.

Posttreatment

The immediate posttreatment phase often involves anger and fear. Contrary to patients' original postdiagnosis expectations, compliance with treatment recommendations initially creates a sense of hope for a long, normal life after breast cancer. Anxiety may be rekindled by the end of treatment and the start of infrequent follow-up appointments (Stanton, 2006). The uncertainty of the future and a lingering sense of sadness elicit periodic flashbacks about the diagnostic process. Patients may experience a heightened sense of vulnerability and a feeling of being abandoned by the medical community. Family and friends have returned to their own lives, expecting that things will be fine now that treatment has ended. It is not over for the person with cancer; it just means that he or she must now handle the cancer alone.

Survivorship

We see many long-term survivors who report diminishing distress as their diagnosis recedes. Life may even return to pre-diagnosis normalcy. Many, however, experience anxiety about the need for routine oncology appointments and tests. Some survivors develop a greater appreciation for life and a new approach to illness. Often, the survivor's need for a community of survivors does not seem to diminish. We have former group members who continue to visit our early-stage group and maintain contact with people they met during treatment.

Some people experience anger over the lingering side effects of lymphedema, neuropathy, hot flashes, and sexual dysfunction. One woman facetiously called breast cancer treatment "the gift that keeps on giving." They may be frustrated because the medical community does not treat these long-term effects with the seriousness and attention given to their cancers (Stanton, 2006). Despite there being many bumps in the road, most people return to their previous lifestyles and feel as if their lives have returned to normal.

Advanced Disease

Those who are rediagnosed or newly diagnosed with metastatic disease experience an overwhelming sense of sadness. Many report feeling betrayed or let down because they had led relatively healthy lives and complied with the recommendations of the medical community. They experience a loss as they relinquish the illusion of having control over their bodies. They are reminded of this loss of control as the illness progresses and increasing physical limitations need to be addressed (Mayer, 2010).

There is also a sense of isolation within the metastatic breast cancer community. The media are flooded with images of breast cancer charity races involving women crossing the finish lines with expressions of glory. Cancer and its treatment are often analogized to a race or battle that is confronted, fought, and completed. People with metastatic disease do not feel victorious. Their treatment never ends; it is given continuously while they are alive. It is not uncommon to feel envy and hostility toward those who are well, along with guilt over having such feelings.

Unlike patients with early-stage breast cancer, those with metastatic disease do not generally experience great anxiety. They do, however, experience profound fear and sadness. In spite of this, they need to find and maintain meaning in their lives. The person with metastatic breast cancer needs to remember who he or she has been and maintain a sense of self, despite often having to give up dearly held dreams, cope with the physical limitations imposed by a progressive illness, deal with tremendous time commitments for appointments, and experience the side effects of ongoing treatment (Breitbart & Heller, 2003).

In 1974, both Betty Ford and Happy Rockefeller (wives of the U.S. president and vice president, respectively) revealed that they had been diagnosed with breast cancer, thrusting the illness into the public forum. Breast Cancer Awareness Month activities in October and greater funding for research have also helped diminish the stigma of cancer. Those with metastatic cancer have not always benefited from this attention. Advanced cancer remains "in the closet," just as it was before Betty Ford and Happy Rockefeller spoke publicly of their illnesses. Advocates have worked to bring needed attention and support to this population. In the words of Arthur Miller (1973) in *Death of Salesman*, "Attention must be paid." The person with metastatic disease is the person we fear we will become. Advocates established an organization dedicated to the needs of people living with chronic breast cancer. Several national conferences focused on their unique issues have been organized. Over the past 10 years, many major breast cancer organizations have included the issue of metastasis in their fund-raising, conferences, and patient support activities.

Psychosocial Programs and Interventions

Psychosocial programs available to breast cancer patients throughout the disease continuum are offered in the following modalities: individual counseling; couples, family, and group work; advocacy; and the patient-to-patient connection. We will focus on the two programs we feel are most beneficial to this population: group work and the patient-to-patient connection.

Due to the large size of the breast cancer population, we have the luxury of offering stage-specific and sometimes stage- and age-specific groups (Daste, 1990; Vilhauer, 2001). Our group program includes an open, ongoing adjuvant support group that encompasses people diagnosed at Stages 0 through 3 and two open, ongoing, age-categorized groups for the metastatic population. The effects of the diagnosis and treatment differ for this population depending on the patient's age.

Research over the past 40 years has examined the benefits of support groups for people with cancer. Initially, studies found evidence that groups improved participants' prognoses. Later research has demonstrated that support groups can improve the cancer patient's quality of life by enhancing adjustment and coping and by providing much-needed information (Goodwin, 2005; Goodwin et al., 2001; Gore-Felton & Spiegel, 1999; Kissane et al., 2007; Spiegel & Classen, 2000; Weis, 2003; Yalom, 1995). Our experiences in facilitating support groups reinforce these findings.

Irvin D. Yalom, MD, a psychiatrist and group therapist, discusses the mechanisms of change in group work: universality, instillation of hope, imparting information, altruism, imitative behavior, desensitization through articulation, existential factors, and group cohesiveness. Though each mechanism of change has its significance in group work, we believe two are invaluable. *Universality* enables group participants to realize that they are not alone and do not have unique issues. Interacting with others with cancer at similar stages reduces isolation. Feelings of anxiety, shame, fear, and sadness can be normalized and reduced. A sense of connection to others can be restorative (Yalom, 1995).

The *imparting of information* by the group facilitator or one of the members through explanation, advice, clarification, or instruction can help reduce confusion, uncertainty, and anxiety. Understanding and clarity can aid decision making and problem solving. It is sometimes less intimidating and more accessible to receive information from a group member, rather than from the medical team, and it can help prepare the person for the journey ahead (Yalom, 1995).

Although support groups are helpful for many people, some are uncomfortable in this setting. A one-to-one, patient-to-patient connection can serve the same purpose for these people. We have a vast network of people with remote or current breast cancer diagnoses from whom we can elicit help. Matching of people with similar diagnoses, treatment regimens, and/or social situations serves as the core of this intervention. These informal volunteers are usually further along in treatment or have completed treatment and are eager to share their experiences with someone who has concerns. This provides the person with breast cancer with an invaluable connection to someone who has "been there." It provides the volunteer with an opportunity to "give back" and instill hope and information.

A typical scenario involves a person who must decide among treatment options. Decision making can be aided by talking to several women who are similar in age and social situation and have chosen one of the options. Both the volunteer and the patient usually feel validated by the experience. Lucille, an older woman with metastatic disease that had progressed, asked to see the social worker because she was unsure whether she wanted to continue with treatment. She was frightened by the potential side effects of the recommended chemotherapy and wondered whether she could tolerate it. Her anxiety and sense of isolation were alleviated by connecting her with someone else undergoing the recommended treatment. She understood that there were other women like her who were indeed able to manage.

Pearls

- The public attention paid to breast cancer has helped diminish its associated shame and stigma. The growing population of patients living with advanced cancers has only recently received the recognition and support it deserves.
- Breast cancer is a commonly diagnosed cancer. As a result, many interventions and resources exist for individuals and families.
- Group work and the patient-to-patient connection are two interventions that have been found to be most helpful to people with breast cancer.

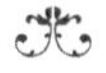

Pitfalls

- Most people diagnosed with breast cancer can expect to contend with some form of psychosocial stress during the diagnostic and treatment process.
- Threats to one's sense of mortality, vulnerability, control, relationships, body image, and integrity contribute to the losses experienced throughout the disease continuum.
- Oncology social workers must maintain an up-to-date understanding of the changing treatments and

prognoses for breast cancer to address the concerns of people with the disease.

People with breast cancer face similar issues and challenges at all stages of the disease continuum. Their emotional state and its intensity change over the course of the illness. Anxiety, fear, and sadness are quite common, and psychosocial interventions must address these emotions throughout the continuum. When patients with early-stage disease complete treatment, they often continue to experience anxiety, fear of recurrence, and feelings of abandonment by family, friends, and the health care team. Those with metastatic disease are distressed by concerns about the uncertainty of the disease trajectory. As the disease progresses, fears of suffering and dependence on others may dominate their thoughts. Group process and patient-to-patient connections are two helpful interventions. Adaptive coping skills and strategies are promoted by validation and normalization of feelings, the sharing of information, and the experience of universality.

Social workers, as integral interdisciplinary team members, must have an adequate understanding of breast cancer care. The oncology social worker must be acquainted with the diagnostic process, disease stages and their impact, and treatment options if he or she is to be able to understand and address the concerns of someone with breast cancer.

Advances in breast cancer treatment have contributed to shorter hospital stays, the development of targeted treatment options, and shorter overall treatment times for some diagnoses. Genomic research has yielded helpful information concerning treatment decisions. Innovations in the field of infertility have provided previously unavailable options. These trends have implications for oncology social workers who are developing time-sensitive and practical interventions.

ADDITIONAL RESOURCES

Readings

Frankl, V. (2006). *Man's search for meaning.* Boston, MA: Beacon Press.

Groopman, J. (2004). *The anatomy of hope.* New York, NY: Random House.

Silver, M. (2004). *Breast cancer husband.* Emmaus, PA: Rodale Books.

Online Resources

BreastCancer.org: http://www.breastcancer.org

Fertile Hope: http://www.fertilehope.org

Memorial Sloan-Kettering Cancer Center, Department of Integrative Medicine: http://www.mskcc.org/cancer-care/integrative-medicine/

Metastatic Breast Cancer Network: http://www.mbcn.org

Triple Negative Breast Cancer Foundation: http://www.tnbcfoundation.org

REFERENCES

American Cancer Society. (2012). *Cancer facts & figures 2012.* Atlanta, GA: Author.

Block, S. (2001). Psychological considerations, growth, and transcendence at the end of life. *Journal of the American Medical Association, 285*(22), 2898–2905.

Breitbart, W., & Heller, K. S. (2003). Reframing hope: Meaning-centered care for patients near the end of life. *Journal of Palliative Medicine, 6*(6), 979–988.

Breitbart, W., Rosenfeld, B., Gibson, C., Pessin, H., Poppito, S., Nelson, C., ... Olden, M. (2010). Meaning-centered group psychotherapy for patients with advanced cancer: A pilot randomized controlled trial. *Psycho-Oncology, 19*, 21–28. doi:10.1002/pon.1556

Christ, G., & Sormanti, M. (2000). Advancing social work practice in end-of-life care. *Social Work in Health Care, 30*(2), 81–99.

Daste, B. (1990). Important considerations in group work with cancer patients. *Social Work With Groups, 13*(2), 69–81.

Fobair, P., & Spiegel, D. (2009). Concerns about sexuality after breast cancer. *Cancer Journal, 15*(1), 19–26.

Goodwin, P. J. (2005). Support groups in advanced breast cancer. *Cancer Supplement, 104*(11), 2596–2601.

Goodwin, P. J., Leszcz, M., Ennis, M., Koopmans, J., Vincent, L., Guther, H., ... Hunter, J. (2001). The effect of group psychosocial support on survival in metastatic breast cancer. *New England Journal of Medicine, 24*(345), 1719–1726.

Gore-Felton, C., & Spiegel, D. (1999). Enhancing women's lives: The role of support groups among breast cancer patients. *Journal for Specialists in Group Work, 24*(3), 274–287.

Holland, J. (2002). History of psycho-oncology: Overcoming attitudinal and conceptual barriers. *Psychosomatic Medicine, 64*(2), 206–221.

Kissane, D. W., Grabsch, B., Clarke, D. M., Smith, G. C., Love, A. W., Bloch, S., ... Li, Y. (2007). Supportive-expressive group therapy for women with metastatic breast cancer: Survival and psychosocial outcome from a randomized controlled trial. *Psycho-Oncology, 16*, 277–286. doi:10.1002/pon.1185

Mayer, M. (2010). Lessons learned from the metastatic breast cancer community. *Seminars in Oncology Nursing, 26*(3), 195–202.

Messner, C., & Patterson, D. (2001). The challenge of cancer in the workplace. *Cancer Practice, 9*(1), 50–51.

Miller, A. (1973). *Death of a salesman.* New York, NY: Viking Press.

Schover, L. (1997). *Sexuality and fertility after cancer.* New York, NY: John Wiley & Sons.

Senkus, E., Gomez, H., Dinx, L., Jerusalem, G., Murray, E., Tienhoven, G., ... Neskovic-Konstantinovic, Z. (2014). Attitudes of young patients with breast cancer toward fertility loss related to adjuvant systemic therapies. EORTC study 10002 BIG 3-98. *Psycho-Oncology, 23*, 173–182.

Spiegel, D. (1997). Psychosocial aspects of breast cancer treatment. *Seminars in Oncology, 24*(1), S1-36–S1-47.

Spiegel, D., & Classen, C. (2000). *Group therapy for cancer patients: A research-based handbook of psychosocial care.* New York, NY: Basic Books.

Stanton, A. (2006). Psychosocial concerns and interventions for cancer survivors. *Journal of Clinical Oncology, 24*(32), 5132–5137.

Vilhauer, R. (2001). "Them and us": The experiences of women with metastatic disease in mixed-stage versus stage-specific breast cancer support groups. *Psychology and Health, 26*(6), 781–797.

Wefel, J., Lenzi, R., Theriault, R., Buzdar, A., Cruickshank, S., & Meyers, C. (2004). "Chemobrain" in breast carcinoma? *Cancer, 101*(3), 466–475.

Weis, J. (2003). Support groups for cancer patients. *Support Care Cancer, 11*, 763–768.

Yalom, I. (1995). *The theory and practice of group psychotherapy.* New York, NY: Basic Books.

Zabora, J., Blanchard, C., Smith, E., Roberts, C., Glajchen, M., Sharp, J., … Hedlund, S. (1997). Prevalence of psychological distress among cancer patients across the disease continuum. *Journal of Psychosocial Oncology, 15*(2), 73–87.

15

Kate Pederson, Brian Tomlinson, and Lisa O'Brien

Hematologic Cancers: Patients' Needs for Special Care

Key Concepts

- *Hematologic (blood) cancers include a wide variety of cancers that affect the blood-producing system.*
- *Treatment and decision making for hematologic cancers is very specialized and, based on subtype, is best done in partnership with a multidisciplinary cancer treatment team with leukemia, lymphoma, multiple myeloma, or myelodysplasia expertise.*
- *Treatments vary greatly from "watchful waiting" to intensive bone marrow transplantation, and adjustment to these situations is equally varied.*
- *Long-term survivorship comes with a fear of relapse and a need for specialized monitoring, offering important opportunities for oncology social work intervention.*

Hematologic malignancies (blood cancers), such as leukemia, lymphoma, multiple myeloma, and myelodysplasia, are groupings of diseases with many subtypes, making it difficult for patients and families to feel that they can find experts to address their disease. Locating an oncology team who can accurately diagnose and treat these diseases is a first priority for the patient and family, which often requires consultation or care away from home. For the social workers in this field of oncology, subspecialty-level knowledge about prognosis, treatment, and cost can help clarify questions that patients may pose. This chapter provides oncology social workers with the fundamentals of hematologic malignancies and an overview of the challenges or issues this patient population may face.

Overview of Hematologic Malignancies

As defined by the Leukemia and Lymphoma Society, blood cancers represent a group of heterogeneous diseases affecting bone marrow, blood cells, lymph nodes, and other parts of the lymphatic system and include lymphoma, leukemia, multiple myeloma, and myelodysplastic syndromes (LLS, 2013). More than 1 million Americans are currently living with one of these diseases.

Types of Hematologic Malignancies

Lymphoma is the most common blood cancer. Lymphomas begin in the lymphatic system (i.e., lymph nodes, spleen, bone marrow, blood, or other organs) and represent a complex group of closely related cancers. They are divided into two main forms: non-Hodgkin lymphoma (NHL) and Hodgkin lymphoma (HL). Generally categorized as aggressive (fast growing) or indolent (slow growing), each has different treatment options and related outcomes (LRF, 2012a, 2012b).

Leukemia is the second most common blood cancer (LLS, 2013). Leukemia is a general term used to describe cancers that begin in the bone marrow and are categorized as either acute (rapidly growing) or chronic (slow growing). The four most common types of leukemia are acute lymphocytic (lymphoblastic) leukemia (ALL), acute myelogenous (myeloid) leukemia (AML), chronic lymphocytic leukemia (CLL), and chronic myelogenous leukemia (CML). Each of these four main types also has subtypes (LLS, 2012).

Multiple myeloma is the most common type of plasma cell tumor. It begins in plasma cells, which help protect the body from germs and other harmful substances. When these cells become abnormal, they can cause damage to the bone and other tissues and organs, so the very cells that are supposed to protect the body become harmful (NCI, 2008). Myelodysplastic syndromes (MDSs) are diseases of the bone marrow that occur when the bone marrow stops making enough healthy blood-forming stem cells, generally resulting in anemia. MDS can also grow more severe and develop into AML (Be the Match, 2014).

Treatment Options for Hematologic Malignancies

A variety of treatment options are available for patients with hematologic malignancies, including but not limited to chemotherapy, radiation therapy, watchful waiting, targeted treatments, new drug therapies, and transplantation (LLS, 2013). The goal of treatment varies from disease to disease. For some, the goal is cure; for others, it is chronic disease management. Because of the complicated nature of blood cancers and the variability in treatment choices, an accurate diagnosis is critical during treatment planning. It is also important for patients to see a hematologist or oncologist who specializes in the treatment of the patient's specific disease and is knowledgeable about new drugs and clinical trials, even when the patient receives ongoing treatment and disease management by his or her local oncologist.

Although chemotherapy is often used in the treatment of blood cancers, there are several other standard regimens including radiation therapy, biologic therapy, transplantation, and the watchful waiting approach for slow-growing hematologic cancers (LRF, 2014). The patient with slow-growing lymphoma who undergoes watchful waiting does not receive any active treatment to fight the disease but rather is "actively observed" for disease progression, which, when it occurs, may or may not require treatment. The psychological side effects of such an approach can be daunting, which is why patients often describe it as "watch and worry."

Another treatment option for a serious blood cancer or disorder is a marrow or cord blood transplant—also called a bone marrow transplant (BMT) or stem cell transplant. The object of a marrow or cord blood transplant is to replace diseased cells with healthy blood-forming cells, either from oneself (autologous transplant) or from a matched donor or cord blood unit (allogeneic transplant; Be the Match, 2011).

The development of new drugs used to treat blood cancers has also had a profound impact on the outcomes of these diseases (LLS, 2013). These new agents often have fewer side effects and are generally tolerated well by patients.

Treatment Decision Making

Research shows that patients are becoming more active and involved in the treatment decision-making (TDM) process (Poe, Hayslip, & Studts, 2012), with many patients and their caregivers educating themselves to engage in meaningful discussions with the oncology team. One article found that the majority of participants wanted to be actively involved in the decision-making process; the study looked at adults diagnosed with follicular lymphoma (the second most common type of lymphoma) and found that patients were engaged in the TDM process with their health care team and actively spoke with family members (spouse, children, and others) about their treatment options. The participants reported high levels of satisfaction with their most recent treatment decision, but the study also found that the majority of the participants experienced moderate amounts of anxiety and moderate to severe levels of cancer-specific distress (Poe et al., 2012). Awareness of the anxiety accompanying TDM is particularly important when working with hematologic cancer patients because most will require more than one treatment during their cancer journey as they go between being "on treatment" and "off treatment."

Survivorship

Just as it is difficult for the patient to accept and adjust to the diagnosis of a blood cancer, undergoing treatment and the subsequent length of recovery also present challenges. For example, recovery after allogeneic transplant may take a year or longer depending on the severity of long-term complications. Patients can experience a host of physical and emotional survivorship issues, including worry about relapse; chronic graft-versus-host disease; susceptibility to infections; infertility; sexual problems; feelings of depression, anger, or guilt; fatigue; and memory and concentration problems.

Pediatric transplant patients can have growth and development late effects, including learning difficulties, delayed skeletal growth, growth hormone deficiency, and late onset of puberty. The patient's parent/guardian may also experience both short- and long-term emotional turmoil due to disruptions in the family's life cycle (Be the Match, 2011).

Patient Psychosocial Challenges

The uncertainty of the prognosis may intensify the psychosocial distress and adjustment to a hematologic malignancy. In addition to the uncertainty of cure and survival, a prolonged treatment course often involves many hospitalizations and clinic visits. An additional challenge is that many patients have never heard of their particular disease, nor do they know anyone with a similar diagnosis. Social work interventions with this group of cancer survivors must take into account these multiple patient stressors, yet the assessment and counseling techniques that are used in other oncology social work settings apply equally to this patient population: identifying the patient's understanding and adjustment to illness, screening for depression and anxiety, providing individual and family support and therapy as needed, and connecting the patient to resources. Education is crucial on the usual and expected course of recovery and emotional adjustment. Patients who are advised that watchful waiting is optimal often have difficulty accepting this approach. An understanding that potential side effects may overshadow potential benefits can seem incongruous to fearful patients and families with diseases such as slow-growing lymphomas, CLL, or early-stage multiple myeloma. The need for professional support opens the opportunity for counseling and education from the whole treatment team, often led by social workers.

A 79-year-old man was diagnosed with non-HIV-related indolent B-cell lymphoma while asymptomatic after undergoing a computed tomography scan before hip replacement for severe osteoarthritis. Having had a brother who died after many years' survivorship of colon cancer, he believed that the best approach to control cancer was to "hit it early and hit it hard." Such a tactic fit in with his general worldview as a retired police detective. When his first- and second-opinion oncologists, both experts in lymphoma, gave him identical advice about watchful waiting, he remained uncomfortable with the idea that he was doing nothing to fight his cancer. After the health care team listened to his ongoing reservations about watchful waiting, he was referred for a clinical trial that randomized a novel targeted chemotherapy. Counseling with the social worker helped this gentleman express his concerns about watchful waiting and the health care team was able to address this through enrollment in a clinical trial.

Social workers assist the interdisciplinary team by identifying challenges that may hinder compliance with care, such as the availability of housing or a caregiver, financial concerns that impact transportation, or prescription coverage. Due to the life-threatening nature of many of the blood cancers, social workers will also assist the family through stages of fear, hope, grief, and loss. Families enduring aggressive treatment are sometimes hit with a sudden downturn in prognosis and face making end-of-life decisions quickly. Because of this, advance care planning is best introduced at the initial assessment. When these discussions are a routine part of care planning, it is more likely that the individual and family will have better clarity for making such decisions when the outcome is not a cure. Other common emotional issues social workers may help patients address include diminished physical functioning, loss of social identity associated with work or school, and changing family roles and relationships.

Although most studies have focused on the negative impacts of the patient's experience—especially the downsides of BMT on quality of life—some studies report positive outcomes as well. In a study of 662 survivors of BMT who were compared to a control group matched for age and gender, the survivors experienced expected deficits in physical, psychological, social, and relationship functioning, yet they also reported positive outcomes that could be described as posttraumatic growth across psychological, interpersonal, and spiritual domains (Andrykowski et al., 2005). The long-term late effects of transplant indicate that this group of patients and caregivers would benefit from interventions for many years after treatment, even when the patient is considered to be cured of the underlying disease. Potential social work interventions include individual and group counseling and provision of information on survivorship issues, with the chance to participate in interactive events geared toward BMT survivors that allow for discussion and connection with others who are dealing with similar late effects. Although face-to-face events are available for some survivors, online support via chat rooms and webcasts allows those who are geographically distant to connect with peers and professionals.

Caregiver Assessment and Intervention

Family members also share in the impact of the cancer diagnosis. Siblings, spouses, children, and parents are all affected, and for this reason, they are called cosurvivors. Many studies have documented the need for more support of family caregivers and family members. Family caregivers for oncology patients often face increased health concerns of their own (Bevans & Sternberg, 2012). Although the focus in the medical setting is on the person with cancer, the patient's well-being is dependent on his or her family care provider's well-being and ability to be present and provide care (Stenberg, Ruland, & Miaskowski, 2010). Helping the family designate a primary caregiver, as well as finding ways to support that person's physical and social/emotional needs, is part of the social work task. Often due to competing demands, the needs of the caregiver may not be addressed in the hospital/clinic setting. When family social support networks are limited, it is important to link the family to community and national health partner organizations with services (see additional resources at the end of the chapter) that provide programs such as peer support, online support, information, and connection.

Financial Barriers to Care

Financial impact is one of the biggest difficulties faced by families who undergo extensive treatment for blood disorders. The distance to treatment facilities from small towns and frontier communities can span hundreds of miles, creating financial barriers to treatment for patients who cannot afford gas and physical barriers to treatment for patients with no reliable transportation. Patients and caregivers often need lodging for extended periods during chemotherapy, radiation therapy, and transplant. The length of time it takes for treatment of the underlying disease will determine how much the family spends on out-of-pocket medical expenses at a time when they experience lost income due to missed work. These expenses accumulate while the patient goes through treatment, and the patient may need to go on extended leave or medical disability. Helping the family assess their financial needs and what insurance and other programs will pay for treatment and expenses is yet another way that the social worker provides much-needed assistance (Wagner & Lacey, 2004).

Pearls

- Optimal management of hematologic malignancies requires cancer treatment team members with specialized experience, including oncology social work.
- Worry about relapse is common among survivors of hematologic malignancies.
- Watchful waiting is often psychologically uncomfortable for patients and families who would prefer a more aggressive treatment plan.

Pitfalls

- Believing that all patients with leukemias, lymphomas, multiple myeloma, or myelodysplasia are treated in the same way.
- Thinking that the most aggressive treatment at the time of diagnosis may lead to improved survival or quality of life.
- Thinking that it's not necessary to address advance care planning until after treatment has begun or the patient's condition deteriorates.

Social workers working with patients with a hematologic malignancy can help the patient and family gain mastery of the language of their disease and help them form the questions to ask the physician and nurse. The social worker provides links to patient disease organizations where patients and caregivers can find others with similar situations and find information about disease and treatment at an appropriate level of health literacy. The social worker provides concrete resources at a time of financial stress that may assist with travel, lodging, and prescription co-pays, as well as information about social security and insurance. Social work is the discipline that remembers and addresses the needs of the caregiver and other family members. For the many psychosocial challenges faced by the patient and family, the social worker is a sounding board, assisting the family as they navigate the continuum of treatment and regain a sense of balance and hope for the future.

ADDITIONAL RESOURCES

Be the Match: http://www.BeTheMatch.org

ExploreBMT: an easy-to-search web portal to browse resources and services from many respected organizations and allow you to connect to the resources that you or your patients need most throughout the transplant journey, from diagnosis through survivorship: http://www.Explorebmt.org

Leukemia & Lymphoma Society: http://www.lls.org

Lymphoma Research Foundation: http://www.lymphoma.org

Multiple Myeloma Research Foundation: http://www.multiple-myeloma.org

REFERENCES

Andrykowski, M. A., Bishop, M. M., Hahn, E. A., Cella, D. F., Beaumont, J. L., Brady, M. J., & Wingard, J. R. (2005). Long-term health-related quality of life, growth, and spiritual well-being after hematopoietic stem-cell transplantation. *Journal of Clinical Oncology*, 23(3), 599–608. doi:10.1200/JCO.2005.03.189

Be the Match. (2011). *Your introduction to marrow and cord blood transplant.* Minneapolis, MN: National Marrow Donor Program.

Be the Match. (2014). Myelodysplastic syndromes. Retrieved from http://bethematch.org/For-Patients-and-Families/Learning-about-your-disease/Myelodysplastic-syndromes-(MDS)/

Bevans, M., & Sternberg, E. M. (2012). Caregiving burden, stress, and health effects among family caregivers of adult cancer patients. *JAMA: Journal of the American Medical Association, 307*(4), 398–403. doi:10.1001/jama.2012.29

Leukemia and Lymphoma Society (LLS). (2012). Understanding leukemia. Retrieved from http://www.lls.org/content/nationalcontent/resourcecenter/freeeducationmaterials/leukemia/pdf/understandingleukemia.pdf

Leukemia and Lymphoma Society (LLS). (2013). Facts 2013. Retrieved from http://www.lls.org/content/nationalcontent/resourcecenter/freeeducationmaterials/generalcancer/pdf/facts.pdf

Lymphoma Research Foundation (LRF). (2012a). Understanding Hodgkin lymphoma: A guide for patients. Retrieved from http://www.lymphoma.org/atf/cf/%7Baaf3b4e5-2c43-404c-afe5-fd903c87b254%7D/LRF%20UNDERSTANDING%20HL%20GUIDE1.PDF

Lymphoma Research Foundation (LRF). (2012b). Understanding non-Hodgkin lymphoma: A guide for patients. Retrieved from http://www.lymphoma.org/atf/cf/%7Baaf3b4e5-2c43-404c-afe5-fd903c87b254%7D/LRF%20UNDERSTANDING%20NHL%20GUIDE2.PDF

Lymphoma Research Foundation (LRF). (2014). Lymphoma treatments. Retrieved from http://www.lymphoma.org/site/apps/s/content.asp?c=bkLTKaOQLmK8E&b=6298135&ct=8806721

National Cancer Institute (NCI). (2008). What you need to know about multiple myeloma. NIH Publication. U.S. Department of Health and Human Services. Retrieved from http://www.cancer.gov/cancertopics/wyntk/

Poe, J. K., Hayslip J. W., & Studts, J. L. (2012). Decision making and distress among individuals diagnosed with follicular lymphoma. *Journal of Psychosocial Oncology, 30*, 426–445. doi:10.1080/07347332.2012.684853

Stenberg, U., Ruland, C. M., & Miaskowski, C. (2010). Review of the literature on the effects of caring for a patient with cancer. *Psycho-Oncology, 19*(10), 1013–1025. doi:10.1002/pon.1670

Wagner, L., & Lacey, M. D. (2004). The hidden costs of cancer care: An overview with implications and referral resources for oncology nurses. *Clinical Journal of Oncology Nursing, 8*(3), 279–287. doi:10.1188/04.CJON.279-287

16

Elizabeth Ezra and Maria Chi

When the Other Shoe Drops: Unique Fears and Challenges of Recurrent Disease

This is the placing of one foot before the other. Not the free stride of the unencumbered but the careful tread of the initiated foot.

—*Maude Meehan (1997)*

Key Concepts

- *A recurrence of cancer denotes a major crisis point along the illness trajectory.*
- *Recurrence is a very vulnerable time, and it is important to be cognizant of the depth of the psychological injury and the force of the ensuing emotional wave.*
- *Understanding the high mortality rates associated with most recurrent cancers, the oncology social worker must help clients reactivate strengths and mobilize the inner and outer resources they may already possess.*
- *Oncology social workers have the special opportunity to help patients with recurrent or relapsed cancer to re-evaluate their coping strategies in the face of renewed crisis and identify steps that will help them actualize their new goals.*

Oncology social workers work with other members of the treatment team to help cancer survivors nurture their resilience and more effectively cope with recurrence (note: *recurrence* is used as an inclusive term for *recurrence* of solid tissue cancers and *relapse* of blood or lymphatic cancers unless otherwise specified). Clinicians support survivors in making sense of a diagnosis and focusing on what is essential in their lives. This process helps clients maximize the ability to live a meaningful life, whatever the path or duration.

A recurrence of cancer denotes a major crisis point along the illness trajectory, reactivating the cycle of disruption, stabilization, resolution, and integration that Fennell (2003) identifies in her Four-Phase Model of chronic illness. Discovery of a recurrence compels survivors to once again face their mortality as at initial diagnosis, making it harder to absorb the shock, mourn the formerly healthy self, sustain hope, and reorganize one's life to accommodate the disease. In addition to the increased sense of vulnerability that a recurrence elicits are the cumulative practical and financial challenges, continuous role disruptions, exhaustion of social support, repeated adjustment of goals and dreams, and a constricted focus on disease (Fennell, 2003).

Role of the Oncology Social Worker

Congruent with a crisis-intervention approach (Greene, Lee, Trask, & Rheinscheld, 2000), an oncology social worker's role starts with an assessment of what clients understand about their illness in an attempt to stabilize their immediate experience. Questions to have patients ask themselves include:

- How much do I need or want to know about the progression of my cancer?
- Can I survive another course of treatment?
- Have I depleted all my resources?

- Who can I count on for support?
- What can I still control in my life?
- How far ahead can I make plans?

Clinicians provide active guidance around these questions and facilitate a survivor's ability to integrate the diagnosis into everyday life.

Engagement and the Therapeutic Alliance

A strong, trusting relationship is essential to building a safe space in which a patient can hear and answer frightening questions candidly (Woods & Robinson, 1996). Being genuine and compassionate makes an enormous difference and entails active listening, which allows the clinician to hear what is said and what is hidden beneath these words. Understanding manifest and latent meaning is crucial to grasping the client's emotional readiness and how best to tailor interventions. The oncology social worker should strive to leave assumptions at the door and wait to hear what clients say about what they are feeling. Clinicians need self-awareness concerning the issues of treatment choices, stopping treatment, and dying so that countertransference does not hinder or detour the clinical work. Otherwise, the client will sense insincerity.

Mary started counseling after extensive surgery and very burdensome treatment, feeling as if she was drowning in emotions and fear. A 65-year-old lesbian with pancreatic cancer, Mary was able to clearly and concisely relate how her life had been turned upside down. Mary told her story eloquently with generous self-awareness and humility. She appeared calm and even a little distant. The social worker posed a few reflective questions to let her know that she was being heard and helped her overcome a history of personal rejection after the disclosure of her sexual orientation 40 years ago. The social worker built a foundation of trust by affirming Mary's request for help as a sign of strength and expression of faith.

Any cancer diagnosis can be perceived as numbing and surreal, but those with the highest mortality rates, such as pancreatic cancer, can be particularly alarming. One of the most paralyzing challenges of a pancreatic cancer recurrence is the potential catastrophic reaction of friends and family, who sense that the risk of death is high. Mary has a fighting spirit and tried very hard to cast off the negativity around her. Normalizing Mary's frustrations and encouraging her to be active for as long as possible reinforced her perseverance during treatment.

Ego-Supportive Pacing

Knowing when to ask certain questions is as important as knowing which ones to ask. When listening to a client, it is sometimes best to wait before commenting. One must assess the client's ability to tolerate the information and integrate the message outside of the session. Knowing what and when to support first involves an evaluation of the client's ego strengths (Goldstein, 1995). Clinicians must pace the work and not be impatient for change. Insights take time to emerge and need to be handled carefully. Recurrence is a very vulnerable time, and it is important to be cognizant of the depth of the injury and the force of the ensuing wave of emotion.

Casey is a 46-year-old single woman with metastatic colon cancer involving her liver. In counseling, Casey was first worried about concrete issues such as paying her rent but then began to share her worries about how long she would survive. After building a therapeutic alliance, Casey was able to approach the existential issues a little at a time.

The challenge for practitioners is not to force conversations that clients are not ready to have, or conversely, to ignore something that they are reluctant to bring up. Their silence may be saying: "I don't know how to start this conversation." Allowing clients to set the pace in the initial phase of work enables the clinician to guide them to more emotional and potentially frightening topics later on.

Strengths-Based Approach

Understanding the high mortality rates associated with most recurrent cancers, the oncology social worker must help clients reactivate strengths and mobilize the inner and outer resources they may already possess. The beauty of a strengths-based assessment is that it can be utilized throughout the continuum of care (Graybeal, 2001). A clinician might ask: "What has changed since your last experience with cancer?" This question can elicit feelings of well-earned personal satisfaction and self-worth, as clients reorganize their thoughts and see the changes they have accomplished, no matter how small. There is recognition of one's resilience in the face of a stressful experience (Folkman, 1997). This is a powerful process that helps clients set new goals and move forward, even in the midst of a recurrence.

After an initial round of effective treatment, Mary could once again engage more fully in her life. When her cancer first recurred, she was momentarily stifled by the thought of having to re-start treatment. Although better prepared, she felt depressed and shaken by the news and isolated herself from friends. She questioned her initial treatment plan and her lifestyle changes. She searched for what went wrong. Counseling helped Mary identify how her strengths could help her manage her fears and concerns. Gradually, she affirmed her self-worth and passion for life.

Changes in Body Image and Intimacy

Both men and women may feel that cancer has changed their bodies forever and that the body that has been their residence for a lifetime is no longer home. With disfiguring surgeries, one emotional challenge is to acknowledge their discomfort and shame (Begovic-Juhant, Chmielewski, Iwuagwu, & Chapman, 2012). Sometimes clients feel safe enough to reveal their physical scars. There is a tremendous amount of significance in this small gesture. Often clients arrive in wigs and once the door is closed they remove them and sit proudly with their bald heads. The clinician must portray a calm and understanding response.

Casey's fear of intimacy is interwoven with her feelings about her appearance. She chose not to reveal her body because she did not like the way she looked and was fearful of being hurt. The echoes of her previous self-loathing got louder.

The unmasking of these psychological wounds can occur in a nonjudgmental atmosphere with an open mind and heart. A clinician must look for both latent and manifest messages. One of Casey's strengths is her energy reserve, or as she puts it, "I refuse to stop." She manages to push through her fatigue and pain. This strength is also an adaptive defense mechanism. She doesn't have time to think about what is going on in her body when she keeps herself busy.

Respecting Client Autonomy

Helping clients maintain some autonomy over their recurrent cancer experience means respecting their choices and values. Recurrent cancer has the potential to strip away someone's sense of self that may have been recovered after the initial cancer treatment. Loss of bodily integrity, reduced treatment choices, and decreased energy are all features of recurrent cancer that constrict one's life. Recurrent cancer heightens the eight emotional challenges of chronic illness described by Pollin and Kanaan (1995): anger, loss of control, stigma, shattered self-image, fear of dependency, abandonment, isolation, and death. With all the indignities that someone can suffer with recurrent cancer, preserving autonomy becomes even more important.

Ellen is a 50-year-old single woman with ovarian cancer. Three years after an effective first course of treatment, she developed a recurrence. With her latest cycle of treatment, she reached a point of crisis when cumulative side effects began to take their toll. Ellen was weak, fatigued, and in pain. She could no longer work or visit friends.

Deciding whether to continue treatment was difficult for Ellen. Her family, seeing her suffering, wished she would stop. However, Ellen's oncology social workers helped her navigate these conflicting and emotional choices using a helpful, motivational interviewing approach. Specifically, they asked "evocative questions" in relation to Ellen's goals to distill her values and the impact of her various decisions (Rosengren, 2009, p. 95). With Ellen, this meant asking the following questions:

- *How would things change, for better or worse, if you continued treatment? If you stopped?*
- *What in your life is most important to you?*
- *How would your decision about treatment affect that?*

Ellen emerged from this process still wanting to pursue more treatment. She had a strong "fighting spirit," a common coping style that people use to deal with cancer (Moorey & Greer, 2002). Viewing her recurrence as a challenge to overcome, Ellen was optimistic about her situation while never denying how serious it was.

In counseling, the oncology social worker honors and enhances a client's capacity to choose his or her own path. As Folkman and Moskowitz (2004) note, there are no right or wrong coping styles, only more or less effective ones. Seeking new treatment helped Ellen maintain a sense of purpose and self-efficacy that directly enhanced her quality of life. Ellen was hopeful that new treatment would give her more time with the family she loved. She also realized that more treatment might hasten her death. This balance of hope and reality is essential; it releases the mental and emotional energy within a person and mobilizes his or her coping efforts (Folkman, 2010).

Using Cognitive Tools

A cancer recurrence forces clients to make life role changes once again after having done so during the initial treatment course. Oncology social workers provide valuable problem-solving support by helping clients perform the life roles that are most vital to them, even in altered form (Nezu, Nezu, Felgoise, McClure, & Houts, 2003).

Cognitive behavioral therapy is an effective means of preventing or decreasing depression in people with recurrent cancer (Jacobsen & Jim, 2008). When a client starts to think in distorted ways, a key question to ask is, What is the evidence to support your belief? (Moorey & Greer, 2002). After

Most disheartening to Ellen since her cancer recurrence was the change in roles within her family and community. She had been taking care of her elderly parents, but as her health deteriorated, she needed them to take care of her. She had long cherished her career as a teacher and now felt that she could no longer contribute to society. Validation of these changes had to precede any effort to help her move forward. She could then start addressing the unhelpful belief that she was a failure.

Ellen fully considered this question, she recognized that her physical frailty did not negate her value as a member of her family or community. She soon reframed the situation and developed more helpful beliefs, such as "These are changes, not failures. My present limitations do not negate my past contributions."

Spirituality

Just as medical teams try to heal the body and diminish physical pain, oncology social workers try to identify ways to heal the psychic wounds and pain of a recurrence. Social workers have a long history of looking at clients holistically—as individuals and as members of families, communities, and all that surrounds them (Canda & Furman, 1999). Within these surrounding fields, one finds the special connections that form the basis of one's spiritual side. Oncology social workers have an important role in providing the space for discussions about spirituality to occur.

> *As Mary managed her symptoms and felt better physically, she was able to explore more existential issues in counseling, such as the meaning of life and spirituality. Her life was constricted by the recurrence but her perspective had broadened. Mary had been a member of a 12-step program for many years, so the Serenity Prayer was a big comfort for her. The phrase "finding peace" or acceptance became a benchmark.*

Oncology social workers can encourage clients to use this time to discover and explore how their changed circumstances affect their outlook. In speaking with them, oncology social workers might substitute the word *whole* for *healthy*, because patients with advanced cancer strive to feel whole and complete rather than physically healthy. Wholeness and quality of life include spiritual and emotional components, as well as one's feelings toward the physical body. Patients reconsider what they hope for in this new phase and the social worker helps them identify specific ways to actualize these goals (Rummans et al., 2006).

> *A recurrent fear for Casey is that she will die alone. The latent message is that her life did not turn out the way she had hoped it would. There will be no loving partner holding her hand when she feels scared, and no children to grieve her passing. These are tremendous losses for anyone and impossible to dismiss. Instead, the clinician looks for other connections that have been made, such as pursuing a life's passion, simple acts of loving kindness, or a life lived with dignity—something that reinforces a client's feelings of self-worth and mastery.*

Pearls

- Oncology social workers have the special opportunity to help patients with recurrent or relapsed cancer to re-evaluate their coping strategies in the face of renewed crisis. They help patients identify new meanings of hope.
- It is most helpful for clients to use a diverse range of coping styles when facing recurrent cancer.

Pitfalls

- Clinicians are often tempted to avoid what makes them uncomfortable. Develop enough self-awareness so as not to let your own feelings and beliefs about cancer and death prevent you from addressing emotional issues with your clients.
- Beware of overidentifying with a client's sense of hopelessness and fear, thus becoming unable to offer the client different or more hopeful and adaptive perspectives.

Whenever one talks about a cancer diagnosis, death comes in the room. It is the uninvited visitor. If this is true with any cancer diagnosis, imagine the impact at the time of a recurrence. The cancer has defied the standard treatment and the client has the feeling of being betrayed again. Similar to someone diagnosed with a traumatic stress response, a patient with a recurrence becomes suspended in a haunting, recurring nightmare where sights, sounds, and especially smells elicit fearful and dramatic responses (Lin & Bauer-Wu, 2003). The clinician's role is to normalize and validate these feelings, whereas friends and family might try to suppress them. The oncology social worker's role is to directly and sensitively help the client re-establish a semblance of control. It is a time to encourage a step-by-step approach because the client's reality can be harsh and foreboding. This will help desensitize clients to whatever triggers such strong reactions. An effective counseling intervention can help clients feel less alone and more capable of facing both practical and existential issues. Oncology social workers help clients with recurrent cancer put one foot in front of the other, living in smaller steps on a shorter road, but with an eye toward the horizon.

ADDITIONAL RESOURCES

American Society of Clinical Oncology:http://www.cancer.net

Cancer*Care*: http://www.cancercare.org

Given, B. A., Given, C. W., & Sherwood, P. R. (2012). Family and caregiver needs over the course of the cancer trajectory. *Journal of Supportive Oncology, 10*(2), 57–64.

Helgeson, V. S., Reynolds, K. A., & Tomich, P. L. (2006). A meta-analytic review of benefit-finding and growth. *Journal of Consulting and Clinical Psychology, 74*(5), 797–816.

Hick, S. F. (2009). *Mindfulness and social work*. Chicago, IL: Lyceum Books.

Holland, J., & Lewis, S. (2000). *The human side of cancer: Living with hope, coping with uncertainty*. New York, NY: HarperCollins Publishers.

National Cancer Institute: http://www.cancer.gov

Pargament, K. I. (2007). *Spiritually integrated psychotherapy: Understanding and addressing the sacred*. New York, NY: Guilford Press.

Tedeschi, R. G., & Kilmer, R. P. (2005). Assessing strengths, resilience, and growth to guide clinical interventions. *Professional Psychology, Research, and Practice, 36*(3), 230–237.

Yalom, I. (1980). *Existential psychotherapy*. New York, NY: Basic Books.

Yalom, I. (2009). *Staring at the sun: Overcoming the terror of death*. San Francisco, CA: Jossey-Bass.

REFERENCES

Begovic-Juhant, A., Chmielewski, A., Iwuagwu, S., & Chapman, L. A. (2012). Impact of body image on depression and quality of life among women with breast cancer. *Journal of Psychosocial Oncology, 30*, 446–460.

Canda, E. R., & Furman, L. D. (1999). *Spiritual diversity in social work practice: The heart of helping*. New York, NY: Free Press.

Fennell, P. A. (2003). *Managing chronic illness using the four-phase treatment approach: A mental health professional's guide to helping chronically ill people*. New York, NY: Wiley & Sons.

Folkman, S. (1997). Positive psychological states and coping with severe stress. *Social Science and Medicine, 45*(8), 1207–1221.

Folkman, S. (2010). Stress, coping, and hope. *Psycho-Oncology, 19*, 901–908.

Folkman, S., & Moskowitz, J. T. (2004). Coping: Pitfalls and promise. *Annual Review of Psychology, 55*, 745–774.

Goldstein, E. G. (1995). *Ego psychology and social work practice*. New York, NY: Free Press.

Graybeal, C. (2001). Strengths-based social work assessment: Transforming the dominant paradigm. *Families in Society: The Journal of Contemporary Human Services, 82*(3), 233–242.

Greene, G. J., Lee, M.-Y., Trask, R., & Rheinscheld, J. (2000). How to work with clients' strengths in crisis intervention: A solution-focused approach. In A. R. Roberts (Ed.), *Crisis intervention handbook: Assessment, treatment, and research* (pp. 31–51). New York, NY: Oxford University Press.

Jacobsen, P. B., & Jim, H. S. (2008). Psychosocial interventions for anxiety and depression in adult cancer patients: Achievements and challenges. *CA: A Cancer Journal for Clinicians, 58*(4), 214–230.

Lin, H.-R., & Bauer-Wu, S. M. (2003). Psycho-spiritual well-being in patients with advanced cancer: An integrative review of the literature. *Journal of Advanced Nursing, 44*, 69–80.

Meehan, M. (1997). Coin of this realm. In S. Heinlein, G. Brumett, & J.-E. Tibbals (Eds.), *When a lifemate dies: Stories of love, loss, and healing*. Minneapolis, MN: Fairview Press.

Moorey, S., & Greer, S. (2002). *Cognitive behaviour therapy for people with cancer*. Oxford, England: Oxford University Press.

Nezu, A. M., Nezu, C. M., Felgoise, S. H., McClure, K. S., & Houts, P. S. (2003). Project genesis: Assessing the efficacy of problem-solving therapy for distressed adult cancer patients. *Journal of Consulting and Clinical Psychology, 71*(6), 1036–1048.

Pollin, I., & Kanaan, S. B. (1995). *Medical crisis counseling: Short-term therapy for long-term illness*. New York, NY: W. W. Norton & Company.

Rosengren, D. B. (2009). *Building motivational interviewing skills: A practitioner workbook*. New York, NY: Guilford Press.

Rummans, T. A., Clark, M. M., Sloan, J. A., Frost, M. H., Bostwick, J. M., Atherton, P. J., ... Hanson, J. (2006). Impacting quality of life for patients with advanced cancer with a structured multidisciplinary intervention: A randomized controlled trial. *Journal of Clinical Oncology, 24*(4), 635–642.

Woods, M. E., & Robinson, H. (1996). Psychosocial theory and social work treatment. In F. J. Turner (Ed.), *Social work treatment: Interlocking theoretical approaches* (pp. 555–580). New York, NY: Free Press.

IV

Implementing Distress Screening Initiatives in Oncology

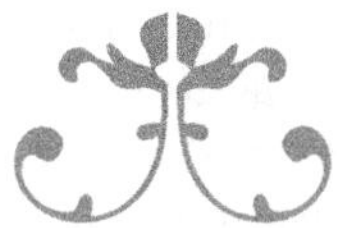

Grace Christ

Psychosocial screening has been a central function of oncology social work since the beginning of the specialty. Social workers developed education, group, and brief psychotherapies for meeting the needs of their assigned patients and their patients' families. However, with staffing ratios limited and psychosocial needs evident, social workers are constantly challenged to find ways to determine which individuals are at higher risk for adverse consequences and need more intensive and timely intervention. All patients have psychosocial problems and support needs. Social workers, as committed advocates, are also asked to help with "outliers"—unusual patient situations such as severe mental illness or cultural, linguistic, or economic challenges—and those with advanced diseases or undergoing high-risk treatments. Therefore, oncology social workers approach distress screening with a sense of familiarity and confidence supported by the early research in screening by oncology social work leaders described in this section. The American College of Surgeons' new requirements for distress screening, which are to be in place by 2015 in all cancer treatment programs (American College of Surgeons, 2014), have vastly increased the visibility of and opportunities to be found in oncology social work.

This section describes the problems social workers confront when implementing distress screening programs and the innovative ways they have found to solve them. Because Canada developed distress screening as the 6th vital sign 10 years ago within its national health care system, we include three chapters from its earlier implementation processes.

In "Distress Screening Guidelines for Oncology Social Workers," James R. Zabora identifies the essential components of a distress screening program, including the range of appropriate follow-up communications and interventions for responding to high levels of distress. These components include a reliable and valid screening tool, integration into the electronic medical record, and evidence-based interventions for higher levels of distress and problems. In addition, he describes the work of the cancer program he directs on developing and testing a reliable, valid, and accessible measure of distress.

In "Development of a National Canadian Program for Oncology Stress as the 6th Vital Sign," Barry D. Bultz, Matthew Loscalzo, and Shannon Groff discuss the development of this Canadian initiative. When the program was implemented there 10 years ago, it included the promotion of an interdisciplinary management model for psychosocial services. Because it has a nationalized health care system, Canada was able to require providers to use a problem checklist and various other measures to screen for distress. Regulatory groups also developed a set of algorithms for interventions with different distress levels and with different problems.

In "Touch-Screen Technology: Using a Problem Checklist for Psychosocial Oncology Screening," Karen Clark, Matthew Loscalzo, and Barry D. Bultz describe lessons learned from their process of implementing a 36-item problem checklist that relates distress levels to specific problems that cancer patients self-identify. The information is obtained by using touch-screen technology in an outpatient cancer treatment center. They advocate a screening program accessible to patients and acceptable to medical and administrative staff from its inception, as well as variable criteria that address items and interventions tailored to the particular services that are participating in the program.

In "Implementation and Evaluation of Distress Screening and Responding in an Ambulatory Cancer Center," Jill Taylor-Brown and Heather Campbell-Enns describe a paper-and-pencil distress screening and responding program in Canada. Screening is conceptualized as a strategy to open the conversation with patients about distress, give direction for further assessment, increase awareness of clinical practice guidelines and best practices, and recognize criteria for referral to specialized service. Ongoing responsiveness to feedback and evaluation are critical to the success of the program. Failing to acknowledge patients' completion of the screening may increase patient distress. Evaluation of educational initiatives includes staff satisfaction with practice change, patient satisfaction, and perception of effect on care.

The elevated risk of suicide in cancer patients and the effectiveness of preventive intervention support consideration of including related items on a distress screen. In "Screening and Assessment of Suicide Risk in Oncology," Mark E. Anderson, Margrett R. Myhre, Donna Suckow, and Angela McCabe discuss the challenges of assessment, communication within the family, referral, and follow-up within the cancer program and with mental health professionals the patient may be working with in the community. The experience of one cancer distress screening program suggests guidelines for assessment of at-risk patients following screening.

In "Using Telehealth to Respond to Distress in Rural and Remote Chemotherapy Clinics," Carole Mayer and Sheila Damore-Petingola describe a quality improvement initiative to develop distress screening in 13 chemotherapy clinics connected to a regional cancer center in Canada. Extensive development of clinical pathways and easier access to resources was essential to sustain psychosocial screening efforts. Videoconferencing as part of telehealth technology has emerged as an effective venue for providing access to education and professional support services in this rural and remote area.

In "Next Steps for Psychosocial Screening in Oncology," Lynne E. Padgett, Carly Parry, and Stephen Taplin describe some of the questions and controversies surrounding the implementation of distress screening at the National Cancer Institute. They suggest that conceptualizing distress management as a process of psychosocial care will affect the choice of measures used by practitioners and argue that *detection* and *assessment* are more accurate terms than *screening*. Ultimately, they show that developing consensus on appropriate measures to detect and assess distress, determine optimal implementation approaches, and evaluate these processes is an important research priority going forward.

REFERENCE

American College of Surgeons. (2014). Cancer program standards 2012: Ensuring patient-centered care. Retrieved from http://www.facs.org/cancer/coc/programstandards2012.html

17 James R. Zabora

Distress Screening Guidelines for Oncology Social Workers

Key Concepts

- *Because the American College of Surgeons' (ACOS, 2014) Standard 3.2 (Psychosocial Distress Screening) and Standard 3.3 (Cancer Survivorship Care Plan) require not only screening for distress but also referral for appropriate psychosocial care, oncology social workers should consider what evidence-based interventions could be provided for patients with varying levels of distress.*
- *The implementation of distress screening, originally and currently championed in the United States by social work leaders, has been advanced considerably by these new standards.*
- *Types of evidence-based interventions used with cancer patients with varying levels of distress include psychoeducation, cognitive behavioral therapy, disease management groups, and time-limited psychotherapy. Problem-solving education is presented as one example of an evidence-based intervention for high-distress patients.*
- *Essential components of an effective distress screening program are a reliable and valid screening tool, integration of the screening tool into the electronic medical record, algorithms that define evidence-based interventions based on levels of distress, and a database.*
- *Screening to identify high stress for intervention does not mean that moderate- to low-distress patients do not need any type of psychosocial care.*

Medical costs related to cancer are staggering, but the psychological and social consequences of cancer are also great. Despite the development of Distress Management Guidelines by the National Comprehensive Cancer Network (NCCN) in 1999 (with several revisions since then; NCCN, 2013) and two reports by the Institute of Medicine (IOM, 2006, 2007), availability and access to formalized and structured psychosocial programs for patients, survivors, and families are limited. The most comprehensive psychosocial programs tend to be located in National Cancer Institute–designated comprehensive cancer centers. However, 85% of all cancer patients receive treatment through a range of community-based programs and settings (IOM, 2007). A critical goal for oncology social workers is to develop and implement distress screening strategies coupled with interventions and programs that are responsive to the variations in each patient's attempt to manage this chronic illness. Models need to be brief and effective at the community level, as well as in the major centers.

At the time of diagnosis, cancer generates a sense of vulnerability, fear, and uncertainty for virtually all cancer patients. Evidence indicates that most newly diagnosed cancer patients gradually adapt to this crisis, their diagnosis, and related treatments and begin to incorporate cancer into their daily lives and effectively address problems or concerns created by a life-threatening condition (Weisman, 1976).

Time Points for Screening

Based on the early work of Weisman (1976), Christ (1991), Holland (1991), and others, the study of psychological responses to cancer and effective interventions has expanded to include time points beyond the initial diagnosis. Survivorship begins on the day of diagnosis, as cancer patients gain experience and begin to redefine all aspects of their lives. Three primary transition points exist in the adaptation process. First, patients experience an "existential plight" (Weisman, 1976) during the first 3 months following their diagnosis. While they strive to regain a sense of normalcy, many experience intense feelings of distress exacerbated by the physical trauma associated with cancer therapies. For the most part, patients are forced to acknowledge that their lives will never again be the same. Second, if a remission occurs, patients learn to live with their cancer, incorporating disruptions into their day-to-day routines. Third, the fear of recurrence or the actual event further complicates the psychosocial course for each patient. Although many health care providers assume that patients may experience recurrence as the point of highest distress, this may not be the case (Weismann & Worden, 1986; Zabora et al., 1997). Patients gain critical information and knowledge concerning their disease and treatments from supportive relationships with members of the health care team, as well as from other patients, family, and friends. This knowledge and support enable patients to anticipate and understand their course of treatment following recurrence and solve problems associated with this phase (see Chapters 54 and 58).

Given these three critical points in time, the first 100 days following diagnosis provides the best opportunity to intervene early and integrate effective problem-solving approaches to disease management based on the patient's level of distress and through the integration of the family.

Definition of Distress

Psychological distress has been defined as follows:

> *a multifactorial unpleasant emotional experience of a psychological (cognitive, behavioral, emotional), social, and/or spiritual nature that may interfere with the ability to cope effectively with cancer, its physical symptoms, and its treatment. Distress extends along a continuum, ranging from common normal feelings of vulnerability, sadness, and fears to problems that can become disabling such as depression, anxiety, panic, social isolation, and existential and spiritual crisis. (NCCN, 2014, p. DIS-2)*

Distress was chosen because it was a term that was more acceptable to patients and less stigmatizing than clinical diagnostic categories such as depression, anxiety, or posttraumatic stress. Diagnostic language may be felt to imply that patients are weak, mentally ill, or failing to cope adequately rather than confronting illness and treatment-related problems for which they need professional assistance. Often, the distress associated with these problems does not manifest to the health care team until the patient reaches an observable crisis event. Studies indicate that oncologists and oncology nurses often do not identify patients with elevated levels of anxiety and depression symptoms in a timely manner (Newell, Sanson-Fisher, Girgis, & Bonaventura, 1998). Referrals to psychosocial providers occur only when the patient is severely depressed or anxious, experiences conflicts within the family, or is suicidal (Zabora, Loscalzo, & Smith, 2000).

Screening and early detection of vulnerability can enable oncology social workers to provide preventive interventions that are problem focused, are related to disease management, and can effectively reduce distress, increase quality of life, and enhance cancer treatment outcomes.

Given these issues, what are the essential components of an effective distress screening program? How does one choose the right screening measure? What evidence-based interventions best match the varying levels of distress that a patient exhibits?

Essential Components of an Effective Distress Screening Program

To establish a distress screening program, the essential and ideal components are a reliable and valid screening tool, integration of the screening tool into the electronic medical record, algorithms that define evidence-based interventions based on levels of distress, and a database. At a minimum, the database should include the following elements: patient number, date of screening, cancer diagnosis, gender, age, race/ethnicity, marital status, educational level, occupation, date of assessment, and list of interventions (Zabora, BrintzenhofeSzoc, Curbow, Hooker, & Piantadosi, 2001). The addition of outcome measures should also be considered. The distress screening tool could possibly serve as a repeated measure for outcome assessment. In this way, oncology social workers could demonstrate the reduction of distress over time. Other potential outcome measures might include the Condensed Memorial Symptom Assessment Scale (Chang, Hwang, Kasimis, & Thaler, 2004) and the Satisfaction With Life Domains Scale as a measure of quality of life (Baker, Curbow, & Wingard, 1992).

Distress Screening Measures

Of all the measures of distress in psychosocial oncology, the Brief Symptom Inventory (BSI) has been used more frequently to measure distress than any other instrument (Gotay & Stern, 1995). Social work investigators developed the cancer norms for the BSI-18 to use this shorter form of the BSI as a screening instrument to identify patients at elevated risk for distress (Zabora, BrintzenhofeSzoc, Jacobsen, et al., 2001). As a screening instrument, the BSI-18 performs with higher levels of sensitivity and specificity than other measures such as the Distress Thermometer (DT) or the Hospital Anxiety and Depression Scale (HADS). Sensitivity is the ability of any screening tool to identify high-distress patients accurately, whereas specificity describes the tool's ability to correctly identify low-distress patients as low distress. Furthermore, the BSI-18 possesses high levels of reliability and validity in that it measures distress in a consistent manner and has been shown to accurately measure distress among cancer patients. Finally, with increased use of the DT, it should be emphasized that its levels of sensitivity and specificity are as low as 0.77 and 0.68 for the DT versus 0.91 and 0.92 for the BSI-18. Essentially, the DT is only correct 77% of the time in identifying high-distress patients, whereas the BSI-18 is correct 91% of the time (Zabora, BrintzenhofeSzoc, Jacobsen, et al., 2001).

Finally, investigators at the Inova Health System are developing the Chronic Illness Distress Scale (CIDS), which is a 7-item tool to screen patients for their levels of distress at the time of entry into treatment. While the CIDS is still under development, preliminary results after 40 patients indicate that the Cronbach alpha, inter-item correlations, and the correlation with the BSI-18 are .80 and above. The CIDS may be a viable screening tool that is built on the original instruments developed by Weisman, Worden, and Sobel (1980).

Evidence-Based Interventions for Varying Levels of Distress

Because the ACOS Standard 3.2 (Psychosocial Distress Screening) and Standard 3.3 (Cancer Survivorship Care Plan) requires not only screening for distress but also referral for appropriate psychosocial care, oncology social workers should consider what evidence-based interventions could be provided for patients with varying levels of distress (ACOS, 2014). The research literature in psychosocial oncology is the most extensive of all of the chronic diseases, and evidence-based intervention studies date back to the 1970s. Fawzy, Fawzy, Arndt, and Pasnau (1995) reviewed more than 200 of these types of studies and, through their analysis, categorized all of the interventions into the following four major categories: psychoeducation, cognitive behavioral therapy, disease-management groups, and psychotherapy. Consequently, these interventions are based on evidence and research and can be used with newly diagnosed cancer patients with higher levels of distress. Later research has shown that "problem-solving therapy" (PST) or "problem-solving education" (PSE) also possesses strong evidence for use among distressed patients. PSE is a blend of "psychoeducation," where patients are taught a specific skill to increase knowledge and control, and "cognitive" techniques, which enable them to consider alternative solutions to solve a specific problem that may be causing distress (Bucher et al., 2001; Houts, Nezu, Nezu, & Bucher, 1996).

Screening to identify high-distress patients for intervention does not mean that moderate- to low-distress patients do not need any type of psychosocial care. Although these patients may have more internal and external coping resources than high-distress patients, specific programs might enhance their level of adaptation. Most often, these patients will benefit from psychoeducational programs about symptom management, nutritional approaches, and varying levels of exercise. These patients might benefit from cognitive behavioral interventions that focus on specific symptoms such as insomnia or pain. They may also benefit from short-term, time-limited psychotherapy interventions (Nissim et al., 2011).

Problem-Solving Education as an Example of Evidence-Based Intervention for High-Distress Patients

To enable patients with higher levels of distress to manage their disease more effectively, problem-solving theory as conceived by D'Zurilla and Nezu (1982) and others defines problem solving as a series of skills that can be provided to patients in a therapeutic relationship or through a psychoeducational format. According to the theoretical model, successful problem solving requires five component processes, each of which contributes directly to effective problem resolution (D'Zurilla & Nezu, 1982): (1) problem orientation, definition, and formulation; (2) generation of alternatives; (3) decision making; (4) solution implementation; and (5) verification. Problem orientation involves a motivational process; the other components consist of specific skills and abilities that enable a person to effectively solve a particular problem. Because problem solving is a set of skills, this approach lends itself to being provided in an educational format.

Problem-solving theory has led to the development of problem-solving education that adapts the five components for use with the special needs of cancer patients and their family caregivers (Houts et al., 1996). The acronym COPE summarizes the four essential elements of the motivational approach: creativity, optimism, planning, and expert information. These four elements are essential in the development and implementation of a course of action that results in control, direction, and hope for patients and family caregivers.

The basic notion underlying the relevance of problem solving for cancer patients and family caregivers lies in the moderating role that problem solving serves to enhance coping in the general stress-distress relationship. The more effective people are in resolving or coping with stressful problems, the more likely it is that they will experience a higher level of quality of life as compared with those persons facing similar problems who do not have an established way of addressing difficult cancer-related challenges. Families also require guidance and support for how to manage the multiple problems associated with cancer, related treatments, adverse reactions, and rehabilitation. Following the diagnosis of cancer, families need to have honest, intelligible, and timely information while being reassured that competent and compassionate health care professionals are caring for their family member (Houts et al., 1996).

Pearls

- A highly reliable and valid tool should always be used for distress screening.
- There are several interventions for cancer patients who experience elevated levels of distress.
- There are four categories of evidence-based interventions identified in the literature: psychoeducation, cognitive behavioral therapy, disease management groups, and short-term psychotherapy.

Pitfalls

- Using screening instruments that possess lower levels of predictability in detecting the most vulnerable patients may fail to identify those in need of assessment.
- Intervention options should be accessible for low and moderately distressed individuals confronting disease-related problems and for highly distressed patients.

The obvious next step is the implementation of the American College of Surgeons' Standard 3.2 (Psychosocial Distress Screening) and Standard 3.3 (Cancer Survivorship Care Plan) as cancer centers and programs attempt to develop mechanisms to ensure that all patients receive this new level of psychosocial and survivorship care. Relating to the chapter in this section on instrumentation (Chapter 23), as previously stated, investigators at the Inova Health System (Zabora and colleagues) are testing a new 7-item distress screening tool, the CIDS, and aim to complete the study in 2014. Preliminary analyses after the first 40 patients are encouraging regarding reliability and validity, as well as test–retest reliability. These questions about instrumentation should encourage other investigators to develop new distress screening tools as well.

Interestingly, the new distress screening instruments do not specifically mention pediatric cancer patients. These patients also need to be screened so that more vulnerable children receive more immediate psychosocial care. Wiener, of the National Cancer Institute in Bethesda, Maryland, has developed a pediatric screening tool currently used with pediatric patients at the National Cancer Institute. Also, the standards do not mention family caregivers. Given the distress associated with caregiving and how this might also contribute to the patient's distress, appropriate screening strategies should be developed for caregivers in the future. Finally, consideration should be given to screening families for their level of functioning. Past research has documented how family functioning can play a positive or negative role in the overall care of the patient. Families with lower levels of functioning can be highly problematic and can interfere with the delivery of care, be unsupportive to the patient, or encourage the patient to be noncompliant with treatment procedures or regimens.

This is an exciting time that presents opportunities for oncology social workers to provide leadership in the development of distress screening programs that include clinical pathways for intervention. The concept of psychosocial screening for distress is not a new concept, dating back to the late 1970s when Weisman and colleagues (1980) developed the first distress screening tool at the Massachusetts General Hospital. Since that time, guidelines and recommendations have been developed and implemented, but few cancer centers or programs have actually instituted screening protocols. New standards of care change everything and truly move the field forward.

REFERENCES

American College of Surgeons (ACOS). (2014). *Cancer program standards 2012: Ensuring patient-centered care*. Retrieved from http://www.facs.org/cancer/coc/programstandards2012.html

Baker, F., Curbow, B. A., & Wingard, J. R. (1992). Development of the Satisfaction with Life Domains Scale for cancer. *Journal of Psychosocial Oncology*, *10*(3), 75–90.

Bucher, J. A., Loscalzo, M., Zabora, J., Houts, P. S., Hooker, C., & BrintzenhofeSzoc, K. (2001). Problem-solving cancer care education for patients and caregivers. *Cancer Practice*, *9*(2), 66–70.

Chang, V. T., Hwang, S. S., Kasimis, B., & Thaler, H. T. (2004). Shorter symptom assessment instruments: The Condensed Memorial Symptom Assessment Scale (CMSAS). *Cancer Investigations*, *4*(22), 526–536.

Christ, G. (1991). Principles of oncology social work. In A. Holleb, D. Fink, & G. Murphy (Eds.), *American Cancer Society textbook of clinical oncology* (pp. 594–605). Atlanta, GA: American Cancer Society.

D'Zurilla, T. J., & Nezu, A. M. (1982). *Social problem-solving in adults*. In P. Kendall (Ed.), *Cognitive-behavioral research and therapy*. New York, NY: Academic Press.

Fawzy, F. I., Fawzy, N. W., Arndt, L. A., & Pasnau, R. O. (1995). Critical review of psychosocial interventions in cancer care. *Archives of General Psychiatry*, *52*, 100–113.

Gotay, C. G., & Stern, J. D. (1995). Assessment of psychological functioning in cancer patients. *Journal of Psychosocial Oncology*, *13*(1–2), 123–160.

Holland, J. C. (1991). Progress and challenges in psychosocial and behavioral research in cancer in the twentieth century [Review]. *Cancer*, *67*(3 Suppl.), 767–773.

Houts, P. S., Nezu, A. M., Nezu, C. M., & Bucher, J. A. (1996). A problem-solving model of family caregiving for cancer patients. *Patient Education and Counseling*, *27*, 63–73.

Institute of Medicine (IOM). (2006). *From cancer patient to cancer survivor: Lost in transition*. Washington, DC: National Academies Press.

Institute of Medicine (IOM). (2007). *Cancer care for the whole patient: Meeting psychosocial health needs*. Washington, DC: National Academies Press.

National Comprehensive Cancer Network (NCCN). (2014). *NCCN clinical practice guidelines in oncology,: Distress management*. Retrieved from http://www.nccn.org/professionals/physician_gls/pdf/distress.pdf

Newell, S., Sanson-Fisher, R. W., Girgis, A., & Bonaventura, A. (1998). How well do medical oncologists' perceptions reflect their patients' reported physical and psychosocial problems? *Cancer, 83*(8), 1640–1651.

Nissim, R., Freeman, E., Lo, C., Zimmermann, C., Gagliese, L., Rydall, A., . . . Rodin, G. (2011). Managing Cancer and Living Meaningfully (CALM): A qualitative study of a brief individual psychotherapy for individuals with advanced cancer. *Palliative Medicine, 26*(5), 713–721.

Weisman, A. D. (1976). The existential plight in cancer: Significance of the first 100 days. *International Journal of Psychiatry in Medicine, 7*(1), 1–15.

Weisman, A. D., Worden, J. W., & Sobel, H. J. (1980). *Psychosocial screening and intervention with cancer patients: A research report*. Boston, MA: Harvard Medical School.

Weismann, A. D., & Worden, W. (1986). The emotional impact of recurrent cancer. *Journal of Psychosocial Oncology, 3*(4), 5–16.

Zabora, J., Blanchard, C., Smith, E., Roberts, C. S., Glajchen, M., Sharp, J. W., . . . Hedlund, S. C. (1997). Prevalence of psychological distress across the disease continuum. *Journal of Psychosocial Oncology, 15*(2), 73–87.

Zabora, J., BrintzenhofeSzoc, K., Curbow, B., Hooker, C., & Piantadosi, S. (2001). The prevalence of psychological distress by cancer site. *Psycho-Oncology, 10*, 19–27.

Zabora, J., BrintzenhofeSzoc, K., Jacobsen, P., Curbow, B., Piantadosi, S., Hooker, C., . . . Derogatis, L. (2001). Development of a new psychosocial screening instrument for use with cancer patients. *Psychosomatics, 42*(3), 19–24.

Zabora, J. R., Loscalzo, M. L., & Smith, E. D. (2000). Psychosocial rehabilitation. In M. D. Abeloff, J. O. Armitage, A. S. Lichter, & J. E. Neiderhuber (Eds.), *Clinical oncology* (2nd ed., pp. 2845–2865). New York, NY: Churchill Livingstone.

18

Barry D. Bultz, Matthew Loscalzo, and Shannon Groff

Development of a National Canadian Program for Oncology Stress as the 6th Vital Sign

Key Concepts

- *Currently, hospitals are moving toward integrating psychosocial, mental health, and a broad range of other patient services.*
- *This chapter discusses national initiatives of distress as the 6th vital sign in international societies and cancer care programs.*
- *It is important to use standardized measures and evaluate outcomes.*
- *Implementation of psychosocial screening can increase psychosocial resources and improve patient-centered care.*
- *Future directions for distress screening are discussed.*

Ever since social work, psychology, and psychiatry started being integrated into the medical practices surrounding oncology, there has been a steady shift in how cancer patients are approached, how information is communicated, and how care for the whole patient is provided. Even though cancer care has progressed beyond the traditional biomedical perspective to the modern person- and family-centered approach of viewing the patient as an integrated whole, providers today still remain very much isolated in their own professional silos with very little discussion about the whole person or understanding of the health system's impact. Largely, health care providers proverbially still "talk the talk" about the benefits of integrated interdisciplinary care models, but little evidence exists that any formal culture shift is taking place. Additionally, social work programs, along with psychology and psychiatry programs, or departments globally, remain poorly funded.

However, one major change in many cancer programs has been the integration of specialized mental health workers (social workers, psychologists, and psychiatrists) into a single department called Psychosocial Oncology (Canada) or Patient and Family Support, Counseling and Support Services, or Patient and Family Resource Centers (United States; Loscalzo, Bultz, & Jacobsen, 2010).

The integrated interdisciplinary model began in Canada in the 1980s, resulting in the creation of the Canadian Association of Psychosocial Oncology (CAPO). The United States, however, has been slower in developing integrated interdisciplinary models, with more variation in how the integration is structured and administered. In addition, U.S. programs often include a broad range of services beyond traditional mental health, for example, patient education, complementary medicine, and family advisory councils (see Chapter 19). Several successfully integrated programs in the United States have been described and are being disseminated (Loscalzo et al., 2010).

With the move away from discipline-centric mental health programs, a new Canadian definition of psychosocial oncology explains this evolving clinical perspective. Psychosocial oncology is a specialty in cancer care concerned with understanding and treating the social, psychological, emotional, spiritual, quality-of-life, and functional aspects of cancer, from prevention through bereavement.

A whole-person approach to cancer care addresses a range of human needs that can improve quality of life for people affected by cancer (CAPO, 1999).

By evolving from a discipline-specific focus, psychosocial oncology seeks to depathologize, and remove the stigma of, a psychiatric diagnosis by *normalizing* the cancer patient experience. The U.S. National Comprehensive Cancer Network (NCCN) attempted to reframe the cancer experience by employing the word *distress* to explain the challenges facing the oncology patient (NCCN, 1999): Distress is an emotional experience of a psychological, social, and/or spiritual nature that extends on a continuum from normal feelings of vulnerability, sadness, and fear to disabling problems such as depression, anxiety, panic, social isolation, and spiritual crisis (NCCN, 1999).

Merging mental health disciplines into a single integrated service and redefining the cancer experience as distress (with the acceptance of a fuller range of human responses) represented two major shifts toward the development of a person-centered cancer care framework. These concepts also represented the beginning of a culture shift toward greater interdisciplinary teamwork in approaches to patient care (Wood, Flavell, Vanstolk, Bainbridge, & Nasmith, 2009).

Research as a Driver for Change

> *There are two drivers of change: science and opinion; the former begets knowledge, the latter ignorance.*
>
> —*Hippocrates*

Although the research into the prevalence of patient concerns is well documented (Carlson et al., 2004; Zabora, BrintzenhofeSzoc, Curbow, Hooker, & Piantadosi, 2001), it is becoming clear that distress is complex and multifactorial and that the unmet needs identified by biopsychosocial screening are important in and of themselves and in combination with each other. Therefore, any screening-for-distress program must take into account not only the identified symptom or concern but also each identified concern. Identification must then lead to a conversation between the health professional and the patient and, when possible, to an evidenced-based intervention. In our experience, without a standardized screening tool and because of time pressures or lack of training, health care providers are unable to take time to better understand the concerns and needs of patients systematically. In fact, research indicates that relying on unstructured interviews is insufficient because patients either are reluctant or generally fail to report their concerns (Homsi et al., 2006). The literature also supports (and we believe that this is much more of a barrier) that health care providers fail to understand the specific concerns patients experience (Mitchell, Meader, Bird, & Rizzo, 2012; Mitchell, Vahabzadeh, & Magruder, 2011) and do not appreciate the full impact that concerns may have on their patients' ability to regulate emotions, navigate the health system, and maintain an acceptable quality of life (Fallowfield, Ratcliffe, Jenkins, & Saul, 2001).

In medical care, the measurement of the patient's health status is a standard known as a *vital sign*. Historically there were four vital signs—blood pressure, heart rate, temperature, and respiration rates—but because of its prevalence in the cancer patient population, pain too became seen as a key indicator of the patient's well-being and, in 1999, was added to the list (NCCN, 2011). This was the model that was used in Canada to elevate distress to the 6th vital sign (Bultz & Carlson, 2005; Rebalance Focus Action Group, 2005) and is the concept now endorsed by the International Psycho-Oncology Society (IPOS) and 75 other international societies and cancer care programs worldwide (IPOS, 2014).

Given the research on what is becoming a true "science of caring" (applying scientific principles to enhance the humanistic aspects of serious illness), all of cancer care is increasingly focused on improving the patient experience. Additionally, expectations of obtaining psychosocial information and using standardized measurements are much higher. A report by the Institute of Medicine and National Research Council of the National Academies (2007) carefully reviewed the literature on supportive care interventions and found benefit to most psychosocial interventions as practiced today. More recently, both quality of life and length of life were improved in two randomized control trials: Carlson, Groff, Maciejewski, and Bultz (2010) showed the impact of screening integrated with education and referral, and Temel, Pirl, and Lynch (2006) showed the impact of a coordinated palliative care program. There is also an international movement away from merely monitoring process outcomes (where guidelines and standards are documented as being followed) to routinely monitoring patient-reported outcomes. At the heart of the demand for improved patient outcomes is the expectation that interventions will be evidence based and cost-effective—responses to the large and rapidly increasing aging populations in all of the industrialized nations with a high incidence of cancer diagnoses—while being aware that there are limits to what health care can effectively provide. At the same time, however, in many countries there are consumer movements by cancer survivors and their families to humanize the cancer experience and to attend to the supportive care needs of both the patient and the family.

Branding Distress as the 6th Vital Sign

Given the prevalence of distress (physical, psychosocial, spiritual, and practical) that patients experience from the time of diagnosis through survivorship and the challenges in detecting patient problems and unmet needs, it became clear that distress needed to be monitored. However, to be diagnosed, assessed, and treated, distress must be monitored not by clinical acumen alone but also by standardized measures because "what you measure is what you act on" (McMurtry & Bultz, 2005, p. 699). This is a core value in biomedical care and should be the same principle that guides psychosocial care.

Asking the patient, "How are you doing?" and relying on the patient's response adds little to improving the health care teams' understanding of how the patient is coping with his or her cancer treatment or diagnosis (Fallowfield et al., 2001; Pirl et al., 2007). Patients and their families need to be guided through what they can expect within and throughout the cancer experience. Screening for distress at the beginning of treatment and across the cancer trajectory helps educate and focus patients and raises the expectation that there is assistance for common cancer-related problems.

Acknowledging the need for a more thorough understanding of the issues and concerns of the cancer experience, Weisman, Worden, and Sobel (1980), early psychosocial oncology pioneers of screening for distress in cancer patients, developed the Omega Project; they subsequently began advocating for routine screening. However, despite numerous prevalence studies highlighting patient concerns (Carlson et al., 2004; Zabora et al., 2001) and NCCN guidelines (NCCN, 1999), screening for distress, until recently, had very limited uptake (Jacobsen & Ransom, 2007).

Development of a Canadian National Strategy

Following the endorsement of distress as the 6th vital sign by the Rebalance Focus Action Group of the Canadian Strategy for Cancer Control (2005), a national meeting was held to discuss how to move screening for distress forward across the country. The meeting was successful in establishing key recommendations for moving screening for distress forward, including (1) establishing national standards and guidelines; (2) raising the profile of screening for distress, the 6th vital sign; and (3) securing sufficient resources for nationwide screening-for-distress implementation (Bultz et al., 2011).

Following this meeting, the Canadian Partnership Against Cancer (2008) endorsed screening for distress as a driver toward a vision of person-centered care and supported the development of national recommendations and the implementation of screening for distress in nine jurisdictions representing eight provinces (Bultz, Groff, Fitch, & Screening for Distress Toolkit Working Group, 2009). The national recommendations state that all patients should be routinely screened for distress and that any screening program should include psychosocial, practical, and physical concerns (Bultz et al., 2009). Additionally, there was a national consensus on a minimum data set and it was recommended that all sites, at a minimum, screen patients with the Edmonton Symptom Assessment System (ESAS; more recently the ESAS-revised has been

18.1). The group also advocated that screening alone would not be useful or sufficient and that any screening program must consist of screening, assessment, and intervention, as well as a conversation between the patient and health care provider (Figure 18.2).

Implementing Screening for Distress

Although developing a national strategy and recommendations was challenging, it was recognized that changing practice to incorporate screening for distress was another area that required attention and resources. As sites began implementing screening-for-distress protocols, a national group—the Screening for Distress Implementation Group—was formed, consisting of two representatives from each jurisdiction. The group's focus was to enhance and accelerate all implementations by sharing strategies to implement screening, overcome challenges, and share educational resources; the group was central to facilitating the successful uptake and sustainability of screening-for-distress concepts.

Despite differences in size and location, implementation generally followed five key steps (Bultz et al., 2011):

1. Engage high-level stakeholders and establish steering groups.
2. Provide widespread education about screening for distress.
3. Establish teams that would drive the implementation.
4. Provide targeted training on screening for distress.
5. Roll out screening in a phased approach (tumor site by tumor site).

The Screening for Distress Implementation Group also developed minimum requirements for reviewing screening results with patients. Regardless of scores on the screening tools, the group noted that the following should occur:

1. Acknowledge scores.
2. Discuss meaning of score with patient.
3. Document conversation.
4. Follow through on action plan.

Additionally, the group emphasized the importance that the patient, in collaboration with the health care team, should drive the assessment and that any intervention should be chosen in conjunction with the patient's needs and values.

Overcoming Challenges to Screening for Distress: Time, Buy-In, and Resources

Numerous challenges were noted and addressed throughout the course of the implementations, the most common being time limitations, lack of staff buy-in, and limited

Completed by:
- ❒ Patient
- ❒ Family
- ❒ Health Professional
- ❒ Assisted by family or health

Date of Completion:_______________ **Time:** ___________

1. Edmonton Symptom Assessment System (ESAS):

Please circle the number that best describes:

No pain	0	1	2	3	4	5	6	7	8	9	10	Worst possible pain
Not tired	0	1	2	3	4	5	6	7	8	9	10	Worst possible tiredness
Not nauseated	0	1	2	3	4	5	6	7	8	9	10	Worst possible nausea
Not depressed	0	1	2	3	4	5	6	7	8	9	10	Worst possible depression
Not anxious	0	1	2	3	4	5	6	7	8	9	10	Worst possible anxiety
Not drowsy	0	1	2	3	4	5	6	7	8	9	10	Worst possible drowsiness
Best appetite	0	1	2	3	4	5	6	7	8	9	10	Worst possible appetite
Best feeling of well-being	0	1	2	3	4	5	6	7	8	9	10	Worst possible feeling of well-being
No shortness of breath	0	1	2	3	4	5	6	7	8	9	10	Worst possible shortness of breath
Other problem	0	1	2	3	4	5	6	7	8	9	10	

2. Canadian Problem Checklist:

Please check all of the following items that have been a concern or problem for you in the past week including today:

Emotional:
- ❒ Fears/Worries
- ❒ Sadness
- ❒ Frustration/Anger
- ❒ Changes in appearance
- ❒ Intimacy/Sexuality

Practical:
- ❒ Work/School
- ❒ Finances
- ❒ Getting to and from appointments
- ❒ Accommodation

Informational:
- ❒ Understanding my illness and/or treatment
- ❒ Talking with the health care team
- ❒ Making treatment decisions
- ❒ Knowing about available resources

Spiritual:
- ❒ Meaning/Purpose of life
- ❒ Faith

Social/Family:
- ❒ Feeling a burden to others
- ❒ Worry about family/friends
- ❒ Feeling alone

Physical:
- ❒ Concentration/Memory
- ❒ Sleep
- ❒ Weight

**Questionnaire from the Cancer Journey Advisory Group, Canadian Partnership Against Cancer's Minimum Data Set*

Figure 18.1. Screening for Distress Minimum Data Set

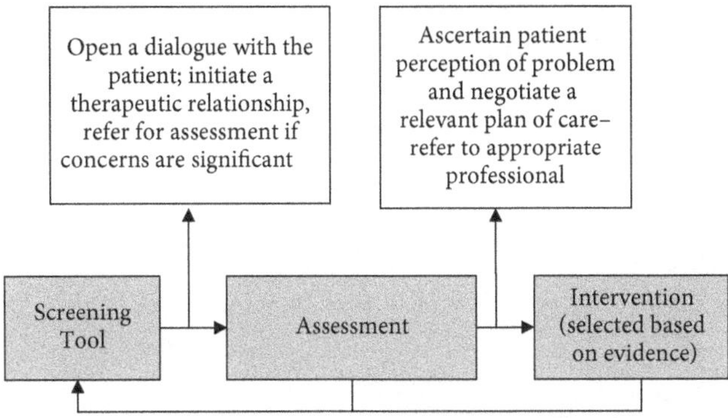

Figure 18.2. Model of Screening for Distress

care delivery, particularly when required by a change in practice. We found that the implementation of screening for distress may result in an initial time increase but that as health care providers become familiar with the process, their assessment and intervention times may decrease as the tool helps them and the patient identify in a standardized way what is of greatest concern. This approach is consistent with person-centered care, in which the patient is an active participant in his or her care. If time remained an issue after approximately 6 weeks of implementation, the implementation team explored staff concerns and scheduled additional training on how to use the screening tool more effectively and efficiently.

The second concern, lack of buy-in, was often found to be a result of misunderstandings about the process or a general resistance to change. Previous papers by our group and other colleagues outline effective strategies for overcoming this challenge, including ensuring administrative support, acknowledging resistance, actively listening to concerns, showing interest and understanding toward culture/work organization, openly communicating with the implementation team, ensuring sufficient time for field preparation, and tailoring education and training materials to each professional group (Bultz et al., 2011; Loscalzo, Clark, & Holland, 2011).

Elucidated by questions such as "How will we help the patient if we have nothing to offer them?" the third most common concern among social workers implementing screening for distress was a lack of resources. Most sites that implemented screening found that although resources may be limited, there were often resources available of which staff were not aware. Much of the work to address this concern involves doing an environmental scan or resource inventory of what is available, coordinating access to resources, and educating staff on how and when to refer and how to manage the symptoms that are within their scope of practice. We found that despite the initial concern raised, staff quite often had many of the skills and resources available to help improve the patient experience.

Sustainability/Integration

A key focus of any screening-for-distress implementation program should be sustainability. Sustainability is only possible when all stakeholders feel and can easily see the direct benefits to themselves or to their patients and recognize that the enhanced outcomes are linked to quality and cost (in other words, value). If sustainability is not at the forefront of thinking early in the implementation, key opportunities to structure the program in a sustainable format are likely to be missed. Additional strategies to enhance sustainability include (1) embedding responsibilities related to screening for distress into job descriptions, (2) including screening for distress training programs and orientations, and (3) conducting regular quality improvement checks on how screening for distress is being implemented and used in the clinical setting.

Current Status

In March 2012, at the completion of the first mandate of the Canadian Partnership Against Cancer, nine Canadian jurisdictions representing eight provinces had begun screening for distress. Figure 18.3 indicates the locations of the cancer centers where screening for distress was implemented. Since 2009, over 42,000 screens have been completed and over 1,400 providers trained. At present, all jurisdictions have continued to meet and many continue to expand their screening-for-distress programs. As well, with Accreditation Canada naming distress as the 6th vital sign and requiring distress as an accreditation standard (Accreditation Canada, 2008), new funding is being made available to ensure that institutions are in compliance. More important, both patients and staff are seeing real value in screening for distress.

The Future of Screening for Distress

Although only briefly described here, implementing screening for distress, which requires a change in practice, is a complex and difficult process. Underestimating the resources required to implement not only the tool but also the processes and supports to facilitate assessment and intervention will likely result in an unsuccessful program. However, with the proper resources and institutional support, screening for distress can be implemented successfully, resulting in improved person-centered care. To support others in this process, the Canadian Partnership Against Cancer, in

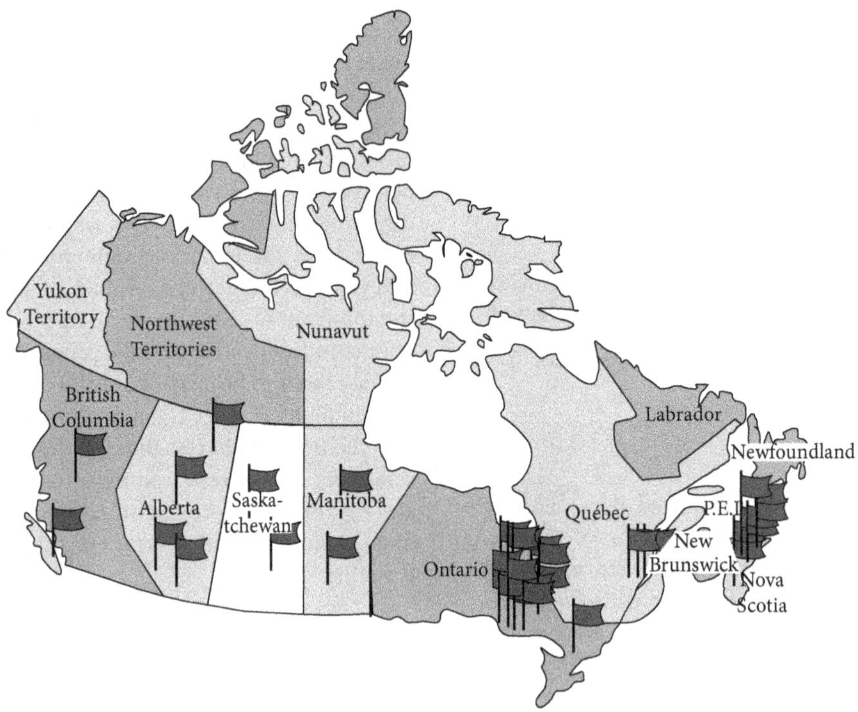

Figure 18.3. Map of Screening Sites in Canada

collaboration with the jurisdictions that implemented screening for distress, has developed a guide to screening for distress that is available on its website (http://www.cancerview.ca/idc/groups/public/documents/webcontent/guide_implement_sfd.pdf).

Distress continues to be endorsed as the 6th vital sign in cancer care on a regular basis by national and international organizations, such as the IPOS, the Union for International Cancer Control, and CAPO. As mentioned earlier, to date, 74 organizations have endorsed the IPOS Statement on Quality Cancer Care. This momentum is likely to continue as both patients and providers recognize the importance of screening for distress. The collaboration that occurred in Canada to facilitate the successful implementation of screening for distress in nine jurisdictions was impressive and benefited all involved. We would encourage this type of collaboration across all cancer institutions, because ultimately this will help us achieve our goal of systematic comprehensive routine screening, assessment, and intervention for all cancer patients. With cancer centers and psychosocial professionals working together, we are likely to see a culture shift that truly embraces cancer care for the whole person.

Pearls

- Having distress recognized as the 6th vital sign to be monitored in cancer patients helped mobilize resources for the development of broadly applied screening measures in Canada.
- Integrated interdisciplinary screening programs have shown success in implementing screening, although their structure and leadership show more variation in the United States.
- Interventions must be evidenced based and cost-effective going forward.

Pitfalls

- Underestimating the resources required to implement the screening tool and the processes and supports to facilitate assessment and intervention will likely result in an unsuccessful program.
- Failure of the implementation team to engage in a process of ongoing communication and education about screening with all administrative and professional groups—including tailoring education and training materials to the interests and concerns of each group—will likely limit the effectiveness of the screening program.

REFERENCES

Accreditation Canada. (2008). *Qmentum Program 2009 Standards: Cancer Care and Oncology Services*; Version 2. In author's possession.

Bultz, B. D., & Carlson, L. E. (2005). Emotional distress: The sixth vital sign in cancer care. *Journal of Clinical Oncology, 23*(26), 6440–6441.

Bultz, B. D., Groff, S. L., Fitch, M., Claude-Blais, M., Howes, J., & Levy, K. (2011). Implementing screening for distress, the 6th vital sign: A Canadian strategy for changing practice. *Psycho-Oncology, 20*(5), 463–469.

Bultz, B. D., Groff, S. L., Fitch, M., and Screening for Distress Toolkit Working Group. (2009). *Guide to implementing screening for distress, the 6th vital sign, part A: Background, recommendations, and implementation.* Cancer Journey Action Group, Canadian Partnership Against Cancer. Retrieved from http://www.partnershipagainstcancer.ca/download/2.4.0.1.4.5-Guide_CJAG.pdf

Canadian Association of Psychosocial Oncology (CAPO). (1999). *Canadian Association of Psychosocial Oncology standards.* Toronto, Canada: Author.

Canadian Partnership Against Cancer. (2008). *Canadian Partnership Against Cancer annual report 2007–2008.* Retrieved from http://www.partnershipagainstcancer.ca/download/3.1.4-CPAC_ENG_AR07_08_web.pdf

Rebalance Focus Action Group. (2005). A position paper: screening key indicators in cancer patients: Pain as a 5th vital sign and emotional distress as a 6th vital sign. *Canadian Strategy for Cancer Control Bulletin*, 7 (suppl 4).

Carlson, L. E., Angen, M., Cullum, J., Goodey, E., Koopmans, J., Lamont, L., ... Bultz, B. D. (2004). High levels of untreated distress and fatigue in cancer patients. *British Journal of Cancer, 90*(12), 2297–2304.

Carlson, L. E., Groff, S. L., Maciejewski, O., & Bultz, B. D. (2010). Screening for distress in lung and breast cancer outpatients: A randomized controlled trial. *Journal of Clinical Oncology, 28*(33), 4884–4891.

Fallowfield, L., Ratcliffe, D., Jenkins, V., & Saul, J. (2001). Psychiatric morbidity and its recognition by doctors in patients with cancer. *British Journal of Cancer, 84*(8), 1011–1015.

Homsi, J., Walsh, D., Rivera, N., Rybicki, L. A., Nelson, K. A., Legrand, S. B., ... Hahm, P. (2006). Symptom evaluation in palliative medicine: Patient report vs. systematic assessment. *Supportive Care in Cancer, 14*(5), 444–453.

Institute of Medicine and National Research Council of the National Academies. (2007). *Cancer care for the whole patient: Meeting psychosocial health needs.* Washington, DC: National Academies Press.

International Psycho-Oncology Society (IPOS). (2014). IPOS standard of care—endorsements. Retrieved from http://www.ipos-society.org/about-ipos/ipos-standard-of-care-endorsements/

Jacobsen, P. B., & Ransom, S. (2007). Implementation of NCCN distress management guidelines by member institutions. *Journal of the National Comprehensive Cancer Network, 5*(1), 99–103.

Loscalzo, M. J., Bultz, B., & Jacobsen, P. B. (2010). Building psychosocial programs: A roadmap to excellence. In J. C. Holland, W. S. Breitbart, P. B. Jacobsen, M. S. Lederberg, M. J. Loscalzo, & R. S. McCorkle (Eds.), *Psycho-oncology* (2nd ed., pp. 569–574). New York, NY: Oxford University Press.

Loscalzo, M., Clark, K. L., & Holland, J. C. (2011). Successful strategies for implementing biopsychosocial screening. *Psycho-Oncology, 20*(5), 455–462.

McMurtry, R., & Bultz, B. D. (2005). Public policy, human consequences: The gap between biomedicine and psychosocial reality. *Psycho-Oncology, 14*(9), 697–703.

Mitchell, A. J., Meader, N., Bird, V., & Rizzo, M. (2012). Clinical recognition and recording of alcohol disorders by clinicians in primary and secondary care: Meta-analysis. *British Journal of Psychiatry, 201*, 93–100. doi:10.1192/bjp.bp.110.091199

Mitchell, A. J., Vahabzadeh, A., & Magruder, K. (2011). Screening for distress and depression in cancer settings: 10 lessons from 40 years of primary-care research. *Psycho-Oncology, 20*(11), 572–584.

National Comprehensive Cancer Network (NCCN). (1999). *NCCN practice guidelines for the management of psychosocial distress.* Williston Park, NY: Author.

National Comprehensive Cancer Network (NCCN). (2011). *NCCN clinical practice guidelines in oncology: Adult cancer pain.* Retrieved from http://www.nccn.org/professionals/physician_gls/pdf/pain.pdf

Pirl, W. F., Muriel, A., Hwang, V., Kornblith, A., Greer, J., Donelan, K., ... Schapira, L. (2007). Screening for psychosocial distress: A national survey of oncologists. *Journal of Supportive Oncology, 5*(10), 499–504.

Rebalance Focus Action Group. (2005). A position paper: Screening key indicators in cancer patients: Pain as a 5th vital sign and emotional distress as a 6th vital sign. *Canadian Strategy for Cancer Control Bulletin, 7*(Suppl.), 4.

Temel, J. S., Pirl, W. F., & Lynch, T. J. (2006). Comprehensive symptom management in patients with advanced-stage non-small-cell lung cancer. *Clinical Lung Cancer, 7*(4), 241–249.

Weisman, A., Worden, J., & Sobel, H. J. (1980). *Psychosocial screening with cancer patients: A research report.* Boston, MA: Project Omega, Department of Psychiatry, Harvard Medical School, Massachusetts General Hospital.

Wood, V., Flavell, A., Vanstolk, D., Bainbridge, L., & Nasmith, L. (2009). The road to collaboration: Developing an interprofessional competency framework. *Journal of Interprofessional Care, 23*(6), 621–629.

Zabora, J., BrintzenhofeSzoc, K., Curbow, B., Hooker, C., & Piantadosi, S. (2001). The prevalence of psychological distress by cancer site. *Psycho-Oncology, 10*(1), 19–28.

19

Karen Clark, Matthew Loscalzo, and Barry D. Bultz

Touch-Screen Technology: Using a Problem Checklist for Psychosocial Oncology Screening

Key Concepts

- *Social workers are leaders in the biopsychosocial screening field.*
- *Cancer patients' unmet clinical and educational needs are directly relevant to social work.*
- *Effective practical strategies for implementing touch-screen technology in biopsychosocial screening should be developed.*
- *Important lessons can be learned when implementing distress screening in a cancer center.*

The health care system can be intimidating, confusing, and challenging to navigate for patients and their families, who may not know what symptoms and psychosocial needs are acceptable to discuss and may have difficulty sharing vulnerabilities. As such, patients with the most unmet needs or psychosocial problems, and those who are members of stigmatized or marginalized groups, are the core of social work practice. Biopsychosocial screening gives these high-risk groups a voice to share their concerns as an essential part of their cancer care. Although integrated triage, patient/caregiver education, and follow-up can be central to successful patient-centered care across the cancer treatment trajectory, it is biopsychosocial screening that optimizes communication among the patient, family, and health care team by prospectively identifying the patient's physical, psychosocial, spiritual, financial, and practical problems. Although biopsychosocial screening guidelines have been endorsed by the National Comprehensive Cancer Network (NCCN) and the Institute of Medicine (IOM), and new accreditation standards have been developed by the American Society of Clinical Oncology (ASCO) and the American College of Surgeons' (ACOS) Commission on Cancer (COC), they have not been widely implemented. We have a track record of successfully implementing comprehensive biopsychosocial screening programs across diverse settings and within integrated, interdisciplinary, patient- and family-centered programs (Clark, Bardwell, Arsenault, DeTeresa, & Loscalzo, 2009; Loscalzo et al., 2010; Loscalzo, Clark, & Holland, 2011).

This chapter addresses the pressing need for a practical road map that social workers can use to understand and obtain necessary resources and to implement biopsychosocial screening programs using touch-screen technology.

Biopsychosocial Screening

Definition of Biopsychosocial Screening

Biopsychosocial screening is the identification of a patient's physical, psychosocial, spiritual, financial, and practical problems, designed to improve communication between the patient, family, and care team (Patlak, Balogh, & Nass, 2011). As a result, it promotes an understanding of the patient within his or her social context and results in improved treatment adherence, quality of life, and overall satisfaction (Adler & Page, 2008; Bultz & Johansen, 2010; Carlson, Groff, Maciejewski, & Bultz, 2010).

Screening helps guide the care plan and creates a sense of trust and hope by revealing the patient's relevant problem areas, unmet needs, and strengths. Common problems in adaptation are identified by integrating the unmet psychosocial and other supportive care needs into standard cancer care and normalizing the helping process. Within this context, the patient and family are able to identify and share their problems and concerns from the very beginning of medical care, which enables them to partner with the health care team in a more effective way.

Particularly for social workers, biopsychosocial screening of cancer patients is extremely beneficial. The ability to monitor and anticipate unmet needs in *any* given population creates an opportunity for greater specialization, coordination, and professional satisfaction. The incorporation of psychosocial and medical data allows patients' needs to be clearly documented and encourages social work departments to tailor their services to their patient populations. Last, biopsychosocial screening clearly highlights the value of social workers' depth of understanding of patients' needs and documented skills in providing help with a range of patient and family concerns.

One such biopsychosocial screening program—You, Your Family, and City of Hope Are a Team—has been implemented at the City of Hope Cancer Center. Here, it was integrated with triage, patient/caregiver education, and follow-up to promote successful patient-centered care across the cancer treatment trajectory. It included the following:

- A 36-question problem list addresses physical, practical, social, psychological, and spiritual concerns. (The content and number of questions can also be altered for each individual diagnosis—for example, in our gynecology clinic, the screening includes an additional question on vaginal dryness, which is a common problem for gynecological cancer patients.) This survey is given to all patients during their second visit to the outpatient clinic for their cancer diagnosis. Patients (and in some clinics family members as well) are asked to use an automated touch screen to rate the severity of each problem on a scale of 1 to 5. They are also given the opportunity to rate their necessary level of assistance by providing written information, talking with a member of the team, or both.
- Updates have included a specific item on suicidal ideation. Because the suicide rate is higher in cancer patients than in the general and other medically ill populations (Breitbart, Pessin, & Kolva, 2010), it is important to screen for suicidal ideation and/or intent. Research indicates that it is unethical not to screen for a known danger, especially because in many situations, the suicide can be prevented with intervention (Leung et al., 2013). Although health care professionals may be hesitant to screen for or ask about suicide because of the perception of enhanced liability or because the topic is so emotionally charged, there is no data to support the link between asking about suicide and increasing the risk of suicide by asking about it.
- This information is transmitted electronically to the appropriate doctor, nurse, or psychosocial/spiritual professional. Notification for intervention is triggered if a patient ranks the severity of a problem at a level greater than an established cutoff point. For example, some items, such as the item screening for suicidality, trigger an intervention at a lower score than do other items and are given immediate attention. The cutoff point for specific social work services may be triggered by higher scores, determined in part by staffing levels. That is, if there are few resources to address particular problems areas, patients indicating mild or moderate concerns in an area may not be referred for individual services, but rather provided educational and resource materials.
- Available interventions include the primary care team and encompass a full range of supportive care services, from information and education, to pain and palliative care, to psychiatric support. These interventions are consistent with NCCN distress management guidelines.

Table 19.1 displays the top five unmet needs reported by over 2,000 cancer outpatients on the touch screen at the City of Hope. A more complete discussion of the importance of screening can be found in Chapter 17 in this book and in three key peer-reviewed articles (Bultz & Johansen, 2010; Carlson et al., 2010; Zabora, Loscalzo, & Weber, 2003).

History of Biopsychosocial Screening

In the 1990s, two social workers at the Johns Hopkins Oncology Center began the first universal prospective biopsychosocial screening program in the United States. From the beginning, it was clear that a psychological screen would require the inclusion of information that physicians valued—for example, physical symptoms, especially pain—for it to be perceived as having direct, immediate, and visible benefits to physicians and, therefore, their patients. Successful screening programs have been based on the principle that every part of screening has to have a clearly identifiable link with improved patient/family outcomes and/or direct benefits to physicians and/or the institution. We know of no successful clinical screening program that has not included participation by physicians from the start, and it is extremely doubtful that there would have been

Table 19.1.
Touch-Screen Data: Most Common Unmet Needs Rated as Sources of High Distress and Requests to Talk With a Member of the Team (N = 2,177)

Top 5 Unmet Needs Rated as Sources of High Distress	%	Top 5 Unmet Needs That Prompted a Request to Talk With a Member of the Team	%
Sleeping	37.52%	Understanding my treatment options	27.55%
Fatigue	34.12%	Needing help coordinating my medical care	22.69%
Worry about the future	33.06%	Fear of medical procedures	17.83%
Pain	31.12%	Sleeping	16.00%
Finances	31.88%	Walking, climbing stairs	13.79%

such rapid and universal uptake and support for the earliest reported screening program if it had only included the psychosocial aspects of care (Zabora, Loscalzo, & Weber, 2003).

Current Screening Guidelines and Standards

Barriers to comprehensive biopsychosocial screening are well documented, including the fact that few oncologists provide any screening (Pirl et al., 2007) and, as a result, may not recognize high patient distress and unmet needs (Fallowfield, Ratcliffe, Jenkins, & Saul, 2001). Patient and institutional barriers have also been widely reported (Adler & Page, 2008; Clark et al., 2009; Patlak et al., 2011). Many so-called barriers are in fact iatrogenic to any health care system that is hierarchical in structure and myopic in focus.

Box 19.1
Lessons Learned

1. Patients and families are not the barrier.
2. Screening for distress alone is not adequate.
3. Screening is a team endeavor.
4. Do not assume screening by itself will lead to better outcomes.
5. Be clear about why you are screening and what you are trying to detect.
6. Do not assume one screening model will meet all institutional needs.
7. Carefully consider resources that are needed and available to implement screening.
8. Be prepared to meet expected demand before implementing screening.
9. Document processes and evaluate outcomes related to screening and delivery of care.
10. Tension between research- and patient-centered clinical care is an opportunity for collaboration.

The aim of such barriers is to protect turf and specialty- or profession-specific focus, rather than to expand the recognition of distress and unmet needs. Our experience has shown that giving patients a real voice promotes a wider long-term view of overall cancer care and quickly identifies people and systems that do not support patient- and family-centered care.

The biggest concern of social workers and other frontline clinicians has been the potential "increase" in workload and the need to clearly define responsibilities. Once a sense of identity and service scope has been clarified, communicated, and demonstrated, it is our opinion that the work does change and becomes more focused on pushing social workers (and others) to the "top of their licenses" (i.e., the point at which they are fully using their training and skills to improve practice outcomes). Because they are not performing tasks that can be accomplished by individuals with less training, professionals who are at the top of their licenses are constantly extending the limits of their expertise. At City of Hope, we have jointly developed the following script for social workers: "I provide for the psychological, social, practical, and emotional needs of cancer patients and their families." Ultimately, we are in the midst of a culture change in health care across North America and Europe. There is no going back. Existing guidelines have now become standards that will have to be met for program accreditation. Canada has accepted distress as the 6th vital sign (Bultz et al., 2011). These changes will have a dramatic impact on the promotion of patient- and family-centered care.

Comprehensive biopsychosocial screening guidelines have been endorsed by the NCCN since 1998 (Holland et al., 2007), and more recently by the IOM (Adler & Page, 2008). New accreditation standards from ASCO (2011) and from the ACOS COC (ACOS, 2012) are imminent. The current screening guidelines and standards for patient care highlight the need for road maps *on how to* meet them. Several empirical publications have focused on screening (e.g., the

2011 special issue *of Psycho-Oncology* dedicated entirely to screening research [Bultz & Johansen, 2011] and the 2012 *Journal of Clinical Oncology* special series [Jacobsen, Holland, & Steensma, 2012]). Few published research studies have specifically evaluated large-scale clinical *implementation.* Two peer-reviewed reports on implementation published by our team constitute, in large part, the foundation for implementation strategies in the field (Bultz et al., 2011; Loscalzo et al., 2011). The emerging literature has shown that patients will actively participate in biopsychosocial screening if it is presented as part of standard cancer care (Kadan-Lottick, Vanderwerker, Block, Zhang, & Prigerson, 2005). Therefore, any serious effort to implement comprehensive screening must include health care professionals and be conducted within an organizational structure (Sanson-Fisher, Grimshaw, & Eccles, 2004).

Applying Touch-Screen Technology for Implementing Biopsychosocial Screening

Despite major advances in computer technology, neither the health care system overall nor medical care specifically have maximized the potential benefits of electronic transfer and documentation of clinical encounters. The Obama administration has mandated the use of electronic medical records to improve safety, efficiency, and quality of care, yet only 1.5% of U.S. hospitals use a comprehensive health record (Jha et al., 2009). Several studies suggest that electronic methods of data collection are easy, quick, reliable, and acceptable to patients, all of which are important components for integration into routine oncology practice (McLachlan et al., 2001; Newell, Sanson-Fisher, & Stewart, 1997; Taenzer et al., 1997; Taenzer et al., 2000; Velikova et al., 1999).

Innovative computer touch-screen technology is one of the more popular methods, and its application to patient care is gaining attention within the health care community (Allenby, Matthews, Beresford, & McLachlan, 2002; Holzner et al., 2004). A touch-screen system implemented at the City of Hope called SupportScreen is a patient-friendly automated process that identifies, triages, and provides educational information all in real time. SupportScreen covers the entire process of biopsychosocial screening—from initiation of patient responses to the generation of referrals and provision of educational information. SupportScreen also facilitates patient, physician, and multispecialist communication and is used to maximize the effectiveness of clinical encounters and overall cancer care (Loscalzo et al., 2010). Velikova, Brown, Smith, and Selby (2002) found that the touch screen was well accepted and that this method of accessing information from patients provided complete and quality data while minimizing missing responses and the need to decipher ambiguous data. Allenby et al. (2002) found in a study of 450 cancer patients that 99% of the patients found the touch screen easy to use, even though half the patients reported having no prior computer experience. Specific steps for implementing a touch-screen biopsychosocial screening program are discussed next. Selected resources are also listed.

Steps for Implementing Biopsychosocial Screening Using Touch-Screen Technology

Almost 20 years of screening experience in academic cancer centers and a small community hospital in both the United States and Canada have helped us identify the specific steps necessary for implementing a successful biopsychosocial screening program using touch-screen technology. These steps and strategies for success can be used as guidelines for implementation of biopsychosocial screening, but each program will need to be tailored to the individual institutional setting.

The content and processes of the biopsychosocial screening programs we developed were created by interdisciplinary teams of social workers, psychologists, psychiatrists, child life specialists, oncologists, health educators, nurses, rehabilitation therapists, chaplains, clinical nutritionists, researchers, and patient navigators. The touch-screen technology was created in a process of concurrent (not serial) development with the information technology department. This process of true engagement and leveraging is an essential part of the culture change that is necessary to implement a biopsychosocial screening program. The clinical screening programs in both the United States and Canada go well beyond merely identifying symptoms or problems and include triage, tailored education, community resources, and data integration for program development and research (see Table 19.2).

Lessons Learned

Biopsychosocial screening is an idea whose time has come, and there is considerable leverage to implement such programs. Fortunately, most settings will not have to repeat the errors of the pioneers but can instead benefit from lessons learned by the social workers and other psychosocial professionals who have implemented screening programs.

Biopsychosocial screening has the potential to identify the most pressing problems of patients and their caregivers and to furnish data that demonstrates the need for social work services. Social workers must continue to play a leadership role in screening that gives patients a voice and leads to meaningful professional coordination and outcomes. The 6th vital sign measure adopted in Canada has been a major accomplishment, and the data from related distress screening studies has led to a much greater understanding of the need for screening to be patient centered. Model biopsychosocial clinical screening programs presently in place

Table 19.2.
Steps in Implementing Touch-Screen Technology for Biopsychosocial Screening

Steps	Strategies for Success
1. Engage interdisciplinary team	*Social workers and other psychosocial team members* • Define biopsychosocial screening and the areas specific to social workers (unmet needs). • List the fears and opportunities related to screening. • Invite the psychosocial team to have input into the instrument content, the triage process, and the selection of the first physicians to be approached about actively participating in a pilot. *Patients* • Create a patient advisory council to engage patients and their family caregivers in the process. • Test everything with patients and their family caregivers. *Physicians* • Ask the physicians, "What information do you need to know to provide the best care?" • Share the data. Physicians highly value the data that comes from screening and its specificity to the populations served. *Nurses* • Ask the nurses, "What information do you need to know to provide the best care?" • Involve nurses from the inception of the screening program and allow them to have input into the process. *Hospital Administrators* • Teach key hospital administrators to understand the value of screening (using written scripts—a mantra that is used with every patient). • As clinicians, apply your clinical skills to engage and motivate administrators. • Share the data to demonstrate unmet needs.
2. Define scope (includes patient population, who is screened, and when they are screened)	• Start slow. • Address problems quickly. • Address control and turf issues up front. • Know that culture change takes time, vision, and persistence.
3. Determine content (includes items, triage, and educational materials)	• Establish objective criteria to determine which items will be included. This helps to ensure that the decisions are professional rather than personal. • Include the interdisciplinary team in the selection of items, triage, and education materials.
4. Engage operational team members in the clinics	• Share the importance of screening and teach them about the big picture. • Reinforce how critical their role is in taking care of the whole patient. • Give them food and small incentives.
5. Determine operational processes for the clinic screening	• Understand the culture of the clinic. • Understand specific staff hierarchy. • Understand standard clinic processes. • Determine how and with whom you will partner to lead the screening program (typically a nurse administrator). • Get introduced to and learn how to engage the clinic staff (front desk administrative staff, schedulers, medical assistants). • Receive guidance in how to integrate screening into standard clinical care.
6. Conduct back-end operational system preparations (ordering tablets, entering content, etc.)	• Engage an information technology person to help set up the hardware. • Have an administrative assistant enter and manage the content in the system.

Table 19.2. (Continued)

7. Staff training and education	• Educate the clinic staff through a series of in-service sessions. • Create tailored orientation sheets, scripts, screening support staff contact information sheets, and protocols for screening refusals and high-risk patient follow-up. • Teach the clinic staff about screening, why it is important, their crucial role, and the specific clinic procedures. • Use role-playing and administering the screening tool as a part of these in-service sessions. • Provide food and beverages at all in-service sessions.
8. Pilot phase	• Start with a few champion physicians and expand slowly over time. • Have a member of the team present during all screenings for at least the first week. • Let the clinic staff know that problems are inevitable.
9. Evaluation phase	• Test questions with patients. • Test processes with clinic staff. • Continually evaluate.
10. Revise processes/content if necessary	• Meet regularly with all users to obtain feedback on the content and processes. • Share updates on the content and processes.
11. Data dissemination	• Share data with interdisciplinary team members and clinic staff. • Publish results at conferences and in peer- reviewed journals (after obtaining institutional review board approval).

around the world have implemented procedures that prospectively, systematically, and efficiently identify distress, unmet needs, and related problems; triage cancer patients and their families to the appropriate professionals; and provide tailored educational information and resources. As the demand for psychosocial cancer services increases, it is critical that these services be provided in a manner that is resource efficient, integrated into practice as the standard of clinical care, and evidence based.

Touch-screen technology creates another opportunity for social workers to serve more patients more efficiently, effectively provide resources, and focus on those patients and families who most need assistance. Technology will allow social workers to practice at the top of their licenses and skill levels, just as it will for physician, nurse, and psychologist colleagues.

Screening inevitably impacts patients, families, psychosocial providers, the primary health care team, the institution, and clinical systems. Understanding how key stakeholders perceive the direct benefits to them, as well as to patients and families, is essential in implementing a successful screening program. This chapter has provided a framework for screening programs that is based on consultation with international leaders, review of the literature, and 18 years of creating clinical screening programs; it can be tailored for use in a variety of clinical settings. Although the process is simple, it is seldom easy. Implementation of a successful screening program creates culture change, and culture change takes time, perseverance, and vision.

The present health care environment provides a unique opportunity for social workers to be at the forefront of positive change, creating whole-patient-centered programs that integrate technology and a science of caring based on humanistic values. Screening can be the connective tissue of fragmented health care systems that helps to coordinate the efforts of the very busy, highly trained multispecialists who strive to provide compassionate expertise in demanding cancer settings. Although high-quality research results have supported the importance of screening, there is a dearth of road maps for effective implementation. It is time to translate the knowledge gleaned from research and existing model programs into strategies that improve clinical practice and quality of life for patients, their families, and our colleagues.

Pearls

- Never wait until all of the resources are in place—start screening with what you have today.
- Explicitly identify the ways in which each professional and patient will personally benefit from the screening program.
- Have clear criteria for what is included in the screening tool and tailor these criteria to the particular services and interventions that can be provided.
- Be realistic about the instruments you use. No single tool can accomplish the goals of both research and clinical care.
- Start small, go slow, recognize the potential for problems, and expand only after you work out the bugs.

Pitfalls

- Not taking a leadership role in a screening program.
- Not including physicians and nurses until late in the process.
- Not openly addressing colleagues' fears of being overwhelmed by the workload.
- Having a screening process that takes too long for patients to complete or is not specific to their cancer diagnosis and treatment.

REFERENCES

Adler, N. E., & Page, A. (2008). Institute of Medicine, Committee on Psychosocial Services to Cancer Patients/Families. In *Cancer care for the whole patient meeting psychosocial health needs*. Washington, DC: National Academies Press.

Allenby, A., Matthews, J., Beresford, J., & McLachlan, S. A. (2002). The application of computer touch-screen technology in screening for psychosocial distress in an ambulatory oncology setting. *European Journal of Cancer Care, 11*, 245–253.

American College of Surgeons (ACOS). (2012). Cancer Program Standards 2012. Version 1.2: Ensuring patient-centered care (2013). Retrieved from http://www.facs.org/cancer/coc/programstandards2012.html

American Society of Clinical Oncology (ASCO). (n.d.). ASCO-ONS standards for safe chemotherapy administration. Retrieved from http://www.asco.org/institute-quality/asco-ons-standards-safe-chemotherapy-administration

Breitbart, W., Pessin, H., & Kolva, E. (2010). Suicide and desire for hastened death in people with cancer. In D. Kissane, M. Maj, & N. Sartorius (Eds.), *Depression and cancer* (pp. 125–150). Hoboken, NJ: John Wiley & Sons.

Bultz, B. D., Groff, S. L., Fitch, M., Blasis, C., Howes, J., Levy, K., & Mayer, C. (2011). Implementing screening for distress, the 6th vital sign: A Canadian strategy for changing practice. *Psycho-Oncology, 20*, 463–469.

Bultz, B. D., & Johansen, C. (2010). Call for papers: Special issue of *Psycho-Oncology* on screening for distress, from research to practice. *Psycho-Oncology, 19*, 113.

Bultz, B. D., & Johansen, C. (2011). Screening for distress, the 6th vital sign: Where are we, and where are we going? *Psycho-Oncology, 20*, 569–571.

Carlson, L. E., Groff, S. L., Maciejewski, O., & Bultz B. D. (2010). Screening for distress in lung and breast cancer outpatients: A randomized controlled trial. *Journal of Clinical Oncology, 28*, 4884–4891.

Clark, K., Bardwell, W. A., Arsenault, T., DeTeresa, R., & Loscalzo, M. (2009). Implementing touch-screen technology to enhance recognition of distress. *Psycho-Oncology, 18*, 822–830.

Fallowfield, L., Ratcliffe, D., Jenkins, V., & Saul, J. (2001). Psychiatric morbidity and its recognition by doctors in patients with cancer. *British Journal of Cancer, 20*, 1011–1015.

Holland, J. C., Breitbart, W. S., Anderson, B., Dabrowski, M., Dudley, M. M., Fleishman, S., ... Greiner, C. B. (2007). The NCCN distress management clinical practice guidelines in oncology. *Journal of the National Comprehensive Cancer Network, 5*(1), 66–98.

Holzner, B., Zabernigg, A., Kemmler, G., Baier, S., Kopp, M., & Sperner-Unterweger, B. (2004). Computerized assessment of quality of life in patients undergoing chemotherapy. *Quality of Life Research, 13*, 1523.

Jacobsen, P. B., Holland, J. C., & Steensma, D. P. (2012). Caring for the whole patient: The science of psychosocial care. *Journal of Clinical Oncology, 30*, 1151–1153.

Jha, A. K., Desroches, C. M., Campbell, E. G., Donelan, K., Rao, S. R., Ferris, T. G., ... Blumenthal, D. (2009). Use of electronic health records in U.S. hospitals. *New England Journal of Medicine, 360*, 1628–1638.

Kadan-Lottick, N. S., Vanderwerker, L. C., Block, S. D., Zhang, B., & Prigerson, H. G. (2005). Psychiatric disorders and mental health service use in patients with advanced cancer: A report from the coping with cancer study. *Cancer, 104*, 2872–2881.

Leung, Y. W., Li, M., Devins, G., Zimmermann, C., Rydall, A., Lo, C., & Rodin, G. (2013). Routine screening for suicidal intention in patients with cancer. *Psycho-Oncology, 22*(11), 2537–2545. doi:10.1002/pon.3319

Loscalzo, M., Clark, K., Dillehunt, J., Rinehart, R., Strowbridge, R., & Smith, D. (2010). SupportScreen: A model for improving patient outcomes at your fingertips. *Journal of the National Comprehensive Cancer Network, 8*, 496–504.

Loscalzo, M., Clark, K. L., & Holland, J. (2011). Successful strategies for implementing biopsychosocial screening. *Psycho-Oncology, 20*, 455–462.

McLachlan, S. A., Allenby, A., Matthews, J., Wirth, A., Kissane, D., Bishop, M., ... Zalcberg, J. (2001). Randomized trial of coordinated psychosocial interventions based on patient self-assessments versus standard care to improve the psychosocial functioning of patients with cancer. *Journal of Clinical Oncology, 19*, 4117–4125.

Newell, S. G., Sanson-Fisher, R., & Stewart, J. (1997). Are touch-screen computer surveys acceptable to medical oncology patients? *Journal of Psychosocial Oncology, 15*, 37–46.

Patlak, M., Balogh, E., & Nass, S. J. (2011). National Cancer Policy Forum (U.S.), National Coalition for Cancer Survivorship, Institute of Medicine. *Patient-centered cancer treatment planning: Improving the quality of oncology care: Workshop summary*. Washington, DC: National Academies Press.

Pirl, W. F., Muriel, A., Hwang, V., Kornblith, A., Greer, J., Donelan, K., ... Schapira, L. (2007). Screening for psychosocial distress: A national survey of oncologists. *Journal of Supportive Oncology, 5*, 499–504.

Sanson-Fisher, R. W., Grimshaw, J. M., & Eccles, M. P. (2004). The science of changing providers' behaviour: The missing link in evidence-based practice. *Medical Journal of Australia, 80*, 205–206.

Taenzer, P., Bultz, B. D., Carlson, L. E., Speca, M., DeGagne, T., Olson, K., ... Rosberger, Z. (2000). Impact of computerized quality of life screening on physician behavior and patient satisfaction in lung cancer patients. *Psycho-Oncology, 9*, 203–213.

Taenzer, P. A., Speca, M., Atkinson, M. J., Bultz, B. D., Page, S., Harasym, P., & Davis, J. L. (1997). Computerized quality of life screening in an oncology clinic. *Cancer Practice, 5*, 168–175.

Velikova, G., Brown, J. M., Smith, A. B., & Selby, P. J. (2002). Computer-based quality of life questionnaires may contribute to doctor-patient interaction in oncology. *British Journal of Cancer, 86*, 51–59.

Velikova, G., Wright, E. P., Smith, A. B., Cull, A., Gould, D., Forman, T., ... Selby, P. J. (1999). Automated collection of quality of life data: A comparison of paper and computer touch screen questionnaires. *Journal of Clinical Oncology, 17*, 998–1007.

Zabora, J. R., Loscalzo, M. J., & Weber, J. (2003). Managing complications in cancer: Identifying and responding to the patient's perspective. *Seminars in Oncology Nursing, 19*, 1–9.

20

Jill Taylor-Brown and Heather Campbell-Enns

Distress Screening and Responding in an Ambulatory Cancer Center

Key Concepts

- *Screening for distress is a strategy used to improve patient care and move health care systems toward person-centered, multidimensional, and interprofessional care.*
- *To respond effectively to identified unmet patient needs, the social worker must develop knowledge about and skills in opening conversations about distress, provide a targeted assessment of identified needs, understand clinical practice guidelines and best practices applicable to a broad range of needs, and recognize criteria for referral to specialized services.*
- *Models and theories of knowledge translation are useful foundations to drive changes in practice. Planned action (Ellis & Kiely, 2000), a process concerned with translating knowledge into action at the local level, was used to implement screening across multiple professional groups and patient services.*
- *Ongoing evaluation is critical to the success of screening-for-distress programs. This includes evaluation of educational initiatives, staff satisfaction with practice change, patient satisfaction, and perception of effect on care.*
- *Responding to feedback from patients, families, and staff about the screening and addressing the particular culture and idiosyncrasies of the clinical practice environment are critical.*

Screening for (and responding to) distress is one strategy to help ensure integrated and interprofessional whole-person care for those experiencing cancer (Bultz, Groff, & Fitch, 2009). For more than 30 years, it has been known that a cancer diagnosis and its subsequent treatment may result in high levels of psychosocial and physical distress. North American studies indicate that during any point in the cancer trajectory, 35% to 45% of patients require specialized or intensive professional intervention or both for this distress (Bultz, 2005; Vodermaier, Linden, & Siu, 2009; Zabora, BrintzenhofeSzoc, Curbow, Hooker, & Piantadosi, 2001). Although there are variations in the methods used to screen for distress, the initiatives addressed in this chapter draw from common elements found in *Screening for Distress, the 6th Vital Sign: A Guide to Implementing Best Practices in Person-Centered Care* (Cancer Journey Portfolio, 2012).

This chapter focuses on the implementation and preliminary evaluation of a programmatic screening-for-distress initiative at a tertiary provincial adult ambulatory cancer care (ACC) center. The center is located at two sites in a Canadian city with a population of 750,000, with 17 rural community cancer program satellites spread across a large geographical area (250,946 square miles) with an additional population of about 500,000. The center sees approximately 6,000 new patients annually. In the urban setting, delivery of care is organized into cancer disease site groups. The center is currently transitioning to a completely electronic health record. In the interim, some paper documents remain as part of the patient's chart.

The screening-for-distress practice change was initiated by the Patient and Family Support Services program, which is made up of six distinct but related services: psychosocial oncology (social work, psychology, psychiatry, spiritual health), nutrition services, speech language pathology, and three resource centers focused on patient and family education and support.

As part of the pan-Canadian National Screening for Distress Implementation Group described in Chapter 18 by Bultz, Loscalzo, and Groff, funding was received that allowed the ambulatory care center to hire a project manager and an implementation facilitator for the first 16 months of this ongoing initiative. After an environmental scan of tools currently in use across Canada, including a series of nationally developed "Guides for Implementing Screening for Distress," the project group recommended the Edmonton Symptom Assessment Scale (ESAS; Bruera, Kuehn, Miller, Selmser, & Macmillan, 1991) plus an adaptation of the Canadian Problem Checklist (CPC; Bultz et al., 2009) as the minimum database tools. Principles of knowledge translation and planned action were utilized in implementing programmatic screening for distress at the ACC, including the engagement of various stakeholders. This chapter highlights the educational strategies that were used.

The role of oncology social workers in implementing and evaluating screening for and responding to distress

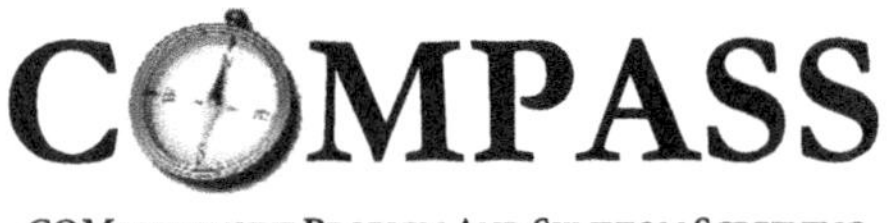

Patient Label

COMPREHENSIVE PROBLEM AND SYMPTOM SCREENING

Date of Completion:__________ **Name:**____________________ **Date of Birth**__________

1. Edmonton Symptom Assessment System (ESAS):

Please circle the number that best describes:

1.	No pain	0	1	2	3	4	5	6	7	8	9	10	Worst possible pain
2.	Not tired	0	1	2	3	4	5	6	7	8	9	10	Worst possible tiredness
3.	Not nauseated	0	1	2	3	4	5	6	7	8	9	10	Worst possible nausea
4.	Not depressed	0	1	2	3	4	5	6	7	8	9	10	Worst possible depression
5.	Not anxious	0	1	2	3	4	5	6	7	8	9	10	Worst possible anxiety
6.	Not drowsy	0	1	2	3	4	5	6	7	8	9	10	Worst possible drowsiness
7.	Best appetite	0	1	2	3	4	5	6	7	8	9	10	Worst possible appetite
8.	Best feeling of well-being	0	1	2	3	4	5	6	7	8	9	10	Worst possible feeling of well-being
9.	No shortness of breath	0	1	2	3	4	5	6	7	8	9	10	Worst possible shortness of breath
10.	Other problem: ________	0	1	2	3	4	5	6	7	8	9	10	

2. Canadian Problem Checklist:

Please check all of the following items that have been a concern or problem for you in the past week including today:

Emotional:
- ❐ Fears / Worries
- ❐ Sadness
- ❐ Frustration/Anger
- ❐ Changes in appearance
- ❐ Intimacy / Sexuality
- ❐ Coping
- ❐ Change in sense of self
- ❐ Loss of interest in everyday things

Spiritual:
- ❐ Meaning / Purpose of life
- ❐ Faith

Practical:
- ❐ Work / School
- ❐ Finances
- ❐ Getting to and from appointments
- ❐ Accommodation
- ❐ Child / Family / Elder care

Physical:
- ❐ Concentration / Memory
- ❐ Sleep
- ❐ Weight
- ❐ Constipation / Diarrhea
- ❐ Swallowing
- ❐ Falling / Loss of balance

Informational:
- ❐ Understanding my illness and/or treatment
- ❐ Talking with the health care team
- ❐ Making treatment decisions
- ❐ Knowing about available resources
- ❐ Quitting smoking
- ❐ Medications

Social/Family:
- ❐ Feeling a burden to others
- ❐ Worry about family / friends
- ❐ Feeling alone
- ❐ Relationship difficulties

Additional Question:

Have you smoked in the past six weeks? ❐ Yes ❐ No

*FINAL November 2011, adapted from: *Cancer Journey Action Group, Canadian Partnership Against Cancer's recommendations for screening for distress, May 2009*

Figure 20.1. COMPASS Screening Tool

is multidimensional. Oncology social workers bring their skills and understanding of principles of change to knowledge translation initiatives, as well as clinical acumen in responding to distress.

Implementation and Evaluation of Screening for Distress

> *The Distress Management Guidelines Panel of the National Comprehensive Cancer Network (2002, p. 5) defines distress as follows:A multifactorial unpleasant emotional experience of a psychological (cognitive, behavioral, emotional), social and/or spiritual nature that may interfere with the ability to cope effectively with cancer, its physical symptoms and its treatment. Distress extends along a continuum, ranging from common normal feelings of vulnerability, sadness, and fears, to problems that can become disabling such as depression, anxiety, panic, social isolation, and existential and spiritual crisis.*

Programmatic Screening for Distress in the clinical oncology setting includes not only identifying symptoms and concerns as reported by the patient but also responding to distress as soon as possible (Bultz et al., 2009). Use of a screening tool is not an end in itself; it is the "red flag" that leads to opening meaningful conversations between providers and patients for further assessment, intervention, or referral based on best practices, clinical practice guidelines, and care pathways (Carlson, Waller, & Mitchell, 2012).

Since 1999, the ACC has used the ESAS as a paper screening tool in almost every disease site group. At every physician visit, patients are handed a clipboard with a paper copy of the ESAS to complete. The ESAS was rarely used in the rural satellite centers. In 2004, random chart audits in two clinics that had implemented the ESAS identified many successes and challenges. These included an uneven use of the ESAS, lack of clarity about charting expectations around the ESAS, lack of ongoing education about responding to distress, screening results not available in the electronic health record, clinic workload (lack of time available for postscreening conversation in clinic), and staff changes. In collaboration with the National Screening for Distress Implementation Group and building on lessons learned locally and by other Canadian jurisdictions, the ACC began implementing an enhanced screening-for-distress tool and postscreening practice change.

Conceptualization and Development of the Updated Screening Tool

To demarcate the new screening tool and refocus on postscreening interventions, the acronym COMPASS was developed for the screening tool—*Com*prehensive *P*roblem *a*nd *S*ymptom *S*creening. COMPASS complies with the national recommended minimum data set and consists of the ESAS, an adapted CPC, and an additional question related to smoking (Figure 20.1). Its name or logo appears on all resources and documents related to the distress screening initiative.

Like the ESAS, a paper copy of the COMPASS tool is to be completed by patients at every physician visit. Initially the plan was to have patients complete the tool electronically, either with tablets or kiosks, so that the results would automatically be included in the electronic health record. Unfortunately, due to current technological and financial constraints, this is not possible at this time. Instead, patients' paper scores are entered into an electronic comprehensive charting tool that was developed to document postscreening interventions and referrals and allows for the mining of data on frequency of symptoms, problems, and concerns.

Strategy for Implementing Knowledge Translation

Howell and Pathak (2011) conceptualized *knowledge translation* as a series of strategies that make knowledge "relevant and accessible to patients and practitioners" (p. 7). The theory of *planned action* (Ellis & Kiely, 2000; Howell & Pathak, 2011) was used in this implementation.

Planned action is particularly suitable for local-level programmatic changes because the theory is respectful of individual expertise, which may differ between locations, and strives to solve local challenges so that meaningful change will result (Figure 20.2). Table 20.1 provides a summary of

- Individuals in the practice setting are the experts about their setting and its ways.
- It is a process that embraces the concepts of action and reflection to bring about understanding and enable change.
- Respect of individuals' "personal knowledge" gained from practical or theoretical knowledge is acknowledged.
- It involves the interplay of practical wisdom and theoretical concepts.
- The end product is uncertain and the road may lead to unexpected discovery.
- It is a dynamic process that solves real issues and enables meaningful change.
- Most important, it is a process that is concerned with knowledge that is created in and for action at the local level.

Figure 20.2. Tenets of Planned Action (Ellis & Kiely, 2000, in Howell & Pathak, 2011)

Table 20.1.
Summary of Screening for Distress Implementation Strategies

Specific Strategy	Activity to Meet Strategy	Example
1. Establish connections within the ACC.	• Engage stakeholders.	• Invite to steering committee.
2. Capitalize on coexisting initiatives.	• Meet with steering committee to identify coexisting initiatives. • Meet with leaders of coexisting initiatives. • Present opportunities to help each initiative to move forward by working together.	• Opening of new CCP. • Development of guidelines within ACC. • Ongoing opportunities to facilitate nursing professional development.
3. Adapt work to the local setting.	• Communicate with stakeholders.	• Develop COMPASS tool. • Develop clinical aids. • Work with EHR. • Tailor national CPGs.
4. Develop and provide education.	• Develop and provide leadership presentations. • One-on-one training. • Group education sessions. • Clinical aids. • Online learning. • Train-the-trainer. • Nurse orientation.	• Invite national experts to present about programmatic screening and linkage to national initiative. • As needed with early adopters or staff with specific needs. • Introduction to Screening for Distress. • Responding to Distress. • The Clinic Process. • Clinical Practice Guidelines. • Receptionist Guide. • *ASK Conversation Guide* • Resource list. • Clinic flowcharts. • EHR instructions. • Preexisting self-directed learning. • Engage and train nurse managers, clinical resource nurses, rural patient navigators, and CCP management. • Facilitated by nurse educator.
5. Evaluate progress.	• Screen for early identification of distress including screening rates, frequency of symptoms and problems, severity of symptoms. • Provide staff education and training to determine learning needs and evaluate if needs were met. • Facilitate teamwork and collaboration to ensure adherence to best practices. • Assess for patient engagement and satisfaction.	• Survey of clinic staff (baseline data). • Monthly report through EHR (change). • Preeducation survey (baseline). • Posteducation survey (change). • Ongoing chart audit. • Staff satisfaction survey. • Patient satisfaction survey.
6. Identify, assess, and address barriers.	• Identify barriers via evaluation processes. • Utilize PDSA cycles to assess and address barriers.	• Add COMPASS to the EHR. • Train leaders in COMPASS implementation. • Increase clinician understanding of benefits of using COMPASS. • Implement COMPASS in a large rural CCP, charting electronically.

Note: *ACC* = ambulatory care center; *CCP* = community cancer program; *EHR* = electronic health record; *CPG* = clinical practice guidelines; *PDSA* = Plan, Do, Study, Act.

the strategies, the activities used to meet each strategy, and specific examples. These include engaging key stakeholders, capitalizing on concurrent initiatives, being mindful of adapting to the local setting, providing education to leaders and clinic staff, evaluating progress, and identifying, assessing, and addressing barriers throughout the implementation.

A key strategy for knowledge translation is the engagement of stakeholders and change agents in the hopes that they become supporters of the initiative and enablers of change (Buonocore, 2004; Carlson et al., 2012; Harvey et al., 2002). Engagement with staff from all disciplines who would either influence implementation or be directly impacted by it was sought and gained, with particular emphasis on the department of nursing, including frontline nurses, unit managers, and senior nursing leadership. A cross-department, interdisciplinary screening-for-distress steering committee was formed that included representation from frontline and managerial staff. This committee helped identify coexisting initiatives that could mutually benefit from working with the screening-for-distress initiative and was integral

ELECTRONIC CHARTING OF COMPASS

Aim: Have the COMPASS tool entered into the patient's electronic chart, so can be viewed by all involved health care providers.

Objective for this PDSA cycle: Implement an efficient and effective way to add the COMPASS tool to the electronic chart that also allows for analysis and reporting of results.

CYCLE 1 — QUESTIONNAIRE INTRODUCTION

- **Plan:** Train and support nurses to transcribe patient selections into existing "ESAS and CPC" questionnaire.
- **Do:** All clinic team nurses are trained to use questionnaire, and clinic aids developed for reference. Project Manager made available to assist in clinic or at time of charting, as needed.
- **Study:** Nurses complied with electronic charting to varying degrees at first, but consistency improved with time. Nurses indicated that use of the tool increased charting time, as they were entering the information in the questionnaire, and then re-typing some or all of the "scores" into the progress note. Discussion with nursing leadership revealed that a previous survey indicated that clinic staff do not review questionnaires for patient information, and prefer to see all relevant information posted in the progress note.
- **Act:** Discussion with IS to find solution to increased charting time. Result was to create and implement a template that would pull questionnaire line prompt, patient response and date into progress note.

CYCLE 2 — TEMPLATE INTRODUCTION

- **Plan:** Train and support nurses to use new template to import patient responses into progress notes.
- **Do:** All clinic team nurses are trained to use template to bring information from questionnaire into progress note.
- **Study:** Response from nursing staff was mixed. Based on the existing questionnaire, the prompt for each ESAS item was extremely long and the date appeared on each line. The result was a very busy looking text-based section, where the patient score was hard to find. Some nurses continued to chart in progress note by re-typing "relevant" scores; others used the template and spent time deleting the unwanted text from the prompt and date.
- **Act:** Re-design questionnaire so a data-rich template can pull in concise and easy to read information into the progress note.

CYCLE 3 — QUESTIONNAIRE RE-DESIGN AND LAUNCH

- **Plan:** Working with IS and clinic team nurses to re-design, test and launch new COMPASS questionnaire.
- **Do:** The existing "ESAS and CPC" questionnaire was updated in various design and testing phases, including renamed "COMPASS: ESAS and CPC Distress Screening." The paper tool had additional items added and this was integrated into the re-design which included more succinct prompts, and an additional charting section. A corresponding data-rich template was developed that pulled all the information from the questionnaire into the progress note, in a clean, succinct and standardized way.
- **Study:** Clinic team nurses indicated high levels of satisfaction with new questionnaire and data-rich template. Nursing leader ship supported use as a standard for charting COMPASS in the progress notes.
- **Act:** Promote the existence and use of the electronic charting tools to the CCMB community. Re-evaluate the questionnaire and template as new technologies or equipment become available. Ultimate goal would have the patient enter scores electronically themselves through use of tablets, kiosks and/or the internet.

Figure 20.3. Plan, Do, Study, Act Cycle to Add COMPASS Tool to the Electronic Health Record

to identifying clinics and clinicians for early adoption of COMPASS.

A stepwise implementation began with low-patient-volume clinics that had previously used the ESAS and that were willing to alter their practice to adopt the COMPASS tool. The strategy was to "start small" with motivated staff and work through inevitable problems and barriers to change. At this early phase, the implementation team provided one-on-one or small-group education (Table 20.1). Education sessions in larger groups for all nursing staff and clerks were also offered without implementing the COMPASS in all clinics (Table 20.1). In addition, although their clinics had not yet been identified for implementation, some nurses began using the COMPASS after attending these sessions. Likewise, some nurses assigned to multiple clinics implemented it in other clinics as they gained experience. This organic uptake of the COMPASS occurred concurrently with the planned stepwise approach of moving from low-volume to high-volume clinics. These early adopter nursing and clerical staff became mentors to late adopters.

Barriers to Practice Change

As is common in planned-action activities (Ellis & Kiely, 2000; Howell & Pathak, 2011), barriers were encountered throughout the implementation (Table 20.1). Some barriers, such as staff turnover, competing demands of other initiatives, and time-limited funding for implementation facilitation and project management staff, were unable to be controlled. However, as other barriers were identified, Plan, Do, Study, Act (PDSA) cycles (Langley et al., 2009) were utilized for problem solving. PDSA cycles are rapid cycles in which small-scale changes are tested using four steps. At least four PDSA cycles were used in the first 15 months of implementation. For example, recognizing that the minimum data-set tool needed to be clinically relevant to care providers and understanding that there would be a challenge moving from paper and pencil only to entry into the electronic health record, the implementation team worked closely with frontline clinic staff to create at least three iterations of the COMPASS during the initial stepwise implementation (Figure 20.3). Work with the technology department and ongoing consultation with clinic staff ultimately resulted in the current version in use.

Providing Education for Screening for Distress

Education was a key component in the uptake of screening for distress (Table 20.1). Overall, 36 group education sessions were presented with approximately 350 staff. Education sessions were primarily didactic in nature with effort made to make them interactive and engaging by also using audience response systems, small- and large-group discussion, and role-play. The sessions built upon the current knowledge and skill set of clinicians—primarily nurses—recognizing that screening and responding to distress are within their scope of practice.

Three presentations were developed and continue to be used in screening-for-distress education (Table 20.1). The ultimate goal of screening is to respond to distress revealed through the tool. Thus, the second session, which focused on responding to distress, became a focal point for educational efforts so that the focus would move away from the logistics of the tool and toward opening patient conversations. Clinical aids were developed, such as the *ASK Conversation Guide,* that provided a structure for a conversation to respond to distress in a short appointment with a patient. The acronym ASK is a mnemonic device: *acknowledge* the person and the COMPASS tool even when the patient is not experiencing symptoms or problems; *support* the patient through showing empathy, uncovering feeling states, and narrowing in on the problem that concerns him or her most; and use your *knowledge* to provide patient education and make appropriate referrals. By using the *ASK*

Scenario 1:

A 52-year-old woman being treated for primary breast cancer marked "7" for anxiety on the COMPASS tool. The clinic nurse opened the conversation by asking what was troubling the woman most. After further assessment, the nurse referred the patient to the oncology social worker. The social worker met with the woman for three sessions over a period of 3 weeks, providing supportive counseling. Further assessment by the social worker indicated that the client was struggling with managing uncertainty and was feeling isolated and lonely. The social worker encouraged her to speak openly with her life partner about her fears, and they worked on other strategies to manage her anxiety. Four weeks later, at her next physician visit, she marked "2" for anxiety on the COMPASS tool.

Scenario 2:

A 63-year-old widower being seen for palliative treatment for an advanced lymphoma marked "feeling a burden to others" on the COMPASS tool. The nurse asked him gently, in the presence of his adult daughter, if he could say a bit more about this. The man went on to talk about how he had been feeling like such a burden to his daughter, who had to take time off work to take him to his appointments. He worried about the stress and strain on his daughter. The daughter tearfully explained to her father that she had no idea he felt this way. She told him that she often felt very helpless about his situation and that being able to take him to his appointments made her feel useful and that she liked their one-on-one time together. The nurse reported that this encounter took less than 4 minutes and was healing to all present. She indicated that she saw the COMPASS tool as the catalyst for opening this meaningful conversation.

Figure 20.4. Case Scenarios Using COMPASS Tool

Table 20.2.
Most Common Symptoms and Problems Captured by the COMPASS

ESAS Item	%	CPC Item	%
Tiredness	47.7	Sleep	22.2
Well-being	34.6	Fears/worries	21.8
Appetite	32.2	Constipation/diarrhea	18.7
Pain	27.6	Weight	17.4

Note: Percentage indicates the proportion of patients scoring 4 or higher on the ESAS item or selecting item on the CPC. *ESAS* = Edmonton Symptom Assessment Scale; *CPC* = Canadian Problem Checklist.

Conversation Guide in role-play, staff practiced the critical piece of acknowledging the patient and the COMPASS tool before moving on with the remainder of the appointment, even when the patient was not experiencing distress. Relevant clinical practice guidelines and algorithms developed by both Cancer Care Ontario (2012) and the Canadian Association of Psychosocial Oncology (Howell et al., 2010) were also presented to clinical staff.

Anecdotal and questionnaire feedback from patients indicated that if staff did not acknowledge completion of the tool directly with the patient, the patient was not inclined to complete it ("What's the point? Nobody pays any attention to it."). At all education sessions, the idea was emphasized that screening was not benign and that psychological harm (e.g., patients feeling uncared for) could result if the completed tool was not acknowledged. Example scenarios of responding to the COMPASS tool are found in Figure 20.4.

Evaluating the Implementation of Screening for Distress

Evaluation is critical to any planned-action practice implementation because it helps determine if the initiative is meeting its stated objectives. Approval for the evaluation protocol was received from the University of Manitoba Health Research Ethics Board. Overall, the evaluation plan included four domains (Table 20.1): Screening for Early Identification of Distress, Staff Education and Training, Teamwork and Collaboration, and Patient Engagement (Cancer Journey Action Group, 2010).

Screening for Early Identification of Distress

An aggregate report was created from the electronic health record, recording the total number of COMPASS screens completed in a given clinic over a given time period. Specific responses on completed COMPASS questionnaires were also collected from the electronic health record, offering frequency counts of the ESAS symptoms and problem checklist reported by patients (Table 20.2).

Systems are in development to mine data sorted by disease site groups to determine if the interventions and referrals captured on the electronic charting tool aligned with COMPASS scores and clinical practice algorithms. This data could provide valuable information for allocation and development of resources.

Staff Education and Training

Pre- and posteducation surveys were developed and completed by 95 staff members. The surveys assessed staff confidence levels when screening and responding to patient symptoms and concerns by using a 6-point scale. The results show that confidence among staff in identifying patient distress and in addressing emotional and psychosocial patient needs increased from the time of completing the preeducation survey to the posteducation survey. On average, surveyed staff agreed or strongly agreed that the content and format of the education session was beneficial. The surveys also showed that, on average, staff agreed that they would benefit from further training. These results were used to guide further learning opportunities.

Teamwork and Collaboration

Ten charts per month were randomly audited over 8 months from the early adopter implementation sites to determine if the COMPASS had been completed and if interventions occurred based on COMPASS scores. Eighty-two charts were audited that involved both the paper chart and the electronic health record. Results of the audits helped inform ongoing implementation strategies.

A 1-month postimplementation survey was developed and administered to all staff using the COMPASS at the clinic pilot sites to determine satisfaction with the implementation process and the perceived value of screening for distress in patient care. Among 26 completed surveys, 61% were completed by nurses, 23% by physicians or oncologists, and 16% by others including clerks, dietitians, and social work staff. Although most staff indicated that implementing the COMPASS resulted in staff perception of longer appointments, only 8% indicated that additional time was more than 10 minutes. A majority reported that the benefit of screening outweighed the time increase, with 73% indicating that the COMPASS provided a more comprehensive picture of how the patient is doing, 54% remarking that they obtained a more focused assessment of the patient's situation, and 39% reporting that patient symptoms were managed more effectively. Many staff indicated that they felt communication was better focused and that more timely referrals were made with more detailed assessments. Others mentioned wanting to see direct electronic entry by patients and noted that increased appointment time was a positive thing. Staff also asked for minor changes to the tool. Repeating this survey in the future will be important because it may be that some of the results reflect the beginning phase of practice change. Surveys at 6 months and 1 year after implementation are planned.

Patient Engagement/Patient Satisfaction

A survey was also developed to assess patients' satisfaction with their experience of completing the COMPASS and their perceptions of the added care they received for self-identified problems. Invitation letters were given to 250 patients at their physician visits, and 135 patients indicated that they would be willing to participate in the study. Sixty-eight participants completed and returned the survey.

Survey results revealed that most patient respondents found the tool easy to use and complete. Only 7% indicated that they were not able to discuss all of their symptoms and concerns. Sixty-two percent of respondents felt the tool improved the care they received. Many patients commented on better communication with health care providers, as exemplified by this patient's comment: "I think the questionnaire is a great way for patients to reflect on all parts of their well-being not just the affected areas per se. It helped me focus on getting better on all fronts and I was able to better communicate with the caregivers!" Another patient highlighted that completing the tool is not a benign event: "I personally found it very difficult to complete the problem checklist. Tried to answer honestly, but did not want to discuss any of my emotional concerns. . . . Chemo has required me to dig deep for the strength to cope with treatment and after-treatment symptoms. Could not afford to become emotionally vulnerable. I live alone and need to focus on the physical aspects of my 'journey.'"

Building Sustainability and Moving Forward

Sustaining practice change over time is always challenging. The following strategies are underway: (1) engaging key frontline and managerial staff for continued and shared interdisciplinary initiative ownership; (2) developing the capacity to provide specific feedback about the frequency of symptoms and concerns reported in a particular disease site group and/or clinic to appropriate nurses, oncologists, and other health care providers, including social workers; (3) ongoing evaluation of patient and staff satisfaction; and (4) ongoing education about responding to distress based on available clinical practice guidelines and evidence-based best practices.

Further strategies are needed for true sustainability and continuous quality improvement. These will involve developing and engineering systems to allow patients to input their COMPASS scores directly into the electronic health record via tablets or kiosks, having the ability to trend patient-reported data as a flowchart so that it is more easily accessible to clinic staff for quick reference, developing and/or adopting clinical practice guidelines for all symptoms, managing and reporting on data collected through the COMPASS charting tool, ensuring that every patient at the ambulatory care center is screened for distress at every physician visit, and comparing findings with other jurisdictions across Canada.

Pearls

- Emphasize that screening for (and responding to) distress will improve the patient's experience and promote whole-person rather than tumor-focused care.
- Use case examples from patient and staff experiences to highlight benefits.
- Engage staff early and have them be part of the implementation team. Find local champions.
- Implementation and evaluation are interrelated when working toward practice change.

Pitfalls

- Failing to acknowledge the patient's completion of the screening tool may increase patient distress.
- Failing to engage staff and decision makers early in the process in real and meaningful ways may result in an inability to implement change.
- Failing to engage all members of the team, including nurses, physicians, social workers, receptionists/clerks, and allied health workers, compromises ongoing sustainability.

Implementing, evaluating, and sustaining practice change takes commitment and tenacity and involves almost all departments and disciplines in a cancer treatment center. Using principles of knowledge translation and planned action to guide the process of practice change proved invaluable. Implementation focused on integrated interprofessional care and education that requires staff engagement across professions and from the front lines to management. Whatever one's discipline, improving the cancer patient's experience and providing person-centered care are priorities for care providers and a rallying point from which to work.

Although the logistics of using the screening tool in the clinic environment required concerted effort, especially at the beginning, it is important not to focus too much on this aspect of implementation. Rather, emphasize the purpose of the tool; that is, open the conversation with the patient for further assessment, which can lead to improved whole-person care. With shrinking resources in health care, increasing numbers of patients attending cancer centers, and more complex treatments, it is critical to address worries about increased workloads. It is also helpful to focus on working to the full scope of practice because opening the conversation with patients and responding to distress are what many health care providers find most meaningful in their work. Finally, it is imperative to understand that harm may result if patients are asked to complete a screening tool that is not acknowledged by staff, regardless of scores, and that results must be acted upon appropriately based on best-practice evidence.

ADDITIONAL RESOURCES

Guide to Implementing Screening for Distress: http://www.cancerview.ca/idc/groups/public/documents/webcontent/guide_implement_sfd.pdf (for more information contact cpaccinfo@cpacc.net)

IPODE, Screening for Distress: http://www.capo.ca/ipode-project/screening-for-distress/

Watanabe, S. M., Nekolaichuk, C., Beaumont, C., Johnson, L., Myers, J., & Strasser, F. (2011). A multicenter study comparing two numerical versions of the Edmonton Symptom Assessment System in palliative care patients. *Journal of Pain and Symptom Management, 41*(2), 456–468. doi:10.1016/j.jpainsymman.2010.04.020

REFERENCES

Bruera, E., Kuehn, N., Miller, M. J., Selmser, P., & Macmillan, K. (1991). The Edmonton Symptom Assessment System (ESAS): A simple method for the assessment of palliative care patients. *Journal of Palliative Care, 7*(2), 6–9.

Bultz, B. D. (2005). Distress—the sixth vital sign in cancer care: Implications for treating older adults undergoing chemotherapy. *Journal of Clinical Oncology, 23*(26), 6440–6441. doi:10.1200/JCO.2005.02.3259

Bultz, B. D., Groff, S. L., & Fitch, M. I. (2009). *Guide to implementing screening for distress, the 6th vital sign, Part A: Background, recommendations, and implementation.* Toronto, Ontario: Canadian Partnership Against Cancer. Retrieved from http://www.partnershipagainstcancer.ca/wp-content/uploads/2.4.0.1.4.5-Guide_CJAG.pdf

Buonocore, D. (2004). Leadership in action: Creating a change in practice. *AACN Clinical Issues, 15*(2), 170–181.

Cancer Care Ontario. (2012). Symptom management tools. Retrieved from http://www.cancercare.on.ca/toolbox/symptools/

Cancer Journey Action Group. (2010). *Guide to implementing screening for distress, the 6th vital sign, Part B: Quality improvement and evaluation.* Toronto, Ontario: Canadian Partnership Against Cancer.

Cancer Journey Portfolio. (2012). *Screening for distress, the 6th vital sign: A guide to implementing best practices in person-centered care.* Retrieved from http://www.cancerview.ca

Carlson, L. E., Waller, A., & Mitchell, A. J. (2012). Screening for distress and unmet needs in patients with cancer: Review and recommendations. *Journal of Clinical Oncology, 30*(11), 1160–1177. doi:10.1200/JCO.2011.39.5509

Ellis, J. H. M., & Kiely, J. A. (2000). Action inquiry strategies: Taking stock and moving forward. *Journal of Applied Management Studies, 9*(1), 83–94. doi:10.1080/713674360

Harvey, G., Loftus-Hills, A., Rycroft-Malone, J., Titchen, A., Kitson, A., McCormack, B., & Seers, K. (2002). Getting evidence into practice: The role and function of facilitation. *Journal of Advanced Nursing, 37*(6), 577–588.

Howell, D., Keller-Olaman, S., Oliver, T., Hack, T., Broadfield, L., Biggs, K., . . . Syme, A. (2010). *A Pan-Canadian practice guideline: Screening, assessment, and care of psychosocial distress (depression, anxiety) in adults with cancer.* Toronto, Ontario: Canadian Partnership Against Cancer (Cancer Journey Action Group) and the Canadian Association of Psychosocial Oncology.

Howell, D., & Pathak, E. (2011). *Guide to implementing screening for distress, the 6th vital sign, Part C: Improving patient outcomes through the implementation of clinical practice guidelines.* Toronto, Ontario: Canadian Partnership Against Cancer.

Langley, G. J., Moen, R., Nolan, K. M., Nolan, T. W., Norman, C. L., & Provost, L. P. (2009). *The improvement guide: A practical approach to enhancing organizational performance* (2nd ed.). San Francisco, CA: Jossey-Bass.

National Comprehensive Cancer Network. (2002). *Distress management: Practice guidelines in oncology, Version 1.2002.* Fort Washington, PA: Author.

Vodermaier, A., Linden, W., & Siu, C. (2009). Screening for emotional distress in cancer patients: A systematic review of assessment instruments. *Journal of the National Cancer Institute, 101*(21), 1464–1488. doi:10.1093/jnci/djp336

Zabora, J., BrintzenhofeSzoc, K., Curbow, B., Hooker, C., & Piantadosi, S. (2001). The prevalence of psychological distress by cancer site. *Psycho-Oncology, 10*(1), 19–28. doi:10.1002/1099-1611(200101/02)10:1<19::AID-PON501>3.0.CO;2-6

21

Mark E. Anderson, Margrett R. Myhre, Donna Suckow, and Angela McCabe

Screening and Assessment of Suicide Risk in Oncology

Key Concepts

- *The elevated risk of suicide in cancer patients and effectiveness of preventive interventions support including questions about this area on distress screening measures.*
- *Two questions have been used in distress screening to indicate presence of risk: One asks about the patient's concerns about thoughts of ending his or her life, and the second asks about the level of depression.*
- *It is important to distinguish between suicidal ideation and suicidal intent.*
- *Guidelines for assessment of at-risk patients in one cancer treatment program following screening are presented.*

The following is a composite case of an individual presenting with despair and thoughts about dying:

A 72-year-old man presented in the emergency department complaining of pain and shortness of breath. His medical history showed that he had been diagnosed with lung cancer 2 weeks previously. He disclosed to the medical team that "it would be much simpler if he could just die." A psychosocial professional was asked to see the patient to assess for possible suicidal ideation.

In talking with the patient, the psychosocial professional discovered that he was a widower. His wife had died a little over a year before after a long illness. He lived alone. His adult daughter and her family lived close by. He told them about his symptoms and they offered to help. He would rather not burden them as "they have their own lives to live." When asked about his statement to the medical team about dying, he said that he had watched friends waste away from cancer and that he couldn't stop thinking how much easier it would have been for them and their families if they had just been hit by a car or had a heart attack. The psychosocial professional explained that it is normal for cancer patients to think about death and encouraged him to talk with his family. Before discharge, he was presented with a community support option and an appointment was made for him to see a local psychiatrist. Some time during the next several days, he went into the garage attached to his home, shut all of the doors, and shot himself in the head.

The question for anyone involved in such a situation would be: "What went wrong?" The most important missteps were the failure to recognize suicide risk factors in a cancer patient and the failure to adequately explore the patient's thoughts about death and assess his intention to act on his thoughts. Had the professional done so, it might have been discovered that this patient had gone well beyond the exploration of death issues that usually occurs in cancer patients (Maderia, Albuquerque, Santos, Mendes, & Roque, 2011). The patient displayed several important risk factors for suicide in both cancer patients and the general population: a diagnosis of lung cancer, an older male confronting the first anniversary of the death of his spouse, the deaths of multiple other friends, and the perception of being burdensome to family and friends.

These issues may have been addressed more openly if the individual had not been a cancer patient. Joiner (2005, p. 18) suggests that clinicians often adopt an "alarmist" position in assessing suicide risk. This position tends to be reversed with cancer patients, however, as depression is viewed as a normal response to their diagnosis and prognosis (Filiberti & Ripamonti, 2002). The assessment guidelines discussed in this chapter are aimed to be neither "alarmist" nor "dismissive" (Joiner, 2005), but to help clinicians accurately gauge risk of self-harm and suicide and work toward a treatment plan that can meet their patients' needs. The guidelines are followed by the description of a distress screening program that inquires about a patient's thoughts of suicide, suggests guidelines for the follow-up assessment of the patient's risk, and provides an appropriate intervention.

Definition and Demographics

It is important to distinguish between suicidal ideation and suicidal intent. This distinction becomes especially challenging when a cancer diagnosis is involved. There is a consensus among mental health professionals that cancer patients may often bring up the subject of suicide as a way of broaching the subject of death (Maderia et al., 2011, p. 637; Johnson, Garlow, Brawley, & Master, 2011). One study included a follow-up question for those who had previously evidenced suicidal ideation: "Is there a chance you would do something to end your life?" Only 7% of patients reporting suicidal ideation reported suicidal intention. Those with suicidal ideation and intention were more likely to be male and have more physical disability, both risk factors for suicide in cancer patients (Leung et al., 2013). As the composite case demonstrates, it is crucial that we explore these thoughts and feelings to see whether the patient is trying to come to terms with his or her mortality or is actively contemplating suicide. This can be done by asking whether there is a plan in place and whether the patient has the means to execute the plan. This practice is called "exploring intent."

Each year, suicide claims the lives of approximately 30,000 Americans and 1 million persons worldwide (Joiner, 2005). As a general rule, women attempt suicide more often than men, but men are much more likely to complete suicide. Caucasians and Native Americans have higher suicide rates than African Americans and Hispanics. Fewer individuals over age 65 attempt suicide, but those who do are more likely to complete suicide (Joiner, 2005). Chronic diseases, pain, depression, older age, youth, living alone, and unemployment are risk factors associated with suicide in the general population (NIMH, 2009). Other factors associated with suicide in the general population are a history of self-harm or previous attempts; a diagnosed mental health problem, specifically mood disorders and personality disorders; addiction problems; family history of suicide; gender (higher for men); death of a friend or spouse; and few social supports (Anguiano, Mayer, Piven, & Rosenstein, 2012; Joiner, 2005; Robson, Scrutton, Wilkinson, & MacLeod, 2010). These risk factors can be extended to the cancer population. There are also many risks that are specific to cancer patients, which include a range of psychosocial and medical issues.

The incidence of suicide in the cancer patient population is approximately double that in the general population (Misono, Weiss, Fann, Redman, & Yueh, 2008; Robson et al., 2010). Because suicide prevention is a key targeted area in the provision of health and mental health care, it is vital that clinicians working with cancer patients be able to identify both general and disease-specific risk factors. Additional suicide risk factors associated with patients with cancer include depression; hopelessness; physical, psychological, and social impairments; a diagnosis of cancer; and specific cancer type. Disease factors that increase risk of suicide include prostate, lung, head, and neck cancers; advanced stage of disease and poor prognosis; confusion/delirium; inadequately controlled pain; presence of deficit symptoms (e.g., loss of mobility, loss of bowel and bladder control, amputation, sensory loss, inability to swallow and eat, exhaustion, and fatigue; Robson et al., 2010).

Cancer and Suicide

A 42-year-old single woman was seen in her oncologist's office following a diagnosis of ovarian cancer with metastases to the liver. Her medical team asked for a social work consult, reporting that she was crying and refusing to discuss treatment options. She told the social worker that she had been having abdominal pain for some time but "didn't think it was anything." A couple of weeks ago it became severe. She was afraid she might have appendicitis and drove herself to the emergency room. She couldn't believe she had cancer. Her medical record indicated a history of major depression with at least one suicide attempt and subsequent psychiatric hospitalization. She was not interested in discussing anything but the immediate diagnosis, asking the social worker, "Am I going to die?"

In this situation, the social worker responded honestly that she did not know if the patient was going to die but wanted to know what she could do to help her in the moment. She then proceeded to evaluate the woman, asking whom she relied on for support, if she was going home and if she would be alone, and if she had told anyone about her cancer diagnosis—a full assessment for safety and supports including existing therapeutic relationships, followed by plans to implement ongoing interventions.

The intervention plan in such a case would likely include weekly sessions, referral to art therapy or holistic therapies, and an assessment of whether a support group might be helpful. The social worker in this situation would do as full an assessment of safety (including suicide ideation and intention) as the patient permits; if the patient says she doesn't want to discuss these things, the social worker would try as much as possible to determine current risk status to guide next steps.

A growing body of research has documented the interaction of cancer and suicide. A 2010 Swedish cohort study found an increased risk of suicide among U.S. men diagnosed with prostate cancer. The study further revealed that the risk was highest during the first 3 months following diagnosis and that "being single, separated, divorced, or widowed was associated with a higher risk of suicide than being married" (Fang et al., 2010, pp. 309–310). In another study, the same authors found an increased risk of suicide across all cancer diagnoses. Specifically, "the risk of suicide was 2.6 times as high in the 52 weeks after a cancer diagnosis" (Fang et al., 2012, p. 1315). This risk was highest in the first weeks following diagnosis. They also found that the risk increased with the lethality or perceived lethality of the cancer involved (p. 1316). A 2011 study by Johnson et al. found that approximately one third of completed suicides occur within 1 month of diagnosis. Breitbart (1987) also identified pain, delirium, and exhaustion as factors increasing risk of suicide in cancer patients.

In summary, these studies suggest that the risk of suicide rises with the lethality of the cancer, is greater in the weeks following diagnosis, is exacerbated by side effects of disease and treatment, and is inversely related to the strength of the person's support system. In general, suicide risk increases with stress. Thus, cancer patients need to be monitored more closely during points of disease change and times of higher stress related to their disease and treatment or personal circumstances. The social work assessment also needs to take into account non-cancer-related risk factors, the most important of which are a history of mental health issues and past suicide attempts. It should be clear that the 42-year-old woman in the case described previously would need suicide assessment, psychiatric referral, close follow-up care, and development of a support system. The fact that she is newly diagnosed with metastatic disease and is visibly distraught, is single, and has a history of suicide attempts puts her at risk.

Areas of Stress for Cancer Patients and Related Interventions

It is rare to find an oncology social worker who has not worked with a person who has experienced suicidal ideation during the cancer journey. It is natural for people to think of death when faced with a cancer diagnosis. Sometimes patients feel so overwhelmed with treatment that suicide seems to be a reasonable option—for example, patients with head and neck cancers who are facing surgeries that cause major disfigurement. Many patients will find relief in talking about these feelings if they are given the opportunity. Thinking about suicide may provide hope for relief from physical or emotional pain or a way to control pain and discomfort if it becomes too great. Discussing distress enables patients to focus on realistic ways of obtaining comfort and control.

Joiner's interpersonal-psychological theory of suicidal behavior (2005) seems useful in targeting particular areas of stress for cancer patients. It identifies two emotions shared by persons contemplating suicide that are germane to the cancer patient's experience: a perceived sense of burdensomeness and thwarted belongingness. People are thought to commit suicide when they have the desire and the ability to commit suicide. The *desire* to commit suicide stems from a perceived sense of burdensomeness and thwarted belongingness.

Burdensomeness

It is common for oncology social workers to hear patients say they feel a profound sense of burdensomeness to their loved ones. Patients often make statements that others would be better off if they were dead. For example, patients might discuss feeling ineffective due to possible disability or limitations on mobility. Statements of helplessness and hopelessness can also be veiled statements of burdensomeness. Social workers may discover that the person is experiencing thoughts of suicide by asking the simple question, "Where do you find your hope?"

Interventions for helping patients cope with a sense of burdensomeness begin by allowing them to ventilate their feelings. A strengths-based approach that explores past coping strategies can be helpful in building a patient's level of hope for the future. The oncology social worker should help patients partialize and prioritize overwhelming feelings and tasks during the crisis situations that cancer patients frequently confront. Patients can be overcome with cumulative physical and psychological stresses that require help through understanding and problem solving. During these interventions, it is crucial that the oncology social worker allow the patient to vent feelings without attempting to take away the option of suicide. At this vulnerable time, suicide is often experienced as a way of ending emotional pain. Another helpful strategy is to explore activities that can help the person feel more effective, connected, and hopeful. Social workers' role is to explore alternative options for coping with profound emotional pain. To follow is an example of an intervention with a young man who was diagnosed with large B-cell lymphoma:

A 36-year-old patient went to his primary care physician for a regular checkup and by the end of the week, he had been diagnosed with lymphoma, hepatitis C, and HIV. Months later, after several rounds of chemotherapy and two surgeries, he began to feel like he had lost everything that had once made him feel effective. Always an independent person, he had raised himself since age 15. Now he had to rely completely on a family member for transportation, financial assistance, and, at times, activities of daily living. At one point, he had been a model. Now he saw himself as "ugly, bald, skinny. I don't even look human anymore."

Gentle probing by his social worker led this patient to share a lifetime of traumatic experiences. During one visit he revealed that over the past few weeks he had been having intrusive thoughts of suicide. He said that he felt like a burden on his family, had made a prior suicide attempt, and simply felt like life was not worth living anymore. While this discussion was being held, the patient began to draw on a piece of paper. When the social worker asked about his drawing, the patient began to smile and talk about his art. He stated that after his triple diagnosis, he had stopped drawing because he didn't see the purpose anymore. Ultimately, however, his art helped him cope with his suicidal thoughts because it made him feel like he was contributing and also led him to develop a legacy.

Thwarted Belonging

Throughout the cancer journey, a sense of belonging can begin to fade. Thwarted belonging can be seen when there is an absence of caring or meaningful connections with others. Some risk factors that may lead to a lowered sense of belonging are recent losses, such as death or divorce. Some common themes that can lead a person to feel isolated because of a cancer diagnosis are that loved ones' lives continue and frequent visits with loved ones may begin to diminish because of other responsibilities. Many loved ones have stated that they distanced themselves from the patient because they feared they would say the wrong thing. Cancer treatment may cause fatigue, regular nausea and vomiting, and physical pain that make it difficult, if not impossible, to engage in activities that the patient once enjoyed. This can seem overwhelming and very lonely at times. A social worker's role during this time is to be willing to listen to the person's despair. This may be the first time that the person has felt connected to someone in quite some time, which makes authenticity very important. A thorough assessment of the patient's support network and other resources is necessary. Some helpful questions are: "Who is the person you could call at 3:00 a.m. and you know he or she would be there?" Sometimes it seems as though there is absolutely no support for when a person is suicidal. Asking, "Who would find you?" may reveal people in their lives. Again, generally speaking, when a person is feeling suicidal, he or she is experiencing ambivalence about death. Many will feel a reduced sense of anxiety and loneliness after talking.

Providing access to supportive resources available to cancer patients is an effective intervention for thwarted feelings of belonging. Many patients are unaware of these resources because medical teams are focused on treatment rather than the patient's psychosocial needs. Social workers connect patients to resources such as support groups (in person, online, or via telephone) or communication with a person who has gone through a similar cancer diagnosis and treatment and/or is of a similar age. This sense of connectedness can become an effective coping strategy for patients experiencing suicidal ideation.

Example of a Follow-Up Assessment After a Patient Indicates Suicide Risk During a Psychosocial/Distress Screen

Given the commonality of thoughts of death when a person is diagnosed with cancer, his or her elevated suicide risk, and the possibility of preventive interventions, it is important to include items related to suicide on the distress screen measure used by the cancer program. For those who indicate greater severity, the screen is followed by an assessment process that allows the clinician to have a conversation with these patients to understand their level of intention, their current concerns, and their risk factors for suicide and then to problem solve around ways and means to better cope with their situation. To follow are one hospital's assessment guidelines to determine the risk of a patient's intention to act on these thoughts.

A community cancer program on the East Coast selected the City of Hope (COH) Support Screen described in Chapter 19 in this section as a model for its distress screening approach. The program's administrators partnered with the COH for consultation in November 2012 to implement the psychosocial screening program. Following the COH recommendations, they included two questions in their overall screening form to assess suicide risk. One asks about the patient's concerns about thoughts of ending his or her life. The second asks about the level of depression the patient is experiencing. The depression question was added because it was found that patients might talk about suicide without necessarily endorsing depression.

Questions used for screening for suicide risk and system responses:

How much of a problem is this for you?

1. *Thoughts of ending my own life now or in the future?* Yes/No
   An answer of "yes" indicates that it is a problem for them and triggers referrals to social work, nursing, and/or physician for further assessment.
2. *Feeling down or depressed?Level of severity and need for assistance with depression is rated from 1 to 5 or marked "prefer not to answer" or "do not know." If the patient indicates moderate to severe (i.e., 3–5) level of depression, he or she is asked to answer the following questions:*
   a) *Are you feeling hopeless or that life has little or no meaning for you?*
   b) *Has anyone in your family ever tried or committed suicide?*
   c) *Have you ever tried to take your own life?*
   d) *Are you seriously considering taking your own life now or in the future?*
   e) *Do you ever take actions quickly without giving them much thought?*

A response of "yes," "prefer not to answer," or "do not know" to any of these questions is an automatic trigger for a social work assessment.

Assessment Guidelines for the Oncology Social Worker

The following statements can be used to guide the social work assessment of patients' intentions to self-harm and their risks:

Understand the person and his or her view of his or her situation.

The social worker begins the interview by developing an understanding of who this person is in the medical, familial, and psychosocial contexts.

Clarify diagnosis of cancer and staging of disease.

a. Determine patient's understanding of diagnosis, treatment plan, and prognosis.
b. Evaluate symptoms and current management (e.g., pain, insomnia, nausea).

Determine if the patient is being followed by a psychiatrist or other mental health specialist.

If the patient is being followed by a psychiatrist or other mental health professional, ask if he or she would sign a release so that the social worker can collaborate with the professional around the patient's medical and psychiatric treatment. Is the patient taking any psychotropic medications?

Explore the patient's social context and support.

a. Is he or she single, married, divorced? Does he or she live alone?
b. Complete the following exercise: Draw a circle and ask who the patient would put in the circle. Identify each person by name and relationship (family, friends, colleagues, boss, pastor, neighbor, etc.). Ask if the patient would be willing to provide the social worker with the phone numbers of these individuals. If the patient is hesitant, ask for the number of at least one person. Ask who would be outside of the circle. Explore who these individuals are and nature of their relationships with the patient. If the patient identified one person, ask how that individual would feel about hearing the patient's concerns today. Ask, "Have you discussed these feelings with him or her before? How do you think he or she would feel/react to hearing that you are thinking about taking your life?"
c. If the patient has made a suicide attempt, inquire about what led to this, how he or she handled it, what stopped him or her, and who was helpful.
d. The social worker should ask, "Can I have permission to call this one person while you are here with me to share what is going on with you?" If the patient will not do this and the social worker assesses him or her to be at risk, the social worker is instructed to not let the person leave the clinic or office. The social worker should call a physician and nurse to assist with escorting the patient to the emergency department for observation until a member of the crisis team/psychiatrist can evaluate the patient.

Assess hopefulness and review the patient's responses on the Support Screen.

a. Do you have anything to look forward to?
b. What would help to make you feel differently today?
c. Review the questions on the Support Screen and this patient's individual responses.

Ask whether the patient has a plan to commit suicide.

Get a description and determine the level of intention to complete the plan.

Secure safety.

Following the assessment, the social worker secures a safe place for the patient to stay, perhaps with a nurse, secretary, or administrator. The social worker then contacts his or her supervisor to review this information, as well as to report the his or her intuitive assessment. If there are any doubts or concerns, the patient is escorted to the emergency department where one-on-one observation is arranged until a member of the crisis team/psychiatrist can evaluate the patient.

Approximately 6% of 4,775 patients in one study reported suicidal ideation, and only 10.8% of these individuals indicated suicide intention (Leung et al., 2013). Social workers at Saint Barnabas found, however, that many more patients indicate in clinical interviews that they have thoughts about suicide and struggle with these thoughts.

Referral Information From the Distress Screen

The physician, nurse, and social worker receive the following email as a request for assessment upon the patient's completion of the questionnaire:

Results of screening for your patient: Patient Smith

MD: Problems identified by your patient:

Required information on clinical trials

Side effects of treatment

RN: Problems identified by your patient:

Fatigue

MSW: Problems identified by your patient:

Requested information about courses and events

Feeling down or depressed

Feeling irritable or angry

Feeling unsupported by partner

Worry about the future

A social worker met with a patient and her husband. The patient stated that she had been feeling depressed and irritable for the past 2 to 3 days after her chemotherapy treatment. She reported that she had a history of depression, which began in 2005 with one related hospitalization. She was under psychiatric care at another facility. The patient indicated that she had been doing well emotionally before her breast cancer diagnosis and beginning chemotherapy. She noted, "I was even beginning to decrease my antidepressant medication." Since starting cancer treatment, she had been advised to stay on her current dose of antidepressants. The patient informed the social worker that her husband often lost his patience when she was depressed and irritable. The patient's husband agreed that he did and said, "I will try to be more patient." The social worker reviewed the support services available to them and encouraged the couple to schedule follow-up appointments to continue to discuss these issues and feelings as a couple, and if the patient preferred they could also meet individually, normalizing the increase in anxiety with the cancer diagnosis. Both the patient and husband declined at that time, saying, "We will call if the need arises." The social worker provided contact information and a calendar of events for programs and support services.

One month later, the patient called her cancer physician's office and told the secretary that she was feeling very depressed and anxious. Referral was made to the social worker, who conducted an initial telephone interview. The patient tearfully described anxiety related to her overall medical and social situation and shared that she had stopped taking her anxiety medicine and was not sure what dose to take of the antidepressant. She reported that she was not alone; her husband was with her. She did not want to come to the hospital but was seeing her psychiatrist the following week. The patient agreed to restart her anxiety medication. The social worker called the patient 2 days later and learned that she had restarted her anxiety medication but was still feeling anxious. The social worker offered to meet her in the emergency department, but the patient declined. The social worker encouraged the patient to call and update her psychiatrist.

The psychiatrist called the social worker 3 days later. He said he had offered to see the patient but that she had declined. The social worker followed up with the patient, who stated, "I am okay. I am here with my family. I will see my psychiatrist on my regularly scheduled appointment." One week later, the family reported that the patient had overdosed on pills and had been admitted to a psychiatric unit.

The social worker followed the patient throughout the remainder of her chemotherapy treatments. Once treatment ended and her symptoms lessened, the patient embraced the life that she knew, the life that she missed. The team and, of course, her family were grateful that she had not been successful in her suicide attempt.

The patient did not identify suicide intent or ideation on the Support Screen, but she did identify depression and worries about the future. The inability to acknowledge suicidal thoughts in the context of a previous hospitalization/suicide attempt can be seen as an additional risk factor.

Pearls

- Knowledge of general population risk factors and cancer-specific risk factors for suicide is essential for conducting effective assessment of suicide intention.
- The oncology social worker may be the first to "listen to the patient's story" about thoughts of suicide, provide some relief for the intolerable pain and isolation the patient is experiencing, and facilitate communication with the medical and psychiatric teams as indicated.

Pitfalls

- Clinicians may fear that inquiring about suicide will encourage the patient to act on those thoughts. There is no data to support this.
- Often the oncology social worker may be meeting with the patient for the first time while the patient is distressed and will have to manage interruptions and will have limited opportunities to develop rapport and conduct a thorough assessment.
- Interventions are time limited and crisis focused, and follow-up can be a challenge.

Though not always openly acknowledged, clinician anxiety and fear around the issue of suicide can be a practice barrier. One common clinical myth is that "asking the question plants the idea" and could leave a clinician open for legal action if suicide should occur. Once again, such a response is not supported by research. Suicidal individuals are already struggling with intolerable isolation and despair. Therefore, not assessing and not asking the question may leave suicidal individuals even more alone and vulnerable to their pain and misperceptions. Knowing the risk factors for suicide in cancer patients and the general population is critical to an effective assessment.

REFERENCES

Anguiano, L., Mayer, D. K., Piven, M. L., & Rosenstein, D. (2012). A literature review of suicide in cancer patients. *Cancer Nursing*, 35(4), 14–26.

Breitbart, W. (1987). Suicide in cancer patients. *Oncology*, *1*, 49–55.

Fang, F., Fall, K., Mittleman, M. A., Sparen, P., Ye, W., Adami, H., & Valdimarsdottir, U. (2012). Suicide and cardiovascular death after a cancer diagnosis. *New England Journal of Medicine*, *366*(14), 1310–1318.

Fang, F., Keating, N. L., Mucci, L. A., Adami, H., Stampfer, M. J., Valdimarsdottir, U., & Fall, K. (2010). Immediate risk of suicide and cardiovascular death after a prostate cancer diagnosis: Cohort study in the United States. *Journal of the National Cancer Institute*, *102*(5), 307–314. doi:10.1093/jnci/djp537

Filiberti, A., & Ripamonti, C. (2002). Suicide and suicidal thoughts in cancer patients. *Tumori*, *88*, 193–199.

Johnson, T. V., Garlow, S. J., Brawley, O. W., & Master, V. A. (2011). Peak window of suicides occurs within the first month of diagnosis: implications for clinical oncology. *Psycho-Oncology*, *21*(4), 351–356. doi:10.102/pon.1905

Joiner, T. (2005). *Why people die by suicide*. Cambridge, MA: Harvard University Press.

Leung, Y., Li, M., Devins, G., Zimmermann, C., Rydall, A., Lo, C., & Rodin, G. (2013). Routine screening for suicidal intention in patients with cancer. *Psycho-Oncology*, *10*, 3319.

Maderia, N., Albuquerque, E., Santos, S., Mendes, A., & Roque, M. (2011). Death ideation in cancer patients: Contributing factors. *Journal of Psychosocial Oncology*, *29*, 636–642. doi:10.1080/07347332.2011.615381

Misono, S., Weiss, N. S., Fann, J. R., Redman, M., & Yueh, B. (2008). Incidence of suicide in persons with cancer. *Journal of Clinical Oncology*, *26*(29), 4731–4738.

National Institute of Mental Health (NIMH). (2009). Suicide statistics 2009 resources page. Retrieved from http://www.nimh.nih.gov/health/publications/suicide-in-the-us-statistics-and-prevention/index.shtml

Robson, A., Scrutton, F., Wilkinson, L., & MacLeod, F. (2010). The risk of suicide in cancer patients: A review of the literature. *Psycho-Oncology*, *19*, 1250–1258.

22

Carole Mayer and Sheila Damore-Petingola

Using Telehealth to Respond to Distress in Rural and Remote Chemotherapy Clinics

Key Concepts

- *Funded as a quality improvement project, distress screening was implemented by two experienced social work researchers and administrators in 14 chemotherapy clinics affiliated with community hospitals in remote and/or rural Canadian communities.*
- *A knowledge translation strategy and principles of participatory action research were applied to ensure a collaborative, successful outcome.*
- *The development of clinical pathways and creation of easy resource access was required to sustain clinic screening efforts.*
- *The improvement model included Plan, Do, Study, Act cycles to solve challenges.*
- *Videoconferencing as part of telehealth technology emerged as an important and effective venue for providing access to education and professional support services to patients and families in rural and remote areas.*

This chapter describes a quality improvement initiative—a psychosocial distress screening program implemented by the authors, who are social work administrators, clinicians, and researchers—within 14 chemotherapy clinics in community hospitals affiliated with a tertiary cancer center in a rural Canadian region serving approximately 565,000 people across 400,000 square kilometers (Figure 22.1; North East Local Health Integration Network, Ontario Local Health Integration Network, 2014). A strong knowledge-translation strategy and principles of participatory action research were applied to facilitate collaboration to successfully implement distress screening in these clinics. Evaluative research methods included the collection of quantitative and qualitative data. The model of improvement that includes Plan, Do, Study, Act (PDSA; Langley et al., 2009) was also applied to address critical barriers to implementation.

Policy in Canada and the Province of Ontario

The concept to screen for psychosocial distress was endorsed in 2004 by the Council of the Canadian Strategy for Cancer Control, known today as the Canadian Partnership Against Cancer (CPAC), in recognition that very few patients were being referred for psychosocial or supportive care services (Bultz, 2004). To have it recognized as part of the cancer experience, in 2006, distress was added as the 6th vital sign following temperature, respiration, heart rate, blood pressure, and pain (Bultz & Carlson, 2006). In 2008, researchers, policymakers, and clinicians met to build consensus for a national strategy to implement screening for distress that would include the development and implementation of practice guidelines and standards to support clinical practice (CPAC, 2008). In 2008, a toolkit outlining recommendations to implement screening for distress as the 6th vital sign was released under the CPAC, Cancer Journey Action Group (2012).

The Ontario Cancer Symptom Management Collaborative, a program of Cancer Care Ontario (CCO), was established to expand symptom screening to all cancer patients in Ontario at all 14 regional cancer centers in the province, promoting

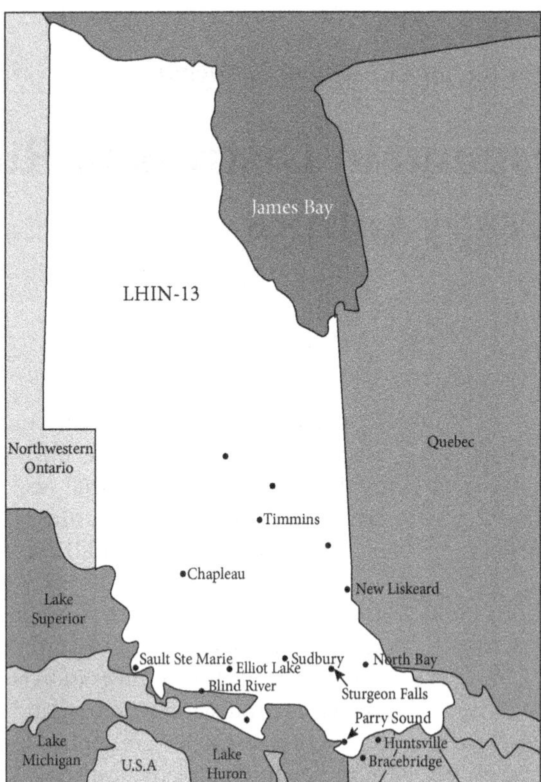

Figure 22.1. Map of Community Oncology Clinic Network and Northeast Local Health Integration Network

earlier identification, documentation, and communication of patients' symptoms. Electronic kiosks in each center allow patients to complete the Edmonton Symptom Assessment System (ESAS), which in turn allows data to be collected for the entire province, permitting quarterly tracking and public reporting of the performance indicator for each cancer center (Dudgeon et al., 2012). Unlike the CPAC, CCO does not require that the Canadian Problem Checklist (CPC) be incorporated into routine screening, and hence the screen is restricted to physical and emotional domains. Screening for distress is a standard of care that must be met by any Canadian health care organization providing cancer services that seeks accreditation (Accreditation Canada, 2008).

Methodological Framework to Implement Screening for Distress as a Quality Improvement Project

Description of Project

Since 2009, nine jurisdictions have been funded to implement screening for distress in Canada utilizing the minimal dataset of the ESAS and CPC (Bultz et al., 2011). Our jurisdiction was one of the early adopters, funded for 2 years to implement screening for distress at 14 chemotherapy clinics in community hospitals affiliated with one cancer center.

The project description answered the following questions: Who should we screen? (All patients receiving chemotherapy at a community chemotherapy clinic site.) When should we screen? (Once per cycle of chemotherapy, preferably before the patient receives chemotherapy.) How should we screen? (For the project, all screens were collected on paper and faxed to the cancer center for data to be entered in relevant databases; the practice today is that most clinics screen electronically.)

Screening Domains (Psychosocial, Practical, and Physical) and Tool Selection (Edmonton Symptom Assessment System and Canadian Problem Checklist)

Cancer patients are able to identify the severity of their symptom(s) on the ESAS, a 9-item visual analog scale (Bruera, Kuehn, Miller, Selmser, & Macmillan, 1991). Patients rate their pain, fatigue, nausea, depression, anxiety, drowsiness, appetite, overall feeling of well-being, and shortness of breath, with an optional 10th item to identify other problem(s). Each symptom is scored on a scale of 0 to 10 with 10 indicating the highest severity. The ESAS scale was originally validated with palliative care populations (Bruera et al., 1991) and has been found to be a reliable scale when used with other disease sites (Chang, Hwang, & Feuerman, 2000). Normal or tolerable distress reflects a score of 1 to 3; moderate distress reflects a score of 4 to 6, requiring further

Northeast Cancer Centre
Health Sciences North

Centre de cancérologie du Nord-Est
Horizon Santé-Nord

Nursing Outcome Sheet

COCN Site Location: Name of Community
Date completed: ____________________

1. Reviewed scores with patient ☐YES ☐NO	2. Compared scores with the Canadian Problem Checklist ☐YES ☐NO
3. Compared scores with previous scores ☐YES ☐NO	4. Screening identified a concern(s) related to cancer ☐YES ☐NO
5. Provided information/teaching ☐YES ☐NO	6. Provided support counselling ☐YES ☐NO
7. Monitored score over cycle of chemotherapy ☐YES ☐NO	8. Follow with patient by telephone ☐YES ☐NO

9. Consulted by phone or face to face:
   a. Pharmacist: ☐YES ☐NO *Date:
      - ☐ At COCN site
      - ☐ In Community
      - ☐ In Sudbury
   b. Family physician/hospitalist ☐YES ☐NO *Date:
   c. Traditional healer ☐YES ☐NO *Date:
   d. Nurse/Oncologist in Sudbury ☐YES ☐NO *Date:
   e. Other Health Care Professional ☐YES ☐NO *Date:
      - ☐ COCN Site Specify Discipline: ____________ *Date:
      - ☐ Cancer Centre/Sudbury Specify Discipline: ____________ *Date:
      - ☐ CCAC Specify Discipline: ____________ *Date:
      - ☐ Family Health Team: Specify Discipline: ____________ *Date:
      - ☐ Mental Health Team: Specify Discipline: ____________ *Date:
      - ☐ Emergency Dept.: Specify Discipline: ____________ *Date:
      - ☐ Other: Specify Discipline & Agency: ____________ *Date:

10. Referred to:
   a. Pharmacist: ☐YES ☐NO *Date:
      - ☐ At COCN site
      - ☐ In Community
      - ☐ In Sudbury
   b. Family physician/hospitalist ☐YES ☐NO *Date:
   c. Traditional healer ☐YES ☐NO *Date:
   d. Nurse/Oncologist in Sudbury ☐YES ☐NO *Date:
   e. Other Health Care Professional ☐YES ☐NO *Date:
      - ☐ COCN Site Specify Discipline: ____________ *Date:
      - ☐ Cancer Centre/Sudbury Specify Discipline: ____________ *Date:
      - ☐ CCAC Specify Discipline: ____________ *Date:
      - ☐ Family Health Team Specify Discipline: ____________ *Date:
      - ☐ Mental Health Program Specify Discipline: ____________ *Date:
      - ☐ Emergency Dept. Specify Discipline: ____________ *Date:
      - ☐ Other Specify Discipline: ____________ *Date:

Patient Accepted referral(s) ☐ YES ☐ NO If no, and you know why, explain below in comment section.

11. For patients scoring 4+ on any symptom for ESAS, were you able to address the distress to achieve a reduced score during this cycle of chemotherapy? ☐YES ☐NO ☐N/A	12. Did you re-administer the ESAS tool during this cycle of chemotherapy? ☐YES ☐NO ☐N/A

13. Screening identified a concern not related to cancer. ☐YES ☐NO
If yes, what was it? What did you do? Add in comment section.

* Date: if the intervention date is different than when you completed the form, please specify date.
Comments you wish add: ____________________

Please fax completed form to (705) 523-7357 Attention: Sheila Damore-Petingola
Please acknowledge the Supportive Care Program, Regional Cancer Program, Hôpital régional de Sudbury Regional Hospital if adapting for your own use. Not to be duplicated without permission - please contact cmayer@hrsrh.on.ca

Figure 22.2. The Nursing Outcome Form

assessment and possibly intervention; and severe distress reflects a score of 7 to 10, where immediate assessment and intervention are required (CPAC, Cancer Journey Action Group, 2012). All forms to be completed by patients (ESAS, CPC, and the Cultural Demographic Form) were provided in English and French. The CPC self-rating tool has six headings for cancer patients to identify their emotional, spiritual, practical, social/family, informational, and physical needs (CPAC, Cancer Journey Action Group, 2012). The CPC complements the ESAS tool to screen for the three required domains. Data for the project was collected from the ESAS, the CPC, the Cultural Demographic Form, and the Nursing Outcome Form (Figure 22.2).

Social Workers Have the Ethics, Knowledge, and Skill Set to Implement Distress Screening Programs

Given their understanding of the cancer disease trajectory, social workers—as patient and community health care advocates providing therapeutic interventions and as valued members of the interdisciplinary team—are equipped to implement screening-for-distress programs (Fobair, 2009; Zebrack, Burg, & Vaitones, 2012). Social work administrators also bring leadership skills, including vision for the organizational context, the ability to set direction while being cognizant of the political and economic climates, and application of professional values of holistic care, to their work (Mizrahi & Berger, 2001). Social workers in the field of psychosocial oncology have been pioneers in developing research programs (Christ, Siegel, & Weinstein, 1995), participating in research initiatives for developing therapeutic interventions, and contributing to the knowledge base of the field through publication of their research and clinical practices (Fobair, 2009).

A Framework for a Quality Improvement Initiative

From our experience of implementing the ESAS in the cancer center, we knew that a top-down management approach would be ineffective in implementing screening for distress at the community chemotherapy clinics. We used principles of participatory action research (PAR) to engage our stakeholders in the project. PAR frameworks build on empowering participants to engage in change (Ristock & Pennell, 1996), and the participants in this project were the nurses and their managers at each site. It was important to equalize the power imbalances within the implementation team to facilitate a collaborative process. Further, we knew that the clinical pathways required to sustain screening practices would need support by an interprofessional team, as opposed to an individual. The nurses, who were most impacted by this initiative, would require the necessary tools to support their clinical practice to screen, assess, and intervene when necessary.

Implementation Process

Engaging Chemotherapy Clinics Through Education

The project received endorsement from senior leadership before the 14 chemotherapy clinics were contacted to ensure support for the initiative. In May 2009, a forum was held for the chemotherapy clinics to collectively learn about screening for distress as the 6th vital sign. The current state of Canadian knowledge and experience in implementing screening for distress was presented by national leaders and attendees, who discussed how screening for distress could address the needs of remote and/or rural community patients, and key recommendations were gathered for implementation. Communities with an interest in implementing screening for distress were identified. The nurses providing the chemotherapy treatment in the clinics—skilled, experienced, and who practice according to evidence-based standards—were prepared to consider the implementation of tools and systematic processes that would improve patient-centered care and enhance their clinical practices. At the conclusion, all sites agreed to provide representation on the working committee that would meet monthly for the duration of the 2-year project. The commitment of the 12 clinics in attendance to implement screening for distress created momentum for the project. Two sites that were not in attendance at the workshop later committed to the project.

Role of the Working Committee

For this project, a working committee was established, terms of reference were developed, and members met monthly via teleconferencing beginning in October 2009. In addition to representation from each of the clinics, members of the working committee included representation from First Nations, Inuit, and Métis leaders; the director of rehabilitation services for the publicly funded home care program; clinical nurse educators; clinical leads and managers from the cancer center; a member from CPAC; a biostatistician; and the leader of and coordinator for the project. The authors cochaired the monthly working committee meetings, where implementation processes and challenges were addressed and input received.

As a result of the working committee's varied expertise and perspectives, a cultural identification tool was incorporated into the project's design. Given their experience and identification of the needs and issues that cancer patients experience in this region, members added the items of legal, child care, and awareness of traditional healing practices to the CPC. The working committee also provided the venue for (1) nurses to share experiences in implementing clinical practice change, (2) the introduction and review of newly launched symptom management guides to practice, and (3) guest presenters to provide information on new initiatives and resources. The project lead and project coordinator met weekly to track all activities of the project according to timelines set by the committee and to keep the project on budget.

The Role of Site Visits

Site visits were conducted over 8 months to educate the project leaders on how chemotherapy was delivered at each clinic. Importantly, they came to understand the multiple roles that chemotherapy nurses assume in community hospitals. Many nurses were assigned to work in various areas of the hospital with the expectation that they maintain competency in different fields (e.g., the chemotherapy clinic, the emergency department, obstetrics). Therefore, processes to implement screening for distress had to be simple, with the nurses being provided all the necessary tools to facilitate screening for distress. The site visits also permitted the nurses and nurse managers to describe how they envisioned the screening process and anticipated barriers. The project leaders were to problem solve these issues with them and support their vision of how the screening would occur.

At these site visits, community and hospital resources were reviewed in terms of their capacity to respond to identified patient needs. Their readiness to roll out screening for distress was determined and a date established.

Working With Champions

All 14 clinics implemented screening for distress between November 16, 2009, and June 1, 2010. In advance of each rollout date, a package of materials was prepared and sent to each clinic. The project coordinator met with each site on the rollout date by teleconference. The materials distributed included a laminated nurse's instruction sheet to be kept at the chemotherapy clinic workstation for reference and copies of all tools that were necessary to implement screening for distress. Completed screens and nursing outcome forms were faxed to the cancer center in Sudbury.

Responding to Findings From the Data

Data reports, specific to each of the 14 clinics, were prepared and provided to each clinic over the following year to track their progress. These reports detailed the number of screens completed for patients and the types of problems reported as compared to those reported by other clinics overall. These reports informed managers and clinicians about the reported needs of their patient population, and they could be used to plan staffing and develop programs to ensure patient-centered care at each site. For example, similar to the findings at the cancer center, tiredness was the symptom most identified on the ESAS for all clinics. As a result of these findings, an interdisciplinary psychoeducational patient session entitled Fighting Fatigue: What Can You Do about It? was developed for patients to attend in person or by videoconferencing through a telehealth network depending on their location.

We noticed that very few referrals were being made to other health care professionals for patients with high distress scores or when problems were identified on the CPC. Parallel to this finding were the concerns by clinic managers and nurses about the limited resources available to respond to patient needs. In response to this repeatedly expressed concern, a workshop was held for the clinic nurses in May 2010 to improve knowledge of supportive care resources in northeastern Ontario for cancer patients and their families. Included was an introduction to established national guidelines and algorithms in addressing distress symptoms. This provided the opportunity for clinic managers and nurses to understand the resources available and the referral processes for patients in northeastern Ontario. These included community resources offered through the provincial home care program and the services of the supportive care program of the cancer center, many of which are available using videoconferencing. Each of the six supportive care program disciplines (dietitian, social worker, neuropsychologist, physiotherapist, speech language pathologist, and pediatric interlink nurse) presented the types of concerns cancer patients experience and the range of professional services provided. This increased awareness of the scope of practice of various health care professionals and the supportive care services available for cancer patients and their family members living in remote and/or rural settings in northeastern Ontario. For many of the clinic managers and nurses, this was new and very welcomed information.

In an October 2011 workshop for clinic managers, chemotherapy nurses, working committee members, and stakeholders, the results of the project were shared and successes celebrated. At this meeting, (1) a review of the data for the 2-year project was provided, (2) processes and best practices in sustaining the screening process were shared, (3) how often to screen for distress in this patient population was discussed, (4) understanding of the application of evidence-based algorithms and guidelines to respond to distress scores in routine practice was increased, and (5) the resources available to cancer patients and families were reviewed.

Providing Tools to Know Where to Refer

In direct response to the clinic nurses' expressed need for better awareness and access to services for cancer patients, a *Directory of Outpatient Oncology Resources* was prepared for each clinic by an advanced social work student. This directory provided an easy-to-use reference list of services so that highly distressed patients could be engaged quickly in understanding the next steps in addressing their elevated scores. The directory identifies the services available (1) within the community hospital at the clinic, (2) within the community at large, and (3) at the cancer center in Sudbury. The resource directories were completed and provided to each clinic in July 2011 and continue to be updated. This reference strengthened the confidence of nurses in continuing the practice of screening for distress.

In addition to the *Directory of Outpatient Oncology Resources*, in July 2011, each clinic received a binder containing national and provincial evidence-based documents and other supporting documents on the ESAS scale and the CPC, as well as guides to managing such symptoms as anxiety, depression, fatigue, loss of appetite, mouth care, bowel care, pain, nausea and vomiting, dyspnea, and delirium. The binder also provides clinical practice guidelines on assessment and referral for the psychosocial health care needs of the adult cancer patient. This resource binder is dynamic, and when updated guides to practice are endorsed by the provincial agency and added to the binder, it is then sent to the clinics for interprofessional teams to reference. In-services are also offered on these clinical practice guidelines as part of the knowledge translation strategy.

Providing Patients With Access to Psychosocial Oncology Specialists

The supportive care program was gifted with videoconferencing technology as part of its telehealth program to further ensure that access to psychosocial oncology services and specialists is available for cancer patients and their families in northeastern Ontario. Telehealth is the use of various forms of telecommunication to deliver health care services such as clinical care, professional and patient consultations, and education from a distance (Stenlund, 2012). As part of telehealth, videoconferencing technology permits the use of video technology to transmit images, voice, and data between two or more locations in real time (Fortney et al., 2013). Each of the clinics has videoconferencing technology as part of a telehealth network, and as cancer patients return to their home communities, they may continue therapeutic intervention and monitoring with their specialists at the cancer center by utilizing this equipment. When possible, patients receive face-to-face services in their home community. In rural and isolated communities, however, where there may not be access to supportive care services, the distress screening project has raised awareness in chemotherapy clinics regarding services available for cancer patients and families through the telehealth network using videoconferencing.

How to Track Change in a Quality Improvement Project

A framework of Plan, Do, Study, Act—called the PDSA cycle—permits a trial of an intervention and implementation of the intervention, leading to a desirable change or outcome. More than one PDSA cycle may be required to track change. To *P*lan is to state the objective of the cycle, make a prediction, and develop a plan to carry out the cycle—who, what, where, and when. To *D*o is to carry out the test, document the problem(s), identify unexpected observations, and begin the data analysis. To *S*tudy is to complete the analysis of the data, compare with predictions, and summarize what was learned. To *A*ct is to determine what changes are to be made next and possibly plan for another cycle (Langley et al., 2009). The following example illustrates the use of a PDSA cycle in the quality improvement process of the project.

On an initial visit to a community chemotherapy clinic, administrators and nurses indicated that they agreed with the principle of distress screening but were not committed to implementing the program. The social work administrators found the clinic had limited psychosocial/supportive care services in place and the nurses were not certain of the services available in the community and how to refer patients to these services. They were not prepared to start screening patients for distress while not knowing where patients could access services if required. The PDSA cycle was used to track the desired change.

The goal was for the clinic to engage in screening patients for distress. Progress could be tracked based on the number of patients receiving chemotherapy and the number screened for distress. The required change was for the nurses to feel confident in their knowledge of clinical pathways and to refer those patients with high distress scores and identified problems to other services. An education workshop was developed in the community of the clinic. It was predicted that if nurses understood how cancer patients could access services to address symptoms of distress, the nurses would feel comfortable with screening. Members of the interdisciplinary team, administrators of the clinic, and members of the local home care program attended. The team identified the services available within their own hospital and where gaps existed. The nurses learned of the services available in the community and how they could refer patients to the publicly funded home care program. The project coordinator also spoke about the services available at the cancer center and how patients could access these services via telehealth using videoconferencing.

After the workshop was held, the nurses agreed to an implementation date. The project coordinator worked with them to establish processes and provide the necessary tools to screen for distress. After 1 month of implementing screening for distress, the screening rate for this clinic was 90.5%. The overall screening rate for the duration of the project was 82.3%, with a range of 71.6% to 91.7%. The PDSA cycle was helpful to develop a plan of action and to work toward a positive resolution.

Program Development and Telehealth for Rural and Remote Communities

Cancer-related fatigue in adults with cancer is the most commonly reported symptom (Barbera et al., 2013; Curt et al., 2000; Jacobsen et al., 1999; Watson & Mock, 2004). Patients receiving chemotherapy at the clinics consistently reported elevated ESAS scores for the symptoms *tired* (lack of energy) and *drowsy* (feeling sleepy). A 90-minute patient education workshop entitled Fighting Fatigue: What Can You Do about It? was developed by an interdisciplinary team in the supportive care program to increase patient knowledge and competency in the self-management of cancer-related fatigue in adults with cancer. This interactive workshop was designed for patients to fight cancer fatigue with nutrition, exercise, and cognitive strategies and is offered through telehealth using videoconferencing throughout northeastern Ontario. In addition to psychoeducation programs such as the fatigue workshop, telehealth technology is utilized for individual and group practice throughout the region. It affords the clinician the ability to observe patients versus the audio-only telephone. Such programs and interventions facilitate clinician confidence in sustaining screening for distress, because there are resources for community clinic patients to access.

Pearls

- To ensure the continuation of screening for distress in this population, the importance of continued knowledge translation exchange and communication between the social work project leaders and the clinics cannot be overstated.

- It was necessary to provide education about the roles of different health care professionals such as social workers, psychologists, physiotherapists, and others so nurses and other health care providers understood how these professionals can provide interventions to cancer patients to manage identified distress symptoms and problems.
- Nurses and managers required data specific to their sites to understand the needs of their patient population and to validate the progress made in screening for distress.
- Telehealth using videoconferencing has become an integral and effective method for providing supportive care and psychosocial services to patients living in rural and/or remote communities.
- It is important to remain current with the scientific evidence and latest trends when implementing a quality improvement project and to ensure that necessary changes are executed accordingly. In February 2013, CCO transitioned the regional cancer centers in Ontario from the ESAS to the ESAS-Revised (ESAS-r) (Watanabe, Nekolaichuck, & Beaumont, 2012) in screening patients for symptoms. Patients have identified their preference for the ESAS-r over the ESAS primarily because definitions are provided for certain items such as tiredness, drowsiness, depression, anxiety, and well-being (Watanabe et al., 2012). We are now screening with the new ESAS-r at our community oncology clinics.

Pitfalls

- Without external funding, this project would not have proceeded.
- Although community clinic nurses and other health care managers were highly committed to this change in practice, competing demands did limit their participation; for example, they were challenged with learning a new electronic workload system, at which time distress screening rates dropped.
- Although the problem checklist has not been implemented as a standard tool in the province, we continue to use it as part of screening for distress as recommended by the nurses and managers of the clinics who like the tool because it guides the discussion for further assessment. We continue to advocate for screening for three domains: physical, practical, and psychosocial.

Two social work administrators were successful in implementing screening for distress at 14 chemotherapy clinics affiliated with community hospitals where patients were not previously being screened, ensuring that patients from rural and remote areas received care consistent with the patient care provided at the tertiary cancer center.

Screening for distress has changed practice for health care professionals working at chemotherapy clinics in northeastern Ontario. The symptom management guides support the clinical practice of nurses to address symptoms such as depression, nausea, vomiting, and cancer-related fatigue. However, the chemotherapy setting does not always allow nurses and other managers to provide the depth of intervention required to address elevated distress scores. The importance of reinforcing the scope of practice of other health care professionals, especially mental health professionals; the services and resources they afford to cancer patients; and methods for referral to them cannot be overstated. Telehealth using videoconferencing will continue to be promoted and utilized in the provision of supportive care and psychosocial oncology services. This venue continues to provide important access to specialists in the supportive care program at the cancer center in Sudbury for cancer patients and their families living in rural and isolated communities.

REFERENCES

Accreditation Canada. (2008). Qmentum accreditation program. Service excellence sector and service-based standards. *Cancer Care and Oncology Services 7.9 Guidelines*. Retrieved from http://www.accreditation.ca

Barbera, L., Atzema, C., Sutradhar, R., Seow, H., Howell, D., Husain, A., . . . Dudgeon, D. (2013). Do patient-reported symptoms predict emergency department visits in cancer patients? A population-based analysis. *Annals of Emergency Medicine, 61*(4), 427–437.

Bruera, E., Kuehn, N., Miller, M. J., Selmser, P., & Macmillan, K. (1991). The Edmonton Symptom Assessment System (ESAS): A simple method of the assessment of palliative care patients. *Journal of Palliative Care, 7*(2), 6–9.

Bultz, B. D. (2004). Emotional care takes centre stage [Notes from the Co-editor in Chief]. *Oncology Exchange, 3*(3), 3.

Bultz, B. D., & Carlson, L. E. (2006). Emotional distress: The 6th vital sign—Future directions in cancer care. *Psycho-Oncology, 15*, 93–95. doi:10.1002/pon.1022

Bultz, B. D., Groff, S. L., Fitch, M., Blais, M. C., Howes, J., Levy, K., & Mayer, C. (2011). Implementing screening for distress, the 6th vital sign: A Canadian strategy for changing practice. *Psycho-Oncology, 20*, 463–469. doi:10.1002/pon.1932

Canadian Partnership Against Cancer (CPAC). (2008). *Screening for distress workshop-5th & 6th Vital Sign: Rebalance focus action group*. Calgary, Alberta: Author.

Canadian Partnership Against Cancer (CPAC), Cancer Journey Action Group. (2012). *Screening for distress, the 6th vital sign: A guide to implementing best practices in person-centered care*. Retrieved from http://www.cancerview.ca/idc/groups/public/documents/webcontent/guide_implement_sfd.pdf

Chang, V. T., Hwang, S. S., & Feuerman, M. (2000). Validation of the Edmonton Symptom Assessment Scale. *Cancer, 88*(9), 2164–2171.

Christ, G. H., Siegel, K., & Weinstein, L. (1995). Developing a research unit within a hospital social work department. *Health and Social Work*, *20*(1), 60–69.

Curt, G. A., Breitbart, W., Cella, D., Groopman, J. E., Horning, S. J., Itri, L. M., . . . Vogelzang, N. J. (2000). Impact of cancer-related fatigue on the lives of patients: New findings from the Fatigue Coalition. *The Oncologist*, *5*, 353–360. doi:10.1634/theoncologist.5-5-353

Dudgeon, D., King, S., Howell, D., Green, E., Gilbert, J., Hughes, E., . . . Sawka, C. (2012). Cancer Care Ontario's experience with implementation of routine physical and psychological symptom distress screening. *Psycho-Oncology*, *21*(4), 357–364. doi:10.1002/pon.1918

Fobair, P. (2009). Historical threads in the development of oncology social work. *Journal of Psychosocial Oncology*, *27*(2), 155–215. doi:10.1080/07347330902775301

Fortney, J. C., Pyne, J. M., Mouden, S. B., Mittal, D., Hudson, T. J., Schroeder, G. W., . . . Rost, K. M. (2013). Practice-based versus telemedicine-based collaborative care for depression in rural federally qualified health centers: A pragmatic randomized comparative effectiveness trial. *American Journal of Psychiatry*, *170*, 414–425.

Jacobsen, P. B., Hann, D. M., Azzarello, L. M., Horton, J., Balducci, L., & Lyman, G. H. (1999). Fatigue in women receiving adjuvant chemotherapy for breast cancer: Characteristics, course, and correlates. *Journal of Pain and Symptom Management*, *18*(4), 233–242.

Langley, G. J., Moen, R. D., Nolan, K. M., Nolan, T. W., Norman, C. L., & Provost, L. P. (2009). *The improvement guide: A practical approach to enhancing organizational performance* (2nd ed.). San Francisco, CA: Jossey-Bass.

Mizrahi, T., & Berger, C. S. (2001). Effect of a changing health care environment on social work leaders: Obstacles and opportunities in hospital and social work. *Social Work*, *46*(2), 170–182.

North East Local Health Integration Network, Ontario Local Health Integration Network. (2014). *About our LHIN*. Retrieved from http://www.nelhin.on.ca/aboutus.aspx

Ristock, J. L., & Pennell, J. (1996). *Community research as empowerment: Feminist links, postmodern interruptions*. Toronto, Ontario: Oxford University Press.

Stenlund, D. (2012). Videoconferencing and dietitian services in rural Ontario communities. *Canadian Journal of Dietetic Practice and Research*, *73*, 176–180.

Watanabe, S. M., Nekolaichuk, C. L., & Beaumont, C. (2012). The Edmonton Symptom Assessment System, a proposed tool for distress screening in cancer patients: Development and refinement. *Psycho-Oncology*, *21*, 977–985. doi:10.1002/pon.1996

Watson, T., & Mock, V. (2004). Exercise as an intervention for cancer-related fatigue. *Physical Therapy*, *84*(8), 736–743.

Zebrack, B., Burg, M. A., & Vaitones, V. (2012). Distress screening: An opportunity for enhancing quality cancer care and promoting the oncology social work profession. *Journal of Psychosocial Oncology*, *30*, 615–624. doi:10.1080/07.2012.721485

23

Lynne E. Padgett, Carly Parry, and Stephen Taplin

Next Steps for Psychosocial Screening in Oncology

Key Concepts

- *The multidimensional construct of distress emphasizes inclusiveness of conditions and nonstigmatizing language.*
- *The term* distress screening *is not concordant with the use of the term screening in the medical literature.*
- *Conceptualizing distress management as a process of psychosocial care affects the choice of measures used in distress detection and assessment.*
- *Consensus on appropriate measures to detect and assess distress, determine optimal implementation approaches, and evaluate these processes is an important research priority.*

The past two decades have witnessed increased recognition of the psychosocial sequelae of cancer as evidenced by recommendations offered by the National Comprehensive Cancer Network (NCCN) and in the Institute of Medicine (IOM) report *Cancer Care for the Whole Patient* (Adler & Page, 2008; Holland et al., 2010). IOM and NCCN recommendations for psychosocial care delivery have been augmented by practice guidelines from the American Society of Clinical Oncology's Quality Oncology Practice Initiative (QOPI) and the 2012 American College of Surgeons' Commission on Cancer standards (ACOS COC, 2012; Siegel, Clauser, & Lynn, 2009). The ACOS COC standards call for incorporation of distress screening into oncology care and referral for psychosocial care at a minimum of one critical point in the survivorship continuum (e.g., time of diagnosis, end of treatment).

The implementation of distress screening into practice has been inconsistent and hampered by difficulties in definition, lack of measurement consensus, and usability and acceptability barriers (Bultz & Johansen, 2011; Loscalzo, Bultz, & Jacobsen, 2010; Parry, Padgett, & Zebrack, 2012; Rohan, 2012). Based on these challenges, there are several relevant issues to consider: whether distress screening meets the criteria for screening as defined in medical practice (U.S. Preventive Services Task Force [USPSTF], 2008), whether distress "detection" might constitute more precise terminology, and whether distress management might be better conceptualized as a process of psychosocial care within medical practice, composed of detection, assessment, and management. The purpose of this chapter is to address these issues, beginning by exploring some of the challenges associated with the current conceptualization of distress screening.

Distress and Distress Screening

Distress: Construct and Complications

Distress was selected as a target condition for psychosocial care assessment and delivery because of the multidimensionality, inclusiveness, and nonstigmatizing nature of the construct. The construct includes clinical conditions, such as anxiety and depression, as well as nonpathological emotional distress and indicators of financial or social adjustment. As it is currently conceptualized, distress can be understood as the result of *multiple* conditions, creating a challenging scenario for its assessment and management. This challenge is reflected in difficulties selecting measures and implementing processes for the detection, assessment, and treatment of distress. The complications multiply as we link the concept of distress with the process of screening.

The Meaning of Screening: Medical Conceptualization of Screening

The phrase *distress screening* was selected to be concordant with definitions of other types of screening (e.g., pain), thereby promoting the acceptability and integration of psychosocial care within the medical context (Holland et al., 2013). Subsequently, distress screening became integrated into accreditation standards and has been widely promulgated. However, the pairing of distress with screening terminology creates a problem—"distress screening" is not concordant with the medical concept of "screening." We suggest that this discord creates confusion and impedes implementation and elaborate on this later.

Screening has a long tradition in the practice of medicine and has been used since the 1940s (Taplin, Dash, Zeller, & Zapka, 2006). The USPSTF currently recommends screening average-risk people for breast, cervical, and colon cancer. The USPSTF states that conditions must meet three criteria to be eligible for screening: (1) the condition is deemed important, (2) there is a presymptomatic state to the condition, and (3) treatment in the presymptomatic state has advantages over treatment once the condition has become symptomatic (USPSTF, 2008).

Recommendations for which cancers merit screening and at what age to commence screening have been a source of controversy in the medical community for over 30 years. Screening debates have educated the medical community and reinforced the principle that screening is a specific and evidence-based process that is not to be recommended lightly. Any recommendation to undertake screening in medical practice (whether the proposed screening is medical or psychosocial in nature) will be understood by medical practitioners within the historical context and rubric of the definitions and debates presented earlier.

Distress and Screening: An Uneasy Marriage

The construct of distress does not meet the USPSTF criterion that screening is beneficial. As noted earlier, "distress" includes multiple conditions, each of which may have separate presymptomatic states and warrant different interventions or no intervention at all. The presence of multiple conditions and presymptomatic states underlying distress creates a complex scenario for determining whether the process of screening improves outcomes. That poses challenges to the marriage of the construct of distress and the process of screening.

Specifically, it is unclear whether distress is the target condition or a presymptomatic state for another condition, such as depression or anxiety, and whether treatment of distress (vs. treatment of anxiety or depression) offers benefits (Thombs & Coyne, 2013). The conceptualization of distress as a nonstigmatizing descriptor of a range of psychological responses that can include both "normal" emotional distress and clinical diagnoses such as depression and anxiety disorders argues against conceptualizing distress as a presymptomatic state of a more serious disorder. If elevated distress can be expected without the presence of depression or anxiety (because it is a precursor to such conditions or because the observed distress may reasonably be expected to diminish on its own over time), what are the implications for intervention? If some distress resolves without intervention, does it make sense to intervene for distress alone, or does it make more sense to intervene for subsequent depression or anxiety? The lack of clarity around these issues makes it questionable to use the term *screening* to apply to the process of detecting and managing distress and related conditions.

Distress Detection

Because it can be argued that distress does not meet two of the three criteria for screening, distress *detection* may be a more accurate term than distress *screening* to use in this context. We define distress detection as the identification of whether the condition's presence exists and, as such, will use the term *distress detection* throughout the remainder of the chapter for that reason.

Although a term such as *distress detection* avoids confusion with accepted medical interpretations of the term *screening*, it does not address measurement and intervention difficulties associated with the complexity of the construct of distress. It may be worth disaggregating and identifying those conditions for which identification and treatment have proven effective to better assess and address the multiple symptoms and conditions under the distress umbrella. Furthermore, it is important to remember that distress detection, by any name, is not the end point but the starting point for a process of psychosocial care delivery that includes detection, assessment, intervention, and follow-up.

Distress Management as a Process of Care

As noted in the introduction to this chapter, distress screening was intended to identify patients with high levels of psychosocial morbidity for subsequent in-depth assessment and referral to appropriate services (Adler & Page, 2008; Holland, Greenberg, & Hughes, 2006; Holland et al.,

2010). Thus, detection of distress was not envisioned as a stand-alone activity but as the first of several components in a process of psychosocial care delivery. This process encompasses distress detection, assessment, intervention, and ongoing surveillance and management across the cancer continuum (Parry et al., 2012). The assessment process is used to identify the specific condition that is causing the distress and determine whether this condition can be treated. Distress detection and management involves coordinating the care that is necessary to establish the underlying diagnosis and arrange the treatment. As such, it is a process best shared across the provider team and may involve a social worker, primary care physician, oncologist, psychologist or psychiatrist, and their respective staffs. The process is therefore best conceived as occurring within and between teams of providers in diverse settings. Distress management could also intersect with models of oncology care delivery (e.g., shared care, the patient-centered medical home) and benefit from strategies such as patient navigation and survivorship care planning. As the field of psychosocial care delivery moves ahead, it will be important to consider how we can thoughtfully and meaningfully integrate psychosocial care delivery into these models and platforms for care delivery.

Measurement: Challenges and Implications Within the Process Paradigm

Given the breadth of the construct of distress and the lack of clarity about the meaning and practice implications of "elevated distress," it should come as no surprise that measurement challenges are endemic and present difficulties for evaluating distress in both research and clinical settings. Measurement challenges fall into two categories: difficulty determining appropriate measurement characteristics for the detection *and* assessment of distress and difficulty addressing the differing priorities, approaches, and values of researchers and clinicians who use distress measures.

Based on the results of the initial distress detection process, further assessment might utilize diagnostic screeners (e.g., Patient Health Questionnaire-9 [PHQ-9] for depression or clinical interview) tailored to the patient's report and/or a detailed side effects profile or interview during the medical visit (e.g., Functional Assessment of Cancer Therapy for Breast Cancer [FACT-B] or addressing the issue during the visit). After detection and assessment have been completed, oncology staff could employ direct intervention and document detection and assessment activities before recommending follow-up actions.

The working assumption is that detection and assessment are linked to accurate identification of clinical disorders with empirically validated treatments. Thus, it may be helpful to focus assessment on psychiatric diagnoses such as depression and anxiety. In addition to determining clinical diagnoses, the distress detection and assessment process should seek to understand patients' mental health histories (including prior diagnoses, treatments, medications, and therapies) and elicit patient reports of unmet needs, including treatment side effects. Findings indicate that cancer patients often cite a mixture of anxiety, worry about loved ones, concerns about recurrence, and fatigue as unmet needs during and after treatment, illustrating the importance of detection and assessment (Armes et al., 2009). Both researchers and clinicians would benefit from understanding the psychometric properties and pragmatic strengths and weaknesses of existing instruments to choose appropriate measures to evaluate the process of psychosocial care (from detection to assessment to management). Several careful reviews of the psychometric properties and clinical relevance/usability of extant distress measures are available, including preceding chapters in this handbook (Carlson, Walker & Mitchell, 2012; Rohan, 2012; Vodermaier, Linden, & Siu 2009; Chapters 17 and 18) and the National Cancer Institute's (NCI's) Grid-Enabled Measures Distress Measurement initiative, which seeks to promote standardized measurement in distress (NCI, n.d.). We address how measures may be used in concert with one another across the distress management continuum in the measurement discussion that follows.

The implications for measurement change when distress detection is considered within the context of a broader process of psychosocial care delivery (encompassing detection, assessment, intervention, monitoring, and follow-up). Required measures include instruments for detecting distress and standard clinical assessment instruments, such as the Hospital Anxiety and Depression Scale (HADS), Brief Symptom Inventory-18, or PHQ-9 for anxiety and depression. Such instruments can be used in initial interviews and follow-up assessments. Moreover, instrument selection criteria may change when the focus shifts from distress detection to distress management. Brief screening instruments are preferred for the detection of distress in clinical settings (due to ease of administration and scoring). A longer, more specific and psychometrically rigorous instrument will ultimately generate more useful information and be judged as more salient to practice needs when the detection and assessment process begins. For example, a practice may use the Distress Thermometer and problem list (1 item and checklist, less than 2 minutes to complete) for its brevity and then follow up with the PHQ-9 for depression (9 items, less than 5 minutes) and then an assessment (Holland et al., 2010; Kroenke, Spitzer, & Williams, 2001). Another setting may elect to use a more comprehensive instrument, such as the Psycho-Oncology Screening Tool (POST; 33 items, less than 5 minutes), that incorporates detection and assessment (Kilbourn et al., 2011).

Some suggest that research and clinical practice are in conflict because research requires longer, more detailed surveys and documentation. This may not be the case for distress detection. In fact, the evaluation of cancer patients with distress must be done carefully to make the appropriate diagnosis and choose the best intervention. Depression differs from anxiety, as well as from concern about insurance coverage and financial challenges; therefore, treatment will differ in each of these scenarios. The field of distress detection is growing. We suggest that distress detection will become more useful as a concept in practice if we move away from thinking of it as a test and move toward understanding it as a process fundamental to easing the burden of cancer.

Pearls

- Use of the term *screening* to describe the process of distress management can lead to confusion between medical and psychosocial providers.
- Distress detection is the identification of the presence of psychosocial distress and more precisely describes the activity than the term *screening.*
- The psychosocial process of care is composed of detection, assessment, intervention, and follow-up.

Pitfalls

- Co-opting the language of medical screening creates a lack of clarity between psychosocial and medical practitioners because their definitions of terms often differs.

The focus on whole-patient care and the imminent Commission on Cancer deadline for the implementation of distress screening highlight the need for evidence-based approaches to the detection and management of psychosocial morbidity among cancer survivors.

Research is needed to establish consensus on appropriate instrumentation to detect psychosocial morbidity, determine optimal approaches to implementing and integrating the psychosocial care process into standard oncology care, evaluate processes that will support the delivery of integrated psychosocial care across the survivorship continuum, and determine whether distress management that is executed in accordance with recommended guidelines will result in higher quality care and improved psychosocial outcomes (Parry et al., 2012). Prospective studies are also needed to evaluate the efficacy of models and processes of psychosocial care in a variety of delivery settings.

A growing literature on models and processes of care offers guidance for care delivery for cancer survivors (Howell et al., 2012; Taplin, Clauser, Rodgers, Breslau, & Rayson, 2010; Taplin & Rodgers, 2010). The literature has not yet linked the processes of medical and psychosocial care delivery, nor has it provided an evidence base to guide best practices in psychosocial care delivery. There are still questions as to what constellation of providers is best equipped and prepared to provide and coordinate psychosocial care across the survivorship continuum. Oncology social workers function as facilitators, communicators, and care coordinators within health care systems. As such, they stand primed to make important contributions to the coordination of psychosocial care. Distress detection and management offer an opportunity for social workers to move beyond the view of distress detection as a Commission on Cancer directive. They should serve as leaders in the conceptualization, evaluation, implementation, and integration of innovative new models of care delivery for cancer survivors.

REFERENCES

American College of Oncology Surgeons' Commission on Cancer (ACOS COC). (2012). *Cancer program standards 2012: Ensuring patient-centered care* (pp. 76–77). Retrieved from https://www.facs.org/~/media/files/quality%20programs/cancer/coc/programstandards2012.ashx

Adler, N., & Page, A. (2008). National Institute of Medicine Committee on psychosocial services to cancer patients/families in a community setting. In *Cancer care for the whole patient: Meeting psychosocial health needs.* Washington, DC: National Academies Press.

Armes, J., Crowe, M., Colbourne, L., Morgan, H., Murrells, T., Oakley, C., . . . Richardson, A. (2009). Patients' supportive care needs beyond the end of cancer treatment: A prospective, longitudinal survey. *Journal of Clinical Oncology, 27*(36), 6172–6179.

Bultz, B. D., & Johansen, C. (2011). Screening for distress, the 6th vital sign: Where are we, and where are we going? *Psycho-Oncology, 20*(6), 569–571.

Carlson, L. E., Walker, A., & Mitchell, A. J. (2012) Screening for distress and unmet needs in patients with cancer: Review and recommendations. *Journal of Clinical Oncology, 30*(11), 1160–1177.

Holland, J. C., Greenberg, D. B., & Hughes, M. K. (Eds.). (2006). *Quick reference for oncology clinicians: The psychiatric and psychological dimensions of cancer symptom management.* Charlottesville, VA: IPOS Press.

Holland, J. C., Andersen, B., Breitbart, W. S., Buchman, L. O., Compas, B., DeShields, T. L., . . . Freedman-Cass, D. A. (2013). Distress management: Clinical practice guidelines in oncology. *Journal of the National Comprehensive Cancer Network, 13*(11), 190–209.

Holland, J. C., Andersen, B., Brietbart, W. S., Compas, B., Dudley, M. M., Fleishman, S., . . . Zevon, M. A. (2010). Distress management. *Journal of the National Comprehensive Cancer Network, 8*, 448–485.

Howell, D., Hack, T. F., Oliver, T. K., Chulak, T., Mayo, S., Aubin, M., & Sinclair, S. (2012). Models of care for post-treatment follow-up of adult cancer survivors: A systematic review and quality appraisal of the evidence. *Journal of Cancer Survivorship, 6*(4), 359–371.

Kilbourn, K. M., Bargai, N., Durning, P. E., Deroche, K., Madore, S., & Zabora, J. (2011). Validity of the

Psycho-Oncology Screening Tool (POST). *Journal of Psychosocial Oncology*, *29*(5), 475–498.

Kroenke, K., Spitzer, R. L., & Williams, J. B. (2001). The PHQ-9: Validity of a brief depression severity measure. *Journal of General Internal Medicine*, *16*(9), 606–613.

Loscalzo, M. J., Bultz, B. D., & Jacobsen, P. B. (2010). Building psychosocial program: A roadmap to excellence. In J. Holland, W. Breitbart, P. Jacobsen, M. Lederberg, M. Loscalzo, & R. McCorkle (Eds.), *Psycho-oncology*. New York, NY: Oxford University Press.

National Cancer Institute (NCI). (n.d.). Distress Measurement Initiative (GEM-DM) (NCI). Retrieved from http://www.gem-beta.org/Public/wsoverview.aspx?wid=15&cat=8

Parry, C., Padgett, L., & Zebrack, B. (2012). What now? Toward an integrated research and practice agenda in distress screening. *Journal of Psychosocial Oncology*, *30*(6), 715–727.

Rohan, E. A. (2012). Removing the stress from selecting instruments: Arming social workers to take leadership in routine distress screening implementation. *Journal of Psychosocial Oncology*, *30*(6), 667–678.

Siegel, R., Clauser, S., & Lynn, J. (2009). National collaborative to improve oncology practice: The National Cancer Institute Community Cancer Centers Program Quality Oncology Practice Initiative experience. *Journal of Oncology Practice*, *5*(6), 276–281.

Taplin, S. H., & Rodgers, A. B. (2010). Toward improving the quality of cancer care: Addressing the interfaces of primary and oncology-related subspecialty care. *Journal of the National Cancer Institute Monograph*, *40*, 3–10.

Taplin, S., Clauser, S., Rodgers, A., Breslau, E., & Rayson, D. (2010). Interfaces across the cancer continuum offer opportunities to improve the process of care. *Journal of the National Cancer Institute Monographs*, *40*, 104–110.

Taplin, S., Dash, S., Zeller, P., & Zapka, J. (2006). Screening for cancer. In A. E. Chang, D. F. Hayes, H. I. Pass, R. M. Stone, P. A. Ganze, T. J. Kinsella, . . . V. J. Strecher (Eds.), *Oncology: An evidence-based approach*. New York, NY: Springer Science + Business Media.

Thombs, B. D., & Coyne, J. C. (2013). Moving forward by moving back: Re-assessing guidelines for cancer distress screening. *Journal of Psychosomatic Research*, *75*(1), 20–22.

U.S. Preventive Services Task Force. (2008). Procedure manual. AHRQ Publication No. 08-05118-EF. Retrieved from http://www.uspreventiveservicestaskforce.org/uspstf08/methods/procmanual.htm

Vodermaier, A., Linden, W., & Siu, C. (2009). Screening for emotional distress in cancer patients: A systematic review of assessment instruments. *Journal of the National Cancer Institute*, *101*(21), 1464–1488.

V

Social Work Research: Challenges and Opportunities

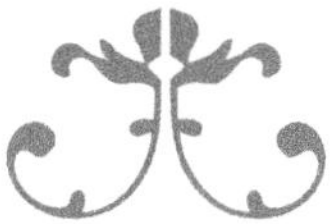

Karen Kayser

Research conducted by social workers can play a critical role in improving the quality of psychosocial services in oncology. Social work research aims to develop innovative programs and treatment models and to assess the effectiveness of programs and interventions. Furthermore, a major tenet of the social work profession is to ensure that evidence-informed interventions are accessible to all survivors and caregivers. Despite the tremendous efforts in developing this empirical knowledge base, many of our practices in psychosocial care are moderately supported by empirical evidence. One remedy for this problem is bringing together oncology social work researchers with the practitioners who are working directly with the myriad issues (financial, social, emotional, spiritual, and physical) that can accompany a cancer diagnosis. This section of the *Handbook* attempts to bridge the divide between research and practice by presenting five chapters that illustrate how practitioners can conduct and utilize research to inform practice and how researchers can implement practice-relevant studies.

In the first chapter in this section, "An Agenda for Oncology Social Work Research: From Bench to Bedside to Trench," Karen Kayser sets an agenda for oncology social work research. She encourages researchers to use a paradigm that transforms their research into results that can be understood and used by practitioners—across disciplines and across cultures.

In "Practice-Relevant Research in Oncology: Science Is What You Do When You Don't Know What to Do," Taryn Lindhorst helps us view the relationship of research and practice through a new lens. She proposes that these are not separate endeavors but can be an integrative process of practice and research. In short, social work practitioners can be effective utilizers of knowledge through integrating evidence-based practice into their work *and* generators of knowledge through practice-based research. Practitioners need research that is relevant to their daily needs and researchers need knowledge of the challenges and opportunities of the practice environment.

Mary Ann Burg's chapter, "Finding Funding for Oncology Social Work Research," provides information about the processes required to conduct research in a practice setting. Burg clearly describes how to develop a good researchable question and how to look for research funding and offers practical tips for writing grant proposals.

In "Writing Proposals for Foundations and Governmental Agencies," Guadalupe R. Palos goes further in-depth with a focus on grant writing. She provides information on a variety of funding resources, navigates the reader through the somewhat overwhelming process of a grant application, and illustrates writing a well-crafted proposal.

In "Opportunities for Social Work Research in Oncology," Carly Parry and G. Stephane Philogene conclude the section with a road map for future social work research. They highlight the elements of success involved in obtaining funding within the large system of the National Institutes of Health and focus on the strategic elements of positioning, partnering, and packaging.

Each chapter in this section provides web-based resources and strategies to assist researcher-practitioners in their endeavors to build a knowledge base that responds to the changing health care service delivery context and the increased need for patient-centered care.

24 An Agenda for Oncology Social Work Research: From Bench to Bedside to Trench

Karen Kayser

Key Concepts

- *Psychosocial and social work research needs to be applied to the "real world" of cancer care to improve psychosocial care.*
- *Interdisciplinary research teams are required to address complex problems, such as disparities in cancer.*
- *Cross-cultural research can inform practitioners about culturally sensitive assessment tools and interventions.*

Although advances in medical research have dramatically changed health care over the past decades, research in psychosocial care has not seen similar advances.[1] It is therefore unsurprising that a recent Institute of Medicine report on cancer care for the *whole* patient concluded: "Cancer care today often provides state-of-the-science biomedical treatment, but fails to address the psychological and social (psychosocial) problems associated with the illness" (IOM, 2008, p. 1). This failure may be partially due to inadequate funding for research on health services, models of care, and service innovations (Colditz, 2012). It has been estimated that only 1.5% of all biomedical research funding (federal and foundations) is spent on health care services and how to best implement them (Woolf, 2008). Oncology social workers have had to adapt and respond to a rapidly changing medical environment, often without the benefits of an empirical basis and scientific knowledge to inform their practice.

Oncology social work research has primarily focused on two aims over the past two decades: (1) furthering our understanding of the psychosocial needs of patients and families and (2) determining whether our interventions make a difference in the quality of patients' and families' lives. Social work practitioners and researchers need to work together to focus and deliberate on planning an agenda for future research. New standards and greater demands for psychosocial services in cancer care are forcing us to transform our practices. Social workers need to do more than merely validate their profession; rather, they need to show how their work adds value to the care of patients while also reducing medical costs. Furthermore, their research needs to inform practitioners on how best practices can be implemented to care for *all* patients. Social workers need to think differently about how to conduct their research and practice because new paradigms for research are needed if they expect to meet new challenges.

Social workers' psychosocial research must be transformative to keep up with the rapidly changing medical system and advances in medical technology. By *transformative*, I mean that research should produce second-order change (change on the systemic level) and must be innovative (advancing knowledge). How do we use new research paradigms to transform our social work practice and policies? How can social work practitioners participate in our research endeavors? In this chapter, I describe three approaches for transformative research: (1) translational, (2) transdisciplinary, and (3) transcultural.

Translational Research: Applying Science to Practice

Producing research does not mean that practitioners are actually using research results in their practice. Little of the psychosocial research that social workers produce will be used in their practice unless researchers take responsibility for translating results to practice areas and demonstrating how to apply the findings to practice problems. Translational research aims to correct this situation by applying scientific knowledge to meet a particular need or address a problem. In the past, this type of research was known as applied research and was depicted as separate from basic research. Instead of dichotomizing research, we need to integrate the two types.

Translational research involves three phases that build on one another: (1) basic research (bench), (2) applied research (bedside), and (3) dissemination research (trench). Each box in Figure 24.1 was purposefully drawn the same size, indicating that none is more critical than any other. Stefanek (2010) states that all three are needed to maximize the impact of evidence-based psychooncology research on the cancer community.

Oncology social work researchers help us understand basic behavioral and social phenomena related to the cancer experience (basic research). Basic research explains how certain individual or social factors are related to cancer-related outcomes, such as quality of life, access to medical care, or adherence to treatment. It can focus on individual levels (e.g., looking at a patient's decision-making process about treatment) or on organizational or community levels (e.g., access to palliative care in a rural community). Examples include studies on the impact of a mother's breast cancer on daughters (Oktay, 2005); adolescent and young adult cancer survivors' quality of life (Jones et al., 2010; Zebrack, Ganz, Bernaards, Petersen, & Abraham, 2006); African American breast cancer survivors (Davis, Rust, & Darby, 2013); and cancer screening among Asian American women (Lee, Ju, Vang, & Lundquist, 2012). Most of these studies involve survey designs that use either standardized instruments (quantitative) or in-depth interviews (qualitative) to collect data. Intervention research is another type of research that falls under the category of applied (bedside) research. This research involves developing and testing psychosocial interventions using designs such as the single-system evaluation or the randomized controlled trial (RCT); RCT is considered the gold standard of best practices.

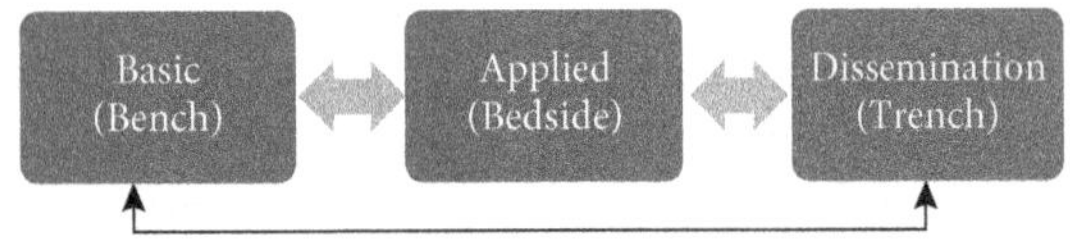

Figure 24.1. Translational Research Paradigm (Stefanek, 2010)

When a large number of studies on a particular cancer-related issue or practice already exist, researchers will review and critique them in one article known as a systematic review or meta-analysis. Review articles enable the practitioner to sift through numerous studies and draw inferences about effective interventions and policies, thus being able to apply the results of several studies in making practice decisions. Furthermore, these articles are informative to the practitioner who wants to use an evidence-based intervention but has neither the time nor funding to conduct bedside research.

How to Use Meta-Analyses or Systematic Reviews in Your Practice

Before developing and implementing a couple-based intervention for breast cancer patients, I wanted to find out whether any researchers or practitioners had developed and tested a similar type of intervention for couples. There were two ways that I could gather this information. I could search for all of the articles that had been written about psychosocial interventions for cancer patients, or I could look for a meta-analysis or systematic review that would summarize and review all of the articles on this topic. A meta-analysis differs from a "literature review" in that the meta-analysis is a systematic review that uses quantitative methods to analyze, synthesize, and summarize the results of a large number of research studies on one particular topic. This allows decisions to be made regarding the effectiveness of an intervention and suggests best practices for particular problems. The following are the steps to conducting a search for a meta-analysis or systematic review:

- *State your practice question or the issue of interest.*
    - *Example: What evidence-based psychosocial interventions have been developed for couples dealing with the cancer of a spouse/partner?*
- *Find databases that contain social science and medical journals. These types of databases are available at university libraries or at teaching hospitals (e.g., PsychINFO, Social Work Abstracts, MEDLINE, and PubMed).*
- *Select key words including meta-analysis or systematic review to use in your search of the database. For my question about interventions for couples, I used the following key words: psychosocial intervention, cancer, couples, meta-analysis.*
- *If one or more meta-analyses result from your search, read the abstracts to make sure the articles will address your issue. If no meta-analyses or systematic reviews result from your search, try another database or broaden your search. If these searches are still not fruitful, remove the key words meta-analysis and systematic review and search for individual articles.*
    - *Example: When I conducted my search for articles on couple-based interventions 10 years ago, there were no meta-analyses specific to couple-based interventions. I broadened my search using the key word psychosocial*

interventions. I found meta-analyses that included all types of interventions (support groups, individual counseling, etc.); two studies on interventions that included spouses were in the results. There are currently at least four systematic reviews of couple-based interventions.

- *If you are reading meta-analyses on outcome studies, you will be interested in the effect size (ES) of the interventions that are reported in the studies. Some meta-analyses specifically review outcome studies (studies that evaluate the effectiveness of interventions). The ES is an index that tells you the amount of change that resulted from the intervention.*
  - *Example: The findings of a systematic review of couple-based interventions for cancer patients (Regan et al., 2012) revealed that ESs for couple-based interventions ranged from.35–.45. This result is within the medium range of effectiveness and is similar to the ES of patient-only or caregiver-only interventions. A glossary or handbook of research, such as the Pocket Glossary for Commonly Used Research Terms (Holosko & Thyer, 2011), can be useful in understanding the research concepts and interpreting the results of studies.*

As part of a larger research team, I developed a psychosocial intervention for breast cancer patients and their partners called "Partners in Coping" (Kayser, Feldman, Borstelmann, & Daniels, 2010), which was based on a prior study of basic research that examined supportive relationships of mothers who were coping with cancer (Kayser, Sormanti, & Strainchamps, 1999). In addition, findings from meta-analyses of psychosocial interventions with cancer patients helped us identify the gaps and needs in services for cancer patients and their family members.

Both basic and applied research studies are important to oncology social work. Dissemination research is equally important but has been largely overlooked and underfunded. This is unfortunate because dissemination is critical to linking research with practice in a broader context, enabling other researchers, practitioners, policymakers, and consumers to use it to inform practice. The process of dissemination occurs in three ways:

1. *Diffusion:* Making research findings available to a clinical audience primarily through publications in peer-reviewed journals.
2. *Dissemination:* Actively distributing information relevant to practice to a targeted audience.
3. *Implementation:* A more active process designed to enable health care providers to deliver care in a manner consistent with research evidence.

What is dissemination and implementation research? The National Cancer Institute defines it as "the use of strategies to adopt and integrate evidence based health interventions and change practice patterns within specific settings" (as cited in Colditz, 2012, p. 4). In other words, it is research that actively supports the movement of evidence-based, effective health care and prevention interventions from the clinical knowl-

Dissemination and implementation research is a new area with implications and applications to social work practice. It often focuses on how to implement psychosocial interventions in the community so that all patients have access to psychosocial care. If our research results are to be transformative, developing effective strategies for dissemination and implementation is essential.

Websites and Tools for Translational Research

Cancer Control P.L.A.N.E.T.: http://cancercontrolplanet.cancer.gov/index.html

This website provides access to data and resources for designing, implementing, and evaluating evidence-based cancer control programs.

Cochrane Collaboration: http://www.cochrane.org/

The Cochrane Collaboration is an international network of people from over 100 countries who prepare, update, and promote the accessibility of systematic reviews or meta-analyses to help people make decisions about health care practices and policies. The collaboration publishes the Cochrane Database of Systematic Reviews and also prepares the largest collection of records of randomized controlled trials in the world (CENTRAL).

RE-AIM: http://www.RE-AIM.org/

The acronym refers to Reach, Effectiveness, Adoption, Implementation, and Maintenance, the five steps of the RE-AIM framework to enhance the quality, speed, and public health impact of research into practice.

D-cubed: http://www.uq.edu.au/evaluationstedi/Dissemination/?q=dissemination

This site provides a review of dissemination strategies used by projects funded by the Australian Learning and Teaching Council. A useful framework for dissemination and a guide to use are provided.

Research to Reality: http://www.researchtoreality.cancer.gov

This is an online community that brings together practitioners and researchers in cancer care and provides opportunities for discussion, learning, and collaboration on moving research to practice.

Transdisciplinary Research: Bridging Disciplines

What do we mean by transdisciplinary research? The term first appeared in the 1980s and is probably best defined by Sarah Gehlert and her colleagues as a means of collaboration in which investigators from different disciplines operate outside their disciplines and form a perspective about a problem that reflects the complexity of the entire problem rather than just a

2010). This approach emerged from the realization that solutions to complex health problems require research from more than one discipline. The transdisciplinary approach is particularly critical in research on the problem of health disparities.

Disparities in health have been and continue to be a challenge that social work researchers take seriously. One example of disparities can be found among women with breast cancer. Although the national rate of breast cancer incidence is much lower among African American women (compared to Caucasian women), the reverse is true for the death rate between these two groups. Why do many more African American women die from breast cancer? Is it related to poor quality of treatment? Access to treatment? How treatment decisions are made? Environmental stress? Social determinants (poverty or lack of education)? Different racial genotypes? Gehlert and colleagues (2010) believe the answers will not be discovered by using a monodisciplinary approach; solutions will require the expertise of researchers who can study genetic factors, pathophysiological pathways, individual risk factors, social relationships, living conditions, neighborhoods and communities, institutions, and social and economic policies. Researchers can no longer work within their discipline-specific silos and must start communicating with each other and with members of other disciplines to make research transformative. As one of the first centers funded by the National Institutes for Health as part of the Centers for Population Health and Health Disparities initiative, the Center for Interdisciplinary Health Disparities Research at the University of Chicago has been a leader in this type of research.

Although cancer care requires interdisciplinary teamwork, physicians, nurses, and social workers have not been taught how to conduct their practices as a team. The same situation exists for an oncology social work research agenda. Studies will not be using a transdisciplinary approach to the research problem if no effort is made to seek out other disciplines to be on the research team. Social work researchers should not wait to be invited to join an interdisciplinary team; they should take the lead by inviting others to participate in their psychosocial research. Because social workers are more likely than physicians and nurses to be left out of such research and because such gaps limit research effectiveness by omitting critical areas of knowledge and expertise—for example, public health, psychology, medicine, nursing, anthropology, and bioethics—social workers must assume a leadership role in research.

Transcultural Research: Advancing Cultural Competence

The Social Work Code of Ethics was revised in 2008 to emphasize the obligation of social work practitioners to be culturally competent. It states that

> *social workers should obtain education about and seek to understand the nature of social diversity and oppression with respect to race, ethnicity, national origin, color, sex, sexual orientation, gender identity or expression, age, marital status, political belief, religion, immigration status, and mental or physical disability.*
>
> *(NASW, 2008)*

As social workers, we have a moral obligation to work toward social justice and health care equity for everyone.

The American Cancer Society calls cancer an "enormous global health burden" that accounts for one in every eight deaths worldwide and is growing at a fast pace. Social work practice has no national boundaries; nor should its research. It is alarming, however, that most of the social science research (particularly psychology) is based on studies of narrow and small samples of human diversity (Diamond, 2012). According to cultural anthropologist Jared Diamond, the problem is the monocultural perspective of social science research:

> *Among the human subjects studied in a sample of papers from the top psychology journals surveyed in the year 2008, 96% were from Westernized industrial countries (North America, Europe, Australia, New Zealand, and Israel), 68% were from the U.S. in particular, and up to 80% were college undergraduates enrolled in psychology courses, i.e., not even typical of their own national societies. . . . Most of our understanding of human psychology is based on subjects who may be described by the acronym WEIRD: from Western, educated, industrialized, rich, and democratic societies.*
>
> *(Diamond, 2012, pp. 8–9)*

Since 70% of the world's population lives in non-Western countries, how can we generalize our Western-based research results to the world? We need to broaden the population of study participants to include people from a much wider range of cultures.

Social work colleagues and I conducted a systematic review of distress screening instruments for cancer to assess the cultural equivalence of screening across diverse samples of cancer patients. One measure of cultural equivalence is that the word *distress* is understood and reported similarly by patients from different cultures. For example, researchers in one study (Noguera et al., 2009) were trying to find a word for depression that they could use in screening Spanish-speaking patients. Direct translation of the word *depression* into Spanish was not understood and did not mean the same thing as in English. The investigators found that the term *desanimado* (discouraged) was more suitable in screening for depression than the word *deprimido* (depressed). Understanding the nuances of language is essential because if a patient does not understand the screening tool's language or if a translated word has a different conceptual meaning than was intended by the person authoring the screening tool, the results of the screening will be biased; as a result, true distress may be undiagnosed and needed services may not be offered.

Conducting transcultural research can be humbling because it quickly becomes evident that Westerners' knowledge base is narrow and ethnocentric. When I was training practitioners in the Partners in Coping Program, a Hong Kong Chinese social worker informed me that parts of the intervention protocol would not be appropriate for Chinese couples. For example, Chinese couples would be unlikely to disclose personal information (e.g., a previous divorce) in an assessment interview. In addition, Chinese couples seemed to have different cancer-related concerns than did American couples in my study sample. My Chinese colleague suggested that we return to basic research and examine how Chinese couples in Hong Kong cope with breast cancer. We conducted a study comparing American couples to Chinese couples and then added couples from India as another subsample. We proposed that cultural contexts that vary on collectivism and individualism would influence how couples cope with a spouse's cancer diagnosis. One finding from our study was that couples in collectivistic cultures included many of their family members (including parents, children, aunts, and cousins) in making decisions about medical treatments and often relied on them for such practical needs as child care, meals, and financial help. Findings from our study and other similar studies assisted us in modifying our interventions to be more relevant and culturally sensitive with couples from non-Western cultures.

Pearls

- Collaborate with a school of social work on a small practice-related study.
- Educate yourself in another discipline (e.g., free online courses are offered by the Massachusetts Institute of Technology through MIT Open Courseware).
- Attend meetings of multidisciplinary professional organizations (American Psycho-Oncology Society, International Psycho-Oncology Society, National Council on Family Relations).
- Participate in a service-learning trip to a developing country.
- Conduct a focus group in an underserved community.
- Read a meta-analysis or systematic review related to a practice problem.
- Start a journal club at your cancer care setting.
- Write about your practice experiences. Practice wisdom can be used to write treatment manuals, protocols, and educational materials for patients and families.

Pitfalls

- Attempting to conduct a research study alone.
- Speaking in the language of only one discipline when you are working on a multidisciplinary team.
- Implementing an evidence-based intervention that is not sensitive to the cultural context.
- Not addressing institutional barriers that prevent working across disciplines.

A world of social work that includes transformative research will advance psychosocial care to meet future needs. Without translational research, our findings will be lost in translation by practitioners. Without transdisciplinary research, our findings will lose their impact on complex problems. Without transcultural research, our findings will lose relevance to diverse cultures. Without translational, transdisciplinary, and transcultural research, oncology social work practice will not be transformative.

NOTE

1. This chapter is based on the author's 2012 American Cancer Society Quality of Life Award Lecture, "Building Bridges Between Oncology Social Work Practice and Research," presented at the 28th Conference of the Association of Oncology Social Work, Boston, MA.

REFERENCES

Colditz, G. A. (2012). The promise and challenges of dissemination and implementation research. In R. C. Brownson, G. A. Colditz, & E. K. Proctor (Eds.), *Dissemination and implementation research in health: Translating science to practice* (pp. 3–22). New York, NY: Oxford University Press.

Davis, C., Rust, C., & Darby, K. (2013). Coping skills among African-American breast cancer survivors. *Social Work in Health Care*, 52(5), 434–448.

Diamond, J. (2012). *The world until yesterday: What can we learn from traditional societies?* New York, NY: Viking.

Gehlert, S., Murray, A., McClintock, M., Conzen, S., & Olopade, O. (2010). The importance of transdisciplinary collaborations for understanding and resolving health disparities. *Social Work in Public Health*, 25, 408–422.

Holosko, M. J., & Thyer, B. A. (2011). *Pocket glossary for commonly used research terms*. Los Angeles, CA: Sage.

Jones, B., Volker, D., Vinajeras, Y., Butros, L., Fitchpatrick, C., & Rosetto, K. (2010). The meaning of surviving cancer for Latino adolescents and emerging young adults. *Cancer Nursing: An International Journal for Cancer Care*, 33(1), 74–81. doi:10.1097/NCC.0b013e3181264ab8f.

Institute of Medicine (IOM). (2008). *Cancer care for the whole patient: Meeting psychosocial health needs*. Washington, DC: National Academies Press.

Kayser, K., Feldman, B. N., Borstelmann, N., & Daniels, A. (2010). The effects of a randomized couple-based intervention on the quality of life of breast cancer patients and their partners. *Journal of Social Work Research*, *34*(1), 20–32.

Kayser, K., Sormanti, M., & Strainchamps, E. (1999). Women coping with cancer: The impact of close relationships on psychosocial adjustment. *Psychology of Women Quarterly*, *23*, 725–739.

Lee, H., Ju, Z. S., Vang, P. D., & Lundquist, M. (2012). Breast and cervical cancer screening disparity among subgroups of Asian American women: Does race/ethnicity matter? *Journal of Women's Health*, *19*(10), 1877–1884. doi:10.1089/jwh.2009.1783.

National Association of Social Workers (NASW). (2008). *Code of ethics*. Washington, DC: NASW Press. Retrieved from http://www.socialworkers.org/pubs/code/

Noguera, A., Centeno, C., Carvajal, A., Tejedor, M. A. P., Urdiroz, J., & Martinez, M. (2009). "Are you discouraged? Are you anxious, nervous, or uneasy?": In Spanish some words could be better than others for depression and anxiety screening. *Journal of Palliative Medicine*, *12*, 707–712. doi:0.1089/jpm.2009.0024.

Oktay, J. S. (2005). *Breast cancer daughters tell their stories*. New York, NY: Haworth Press.

Regan, T., Lambert, S., Girgis, A., Kelly, B., Kayser, K., & Turner, J. (2012). Do couple-based interventions make a difference for couples affected by cancer?: A systematic review, *Biomedical Cancer*, *12*, 279. doi:10.1186/1471-2407-12-279.

Rubenstein, L. V., & Pugh, J. (2006). Strategies for promoting organizational and practice change by advancing implementation research. *Journal of General Internal Medicine*, *21*(Suppl. 2), S58–S64.

Stefanek, M. (2010). Basic and translational psycho-oncology research. In J. C. Holland, W. S. Breitbart, P. B. Jacobsen, M. S. Lederberg, M. J. Loscalzo, & R. McCorkle (Eds.), *Psycho-oncology*. New York, NY: Oxford University Press.

Woolf, S. H. (2008). The meaning of translational research and why it matters. *Journal of the American Medical Association*, *299*(2), 211–213.

Zebrack, B. J., Ganz, P. A., Bernaards, C. A., Petersen, L., & Abraham, L. (2006). Assessing the impact of cancer: Development of a new instrument for long-term survivors. *Psycho-Oncology*, *15*, 407–421. doi:10.1002/pon.963.

25 Practice-Relevant Research in Oncology: Science Is What You Do When You Don't Know What to Do

Taryn Lindhorst

Key Concepts

- *Evidence-based practice uses systematically gathered information to inform clinical decision making. "Evidence" can be generously or narrowly defined, arranged in hierarchies, or a more inclusive evidence "house."*
- *Practice-based research includes both the efforts of individual clinicians to evaluate their work and the creation of research from practice rather than academic settings.*
- *This chapter presents an integrated model of research and practice to guide research development.*

Social work (like other practice professions) has been plagued with dueling dualisms, particularly in understanding the relationships between research and practice. "Practice and research, agency and university, practice wisdom and research-based knowledge, positivist and interpretivist research methods, relevance and rigor, science and art" are often discussed as mutually exclusive endeavors (Epstein, 2009, p. 216). The gap between research and practice is persistent and has been likened by others to a war of worldviews ultimately involving money and livelihoods (Milne & Reiser, 2012; Tavris, 2003). As a social work practitioner turned mixed-methods researcher, I have a pluralistic view toward "evidence" that focuses on its usefulness for the work of alleviating human inequality and suffering. I have chosen to focus this chapter from a more harmonious frame (Epstein, 2009) to encourage oncology social work research that addresses issues of relevance and participation and considers knowledge needs from both practice and research vantage points.

As the title to this chapter suggests, *science* (from the Latin word for *knowledge*) is an activity that we undertake in the face of uncertainty. We live in a world in which ambiguity abounds and equally plausible interpretations of people and events are commonplace, even within the scientific endeavor (Harari, 2001). What the practice of research offers is a way to develop skills in systematic reasoning (Wallace & Wray, 2011) that drive us to explore alternative possibilities in the search for guidance in the situations we face each day in social work. To situate this conversation, I review discussions of evidence-based practice and practice-based research and then suggest directions for future oncology social work research.

Evidence-Based Practice

Evidence-based practice (EBP) refers to the systematic use of current research for clinical decision making (Straus & McAlister, 2000). Research on medical practice has shown that effective treatments are not reliably implemented in practice (Kravitz, 2005) and that enhancing application of these validated interventions could save more lives than creating new therapies (Woolf & Johnson, 2005). Discussions of

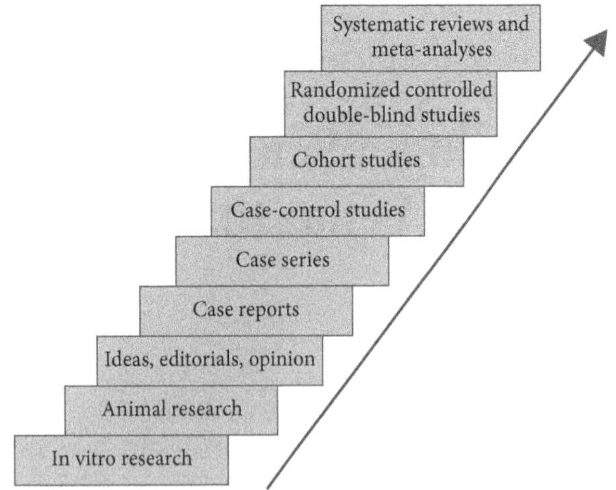

Figure 25.1. Hierarchy of Evidence in Cancer Research

aligning professional practice with research evidence have circulated for decades, but in the 1990s, new calls were issued in medicine for evidence-based practice (Sackett, Rosenberg, Gray, Haynes, & Richardson, 1996) and quickly spread to other professions within and outside health services (A. M. Cohen & Hersh, 2004; Thomas & Pring, 2004). The first article on EBP in social work appeared in the late 1990s (Gambrill, 1999), and a vigorous debate has since developed in the profession over its meaning, role, and implementation (see Drisko & Grady, 2012; Gray, Plath, & Webb, 2009; and Vaughn, Howard, & Thyer, 2009).

As these discussions evolved, efforts were made to differentiate levels of evidence and to understand how much guidance they gave to practice. For example, Figure 25.1 shows an adaptation of Sackett and colleagues' discussion of levels of evidence to the world of cancer research. The best evidence, by this argument, is to be found in the meta-analysis of multiple randomized controlled trials (RCTs), with all other forms of evidence considered to be inferior to this gold standard. RCTs hold this esteemed position because of their ability to control for potential alternative hypotheses and biases of the researchers, increasing the confidence that an intervention works, in those cases where a positive significant difference is found between the control and experimental groups.

With the proliferation of RCTs in medicine, education, mental health treatment, and other areas, new organizations, such as the Cochrane Reviews in medicine and the Campbell Collaboration (focused on education, crime, and social welfare), have developed to synthesize research evidence through meta-analyses and systematic research reviews (see Table 25.1 for a listing of web-based resources on EBP). The National Association of Social Workers has also developed online resources to guide social work intervention development and delivery. In addition to these general review sites, the National Cancer Institute has collaborated with other federal agencies to develop two cancer-specific web portals for information on empirically supported treatments and systematic reviews of psychosocial and other research. The Research Tested Intervention Program (RTIP) is an online resource that currently lists over 130 interventions tested through RCTs or quasi-experimental designs in areas such as cancer screening, behavior change, and informed decision making. These results and others are used to create research syntheses and meta-analyses that are available for oncology practitioners and researchers through Cancer Control P.L.A.N.E.T. (Plan, Link, Act, Network with Evidence-based Tools), an online resource that provides information on cancer-related systematic reviews and research syntheses.

In the midst of these efforts to develop and streamline research evidence to make it more relevant to practitioners, critiques of evidence-based practice have grown, especially the EBP focus on RCTs as the dominant form of evidence. In general, although RCTs are useful in controlling confounding factors and minimizing bias, they do so at the cost of complexity and context. The origin of the modern RCT can be traced to the 1940s, when randomization was employed to study the effects of immunization and drug treatment

Table 25.1.
Evidence-Based Practice Websites

Organization	Website
American Psychological Association, Society of Clinical Psychology	http://www.psychologicaltreatments.org/
Campbell Collaboration	http://www.campbellcollaboration.org
Cancer Control P.L.A.N.E.T.	http://cancercontrolplanet.cancer.gov/index.html
Cochrane Reviews	http://www.cochrane.org
National Association of Social Workers, Social Work Policy Institute	http://www.socialworkpolicy.org/research/evidence-based-practice-2.html#further
National Cancer Institute—Research-Tested Intervention Programs	http://rtips.cancer.gov/rtips/index.do

(Doll, 1998). Administering a drug is a much simpler and more standardized intervention than implementing a psychosocial intervention, and measuring what matters is difficult in psychosocial research. As McKenna (2010, p. 86) notes, "Many of the issues of importance to health care and to patients defy quantification: how do you calibrate kindness, how do you quantify concern and how do you measure compassion?" RCTs also minimize complexity through criteria for inclusion in the study. For example, RCTs routinely exclude people with comorbid conditions or who are receiving other treatments; children, the elderly, and pregnant women; those with mental illness, substance use, or confusion; and people who do not speak English (Aoun & Kristjanson, 2005). Because of the disproportionate representation of racial and ethnic minorities among these groups, people of color are underrepresented in RCT research (Aisenberg, 2008). These excluded categories form the core constituencies of social work practice.

The lack of inclusion of people of color in much clinical research has raised important questions about the issues of context and generalizability in RCTs and EBPs more broadly. Many EBPs have been normed on white, non-Latino populations, so contextual factors such as differences in histories, language, and values are not incorporated into the intervention (Aisenberg, 2008). Most efforts to understand cultural differences rely on problematic notions of broad racial groupings (such as Asian American) that do not account for heterogeneity within different groups (Cardemil, 2010). For example, a study of a guided imagery exercise found that imagery focused on oneself resulted in a diminished effect of the intervention among Latinos, who endorsed more relational values (LaRoche, D'Angelo, Gualdron, & Leavell, 2006). Findings such as this emphasize the need to ensure the inclusion of diverse groups of persons in research studies (Aisenberg, 2008), the adaptation of tested interventions to account for differences in cultural views (Cardemil, 2010), and the operationalization of cultural factors beyond racial groupings (LaRoche & Lustig, 2010).

In addition to these critiques, two other criticisms of EBPs are particularly relevant to oncology social work researchers and practitioners. First, the application of RCTs to test increasingly complex interventions has raised uncertainties about the "black box" of interventions—that is, what is the mechanism responsible for any improvements seen? In psychosocial research, questions are emerging about the interplay among common factors across all psychosocial interventions and the effects of a particular treatment modality (Barth et al., 2012). For example, some portion of the effect of any psychological intervention is related to aspects of the therapist (e.g., warmth, empathic communication), characteristics of the client (e.g., motivation for treatment, expectations), and the quality of the therapeutic alliance. In this context, questions of fidelity to a particular treatment approach (D. J. Cohen et al., 2008) become less important than ensuring that the provision of any treatment accounts for these common factors.

Second, RCTs are difficult to implement in research that focuses on end-of-life and palliative care concerns. Palliative-care interventions tend to be holistic (focused on more than one point of intervention), tailored to the individual, and lacking in uniformity in their timing because of differences in life expectancy (Aoun & Kristjanson, 2005). Generally, RCTs measure clinical outcomes that relate to decreased morbidity or mortality, but these end points are not relevant in research where the person is expected to die. Instead, palliative research

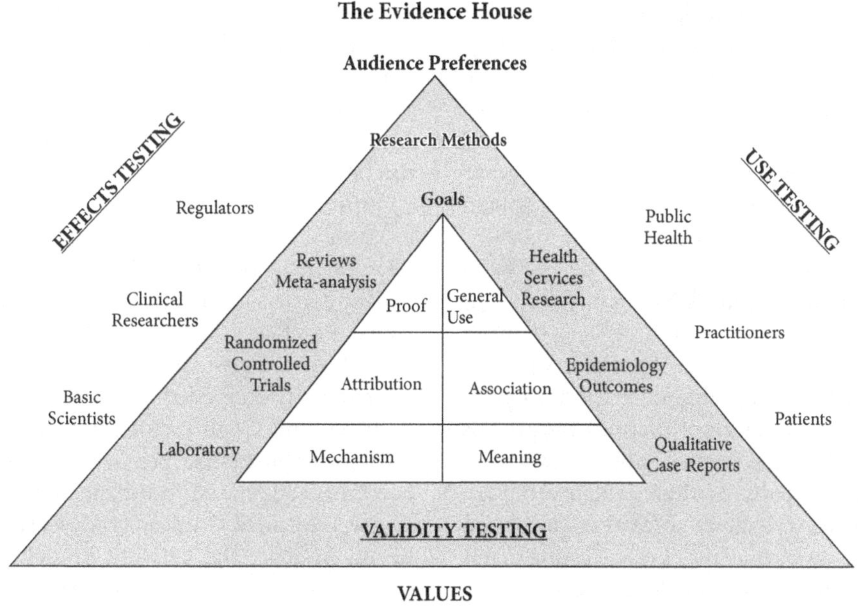

Figure 25.2. The Evidence House as an Alternative to the Evidence Hierarchy

tends to focus on psychosocial outcomes such as quality of life, dignity, or symptom relief, but RCTs that require control groups may be difficult to mount when life expectancy is short.

Alternative conceptualizations of EBP have begun to develop in response to these varying critiques. For instance, Figure 25.2 shows a novel re-visioning of the evidence hierarchy by the former director of the Office of Alternative Medicine at the National Institutes of Health (Jonas, 2001). Here, the evidence "house" is divided into understanding causal relationships (a focus of basic science and clinical researchers, the traditional ground of EBP), and focusing on what happens in practice and its relevance to patients and practitioners. Jonas encourages a balanced approach to the development of evidence, saying, "if resources are disproportionately invested in certain rooms of the house to the neglect of others, it is not possible to obtain the evidence needed for full public participation in clinical decisions" (2001, p. 80). Within social work, theorists have suggested a shift from EBP to evidence-*informed* practice (Epstein, 2009; Nevo & Slonim-Nevo, 2011). This modification encourages knowledge of research coupled with consideration of client values and preferences, the context of work, and the social worker's professional judgment. These differences in wording reflect not only shifts in conceptualization but also expansion of the epistemological underpinnings of what is considered evidence beyond a solely postpositivist frame (Carter & Little, 2007; A. M. Cohen & Hersh, 2004; McKenna, 2010).

Practice-Based Research

Underlying the discussion of EBP is an implicit assumption that academic researchers are knowledge *generators* whereas practitioners are knowledge *implementers* (Epstein, 2009). Even though we teach research skills at the master's level, most research that is published in peer-reviewed journals is conducted by PhD-trained researchers in academic settings. The lopsided, top-down, and frequently condescending discussion (see Epstein, 2009) of EBP has contributed to the skepticism among practitioners about the relationship of research to practice. The "artificial divide between researcher and practitioner" (Wade & Neuman, 2007, p. 51) is overcome in practice-based research with systematic techniques that investigate phenomena of practice within its existing structure and logic. Engaging in research in practice can foster greater conceptual clarity because the process of research requires making the implicit explicit and understanding the presence of patterns that structure human problems and responses (Henton, 2012). Practice-based research (PBR) also moves beyond the efficacy testing that is characteristic of RCTs into the real world, addressing complex questions of practice effectiveness in ever-changing social contexts (Epstein, 2009).

Early efforts to encourage the development of the "scientific-practitioner" (Barlow, Hayes, & Nelson, 1984) in social work practice focused on the use of single-system research designs and standardized assessment instruments (Wakefield & Kirk, 1996). Most single-system designs track some outcome of interest to the client and practitioner over time; in more sophisticated models, an intervention is applied and withdrawn (ABA designs; Babbie, 2007). Client problems that are not amenable to traditional RCTs are often the focus of single-system, or "*n*-of-1," investigations. For instance, practitioners in palliative care (Mitchell, 2010) and complementary medicine (Sagar, 2008; Sung & Feldman, 2006) have advocated the use of *n*-of-1 trials. With advances in statistical practices, *n*-of-1 studies can be aggregated to produce results that may be generalizable beyond the practitioner's clinical work (Mitchell, 2010). Although frequently taught in social work research classes, single-system designs remain underutilized in practice, even though their use is consistent with the case-based approach of social work.

Defining PBR can be slippery, because the term has been used to refer to nonexperimental research (i.e., not an RCT), research conducted by practitioners or within routine practice settings, and certain research designs such as case-study research (Henton, 2012). PBR's approach to knowledge development tends to be more inclusive of varying epistemologies, seeing value in research that illuminates cultural meanings and lived experiences that are critical to relationship development. PBR is both nomothetic (focused on generalized understanding–based groups of situations or events) and idiographic (interested in the fullest possible explanation of a particular situation or experience; Babbie, 2007). Tacit knowledge that is difficult to articulate (Berg, 2008) is sought through deep immersion in the practice environment, observation, and interaction with clients and practitioners. Because of its location within practice, PBR often shares values with other community-based approaches such as community-based participatory research. Common values include sharing power and decision making among participants, developing long-term relationships, and emphasizing local expertise (Westfall et al., 2009).

Primary care research in medicine has been at the forefront of the development of PBR through the creation of networks of physicians who collaboratively study patient-care issues (Fagnan, Davis, Deyo, Werner, & Stange, 2010). Practice-based research networks (PBRNs) have existed in medicine since the 1970s, and over 130 networks are currently funded through the Agency for Healthcare Research and Quality (2013). Like primary care medicine, substance-abuse treatment researchers and practitioners have also cooperated in the creation of the National Drug Abuse Treatment Clinical Trials Network (Tai et al., 2010). Begun in 1999, the network brought academic researchers together with community drug-treatment providers to develop and test new approaches to substance-abuse treatment. This effort has resulted in the community-based treatment of over 11,000 people through the completion of 20 clinical trials.

With the evolution of the electronic medical record, the potential exists to more efficiently capture information that can be used in practice-based research. In the past decade, the Robert Wood Johnson Foundation funded primary care PBRNs to test interventions that could be integrated into health care that would help patients change behaviors related to tobacco and alcohol use, diet, and physical inactivity (Green, Cifuentes, Glasgow, & Stange, 2008). Through this effort, participating PBRNs collected common measures of patient behavior. These measures were chosen based on their practicality, relationship to clinical goals and behavioral interventions, and validity and sensitivity to change (Glasgow et al., 2005). Social work researchers have reported a similar effort to mine data from electronic medical records to understand practice-related issues in hospital-based social work (Plath & Gibbons, 2010). By drawing on the infrastructure of the PBRNs and combining it with the efficiency of the electronic medical record, these inquiries have the possibility of informing both practice and research efforts in the future.

To date, no similar efforts have been made to draw together psychosocial oncology practitioners into a PBRN, yet the potential of such an effort is alluring. For example, the Commission on Cancer (the accrediting body of the American College of Surgeons) has required affiliated cancer treatment centers to routinely screen patients for psychological distress by 2015 (Commission on Cancer & American Cancer Society, 2012). The evaluation of distress screening through a PBRN could potentially produce information that is highly generalizable for practice, if a broad group of practitioners participated. Practice-based research requires infrastructure, including an educated workforce, financial resources for information management, collaboration between practitioners and researchers, mentorship, and research consultation (Wade & Neuman, 2007). Without infrastructure investment, practice-based research in oncology social work will struggle to move beyond limited local relevance.

Practice-Based Research and Research-Based Practice in Oncology Social Work

> *A truly scientific attitude is always inquiring, always curious about the things that do not fit in.*
>
> —*Berg, 2008, p. 156*

Every method humans have created to understand ourselves in the context of our world has strengths and limitations that reflect differences in worldviews. These ontologies and epistemologies prescribe what is important, what is knowable, and how we can go about discovering new knowledge (Carter & Little, 2007). For social work practitioners in oncology or researchers focused on psychosocial concerns related to cancer, a diversity of methods will be necessary to understand both particular and general experiences of patients, practitioners, and health systems. Critical realism, as noted by one of its primary methodological proponents, can create the philosophical space that values multiple forms of research:

> *Critical realism combines a realist ontology (the belief that there is a real world that exists independently of our beliefs and constructions) with a constructivist epistemology (the belief that our knowledge of this world is inevitably our own construction, created from a specific vantage point, and that there is no possibility of achieving a purely "objective" account that is independent of all particular perspectives).*
>
> *(Maxwell, 2012, p. vii)*

Instead of creating a hierarchy of preferred research, critical realism focuses on the question of what needs to be researched (McKenna, 2010), understanding that some questions require attention to unpacking issues of meaning and culture, whereas others call for investigation of causal processes and their mechanisms. Problems we encounter have patterns and particularities that reflect both quantitative and qualitative aspects of the same problem (Erickan & Roth, 2006). Assuming that one form of research will be responsive to all of these concerns is unrealistic.

Efforts have been made in the past decade to develop research agendas for mental health services, palliative care, and oncology social work (Table 25.2). These outlines are expansive yet focused on issues of direct interest to oncology social work. Common areas of concern include health disparities, the effects of policy on practice, mental health concerns, communication, and quality of life. In oncology, cancer research has been defined as a continuum that includes prevention, detection, diagnosis, treatment, and survivorship (NCI, 2011). Notably, social workers have produced research in each of these areas in the past decade (Institute for the Advancement of Social Work Research, 2003). Although relatively few social work researchers have been funded by the National Cancer Institute directly, social work research by practitioners and academics contributes to the knowledge base.

As noted earlier by Berg, practitioners benefit from an attitude of curiosity and engagement with questions that require systematic inquiry to answer. Likewise, researchers also need the clinician's awareness of "meaning, context, narratives, subjectivity and dialogue" (Berg, 2008, p. 156) to craft research that is likely to make a difference in the alleviation of human suffering. Drawing from Epstein's (2009) discussion of practice-based research and research-based practice and from the previous discussions of EBP and PBR, Figure 25.3 provides a heuristic to help guide the development

Table 25.2.
Research Agendas in Areas Relevant to Oncology Social Work

Practice-Based Research Agenda for Mental Health Services[a]	National Agenda for Social Work Research in Palliative and End-of-Life Care[b]	Social Work and Research on Cancer[c]
What really happens in practice?	Continuity, gaps, fragmentation, and transitions in care	Health status and quality of life in cancer survivorship
Do specified evidence-supported interventions or practice guidelines work when implemented in frontline care?	Diversity and health care disparities	The interface of cancer and aging
What are the real life challenges to implementation?	Financing and the policy practice nexus	Elimination of health disparities
How can practitioner behavior best be modified and maintained?	Mental health concerns and services	Improving the quality of cancer care
Are practice-based research networks effective dissemination vehicles for evidence-supported interventions?	Individual and family care needs and experiences	Enhancing cancer communications to health care providers
How do policy changes affect everyday practice?	Communication	Genetic factors and cancer
	Quality of care and services	Strengthening interdisciplinary research
	Decision making, family conferencing, and family caregiver support	Improving palliative care
	Grief and bereavement	
	Pain and symptom management	
	Curriculum development, training, and evaluation	

[a] McMillen, Lenze, Hawley, and Osborne (2009).

[b] Kramer, Christ, Bern-Klug, and Francoeur (2005).

[c] Institute for the Advancement of Social Work Research (2003).

of research for practice. This diagram describes two main dimensions of the level of relevance of the research: whether intended primarily to influence local practice (top) or to contribute more generally to knowledge development (bottom), and whether it is primarily initiated by researchers (left side) or practitioners (right side). By considering these dimensions, four domains are identifiable: locally relevant research conducted by practitioners (professional development), locally relevant research that is more likely to be conducted by researchers (program development), generally relevant research conducted primarily in practice (idiographic research), and generally relevant research primarily conducted by researchers, predominantly in academic settings (nomothetic research). Some activities reside exclusively in the domain, whereas others may straddle areas. For example, participatory action research may be conducted by researchers or practitioners, but generally, its goals are not to generate broadly relevant knowledge; instead, it seeks to empower participants with specific, locally relevant information (Kemmis & McTaggert, 2003).

At the center of this diagram are systematic case studies and $N = 1$ studies. These two forms of research can be locally or generally relevant and initiated by researchers or practitioners. They differ from each other primarily in their attention to outcomes ($N = 1$ studies) or processes (case studies). McLeod and Elliott (2011) provide an in-depth discussion of the importance of case-study research in the development of theory for practice. Case studies can contribute distinctive knowledge that is relevant to oncology social work because this form of research collects a large amount of contextually rich data about a single case over time. These aspects of the research allow for "the identification and analysis of complex patterns of interplay between different factors or processes . . . [and how]

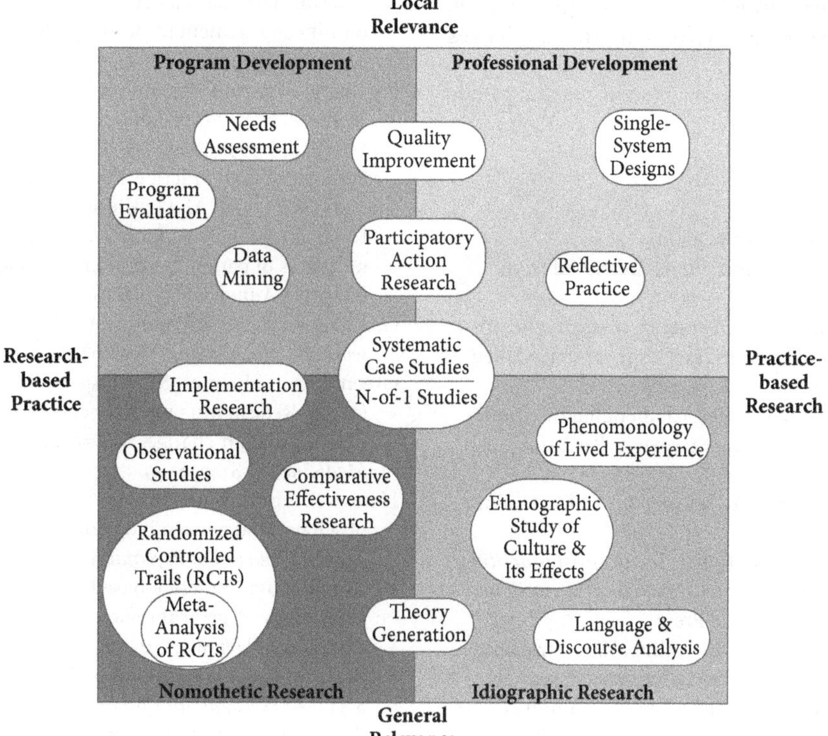

Figure 25.3. An Integrated Model of Research and Practice

change unfolds over time" (McLeod & Elliott, 2011, p. 3). Because case studies are described in a narrative format that is memorable to practitioners who are engaged in the collection of stories from clients, case studies may more easily be useful in practice. Through the selection of "critical" cases (Flyvbjerg, 2006; Lee, Mishna, & Brennenstuhl, 2010)—those that are most likely to provide rich information about the phenomenon under study—practitioners and researchers are able to identify processes that may reflect theoretically important areas in understanding the practice of oncology social work.

Pearls

- The quest for evidence on which to base clinical practice should focus on an expansive view of what constitutes evidence.
- With new developments in technology, practice-based research can address questions that are relevant to both the local practice community and the larger area of scientific inquiry in psychosocial oncology.
- Considering both the level of relevance of the research and who initiates it will help practitioners and researchers to value a variety of knowledge-generating enterprises.

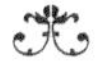

Pitfalls

- Research processes are based on underlying philosophies of what constitutes science. These debates have a long history and are important for both researchers and practitioners to understand.
- A divide often exists between academic and practice-based researchers. An interest in the worldviews of each group is necessary to promote meaningful collaboration.
- When evidence is defined solely as the accumulation of randomized, controlled experiments, much of the knowledge generated in practice may not be considered.

A recursive relationship is needed between practice and research in oncology social work—practitioners need research that is relevant to their daily needs, and researchers need knowledge of the practice environment and its challenges and opportunities. By arguing that a plurality of research methods is essential to knowledge development in oncology social work, I hope that this chapter provides encouragement for knowledge development across a broad range of areas that would be relevant to people with cancer, their families, and the health care systems in which they receive care. Dualistic debates that seek to privilege one form of research over another divert energy from the vital work that is necessary in confronting the challenges cancer poses.

REFERENCES

Agency for Healthcare Research and Quality. (2013). Practice-based research networks. (2013). Retrieved from http://pbrn.ahrq.gov

Aisenberg, E. (2008). Evidence-based practice in mental health care to ethnic minority communities: Has its practice fallen short of its evidence? *Social Work, 53,* 297–306.

Aoun, S. M., & Kristjanson, L. J. (2005). Challenging the framework for evidence in palliative care research. *Palliative Medicine, 19,* 461–465.

Babbie, E. (2007). *The basics of social research* (4th ed.). Belmont, CA: Thompson.

Barlow, D., Hayes, S., & Nelson, R. (1984). *The scientist practitioner: Research and accountability in clinical and educational settings.* New York, NY: Pergamon Press.

Barth, R. P., Lee, B. R., Lindsey, M. A., Collins, K. S., Strieder, F., Chorpita, B. F., . . . Sparks, J. A. (2012). Evidence-based practice at a crossroads: The timely emergence of common elements and common factors. *Research on Social Work Practice, 22,* 108–119.

Berg, E. M. (2008). Clinical practice: Between explicit and tacit knowledge, between dialogue and technique. *Philosophy, Psychiatry, and Psychology, 15,* 151–157.

Cardemil, E. V. (2010). Cultural adaptations to empirically supported treatments: A research agenda. *Scientific Review of Mental Health Practice, 7,* 8–21.

Carter, S. M., & Little, M. (2007). Justifying knowledge, justifying method, taking action: Epistemologies, methodologies, and methods in qualitative research. *Qualitative Health Research, 17,* 1316–1328.

Cohen, A. M., & Hersh, W. R. (2004). Criticisms of evidence-based medicine. *Evidence-Based Cardiovascular Medicine, 8,* 197–198.

Cohen, D. J., Crabtree, B. F., Etz, R. S., Balasubramanian, B. A., Donahue, K. E., Leviton, L. C., . . . Green, L. W. (2008). Fidelity versus flexibility: Translating evidence-based research into practice. *American Journal of Preventive Medicine, 35,* S381–S389.

Commission on Cancer & American Cancer Society. (2012). *Cancer program standards 2012: Ensuring patient-centered care.* Retrieved from http://www.facs.org/cancer/clp/collaborative-action-plan-guide.pdf

Doll, R. (1998). Controlled trials: The 1948 watershed. *British Medical Journal, 317,* 1217–1220.

Drisko, J. W., & Grady, M. D. (2012). *Evidence-based practice in clinical social work.* New York, NY: Springer.

Epstein, I. (2009). Promoting harmony where there is commonly conflict: Evidence-informed practice as an integrative strategy. *Social Work in Health Care, 48,* 216–231.

Erickan, K., & Roth, W. M. (2006). What good is polarizing research into qualitative and quantitative? *Education Researcher, 35,* 14–23.

Fagnan, L. J., Davis, M., Deyo, R. A., Werner, J. J., & Stange, K. C. (2010). Linking practice-based research networks and clinical and translational science awards: New opportunities for community engagement by academic health centers. *Academic Medicine, 85,* 476–483.

Flyvbjerg, B. (2006). Five misunderstandings about case study research. *Qualitative Inquiry, 12,* 219–245.

Gambrill, E. (1999). Evidence-based practice: An alternative to authority-based practice. *Families in Society, 80,* 341–350.

Glasgow, R. E., Ory, M. G., Klesges, L. M., Cifuentes, M., Fernald, D. H., & Green, L. A. (2005). Practical and relevant self-report measures of patient health behaviors for primary care research. *Annals of Family Medicine, 3,* 73–81.

Gray, M., Plath, D., & Webb, S. A. (2009). *Evidence-based social work: A critical stance.* New York, NY: Routledge.

Green, L. A., Cifuentes, M., Glasgow, R. E., & Stange, K. C. (2008). Redesigning primary care practice to incorporate health behavior change. *American Journal of Preventive Medicine, 35,* S347–S349.

Harari, E. (2001). Whose evidence? Lessons from the philosophy of science and epistemology of medicine. *Australian and New Zealand Journal of Psychiatry, 35,* 724–730.

Henton, I. (2012). Practice-based research and counseling psychology: A critical review and proposal. *Counselling Psychology Review, 27,* 11–28.

Institute for the Advancement of Social Work Research. (2003). *Social work's contribution to research on cancer prevention, detection, diagnosis, treatment and survivorship.* Washington, DC: Author.

Jonas, W. B. (2001). The evidence house. *Western Journal of Medicine, 175,* 79–80.

Kemmis, S., & McTaggart, R. (2003). Participatory action research. In N. K. Denzin & Y. S. Lincoln (Eds.), *Strategies of qualitative inquiry* (pp. 336–396). Thousand Oaks, CA: Sage.

Kramer, B. J., Christ, G. H., Bern-Klug, M., & Francoeur, R. B. (2005). A national agenda for social work research in palliative and end-of-life care. *Journal of Palliative Medicine, 8,* 418–431.

Kravitz, R. L. (2005). Doing things better vs. doing better things. *Annals of Family Medicine, 3,* 483–485.

LaRoche, M. J., D'Angelo, E., Gualdron, L., & Leavell, J. (2006). Culturally sensitive guided imagery for allocentric Latinos: A pilot study. *Psychotherapy: Theory, Research, Practice, Training, 43,* 555–560.

LaRoche, M. J., & Lustig, K. (2010). Cultural adaptations: Unpacking the meaning of culture. *Scientific Review of Mental Health Practice, 7,* 26–30.

Lee, E., Mishna, F., & Brennenstuhl, S. (2010). How to critically evaluate case studies in social work. *Research on Social Work Practice, 20,* 682–689.

Maxwell, J. A. (2012). *A realist approach for qualitative research.* Thousand Oaks, CA: Sage.

McKenna, H. (2010). Critical care: Does profusion of evidence lead to confusion in practice? *Nursing in Critical Care, 15,* 285–290.

McLeod, J., & Elliott, R. (2011). Systematic case study research: A practice-oriented introduction to building an evidence base for counseling and psychotherapy. *Counselling and Psychotherapy Research, 11,* 1–10.

McMillen, J. C., Lenze, S. L., Hawley, K. M., & Osborne, V. A. (2009). Revisiting practice-based research networks as a platform for mental health services research. *Administration & Policy in Mental Health & Mental Health Services Research, 36,* 308–321.

Milne, D., & Reiser, R. P. (2012). A rationale for evidence-based clinical supervision. *Journal of Contemporary Psychotherapy, 42*, 139–149.

Mitchell, G. K. (2010). Generating high-quality clinical evidence in palliative care using n-of-1 trials. *Journal of Palliative Medicine, 13*, 1185–1186.

National Cancer Institute (NCI). (2011). Cancer control continuum. Retrieved from http://cancercontrol.cancer.gov/od/continuum.html

Nevo, I., & Slonim-Nevo, V. (2011). The myth of evidence-based practice: Toward evidence-informed practice. *British Journal of Social Work, 41*, 1176–1197.

Plath, D., & Gibbons, J. (2010). Discoveries on a data-mining expedition: Single session social work in hospitals. *Social Work in Health Care, 49*, 703–717.

Sackett, D. L., Rosenberg, W. M., Gray, J. A., Haynes, R. B., & Richardson, W. S. (1996). Evidence based medicine: What it is and what it isn't. *British Medical Journal, 312*, 71–72.

Sagar, S. M. (2008). How do we evaluate outcome in an integrative oncology program? *Current Oncology, 15*, s78–s82.

Straus, S. E., & McAlister, F. A. (2000). Evidence-based medicine: A commentary on common criticisms. *Canadian Medical Association Journal, 163*, 837–841.

Sung, L., & Feldman, B. M. (2006). N-of-1 trials: Innovative methods to evaluate complementary and alternative medicines in pediatric cancer. *Journal of Pediatric Hematology and Oncology, 28*, 263–166.

Tai, B., Straus, M. M., Liu, D., Sparenborg, S., Jackson, R., & McCarty, D. (2010). The first decade of the National Drug Abuse Treatment Clinical Trials Network: Bridging the gap between research and practice to improve drug treatment. *Journal of Substance Abuse Treatment, 38*, s4–s13.

Tavris, C. (2003). Mind games: Psychological warfare between therapists and scientists. *Chronicle Review, 49*(25), B7.

Thomas, G., & Pring, R. (Eds.). (2004). *Evidence-based practice in education*. New York, NY: Open University Press.

Vaughn, M. G., Howard, M., & Thyer, B. A. (Eds.). (2009). *Readings in evidence-based social work: Synthesis of the intervention knowledge base*. Thousand Oaks, CA: Sage.

Wade, K., & Neuman, K. (2007). Practice-based research: Changing the professional culture and language of social work. *Social Work in Health Care, 44*, 49–64.

Wakefield, J. C., & Kirk, S. A. (1996). Unscientific thinking about scientific practice: Evaluating the scientist-practitioner model. *Social Work Research, 20*, 83–95.

Wallace, M., & Wray, A. (2011). Scholarly reading as a model for scholarly writing. In T. S. Rocco & T. Hatcher (Eds.), *The handbook of scholarly writing and publishing* (pp. 44–61). San Francisco, CA: Jossey-Bass.

Westfall, J. M., Fagnan, L. J., Handley, M., Salsberg, J., McGinnis, P., Zittleman, L. K., & Macaulay, A. C. (2009). Practice-based research is community engagement. *Journal of the American Board of Family Medicine, 22*, 423–427.

Woolf, S. H., & Johnson, R. E. (2005). The break-even point: When medical advances are less important than improving the fidelity with which they are delivered. *Annals of Family Medicine, 3*, 545–552.

26

Mary Ann Burg

Finding Funding for Oncology Social Work Research

Key Concepts

- *A practice-based "researchable" question is one that is stated as an expectation of what outcome(s) might be achieved by instituting a new intervention technique.*
- *Getting research done in a clinical setting is often enhanced by seeking collaboration with other staff and/or local academic researchers.*

Why *You* Are the Right Person to Start a Practice-Based Research Project

Admit it: Some of you are itching to do practice-based research but are afraid to take the plunge. You may think you don't have the expertise to carry out a research study, worry that your research questions are too practical or simplistic, or believe you have a great research question but can't pitch it convincingly to others. Moreover, you may think that you could never convince your administration or supervisor to allow you to spend work time carrying out a research study. Finally, you may have no idea how to get financial support. However, you, the practicing oncology social worker, are *exactly* the right person to generate great practice-based research questions: You work in the oncology setting, have direct knowledge of how patients and families experience cancer care, and are an expert on how the health care system can help or hinder opportunities for cancer patients. These are the critical vantage points that spawn good practice-based research questions—questions that can lead to funded research projects and produce relevant data for improving cancer care. This chapter addresses how to plan and find funding for your practice-based research project.

Wresting Your Practice-Based Passion into a "Researchable" Question

What's a good practice-based research question? The answer is in the following four simple components:

- It can be posed as a researchable question.
- The answer(s) generated from the research question will have practical implications for improving cancer care and/or meeting unmet needs of patients and their families.
- There are precise ways to implement and measure the ideas in your research question.
- It is feasible to carry out the research in your practice setting.

Many of us become interested in, even fascinated with, a particular part of our work, leading us to contemplate research. Sometimes this passion emanates from witnessing care gaps in cancer settings or missed opportunities for helping patients, then wishing we could try new or better ways to deliver psychosocial care. These are great places to start, since seeing a research project from start to finish requires passion. However, to write a convincing research proposal to sell to your administration and potential collaborators and funders, your idea first needs to be developed into a *researchable question*.

A researchable question is usually stated as an expectation about what might happen if something were changed. For example, Olga Arias, an oncology social worker in an outpatient breast cancer treatment clinic, has had patients say they experience an unexpected and strong sense of isolation and depression after completing treatment. Olga did research online and found that this experience is not uncommon for cancer survivors: Once leaving active treatment, they expect to feel relieved and happy but sometimes feel scared and isolated—feelings compounded by friends and family members who are relieved the treatment phase is complete and expect the cancer survivor to happily resume his or her normal life.

Olga doesn't see her patients once they complete treatment, but she has wondered what she could do after treatment to help survivors prepare for and cope with this isolation. She brought the topic up in a staff meeting, and her social work colleagues agreed that it would be great to help prepare their patients for posttreatment mood problems. The group then came up with the idea that if the survivor has a friend or significant other who can be educated about this potential posttreatment isolation, that person could be trained to serve as a coping partner or coach. Therein lay the ideas needed for a researchable question.

The Researchable Question: Does an intervention to train a caregiver or close friend of a breast cancer patient about ways to support the patient in the posttreatment phase help reduce the sense of posttreatment isolation some patients experience?

The second part of developing a good research question is making sure the answer(s) generated from the research will have practical implications. In other words, how will the answers help staff meet unmet patient needs in your facility (e.g., posttreatment isolation)?

First, find a way to document that the unmet need exists—your "need statement." This might be supported by anecdotal data (e.g., patient and caregiver testimonials); through interviews or surveys of patients, caregivers, and hospital staff; with relevant electronic medical records or utilization data; and with evidence from a targeted literature review that supports the need for improved care in your proposed area. You should also be able to argue that this unmet need falls within the mission of your cancer center. Better yet, consider how it may create efficiencies at your workplace from the administration's point of view (e.g., decreased posttreatment phone calls from patients or fewer follow-up appointments). Finally, clearly articulate who would benefit from the project and what the specific benefits would be.

A researchable question also requires that you have considered a precise and consistent method to pilot test the efficacy of the proposed intervention and specific ways to measure its outcome(s) in your setting. The first part of this entails showing your capacity and expertise to deliver the intervention and adequately describing the details of implementation (the who, what, when, where, and how of the intervention). In Olga Arias's example, she would need to work closely with her staff to (1) develop a detailed model of the components of the partner-based posttreatment support training, (2) describe how it would be delivered within the context of their patient care flow and by whom, (3) clearly articulate how patients and their partners would be recruited for the intervention, and (4) decide how many patient–partner dyads would be trained and over what time period.

Olga and her staff would also need to consider ways to measure the outcome(s) of the intervention. Including more than one outcome in your research proposal to provide sufficient evidence to support its usefulness is a good idea. For example, in Olga's case, we know she wants to find out if the partner training intervention decreases the chances of breast cancer patients experiencing posttreatment feelings of isolation. She might work with staff to develop a survey that asks previous patients and their partners about how problematic this isolation was. This data would then serve as a baseline to compare to the same data gathered from patients and partners after they go through the intervention. She might want to add open-ended questions that elicit their opinions about how useful the intervention was for them, perhaps adding a second outcome measure specific to how the breast cancer survivor's mood was affected by being a participant in the intervention project. Olga could then review the research literature to see if there is a standardized scale that measures isolation, loneliness, or related moods. This scale could be incorporated into the set of questions asked of the patients who participate in the project.

Finally, she might consider what available data could be used to demonstrate the effects of her intervention project. Called "clinical data mining," this is the use of patient data routinely collected in the hospital systems (including social work documentation, medical chart records, intake forms, financial statements, treatment plans, patient satisfaction surveys, and hospital tumor registry data) for use in practice-based research (Epstein, 2010). Olga could potentially utilize available hospital records to find out how often oncology patients attempt to contact their oncology providers after treatment. This data could be collected for the patients participating in the intervention to see if they have fewer follow-up phone calls than similar patients who did not receive the intervention.

Once their outcome measures are selected, Olga and her colleagues will have to consider (1) a method to administer surveys or scales to the patient–partner dyads who go through the intervention, (2) a reasonable timeframe and method for following up with the participants after the intervention, and (3) the possibility of having a "usual care" group of patients in her study (a comparison group) who do not get the intervention to compare them to patients who have the intervention.

The final component of developing the researchable question is feasibility. Support for the project from key stakeholders within the cancer center is essential to the feasibility of undertaking a research project. This buy-in is essential to being able to complete the research project. The level of support from administration, social work and nurse supervisors, and staff colleagues will determine the "research readiness" of your workplace. Securing support may require a series of meetings with your stakeholder groups to promote your research idea. It is useful to have a written project summary—also called an "executive summary"—to give to key stakeholders. The summary should clearly outline the need the project serves, the impact it might have (including impacts on patient care, patient satisfaction with care, and facility reputation in the community), how it fits within the mission of your facility, and a description of the intervention and follow-up measures. You will need stakeholder buy-in before requesting letters of support from your administration to include in grant applications for funding agencies and before approaching your facility's human subjects' committee (also called the institutional review board) for securing permission to conduct the research.

Project feasibility also requires that you have given careful thought and have done your fact-checking to ensure that you have access to the subjects, data, staff time, physical facilities, and technical support needed to carry out the research. Feasibility can be enhanced by partnering with experts within your institution (e.g., physicians, nurses, or other professionals with interest and expertise in psychosocial oncology and patient care) or experts in local area universities interested in collaborating with you on your research project who can also provide technical expertise (such as helping you develop the project protocol, providing data analysis support, helping you disseminate project findings through presentations at meetings, and publishing the project outcomes in clinical journals). Universities with graduate programs often have faculty and graduate students looking for potential research projects. A graduate school of social work is a great place to look for research partners. Also, look for partnerships with faculty and students in schools of nursing, medicine, public health, psychology, and health care administration.

Funding Your Practice-Based Research Proposal

Some small research projects can be conducted without complete the project by paying for training materials, overhead expenses (e.g., telephone, postage, and computer hardware, if needed), and salary support for a research assistant or consultant to complete data collection, data management, and analysis. You may also be able to fund part of your own salary or to pay for travel to professional meetings to present your research findings. Some research grants require a line-item budget with every expense for the project detailed; other grants are given as a lump sum based on your best estimate of the costs of your project or the award amount set by the funding agency.

Government and foundation grants are the two major categories of grant-funding agencies. Government grants emanate from some level of government and include federal grants (e.g., National Cancer Institute [NCI] and Centers for Disease Control and Prevention), grants from state agencies (e.g., state Cancer Control offices), or county or city grants (usually special funds from taxpayer initiatives that are released for targeted reasons or community foundations). Government research grants such as those from the NCI are competitive—only 10% to 15% are funded (U.S. Department of Health and Human Services, National Institutes of Health, Research Portfolio Online Reporting Tool, 2009)—and intended for highly technical academic researchers. Foundation grants include those from national private or nonprofit charitable organizations (e.g., the American Cancer Society [ACS] and Susan G. Komen for the Cure) and those from regional and local nonprofit and not-for-profit charitable foundations (e.g., regional cancer charities or Blue Foundations). Many private for-profit corporations, including banks (e.g., Bank of America), pharmaceutical companies (e.g., Eli Lilly and Novartis), and other national and international corporations (e.g., Exxon, Kroger, and Walmart) also have foundations with dedicated grants for health care.

Grants can be peer reviewed or non–peer reviewed. Peer-reviewed grants are reviewed and scored by a panel of experts in the particular field of research, and after review, some proportion of the high-scoring grants are funded depending on the grant agency's budget and how closely the grants fit into the mission of the funding agency. This is the typical process used by the funding programs of federal agencies, including the NCI and ACS.

Although foundations have a wide range of grant-funding processes, many foundations, particularly regional, corporate, and individual, have a board that reviews grant applications; sometimes, applications are reviewed on an ongoing basis over the year rather than at specific application deadlines. Typically, grants from foundations will have very specific types of projects they look to fund (e.g., short demonstration projects or projects for only certain types of cancers) and will have very specific eligibility criteria for grantees (e.g., they will fund programs only in particular geographic areas). Moreover, foundation grants tend to require less rigorous applications (shorter and not as technically sophisticated as federal grants), taking less time to

interest rather than a full-blown application. The grant officer will review the letter to determine whether your idea falls into a fundable category in his or her agency; if it does, he or she will ask you to complete a full grant application.

So what type of grant would someone like Olga Arias look for to fund her patient–partner dyad training intervention project? First, many health care systems, including hospital-based cancer centers, have in-house foundations that receive philanthropic donations (often from grateful patients), and the foundation boards will sometimes look for great patient care projects to support with some of the donated money. Or Olga could pitch her grant to her hospital administration as a "quality improvement" (QI) project to garner in-house funding dedicated to QI efforts. Hospitals and services within hospitals are required to demonstrate accountability: for example, who is being served, what services are being received, the outcomes of patient services, how patient services can be improved, and the cost effectiveness of patient services (Epstein & Blumenfield, 2001). Especially in the case of hospital social service departments, there is a continual need to justify services and their costs, because social services are typically not separately billable to third-party insurers (as are physician fees, for example) but are instead bundled into the overall hospital budget. For example, QI departments are often interested in solving problems in "transitions" for patients—moving from one phase of treatment to the next or to off treatment. Framing the patient–dyad intervention project this way will more likely engage interdisciplinary collaboration and potentially some practical support from the hospital for the project.

Second, Olga can search for local and regional foundations for funding. There are a variety of Internet search engines that work with key words (e.g., breast cancer, survivor, patient care, see Table 26.1) to identify foundations with monies to fund related projects. A great place to start is the Grantsmanship Center, which includes many resources, grant-writing tips, and a search engine that allows you to search for grants by type, locality, and topic. Third, Olga can look at the websites of the national cancer foundations, including the ACS, Susan G. Komen for the Cure, Lance Armstrong Foundation, and Avon Foundation, and some of the pharmaceutical company foundations to see what types of grants they offer and if her project might fit within these foundations' interests.

You can find important tips for searching for foundation grants in multiple sources, including some of the books included in the bibliography and through some valuable Internet sites, such as the University of North Dakota Center for Rural Health website (Center for Rural Health, University of North Dakota School of Medicine and Health Sciences, 2012).

Before you choose an agency to submit your grant to, understand the agency's mission and be sure that your project fits within it. Review the foundation's criteria for funding projects, their deadlines for submission of applications, and their review processes. Review examples of previously funded projects if they list them on their website. And before you take the plunge to begin the grant application, first call the foundation's grant officer or program officer—most foundations have a key staff person who is charged with providing information and answering questions about his or her foundation's grant-making policies. Usually, you can discuss your project idea with this person and get feedback about whether the board would be interested in your project.

Finally, if you identify a potential funder, the most important rule for writing the grant application is to follow

Table 26.1.
Select Search Engines for Funding Tips and Grant Searches

Grant Search Engine	Website Address
Charity Net	http://www.charitynetusa.com/
Chronicle of Philanthropy	http://www.philanthropy.com/section/Home/172
College of Science Pivot	http://pivot.cos.com/
Council on Foundations	http://www.cof.org
Federal Register	http://www.federalregister.gov
Foundation Center Directory	http://www.fdncenter.org/funders
Grant Advisor	http://www.grantadvisor.com
Grantsmanship Center	http://www.tgci.com
IRS website Publication 78	http://www.irs.gov/Charities-&-Non-Profits/Search-for-Charities

Table 26.2.
Questions Funders Ask About Grant Proposals

- Why is this program or research project important (the "so what?" question)?
- Do the problem and request meet our funding mission?
- Does it assist a small group of people or does it have a more expansive social mission?
- Does the applicant appear to have the ability, skill, time, and technical knowledge to carry out the program in the stipulated time and within the proposed budget?
- What real difference will this project make to the cancer community?

Source: Center for Rural Health, University of North Dakota School of Medicine and Health Sciences (2012).

Table 26.3.
Tips for Writing Foundation Grants

• Discuss your project with the foundation grant's officer before you start the application to make sure your idea fits well with the funding agency's mission. • Use perfect spelling and grammar. • Follow the funder's guidelines for content and format exactly. • Avoid jargon that reviewers may not understand.

the funding agency's application instructions precisely, giving them everything they ask for in your application and nothing more (see Tables 26.2 and 26.3). Often, details such as page limits, budget limitations, and timelines are critical to just getting your application through the door of the foundation for review, and failing to follow grant application instructions is a major mistake new grant applicants make. The second most important rule for practicing social workers looking to fund a research project is to keep trying! Even the most seasoned academic researchers often have to pitch research ideas multiple times to different funding agencies before receiving a favorable response.

Pearls

- Practice articulating your research plan in layperson's terms to be sure you can clearly describe it and make it compelling to potential partners and funders.
- Work at getting buy-in from all stakeholders (coworkers, administration, community partners, and patients) to prevent future roadblocks to completing your research.
- Always consult with a program officer from the granting agency to make sure your concept fits with the agency's mission.
- Keep working at it: Even an unfunded grant proposal can be used to seed a new grant proposal in a similar area of practice-based research.

Pitfalls

- A complex research plan may be difficult to complete in the real world of oncology practice.
- Lack of clarity about practice implications of research proposals lessens your chances of obtaining support.
- Failure to follow the fine print in grant application guidelines may result in disqualification of your application.

There are some great benefits to complementing your oncology social work practice with research. First, we know from the National Association of Social Workers' Code of Ethics that evidence-based practice is an obligation of the practicing social worker. This includes utilizing evidence-based literature to inform your practice and generating evidence from your practice to contribute to the evidence for social work interventions.

As is true with all social work practice, developing a practice-based research project and writing grants involves a set of skills that can be learned but also requires some art as well. The art includes managing to present your ideas in a logical but compelling fashion and persuading key stakeholders to support your efforts to include practice-based research in your work as an oncology social worker.

You and your colleagues will find that investing some time and effort to do practice-based research will help to renew your excitement about your work with patients. The process of posing critical questions about ways to improve patient care in your workplace and testing new patient care approaches makes the daily grind more interesting and, even more important, may yield improved cancer care outcomes for your patients. As you recruit cases or information for your study, colleagues become more aware of the psychosocial problem you are trying to address and may become champions of your approach. The research process stretches your mind and may stretch your horizons too, especially if in the process you manage to connect with new sets of colleagues, including university-based researchers to consult on your research projects and practitioners in other cancer settings who may want to collaborate on your project. Furthermore, when the project is complete, you may have the opportunity to present your results at professional meetings on a local, state, or national level, and you may be able to utilize your research findings to advocate for improved patient care in some influential venues in your workplace, community, and policymaking settings.

ADDITIONAL RESOURCES

Arnett, D. K. (2009). Writing effective grant applications. *Circulation, 120*, 2607–2612.

Burke, J., & Prater, C. A. (2000). *I'll grant you that: A step-by-step guide to finding funds, designing winning projects, and writing powerful grant proposals.* Portsmouth, NH: Heinemann.

Carlson, M., & O'Neal-McElrath, T. (2008). *Winning grants step by step.* San Francisco, CA: Jossey-Bass.

Karsh, E., & Fox, A. S. (2009). *The only grant-writing book you'll ever need: Top grant writers and grant givers share their secrets.* New York, NY: Basic Books.

Lyons, K. J., & Gitlin, L. N. (2008). *Successful grant writing: Strategies for health and human service professionals.* New York, NY: Springer.

Pequenet, W., Boyce, C. A., & Stover, E. (Eds.). (2011). *How to write a successful grant application: A guide for social scientists.* New York, NY: Springer.

Robbins, V. (2010). *101 tips for aspiring grant writers.* Woodland, CA: Creative Resources and Research.

U.S. Department of Health and Human Services, Office of Extramural Research, National Institutes of Health. (n.d.). *Types of grant programs.* Retrieved from http://grants.nih.gov/grants/funding/funding_program.htm

Yuen, F. K. O., Terao, K. L., & Schmidt, A. M. (2009). *Effective grant writing and program evaluation for human service professionals.* Hoboken, NJ: John Wiley & Sons.

REFERENCES

Center for Rural Health, University of North Dakota School of Medicine and Health Sciences. (2012). *Center for rural health grant writing tips.* Retrieved from http://ruralhealth.und.edu/projects/flex/pdf/grantwriting_tips.pdf

Epstein, I. (2010). *Clinical data-mining: Integrating practice and research (pocket guides to social work research methods).* New York, NY: Oxford University Press.

Epstein, I., & Blumenfield, S. (2001). *Clinical data mining in practice-based research: Social work in hospital settings.* New York, NY: Haworth Press.

U.S. Department of Health and Human Services, National Institutes of Health, Research Portfolio Online Reporting Tool (RePORT). Research project success rates by NIH Institute for 2008. Retrieved from http://report.nih.gov/success_rates/Success_ByIC.cfm

27

Guadalupe R. Palos

Writing Proposals for Foundations and Governmental Agencies

Key Concepts

- *As the demand for evidence-based social work practice, interventions, and outcomes increases, social workers should assume responsibility for writing research grants to generate new knowledge in the field.*
- *The social work profession has firsthand knowledge of and experience with psychosocial interventions and services. Social workers are qualified to write grants for programs and research studies that will fit the current and projected needs of our nation's health care system.*
- *Social workers must become adept at writing and submitting grants. They must also publish the results of their research in scientific journals outside their profession so that the findings may be disseminated across the disciplines.*

After working for years with patients and their families in a large academic cancer center, I, a master's-prepared social worker, became interested in how caring for a loved one diagnosed with advanced cancer affected the physical and emotional health of family caregivers. I was particularly concerned about the intensity and types of symptoms caregivers reported, such as sadness, tiredness, or sleep disturbances. The desire to conduct my own research prompted me to return to school and obtain my doctoral degree. As I began my research career, I realized grant funding was required to conduct research on caregiver burden. After meeting with different researchers and mentors, I decided to apply for a federal grant from the National Cancer Institute. I had no experience in writing such a grant and quickly realized that reaching my goal would require a substantial amount of work, knowledge, skills, patience, and perseverance. Nonetheless, I was ready to begin my journey toward obtaining federal funding.

Several national trends will increase the need for social workers to become adept at writing grants for program and research funding. First, it is unknown how health and related social services under the 2010 Affordable Care Act will be delivered to America's population (U.S. Department of Health and Human Services, 2012). Second, the current economic turmoil has contributed to high unemployment rates, cutbacks in social services, loss of housing, and several other similarly difficult consequences (U.S. Department of Commerce, Bureau of Economic Analysis, 2013). Third, social work practice continues to be influenced by the dramatic increase in America's cultural, racial, and ethnic diversity. Fourth, the projected growth of the U.S. population aged 65 years and older will increase the need for social workers with expertise in gerontology (Federal Interagency Forum on Aging-Related Statistics, 2012). Last is the changing definition of U.S. families, which requires social workers to better understand the nontraditional roles, support, and structures of families in crisis. These can have an impact on the types of services and interventions social workers provide for America's individuals, families, and other vulnerable populations and may limit or increase the need for innovative social services, interventions, and programs. However, these may not be available due to economic constraints or the lack of evidence to show which services or programs are the most effective in outcomes and cost.

The social work profession is recognized and respected for its proactive response to problems impacting society. In fact, a National Institutes of Health (NIH) report acknowledged that "social work was one of the largest allied health professions . . . that worked within and across systems of care and services on a variety of levels and in direct practice with diverse and/or multi-problem populations" (Office of Behavioral and Social Sciences Research, 2003). One way social workers demonstrate the truth in the NIH statement is by writing grants successful in obtaining funding for program services or research studies. Successful grant writing is an art and a science that requires patience, perseverance, and resilience, and few social workers have the expertise necessary to write well-crafted proposals and grant applications. The NIH has recognized the need to increase social workers' participation in "developing innovative theory driven research on social work practice, concepts, and theories . . . and to increase the submission of research relevant to social work practice" (Office of Behavioral and Social Sciences Research, 2003; Figure 27.1). Despite this acknowledgment, a study conducted by the Institute for the Advancement of Social Work Research (IASWR, 2009) found that few social workers have received funding for research-based grants that promote the science of social work practice.

This chapter provides an overview of federal and other sources that fund social work research studies or career development grants. Discussed are the essential elements of a well-crafted proposal, the research grant application process, and tips for writing grants. Finally, the chapter chronicles the author's personal experience as the awardee of a 5-year K07 career development grant from the NCI to study the effects of symptoms on underserved, minority caregivers.

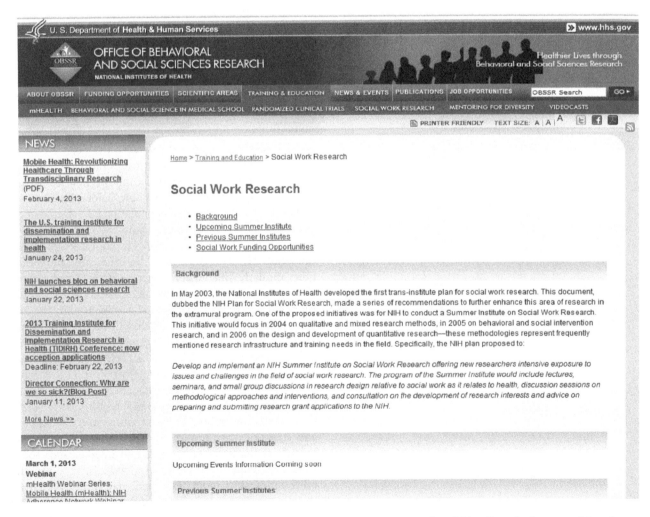

The Mystery of Funding

The global economic crisis has curtailed funding and increased the challenges involved in obtaining grants.

U. S. Department of Health & Human Services
www.hhs.gov
OFFICE OF BEHAVIORAL AND SOCIAL SCIENCES RESEARCH
NATIONAL INSTITUTES OF HEALTH
Healthier Lives through Behavioral and Social Sciences Research
ABOUT OBSSR | FUNDING OPPORTUNITIES | SCIENTIFIC AREAS | TRAINING & EDUCATION | NEWS & EVENTS | PUBLICATIONS | JOB OPPORTUNITIES | OBSSR Search | GO
mHEALTH | BEHAVIORAL AND SOCIAL SCIENCE IN MEDICAL SCHOOL | RANDOMIZED CLINICAL TRIALS | SOCIAL WORK RESEARCH | MENTORING FOR DIVERSITY | VIDEOCASTS
PRINTER FRIENDLY TEXT SIZE: A | A | A

NEWS

Mobile Health: Revolutionizing Healthcare Through Transdisciplinary Research (PDF)
February 4, 2013

The U.S. training institute for dissemination and implementation research in health
January 24, 2013

NIH launches blog on behavioral and social sciences research
January 22, 2013

2013 Training Institute for Dissemination and Implementation Research in Health (TIDIRH) Conference: now acception applications
Deadline: February 22, 2013

Director Connection: Why are we so sick?(Blog Post)
January 11, 2013

More News >>

CALENDAR

March 1, 2013
Webinar
mHealth Webinar Series:
Mobile Health (mHealth): NIH

Home > Training and Education > Social Work Research

Social Work Research

- Background
- Upcoming Summer Institute
- Previous Summer Institutes
- Social Work Funding Opportunities

Background

In May 2003, the National Institutes of Health developed the first trans-institute plan for social work research. This document, dubbed the NIH Plan for Social Work Research, made a series of recommendations to further enhance this area of research in the extramural program. One of the proposed initiatives was for NIH to conduct a Summer Institute on Social Work Research. This initiative would focus in 2004 on qualitative and mixed research methods, in 2005 on behavioral and social intervention research, and in 2006 on the design and development of quantitative research—these methodologies represent frequently mentioned research infrastructure and training needs in the field. Specifically, the NIH plan proposed to:

Develop and implement an NIH Summer Institute on Social Work Research offering new researchers intensive exposure to issues and challenges in the field of social work research. The program of the Summer Institute would include lectures, seminars, and small group discussions in research design relative to social work as it relates to health, discussion sessions on methodological approaches and interventions, and consultation on the development of research interests and advice on preparing and submitting research grant applications to the NIH.

Upcoming Summer Institute

Upcoming Events Information Coming soon

Previous Summer Institutes

Figure 27.1. Screenshot of the Social Work Research Website of the National Institutes of Health's Office of Behavior and Social Sciences Research

In fact, the American Cancer Society cancelled its 2013 funding cycle (American Cancer Society, 2013). During this curtailing, social workers can prepare themselves by obtaining the skills needed to write successful grants. Grant applications focus on three areas of funding: (1) direct services or evaluations, (2) research studies, and (3) career development. Although grant applications have several elements in common, each has its own set of requirements. Social workers have historically been most familiar with writing grants for direct services or program evaluation. Funding for these comes from foundations, nonprofit organizations, corporate sponsors, or governmental agencies. The following discussion focuses on funding from foundations and federal agencies.

Philanthropic Sources

The Robert Wood Johnson Foundation (RWJF) is an example of a philanthropic group that funds program and research on diverse populations and social issues. Because it is involved in varied facets of health care, the RWJF is an ideal source of funding for social work applications. The foundation targets vulnerable populations and areas such as addiction, substance abuse, and access/barriers to care. The RWJF funds evaluation, research, direct services demonstrations, and several other types of research in seven program areas. The foundation supports tax-exempt public agencies, universities, and public charities.

Social workers are noted for identifying gaps in direct services and supporting changes in public policies. The RWJF funds applications that promote change in communities and corporate practice through public policy. One example is the Supporting a Convening of Policy-Makers at the Latino Legislative Summit on Health grant. The purpose of this grant was to work with elected and appointed officials to create and promote healthy communities. The RWJF website provides detailed information on the grants, topics, and current calls for proposals (RWJF, 2014). Other sources of private funding from foundations or corporations may be found on the Foundation Center (http://foundationcenter.org/) and the Council on Foundations (http://www.cof.org/) websites.

Federal Agencies

The Agency for Healthcare Research and Quality (AHRQ) and NIH are two federal agencies that provide funding for research, training, and small business ventures. Additional sources of federal funding include the Centers for Disease Control and Prevention (CDC) and Health Resources and Services Administration (HRSA). Each agency's website provides information about the research priorities, guidelines, and other pertinent information for the grant writer.

Agency for Healthcare Research and Quality

The AHRQ provides diverse intramural and extramural pre- and postdoctoral educational and career development grants and opportunities in health services research. The agency also supports the development of health services research infrastructure through emerging centers of excellence and works with federal and academic partners to develop innovative educational initiatives.

The AHRQ also provides funding through the American Recovery and Reinvestment Act (ARRA) to provide patients, clinicians, and others with evidence-based information to make informed decisions about health care (AHRQ, 2010). One innovative adaptation and dissemination grant awarded through ARRA funding is entitled Story Guides: Making Comparative Effectiveness Useful for Vulnerable Patients (Grant No. R18HS19353-01). Social workers have long delivered services and interventions to high-risk and vulnerable populations such as the aged, children, and the underserved and are in ideal positions to assess whether a patient or client understands the services, interventions, or guidelines. Through collaborative networks, this type of research could be led by a social worker with research experience. The AHRQ also provides excellent resources for those seeking research, educational (pre- and postdoctoral grants), and career (career development awards for emerging scientists) opportunities in health service research. Brief descriptions and instructions for grants at the individual and institutional levels are available at http://www.ahrq.gov/funding/training-grants/index.html.

National Institutes of Health

In 2009, the IASWR developed the *Directory of Social Work Research Grants Awarded by the National Institutes of Health* to identify social work researchers funded by the NIH, their topics of study, and funding sources (IASWR, 2009). The directory reflects the results of a study to determine the number of social work researchers receiving grants as principal investigators over the past decade and a half. The IASWR goal was to highlight the robustness of social work research, which made important contributions to America's public health priorities. The IASWR study found that between 1993 and 2009, social workers received only 680 NIH grants. This low statistic is both encouraging and disheartening. Despite some NIH funding, support for social work research remains limited. The NIH Research Agenda for Social Work was a major advancement for expanding the science and knowledge of evidence-based social work practice. The full "NIH Plan for Social Work Research" is available at http://obssr.od.nih.gov/news.html.

Despite these opportunities, there continues to be a gap in social work research as reflected by the current absence of funding announcements focused specifically on social work practice or research. Social workers must become adept at writing grants and submitting them for funding. Social workers must also publish the results of their research in peer-reviewed scientific journals outside the social work profession so the findings may be disseminated across the disciplines.

National Institutes of Health Career Development and Research Awards

The NIH offers a variety of research grant awards for early career investigators. Although the number of different awards can be somewhat daunting to new researchers, the NIH provides excellent resources on writing grants that can be accessed online (NIH, 2014). Figure 27.2 provides a snapshot of the types of grants available, provides links to instructions on how to apply, and outlines steps explaining the grant process. These resources provide invaluable information and tips specific to each agency and grant. Funding is available for social work research and program initiatives if social workers look for the sources and have innovative ideas that will contribute to the body of knowledge needed for evidence-based social work practice (Langhorst & Svikis, 2007).

Elements of a Well-Crafted Proposal

Regardless of which funding source is selected, there are shared elements across these three funding sources and others and a plethora of literature available on grant writing from the perspective of different disciplines (Hasche, Perron, & Proctor, 2009; Stein et al., 2012; Taylor, 2010; Wescott & Laskofski, 2012). This section describes common elements and steps integral to writing a grant application.

Preplanning

Preplanning entails getting organized and being prepared. Before initiating literature reviews or making contact with grant sources, one must develop a draft of an abstract. In this context, the abstract provides a general idea of the research question, design, target population, setting, methodology, statistical analysis, and resources needed. A dynamic document that evolves over time, the abstract can be used by the grant writer as he or she conducts literature/funding reviews, contacts prospective collaborators, and speaks with appropriate grant officers. This type of preparation shows the grant or program officer, potential partners, and others that the research is being carefully planned and monitored.

A general consensus exists among funders that collaborative research—interdisciplinary, multidisciplinary, and transdisciplinary—is the best way to maximize resources and support successful implementation of the program or research study. Each team member provides his or her own set of tools, expertise, and knowledge of an area needed to support the application. For example, social workers bring to the team their expert knowledge of working with diverse and vulnerable families. They are skilled in providing psychosocial interventions and services across populations. Other key partners include statisticians, epidemiologists, physicians, nurses, economists, or other professionals whose expertise will increase the robustness of the grant application. It is also crucial to include representatives from the target population (e.g., patients, clients, and community members). The social worker can lead the team as the principal investigator and maximize the expertise of each member.

Mentors are also needed for career development grants to provide guidance and teaching in an area the candidate may wish to further develop or learn. Once again, it is more beneficial to involve members of diverse professions to add to the robustness of a career plan. Mentors do not always have to be in the same geographic region as the candidate; the applicant must simply justify why the proposed mentor

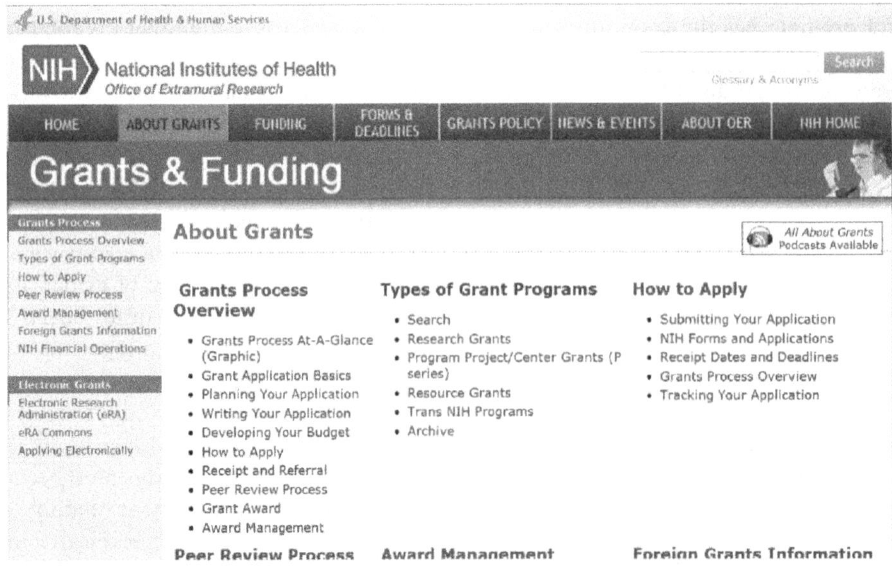

Figure 27.2. Screenshot of the Grants and Funding Website of the National Institutes of Health's Office of Extramural Research

is best qualified to be a team member. Working with the grant officer to determine the best strategies for the specific grant is also useful.

Developing a tentative timeline for activities related to grant preparation and a checklist to keep track of which tasks have been accomplished or still need to be completed is another helpful preproposal activity. "An Evidence-Based Guide to Writing Grant Proposals for Clinical Research" is an excellent article by Inouye and Fiellin (2005).

Review Relevant Literature and Potential Funding Sources

It is critical to conduct an in-depth literature review of the topic before a funding source is identified. Also beneficial is determining whether research in the area has been funded previously. The NIH Research Portfolio Online Reporting Tools (RePORT) is an online source for information about NIH-funded research projects that also includes access to publications and patents resulting from the funding (http://report.nih.gov/index.aspx). The directory provides the name of the principal investigator, grant number, institute awarding the grant, grant mechanism, grant title, and the years for which funding was obtained.

Know Program Officers, Guidelines, and Forms

The grant officer or program manager responsible for the particular call for funding is one of the most underutilized resources. Although potential investigators are advised to contact a program manager, many do not. The grant officer can become an applicant's best resource, providing information on the specifics of the call, helping determine whether your topic or career level fits the call, and providing a wealth of other information that investigators often don't even think about. Also, if the program manager is familiar with your research and its aims, design, and outcomes, he or she can provide information to the review committee if questions come up during the sessions.

Another critical step is to become familiar with the details of the guidelines and identify the most current application forms to use. Most funding agencies require an electronic application submission process, so understanding both the forms and the electronic program used to download and submit the application is key. Many systems require agency-specific user names, passwords, and other credentialing steps. Because many of these requirements seem so basic, individuals may assume that they will be able to understand or learn the systems without any problems. One such system is the Electronic Research Administration (eRA), which provides applicants, grantees, and federal staff with the tools necessary for electronic processing of grants. This system is used by most federal agencies, including those listed earlier, such as the NIH, AHRQ, HRSA, and CDC. The eRA Commons and IMPAC II systems support the full grant life cycle from receipt of the application to award to closeout (NIH, 2013b).

Writing

Applicants must describe their research in clear and concise terms that the reviewers and other scientists can easily understand. It is important to follow the outline provided by the funding agency. Reviewers are accustomed to having grant applications written in a certain manner. Compliance with protocol is one of the first evaluation criteria because it reflects the applicant's ability to follow instructions precisely. You should also be aware of such seemingly minor details as preferred spacing, font, and size and required margins. The following sections highlight different elements of the grant application that must be addressed in the applicant's written plan. There are numerous publications available on grant writing from the perspectives of different disciplines (Lee, 2010; Long & Shobe, 2010; Marshall, 2012; Powers & Swick, 2011; Proctor, Powell, Baumann, Hamilton, & Santens, 2012; Wurmser & Hedges, 2009).

Cover Letter

The cover letter is helpful and can be used to request a specific institute or study section or to recommend reviewers if your research topic focuses on a rare scientific issue or unusual methodology (e.g., grounded qualitative research). It will also help staff assign the application to the most appropriate review committee. Each institute or funding announcement has a program officer (PO) assigned to that particular agency or item. Due to the number of institutes, announcements, and complexities associated with writing grants, it is strongly recommended that the PO be an essential member of your team. For example, it is beneficial to make an appointment to speak with the PO; before the appointment, you should prepare a draft of your abstract (or even e-mail the abstract before your meeting) and have your list of questions available to discuss.

Title

The title is an important part of the application and must immediately capture the reader's attention. The title needs to convey the research focus in a novel and brief manner. It is useful to write down several versions of a title and have a group of colleagues read, help edit, refine, or change it as needed. This is a time to be appreciative of feedback—positive or negative, as it can be used to strengthen your application. In general, there is a word limitation on the title, so plan for a full title and a running title for the proposal.

Research Design

The majority of grant applications follow the same outline for writing the proposal: (1) abstract; (2) specific aims;

(3) background and significance; (4) research design and methods; and (5) implications of the proposed research for public health, social work, or whichever discipline the research focuses on. Proposals may vary in their requests for other supporting documents, such as biographical information on key study personnel, evidence that the appropriate resources to conduct the study are available to the researcher, or strategies that will be used to protect the confidentiality of all human subjects needed for a study.

Review Process

Once the funding source has been identified, the applicant must become familiar with the review process. In particular, applicants should study the different review committees, guidelines, and committee members. The NIH provides the Center for Scientific Review (CSR), a website for NIH grant applications and their review for scientific merit (NIH, 2013a). Other funding sources will have similar resources available for applicants to review before submitting their applications.

The applicant should participate in review activities to become knowledgeable about the process or questions that may arise during the review. For example, an applicant can volunteer to be a member of the institutional scientific review committee or board or participate in scientific reviews conducted by professional organizations. The applicant will also benefit from the following strategies: ask senior investigators to review the research design for scientific merit; have scientific editors assess the writing style, organization, clarity, spelling, and grammar; and contact institutional research departments, such as grants and contracts and research administrations, to ensure all federal and institutional guidelines have been addressed.

Once the review has been completed, the applicant will receive written critiques from the assigned reviewers, a summary of the discussion, scores for each review criterion, and any type of administrative notes of special consideration.

Dissemination of Results

Once a grant application has been funded and is underway, the principal investigator must develop a publication plan. Preliminary data can be used for abstracts or poster presentations. The literature review used in the grant application can be the principal investigator's first step in building or strengthening his or her publication record. High-impact journals are preferred in the scientific world. It is important, however, for a novice researcher to get published in a peer-reviewed and scientific journal, regardless of the impact score. Additional information on impact factors can be found in a series of publications covering writing grants and publishing results (Eastwood et al., 2012). An excellent series of publications describing strategies for writing research grant applications and papers is available to readers at no charge from http://www.ncbi.nlm.nih.gov/pubmed/22452595.

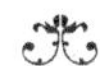

Pearls

- Develop a team of formal and informal mentors with knowledge and expertise in conducting successful research; working with budgets, restrictions, and allowable expenses specific to research studies; and collaborating with other researchers within and outside your institution.
- After consultations with my department chair, senior investigators, and NIH program officers from the National Cancer Institute and the National Institute of Nursing Research, it was determined that a career development grant would be the most strategic way to move my research career forward and build a research portfolio around the topic of caregiver burden. Through a K07 award, I would have 5 years of protected time to develop my research and career.
- Focus on an area that has a gap in knowledge and demonstrate how your innovative research will answer that gap.
- A review of the literature on cancer caregiving indicated there were few studies on underserved ethnic minority populations. Based on my experience in working with underserved Black, White, and Latino communities, I developed an interest in studying caregiver burden in the dyads of caregivers and cancer patients.
- Submit literature reviews, preliminary results, and final results to scientific meetings for poster presentations, peer-reviewed scientific journals (even those with low-impact factors), or book chapters.
- During the 2 years I spent rewriting the grants, I enrolled in scientific writing and grants-writing classes, volunteered to review colleagues' applications, and worked with editors from the institution's scientific publications department. To date, the study results have been published in high-impact journals and presented as podium or poster presentations at numerous scientific conferences, including the American Society of Clinical Oncology, the American Society of Psychosocial Oncology, and the Oncology Nursing Society.

Pitfalls

- Limitations and obstacles can prevent submission of applications, so identify them and negotiate viable solutions.

- The process of securing research funding from any source is extremely competitive. It was also evident that my limited research experience and limited publication record were major obstacles in my attempts to seek funding. Expect to have resubmission requested; it is extremely rare to have an application accepted on the first submission.
- The K07 consisted of a research and career plan. At that time, investigators were allowed three submissions (currently limited to two submissions). In my case, it took three attempts to obtain funding. The first application was rejected because the reviewers felt the research plan was too ambitious, but the career plan was well received. In the second submission, the reviewers approved of the research plan but felt the career plan was limited. The third attempt was scored favorably by the reviewers in both areas. I was awarded funding from 2005 to 2010 for the study entitled "Effects of Symptoms on Minority Caregivers," K07 CA102482, National Cancer Institute.
- Learn from mistakes, expect challenges, and enjoy the experience.

Over the past 5 years, I gained valuable experience as the study's principal investigator. I led a team of collaborators from different institutions and internal departments, research interviewers, and statisticians and worked with grant administrators from four different organizations and mentors located across the United States. From my research, I gained insight into the unique experience of cancer patients, their caregivers, and their families as they dealt with a cancer diagnosis and limited resources. For example, we learned that caregivers report symptom burden as moderate to severe psychosocial symptoms including sadness, distress, worry, or anxiety. On the other hand, patients report physical symptoms such as pain, fatigue, or sleep disturbances. This data is being used to tailor interventions to caregivers and patients. The narrative in this chapter reflects one social worker's experience in writing grants and seeking funding. I hope that this information has piqued the interest of other social workers to conduct their own research and contribute to the science and knowledge of evidence-based social work practice.

REFERENCES

Agency for Healthcare Research and Quality. (2010). American Recovery and Reinvestment Act investments in comparative effectiveness research for evidence generation. Retrieved from http://archive.ahrq.gov/funding/arra/factsheets/cerfsevgen.pdf

American Cancer Society. (2013). Funding opportunities: Cancellation of the 2013 grants cycle. Retrieved from http://www.cancer.org/research/researchprogramsfunding/fundingopportunities/index

Eastwood, P. R., Naughton, M. T., Calverley, P., Zeng, G., Beasley, R., Robinson, B., & Lee, Y. C. G. (2012). How to write research papers and grants: 2011 Asian Pacific Society for Respirology Annual Scientific Meeting Postgraduate Session. *Respirology, 17*(5), 792–801. doi:10.1111/j.1440-1843.2012.02175.x

Federal Interagency Forum on Aging-Related Statistics. (2012). *Older Americans 2012: Key indicators of well-being.* Retrieved from http://www.agingstats.gov/agingstatsdotnet/Main_Site/Data/2012_Documents/Docs/EntireChartbook.pdf

Hasche, L. K., Perron, B. E., & Proctor, E. K. (2009). Making time for dissertation grants: Strategies for social work students and educators. *Research on Social Work Practice, 19*(3), 340–350. doi:10.1177/1049731508321559

Inouye, S. K., & Fiellin, D. A. (2005). An evidence-based guide to writing grant proposals for clinical research. *Annals of Internal Medicine, 142*(4), 274–282.

Institute for the Advancement of Social Work Research (IASWR). (2009). *Directory of social work research grants awarded by National Institutes of Health: 1993–2009.* Washington, DC: Author.

Langhorst, D. M., & Svikis, S.S. (2007). The NIH R03 award: An initial funding step for social work researchers. *Research on Social Work Practice, 17*(3), 417–424.

Lee, S. J. (2010). Tips for writing successful patient-oriented research career development awards. *Hematology: American Society of Hematology Education Program, 2010*, 185–188.

Long, D. D., & Shobe, M. A. (2010). Lessons learned from preparing social workers for grant writing via connected learning. *Administration in Social Work, 34*(5), 392–404. doi:10.1080/03643107.2010.512837

Marshall, L. S. (2012). Research commentary: Grant writing: Part 1: First things first. *Journal of Radiology Nursing, 31*(4), 154–155. doi:10.1016/j.jradnu.2012.10.001

National Institutes of Health (NIH). (2013a). Centers for review. Retrieved from http://public.csr.nih.gov/Pages/default.aspx

National Institutes of Health (NIH). (2013b). Electronic research administration. Retrieved from http://era.nih.gov/

National Institutes of Health (NIH). (2014). Grants and funding. Retrieved from http://grants.nih.gov/grants/about_grants.htm

Office of Behavioral and Social Sciences Research. (2003). *NIH plan for social work research.* Washington, DC: National Institutes of Health, U.S. Department of Health and Human Services. Retrieved from http://obssr.od.nih.gov/pdf/SWR_Report.pdf

Powers, J. D., & Swick, D. C. (2011). Straight talk from recent grads: Grant writing tips for new investigators. *Academic Leadership, 9*(2), 166–168.

Proctor, E. K., Powell, B. J., Baumann, A. A., Hamilton, A. M., & Santens, R. L. (2012). Writing implementation research grant proposals: Ten key ingredients. *Implementation Science, 7*(1). Retrieved from http://www.implementationscience.com/content/7/1/96

Robert Wood Johnson Foundation (RWJF). (2014). Grants. Retrieved from http://www.rwjf.org/en/grants.html#q/maptype/grants/topics/topics:508/ll/39.994,-75.067/z/5

Stein, L. A. R., Clair, M., Lebeau, R., Prochaska, J. O., Rossi, J. S., & Swift, J. (2012). Facilitating grant proposal writing in health behaviors for university faculty: A descriptive study. *Health Promotion Practice, 13*(1), 71–80. doi:10.1177/1524839910385895

Taylor, C. (2010). Thinking out of the box: Fundraising during economic downturns. *Serials Librarian, 59*(3), 370–383. doi:10.1080/03615261003623120

U.S. Department of Commerce, Bureau of Economic Analysis. (2013). GDP and the economy. Advance estimates for the fourth quarter of 2012. Retrieved from http://www.bea.gov/scb/pdf/2013/02%20February/0213_gdpecon.pdf

U.S. Department of Health and Human Services. (2012). Read the law: The Affordable Care Act, section by section. The health care law and you. Retrieved from http://www.healthcare.gov/law/full/index.html

Wescott, L., & Laskofski, M. (2012). Grant writing tips for translational research. *Molecular Profiling: Methods and Protocols, 823*, 379–389. doi:10.1007/978-1-60327-216-2_25

Wurmser, T., & Hedges, C. (2009). Primer for successful grant writing. *AACN Advanced Critical Care, 20*(1), 102–107. doi:10.1097/NCI.0b013e3181945

28

Carly Parry and G. Stephane Philogene

Opportunities for Social Work Research in Oncology

Key Concepts

- *In the context of trends supporting interdisciplinary and team science, social work has an opportunity to position itself to help solve major public health problems.*
- *Social work's unique contributions include its combined behavioral, contextual, and systems focus and social workers' ability to work across lines of difference.*
- *Success in social work research involves the use of strategic positioning, partnering, and packaging of one's work in the biomedical and public health milieu, as well as solid grantsmanship.*

The preceding chapters in this section have described the contributions of social work research to the oncology social work knowledge base. In this closing chapter, we provide a brief commentary and road map for future social work research, highlighting the successful elements involved in obtaining funding and in positioning social work researchers to make contributions to the fields of oncology and health and population health. These elements include strategic positioning and packaging of social work research within biomedical and public health frameworks, and partnering with researchers with complementary expertise and strong grantsmanship. Although we speak from the perspective of the National Institutes of Health (NIH), the themes and suggestions we offer transcend the priorities of our institution.

In a July 19, 2013, *New York Times* editorial, Nicholas A. Christakis noted that science has evolved rapidly over the past few decades. Whether one accepts the argument that the natural sciences have outpaced the social sciences in this process of development is up for debate, but there can be no doubt that transformation has occurred in many scientific areas, including the behavioral and social sciences. In fact, the NIH and its Office of Behavioral and Social Sciences Research have been leaders in this transformation. Consequently, social work schools and the investigators they produce must not only embrace these changes but also position themselves as leaders or change agents possessing a unique perspective and contribution to solving major population health challenges.

Too often, social work practitioners and researchers perceive a false dilemma, striking allegiance to either social work practice or social work research. However, for the field to thrive and optimize its contribution to population health and well-being, researchers and practitioners must work together. There is no denying that social work interventions need to be evidence based, that scientific and technological advances are changing the health care enterprise, and that social work practitioners and researchers are affected by this changing landscape. But how are social workers affecting this landscape in turn? Nurius and Kemp (2012) also posed the following question: "What is lost if social workers are not active voices and productive contributors in the contemporary enterprise of science focusing on 21st-century social, health, and welfare challenges?" In our view, much would be lost, including the unique combination of behavioral, contextual, and systems foci of social work. So, social workers should not buy into this false choice but should instead cast a wide net, welcoming rigorously trained researchers and practitioners from multiple disciplines and perspectives and jointly focusing on solving problems and improving population health and well-being.

Social Work Research and the National Institutes of Health: Where Are We Now?

It has been a decade since the U.S. Congress asked the NIH to "develop a social work research plan that outlines research priorities, as well as a research agenda, across NIH Institutes and Centers" (NIH, 2003, p. 2). The NIH Office of Behavioral and Social Sciences Research, which coordinates and stimulates behavioral and social sciences research across the NIH, led the development of this plan, signed by the NIH director in May 2003. Since that time, positive steps have been taken, including a consistent presence by NIH scientific program officers at the Society for Social Work and Research annual meetings, the issuance of a funding opportunity announcement entitled "Developmental Research on Social Work Practice and Concepts in Health," and the establishment of an annual NIH summer research training institute on social work research. These important steps stemmed from recognizing the important role social workers play in the nation's health care enterprise. Indeed, social work is one of the largest allied health professions in the United States, and social workers provide more social services to populations across the life span than any other human service profession (Brekke, 2012; Center for Health Workforce Studies & Center for NASW Workforce Studies, 2006). Clinical social workers are a major component of the mental health workforce, and approximately 60% of mental health professionals are clinically trained social workers (NASW, 2013). However, social work researchers and professionals remain underrepresented in the research enterprise. For social work researchers operating in the health arena, success involves strategically thinking beyond the bounds of social work research and practice. We propose a three-pronged strategy to this end: positioning the science in priority areas, partnering with other disciplines and with funders to develop your area of research, and packaging the science in language that will be accessible to audiences beyond social work.

Introduction to Strategic Elements: The Three Ps (Positioning, Partnering, and Packaging)

Although solid grantsmanship is necessary to succeed in research, a well-written proposal may not be sufficient for funding success in the current constrained fiscal environment. An investigator's work must be deemed innovative, with a high potential to have an impact on the problems it purports to address. In addition, proposed projects must be closely aligned with the state of the science, funders' priorities, developments in the policy and clinical areas of a topic area, and broader trends in health policy.

Positioning

Positioning one's work involves aligning the focus of the proposed project with the priorities of the field of science, with more macrolevel practice and policy trends, and with the funder's priorities and mission—in short, positioning oneself in the flow of science and trends that are accelerating. Consideration of the relationship between the extant scientific evidence base and policy and clinical practice trends may inform researchers about areas for future research, as well as areas of practice and policy that could benefit from the insights of research in the present. For example, in the area of cancer survivorship, cutting-edge science as of this writing might consider the contexts of Institute of Medicine reports on follow-up care and whole-patient care, the American College of Surgeon's Commission on Cancer's call for implementation of survivorship care plans and distress management protocols, the Affordable Care Act and Accountable Care Organizations for financing cancer care delivery, and the priority areas defined for research by entities such as the NIH, the American Cancer Society, the Patient-Centered Outcome Research Institute, and other funders supporting work in this area.

Scientific areas that overlap philosophically or pragmatically with the core values and tenets of social work may be promising targets for social work researchers. For instance, implementation science shares commonalities in its approach and methods with social work's applied ethos and expertise in formative and summative program evaluation. Likewise, the person-in-environment perspective that undergirds social work practice and training is a systems approach to understanding social problems that attends to multiple levels of context and the interactions between these levels. Leveraging this perspective, social work researchers may be well suited to develop systems science and design multilevel interventions to address challenges in behavioral and health services research. In addition, the focus on diversity and culturally competent practice that is core to social work training has much to offer a research milieu striving to understand and intervene to achieve optimal outcomes among diverse populations of cancer survivors. Finally, other areas of scientific inquiry that are natural partners with social work research include areas in which social work already plays a clinical care delivery role, such as patient navigation, distress management, and survivorship care planning.

Partnering

Approximately half the United States' burden of disease, disability, and premature death is driven by social and behavioral factors (McGinnis & Foege, 1993; Mokdad, Marks, Stroup, & Gerberding, 2004; Oxford Health Alliance, 2012). Additionally, most major population health threats are complex and arise from a mix of behavioral, social, and biological factors interacting over the life span and across an array of settings. Consequently, solving our most pressing health problems requires a greater understanding of the full range of factors that determine health (i.e., biological, medical, behavioral, social, and environmental) and of their complex relationships. The traditional approach of tackling big population health challenges from a single research discipline's perspective is inadequate and dated. Moreover, with the advent of high-speed computing, mobile technology, the era of big data, and new analytical approaches and techniques and their application to health care and biomedical research, there is tremendous potential to address hitherto unapproachable research questions and population health problems. The NIH has long recognized this trend and has facilitated a research framework that emphasizes uniting researchers from different disciplines at both the frontiers and the intersections of those disciplines. The intent of this collaborative approach is to pool diverse knowledge and foment new discoveries and innovative solutions to the most pressing population health challenges.

One of the ways the NIH sought to facilitate the move to team science was by establishing the multiple-principal -investigator option in 2006 as a means to support investigators proposing new projects or activities that require a team science approach. This option is targeted specifically to projects that do not fit the single-investigator model. The goal of this policy change is to maximize the potential of team science efforts to be responsive to the scientific challenges and opportunities of the 21st century. When working in the biomedical and public health realms, partnerships with scientists from other disciplines may help strengthen social workers' research proposals by creating an investigative team with greater breadth and diversity of approaches to addressing health problems. Furthermore, it seems that social work, because of its emphasis on science, context, complexity, and policy, is uniquely positioned to catalyze the creativity and productivity of scientific teams when considering research projects that integrate multiple levels of analysis—from cells to behavior to society.

For social work to position itself as suggested earlier, we are not proposing that the field surrender its unique philosophical identity and social concerns. Rather, we are suggesting that leaders in the field (deans and directors of schools of social work) take steps to buttress the research capacity in their master's- and PhD-level faculty development programs to enable their graduates to engage and challenge their collaborators and help move forward a wider range of [illegible]. The scientist who is most prepared to collaborate on interdisciplinary teams is not someone who has a superficial knowledge of a variety of different fields, but one grounded with a solid background and an in-depth training in his or her field's theories, approaches, and research methods and techniques. But this scientist must also possess the capacity to maintain an open mind and willingness to collaborate with other scientists who may view the world differently. The key is to be well trained in the perspective, approaches, and techniques that one brings to the table and have a willingness to listen and learn new ways of approaching a research problem and to collaborate with others who share one's interest in solving that problem.

Packaging

In addition to positioning one's research in alignment with scientific, policy, and funding priorities and partnering with complementary disciplines, the "packaging" of one's research proposal is an essential strategic skill for social work researchers. By packaging, we mean the framing and language used to relay one's ideas. Using the right language is not the same as being well written. A proposal could be well written and well organized but still not readily accessible to reviewers for reasons outlined later.

The process of applying for research funding can be a multidisciplinary and cross-cultural exercise. As such, applying for funding may involve navigating a context that relies on different values, framing, and language than social work. Funders of health research often support science from multiple disciplines (not just social work) and may rely implicitly or predominantly on biomedical or public health paradigms in their framing and approach to health-related issues. Attention to the language and approach used by funders in their mission and priorities may be helpful in determining how to frame one's research in a manner that will be most accessible to reviewers of the science. For example, although a social work entity may use the language of diversity, social justice, or culturally competent practice to discuss health equity issues, health and public health entities may use the language of health disparities in underserved or low-resource populations. Similarly, core concepts of the person-in-environment approach in social work may be represented under the rubric of the socioecological model or research on multilevel systems in health and public health contexts.

The language and framing used in one's proposal is essential in determining the reviewers' accessibility to the science. As in any cross-cultural situation, successful navigation of interdisciplinary differences in framing and language is premised on learning to speak the language of the culture one hopes to engage in dialogue. Several strategies that may be helpful include asking readers from outside the social work discipline to review the proposal and using models and figures, which transcend the limits of language. Social workers are perhaps uniquely suited to traverse and facilitate understanding across this chasm of culture, language, and understanding if these skills are actively applied in the research context.

The Role of Grantsmanship

Because solid grantsmanship is necessary to be successful in research, we begin with a brief review of the core tenets in grant getting and grant writing. A more thorough discussion is found in volumes dedicated to grant writing, including a booklet produced by the National Cancer Institute (U.S. Department of Health and Human Services, National Institutes of Health, National Cancer Institute, 2005). Foremost, it is important to understand the funder's mission and priorities and the scope and types of research the funder has supported in the past and hopes to support in the future. For example, the NIH is composed of 27 institutes and centers (called ICs), with a $31 billion budget in fiscal year 2012, of which approximately 80% is used to support extramural research through grants and contracts. The NIH's mission is to "seek fundamental knowledge about the nature and behavior of living systems and the application of that knowledge to enhance health, lengthen life and reduce illness and disability" (NIH, 2013). More specific funding priorities are delineated for each of the ICs and for divisions, programs, and branches within those ICs. Foundations and other funding entities are, likewise, mission driven and will generally highlight current grantee projects and articulate funding priorities through their promotional platforms. Spending time exploring funders' websites and written materials, reviewing funding opportunity announcements or requests for proposals, attending funder presentations, and developing relationships with program officers in funding agencies can assist investigators in assessing the fit between their research agenda and funders' missions and priorities. Speaking with program officers at funder institutions is particularly important for understanding which topics or areas a funder hopes to build and which are waning.

Numerous resources exist to advise researchers on successful grant writing, centered on the goal of making one's ideas as accessible as possible to the individuals who will review the grant proposal. Key tips for successful grant writing at the NIH include using the allotted page limit wisely and helping reviewers understand and locate the information needed to evaluate the proposed science. This can be accomplished by using brief, clear headers and subheaders to organize the text; using explanatory graphics (such as conceptual models and timelines) to relay complex information; and highlighting important information in the body of the grant application rather than the appendices, where it may be overlooked. The application should anticipate any questions the proposal might raise for reviewers and address these questions. A scientific grant application should tell a story that outlines the problem to be solved, identifies the question to be answered, specifies how that question will fill a gap in scientific knowledge, explains the significance of the science proposed, and illustrates how the research question will be answered. The grant application should convey enthusiasm for the proposed project, identify and propose solutions to any substantive or methodological dilemmas, and provide evidence for assertions. Research aims should be driven by the research question, have a clear and testable focus, address the significance (or the "so what?") question, and be realistic in scope (e.g., the aims should outline a project, rather than the work of an entire career). The application should also demonstrate congruence between the research question, aims, conceptual model, methods, and measures used; use a sound data analysis plan and a research design that will answer the research question; and demonstrate the investigator's ability, support, and connections to accomplish the proposed project.

Pearls

- For social work researchers operating in the health arena, success involves thinking beyond the bounds of social work research and practice.
- Utilize a three-pronged strategy for acquiring funding and generating relevant work: positioning the science in priority areas, partnering with funders and investigators from other disciplines, and packaging the science in language that will be accessible to audiences beyond social work.
- Solid grantsmanship involves aligning one's work with funders' priorities; developing relationships with program officers; using figures and tables to convey complex information; addressing gaps in the research; demonstrating congruence between the research question, aims, model, methods, and measures used; and demonstrating the investigator's ability to accomplish the proposed project.

Pitfalls

- Failing to work across boundaries and frame social work research in the context of interdisciplinary language and priorities could prevent the insights and contributions of social work from being leveraged in the broader health domains.
- Common problems in grant writing include failure to explain the significance of the work; inconsistency between aims, models, methods, and/or measures used; and proposal of a study that is overly ambitious in scope or beyond the investigator's ability to accomplish.

This chapter has provided a brief commentary on and road map to success for principal investigators seeking funding for social work research projects. Specifically, we presented the elements of success involved in obtaining funding, including strategic positioning and packaging of social work research projects within biomedical research and population health, partnering with investigators with expertise in other complementary fields working on similar or related research problems, and developing grant applications that are strategic and relevant. These elements, we suggest, are the keys that will enable social work researchers to position themselves to make contributions to the fields of oncology, health, and population health.

This chapter should make clear for social work researchers that successfully competing for an NIH grant is not simply a matter of grantsmanship. A great idea that is too far ahead of its time will have difficulty winning NIH support, as will an idea that duplicates projects already benefiting from support. Smartly positioning one's work within the scientific priorities of one's field and the targeted NIH ICs is an important element. An important second element is to embrace the fact that science has become increasingly more interdisciplinary and that working in scientific silos is a thing of the past. We now have the tools to consider and analyze the full context of a health condition. The future is in team science, which calls for establishing partnerships to tackle research problems that transcend a single paradigm. We are not suggesting that social workers become geneticists, economists, or experts in informatics and systems modeling. Rather, we are proposing that the successful social work researcher of the future has a firm grasp of social work theory and practice, a solid foundation in research methods, a facility to quickly grasp methodological elements that cut across scientific areas, and an ability to cultivate connections across those areas. Finally, we stress the importance of considering the audience when pulling it all together. Using appropriate language is just as important as one's methodology.

Although they cannot mitigate the tight budget constraints and limited resources faced by all grant applications to the NIH, the suggested strategies are intended to support the determined social work research applicant in competing successfully for those scarce resources.

REFERENCES

Brekke, J. S. (2012). Shaping a science of social work. *Research on Social Work Practice, 00*(0), 1–10.

Center for Health Workforce Studies & National Association of Social Workers (NASW) Center for Workforce Studies. (2006). National study of licensed social workers. Retrieved from http://workforce.socialworkers.org/studies/natstudy.asp

Christakis, N. A. (2013, July 19). Let's shake up the social sciences. *New York Times*. Retrieved from http://www.nytimes.com/2013/07/21/opinion/sunday/lets-shake-up-the-social-sciences.html

McGinnis, J. M., & Foege, W. H. (1993). Actual causes of death in the United States. *Journal of the American Medical Association, 270*(18), 2207–2212.

Mokdad, A. H., Marks, J. S., Stroup, D. F., & Gerberding, J. L. (2004). Actual causes of death in the United States, 2000. *Journal of the American Medical Association, 291*(10), 1238–1245.

National Association of Social Workers (NASW). (2013). Mental health. Retrieved from http://www.socialworkers.org/pressroom/features/issue/mental.asp

National Institutes of Health (NIH). (2003). NIH plan for social work research. Retrieved from http://obssr.od.nih.gov/pdf/SWR_Report.pdf

National Institutes of Health (NIH). (2013). Mission. Retrieved from http://www.nih.gov/about/mission.htm

Nurius, P. S., & Kemp, S. P. (2012). Social work, science, social impact: Crafting an integrative conversation. *Research on Social Work Practice,* 00(0), 1–5.

Oxford Health Alliance. (2012). 3Four50: Connect collaborate create. Retrieved from http://www.3four50.com

U.S. Department of Health and Human Services, National Institutes of Health, National Cancer Institute. (2005). *Everything you wanted to know about the NCI Grants Process, but were afraid to ask*. NIH Publication No. 05-1222. Retrieved from http://www3.cancer.gov/admin/gab/2005GPB/GPB05-LowRes.pdf

VI

Complex Issues Affecting Quality of Life and Quality of Care

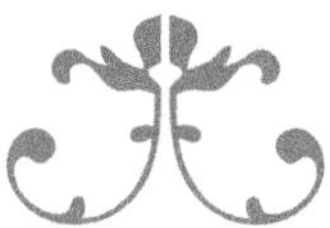

Shirley Otis-Green

Oncology social workers recognize the complex, multisystem issues that affect people with cancer, which require specialized knowledge and skills. This perspective is a core social work conceptual framework that directs the integration of a broad range of contextual issues and related skills that affect patients, families, and professionals in our rapidly evolving health care system.

In "The Convergence of Oncology and Palliative Social Work," Terry Altilio and Bridget Sumser encourage oncology social workers to take leadership roles in incorporating the key principles of palliative care within oncology practice, in collaboration with palliative social work specialists. Palliative care is an interdisciplinary, person-centered, and family-focused approach congruent with current oncology treatment standards. However, barriers to integrating palliative care in oncology treatment programs continue. Palliative care seeks to address the quality-of-life concerns associated with cancer and its treatment throughout the illness trajectory, not just at the end of life. The authors review the evidence in support of this broader understanding of palliative care and demonstrate how it provides a solid foundation for a comprehensive and collaborative biopsychosocial-spiritual approach to care delivery that seamlessly integrates the role of social work in the provision of services.

Brian Giddens, in "Treatment Adherence," provides readers with practical guidance regarding the fundamental role of oncology social work in addressing increasingly complex treatment adherence issues. Differentiating the complex socioeconomic, political, and cultural factors that influence adherence requires skillful assessment. As such, helping health care teams understand why a patient is unable (or unwilling) to follow recommendations has historically been a key task for social workers.

In "The Impact of Comorbidities on Cancer Care," Barbara Head brings insights from her experience as a nurse and social worker to our understanding of the issues that occur when managing multiple physical and psychiatric conditions. As our population ages, the challenges of comorbidities are increasing in the management of a cancer diagnosis and conditions such as heart disease, diabetes, arthritis, and depression. An overview of polypharmacy issues demonstrates how multiple health treatments can be related to lower quality of life and may contribute to an inability to adhere to health recommendations. Oncology social work's well-honed skills in assessment, care coordination, and communication with the interdisciplinary team are essential in helping to effectively manage comorbidities in patients.

Allison Werner-Lin provides two related chapters. The first, "Social Work Practice With Families Affected by Hereditary Cancer," describes ways in which the scientific knowledge about genetics and related technologies has outpaced the development of cancer treatments and preventive therapies. It has also challenged individuals' and families' abilities to cope with the psychological and social impact of the information and to make informed decisions about genetic testing and treatments. Described are the significant personal, relational, and familial issues patients confront. Oncology social work guidelines for supporting family communication and coping include maintaining fluency in technological, psychosocial, and decision-making issues related to this advancing science.

In "Pain and Symptom Management," Terry Altilio and Laurel Eskra Tropeano remind us of our professional obligation to address the multidimensional aspects of patient suffering and distress associated with cancer and its treatment. Skilled oncology social workers are needed to provide a holistic, biopsychosocial-spiritual perspective to the management of symptoms such as pain or fatigue. The authors discuss the use and misuse of pain medications and highlight opportunities for oncology social workers to provide education to address myths and concerns related to their use.

Oncology care addresses every dimension of a person's quality of life. In "Sexuality and Cancer," Sage Bolte and Christopher Anrig provide concrete and practical suggestions of ways to assist patients and their partners with the impact of a cancer diagnosis and treatment on sexuality and intimacy. Oncology social workers need to have the expertise and comfort level to address issues of sexual function and fertility, as well as body image and sexual abuse. Strategies to aid in the collection of a comprehensive sexual history are provided.

Alison Werner-Lin's second chapter, the final in this section, is entitled "The Oncology Social Worker and Genomics." In it, Werner-Lin provides in-depth overviews of the current science of genetics for oncology social workers and a glossary of terms, additional resources, and patient-rich examples. Described are opportunities for oncology social workers to skillfully assist patients and families in understanding social, political, and ethical complexities.

29

Terry Altilio and Bridget Sumser

The Convergence of Oncology and Palliative Social Work

Key Concepts

- *Oncology and palliative social work have the potential to ensure the integration of palliative care principles and values into the ongoing care of cancer patients and their families.*
- *The 2012 Commission on Cancer Program Standards and the 2001 and 2007 Institute of Medicine reports are invaluable tools to enhance advocacy for the holistic care integral to oncology and palliative social work.*
- *The 2012 American Society of Clinical Oncology provisional clinical opinion produced the following consensus: "combined standard oncology care and palliative care should be considered early in the course of illness for any patient with metastatic cancer and/or high symptom burden" (Smith et al., 2012, p. 880).*
- *As additional research documents the benefit of oncology and palliative care integration, social workers are ideally placed to lead their teams beyond proprietary interests to collaborative, cost-effective processes that converge around the best interest of patients and families.*

The Commission on Cancer (COC) Cancer Program Standards 2012, Ensuring Patient-Centered Care, emanates from the American College of Surgeons (ACOS) and creates a structure to ensure that cancer programs seeking accreditation "provide all patients with a full range of diagnostic, treatment, and supportive services" (ACOS, 2012, p. 13). Highlighting the 2007 Institute of Medicine (IOM) report, "Cancer Care for the Whole Patient: Meeting Psychosocial Health Needs," the COC validates its historical commitment to providing the standards, data systems, quality metrics, and multidisciplinary programs to help its accredited programs address the IOM's recommendations. The 2012 report adds new standards that "enhance patient centered functions and define performance criteria in quality measures and outcomes" (ACOS, 2012, p. 15). One of these is Standard 2.4: "palliative care services are available to patients either on site or through referral" (ACOS, 2012, p. 70). Congruent with the scope defined in the National Consensus Project on Quality Palliative Care, services are described as an "essential component of cancer care beginning at the time of diagnosis and being continuously available throughout treatment, surveillance and, when applicable, during bereavement" (ACOS, 2012, p. 70). Before the publication of either of these reports, the Institute of Medicine wrote compellingly:

> *It is innately human to comfort and provide care to those suffering from cancer, especially those close to death. Yet what seems self-evident at an individual, personal level, has, by and large, not guided policy at the level of institutions in this country. There is no argument that palliative care should be integrated into cancer care from diagnosis to death but significant barriers—attitudinal, behavioral, educational, economic, and legal—still limit this needed care for a large proportion of people with cancer. We have also ignored palliative care in cancer research in accepting a single-minded focus on research toward cure, we have inadvertently devalued this critical need to care for and support patients with advanced disease.*
>
> *(IOM, 2001, p. 1)*

For those practicing oncology social work and those specialized in palliative social work, these reports validate the voice of our specialties and skill sets. This chapter invites consideration of the challenges and opportunities and the potential risks and rewards as we fashion collaborations that enhance the services provided along the continuum of illness for patients living with cancer and their families.

The Challenge

Integration and Enrichment

How, then, will the vision of palliative care integration evolve? What are the similarities and differences within oncology and palliative care teams? With role boundaries, duplication, and blurring *within* interdisciplinary teams already challenging to navigate, what about boundaries, duplication, and blurring *across* teams if, in fact, a separate palliative care team joins the constellation of clinicians already providing services? As social workers, how do we model collaboration rather than competition? Additionally, how do we model an approach that honors our specialist skill sets and recognizes when the skill or the objective view of another may serve our patients families and ourselves well? An introduction to the scope and vision of palliative care follows to build a context within which collaboration and sharing may take place.

Palliative Care Defined

The intention of palliative care specialists is to ease the burden of advancing illness and to improve quality of life by treating pain and symptoms, promoting communication, advancing discussions about personal and medical goals, and addressing the complex emotional, psychological, social, and spiritual needs that arise throughout illness and during bereavement. First recognized as a medical specialty 20 years ago, palliative care can be offered along with life-prolonging therapies or as the primary focus of care. It challenges the traditional medical model that has been fueled by the growth of technology and a reimbursement system that disincentivizes communication while rewarding interventions and treatments that focus on the body and the disease, often to the exclusion of the person at the center of care.

Like our colleagues in oncology, palliative care social workers are guided by many similar precepts, including patient and family as the unit of care; provision of services informed by patient and family values, preferences, cultural backgrounds, and expressed needs; integrated care achieved by enhancing communication among medical teams and within family systems; informed consent processes; and shared decision making and support along the trajectory of illness from pre-diagnosis through the end of life.

Patients and families have historically interfaced with palliative care through inpatient consultation services and specialized units. Increasingly, palliative care teams are offering outpatient services, affording physicians the opportunity to refer patients earlier in the evolution of illness who may never require hospitalization (Bruera & Hui, 2010). Literature is emerging that demonstrates early integration of palliative care can improve the patient's quality of life and reduces interventions that have no benefit at the end of life (Temel et al., 2010). This nascent research, along with documents such as the IOM report, is encouraging more oncologists to utilize palliative care services across settings; the ASCO projects full integration of palliative care into oncology by 2020 (Ferris et al., 2009).

Palliative Social Work

Historical Perspective

The burgeoning specialty of palliative social work has followed in the footsteps of the fields of palliative medicine and nursing. The Project on Death in America's social work leadership initiative in 1999 and the Center for the Advancement of Palliative Care's validation of social workers as core palliative team members are only two of many institutional actions that have affirmed the contributions of specialist social work. The publication of the *Oxford Textbook of Palliative Social Work* (Altilio & Otis-Green 2011), a companion to the larger compilation of *Oxford Texts of Medicine and Nursing*, set a standard and scope that affirms the specialty, as does the certification available through the National Association of Social Workers and National Hospice and Palliative Care Organization. The Social Work Hospice and Palliative Care Network was formed in 2008 to advance palliative social work and integrate palliative social work–related initiatives, organizations, and key stakeholders. Oncology social workers have had a professional organization since 1984 and a certification that began in 2002. The following section discusses the role of specialist palliative care and then offers a perspective to enhance the collaboration with specialist oncology social work clinicians.

Similarities and Differences With Oncology Social Work

Quite similar to oncology social workers, palliative social workers function as frontline members of teams across various practice settings, providing expert psychosocial assessment and intervention to patients and families facing serious or life-limiting illness. With a background in both social work and palliative care, the palliative social worker is able to tailor interventions based on need, providing both a "generalist" level of clinical intervention and a more focused expertise relevant to the complexities and nuances of serious and life-limiting illness (Altilio & Otis-Green, 2011; Gwyther et al., 2005; McCormick, Engelberg, & Curtis, 2007; Raymer & Gardia, 2007). Christ and Blacker (2005) summarized the role of the palliative social worker:

> *Social workers possess expert knowledge about navigating medical and social systems that frequently present barriers to terminally ill clients. They fully embrace the role of patient advocate to assist with obtaining resources. They are experts in the art and science of communication with families, but also between clients and the health care team. Drawing on knowledge of family systems and interpersonal dynamics, the social worker is able to examine the family's experience in a unique way that can guide the team toward more informed and effective interactions with highly distressed individuals. (p. 415)*

The palliative social worker's role may range, depending on the configuration and nature of the team, from direct therapeutic interventions, to education and program planning, to a major role in family meetings, advance care planning, and enhancing relationships across specialties (Altilio, Otis-Green, & Dahlin, 2008). Underlying this work is an awareness of the complex ethical considerations and legal aspects that converge in the treatment of life-limiting illness and the decisions that are often subsumed under the phrase "goals of care." This facet of the work may revolve around proxy decision making, prognostication, informed consent, physician aid in dying, and the right to accept, refuse, or withdraw treatments such as dialysis, artificial hydration, and nutrition (NASW, 2014).

Affirming each individual's right to determine the direction of his or her own care is often complicated as patients decline physically and cognitively. Discovering values related to self-determination, or advocating for patients and families whose cultures do not define individual autonomy as the dominant value, requires knowledge, courage, and critical assessment to ensure that the beliefs and history of individual patients are honored. This intersection powerfully illustrates the benefits of collaboration between oncology and palliative social workers. Palliative specialists often engage with patients and families when goals of care are in flux. Palliative social workers' understanding of the ongoing patient and family care is enriched by the historical knowledge that comes from having preexisting relationships with oncology social workers.

In palliative social work, as well as in oncology social work, communication across disciplines, within and beyond teams and families is a core skill. Just as a physical exam centers the practice of medicine, listening is essential to the practice of social work. Although all disciplines in palliative care are expected to respond to psychological and spiritual distress, the way practitioners in each discipline listen is unique and based in specialized training. This is consistent across social work specialties, another aspect where oncology and palliative social work converge.

The skill sets of oncology and palliative social work may have areas of commonality and difference. Pain and symptom management, ethical inquiry, and goals of care receive primary attention in palliative care. Chapter 33 captures the ethical mandate and skills relative to the potential for social work to engage with interdisciplinary colleagues in the treatment of suffering consequent to pain and other symptoms.

The following narrative reflects the integration of palliative clinicians as a diagnosis of a serious illness is established, illustrating how pain and symptom management opens doors for social workers to connect with patients and families, potentially establishing a relationship that may provide continuity of care throughout the evolution of illness. Developing a relationship amid profound ambiguity, and a time of many unknowns, lends itself to the creation of a therapeutic alliance that transcends specific stages of illness and integrates psychosocial care from the outset. Psychosocial care becomes rooted in the expectation of the person and family before they become identified with a diagnosis, building a foundation that can support them as they traverse care teams and settings. The narrative also illustrates the opportunity and potential for skilled social workers, whether they are working within the specialty of oncology or palliative care. Both specialties have the honor of joining with others as they integrate serious illness and work to weave the experience into the tapestry of their lives.

Mr. Henson, a 39-year-old African American man, had been treated for severe back pain thought to be related to a bulging disc, which, over months, had greatly reduced his mobility and capacity to navigate his professional, personal, and familial life. Mr. Henson was admitted to an inpatient oncology service to complete a diagnostic workup and for pain management after an initial outpatient study revealed lesions in the pelvis. An inpatient computed tomography scan revealed a lung mass, left kidney mass, and iliac muscle lesion. A palliative care consult was requested from the oncologist, specifying that the team's focus should be pain and symptom management.

Mr. Henson is a married father of two children aged 8 and 10. His extended family was highly involved in his care and hospitalization, negotiating the hospital system and attempting to protect him from the flood of evolving information and the many clinicians who presented new and sometimes discrepant results and opinions. This highly resourceful family utilized the Internet, working actively to research and master large amounts of medical information during an extended process of diagnosis and treatment planning. Pain management involved complex pharmacological and psychosocial interventions, and the palliative care team provided essential continuity through an admission that lasted for 3 weeks. Various oncology specialists entered the life of the patient and family, but the palliative social worker became a stabilizing relationship within which opinions, feelings, and frustrations could be expressed, tested, and focused to support efficacy and effective communication.

Pain management was the reason for referral and the foundation of the work with Mr. Henson and his family. Although Mr. Henson and his family were open and communicative, there was an underlying mistrust emanating from months of medical care that may have missed discovery of a lung cancer that presented with early symptoms of back pain. Receptivity to ongoing social work interventions was enhanced by the vigilant efforts of the palliative care team to effectively manage ongoing and debilitating pain and further strengthened after an early test of trust related to racial and generational differences. Consequent to the skill set of the palliative social worker, Mr. Henson utilized this relationship as a conduit to information about side effect profiles of different opioid therapies, working to find the balance between pain reduction and desired functional and cognitive capacity. The introduction of a pain journal allowed Mr. Henson to objectify his own experience of pain over time for both self-knowledge and improved collaboration with the treatment team. By charting medicine use and capturing the anticipatory anxiety related to movement and his worries about pain exacerbations, Mr. Henson was able to have interventions tailored to his physical self and his cognitive and emotional self. Additionally, the journal provided important data to inform a hypothesis that Mr. Henson was using opioids to treat mood and anxiety, as well as pain. When complemented by ongoing assessment and inquiry, this therapeutic tool helped the team address the patient's goals, which included reduced mental clouding and increased function. Cognitive behavioral interventions implemented by the palliative social worker focused on pain and anxiety reduction, supported Mr. Henson's internal locus of control, and enhanced autonomy and self-efficacy in the setting of limited mobility and a body that was sorely disappointing him. This work combined with psychoeducation provided the foundation to move beyond pain and add interventions to assist Mr. Henson and his family through the process of diagnosis to treatment planning, discharge, and beyond.

Although the interventions that follow might well have been the focus of the oncology social worker, they flowed naturally from the palliative care team's attention to pain management over the course of diagnosis. In the setting of initial mistrust and distress related to multiple clinicians, the decision was made to support the continuity of the palliative social work relationship and engage the oncology social worker as discharge planning was introduced. This discrete topic became a vehicle for the oncology social worker to focus further on concerns related to disability, family discord, and Mr. Henson's desire to maximize his participation in the lives of his children.

Interventions

- *The palliative social worker solicited, explored, and validated the concerns, hopes, and spiritual and emotional responses of the patient and family as they dealt with the uncertainty of the evolving diagnosis.*
- *Supportive and family counseling focused on acknowledging the impact that weeks of pain and uncertain diagnosis had on the nuclear and extended family, creating an environment of crisis and disequilibrium; highlighting engagement and communication with children; offering coping strategies to the patient and family; meaning making; and managing stress.*
- *Psychoeducation reinforced the integration of palliative services into the oncology care plan in conjunction with disease-modifying therapies, taught strategies for self-care, and explored developmentally appropriate resources and supports for children.*
- *Family systems interventions focused on supporting Mr. Henson as he explored the risks and benefits of tailored and assertive communication with clinicians and family members designed both to recognize his family's suffering and to assert an essential need to recover his voice, autonomy, and adjusted role within the family.*
- *Linkages to community resources were provided for child and family counseling.*
- *Ongoing collaboration with consulting teams and oncology clinicians focused on reducing confusion and inconsistent messages and negotiating complex dynamics that often evolve in the setting of young patients, active families, and long hospitalizations.*
- *Discharge planning further integrated the oncology social worker and created an opportunity for seamless transition to the outpatient oncology social worker.*

Transitions in Care: An Essential Social Work Focus

Although this vignette illustrates work over a long period of hospitalization, it begins with a focus on pain and is enhanced by critical thinking and clinical skills that can be employed both during short periods of crises and during clinical care over weeks and months in inpatient or outpatient settings. A respect for the importance of transitions is a central focus in both oncology and palliative social work. It involves anticipatory thinking, problem solving, and planning. Depending on the structure of the medical system, patients move across settings and often lose continuity of relationships.

New beginnings are a feature, for better or worse, of our fractured health care system. Under the best of circumstances and in mutually respectful relationships, social workers can prioritize nonabandonment and model seamless transitions as a goal of practice. The collaborative work of oncology and palliative social workers can serve to model specialist clinicians capable of enhancing the life of patients and families across the continuum of illness. In some hospital settings, palliative social work clinicians provide continuity by traveling with patients and families as illness and systems force transfers from the oncology unit to the intensive care unit and beyond. This freedom potentially benefits patients and families and may also relieve clinicians who are conflicted when the institutional mandate does not allow for such continuity of care. At times, the palliative consultation service in a hospital may be the only team that maintains relationship and continuity, becoming the repository of the patient's medical, psychological, social, and spiritual history.

Capturing and Celebrating Synergy

The guiding principles, standards, and skill sets of palliative and oncology social work are powerfully congruent. For oncology and palliative care, the patient and family are the unit of care, a principle so basic to the work that its importance can easily be overlooked. Cancer is frequently considered a systemic illness rather than the malfunction of a specific body part, as is often the focus in such specialties as cardiology or nephrology. Cancer has evolved from being frequently fatal to a disease that may be curable, remittable, or chronic. Often, oncology and palliative care teams are the first health care providers interested in the well-being of the family *and* the patient, in the present and over time. There is a shared commitment to family systems and often services are guided by patient and family values, preferences, and cultural backgrounds, as well as assessed, expressed, and observed needs.

Although the emergence and development of the specialty of palliative care followed the specialty of oncology, there is a shared mission focused on providing comprehensive service for whole persons. Many patients look to their oncology physicians to achieve cure or remission, yet cancer is an illness where, in many settings, interdisciplinary teams focus services on the person living with the disease.

There is also a large body of research focused on the patient and family experience, and an extensive network of resources and specialists has developed to respond to biopsychosocial-spiritual needs. This research has served to guide social workers and colleagues in oncology and palliative care who have created programs and practices responsive to the needs identified by screening tools and assessment processes, as well as a constantly growing literature.

Modeling an Extended Interdisciplinary Team

As social workers who generally practice in interdisciplinary teams and do not directly generate income, we are challenged to clearly represent and reflect our expertise and efficacy within the team, across disciplines, and across teams as we provide consultation to others. This same process of reflection can be helpful to social workers from oncology and palliative care, who may be asked to share patients and families, in a manner that enriches rather than fractures preexisting relationships. As palliative care is introduced into the world of oncology, health care providers who keep "good care" for individual patients and families central to program planning may be able to create systems that, in fact, enrich care while enhancing satisfaction for practitioners. Assuming that providers might find a way to acknowledge and value the skills of the other and those of the self, care decisions may emanate from the needs of patients and families.

Pain management and prognostication are two aspects of care where the convergence of oncology and palliative care may enhance conversation and mutual understanding. Social workers who have long negotiated teams and systems within medical settings have the opportunity to engage in these discussions and work to design creative and effective ways to enhance care and stimulate mutual education and thoughtfulness.

Pain Management

There is a current and historical literature related to the pain treatment skills of oncologists. A 2011 survey of U.S. oncologists published in the *Journal of Clinical Oncology* revealed that although physicians rated their pain management skills as "fairly good," less than 50% selected appropriate interventions when presented with clinical scenarios (Breuer, Fleischman, Cruciani, & Portenoy, 2011). Perhaps in the area of pain and symptom management, palliative clinicians will enhance care while informing and improving the skills sets of interdisciplinary colleagues in this focused and important aspect of oncology practice. Curiously, in certain patients the risk of pain or other side effects is accepted as a possible consequence of some cancer treatments in exchange for an anticipated positive outcome. Reporting and managing symptoms within this context is complex, and perhaps the emotions and thoughts around this dynamic are more easily expressed with clinicians who have not participated in this decision-making process or provided the treatment that caused the symptom.

Prognostication

An important focus of palliative clinicians is prognostication. A patient cannot make informed decisions without some sense of where he or she stands in a disease process. There is evidence that errors in prognostication relate to length of relationship. The better the physician knows the patient, the more likely the error tends toward overoptimism, with the result that patients and families may lose the opportunity to focus on activities that enhance meaning and legacy and to make medical choices that have little or no benefit rather than choosing options that might improve quality of life (Christakis & Lamont, 2000). Oncology teams may work with patients and families over long periods, and it may be that access to palliative care clinicians will afford expert and objective opinion that emanates from a lack of personal and professional history, as well as a distinct interest in this complex skill. Palliative care experts may be called in and, without personal and professional history or attachment, offer an objective view to clinicians whose continuity and history may blur the present. Shared prognostication has the potential to inform and enrich the oncologist–patient relationship rather than build in an inadvertent abandonment that comes from transferring the work of difficult conversations to another.

Social workers have advocated models of care for patients and families that tend to their body, mind, heart, and spirit. We are practicing in a turbulent time replete with opportunities and challenges. That is not new for our discipline because our roots rest in environments of overcoming obstacles and maximizing strengths and resilience. It appears most likely that palliative care will integrate oncology care with varied levels of enthusiasm and wide-ranging skill sets. This is an occasion for social workers to demonstrate collaboration and mutual respect. It is also an occasion to build processes that do not duplicate, add needless expense, confuse the patients and families we seek to serve, or fracture preexisting and valued relationships.

Our current health care system consistently asks patients and families to engage in new beginnings and new relationships. Strengthening the network and connection between oncology and palliative social work may mitigate the impact of new beginnings. Fostering professional relationships and understanding and working together in shared responsibility for patient and family well-being may reduce the psychosocial burden that comes from transitions in settings and as changing goals and plans of care threaten personal and family equilibrium.

Pearls

- Numerous opportunities exist for oncology and palliative social workers to collaborate, enhancing psychosocial care to patients and families along the continuum of illness.
- Understanding similarities and differences in skill sets promotes an ethic of collaboration and open communication, enhancing whole-patient care while reducing duplication of psychosocial services.
- Respect for preexisting relationships creates a platform upon which continuity of care and quality transitions may occur that support patients and families as illness evolves.
- Palliative care consultation may provide objective perspectives helpful to oncology clinicians who have been intimately involved with unique patients over long periods of time.

Pitfalls

- Clinical involvement by oncology and palliative social workers has the potential to duplicate service and blur boundaries.
- Environments of competition and conflict diminish each of us and confuse patients, families, and interdisciplinary clinicians.
- As patients and families move across systems, beware of establishing processes that constantly create "new beginnings."

ADDITIONAL RESOURCES

Advanced Certified Hospice and Palliative Social Worker (ACHP): http://www.socialworkers.org/credentials/credentials/achp.asp

Certified Hospice and Palliative Social Worker (CHP-SW): http://www.socialworkers.org/credentials/credentials/chpsw.asp

Association of Oncology Social Work Specialty Certification: http://www.aosw.org/html/resources.php

National Association of Social Workers: NASW Standards for Social Work Practice in Palliative and End-of-Life Care: http://www.socialworkers.org/practice/bereavement/standards/

National Consensus Project: Clinical Practice Guidelines for Quality Palliative Care: http://www.nationalconsensusproject.org/guideline.pdf

National Quality Forum: A National Framework and Preferred Practices for Palliative and Hospice Care Quality: http://www.qualityforum.org/Publications/2006/12/A_National_Framework_and_Preferred_Practices_for_Palliative_and_Hospice_Care_Quality.aspx

REFERENCES

Altilio, T., & Otis-Green, S. (Eds.). (2011). *Oxford textbook of palliative social work*. New York, NY: Oxford University Press.

Altilio, T., Otis-Green, S., & Dahlin, C. (2008). Applying the National Quality Forum Preferred Practices for Palliative and Hospice Care: A social work perspective. *Journal of Social Work in End-of-Life and Palliative Care*, *4*(1), 3–16.

American College of Surgeons (ACOS). (2012). Cancer program standards: Ensuring patient-centered care. http://www.facs.org/cancer/coc/cocprogramstandards2012.pdf

Breuer, B., Fleishman, S. B., Cruciani, R., & Portenoy, R. K. (2011). Medical oncologists' attitudes and practice in cancer pain management: A national survey. *Journal of Clinical Oncology*, 29, 4769–4775.

Bruera, E., & Hui, D. (2010). Integrating supportive and palliative care in the trajectory of cancer: Establishing goals and models of care. *Journal of Clinical Oncology*, *28*(25), 4013–4017.

Christ, G. H., & Blacker, S. (2005). The profession of social work in end-of-life and palliative care. *Journal of Palliative Medicine*, *8*(4), 415–417.

Christakis, N. A., & Lamont, E. B. (2000). Extent and determinants of error in physicians' prognoses in terminally ill patients. *Western Journal of Medicine, 172*(5), 310–313.

Ferris, F. D., Bruera, E., Cherny, N., Cummings, C., Currow, D., Dudgeon, D.,. . . Von Roenn, J. H. (2009). Palliative cancer care a decade later: Accomplishments, the need, next steps—from the American Society of Clinical Oncology. *Journal of Clinical Oncology, 27*(18), 3052–3058. doi:10.1200/JCO.2008.20.1558

Gwyther, L. P., Altilio, T., Blacker, S., Christ, G., Csikai, E. L., Hooyman, N., . . . Howe, J. (2005). Social work competencies in palliative and end-of-life care. *Journal of Social Work in End-of-Life and Palliative Care, 1*(1), 87–120.

Institute of Medicine (IOM). (2001). *Improving palliative care for cancer.* Washington, DC: National Academies Press. Retrieved from http://www.nap.edu/openbook.php?isbn=0309074029

Institute of Medicine (IOM). (2007). *Cancer care for the whole patient: Meeting psychosocial health needs.* Washington, DC: National Academies Press. Retrieved from http://www.iom.edu/CMS/3809/34252/47228.aspx

McCormick, A. J., Engelberg, R., & Curtis, J. R. (2007). Social workers in palliative care: Assessing activities and barriers in the intensive care unit. *Journal of Palliative Medicine, 10*(4), 929–937.

National Association of Social Workers (NASW). (2014). *NASW Standards for palliative and end-of-life care.* Retrieved from https://www.socialworkers.org/practice/bereavement/standards/standards0504New.pdf

Raymer, M., & Gardia, G. (2007). *What social workers do: A guide to social work in hospice and palliative care.* Alexandria, VA: National Hospice and Palliative Care Organization.

Smith, T. J., Temin, S., Alesi, E. R., Abernathy, A. P., Balboni, T. A., Basch, E. M., . . . Von Roenn, J. H. (2012). American Society of Clinical Oncology provisional clinical opinion: The integration of palliative care into standard oncology care. *Journal of Clinical Oncology, 30*(8), 880–887.

Temel, J. S., Greer, J. A., Muzikansky, M. A., Gallagher, E. R., Sonal Admane, M. B., Jackson, V. A., . . . Lynch, T. J. (2010). Early palliative care for patients with metastatic non-small-cell lung cancer. *New England Journal of Medicine, 363*(8), 733–742.

30 Treatment Adherence

Brian Giddens

Key Concepts

- *Adherence to preventive care and to active treatment is a multifactorial issue.*
- *There are both tangible and psychosocial barriers to treatment adherence.*
- *Oncology social workers can help patients improve adherence, resulting in better health outcomes.*

An important role for an oncology social worker is helping a person with cancer adhere to the recommended treatment plan. Whether serving as a liaison between the interdisciplinary team and the patient, helping to facilitate a family conference, serving as an educator to the team or patient, or advocating for more resources, social workers can have an enormous influence on shared patient and team treatment goals.

For some medical providers, a person is adherent if he or she does what the doctor recommends (DiMatteo, 2004). Adherence has been defined as narrowly as "the extent to which patients take their medications as prescribed by their health care providers" (Osterberg & Blaschke, 2005, p. 487). Complying with medications is an essential component of treatment, but for the purposes of this chapter, the broader definition of adherence goes beyond just medications or the request of one provider. Adherence can also be defined as "the extent to which patients follow the instructions they are given for a prescribed treatment" (Haynes, McDonald, Garg, & Montague, 2002, p. 2). The term *adherence* is now used more frequently than *compliance*, which can suggest passivity on the part of patients and can be unfairly judgmental of their behavior. Adherence recognizes that patients also play a role in shaping and following goals of care (Lutfey & Wishner, 1999) and emphasizes patient autonomy and the need for patient/provider collaboration. Yet just as "noncompliance" became a pejorative label for patients not following treatment, "nonadherence" can also be seen as the patient's fault unless the medical team recognizes that the treatment reflects an agreed-upon partnership with the patient.

There is an important distinction to be made between intentional nonadherence and unintentional nonadherence (Figure 30.1). Intentional nonadherence is when a person does not believe in the plan—when it conflicts with his or her beliefs, values, or resources (Beni, 2011; Martin, Williams, Haskard, & DiMatteo, 2005). Social work may be referred a client because he or she is "resistant to treatment," but on further examination, the social worker may find that the patient doesn't understand the treatment, believes it won't make a difference, or thinks it is not affordable. There may also be practical obstacles that interfere, such as care for dependent children or elders or transportation. Intentional nonadherence is more complicated than someone unintentionally forgetting to take a medication or missing an appointment and requires more in-depth interviewing to

Tangible Resources	Psychological/Emotional Support	Health System	Cultural
Housing: A safe and secure place to recover or rest	Preexisting emotional or behavioral problem	Ability to understand verbal, written instructions	How does individual culture view illness?
Financial needs: Money to pay for care needs or to manage basic necessities	Substance abuse	Personal learning style	What role does the person have in the family? Who makes decisions?
Transportation: Access to dependable, convenient, and affordable transport	Previous history of illness: Personal or familial experiences	Language	What are the cultural beliefs relating to treatment decisions?
Health insurance: A plan that covers the types of care needed, without unmanage-able out-of-pocket expenses	Perception of self-efficacy	Literacy level	Cultural expectations of treatment providers
Practical in-home supports: Meal assistance, chore assistance, accessibility options	Availability of friends and family	Provider/patient relationship	Issues relating to provider/patient interactions (touch, asking questions, self-advocacy)
	Role change due to illness	Access to care	
		"Patient-friendly" instructions and information	

Figure 30.1. Barriers to Adherence

understand the discordance between the patient and provider. Adherence to treatment is important for many reasons. Not following medical treatment plans may result in poor outcomes for the patient and can be wasteful and costly to the health care system.

Common Barriers to Adherence

Barriers to adherence generally fall into four categories: tangible resources, psychological and emotional support, health system barriers, and cultural and language barriers (Figure 30.1). Social workers have the skills and knowledge to make a difference in all of these areas.

With the development of targeted oral chemotherapies and more effective antiemetics, one of the most significant resource barriers is the cost of medications used in the ambulatory setting. As more people become eligible for insurance under health care reform, prescription coverage should also expand. At the same time, many prescription assistance programs only provide help if a patient is not eligible for Medicaid coverage. As expansion of Medicaid makes more persons eligible for prescription coverage, assistance programs should also be able to alter their criteria to consider assistance for co-pays or for drugs not on a state's Medicaid formulary. Talking with the pharmaceutical company is a good place to start, as is working with the medical team and hospital/clinic administration. If it can be shown that having the health system help with the cost of medications can decrease lengths of stays or reduce readmissions, then health systems may become more open to helping with such costs through charity programs. In addition, home infusion companies often have patient assistance programs to assist with pharmaceutical costs.

Unique Concerns for Persons With Cancer

Adherence is an issue for most health care conditions, but for those who work in oncology, some key issues need to be considered:

- Emotional distress can block understanding of useful information. The words "you have cancer" elicit distress, and reduction of anxiety and repetition of critical treatment information become important interventions.
- Adherence is important not just at the time of active treatment but also in prevention. Adjuvant therapies, cancer screenings, and lifestyle changes all require adherence to a suggested plan or guideline. Adherence can be doubly difficult in prevention when there is no imminent, apparent threat.
- Cancer is complicated. All disease is complex, but oncology is one of the most dynamic in the health care field, with new treatments and clinical trials constantly emerging. In addition, there is usually more than one provider (primary care doctor, medical oncologist, surgical oncologist, radiation oncologist, etc.), and many interdisciplinary team members are involved in the patient's care. This requires more appointments,

contacts, and information. As complexity increases, chances of adherence decline.

- Cancer may not be the only medical issue that needs to be managed. Many patients have comorbid conditions that require attention (see Chapter 31). The intensity of the treatment may exacerbate existing conditions or lead to new medical conditions and subsequent treatments.
- Cancer takes time and resources. Treatments are expensive and, increasingly, insurance plans are requiring more in co-pays or up-front costs. Having cancer takes time away from work (which, for some, further depletes finances) and family. In many cases, ongoing monitoring is required after the initial stages of treatment, which in turn requires more resources.
- Some cancers become terminal and conflicts can occur regarding goals of care. The oncologist may want to continue curative treatment, whereas the patient and family may be ready to focus on palliative or comfort measures. The family may discuss this with the social worker but not the physician, whom they do not want to offend or disappoint. They may fear losing their relationship with the treatment team they have worked with for many months and years if they request a primary focus on symptom management and comfort care. Recognizing that a cancer is terminal provides an important opportunity for the social worker to bring the treatment team and the patient/family together to reconsider goals of care, recognize abandonment fears, and develop a mutually agreed-upon plan for transitioning into palliative care.

Intervention Approaches to Increase Adherence

Policy and program changes currently occurring in health care may help increase adherence. Hospitals, for example, are increasingly expected to avoid unnecessary readmissions by improving transitions from inpatient to outpatient care. This requires greater collaboration between the old "silos" of inpatient and outpatient care. Improved case management and care coordination are expected to reduce costs and improve quality.

Adherence Counseling and Case Management

Insurers have been moving toward managing high utilizing consumers, and hospitals have been doing more follow-up after discharging patients. "Case management," "care management," or "transitions management" refers to a growing attempt to identify best practices to reduce unnecessary costs and readmissions by ensuring that patients understand their discharge instructions, are aware of follow-up appointments, have obtained and are correctly taking medications, and have the ability to ask further questions (Rutherford, Nielsen, Taylor, Bradke, & Coleman, 2012). Much of the focus on reducing costs relates to improving adherence. Although many of these positions are filled by nurses, largely due to nursing's ability to assess physical symptoms and medication side effects, there is also extensive listening, assessing, and problem solving involved that is very appropriate for social work.

Incorporating Adherence Questions Into Existing Assessments

Assessing for adherence barriers does not have to be complicated and can be integrated into regular health screening questions that social workers ask. Giddens and Ka'opua (2006) provide examples of questions that may trigger further interventions:

- Does the patient have a way to pay for medications?
- Is English the primary language? If not, is an interpreter needed?
- Can the patient "teach back" instructions? (Teach-back is a valuable tool that asks the patient to repeat back to the provider/educator what it was that he or she was told [i.e., who would you call if you did not remember which medications to take?]. This practice also provides clues about whether the individual can truly read and understand the information.)
- Whom would the patient call if he or she was in need of assistance? (By asking this question, the social worker confirms whom the patient views to be a primary support person, or if there truly is someone who can help the patient. A name may be listed on the patient's chart as contact person, but that does not signify the level of support available.)
- Are there other community providers or services currently working with the patient? If so, can they be informed of, and included in, the plan? (This is another example of how the social worker can create collaborations, build a larger team, and share the goal of ensuring adherence.)
- What does the patient perceive about the illness and what does the patient perceive needs to be done to treat it or prevent a recurrence?

The Role of Technology and Practical Applications

There is an ever-growing dependence on technology that can be used to help with adherence, especially where lifestyle changes are concerned. For a tech-savvy health care consumer, not only is there extensive information that can be found on the Internet (which can also be overwhelming and require consultation from health care providers) but also there are countless smartphone and computer applications that allow the user to engage in care. Applications allow a person to track meals and calculate the calories and nutritional aspects of a meal. Many of the new devices do not require a person to be tech savvy. For example, there are electronic pill dispensers that a caregiver or home health nurse can preload, which autodispense medications and sound an alarm when it's time to take the medications (also good for those with language barriers or visual impairments). Increasingly, health systems are setting up electronic access to health records that allow patients to see test results and communicate with their providers by e-mail.

Other practical ideas are simple yet effective. Color-coding prescription bottles, asking the pharmacist to provide large-print prescription information, and, if children are not present, using easy-open prescription bottles are just some examples relating to medications for those who are visually impaired or challenged by low literacy or other physical impairments. Utilizing one's interdisciplinary team can be very helpful. Occupational therapists have the latest information on practical solutions to physical or cognitive impairments, and a strong interpreter services program can help with practical solutions to counter language barriers.

The Social Work Role in Improving Adherence

Social workers can be an important force in helping improve adherence related to their knowledge and skill base. Depending on the setting and scope of the position, the social worker can play a part in improving adherence in almost all situations.

Relationship With the Interdisciplinary Team

Social workers understand how to communicate difficult information and how to raise questions while keeping relationships intact. They understand team dynamics and demonstrate the valuable skills of facilitation, relationship building, and problem solving (Figure 30.2). Some of the roles social workers play are as follows:

- Liaison: The social worker arranges family conferences, helps the patient find ways to communicate needs to the team, and guides the team in how best to approach the patient.
- Advocate: Encouraging the team to consider aspects of the patient's needs or culture that they have not noticed or helping the patient to better understand a team or treatment goal can ensure that both parties are heard and understood.
- Educator: The social worker informs people about how health care or social service systems work, reviews the value of community services, counsels patients and caregivers about how to seek help when needed, informs the team about cultural issues affecting the patient, and translates the impacts of an illness into commonly understood language.
- Counselor/consultant: In some situations, the social worker may be the only one whose role it is to listen rather than "doing something" to the patient. Social workers are skilled at engaging quickly and facilitating services while monitoring for further needs or for a shift in emotion. Listening, watching, being empathic, or sometimes just sitting with a person is a stark and welcome contrast to the chaos of a clinic or hospital.
- Coordinator: Moving the plan to implementation is often the social worker's role. This work is detail oriented and requires creativity and resourcefulness. How will a patient get to radiation therapy 5 days per week if the caregiver does not drive? If the patient needs a new prescription that is still in clinical trials, how will it be paid for? What if the patient is refusing further treatment unless a temporary home can be found for her canine companion? These examples demonstrate the variety of requests an oncology social worker may receive that would affect adherence if not resolved. They also demonstrate how a social worker builds trust with the patient and the team.

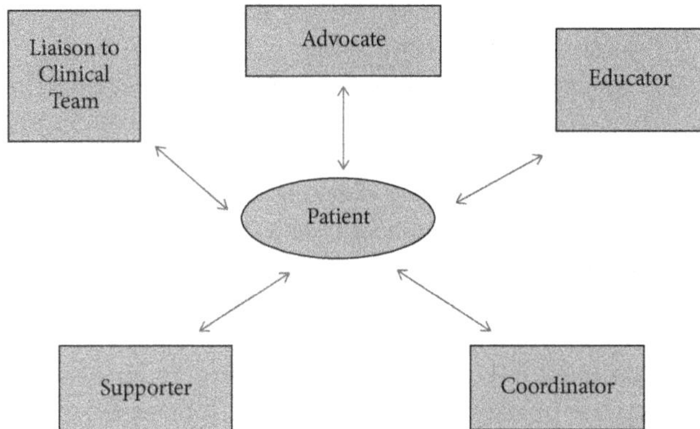

Figure 30.2. Social Work Roles in Improving Adherence

Family and interdisciplinary team conferencing can be one venue for fulfilling all of these roles. Bringing the team together with the focus on the patient can help ensure that everyone is clear about the plan of care and prevent potential misunderstandings (see Chapter 58). These roles and functions convey the strength of the profession and serve to make the discipline of social work indispensable within a care team.

The Value of a Systems Perspective

Social workers can also improve adherence by helping patients understand and negotiate systems, especially dysfunctional ones. Just as social workers can identify the cracks in the foundation of a troubled family, they can also spot potential problems within systems and have the problem-solving ability to bridge the gaps. By viewing the larger context, social workers can bring together all the players involved in a plan of care, facilitate communication among them, and ensure that there is one clear, coherent plan that also incorporates the patient's perspective and needs.

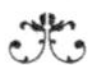

Pearls

- Get the person's story: Does he or she understand the plan and the consequences if the plan is not followed?
- Look for red flags in your assessment and interventions that might suggest difficulties the patient may have in following the treatment plan. Will the patient be able to keep his or her job and thus his or her health insurance? Will responsibilities such as child care or family caregiving prevent the patient from self-care?
- Is the team talking about one plan and the patient another? If so, talk with your team and let them know of the discordance, find out how the miscommunication occurred, and discuss with the team how future communication can be improved. Does the treatment plan seem realistic based on your knowledge of the patient?
- Never assume that what seems obvious to you is obvious to your medical team. The joy of an interdisciplinary team is the combined power of different perspectives and skills. Your contribution as a social worker includes being able to see the larger context for the patient and family and knowing what is possible and best for the patient.

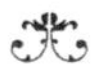

Pitfalls

- Do not get trapped in the middle of a dispute between the team and the patient. Help facilitate communication of treatment needs rather than taking on the provider's tasks.
- Maintain objectivity, and if something appears to be a crisis from the perspective of either the medical team or the patient, stay calm to get the facts and forge ahead with problem solving. Most crises are manageable, but if they are not, they probably need to involve the entire team.
- Watch for signs of compassion fatigue. All problems seem to take on an exhausting sameness when burnout exists, patients can start to be negatively stereotyped ("Not another one of those again!"), and the essential qualities of objectivity and compassion can be replaced by blaming and one-way communication. Consider that perhaps the patient's needs have changed or that the plan is no longer working and needs to be reassessed. Adherence can be as dynamic as the disease. As priorities change for the team, they may also change for the patient.
- In the event of negative team dynamics, remember that the center of the team is the person with cancer. The focus of the work revolves around the individual and his or her support system. Use social work skills to manage communication or personality differences within the team so that full attention goes to the person who needs it the most.

Social workers should not be afraid of tackling issues of adherence. Much of what social workers do in screening and assessment provides crucial information relating to a person's ability to adhere to treatment and outline solutions to possible barriers to adherence. The next step is for social workers to own this important work as part of their repertoire and to speak to team members and patients using the language of adherence.

Janae, a social worker for a major urban hospital system, was referred to see Maria, a 23-year-old patient transferred from a rural farming community 2 hours away. The referral indicated that the patient was "resistant to treatment."

Janae found Maria with a 2-year-old child on the bed with her and her 4- and 6-year-olds playing on the floor. Another woman introduced herself as Delores, Maria's sister. Delores had traveled to the hospital to allow Maria some time with her children, whom she was taking care of temporarily. Maria had been sent to the hospital because she had a "bad cancer" (leukemia). She spoke haltingly in English but claimed to understand English and declined an interpreter. Maria stated that her husband was working as a farm laborer. Delores stated that the doctors had told her that Maria needed to stay at the hospital to receive medication that was part of a clinical trial and unavailable through their local hospital.

Worried about her children and about the burden to Delores, Maria was refusing further care. Transportation and temporary living costs were expensive in an urban area, and to Maria, living in the city, even temporarily, was "scary." Maria also wanted to get back to her husband and was very worried about health care costs. When asked what she thought would happen if she left without further treatment, she stated, "God will take care of me."

Maria had no insurance, and Janae noted that she was not eligible for Medicaid due to lack of proof of in-state residency status. Janae knew that her hospital would continue to treat Maria as a charity care patient but also knew that other community hospitals might not be willing to care for someone without insurance.

- *What are the adherence barriers in this situation? What could be done to help Maria maintain her treatment while still addressing her concerns?*
- *Can funds be found to help with transport, through a community cancer program or one that helps undocumented persons?*
- *Can funds be found to pay for a bus ticket for an out-of-state family member to come and care for the kids and assist Delores and Maria?*
- *Maria is religious. Can the church help?*
- *Has every possibility of offering the treatment locally been considered? (Never assume this has been considered.)*
- *Is the plan realistic, given the burden imposed on Maria? There may be alternatives to treatment that, although not the provider's first choice, could be done locally so that Maria can participate in treatment.*
- *Has Maria, as well as her family, been appropriately educated as to the impact of not continuing treatment?*

ADDITIONAL RESOURCES

Centers for Disease Control and Prevention: http://www.cdc.org
World Health Organization: http://www.who.int/en/
Robert Wood Johnson Foundation: http://www.rwjf.org/

REFERENCES

Beni, J. (2011). Technology and the healthcare system: Implications for patient adherence. *International Journal of Electronic Healthcare, 6*(2–4), 117–137.

DiMatteo, M. R. (2004). Variations in patients' adherence to medical recommendations: A quantitative review of 50 years of research. *Medical Care, 42*(3), 200–209.

Giddens, B., & Ka'opua, L. (2006). Promoting adherence through collaborative teams (PACT): A practice model. In W. T. O'Donohue & E. R. Levensky (Eds.), *Promoting treatment adherence* (p. 171). Thousand Oaks, CA: Sage.

Haynes, R. B., McDonald, H., Garg, A. X., & Montague, P. (2002). Interventions for helping patients to follow prescriptions for medications. *The Cochrane Database of Systematic Reviews*, 2, CD000011. doi:10.1002/14651858. CD000011

Lutfey, K. E., & Wishner, W. J. (1999). Beyond compliance is adherence: Improving the prospect of diabetes care. *Diabetes Care, 22*(4), 635–639.

Martin, L. R., Williams, S. L., Haskard, K. B., & DiMatteo, M. R. (2005). The challenge of patient adherence. *Therapeutics and Clinical Risk Management, 1*(3), 189–199.

Osterberg, L., & Blaschke, T. (2005). Adherence to medication. *New England Journal of Medicine, 353*(5), 487–497.

Rutherford, P., Nielsen, G. A., Taylor, J., Bradke, P., & Coleman, E. (2012). *How-to guide: Improving transitions from the hospital to community settings to reduce avoidable rehospitalizations.* Cambridge, MA: Institute for Healthcare Improvement.

31 The Impact of Comorbidities on Cancer Care

Barbara Head

Key Concepts

- *Many cancer patients have one or more comorbidities concurrent with their cancer diagnosis.*
- *The impact of comorbidities on treatment decisions, responses, and outcomes must be considered when developing a care plan.*
- *The oncology social worker's role includes the complete assessment of comorbidities' impact on the patient's cancer diagnosis and care. The social worker functions as a patient navigator in facilitating the coordination and continuity of health services and providing resources for both the cancer diagnosis and comorbid conditions.*
- *Comorbidities are more common and numerous in the elderly, who may feel burdened by them but who may also have considerable knowledge and skills for managing their illness conditions.*
- *The presence of patient comorbidities adds substantially to caregiving responsibilities.*

Although often the patient's focus, a cancer diagnosis is only part of his or her health care profile when comorbidity—one or more additional health conditions in a patient diagnosed with a particular condition or disease—is present (Satariano, Silliman, & Lash, 2006). Comorbidities are essential pieces of the total puzzle, impacting the diagnosis, treatment options (including reactions to and outcomes), prognosis, and quality of life along the cancer trajectory. Often, patients and their caregivers have managed comorbid conditions for years before the cancer diagnosis. Some may respond with a sense of despair and hopelessness, viewing the new diagnosis as an additional financial, social, physical, psychological, or spiritual burden. Conversely, those who have mastered day-to-day coping with previous illnesses may be confident and resilient and view it as one more problem to be solved. A comprehensive assessment of the impact of the diagnosis on the patient and caregiver will enable the social worker to plan care that builds on existing strengths and resilience for effective coping.

The Social Worker's Role in Managing the Impact of Comorbidities on the Cancer Patient and Family Caregivers

Assessment

The social worker assesses the impact of comorbidities on the psychosocial care of every cancer patient and caregiver, assisting them in navigating the health care system to ensure that both the cancer and comorbid conditions are addressed and optimally treated.

Every patient assessment should include a comprehensive health history (after ascertaining if one is already available to avoid unnecessary history taking). This should assess all co-occurring conditions including date of diagnoses, severity, medications prescribed (those that work and are continued, as well as those tried that failed), symptoms (including related pain) and complications experienced, and impact on functional level and quality of life.

Physicians and nurses often gather historical information about diseases and related treatment. However, the social worker is responsible for assessing the patient's reactions to the conditions, understanding of the illness, ability or willingness to be adherent with treatment plans, and quality-of-life issues.

The meaning of each condition to the patient is explored, as well as the patient's adherence to the treatment plan, with his or her past responses to illnesses and treatments used to provide clues as to how he or she will cope with the cancer. The social worker assesses the presence and/or history of comorbid conditions by inquiring about the areas identified to follow. If new comorbidities develop during cancer care, the social worker should assess these factors related to the new diagnosis.

Components of the Social Work Assessment of Patient Comorbidities

- *The patient's and family's understanding of the patient's comorbid condition(s) and the impact of those conditions on the current diagnosis and treatment plan*
- *Past patterns of adherence/nonadherence with treatment regimens*
- *Reasons for any nonadherence including economic, environmental, and intellectual deficits*
- *Impact of the comorbid condition(s) on functionality, ability to work, activities of daily living, and independence*
- *Impact of the comorbid condition on quality of life*
- *Symptom burden related to comorbid condition(s)*
- *Resource needs related to both the comorbid conditions and the current cancer diagnosis*
- *Caregiving needs, availability, issues, and concerns*
- *Caregiver coping skills, previous experience with caregiving, fatigue, and potential for burnout*
- *Impact of comorbid condition(s) on family members*
- *Ability of patient and caregiver to express and address emotional needs and feelings*

After assessment, the social worker shares findings with the medical team members (physicians, nurses, allied therapists), who can assist with the social worker's understanding of the comorbid condition(s), its impact on care and treatment, and the impact of cancer treatment on the comorbid condition. In exchange, the social worker conveys insights helpful to the medical team members' understanding of the impact of the comorbidity, related coping skills, resource limitations, caregiving issues, and the patient's mental health history.

However, perhaps the most important social work intervention is helping patients and families organize and prioritize the various conditions and their treatment and developing a comprehensive care plan to share with the medical team. As care planning proceeds, the social worker advocates for the patient and seeks resources and supports related to both cancer care and the comorbid condition.

Measurement of Comorbidities

By its nature, comorbidity assessment is complicated because it is multidimensional, requiring consideration of multiple conditions, as well as each one's prognostic impact (Lee, Cheung, Atkinson, & Krzyzanowska, 2011). Several instruments help in evaluating the presence and impact of comorbidities and are briefly described here. If the oncology team utilizes a comorbidity measurement instrument such as those described, results may be noted in the patient's medical history and the social worker should note the patient's score and its possible implications for functioning. However, such measurement should be coupled with consideration of the patient's functional and performance status, as well as psychosocial factors.

Adult Comorbidity Evaluation (ACE-27): This instrument was developed specifically to measure comorbidity in the cancer patient (Jorgensen, Hallas, Land, & Herrstedt, 2010). Presence and severity (1 = mild, 2 = moderate, or 3 = severe decompensation) of 27 health diagnoses and conditions are rated within 11 categories: cardiovascular, respiratory, gastrointestinal, endocrine, neurological, psychiatric, rheumatological, immunological, malignance, substance abuse, and body weight.

Charlson Comorbidity Index (CCI): Developed and validated in 1987 (Charlson, Pompei, Ales, & MacKenzie, 1987), this instrument is the most extensively studied (De Groot, Beckerman, Lankhorst, & Bouter, 2003) and widely used (Satariano et al., 2006) measure of comorbidity. The index includes 19 diseases weighted according to their association with 1-year mortality risk. The CCI accounts for both the number and the seriousness of comorbid diseases (Jorgensen et al., 2010).

Cumulative Illness Rating Scale (CIRS): Intended to be a measure of overall health, this scale is based on a systematic assessment of separate organ systems. A scale of 0 to 4 is used to rate each disease according to severity. The disease with the highest score in each organ system is counted. Total score is the sum of scores across the organ systems.

With each of these scales, the higher the level of comorbidity is, the greater the risk is of dying. The summary score reflects the severity of conditions, with the index condition, cancer, excluded from the score. The possibility of synergistic or multiplicative relationships among conditions is also not considered in the scoring (Satariano et al., 2006), though such relationships further complicate the prognosis.

It is difficult to determine the best comorbidity measure. No matter which one is chosen, however, users need to familiarize themselves with that instrument and use it consistently when evaluating and comparing patients, meaning if a tool is used by the oncology team to measure patient morbidity, the social worker must become familiar with that particular instrument and the implications of the patient's score.

For geriatric patients, the Comprehensive Geriatric Assessment (CGA), a multidisciplinary evaluation, may be used to assess the problems, resources, and strengths of the patient. It includes comorbidities and functional, physical, psychological, nutritional, and cognitive functioning and status (Rodin & Mohile, 2007) and also reveals polypharmacy concerns.

Assisting With Decision Making

The presence of comorbid conditions may impact patients' decisions about treatment and ongoing therapy. The social worker assists the patient and family in processing information about treatment options, potential outcomes, and decision making. Quality-of-life issues may outweigh the potential benefits of intensive cancer treatment, especially in the elderly. Because of the burden of comorbid disease, a patient may make treatment choices that are less than optimal but reduce quality-of-life impacts. However, some patients accustomed to illness and treatment may wish to continue treatment beyond what is medically recommended.

When patient choice contradicts medical team recommendations or family preferences, the social worker should develop an understanding of the patient's rationale, clarify patient choices with the medical team, and act as patient advocate with the medical team and family. In situations where the patient's involvement with the oncology team is terminated because treatment is not chosen, the social worker seeks to ensure that the patient is not abandoned while other sources of care and support are initiated. In some instances, hospice may be the preferred service for ongoing care, and the social worker can facilitate that referral process.

The Prevalence of Comorbidities in Cancer

Aging populations and advances in treatment of chronic conditions contribute to the propensity of comorbid conditions in today's cancer patient. However, aging remains the most important risk factor for cancer and, as the population ages, there will be more older patients with cancer—patients with histories of chronic disease *and* the ongoing development of comorbid conditions during and after their cancer care (Extermann, 2007).

Studies have shown that older cancer patients have an average of three comorbidities (Extermann, 2007; Jorgensen, Hallas, Friis, & Herrstedt, 2012; Jorgensen et al., 2010), with the most frequent being hypertension; cardiovascular, respiratory, and cerebrovascular diseases; diabetes; and arthritis (Jorgensen et al., 2012).

Comorbidities occur not only in patients who develop cancer but also in cancer survivors. In a study comparing 964 long-term cancer survivors to 14,330 persons with no history of cancer, Keating, O'Malley, Freedland, and Smith (2012) found the survivors to be more likely to be diagnosed with lung or heart disease, arthritis, or diabetes and to have more frequent pain, urinary infections, and limitations in activities of daily living. Additionally, cancer treatment can result in comorbid conditions such as neuropathy, muscular aches and pains, decreased mobility, and cardiac disease. Therefore, the oncology social worker's role in facilitating effective coping with multiple health conditions extends into cancer survivor work. Comorbidities that developed before, during, and after cancer care must be considered when developing survivorship plans of care.

The Impact of Comorbidities on the Patient With Cancer

A systematic review of the impact of comorbidity on chemotherapy use and patient outcomes reported decreased chemotherapy use, reduced survival independent of treatment, increased toxicity among those receiving chemotherapy, and increased treatment delay for patients with comorbidities (Lee et al., 2011).

Research findings related to the impact of comorbidities on cancer care include the following:

- The presence of comorbid conditions has been shown to negatively impact the survival of patients with cancers of the prostate (Lund, Borre, Jacobsen, Sorensen, & Norgaard, 2008), colon (Koroukian, 2009), ovary (Tetsche, Norgaard, Jacobsen, Wogelius, & Sorensen, 2008), and breast (Cronin-Fenton et al., 2007).
- Cancer patients aged 65 or over report more comorbid conditions and poorer physical and mental health compared to older patients without cancer (A. W. Smith et al., 2008).
- Women with comorbidity are less likely to receive chemotherapy and radiation.
- Failure to manage comorbidities may impact longevity among breast cancer survivors (Braithwaite et al., 2012).
- Patients with metastatic cancer continue to take medications for their comorbidities even when the medications are no longer appropriate and cause inconvenience and side effects (Cashman, Wright, & Ring, 2010).
- For patients (especially the elderly) diagnosed with less lethal cancers, their comorbid condition may well be the eventual cause of death (Braithwaite et al., 2012; Kendal, 2008; Terret, Castel-Kremer, Albrand, & Droz, 2009).

There is less in the literature about the impact of comorbidities on quality of life (QOL) in patients with cancer and comorbidities. Unfortunately, routine QOL measurement is not done because it is time-consuming and the clinical implication of such measurement is not well understood (Jacot et al., 2008). However, QOL has been shown to have prognostic impact for many cancer diagnoses (poorer QOL is associated with poorer prognosis; Jacot et al., 2008; Karvonen-Gutierrez et al., 2008; A. W. Smith et al., 2008). The presence of comorbidities contributes to increased frailty and disability, important variables impacting QOL scores.

Polypharmacy: An Additional Complicating Factor

Increased comorbidity results in treatment with multiple medications (polypharmacy), with older patients taking an average of six concomitant drugs (Extermann, 2007). The treatment of cancer may include multiple anti-cancer agents coupled with supportive medication such as anti-nausea drugs and analgesics. Such polypharmacy can contribute to adverse drug reactions, drug–drug interactions, nonadherence to medication protocols, and a related increased risk of hospitalization. However, the fact that patients with comorbidities are not included in clinical trials limits knowledge related to the influence of comorbidity and polypharmacy on patients' response to and tolerance of antineoplastic treatment (Jorgensen et al., 2010). Additionally, changes in organ functioning, alterations in the gastrointestinal system, altered metabolic processes, and reduced drug clearance in the elderly can contribute to serious medication-related complications.

Jim, a 59-year-old patient diagnosed with Stage 2 colon cancer, received a bowel resection, and the oncologist believes he has a good chance of long-term survival with chemotherapy. In your conversation with him and his wife, you learn he was diagnosed with diabetes 5 years ago. Initially, it was thought to be treatable with diet and oral medications, but his nonadherence intensified his condition and he was placed on insulin 2 years ago. He is supposed to check his glucose levels four times a day and take sliding-scale insulin. His wife states that he usually checks his glucose levels in the morning and takes his shot, but he often ignores it during the day because he is busy at work and often works overtime.

Although Jim's long-term prognosis is good, he must maintain optimal treatment for his diabetes if he is to do well during chemotherapy. His cancer treatment can affect his appetite, and he may have nausea and vomiting, requiring additional medications. Poor intake or vomiting can have negative consequences for his diabetes. He will also be at high risk for toxicities during his cancer treatment.

Important interventions of the social worker might include the following:

- *Explore Jim's history of nonadherence related to his diabetes. Did he fully understand that diagnosis and the negative health consequences of nonadherence? Did he have adequate resources to care for his diabetes (e.g., coverage for syringes and insulin)?*
- *Explore financial resources to help with coverage of his diabetes treatment as appropriate to his situation.*
- *Ensure that the patient and his wife understand the importance of adequate diabetes treatment during his treatment for cancer. Involve others, such as a diabetes educator and the team nurse, in providing patient/family information/education and validating that the patient comprehends the education and his role/responsibility in self-management.*
- *Facilitate a discussion/meeting with the patient, his wife, and the physician to develop a shared understanding of how the diabetes can best be managed during his treatment for cancer and beyond.*
- *Involve his wife in an active caregiving role. Encourage the patient to involve his wife as a partner in his care and include her in discussions with the physician.*
- *Secure home health resources to reinforce teaching about diabetes and teach methods for ensuring adherence.*
- *Offer emotional support to his wife as his caregiver. Allow her to vent her frustration with his nonadherence. Explore techniques she can use to encourage adherence.*
- *Encourage the couple to talk together about feelings related to his illnesses and the impact of his health on their lives.*

Common Comorbidities Impacting a Cancer Diagnosis

There are certain comorbidities that are closely associated with cancer. In this section, several of these common associations will be described.

Aging and Cancer

As previously stated, cancer is a disease of the aging. Most cancer diagnoses and related deaths occur in people over age 65, and it is estimated that patients 65 or older will account for 70% of all cancer diagnoses by 2030 (B. D. Smith, Smith, & Hurria, 2009).

Optimal supportive care is recommended in the elderly cancer patient with comorbidities because these patients are at increased risk of toxicity when receiving antineoplastic agents (Jorgensen et al., 2010). Myelosuppression, anemia, and mucositis are more prevalent in this population. Renal function declines with aging and can place the patient at increased risk for treatment-related toxicities. However, elderly patients are at less risk for chemotherapy-induced nausea and vomiting.

Chronic Obstructive Pulmonary Disease and Lung Cancer

Lung cancer is a frequent cause of death in patients with chronic obstructive pulmonary disease (COPD; Barnes & Adcock, 2011). An Italian study found that after adjustment for smoking and other factors, chronic bronchitis, emphysema, and COPD were associated with an approximately twofold increased risk of lung cancer. Family history of chronic bronchitis and emphysema are associated with increased risk of lung cancer (Koshiol et al., 2009). One study found the prevalence of lung cancer in COPD patients to be greater than 16 per 1,000 person-years, which compares with 1 to 1.5 per 1,000 person-years in smokers without COPD (De Torres et al., 2011). This strong association may be due to one or more of the following factors: both diseases result from cigarette smoking, abnormalities in the COPD lung (such as impaired pulmonary function) favor the development of lung cancer beyond the effect of smoking alone, and/or there is a genetic susceptibility to both diseases (Barnes & Adcock, 2011; Carrozzi & Viegi, 2011).

Patients with COPD already experience a high symptom burden comparable to that of patients with lung cancer (Joshi, Joshi, & Bartter, 2012), but patients with COPD alone tend to live longer than those with cancer. Symptoms for both diseases include dyspnea, fatigue, dry mouth, cough, anxiety, irritability, nervousness, pain, and depression. COPD sufferers are often dependent on others, which places a substantial burden on caregivers over time. Palliation of symptoms should be the standard of care with either diagnosis. Patients with either disease have diminished quality of life, which is compounded when both diseases are present.

Obesity, Diabetes, and Cancer

An Institute of Medicine report concluded that obesity and excess weight play a role in the development and progression of various cancers; obesity and cancer may both be fueled by energy intake that is higher than energy expenditure (Patlak & Nass, 2011). Fat tissue generates hormones and growth factors and fosters inflammation, which fuels the growth of tumors, resulting in increased cancer incidence, progression, and recurrence and decreased survival rates. Evidence has linked obesity to increased risk of endometrial, colorectal, esophageal, kidney, pancreatic, and postmenopausal breast cancer (Patlak & Nass, 2011).

The presence of diabetes may negatively impact both cancer risk and the outcomes of cancer treatment (M. Singer, 2007). Studies have shown that individuals with type 2 diabetes are more likely to both develop and die from cancer (U. Smith & Gale, 2009). Cervical and stomach cancers are associated with type 1 diabetes, whereas breast, colon, endometrial, pancreatic, liver, and bladder cancers, as well as non-Hodgkin and Hodgkin lymphomas, have been associated with type 2 diabetes (M. Singer, 2007).

Obese and overweight cancer patients are at high risk for developing type 2 diabetes. If diabetes was undiagnosed before the cancer, its diagnosis and treatment add burden. Patients with diabetes receiving treatment are at high risk of such toxicities as peripheral neuropathy, nephropathy, and cardiomyopathy and therefore require close medical monitoring. Meticulous monitoring of glucose levels, renal function, and signs/symptoms of toxicity is essential and may be overwhelming to the patient and family. Death in patients with cancer and diabetes can be the result of various causes including myocardial infarction, other bacterial disease, urinary system disease, hypertensive disease, or arterial disease (Liu, Ji, Sundquist, Sundquist, & Hemminki, 2012).

Human Immunodeficiency Virus and Cancer

Antiretroviral therapy has changed HIV from a terminal condition into a long-term chronic disease, and HIV patients treated with such therapy now have a near-normal life expectancy (Perry et al., 2013). As persons with HIV grow older, they too will experience increasing rates of all diseases related to aging, including cancer. However, the specific cancer diagnosis may be more related to the chronic effects of certain oncogenic infections that accelerate aging in the patient with HIV (Grulich, Jin, Poynten, & Vajdic, 2011). People with HIV also have higher risks for cancers associated with lifestyle factors such as smoking and alcohol usage. The incidence of lung cancer is increased 1.7 times in persons with HIV infection and at least threefold among those with AIDS compared to demographically similar populations (Sigel et al., 2012).

When assessing and working with the HIV patient with cancer, it is important to consider the symptom burden that may be already present. Adding the side effects of cancer and its treatment to an already burdensome symptom profile may overwhelm the patient and seriously impact an already diminished quality of life.

Psychiatric Comorbidities and Cancer

Estimates of psychiatric comorbidities among cancer patients vary. Meta-analyses evaluating the overall prevalence of mental disorders among cancer patients have found ranges from 9.8% to 38.2% in various cancer settings (Mehnert et al., 2012; Mitchell et al., 2011; S. Singer, Das-Munshi, & Brahler, 2010). In advanced-cancer patients, approximately 50% meet criteria for a psychiatric disorder (Miovic & Block, 2007).

Such comorbidities may be present at diagnosis or may develop during cancer care and survivorship. A study of 1,323 cancer survivors in Australia found the prevalence of psychological morbidity to be 28% at 6 months after diagnosis. Mental health history, modifiable health behaviors, and psychological and social characteristics were found to be stronger indicators of psychological morbidity than individual or disease characteristics (Boyes, Girgis, D'Este, & Zucca, 2011). Preexisting psychiatric disorders may be exacerbated by a serious cancer diagnosis (Miovic & Block, 2007). However, an analysis of data from the National Health Interview Survey found that long-term cancer survivors (5 years or more postdiagnosis) do not have elevated rates of major depressive disorders when compared to those with no previous cancer diagnosis (Pirl, Greer, Temel, Yeap, & Gilman, 2009).

Too often, a mental health history may be overlooked by the medical treatment team. Social workers, therefore, must address coping difficulties and mental health issues/history as part of the comprehensive assessment of a cancer patient. When problems are present, the social worker should advocate for treatment of any psychiatric comorbidities. Untreated anxiety and depression can seriously impact a patient's quality of life and the treatment experience.

The Impact of Comorbidities on Family Caregivers

Caregivers of patients with comorbidities and cancer may have already been stressed by the demands and hardships entailed in the care of their loved one. Although some caregivers have ample coping skills and personal, social, and economic resources, others may feel totally overwhelmed by the additional burden of a cancer diagnosis and related treatment. In one study of cancer caregivers, half reported not getting training perceived as necessary for their caregiving (Van Ryn et al., 2011); this points to the need for adequate information, education, and resources related to the care of both the cancer and the comorbidities present. The social worker should not assume that the caregiver and patient received adequate information, training, and resources related to a previous diagnosis.

Knowing that the "emotional work" of caring may be the most challenging aspect for a caregiver (Thomas, Morris, & Harman, 2002), the social worker must assess the caregiver's ability to effectively regulate and communicate about emotions and the personal impacts of the diseases affecting the patient. Caregivers may benefit from support groups for caregivers and/or short-term counseling, and, as with patients, caregiver needs extend beyond the period of active treatment (Given, Sherwood, & Given, 2013).

The oncology social worker's role when working with the cancer patient with comorbidities includes comprehensive assessment; patient/family education; assistance with exploring treatment options and making decisions; advocating for patients' informed decisions; assisting with procurement of adequate financial, environmental and caregiving resources needed for all conditions; and ensuring that patients are not abandoned should they opt for no or limited cancer care.

Assessment of and intervention with the family caregiver is also essential to the psychosocial care of cancer patients with comorbidities. Intervening to support the caregiver, alleviate the caregiver's stress, address relationship issues, and facilitate effective dyadic coping may be key to facilitating improved quality of life and decreased mental distress.

Pearls

- A comprehensive assessment of comorbid conditions is essential when planning care for the cancer patient.
- Comorbidities can exist before diagnosis or they may be first identified or may develop after the cancer diagnosis. Assessment must therefore be ongoing.
- How patients have coped with comorbidities and their adherence with treatment of those conditions are important considerations when developing a plan of care for the cancer patient.
- The social worker is uniquely qualified to facilitate effective coping of patients with multiple comorbidities—both during cancer care and into survivorship.

Pitfalls

- The team focuses on the cancer diagnosis to the exclusion of comorbidity management.
- The team fails to continually reassess the impact of comorbidities during cancer care and throughout survivorship.
- Inadequate resources and support are provided to assist the patient and family in managing comorbidities of cancer and its treatment.

REFERENCES

Barnes, P. J., & Adcock, I. M. (2011). Chronic obstructive pulmonary disease and lung cancer: A lethal association. *American Journal of Respiratory and Critical Care Medicine, 184*(8), 866–867. doi:10.1164/rccm.201108-1436ED

Boyes, A. W., Girgis, A., D'Este, C., & Zucca, A. C. (2011). Flourishing or floundering? Prevalence and correlates of anxiety and depression among a population-based sample of adult cancer survivors 6 months after diagnosis. *Journal of Affective Disorders, 135*(1–3), 184–192. doi:10.1016/j.jad.2011.07.016

Braithwaite, D., Moore, D. H., Satariano, W. A., Kwan, M. L., Hiatt, R. A., Kroenke, C., & Caan, B. J. (2012). Prognostic impact of comorbidity among long-term breast cancer survivors: Results from the LACE study. *Cancer Epidemiology, Biomarkers, and Prevention*, *21*(7), 1115–1125. doi:10.1158/1055-9965.epi-11-1228

Carrozzi, L., & Viegi, G. (2011). Lung cancer and chronic obstructive pulmonary disease: The story goes on. *Radiology*, *261*(3), 688–691. doi:10.1148/radiol.11111950

Cashman, J., Wright, J., & Ring, A. (2010). The treatment of co-morbidities in older patients with metastatic cancer. *Support Care Cancer*, *18*(5), 651–655. doi:10.1007/s00520-010-0813-1

Charlson, M. E., Pompei, P., Ales, K. L., & MacKenzie, C. R. (1987). A new method of classifying prognostic comorbidity in longitudinal studies: Development and validation. *Journal of Chronic Disease*, *40*, 373–383.

Cronin-Fenton, D. P., Norgaard, M., Jacobsen, J., Garne, J. P., Ewertz, M., Lash, T. L., & Sorensen, H. T. (2007). Comorbidity and survival of Danish breast cancer patients from 1995 to 2005. *British Journal of Cancer*, *96*(9), 1462–1468. doi:10.1038/sj.bjc.6603717

De Groot, V., Beckerman, H., Lankhorst, G. J., & Bouter, L. M. (2003). How to measure comorbidity: A critical review of available methods. *Journal of Clinical Epidemiology*, *56*(3), 221–229.

De Torres, J. P., Marin, J. M., Casanova, C., Cote, C., Carrizo, S., Cordoba-Lanus, E., & Celli, B. R. (2011). Lung cancer in patients with chronic obstructive pulmonary disease—incidence and predicting factors. *American Journal of Respiratory and Critical Care Medicine*, *184*(8), 913–919. doi:10.1164/rccm.201103-0430OC

Extermann, M. (2007). Interaction between comorbidity and cancer. *Cancer Control*, *14*(1), 13–22.

Given, B. A., Sherwood, P., & Given, C. W. (2013). Support for caregivers of cancer patients: Transition after active treatment. *Cancer Epidemiology, Biomarkers, and Prevention*, *20*(10), 2015–2021.

Grulich, A. E., Jin, F., Poynten, I. M., & Vajdic, C. M. (2011). HIV, cancer, and aging. *Sex Health*, *8*(4), 521–525. doi:10.1071/sh11048

Jacot, W., Colinet, B., Bertrand, D., Lacombe, S., Bozonnat, M. C., Daures, J. P., & Onco, L. R. (2008). Quality of life and comorbidity score as prognostic determinants in non-small-cell lung cancer patients. *Annals of Oncology*, *19*(8), 1458–1464. doi:10.1093/annonc/mdn064

Jorgensen, T. L., Hallas, J., Friis, S., & Herrstedt, J. (2012). Comorbidity in elderly cancer patients in relation to overall and cancer-specific mortality. *British Journal of Cancer*, *106*(7), 1353–1360. doi:10.1038/bjc.2012.46

Jorgensen, T. L., Hallas, J., Land, L. H., & Herrstedt, J. (2010). Comorbidity and polypharmacy in elderly cancer patients: The significance on treatment outcome and tolerance. *Journal of Geriatric Oncology*, *1*, 87–102.

Joshi, M., Joshi, A., & Bartter, T. (2012). Symptom burden in chronic obstructive pulmonary disease and cancer. *Current Opinion in Pulmonary Medicine*, *18*(2), 97–103. doi:10.1097/MCP.0b013e32834fa84c

Karvonen-Gutierrez, C. A., Ronis, D. L., Fowler, K. E., Terrell, J. E., Gruber, S. B., & Duffy, S. A. (2008). Quality of life scores predict survival among patients with head and neck cancer. *Journal of Clinical Oncology*, *26*(16), 2754–2760.

Keating, N. L., O'Malley, A. J., Freedland, S. J., & Smith, M. R. (2012). Does comorbidity influence the risk of myocardial infarction or diabetes during androgen-deprivation therapy for prostate cancer? *European Urology*, *64*(1), 159–166. doi:10.1016/j.eururo.2012.04.035

Kendal, W. S. (2008). Dying with cancer: The influence of age, comorbidity, and cancer site. *Cancer*, *112*(6), 1354–1362. doi:10.1002/cncr.23315

Koroukian, S. M. (2009). Assessment and interpretation of comorbidity burden in older adults with cancer. *Journal of the American Geriatric Society*, *57*(Suppl. 2), S275–S278. doi:10.1111/j.1532-5415.2009.02511.x

Koshiol, J., Rotunno, M., Consonni, D., Pesatori, A. C., De Matteis, S., Goldstein, A. M., . . . Caporaso, N. E. (2009). Chronic obstructive pulmonary disease and altered risk of lung cancer in a population-based case-control study. *PLOS One*, *4*(10), e7380. doi:10.1371/journal.pone.0007380

Lee, L., Cheung, W. Y., Atkinson, E., & Krzyzanowska, M. K. (2011). Impact of comorbidity on chemotherapy use and outcomes in solid tumors: A systematic review. *Journal of Clinical Oncology*, *29*(1), 106–117. doi:10.1200/jco.2010.31.3049

Liu, X., Ji, J., Sundquist, K., Sundquist, J., & Hemminki, K. (2012). Mortality causes in cancer patients with type 2 diabetes. *European Journal of Cancer Prevention*, *21*(3), 300–306.

Lund, L., Borre, M., Jacobsen, J., Sorensen, H. T., & Norgaard, M. (2008). Impact of comorbidity on survival of Danish prostate cancer patients, 1995–2006: A population-based cohort study. *Urology*, *72*(6), 1258–1262. doi:10.1016/j.urology.2007.12.018

Mehnert, A., Koch, U., Schulz, H., Wegscheider, K., Weis, J., Faller, H., . . . Harter, M. (2012). Prevalence of mental disorders, psychosocial distress, and need for psychosocial support in cancer patients: Study protocol of an epidemiological multi-center study. *BMC Psychiatry*, *12*(1), 70. doi:10.1186/1471-244x-12-70

Miovic, M., & Block, S. (2007). Psychiatric disorders in advanced cancer. *Cancer*, *110*(8), 1665–1676. doi:10.1002/cncr.22980

Mitchell, A. J., Chan, M., Bhatti, H., Halton, M., Grassi, L., Johansen, C., & Meader, N. (2011). Prevalence of depression, anxiety, and adjustment disorder in oncological, haematological, and palliative-care settings: A meta-analysis of 94 interview-based studies. *Lancet Oncology*, *12*, 160–174.

Patlak, M., & Nass, S. J. (2011). *The role of obesity in cancer survival and recurrence*. Washington, DC: Institute of Medicine.

Perry, B. A., Westfall, A. O., Molony, E., Tucker, R., Ritchie, C., Saag, M. S., & Merlin, J. S. (2013). Characteristics of an ambulatory palliative care clinic for HIV-infected patients. *Journal of Palliative Medicine*, *16*(8), 1–4.

Pirl, W. F., Greer, J., Temel, J. S., Yeap, B. Y., & Gilman, S. E. (2009). Major depressive disorder in long-term cancer survivors: Analysis of the National Comorbidity Survey Replication. *Journal of Clinical Oncology*, *27*(25), 4130–4134. doi:10.1200/jco.2008.16.2784

Rodin, M. B., & Mohile, S. G. (2007). A practical approach to geriatric assessment in oncology. *Journal of Clinical Oncology*, *25*, 1936–1944.

Satariano, W. A., Silliman, R. A., & Lash, T. L. (2006). Comorbidity and cancer treatment in older populations. In H. B. Muss, C. P. Hunter, & K. A. Johnson (Eds.), *Treatment and management of cancer in the elderly* (pp. 471–482). New York, NY: Taylor and Francis.

Sigel, K., Wisnivesky, J., Dubrow, R., Justice, A., Gordon, K., & Brown, S. T. (2012). HIV is an independent risk factor for incident lung cancer. *AIDS, 26*, 1017–1025.

Singer, M. (2007). Management of comorbid diabetes and cancer. *Oncology, 21*(8 Suppl.), 26–37.

Singer, S., Das-Munshi, J., & Brahler, E. (2010). Prevalence of mental health conditions in cancer patients in acute care—a meta-analysis. *Annals of Oncology, 21*, 925–930.

Smith, A. W., Reeve, B. B., Bellizzi, K. M., Harlan, L. C., Klabunde, C. N., Amsellem, M., . . . Hays, R. D. (2008). Cancer, comorbidities, and health-related quality of life of older adults. *Health Care Financial Review, 29*(4), 41–56.

Smith, B. D., Smith, G. L., & Hurria, A. (2009). Future of cancer incidence in the United States: Burdens upon an aging, changing nation. *Journal of Clinical Oncology, 27*, 2758–2765.

Smith, U., & Gale, E. A. (2009). Does diabetes therapy influence the risk of cancer? *Diabetologia, 52*, 1699–1708.

Terret, C., Castel-Kremer, E., Albrand, G., & Droz, J. P. (2009). Effects of comorbidity on screening and early diagnosis of cancer in elderly people. *Lancet Oncology, 10*(1), 80–87. doi:10.1016/s1470-2045(08)70336-x

Tetsche, M. S., Norgaard, M., Jacobsen, J., Wogelius, P., & Sorensen, H. T. (2008). Comorbidity and ovarian cancer survival in Denmark, 1995–2005: A population-based cohort study. *International Journal of Gynecologic Cancer, 18*(3), 421–427. doi:10.1111/j.1525-1438.2007.01036.x

Thomas, C., Morris, S. M., & Harman, J. C. (2002). Companions through cancer: The care given by informal carers in cancer contexts. *Social Science and Medicine, 54*, 529–544.

Van Ryn, M., Sanders, S., Kahn, K. L., van Houtven, C., Griffin, J. M., Martin, M., . . . Rowland, J. (2011). Objective burden, resources, and other stressors among informal cancer caregivers: A hidden quality issue. *Psycho-Oncology, 20*, 44–52.

32

Allison Werner-Lin

Social Work Practice With Families Affected by Hereditary Cancer

Key Concepts

- *The ability to identify genetic contributions to cancer continues to outpace the development of effective and targeted therapies, marking a therapeutic gap.*
- *Family histories with familial cancer inform perceptions of cancer risk and vulnerability, health behaviors, and expectations about diagnostic and treatment outcomes.*
- *Disclosure of cancer risk information within families must be viewed as an ongoing process, particularly as novel therapies become available and as younger family members become eligible for testing.*
- *Motivation for and reactions to genetic testing vary across the life cycle as individuals and families face distinct challenges and transitions.*

The identification of genetic variants that increase cancer risk or that shape treatment response means that social work settings must not only contend with a new risk concept but also broaden our person-in-environment lens to include consideration of genetic variation as a core feature of assessment of cancer patients and their families (Werner-Lin & Reed, 2011). The identification of genetic contributions to cancer continues to outpace the development of effective and targeted therapies, marking a *therapeutic gap* (Holtzman & Watson, 1997). As a result, social work must now contend with a new "at risk" patient population: asymptomatic individuals with genetic variants linked to elevated cancer risk confirmed through genetic testing who may be actively involved in the cancer world by caregiving for ill loved ones, pursuing measures to screen for or prevent cancer from developing, or regularly visiting physicians.

The strain of living with cancer risk has been explored, particularly concerning cancer-linked gene mutations identified early in the Human Genome Project. Yet more work is needed to fully explore the impact of emerging genetic technologies on families and communities affected by cancer, particularly those with limited access to genetic services and poor cancer care. This chapter presents the rapidly evolving empirical base regarding the impact of hereditary cancer syndromes across the life cycle. (For an introduction to cancer genetics, see Chapter 35).

A Role for Social Work in Genetic Medicine

Social workers possess many of the skills critical to working with individuals, families, and communities affected by hereditary cancer syndromes. Social workers regularly facilitate patient-driven decision making in complex medical contexts. Across settings and populations, social workers help clients identify family expectations about disease risk and separate these expectations from individual beliefs about one's own susceptibility. The strengths perspective and person-in-environment lens suggest a potent role for social workers to participate in designing information-sharing models and approaches to genomic services in oncology care settings that are tailored to the specific needs of individuals, families, and communities (Werner-Lin & Reed, 2011). However, additional knowledge and skills in genetics risk assessment and counseling are required for oncology social workers, as well as other professionals who want to participate in specialized genetic services (Robson, Storm, Weitzel, Wollins, & Offit, 2010; Weltzel, Blazer, MacDonald, Culver, & Offit, 2011).

Essential Skills for Social Workers in Cancer Genetics

Knowledge Base

- *Acquire a basic understanding about hereditary cancer genetics as a science and a field of study, including its biological, psychosocial, ethical, and legal aspects.*
- *Obtain current information about hereditary cancer from reliable sources for self, clients, and colleagues.*
- *Develop specialized knowledge and understanding about the history, traditions, values, and family systems of client groups as they relate to cancer and genetics.*

Direct Practice

- *Gather relevant family history information focused on cancer and genetics and including a multigenerational family history that includes parents, children, siblings, grandparents, aunts/uncles, and cousins.*
- *Identify clients who might benefit from a referral for genetic services.*
- *Properly communicate to clients the purpose of genetic services and the role of various genetic professionals in oncology settings.*
- *Discuss costs of genetic services and insurance benefits.*
- *Provide culturally sensitive services to clients with or at risk of developing hereditary cancers.*
- *Explore with clients the possible range of emotional effects they and family members may experience as a result of receiving or refusing cancer genetic information.*
- *Assist clients and their families in the genetic decision-making process and in adapting to genetic information throughout the life cycle.*

Advocacy

- *Facilitate the creation and maintenance of support resources for clients with hereditary cancer syndromes.*
- *Educate clients, professionals, and the community about policy issues regarding cancer genetics.*
- *Advocate for client-focused public policy in genetics.*
- *Assist clients in understanding the limitations and benefits of participating in cancer genetics research and the importance of informed consent.*

Interdisciplinary Collaboration

- *Seek assistance from and refer to appropriate cancer genetics experts and peer support resources.*
- *Safeguard privacy and confidentiality of genetic information of clients to the extent possible.*
- *Participate in multidisciplinary teams that deliver comprehensive cancer services and conduct genetics research.*
- *Contribute to the development of research-based and practice-relevant knowledge of the psychosocial, cultural, economic, and ethical implications of cancer genetics on individuals, families, and society.*

Adapted from Weiss et al. (2003).

Understanding Family Histories

Fluency with family history information is critical to making informed choices about genetic testing and cancer risk management. Family histories with familial cancer inform perceptions of cancer risk and vulnerability, health behaviors, and expectations about diagnostic and treatment outcomes (Kenen, Ardern-Jones, & Eeles, 2003; Werner-Lin, 2007). For providers, family histories are critical to identifying groups that might benefit from genetic services, shaping their understanding of a family's anticipated disease course and, as a result, offering recommendations for prevention and early detection.

Pedigree

A pedigree is a clinical tool used by the genetic service provider to map patterns of disease expression over multiple generations in a family (Figure 32.1). A pedigree uses a set of common symbols to collect and annotate information about a family's geographic origins, births and deaths, medical diagnoses, birth defects, and developmental delays (Bennett, 1999). Oncology social workers may interact with clients who are struggling to interpret pedigree information to make sound medical decisions about cancer care.

Genogram

Genograms start with the same basic structure of the pedigree yet extend its utility to capture multigenerational family patterns of coping, caregiving, and loss. Social workers who use genograms in their work recognize that although one family member may be diagnosed with cancer (referred to clinically as *affected*), everyone in the family's intimate social system is impacted by the emotional and pragmatic demands of a cancer diagnosis. Translating a pedigree into a genogram (shown in Figure 32.2 with the Steuben family) shows the family dynamics and the impact of illness on activities of daily life to provide a holistic picture of the illness experience. To capture this, a medically oriented genogram incorporates developmental, familial, community,

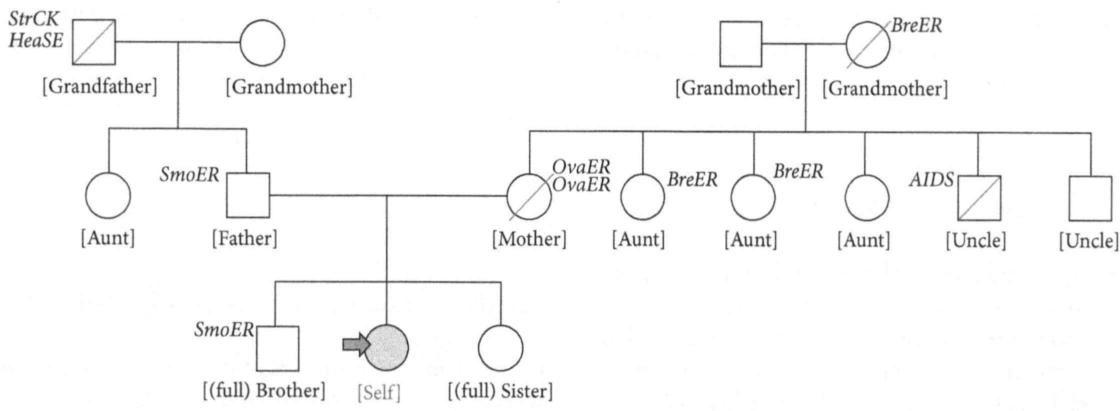

Figure 32.1. Pedigree of Steuben Family (With Hereditary Breast and Ovarian Cancer)

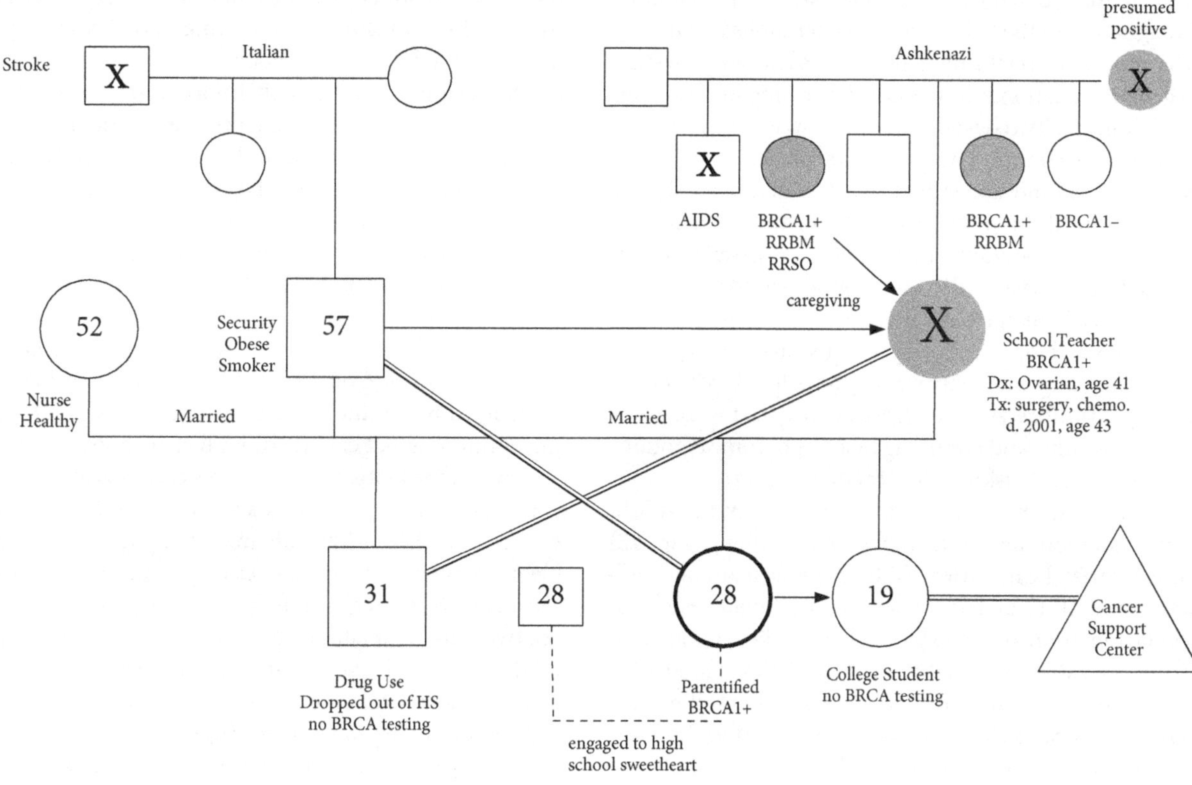

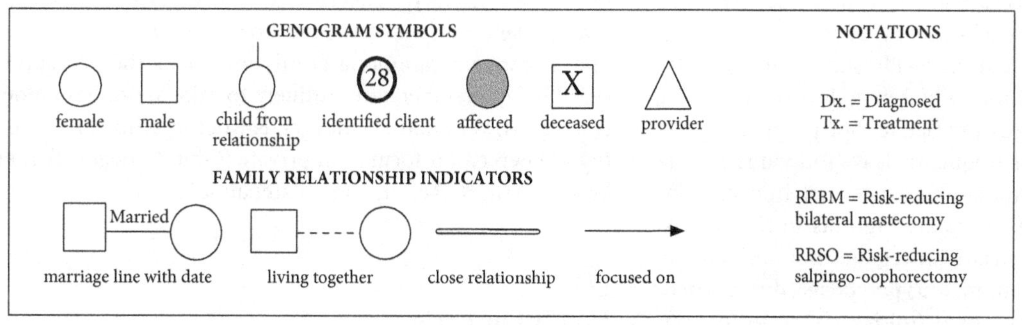

Figure 32.2. Genogram of Steuben Family (With Hereditary Breast and Ovarian Cancer)

and social factors (McGoldrick, Gerson, & Shellenberger, 1999) that influence and are affected by cancer expression, treatment, and future risk management.

Reactions to Genetic Testing Results

Professional guidelines are in place to help families and providers make decisions about when to get cancer genetic testing and how to use test results (NSGC, 2012). Beyond that, each hereditary cancer syndrome has a set of evolving management guidelines for screening and risk reduction. Many hereditary cancer syndromes are inherited in a pattern of autosomal dominance, which means each child of a mutation carrier has a 50% chance of inheriting the mutation. Both men and women can carry and inherit the mutation, and diagnoses are likely in multiple generations in a family.

The process of pursuing genetic counseling and testing for a genetic mutation is frequently distressing for individuals and families. Two decades of research demonstrate that this distress is common and does not produce anxiety or depression over and above that which individuals already experience in their daily lives (Broadstock, Michie, & Marteau, 2000). Individuals who carry a genetic mutation may experience elevated distress around periods of screening, particularly as false positives are common and often lead to regular biopsies. Younger individuals who pursue regular screening may experience *surveillance fatigue*, in which regular office visits, distress experienced while waiting for test results, and recurring biopsies become emotionally burdensome (Hoskins, Roy, & Greene, 2012).

Because each child has a 50% chance of inheriting a parent's mutation, not all members of a sibling group will definitely carry the mutation. Sibling groups may come into genetic counseling or testing with beliefs about who will carry the mutation and who will not. These beliefs are often based on visual or personality characteristics shared with affected parents and are not always borne out in test results. Social workers can help family members adjust to their test results; however, those who "escape" the family's mutation by testing mutation negative may feel survivor's guilt as potent as the distress and resentment experienced by those who are mutation positive (Cumming, 2000).

Genetic testing information yields statistical risk estimates about whether an individual may develop a specific kind of cancer and is thus predictive, not prophetic. As a result, genetic test results frequently leave individuals, couples, and families with ambiguous cancer risk information. Ironically, when risk estimates are high (as in the case of hereditary breast and ovarian cancer) but not absolute (as in the case of familial adenomatous polyposis), distress may be higher. In the absence of definitive risk information, individuals may lean on heuristics, or cognitive shortcuts, embedded in their family histories with cancer (Kenen et al., 2003; Werner-Lin, 2007) to interpret cancer risk information, and these interpretations may become central to the ways cancer risk information is shared in family networks (Erblich, Bovbjerg, & Valdimarsdottir, 2000). Thus, distress about how best to interpret cancer risk information is tied intimately to the family's history of cancer, caregiving, and loss.

Family Communication About Inherited Cancer Risk

Family communication about inherited cancer risk serves several purposes. At-risk individuals share genetic risk information with relatives to seek support and advice, to enable others to engage in risk management and prevention, to discharge the burden of knowing the family carries a mutation (Gaff et al., 2007), and to obtain family history information to facilitate counseling and risk management decisions (Hallowell et al., 2002).

Disclosure of cancer risk information within families must be viewed as an ongoing process, particularly as novel therapies become available and as younger family members become eligible for testing. Discussions about genetic risk information may be emotionally charged, particularly when an individual hearing the information may also be at risk of carrying a genetic mutation. In some families, individuals may choose not to learn their genetic testing status and may prefer not to know about or be involved in the genetic testing of loved ones. Communication in these families may be challenged by strained loyalties, fragile trust, and competing opinions about care (Hallowell et al., 2003).

Beyond the matter of *who* shares cancer risk information is the issue of *what* relatives are told about hereditary cancer risk. At-risk individuals may give incorrect or incomplete information to loved ones (Seymour, Addington-Hall, Lucassen, & Foster, 2010), tailored to perceptions of the relatives' need or ability to understand risk information (Hallowell et al., 2003). Individuals are likely to share cancer risk information when they feel a sense of responsibility, or if they anticipate regret at not having shared potentially lifesaving information. Barriers to sharing cancer risk information in families include feelings of guilt, burden, or anxiety; concern that sharing risk information may cause emotional harm or financial strain for a loved one; estrangement among family members; the perception that family members are unlikely to take action (Seymour et al., 2010; Wiseman, Dancyger, & Michie, 2010); and wanting to keep risk information private (Offit, Groeger, Turner, Wadsworth, & Weiser, 2004; Patenaude, 2004).

Family Life Cycle

A family life cycle perspective suggests that human development progresses through normative, sequential stages with anticipated psychosocial challenges and changes (Carter & McGoldrick, 1999). As normative developmental pathways intersect with exposure to genetic information, consumers face distinct challenges.

Hereditary Cancer in Children and Adolescents

Approximately 5% of childhood cancers are believed to originate from inherited gene mutations or combinations of mutations (Downing et al., 2012). Lively ethical debate exists about the medical necessity and ethical challenges of testing children and adolescents for genetic mutations. When a hereditary cancer syndrome is likely to present in childhood, genetic testing before the child is symptomatic or as the child becomes symptomatic may help physicians manage the condition (Field, Shanley, & Kirk, 2007). Many familial cancer syndromes presenting in childhood have implications for siblings, and as a result, reproductive counseling may be indicated to support future childbearing of parents with affected children.

Of major concern is the inability of the minor to fully appreciate and autonomously elect to undergo genetic testing. The professional ethics of both geneticists and genetic counselors do not support testing children for adult-onset genetic disorders, particularly when treatments do not exist for children, as they believe that a child should have the right to decide about testing when he or she reaches adulthood (NSGC, 2012).

Hereditary Cancer Risk in Early Adulthood

Young adulthood, perhaps more than any other period of development, may be the most critical time to consider the impact of genetic testing on coping and quality of life due to the normative developmental tasks associated with identity development, the creation of lifelong partnerships, and the formation of family life (Werner-Lin, Hoskins, Doyle, & Greene, 2012). Health literacy and health behaviors are developing properties of young adults' increasingly autonomous life. Yet higher order brain function associated with frontal lobe development is not complete (Leisman, Machado, Melillo, & Maulem, 2012). This means that young adults are still developing the capacity to understand and responsibly act on the chronic and persistent threat genetic mutation presents. Lingering adolescent impulsivity may push young adults toward genetic testing before they are ready to elect it autonomously, particularly if the family's emotional life is burdened by grief over cancer-related loss (Hoskins & Werner-Lin, 2013).

After completing cancer genetic testing, young women and men face psychosocial challenges in managing their cancer risk while adequately attending to tasks that are developmentally appropriate to early adulthood. Among these challenges, particularly for adult-onset hereditary cancer syndromes, is mapping out a plan for surveillance and risk reduction that attends to young adults' cancer risk, addresses their concerns with respect, and facilitates decision making in an empirical context within which evidence-based practices are still developing. Due perhaps in part to generational differences, young adults may encounter providers who minimize their concerns or do not take their wishes seriously.

Developing Lifelong Partnerships: Family Formation and Hereditary Cancer Risk

Although the phrase "in sickness and in health" has made its way into the common vernacular of Western wedding vows, attending to chronic and life-threatening illness at the start of a relationship is fairly uncommon among individuals of reproductive age. Yet for individuals approaching lifelong partnerships with a known cancer mutation, the need to set expectations about illness may drive partner selection. When young adults are aware they are living with elevated cancer risk, they must make accommodations (Hallowell, Foster, Ardern-Jones, Eeles, & Watson, 2004) for that risk as they plan for family life. They may actively and rapidly seek out a life partner who has demonstrated the capacity to traverse the terrain of the cancer world with compassion, understanding, and openness. Some may be challenged by perceptions of themselves as imperfect or damaged by the genetic mutation, leading them to believe they have less to offer a prospective partner (Werner-Lin, 2007).

When young adults in committed relationships consider cancer risk assessment, an established partnership may allow them to pursue gene testing and cancer risk reduction in the context of an emotional and sexual relationship, replete with plans for family and career development. In this case, discussion about how best to integrate cancer risk and risk management into family life may require renegotiation of treasured goals. Anticipating a cancer diagnosis jointly may support partner bonding (Hoskins, Roy, Peters, Loud, & Greene, 2008) if couples frame cancer risk as a joint health issue that both must work together to address (Rolland & Werner-Lin, 2006).

Disclosure to Partners

Young adults may need support in deciding when and how best to share their mutation status and lifetime risk information with prospective partners. Early in the development of romantic attachments, individuals commonly share the details of their lives to build intimacy and enhance connection. At-risk individuals may anxiously anticipate sharing their mutation status with romantic partners (Hoskins et al., 2008) out of fear that such a conversation may signal the end of a fledgling relationship. Concern that a mutation may complicate a relationship or "scare away" a new partner may push young adults to postpone disclosure until the couple has developed a sense of intimacy within which cancer risk may be discussed evenly and openly.

Reproductive Health and Fertility

Genetic information about inherited cancer risk frequently becomes salient for individuals and couples considering pregnancy or anticipating the birth of a child (Ehrich & Williams, 2010). Beyond the risk of a child inheriting a genetic mutation linked to elevated cancer risk, mutation-positive parents may be concerned that they will develop cancer either during a pregnancy or early in their child's lifetime (Biank & Werner-Lin, 2011).

Pearls

- Oncology social workers have the ability to carve out a distinct and indispensable niche for themselves in the practice of cancer genetics by applying their unique practice knowledge to the psychosocial implications of hereditary cancer syndromes for individuals, families, and communities.
- Additional knowledge and skills in genetic risk assessment and counseling are required for oncology social workers who want to participate in specialized genetic services.
- Social workers are ideally situated to help individuals, families, and communities distinguish important decisions from urgent decisions.

Pitfalls

- The ethical, legal, and social implications of translating genomic technologies into clinical practice remain underexplored and unregulated, creating disparities in the ways technologies are discussed with, and accessed by, patients.
- Social workers may be called upon to support families whose communication is complicated by grief or spiritual concerns and families whose aims are at odds with the capacity of genetic technology to answer painful questions. Social workers, like other professionals working in genomics, must maintain fluency in what new tools can and cannot do.

REFERENCES

Bennett, R. (1999). *The practical guide to the genetic family history.* Indianapolis, IN: Wiley.

Biank, N. M., & Werner-Lin, A. (2011). Growing up with grief: Revisiting the death of a parent over the life course. *OMEGA: Journal of Death and Dying, 63*(3), 271–290.

Broadstock, M., Michie, S., & Marteau, T. (2000). Psychological consequences of predictive genetic testing: A systematic review. *European Journal of Human Genetics, 8*(10), 731–738.

Carter, E. A., & McGoldrick, M. (1999). Overview: The expanded family life cycle: Individual, family, and social perspectives. In E. A. Carter & M. McGoldrick (Eds.), *The expanded family life cycle: Individual, family, and social perspectives* (3rd ed., pp. 1–26). Boston, MA: Allyn & Bacon.

Cumming, S. (2000). The genetic testing process: How much counseling is needed? *Journal of Clinical Oncology, 18*(Suppl.), 60s–64s.

Downing, J. R., Wilson, R. K., Zhang, J., Mardis, E. R., Pui, C. H., Ding, L., . . . Evans, W. E. (2012). The pediatric cancer genome project. *Nature: Genetics, 44*(6), 619–622.

Erblich, J., Bovbjerg, D. H., & Valdimarsdottir, H. B. (2000). Looking forward and back: Distress among women at familial risk for breast cancer. *Annals of Behavioral Medicine, 22,* 53–59.

Ehrich, K., & Williams, C. (2010). A "healthy baby": The double imperative of preimplantation genetic diagnosis. *Health, 14*(1), 41–56.

Field, M., Shanley, S., & Kirk, J. (2007). Inherited cancer susceptibility syndromes in paediatric practice. *Journal of Paediatrics and Child Health, 43*(4), 219–229.

Gaff, C. L., Clarke, A. J., Atkinson, P., Sivell, S., Elwyn, G., Iredale, R., . . . Edwards, A. (2007). Process and outcome in communication of genetic information within families: A systematic review. *European Journal of Human Genetics, 15,* 999–1011. doi:10.1038/sj.ejhg.5201883

Hallowell, N., Foster, C., Ardern-Jones, A., Eeles, R., Murday, V., & Watson, M. (2002). Genetic testing for women previously diagnosed with breast/ovarian cancer: Examining the impact of BRCA1 and BRCA2 mutation searching. *Genetic Testing, 6*(2), 79–87.

Hallowell, N., Foster, C., Eeles, R., Ardern-Jones, A., Murday, V., & Watson, M. (2003). Balancing autonomy and responsibility: The ethics of generating and disclosing genetic information. *Journal of Medical Ethics, 29,* 74–79.

Hallowell, N., Foster, C., Ardern-Jones, A., Eeles, R., & Watson, M. (2004). Accommodating risk: Responses to BRCA1/2 genetic testing of women who have had cancer. *Social Science and Medicine, 59*(3), 553–565.

Holtzman, N. A., & Watson, M. S. (1997). *Promoting safe and effective genetic testing in the United States: Final report of the Task Force on Genetic Testing.* Retrieved from http://www.genome.gov/10001733

Hoskins, L. M., Roy, K., & Greene, M. H. (2012). Toward a new understanding of risk perception for young female BRCA1/2 "previvors." *Families, Systems, and Health, 30*(1), 32–46.

Hoskins, L. M., Roy, K., Peters, J. A., Loud, J., & Greene, M. H. (2008). Disclosure of positive BRCA 1/2-mutation status in young couples: The journey from uncertainty to bonding through partner support. *Families, Systems, and Health, 26,* 296–316.

Hoskins, L., & Werner-Lin, A. (2013). A multi-case report of the pathways to and through genetic testing and cancer risk management for BRCA1/2 mutation positive women aged 18–25. *Journal of Genetic Counseling, 22*(1), 27–38.

Kenen, R., Ardern-Jones, A., & Eeles, R. (2003). Family stories and the use of heuristics: Women from suspected hereditary breast and ovarian cancer (HBOC) families. *Sociology of Health and Illness*, *25*, 838–865.

Leisman, G., Machado, C., Melillo, R., & Maulem, R. (2012). Intentionality and "free-will" from a neurodevelopmental perspective. *Frontiers in Integrative Neuroscience*, *6*(36), 3–12.

McGoldrick, M., Gerson, R., & Shellenberger, S. (1999). *Genograms: Assessment and intervention*. New York, NY: Norton.

National Society of Genetic Counselors (NSGC). (2012). Position statement: Genetic testing of minors for adult-onset conditions. Retrieved from http://nsgc.org/p/bl/et/blogid=47&blogaid=28

Offit, K., Groeger, E., Turner, S., Wadsworth, B., & Weiser, M. A. (2004). The "duty to warn" a patient's family members about hereditary disease risk. *Journal of the American Medical Association*, *292*(12), 1469–1473.

Patenaude, A. (2004). *Genetic testing for cancer: Psychological approaches for helping patients and families*. Washington, DC: American Psychological Association Press.

Robson, M., Storm, C., Weitzel, J., Wollins, D. S., & Offit, K. (2010). American Society of Clinical Oncology policy statement update: Genetic and genomic testing for cancer susceptibility. *Journal of Clinical Oncology*, *28*(5), 893–901.

Rolland, J. S., & Werner-Lin, A. (2006). Families and illness. In S. Gehlert & T. Arthur (Eds.), *Handbook of health social work* (pp. 305–334). Indianapolis, IN: Wiley.

Seymour, K. C., Addington-Hall, J., Lucassen, A. M., & Foster, C. (2010). What facilitates or impedes family communication following genetic testing for cancer risk? A systematic review and meta-synthesis of primary qualitative research. *Journal of Genetic Counseling*, *19*, 330–342.

Weiss, J., Black, P. N., Weissman, N., Oktay, J., Rodriguez, G., Johnson, A. M., & Whittemore, V. H. (2003). *NASW standards for integrating genetics into social work practice*. Washington, DC: NASW Press.

Weltzel, J., Blazer, K., MacDonald, D., Culver, J., & Offit, K. (2011). Genetics, genomics, and cancer risk assessment. *CA: A Cancer Journal for Clinicians*, *61*(5), 327–359.

Werner-Lin, A. (2007). Danger zones: Risk perceptions of young women from families with hereditary breast and ovarian cancer. *Family Process*, *46*, 335–349.

Werner-Lin, A., Hoskins, L. M., Doyle, M. H., & Greene, M. H. (2012). "Cancer doesn't have an age": Genetic testing and cancer risk management in BRCA1/2 mutation-positive women aged 18–24. *Health: An Interdisciplinary Journal for the Social Study of Health, Illness, and Medicine*, *16*(6), 636–654.

Werner-Lin, A., & Reed, K. (2011). Social work and genetics. In S. Gehlert & T. Arthur Browne (Eds.), *Handbook of health social work* (2nd ed., pp. 557–589). San Francisco, CA: Wiley & Sons.

Wiseman, M., Dancyger, C., & Michie, S. (2010). Communicating genetic risk information within families: A review. *Familial Cancer*, *9*, 691–703.

33 Pain and Symptom Management

Terry Altilio and Laurel Eskra Tropeano

Key Concepts

- *Pain and symptoms, such as fatigue and shortness of breath, impair the quality of life of cancer patients along the continuum of illness, resulting in distress and suffering that may ripple outward from the patient to those in his or her intimate network.*
- *Research and clinical experience demonstrate that psychosocial and mind–body interventions have positive effects on symptoms and quality of life.*
- *Social workers share an ethical responsibility to develop the skills needed to ensure that patients receive expert, comprehensive symptom management by being leaders in assessment, advocacy, and interventions based in a biopsychosocial-spiritual model.*
- *Pain is unique and immersed in a political, legal, socioeconomic, and ethical quagmire emanating from the public health concerns regarding the abuse of prescription medication.*

In cancer patients and across disease states, pain prevalence is estimated at 53% (van den Beuken-van Everdingen et al., 2007) with 70% to 90% of hospitalized patients suffering severe pain (Saskia et al., 2007). There is also historical evidence of the undermanagement of pain in cancer patients, with a 2008 review by Deandrea, Montanari, Moja, and Apolone suggesting that 43% of cancer patients receive inappropriate care for pain. In addition, cancer is often accompanied by other symptoms such as fatigue, dyspnea, and loss of appetite, though suffering and distress may occur independent of symptoms, be exacerbated by their presence, or evolve purely from the anticipation that symptoms may develop.

Because it has been well studied, pain serves as a model for understanding the comprehensive and multidimensional perspectives that infuse the assessment and interventions of other symptoms. Because pain is universal, the experience of those who live with chronic pain is the focus of considerable research from which we might extrapolate concepts and understandings to enhance the thoughtfulness and skill sets of oncology social workers (Turk, Monarch, & Williams, 2002). Additionally, pain management is complicated by social, political, and ethical considerations. Opioids are often mainstay medications, and their status as controlled substances attracts the attention of regulatory agencies who seek to minimize their abuse. These are some of the contextual factors that influence clinicians and institutions who treat pain and symptoms safely and effectively to ameliorate suffering while struggling to honor the ethical principles of beneficence toward, respect for, and honoring of the dignity of people. This chapter explores the environmental framework in which symptoms are managed to reveal the many opportunities social workers have to influence the quality of symptom management for patients from diagnosis through survivorship and end of life, and also provides concrete tools and assessments for everyday use in oncology settings.

Laying the Groundwork

In 1977, social worker Alletta Hudgens authored "The Social Worker's Role in a Behavioral Management Approach to Chronic Pain," which was published in *Social Work in Health Care*. Although the article was not specific to cancer pain, Hudgens may have been the first social worker to assert an awareness of social workers' role in providing—and indeed, their responsibility to provide—service to those living with pain. Around the same time, medical literature was advocating an ethical and humane mandate to treat pain in cancer amid controversy related to the use of opioids (controlled substances called "narcotics" in the world of law enforcement). In the late 1960s, Dame Cicely Saunders introduced the concept of "total pain," which continues as a model inviting clinicians to consider the interface of the physical, social, psychological, and spiritual aspects of the experience of illness and end of life (Saunders, 1964). Soon thereafter, research began to document the undertreatment of pain and to discuss factors that were contributing to inadequate pain management (Marks & Sachar, 1973). At St. Christopher's Hospice in England, diamorphine, also known as heroin, was studied to assess its efficacy in the treatment of pain at end of life (Twycross, 1975).

The Nature of Related Evidence

Symptom Prevalence, Etiology, and Illness Context

In 2007, a systematic review of symptom prevalence in patients with advanced cancer included 44 studies (Group 1: 25,074 patients) on overall symptom prevalence and six studies (Group 2: 2,219 patients) that focused on patients during the last 1 to 2 weeks of life (Saskia et al., 2007). The authors identified 37 symptoms assessed in at least five studies. Five symptoms (fatigue, pain, lack of energy, weakness, and appetite loss) occurred in more than 50% of the Group 1 patients. Weight loss occurred significantly more often in Group 2 than in Group 1, and pain, nausea, and urinary symptoms occurred significantly less often in Group 2 than in Group 1. Implicit in this prevalence data is an expectation that symptoms are seldom isolated problems but, rather, situated within a framework of related and reciprocal impacts and influences.

At the same time that the prevalence data continues to accumulate (Table 33.1), oncology clinicians are challenged to understand the changing circumstances in which symptoms present. For many, cancer has become a chronic illness; symptoms are consequent to treatments they chose to extend their lives or enhance quality, often knowing—in the abstract—that potentially lifelong symptoms such as neuropathic pain or dry mouth were a possibility. For others, pain or shortness of breath might have heralded the diagnosis. And at other times, symptoms represent progression of disease. Treatment options include consideration of the goals of care, anticipated outcome, and prognosis. Sometimes clinicians cause pain by such interventions as lumbar punctures or searching for a vein to begin an intravenous medication, doing immediate harm for the sake of a longer term benefit. Subsequently, the

Table 33.1.
Symptom Prevalence

Symptom and Estimate of Prevalence	Contributing Factors	Social Work Interventions: A Sampling
Pain[a]		
Receiving treatment 59% Despite cure 33%	• Multifactorial	• Family caregivers may misestimate rating of pain • Explore any discrepancy in reports of symptoms; intervene accordingly • Assess fears, anxiety, and depression • Advocate for management of procedure-related pain[b] • Identify themes related to suffering and spiritual and cultural components • Teach mind–body and cognitive behavioral techniques, such as relaxation and imagery[c]
Metastatic cancer 64%	• Directly due to tumors	
Treatment related 20%	• Heightened by tension, fear, and anxiety	
Breakthrough pain 65%[d]	• Unpredictable and disruptive to emotional and physical function	
Fatigue[e]		
Overall, of patients receiving treatment 80% Metastatic cancer 75%	• Multifactorial—treatment of other symptoms can improve fatigue • Hard to discern between tiredness, fatigue, and exhaustion • Can persist for months or even years after completion of treatment	• Some research indicates this is the most distressing symptom as it impacts overall quality of life and treatments lack efficacy • Discuss with oncologist if exercise regimen or psychostimulants are indicated • Educate on energy-saving strategies • Ensure accurate understanding of medical etiology of fatigue

(continued)

Table 33.1. (Continued)		
Symptom and Estimate of Prevalence	**Contributing Factors**	**Social Work Interventions: A Sampling**
Nausea[f] Treatment related 90% With proper intervention, only 30% will become emetic Anticipatory nausea and/or vomiting 18%–57%	After: • Disease: bowel obstruction, brain metastases, electrolyte imbalances • Chemotherapy or radiation therapy • If not adequately addressed, can disrupt treatment cycles[g]	• Provide strategies to prevent anticipatory nausea • Goal is prevention of nausea and vomiting • Lifestyle changes can improve (i.e., eating small meals) • Advocate for appropriate antiemetic pretreatment • Offer cognitive behavioral interventions
Dyspnea[h] General cancer population 49% Lung cancer 62%	• Most typically noted in lung cancer, but also with concomitant COPD and asthma • Related to history of smoking or inhalation of irritants as well • Side effect of fluid buildup when liver or cardiac function is failing	• Advocate for appropriate medication management • Address relationship between anxiety and dyspnea • Educate on cognitive behavioral and environmental strategies accordingly • This can result in social isolation as patients limit activities and events
Constipation[i] Overall 50% Occurs in majority of patients treated with opioids	After: • Opioid use for pain • Bowel obstruction due to disease	• This should be anticipated with use of opioids and treated prophylactically • If opioid related: advocate for better bowel regimen. • This requires close monitoring • Assess impact on mood, sense of self, and loss of privacy
Anorexia-cachexia Malnutrition present in up to 80%	• Anorexia: loss of desire to eat • Cachexia: progressive wasting of muscle mass[j] After: • Treatment • Disease-related bowel obstruction • Malabsorption due to disease • Tumors affect metabolism by interfering with immune system	• This is a common and devastating symptom to patients and families • Assess conflict and tension related to "eating" and "starvation," with attention to cultural and family factors[k] • Ensure that best medical information regarding nutrition and hydration and safe options for eating are provided[l] • Explore impact on body image, intimacy, and socialization • Assist patient and family to integrate symbolic significance of symptom when indicative of end-stage cancer

[a] van den Beuken-van Everdingen et al. (2007).
[b] NCCN (2014).
[c] Deng and Cassileth (2005).
[d] Caraceni et al. (2004).
[e] NCCN (2014).
[f] NCCN (2014).
[g] Brearley, Clements, and Molassiotis (2008).
[h] Dudgeon, Kristjanson, Sloan, Lertzman, and Clement (2001).
[i] NCCN (2014).
[j] Laviano, Meguid, Inui, Muscaritoli, and Rossi-Fanelli (2005).
[k] McClement (2005).
[l] Brown (2002).

meaning that patients attribute to symptoms in these varying contexts may either exacerbate or diminish the level of concurrent distress and may influence relationships with clinicians. Hence, attributed meaning becomes an essential facet of psychosocial-spiritual assessment and interventions.

Most symptoms may be attributed either to disease itself or to treatment for the disease. Research indicates that the three most distressing symptoms to patients and families are pain, fatigue, and anorexia-cachexia. Often interrelated, these symptoms can greatly exacerbate one another when they present in clusters. For example, a lack of appetite due to treatment-related nausea will likely result in fatigue and, over time, anorexia-cachexia. In addition to the physical manifestations of symptoms, there are often emotional, social, and spiritual effects requiring ongoing social work assessment and interventions that focus on such aspects as attributed meaning, impact on relationships, and quality of life (McClement, 2005). Beyond the immediate clinical relationship, encouraging patients and families to keep a log or journal of symptoms, patterns, and timing—as well as related emotions and thoughts—can inform ongoing clinical work while empowering patients and family and providing a transitional connection to the team (Cagle & Altilio, 2011).

Data Related to Assessment and Interventions

Just as there is historical data related to the prevalence of cancer pain and other symptoms, so too is there data related to the treatment skills of oncology clinicians. As early as 1990, a survey of 1,800 U.S. oncologists revealed that only 51% believed that pain management in their practices was good or very good, and a large majority expressed dissatisfaction with their training (Von Roenn, Cleeland, Gonin, Hatfield, & Pandya, 1993). Despite proliferation of standards and guidelines, as well as access to online learning, a 2011 survey of U.S. oncologists published in the *Journal of Clinical Oncology* revealed that, while they rated their pain management skills as "fairly good," less than 50% selected appropriate interventions when presented with clinical scenarios (Breuer, Fleischman, Cruciani, & Portenoy, 2011).

This data, coupled with well-established evidence of the undertreatment of pain based in gender, age, ethnicity, and socioeconomic status, creates an irrefutable mandate for oncology social workers to act as informed clinicians, advocates, and leaders in ensuring state-of-the-art management of pain and other symptoms. Integrating evidence, guidelines, and standards from the oncology community is a strategy and an avenue to encourage collective and collaborative responsibility and expertise across disciplines on the oncology team. A comprehensive assessment guides clinicians as they triage patient and family needs, be they psychological, spiritual, or of a more physical nature. To that end, Table 33.1 illustrates the prevalence of symptoms, contributing factors, and a beginning direction for social work advocacy, assessments, and interventions.

Social Work Principles and Practices

As astonishing as it may seem, professional and patient voices have had to plead with clinicians for over four decades to honor their commitment to attend to suffering, no matter the etiology. A small cadre of social work authors and leaders has encouraged the potential for professional contribution and advocacy, which so naturally flows from the profession's historical commitment to service, vulnerable populations, and social justice.

The social work model of care honors the central importance of relationship and is based in an assessment of the "person in environment," which might include social, economic, emotional, cultural, and spiritual aspects of one's experience. Social work training in and attunement to family and interpersonal dynamics uniquely position the profession to recognize the interplay of these factors in medical care. One example of this is assessment of a family's history with cancer and the outcomes of previous experiences. Within this framework, families may hold a belief and expectation that all cancers are fatal, or the opposite—that by being a "fighter," a patient can discover the internal strength to overcome cancer. Another example involves the comprehensive management of pain and other symptoms, which are often interwoven with dynamics inherent in one's culture of origin. The cultural and spiritual context may lead an individual, whether patient or clinician, to attribute meaning to pain that extends beyond the physical to such values as suffering, redemption, sacrifice, or punishment. A social worker's attention to these themes provides necessary insight to treatment teams and leads to exploration, mediation, and interventions that extend much beyond pharmacology. The direction provided by this person-in-environment construct is invaluable, because the care of symptomatic persons has moved beyond the medical model to a multidimensional focus within the political, regulatory, and legislative arenas. By familiarizing themselves with the variety of symptom assessment tools available and their appropriate uses (Table 33.2), social workers position themselves to become indispensible members of the treatment team.

Beyond the perspective of person in environment, there are several other essential aspects of a social work worldview that further infuse the engagement and intervention process when working with patients and their symptoms. Efforts to assess and manage symptoms begin with the patient's report. This description is enhanced and guided by the expertise of the clinician who seeks to discover etiology and characterize multiple dimensions of the patient's experience, such as components of suffering, depression and anxiety, impact on quality of life, and distress related to psychosocial and/or spiritual concerns. Compassionate and competent assessment begins with an acceptance of patients' reports of their symptom and broadens beyond medical management to an understanding of its meaning and impact in their lives and the lives of their families.

Table 33.2.
Symptom Assessment Tools

Assessment	Developed By and How to Access	What It Includes
Psychosocial Pain Assessment Form	• Otis-Green, City of Hope • http://prc.coh.org/pdf/PS%20Pain%20Assess10-09.pdf • English and Spanish	• Measures distress related to various factors across five domains: economics, social support, activities of daily living, emotional problems, and coping behaviors • Elicits ratings from patient and caregiver/family member, as well as subjective impressions of interviewer
Pain Assessment in Advanced Dementia (PAINAD)	• Warden, Hurley, and Volicer (2003) • http://www.healthcare.uiowa.edu/igec/tools/pain/PAINAD.pdf	• Following visual assessment, clinician assesses for various behaviors that indicate if an adult with cognitive impairment is experiencing pain
Memorial Symptom Assessment Scale (MSAS)	• Memorial Sloan-Kettering Cancer Center • http://www.npcrc.org/files/news/memorial_symptom_assessment_scale.pdf • English and Chinese	• Measures frequency, severity, and level of distress of 24 symptoms over the past week • Utilizes everyday language • Available in short and condensed form • Distress ratings assist in triaging interventions
Brief Pain Inventory (BPI)	• MD Anderson Cancer Center • http://www.mdanderson.org/education-and-research/departments-programs-and-labs/departments-and-divisions/symptom-research/symptom-assessment-tools/bpilong.pdf • Translated into 50 languages	• Long and short versions available • 0–10 rating over past week, as well as comparison to pain scores over time • Elicits understanding of extent to which pain interferes with everyday living

Evelyn is a 43-year-old mother of two children, ages 5 and 8 years. Diagnosed with Stage 4 breast cancer, she is admitted for exacerbation of pain, which has historically been managed by her oncologist, who now requests specialist consultation from the palliative care team. She is anxious and tearful, rolled up in a fetal position in her bed. The initial assessment focuses on pain quality and frequency, temporal characteristics, relieving and exacerbating aspects, hypothesized etiology, and review of the prior medications, doses, and side effects. Evelyn offers that her suffering has created fear and anxiety in her children and she believes that the exacerbation of pain indicates that she is coming to the end of her life. She is assured that as her pain is better managed, her oncologist will help her understand its prognostic significance and her social worker will work with her to address her concerns as a parent. Evelyn quickly leads the palliative care clinicians to a nascent understanding of the meaning and impact of her pain, her worries, and the needs of her children. Medications will touch one aspect of her suffering, which is an essential beginning. As Johnson (2001, p. 11) writes, "Severe or chronic pain blocks or seriously impedes the realizations of all other human values. Relief of unrelenting pain is required to allow the human being to reflect, enjoy human relationships, and even to think and function on a most basic level." Along with medications to relieve her pain, the clinical team may introduce relaxation techniques to mitigate anxiety and physiological tension. Pain relief is essential to establish the credibility of the team and to begin to restore Evelyn's ability to negotiate her world.

The assessment process requires that clinicians listen for discrepancies or disconnects exemplified in symptom descriptions, whether from staff, family, or friends. Although it is important to enlist the observations, insight, and history of family and friends, the work of experts includes assessing symptoms directly from the patient's behavior or report to create a plan of care that responds to the patient's unique and identified needs. For example, a patient may protect family by minimizing the symptom or the related distress. A family may underrate a symptom for fear that it symbolizes progression of disease or may—from a place of beneficence—interpret a facial grimace as pain rather than agitation, leading them to advocate for increased pain medication. In the setting of a history of addictive disease or fears related to creating an opioid addiction (or threatening a stable recovery), minimizing the pain and suffering of the patient may be proxy behavior for undisclosed worries.

In such scenarios, the interventions of specialist clinicians include a multidimensional response that includes psychoeducation and interdisciplinary attention to the suffering of the family rather than an automatic adjustment in medications. In these instances, the social worker's role may include reframing the perception of a symptom to validate that family perspectives have been respected as one aspect of the data needed to choose appropriate interventions.

Another principle that infuses social work practice relates to discovering a patient's and family members' strengths and competencies, which is often key to assisting people who feel disempowered and devastated by pain and other symptoms. Concurrent with expert medical and nursing interventions, patients and families can be helped over time to recover their voice, restore a sense of self and direction, and re-create avenues of hopefulness and meaning in their lives. Interventions that enhance this process may range from the practical, such as providing modes of communication for those who are impacted by symptoms such as shortness of breath or dysphasia, or problem solving or therapeutic techniques, such as relaxation or imagery designed to distract or enhance feelings of self-efficacy, coherence, or control.

Kim is a 27-year-old woman, newly diagnosed with acute myeloid leukemia. Upon each cycle of chemotherapy, Kim is re-admitted to the oncology unit. Kim feels that her pain—ever present but prominent particularly during lumbar punctures and other procedures—is poorly managed and misunderstood, because it was initially attributed to a diagnosis of fibromyalgia. She and her family struggle to put a life-threatening illness into the context of their culture, developmental stage, and family system and silently settle on a dynamic wherein her mother works to create a soothing environment and protect Kim, whose work is to focus on "healing." With each hospital admission, Kim's very-involved family transforms her hospital room in an attempt to draw a boundary between the sterility of the hospital and the intimacy of home. The ritual of hanging her bright-pink curtains, spreading out lush pillows, and laying out new pajamas upon each admission results in the unintended consequence of blurring the distinction between home and medical spaces, because Kim is in neither space exclusively. The combined factors of developmental stage, staff's countertransference, the complexity of her symptom presentation, frequent hospitalizations, and the integral and intimate participation of family create a complex dynamic further exacerbated by a large cadre of providers. Kim's care further fragments and she consequently feels as if she has lost control and her sense of self. Social work interventions focus on acknowledging these complex dynamics and educating Kim on ways to rebalance her internal and external locus of control and assert her needs. In collaboration with the oncology team, a family meeting is organized with the explicit purpose of reinforcing Kim as the center of care and eliciting her voice while recognizing the suffering of family members and balancing their need to help with Kim's need for autonomy. Integrative therapies are introduced and, although most of them frustrate Kim, she is receptive to music therapy. This process of accepting and refusing treatments inadvertently serves to help her recover authority over her body, mind, and emotions. The oncology social worker introduces mind–body techniques to minimize anxiety and pain due to procedures and to enhance Kim's internal locus of control. These techniques, combined with the support of a spiritual care clinician, allow Kim to more readily transcend the hospital environment. Kim continues to allow her family to speak on her behalf but begins to restore a sense of self-efficacy as she makes treatment-related decisions. Ongoing work includes advocating for appropriate pain management and encouraging the prescribing clinicians to deconstruct symptoms rather than delegitimize her experience by simply attributing a psychological etiology. Additionally, facilitating communication across settings serves to unify clinicians around the cause of empowerment and self-efficacy.

Last, at the core of social work values lies the commitment to professional competence. In the setting of symptom management, specialized oncology social workers acquire basic knowledge related to common symptoms and disease trajectories, seek ongoing educational opportunities, and keep abreast of advances in research (Gorin et al., 2012). They learn to distinguish addiction, physical dependence, and tolerance so they can assist patients and families with their fears and participate with their teams to assess and treat with confidence and safety, balancing ethical principles of harm and benefit. See the additional resources toward the end of the chapter for a sampling of links to best practices literature and electronic resources that contribute to a foundation for competence. This ongoing passion for development and expansion of skills is critical to direct work with patients and families and also ensures that interdisciplinary colleagues have an understanding of the scope of social work practice and capabilities.

Pearls

- Psychoeducation, crisis intervention, supportive counseling, and cognitive behavioral interventions are essential symptom management skills.
- Exploring the tapestry of patients' experiences with enhanced symptom management expertise leads to enriched understanding and collaboration between individuals and their providers who seek to respond to suffering.

Pitfalls

- Beware the illusion of working in a silo; implicit in the mandate to act as informed clinicians, advocates, and leaders is the responsibility to recognize opportunities for collaboration, rather than competition, across and within disciplines.
- Those who lose sight of objectivity and expertise in assessment of symptoms run the risk of colluding with either patients, families, or providers exclusively.

Oncology social workers are uniquely trained and positioned to identify and address the myriad effects that cancer—whether in the acute setting or as a chronic disease—has on an individual and his or her extended intimate network. Undoubtedly, social workers have a personal, ethical, and professional responsibility to contribute to the assessment of the whole person that includes the rippling impact of symptoms such as pain, dyspnea, constipation, and fatigue. Woven—often invisibly—into the responses of patients are unique attributes, meanings, and emotions informed by history, culture, and community.

Although a common challenge in the practice of social workers is a perceived lack of recognition within the traditional hierarchical medical system, developing skills in this aspect of care affirms the shared mandate across disciplines to respond to the suffering of patients and their families. Rather than waiting for an invitation, inherent in the profession's ethics and values are the mandates to assert leadership, curiosity, and compassion—in combination with evidence-informed knowledge. Social workers can learn from interdisciplinary colleagues and can collaborate, model, or lead in the shared process of enhancing the quality of symptom management. The vast resources afforded electronically—through medical journals, webinars, and multiple online databases—remove former barriers to learning as there is now opportunity for ongoing education and collaboration worldwide. By advancing one's knowledge base, joining with interdisciplinary colleagues in research, and ultimately contributing to the literature, social workers will expand the small cadre of leaders and advocates representing the profession in this essential aspect of care.

Learning Exercises

1. Explore the work of persons who choose art as a method of expressing their pain experience.Art and the Pain Experience: http://www.painexhibit.com/art_painexperience
2. Review the assessment instruments listed in Table 33.2. Choose one and, in consultation with your team, become familiar with its use.
3. Consider the composition of the teams in your setting. Imagine the response of various team members as you expand your expertise and participation in the care of symptomatic patients. Who will be your advocates, and who will obstruct? Prepare a response, immediate and over time, that validates the shared responsibility both for clinical intervention and for ongoing learning.
4. Peruse the Internet for lawsuits related to pain management and consider how you might use information about litigation in the field of pain to enhance the practice expertise of you and your prescribing colleagues.

ADDITIONAL RESOURCES

American Pain Society: http://www.americanpainsociety.org
City of Hope Pain & Palliative Care Resource Center: http://prc.coh.org/pain_assessment.asp
Institute of Medicine Reports: http://www.iom.edu
National Comprehensive Cancer Network Clinical Practice Guidelines in Oncology: http://www.nccn.org

REFERENCES

Brearley, S., Clements, C., & Molassiotis, A. (2008). A review of patient self-report tools for chemotherapy-induced nausea and vomiting. *Support Care Cancer, 16*(11), 1213–1229.

Breuer, B., Fleishman, S. B., Cruciani, R., & Portenoy, R. K. (2011). Medical oncologists' attitudes and practice in cancer pain management: A national survey. *Journal of Clinical Oncology, 29*, 4769–4775.

Brown, J. (2002). A systematic review of the evidence on symptom management of cancer-related anorexia and cachexia. *Oncology Nursing Forum, 29*(3), 517–532.

Cagle, J., & Altilio, T. (2011). The social work role in pain and symptom management. In T. Altilio & S. Otis-Green (Eds.), *Oxford textbook of palliative social work* (pp. 271–287). New York, NY: Oxford University Press.

Caraceni, A., Martini, C., Zecca, E., Portenoy, R. K., Ashby, M. A., Hawson, G., . . . Lutz, L. (2004). Breakthrough pain characteristics and syndromes in patients with cancer pain: An international survey. *Journal of Palliative Medicine, 18*(3), 177–183.

Deandrea, S., Montanari, M., Moja, L., & Apolone, G. (2008). Prevalence of undertreatment in cancer pain. A review of published literature. *Annals of Oncology, 19*(12), 1985–1991.

Deng, G., & Cassileth, B. (2005). Integrative oncology: Complementary therapies for pain, anxiety and mood disturbance. *A Cancer Journal for Clinicians, 55*(2), 109–116.

Dudgeon, D., Kristjanson, L., Sloan, J., Lertzman, M., & Clement, K. (2001). Dyspnea in cancer patients: Prevalence and associated factors. *Journal of Pain and Symptom Management, 21*(2), 95–102.

Gorin, S. S., Krebs, P., Badr, H., Janke, E. A., Jim, H. S. L., Spring, B., . . . Jacobsen, P. B. (2012). Meta-analysis of psychosocial interventions to reduce pain in patients with cancer. *Journal of Clinical Oncology, 30*(5), 539–547.

Hudgens, A. (1977). The social worker's role in a behavioral management approach to chronic pain. *Social Work in Health Care*, *3*, 149–157.

Johnson, S. H. (2001). Relieving unnecessary treatable pain for the sake of human dignity. *Journal of Law, Medicine, and Ethics*, *29*, 11–12.

Laviano, A., Meguid, M., Inui, A., Muscaritoli, M., & Rossi-Fanelli, F. (2005). Therapy insight: Cancer anorexia-cachexia syndrome—when all you can eat is yourself. *Nature Clinical Practice Oncology*, *2*(3), 158–165.

Marks, R. M., & Sachar, E. J. (1973). Undertreatment of medical inpatients with narcotic analgesics. *Annals of Internal Medicine*, *78*(2), 173–181.

McClement, S. (2005). Cancer anorexia-cachexia syndrome: Psychological effect on the patient and family. *Journal of Wound, Ostomy, and Continence Nursing*, *32*(4), 264–268.

National Comprehensive Cancer Network (NCCN). (2014). NCCN Clinical Practice Guidelines in Oncology: Supportive care guidelines. Retrieved from http://www.nccn.org/professionals/physician_gls/f_guidelines.asp

Saskia, C. C. M., Teunissen, S. C., Wesker, W., Kruitwagen, C., de Haes, H. C. J. M., Voest, E. E., & deGraff, A. (2007). Symptom prevalence in patients with incurable cancer: A systematic review. *Journal of Pain and Symptom Management*, *34*(1), 94–104.

Saunders, C. (1964). The symptomatic treatment of incurable malignant disease. *Prescribers Journal*, *4*, 68–73.

Turk, D. C., Monarch, E. S., & Williams, A. D. (2002). Cancer patients in pain: Considerations for assessing the whole person. *Hematology/Oncology Clinics in North America*, *16*, 511–525.

Twycross, R. G. (1975). The use of narcotic analgesics in terminal illness. *Journal of Medical Ethics*, *1*, 10–17.

van den Beuken-van Everdingen, M. H. J., de Rijke, J. M., Kessels, A. G., Schouten, H. C., van Kleef, M., & Patijn, J. (2007). Prevalence of pain in patients with cancer: A systematic review of the past 40 years. *Annals of Oncology*, *18*, 1437–1449.

Von Roenn, J. H., Cleeland, C. S., Gonin, R., Hatfield, A. K., & Pandya, K. J. (1993). Physician attitudes and practice in cancer pain management: A survey from the Eastern Cooperative Oncology Group. *Annals of Internal Medicine*, *119*, 121–126.

Warden, V., Hurley, A. C., & Volicer, L. (2003). Development and psychometric evaluation of the Pain Assessment in Advanced Dementia (PAINAD) scale. *Journal of the American Medical Directors Association*, *4*(1), 9–15.

34 Sexuality and Cancer

Sage Bolte and Christopher Anrig

Key Concepts

- *This chapter identifies how cancer and its treatments directly and indirectly affect the human sexual response cycle.*
- *Through this chapter, social workers will gain an understanding of the sexual self-conceptual model.*
- *Social workers should increase their knowledge about how changes in the sexual self and intimate relationships can affect quality of life.*
- *This chapter explains how to engage in assessing and addressing sexual health concerns utilizing an assessment model.*

Growth in cancer survivorship has shifted the focus of patient care to include a wide range of quality-of-life concerns, among which sexual health is an issue across the disease trajectory and throughout the life span (Bolte, 2010; Katz, 2005; Tan, Waldman, & Bostick, 2002). This chapter examines complex issues related to how cancer and its treatment may affect sexual health. A framework is given for assessing sexual health concerns, and brief interventions and psychoeducation for enhanced sexual health and intimacy are provided. With over 11 million people now identified as cancer survivors, estimates indicate that anywhere from 10% to 100% of these individuals will experience some form of sexual dysfunction (Ofman & Auchincloss, 1992; Roth, Carter, & Nelson, 2010). Oncology social workers are challenged to develop their own expertise on sexual issues and to address these concerns for patients throughout the disease continuum, regardless of cancer site, age, sexual orientation, or relationship status.

Sexuality and Cancer

Cancer and its treatment can impact sexuality and sexual function in any of the commonly used five phases of the human sexual response cycle (HSRC) and throughout the three domains of the sexual self. For the purpose of this chapter, desire, arousal, stimulation, orgasm, and resolution represent the five interactive, nonlinear phases of the human sexual response cycle (Basson, 2005). The HSRC is used to describe the emotional and physiological processes the body goes through as a person becomes sexually aroused and participates in sexually stimulating activities—a process unique to each individual. Sexual dysfunction, as described by the *Diagnostic and Statistical Manual of Mental Disorders*, fifth edition (DSM-5; American Psychiatric Association, 2013), is a disorder that may affect one or more phases of the HSRC and negatively influence sexual functioning, resulting in psychological or relational distress. However, not all changes in sexual function will lead to distress or stress within a relationship (Bancroft, Loftus, & Long, 2003).

As reported by cancer survivors, the most common sexual dysfunctions described as negatively influencing quality

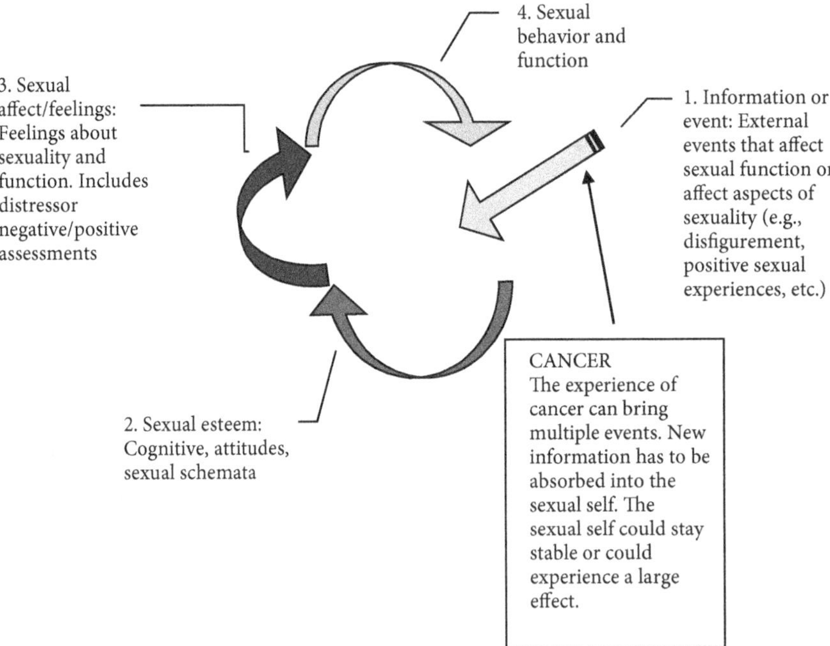
4. Sexual behavior and function
3. Sexual affect/feelings: Feelings about sexuality and function. Includes distressor negative/positive assessments
1. Information or event: External events that affect sexual function or affect aspects of sexuality (e.g., disfigurement, positive sexual experiences, etc.)
CANCER
The experience of cancer can bring multiple events. New information has to be absorbed into the sexual self. The sexual self could stay stable or could experience a large effect.
2. Sexual esteem: Cognitive, attitudes, sexual schemata

Figure 34.1. The Sexual Self When Affected by Cancer

of life are sexual pain disorders, such as vaginal stenosis and dyspareunia; erectile dysfunction; and changes in sexual desire (Bolte, 2010; Schover, 1999).

The sexual self-concept includes sexual esteem, sexual affect, and sexual function as influenced by the actual disease and treatment process, and the subjective meaning of that experience for patients (Figure 34.1; Bolte, 2010). Objectively, people with cancer will experience hair loss, fatigue, neuropathy, organ loss or scarring, loss of libido, and/or erectile dysfunction, which directly impact all domains of the sexual self. Subjectively, the meaning for the individual who experiences sexual side effects can vary across the domains. The understanding or meaning made of cancer/treatment effects on sexual function, sexual history, relationship status, spiritual beliefs, and support systems in the social environment can have a positive or negative effect on the sexual self. The HSRC and the sexual self will be used in this chapter to describe how sexual problems are experienced in cancer survivors with a range of diagnoses and varied treatment modalities. A positive sexual self is contingent upon the ability of patients (and their partner[s] if relevant) to communicate their changing sexual needs and preferences across multiple domains (Flemming & Kleinbart, 2001).

Disease and Treatment Effects

The most common complaint by women and men treated for cancer is a decrease in sexual desire or libido (Frumovitz et al., 2005). Sexual desire is shaped by the interplay of biopsychosocial-spiritual domains and is threatened on all fronts by a cancer diagnosis, its treatment, and its prognostic implications. The impact of the disease and treatment on desire is both direct and indirect. Cancers and treatments that disrupt the endocrine production of the hormones responsible for sexual desire, testosterone, and androgen, for example, have a direct biologic effect resulting in low desire. Further, cancers and treatments that impact neural and vascular systems may also result in low desire by virtue of the interplay between physiological systems. For example, desire can diminish due to increases in the amount of time and type of stimulation required for adequate penile or clitoral arousal. Sexual discomfort and pain can also result in sexually avoidant behavior. Keeping in mind that low desire is also mediated by prior sexual experience, relational factors, and sexual esteem and affect, the effects of a cancer diagnosis/treatment can be profound even when hair loss is the only precipitating cause for sexual changes. When treatment is finished, the physical, mental, emotional, and spiritual effects may linger and continue to affect one's sexual self.

Cancers of the sexual organs have a direct impact on sexual function. Breast and cervical cancer in women and prostate and testicular cancer in men have all received attention in the literature due to their clear and often direct effect on sexual physiology, function, and intimacy. Perhaps less obvious are the sexual dysfunctions that may result secondary to the diagnosis and treatment impacts of other cancers. For example, colorectal, bladder, thoracic, head and neck, melanoma and sarcomas, and neurological and blood cancers can have effects on sexual function throughout the HSRC and across the domains of the sexual self. Although blood cancers are not often associated with sexual dysfunction, they are used here to illustrate how the disease and treatment process can interfere with intimacy and sexual relations with self or partner(s) in all cancer diagnoses.

Blood and marrow stem cell transplant protocols are both physically and emotionally demanding treatment processes that can have sexual side effects. Despite the fact that blood and marrow stem cell transplantation are not commonly associated with sexual side effects, the reality for patients is one in which they experience a hiatus from intimate contact and sexual relations and for which resuming sexual activity can be challenging due to both medical and psychosocial issues. Beyond the emotional and physical isolation that can occur during and after transplant, graft-versus-host disease (GVHD) can contribute to sexual problems. GVHD in the female genital track can cause a loss of depth in the vagina, scarring, and ulcers (National Cancer Institute, n.d.). Gynecological exams, sexual intercourse, or many types of sexual play can be extremely painful to women experiencing GVHD in the vaginal area. Loss of vaginal depth causes painful vaginal intercourse, which may lead to sexual aversion or a decrease in desire (for both patient and partner) due to fear of causing pain. However, loss of vaginal depth may not impact the sexual self if the female has been able to establish other means of sexual intimacy. Long-term skin sensitivity, dryness, and changes in the skin's flexibility may also occur, and persons with GVHD have to take numerous precautions to prevent infection and maintain a healthy immune system. Sexual activities may be limited due to skin tightness and sensitivity, vaginal pain, and fatigue. Even kissing may be challenging and less pleasurable due to affected saliva glands. Studies also indicate that young men may have lower testosterone levels after transplant, affecting libido, erectile function, and mood (Savani, Griffith, Jagasia, & Lee, 2011).

In a study exploring the sexual selves of young adults, one man reported: "I'm talking physical limitations [around sexual health] as basically the main thing that cancer introduced for me. It also introduced, I suppose, some mental limitations. . . . Well, obviously, the physical limitations are, you know, hammering down on my mental state of mind because, okay, I can't perform, you know, because of this, this, and this. And so, I mean, it's bogging me down like emotionally sometimes I just don't—I don't even feel like trying" (Bolte, 2010). Although this young man was 3 years posttreatment, the impact on his sexual self was still evident in his performance anxiety and level of desire. As oncology social workers, we must explore the many different ways in which cancer and its treatment affect desire, whether through the domains of the sexual self or via the direct impact of the disease or treatment modality.

Surgical Treatment

Changes in anatomy secondary to surgery have both subtle and overt sexual effects. Surgery is often the initial treatment modality, certainly in early-stage cancers, and is still the only potentially curative treatment for many cancers. The adjustment to changes in postoperative anatomy is important in the context of sexual self-concept and body image regardless of the surgical site. Long-term problems that may result include lymphedema, menopause, erectile dysfunction (ED), vaginal stenosis, dryness, and foreshortening of the vaginal wall. There is much literature on the impact of mastectomies on sexual function in women. Whether a radical mastectomy, modified radical mastectomy, or breast-conserving therapy, with or without immediate or delayed reconstruction, for many, these surgeries do not cause significant physiological changes but do have an impact on the domains of the sexual self and sexual behavior. For many survivors, the consequences of cancer treatment(s), and the changes the body experiences, have a more profound impact on the sexual self than the cancer diagnosis itself.

As one patient described: "Much of my problem was caused by anxiety and fear of rejection rather than actual physical effects. I imagined that sex would be the big hurdle to get over, and I discovered that it was not. I found that the more difficult hurdle was nudity. I feel it was the loss of my femininity and self-image. When I slept at night and my hands touched my chest, I was startled when I was able to feel my ribs, feeling something hard instead of something soft. I found that I needed to wear my prosthesis when sleeping, not for my husband, but for myself. The grief I felt from losing my sexual pleasure has been more difficult than the cancer" (Tan et al., 2002, p. 311).

Similarly, ostomy surgeries represent a profound anatomical change that has an impact on the sexual self and interferes with sexual function. A cystectomy is a common surgery in the treatment of bladder cancer that involves resection of the bladder and prostate in men and a hysterectomy and oophorectomy in women. Both surgeries result in creation of a continent urinary diversion terminating in an ostomy or opening. Postoperatively, urine drains out through the urostomy into an external bag. The urostomy bag itself is the most visible change and represents an acute challenge to postoperative quality of life. In the example of a male patient after radical cystectomy and urostomy surgery, consider the various factors across the domains of the HSRC and sexual self that might result in sexual problems:

HSRC: The radical prostatectomy results in damage to the nerve bundle responsible for penile stimulation, damage to the accessory blood vessels arising at the prostate responsible for penile blood flow, surgical adhesion of the urethra, and penile foreshortening and/or curvature, which may result in low desire, poor stimulation and arousal, dry ejaculation, and ejaculatory pain.

Sexual self: The urostomy bag may create negative sexual esteem based on the visual presence of the external bag and urine and its interpretation as antisexual.

Table 34.1.
Sensate Focus Exercise Example

Phase 1: Each partner takes a turn touching and being touched. Try many types of touching, varying light stroking and a firmer touch, as in a massage.

- One partner lies face down on the bed, allowing the other partner to touch the entire back, from toes to scalp.
- Turn over (after ~15 minutes) so the front of the body can be touched.
- While being touched, pay attention to your own feelings.
- When you are doing the touching, enjoy the shape and texture of your partner's body.
- The first touching session should avoid genitals and breasts. Your goals are to feel relaxed and to experience sensual pleasure. It is not important to get sexually excited.

Phase 2: If you both feel relaxed during the first touching session, you can add some genital touching the next time.

- Over several sessions, partners can slowly spend more time on genital touching, until each one can reach an orgasm.
- Stroke with a hand or through oral sex, if that is comfortable for both of you. Penetration is not necessary or recommended for several sessions, if at all.

It is difficult to predict all of the possible ways in which post-operative anatomy changes may interface with sexuality and intimacy. However, oncology social workers are in a unique position to help patients and their partners talk about these problems and compensate in ways that will allow them to sustain fulfilling sexual relations and intimacy throughout their survivorship.

Chemotherapy

The secondary effects of systemic therapy, such as nausea, fatigue, hair loss, weight loss (or gain), skin changes, pain, mucositis, and concentration and memory problems, can immediately interfere with intimacy and sexual relations and result in a negative sexual self-concept. Although many of these treatment effects are short term, pain, decreased desire, menopause, vaginal dryness, and sensitivity are common long-term, delayed effects from treatment. The impact of neuropathy on sexual function has not been well studied, but tactile sensation contributes dramatically to sexual arousal and stimulation. Similarly, changes in olfactory and taste sensitivities common for people in chemotherapy may make sexual activities aversive. Premature menopause is a common sexual side effect in young women receiving all modes of treatment. This again represents change across the board in terms of the sexual self and the HSRC. Among those changes, infertility resulting from chemotherapy, although not a sexual dysfunction per se, is a major concern for many people with cancer and can impact intimacy and sexual relations.

The effects of early menopause can be hard to predict; although everyone experiences their menstrual periods differently and changes in hormonal levels and other symptoms may vary, cancer patients with early menopause often experience these changes suddenly and severely. Hot flashes, night sweats, sleep disturbances, and urinary pain and incontinence are common symptoms related to early menopause. Vaginal changes resulting from lower estrogen levels include thinning of the vaginal lining, dryness, and inelasticity. Vaginal itching, discharge, and irritation often result. Some women also report reduced sexual desire during menopause. This may be due to hormonal changes, the cancer or treatment, and painful intercourse. Mood swings, depression, and anxiety are common during menopause as well. Although the loss of fertility and other biopsychosocial changes resulting from menopause are significant, some women will be relieved to no longer have periods or to worry about pregnancy. Vaginal moisturizers may provide relief from menopausal symptoms. Lubricants are often helpful in making penetrative sexual activity more comfortable. Further, hormone replacement therapy (HRT) is common in the treatment of menopause, although it is contraindicated for some cancers.

HSRC: Hormonal changes in a young woman resulting in hot flashes, mood changes, and vaginal dryness can cause low desire, painful intercourse, and changes in sensitivity, which typically have negative consequences on arousal, stimulation, and orgasm.

Sexual self: A woman's negative sense of self, or negative thoughts about oneself, due to weight gain or other body changes caused by menopause can influence sexual desire. And let's not forget the very powerful effect that the loss of fertility can have on some women, who may have an altered sense of femininity related to this loss.

Radiation

Because external beam radiation therapy will damage all tissue within the radiation field, targeting the tumor site for maximum radiation can result in more generalized effects. For example, gastrointestinal dysfunction is a common side effect of radiation of the prostate, as is ED secondary to destruction of the microvasculature of the surrounding area contributing to poor venal circulation. The often long-term, chronic effects of external beam radiation therapy include fatigue, mucositis, infection, genitourinary dysfunction, postcoital bleeding, and premature menopause. Consider the following patient example for how external beam radiation may cause sexual dysfunction throughout all phases of the HSRC and in the domains of the sexual self.

James is a 52-year-old man with a history of prostate cancer status post–external beam radiation to the prostate bed. He is meeting with the social worker after his 6-month follow-up appointment during which his oncologist told him that there was no evidence of disease and that he would repeat scans in another 6 months. At the time of the appointment, James and his wife were happy with the news and inquired if it was okay to resume sexual activity. James had not inquired about treatment for his ED despite his awareness that ED is a common problem from external beam radiation. He did not talk about it with his wife either, because he felt afraid and ashamed. As a result, he avoided making any physical expressions of intimacy with his wife for fear that it would lead her to want more sexual contact. She was also afraid to raise the issue with her husband because she did not want to put added pressure on him during his recovery. While trying to be supportive, she was quietly condoning his silence around his sexual health and their lack of intimacy despite feeling its loss in their relationship. The social worker started by asking, "Is it okay if we start talking about how you want to resume sexual activity now?" Both the patient and his wife were eager to discuss what they might do to begin slowly becoming more intimate after so much time had passed since they last had sex and they were both feeling anxious. After gathering a brief sexual history on their previous sexual activities and what they enjoyed before the diagnosis and after, the social worker first offered them some suggestions on sensate focus exercises (Table 34.1). These exercises help get individuals/couples back to simple and sensual touch and explore the sensations that might feel good or arouse each of them without the pressure of sexual play or intercourse. She then scheduled a follow-up appointment with them to revisit their success and further explore additional treatment options as they related to reclaiming their intimacy and sexual relationship.

Beyond Cancer Treatment

Sexual function can also be affected by the medications given to counteract other physical health problems, side effects, late effects, or mental health problems. Effects of medications such as antidepressants, antihypertensives, corticosteroids, hormone treatments such as tamoxifen, or aromatase inhibitors can range from a direct impact on sexual function, such as lowered libido or delayed orgasmic response, to indirect effects such as weight gain and mood changes.

Beyond sexual function and changes in the way one feels about his or her body, fertility is an area that is commonly impacted by cancer and its treatments in both men and women. Although some survivors may not place great value on their fertility, for others the mere threat of the loss of fertility can have a profound impact on the way they view their sexual self and, as a result, their quality of life. Infertility, regardless of whether or not the survivor was planning to have children, has been shown to be correlated with higher distress, greater depression, and lower reported quality of life related to relationships and sexuality (Carter et al., 2005).

Assessment

Oncology social workers should assess the various dimensions of sexuality and gather a basic sexual history on each patient as part of the biopsychosocial-spiritual assessment. Cultural and religious factors may influence the taking of a sexual health history. For example, in some cultures, it would not be sensitive to take a sexual history in front of another family member, even a partner. Oncology social workers need to educate themselves and other team members about cultural and religious norms that may influence how interviews and care should be provided. Initiating a sexual history can be as simple as offering a close-ended question: "It is important we gather enough information about you to ensure that you have all the resources and support you need while being treated. This includes gathering information on any previous trauma or experience you have had that is important for the team to know about in the care we provide you, as we want you to feel comfortable and safe. For example, have you ever experienced nonconsensual sexual touch or been in an abusive relationship?" Such information allows the team to be sensitive to triggers of past trauma. For example, an unexpected touch in the provision of care may cause a traumatic response and have other negative consequences in the patient/provider relationship (Bolte, 2010).

Models of Assessment

Two commonly used models of assessment include BETTER and Expanded PLISSIT or Ex-PLISSIT. In the assessment process, it is essential to utilize neutral language around sexual preference. Demographic questions about "relationship status" such as "Do you have a partner?" allow respondents who have a partner of the same or opposite sex to define their relationship and sexual orientation in their own language. Once relationship status is disclosed, always utilize gender-neutral language about the partner until the patient clearly identifies the partner as male or female.

The BETTER model was created to assist health care providers in bringing sexual health assessments into daily practice (Mick, Hughes, & Cohen, 2004). It begins by *B*ringing up the topic of sexuality and *E*xplaining to the patient and care partner that sexuality is an important part of quality of life. The healthcare provider then *T*ells the patient and partner that information will be made available at the *T*ime(s) when they are ready to receive it. The patient and partner should be well *E*ducated about the cancer treatment and its side effects as they pertain to sexual function and sexual health. Last, *R*ecord any education or referrals provided and ongoing resources needed by the patient (for an example of the BETTER model, refer to Mick et al. [2004]).

The PLISSIT model was originally developed in 1976 (Annon, 1976) to assist mental health providers in assessing and addressing sexual health needs and concerns in persons with mental illness. The PLISSIT model is widely supported and promoted as a guide for assessment and intervention for sexual health by the American Association of Sex Educators, Counselors, and Therapists (2004). This model has since been used in a variety of settings and illnesses and expanded (Ex-PLISSIT) where permission is gathered in every step of the model (Davis & Taylor, 2006). Additionally, the model allows for flexibility as to when each step is taken and encourages referrals to professionals when the information or support needed is beyond the practitioner's scope of practice. For example, a social worker will offer/ask for *P*ermission at every interaction he or she has with a patient while offering *L*imited *I*nformation as needed. When *S*pecific *S*uggestions are needed, the social worker can set up a separate appointment with the patient or partner to address them, allowing more time and privacy for the discussion to take place. *I*ntensive *T*herapy is a referral to a trusted professional who can provide more time and further assessment of the sexual problem, such as a referral to a certified sex therapist, pelvic floor therapist, gynecologist, or urologist. It is essential for the oncology social worker to work within his or her training, knowledge, and skill sets and refer to a professional when the problems exceed these areas.

In the example that follows, the identified problem is lowered libido in a young woman. The Ex-PLISSIT model is used to identify how an oncology social worker might incorporate this assessment into practice.

STEP	EXAMPLE
Permission	
Offer Permission for sexual difficulties to exist and obtain Permission from the patient and partner to initiate sexual discussion and legitimize sexual concerns. Permission happens at every step of the Ex-PLISSIT model and can be offered at every assessment to build trust and provide culturally relevant materials and culturally sensitive interventions to assist in building a strong therapeutic alliance (Ayonrinde, 2003). The opportunity for addressing any concerns the woman may have is provided by generalizing common sexual concerns and offering permission to be sexual and discuss sexuality (McInnes, 2003).	"Oftentimes, after numerous treatments or disease progression, a woman's thoughts about herself and her sexual relationship(s) may be impacted. This might mean a loss of desire for sex, feelings of guilt, or extreme fatigue. Unfortunately, many people mistakenly believe that they 'shouldn't' think about their sexual needs during cancer. How has cancer affected your thoughts about your sexual relationship with yourself or your partner?"
Limited Information	
Begin with both providing and obtaining Permission to explore and offer Limited Information. Provide Limited Information for the patient to be able to perform sexually, with brief education or resources. Address myths the patient may have regarding sexuality and gently re-educate.	"Many women experience lowered libido and fatigue and may be concerned about their ability to engage in any sexual activity. This may be due to fear of pain or failure to please their partner, thereby decreasing or stopping sexual activity altogether. Water-based lubricants, the use of vaginal dilators, and experimenting with more touch and caress can often assist with managing anxiety or pressure to perform. Would you like to explore more approaches to help you manage your fatigue or anxiety around performance as it relates to your sexual relationship with yourself or your partner?" Offer the patient a list of resources for the management of fatigue as it relates to desire and sexual function, such as the American Cancer Society's *Sexuality for the Woman With Cancer: Cancer, Sex, and Sexuality* (American Cancer Society, 2013), along with literature on managing fatigue.

STEP	EXAMPLE
Specific Suggestions	
Begin with both providing and obtaining Permission to explore and offer Specific Suggestions.	The goal might be to help the individual, or couple, redefine the "new normal" or expectations for sexual intimacy.
Provide specific suggestions for the patient or partner to proceed with sexual relationships and enhance intimacy.	Describe sensate focus exercises she may do with her partner, to assist in re-establishing sensual touch.
First understand how the patient expressed and explored sexuality before having cancer and how sexual pleasure was achieved.	Discuss with the team a variety of approaches to assist in improving fatigue before intimate engagements (sexual and nonsexual).
Reinforce that an orgasm does not need to be present to have an enjoyable sexual experience.	The couple may need to redefine sexual intimacy such as mutual masturbation or time touching and caressing one another. Sex as they once enjoyed it may not be possible. It is the social worker's job to either help them explore other ways of maintaining sexual and intimate moments or refer them to a professional who can.
Understand the patient's definitions of sexuality and intimacy and the cultural and religious implications that may influence these.	
Do not use medical jargon.	One may also address the partner's concerns, fears, feelings of loss, or ambivalence as the lack of intimacy may create thoughts of being unloved or unappreciated.
Intensive Therapy	
An estimated 30% of patients will need additional and more specialized or ongoing assistance with their sexual health concerns (Derogatis & Kourlesis, 1981).	Refer to a trusted network of colleagues who can further address your patient's sexuality concerns.
Know your own skill level, comfort level, and ability to provide further assistance.	Other professionals may include, but are not limited to, the following:
	Physical therapist specializing in pelvic floor exercises or capable of helping patient with creative movement/positioning (http://www.womenshealthapta.org)
	Certified sex therapist (http://www.aasect.org)
	Oncology certified social worker
	Gynecologist
	Urologist
	Endocrinologist

Pearls

- Sexual health and intimate relationships are an important and often underaddressed area of quality of life in persons diagnosed with cancer, both during and after treatment.
- Utilizing a model of assessment (e.g., Ex-PLISSIT) will convey to all patients and their loved ones that their sexual health and relationships are valued.
- Oncology social workers need to create and collaborate with a referral network of specialists for patients who may need more specific, ongoing support on issues related to their sexual health.

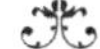

Pitfalls

- Limited awareness of cultural and religious values around discussing sexuality may reduce the effectiveness of an assessment of sexual issues.
- Difficulty managing one's own feelings of discomfort or embarrassment about addressing sexual health issues can also limit effectiveness of assessment and intervention.

Studies demonstrate that between 10% and 100% of persons diagnosed with cancer will experience some form of sexual dysfunction (Roth et al., 2010; Sryjala et al., 2000).

Additionally, 78% of oncology patients reported believing that sexual health discussions with the oncology providers were important; however, only 45% reported receiving any information from their providers (Flynn et al., 2011). Given these statistics, it is essential that oncology social workers incorporate the assessment of a patient's sexual self into their psychosocial-spiritual assessments and distress screening. Through normalizing the practice of asking all patients about sexual health, providers may be able to decrease the stigma about having sexual concerns. Assessing sexuality can occur at multiple points across the continuum of care. By addressing patients' sexual health needs, oncology social workers demonstrate that sexual problems are common, that their experiences are normal, and that we are comfortable discussing all issues that impact quality of life.

REFERENCES

American Association of Sex Educators, Counselors, and Therapists. (2004). Certification types: Distinguishing sexuality educators, counselors, and therapists. Retrieved from http://www.aasect.org/certification-types-distinguishing-sexuality-educators-counselors-and-therapists

American Cancer Society. (2013). Sexuality for the woman with cancer: Cancer, sex, and sexuality. Retrieved from http://www.cancer.org/acs/groups/cid/documents/webcontent/002912-pdf.pdf

American Psychiatric Association. (2013). *The diagnostic and statistical manual of mental disorders* (5th ed.; DSM-5). Arlington, VA: Author. Retrieved from http://dsm.psychiatryonline.org/dsmLibrary.aspx?bookid=22. doi:10.1176/appi.books.9780890425596.125889

Annon, J. (1976). The PLISSIT model: A proposed conceptual scheme for the behavioral treatment of sexual problems. *Journal of Sex Education Therapy*, *2*(1), 1–15.

Ayonrinde, O. (2003). Importance of cultural sensitivity in therapeutic transactions: Considerations for healthcare providers. *Disability Management and Health Outcomes*, *11*(4), 234–246.

Bancroft, J., Loftus, J., & Long, L. S. (2003). Distress about sex: A national survey of women in heterosexual relationships. *Archives of Sexual Behavior*, *32*(3), 193–208.

Basson, R. (2005). Women's sexual dysfunction: Revised and expanded definitions. *Canadian Medical Association Journal*, *172*(10), 1327–1333.

Bolte, S. (2010). *The impact of cancer and its treatments on the sexual self of young adult cancer survivors as compared to their healthy peers* (Doctoral dissertation, Catholic University of America). Retrieved from http://aladinrc.wrlc.org/bitstream/handle/1961/9180/Bolte_cua_0043A_10082display.pdf?sequence=1

Carter, J., Rowland, K., Chi, D., Brown, C., Abu-Rustum, N., Castiel, M., & Barakat, R. (2005). Gynecologic cancer treatment and the impact of cancer-related infertility. *Gynecologic Oncology*, *97*, 90–95.

Davis, S., & Taylor, B. (2006). Using the extended PLISSIT model to address sexual healthcare needs. *Nursing Standard*, *21*(11), 35–40.

Derogatis, L., & Kourlesis, S. (1981). An approach to the evaluation of sexual problems in the cancer patient. *Canadian-American Cancer Journal for Clinicians*, *31*(1), 46–50.

Fleming, M., & Kleinbart, E. (2001). Breast cancer and sexuality. *Journal of Sex Education and Therapy*, *26*(3), 215–224.

Flynn, K., Reese, J., Jeffery, D., Abernathy, A., Lin, L., Shelby, R., . . . Weinfurt, K. (2011). Patient experiences with communication about sex during and after treatment for cancer. *Psycho-Oncology*, *21*, 594–601. doi:10.1002/pon.1947

Frumovitz, M., Sun, C. C., Schover, L. R., Munsell, M. F., Jhingran, A., Wharton, J. T., . . . Bodurka, D. C. (2005). Quality of life and sexual functioning in cervical cancer survivors. *Journal of Clinical Oncology*, *23*(30), 7428–7436.

Katz, A. (2005). The sounds of silence: Sexuality information for cancer patients. *Journal of Clinical Oncology*, *23*(1), 238–241.

McInnes, R. (2003). Chronic illness and sexuality. *Medical Journal of Australia*, *179*, 263–266.

Mick, J., Hughes, M., & Cohen, M. (2004). Using the BETTER model to assess sexuality. *Clinical Journal of Oncology Nursing*, *8*(1), 84–86.

National Cancer Institute. (n.d.). GVHD. In *NCI Dictionary of Cancer Terms*. Retrieved from http://www.cancer.gov/dictionary?cdrid=46376

Ofman, U. S., & Auchincloss, S. S. (1992). Sexual dysfunction in cancer patients. *Current Opinions in Oncology*, *4*(4), 604–613.

Roth, A. J., Carter, J., & Nelson, C. J. (2010). Sexuality after cancer. In J. C. Holland, W. S. Breitbart, P. B. Jacobsen, M. S. Lederberg, M. J. Loscalzo, & R. McCorkle (Eds.), *Psycho-oncology* (2nd ed., pp. 245–250). New York, NY: Oxford University Press.

Savani, B. N., Griffith, M. L., Jagasia, S., & Lee, S. J. (2011). How I treat late effects in adults after allogenic stem cell transplantation. *Blood*, *117*(11), 3002–3009.

Schover, L. R. (1999). Counseling cancer patients about changes in sexual function. *Oncologist*, *13*(11), 1585–1591.

Syrjala, K., Schroeder, T., Abrams J., Atkins, T., Brown, W., Sanders, J., . . . Heiman, J. (2000). Sexual function measurement and outcomes in cancer survivors and matched controls. *Journal of Sex Research*, *37*(3), 213–225.

Tan, G., Waldman, K., & Bostick, R. (2002). Psychosocial issues, sexuality, and cancer. *Sexuality and Disability*, *20*(4), 297–318.

35 The Oncology Social Worker and Genomics

Allison Werner-Lin

Key Concepts

- *All cancers arise from changes, or mutations, to the genetic code that impair normal cellular function.*
- *Genetic tests to identify mutations associated with inherited cancer syndromes are included in a class of gene tests called predictive tests.*
- *Providing genetic services brings specialists together to address different aspects of sporadic and inherited cancer risk.*
- *Genomic discovery offers the promise of personalized medicine, yet health disparities are likely to grow with the translation of genomic science from laboratories to communities.*

The Human Genome Project, launched in 1990 and completed in 2003, sought to move cutting-edge science beyond the understanding of single genes and their effects (*genetic science*) to an understanding of the exact makeup of the human genome and the ways the human genome interacts with environments (*genomic science*). The goals of the Human Genome Project were to improve health and disease outcomes by identifying genetic variants that contribute to disease, including many cancers. Scientists have made great strides in identifying genetic mechanisms and variants that contribute to cancer expression, opening the door for improved methods of understanding cancers and for the development of effective interventions for both rare and common cancers with identifiable genetic components.

The genomic revolution offers a variety of opportunities for social workers to participate in the comprehensive care of patients and families in oncology settings. A social work voice is critical to ensure the appropriate application of rapidly emerging technologies to the interdisciplinary, and often fragmented, practice of oncology. Social workers may provide supportive and educational services that help clients identify risk factors in their families, environments, and health behaviors. To support these services, this chapter introduces readers to basic concepts and processes associated with cancer genetics, including a focus on genetic mutations linked to complex, hereditary cancer syndromes. Important terms are italicized and definitions may be found in a glossary. Patient scenarios illustrate increasingly common challenges to providing evidence-based services.

This chapter also discusses the ways in which social workers' integrated theoretical and practice foundation enable them to support clients in seeking out reliable resources, advocate for rare disease groups and marginalized communities, collaborate across disciplines to provide holistic services to patients, and provide high-quality support services to individuals, families, and communities affected by cancer. An exploration of family dynamics of coping, caregiving, and grief with respect to inherited cancer risk can be found in Chapter 32.

Cancer Genetics Primer

All cancers arise from changes, or mutations, to the genetic code that impair normal cellular function. These changes occur at the DNA level, which carries genetic information encoded in four different chemicals bases—adenine, thymine, cytosine, and guanine, or, more familiarly, A, T, C, and G—which pair (A-T and C-G) together. Genes are segments of DNA with a unique combination of base pairs that contain instructions for making a specific protein required for cell growth, development, and/or maintenance. Human beings have about 20,000 to 25,000 genes. All human beings have roughly the same genes, but no two people, except identical twins, have the same versions (*alleles*) of each of those genes. Each person generally has two copies of each gene, one inherited from each parent.

Approximately 90% of all cancers are currently understood to be the result of gene change caused by *sporadic, somatic*, or *acquired* mutations, which occur during one's life (Garber & Offit, 2005). Ten percent of cancers are considered *hereditary* and are linked to mutations passed from parent to child in genetic blueprints encoded in a parent's egg or sperm. They are present in every cell in the body, including reproductive cells that are passed on to children during conception.

Resources and Consultation to Communities Affected by Cancer

An old friend from social work school calls to ask for your help. He runs a weekly support group for parentally bereaved adolescents at a school in the rural Midwest, where the science teacher was recently diagnosed with glioblastoma. The parent of one support group participant died of brain cancer (he has no other information about the malignancy), and the students are now worried about carcinogens in their environment. Your friend is unsure what to tell his students. He knows you work in a large cancer center with access to up-to-date research and preeminent oncologists, and he asks for your help in educating—and relieving—the students.

Your first step is to send your friend a list of well-regarded and peer-reviewed resources written for consumers so that he can become acquainted with the basics of brain cancer, including environmental and hereditary factors in brain cancer expression. You offer to speak with him directly about your experience with adolescents, who are technologically savvy and able to find all sorts of information on the Internet, yet who are not mature enough to interpret it adequately. However, you recognize the limits of your expertise and offer to consult with a genetic counselor. You suggest setting up a meeting time when you or the genetic counselor and your colleague can Skype with the bereavement group to answer questions and discuss their concerns.

Understanding Gene × Environment Interactions

In the context of cancer genetics, the presence of a single mutation alone may not be sufficient to cause disease, but when environmental risk factors are also present (e.g., high-fat diet, smoking), an individual may develop cancer. For this reason, researchers and clinicians commonly refer to cancer *genomics*, which represents the integration of genetics and environments (represented as gene × environment). For example, interaction between genes that control skin pigment, such as melanin, and exposure to sunlight may lead to the development of skin cancer. In this case, the genetic variant causes the body to produce insufficient pigment to protect itself during exposure to ultraviolet rays.

Epigenetics

Perhaps most exciting for social workers and others who seek to measure and modify environments to improve the health and mental health of individuals, families, and communities is the field of *epigenetics*. Epigenetics is the study of how environmental factors impact gene expression. Even though these changes are *acquired* during an individual's life, that individual's children may *inherit* them. Epigenetic factors may impact the onset and expression of cancer. For example, social work–driven research linked social environments and hypervigilance to increased early breast cancer risk for African American women on Chicago's South Side (Gehlert et al., 2008). Living in an environment that requires heightened vigilance impacts hormone levels because of an increased and ongoing need to modulate response to stress (McClintock, Conzen, Gehlert, Masi, & Olopade, 2005). Hormone levels impact breast cancer risk. Epigenetic research such as this has implications for population- and community-based interventions designed by social workers to identify environmental risk for cancer prevention.

Genetic Education, Counseling, Testing, and Referrals

Who Is on the Team?

Providing genetic services brings specialists together to address different aspects of sporadic and inherited cancer risk (Quillin, Miller, & Bodurtha, 2011; Werner-Lin & Reed, 2011). Should an individual present for care after a cancer diagnosis, these specialists' role will be to diagnose, treat, and manage specific cancer care. Although genetics professionals may typically take the lead on patient care coordination, patient management is a shared responsibility among these professionals. *Clinical geneticists* are physicians with advanced training in medical genetics who provide care for patients affected by genetic disorders. *Genetic counselors* and *oncology nurses* with advanced training in genetics provide education and counseling about the medical risks associated with a gene mutation that might be implicated in a family's cancer history. These providers help individuals, couples, and families make decisions about genetic testing, adapt to genetic testing information, and make decisions about risk management. Individuals with training in *public health genomics* work to improve population-based health through initiatives that integrate genetic concepts and tools into research, policy, and educational campaigns.

Master's-prepared *social workers* are trained to understand the client and family in their social and historical milieu by eliciting family narratives of illness, caregiving, and loss; addressing outstanding emotional concerns; fostering active client participation in counseling and decision making; and bolstering client self-awareness. They may collaborate with or work alongside psychologists and psychiatrists to conduct research and to provide a variety of psychosocial services to individuals and families with hereditary cancer risk. These services include referrals, individual and family counseling, and consultation and ongoing supports for individuals, families, and groups coping with genetic conditions. They may also conduct family meetings about genetic testing, support medical decision making about risk management, and facilitate adjustment to cancer treatment.

Applying Social Work Skills to Practice in Cancer Genetics

Social work practice across disparate populations, settings, and geographies requires practitioners to master basic skills of engagement, advocacy, collaboration, and research. Essential social work skills that may be easily translated into practice in the cancer genetics setting include the following:

- *Facilitate family communication.*
- *Map family histories, expectations, and scripts about illness and loss.*
- *Address beliefs about susceptibility separately from empirical data about risk.*
- *Separate individual from family scripts about caregiving and illness roles.*
- *Develop a network of skilled providers to whom referrals can be made.*
- *Identify and ameliorate challenges to effective communication with providers.*
- *Distinguish important decisions from urgent decisions.*
- *Enhance self-efficacy to enable satisfactory choice.*
- *Identify reputable resources to facilitate informed decision making.*
- *Connect individuals and families with supportive communities.*

For a more comprehensive set of essential social work skills for competent practice in cancer genetics, see Chapter 32.

Referrals

Provider familiarity with genetic concepts and services increases the likelihood that consumers will learn about, be referred to, and pursue genetic testing (Suther & Goodson, 2003). This is particularly evident in well-resourced medical and social environments and with privileged groups that providers believe will act on genetic information. Provider comfort with genetic information increases patient trust and promotes information seeking and behavioral change.

Social workers frequently ask clients with physical and mental illness about family history and may therefore be in a good position to identify families that could benefit from genetic counseling. Cancer genetic testing raises psychosocial and sometimes ethical issues for patients. Such issues require knowledgeable professionals, including social workers, to facilitate decision making that is congruent with patient values and priorities. Social workers should be prepared to provide reliable referrals and resources to clients interested in pursuing genetic consultation. Referrals are appropriate when factors are present in the individual or family that suggests an increased risk for a genetic condition. Resources should include connections to providers who specialize in genetic education and counseling in addition to online resources that can link clients to supportive and informative communities, particularly for rare genetic conditions (see Additional Resources toward the end of this chapter). Due to the vast amount and variable quality of information available online, especially with respect to rare conditions, social workers should prepare to help patients interpret and assess the quality of information.

Learning About Genetics After a Cancer Diagnosis

A 41-year-old woman recently diagnosed with cancer in her left breast calls the hospital social worker to discuss her oncologist's recommendation that she complete rapid genetic testing to identify whether she carries a mutation to the BRCA gene. Her maternal grandmother and aunt died of breast cancer at ages 42 and 38, respectively. Her surgeon recommends testing to inform her course of treatment. Should she test BRCA-mutation positive, the recommendation includes bilateral mastectomy, removing the cancerous tissue of the left breast and the healthy tissue of the right breast, followed by risk-reducing salpingo-oophorectomy to remove her ovaries and fallopian tubes. Should she test negative, she may elect for lumpectomy or mastectomy.

The client is unsure about why she should remove her ovaries if the cancer is in her breast, and she is confused about how her genes could impact the course of her treatment. She is also worried about whether genetic testing and risk-reducing surgery are covered by her insurance. She's heard a lot about BRCA in the news but is unsure about how these stories impact her. She comes to you asking what she should do.

Your first step is to teach the client about the BRCA mutation she carries if you are knowledgeable (there are several mutations) and/or to provide resources and educational materials so that she can revisit her questions with a certified genetic counselor. You connect her with the Internet-based advocacy group FORCE: Facing Our Risk of Cancer Empowered (http://www.facingourrisk.org) and suggest she attend a local support group for women who have breast cancer to learn more about their experiences and challenges. You suggest she continue to schedule visits with you until she has arrived at a decision about genetic testing and treatment for her breast cancer.

Ensuring Equal Access to Genomic Services

Genomic information now has relevance for a large and increasing percentage of persons who may be considered "at risk" for cancer in complex ways as a result of the particular combination(s) of common genes they carry and the interaction of those genes with the environment. Although discoveries associated with genomic information offer the promise of personalized medicine, health disparities are likely to grow with the translation of genomic science from "bench to trench." For example, physicians treating low-income patients or patients of color are less likely to be familiar with genetic services, to have fluency in genetic concepts and skills, to refer patients to genetic services, or to provide adequate counseling to support informed decision making (Suther & Kiros, 2009). Even when providers are well versed in genetics, consumers from marginalized groups are referred less frequently for genetic services due, in part, to the perception that uptake and comprehension are less likely (Graves, Christopher, Harrison, Peshkin, & Isaacs, 2011).

Consumer-Driven Information Seeking

Increasingly, our consumer-driven health care culture relies on patients to seek out information from a variety of sources, to understand this information, and to present it for discussion with providers. With a national shortage of genetic counselors, many computer-based decision aids have been developed to facilitate information sharing across wide geographic distances by increasing access to genetic services.

A blended family schedules a visit with a private practice social worker specializing in medical family therapy to discuss disagreement over whether to pursue genetic testing. The father of two adolescent daughters recently went into remission following Stage 3 colon cancer. His elder daughter, who recently turned 18, is planning to attend college in the fall and wants to know whether her father carries a mutation that predisposes him to elevated risk of Lynch syndrome, also known as hereditary nonpolyposis colon cancer. The younger daughter, age 16, believes her father is "cured" and does not want him to pursue testing, which she believes would "reopen the wound" of his diagnosis. In confidence, the elder daughter admits to you that, using her own money, she sent a DNA sample to an online genome sequencing company. She reasoned that online testing costs a fraction of laboratory testing through the hospital and provides some anonymity. She can choose to share the information with her siblings should they choose to ask for it. She asks for your advice about whether to share the results, still forthcoming, with her father.

Your first step is to educate this young woman about information she wants to know versus what she needs to know to inform current health behaviors. Good gastrointestinal health is important throughout the life cycle. For more specific information about Lynch syndrome, you refer her to a local genetic counselor to interpret her results, to confirm the legitimacy of the findings, and to discuss formal genetic testing. Once an appointment with the genetic counselor has occurred, you sit down with the father and eldest daughter to facilitate a discussion about their responses to the information they have obtained and issues around disclosure.

Increasingly, genetic tests associated with cancer risk are being marketed, and in some instances sold, directly to consumers (direct-to-consumer advertising [DTCA]). These tests can identify variants linked to specific high-risk cancer syndromes for which recommendations exist for screening and prevention, and those linked to low or unknown cancer risk for which limited research exists about cancer penetrance and prevention. DTCA may increase knowledge of genetic services for individuals who otherwise would not be able to learn information about their cancer risk. Yet, DTCA circumvents health care professionals, who can provide a balanced explanation of the risks and benefits of genetic testing and cancer risk management. Ideally, DTCA empowers patients to be educated and to support decisions consistent with their preferences and values. Yet DTCA may actually increase health disparities, because most information provided directly to consumers is incomplete and requires higher health literacy and numeracy than is common in the general population (Lea, Kaphingst, Bowen, Lipkus, & Hadley, 2011), much less marginalized subpopulations (Kontos & Viswanath, 2011).

The Ethics of Privacy and Control: Who "Owns" Genetic Information?

Hereditary cancer syndromes present a set of unique challenges for patients and providers. The familial implications of identifying hereditary cancer syndromes shift the existing biomedical paradigm that focuses on the rights of the individual patient to a broader focus on the rights of family members. Providers may encourage patients to share genetic testing information with family members and to support them in deciding whom to tell, what to tell, and how best to tell relatives about cancer risk.

Early genetic counseling protocols led to ethical questions about the ownership of genetic material and about who should benefit from genetic discoveries (Kent, 2003; Skloot, 2010). Because genetic testing reveals cancer risk information for an entire family line, individuals who do not know they may have inherited disease risk do not have the opportunity to engage in treatment or prevention. If available treatments may prevent an early death, improve quality of life, and prevent suffering, are doctors obligated to share genetic information with other members of the bloodline? Are family members? Although some hereditary cancers follow predictable patterns of expression, others are ambiguous, leaving a gray area in interpreting medical guidelines about disclosure. Oncology social workers can support families as they make decisions about whether and how to share genetic information with family members so that decisions are ethically and relationally sound. This requires attention to the emotional and medical needs of family members including, in many cases, those beyond the scope of the therapeutic relationship.

Protecting Genetic Information

The Health Insurance Portability and Accountability Act (HIPAA) of 1996 protects consumer health information from disclosure to third parties and provides governance over the ways providers and insurers can access and use health information. HIPAA struck a balance between the rights of the consumer to control his or her own health information and the needs of health care providers to access medical records to provide quality care. HIPAA has had implications for individuals with identified mutations linked to hereditary cancer syndromes because it enables physicians to breech patience confidentiality to "prevent or lessen a serious and immediate threat" (U.S. Department of Health and Human Services, 2005). The Institute of Medicine (2009) concurred that when failure to communicate genetic information can result in serious, imminent harm or death, the physician may contact the family if the patient has not done so.

Genetic Information Nondiscrimination Act

The Genetic Information Nondiscrimination Act (GINA) of 2008 was designed to protect genetic information from health insurance and employment discrimination. GINA, which became effective in November 2009, ensures that health insurance companies cannot require prospective clients to undergo genetic testing, nor can they use known genetic testing information to exclude individuals from coverage or to set premiums. With respect to employment practices, GINA prohibits the use of genetic information to inform decisions in hiring or termination of employment, in assignment of job tasks, or in promotions. The scope of protection includes an individual's family medical history, genetic testing results for carriers, prenatal or predictive testing, and any DNA spectrum analysis (NCHPEG, 2010).

Before the passage of GINA, such protections varied by state and no umbrella legislation covered all Americans. As a result, GINA marked a huge step toward reducing barriers to genetic testing. Yet GINA has limitations. If a genetic condition has already manifested in symptoms leading to a diagnosis, GINA does not apply. Although the legislation applies to health insurance companies, it does *not* apply to life, disability, or long-term care insurance (NCHPEG, 2010). Finally, the provisions of GINA do not apply to certain groups of individuals receiving federal benefits for which legislation was put in place in 2000 by President Clinton's administration. These groups include the U.S. military, veterans obtaining health care through the Veteran's Administration, individuals using the Indian Health Service, and individuals enrolled in the Federal Employees Health Benefits program (NCHPEG, 2010).

The United States' social history of institutionalized racism, misuse of health information, and exploitation of poor individuals with chronic conditions has led many marginalized groups, particularly those of African ancestry, to distrust how genetic information will be used (Sussner et al., 2011). Concerns that genetic information may provide another potent vehicle to stigmatize and exploit populations or to refuse coverage or care for chronic and life-threatening conditions are well founded (Skloot, 2010). As a result, marginalized groups may not see the benefit of genetic testing to their families or their communities, and uptake of genetic services is less likely as perceived benefit decreases (Suther & Kiros, 2009; Thompson, Valdimarsdottir, Jandorf, & Redd, 2003).

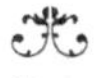

Pearls

- Social work education prepares professionals to lead effective and productive collaborations with a host of oncology care providers, as well as to design and implement innovative and empirically informed services across cancer care settings.
- Social work's biopsychosocial approach to assessment and intervention fits well with models of multifactor genetic diseases, such as cancer, in which genetic mutations interact in yet unknown ways with other genes, the environment, and a host of other factors to increase disease risk.
- As genetic technologies mature, social workers will be in a unique position to develop and implement relevant programming and to provide ongoing support as families reach new milestones and face new dilemmas in their cancer care.

- Our rich history of innovative and applied research will facilitate ethical translation of genetic discovery into tangible products to support vulnerable and marginalized groups.

Pitfalls

- As our understanding of both sporadic and hereditary cancers explodes, geneticists will need to partner with social scientists trained to assess environments, hypothesize links between environmental strengths and constraints and health outcomes, and design research to test these links. Although complementary knowledge and skills across collaborators can potentiate research impact, disparate professional lexicons, beliefs about standard and rigorous research methodology, and perceptions about important targets of research may threaten collaboration.
- Social workers' immeasurable contribution to these partnerships lies in their expertise in understanding the impact of familial and social conditions on human development throughout the life cycle and across diverse and dynamic environments. Yet, social workers must navigate complex and hierarchical medical systems to be heard and to advocate for improved patient care.

ADDITIONAL RESOURCES

American College for Medical Genetics: http://www.acmg.net
Duke Center for Human Genome Variation: http://humangenome.duke.edu/home
Genetic Alliance: http://www.geneticalliance.org
Genetic and Rare Conditions Site: http://www.kumc.edu/gec
Genetics and Public Policy Center: http://www.dnapolicy.org
Genetics Science Learning Center: http://learn.genetics.utah.edu
Michigan Cancer Consortium: http://www.michigancancer.org
National Cancer Institute: http://www.cancer.gov/cancertopics/genetics
National Coalition of Health Professional Education in Genetics: http://www.nchpeg.org
National Human Genome Research Institute at the National Institutes of Health: http://www.genome.gov
Personal Genomics Education Project: http://www.pged.org

REFERENCES

Garber, J. E., & Offit, K. (2005). Hereditary cancer predisposition syndromes. *Journal of Clinical Oncology, 23*(2), 276–292.

Gehlert, S., Sohmer, D., Sacks, T., Mininger, C., McClintock, M., & Olopade, O. (2008). Targeting health disparities: A model linking upstream determinants to downstream interventions. *Health Affairs (Millwood), 27*(2), 339–349.

Graves, K. D., Christopher, J., Harrison, T. M., Peshkin, B. N., & Isaacs, C. (2011). Providers' perceptions and practices regarding BRCA1/2 genetic counseling and testing in African American women. *Journal of Genetic Counseling, 20*(6), 674–689.

Institute of Medicine. (2009). Beyond the HIPAA privacy rule: Enhancing privacy, improving health through research. In S. J. Nass, L. A. Levit, & L. O. Gostin (Eds.), *Committee on Health Research and the privacy of health information: The HIPAA privacy rule.* Washington, DC: National Academies Press.

Kent, A. (2003). Consent and confidentiality in genetics: Whose information is it anyway? *Journal of Medical Ethics, 29*(1), 16–18.

Kontos, E. Z., & Viswanath, K. (2011). Cancer-related direct-to-consumer advertising: A critical review. *Nature Reviews Cancer, 11*, 142–150. doi:10.1038/nrc2999

Lea, D. H., Kaphingst, K. A., Bowen, D., Lipkus, I., & Hadley, D. W. (2011). Communicating genetic and genomic information: Health literacy and numeracy considerations. *Public Health Genomics, 14*(4–5), 279–289.

McClintock, M. K., Conzen, S. D., Gehlert, S., Masi, C., & Olopade, F. (2005). Mammary cancer and social interactions: Identifying multiple environments that regulate gene expression throughout the life span. *Journals of Gerontology, 60B*(Special Issue 1), 32–41.

National Coalition of Health Professional Education in Genetics (NCHPEG). (2010). The Genetic Nondiscrimination Act (GINA). Retrieved from http://www.nchpeg.org/index.php?option=com_content&view=article&id=97&Itemid=120

Quillin, J. M., Miller, J., & Bodurtha, J. N. (2011). Social work and genetics. In T. Altillio & S. Otis-Green (Eds.), *Oxford textbook of palliative social work* (pp. 489–449). New York, NY: Oxford University Press.

Skloot, R. (2010). *The immortal life of Henrietta Lacks.* New York, NY: Crown.

Sussner, K. M., Edwards, T. A., Thompson, H. S., Jandorf, L., Kwate, N. O., Forman, A., . . . Valdimarsdottir, H. B. (2011). Ethnic, racial, and cultural identity and perceived benefits and barriers related to genetic testing for breast cancer among at-risk women of African descent in New York City. *Public Health Genomics, 14*, 356–370.

Suther, S., & Goodson, O. (2003). Barriers to the provision of genetic services by primary care physicians: A systematic review of the literature. *Genetics in Medicine, 5*, 63–65.

Suther, S., & Kiros, G. (2009). Barriers to the use of genetic testing: A study of racial and ethnic disparities. *Genetics in Medicine, 11*(9), 655–662.

Thompson, H. S., Valdimarsdottir, H. B., Jandorf, L., & Redd, W. (2003). Perceived disadvantages and concerns about abuses of genetic testing for cancer risk: Differences across African American, Latina, and Caucasian women. *Patient Education and Counseling, 51*(3), 217–227.

U.S. Department of Health and Human Services. (2005). Understanding HIPAA. Retrieved from www.hhs.gov/ocr/privacy/hipaa/understanding/summary/index.html

Werner-Lin, A., & Reed, K. (2011). Social work and genetics. In S. Gehlert & T. Arthur Browne (Eds.), *Handbook of health social work* (2nd ed., pp. 557–589). San Francisco, CA: Wiley & Sons.

VII

Sociocultural and Economic Diversity: Improving Access and Health Outcomes

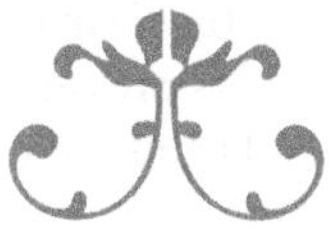

Yvette Colón

Oncology social workers work with diverse cancer patients and families facing barriers to care, devastating illnesses, and difficult treatments. This section on working with social and cultural diversity is not meant to be comprehensive—in other words, we are not suggesting that all patients and families are reflected. When we talk about Hispanic/Latino patients, it is useful to remember that there are multiple Hispanic/Latino cultures with overlapping characteristics but each with distinct cultural practices, language differences, and histories. This perspective is the same for members of African American, American Indian/Alaska Native, and Chinese cultures. The experiences of lesbian, gay, bisexual, and transgender patients and families are also not uniform and similar, as is true of immigrants, refugees, and asylum seekers whose experiences must be understood individually. All individuals' life experiences are unique and complex and include cultural, spiritual, and social practices that can bring discrimination, current and historical oppression, and poverty. Oncology social workers are challenged to understand their patients' sociocultural and diverse economic experiences in a whole-person context.

In "Working With Sociocultural and Economic Diversity," Yvette Colón provides a broad view of racial, ethnic, socioeconomic, disability, gender identity, and sexual orientation diversity in the United States. She discusses the influence of culture in all aspects of illness, discusses the problem of persistent health care disparities, and highlights the importance of cultural competence, proposing cultural humility as the perspective for enhancing culturally sensitive psychosocial oncology care.

In "Support for Immigrants, Political Refugees, and Patients Seeking Asylum Who Have Cancer," Amanda Amodio and Upal Basu Roy state that immigrants, refugees, and asylum seekers are minority populations whose health care needs are traditionally underserved in the United States. Oncology social workers must possess knowledge of community resources serving these vulnerable populations and play a critical role in assisting them navigate health and mental health systems.

In "Gay, Lesbian, and Bisexual Individuals Diagnosed With Cancer," Kathryn M. Smolinski and William Goeren help us understand how members of lesbian, gay, and bisexual communities encounter additional barriers to accessing care, receiving treatment, and feeling comfortable within the health care system. They propose that oncology social workers can cultivate an environment that is responsive to these patients' critical needs by developing excellent educational materials, clinical models of care, and research protocols focused on improving their health care service delivery.

In "Transgender Individuals and Families Affected by Cancer," Max Rorty provides a much-needed and progressive view of oncology social work with transgender cancer patients. Members of transgender communities are among society's most discriminated and disadvantaged individuals; they are often included as an afterthought or overlooked altogether in any discussion of gay, lesbian, bisexual, and transgender concerns. Rorty offers a sensitive discussion of the specific concerns that transgender cancer patients bring to health care interactions and the psychosocial interventions that can be undertaken by oncology social workers and others to address these concerns.

In "Alaska Native, Native American, and First Nation People: Outreach, Screening, and Assessment," Karina L. Walters, Teresa Evans-Campbell, Matthew A. Town, Katie Schultz, Jessica H. L. Elm, and Ramona E. Beltrán introduce an indigenous-centered approach to wellness, cancer prevention, and care that should be used with American Indian and Alaska Native patients and families. Oncology social work practice includes cultural issues that should be addressed throughout their continuum of care.

In "Access to Medical Treatment for African Americans Diagnosed With Cancer: The Current Evidence Base," Karen Bullock and Hannah Allison outline the significant cancer disparities and poor survival rates faced by African American cancer patients. They highlight social supports important to the African American community and discuss oncology social workers' obligation to treat individuals and families according to their preferences when possible.

In "Hispanic/Latino Individuals and Families Affected by Cancer: Outreach, Screening, and Assessment," Guadalupe R. Palos discusses the need to understand Hispanic/Latino cultural values and worldviews, to recognize that appropriate psychosocial oncology services are delivered to populations with great diversity in sociodemographic characteristics, and to recognize preferences relevant to health, family, community, and environment.

In "Working With Chinese Families Impacted by Cancer: An Integrative Body–Mind–Spirit Approach," Pamela Pui-Yu Leung and Cecilia L. W. Chan explore how Chinese culture influences patients' and families' reactions to cancer and their coping in the face of serious illness. They introduce an integrative body–mind–spirit practice model that can bring together Eastern philosophies and traditional Chinese medicine with oncology social work practice.

Each chapter in this section provides strategies, case vignettes, additional readings, and resources to build oncology social workers' knowledge and skills in working with diverse cancer patients and families to enhance culturally sensitive practice. Each makes a compelling case that learning about culture can help oncology social workers provide appropriate psychosocial services to their patients and their families.

36

Yvette Colón

Working With Sociocultural and Economic Diversity

Of all the forms of inequality, injustice in health is the most shocking and the most inhumane.

—*Dr. Martin Luther King Jr. (1966)*

Key Concepts

- *Culture influences all aspects of individuals' lives.*
- *There is great diversity among the patients and families oncology social workers serve.*
- *Cultural competency and cultural humility must be used to provide ethical, supportive, and whole-person services to cancer patients and families.*

The richness of oncology social workers' professional lives lies, in part, in the diversity of the patients and families they serve. Oncology social workers spend their careers working with many cancer patients and families who are different from them. The patients and families present not just racial and ethnic diversity but also differences due to language, socioeconomic status, education, literacy, age, gender, spirituality, disability, sexual orientation, gender identity, and more. Yet the community of professional social workers is much less diverse than the clients they serve: 86% of all licensed social workers in the United States are non-Hispanic Caucasians (NASW, 2006). Given the possibility for there to be a racial disparity between social workers and their clients, developing cultural competence is important.

All professional health and mental health organizations recognize the importance of cultural competence. The National Association of Social Workers (2001, pp. 4–5) provides the most extensive standards for cultural competence in social work practice that stress the importance of ethics and values, self-awareness, cross-cultural knowledge and skills, service delivery, empowerment and advocacy, diverse workforce, professional education, language diversity, and cross-cultural leadership. Although published in 2001, these remain current standards to guide social work practice. The Association of Oncology Social Work also recognizes that in embracing patient and family-centered care at all levels of practice, oncology social workers must provide coordinated and integrated culturally competent care. Psychosocial assessments should include information about "race, ethnicity, religion, culture, language, physical or mental disability, socio-economic status, sex, sexual orientation, and gender identity or expression" (AOSW, 2012).

A Snapshot of Diversity

In 2012, minority individuals composed approximately 22% of the U.S. population, of which 12.9% were foreign born (U.S. Census Bureau, 2014). By 2023, more than half of all U.S. children will likely be from ethnic minority groups (Columna, Foley, & Lytle, 2010). Minorities are expected to become the majority by 2050 (Cohn & Taylor, 2012).

By 2030, there will be approximately 70 million people older than 64 in the United States. This is nearly 22% of the total population. This group will be more racially and ethnically diverse, with almost 26% ethnic minorities. Also, the number of those over age 85 will increase from 4.2 million to 8.9 million (U.S. Department of Health and Human Services Administration on Aging, 2011).

According to the National Poverty Center (2014), in 2010, 15.1% of the U.S. population lived in poverty. Children were 24% of the U.S. population, but 36% of them lived in poverty. There is considerable variation between racial and ethnic subgroups. Poverty rates for African Americans and Latinos are much higher than the national average. In 2010, 27.4% of African Americans and 26.6% of Latinos lived in poverty, compared to 9.9% of non-Latino Caucasians and 12.1% of Asian Americans. Poverty rates were highest for families headed by single women, especially if they were African American or Latino; 31.6% of households headed by single women were poor, whereas 15.8% of households headed by single men were poor. Foreign-born residents had a higher incidence living in poverty compared to residents born in the United States. Foreign-born noncitizens had even higher rates of poverty. Many adults and children, especially those in poverty, do not have health insurance (Centers for Disease Control and Prevention, 2011).

Approximately 18.7% of the U.S. population are disabled (U.S. Census Bureau, 2012). Approximately 4% of Americans are lesbian, gay, bisexual, and/or transgender (Williams Institute, 2011).

Cultural Influences

The familial, psychological, social, and spiritual consequences of having cancer can be great. Culture influences the perception and expression of illness, symptoms, and the language used to communicate illness information. Cultural meanings assigned to a diagnosis of cancer, its treatment, and associated pain and suffering can guide emotional responses to illness.

Culture also can define what is considered a health problem, how cancer information is received, how symptoms are expressed, what type of treatment should be given or will be accepted, who should provide treatment and supportive care, and how patient rights and protections are exercised. Spirituality, faith, and/or a life philosophy can be culturally determined, as can health beliefs and practices. Family and kinship networks may be different than those in which majority-culture patients feel most comfortable. Levels of acculturation (the degree to which one's own culture and the dominant culture are combined) and assimilation (the putting aside of one's original culture in favor of the dominant culture) need to be assessed. Patients and their families may hold non-Western health beliefs that are vitally important to them but may clash with the Western health philosophy of U.S. hospitals and oncology centers.

The Role of the Oncology Social Worker

Oncology social workers can provide a culturally competent perspective that can affect the care that patients and families receive. In combining cultural awareness with psychosocial assessments and interventions, oncology social workers and other cancer care providers can understand their patients' holistic experiences in the health care system and advocate for their well-being. Oncology social workers understand the cancer care process and the psychosocial experiences of patients and families throughout the cancer continuum, ranging from diagnosis to survivorship or from early-stage cancer to metastatic or advanced disease to end of life. They understand oncology care in the real world.

For people with cancer, oncology social workers may function as mental health or psychosocial clinicians, educators, patient navigators, case managers, or resource coordinators. They can play an important role in helping patients access appropriate treatments and other services and in supporting them, their families, and their caregivers. They can provide information about and access to pain and symptom management. They can help find resources for insurance coverage issues, child care, transportation to and from appointments, treatment sessions, and other responsibilities. Oncology social workers can teach strategies to enhance coping, help patients and families communicate more effectively, and think through important decisions.

For patients and families with limited English proficiency, oncology social workers can help overcome communication barriers. Clearly, there are advantages to having bilingual and bicultural staff who speak patients' languages. When they are not available, using professional interpreters as much as possible rather than family members is important. Using visual aids rather than text-only information increases a patient's understanding of his or her diagnosis and treatment. Simplifying medication schedules helps with adherence to the treatment plan.

As valued members of interdisciplinary teams, oncology social workers also provide support and information to their colleagues in the service of strengthening and enhancing the team's ability to provide the best possible oncology care to patients.

Factors in Health Care Disparities

Smedley, Stith, and Nelson (2002) in a review of the literature found that racial and ethnic minority individuals often received lower quality health care services than nonminority individuals. Even when things like insurance and income were controlled, equal access was limited. Their report, *Unequal Treatment: Confronting Racial and Ethnic Disparities in Health Care*, was requested by the U.S. Congress because of documented differences in morbidity and mortality between minority and nonminority populations. The report focused on the operation of health care systems, legal fairness, and conscious and unconscious discrimination and bias.

Factors such as difficulty in communicating, low socioeconomic status, and inadequate health insurance created barriers to obtaining adequate health care. Provider bias, cultural insensitivity, or stereotypical beliefs about minority health or behavior were found to contribute to barriers. Disparities were consistent across disease areas, clinical settings, and clinical services.

The report made specific recommendations for legal, regulatory, policy, and health system interventions; better data collection and monitoring; and more specific research about how patients might influence clinical encounters with providers. It identified the importance of patient education and empowerment and cross-cultural education about attitudes, knowledge, and skills in health professions as strategies to help eliminate disparities in health care. The Institute of Medicine (2012) highlighted the continuing difficulties in reducing U.S. health disparities. More research on the social determinants of health disparities and effective culturally sensitive interventions is very much needed.

Research has proposed several reasons for poorer health outcomes of racial and ethnic minority populations compared to the Caucasian population. However, even when these factors have been accounted for, disparities in health outcomes persist. In its *National Healthcare Disparities Report 2012*, the Agency for Healthcare Research and Quality (2012) consistently found that there is inequality in the quality of care in the United States. Examples include the following:

- Adults aged 50 to 64 who were uninsured were less likely to receive colorectal cancer screening than those with private insurance.
- Worsening disparities were in the differences between African Americans and Caucasians in the rates of advanced-stage breast cancer.

The American Cancer Society has long looked at cancer disparities and wants to eliminate disparities in the burden of cancer among different U.S. groups. Included in the identified disparities are the following (ACS, 2013):

- Persons in lower socioeconomic levels have much higher cancer death rates than those in higher socioeconomic levels, regardless of race or ethnicity.
- Among racial and ethnic groups, African American men and women have much higher cancer incidence and mortality rates than Caucasian Americans.
- Information on cancer incidence and mortality for Native Americans/Alaska Natives is considered to be incomplete because their racial and ethnic status is often not identified correctly in health records.
- Although Latinos, Asian Americans, and Pacific Islanders have lower incidence rates of cancer overall, they have much higher rates of specific cancers (Latinos have higher rates of liver, stomach, and cervical cancers; Asian Americans and Pacific Islanders have much higher incidence of liver cancer and the highest mortality rates of any racial/ethnic group).

As a result of these and other recognized differences, cultural competence is developed as a strategy to reduce racial and ethnic disparities in U.S. health care.

Cultural Humility: A Perspective for Enhancing Culturally Sensitive Psychosocial Care

Although it is always helpful to know something about the culture of one's cancer patients and families, it is not enough. When the concept of culture is broad, it may be difficult to identify when competence is achieved. Cultural competence is not an end point; it is a process that can never reach an end. Perhaps a different perspective to enhance culturally sensitive psychosocial care can be used.

Tervalon and Murray-García first argued for cultural humility, as a "more suitable goal in multicultural medical education" (1998, p. 117). To make cultural competence training more effective, they proposed adding two additional factors: (1) an awareness of the ever-changing quality of culture that is neither a behavioral representation nor a fixed identity and (2) the practice of cultural humility. They view cultural humility as health care providers' acknowledgment that they bring their own cultural differences to the interactive relationship with patients (and families) and that this acknowledgment is part of a lifelong process of self-reflection and self-critique. Providers must recognize that it is impossible to ignore subtle and overt misinformation about different cultures. Thus, providers are aware that their own cultural beliefs or biases may affect the care of their patients and they engage in active exploration of the differences that they *and* their patients bring to their interactions with each other. This puts the burden of cultural sensitivity and efforts to navigate real and perceived differences rightly on the provider and not on the person with cancer who may be perceived as culturally "other."

Cultural humility research and education continue in various areas as, for example, educating medical residents (Shapiro, Lie, Gutierrez, & Zhuang, 2006), using it with community-based participatory research (Ross, 2010), and combining cultural humility with cultural philosophies (Chang, Simon, & Dong, 2012).

Oncology social workers and other care providers must reach beyond their comfort level in providing culturally sensitive care to their patients and families.

Marta is a 38-year-old woman born in the Dominican Republic and recently diagnosed with cervical cancer. She is married to a Dominican man and they have several children, all of them U.S. citizens. She feels fortunate to be a stay-at-home mother; her husband's income is sufficient so that she doesn't have to work, and his employer provides a family health insurance plan. Although Marta knows some conversational English, she is much more comfortable speaking Spanish. Her physician involved the oncology social worker in Marta's care because she wasn't sure if Marta understood her options and seemed hesitant to make decisions about surgery and chemotherapy.

The oncology social worker did not speak Spanish, so she used the services of a professional interpreter on several occasions. She spoke in plain and simple terms, avoiding medical language and jargon. She asked Marta many questions to elicit her understanding of her diagnosis and possible treatment; she asked about health beliefs and learned about the important decision makers in Marta's family who needed to be involved. Most important, the oncology social worker shared some of her perspectives about being different from Marta; she invited Marta to share what the oncology social worker and doctor needed to know about her culture, family, and community to provide the best help and support possible. The two developed a good working relationship and Marta felt acknowledged and supported by the oncology team.

Pearls

- Taking time to learn about culture can help oncology social workers provide the most culturally sensitive psychosocial services to their patients and their families during their cancer care.
- Cultural competence and cultural humility are essential lifelong skills that can enhance oncology social workers' relationships with people affected by cancer.

Pitfalls

- Relying on cultural generalizations or stereotypes will interfere in the helping relationship between oncology social workers and their patients.
- Making assumptions about a patient's culture can have a potentially negative impact on providing culturally sensitive interventions.

Oncology social workers are exceptional at educating and collaborating with the patients and families they serve and building and maintaining good cancer care teams. They are excellent problem solvers, effective advocates, and skilled at looking at the big picture. They serve on the front lines of oncology care, know about problems and barriers experienced by their patients, care deeply about those patients, and are passionate about the psychosocial care of individuals and families affected by cancer. In using their cultural skills and knowledge and taking a culturally humble perspective, oncology social workers can continue to provide psychosocial care that acknowledges and honors diversity in all of its forms.

ADDITIONAL RESOURCES

Altilio, T., & Otis-Green, S. (Eds.). (2011). *Oxford textbook of palliative social work*. New York, NY: Oxford University Press.

Institute of Medicine. (2008). *Cancer care for the whole patient: Meeting psychosocial health needs*. Washington, DC: National Academies Press.

U.S. Department of Health and Human Services Office of Minority Health. (2013). *National culturally and linguistically appropriate services standards in health and health care*. Retrieved from http://minorityhealth.hhs.gov/templates/browse.aspx?lvl=2&lvlID=15

REFERENCES

Agency for Healthcare Research and Quality. (2012). *National healthcare disparities report 2012*. Rockville, MD: U.S. Department of Health and Human Services.

American Cancer Society (ACS). (2013). *Cancer facts and figures 2013*. Atlanta, GA: Author.

Association of Oncology Social Work (AOSW). (2012). *AOSW standards of practice in oncology social work*. Retrieved from http://aosw.org/standards-of-practice/

Centers for Disease Control and Prevention. (2011). *Health insurance coverage: Early release of estimates from the national health interview survey, 2011*. Retrieved from http://www.cdc.gov/nchs/data/nhis/earlyrelease/insur201206.pdf

Chang, E. S., Simon, M., & Dong, X. (2012). Integrating cultural humility into health care professional education and training. *Advances in Health Science Education, 17*(2), 269–278.

Cohn, V., & Taylor, P. (2012). A milestone en route to a majority minority nation. Washington, DC: Pew Research Social & Demographic Trends. Retrieved from http://www.pewsocialtrends.org/2012/11/07/a-milestone-en-route-to-a-majority-minority-nation/

Columna, L., Foley, J. T., & Lytle, R. K. (2010). Physical education teachers' and teacher candidates' attitudes toward cultural pluralism. *Journal of Teaching in Physical Education, 29*(3), 295–311.

Institute of Medicine. (2012). *How far have we come in reducing health disparities?: Progress since 2000: Workshop summary*. Washington, DC: National Academies Press.

King, M. L., Jr. (1966, March 25). Keynote address. Speech presented at the Second National Convention of the Medical Committee for Human Rights, Chicago, IL.

National Association of Social Workers (NASW). (2001). *NASW standards for cultural competence in social work practice*. Washington, DC: Author. Retrieved from http://www.naswdc.org/practice/standards/NASWculturalstandards.pdf

National Association of Social Workers (NASW). (2006). *Assuring the sufficiency of a frontline workforce: A national study of licensed social workers.* Retrieved from http://workforce.socialworkers.org/studies/nasw_06_execsummary.pdf

National Poverty Center. (2014). Poverty in the United States: Frequently asked questions. Retrieved from http://www.npc.umich.edu/poverty/

Ross, L. (2010). Notes from the field: Learning cultural humility through critical incidents and central challenges in community-based participatory research. *Journal of Community Practice, 18*(2–3), 315–335.

Shapiro, J., Lie, D., Gutierrez, D., & Zhuang, G. (2006). "That never would have occurred to me": A qualitative study of medical students' views of a cultural competence curriculum. *BMC Medical Education, 6*, 31.

Smedley, B. D., Stith, A. Y., & Nelson, A. R. (2002). *Unequal treatment: Confronting racial and ethnic disparities in health care.* Washington, DC: National Academies Press.

Tervalon, M., & Murray-García, J. (1998). Cultural humility versus cultural competence: A critical distinction in defining physician training outcomes in multicultural education. *Journal of Health Care for the Poor and Underserved, 9*(2), 117–125.

U.S. Census Bureau. (2012). *Americans with disabilities: 2010.* Retrieved from http://www.census.gov/prod/2012pubs/p70-131.pdf

U.S. Census Bureau. (2014). State and county quick facts. Retrieved from http://quickfacts.census.gov/qfd/states/00000.html

U.S. Department of Health and Human Services Administration on Aging. (2011). *A profile of older Americans: 2011.* Retrieved from http://www.aoa.gov/Aging_Statistics/Profile/2011/docs/2011profile.pdf

Williams Institute. (2011). *How many people are lesbian, gay, bisexual, and transgender?* Retrieved from http://williamsinstitute.law.ucla.edu/wp-content/uploads/Gates-How-Many-People-LGBT-Apr-2011.pdf

37 Support for Immigrants, Political Refugees, and Patients Seeking Asylum Who Have Cancer

Amanda Amodio and Upal Basu Roy

Key Concepts

- *Immigrants, refugees, and asylum seekers are unique minority populations whose health care needs are traditionally underserved in the United States and globally.*
- *They face similar structural barriers and psychosocial challenges when confronted with a cancer diagnosis and express their own cultural beliefs and attitudes toward illness. This may influence their health-seeking behavior across the disease trajectory, from preventive screening to palliative care.*
- *Access to care, potential trauma history, migration status, and immediate versus distant needs following a cancer diagnosis impact social work intervention.*
- *The social-ecological framework can guide oncology social work intervention geared toward this population.*

This chapter describes the cancer experience in a unique minority population in the United States of America—immigrants, refugees, and asylum seekers—often called aliens (despite the unsupportive connotation of the word) or noncitizens by the U.S. Citizenship and Immigration Services (USCIS). It explains the fundamental differences among these groups and highlights important concepts that social workers need to be mindful of when planning social work interventions and program development for these distinct groups.

Oncology social workers must possess basic tenets of cultural competence and have knowledge of community resources serving various immigrant groups and vulnerable populations, such as refugees. There exists a critical role for social workers to assist immigrants and refugees navigating the health and mental health systems. An astute awareness of oncology-related health and support services and knowledge of sources of financial assistance are core components of the role.

Cancer Disparities in Immigrants, Asylum Seekers, and Refugees

Although there is increasing evidence that minorities and underserved populations share a large proportion of the cancer burden, there is little social work literature devoted uniquely to the needs of noncitizens. The USCIS defines an immigrant as a foreign national who voluntarily declares his or her intent to take up permanent residence in the United States for purposes of employment or family union (USCIS, 2012). Refugees are persons who, owing to a well-founded fear of being persecuted for reasons of race, religion, nationality, membership in a particular social group, or political opinion, are outside the country of their nationality and unable (or, owing to such fear, is unwilling) to avail themselves of the protection of that country (UNHCR, 2011). According to the USCIS (2012), refugee status is often granted as a form of protection to those who meet the definition of a refugee and are of special humanitarian concern to the United States. Asylum status is a form of protection available to those who meet the definition of refugee, are already in the United States, and are seeking admission at a port of entry (USCIS, 2012). For refugees seeking asylum, a detailed health examination by physicians and mental health professionals, such as licensed clinical social workers, documenting the aftermath of physical and emotional trauma has been demonstrated to increase asylum grant rates (Lustig, Kureshi, Delucchi, Iacopino, & Morse, 2008). These evaluations or affidavits are often considered to be critical components of the asylum application as part of the documentation submitted for judicial review (Physicians for Human Rights, 2012). Though health screening is often conducted overseas, many screening practices are often cursory and geared toward contagious diseases (Smith, 2006). Thus, a cancer diagnosis might come as a surprise to an asylee, especially if the person has previously been screened in his or her home country. This may be an especially traumatic experience because the patient is potentially dealing with multiple stressors at the same time.

Most studies that discuss the cancer experience in this population (immigrants, refugees, and asylum seekers) tend to focus primarily on immigrants. As evident from their classification, these three groups experience similar and unique barriers in navigating and accessing the health care system in the United States. Although there has been a steady decline in the overall incidence and mortality of cancer in the United States, noncitizens continue to experience disparities in incidence, prevalence, mortality, and burden of cancer (ACS, 2012).

In 2011, 39,955,854 foreign-born persons (12.9% of the total U.S. population) lived in the United States, including 264,263 refugees and asylum seekers and those who are awaiting formal refugee and asylum status (MPI, 2010; UNHCR, 2011). Foreign-born persons include naturalized citizens, lawful permanent residents, certain legal nonimmigrants (e.g., persons on student or work visas), those admitted under refugee or asylum status, and persons illegally residing in the United States (MPI, 2010). Several studies have demarcated the incidence of cancer among various immigrant and ethnic minority groups living in the United States, but these statistics often consider aggregated data and do not include specific statistical information about refugees and asylum seekers. This makes it difficult to estimate accurately the true cancer burden among immigrants and refugees, further exacerbating the unmet needs of this population.

Socioecological Framework: The Role of Oncology Social Workers

Though suffering is an individual experience, one's perspective is often influenced by one's personal history, culture, religious beliefs, and socioeconomic status and the sociopolitical structure of one's community and country (Barton-Burke, Barreto, & Archibald, 2008). The multidimensional impact of a cancer diagnosis and its sequelae may be understood by using the lens of the socioecological model. This model provides the oncology social worker with an effective conceptual framework to understand the interaction among various factors that influence the patient's behavior and experience across the disease continuum, from prevention to diagnosis to palliative care (Ockene et al., 2007). These factors can be categorized into the following elements (micro-, meso-, macro-), which come together to provide an in-depth analysis that should inform social workers and other multidisciplinary health professionals who interact with people living with cancer who are classified under this group (Figure 37.1).

Micro-Level Factors

The current cultural and demographic landscape in the United States is constantly shifting. Ethnic minorities make up 100 million of the approximately 300 million Americans. With over 100 million immigrants entering the country annually, the United States is becoming increasingly more diverse in terms of language, ethnicity, and religion. It is predicted that the United States won't have any categorized racial or ethnic majority at some point between 2050 and 2100 (NASW, 2005).

Demographic change and migration are strong predictors that health care providers will increasingly care for

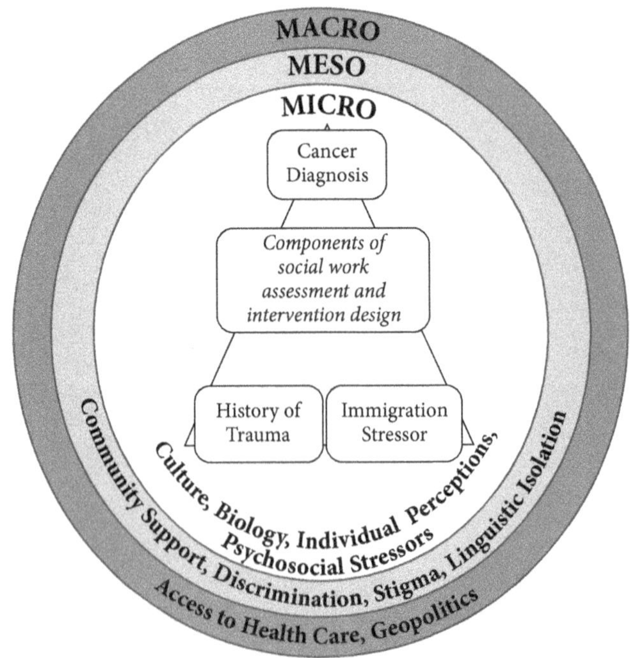

Figure 37.1. Applying the Social-Ecological Framework to Oncology Social Work Intervention for Noncitizens
This figure provides a framework to understand mental health needs and design effective social work programs and interventions for immigrants, refugees, and asylum seekers.
(Amodio and Basu-Roy, used with permission).

patients from cultural backgrounds other than their own (Crawley, Marshall, Lo, & Koenig, 2002). Although social workers are trained to adapt interventions to a particular population, they often work as part of a multidisciplinary team, and part of their role is to educate other staff and advocate for patients in accordance with their needs and wishes.

In the United States, the larger, dominant European American society is the milieu through which the biopsychosocial-cultural model occurs at each stage on the continuum of cancer care. Some core values of Northwestern European philosophy view the individual as autonomous, egalitarian, rational, self-assertive, and self-aware. These values, however, are not held in the same regard, if at all, by members of cultures that follow more sociocentric or community-centered lifestyles. Members of cultural groups have varying degrees of adherence to cultural beliefs and practices (Kagawa-Singer, Dadia, Yu, & Surbone, 2010). For the purposes of this chapter, it is imperative to consider the potential impact of culture on individual and community illness behavior (defined as how patients think, react, and cope when they suffer from illness) while taking care not to generalize an individual's belief to the entire community of a particular group. A common example in oncology care is the role that family members play in assisting patients with care decisions and care planning. They may take on the responsibility of deciding on treatment options, withholding sensitive information from patients, or making decisions around goals of care without consulting the patient in accordance with cultural values and norms. Disagreements about truth telling are common because practices of nondisclosure persist in many countries, despite a shift toward more open communication with cancer patients worldwide (Kagawa-Singer et al., 2010). Often, the social worker collects important data about the patient's and family members' preferences, wishes around goals of care, styles of coping, and relationship patterns that may inform team members and influence care planning.

An understanding of the unique and varied mental health considerations affecting immigrants and refugees is critical to the success of social work assessment, selection of appropriate interventions, and overall practice models (Burnett & Peel, 2001). Immigrants, refugees, and asylum seekers may share commonalities in their cancer experience in a new country, but differences due to the nature of departure from the home country might surface. Unlike the voluntary nature of departure for immigrants, refugees and asylum seekers may have inevitably endured various forms of torture, trauma, and fear of execution, forcing them to flee their home countries or live in exile. Such populations have been found to exhibit symptoms of posttraumatic stress disorder and other psychiatric comorbidities (APA, 2000). Undergoing invasive procedures or treatments and living with the uncertainty of progression of disease or overall prognosis—all parts of a patient's cancer experience—may or may not exacerbate already existing psychological symptoms. Often, the role of the social worker in a health care setting is to advocate for the expansion of or increased access to more specialized mental health services such as referral to psychiatry or advocacy and referral for ongoing psychotherapeutic services (Murray, Davidson, & Schweitzer, 2010).

Meso-Level Factors

Immigrants, refugees, and asylum seekers face many health care challenges, including but not limited to facing linguistic barriers, dealing with physical and/or emotional traumas, resettling in a foreign environment, and having few medical services, especially preventive screening, before their arrival to the United States (Saadi, Bond, & Percac-Lima, 2012). A study by Barnes and Harrison (2004) conducted among Vietnamese, Cuban, and Bosnian refugee women revealed that 86% of them had never had a mammogram in their lifetime, compared to 33% of American-born women.

Linguistic isolation, lack of social support, and stigmas that may be associated with a chronic and debilitating illness such as cancer (Porter & Haslam, 2005) are of interest to the social worker in any setting. A study by Percac-Lima, Milosavljevic, Oo, Marable, and Bond (2012) found that patients who spoke Serbo-Croatian were less likely to have had preventive mammograms as compared to English- and Spanish-speaking patients. Similarly, other studies (Redwood-Campbell, Fowler, Laryea, Howard, & Kaczorowski, 2011; Sussner et al., 2009) have demonstrated that the stigma associated with screening for and having cancer influence the health-seeking behavior of women during breast and cervical cancer screening. Although health care professionals receive training in cultural competency geared toward ethnic minorities residing in the United States, they should recognize how services they provide might need to be tailored toward immigrants and refugees, many of whom might have limited English proficiency (Yakushko, 2010). An important part of the social work role is to reduce the stigma associated with membership in a particular ethnic group, limited English proficiency, or migration status and facilitate effective communication with health care professionals.

Macro-Level Factors

Macro-level factors typically include the geopolitical and social context of the population and typically cannot be changed or controlled easily. When working with asylum seekers and refugees, it is especially important to be aware of these factors.

Typically, the United States allows the admission of a fixed number of refugees and asylum seekers each year. This number is often controlled by the current political climate of the United States and the foreign policy stipulations and the ties that the United States shares with the country from which refugees are seeking asylum. Another factor that controls the profile of refugees being settled in the United States is the representations from the United Nations High Commissioner for Refugees to the U.S. government (Smith, 2006). Refugees from a country with strained ties with the United States might harbor suspicion and mistrust toward U.S. health care professionals (Hadley & Patil, 2009). Such biases might also exist toward refugees. Discrimination has been documented toward the Iraqi refugee population, for example, and is a severe impediment to accessing health care (Inhorn & Serour, 2011).

Other factors governed by the political climate are access to health care and changes to immigration reform. The Patient Protection and Affordable Care Act (2010) stipulates insurance coverage for the 32 million uninsured Americans, improvement in affordability and stability of insurance for the already insured, and decreased health care costs to improve the federal budget deficit (Tuma, 2012). Lack of health insurance and fear of deportation might influence the health-seeking behavior of the patient. The social worker may participate in lobbying efforts to influence legislation that may affect immigration policy or affect expansion of access to health care and raise awareness of barriers affecting marginalized populations.

A 79-year-old man is receiving specialized inpatient oncology care and is referred to social work for assessment of anxiety. A psychosocial history is performed and the social worker learns that one source of anxiety for his patient is the care of his wife, who has a neurological condition. His adult son is filling the role of caregiver temporarily. He further reflects on his cancer diagnosis and the significance of it in the context of his life span to date. He becomes tearful, explaining that he and his brother had together been business owners and later prisoners of war, captured and imprisoned in a nearby country for their presumed political views. The patient's brother died of starvation in the prison. The patient recalls the suffering endured and his decision to start a new life in the United States. Clearly, the feelings associated with this traumatic life experience have surfaced during his inpatient stay for oncology care.

Possible Assessment Questions

- *What do you want to know about your condition?*
- *Do you feel that your medical team understands your wishes? How do you think your medical team can better serve you?*
- *Does anyone know about your condition? With whom may we speak about your treatments and potential outcomes?*
- *Whom do you want to make health care decisions for you now or if you are unable to do so in the future?*
- *How are you coping with your diagnosis?*
- *Is your immigration status of primary concern at this time? Do you feel safe here? (Reassure the patient about social workers' neutrality related to immigration policies.)*
- *Are you able to communicate with family or friends in your country of origin? Is this important for you?*
- *Do you have a cultural or spiritual practice that you wish to observe?*

Pearls

- Social workers are in a unique position to help noncitizens navigate a complex and sometimes highly structured health care system and to assist those who are at high risk for poor outcomes due to potential inability to access specialized care or resources needed to support care.
- The advocacy and education roles social workers perform may be heightened as increased awareness of new health care policies and changes related to immigration reform have emerged and may be relevant to this population.

Pitfalls

- Immigrants, refugees, and asylum seekers have often been studied as an aggregate group along with other ethnic minority patients. While this approach was feasible when group-level data was unavailable, such an approach needs to be revised because aggregation of these three populations into one category of "ethnic minorities" underestimates the needs of the most vulnerable groups.
- At the time of publication of this chapter, the fate of health care coverage of undocumented immigrants and asylum seekers remains to be seen, as it is unlikely that access to health insurance coverage will readily be available to noncitizens or those who have been residents for a short period of time.

The social work profession's commitment to social justice will inevitably bring oncology social workers into contact with the vulnerable populations described in this chapter. It is therefore critical for social workers to have an awareness of their own ethnic and cultural heritage juxtaposed with a working knowledge of immigration and health policies within their current sociopolitical climate. Furthermore, an oncology social worker who deals with immigrants, refugees, and asylum seekers should make special efforts to avoid potential bias in assessment instruments and diagnostic systems Finally, creative approaches to navigate institutional and systemic barriers will be essential for the development and implementation of culturally appropriate interventions.

Tips

- The oncology social worker well versed in community and national resources for noncitizens will be best able to refer clients to appropriate agencies.
- The oncology social worker's advocacy role and investment in continuity of care may help refugees or asylum seekers connect with resources that they would not be able to access or navigate on their own.
- The oncology social worker may facilitate and serve as a navigator for the mandatory health examination required for immigration.

ADDITIONAL RESOURCES

Books/Reports

Akhtar, S. (1999). *Immigration and identity: Turmoil, treatment, and transformation*. Northvale, NJ: Jason Aronson.

Feser, L. (2003). Cultural competence and cross cultural care at the end of life. Retrieved from http://virtualhospice.ca/Assets/loreen%20feser%20-%20culture_20081127165937.pdf

Websites

Bellevue/NYU Program for Survivors of Torture: http://www.survivorsoftorture.org/files/pdf/psot_resource_book.pdf

HealthRight International: http://www.healthright.org

Human Rights Watch: http://www.hrw.org

Immigration Law Help: http://www.immigrationlawhelp.org/

National Network for Immigrant and Refugee Rights: http://www.nnirr.org/drupal/

Refugee & Immigrant Fund (RiF): http://www.rifnyc.org/

U.S. Citizenship and Immigration Services: http://www.uscis.gov/humanitarian/refugees-asylum/asylum

U.S. Department of Health and Human Services Office of Refugee Resettlement: http://www.acf.hhs.gov/programs/orr/

U.S. Department of Justice Free Legal Services Providers: http://www.justice.gov/eoir/probono/states.htm

REFERENCES

American Cancer Society (ACS). (2012). *Priority focus in cancer control and prevention research program: Health disparities research*. Retrieved from http://www.cancer.org/Research/ResearchProgramsFunding/FundingOpportunities/IndexofGrants/NewInitiatives/priority-focus-in-cancer-control-and-prevention-research-program- health-disparities-research

American Psychiatric Association (APA). (2000). *Diagnostic and statistical manual of mental disorders* (4th ed., text revision). Arlington, VA: Author.

Barnes, D. M., & Harrison, C. L. (2004). Refugee women's reproductive health in early resettlement. *Journal of Obstetric, Gynecologic, and Neonatal Nursing, 33*(6), 723–728.

Barton-Burke, M., Barreto, Jr., R. C., & Archibald, L. I. (2008). Suffering as a multicultural cancer experience. *Seminars in Oncology Nursing, 24*(4), 229–236.

Burnett, A., & Peel, M. (2001). Health needs of asylum seekers and refugees. *British Medical Journal, 322*(7285), 544–547.

Crawley, L. M., Marshall, P. A., Lo, B., & Koenig, B. A. (2002). Strategies for culturally effective end-of-life care. *Annals of Internal Medicine, 136*(9), 673–679.

Hadley, C., & Patil, C. (2009). Perceived discrimination among three groups of refugees resettled in the U.S.: Associations with language, time in the U.S., and continent of origin. *Journal of Immigrant and Minority Health, 11*(6), 505–512.

Inhorn, M. C., & Serour, G. I. (2011). Islam, medicine, and Arab-Muslim refugee health in America after 9/11. *Lancet, 378*(9794), 935–943.

Kagawa-Singer, M., Dadia, A. V., Yu, M. C., & Surbone, A. (2010). Cancer, culture, and health disparities: Time to chart a new course? *CA: A Cancer Journal for Clinicians, 60*(1), 12–39.

Lustig, S. L., Kureshi, S., Delucchi, K. L., Iacopino, V., & Morse, S. C. (2008). Asylum grant rates following medical evaluations of maltreatment among political asylum applicants in the United States. *Journal of Immigrant and Minority Health, 10*(1), 7–15.

Migration Policy Institute (MPI). (2010). *2011 American community survey and census data on the foreign born by state*. Retrieved from http://www.migrationinformation.org/DataHub/acscensus.cfm

Murray, K. E., Davidson, G. R., & Schweitzer, R. D. (2010). Review of refugee mental health interventions following resettlement: Best practices and recommendations. *American Journal of Orthopsychiatry, 80*(4), 576–585.

National Association of Social Workers (NASW). (2005). *Practice update: Multiculturalism*. Retrieved from http://www.socialworkers.org/practice/equity/multiculturalism-PU0505.pdf

Ockene, J. K., Edgerton, E. A., Teutsch, S. M., Marion, L. N., Miller, T., & Genevro, J. L. (2007). Integrating evidence-based clinical and community strategies to improve health. *American Journal of Preventive Medicine, 32*(3), 244–252.

Percac-Lima, S., Milosavljevic, B., Oo, S. A., Marable, D., & Bond, B. (2012). Patient navigation to improve breast cancer screening in Bosnian refugees and immigrants. *Journal of Immigrant and Minority Health, 14*(4), 727–730.

Physicians for Human Rights. (2012). Examining asylum seekers: A clinician's guide to physical and psychological evaluations of torture and ill-treatment. Retrieved from http://physiciansforhumanrights.org/library/reports/examining-asylum-seekers-manual-2012.html

Porter, M., & Haslam, N. (2005). Predisplacement and postdisplacement factors associated with mental health of refugees and internally displaced persons: A meta-analysis. *Journal of the American Medical Association, 294*(5), 602–612.

Redwood-Campbell, L., Fowler, N., Laryea, S., Howard, M., & Kaczorowski, J. (2011). "Before you teach me, I cannot know": Immigrant women's barriers and enablers with regard to cervical cancer screening among different ethnolinguistic groups in Canada. *Canadian Journal of Public Health, 102*(3), 230–234.

Saadi, A., Bond, B., & Percac-Lima, S. (2012). Perspectives on preventive health care and barriers to breast cancer screening among Iraqi women refugees. *Journal of Immigrant and Minority Health*, *14*(4), 633–639.

Smith, M. M. (2006). Refugees in Australia: Changing faces, changing needs. *Medical Journal of Australia*, *185*(11–12), 587–588.

Sussner, K. M., Thompson, H. S., Jandorf, L., Edwards, T. A., Forman, A., & Brown, K. (2009). The influence of acculturation and breast cancer-specific distress on perceived barriers to genetic testing for breast cancer among women of African descent. *Psycho-Oncology*, *18*(9), 945–955.

Tuma, P. A. (2012). An overview of the intentions of health care reform. *Journal of the Academy of Nutrition and Dietetics*, *112*(3 Suppl.), S56–S63.

United Nations High Commissioner for Refugees (UNHCR). (2011). *Global trends 2011—A year of crisis*. Retrieved from http://www.unhcr.org/4fd6f87f9.html

U.S. Citizenship and Immigration Services. (2012). *U.S. Citizenship and Immigration Services*. Retrieved from http://www.uscis.gov/portal/site/uscis

Yakushko, O. (2010). Clinical work with limited English proficiency clients: A phenomenological exploration. *Professional Psychology: Research and Practice*, *41*(5), 449–455.

38

Kathryn M. Smolinski and William Goeren

Gay, Lesbian, and Bisexual Individuals Diagnosed With Cancer

Key Concepts

- *Members of the lesbian, gay, and bisexual[1] community historically have experienced discrimination within society in general and in health care settings more specifically, often facing insensitive, uninformed providers who fail to recognize the unique discrimination these individuals face due to institutional, internalized, and cultural homophobia.*
- *Although treatment issues for cancer patients can vary, members of the lesbian, gay, and bisexual community encounter additional barriers to accessing care, receiving treatment, and feeling comfortable within the health care system.*
- *Oncology social workers can cultivate an environment that is responsive to critical needs by developing excellent educational materials, clinical models of care, and research protocols focused on improving health care service delivery to lesbian, gay, and bisexual persons.*

Cancer is a disease that does not discriminate when it comes to individuals who identify as lesbian, gay, or bisexual (LGB). However, the health care system that treats them often does. Knowing the historical, cultural, social, and psychological context of health care disparities among LGB individuals in the United States is important when providing psychosocial care and services in the oncology setting. For LGB cancer patients, the effects of institutional, internalized, and cultural homophobia on the quality of and access to health care are additional stressors. Fortunately, trends in society and health care delivery have started to include education and interventions responsive to the needs of the LGB community. Oncology social workers need to be advocates to help eliminate health care disparities by providing care that is culturally sensitive and a health care environment that is welcoming and responsive. To do so, however, oncology social workers need to be aware of the unique cancer risks in the LGB community.

Cancer Incidence and Risk in the Lesbian, Gay, and Bisexual Community

For lesbians and gay men affected by cancer in the United States, there is scant recent research on cancer diagnoses, survivorship, and morbidity. However, available data reflect a higher rate of incidence within the LGB population of certain cancers. For example, the American Cancer Society (ACS) reported a general overall increased risk and higher rates of lung, breast, cervical, anal, and liver cancers within the LGB population (ACS, California Division, 2009). Human papilloma virus (HPV), a precursor to anal cancer, is found more often in gay men than in heterosexual men, and HIV infection, also seen more often in gay men, increases their risk for developing testicular cancer (ACS, California Division, 2009). Given its correlation with AIDS, Kaposi's sarcoma is more prevalent in gay and bisexual men than the general population, and the risk for AIDS-related non-Hodgkin lymphoma is increased in HIV-positive men. Lesbian women have higher rates of breast cancer and increased risks for cervical and ovarian cancers when compared to heterosexual women (ACS, 2013; Meyer & Northridge, 2007). Possible factors responsible for these increases are a lower frequency of childbearing, lack of contraceptive use, and possible use of fertility drugs among lesbian and bisexual women (ACS, 2013). Lesbians tend not to participate in cancer screenings, putting them at a higher risk for later-stage diagnoses (Boehmer, Miao, Linkletter, & Clark, 2012).

Risk factors such as obesity, high-fat diet, smoking, alcohol consumption, and recreational drug use most closely associated with a cancer diagnosis, especially lung and colon cancers, are more prevalent in the LGB community than among heterosexuals (Boehmer, Miao, & Ozonoff, 2012). The ACS reports that lesbians and bisexual women are more than twice as likely to smoke as heterosexual women (Boehmer, Miao, Linkletter, et al., 2012). Additionally, 42% of gay and bisexual men report being current tobacco users, greatly exceeding the national average of 29% (ACS, 2009; Boehmer, Miao, Linkletter, et al., 2012). Similar to lesbians, gay men do not participate in routine cancer screening, resulting in late-stage diagnoses. In fact, LGB individuals participate far less frequently in routine health care visits than heterosexual individuals. Oncology social workers who provide community outreach and education to the LGB population will want to stress the importance of routine screening and follow-up.

Psychosocial Stressors of Lesbian, Gay, and Bisexual Persons and the Role for Oncology Social Workers

Members of the LGB community historically have been discriminated against when seeking health care services. Although discrimination may be more passive than active, fear of and the perception of the existence of such discrimination can have a negative impact on seeking services. Delays in seeking health services for symptoms inevitably result in late-stage cancers at diagnosis (ACS, 2013; Harding, Epiphaniou, & Chidgey-Clark, 2012; Hutchinson, Thompson, & Cederbaum, 2006). Homophobia, the "dread of being in close quarters with homosexuals," and a "fear or hatred of anyone or anything connected with homosexuality" (Herek, Gillis, & Cogan, 2009, p. 1; Levine, 2001, p. 257) becomes socialized generationally into the fabric of cultural attitudes and actions. LGB persons aware of homophobia are more guarded during discussions about their health, for fear that "coming out" (disclosing one's sexual orientation) will lead to discrimination in the quality of care they receive. LGB persons tend not to disclose their sexual orientation and so forfeit the ability to access all supports that may be available.

Oncology social workers want to be aware of the possibility of this fear when working with clients they suspect may be members of the LGB community. Social workers may be the only persons who take the time to elicit information about the LGB patient's relationships and complete support system (Smolinski & Colón, 2006, 2011). Therefore, social workers will want to ask questions such as "How long have you been together?" rather than "How long have you been married?" Similarly, using "partner" versus "spouse" allows the client to define the relationship as he or she feels comfortable.

Language has been and always will be a very powerful tool for oncology social workers. In working with LGB persons, language can influence how the patient perceives the openness of the health care facility and whether it is a safe place to fully be "out." By using the same language as patients, asking about their support system rather than about children, and adopting open-ended, gender-neutral questions about supportive relationships and next of kin, social workers can create an inclusive environment. Such questions provide verbal cues of an accepting environment for the cancer patient to be more comfortable in defining the scope of any relationship. When sexual orientation or gender identity are unknown and a social worker's attitude and language do not express openness, it can be actively, if unwittingly, painful and alienating to the patient.

Oncology social workers at the provider level can incorporate effective education, inclusive language, and affirmative psychotherapy within their practice with LGB persons by affirming the strengths and healthy psychological core a client possesses. Inclusive language and education specifically geared toward LGB individuals have proven effective. In fact, screening for cervical and breast cancer increased in lesbians who participated in tailored risk counseling (Brown & Tracy, 2008) and tailored interventions improved the mental health of lesbian breast cancer patients (Fobair et al., 2002).

On a broader level, "institutional homophobia" manifests itself within systems like health care organizations when they "systematically discriminate on the basis of sexual orientation or identity" (Blumenfield, 1992, p. 5). Heterosexism perpetuates the belief that "heterosexuality is or should be the only acceptable sexual orientation" (Blumenfield, 1992, p. 15). Consequently, when LGB individuals incorporate these biases, they often experience diminished self-esteem, problematic intimate and relational attachments, and anticipatory rejection. Internalized homophobia aims to describe a "sexual identity characterized by persistent, structured negative feelings, particularly shame and self-loathing" (Allen & Oleson, 1999, p. 34). Oncology social workers need to assess whether an LGB cancer patient may be experiencing such feelings and provide the appropriate supportive therapy to combat low self-esteem.

Interventions at the health care institutional level are just as critical as those at the provider level. This is because the clinic environment, from intake forms to welcome signs to waiting room literature and images, is the first impression patients have about a health care setting. Unfriendly and noninclusive policies and practices may prevent a patient from completing a screening test or returning for follow-up. Social workers must be keenly aware of the environment in which patients are being treated. They can then advocate for inclusive forms and documentation that are LGB friendly, as well as making LGB-friendly fliers, magazines, and other materials available in public areas and treatment rooms (Wilkerson, Rybicki, Barber, & Smolenski, 2011). They can insist on visitation policies that include partners, public postings of nondiscrimination declarations that include language about sexual orientation, professional sensitivity training for all staff, and a transparent avenue for complaints when discrimination does exist (Hutchinson et al., 2006; Wheeler & Dodd, 2011).

The HIV/AIDS epidemic had a unifying and mobilizing effect for gay men and fostered an increase in attention to their medical and psychosocial needs, but the stigma of HIV continues. For lesbians, fear of homophobia could be one explanation for a review study's finding that lesbian and bisexual female cancer survivors reported fair or poor health when compared to heterosexual female cancer survivors (Boehmer, Miao, & Ozonoff, 2011; Boehmer, Miao, Linkletter, et al., 2012). However, there was no difference in the prevalence of cancer among the heterosexual and lesbian participants in the study. The authors suggest that psychosocial interventions focused on helping lesbians change their perception of care may be invaluable in helping them achieve better health outcomes.

LGB cancer patients must receive medical care in knowledgeable, safe, and welcoming environments. Fears of adverse reactions and ostracism; lack of gay-positive or homosexual-normative medical literature, such as intake and assessment forms; and limited or nonexistent cultural competence training result in poorer treatment and health outcomes for LGB individuals. Fearing negative interactions with health care providers, complicated by previous discrimination, some members of the LGB community will delay treatment or avoid maintaining health care. Other LGB individuals may pursue health care in an active and timely manner but not disclose their orientation.

Paul, a 35-year-old gay man, arrived at a New York City cancer support organization inquiring about counseling services. Having just completed surgery and radiation for his Stage 2 salivary gland cancer, Paul stated that searching out emotional support for his cancer had been unexpectedly and painfully stalled because of a negative and upsetting experience during his radiation treatment. He reported that during his series of radiation treatments, he had established an easy, conversational rapport with the technician. When he came out (disclosed his sexual orientation) to the technician, the tenor of the relationship completely shifted. The technician from that session became cold, rude, brusque, and professionally inconsiderate. He occasionally made Paul wait for extended periods to receive his treatment for no understandable reason. Paul attributed this blatant attitude change to homophobia.

LGB cancer patients endure more psychosocial stressors in addition to the fear and stress associated with homophobia. Issues regarding support and legal and financial security can impact LGB cancer individuals because relationships for LGB individuals involve more than just those with their health care providers. Familial and caregiver support are instrumental in helping cancer patients navigate treatment. However, fear of discrimination or lack of acceptance within an LGB patient's own family and community can be just as detrimental in coping with cancer as experiencing it within the health care setting. LGB seniors, for example, are at the greatest risk because they are more likely to live alone, endure poverty, and be reluctant to disclose to health care providers (Brennan-Ing, Karpiak, & Seidel, 2011; Lee & Quam, 2013). The documentary *Gen Silent* captures eloquently the fear and dread with which LGB seniors are living as they age and need access to more health care services from providers who want to "heal" them of their sexual orientation or bully them into silence (Maddux, 2011). LGB individuals whose families are not accepting and not connected with the LGB community may be especially at risk for poor coping and adjustment.

Finally, basic legal and financial supports available to heterosexual cancer patients are not as easily accessible for LGB individuals. For example, LGB individuals tend to avoid care due to inadequate insurance coverage and insufficient financial and legal resources (ACS, 2013; Harding et al., 2012). Many corporate and state employers still do not extend health insurance and other benefits to partners of LGB employees. Completing state and federal benefit forms that are not LGB friendly can be further alienating for LGB persons. In states where same-sex marriages are not recognized, LGB cancer patients have to be extremely diligent in preparing powers of attorney for health care and finances, among other arrangements, because state law does not automatically grant those protections.

Renée was diligent in her care and attention of Samantha, who had been diagnosed with breast cancer. After surgery, recovery, and treatment, Samantha had been doing well and they enjoyed living in the home Samantha solely owned. Because of the intense schedule of treatment, the couple never got around to preparing advance directives or wills or done any legal planning. Unexpectedly, Samantha was hospitalized with a serious infection. Samantha's parents, who never sanctioned the couple's relationship, were devastated that she was so ill. Exercising their rights under the law, they became decision makers for Samantha's care, leaving Renée out of the conversations and discussions. Upon Samantha's death, Renée was asked to move out by the family and she had no legal recourse to preserve the home she and Samantha had made.

Oncology social workers need to be aware of their own biases when working with LGB persons, as well as any bias among members of the health care team. Being aware of personal feelings is important in identifying how it may impact interventions with LGB persons. Inquiring whether a patient holds beliefs that are prevalent within the LGB culture is helpful, but the social worker must be aware of what beliefs are in the local LGB community. It is important to know what LGB resources are available nationally and locally. If patients disclose being LGB, staff need to inform them of services and resources with which they may not be familiar. Finally, being cognizant of state laws, especially those regarding family, custody, marriage, and advance directives, can be very helpful when trying to assist LGB persons in decision making and long-term planning that is routine during cancer treatment. Hopefully, oncology social workers will be inspired by society's increasing acceptance of LGB individuals.

Affirmative Trends in Society and Health Care for the Lesbian, Gay, and Bisexual Community

Education, advocacy, awareness, and action initiate and institute improvement and evolution of health care policies and practices. In 1996, the American Medical Association recommended that medical students and physicians receive better medical training to address resolving the health care disparities experienced by LGB persons (Sanchez, Rabatin, Sanchez, Hubbard, & Kalet, 2006). In 2012, Kathleen Sebelius, secretary of the Health and Human Services Department, cosponsored the first White House LGBT Conference to provide advocates, community leaders, and health care providers the first federally sponsored opportunity to discuss the health care needs of lesbian, gay, bisexual, and transgender (LGBT) American citizens (U.S. Department of Health & Human Services, 2012).

Before this historic event, the National Association of Social Workers (NASW) had written clear guidelines that established directives for professional social work policy with LGB clients. The NASW's statement can be viewed as a "blueprint" for social work's role in addressing the concerns and strengths of LGB clients and communities. The NASW strongly advocates for the availability of culturally appropriate comprehensive health and mental health services for LGB populations across the life span (NASW, 2009). Additionally, the Institute of Medicine (2011) provided a report that is exclusive to the health status of LGBT populations, identifies research gaps, and discusses opportunities to conduct research in the future.

Finally, legal supports for LGB persons have increased. The increase in state-sanctioned same-sex marriages, coupled with federal recognition of those marriages, has allowed LGB persons to access resources for and attain social recognition for their relationships. The cultural and psychosocial consequences were immediately noticeable in news reports showing throngs of LGB persons celebrating in city streets and state capitols. In 2013, the U.S. federal government began to extend benefits, including health insurance and veterans and retirement benefits, to partners of those LGB couples affected by the Supreme Court's decision to strike down the Defense of Marriage Act and recognize same-sex marriages on a federal level for those individuals who are recognized in their state.

In addition to trends in the United States, the needs of LGB persons within health care have been addressed abroad. In Britain in 2012, the National Council for Palliative Care and the Consortium of Lesbian, Gay, Bisexual, and Transgendered Voluntary and Community Organizations published a report after surveying over 700 health care providers, service organizations, and consumers (Dying Matters, 2012). The report makes numerous recommendations for institutions and providers in end-of-life care. Suggestions include increasing the links between care providers and the LGBT community, reviewing staff training, and ensuring appropriate language and use of positive images of LGBT people in promotional materials. Subsequently, Britain held the first-ever national conference specifically focused on end-of-life care for LGBT persons (National Council for Palliative Care, 2012). It can be surmised that health care providers are beginning to understand the unique needs of LGB individuals.

Pearls

- As societal trends and laws continue to reflect a greater acceptance of LGB persons, relationships, and families, oncology social workers need to ensure that laws and policies are proactively institutionalized and enforced in their own health care setting.
- Social workers can lead the training of oncology colleagues on LGB issues, disseminating information and being catalysts for dialogue when homophobia, discrimination, and prejudice are present.
- Oncology social workers are the voice of all people, including sexual minorities. As they promote client advocacy, policy change, and procedural transformation for their LGB clients, they must also promote professional self-awareness.

Pitfalls

- Social workers must take the time to consult the professional literature, attend continuing education training, and use supervision to provide optimal psychosocial care to LGB individuals.
- Homophobia is individually, socially, and culturally damaging to all people. Health care providers still may continue with biased attitudes and discriminatory behaviors against LGB cancer patients despite societal trends indicating acceptance of LGB persons.

- Individual health care providers and health care institutions may unintentionally enable biased attitudes and discriminatory behaviors against LGB patients. Documents and institutional forms that do not include LGB options can be interpreted as passively prejudiced and be the catalyst for unrealized health care disparity.

Oncology social workers are in a uniquely responsible position to be professional catalysts for institutional, organizational, and policy change by identifying existing health disparities and institutional homophobia. Social workers must model for other health care team members the most culturally respectful way to respond to the needs of gay men, lesbians, and bisexual individuals coping with a cancer diagnosis. By responding actively to homophobic reactions on the part of staff or colleagues, dispelling myths about homosexuality, and advocating for clients, social workers can effect change within their health care setting. Oncology social workers must be leaders within institution-wide committees focused on patient diversity, education, and outreach; incorporate gender-neutral patient forms and materials; and make visible nondiscrimination policies. Finally, oncology social workers must support funding research that seeks not only to examine the health disparities within the LGB cancer population but also to understand and train providers in providing sensitive and competent care to this community.

NOTE

1. The authors have not specifically addressed the needs of transgendered individuals as those are discussed in Chapter 39.

ADDITIONAL RESOURCES

Advancing Effective Communication, Cultural Competence, and Patient- and Family-Centered Care for the Lesbian, Gay, Bisexual, and Transgender (LGBT) Community—A Field Guide: http://www.jointcommission.org/assets/1/18/LGBTFieldGuide.pdf
Bisexual Invisibility: Impacts and Recommendations: http://www.sf-hrc.org/modules/showdocument.aspx?documentid=989
Centers for Disease Control and Prevention Lesbian, Gay, Bisexual, and Transgender Health Resources: http://www.cdc.gov/lgbthealth/links.htm
Gay and Lesbian Medical Association: http://www.glma.org/
Healthy People 2020 LGBT Companion Document: http://healthypeople.gov/2020/topicsobjectives2020/objectiveslist.aspx?topicId=25
Human Rights Campaign: http://www.hrc.org/
Journal of Gay and Lesbian Social Services: http://www.tandfonline.com/loi/wgls20
Lambda Legal: http://www.lambdalegal.org/
Mautner Project of Whitman-Walker Health: http://www.whitman-walker.org/mautnerproject
National Coalition of LGBT Health: http://lgbthealth.webolutionary.com/
National Gay and Lesbian Task Force: http://thetaskforce.org/
National LGBT Cancer Network: http://www.cancer-network.org/
National LGBT Cancer Project: http://lgbtcancer.com/
National LGBT Tobacco Control Network: http://www.lgbttobacco.org/
National Resource Center on LGBT Aging: http://www.lgbtagingcenter.org
Network for LGBT Health Equity: https://lgbthealthequity.wordpress.com/
Out with Cancer Social Network: http://www.outwithcancer.com/

REFERENCES

Allen, D., & Oleson, T. (1999). Shame and internalized homophobia in gay men. *Journal of Homosexuality*, *37*(3), 33–43.
American Cancer Society (ACS). (2013). Cancer facts for lesbians and bisexual women. Retrieved from http://www.cancer.org/healthy/findcancerearly/womenshealth/cancer-facts-for-lesbians-and-bisexual-women
American Cancer Society (ACS), California Division. (2009). *California cancer facts and figures 2010*. Retrieved from http://www.ccrcal.org/pdf/Reports/ACS2010-9-29-09.pdf
Blumenfield, W. (Ed.). (1992). *Homophobia: How we all pay the price*. Boston, MA: Beacon Press.
Boehmer, U., Miao, X., & Ozonoff, A. (2011). Cancer survivorship and sexual orientation. *Cancer*, *117*(16), 3796–3804.
Boehmer, U., Miao, X., & Ozonoff, A. (2012). Health behaviors of cancer survivors of different sexual orientations. *Cancer Causes and Control*, *23*(9), 1489–1496.
Boehmer, U., Miao, X., Linkletter, C., & Clark, M. A. (2012). Adult health behaviors over the life course by sexual orientation. *American Journal of Public Health*, *102*(2), 292–300.
Brennan-Ing, M., Karpiak, S., & Seidel, L. (2011). *Health and psychosocial needs of LGBT older adults*. Retrieved from http://www.lgbtagingcenter.org/resources/pdfs/COH%20Study%20Final%20Report%20091911.pdf
Brown, T., & Tracy, J. K. (2008). Lesbians and cancer: An overlooked health disparity. *Cancer Causes and Control*, *19*(10), 1009–1020.
Dying Matters. (2012). LGBT people "let down" by end-of-life care services. Retrieved from http://dyingmatters.org/page/lgbt-people-let-down-end-life-care-services
Fobair, P., Koopman, C., DiMiceli, S., O'Hanlan, K., Butler, L. D., Classen, C., . . . Spiegel, D. (2002). Psychosocial intervention for lesbians with primary breast cancer. *Psycho-Oncology*, *11*(5), 427–438.
Harding, R., Epiphaniou, E., & Chidgey-Clark, J. (2012). Needs, experiences and preferences of sexual minorities for end-of-life care and palliative care: A systematic review. *Journal of Palliative Medicine*, *15*(5), 602–611.
Herek, G., Gillis, J. R., & Cogan, J. (2009). Internalized stigma among sexual minority adults: Insights from a psychological perspective. *Journal of Counseling Psychology*, *56*(1), 32–43.
Hutchinson, M. K., Thompson, A. C., & Cederbaum, J. A. (2006). Multisystem factors contributing to disparities in preventive health care among lesbian women. *Journal of Obstetric, Gynecologic, and Neonatal Nursing*, *35*(3), 393–402.

Institute of Medicine. (2011). *The health of lesbian, gay, bisexual, and transgender people: Building a foundation for better understanding.* Washington, DC: National Academy of Sciences.

Lee, M., & Quam, J. (2013). Comparing supports for LGBT aging in rural versus urban areas. *Journal of Gerontological Social Work, 56*(2), 112–126.

Levine, E. (2001). Special issues for gays and lesbians with cancer. In M. Lauria, E. J. Clark, J. F. Hermann, & N. M. Stearns (Eds.), *Social work in oncology: Supporting survivors, families, and caregivers.* Atlanta, GA: American Cancer Society.

Maddux, S. (Producer and Director). (2011). *Gen silent* [DVD]. United States: Interrobang Productions.

Meyer, I. H., & Northridge, M. E. (Eds.). (2007). *The health of sexual minorities: Public health perspectives on lesbian, gay, bisexual, and transgender populations.* New York, NY: Springer.

National Association of Social Workers (NASW). (2009). Lesbian, gay, and bisexual issues. In *Social work speaks: National Association of Social Workers policy statements 2009–2012.* Washington, DC: NASW Press.

National Council for Palliative Care. (2012). First ever national conference on end of life care for lesbian, gay, bisexual, and transgender people. Retrieved from http://www.ncpc.org.uk/news/first-ever-national-conference-end-life-care-lesbian-gay-bisexual-and-transgender-people

Sanchez, N. F., Rabatin, J., Sanchez, J. P., Hubbard, S., & Kalet, A. (2006). Medical students' ability to care for lesbian, gay, bisexual, and transgendered patients. *Family Medicine, 38*(1), 21–27.

Smolinski, K. M., & Colón, Y. (2006). Silent voices and invisible walls: Exploring end of life care with lesbians and gay men. *Journal of Psychosocial Oncology, 24*(1), 51–64.

Smolinski, K. M., & Colón, Y. (2011). Palliative care with lesbian, gay, bisexual, and transgender persons. In T. Altilio & S. Otis-Green (Eds.), *Oxford textbook of palliative social work.* New York, NY: Oxford University Press.

U.S. Department of Health & Human Services. (2012). *Announcing the White House LGBT conference series.* Retrieved from http://www.whitehouse.gov/blog/2012/02/02/announcing-white-house-lgbt-conference-series

Wheeler, D., & Dodd, S. J. (2011). LGBTQ capacity building in health care systems: A social work imperative. *Health and Social Work, 36*(4), 307–309.

Wilkerson, J. M., Rybicki, S., Barber, C. A., & Smolenski, D. J. (2011). Creating a culturally competent clinical environment for LGBT patients. *Journal of Gay and Lesbian Social Services, 23*(3), 376–394.

39 Transgender Individuals and Families Affected by Cancer

Max Rorty

Key Concepts

- *Transgender oncology patients encounter many barriers to good medical care, including provider anxiety, diagnosis-specific hazards, and institutional abandonment or mistreatment.*
- *Oncology social workers are in an excellent position to navigate the difficulties and uncertainties both patients and the medical team face.*
- *Medical team members can make hurtful mistakes, which can be compounded by poor apologies. Apologizing is an important clinical intervention that requires awareness and practice.*
- *Some institutional barriers are easy to fix—for example, demographics collection and bathroom signage—and, once changed, can make a positive impact on the health and safety of transgender patients.*

The oncology social worker who provides services to transgender patients must be aware of some particular issues for which a patient's transgender status puts him or her at risk in medical settings. This chapter explores the negative personal and bureaucratic consequences that can occur when a patient's body, name, or legal gender status doesn't meet care providers' expectations. Transgender oncology patients need oncology social workers who meet them with an attitude of respectful acceptance.

This chapter discusses the specific concerns that transgender oncology patients bring to the health care interaction, as well as the specific interventions that can be undertaken in health care institutions to address these concerns, which include the following:

- Anatomy-specific oncology diagnoses and/or anatomy-exposing diagnostics or treatment
- Undereducation or miseducation by providers who make assumptions about anatomy or sexual behavior
- Risk of assumptions or harassment because of non-normative gender presentation
- Public administrative spaces, including waiting rooms, where legal names and documentation are a precondition to health care access

Transgender people have different concerns than gay, lesbian, and bisexual people, and interventions for transgender people need to be specific to these concerns. This chapter presents micro-level or individual assessments and interventions, meso-level interventions on the team level, and macro-level or institutional and organizational interventions that can increase the health and safety of transgender patients.

Terminology

The following definitions come from Transgender Terminology (National Center for Transgender Equality, 2009):

Gender Nonconforming: *A term by some individuals whose gender expression is different from societal expectations related to gender.*

Transgender: *An umbrella term for people whose gender identity, expression, or behavior is different from those typically* *associated with their assigned sex at birth, including but not limited to transsexuals, cross-dressers, androgynous people, genderqueers, and gender nonconforming people.* Transgender *is a broad term and is good for nontransgender people to use.* Trans *is shorthand for transgender.*

Transsexual: *A term for people whose gender identity is different from their assigned sex at birth. Often transsexual people alter or wish to alter their bodies through hormones or surgery to make it match their gender identity.*

Do not make assumptions about sexual orientation. Neither gender nonconforming presentation nor transsexualism is a sexual identity or indication of sexual orientation or behavior. Rather, gender identity, the feeling that one is essentially male or essentially female or a combination of both, is a fundamental aspect of selfhood, regardless of relationship with others. Gender identity is an "all the time" quality of self.

Oncology Social Work Interventions

The oncology social worker is ideally situated to provide mediation and communication between the patient and the medical team. This role of communicator is consistent with most of our job descriptions and, especially in the case of transgender patients, truly needed. This chapter will suggest appropriate clinical interventions on micro-, meso-, and macro-levels.

A trans woman patient and her female partner are in the hospital room, waiting to see the oncologist. The nurse correctly genders the patient, explaining to the patient's partner, "Her blood pressure is normal and her fever is down." Then the doctor enters the room. The nurse turns to the oncologist and says, "His blood pressure is normal and his fever is down."

Pronouns

This vignette demonstrates the importance of gender pronouns. Correct pronoun use evidences an agreement to accept and relate to patients as they define themselves. Misusing pronouns indicates an unsafe ignorance or an unwillingness to know the patient. Given that the first, most basic thing that defines transgender people is a sense of not being believed, honored, or respected, it is less likely that they will trust the care team with important medical information if they feel misunderstood or misrepresented. The trust essential to medical care depends on practitioners demonstrating their care for the actual person in the room: knowing their name, knowing their gender, and knowing their medical history and current needs. Misgendering someone through something as simple as even pronoun use breaks that trust.

Consistency

This vignette also demonstrates the importance of team consistency. Without it, the patient can feel as if she is being colluded against. In this example, the nurse's correct pronoun use turns out to be a changeable thing, perhaps just a humoring or cajoling performance that ends when the doctor enters the room. The nurse no longer seems reliable because she is inconsistent. The doctor seems immediately unsafe, because the nurse has demonstrated that the doctor can't be trusted with the patient's actual information or identity. The team's inconsistency makes each member unreliable. Team consistency is a good focus of oncology social work interventions. Oncology social workers should use cross-team communication, reminding all staff on all shifts of patients' preferred pronouns. For example, "Mrs. Johnson prefers the pronouns she or her. Please talk to the social worker if you have any questions."

Micro-Level Interventions

Gender Patients Correctly

A skilled oncology social worker will ascertain gender nonconforming patient pronoun preferences and use the pronoun correctly and consistently while apologizing concisely for any mistakes. Misgendering transgender people, whether by reflex, inattention, or misinformation, is a common mistake. However, common is not the same as trivial. Misgendering people, calling a woman "he" or a man "she," demonstrates that one does not accept the patient's gender identity or, worse, that one does not believe the patient is who the patient says he or she is and is consciously (or even unconsciously) refusing to acknowledge the patient's legitimacy and personhood. This mistake is instantly alienating.

Practice Correct Apologies

Well-meaning, conscientious team members may make mistakes when using pronouns. Aware of the magnitude of this mistake, they may inadvertently compound their error by trying to explain the basis of their mistake. For example: "I'm sorry. I didn't mean to say she, but I'm looking at your chart and it has an F where an M should be." Or "I'm sorry. It's just you don't look like I expected." Or "I'm sorry. I've never had a trans patient before." All of these explanations invalidate the preceding apology. Apologies are not explanations.

Social workers are in an excellent position to observe and advise well-meaning team members as they try to do right by transgender patients. Part of this project is learning and practicing apologies. An appropriate apology is an acknowledgment that one has made an error. It is brief—for example, "My mistake"—and is followed by a correction.

Avoid False Affiliation

Gay, lesbian, and bisexual people are often tempted to make a comparison or affiliation with trans people.

For example, a lesbian oncology social worker may feel inclined to reveal to a trans patient that she too is queer, in an attempt to ally with her patient. This is a false affiliation. The political projects and individual journeys of gay people—from unseen to seen—are diametrically different from those of transsexual people and gender nonconforming people.

Although gay, lesbian, bisexual, and trans histories are intertwined, individual lives do not run a similar course, and the social and institutional barriers they face are not the same. Rather than drawing comparisons, an ally will do his or her best to start where the actual trans person is. Oncology social workers know this already: Accept patients as they are.

Meso-Level Interventions

The oncology social worker's focus on the medical team as the subject of intervention is important. Transgender patients have many reasons to distrust medical teams. Team members are responsible for managing their own distress, uncertainty, and discomfort with ambiguity so that the patient does not have to bear the brunt of external anxiety about his or her sexual identity or physiology.

Team Support

The transgender patient, like all patients, is in a position of relative dependence and powerlessness. It is not appropriate to make the patient responsible for the team's misinformation, confusion, or uncertainty. The team is responsible for its own education, behavior, professionalism, and consistency. Oncology social workers can manage team anxiety by using clinical skills on the team as a whole. The medical team is equally deserving of a thorough social work assessment and psychosocial intervention. Some of the members of the team will feel comfortable and confident with transgender patients and some will not. The task of the oncology social worker is to find or create a space where staff can discharge or dispel their concerns, anxieties, questions, or misapprehensions. Some of these conversations will prevent the patient from having to educate staff.

Psychosocial Education

Oncology social workers can take opportunities to provide psychosocial education. For example, "Actually, it's estimated that only 15% of transsexuals have had genital surgery. Many express no interest in the procedure." Or "Would you believe our state doesn't alter the sex on a driver's license without proof of genital surgery?" Or "Unfortunately, our electronic medical record system doesn't let us change the gender of our patients in their records." Or "Just because somebody identifies as male doesn't mean we know anything about his sexual behavior."

> *A 38-year-old transgender man comes in for a routine hysterectomy. His surgeon is familiar with his pronouns, correctly genders him, and sends the patient home with discharge instructions. Routine discharge instructions note the fragility of the newly created vaginal cuff and encourage patients to avoid vaginal penetration for several weeks after surgery. But the nurse caring for this transgender man at discharge fails to go over the prohibition on vaginal penetration. The patient is not warned against premature penetrative sex, possibly because the discharging nurse, in an effort to respect the patient's identity, made assumptions about his sexual activities based on his gender identity and that of his wife. The patient returns to the hospital with a torn vaginal cuff, the result of premature penetration. What could the oncology social worker have done to support the patient and the team in this case? A meso-level intervention, educating the team about its assumptions and responsibilities, can prevent patient harm.*

Macro-Level Interventions

Transgender people in need of any kind of medical care face considerable risks when they approach medical care teams. Some of the areas that present barriers or risks to transgender patients, generally, and potential social work interventions follow.

Legal Documents

Because most states prohibit changing sex on driver's licenses, many transsexual people have identification that does not match their appearance or identity. Most medical offices require patients to show picture ID or proof of insurance before appointments. Many insurance companies require an "M" or an "F" on their insurance card to identify sex. Transsexual people who have IDs that don't match their insurance card or an appearance that doesn't match their ID may face suspicion upon registering for care. Because most insurance companies and health care organizations do not have a mechanism for changing sex on medical records or charting, transsexual patients are left with inaccurate documentation and are therefore at risk of increased scrutiny, curiosity, and confusion well before they actually meet with a physician. Oncology social workers can work with their state policymakers to change the requirements for gender changes on state identification, as well as work with national advocacy and policy organizations on federal-level changes.

Waiting Rooms

Consider the waiting room that uses legal names obtained from driver's licenses to summon patients to their appointments. A phlebotomist calling "Jane Doe" across a crowded waiting room may be met by John Doe, or vice versa. This scenario is quite common, and laboratories are especially likely areas for this kind of mistake, because most people on hormone therapy require frequent testing for the first year of transition. This mistake is embarrassing to the staff and the patient. The staff sees they are mistaken and have been led into a mistake that potentially "outs" their trans patient by a policy that requires the public use of legal names.

These publicly embarrassing moments can be effectively avoided with systemic change in how patients get called up to see their clinician. Using only last names is often not sufficient because many people share last names, but alternatives are possible. For example, each person can have their legal documents reviewed privately and then be given a baseball card or a playing card. When it is time to be seen, the name "Babe Ruth" or the phrase "three of clubs" can be used to call people from across the waiting room. As is often the case when we make policy changes to protect the safety of one group, other groups benefit. This systemic solution protects the privacy of all patients.

Demographics Collection

A standard error in demographic questioning is to ask: "Are you GLBT?" which is as incongruous as: "Are you male, female, or Asian?" One is gay, lesbian, or bisexual (GLB) as well as transgender (T). There is no connection between sexual orientation and gender identity. The correct demographic question would ignore these letters and instead ask: "With whom do you have sex? People with penises, people with vaginas, both, or neither?" And "With what gender do you identify? Male, female, both, or neither?"

Oncology social workers are well situated to address the assumptions of demographic-collecting paperwork and to rewrite it so it "starts where the patient is."

Pathologizing Trans

Aside from waiting rooms, transgender patients often face physicians who are distracted by transgender status and can't see anything else. As a participant says in the film *Diagnosing Difference*, "It's not a trans sore throat" (Ophelian, 2009). Although a full history and physical examination require a discussion of hormone levels, many trans patients report that inexperienced physicians blame hormones for every health problem. Likewise, oncology social workers must remember not to blame psychosocial ills on transition, for lack of a better analysis. Skilled clinicians of all kinds must work to see the full picture of who that person is and what he or she needs.

Gender Nonconforming Patients

Some gender nonconforming people have a binary gender identity (i.e., they identify as either male or female) that may not be immediately perceivable by another person. Gender nonconforming people may be assigned different genders depending on their location, clothing, or context. For example, a woman who appears to someone else as male may find herself threatened or punished for being in a women's restroom. Gender nonconforming people are at risk in restrooms and waiting rooms that are typically organized as single-sex places.

Ask for Pronoun Preference

Medical practitioners should make a practice of asking people what pronoun they use, to ensure they do not embarrass themselves or alienate their gender nonconforming patients by mistakenly referring to someone as "him" rather than "her." This intervention is simple: "What pronoun do you prefer?"

Bathrooms

Transgender patients with genderqueer presentations are just one of the many populations that benefit from single-stall unisex restrooms. People who do not immediately register as male or female in the mind of the observer frequently avoid restrooms, for fear of confrontation or abuse.

Installing unisex signage to single-sex restrooms demonstrates an awareness of a vulnerable population's specific needs and a systemic intervention that can ease suffering. Because many patients require attendants and because many families with young children are in hospitals, there are several excellent reasons to make all single-stall restrooms unisex. Oncology social workers are in an excellent position to advocate for unisex signage on all single-stall restrooms.

Transsexual Oncology Patients

The term *transsexual* used to refer to people who had "had the surgery," but its current use describes people who have altered their appearance by any means, including clothing, mannerisms, hormone therapy, or surgery, and are living their lives in the gender different from that assigned at birth. This full-time identity is most frequently achieved with the help of hormone injections, by which people alter their bodies, appearance, and biological makeup. Hormones are relatively available to insured people; genital surgery is not.

Very few transsexual people who wish to alter their genitals surgically are able to afford it. Few insurers cover this process, and relatively few surgeons are trained to perform it. It is estimated that 15% of all transsexual people have had genital surgery. Therefore, the vast majority of transsexual men, who live their lives as men, have cervixes, ovaries, and uteruses that require oncological screening. Conversely, the vast majority of transsexual women, who live their lives as women, have prostates that require oncological screening.

In both collection of demographic information and service provision, health care teams need to be more explicit in how we differentiate between sexual behavior and gender identity. Conflating sexual orientation with gender identity turns gender identity into an erotic activity instead of an essential part of who one is. Sexual orientation, colloquially put, is who one goes to bed *with*. Gender identity is who one goes to bed *as*. Our vignettes demonstrate the danger to patients when medical professionals make assumptions about sexual behavior from gender identity or presentation.

Barriers to Oncology Care

Inappropriate responses from medical practitioners to transsexualism or nonconforming gender presentations can lead to the avoidance of diagnosis, treatment, or clinical supports.

Screening

Avoiding medical care is particularly dangerous for oncology patients, for whom early detection and treatment can be a matter of life or death. Therefore, it is essential that oncology services provide a safe and supportive environment to transgender people and that the availability of safe and supportive environments be made as public as possible.

For example, an outpatient oncology clinic office could develop a brochure that explains Pap smears, cytology, and treatment surgery options in gender-neutral language, including information for "men and women and anyone who has gynecological needs." Similarly, explanations of testicular or prostate care services can be provided without pictures of men, reference to male pronouns, or sex-specific care. These brochures may be distributed to other clinics or agencies where patients may seek services and thereby increase the likelihood of a transgender patient seeking early care for potential cancer diagnoses to access cancer screenings or services.

Diagnosis

Oncology patients can be "outed" by their diagnoses, because the name of their disease often includes an organ of origin. People with cervixes get cervical cancer, but in the case of a transsexual man who has not been thought of as a woman for many years, this diagnosis brings a large group of people into discussion about his history and journey. Trans women are as vulnerable to prostate cancer as anyone else with a prostate. Because only an estimated 15% of transsexuals (people who are living their lives in the binary gender different from the gender assigned at birth) have had genital surgery, the vast majority of transgender people are vulnerable to cancers of organs that no one knows they have.

Treatment and Clinical Interventions

Cancer treatment can also make transgender patients vulnerable to misgendering. All treatments that cause hair loss strip women of a gender signifier. Inpatient treatment requiring hospital gowns takes away clothing and accessories, other signifiers. Without these signs and symbols of gender, caregivers can struggle to remember the correct gender of their gender-ambiguous patients.

Support groups could present potential hazards to transgender patients. Group members may misgender people in group settings and may make personal inquiries about gender, surgery, or other personal issues. Poorly facilitated groups can make people feel very vulnerable. Oncology social workers can begin groups by introducing themselves using their own preferred pronouns and encouraging the use of each member's preferred pronouns. Groups are an opportunity for oncology social workers to encourage safe sharing of mutual concerns.

Finally, psychosocial support at end of life often includes a life review. Transgender people may have memories and reflections of their life as a little girl or little boy, or an adolescent period in a body that is different from the one they have now. The care team needs to be able to adopt a flexible position on the use of pronouns, the description of self, and the potential variability of a person's identity and perceived identity over time.

National Interventions

As our social work code of ethics demands, "Social workers should act to prevent and eliminate domination of, exploitation of, and discrimination against any person, group, or class on the basis of race, ethnicity, national origin, color, sex, sexual orientation, gender identity or expression" (NASW, 2008). Gender-variant people and transgender patients are among our charges, and their welfare is part of our mandate. Social work advocacy includes ensuring health care access for all people regardless of employment status. Many state and federal policies impede health care access for transgender people. Linking health care insurance to employment imperils the unemployed, the tenuously employed, and, more specifically, transgender persons whose work history is under another name or identity. Therefore, working to decouple employment from health care access is part of transgender advocacy.

Pearls

- Ask people who they are and what they want to be called and then call them that.
- When you make a mistake, say only, "I made a mistake." Then proceed with your correction.
- Recognize and publicize the institutional barriers to health care—for transgender people and all people—to reduce harm and increase access.

Pitfalls

- Don't make assumptions about someone's sexual orientation based on his or her gender presentation or gender identity.
- Don't assume a false affiliation, if you are gay or queer, with someone who is trans. Maintain the caregiver/patient frame in your work.
- Don't essentialize transgender identity. It is one aspect of their lives, and if you are seeing them, then cancer is the main event for them.

Health care institutions, especially providers of long-term treatments such as cancer centers, present numerous obstacles to the safe and supportive treatment of transgender patients. With attention to the needs of the patient and conscious interventions in key institutional practices, oncology social workers can improve the care and treatment of transgender patients. All patients benefit from the previously listed key points: being open to who patients are, seeing them as they see themselves, and taking responsibility for our mistakes when we make them.

ADDITIONAL RESOURCES

Book

Lev, A. I. (2004). *Transgender emergence: Therapeutic guidelines for working with gender-variant people*. New York, NY: Routledge.

Websites

National Center for Transgender Equality: http://transequality.org/
Transgender Law Center: http://transgenderlawcenter.org/
World Professional Association for Transgender Health: http://www.wpath.org

REFERENCES

National Association of Social Workers (NASW). (2008). *Code of ethics*. Retrieved from https://www.socialworkers.org/pubs/code/code.asp

National Center for Transgender Equality. (2009). *Transgender terminology*. Retrieved from http://transequality.org/Resources/NCTE_TransTerminology.pdf

Ophelian, A. (Director). (2009). *Diagnosing difference* [DVD]. San Francisco, CA: Floating Ophelia Productions.

40

Karina L. Walters, Teresa Evans-Campbell, Matthew A. Town, Katie Schultz, Jessica H. L. Elm, and Ramona E. Beltrán

Alaska Native, Native American, and First Nation People: Outreach, Screening, and Assessment

Key Concepts

- *An indigenous-centered approach to wellness should be used and cultural issues should be addressed throughout the continuum of care with American Indian and Alaska Native patients and families, including cultivating relational ways of being, identifying cultural perceptions of disease and healing options, assessing the role of traditional medicines and spiritual supports, and navigating life transitions and survivorship.*
- *Culturally grounded oncology social work practice is desperately needed in Indian Country, not only to address deep historical mistrust and assist in navigating complex tribal and nontribal systems of care but also to bridge cultural barriers in health care services.*
- *Tribal language, worldviews, and meanings associated with cancer have implications for health behaviors, adaptive coping, and identification of culturally relevant healing approaches for American Indian and Alaska Native patients and families.*

This chapter outlines social work practices for American Indian and Alaska Native (AIAN) populations, with a focus on the integration of cultural worldviews into social work cancer prevention and oncology practice.[1] Through the voices and experiences of AIAN cancer survivors, social workers will be introduced to AIAN cancer disparities; historical, cultural, and social determinants of cancer-related health outcomes; indigenous approaches to healing and life transitions; and culturally based practices for the continuum of care.

Cancer Among American Indians and Alaska Natives

Although the 2.3 million AIANs in the United States constitute approximately 1.7% of the total population (U.S. Census, 2012) and have a reportedly lower cancer burden compared to other racial and ethnic groups, they remain disproportionately affected by cancer-related health disparities, with incidences of and mortality rates much higher for selected cancers within specific regions (Kaur & Hampton, 2008).

Among all AIANs, cancer is the third leading cause of death it is the second leading cause of death among AIANs over age 45 (Steele, Cardinez, Richardson, Tom-Orme, & Shaw, 2008). Once AIANs have cancer, their survival rates are much lower than non-Hispanic Whites (NHWs), with AIAN incidence rates consistently exceeding NHW rates for kidney, stomach, liver, and gallbladder cancer. Contributing factors to cancer mortality and morbidity are tied to disparities in AIAN chronic disease risk factors (e.g., high prevalence of tobacco use) and poor access to screening and care (e.g., 30% of AIANs have no insurance). Finally, AIAN communities bear the brunt of environmental carcinogenic contaminant exposure (e.g., hydraulic fracturing or "fracking"). Despite all of this, research addressing AIAN cancer prevention and treatment lags.

American Indian and Alaska Native Health Care Systems

AIANs who are enrolled members of federally recognized tribes have unique political status in the United States, holding dual U.S. and tribal nation citizenship. Through long-standing treaties and Supreme Court, congressional, and executive orders, tribal nations are entitled to health care in perpetuity (Warne, Kaur, & Perdue, 2012), which, today, is delivered by the federal agency Indian Health Service (IHS). However, with congressional IHS appropriations 50% lower per capita than other federally funded health care systems, specialized services, such as radiation treatment, are not funded through the IHS (Warne et al., 2012). Funds are typically exhausted before the end of the fiscal year, forcing tribal clinics to close until the next cycle—hence the tribal saying "Don't get sick after June."

Indian Health Service

In the early 1800s, the U.S. Department of War stationed physicians at military forts to control contagious diseases such as smallpox (Warne et al., 2012). By 1832, the federal government provided health care in exchange for land and resources. In 1955, tribal health care was moved from the Bureau of Indian Affairs to the Department of Health and Welfare, now the Department of Health and Human Services.

Currently, IHS services are administered through 12 regional area offices and 168 tribally managed service units. There are 33 urban programs. IHS-run hospitals and clinics serve any registered AIAN, regardless of tribe or income. Tribal-contract health care facilities serve only their tribal members, with other qualified AIANs being offered care on a space-available basis (Warne et al., 2012). This policy makes it difficult for over two thirds of the AIAN population who now live in cities to receive the health care services to which they are legally entitled.

Contextualizing Cancer

Although classic social determinants of health, such as poor access to care, contribute to health outcomes, these factors alone do not explain the high cancer rates among AIAN populations. Increasingly, AIAN scholars and communities have turned their attention to the complex role of historically traumatic events (e.g., boarding school) and contemporary discriminatory events in undermining AIAN health (Walters, Mohammed, et al., 2011). Emerging work in AIAN health also considers *embodiment* as a primary factor in AIAN health. Embodiment illuminates key processes for identifying the complicated ways social experience is physically integrated into the body and expressed (Krieger, 2005). The concept of embodiment is consistent with AIAN relational worldviews that recognize the interdependency between humans and nature, the physical and spiritual worlds, and ancestors and future generations (Walters, Mohammed, et al., 2011).

Social Work Practice Models

To date, the majority of cancer prevention efforts in Indian Country have focused on eradicating negative health behaviors and risks while ignoring the positive attributes of traditional and contemporary AIAN culture, including its emphasis on physical, mental, emotional, and spiritual balance. Building on available personal and cultural strengths and resources and looking to AIAN communities to identify their own prevention needs are essential strategies for any social work practice model.

Although very few cancer intervention studies have been conducted in AIAN communities, some prevention models, including patient navigator approaches, demonstrate initial efficacy or show promise (Burhansstipanov et al., 2012). Other models could be adapted for cancer control strategies, such as health leadership development frameworks (Kenyon & Hanson, 2012) that focus prevention efforts on "building" positive communal and familial relationships rather than "fixing" individual problems. Finally, the Indigenist Stress-Coping Model (Walters & Simoni, 2002) can be useful for incorporating cultural resiliency factors in social work practice.

Oncology Social Work Practice With American Indians and Alaska Natives

To address historical mistrust, assist in navigating complex care systems, and bridge cultural health care barriers in Indian Country, culturally grounded oncology social work practice is desperately needed throughout the continuum of care. In this section, we provide an overview of key cultural issues to address, incorporating an ecosocial framework, incorporating an indigenous-centered approach to wellness, and expanding on the cultural aspects of traditional biopsychosocial-cultural approaches while weaving in stories from AIAN cancer survivors (NACES, 2012) to illustrate key themes.

Appreciate Competing Life Issues

Given the high levels of poverty and health disparity in AIAN communities, cancer-related concerns are not likely a priority for most AIAN individuals or families. Pressing issues such as meeting basic needs with respect to food and shelter or navigating other health priorities such as familial deaths sometimes take precedence.

Consider Cancer Conceptualizations

Over 217 AIAN languages are actively spoken within the United States, and many tribes have no equivalent word for "cancer," though for some, their approximated word roughly translates into "the disease for which there is no cure" (Native American Cancer Research Corporation, 2014). As a result, such translations may unintentionally stigmatize individuals living with cancer or instill fear or hopelessness.

Assess Perceptions of "Dis-ease" and Healing Approaches

For AIANs, disease, or literally, "dis-ease" ("out of balance"), is tied to the holistic understanding of the interconnected mind, body, emotion, spirit, and land. Although varied among tribal cultures, wellness is generally experienced by AIANs as a state of living balanced among these elements and the greater world (Walters, Beltrán, et al., 2011). Many AIAN persons, whether living in the city or in remote communities, practice traditional health practices daily to maintain this balance (e.g., smudging with sage). Some AIANs may seek traditional healers (a.k.a. medicine people) to assist them in returning to balance, to heal, or to drive away the illness. Traditional medicines (e.g., teas, plant medicine) or practices may also be used for traditional healing (e.g., sweat lodges). For example, Doug Six-Killer St. Clair (Cherokee/Shoshone) comments:

> *What I did was I contacted a couple of Native healers that I knew from back home. . . . Then there were . . . some things that were given to me so that I could help get myself into balance after being through the rigors of all of those massive amounts of poisons (chemotherapy) that they put into my body.*
>
> *(NACES, 2012)*

More commonly, AIAN patients may access a combination of healing practices but may not discuss them with outsiders, sometimes, in part, to protect the healers and the protocols surrounding the practices. As Abe Conklin (Ponca/Osage) notes about the importance of combining traditional and allopathic healing approaches:

> *I got with the medicine man up there. And I had my son come back and help healing ceremony for me. All this all together along with your spiritualness and faith, never give up on that along with you doctors help, they go together. If you use both of them, they will help you. But you've got to have that inner faith in yourself, let your body help you heal yourself, along with your doctor and whatever they ask of you to do.*
>
> *(NACES, 2012)*

By being open to varying healing practices and letting ceremony details remain private, social workers can establish personal rapport and demonstrate respect. However, as professionals, social workers should note that some teas and medicines might interact with allopathic medicines and should encourage the patient to talk with the doctor about the potential ways in which both medicines could best work together for healing.

Identify Spiritual Supports

Although AIAN spiritual practices are as varied as the tribes themselves—from traditional to Christian to Buddhist, or a blend of all of these—for most, spirituality remains central in relating to health, forming the core of everyday behavioral expressions embodied in health practices. Native American spiritual ways, however, have been systematically attacked over the years by policies of assimilation, including those enacted during the Indian boarding-school era when thousands of AIAN children were forced to learn Western ways and adopt Christianity (Evans-Campbell, 2008). Punishments for attempting to practice traditional spirituality were often harsh, and children quickly learned to keep traditional practices and beliefs secret. As a result, social workers need to be particularly sensitive to discussing spiritual beliefs and practices given the legacy of historical trauma, communities' concern with keeping practices sacred and safe, and families' needs to share their particular views in relation to their healing and journey with cancer. Overall, spirituality forms a core for addressing the initial diagnosis through all stages of care and survivorship. For example, Ruth Bugess (Muscogee/Seminole) eloquently identifies how her faith and spirituality led her to transform the meaning of cancer in her life:

> *I went to a church camp . . . and she gave me this name tag and said put this on and it said "Encourager" and it was like getting a slap on the back and saying don't become discouraged, go out and encourage somebody. . . . I was falling into the dumps and I have not let cancer do that to me and I encourage people to not let that do that to them. There's a purpose for whatever God has placed upon your life.*
>
> *(NACES, 2012)*

For others, a cancer diagnosis provides an opportunity to reflect on their strengths or the gifts they can receive when confronted with such a life-altering diagnosis. As Ralaine M. Hinton (Passamaquod) notes:

> *Cancer was not the worst thing that had happened to me in my life. Cancer really in its own unique way was a gift to me. My life had been troubled at times and I had demons that I was up against, as we all do. But when I was diagnosed with cancer, I realized how inconsequential those demons were to the entirety of what my life was. . . . And for the first time in my life I found an inner peace.*
>
> *(NACES, 2012)*

Social workers can play a unique role in facilitating conversations about the meaning of the journey to diagnosis and healthful coping and providing opportunities to reflect on hope and healing in light of the cancer diagnosis.

Acknowledge Potential Role of Traditional Medicines

Receiving a cancer diagnosis also provides an opportunity for AIANs to reconnect culturally and spiritually to traditional practices, as Dorcas Bloom (Yupik) elder notes:

> *I never used to believe in stuff like that [traditional medicine] and then my friends . . . started bringing me traditional medicine, and I never knew how to use them because I never, I'm from a different village. . . . I find that traditional medicine cleared my esophagus, what the, what the normal medicine couldn't do. . . . I never used to believe it. I believe because it worked on me.*
>
> (NACES, 2012)

Blending Christian and traditional medicines or ceremonies is quite common in treating cancer. Thompson Williams (Caddo/Comanche) provides the following example:

> *I have family who are traditional and have family who are Christian. My sister is a minister and this was the 1st time that there was never a conflict between them, they had come together at prayers and things to assure that my surgery and everything else would go, go good. . . . I think these prayers, these ceremonies, these things that have been gone through for me are allowing me to step up and do this.*
>
> (NACES, 2012)

Cultivate a Relational Orientation

AIANs see all "beings" as connected to the greater "web of life" of which "each and every being has a purpose and relationship to one another that must be honored through ceremony and everyday living" (Walters, Beltrán, et al., 2011, p. 169). This relational orientation reflects an indigenous understanding of the interrelatedness of all beings and leads to a deep understanding of how the power of relationships is inextricably linked to behavior, practices, and wellness. To varying degrees, historically traumatic events disrupted relational ways of being. Behavioral interventions with AIANs should focus on supporting the development of relational ways of being. For example, language such as "living with cancer" acknowledges the relational orientation to the dis-ease state rather than being diseased and can help patients consider how they want to be in relation to cancer.

Family support throughout the continuum of care is critical, and identifying a particular family member that could be engaged when meeting with doctors is beneficial. For example, Michael George (Coeur d'Alene) notes:

> *I was lucky I had family that, mainly a younger brother that stood right next to me. And questions that I was to be shy to ask or maybe afraid to ask, he'd come right out and ask the doctor, "Why—why does my brother have to do this?"*
>
> (NACES, 2012)

No matter how assimilated or culturally immersed AIAN families are, having involved family networks is akin to being wealthy and healthy. It is not uncommon to have extended family involved from diagnosis through continuum of care; for some social workers who have little experience with AIAN families, the amount of familial involvement can at first be a bit overwhelming. As Charlene Capps (Caddo/Cheyenne) explains:

> *As Indian people usually do, they just, it was like a reunion, the next day, a family reunion [at the hospital]. Everybody was there, and was there every day. My children, my sisters were there every day. It was really something.*
>
> (NACES, 2012)

Acknowledge Cultural Perceptions of Responsibilities

Of particular concern to AIANs are perceived responsibilities to ancestors, children, and future descendants. Known as "sequential immortality," this relational orientation links contemporary AIANs inextricably to their ancestral and future relations and means that both action and inaction can have consequences not only for the immediate individual and family but also for future and past generations simultaneously. This relational orientation provides a powerful base on which social workers may build as they support patients in taking action toward health not only for oneself but also for past, present, and future generations. It is also the community's responsibility to learn more about cancer and cancer prevention for the future of its members. Quite often, families and children of parents living with cancer invoke relational responsibilities that can facilitate motivation and return to healthful practices. As Dora Garcia (San Felipe Pueblo) shares:

> *They were all very supportive. . . . They were the ones to tell me that I was okay and doing good. . . . They said, we need you Mom, we need you around, so we're doing everything we can to help you get well. Of course, we said our prayers. . . . We're always asking the spirits to help you get well. So, it's up to you Mom. Just try to get well. . . . We're all rooting for you.*
>
> (NACES, 2012)

Thompson Williams also notes that AIAN fathers play an integral relational role to children and future generations:

> *We talk about who we are as Native men and . . . our responsibilities as fathers. We're here and we take on*

our responsibility as warriors. . . . If I had let this go, there'd be no one to protect my family. I would be selfish, and I would be less than a man because I'd been selfish enough not to do this to protect my family.
(NACES, 2012)

Assess Orientation Toward Death and Dying

AIANs see dying as part of the natural order of life and experience it as "just a change of worlds." As Lorraine Shanaaquet (Potawatomie) explains: "We don't believe in death being final, we just believe it's another step, where we leave this physical earth, to go on . . . to another part of home" (NACES, 2012).

Traditionally, funerary practices were an acknowledgment of the transitioning of the individual into another "world" and as part of the cycle of life. Social work practitioners should honor AIAN funerary practices and ways of caring for the dead and dying and recognize that family and community members have specific roles to fill and may need support in carrying out their duties (e.g., communicating plans to health care providers). If not done properly, the dying person may not be able to move on to the next world or those left behind will not be able to grieve properly. CeCe Whitewolf (Umatilla) notes how she assisted her mom in the transition:

At the end I couldn't figure out what do I have to do to help my mom die. That last day, my sister Judy and I with the hospice person came and we gave her a bath. . . . After we finished cleaning her, within about a minute or so later, she left us. . . . My sister Judy . . . was outside with one of the Medicine Ladies. . . . They looked up and they saw an eagle that was flying around . . . and the Medicine lady said. "See there she goes the Eagles are taking her now, don't cry.
(NACES, 2012)

The loss of any person is difficult for families and communities. However, among AIANs, the loss of certain members carries more significance. Elders, for example, may be the last individual in their family or community to hold stories, language, and history. Sadly, many contemporary AIAN communities are losing elders who are the last to speak their traditional language. Such losses hold profound meaning for tribal culture and future generations. Relatedly, the loss of children to cancer can be particularly devastating to a community as young people symbolize the future and hope of AIAN communities. In small communities that have experienced generational losses, the importance of young people and the losses connected to their deaths cannot be overstated.

Just as funerary rites are culturally distinct, so are the ways that families and communities mourn death. The concept of a "mourning period" based on Western grief frameworks may not make sense to some AIAN people. Many AIAN communities prescribe unique customary practices for family members to follow during the year following the passing of a relative (e.g., cutting one's hair short) and then hold a memorial on the anniversary of the family member's transition. In some tribal communities, it is taboo to say the name of the person who passed. Unfortunately, it is not uncommon for AIAN families or communities to deal with multiple deaths over the course of each year, with each death adding to a greater communal sense of loss. Compounded grief may directly or indirectly impact family functioning after the loss of a loved one.

Recognize Strengths of Survivorship

AIAN survivors often feel energized to give back to their community, share stories, and foster hope. They can serve as powerful role models for other community members. Although survivorship is a blessing, social workers will need to anticipate effective processes that break through once the person transitions from living with to surviving cancer. For example, Margo Boesch (Chippewa) notes that grief frequently emerges after survivorship and embracing this grief is critical to healing:

There is a loss of innocence when you have had cancer. . . . So, one of the things I'd like to say is . . . allow for the pain . . . allow for the tears, because they're all part of the healing process. And that's what comes to make you stronger and better. Because the tears are like the rain in spring that bring the flower.
(NACES, 2012)

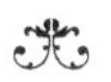

Pearls

- Know AIAN systems of health care—don't make assumptions about coverage or access.
- Recognize that historically traumatic events provide an important backdrop for AIAN health care.
- Explore tribal language, worldviews, and meanings associated with cancer.
- It is critical to incorporate familial supports and culturally sanctioned practices.

Pitfalls

- Do not generalize that all AIAN people want traditional medicines or practices.
- Watch for spiritual hucksters. Work with AIAN leaders to identify trusted community healers when appropriate.

Social work practice across the continuum of care presents a unique opportunity for integrating innovative, culturally based interventions that not only empower clients and families but also assist them in fulfilling their health responsibilities to themselves and to past and future generations. Oncology practice requires ongoing cultural and spiritual consultation and deep engagement with family and tribal systems. Finally, social workers must demonstrate compassion not only for others but also for themselves as they navigate structural inequities and health injustices at the macro-level to multiple traumas and unresolved grief at the individual level. Self-care to avoid compassion fatigue is necessary for social workers to provide healthful practice and healing strategies.

NOTE

1. This research was supported by awards from the National Institute of Mental Health (NIMHD-1P60MD006909 and NIDAK24-PA-10-061).

ADDITIONAL RESOURCES

Article

Espey, D. K., Wu, X., Swan, J., Wiggins, C., Jim, M. A., Ward, E., . . . Edwards, B. K. (2007). Annual report to the nation on the status of cancer 1975–2004: Featuring cancer in American Indians and Alaska Natives. *Cancer, 110*(10), 2119–2152. Retrieved from http://onlinelibrary.wiley.com/doi/10.1002/cncr.23044/full

Websites

Intercultural Cancer Council: http://iccnetwork.org/

The Intercultural Cancer Council promotes policies, programs, partnerships, and research to eliminate the unequal burden of cancer among racial and ethnic minorities and medically underserved populations in the United States and its associated territories.

Native American Cancer Research Corporation: http://www.natamcancer.org/

The Native American Cancer Research Corporation is dedicated to helping improve the lives of Native American cancer patients and survivors, seeks to reduce Native American cancer incidence and mortality, and works to increase survival from cancer among Native Americans.

REFERENCES

Burhansstipanov, L., Krebs, L. U., Watanabe-Galloway, S., Petereit, D. G., Pingatore, N. L., & Eschiti, V. (2012). Preliminary lessons learned from the "Native Navigators and the Cancer Continuum." *Journal of Cancer Education, 27*(Suppl. 1), S57–S65.

Evans-Campbell, T. (2008). Historical trauma in American Indian/Native Alaska communities: A multilevel framework for exploring impacts on individuals, families, and communities. *Journal of Interpersonal Violence, 23*(3), 316–338.

Kaur, J. S., & Hampton, J. W. (2008). Cancer in American Indian and Alaska Native populations continues to threaten an aging population. *Cancer, 113*(5 Suppl.), 1117–1119.

Kenyon, D. B., & Hanson, J. B. (2012). Incorporating traditional culture into positive youth development programs with AIAN youth. *Child Development Perspective, 6*(3), 272–279.

Krieger, N. (2005). Stormy weather: Race, gene expression, and the science of health disparities. *American Journal of Public Health, 95*(12), 2155–2160.

Native American Cancer Education for Survivors (NACES). (2012). *Native Americans and cancer vignettes.* Retrieved from http://www.natamcancer.org/vignettes/vignettes.html

Native American Cancer Research Corporation. (2014). Native Americans and cancer. Retrieved from http://natamcancer.org/page12.html

Steele, C. B., Cardinez, C. J., Richardson, L. C., Tom-Orme, L., & Shaw, K. M. (2008). Surveillance for health behaviors of AIANs-Findings from the Behavioral Risk Factor Surveillance System, 2000–2006. *Cancer, 113*(5 Suppl.), 1131–1141.

U.S. Census. (2012). *Facts for features: American Indian and Alaska Native heritage month: November 2012.* Retrieved from http://www.census.gov/newsroom/releases/archives/facts_for_features_special_editions/cb12-ff22.html

Walters, K. L, Beltran, R., Huh, D., & Evans-Campbell, T. (2011). Dis-placement and dis-ease: Land, place, and health among American Indians and Alaska Natives. In L. M. Burton, S. P. Kemp, M. Leung, S. A. Matthews, & D. Takeuchi (Eds.), *Communities, neighborhoods, and health: Expanding the boundaries of place* (pp. 163–199). New York, NY: Springer.

Walters, K. L., Mohammed, S. A., Evans-Campbell, T., Beltrán, R. E., Chae, D. H., & Duran, B. (2011). Bodies don't just tell stories, they tell histories: Embodiment of historical trauma among American Indians and Alaska Natives. *Dubois Review, 8*(1), 179–189.

Walters, K. L., & Simoni, J. M. (2002). Reconceptualizing Native women's health: An "indigenist" stress-coping model. *American Journal of Public Health, 92*(4), 520–524.

Warne, D., Kaur, J., & Perdue, D. (2012). American Indian/Alaska Native cancer policy: Systemic approaches to reducing cancer disparities. *Journal of Cancer Education, 27*(Suppl. 1), S18–S23.

41

Karen Bullock and Hannah Allison

Access to Medical Treatment for African Americans Diagnosed With Cancer: The Current Evidence Base

Key Concepts

- *Cancer is a leading cause of death among African Americans.*
- *African Americans are less likely than other racial groups to utilize cancer screening and treatment.*
- *Cultural competence is the cornerstone of effective, evidence-based practice with individuals and families living with cancer.*

According to the World Health Organization (2011), advances in cancer detection and treatments have increased chances of survival for people worldwide.[1] However, cancer incidence and death rates vary considerably among racial and ethnic groups. In the United States, for decades, African Americans have retained the highest risk for cancer death (Siegel, Ward, Brawley, & Jemal, 2011; Ward et al., 2004). Increasing access to and increasing participation in early detection screening by racial and ethnic groups are recommended strategies for reducing cancer health disparities (USDHHS, 2012).

African Americans are a particularly important group to target for early detection screening because, according to cancer statistics (Siegel, Naishadham, & Jemal, 2012), African American men have a 15% higher cancer incidence rate and a 33% higher cancer death rate than Caucasian men. Similarly, although African American women have a 6% lower cancer incidence rate, they have a 16% higher death rate than Caucasian women. These data also show that for specific cancer sites, incidence and death rates are consistently higher in African Americans than in Caucasian Americans except for cancers of the breast (incidence) and lung (incidence and mortality) among women and cancer of the kidney (mortality) among both men and women. Access to high-quality screening (breast, cervical, and colorectal cancers) and timely diagnosis and treatment for many cancers are known factors that contribute to racial disparities in mortality (Ghafoor et al., 2002).

The purpose of this chapter is to review the current literature on access to cancer treatment for African American populations and to discuss the application of current evidence-based practice approaches for improving cancer risk and outcomes for African American individuals and families. Recommendations are also made for culturally competent practice approaches.

Differences in Cancer Diagnosis and Prognosis

African Americans are more likely to develop cancer than any other racial or ethnic group (Freeman & Chu, 2005;

Siegel et al., 2012), and for all cancers combined, African Americans have a lower 5-year relative survival rate compared to Caucasians (ACS, 2012; Siegel et al., 2012). Although overall death rates from cancer among African Americans have declined since the early 1990s, African Americans are more likely to die from cancer than any other racial or ethnic group (Altekruse et al., 2010). Though with some individual cancers, such as melanoma of the skin, non-Hodgkin lymphoma, and cancer of the urinary bladder (ACS, 2012), incidence and death rates are lower among African Americans than Caucasians, research nonetheless documents that African Americans bear a higher cancer burden than any other racial or ethnic group.

According to current national data (Siegel et al., 2012), compared with Caucasian Americans, African American men and women have poorer survival rates once cancer is diagnosed. Furthermore, African Americans have a lower 5-year survival rate than Caucasian persons for every stage of diagnosis for nearly every type of cancer and are also less likely than their Caucasian counterparts to be diagnosed with cancer at a localized stage, when the disease may be more easily and successfully treated.

Among African American men, prostate cancer is the most common cancer diagnosis, followed by lung and colorectal cancers (ACS, 2012; Siegel et al., 2012). Moreover, African American men have the highest mortality rates from cancers of the colon and rectum, lung and bronchus, and prostate in comparison to all other race and gender groups (Siegel et al., 2011).

Just as low socioeconomic status poses higher risk for cancer and greater potential for negative outcomes across the boundaries of racial and ethnic identity, so does being elderly (ACS, 2012); therefore, older African American women may be at even greater risk for cancer mortality. A long history of disparities and discrimination in health care, which can affect the individual's and family's beliefs, values, and health care practices, make cancer promotion and outreach particularly challenging for practitioners. Understanding cultural factors that influence health care behavior, often labeled as barriers, can facilitate effective, evidence-based practices (Freeman & Chu, 2005; Snow & Gilbertson, 2011).

Barriers

One major issue in addressing oncology health disparities is the lack of evidence-based practices based on African American communities, in large part due to difficulties in recruiting participants in clinical trials. Barriers to recruitment of African Americans in clinical trials include a history of abuse and distrust, concerns about the ethical conduct and fairness of investigators, and socioeconomic factors related to education, employment, and health insurance status (Branson, Davis, & Butler, 2007). In addition, some may have a limited understanding of the informed consent process (Corbie-Smith, Thomas, Williams, & Moody-Ayers, 1999).

Similar barriers are linked to the nonuse of early screening methods by African Americans. A major barrier is the lack of knowledge, as well as misinformation, about cancer, such as the belief that a cancer diagnosis will result in death, which devalues the early detection of cancer (Matthews, Sellergren, Manfredi, & Williams, 2002; Spurlock & Cullins, 2006). Other barriers include concerns about keeping medical information private, lack of health insurance, and religious beliefs about putting healing in God's hands, all of which may limit participation in help-seeking behaviors for medical symptoms. These cultural beliefs and attitudes may also influence how patients experience and express emotions associated with diagnosis and treatment. There may be fear and stigma associated with seeking emotional support and/or showing emotions related to disease and illness (Matthews et al., 2002).

Strategies for Improving Access to Medical Treatment

Several strategies are recommended for improving access to medical treatment among African Americans, including community involvement, social supports, and culturally competent care plans. Given what has been learned from the literature about disproportionate burden of cancer on African Americans and the barriers to assessment, intervention, or programmatic efforts, oncology social workers should integrate cultural competence into their practice. Formative evaluation of these strategies is an acceptable means of identifying and refining the critical elements of the approaches.

Community Involvement

First, the skill of engaging the African American community in promoting and affirming the need to target their population for cancer research is critical. One of the ways to improve involvement in cancer prevention activities, be it through a clinical trial, through an educational campaign, or in an individual's treatment, is through the involvement of people whom they trust (Branson et al., 2007; Sanders, 2011). One such source is the church, which in African American communities is a respected institution of social change, empowerment, and emotional support, as well as a provider of tangible services.

Social Supports

The Screening Older Minority Women study (Bullock & McGraw, 2013) highlights the importance of designing interventions that strengthen existing social networks of those who have high cancer risk. In other research (Bastani, Gallardo, & Maxwell, 2001) that included high-risk, racially diverse men and women, the most common barrier to screening reported among non-Caucasian participants was the fear of finding cancer. Perceived lack of sensitivity on the part of the physician was another cultural-element finding of this study. Having a strong social support network can help patients feel more at ease and more willing to enter into the health care setting. There are several ways in which a cancer diagnosis can affect the support systems of an individual (Hamilton, Moore, Powe, Agarwal, & Martin, 2010), and these should be considered when developing strategies for improving access to medical treatment among African Americans. The cultural beliefs and attitudes about disclosure, and with whom to share information, may supersede what the medical team may feel is an appropriate and/or typical reaction to the receipt of critical health information. There is an oral tradition among African Americans about when and when not to share information with outsiders, and this cultural norm may cause individuals and families not to disclose their symptoms of cancer and/or side effects of treatments. Moreover, there may be a fear of certain medical interventions that require "opening a person up" and thus refusal of surgical procedures. Yet, the request may be made to otherwise "do all that you can for him or her and let God do the rest." Some older African Americans have passed on certain cultural beliefs and stigmas about cancer from previous generations of older adults who had even less access to formal education, health care, and providers than younger generations of African Americans. These historical realities have become barriers in contemporary society, leading to a shortage of cancer education initiatives in African American communities to dispel the cancer myths. Tailoring cancer screening and intervention programs that include outreach and education with intergenerational families as an enrichment component is recommended for this population (Bullock & McGraw, 2006).

The involvement of spiritual leaders and communities is key to providing social support for African Americans, and including an assessment tool that considers informal supports in the care plan can be beneficial to the patient's and family's well-being (Roff, Simon, Nelson-Gardell, & Pleasants, 2009). Those who are active in their church communities will have an appreciation for the health care provider's sensitivity. Furthermore, there is evidence that the inclusion of spiritual resources and social supports in a client's treatment can be an important factor for older African American cancer survivors (Hamilton et al., 2010).

Mrs. T. Davis, an 84-year-old African American woman, was admitted to the stroke unit of the hospital. In addition, she has a diagnosis of Stage 4 lung cancer that had metastasized to the bladder. She was accompanied by several members of her social support network, including the pastor of her Kingdom Hall, Pastor Jones. Although Mrs. Davis herself was not a "difficult" patient, her family members were labeled "difficult" and challenging to work with. Pastor Jones was seen as the biggest culprit. His first request was to have visiting hours (10 a.m. to 8 p.m.) extended to 7 a.m. to 10 p.m. so that Mrs. Davis could have family members at her bedside at all times. Next, he requested that no blood transfusions be administered to the patient. The medical staff became very frustrated with him. The oncology social worker returned to the nurses' station quickly concluding, "This family is going to be difficult to deal with." Another treatment team member questioned, "Why do they have to be so demanding? It's not even like he is a family member."

What Can Oncology Social Workers Do to Be More Culturally Sensitive in Care?

- At first encounter, ask patient if he or she would prefer to talk with family present or not. Allow the patient the right to consent to have others present or not.
- Try to accommodate the schedules of the patient and members of the social support network.
- Learn to read and understand nonverbal cues and/or language.
- Ask the patient what his or her past experience has been with this type of treatment, care setting, staff, and so forth.

Culturally Competent Practice

Cultural competence is necessary to break down barriers and to ensure that each patient with a cancer diagnosis receives optimal care while coping with serious illness and loss. It is impossible to know everything about every cultural group, but we can be culturally competent in recognizing factors that influence differences in preference for and decisions about end-of-life care. According to the National Association of Social Workers (2008), cultural competence means understanding culture and its function in human behavior and society and recognizing the strengths that exist in distinct cultures.

Practitioners who deliver cancer care have an obligation to treat individuals and families according to their preferences, when possible. The problem for some patients is that they do not feel that enough is done on the part of the practitioner to identify and incorporate the value and norms of the patient's culture (Carrión & Bullock, 2012). This may sometimes cause them to present themselves in ways that treatment team members view as "difficult." Establishing standards of care that are derived from culture-based assessments and community involvement would ensure that there are recommendations that guide activities and policies to support the inclusion of diverse perspectives, as has been recommended from evidence-based practice approaches (Stein, Sherman, & Bullock, 2009). Assumptions about race, structural racism, and power and privilege differentials should be examined in the application of cultural competency strategies and care models.

Using an assessment technique and/or tool that incorporates collective decision making and exploration of care options in the context of cultural norms, values, and beliefs will enable practitioners to do the following:

- Gain knowledge about the family structure and function that can influence health behaviors, as well as practices, values, and attitudes toward the health care system.
- Evaluate the capacity of the patient and members of the informal support network to navigate the health care system and cope with the disease or illness in a culturally acceptable manner.

It is important for practitioners to learn the preferences of the patients and families they care for. Often, African Americans do not prefer the treatment philosophies, approaches, and even care settings that are consistent with Western-based medicine's recommendations (Mazanec, Daly, & Townsend, 2010). An assessment tool tailored to this population should be developed to discern essential quality-of-life factors and assess for social factors such as stigmatizing beliefs about cancer, racial discrimination in care settings, myths and misunderstandings about cancer disease and diagnosis, and faith and spirituality.

Pearls

- Establish cultural competence standards of care derived from evidence-based practice approaches.
- Tailor community-based outreach to African Americans that relies on informal helpers.

Pitfalls

- Excluding trusted members of the patient's social support network will sustain existing barriers to care.
- When conflicts arise between the patient/family's cultural values, beliefs, and attitudes and those of the treatment team, failure to address these through culturally appropriate strategies may result in the patient receiving no care at all.

Current literature on access to cancer treatment for African American populations is inconclusive about best practices for oncology social workers. However, the recommendations made in this chapter are premised upon the available evidence on culturally competent oncology practice approaches.

ADDITIONAL RESOURCES

Websites

African American Breast Cancer Alliance: http://aabcainc.org/
Black Women's Health Imperative: http://www.healthyblackwomen.org/issues-and-resources/black-women-cervical-cancer-the-other-cancer/
Sisters Network Incorporated: http://www.sistersnetworkinc.org/
Witness Project: http://witnessprojectharlem.wordpress.com/resources/support/

Videos/DVD

Prostate health: A guide for African American men [Guidebook & DVD]: https://docs.google.com/document/d/1I2CqUV8GFSU_6r-c4Ed7aRzMtq3TUcgPu-mqcB9Slo4/edit

Book

Rawls, G., & Lloyd, Jr., F. (2006). *Managing cancer: The African American's guide to prevention, diagnosis and treatment* (2nd ed.). Indianapolis, IN: Hilton Publishing.

NOTE

1. We'd like to acknowledge the assistance of Leslie Forrest Ware, MSW student, for research assistance.

REFERENCES

Altekruse, S. F., Kosary, C. L., Krapcho, M., Neyman, N., Aminou, R., Waldron, W., . . . Edwards, B. K. (2010). *SEER cancer statistics review, 1975–2007*. Bethesda, MD: National Cancer Institute.
American Cancer Society (ACS). (2012). *Cancer facts and figures for African Americans, 2011–2012*. Atlanta, GA: Author.
Bastani, R., Gallardo, N., & Maxwell, A. (2001). Barriers to colorectal cancer screening among ethnically diverse and average risk individuals. *Journal of Psychosocial Oncology, 19*(3/4), 65–84.
Branson, R. D., Davis Jr., K., & Butler, K. L. (2007). African Americans' participation in clinical research: Importance, barriers, and solutions. *American Journal of Surgery, 193*(1), 32–39.
Bullock, K., & McGraw, S. A. (2006). A community capacity-enhancement approach to breast and cancer screening among older women of color. *Health and Social Work, 31*(1), 16–25.
Bullock, K., & McGraw, S. A. (2013). Promoting breast and cervical cancer among Hispanic and African American women. *International Journal of Humanities and Social Sciences, 3*(7), 35–47.

Carrión, I. V., & Bullock, K. (2012). A case of Hispanics and hospice care. *International Journal of Humanities and Social Sciences*, 2(4), 9–16.

Corbie-Smith, G., Thomas, S. B., Williams, M. V., & Moody-Ayers, S. (1999). Attitudes and beliefs of African Americans toward participation in medical research. *Journal of General Internal Medicine*, 14(9), 537–546.

Freeman, H. P., & Chu, K. C. (2005). Determinants of cancer disparities: Barriers to cancer screening, diagnosis, and treatment. *Surgical Oncology Clinics of North America*, 14(4), 655–669.

Ghafoor, A., Jemal, A., Cokkinides, V., Cardinez, C., Murray, T., Samuels, A., & Thun, M. J. (2002). Cancer statistics for African Americans. *CA: A Cancer Journal for Clinicians*, 52(6), 326–341.

Hamilton, J. B., Moore, C., Powe, B. D., Agarwal, M., & Martin, P. (2010). Perceptions of support among older African American cancer survivors. *Oncology Nursing Forum*, 37(4), 484–493.

Matthews, A. K., Sellergren, S. A., Manfredi, C., & Williams, M. (2002). Factors influencing medical information seeking among African American cancer patients. *Journal of Health Communication: International Perspectives*, 7(3), 205–219.

Mazanec, P. M., Daly, B. J., Townsend, A. (2010). Hospice utilization and end-of-life care decision making of African Americans. *American Journal of Hospice and Palliative Medicine*, 27(8), 560.

National Association of Social Workers. (2008). *Code of ethics.* Washington, DC: Author. Retrieved from http://www.socialworkers.org/pubs/code/code.asp?print=1&

Roff, L. L., Simon, C. E., Nelson-Gardell, D., & Pleasants, H. M. (2009). Spiritual support and African American breast cancer survivors. *Affilia*, 24(3), 285–299.

Sanders, P. R. (2011). Increase African American enrollment. *Applied Clinical Trials*, 42–50. Retrieved from http://digital.findpharma.com/nxtbooks/advanstar/act_201101/index.php?startid=42#/44

Siegel, R., Naishadham, D., & Jemal, A. (2012). Cancer statistics, 2012. *CA: A Cancer Journal of Clinicians*, 62(1), 10–29.

Siegel, R., Ward, E., Brawley, O., & Jemal, A. (2011). Cancer statistics, 2011: The impact of eliminating socioeconomic and racial disparities on premature cancer deaths. *CA: A Cancer Journal of Clinicians*, 61(4), 212–236.

Snow, A., & Gilbertson, K. (2011). The complexity of cancer in multiple family members: Dynamics of social work collaboration. *Social Work in Health Care*, 50(6), 411–423.

Spurlock, W. R., & Cullins, L. S. (2006). Cancer fatalism and breast cancer screening in African American women. *Association of Black Nursing Faculty Journal*, 17(1), 38–43.

Stein, G. L., Sherman, P. A., & Bullock, K. (2009). Educating gerontologists for cultural proficiency in end-of-life care practice. *Journal of Educational Gerontology*, 35(11), 1008–1025.

U.S. Department of Health and Human Services (USDHHS). (2012). *Healthy people 2020: HHS action plan to reduce racial and ethnic health disparities.* Retrieved from http://minorityhealth.hhs.gov/npa/files/Plans/HHS/HHS_Plan_complete.pdf

Ward, E., Jemal, A., Cokkinides, V., Singh, G. K., Cardinez, C., Ghafoor, A., & Thun, M. (2004). Cancer disparities by race/ethnicity and socioeconomic status. *CA: A Cancer Journal for Clinicians*, 54(2), 78–93.

World Health Organization. (2011). *Global status report on noncommunicable diseases 2010.* Geneva, Switzerland: Author.

42

Guadalupe R. Palos

Hispanic/Latino Individuals and Families Affected by Cancer: Outreach, Screening, and Assessment

Key Concepts

- *Oncology social work practice with Hispanic/Latino patients and their families requires culturally competent skills and experience.*
- *A Latino's country of origin, legal status, and level of acculturation have an impact on patient and family worldviews toward cancer, as well as outreach, screening, and assessment services.*
- *Conceptual models that address Latinos' diversity, sociodemographic characteristics, and preferences relevant to family, community, and environment are the most appropriate ways to achieve evidence-based oncology social work practice with this population.*

By 2050, oncology social work practice in the United States will be impacted by the dramatic increase in the number of Hispanics/Latinos (Taylor, Lopez, Martínez, & Velasco, 2012; U.S. Census Bureau, 2013). Oncology social workers will be asked to use their professional expertise, knowledge, and emotional intelligence to deliver services to a Hispanic/Latino population with a wide, intragroup variation in their reaction to the cancer experience and cancer outcomes. The social work profession is recognized for its innate commitment to integrate cultural competence and awareness into every practice setting (AOSW, 2012; NASW, 2001).

Oncology social work practice has evolved from experiential learning and practitioner expertise to a greater focus on evidence-based practice models, theories, and research (Furman et al., 2009; Organista, 2009). The projected growth and disproportionate cancer burden in Latinos support the need for empirically supported interventions appropriate for heterogeneous Hispanic/Latino cancer patients and their families. The use of conceptually, culturally, and linguistically appropriate interventions can lead to better outcomes in Hispanic/Latino cancer patients (Anderson et al., 2004; Elk et al., 2012).

The purpose of this chapter is to describe how Hispanics and their families are impacted by a diagnosis of cancer, including how unique cultural, demographic, and epidemiological characteristics may influence cancer risk, diagnosis, treatment, and dying. The challenges and opportunities encountered by social workers when working with Latino families are discussed, and the impact of these factors on providing outreach, screening, and assessment services is examined. The chapter closes with the introduction of case studies and exemplars to demonstrate how research and practice may be successfully integrated. In this chapter, we use the terms *Latino* and *Hispanic* interchangeably.

What Have We Learned So Far

Changing Demographic Trends and Other Determinants

Latinos are widely heterogeneous due to the numerous subethnic groups originating from Mexico, Central America,

Latin America, and the Caribbean Islands (Guzmán, 2001; Motel & Patten, 2012). The geographic diversity of Latinos contributes to preferences in their self-classification of their ethnicity (Hispanic vs. non-Hispanic), race (Black, White, mixed), and country of origin (over 20 countries; Motel & Patten, 2012). Table 42.1 provides definitions of key concepts to help the reader understand how these terms are used in this chapter. Social workers who are aware of these hidden, but critically important, nuances can integrate differences into their interactions and overall practice with Latinos.

Identifying Latinos or Hispanics

Confusion and debate surround the question of which term is most appropriate to use when identifying or reporting Hispanic or Latino ethnicity. The term *Hispanic* originated from the 1976 Public Law 94-31, which was revised in the 1997 Office of Management and Budget Directive 15 to include *Latino* in the definition. Currently, a Hispanic or Latino is defined as "a person of Cuban, Mexican, Puerto Rican, South or Central American, or other Spanish culture or origin regardless of race" (Office of Management and Budget, 1997).

Social workers working with Latino families must understand the importance of permitting the individual to self-report his or her ethnicity and race. If an oncology social worker uses his or her own judgment to categorize a person into an ethnic or racial group, misclassification of the individual may occur. Lack of understanding creates a barrier for delivery of culturally competent interventions and, ultimately, the desired treatment outcomes for the person diagnosed with cancer or his or her family.

Cancer Epidemiology in Hispanics

The changing demographics of U.S. Latinos will have an impact on future cancer outcomes (ACS, 2012; Haile et al., 2012; Reuben, Milliken, & Paradis, 2011). Despite the increase and visibility of the Latino population, there are limitations in collecting, analyzing, and reporting cancer data for Latinos.

Table 42.2 lists the top four cancers of highest incidence and mortality rates among Latino men and women. Interestingly, death rates in Latinos exceeded those of non-Hispanic Whites by 50% for four cancers, including acute lymphocytic leukemia and cervical, gastric, and lung cancer (ACS, 2012; Haile et al., 2012). It is important to note that statistics reported collectively for Latinos conceal the wide heterogeneity in cancer rates for Latino subgroups.

Conceptual Models for Social Work Interventions

A review of the literature regarding social work practice reflects the limited availability of theories and models based on empirical evidence. Three conceptual models oncology social workers can refer to are (1) ecological (Kagawa-Singer, 2012), (2) community-based participatory (Strong et al., 2009), and (3) ecosystems matrix (Organista, 2009). Elements of each model are relevant to oncology social work practice, such as building collaboration among the individual and families, social networks, community outreach and partnerships, and the health care system.

Table 42.1.
Definitions to Consider When Delivery Oncology Social Work Interventions to U.S. Latinos

Term	Definition	Source
Ancestry	Refers to a person's ethnic roots, heritage, or the place of birth of the person's parents or ancestors before coming to the United States	U.S. Census Bureau (2012)
Ethnicity	A shared culture and way of life, especially reflected in language, folkways, religious and institutional forms, material culture such as clothing and food, and cultural products such as music, literature, and art	Bryd and Clayton (2003)
First-generation/ foreign-born immigrant	Refers to foreign-born people (those born outside the United States). Born to parents who are not U.S. citizens. Used interchangeably	Taylor et al. (2012)
Second generation	Describes a person born in the United States, with at least one first-generation parent	Taylor et al. (2012)
Third or higher generation	Describes a person born in the United States and with both parents born in the United States	Taylor et al. (2012)
Native born	Describes a person born in the United States or born in other countries but who have at least one parent who is a U.S. citizen	Taylor et al. (2012)

Table 42.2.
Leading Cancer Sites of Incidence and Mortality Among Latinos, 2012 Estimates[a]

	Males	Females
Incidence (new cases)	Prostate, colon and rectum, kidney	Breast, thyroid, lung, uterus
Mortality (deaths)	Lung, colon and rectum, liver, prostate	Breast, lung and bronchus, colon and rectum, pancreas

[a] ACS (2012).

Conflicts in Worldviews

The entire trajectory of the cancer experience and its impact on the Latino patient and his or her family are influenced by multiple factors, including cultural factors. Culture defines reality for its people and, in this reality, forms a worldview for an individual or society (Kagawa-Singer, 2012). Worldview affects the manner in which an individual or society views the world, and the combination of culture and worldviews influences the development of a person's value system, which then guides the lives, beliefs, and practices of a collective group of people. A culturally competent social worker can integrate appropriate practices and beliefs from all worldviews to attain a culturally appropriate intervention.

Latino Cultural Values

Latinos, despite their diversity, have core values that form their worldviews, expectations, and coping methods relevant to the entire cancer trajectory (Table 42.3). The Association of Oncology Social Work's and the National Association of Social Workers' standards of practice stress the need for oncology social workers to continue receiving education to maintain and expand their understanding for delivering culturally competent social work interventions (AOSW, 2012; NASW, 2001).

Table 42.3.
Latino Core Values in Spanish and English[a]

Spanish	English
confianza	trust
compadreo	kinship and friendship
familismo	family
machismo	protector and strength
marianismo	moral strength and sacrifice
respecto	respect
simpatía	harmonious

[a] Palos (1998).

Key Concepts Related to Latinos

The degree that a person believes in these values will be strongly influenced by three key concepts: (1) country of origin, (2) legal status, and (3) acculturation. For example, a first-generation Latina who has recently migrated to the United States may not be familiar with the concept of screening for breast and cervical cancer. This woman's country of origin may have lacked the infrastructure to provide this type of preventive care. Legal status also influences the cancer experience, particularly if the individual is an undocumented immigrant. Access to medical care or social services may be denied due to current policies, such as the Personal Responsibility and Work Opportunity Reconciliation Act of 1996 (U.S. Congress, 1996). These policies will have a profound effect on eligibility requirements for access to necessary cancer care.

Acculturation has been identified as an important process and concept when working with Latino families. Acculturation is often called cultural assimilation and indicates a person changing his or her own cultural worldviews so he or she may be like others in dominant society (Thomson & Hoffman-Goetz, 2009). However, as immigrants try to acculturate, there is also the risk that they can become separated or marginalized from both their culture of origin and the new society they are trying to adopt. The result is that the individual loses both identities and is excluded from both societies. Immigrants may choose to adapt to the dominant society beginning with enculturation and incorporation, and then fully integrate into their new or dominant society. An example of this process can be seen with the growing number of Latino enclaves. There is growing interest in how these communal communities may have a protective factor in moderating distress and helping Latinos better adjust to the acculturation process (Fuentes & Aranda, 2012). Oncology social workers must recognize the impact this process has on a person and his or her family when identifying cancer-related services and planning interventions.

Challenges and Opportunities

A major challenge often experienced by social work practitioners is the risk of forming their own stereotypes, generalizations, and biases about Latinos based on general information such as that presented in this chapter. The following case study provides an example of how stereotyping can impact oncology social workers' interventions.

Spanish or English Mistaken Identity

A Latina woman named Xochi Martinez (pseudonym) receiving chemotherapy for acute lymphocytic leukemia was admitted to the emergency room with high fever and chills. Because of the acuteness of her situation, she was immediately ushered into a treatment room, where the medical team began to work on her. The patient was bombarded with several questions from various members of the team—all in Spanish. The patient was slow to answer any of the questions and the team assumed it was due to her condition. Administration of medications was part of the treatment plan, but before they were administered, the nurse was required to confirm the patient's identity and asked in Spanish, "Is your name Xochi Martinez?" The patient did not reply immediately, but when she did respond, she asked the nurse to speak to her in English because she felt more comfortable with that language. The nurse promptly checked the patient's wristband again and asked, "You are Xochi Martinez, aren't you?" After a brief silence, a team member quipped, "We were only trying to be sensitive to your culture." The social worker spoke to the patient once she was stabilized and discovered that Xochi was a third-generation Hispanic woman, born in the United States and named after her great-great-grandmother, who was born in Mexico. English was the dominant language in her family, and she had not been raised to be proficient in Spanish. She confided that people always assumed she spoke Spanish because of her name, which was embarrassing because she wasn't fluent in Spanish. She asked the social worker, "Why can't people just ask me if I prefer to speak in English or Spanish?"

In this case, the social worker encountered the following challenges: (1) an emergency situation in which the patient's life may have been in danger, (2) lack of information on the patient's demographic or clinical characteristics, and (3) lack of an opportunity to begin a preliminary assessment of the patient's needs. Fortunately, the social worker identified several opportunities to intervene in this situation. First, the social worker noted that the patient was accompanied by several family members, who remained in the waiting room. She approached the eldest member of the group and asked if she could help the family in any way. Based on the values of respecto *(respect) and* familismo *(family), the foundation for trust (confianza) was initiated. Second, the social worker noted that one family member seemed to be the spokesperson for the family and discovered that person was the patient's godmother* (compadreo). *The family trusted her to facilitate communication between the social worker and the family. Third, the social worker realized the family members were conversing primarily in English and made it a point to respond in the same language. Fourth, the social worker sat down with the family and began to ask questions about the various members who were present. This small talk* (plática) *engaged the family even more and they began to share information with more ease and readiness* (personalismo). *In sum, the social worker conducted a multimodal family systems assessment, obtained background information, and planned an intervention for the patient, which would begin by initiating the interview in English when the two met. The social worker did not make assumptions about the family and patient's language preferences, roles, or familiarity with the health care system. Instead, her assessment of this Latino family was a dynamic process of gathering and synthesizing culturally relevant information.*

Cultural Competency in Assessment, Screening, and Outreach

Cultural worldviews must be incorporated into planning assessment, screening, and outreach efforts for Latino families. Oncology social workers have several practice models that have been successfully used with families in crisis.

One approach, as illustrated earlier, is family-based assessment and interventions. Studies have shown that these types of interventions complement Latinos' cultural norms and practices and can increase the reach of the intervention because several family members can be involved at the same time (Furman et al., 2009; Garland, 2012; Miller, 2012). Oncology social workers have been using family-based interventions quite successfully in working with cancer patients and their families. To date, there is no or limited research examining the effectiveness of using family conferences with Latinos during their cancer experience.

The following sections present guidelines that can help the oncology social worker provide quality services and interventions for Latino patients, their caregivers, and their family members (nuclear, blended, or extended) throughout the cancer experience. The guidelines are grouped into three categories of practice essential in oncology social work: assessment, screening, and outreach. Each section provides a brief discussion of key issues to consider when working with Latino families.

Assessment

Generally, oncology social workers are called when patients and families need support in dealing with the impact of a potential or actual diagnosis of cancer. These encounters can take place in diverse locations, including outpatient clinics, inpatient rooms, or even home settings. Although it may be challenging to conduct a detailed cultural assessment, it is a critical element in delivering culturally sensitive oncology social work interventions.

The assessment has two major goals: (1) engage in pláticas (small talk) to establish trust and (2) collect cultural data to help individualize the plan of care for this ethnic group. Pláticas help the oncology social worker in several ways, including determining language preference and, if needed, calling for Spanish-speaking interpreters to participate in the assessment. Establishing trust and rapport with the patient and his or her family (*familismo*) by engaging in pláticas between providers, patients, and families builds personalismo. Learning the family hierarchy of decision making and communication by acknowledging each member with the patient is critical.

Screening

Social workers may be asked to instruct the team about culturally relevant activities or approaches that could increase Latino participation in cancer screening. Key areas to inquire about before an examination include preferences or taboos regarding privacy needs and physical touch needed to perform the examination or procedures, participation of other team members during the examination, and previous traumatic events or medical conditions that may have occurred during their lives. The latter information is of particular importance for female immigrants who left their country for personal safety or political reasons.

Outreach

Oncology social workers become involved in cancer outreach activities in a hospital or community setting for various reasons. One important outreach activity relates to developing and implementing cancer support groups for Latino cancer patients or their families. Several obstacles—including language, transportation, timing of events, a perception that facilitators will be unfamiliar with Latino culture or uncomfortable working with this population, and fear of being identified as undocumented—may limit Latino participation in support groups. However, this trend is changing with the growing access to and availability of Spanish-language support groups, culturally and linguistically competent facilitators, and online support groups offered in Spanish.

Pearls

- Engaging in *pláticas* from the initial visit helps establish language preferences, trust, rapport, and *personalismo* among the Latino client, his or her family, and the oncology social worker.
- Taking time to learn about the family and its dynamics (hierarchies, roles, and functions) will help the oncology social worker when planning interventions to help Latinos through the cancer experience.

Pitfalls

- Professional and personal worldviews based on an oncology social worker's life experiences may contribute to generalizations or stereotypes about Latino clients and families encountered in their practice.
- Misclassification of a client's ethnic or racial identity can have an impact on the delivery of culturally competent interventions and, ultimately, the desired treatment outcomes for the person diagnosed with cancer and his or her family.

Culturally competent social work practice with Latinos can be achieved by acquiring informal and formal knowledge, learning or enhancing assessment and intervention skills based on Latino cultural values and worldviews, and showing commitment to ongoing professional development by participating in academic courses, continuing education, and conferences (Furman et al., 2009; Jani, Ortiz, & Aranda, 2009). This chapter has provided strategies for social workers to assess their own skills, knowledge, and commitment to understanding the Latino culture; identify community-based resources relevant to working with Latinos; use professional standards as resources to support their practice with Latinos; and encourage lifelong learning to become a proactive, culturally competent oncology social worker.

Oncology Social Worker Strategies to Build Skills and Knowledge When Working With Latinos

- Gather a list of Latino cultural experts within your organization or from your local community to contact for advice and collaboration in providing services, interventions, or outreach activities to Latinos.
- Conduct a windshield survey of a local Latino enclave or community; tune in to the types of businesses in the area and environmental details that can impede or facilitate access to cancer care.
- Advocate for funding of oncology research conducted by oncology social workers to establish evidence-based culturally competent practice.

REFERENCES

American Cancer Society (ACS). (2012). *Cancer facts and figures for Hispanics/Latinos 2012–2014*. Atlanta, GA: Author.

Anderson, K. O., Mendoza, T. R., Payne, R., Valero, V., Palos, G. R., Nazario, A., . . . Cleeland, C. S. (2004). Pain education for underserved minority cancer patients: A randomized controlled trial. *Journal of Clinical Oncology, 22*(24), 4918–4925.

Association of Oncology Social Work (AOSW). (2012). Oncology social work standards of practice. Retrieved from http://aosw.org/standards-of-practice/

Bryd, M. W., & Clayton, L. A. (2003). Racial disparities in health care: A background and history. In B. D. Smedley, A. Y. Stith, & A. R. Nelson (Eds.), *Unequal treatment: Confronting racial and ethnic disparities in health care* (pp. 455–527). Washington, DC: National Academies Press.

Elk, R., Morris, A., Onega, T. L., Ganschow, P., Hershmann, D., Brawley, O. W., & Cykert, S. (2012). Disparities in cancer treatment: Factors that impact health equity in breast, colon, and lung cancer. In R. Elk & H. Landrine (Eds.), *Cancer disparities: Causes and evidence-based solutions* (pp. 89–120). New York, NY: Springer Publishing Company.

Fuentes, D., & Aranda, M. P. (2012). Depression interventions among racial and ethnic minority older adults: A systematic review across 20 years. *American Journal of Geriatric Psychiatry*, *20*(11), 915–931.

Furman, R., Negi, N. J., Iwamoto, D. K., Rowan, D., Shukraft, A., & Gragg, J. (2009). Social work practice with Latinos: Key issues for social workers. *Social Work*, *54*(2), 167–174.

Garland, D. R. (2012). A process model of family formation and development. *Journal of Family Social Work*, *15*(3), 235–250.

Guzmán, B. (2001). *The Hispanic population: 2000 Census Brief.* Retrieved from http://www.census.gov/prod/2001pubs/c2kbr01-3.pdf

Haile, R. W., John, E. M., Levine, A. J., Cortessis, V. K., Unger, J. B., Gonzales, M., . . . Boffetta, P. (2012). A review of cancer in U.S. Hispanic populations. *Cancer Prevention Research*, *5*(2), 150–163.

Jani, J. S., Ortiz, L., & Aranda, M. P. (2009). Latino outcomes studies in social work: A review of the literature. *Research on Social Work Practice*, *19*(2), 179–194.

Kagawa-Singer, M. (2012). Applying the concept of culture to reduce health disparities through health behavior research. *Preventive Medicine*, *55*(5), 356–361.

Miller, G. (2012). Application of theory to family-centered care: A role for social workers. *Social Work in Health Care*, *51*(2), 89–106.

Motel, S., & Patten, E. (2012). The 10 largest Hispanic origin groups: Characteristics, rankings, top counties. Washington, DC: Pew Research Center Hispanic Trends Project. Retrieved from http://www.pewhispanic.org/2012/06/27/the-10-largest-hispanic-origin-groups-characteristics-rankings-top-counties/

National Association of Social Workers (NASW). (2001). *NASW standards for cultural competence in social work practice.* Washington, DC: Author.

Office of Management and Budget. (1997). *Revisions to the standards for the classification of federal data on race and ethnicity.* Washington, DC: Federal Register Notice. Retrieved from http://www.whitehouse.gov/omb/fedreg_1997standards/

Organista, K. C. (2009). New practice model for Latinos in need of social work services. *Social Work*, *54*(4), 297–305.

Palos, G. R. (1998). Culture and pain assessment in Hispanic patients. In R. Payne, R. B. Patt, & C. S. Hill (Eds.), *Assessment and treatment of cancer pain* (pp. 35–51). Seattle, WA: IASP Press.

Reuben, S. H., Milliken, E. L., & Paradis, L. J. (2011). America's demographic and cultural transformation: Implications for cancer. In *President's Cancer Panel: 2009–2010 Annual report.* Bethesda, MD: National Cancer Institute.

Strong, L. L., Israel, B. A., Schulz, A. J., Reyes, A., Rowe, Z., Weir, S. S., & Poe, C. (2009). Piloting interventions within a community-based participatory research framework: Lessons learned from the healthy environments partnership. *Progress in Community Health Partnerships: Research, Education, and Action*, *3*(4), 327–334.

Taylor, P., Lopez, M. H., Martínez, J., & Velasco, G. (2012). Why labels don't fit: Hispanics and their views of identity. Washington, DC: Pew Research Center Hispanic Trends Project. Retrieved from http://www.pewhispanic.org/2012/04/04/when-labels-dont-fit-hispanics-and-their-views-of-identity/

Thomson, M. D., & Hoffman-Goetz, L. (2009). Defining and measuring acculturation: A systematic review of public health studies with Hispanic populations in the United States. *Social Science and Medicine*, *69*(7), 983–991.

U.S. Census Bureau. (2012). People and households: Ancestry. Retrieved from http://www.census.gov/population/ancestry/

U.S. Census Bureau. (2013). People and households: Race. Retrieved from http://www.census.gov/population/race/

U.S. Congress. (1996). 104th Congress H.R. 3734: Personal Responsibility and Work Opportunity Reconciliation Act of 1996. Retrieved from https://www.govtrack.us/congress/bills/104/hr3734

43

Pamela Pui-Yu Leung and Cecilia L. W. Chan

Working With Chinese Families Impacted by Cancer: An Integrative Body–Mind–Spirit Approach

Key Concepts

- *Cultural values such as filial piety, social harmony, self-reliance, and self-restraint have implications for the health behaviors, preferences, communication styles, and coping strategies of Chinese patients and families.*
- *Cultural beliefs can be a resource for adaptive coping. The Eastern beliefs and values of Confucianism, Daoism, and Buddhism promote a sense of acceptance, resilience, and harmony in living with cancer.*
- *An integrative body–mind–spirit practice model that brings together Eastern philosophies and traditional Chinese medicine to oncology social work practice is introduced.*

Chinese culture is characterized by a holistic system of thought, collectivism, pragmatism, and respect for family decision making (Chau & Yu, 2010). This chapter explores how Chinese culture influences patients' and families' reactions to cancer and coping, highlights the principles integral to the care of ethnic Chinese patients, and addresses the importance of psychosocial oncology care that speaks to a language of cultural diversity.

Health Beliefs, Practices, and Care Preferences

Traditional Chinese Medicine

Chinese people have used traditional Chinese medicine (TCM) for treatment and fostering health for more than 2,000 years, and it remains a popular treatment in contemporary China (Yu, Wang, Liu, & Lewith, 2012). According to TCM, health is a matter of balance and harmony between yin (representing softness, stillness, cold, and darkness) and yang (representing hardness, movement, heat, and brightness). Illness is caused by a yin–yang imbalance (Beinfield & Korngold, 2003). Prolonged physical or psychological disturbances such as imbalanced diet (excess consumption of either "cold" or "hot" food), unresolved emotions (e.g., chronic worry and extreme fear), interpersonal disharmony, and loss of meaning in life disrupt the smooth circulation of qi and thus cause illness. Therefore, TCM treatment aims at restoring an individual's balance and harmony.

Diet

As diet can affect the yin–yang balance of the body, Chinese people tend to avoid cold and icy drinks because cold food and beverages will deplete qi. They believe that the choice of food taken by an individual should harmonize the yin (cold) and yang (hot) balance within the body (Chui, Donoghue, & Chenoweth, 2005).

Health Care Preferences

Many Chinese patients, including those living in migrant cities, use complementary and alternative medicine along with, or separate from, Western medicine (Ashing, Padilla, Tejero, & Kagawa-Singer, 2003; Chui et al., 2005; Payne, Chapman, Holloway, Seymour, & Chau, 2005; Yu et al., 2012). For example, Chinese Australians use Chinese herbs and acupuncture for alleviating the side effects of cancer treatment and to promote well-being. Chinese patients see the Western approach to cancer treatment as aggressive, whereas they perceive herbal medicine, qigong, and food therapy as restorative (Chui et al., 2005). Patients also regard TCM as the last hope when they find no further active Western treatment available (Chui et al., 2005; Yu et al., 2012). Despite the high prevalence of TCM use, Chinese patients may not discuss this at all or fully with their health care professionals, especially when they believe their health care team may be opposed to TCM.

Implications for Social Work Practice

- Health care facilities could offer both hot and cold water and a microwave so that patients are offered choices. Asian family caregivers would feel more comfortable about bringing food and tonic soup to patients in the hospital.
- Create a supportive environment for health care professionals to discuss with the patients culture-specific practices such as the complementary use of traditional Asian medicine and exercises of yoga or qigong.

Chinese Culture and Its Influence on Coping With Cancer

Stigma and Reluctance to Seek Help

As with cancer patients of other ethnic origins, Chinese patients also feel emotionally overwhelmed upon diagnosis and experience a mixture of shame, guilt, worry, uncertainty, fear, and anxiety (Ashing et al., 2003; Lui, Ip, & Chui, 2009). However, studies show that Chinese immigrants in need of care were much slower to seek medical help and social work services than were Western patients (Armstrong & Swartzman, 2001; Ashing et al., 2003; Lui et al., 2009). Cultural taboo was a major barrier. Traditionally, cancer carries a stigma, with the thinking that it may be caused by evil spirits or related to past bad deeds or even past lives (negative karma) or bad *feng shui* (geomancy). Studies found that these beliefs persist in Chinese immigrant communities (Chui et al., 2005; Lui et al., 2009). Because of the shame associated with cancer, Chinese people prefer to keep the diagnosis within the family and rely solely on family members for support. Ashing et al. (2003) found that Asian Americans are hesitant to share personal feelings and emotional problems about their cancer. Some patients even avoid using the word *cancer* when discussing their illness. There are also strong taboos associated with death, which make it very difficult for Chinese patients and their families to discuss advance care planning and preparation for death (Leung & Chan, 2011).

Traditional Chinese values on self-reliance, perseverance, and filial piety may contribute to the reluctance in help seeking. Chinese people tend to perceive managing their own needs as a personal responsibility. Outside help is sought only when they find that existing kinship networks can no longer cope with the problems (Lui et al., 2009).

Implications for Social Work Practice

- Social workers should be sensitive in communicating with Chinese patients and their family members, as the word *cancer* carries a stigma.
- Many Chinese people are not used to openly talking about their personal problems with strangers, including professionals. Social workers should respect their need for more time to develop the rapport needed to openly share their concerns, especially negative emotions.
- Sharing videos or books on how other Chinese patients cope with and survive cancer is recommended. Support groups for ethnic Chinese patients in their own dialect are also helpful.[1]

Communication Style and Expression of Love and Care

Chinese people value social harmony over individual expression (Russell & Yik, 1996). In a collectivist culture, the constant engagement with the in-group enables individuals to suppress the need for self-expression and be fully dedicated to how others are feeling and thinking (Armstrong & Swartzman, 2001). Chinese people tend to be circumspect and avoid direct expression of negative feelings. They expect others to know their needs or wishes.

Love for others is expressed through actions, not words. Chinese people prepare tonic soup and food and help with daily care of the sick family member (Wong & Chan, 2007). Eating is a very important aspect of quality of life for Chinese patients because food prepared by friends and family carries an important message of love. Taking good care of ill family members and being present at the moment of death are expressions of filial piety, and thus bear great importance. Studies have found that a sense of guilt was evident for family members who were not able to perform their filial role properly (Lui et al., 2009; Wong & Chan, 2007).

Implications for Social Work Practice

- The nonverbal, subtle, and indirect communication style of Chinese patients forms a contrast to the Western style in which an individual assumes the responsibility to express him- or herself clearly if he or she expects to be attended to or understood. Social workers have to be sensitive to the possible needs behind what has been expressed. Paying attention to nonverbal expressions of Chinese patients and family members would be very helpful.
- Family members like to know about the patient's condition daily so they can carry out proper care for their sick family member (Wong & Chan, 2007). Teaching them how to do concrete and specific caring skills, massage, and so forth would be much appreciated.
- Social workers can express appreciation to family members for performing their filial role because they need the cultural affirmation that they have done the best they could.

Somatization and Mind–Body Connection

From a Western perspective, Chinese people tend to somatize emotions. Physical rather than emotional complaints induce social support in Chinese societies (Russell & Yik, 1996). It is easier for Chinese people to express bodily discomfort than to articulate psychological distress. Emotions are often expressed using body organs as metaphors (e.g., a "hot liver" is a metaphor for anger) in Chinese. In TCM, different emotions affect different organs. For example, excessive joy and a state of euphoria can affect the cardiovascular (heart) system, worrying too much can affect the digestive (stomach) system, and intense sorrow and prolonged grief can affect the respiratory (lung) system. Mind and body are intricately connected. Empowering patients to be in touch with their body is effective in helping them connect with their psychological concerns and work toward integrative well-being (Leung, Chan, Ng, & Lee, 2009).

Yanny was a 37-year-old woman diagnosed with metastatic colon cancer and under the care of the palliative home care team. Her symptoms were under control. A few weeks before her death, she experienced shortness of breath and serious discomfort around her chest. However, the symptoms went away during the weekend, when her husband was home. Her condition worsened at the start of the week, when her husband went back to work. In a conversation with the social worker, Yanny said she hoped her husband could have more time with her, but she did not want to tell him this and trouble him. With the social worker's encouragement, Yanny told her husband that she wished for his company during her last days. Her husband immediately took leave from work. The couple had time to celebrate their life together, finish unfinished business, and say good-bye. Yanny passed away in peace 2 weeks later.

Implications for Social Work Practice

- It is helpful to understand the emotional interpretation of physical symptoms, or at least to know that Chinese people tend to use bodily complaints to express psychological concerns.
- As mind–body connectedness is deeply ingrained in Chinese culture, a mind–body approach of intervention is most helpful.

Treatment Goals and Health Decision Making

In a collectivist culture, family welfare and social harmony have priority over individual autonomy. Receiving health care treatment can be instrumental for the attainment of goals geared toward collective wellness, such as to return to work or to the family, thereby fulfilling social obligations and commitments (Armstrong & Swartzman, 2001). Similarly, health decisions Chinese patients make may be based more on their potential impact on family members than on the self. The following patient narrative is a vivid illustration.

Fifty-year-old Thomas's lung cancer returned a year after surgery and chemotherapy. His oncologist said the chance for a cure was minimal, but he could try targeted therapy. In Hong Kong, the government does not sponsor targeted treatment. Thomas did not have any insurance coverage for his treatment. He had some savings, just sufficient to pay for the drugs, but he was determined that he would not opt for treatment. He would rather save the money for his children (who were in high school and college) than spend it on treatment only to prolong his life. When he told his wife and children of his decision, they insisted that he continue treatment. He became very upset. The social worker met with the family and helped them to openly share their concerns, values, and wishes for one another. What appeared to be an undesirable decision was an adaptive decision for Thomas, who valued family collective welfare, especially a good college education for his children. The family finally supported Thomas's decision of investing in his children instead. Thomas used Chinese herbs and practiced qigong to foster his health. The family used some money for a family trip and saved the rest for the children's education. Thomas was able to live his life fully until his death a year later. He had no regrets, because his wishes were honored.

Implications for Social Work Practice

- Sometimes Chinese patients are not looking for individual-oriented goals (e.g., maximizing health outcomes). Social workers have to be cautious not to mistake patients' decisions that focus on the other as unwise before getting an understanding of the patient's concerns and value.

- Social workers can use patients' communal goals (e.g., to learn coping skills so as not to burden others) as a motivation for patients to strive for better outcomes.
- Rather than endorsing individual autonomy, sometimes it may be more appropriate for a social worker to enhance family harmony and acknowledge the interconnectedness of family members (Payne et al., 2005).

Family Support: A Double-Edged Sword

A study on Asian Americans found that Chinese patients regard family as the primary source of support and the most important agent in making illness-related decisions (Ashing et al., 2003). The study by Lui et al. (2009) on Chinese Australians found that family members managed almost every aspect of a patient's life, including daily care, emotional support, and medical decision making. However, a patient's reliance on family members can impose huge pressures on the familial network. It could also become a barrier to seeking "outside" help, delaying professional intervention.

Ashing et al. (2003) found a phenomenon of ambivalence toward seeking help among Asian American female patients. Asian women have been socialized as caretakers, not dependents. They acknowledge the need for assistance but at the same time avoid requesting help because they do not want to burden their families.

Implications for Social Work Practice

- Social workers have to watch for patients who present themselves as capable even though they need help.
- While respecting patients' desire to protect the family, the social worker should encourage them to express their thoughts, feelings, needs, and desires.

Cultural Beliefs and Practices as Coping Resources

The Chinese way of coping with illness emphasizes positive acceptance. Acceptance is not fatalism or passive surrendering but rather an act of taking responsibility and working to restore one's system to balance while being at peace with whatever comes. Chinese cancer patients interpret suffering arising from the illness through their own cultural beliefs. They seek comfort by seeing suffering as the will of Heaven (*tien-ming*; Confucianism, Daoism), the result of karma (Buddhism), or part of normal life (Daoism). These beliefs help transform negative emotions into adaptive coping, such as focusing on living in the moment, accumulating good karma, and engaging in meditative practice (Leung & Chan, 2010). Some patients adopt other cultural strategies such as ancestor worship or rearrange their home environment to attract good feng shui in combating cancer (Ashing et al., 2003; Chui et al., 2005; Lui et al., 2009). Many find the practice of qigong helpful in fostering physical stamina and psychological well-being (Chui et al., 2005; Leung & Chan, 2010). The following patient narratives illustrate how Chinese patients use cultural concepts in adapting to cancer.

Betty, age 54, is a breast cancer survivor. She regarded cancer as Tien's (Heaven's) plan to test her mind and strengthen her resolution: "I conceived of it as a test from Tien. Tien was testing my mind and to see if I would yield to the disease. I won't be defeated by this test. The greater the challenge, the stronger my willpower."

When Ivy, age 44, was first diagnosed with breast cancer, she felt miserable and asked, "Why me?" During her recovery, she learned Buddhist teachings. She attributed her cancer to karma: "Now, there is no need to ask why. . . . I didn't know the 'cause,' as it may have happened in my previous lives. I am just getting the 'consequence.' It's karma. Instead of asking why, I now focus on sowing good seeds of karma for the future. I got an answer for my suffering and am looking at the positive side."

The Integrative Body–Mind–Spirit Model

The integrative body–mind–spirit (IBMS) practice model cross-fertilizes the Eastern philosophies of Daoism, Buddhism, and TCM with Western therapeutic techniques in promoting holistic well-being in individuals and families (Lee, Ng, Leung, & Chan, 2009). When the IBMS model is applied to cancer patients, the cancer experience can be life transforming because the suffering from cancer can be converted into a new journey of personal search for meaning that leads to growth through pain. Learning therapeutic techniques can help alleviate symptoms and promote health. The intervention is designed as a psychoeducational group of five sessions of 3 hours each. Table 43.1 lists the intervention components. Table 43.2 summarizes the themes and objectives of each session.

Each session includes didactic discussion, sharing, and practicing techniques (the intervention protocol is in a manual; see Additional Resources at the end of this chapter). The design fits Chinese patients' expectations of learning techniques and working on the body and the mind. Randomized controlled trials conducted in both Hong Kong and other Asian communities suggested that the approach has been effective in improving mood, improving quality of life, and providing other positive outcomes across different types of cancer populations (Chan et al., 2006; Hsiao, Jow, Kui, & Chang, 2010).

Table 43.1.
The Integrative Body–Mind–Spirit Approach: Intervention Components

Domains	Therapeutic Interventions/Techniques
Body (Physical)	• Breathing (e.g., mindful breathing, breathing qigong) • Therapeutic massage • Acupressure (points to press to enhance energy levels) • Qigong exercises and movements • Relaxation techniques (e.g., body scan, guided imagery)
Mind (Cognitive/Emotional)	• Normalization • Acceptance and validation • Cognitive reframing (e.g., develop new perspective on suffering)
Spiritual (Existential/ Contemplative)	• Meaning searching and reconstruction • Growth and transformation in suffering • Mindfulness and living in the moment • Developing compassion and gratitude

Table 43.2.
The Integrative Body–Mind–Spirit Approach: Session Themes and Objectives

Session Themes	Objectives
Session 1: Cancer and holistic wellness	• Introduce the concept of holistic health. • Develop an awareness of the interconnectedness of physical health, emotions, and spiritual well-being.
Session 2: Acceptance and letting go	• Evaluate the gains and losses from cancer. • Introduce the ideas of gains through losses and new perspective on suffering.
Session 3: Love and forgiveness	• Discuss the idea of forgiveness and self-love as keys to joy and peace of mind. • Develop a readiness to love and forgive and the skills for nurturing one's body, mind, and spirit.
Session 4: Self-transformation	• Develop a deepened connection with self through mindfulness, compassion, and living in the moment. • Make meaning from the cancer experience.
Session 5: Hope for the future	• Share the idea of giving as a means to happiness. • Work on planning and commitment to goals.

Pearls

- Understanding the beliefs, values, preferences, and practices of Chinese patients and families is helpful in offering appropriate support and improving the patient experience.
- Chinese patients prefer practical solutions to problems and like action-oriented guidance. Practical tips (e.g., recommendations on diet, exercise, acupressure, and relaxation techniques) and psychoeducation through "direct instructions" will be greatly appreciated.
- Supportive services to the entire family are most helpful.
- Connecting patients with Internet resources, help lines, and peer support offered by survivors from the same ethnic group is desirable.

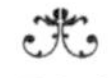

Pitfalls

- There is diversity within Chinese communities and among individuals. A cultural belief can facilitate adaptive coping to some but not all. Insufficient attention to identify individual differences may result in inappropriate support.

- Inquiring directly regarding emotions about cancer and other culturally sensitive or taboo topics (e.g., sex, palliative care, and death) may arouse resentment and denial, leading to withdrawal from service utilization.
- Patients and family members would like to protect each other and seek cooperation from health professionals in regard to disclosure of diagnosis. Patience and working with resistance gently is essential, especially with older and more traditional patients and families.

The values of self-reliance, filial obligations, and family responsibilities are still deeply ingrained in many Chinese people. Culturally competent practice depends, among other things, on understanding and appreciating people's unique concerns, as well as a set of values and attitudes respectful and inclusive of differences (Payne et al., 2005).

Acknowledgments

This work was supported by funding from the General Research Fund, Research Grant Council, Hong Kong SAR Government (Project No. 747910).

ADDITIONAL RESOURCES

Chan, C. L. W. (2001). *An Eastern body-mind-spirit approach: A training manual with one-second techniques.* Hong Kong, China: University of Hong Kong.

Clips of the techniques discussed in this chapter can be found on YouTube: http://www.youtube.com/watch?v=VWGLNqpCSLQ

NOTE

1. Cantonese is spoken by immigrants from Hong Kong and Macau. Mandarin (*Putonghua*) is used by those from Taiwan and mainland China.

REFERENCES

Armstrong, T. L., & Swartzman, L. C. (2001). Cross-cultural differences in illness models and expectations for the health care provider-client/patient interaction. In S. S. Kazarian & D. R. Evans (Eds.), *Handbook of cultural health psychology* (pp. 63–84). London, England: Academic Press.

Ashing, K. T., Padilla, G., Tejero, J., & Kagawa-Singer, M. (2003). Understanding the breast cancer experience of Asian American women. *Psycho-Oncology, 12*(1), 38–58.

Beinfield, H., & Korngold, E. (2003). Chinese medicine and cancer care. *Alternative Therapies in Health and Medicine, 9*(5), 38–52.

Chan, C. L. W., Ho, R. T. H., Lee, P. W. H., Cheng, J. Y. Y., Leung, P. P. Y., Foo, W., . . . Spiegel, D. (2006). A randomized controlled trial of psychosocial interventions using the psychophysiological framework for Chinese breast cancer patients. *Journal of Psychosocial Oncology, 24*(1), 3–26.

Chau, R. C. M., & Yu, S. W. K. (2010). The sensitivity of United Kingdom health care services to the diverse needs of Chinese-origin older people. *Aging and Society, 30*, 383–401.

Chui, Y. Y., Donoghue, J., & Chenoweth, L. (2005). Responses to advanced cancer: Chinese-Australians. *Journal of Advanced Nursing, 52*, 498–507.

Hsiao, F. H., Jow, G. M., Kui, W. H., & Chang, K. (2010). The effects of psychotherapy on psychological well-being and diurnal cortisol patterns in breast cancer survivors. *Psychotherapy and Psychosomatics, 81*, 173–182.

Lee, M. Y., Ng, S. M., Leung, P. P. Y., & Chan, C. L. W. (2009). *Integrative body-mind-spirit social work: An empirically based approach to assessment and treatment.* New York, NY: Oxford University Press.

Leung, P. P. Y., & Chan, C. L. W. (2010). Utilizing Eastern spirituality in clinical practice: A qualitative study of Chinese women with breast cancer. *Smith College Studies in Social Work, 80*(2), 159–183.

Leung, P. P. Y., & Chan, C. L. W. (2011). Palliative care in the Chinese context: An integrated framework for culturally respectful practice. In T. Altilio & S. Otis-Green (Eds.), *Oxford handbook of palliative social work* (pp. 573–578). New York, NY: Oxford University Press.

Leung, P. P. Y., Chan, C. L. W., Ng, S. M., & Lee, M. Y. (2009). Toward body-mind-spirit integration: East meets West in clinical social work practice. *Clinical Social Work Journal, 37*(4), 303–311.

Lui, C. W., Ip, D., & Chui, W. H. (2009). Ethnic experience of cancer: A qualitative study of Chinese-Australians in Brisbane, Queensland. *Social Work in Health Care, 48*, 14–37.

Payne, S., Chapman, A., Holloway, M., Seymour, J. E., & Chau, R. (2005). Chinese community views: Promoting cultural competence in palliative care. *Journal of Palliative Care, 21*, 111–116.

Russell, J. A., & Yik, M. S. M. (1996). Emotion among the Chinese. In M. H. Bond (Ed.), *The handbook of Chinese psychology* (pp. 166–188). Hong Kong, China: Oxford University Press.

Wong, M. S., & Chan, S. W. C. (2007). The experiences of Chinese family members of terminally ill patients: A qualitative study. *Journal of Clinical Nursing, 16*, 2357–2364.

Yu, H., Wang, S., Liu, J., & Lewith, G. (2012). Why do cancer patients use Chinese Medicine? A qualitative interview study in China. *European Journal of Integrative Medicine, 4*, 197–203.

VIII

Assessment and Intervention With Adults Living With Cancer

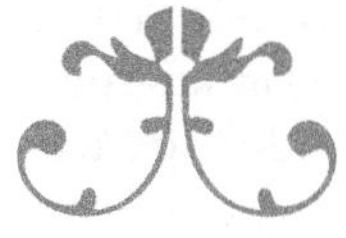

Hester Hill Schnipper

The overwhelming majority of oncology social workers focus on adults living with cancer in the context of their family and support network. Just as the pathology report directs and guides medical care, our assessment becomes the basis of ongoing psychosocial care. Every new patient referral demands that we carefully assess the situation and plan the most appropriate interventions to support the patient and family through the cancer experience. Oncology social workers must be attentive to changing dynamics and medical situations, ready to adapt the treatment plan to best fit the immediate circumstances.

In "Interventions and Ongoing Assessment With People Living With Cancer," Hester Hill Schnipper and Ashley Varner describe the need for knowledge of normative responses and risk factors, as well as for a broad range of specific skills required to assess patient and family needs through the ever-evolving process of cancer treatment. This includes special attention to points of transition and change in the illness and treatment process and within the patient and his or her support network. The authors emphasize the importance of collaborating with colleagues about psychosocial issues and teaching others to respond to patients in more helpful ways.

In "Time Enough to Make a Difference: Helping Patients Live Well With Advanced Cancer," Hester Hill Schnipper describes the often intense and moving content engaged in both individual and group work with this population and reminds us that this is not work to be undertaken within rigid boundaries or tightly held theoretical frameworks. Working with oncology patients with advanced disease may be the most challenging and yet rewarding work that oncology practitioners can do. It is important that social workers do not see themselves as separate from their patients or distance themselves from their own reactions. This is a time to be intellectually and emotionally open, to extend hands and hearts as challenging moments are experienced together.

In "Integrating Spirituality in Oncology Care," Shirley Otis Green and Terry L. Irish explore the importance and meaning of including spirituality in the practice of oncology social work. Defining spirituality as that aspect of humanity focused on meaning and connectedness invites an interdisciplinary response to the spiritual concerns of patients and their families. There is increasing evidence that the patient's quality of life is improved with attention to this important part of human life and spirit, and that the oncology social worker's experience and practice are similarly enriched.

In "Clinical Group Work: Embracing Opportunities, Navigating Challenges," Erin Columbus and Kate Wakelin provide a bicontinental view of this important intervention method. They describe three major group models: face to face, telephone, and online. Each type of group reduces isolation and enables people with cancer to live better than they likely could alone. Although all group models have similar goals, each requires different structures, methods of facilitation and delivery, and technologies. This chapter describes clinical imperatives, philosophical ideals, and the specifics of planning, screening, organizing, and maintaining successful groups.

In "Assessing and Intervening With the Spectrum of Depression and Anxiety in Cancer," Carole F. Seddon and Hester Hill Schnipper discuss working with oncology patients who are dealing with these affects/symptoms in coping with cancer. Patients with preexisting mental illness or substance abuse are especially challenging in the oncology clinic. The authors review current concepts of mental health assessment and intervention during medical illness and provide case vignettes to illustrate effective work with these patients and their caregivers.

In "Using Cognitive and Behavioral Approaches Throughout the Cancer Experience," John G. Cagle and Matthew Loscalzo introduce readers to cognitive behavioral therapy (CBT), its tenets, and its potential for application within oncology settings. The chapter also reviews evidence-supported CBT models that address common problems cancer patients and their families experience, including pragmatic approaches for assessing, addressing, and monitoring cancer-related problems and symptoms. CBT has become an essential clinical skill in oncology social work.

In "Meaning-Making Approaches to Social Work Practice in Oncology," Carrie Lethborg and Lou Harms introduce readers to meaning-making approaches in the Australian context. This cognitive-existential perspective requires the social worker to stand in each patient's shoes and to view the cancer from the patient's perspective, listening carefully to how he or she makes sense of and finds value in living. Meaning-making approaches help the patient understand and shape his or her own unique integration of meaning, purpose, and suffering in effective coping with a cancer illness.

In "Schema Therapy With Oncology Patients and Families," Lissa Parsonnet describes a cognitive model of assessment and intervention extremely useful in working with the oncology population. The schema therapy model can be used to inform clinicians' understanding of a patient's unique responses to a cancer diagnosis and treatment and to guide clinicians' treatment of the patient based on their previous experiences and beliefs. This chapter presents an overview of schema therapy, identifying and explaining the primary early maladaptive schemas patients may present in an oncology setting. Each relevant schema is described, followed by illustrations of how it can be activated by a cancer diagnosis. Coping strategies for dealing with the schema once activated and therapeutic ways to use this knowledge to help patients challenge negative schemas and establish positive ones are elaborated.

In "Practice Issues in Social Work and Psychosocial Oncology in Israel," Shlomit Perry articulates a model of psychosocial care appropriate for this unique population. Oncology social work interventions may often be brief and situation specific, but social workers maintain connections with and accessibility to higher risk patients and families over a long period of time, reflecting the family and community culture of the country. In Israel, the sophisticated crisis management skills of all social workers based on their geopolitical challenge adds to their value within the medical and psychosocial oncology team as well.

In "Oncology Social Work Practice in Integrative Medicine," Cecilia L. W. Chan and Richard R. Dickens explore various forms of complementary and alternative medicine, including integrative body–mind–spirit approaches that oncology social workers can include in their responses to patients' needs. Integrative body–mind–spirit techniques include those that focus on the body (e.g., acupressure, hand and ear massage, and breathing exercises), the mind–body (e.g., stress management, relaxation, imagery, self-hypnotic instructions, acupressure, qigong), and the spirit (e.g., mindfulness, meaning making, life review, appreciation, gratitude, and forgiveness). Recognizing that it is common for cancer patients to adopt complementary medicine alongside Western oncology treatments, social workers are creative in integrating Eastern and Western psychosocial and spiritual practices to empower and support their patients across the continuum of care.

Oncology social workers create and sustain unique and powerful relationships with their clients. Understanding that a clinical lens is frequently needed, oncology social workers view the therapeutic role of the human connection as essential for providing effective guidance of patients through the cancer illness process. Each chapter in this section reinforces this core value while presenting unique therapeutic interventions to consider for the adult oncology population. These chapters also demonstrate that oncology social workers are fully engaged in the challenge of developing an appropriate arsenal of evidence-based interventions that will help them meet the needs of patients with varied problems and different levels of distress within a complex multidisciplinary system.

44

Hester Hill Schnipper and Ashley Varner

Interventions and Ongoing Assessment With People Living With Cancer

Key Concepts

- *Assessment and intervention are vital, ongoing, and dynamic processes in the psychosocial care of people affected by cancer.*
- *Oncology social workers' job responsibilities differ depending on the environment, but all should be competent to assess the cancer patient/family member and meet both brief counseling and resource referral needs.*
- *Educating our medical team members, patients, and family caregivers about our role will increase referrals and opportunities to meet their needs effectively.*
- *The cancer trajectory has well-known psychosocial crisis points including diagnosis, beginning treatment, finishing treatment, early survivorship, recurrence, and progression. These are excellent points at which to assess or reassess clients.*
- *Countertransference is an inevitable part of our practice, and having supports in place to help us manage our own feelings is crucial.*

Assessment and intervention are crucial skills for oncology social workers, and both are dynamic processes. Each time we interact with a patient, we assess his or her situation and understand that needs, strengths, and resources evolve over time. It helps to be cognizant of what is changing in the patient's medical situation, environment, and life. Often, we also have the family members of diagnosed patients as clients (see Chapter 55). Oncology social workers should be prepared to understand and assess any client's coping while offering strategies to him or her and to our colleagues of how best to help him or her manage. The Association of Oncology Social Work (AOSW) *Standards of Practice* (AOSW, 2012; Table 44.1) address the necessary components of a complete assessment under "Services to Patients and Families." Although we may not always be able to address every item in every assessment, the goal should be a full picture of the client in his or her current environment.

In this chapter, we provide an overview of the psychosocial assessment and intervention process, addressing referral sources and initial engagement, predicted crisis points and appropriate interventions during the trajectory of the illness, ways to engage patients, and how to manage our own reactions, feelings, and countertransference.

Referral Sources and Engagement

Referral sources and patterns vary enormously among settings and practices. There are some standard guidelines, but you must begin by assessing your own workplace: How do patients enter your system? Who are their first contacts? Who are your patients? Where do they live? What is the range of diagnoses, ages, and cultures? What is the insurance mix? Do you have a large number of patients with other complex psychosocial needs? Can you develop a bullet list of red flags (Box 44.1) that should automatically trigger referrals? Are your colleagues sensitive to psychosocial issues, or are they focused only on the immediate medical questions? Do your colleagues understand your role and how you can help them? What is possible for you? You do not want to develop a system that will result in a flood of referrals that you can't possibly manage. Not being able to meet expectations will only diminish your effectiveness.

Table 44.1.
Association of Oncology Social Work Standards of Practice for Psychosocial Assessments

Completion of a psychosocial assessment of the patient's and family's response to the cancer diagnosis and treatment to include:

1. Age and stage of human development
2. Knowledge about cancer and its treatment including level of understanding, reactions, goals for care, and expectations
3. Characteristics of the patient's support system, including family, related biologically, legally, or emotionally
4. Patient and family psychosocial functioning including strengths, limitations, and coping skills
5. Race, ethnicity, religion, culture, language, physical or mental disability, socioeconomic status, sexual orientation, and gender identity or expression
6. Identification of barriers to care
7. Source, availability, and adequacy of community resources
8. Patient and family level of interest in participation in care and decision making
9. Development of a case plan with patient and family based on mutually agreed-upon goals to enhance, maintain, and promote optimal psychosocial functioning throughout cancer treatment and its outcome

Increasingly, oncology social workers are including distress screening in their practices and using some screening method as a way of identifying need and generating referrals (Jacobsen & Wagner, 2012). If a system of routine screening exists, you will hear of many patients who are experiencing high levels of distress. However, professionals are cautioned not to rely too much on any one screening tool because, although often useful, they are never a substitute for clinical judgment (Parry, Padgett, & Zebrack, 2012).

Box 44.1
Sample Red Flag List and Script for the Health Care Team

Referring to Oncology Social Work

Research shows if any of the following are true, the patient may benefit from oncology social work services. Please don't hesitate to refer! Verbiage that can be helpful in introducing this opportunity can be, "We have an oncology social worker who knows of many resources and is often helpful at smoothing out the speed bumps that can come with a cancer diagnosis. Her name is ________. I can set up an appointment for you now, or she can give you a call tomorrow."

- *Those with young children (under 18)*
- *Those who are primary caregivers to a family member with great needs (e.g., dementia, severely developmentally disabled adult children)*
- *Those choosing to disclose to no one*
- *Those requesting to see a counselor/social worker*
- *Those who have moved to this area within the past year*
- *Those with very little or no family/friend support*
- *Those who disclose a previous mental health/suicide attempt/substance abuse history*
- *Those about whom you have a concern for domestic violence/abuse*
- *Those with sexuality concerns and/or body image concerns*
- *Those receiving concurrent radiation and chemotherapy*
- *Those who appear highly anxious or depressed*
- *Those who have employment/school or other financial concerns*
- *Those with bulky disease that has been left unaddressed by the patient*
- *Those who present with metastatic disease*
- *Those identified as VIPs (This one may not be obvious, but our experience is that VIPs often receive care that is intended to be respectful and may, instead, preclude some of the normal standards of care that are universally helpful.)*

Family members, friends, or significant others who are having a difficult time coping with their loved one's cancer are also welcome to meet with the oncology social worker, with or without their loved one.

Never underestimate the value of your presence. Being an effective clinician and team member means that you are present and available. In some settings, social workers make daily rounds, usually with colleagues from other disciplines. On an inpatient floor, accompanying the team during rounds will demonstrate your commitment, introduce you to the patients, teach you a lot, and allow you to teach your colleagues about social work.

In ambulatory settings, it is likely impossible to be informed about every patient. Educating your colleagues about what you do is just as important as developing guidelines for referrals. When your referral source is another member of the health care team, always try to follow up with him or her about your interaction with the patient. Keep your documentation current and include enough information to help others care for the patient and demonstrate the value of your involvement.

Referrals can come from many sources. Certainly, physicians and nurses will refer, but so may phlebotomists, front-desk staff, physical therapists, and anyone else in contact with patients. The AOSW has developed excellent, concise materials for patients about the benefits oncology social workers can provide them (Figure 44.1).

Making patient education materials available in waiting rooms and other care areas will increase self-referrals. You may also receive calls from other patients, concerned friends, and more distant relatives about a patient. These can be helpful background conversations in learning about

ONCOLOGY SOCIAL WORKERS

Serving people with cancer and their families worldwide

Empower yourself—we can help. Oncology social workers provide counseling and other services which can reduce stress for you and your family through all phases of your cancer.

We can help you:

- Access information to help you understand your diagnosis and treatments
- Cope with your diagnosis of cancer and the many emotions you may be experiencing
- Consider decisions about treatment options as you think about your work, family and other things in your life
- Understand social security benefits, disability benefits, and insurance coverage
- Apply for programs that offer financial assistance

We offer:

- Counseling for you and your family members
- Support groups and educational programs
- Referrals to community counseling
- Workplace and school education and consultation

We can teach you about:

- Talking with your treatment team members
- Talking with your children, family, friends or co-workers
- Coping with your emotions — sadness, anger, worry and fears
- Reducing stress and using relaxation skills
- How cancer affects sex, intimacy, fertility, and feeling good about your body
- Complementary and alternative medicine
- Clinical trials
- Living with cancer, issues commonly experienced and resources to help you long term
- Planning for your care with the use of advance directives
- Life as a cancer survivor

This brochure was made possible through a grant from the Lance Armstrong Foundation.

AOSW
Family Conferences and Counseling
couples counseling
individual counseling
Support Groups
Communication
ADVOCACY
Educational Information
Stress Management
HOME HEALTH SERVICES
Hospice Care
HOPE
Legal Issues
transportation
Financial Assistance
Coping Strategies
problem solving
workplace issues
living wills

We can help you access:

- Affordable medical care and prescription drug coverage
- Transportation to and from medical care
- Temporary housing during your treatment
- Home health care and hospice care
- Items such as a cane or walker
- Referrals for help at home

How can you find an Oncology Social Worker?

- Ask your doctor, nurse or other healthcare provider
- Visit the Association of Oncology Social Work on the web at www.aosw.org and access POWER (Psychosocial Oncology Worldwide Educational Resource) — an on-line database to locate a clinician who may fit your needs, whether it be resources, counseling or education.

AOSW ASSOCIATION OF ONCOLOGY SOCIAL WORK

Oncology social workers are recognized as experts in providing psychosocial care to those affected by cancer.

Excellence in Psychosocial Oncology www.aosw.org

Figure 44.1. Oncology Social Work Patient Education Materials

a patient, but, keeping in mind Health Insurance Portability and Accountability Act (HIPAA) regulations and social work's commitment to confidentiality, you cannot even acknowledge to these people that the individual is a patient without the patient's permission.

An ongoing need is to market your offerings and your skills to your patient population. We know how valuable our services can be, and if we are doing our job, our colleagues will know it too. Fliers about available groups, support services, psychoeducational programs, and resources that may be helpful should be available. Getting the word out will bring in referrals, increase your visibility and influence, and embed you more deeply as a vital primary caregiver.

Initial Meetings and Assessments

Introductions are not the same as initial meetings. Introductions are brief and may occur anywhere. We meet patients in infusion areas, examination and hospital rooms, hallways, and waiting areas. Your job here is twofold: to respond to a referral or need and to make a connection that will result in a longer meeting. Think of the introduction as a prelude to the work and the moment to establish a time and place to continue. If there is an emergent need, it is most likely a concrete one (e.g., Mrs. X has no way to get home or Mr. Y has immediate financial problems). Addressing these immediate needs builds a foundation for the relationship.

Ideally, initial meetings should be planned to allow for uninterrupted private conversation. This may well be impossible in settings where the patient has a roommate or others receiving infusions nearby, but you may be able to use family rooms, quiet nearby sitting spaces, or a time when a roommate is not present. At the initial meeting, your goal is to conduct a preliminary assessment and to establish a supportive relationship. Most settings have documentation templates that can also guide the interview.

Two things are unique to oncology social work initial assessments. First, remember that a person who has just been diagnosed with cancer, just learned of a recurrence, or is reeling from some kind of medical emergency is *not* the same person you would meet in other circumstances. Many people present as much more anxious, vulnerable, alone, troubled, and even psychiatrically impaired than they truly are. The impact of this crisis is enormous, and no one is at his or her best. Make your preliminary assessment, but allow for the probability that this person is better able to cope and more capable than he or she seems (Härtl et al., 2010; Montgomery & McCrone, 2010).

Second, in making your assessment, you need to include the context of the diagnosis, the likely treatment, and the patient's understanding of diagnosis and treatment. In other words, it is important to include the new characteristics of the patient's environment that the cancer diagnosis and treatment bring. As you consider your patient's coping supports, you integrate an understanding of what the individual's needs and experiences will be.

Parallel to completing an initial assessment will be formulating a treatment plan. In oncology social work, this means thinking about both short- and long-term clinical goals, concrete needs, and appropriate support resources. Again, oncology social workers in diverse settings have different job descriptions. You should tailor your treatment plan formulation based on your role in your setting and the client's needs.

Predicted Crisis Points

Although we know that everyone's experience is unique, we also know that there are predictable moments when cancer is most stressful (Lauria, Clark, Hermann, & Stearns, 2001). From crisis theory, we know that an acute sense of crisis cannot persist for longer than 6 to 8 weeks (Regehr, 2011). People are amazingly resilient and begin to adapt to any circumstance as time passes. Most referrals will likely come during one of these crisis points. The common clinical threads are the need for normalization and education. Concurrent with your assessment of new patients should be normalizing their distressed feelings, assuring them that they will feel better and more in control, and giving them the basic knowledge they need to understand and manage the circumstances. The next section of this chapter further describes how to do this at each stage in the cancer process.

Cancer Diagnosis

Hearing an initial diagnosis of cancer is overwhelming and terrifying. Most people assume that the diagnosis is a death sentence, and most hear very little of whatever the doctor tells them after the first few sentences. The first weeks of having a known cancer, keeping medical appointments, learning the vocabulary and the medical landscape, undergoing various staging tests, and having to make difficult choices about caregivers, institutions or practices, and treatment regimens are all consuming.

The first intervention with a newly diagnosed individual should be to reassure him or her that intense feelings are normal, that everyone feels out of control, and that it will get better. Psychologically, these are among the most difficult days of having cancer, no matter what the future may bring. Be clear that once a treatment plan has been developed, he or she will likely start to feel better. In the meantime, however, it is common to have difficulties with sleep, to either overeat or lose one's appetite entirely, to think only about cancer and its dire possibilities, to be unable to concentrate on usual activities and things, and to experience intense labile feelings with tearfulness, anxiety, and grief.

This is a time when clinical assessment skills are especially valuable. An oncology social worker develops an instinct for what is within the normal range of reactions (most things are) and what is worrisome. The same person may present as "over-the-top anxious" just after diagnosis and quite collected some months later.

In addition to normalizing feelings, it is helpful to offer strategies to help process and manage the situation. Asking a new patient about how much and how he or she prefers to receive information can be helpful. Once a patient has identified whether he or she is someone who wants to know everything or just enough to get to the next step in the journey, he or she should be encouraged to share this with the treatment team. For people who want to know everything possible, be prepared to refer them to solid sources.

Helping patients identify what has helped in other times of crisis can help. Teaching simple breathing and relaxation exercises or meditation techniques may be useful. Remind the patient of the importance and value of moderate exercise, trying to eat, and being with friends. Distraction in the form of movies or outings may help.

Beginning Treatment

Reassuring new oncology patients that the anxiety about surgery, chemotherapy, or radiation therapy is almost always much worse than the reality can be helpful. Taking a tour before the first appointment or participating in an orientation session, which some centers offer, is also a useful way to alleviate a patient's fears.

Many people are more frightened about chemotherapy than about any other aspect of cancer treatment. Too many remember past experiences of friends or family when there were few anti-nausea medications and patients truly suffered. It is wise to ask about others whom they have known who went through cancer treatment. This gives you the opportunity to clarify improved practices and to dispel fantasies and most fears. Be clear that most people feel reasonably well throughout treatment, that the chemo nurse will provide a detailed schedule and instructions, and that someone is available 24/7 for urgent questions or concerns.

Especially for women (although also for some men), hair loss is the most dreaded side effect of cancer treatment. Preparation generally increases one's sense of control, so talk with your patient about what to expect. Encourage a plan and help the patient explore all the possibilities both of managing the loss itself and ways to cover one's head. For some patients, it can also be helpful to talk about the meaning of hair loss. For most women, there are the real losses of femininity and sensuality. Many patients comment that hair loss is the first openly visible sign that they are a cancer patient or even a cancer "victim." Shaved heads have also been associated with imprisonment and punishment in the past; these metaphors can be powerful.

Fatigue is another side effect with which patient's struggle. Simply validating the depth of fatigue that some feel can be a powerful intervention. Teaching patients how to conserve energy and recognize that, for the time being, their energy may be limited is also helpful. Explaining the paradox that gentle exercise is often energizing can also help patients cope with fatigue.

Finishing Treatment

Many people assume they will be relieved or even overjoyed to finish treatment, but research shows that finishing treatment is one of the most common points of psychosocial distress. Preparing a patient for this, so he or she is not caught off guard by feelings of vulnerability and fear and, for some, the symptoms of posttraumatic stress disorder can be another helpful intervention (Waldrop, O'Connor, & Trabold, 2011). It is not unusual for a person to present for social work support at this time. Many people who have coped well with the rigors of treatment have an emotionally difficult time when it is completed. This may be a good time to suggest a support group, especially a group designed for cancer survivors/individuals who have completed treatment.

Remind your patient that the people around him or her will be delighted that treatment is done and may assume that he or she is fully recovered physically and emotionally. Remind the patient that the rule of thumb is that it takes at least as many months to recover as it did to receive treatment. It is also important to reassure patients that the pervasive anxiety and sadness will gradually abate.

Survivorship

The National Coalition for Cancer Survivorship defines a cancer survivor as a person "from the moment of diagnosis through the balance of life. Whether treatment is being received or has been completed, anyone who has received a cancer diagnosis is a cancer survivor" (Clark, 2011). Some people are comfortable with this, and others are never comfortable with the word. Explore the meaning of this term with your patients, encourage their expression of feelings about it, and help them develop other vocabulary if they would prefer different language.

The challenge of this phase is re-creating a comfortable life and moving forward with growing hope and optimism. This may take time, and many people initially experience anxiety, sadness, or a sense of victimization. Helpful interventions may include individual counseling, a support group, participation in a cancer organization, or fund-raising or political effort.

Helping your patients develop a sense of wellness and renewed trust in their body is most important. Several studies (e.g., Rock et al., 2012) suggest that regular moderate exercise and weight control may reduce the risk of recurrence. These are things that someone can control and it is empowering to support these efforts.

Recurrence

Learning that cancer has returned and spread can be an even greater crisis than the first diagnosis (Hjörleifsdóttir & Óskarsson, 2010). No one is ever really prepared to learn that the cancer is back. Metastatic or Stage 4 cancer is, with very few exceptions, not curable. Some talk about cancer as a chronic illness, and, indeed, people do not necessarily die quickly. However, Stage 4 cancer is usually a lethal illness, and calling it "chronic" may minimize the reality.

The two goals of medical treatment for noncurable Stage 4 cancer are prolonging life and maintaining as high a quality of life as possible. Social workers are very helpful with the latter goal. The initial panic will subside after the first weeks, but it often takes months for an individual to adapt to these changed circumstances.

Helpful interventions include counseling sessions to support the expression of complicated feelings that enable people to plan how best to manage life, support groups designed for people living with advanced cancer, anxiety management strategies such as meditation, relaxation techniques, mild exercise, and consideration of any doctor-approved complementary therapies. Meeting the patient where he or she is by respecting his or her own sense of pacing is especially important at this point in the journey.

Progression

People with advanced cancer are usually on one or another kind of systemic treatment for the rest of their lives. Inevitably, any one treatment will stop being helpful at some point, and the oncologist will order a treatment change. This is a crisis point as the patient recognizes that one more option has been exhausted and that time continues to pass quickly. Other chapters in this book deal with end-of-life issues (see, for example, Chapter 10), but helping the patient feel more in control is a primary goal of all clinical work.

This is the time when patients, if they have not already done so, should complete any necessary legal business, consider their end-of-life choices, and begin to plan, as they wish, for their family's future. Although these are difficult topics, you can be confident that you are not suggesting something the patient has not already considered. Conversations with an oncology social worker are often the best way to begin this work and to help patients become more comfortable talking with their doctors and their families.

Working with advanced cancer patients can be one of the most challenging and most rewarding parts of your job. All of your clinical skills will be tested at times, and it is vital to maintain some professional boundaries and perspectives. It is also time to be human. We share the same existential realities as our patients, and being present, bearing witness, sustaining hope, and keeping faith become our major goals and best tools. Never make promises you can't keep, and be very clear with yourself about your own feelings.

Engaging Patients Through Problem Solving

There are innumerable ways that we first engage with our patients. Often the reason for a referral is straightforward, and we can begin where the patient is and proceed toward a shared goal. But sometimes our job is trickier. It is not uncommon to receive a referral from a colleague who has general or vague concerns about someone's coping but cannot be specific and may not have really informed the patient about the referral to social work. This is a moment when we are fortunate to be social workers rather than any other mental health practitioner. We are expert in thinking about the "person in environment" and can always identify something about an individual's situation that can be acknowledged as a problem and discussed. Engaging new patients through problem solving is a core social work skill.

Common problems include financial worries, insurance and disability questions, transportation issues, and questions about community resources that might be available. Be careful with your responses in these areas. There will be things that you know well and others, like Social Security disability compensation, that may be complicated. Be careful not to promise what cannot be delivered; it is always better to refer someone to the experts. It is also important to remember never to take on more of the worry and responsibility for the problem than the patient has. Our job, almost always, is to prepare the way, strategize and identify possible obstacles, and guide our patients toward the best solution. Teaching problem-solving skills allows patients and family members to move forward in the journey and solve issues themselves (Bucher & Zabora, 2010).

Depending on your setting and defined role, you may or may not be the person designated to assist with practical and resource problems. If you are, you likely are comfortable having a conversation about what resources might make the patient's treatment a little easier. If you are not, you can certainly still initiate this discussion, clarify the problems, and then refer the solution to whoever is appropriate. Whether or not you arrange the transportation or work with the insurance company, you will have had a chance to begin a relationship based on support, assistance, and trust. It can be difficult to move this connection to one that is more therapeutically based, but it usually can be done.

If your initial contact was around concrete needs but your goal is something more clinical, you will need to be clear fairly quickly. If you are referring the problems to someone else, it is easy: "Our patient navigator will call you to arrange that ride. I'm glad that you told me about that problem, and really glad that we are starting to know each other. Let's talk a little now about how you and your family are doing with the cancer diagnosis." If you are the resource person *and* the clinical person, be even more direct: "I am glad to make the calls about those rides, and someone will then be in touch with you with the details. Helping with things like this is only one part of my job here. I have been trained as a counselor (or therapist or whatever word seems right in your world) and would like to talk a little now about your kids. What have you told them and how are they doing?"

Another general area of connection can be around treatment team/professional caregiver issues. Patients may well talk to us about problems with their nurses or doctors; they are often afraid to bring these complaints directly to the doctor but may feel safe disclosing them to us. We have the advantage of knowing our colleagues and knowing how to advocate. It should go without saying that we should *never* criticize one of our colleagues to a patient. Instead, we can listen carefully, reflect what we are hearing, and try to normalize the feelings. A commonly expressed complaint may be that the doctor is hard to reach, seems too busy, or does not quickly return calls. You might respond this way: "It is really tough when you are worried about something, make the call, and then have to wait a long time for a response. Have you talked with Dr. X about the best way to reach her? Some of our doctors do well with emails, while others rely on their nurse practitioners or fellows to return most calls. It will work better for you both if you understand the system." It can help to role-play conversations or to suggest language that feels comfortable to the patient.

Our Feelings

Cancer is an equal-opportunity illness, and our patients come from every background, racial and cultural group, and socioeconomic level. On the one hand, social workers often work in settings where they are personally quite different from their clients. On the other hand, many, although certainly not all, of our patients could be and perhaps are our neighbors, friends, or family members. Any real barriers between us are quite artificial, and it can be more difficult to sustain some distance and appropriate boundaries and to manage our own feelings. Countertransference is always present, and the key is to recognize its influence and minimize its power (Peck, 2009).

We work from our hearts and from our brains. Unlike our medical or nursing colleagues who can always fall back on "doing something," there are times when we must just be there. What can feel like "doing nothing" is actually doing a great deal. Our faithful, quiet, nonjudgmental presence is an unusual gift to someone in pain, be it physical pain, emotional pain, or both. We cannot always offer the same close relationship to every one of our patients, and it would not be clinically appropriate to do so. We have to pay close attention to our own feelings, our physical and emotional limits, and our personal coping.

We get tired; we get sad too. We don't like all of our patients, and we certainly feel frustrated and angry with some of them. These are all normal and acceptable feelings. We get into trouble only when we try to deny or suppress them. Clinical supervision is invaluable for social work practitioners to sort out countertransference, share our feelings, and avoid compassion fatigue.

Pearls

- Over time, we all find our own rhythm and style. You must be comfortable with yourself to be helpful to your clients.
- If you are unsure what to do in a moment, say something honest, even if that is "I don't know what to say."
- Show up, dress the part, speak up, and be proud of what you know and what you do.

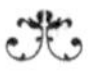

Pitfalls

- Don't shoulder the burden of patient concerns alone. Use your colleagues for support and consultation.
- Don't avoid or be afraid of difficult conversations. Remember the Pearls listed previously.
- Try never to be more engaged in the problem than the patient or the family is. Any time you are feeling irreplaceable, step back.

Psychosocial assessment and appropriate intervention are core skills for oncology social workers. In addition to components of psychosocial assessments that most social work practitioners share, it is important for oncology social workers to consider where in the trajectory of the illness the patient is and his or her understanding of the illness and treatment choices. Common psychosocial crisis points include diagnosis, beginning treatment, ending treatment, survivorship, recurrence, and progression. We engage patients and our fellow team members in myriad ways. It is important for us to attend to our own feelings to identify countertransference and best help our clients.

ADDITIONAL RESOURCES

Reliable Cancer Information Resources

American Cancer Society: http://www.cancer.org
American Society of Clinical Oncology: http://www.cancer.net
Cancer Support Community: http://www.cancersupportcommunity.org
National Cancer Institute: http://www.cancer.gov

REFERENCES

Association of Oncology Social Work (AOSW). (2012). AOSW standards of practice in oncology social work. In *AOSW oncology social work standards of practice*. Retrieved from http://www.aosw.org/iMIS201/AOSWMain/professionals/standards-of-practice/AOSWMain/Professional-Development/standards-of-practice.aspx?hkey=51fda308-28bd-48b0-8a75-a17d01251b5e

Bucher, J. A., & Zabora, J. R. (2010). Building problem-solving skills through COPE education of family caregivers. In J. C. Holland, W. S. Breitbart, P. B. Jacobsen, M. S. Lederberg, M. J. Loscalzo, & R. McCorkle (Eds.), *Psycho-oncology* (2nd ed., pp. 469–472). New York, NY: Oxford University Press.

Clark, E. J. (Ed.). (2011). *Teamwork: The cancer patient's guide to talking with your doctor* (5th ed.). Silver Spring, MD: National Coalition for Cancer Survivorship.

Härtl, K., Engel, J., Herschbach, P., Reinecker, H., Sommer, H., & Friese, K. (2010). Personality traits and psychosocial stress: Quality of life over 2 years following breast cancer diagnosis and psychological impact factors. *Psycho-Oncology, 19*(2), 160–169. doi:10.1002/pon.1536

Hjörleifsdóttir, E., & Óskarsson, G. (2010). Psychological distress in Icelandic patients with repeated recurrences. *International Journal of Palliative Nursing, 16*(12), 586–591.

Jacobsen, P. B., & Wagner, L. I. (2012). A new quality standard: The integration of psychosocial care into routine cancer care. *Journal of Clinical Oncology, 30*(11), 1154–1159.

Lauria, M. M., Clark, E. J., Hermann, J. F., & Stearns, N. M. (2001). *Social work in oncology: Supporting survivors, families, and caregivers.* Atlanta, GA: American Cancer Society.

Montgomery, M., & McCrone, S. H. (2010). Psychological distress associated with the diagnostic phase for suspected breast cancer: Systematic review. *Journal of Advanced Nursing, 66*(11), 2372–2390. doi:10.1111/j.1365-2648.2010.05439.x

Parry, C., Padgett, L., & Zebrack, B. (2012). Now what? Toward an integrated research and practice agenda in distress screening. *Journal of Psychosocial Oncology, 30*(6), 715–727. doi:10.1080/07347332.2012.721486

Peck, M. R. (2009). Personal death anxiety and communication about advance directives among oncology social workers. *Journal of Social Work in End-of-Life and Palliative Care, 5*(1–2), 49–60.

Regehr, C. (2011). Crisis theory and social work treatment. In F. J. Turner (Ed.), *Social work treatment: Interlocking theoretical approaches* (5th ed., pp. 134–143). New York, NY: Oxford University Press.

Rock, C., Doyle, C., Demark-Wahnefried, W., Meyerhardt, J., Courneya, K. S., Schwartz, A. L., . . . Gansler, T. (2012). Nutrition and physical activity guidelines for cancer survivors. *CA: A Cancer Journal for Clinicians, 62*(4), 242–274. doi:10.3322/caac.21142

Waldrop, D. P., O'Connor, T. L., & Trabold, N. (2011). "Waiting for the other shoe to drop": Distress and coping during and after treatment for breast cancer. *Journal of Psychosocial Oncology, 29*(4), 450–473. doi:10.1080/07347332.2011.582638

45 Hester Hill Schnipper

Time Enough to Make a Difference: Helping Patients Live Well With Advanced Cancer

Key Concepts

- *Clinical work demands a special human connection.*
- *Many people are living for extended periods of time with advanced cancers. This is a relatively new phenomenon with minimal research or literature to suggest best clinical practices.*
- *Care for advanced cancer is not the same as end-of-life care.*
- *There are predictable normal crisis points for advanced cancer patients.*
- *There are recommended therapeutic strategies and goals.*
- *Support groups can be valuable.*
- *Understanding countertransference and self-care are critical.*

Almost 20 million Americans have been diagnosed with cancer, and 50% of them will die from the illness. Although it may not be possible to extend longevity, it is always possible to improve the quality of the life that each person with cancer has left to live. Patients sometimes ask their doctors for an educated guess about their longevity. Statistics can be shared, but we know that each experience is unique, and there is no sure answer to the question "How long do I have, Doc?" The best response I have heard was this: "Time enough to make a difference." The most important goal for oncology social workers is to help patients identify and make the right "difference" for themselves. Parallel to this is to give them the agency to achieve their goals under these circumstances.

Cancer patients often find it difficult to initiate contact with or accept a referral to an oncology social worker. People with advanced cancer feel vulnerable and frightened and may feel they have nothing to lose. Taking a risk, they come to us with life's most important existential issue. They trust us to understand, support, and help them map the final chapter of their lives. We must maintain a strong knowledge base, sound clinical skills, good judgment, and an understanding of the goals and strategies we employ. However, nothing matters as much as sharing the experience, bearing witness, keeping faith, sustaining hope, and never hiding behind artificial walls, unnecessary tasks, or jargon. It is a responsibility and honor to accompany someone during the final phase of life, and we do so both as clinicians and as fellow travelers.

Initial Concepts

There is sparse literature about psychosocial issues related to living with advanced cancer. The general societal understanding of cancer is that either you are cured or you are dying. Few people appreciate the middle ground of living on borrowed time. In the not-so-distant past, individuals who were diagnosed with metastatic disease could anticipate dying fairly quickly. Today, however, progress in the treatment of many advanced cancers means that some people live with a terminal diagnosis for a long time. They find themselves in murky and uncharted territory: not healthy, not well, but also not dying in the immediate future. Learning to live with terminal uncertainty, making sound decisions for themselves and their families, and trying to maintain a balanced and positive daily view are very challenging goals. The old adage says that nothing flies in the face of death like a life well lived. Our job is to help create and sustain, as long as possible, that life.

Little has been written about the connection between the patient and his or her environment in the setting of serious illness. Because social work is grounded on the concept of "beginning where the patient is," this seems an important piece to consider. One study from Denmark shows how "the struggle to be a participant in one's own life" is central. The authors outlined four life conditions: adapting to a life-threatening illness, trying to carry on a normal life, learning to live with powerlessness, and finding the courage and strength to continue (Thomsen, Hansen, & Wagner, 2011).

Depression is the most commonly cited psychiatric symptom among patients with advanced cancer, with anxiety a close second. The reported prevalence (0% to 58%) varies enormously, partly because of the difficulties in evaluating mood and the range from normal sadness to an affective disorder to major depression (Massie, 2004). Major depression is most highly associated with lung cancer, pancreatic cancer, breast cancer, and oropharyngeal cancers. Individuals who have a preexisting anxiety disorder or other psychiatric illness are more likely to be depressed and have a more difficult time coping with cancer. Depression often accompanies anxiety and pain, and mood can be difficult to assess in the context of active cancer treatment and normal affective responses to a life-threatening illness and difficult treatments.

Most people with Stage 4 cancer, however, are neither clinically depressed nor likely to benefit from antidepressants, but are sad, scared, and unsure how to think about their lives and their futures. We, who have broad experience working with this population, have an advantage over most other mental health clinicians in this situation. We appreciate the wide range of normal responses to ongoing threats to life and continuing physical side effects from anti-cancer therapies.

Relying on the *Diagnostic and Statistical Manual of Mental Disorders* (DSM-IV), which states that a diagnosis of depression should not be made if the symptoms are related/attributable to a medical condition, is neither straightforward nor simple (American Psychiatric Association, 1994, p. 349). It is challenging to differentiate symptoms caused by the disease, treatments, or depression. When in doubt of the diagnosis, referring a patient to a psychiatrist for consideration of medication is wise. It becomes increasingly correct to trust your instincts the more you gain experience, but always err on the side of caution.

Normal Crisis Points

The first crisis is the diagnosis of metastatic cancer. Many people describe it as the worst day of their lives, and almost everyone can remember exactly where, how, and when they heard the news. The experience is different for people whose initial diagnosis is Stage 4 than it is for those who have a recurrence or a lesser stage. For Stage 4 patients, the shock is great and there may be less understanding of the meaning of the diagnosis. In my experience, many people in this situation speak about "getting this behind me as fast as possible" or wonder how long treatment will last. Returning patients generally are less shocked, although there are exceptions, and have a more realistic perspective of the diagnosis. They also have the advantages of knowing the cancer vocabulary, having relationships with oncology caregivers, and having the experience of coping with earlier treatments. They may, however, be angrier and sometimes cynical about the value of cancer treatments that did not work.

We know from crisis theory that the most intense affect settles after 6 to 8 weeks. That is generally true in patients with advanced cancer, although most take months to find a "comfortable" adaptation. There is so much variability among disease types and treatments that it is impossible to make sound predictions about timing and process. A person with advanced pancreatic cancer may never have the chance to find any kind of routine or normalcy, whereas many women with Stage 4 breast cancer will live quite well with that diagnosis for years. For people who are likely to live for a longer time, it often takes up to a year to settle into the rhythms and challenges of the diagnosis.

The next and recurring crisis is each time treatment must be changed. As patients move from treatment to treatment, they know their list of options is shrinking. If things stabilize and go uneventfully for a while, most people will settle into the coping strategies they have developed. Different treatments bring different side effects, whose severity in turn affects adaptation. Women, especially, and some men find it tough to be bald for extended or repeated periods. Some people even reject chemotherapy options that cause hair loss; I have known several women who insisted that they were not going to die bald.

As a person becomes more ill, decisions will likely have to be made about life responsibilities and roles. Needing to leave work, hiring a nanny, stopping driving, and other major choices trigger emotional crises for many patients.

The decision to stop active treatment and transition to palliative care or hospice is always difficult. Other chapters discuss hospice and end-of-life issues in detail, but they are relevant here. The steady goal of our work remains helping our patients to live their best possible lives in a very difficult time—it is always about living, never only about dying.

Understanding the Diagnosis

Cancer, especially metastatic cancer, is often called a chronic illness. This seems optimistic because most chronic illnesses are not fatal, but there is no other term to describe the months or years of care. It is often shocking how little people understand about their diagnosis. Physicians may or may not have been clear about the situation, or patients may not have really understood (or wished to hear) what their oncologist said. A place for the oncology social worker to begin is always the question "What has your doctor told you and what do you understand about your illness?" The social worker is not typically the first to explain that Stage 4 cancer is incurable, but he or she must never lie to the patient. We must be well informed and understand the medical situation, treatments, likely progression, and problems. Oncology social workers are well positioned to be interpreters and navigators of the "cancer world," and honesty and directness are part of the work. We explain side effects, suggest questions or issues to raise with the doctor, and normalize physical and psychological reactions to treatment. Some people will make it clear that they do not want to know too much about their situation and prefer to operate on a "need to know" basis. Most, however, feel empowered by knowledge and find that this awareness diminishes fear and elicits more of a sense of control.

An important part of the work is helping your patient manage the medical relationships and understand how best to communicate, how to think about important treatment decisions, and where to find and access resources.

Therapeutic Strategies

Individuals who have been diagnosed with advanced cancer, quite simply, will experience physical and psychological distress. Yet hope is an essential resource and just as important as competent medical care and good social support (McClement & Chochinov, 2008). We all know Emily Dickinson's wonderful lines: "Hope is the thing with feathers that perches in the soul, and sings the tune without the words, and never stops at all" (quoted in Franklin, 1999).

The first meeting marks the moment that you can begin to share the burden and instill hope. In even the direst circumstances, there is hope to be had, and the relationship bond and steady hand you offer may be hope enough to allow your new patient to believe that he or she can feel better. At times when hope is hard to find, it can help to make this offer: "Right now, when you are feeling hopeless, I will hold your hope. I will keep it close and safe and will return it to you when you are ready." William Madsen (2007) reminds us of the importance of relationships characterized by the human values of respect, connection, and hope. Any experienced therapist understands that successful therapy is based on the therapist/client relationship, and that bond is the most valuable tool we have. Clients change and grow because of life events, progressive disease, other important relationships, and self-reflection. Without a solid human relationship between therapist and client, healing could not happen. We are repeatedly reminded that we bring ourselves to our clinical encounters and that who we are matters.

The social worker–patient relationship itself is all-important and remains the foundation and centerpiece of any therapeutic strategy. Recognizing the need to adapt techniques and interventions to individual patients and situations, social workers know that the one constant is steady presence and human warmth. For most patients, the most useful framework is a shifting mixture of denial, distraction, and mindfulness. Denial is the bulwark of managing. We are not talking about denial that keeps someone away from medical appointments and appropriate treatments. We are talking about functional denial that enables an individual with a lethal illness to go on with life without daily fear and misery. There is a limit to how much distress anyone can feel and still function. Most people describe a turning point, a moment when they realized that they had gotten through most of a day without tears and had perhaps even enjoyed themselves. This is a good start.

Distraction becomes the order of the day. You may need to become a life coach to think with your patient about daily management. The large questions have to do with work decisions and family time, but staying busy, seeing friends, and organizing activities and projects will help. Suggest keeping two calendars: one for medical appointments and one for everything else. The "everything else" calendar should have at least one entry every single day. Plans can be made in pencil with the understanding that they may need to be canceled, but making them is imperative. Too much time to think and too much time lying on the couch or in bed will never be helpful.

The third leg of our framework is mindfulness. Living in the moment is challenging, but it is the best possible way to cope with so much uncertainty and fear. Over and over, I have said to patients: "You are not going to die today." One patient expanded the mantra to "I am not dying today, and I am not dying this week or this month. Anything else is too far away to worry about." These can become words to live by. Meditation is often useful for ill patients, and a particularly good resource is Elana Rosenbaum's (2012) book, *Being Well (Even When You're Sick)*. Rosenbaum reminds us that the goal of meditation practice is to feel even more alive and present in the moment. Thomsen et al. (2011) describe how "the struggle to be a participant in one's own life" is a central goal in coping with advanced disease. They describe a pattern of four life conditions: some respite from the rigors of serious illness, ways of maintaining a normal life, learning to live with powerlessness, and, simultaneously, finding the courage to face a very uncertain future. This makes sense and gives us clear goals for the work.

Mary was a 49-year-old single mother of a 10-year-old adopted daughter. She had been treated for breast cancer 3 years previously and was doing well. She was shocked when a lingering pain in her head, which she described as "not a headache, a pain," was diagnosed as a recurrence of the cancer in her skull. Suddenly, her hopeful outlook was challenged, and she realized she needed to deal with her new reality. Mary had been in a relationship for several years, and her boyfriend quickly became her fiancé. Not only did he want to marry her but he also wanted to adopt her daughter to ensure that she would always have a parent and a family. We know that the death of an adoptive parent is especially difficult for a child who has already lost her biological mother, and Mary and her fiancé were determined to do everything possible to help their girl.

Her first treatment for the recurrent cancer was radiation therapy and a change in her hormonal therapy. She hoped and believed this strategy would work for a long time. Instead, 6 months later, the pain in her head returned, and scans indicated that the tumor had regrown in her skull and spread to several other bones in her body. Devastated, she made a decision to focus on the present, care for her daughter, and do everything possible to enjoy her life. She planned a trip to New York to take her daughter to the theater. She went out to dinner with friends. She spent more time at her fiancé's vacation home at the beach. She worked less, played more, and willed herself to stay in the moment. The most remarkable thing about her strategy was her ability to simultaneously hold conflicting intense feelings and needs. One marker of good mental health is the capacity to tolerate ambivalence, and Mary took this to a new level. She and her fiancé sent out invitations to their wedding and took enormous delight in planning it.

An e-mail from her described this period: "Today I went to the funeral home to make arrangements. I don't want my daughter to have to walk by the funeral home every day, so I chose one that is actually farther away from home. I am not planning to need any of these arrangements for a long time, but now they are done and I can cross them off the list. This afternoon, we chose the band for our wedding. This all feels like the culmination of everything that my parents, who were Holocaust survivors, taught me: dance and laugh and love while the world ends around you."

Support Groups

Controversy surrounds the possible role of psychosocial interventions in prolonging life with advanced cancer. A study by Barbara Andersen and colleagues at The Ohio State University (Andersen et al., 2010) examined the impact of support group participation on the longevity of women with breast cancer. Some experts are skeptical about their finding of a 45% reduction in the risk of recurrence for women in the intervention (group) arm of the study. The literature about the value of support groups is diverse and not congruent. However, this study does raise the intriguing possibility that psychosocial support may make a difference in more than quality of life.

As is always true, some people with advanced disease will thrive in the right support group, whereas others would never consider participating. Groups are organized in different ways, and some clinicians prefer to facilitate groups that contain participants at different stages of illness. My strong preference is otherwise, which seems particularly important with Stage 4 patients. The problems of someone with early breast cancer may seem minimal, whereas the realities of advanced disease are terrifying for others who are hoping for cure.

In a Stage 4 group, the facilitator's role may be a more active one than is appropriate in some other groups, and it may be necessary to speak the otherwise unspoken thoughts of everyone in the room. If someone has just talked about an unexpectedly bad scan result or a decision to stop treatment, the facilitator may say something like: "We are all so sad to hear this and also scared for ourselves." It may be necessary to name the feelings associated with bad news or, most difficult of all, when a group member dies. Your forthrightness will make others' words possible.

Irvin Yalom and Molyn Lesczc (2005) described factors, which I expand on, that may be relevant:

- Installation of hope: Hope now focuses on quality of life and diminishment of pain.
- Universality: We are all mortal and being with others who are nearing the end of life can be soothing and instructive. We learn from each other.
- Sharing of information: Group members are motivated and informed advocates and medical consumers.
- Altruism: Some years ago, a woman who attended my group made the decision to stop treatment. Because she lived alone and had no family nearby, it was difficult to access hospice care at home. Her group made the decision to jointly become her primary caregiver; they drew up a schedule, were with her 24/7, and made it possible for her to remain in her home. They did this in spite of or because of the fact that they, too, would someday be dying.
- Identifying and reframing: An important hope toward the end of life is to forgive and accept. Others in the same situation can offer perspectives and assurances that may make it possible to change relationships.
- Socialization: Facing similar problems and decisions, group members demonstrate different decisions and strategies, consider varying factors, and often help one another solve behavioral issues or problems.
- Imitative behavior: Group members frequently model their own behaviors after those observed and admired in others.
- Interpersonal learning: Members mirror each other and themselves as they become close and trusting.

- Cohesion: No one understands what it is like to have advanced cancer better than others living the same experience. Being together reduces feelings of isolation, victimization, and aloneness.
- Catharsis: Tears and laughter are more intense and more common than in other conversations. All feelings are accepted and respected.
- Existential factors: These are the theme of the group.

Here are quotations from people who have attended my advanced cancer group:

- "In the group, we can be honest with each other. Believe it or not, we laugh a lot. We share information and teach each other. We can talk about anything and we do."
- "In the group, I know that as each of us decides we've had enough, that decision will be truly respected. On the other hand, since we meet week after week, I also am confident that if they thought I was giving up too soon due to depression, they would be qualified to say so, and I would listen. In this group, I know I will be loved and supported no matter what happens to me and no matter what I decide to do about it. I know I will be heard and accepted no matter what. That is a priceless treasure."

The Social Worker's Feelings

You are allowed to be sad, angry, frustrated, and frightened right along with your patients. It is okay to cry during a session, probably okay to hug goodbye, and necessary to share the intensity. Unlike our colleagues in medicine or nursing who can revert simply to providing medical care when the affect becomes too difficult, we are required and blessed to "just be." As group members learn from one another, we, too, will find that we are acquiring guides and roadmaps for the hard times in our own lives.

No one can be equally involved with every single patient. No one feels the same attachment to each person. As long as we are ethical and responsible professionals and do our job well, we need have no self-doubts or criticisms about the level of caring we bring to each encounter. We must know ourselves and attend to the inevitable countertransference. The difference between our relationships with our very ill patients and all others is this: Our shared mortality trumps everything else. Whenever there is a clinical juncture and choices between interventions or paths, choose the one that brings you closer and knocks down walls.

This most important thing to remember is that we are all human and we are all going to die. We are in this world together. This is not work to be undertaken behind rigid boundaries or held within tight theoretical frameworks. This is not work to separate us from our patients or from ourselves. This is a time to be intellectually and emotionally open, to extend our hands and our hearts as we experience together a most challenging time.

Pearls

- Whenever there is a clinical juncture and choices between interventions or paths, choose the one that brings you closer.
- Do not be afraid of your own feelings.

Pitfalls

- Do not assume normal sadness is major depression.
- You don't always have to do or say something. Just be there.

REFERENCES

American Psychiatric Association. (1994). *Diagnostic and statistical manual of mental disorders* (4th ed.). Washington, DC: Author.

Andersen, B. L., Thornton, L. M., Shapiro, C. L., Farrar, W. B., Mundy, B. L., Yang, H-C., & Carson, W. E. (2010). Biobehavioral, immune, and health benefits following recurrence for psychological intervention participants. *Clinical Cancer Research, 16*(12), 3270–3278.

Franklin, R. W. (Ed.). (1999). *The poems of Emily Dickinson.* Cambridge, MA: Harvard University Press.

McClement, S. E., & Chochinov, H. M. (2008). Hope in advanced cancer patients. *European Journal of Cancer, 44*(8), 1169–1174.

Madsen, W. (2007). *Collaborative therapy with multi-stressed families.* New York, NY: Guildford Press.

Massie, M. J. (2004). Prevalence of depression in patients with cancer. *JNCI Monographs, 32*, 57–71.

Rosenbaum, E. (2012). *Being well (even when you're sick): Mindfulness practices for people with cancer and other serious illnesses.* Boston, MA: Shambhala.

Thomsen, T. G., Hansen, S. R., &Wagner, L. (2011). How to be a patient in a palliative life experience? A qualitative study to enhance knowledge about coping abilities in advanced cancer patients. *Journal of Psychosocial Oncology, 29*(3), 254–273.

Yalom, I. D., & Lesczc, M. (2005). *The theory and practice of group psychotherapy.* New York, NY: Basic Books.

46 Integrating Spirituality in Oncology Care

Shirley Otis-Green and Reverend Terry L. Irish

Key Concepts

- *A biopsychosocial-spiritual perspective is important for providing comprehensive person-centered and culturally congruent oncology care.*
- *Defining spirituality as that aspect of humanity focused upon meaning and connectedness invites an interdisciplinary response to the spiritual concerns of our patients and their families.*
- *There is growing evidence that not addressing spiritual concerns can negatively affect the quality of life of many oncology patients.*
- *Oncology social workers have an important role to play in the assessment of spiritual care and an ethical responsibility to prepare themselves to effectively provide this care.*

Exploring the Importance of Spirituality in the Delivery of Person-Centered and Culturally Congruent Oncology Care

Oncology social workers have an ethical commitment to provide whole-person care if they are to address the wide range of multidimensional quality-of-life concerns common to cancer patients and their families throughout the trajectory of illness (Altilio & Otis-Green, 2011). A comprehensive biopsychosocial-spiritual approach to care requires oncology social workers to possess the necessary skills to address the physical, psychological, social, spiritual, and cultural concerns of those facing cancer (Henoch, Danielson, Strang, Browall, & Melin-Johansson, 2013). Although many patients report interest in spiritual and existential issues from the moment of diagnosis onward (Allman, Tallman, & Altmaier, 2013; Gaudette & Jankowski, 2013)—with increasing attention to these concerns when facing end of life—many oncology social workers feel ill-prepared to respond to the existential and spiritual issues associated with cancer and its treatment.

This topic is not only germane for patients and caregivers but also vital for staff who provide daily care for their oncology patients. Some health care providers come to this work from a sense of "calling" that frequently emerges from a particular faith perspective. Yet few health care professionals report having received formal training in the appropriate delivery of spiritual care or feel confident as to how to integrate spirituality into the scope of their practice (M. J. Balboni et al., 2013). It is not surprising, then, that some report struggling with spiritual and religious boundaries. Additionally, the risks for moral distress and burnout are magnified when ethical issues and spiritual values become conflicted, with important implications for workforce retention (IOM, 2013). This chapter explores the nexus of oncology social work and spiritual care with information and resources to better prepare social workers for the provision of comprehensive, person-centered, and culturally congruent spiritual care.

Laying the Groundwork for Quality Spiritual Care

Major challenges in the provision of spiritual care are the lack of agreement regarding key terms and the lack of education of health care providers to meet these needs. There has been confusion regarding terminology—some equate *spirituality* with *religion*—that may result in the view that one's only responsibility in this manner is the timely referral to chaplains for the provision of religious rituals.

This narrow definition of *religious* care has had several unintended consequences. We know that patients consistently indicate that spiritual, existential, and religious concerns are important, especially so when facing serious and progressive illness. Research into the effectiveness of religious interventions has struggled with how to "operationalize" complex concepts (such as prayer). A lack of consistency in definitions and a lack of clearly operationalized terms (What type of prayer would be appropriate for which patients? How would we determine the appropriate "dose," and how would we measure the effectiveness of the "outcome" of the intervention?) have resulted in conflicting findings from many of the published reports.

A lack of attention to spiritual suffering in cancer patients can be associated with increased distress. Yet the lack of training to address the complex and nuanced nature of this multidimensional concept and the deficiency of clear reimbursement for this work have led to spiritual care becoming marginalized, despite its importance to patients and their families.

Advances within the field of palliative care suggest that health care professionals have an obligation to address the broader spiritual concerns of patients and families. The National Consensus Project for Quality Palliative Care (NCP) developed clinical practice guidelines that included "spiritual, religious, and existential" and "cultural" aspects of care as part of eight "domains" necessary for the provision of quality palliative care (NCP, 2013). Recognition of the interconnectedness of these key concepts opens the door for social workers to use their expertise to address these crucial aspects of quality of life.

The NCP also recommends the integration of palliative care for those with serious illness from the beginning of diagnosis through treatment and into survivorship or bereavement, making these guidelines relevant for oncology care regardless of where the patient is along the illness trajectory. The National Quality Forum (NQF, 2006) developed 38 "preferred practices" related to the eight domains, with specific recommendations related to the importance of having appropriately trained staff able to address patients' spiritual and cultural concerns.

Based on this foundation, a consensus conference was held in 2009 (funded by the Archstone Foundation). Forty prominent thought leaders from differing disciplines (including social work) and a variety of faith traditions came together to develop recommendations regarding the delivery of quality person-centered spiritual care (Puchalski & Ferrell, 2010; Puchalski et al., 2009). A subsequent grant (also funded by Archstone) selected nine hospitals to implement these recommendations through a Spiritual Care Demonstration Project (Otis-Green et al., 2012). Social workers had integral roles in each site, working closely with their chaplain, nursing, and physician colleagues to create a standardized model for the delivery of spiritual care that incorporated systematized screening, history, and assessment resulting in a spiritual care plan and in the development of metrics to measure the impact of this work through quality improvement efforts. An important finding was a consensus definition of spirituality: "Spirituality is the aspect of humanity that refers to the way individuals seek and express meaning and purpose and the way they experience their connectedness to the moment, to self, to others, to nature, and to the significant or sacred" (Puchalski et al., 2009, p. 887).

In this definition, spirituality is seen as a universal human trait focused on meaning making and connectedness. Religion, from this view, is an element *within* spirituality that describes an organized set of prescribed expectations, rites, rituals, and values that provide a framework for members' beliefs and behaviors. Spirituality is about putting the experience of illness into a meaningful context (McEvoy, Gorski, Swiderski, & Alderman, 2013).

This makes spiritual care the concern not just of chaplains but of each member of the team, with importance for oncology social workers due to the field's focus on context, meaning, and relationships (Reese, 2011). An international and interdisciplinary consensus conference was convened (again including social work) to further refine these standards and set recommendations for integrating spiritual care across the wider health care continuum (Puchalski, Vitillo, Hull, & Reller, 2014). This "normalizes" the delivery of spiritual care, treating it like the delivery of other physical, psychological, or social concerns—with all members of the interdisciplinary team responsible for the provision of a certain level of generalist care and able to refer for specialty care when appropriate. Adopting a biopsychosocial-spiritual model of care provides rich opportunities to address the multidimensional concerns of those facing serious illness (Sulmasy, 2002).

Some of what oncology social work normally engages in qualifies as spiritual care (Canda & Furman, 1999). Oncology patients frequently react to their illness with rage, dread, or incomprehension. Questions such as "Why me?" "Why now?" and "Why my family?" can be seen as spiritual questions appropriate for social work exploration. These are reflective questions about the ultimate mystery and meaning of life that require the compassionate presence that social workers are well prepared to provide. The willingness to sit in silence through a struggle with these profound existential questions can be seen as a spiritual act (Roy, 2014). There are patients and caregivers who do not engage in this reflective process. Social work's basic tenet of the client's right to self-determination is important in assessments with patients about their own perceived needs. Assisting patients as they reprioritize what matters most in their life and offering them support as they struggle to cope with the ambiguities of their illness experience are key social work concerns.

Although many spiritual screening and history tools have been developed for research purposes, their use in clinical care has not been routinely adopted. Common research screening tools include the Functional Assessment of Chronic Illness Therapy-Sp-12 (FACIT-Sp-12), consisting of 12 questions in three domains: Meaning, Peace, and Faith (http://www.FACIT.org). FICA is an acronym for a spiritual history-taking tool developed by internist and geriatrician Christina Puchalski that is widely used (Puchalski et al., 2009). Consisting of four basic questions about *F*aith/Belief/Meaning, *I*mportance/Influence, *C*ommunity, and *A*ddress/Action, the FICA is meant to guide the licensed professional in determining a patient's spiritual concerns and strengths (Borneman, Ferrell, & Puchalski, 2010; Puchalski & Romer, 2000). HOPE is another acronym-named spiritual history tool, regarding the patient's sources of *H*ope, the importance of *O*rganized religion in the patient's life, specific aspects of their *P*ersonal spirituality and practices that are most helpful, and the effects of a patient's spirituality and beliefs on medical care and *E*nd-of-life issues (Anandarajah & Hight, 2001).

Advances in technology have led to alternative screening strategies to more efficiently identify patient concerns. For example, at City of Hope, studies are under way to determine the effectiveness of "SupportScreen" technology as a patient-centered screening tool (Loscalzo et al., 2010). Patients complete a customizable questionnaire using a wireless touch screen indicating their level of concern on a wide range of potential "problems" (including spirituality). This information is electronically delivered to the appropriate discipline so that timely follow-up can be provided.

Collaboration: Social Work and Chaplaincy

Because the exploration of spirituality is compatible with social workers' values and skills, there is an emerging role for our field in developing our expertise in this area. Stewart suggests that clinical social workers need to "develop 'spirituality skills' in order to engage in the deeply meaningful existential considerations that arise for some people who are confronted by chronic cancer" (Stewart, 2014, p. 71). Each patient encounter offers the health care provider an opportunity to provide generalist-level spiritual care, but it is important to be mindful of the limits of one's training and scope of practice and know when it is best to refer to spiritual care specialists such as board-certified chaplains (Soltura & Piotrowski, 2011). Because few health care organizations have sufficient numbers to fully meet patient demand, opportunities for social work/chaplaincy collaboration exist.

As a part of the Spiritual Care Demonstration Project described earlier, a clinical social work lecture series was developed to teach participants how to more effectively assess, intervene, triage, and apply basic principles of spiritual care to oncology patients and their families (Irish, McCarty, & Poppito, 2011). This lecture series was divided into two sections, both of which often cause disconnection and disorientation in the patient's life. Sessions 1 through 6 addressed the most common causes of such disconnection and disorientation, and Sessions 7 through 9 focused on strategies to support reconnections and reorientation. Session 10 offered participants opportunities to reflect upon lessons learned and celebrate the conclusion of the educational series over a shared meal.

Clinical Social Work Spiritual Care Lecture Series

The following curriculum was designed to provide clinical social work staff with the skills needed to more effectively address the spiritual concerns of oncology patients and families. Spiritual distress was selected based on the recommendations within the Clinical Practice Guidelines in Oncology: Distress Management (NCCN, 2013).

Section 1: Disconnection and Disorientation

1. *Spiritual distress in cancer and palliative care*
2. *Spiritual pain and suffering*
3. *Spiritual hopelessness and despair*
4. *Spiritual isolation and abandonment*
5. *Spiritual guilt and shame*
6. *Spiritual uncertainty and ambivalence*

Section 2: Reconnection and Reorientation

7. *Presence and peace*
8. *Forgiveness and reconciliation*
9. *Gratitude and appreciation*
10. *Reflections on lessons learned*

Partnerships with local clergy provide additional resources for oncology social workers and chaplains to assist with caring for patients' and caregivers' diverse spiritual care needs (Puchalski et al., 2009). Opportunities exist for social workers to provide education to community clergy regarding the needs and concerns of oncology patients, and clergy can be tapped to offer greater insight for health care professionals into the cultural and religious beliefs of disparate spiritual and religious groups (Cobb, Puchalski, & Rumbold, 2012).

The complex convergence of spiritual, religious, and cultural care in illness requires a sophisticated and nuanced understanding of an individual's values, beliefs, priorities, and affiliations (T. A. Balboni et al., 2013). Especially at end of life, the understanding of the synergies between one's personal, cultural, spiritual, religious, and existential beliefs takes on heightened importance (Doka & Tucci, 2011; Oliviere, Monroe, & Payne, 2011). Addressing end-of-life decision making, discussing the formation of advance directives, and supporting patients in legacy building require sensitivity and curiosity regarding exploration into "what matters most" for those we serve (Bullock, 2011).

Spiritual Care in Action

Offering one's authentic presence is a key social work skill that can be seen as a spiritual intervention (Otis-Green, 2011a). Oncology social workers are called to patients and families in times of distress and are skilled in using active listening skills to create interventions uniquely tailored to the individual being served. Social work's core principles of warmth, compassion, empathy, and genuineness provide a solid foundation for the creation of a safe environment for the exploration of suffering (Otis-Green, 2008). The key to spiritual care is a willingness to compassionately share one's authentic personhood with another. However, this level of sharing invites a certain level of vulnerability. Oncology social workers are well positioned to teach mindfulness, meditation, relaxation exercises, and other stress reduction techniques—all of which can be viewed as spiritual care interventions—as well as listen to where the patient is and learn from each particular patient's focus and needs. Journaling and the use of expressive arts also offer interventions that can be tailored to be compatible with an individual's cultural, personal, and spiritual views.

Attention to spiritual concerns is most important during care at end of life and in bereavement, when spiritual and religious concerns may dominate. Assisting patients with legacy-building strategies and life-review exercises may be important, as may the provision of anticipatory guidance for families as their loved one faces end of life (Steinhauser, Alexander, Byock, George, & Tulsky, 2009). Oncology social workers can facilitate goals-of-care conferences to ensure that the patient's wishes are addressed, and aiding in the discussion of advance directives can assist the patient in minimizing regrets. Other forms of spiritual intervention may include legacy building and life review (Otis-Green, 2011b). Social workers may assist patients with the development of individualized rituals or routines that meaningfully acknowledge the importance of a particular moment or experience (e.g., by advocating for culturally congruent meals for Orthodox Jewish patients).

However, the patient's death does not end the interprofessional team's responsibilities. Systematic bereavement care often is an extension of spiritual care, including the use of bereavement assessment tools to identify needs for support and those at greatest risk for complicated grief (Puchalski et al., 2009).

Professional Practice Implications

Oncology providers are at risk for moral distress and burnout when they face incongruities within their spiritual beliefs and practice. Struggles with ethically "gray" situations occur frequently within this work and can result in compromised values. Dysfunctional team dynamics may escalate symptoms of burnout and have implications for workforce retention (Portnoy, 2011). Novice practitioners frequently struggle to establish appropriate boundaries, and even seasoned staff may be challenged to maintain a healthy work/life balance. Periodic attention to one's own priorities and reflection regarding what truly matters is an important foundation for rigorous self-care practice (Clark, 2011).

Periodic reflection of our own evolution of spiritual and existential beliefs and values is helpful for sustainable work in this challenging field. Working intimately with the chronically ill and dying as an oncology social worker is a relational experience with the potential for mutual transformation and learning (Renz et al., 2013). The experience of facing one's own mortality offers the invitation for enhanced understanding and spiritual development. If we are open to others, we too will experience moments of reflection that may affect our faith, values, and beliefs (Seccareccia & Brown, 2009).

Ensuring the delivery of spiritual care is the responsibility of every member of the health care team. Social work is relational at its core (Browning & Gerbino, 2011), and spirituality is primarily concerned with connectedness. Authentic human interactions based on social work values such as respect and an appreciation of diversity provide opportunities for "sacred encounters" that have the possibility to be truly transformative for both parties. From this perspective, oncology social workers (with proper education and support) are well positioned to provide spiritually sensitive and culturally congruent person-centered care to those they serve.

Pearls

- The delivery of spiritual care requires professionals committed to reflective practice who are thoughtful about their own motivation for this work and give consideration to existential questions about meaning, connectedness, and purpose in life.
- High-functioning, collaborative teams offer support for the exploration of meaning and a "safe" environment for sharing grief and doubt. This level of professional intimacy allows staff opportunities for deep personal and spiritual growth.

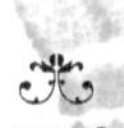

Pitfalls

- Failure to be existentially and spiritually grounded in this work may place one at risk for moral distress and burnout.
- Questions about "boundaries" and "balance" require periodic reconsideration as we mature as clinicians.
- Authenticity in this work requires a willingness to become vulnerable and to "let our humanity show";

however, clinician authenticity may be difficult when one feels the work environment might be critical of addressing spirituality issues.

ADDITIONAL RESOURCE

Association of Professional Chaplains: http://www.professional-chaplains.org

REFERENCES

Allman, A. L., Tallman, B. A., & Altmaier, E. M. (2013). Spiritual growth and decline among patients with cancer. *Oncology Nursing Forum*, *4*(6), 559–565. doi:10.1188.13.onf.599-565

Altilio, T., & Otis-Green, S. (Eds.). (2011). *Oxford textbook of palliative social work*. New York, NY: Oxford University Press.

Anandarajah, G., & Hight, E. (2001). Spirituality and medical practice: Using the HOPE questions as a practical tool for spiritual assessment. *American Family Physician*, *63*(1), 81–88.

Balboni, M. J., Sullivan, A., Amobi, A., Phelps, A. C., Gorman, D. P., Zollfraiik, A., . . . Balboni, T. A. (2013). Why is spiritual care infrequent at the end of life? Spiritual care perceptions among patients, nurses, and physicians and the role of training. *Journal Clinical Oncology*, *31*(4), 461–467. doi:10.1200/JCO.2012.44.6443

Balboni, T. A., Balboni, M., Enzinger, A. C., Gallivan, K., Paulk, M. E., Wright, A., . . . Prigerson, H. G. (2013). Provision of spiritual support to patients with advanced cancer by religious communities and associations with medical care at the end of life. *JAMA Internal Medicine*, *173*(12), 1109–1117. doi:10.1001/jamainternmed.2013.903

Borneman, T., Ferrell, B., & Puchalski, C. M. (2010). Evaluation of the FICA tool for spiritual assessment. *Journal of Pain and Symptom Management*, *40*(2), 163–173. doi:10.1016/j.jpainsymman.2009.12.019

Browning, D., & Gerbino, S. (2011). Navigating in swampy lowlands: A relational approach to practice-based learning in palliative care. In T. Altilio & S. Otis-Green (Eds.), *Oxford textbook of palliative social work* (pp. 673–681). New York, NY: Oxford University Press.

Bullock, K. (2011). The influence of culture on end-of-life decision making. *Journal of Social Work in End-of-Life and Palliative Care*, *7*(1), 83–98. doi:10.1080/15524256.2011.548048

Canda, E., & Furman, L. D. (1999). *Spiritual diversity in social work practice: The heart of helping*. New York, NY: Free Press.

Clark, E. J. (2011). Self-care as best practice in palliative care. In T. Altilio & S. Otis-Green (Eds.), *Oxford textbook of palliative social work* (pp. 495–501). New York, NY: Oxford University Press.

Cobb, M. R., Puchalski, C. M., & Rumbold, B. (2012). *Oxford textbook of spirituality in healthcare*. New York, NY: Oxford University Press.

Doka, K. J., & Tucci, A. S. (Eds.). (2011). *Living with grief: Spirituality and end-of-life care*. Washington, DC: Hospice Foundation of America.

Gaudette, H., & Jankowski, K. R. B. (2013). Spiritual coping and anxiety in palliative care patients: A pilot study. *Journal of Health Care Chaplaincy*, *19*, 131–139.

Henoch, I., Danielson, E., Strang, S., Browall, M., & Melin-Johansson, C. (2013). Training intervention for health care staff in the provision of existential support to patients with cancer: A randomized, controlled study. *Journal of Pain and Symptom Management*, *46*(6), 785–794. doi:10.1016/j.jpainsymman.2013.01.013

Institute of Medicine (IOM). (2013). *Delivering high-quality cancer care: Charting a new course for a system in crisis*. Washington, DC: National Academies Press.

Irish, T. L., McCarty, C., & Poppito, S. R. (2011). Clinical social work spiritual care lecture series. Retrieved from http://prc.coh.org/Spirituality.asp

Loscalzo, M., Clark, K., Dillehunt, J., Rinehart, R., Strowbridge, R., & Smith, D. (2010). SupportScreen: A model for improving patient outcomes at your fingertips. *Journal of National Comprehensive Center Network*, *8*, 496–504.

McEvoy, M., Gorski, V., Swiderski, D., & Alderman, E. (2013). Exploring the spiritual/religious dimension of patients: A timely opportunity for personal and professional reflections for graduating medical students. *Journal of Religion and Health*, *52*, 1066–1072.

National Comprehensive Cancer Network (NCCN). (2013). *Clinical practice guidelines in oncology: Distress management*. Retrieved from http://www.nccn.org/professionals/physician_gls/pdf/distress.pdf

National Consensus Project for Quality Palliative Care (NCP). (2013). *Clinical practice guidelines for quality palliative care* (3rd ed.). Pittsburgh, PA: Author. Retrieved from http://www.nationalconsensusproject.org/NCP_Clinical_Practice_Guidelines_3rd_Edition.pdf

National Quality Forum (NQF). (2006). *A national framework and preferred practices for palliative and hospice care: A consensus report*. Washington, DC: Author. Retrieved from http://www.qualityforum.org/Publications/2006/12/A_National_Framework_and_Preferred_Practices_for_Palliative_and_Hospice_Care_Quality.aspx

Oliviere, D., Monroe, B., & Payne, S. (Eds.). (2011). *Death, dying, and social differences* (2nd ed.). New York, NY: Oxford University Press.

Otis-Green, S. (2008). Health care social work. In T. Mizrahi & L. Davis (Eds.), *Encyclopedia of social work* (20th ed., pp. 348–353). New York, NY: Oxford University Press. Retrieved from http://www.oxfordreference.com/view/10.1093/acref/9780195306613.001.0001/acref-9780195306613-e-176?rskey=gOTasj&result=176

Otis-Green, S. (2011a). Embracing the existential invitation to examine care at the end of life. In S. H. Qualls & J. Kasl-Godley (Eds.), *End-of-life issues, grief, and bereavement: What clinicians need to know* (pp. 310–324). Wiley Series in Clinical Geropsychology. Hoboken, NJ: John Wiley & Sons.

Otis-Green, S. (2011b). Legacy building: Implications for reflective practice. In T. Altilio & S. Otis-Green (Eds.), *Oxford textbook of palliative social work* (pp. 779–783). New York, NY: Oxford University Press.

Otis-Green, S., Ferrell, B., Borneman, T., Puchalski, C., Uman, G., & Garcia, A. (2012). Integrating spiritual care within palliative care: An overview of nine demonstration projects. *Journal of Palliative Medicine*, *15*(2), 154–162. doi:10.1089/jpm.2011.0211

Portnoy, D. (2011). Burnout and compassion fatigue: Watch for the signs. *Journal of the Catholic Health Association of the United States: Health Progress*, 47–50. Retrieved from http://www.compassionfatigue.org/pages/healthprogress.pdf

Puchalski, C., Ferrell, B., Virani, R., Otis-Green, S., Baird, P., Bull, J.,... Sulmasy, D. (2009). Improving the quality of spiritual care as a dimension of palliative care: The report of the consensus conference. *Journal of Palliative Medicine*, *12*(10), 885–904. doi:10.1089/jpm.2009.0142

Puchalski, C., & Romer, A. L. (2000). Taking a spiritual history allows clinicians to understand patients more fully. *Journal of Palliative Medicine*, *3*(1), 129–137. doi:10.1089/jpm.2000.3.129

Puchalski, C. M., & Ferrell, B. (2010). *Making healthcare whole*. West Conshohocken, PA: Templeton Press.

Puchalski, C. M., Vitillo, R., Hull, S. K., & Reller, N. (2014). Improving the spiritual dimension of whole person care: Reaching national and international consensus. *Journal of Palliative Medicine*, *17*(6), 642–656. doi:10.1089/jpm.2014.9427

Reese, D. (2011). Spirituality and social work in palliative care. In T. Altilio & S. Otis-Green (Eds.), *Oxford textbook of palliative social work* (pp. 201–213). New York, NY: Oxford University Press.

Renz, M., Mao, S. M., Omlin, A., Bueche, D., Cerny, T., & Strasser, F. (2013). Spiritual experiences of transcendence in patients with advanced cancer. *American Journal Hospice Palliative Care*. http://www.ncbi.nlm.nih.gov/pubmed/24259402. doi:10.117'7/f049909113512201

Roy, D. J. (2014). Silence in palliative care? *Journal of Palliative Care*, *29*(4), 203–204.

Seccareccia, D., & Brown, J. B. (2009). Impact of spirituality on palliative care physicians: Personally and professionally. *Journal of Palliative Medicine*, *12*(9), 805–809. doi:10.1089=jpm.2009.0038

Soltura, D., & Piotrowski, L. (2011). Teamwork in palliative care: Social work role with spiritual care professionals. In T. Altilio & S. Otis-Green (Eds.), *Oxford textbook of palliative social work* (pp. 495–501). New York, NY: Oxford University Press.

Steinhauser, K. E., Alexander, S. C., Byock, I. R., George, L. K., & Tulsky, J. A. (2009). Seriously ill patients' discussions of preparation and life completion: An intervention to assist with transition at the end of life. *Palliative Support Care*, *7*(4), 393–404. doi:10.1017/S147895150999040X

Stewart, M. (2014). Spiritual assessment: A patient-centered approach to oncology social work practice. *Social Work in Health Care*, *53*, 59–73. doi:10.1080/00981389.2013.834033

Sulmasy, D. P. (2002). A biopsychosocial-spiritual model for the care of patients at the end of life. *The Gerontologist*, *42*(3), 24–33. doi:10.1093/geront/42.suppl 3.24

47

Erin Columbus and Kate Wakelin

Clinical Group Work: Embracing Opportunities, Navigating Challenges

Key Concepts

- *The role of cancer support groups is well established.*
- *There are three major types of groups used for cancer patients: face-to-face, telephone, and online.*
- *Groups have different structures, aims, ways of being facilitated, and modes of delivery.*
- *Groups enable people to achieve outcomes greater than they could in isolation.*
- *There is an opportunity to explore the use of emerging technologies to enhance access to and effectiveness of support groups.*

Background and History

Groups have always been a key feature of human interaction, from families, work teams, and social and sporting clubs to the self-help models of the 20th century (e.g., Alcoholics Anonymous). Groups operate on the common principle that the "whole is greater than the sum of its parts," meaning that group synergies produce outcomes greater than those that could be achieved by individuals in isolation.

Cancer support groups began gaining popularity in the latter part of the 20th century as decreasing mortality and increasing life expectancy led to an increase in cancer diagnoses. Improvements in cancer therapies also led to higher numbers of survivors and people living with cancer as a "chronic" condition. These factors have led to a greater appreciation of the impact of a cancer diagnosis and treatment, both for the person with cancer and for family and friends, encompassing physical, psychological, and spiritual domains.

We now know that cancer brings sequelae beyond the physical. Internationally, there is evidence that most people experience psychosocial distress in the form of anxiety and depression (National Breast Cancer Centre and National Cancer Control Initiative, 2003), with issues such as uncertainty, fear of death, feeling alone, decreased self-esteem, and disruptions to intimate, family, and social relationships.

The role of cancer support groups in assisting people to navigate these very real challenges has been well established. However, the changes in the social climate that the Internet and mobile communications spurred have provided opportunities for service providers to respond and adapt and to explore the adoption of emerging technologies as important tools in the provision of today's cancer support groups.

Future Directions

As our clinical framework, technology, medical model, and societal norms evolve, we can approach the cancer support group model from novel angles. Medical professionals are increasingly aware of the importance of addressing the needs of the "whole person" through the patient-focused model. As a result, cancer support groups will become a more viable and valuable option for physicians in their effort to help patients navigate the emotional aspects of cancer. Most notably, advances in technology such as video chat, which provides a more "intimate" and accessible experience, will allow moderators and members of online support groups to learn more about one another through eye contact, body language, tone, and overall interactive style. The popularity and efficacy of short-term models such as cognitive behavioral therapy have had a profound impact on our approach to group therapy, and there is no doubt that as we learn more about implementing these models in a group setting, this too will change how clients are affected.

Applications of Group Work in Oncology

There are numerous types, models, and applications of oncology group work. Open-ended, "drop-in" groups common in hospital/medical settings offer convenience and immediacy, where both caregivers and patients can benefit. Peer-led groups provide members with an unrestricted forum for self-expression around a common theme, with a largely group-led agenda. Effective training, monitoring, and supervising guidelines for peer group leaders with these vulnerable populations have not yet been developed. Peer support groups may also be professionally facilitated, especially when needs (e.g., advanced cancer) are complex. Key outcomes of peer support groups include increased confidence and sense of control in relation to self, living with cancer, and interactions with others (health professionals, family, and friends; Ussher, Kirsten, Butow, & Sandoval, 2006).

Psychoeducational peer group models have also been found to be effective in improving adjustment and coping, by combining structured information and facilitated group peer support. Outcomes include improved coping, knowledge, and communication and relationships with both significant others and health professionals (Roberts, Black, & Todd, 2002).

There is also a role for professionally led, therapeutic groups in illness. Yalom and Lesczc (2005) describe therapeutic factors that contribute to change and recovery, including the following:

- Instilling hope: encouragement that recovery is possible.
- Universality: seeing others coping with similar situations and corresponding reduction in feelings of isolation.
- Sharing information.
- Altruism: being able to help others in the group context.
- Cohesion: gaining a sense of belonging and acceptance.
- Catharsis: sharing feelings and experiences with the group.

Peer support groups differ slightly from therapeutic models in that the emphasis shifts from the role of the professional facilitator to that of the group. Peer support groups may be professionally facilitated, especially for complex group needs (e.g., advanced cancer), though sessions are guided by the concerns and issues raised by participants themselves. Some of the key outcomes of peer support groups include increased confidence and sense of control in relation to self, living with cancer, and interactions with others. This extends in particular to assisting in managing relationships with medical professionals and family and friends, by providing a safe space for the expression of emotion and thus relieving patients' burden of care (Ussher et al., 2006).

Benefits of Group Participation

Professionally moderated support groups (PMSGs) provide a haven for people struggling with cancer. Talking with peers is a highly beneficial and therapeutic experience that can improve a person's quality of life. A PMSG can have a profound impact on patients' ability to integrate their diagnosis and become oriented in the cancer community while learning the "tricks of the trade" and gaining confidence in their ability to face the emotional, physical, and spiritual intricacies ahead. For a caregiver whose cancer experience can be disenfranchising, a support group is both a welcome respite and a place of empowerment. A PMSG offers those grieving a place of kinship, understanding, and healing when they are feeling most alone. These group spaces enable people to be authentic and to share some of their deepest fears with others who can not only empathize but also "walk in their shoes." When members divulge their deepest fears and anxieties, there is a mutual sense of responsibility—no longer is each individual carrying that heavy weight alone. A support group may also lessen depression, anxiety, and posttraumatic stress. A PMSG can ward off feelings of helplessness and isolation while helping members find meaning and purpose and redirect their focus (Cain, Kohorn, Quinlan, Latimer, & Schwartz, 1986); it can also help members express "unpopular" feelings such as anger, regret, and guilt in a nonjudgmental environment. Because these emotions can be uncomfortable for the general population, they may go unresolved, causing undue stress and complications for the person with cancer (or caregiver/bereaved person). Participants in both professionally led and peer-led groups experienced improvements in psychological functioning, increases in informal support networks, and positive personal changes in handling of the caregiving role when compared with control participants. Professionally led groups produced the greatest improvement in psychological functioning, and peer-led groups produced the greatest increases in informal support networks (Toseland, 1990). Most important, PMSGs provide a sense of community and camaraderie to members enduring a tumultuous, lonely, and frightening time in their lives.

Group Formation

Various criteria for screening patients for group participation are discussed later. But across all modalities, there is an effort to group patients with others with similar types of cancer, similar stages in their disease and treatment process, and similar ages. This is not always possible, and mixed groups can be effective. Open-ended groups, for example, may have limited opportunity to screen by disease but can provide education and mutual support for participants. However, especially with closed time-limited or ongoing groups, patients frequently state their preference for being grouped with others who share their cancer type, stage, and/or life span phase.

Face-to-Face Groups

Time-limited PMSGs contain all the elements of what Yalom terms a *social microcosm*. Although not designed to be psychotherapy per se, group members' roles can mimic those found in a psychotherapy group. While the focus remains largely on the impact of cancer and loss, each individual's personality and life experiences inevitably affect the group's work overtly and covertly. Members may experience transferential reactions—for example, a member may feel a special kinship with certain people in the group while having an aversion to others based on subjective life experiences and relationships. "There is a rich and subtle dynamic interplay between the group member and the group environment. Members shape their own microcosm, which in turn pulls characteristic defensive behaviour from each" (Yalom, 1995, p. 37). Issues discussed in group sessions not only are laden with emotion but also result in differing opinions and perspectives. Some members take on a quasi-leadership role, serving as a sort of "co-leader," whereas others may monopolize or take on an adversarial or "professional patient" role, each of which may serve a protective purpose for the member but can also disturb the collective process (Bogdanoff & Elbaum, 1978).

Moderation/Facilitation

Assessing members for coping mechanisms, family and social supports (or lack thereof), treatment phase, and hopes/expectations for the group, as well as commitment and ability to empathize, will help the facilitator formulate a productive group. Potential members coping with additional life factors such as acute relationship issues, mental health disorders, excessive anger, or social anxiety may not be appropriate and should be referred to additional outside resources. These measures are important for group members to stay focused on the group's "mission" and will help minimize complications that could negatively impact group functioning and safety, as well as help group members relate to one another.

The facilitator's skill is paramount and helps the group feel a sense of safety, allowing members to express themselves, share moments of intimacy, support one another, and strive for cohesiveness and healing. The facilitator must maintain an overall understanding and an awareness of members' roles and how these influence their connection to others, the group, and their task. For health professionals, training and experience in both psychology and group work will enable subtle group dynamic observations that can be identified and navigated in a direct yet therapeutic manner. Facilitators may also have their own countertransference to certain members of the group, or the group as a whole, and therefore must maintain constant levels of self-awareness and continued training, education, and support to navigate these challenges. Clinical supervision helps the facilitator process feelings, maintain attention and responsiveness, and develop strategies to best guide and support the group process.

Training and ongoing support have also been identified as perhaps even more crucial for peer facilitators (Kirsten, Butow, Price, Hobbs, & Sundquist 2006). Research into best practice is at an early stage; however, interventions such as online training and discussion, DVD and printed manuals, and training workshops have been positively evaluated (Zordan et al., 2012).

Telephone Groups

Because not everyone can participate in face-to-face groups, telephone support groups (TSGs) can be a highly effective therapeutic tool, allowing participants the opportunity to explore many issues from the privacy and comfort of home. The aims of TSGs are similar to those of face-to-face groups, including sharing narratives, normalizing experiences, sharing coping strategies and practical information, discussing taboo subjects, and reducing social isolation. TSGs in Australia, for example, commonly utilize two professional facilitators (although peer facilitation models are under development). Groups of six to eight participants meet via teleconference twice a month for an hour.

Potential group members undergo a screening process involving a telephone interview, in which issues such as current health, cancer status and perceived goals of treatment, existing supports, mental health history, previous support group experience, and telephone access are explored. Participants are provided with information including instructions for accessing their group, group aims, and guidelines about confidentiality and respect.

Before meetings, group members receive a check-in call to confirm availability and assess desired discussion topics. Facilitators prepare flexible discussion material; group members are encouraged to discuss issues that are relevant for them. Group newsletters are often provided, summarizing main themes and providing extra information as required. They also provide reflective questions for journaling and further group discussion. Helpful theoretical approaches in group facilitation include mutual aid, narrative, and strengths-based models.

Facilitating a TSG involves many of the skills needed for working with face-to-face groups. Because of the lack of visual cues, there are some special considerations:

- Minimize background noise.
- Say name before speaking to help participants identify others (e.g., "It's Kate speaking; I'm interested to hear others' thoughts").
- Describe the visual (e.g., "Erin and I are nodding our heads").
- Facilitators sit in same location to allow visual and written communication.
- Take notes to assist in keeping track of often complex interactions.
- Establish regular pattern for group sessions by, for example:
    - Refreshing group guidelines (e.g., confidentiality and respect).
    - Providing introductions.
    - Checking in and getting updates from participants.
    - Having a general discussion based on emerging themes.
    - Providing a summary.
    - Asking a closing question to allow participants to return consciousness to present (e.g., "What are you planning to do when we finish our session today?").

Online Groups

Asynchronous (e.g., Forum Based)

An important element for effective online support groups (OSGs) is the presence of a trained facilitator who can elicit dialogue, keep the group focused, offer resources and ideas, and respond to any individual or group needs that may arise. Cancer*Care*'s online support groups are moderated by licensed oncology social workers trained in mental health, oncology, and group work. Each oncology social worker also participates in a tailored training program before moderating an OSG to help them navigate the unique challenges of online group work. The duration of each Cancer*Care* OSG is 3.5 months, at which point all OSGs go on a 2-week hiatus until the next session begins. Prospective group members are carefully screened for appropriateness before being subscribed to their respective groups, which are broken down by category, based on whether the client is a patient, a caregiver, or bereaved, then further specified by cancer type, age, gender, and status (partner or loved one). The groups are conducted in a message board format.

Synchronous (e.g., Live-Chat Based)

Some groups utilize live-chat technology. This allows "real time" text-based conversations. These facilitated, 1-hour group sessions are offered regularly (e.g., once or twice a month) with semistructured conversations similar to those of TSGs. Because of the very limited cues (e.g., no visual or auditory), the written communication skills of facilitators are critical. Engagement with metaphor can be a very powerful tool in allowing group members to more vividly express their thoughts and feelings (Street & Wakelin, 2009). Humor is also an important element in synchronous online group life (Street, Wakelin, Hordern, Bruce, & Horey, 2012).

A different level of consideration is required to craft a response in the online medium, because there is an objective permanence to the words being "spoken," something that both members and professionals can examine more deeply and learn from. The impact of the spoken word is often buffered by fading memory, but written words can be visually recalled and revisited for many purposes.

> *For the patient, the availability of on-line support introduces a new dimension of social connection and access to information. For researchers, the observation of an on-line support group offers a unique window for understanding the kinds of experiences that patients wrestle with, from reluctant insurers to patronizing doctors, as well as histories of suffering, confusion, and misdiagnosis.*
>
> *(Davison, Pennebaker, & Dickerson, 2000, p. 210)*

In the OSG, the moderator needs to listen with a different "ear" and learn and understand each member's moods and emotional responses while encouraging cohesion, empathy, and safety. Finding an authentic "voice" as a moderator in this medium is a complex process requiring patience and the ability to observe and contribute responsively to the group's unique rhythm. Developing a therapeutic alliance through the written word requires the ability to convey warmth and accessibility. The more personal and conversational the moderator's postings are, the more the group members will obtain a sense of the moderator as a source of support, inspiration, and information.

Many clients in desperate need of support may never receive it because of their physical, geographical, or emotional limitations. Participating in an OSG can help clients overcome these limitations in meaningful ways. Reading and rereading the threads of a conversation create a unique and thoughtful connection among members as they discover different elements of the text that may not have been obvious initially. Many members also feel a greater sense of safety online. Because of the lack of physicality, ego defenses are often quickly dissolved, making way for members to become connected with one another more intimately. Members may even use this group as they would journaling and often share more deeply felt emotions, even "secrets." Participating in an OSG can be a gateway to a positive and productive experience in counseling.

Conflict and Vulnerability

Conflict within the group can damage the integrity and functioning of the group if not handled quickly. Members need to know that someone will help them work out their differences or intense feelings. Conflict will often be experienced in an online group as the absence of communication; members may figuratively retreat to the rear and wait for the moderator or another member to interject or smooth hurt feelings. Another important facet to consider is responding to a more vulnerable client. Often, a person posting in the middle of the night will be expressing deeper inner thoughts, and the facilitator should intervene carefully and supportively with this group member. Because there is a public element to the exchange, the moderator should encourage the vulnerable member and reach out to the rest of the group as well, supporting any of the feelings that may come up as a result. Should any member feel he or she is actively in crisis, the moderator should direct members to crisis intervention resources as soon as possible.

Expressive Writing Online Group (Cancer Council Victoria)

The expressive writing group commenced in 2009 to allow sharing of written forms of creative expression (e.g., short stories, poems, and prose). The group has approximately 20 active members and is asynchronous. A striking characteristic of this group is the vivid use of metaphor, which extends to the group's identification of a metaphorical meeting place, the Goat and Quill, a fictitious pub situated on a piece of rugged south Australia coastline. Group members frequently "drop in" for a virtual pint, champagne, chocolate, or other form of indulgence. Group members describe images such as the crackling fire and setting sun, which are interwoven through pieces of creative writing about their cancer experience.

"It's a chilly night outside, but I can feel the warmth of the Goat n' Quill slowly stretching its fingers into my mind, and my heart. Ah, to be amongst kindred spirits again… whether it's in silence or noisy chatter or contemplative word—it's good to be here."

—ZenMoment, group member.

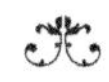

Pearls

- Support groups are an established and effective means of providing psychosocial care to those affected by cancer.
- Support groups utilize the lived experiences of peers, enabling strong therapeutic outcomes.
- A changing social and technological climate is providing opportunities to evolve traditional models and strengthen practice.

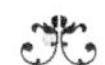

Pitfalls

- Support groups are not a "one size fits all" solution and may be unhelpful for clients with complex needs.
- Training and ongoing clinical supervision are critical for both professional and peer facilitators.

A cancer diagnosis creates for patients and their loved ones far-reaching challenges and consequences, encompassing physical, psychological, and spiritual domains. Groups are a well-established tool for assisting people in adjusting to these challenges and enabling a reduction in depression, anxiety, and social isolation. People who engage in support groups are likely to experience increased confidence and sense of control in relation to self, living with cancer, and their interactions with others.

In a rapidly changing social climate and seemingly shrinking world, it is imperative for those providing psychosocial care to people affected by cancer to respond in ways that explore and utilize emerging technologies. These responses need to encompass research, implications for training and supervision, models of service delivery, and the creation of opportunities for collaborations at national and international levels.

REFERENCES

Bogdanoff, M., & Elbaum, P. (1978). Role lock: Dealing with monopolizers, mistrusters, isolates, helpful Hannahs, and other assorted characters in group psychotherapy. *International Journal of Group Psychotherapy, 28*(2), 247–262.

Cain, E., Kohorn, E., Quinlan, D., Latimer, K., & Schwartz, P. (1986). Psychosocial benefits of a cancer support group. *Cancer, 57*, 183–189.

Davison, K., Pennebaker, J., & Dickerson, S. (2000). Who talks? The social psychology of illness support groups. *American Psychologist, 55*(2), 205–217.

Kirsten, L., Butow, P., Price, M., Hobbs, K., & Sundquist, K. (2006). Who helps the leaders? Difficulties experienced by cancer support group leaders. *Supportive Care in Cancer, 14*, 770–778.

National Breast Cancer Centre and National Cancer Control Initiative. (2003). *Clinical practice guidelines for the psychosocial care of adults with cancer.* Camperdown, NSW: National Breast Cancer Centre.

Roberts, S., Black, C., & Todd, K. (2002). The Living with Cancer Education Programme. II. Evaluation of an Australian education and support programme for cancer patients and their family and friends. *European Journal of Cancer Care, 11*, 280–289.

Street, A., & Wakelin, K. (2009). The use of metaphors in online support groups for people with advanced cancer. *Grief Matters: The Australian Journal of Grief and Bereavement, 12*(2), 40–43.

Street, A., Wakelin, K., Hordern, A., Bruce, N., & Horey, D. (2012). Dignity and deferral narratives as strategies in facilitated technology-based support groups for people with advanced cancer. *Nursing Research and Practice.* http://www.ncbi.nlm.nih.gov/pmc/articles/PMC3317195/. doi:10.1155/2012/647836

Toseland, R. (1990). Long-term effectiveness of peer-led and professionally led support groups for caregivers. *Social Service Review, 64*(2), 308–327.

Ussher, J., Kirsten, L., Butow, P., & Sandoval, M. (2006). What do cancer support groups provide which other supportive relationships do not? The experience of peer support groups for people with cancer. *Social Science and Medicine, 62*, 2565–2576.

Yalom, I. D. (1995). *The theory and practice of group psychotherapy.* New York, NY: Basic Books.

Yalom, I. D., & Lesczc, M. (2005). *The theory and practice of group psychotherapy.* New York, NY: Basic Books.

Zordan, R., Butow, P., Kirsten, L., Juraskova, I., O'Reilly, A., Friedsam, J., . . . Kissane, D. (2012). The development of novel interventions to assist the leaders of cancer support groups. *Support Care Cancer, 20*, 445–454.

48

Carole F. Seddon and Hester Hill Schnipper

Assessing and Intervening With the Spectrum of Depression and Anxiety in Cancer

Key Concepts

- *About half of patients with cancer have a usual and expectable emotional reaction to diagnosis and treatment; others experience multiple psychiatric symptoms (Derogatis et al., 1983).*
- *Sadness and depression are common in varying intensities in cancer. Serious depression is highly associated with certain cancers (Kadan-Lottick, Vanderwerker, Block, Zhang, & Prigerson, 2005), and the suicide rate among cancer patients is higher than in the general population (Anguiano, Mayer, Piven, & Rosenstein, 2012; Misono, Weiss, Fann, Redman, & Yueh, 2008).*
- *Worry is common in cancer; severe anxiety requires a multimodal approach. Substance abuse and alcoholism are among the most complicated challenges faced by the treating staff because opioid medication and other controlled substances are often integral parts of the care.*
- *Oncology social workers must know how to screen for distress and more severe psychiatric conditions and either treat, collaborate to treat, or refer patients to other providers familiar with cancer.*

There are few more frightening words than "You have cancer." Many people manage to move forward and cope with this diagnosis and treatment without special assistance or mental health intervention (Weisman, Worden, & Sobel, 1980). Some, especially those with preexisting depression, anxiety, or other mental illness, will need specialized consultation and treatment. Although feelings of sadness, grief, and anxiety occur with almost all patients and families and are an expectable reaction to this crisis, they usually subside over time. If someone is as acutely distressed weeks after diagnosis as he or she was in the first days, it is appropriate to do an assessment.

This chapter discusses working with oncology patients who experience the usual and expectable reactions, as well as those balancing cancer and psychiatric illness. We include suggestions regarding assessment and intervention and case studies to illustrate successful work in these challenging circumstances.

Usual and Expectable Reactions

Around half of patients diagnosed with cancer experience an expectable reaction when facing life-threatening illness. Whether shared with family and friends or kept in private, many fears emerge: dying, being in pain, becoming dependent on family and the health care system, and being unable to carry on life's usual tasks. As the specifics of the cancer are teased out and treatment routines are established, distress often becomes self-limited, with peaks at certain predictable times of change in treatment modality (surgery, chemotherapy, and radiation therapy) or treatment response. Strong social support, a reliable faith system, and knowledge serve as buffers during this time of crisis. Individual emotional resiliency helps bolster coping (Derogatis et al., 1983; Holland & Rowland, 1990).

Adjustment Disorders: More Significant Reactions

The adjustment disorders, a diagnostic category of the American Psychiatric Association's fifth edition of the

Diagnostic and Statistical Manual of Mental Disorders, are defined as the presence of emotional or behavioral symptoms in response to an identifiable stressor—for example, a cancer diagnosis—that are out of proportion to the severity or intensity of the stressor or result in "significant impairment in social, occupational, or other important areas of functioning" (APA, 2013, pp. 286–287). The emphasis is on the patient's reaction to the stressor. Supportive counseling is the hallmark of treatment. Antidepressants and anxiolytics may be recommended in conjunction via consultation or the primary oncology team.

Patient and Caregiver Distress Signal Consultation

Cancer has been called an "equal opportunity diagnosis." Because cancer patients come from and mirror the general population, there will be some who are able to cope with the diagnosis and treatment with limited impact on functioning. Others, who have been managing satisfactorily, will become less emotionally stable and be unable to adequately cope with the diagnosis of a life-threatening illness. Some patients will present with preexisting mental illness, depression, anxiety, and/or substance abuse that may be exacerbated by the diagnosis. Such patients are especially challenging for primary oncology providers. Oncology social workers' participation in care is a core role, and they work with mental health consultants who may be outside of the primary care team or cancer center. Because part of the oncology social worker's job is to support other colleagues to help them better understand a patient's feelings and behaviors, the social work contribution in this subpopulation of patients with cancer is ever more important.

Patients with serious mental illness bring equally serious challenges to care, including problems not only with the individual's coping, adherence, and behavior but also with the reactions of caregivers. A patient who is disruptive in the hospital or ambulatory setting is a problem, and it is part of the oncology social worker's role to intervene in both arenas.

Oncology social workers are expected to have knowledge and skills in the diagnosis and treatment of common psychiatric illnesses, depression, anxiety, and substance abuse. Having easily accessed and established referral patterns to psychiatrists in one's institution and community facilitates timely consultation and referral when indicated. If a patient has an existing relationship with a psychiatrist, it is crucial to communicate (with the patient's proper consent) early and regularly with that provider. The provider may also need information about usual reactions to a cancer diagnosis, specific treatments, other informational resources, and the availability and limits of supportive services provided by the cancer program. With this information, he or she may be able to determine whether the mental health treatment plan in place is sufficient or should be enhanced and whether the patient may be able to use additional services from the cancer program such as groups, education, and individual counseling.

Mrs. W was a 62-year-old woman with recurrent ovarian cancer. Over the first days of her diagnosis and treatment planning, she became anxious and paranoid. Her husband described a period, before diagnosis, when she began to have panic attacks and to be "not herself." His understandably being upset about her coping created tense relationships with staff as he angrily demanded that more attention, time, and resources than were possible be delivered to them both.

Oncology social work and psychiatry were both involved in her care, but the daily calls and reports of her increasing anxiety did not diminish with their intervention. Her medical oncologist made the decision that she was too psychiatrically fragile to receive the planned chemotherapy; this, of course, escalated the crisis. At this point, it was very clear that her most acute needs were related to her mental, not her physical, health. Several joint meetings were held with the couple, the social worker, and the psychiatrist, and a decision was made to force a psychiatric admission, because she clearly was unable to care for herself and was a danger at home. Mrs. W spent almost 3 weeks as a psychiatric inpatient while being followed by the oncologist as consultant, and she slowly improved with medication and electroconvulsive therapy. Her primary cancer treatment could then be resumed.

Oncology social work was closely involved from the start, expediting the psychiatric evaluation and cotreatment. The cancer treatment providers were very upset about the patient's behavior and frustrated by their inability to make things better for her or her husband. The husband's constant demands overwhelmed their empathy. The oncology social worker had two equally important jobs: direct clinical care of the patient and her husband and supporting and debriefing the medical and nursing staff.

Collaboration With Psychiatrists Experienced With Cancer

When psychiatric consultation is sought, it is imperative that the consultant has experience or training with cancer populations. The value of this experience cannot be overemphasized.

Mr. M was a 55-year-old man with progressive lung cancer. He was facing a life-threatening illness but was still well enough to work and maintain a relatively normal routine. When his wife reported that he was depressed, tearful, not sleeping, and thinking only of dying, a psychiatric consult was ordered. It was clear to his oncology caregivers that his mood had changed and that medication likely would help him. The psychiatrist who evaluated him came out of the exam room shaking his head, saying,

> *"If I were that ill, I would be depressed too." This was entirely unhelpful and reflected the young doctor's inexperience with the oncology population. The medical oncologist prescribed antidepressants, and Mr. M soon was feeling much better.*

Depression and Anxiety

Beyond the expectable sadness, symptoms of depression can emerge: a sense of hopelessness in excess of the survivability from a particular type and stage of cancer, the inability to enjoy even small kindnesses, and changes in sleep, appetite, energy, and concentration not related to the cancer itself. Depression is the most common psychiatric disorder in people diagnosed with cancer (Massie, 2004). Depression is especially associated with certain cancers (oropharyngeal [22% to 57%], pancreatic [33% to 50%], breast [1.5% to 46%], and lung [11% to 44%]) and is more likely in women than in men (Massie, 2004). When screening for distress, it is important to consider these higher risk subgroups.

Major Depressive Disorder

About 15% to 25% of people with cancer report symptoms of a major depressive disorder. This is two to three times the incidence of major depression in the general population (NCI, 2014b). Patients with preexisting major depression are likely to have a recurrence of depression when facing cancer (Kadan-Lottick et al., 2005). They may have an ongoing relationship with a psychopharmacologist or general psychiatrist, and it is important for the social worker (with the patient's signed consent) to speak with that provider. Changes in medication due to chemotherapy or other cancer-related drugs may be indicated, and preemptive consultation is helpful.

Cancer and the Risk of Suicide

A study by Misono et al. (2008) found that patients with cancer in the United States have nearly twice the incidence of suicide as that of the general population. Suicide rates were found to vary among people with different cancers and were highest in people with cancers of the lung and bronchus, followed by stomach cancers and cancers of the oral cavity and pharynx. Suicide risk among all people with cancer was highest in the years immediately after diagnosis but remained elevated for more than 15 years as compared with suicide rates in the general population (Misono et al., 2008). Assessment and identification of people at risk for suicide are crucial issues for any mental health practitioner working with people with cancer. Very little is more terrifying than the thought that suicide risk might be missed and a patient might die. In addition to gathering factual information about risk and intent, the professional is cautioned to listen to his or her own instincts and always err on the side of caution (see Chapter 21).

Remember that almost all cancer patients at some point during their illness may think about suicide as an escape from physical and emotional pain; many feel soothed by holding on to the possibility of suicide as a means of control. This does not mean that any of these people will ever act on the thought. Most do not have a plan and will honestly deny the possibility of ever choosing to end their own life, often commenting on not wanting to leave this legacy for their families (Leung et al., 2013).

Anxiety

Worry or anxiety occurs in varying degrees in virtually all patients with cancer. It is part of the crisis around diagnosis and may increase as the disease progresses or as treatment becomes more aggressive. Investigators have found that 44% of patients with cancer reported some anxiety and 23% reported significant anxiety. Anxiety is a normal reaction to cancer and generally, over time, subsides and becomes manageable. Anxiety reactions that are more prolonged or intense can be adjustment disorders. Generalized anxiety, phobia, and panic disorder are not as common among cancer patients and usually predate the cancer diagnosis. The stress caused by a diagnosis of cancer and its treatment may precipitate a relapse of preexisting anxiety disorders. Whether relapsed or new-onset conditions, anxiety disorders can be disabling and interfere with treatment.

Some medical conditions and interventions have symptoms that present as anxiety disorders, including central nervous system metastases, dyspnea associated with lung cancer or metastasis, and treatment with corticosteroids and other medications. Patients with advanced disease may experience increased anxiety, not because of fear of death, but because of uncontrolled pain or fears of isolation, abandonment, and dependency (Levin & Alici, 2010; Stark et al., 2002).

Anxiety can affect a person's behavior regarding his or her health, thereby contributing to a delay in or neglect of measures that might prevent cancer. Patients can experience moderate to severe anxiety while waiting for the results of diagnostic procedures. For patients undergoing treatment, anxiety can also heighten the expectation of pain or cause difficulties with sleep and appetite, and may be a major factor in anticipatory nausea and vomiting (Friedman, Lehane, Webb, Weinberg, & Cooper, 1994; NIH/NIMH, 2014; NCI, 2014a).

Less commonly associated with cancer, and rarely present in individuals without a preexisting history, are panic attacks or disorder, phobias, and generalized anxiety disorder. None of these conditions responds to reassurance, normal support, or information. It is important to identify and respond to these problems, because they can interfere with care. For example, a patient with phobias or vulnerability to panic attacks may be unable to tolerate a closed magnetic resonance imaging scan or receiving radiation that necessitates wearing a mask. It may be possible to modify the treatment plan in ways that will be less frightening or have anxiolytics prescribed or dosages adjusted.

Assessment

When assessing depression in people with cancer, it is important to remember that some of the side effects of cancer and its treatments are similar to symptoms of major depression and dysthymic depression (e.g., fatigue, lack of energy, sexual disturbance, poor concentration, poor appetite, loss of interest in usual activities, and insomnia or hypersomnia). Checking with the oncologist or nurse helps discern whether these symptoms are noted as treatment side effects. If a patient says that he or she has nothing to look forward to and seems affectively flat, it is especially important to listen carefully and consider depression. Even those who are quite ill usually have events to anticipate. Experience brings competence and confidence in making this diagnosis, and oncology social workers gradually learn how to distinguish between a patient who is clinically depressed and one who is exhausted, sad, and distressed by cancer.

When meeting a new client, it is essential to ask about a history of depression or anxiety and whether he or she is on antidepressant medication. Even if a patient or family member is already taking an antidepressant, the antidepressant dosage may not be sufficient during cancer diagnosis/treatments. If there is no improvement in mood after several sessions, a consultation can be recommended.

Oncology patients who request to see an oncology social worker are generally open and not trying to hide their symptoms and feelings. They have asked for counseling and want help. It is important to normalize their intense feelings, especially at the time of diagnosis, recurrence, or progression. Crying and worry are normal. However, if crying does not give some relief, if sleep is interrupted or takes up much of the day, if no joy is experienced, or if the person doesn't look forward to anything, further consultation is warranted.

Oncology patients with untreated depression may have difficulty adhering to treatment and therefore may have less successful outcomes. Oncology social workers in major medical centers can work with colleagues in psychiatry to secure necessary care. Oncology social workers in the community or in practices without psychiatry need to develop relationships and referral networks that can be accessed quickly and, if necessary, emergently.

Ms. M was a 50-year-old single woman who, within the course of 2.5 years, had three unrelated cancer diagnoses. Each was found early and seemingly successfully treated, but her long-standing major depression deepened. She had tried many medications over the years and found that nothing worked very well. Following the third diagnosis, she became profoundly depressed and expressed passive suicidal ideation to her caregivers.

Fortunately, Ms. M had been self-referred to oncology social work months earlier, so a solid and therapeutically helpful relationship was in place by the time her depression worsened. She reluctantly agreed to meet with a psychiatrist for a medication consult but took an immediate dislike to him and would not consider a second appointment or medication. She was able to promise that she would not harm herself and that a good friend was always available to take her to the emergency room if necessary. She asked for daily telephone contact, which was arranged. Her natural strengths slowly emerged in the context of this relationship, and she clawed her way up from the dark despair that had been threatening her. During each session with the oncology social worker, her safety was reassessed. It was the combined strength of her resilience and determination that helped navigate these days.

Substance Abuse and Alcoholism

Substance abuse and alcoholism are among the more serious and complicated challenges faced by clinicians in an oncology setting, where opioid medication and other controlled substances are the cornerstone of care (Rogak, Starr, & Passik, 2010; Wachter, 2011).

Clinical Challenges

It's important to pay particular attention to people with cancer who have a prior personal or family history of substance abuse. Their experience with those substances may affect their responses to present prescribed medications. The stresses associated with cancer also may possibly result in their using drugs or alcohol again. Ask about their social supports and relationships because they may have been weakened by years of difficult behavior.

New substance abuse is exceptionally rare for people with cancer who do not have a prior history. Opioids and other controlled substances can be prescribed for symptom management without concern about misuse.

When perceived drug-seeking behavior is manifested by such patients, it is often the result of poor pain control, which needs to be addressed by their oncologist (NCI, 2014c). People who are actively abusing alcohol, illicit drugs, or prescription drugs present unique problems, and their behavior needs to be addressed. Individuals who have been previously successful with treatment programs and are alcohol or substance abuse free when diagnosed with cancer may find the idea of taking an addictive substance worrisome. They may fear relapsing, and the social worker should acknowledge and respect these fears. They may need pain medication or steroids as part of the chemotherapy regimen. This is problematic if there is a history of prescription or cocaine addiction. It may help to have a family member or sponsor in Alcoholics Anonymous/Narcotics Anonymous be involved in holding on to and keeping track of the person's medications. Be aware that some members of these groups are strongly against the use of controlled substances for any reason; your patient may experience pushback from others and need particular reassurance and support of the current need for specific drugs (see Chapter 33).

Assessment and Treatment

If a cancer patient is thought to be addicted to alcohol, street drugs, or prescription drugs, it is imperative to promptly conduct a drug assessment. Deterioration in physical or psychosocial functioning that is caused by the cancer and its treatment may be difficult to separate from that caused by substance abuse. Accurate assessment of drug-related behaviors is crucial. Questions to consider include the following: What role might a drug play in the person's life? Is the person being nonadherent with his or her primary therapy? Are there behaviors that jeopardize relationships with physicians, other health care providers, or family members? Do these behaviors include not showing up for appointments, being clearly intoxicated, or being verbally abusive? In doing an assessment of substance abuse, it is crucially important to be respectful and nonjudgmental.

If there is an identified possibility of a substance abuse problem, it is important to refer the patient for a more in-depth assessment by an addictions specialist. Inpatient facilities may not be equipped to medically manage a patient in the midst of treatment, nor may the patient enter a program that may be too far away or prohibits leave for treatment. If the person is unwilling to obtain treatment but continues to be in serious pain because of cancer, the team needs to carefully discuss treatment parameters and entertain a written agreement.

Patients with histories of past or current alcohol/drug abuse continue to struggle. The classic advice to not engage with an alcoholic until he or she is sober is not always feasible or ethical in oncology settings, where the focus is centrally on helping people get through cancer. Drinking may be one of the habits that accompanies the treatment experience. There may need to be adjustments to the treatment or the doses of some drugs, best coordinated with the treatment team.

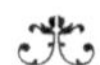

Pearls

- The incidence of mental illness and substance abuse in the general population is mirrored among people with cancer. When making an initial assessment, always be alert to these possibilities.
- Remember that many people appear highly anxious, depressed, and disoriented at the time of diagnosis and then rather quickly return to their baseline function and manage well.
- Develop and maintain solid working relationships with colleagues in psychiatry, ideally both within and outside of your institution or setting. Know when and with whom to partner.

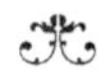

Pitfalls

- People with mental illness or active substance abuse are especially challenging to care for within any oncology setting. Be quick to ask for help.
- Colleagues bring their personal experiences and prejudices to the exam room. The oncology social worker educates and supports their best practices in patient care.
- Community mental health professionals treating patients diagnosed with cancer may need education on cancer and its treatment, prognoses, and expectable emotional and psychological responses.

A cancer diagnosis happens in the context of a life. The incidence of individuals who are dealing with mental health issues is high, and it is assumed that those problems accompany a new patient to cancer treatment. Other caregivers may initially experience such patients as provocative, argumentative, and difficult. The oncology social worker must be alert to the signs and symptoms of mental illness symptoms, able to assess and diagnose common disorders, and develop collaborative relationships and treatment plans with psychiatric and medical colleagues to provide quality care.

REFERENCES

American Psychiatric Association (APA). (2013). *Diagnostic and statistical manual of mental disorders* (5th ed.). Arlington, VA: Author.

Anguiano, L., Mayer, D. K., Piven, M. L., & Rosenstein, D. (2012). A literature review of suicide in cancer patients. *Cancer Nursing*, 35(4), E14–26. doi:10.1097/NCC.0b013e31822fc76c

Derogatis, L. R., Morrow, G. R., Fetting, J., Penman, D., Piasetsky, S., Schmale, A. M., . . . Carnicke, C. L. M. (1983). The prevalence of psychiatric disorders among cancer patients. *Journal of the American Medical Association*, 249(6), 751–757.

Friedman, L. C., Lehane, D., Webb, J. A., Weinberg, A. D., & Cooper, H. P. (1994). Anxiety in medical situations and chemotherapy-related problems among cancer patients. *Journal of Cancer Education*, 9(1), 37–41.

Holland, J. C., & Rowland, J. (1990). *Handbook of psycho-oncology: Psychological care of the patient with cancer.* New York, NY: Oxford University Press.

Kadan-Lottick, N. S., Vanderwerker, L. C., Block, S. D., Zhang, B., & Prigerson, H. G. (2005). Psychiatric disorders and mental health service use in patients with advanced cancer—A report from the coping with cancer study. *Cancer, 104*, 2872–2881.

Leung, Y., Li, M., Devins, G., Zimmermann, C., Rydall, A., Lo, C., & Rodin, G. (2013). Routine screening for suicidal intention in patients with cancer. *Psycho-Oncology, 10*, 3319.

Levin, T. T., & Alici, Y. (2010). Anxiety disorders. In J. C. Holland, W. S. Breitbart, P. B. Jacobsen, M. S. Lederberg, M. J. Loscalzo, & R. McCorkle (Eds.), *Psycho-oncology* (2nd ed., pp. 324–331). New York, NY: Oxford University Press.

Massie, M. J. (2004). Prevalence of depression in patients with cancer. *Journal National Cancer Institute Monographs, 32*, 57–71. doi:101093 jncimonographs/lgh014

Misono, S., Weiss, N. S., Fann, J. R., Redman, M., & Yueh, B. (2008). Incidence of suicide in persons with cancer. *Journal of Clinical Oncology, 28*(29), 4731–4738.

National Cancer Institute (NCI). (2014a). Adjustment to cancer: Anxiety and distress (PDQ). Retrieved from http://www.cancer.gov/cancertopics/pdq/supportivecare/adjustment/HealthProfessional/page1

National Cancer Institute (NCI). (2014b). Depression (PDQ). Retrieved from http://www.cancer.gov/cancertopics/pdq/supportivecare/depression/HealthProfessional

National Cancer Institute (NCI). (2014c). Supportive care statement for health professionals: Substance abuse issues in cancer (PDQ). *Med News*. Retrieved from http://www.meb.uni-bonn.de/Cancernet/CDR0000062835.html

National Institutes of Health, National Institute of Mental Health (NIH/NIMH). (2014). Anxiety disorders. Retrieved from http://www.nimh.nih.gov/health/topics/anxiety-disorders/index.shtml

Rogak, L. J., Starr, T. D., & Passik, S. D. (2010). Substance abuse and alcohol. In J. C. Holland, W. S. Breitbart, P. B. Jacobsen, M. S. Lederberg, M. J. Loscalzo, & R. McCorkle (Eds.), *Psycho-oncology* (2nd ed., pp. 340–347). New York, NY: Oxford University Press.

Stark, D., Kiely, M., Smith, A., Velikova, G., House, A., & Selby, P. (2002). Anxiety disorders in cancer patients: Their nature, associations, and relation to quality of life. *Journal of Clinical Oncology, 20*(14), 3137–3148.

Wachter, K. (2011). Opioid abuse is rising concern in cancer patients and survivors. *Internal Medicine News Digital Network*, April 15.

Weisman, A. D., Worden, J. W., & Sobel, H. J. (1980). *Psychological screening and intervention with cancer patients: A research report.* Boston, MA: Massachusetts General Hospital.

49

John G. Cagle and Matthew Loscalzo

Using Cognitive and Behavioral Approaches Throughout the Cancer Experience

Key Concepts

- *Cancer-related distress is common.*
- *Biopsychosocial problems are an expected part of the cancer experience.*
- *Cognitive behavioral therapy is an effective adjunct for many problems and frontline treatment for others.*
- *Cognitive behavioral therapy is a strengths-based approach with utility throughout the continuum of care.*
- *Cognitive behavioral therapy is relevant to social work practice and is becoming an essential clinical skill.*

This chapter introduces readers to cognitive behavioral therapy (CBT), its tenets, and its potential for application within oncology settings. The chapter also reviews evidence-supported CBT models that address common problems experienced by cancer patients and their families, including pragmatic approaches for assessing, addressing, and monitoring cancer-related problems and symptoms.

Cognitive and behavioral treatment approaches have demonstrated modest efficacy and effectiveness for addressing a variety of problems across diverse populations and settings. In fact, few psychological treatment approaches have withstood extensive empirical scrutiny like CBT. Since its rise in the 1960s, hundreds of studies have been published on the use of CBT in oncology settings. The preponderance of evidence suggests its usefulness as a clinical tool and an essential adjunctive treatment to complement medical and pharmaceutical therapies (Campbell & Campbell, 2012; Preyde & Synnott, 2009; Santin, Coleman, Mills, Cardwell, & Donnelly, 2012). Thus, CBT is an essential treatment modality for oncology social workers to consider in their practice.

Background and History

CBT is a psychotherapeutic approach that explores biopsychosocial connections and associations between thoughts, behaviors, and emotions. By understanding these complex linkages, oncology social workers can identify and change maladaptive thought patterns and behaviors to improve patient/family coping. The underlying premise of CBT is that rational thinking and adaptive behaviors contribute to healthy functioning. Conversely, irrational or self-destructive thoughts and behaviors can lead to emotional distress, poor coping, maladaptive behavior, and deterioration in physical health.

CBT combines the core elements of two well-known psychological treatment approaches: cognitive therapy (CT) and behavioral therapy (BT). Pioneered by psychologist Aaron Beck, cognitive therapy focuses on how a person's beliefs influence his or her mood and reactions. According to Beck, a person's thoughts (i.e., cognitions) are the principal driver of human behavior, and thus a client's thoughts are the primary mechanism for behavioral change and should be the focus of clinical encounters. Under this premise, when social workers work with clients to manage troubling life events, the aim becomes identifying how those events are being perceived and changing clients' patterns of thinking to help them cope in a more adaptive and healthy manner.

Pioneered by Ivan Pavlov, B. F. Skinner, and John Watson, behavioral therapy focuses on a person's actions and aims to systematically identify and change unhealthy behavioral patterns. Behaviorists believe that behavior is modified by manipulating environmental conditions to reinforce or punish a person's actions. Therefore, careful attention to and alteration of the way individual behaviors are being encouraged or discouraged can facilitate behavioral change. Unlike cognitions, behavior and changes in behavior are observable and measurable and therefore amenable to an objective assessment of clinical outcomes.

Both CT and BT have well-established clinical evidence supporting their effectiveness in dealing with a broad range of problems. Within the clinical context, however, the putative differences between CT and BT are less important than the demonstrated benefits of their combined usefulness in the integrated cognitive behavioral therapeutic perspective, which most CBT practitioners now consider a standard of clinical care. This hybrid approach builds from the strengths of both perspectives by helping clients focus on their current problems and developing pragmatic strategies to solve them. Both the patient and therapist are expected to be actively involved in the treatment process, with the therapist partnering with the client to learn how to identify distorted or unhelpful thinking patterns, recognize and change inaccurate beliefs, relate to others in more positive ways, and change behaviors accordingly.

Cancer patients and their families often experience myriad psychosocial stressors and difficult emotions (depression, anxiety, and stress are normal and prevalent reactions) throughout the course of diagnosis, illness, and treatment. Although these may be common responses, their presence may also diminish quality of life and coping as the illness threatens the individual's health, well-being, and personhood. However, the reaction to the illness can be equally threatening. CBT interventionists in cancer care settings can focus their efforts on the patient/family reaction to the illness and to bolster resources, support systems, and coping.

When applied to oncology settings, CBT frequently includes thorough patient/caregiver education, implementation of stress reduction techniques, use of problem-solving strategies, homework assignments, and self-monitoring (APOS, 2006; Horne & Watson, 2011). As Figure 49.1 shows, the underlying conceptual model for CBT users employs an ABC mnemonic, wherein an **A**ctivating event is interpreted cognitively through **B**eliefs about the event, oneself, or the world. These beliefs may be based on pre-established thought patterns or newly formed assumptions. In turn, these beliefs have emotional, behavioral, and social **C**onsequences.

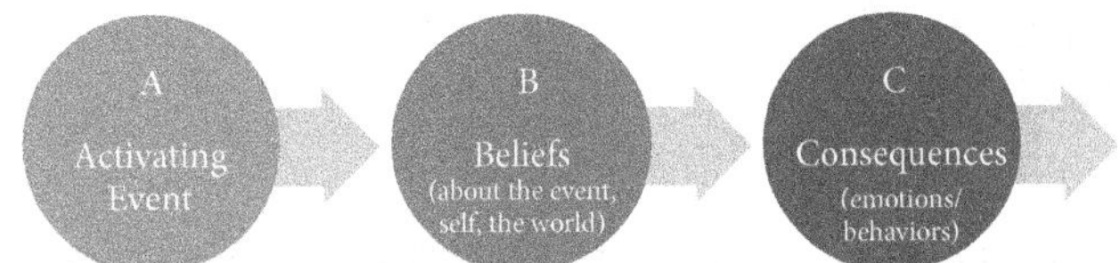

Figure 49.1. The "ABCs" of Cognitive Behavioral Treatment Adapted from Ellis (1991) and David, Freeman, and DiGiuseppe (2009).

Cognitive Behavioral Therapy Interventions

CBT interventions have grown over the years in terms of empirical support, popularity, and sophistication, having been successfully implemented with individuals, couples, and families; in groups; and through a variety of formats (in person, over the phone, or web based), although some research suggests that client–therapist rapport is best facilitated by in-person contact. Contemporary CBT interventions have evolved to embrace the full biopsychosocial model. For example, the importance of emotional regulation (i.e., one's ability to match his or her level of emotional arousal with the reality of the situation) is considered an essential step in the process of encouraging adaptive responses and improved coping. Good emotional regulation fosters positive thoughts and behaviors that serve as self-reinforcing mechanisms of change. In this regard, note that CBT interventions can leverage the multiple dimensions of human potential including the physical, emotional, psychological, and social aspects of health and mental well-being. Although a complete description of the full range of CBT interventions is beyond the limits of this chapter, the following section provides a brief primer on key cognitive and behavioral concepts that are essential knowledge for CBT interventionists. Table 49.1 provides a list of selected clinical tasks appropriate for oncology social workers using a CBT approach.

Key Intervention Concepts

Cognitive Concepts

CBT interventionists should be familiar with several key cognitive-based tools and concepts. *Schemas*, for example, are well-established and reoccurring patterns of thinking. Sometimes, schemas include positive, edifying thoughts; other times they consist of *cognitive distortions*, which are irrational, maladaptive thoughts. Cognitive distortions often involve absolute terms, consisting of words like *should, never, always*, or *must*. For example, a family member caring for

Table 49.1.
Selected Cognitive Behavioral Treatment Tasks for Oncology Settings

- Assess the medical situation and patient/family context.
- Negotiate defined time limits for work together.
- Build trust, rapport, and a parallel client–therapist partnership.
- Focus on the present; prioritize problems.
- Identify modifiable problems.
- Select measurable, realistic outcomes.
- Use sessions to teach skills and strategies for immediate application.
- Have client(s) provide simple, ongoing documentation of progress.

a cancer patient might think, "I must be available 24/7 in case my loved one needs anything." This thinking certainly indicates a strong dedication to the patient, but making oneself indefinitely available is impractical and perhaps a sign of poor self-care on the caregiver's part. Furthermore, a caregiver who dwells on this type of cognitive distortion might be reluctant to accept help from other members within the patient's network of friends, family, and acquaintances. In addition, cognitive distortions can be repetitive and outside of an individual's immediate awareness. When this occurs, the distorted thinking patterns have become established as *automatic thoughts*. CBT practitioners attempt to identify automatic thoughts and cognitive distortions using a *schema analysis* to inquire about an individual's core belief systems. When distorted thinking is identified during the analysis, the clinician then helps the client to develop more positive, reality-based beliefs. Common cognitive distortions voiced by cancer patients and their families include the following:

> *Patient/caregiver:* "I can't handle this—it's too much."
> *Caregiver:* "No one else knows [the patient] as well as I do; therefore, I'm the only one who can provide good care."
> *Patient:* "My life is over now that I have cancer."
> *Patient:* "I must be a bad person because [a higher power] is punishing me with this disease."

Cognitive Restructuring
Cognitive restructuring is the process of challenging a person's cognitive distortions while replacing them with tempered, reality-based, and positive thought patterns. This may include revealing the logical inconsistencies behind one's erroneous thinking and realigning their beliefs to a more realistic, pragmatic way of thinking. Using the previous example of the caregiver who believes that he or she must be available 24/7, a CBT practitioner may tactfully challenge this belief by saying the following:

> *I appreciate your level of commitment, but it probably isn't realistic for you to be present with [the patient] all the time. Plus, if you overcommit yourself, you may end up neglecting other important aspects of your life, including your own health. If you don't take good care of yourself, then you might not be able to provide good care to [the patient] for a sustained period of time. Many families in similar circumstances rely on other friends or family members to provide them with respite from caregiving. Would you be willing to accept some help? And wouldn't you agree that you shouldn't be expected to be available around the clock?*

Cognitive Reappraisal
Cognitive reappraisal occurs when patients and caregivers re-evaluate and alter their thought patterns. Because cognitive restructuring involves educating patients and families about inconsistencies in their thinking, it is important for practitioners to be familiar with common heuristics and flawed thinking. Exposing the erroneous logic behind cognitive distortions can facilitate the cognitive reappraisal process. However, it is essential for clinicians to remember that the primary focus of CBT intervention is not to correct all cognitive distortions, but rather to educate the client about cognitive processes and raise awareness about maladaptive patterns of thinking and distortions that are directly related to the therapeutic work at hand. (For an in-depth review of cognitive distortions, see Beck, Rush, Shaw, and Emery [1979] or Sears and Kraus [2009].)

Reality Testing
Reality testing is an important and frequently used cognitive restructuring approach. In general, reality testing is the process of comparing a person's beliefs with real-world experiences. The goal of reality testing is to create or highlight *cognitive dissonance*, a discomfort felt when an individual's thoughts are incongruent with his or her behavior or reality. This dissonance can facilitate cognitive reappraisals and, ultimately, cognitive restructuring. CBT practitioners often use *self-talk* assignments to facilitate cognitive restructuring and foster adaptive thought patterns. Self-talk refers to the internalized messages that people tell themselves, for example, "Asking for help is not a sign of weakness" or "I can enjoy living despite my cancer." A regimen of positive self-dialogue has been found to improve coping, quality of life, self-worth, and feelings of mastery and control (Moorey & Greer, 2011; Preyde & Synnott, 2009).

Behavioral Concepts

The behavioral component of CBT is based on the premise that the human experience can be improved by reinforcing beneficial (i.e., adaptive) behaviors while discouraging unwanted (i.e., maladaptive) behaviors. The activities we engage in or avoid on a daily basis are often guided by expectations about the consequences of our behaviors. These expectations about punishments and rewards are frequently outside of our immediate awareness.

Behavioral Activation

Behavioral activation occurs when an activity disrupts a dysfunctional pattern of thinking and is aimed at increasing patient activity and access to reinforcements. Activities such as exercise, socializing, playing games, or engaging in household chores may distract a person's attention, allowing his or her mood to be altered (Hopko, Lejuez, Ruggiero, & Eifert, 2003).

Attention to Self-Care Behaviors

Self-care behaviors are activities that facilitate physical health, vitality, and coping. Although specific self-care behaviors will differ from person to person, oncology social workers can partner with their clients to identify and reinforce important healthy habits or other restorative activities. Under stressful circumstances, it can be easy to slip into unhealthy patterns. When pushed to the limits of our coping ability, we may resort to eating junk food, forgoing a full night's sleep, or smoking or drinking excessively. These seemingly maladaptive coping responses may actually help us deal with challenging situations in the short term. However, if these behaviors persist, the negative consequences of neglecting one's self-care may overshadow any short-term benefits. Skipping a planned workout, for example, may give us a few extra hours to manage our schedule on a hectic day, but if the workouts become disrupted on a regular basis, our mental and physical health may suffer as result. Encouraging rejuvenating activities such as daily walks, mediation, healthy cooking, or restful sleep can also provide families with a sense of normalcy, predictability, and routine. Of course, when advising oncology patients about an exercise regimen or other activities, practitioners should collaborate with the patient, family, and other members of the health care team to ensure that the circumstances of the illness will not place the patient at increased risk.

Relaxation Techniques

Progressive muscle relaxation and deep-breathing exercises are prescriptive, physiological strategies that can reduce physical and psychological tension and create a sense of calm and safety. Relaxation is considered the workhorse of CBT and is based on the premise that a person cannot be simultaneously relaxed and afraid.

Homework

Homework is an important behavioral intervention technique and a hallmark of CBT. Homework consists of assigned activities the client agrees to engage in outside of the clinical encounter. These assignments frequently include journaling, keeping a diary, letter writing, self-monitoring, or task-oriented activities. Homework can be a useful assessment tool, self-contained intervention, or a combination of both. Note that the very concept of homework assignments may generate resistance, so any required work outside of the clinical session should be highly focused, of clear benefit to the client, and easy to complete. Progress on homework assignments should be reviewed at the beginning of the session and discussed consistently during each clinical encounter. Any barriers to following through with the assignment(s) should be addressed. See Table 49.2 for an overview of CBT interventions that can be used in oncology settings.

Evaluation of Therapeutic Outcomes

Monitoring client outcomes is essential for modern social work practice. Practitioners in cancer care settings should select outcome measures that are (1) pertinent to the problem of interest and (2) ideally validated for use with diverse oncology populations. Oncology social workers should also be aware that a patient's disease progression,

Table 49.2.
Cognitive Behavioral Interventions Relevant to the Cancer Setting

Intervention	Description
Information and education	Raising client awareness about the linkages between thoughts, emotions, and behavior
Social support	Reinforcing thoughts and behaviors that promote social engagement and support
Progressive relaxation/deep-breathing exercises	Step-by-step processes to reduce stress and anxiety by regulating breathing or tensing and relaxing of select muscle groups
Distraction/behavioral activation	Active diversion of one's attention away from distressing thoughts or activities
Meditation	Mindfulness strategies to enhance focus and attention on the here and now; may include prayer
Cognitive restructuring	The process of replacing maladaptive thinking patterns with positive, reality-based beliefs
Self-talk/coping statements	Positive self-statements to encourage coping and improve self-worth
In-world practice	Employing cognitive behavioral strategies outside of the therapeutic setting

Table 49.2. (Continued)

Intervention	Description
Diaries/journaling	Regular documentation of activating events and accompanying thoughts, behaviors, or responses
Systematic desensitization	Reducing psychological distress by pairing physical relaxation and calming thoughts with progressive exposure to a stress-producing stimulus
Role-playing	Assigning roles and scenarios for the client to play out in the clinical setting; used to highlight cognitive distortions or patterns of reinforcement
Strengths inventory	A guided review of personal resources and successful coping techniques
Social contingency management	A means to manage expectations in social situations by planning cognitive and behavioral responses to a variety of possible scenarios
Time-outs	Intentional disengagement from a situation to assess one's thoughts and develop a response that facilitates adaptive coping
Cognitive behavioral therapy–based hypnosis	Guided suggestion during a deep state of relaxation
Reality testing	Contrasting observations in the real world with one's cognitive schema; used to create cognitive dissonance and to promote thinking that is consistent with reality
Pacing	Prioritizing one's efforts; conserving energy to engage in desirable activities

symptom severity, or treatment side effects may confound the effects of CBT interventions on outcomes of interest. In other words, observable improvements in clinical outcomes may be muted, or even erased, by other factors related to the cancer or treatment. Because CBT concentrates on problem solving, therapeutic progress can usually be easily measured and documented.

Case #1: The Red-Hot Blanket

Shirley, a 29-year-old interior decorator with chronic myelogenous leukemia, reported a deep burning pain in her joints. The pain contributed to insomnia and anorexia. She reported that the pain felt like a "burning red-hot blanket" covering her and that she "felt trapped" because her pain medication made her lethargic. Breathing exercises were attempted but unhelpful. Further exploration of the pain, including in-depth queries about the color, shape, size, texture, taste, and general feel of the pain, produced vivid descriptions of the pain experience; thus, a combination of guided imagery and progressive muscle relaxation was attempted. The patient was directed to imagine the "red-hot blanket" turning into a cool, soothing, healing color. During the guided imagery session, Shirley reported the "red-hot blanket" was changing to a bright cooling purple. She was then instructed to visualize the purple color spreading over her entire body. An audio recording was made of the exercise for her. The patient reported being out of pain for the first time in months and was able to sleep with "actual dreams." Interestingly, the patient said that she still did not believe in this "hocus pocus" but emphasized that it "really worked."

Case #2: Frustrated and Not Sleeping

John was a 42-year-old engineer with lung cancer who had never smoked. His wife, Sarah, had been diagnosed with borderline personality disorder. Together they had three young boys who were homeschooled. Sarah was overwhelmed by the implications of John's disease and refused to come in for a consultation. She was impulsive with frequent emotional outbursts that scared their sons. John was not sleeping and expressed concern about his mounting anger, stating, "I am at my wits' end with Sarah." John reported that his sons were the most important part of his life and he wanted to be a role model for them. John was asked to keep a very briefly worded thought record to track his immediate thoughts about his response to Sarah's outbursts, present behavior, feelings about his present behavior, how he would have liked to respond, and how he would feel about his preferred behavior. This process gave John some insight into how he was responding and how badly this made him feel about himself and what he was teaching his sons. The thought record also enabled him to construct an alternate way of living that was more consistent with who he wanted to be and how he wanted to educate his sons. Not surprisingly, Sarah's behavior also had a therapeutic response from John's new ways of acting. John was able to sleep.

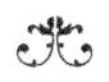

Pearls

- Cancer patients/families especially benefit from interventions that maximize control, predictability, and meaning.
- CBT interventions utilize a biopsychosocial approach to maximize the strengths of patients/families within their unique context.

- The integration of a supportive partnership, tailored education, cognitive behavioral coping skills, and social support creates an optimal therapeutic context.
- Clinical encounters are motivational strategy sessions for real-world activation of skills and meaningful relationships.
- Go with natural inclinations of patients: Ruminators need cognitive coping statements, creative types may benefit from guided imagery, athletic types may be suited for progressive muscle relation, and so on.
- Clinicians who actively use CBT techniques in their own lives make the best CBT therapists.

Pitfalls

- Focusing too much on emotional expression without action or deepening meaning can lead to lack of motivation or behavioral paralysis.
- Asking patients to do too much up front will result in them (and you) accomplishing little but feeling worse.
- Not knowing why you are meeting with a patient who also does not know why you are meeting is the perfect formula for nothing.
- Wanting more for the patient than the patient wants for him- or herself will leave you both wanting.

Cognitive behavioral treatment skills and interventions have much to offer the social worker who aspires to acquire and master the clinical skills essential to help cancer patients, their families, and colleagues.

REFERENCES

American Psychosocial Oncology Society (APOS). (2006). *Quick reference for oncology clinicians: The psychiatric and psychological dimensions of cancer symptom management.* Charlottesville, VA: IPOS Press.

Beck, A. T., Rush, A. J., Shaw, B. F., & Emery, G. (1979). *Cognitive therapy of depression.* New York, NY: Guilford Press.

Campbell, C. L., & Campbell, L. C. (2012). A systematic review of cognitive behavioral interventions in advanced cancer. *Patient Education and Counseling, 89*, 15–124.

David, D., Freeman, A., & DiGiuseppe, R. (2009). Rational and irrational beliefs: Implications for mechanisms of change and practice in psychotherapy. In D. David, S. J. Lynn, & A. Ellis (Eds.), *Rational and irrational beliefs* (pp. 195–217). New York, NY: Oxford University Press.

Ellis, A. (1991). The revised ABCs of rational-emotive therapy (RET). *Journal of Rational-Emotive and Cognitive-Behavior Therapy, 9*(3), 139–172.

Hopko, D. R., Lejuez, C. W., Ruggiero, K. J., & Eifert, G. H. (2003). Contemporary behavioral activation treatments for depression: Procedures, principles, and progress. *Clinical Psychology Review, 23*(5), 699–717.

Horne, D., & Watson, M. (2011). Cognitive-behavioural therapies in cancer care. In M. Watson & D. W. Kissane (Eds.), *Handbook of psychotherapy in cancer care* (pp. 15–26). Chichester, England: John Wiley & Sons. doi:10.1002/9780470975176.ch2

Moorey, S., & Greer, S. (2011). *Oxford guide to CBT for people with cancer* (2nd ed.). Oxford, England: Oxford University Press.

Preyde, M., & Synnott, E. (2009). Psychosocial intervention for adults with cancer: A meta-analysis. *Journal of Evidence-Based Social Work, 6*(4), 321–347. doi:10.1080/15433710903126521

Santin, O., Coleman, H., Mills, M., Cardwell, C. R., & Donnelly, M. (2012). Psychosocial interventions for informal caregivers of people living with cancer. *The Cochrane Library.* doi:10.1002/14651858.CD009912

Sears, S., & Kraus, S. (2009). I think therefore I om: Cognitive distortions and coping style as mediators for the effects of mindfulness meditation on anxiety, positive and negative affect, and hope. *Journal of Clinical Psychology, 65*(6), 561–573.

50

Carrie Lethborg and Lou Harms

Meaning-Making Approaches to Social Work Practice in Oncology

Key Concepts

- *Meaning-making approaches are adopted by social workers in oncology settings in the Australian context.*
- *Patients move between meaning, coping, and suffering throughout their cancer experience.*
- *MaP Therapy is a specific social work approach that enables a patient and his or her family to find meaning and purpose in their illness experience. The term* MaP Therapy *was initially used by Lethborg, Schofield, and Kissane (2012) to reflect both the acronym for "meaning and purpose" and the process of charting (or "mapping") an understanding of meaning through use of a combination of therapies.*

More than 100,000 people are newly diagnosed with cancer each year in Australia (AIHW, CA, & AACR, 2008). Despite increasing survival rates, cancer remains the second most common cause of death for men and women in Australia (AIHW, 2012). Social workers, particularly in many public hospital settings, engage with cancer patients and their families as part of a multidisciplinary support team. Meaning-making approaches are a key focus of this work.

This chapter presents an overview of meaning-making approaches in the Australian context. The particular goals of clinical work are described, that is, encouragement of meaning and purpose while recognizing suffering, promoting coherence, and strengthening meaning in relation to others. This broad discussion of key principles and interventions leads to the introduction of MaP Therapy (Lethborg et al., 2012). This intervention reflects other Australian models of meaning-making approaches, attending particularly to cultural and contextual factors.

What We Have Learned So Far

The notion of "meaning" in both conceptualizing and intervening in the lives of people living with cancer offers a focus that is compatible with a range of social work processes. Speck, Higginson, and Addington-Hall's (2004, p. 124) definition of meaning relates to how a person makes sense of life situations and derives purpose from existence. This definition acknowledges that both cognitive and existential aspects of meaning are equally crucial to understanding the impact of a situation on a person's life and the strengths he or she brings to that situation.

This cognitive-existential perspective provides an opportunity to both understand the individual cancer experience and intervene in a substantial way to improve the adjustment process. This perspective requires the social worker to stand in each patient's shoes and to view the experience of cancer from his or her perspective and in relation to how he or she makes sense of and finds value in living. The existential component of meaning counters the stressful and negative aspects of life experiences, whereas the cognitive component provides a framework for understanding these negatives. From this perspective, then, one can access (1) the lens from which a patient assesses his or her life situations and (2) the sustenance that meaningful aspects of his or her life provide in managing times of difficulty.

The Cognitive Aspect of Meaning

A person approaches a challenge like cancer with a preconceived viewpoint about how events are regulated and where his or her energies should be directed. The belief system that makes up their assumptive world guides the way one leads his or her life and directs one's expectations, one's anticipated future, and what is important on a daily basis (Janoff-Bulman, 1989, p. 114). One's worldview also directs the ways in which individuals interpret new information and understand the impact of their cancer diagnosis.

Thus, two women of different ages who have been diagnosed with the same stage and type of cancer may view their situations differently because of their assumptive worlds. For example, in Gemmel's (2013, p. 117) study of older women with ovarian cancer, one woman said, "I am quite happy to just go along as I am and accept what fate brings, that is all you can do," whereas another stated, "I get better because I've got a plan I can attack and I do something positive about it.... I find I'm more in control then. I'm meant to be a little bit in control." This concept encourages the clinician to have a sense of curiosity about what influences the individual patient's view of his or her cancer and how he or she sees the possible outcomes. It requires an understanding of the impact of cultural and family background, socioeconomic status, other life stressors, past experiences with cancer, religious beliefs, and so on. Understanding the cognitive aspect of meaning for each person does not mean, however, that all these aspects of his or her life need to be explored as such. Insight into a person's unique perspective can be gained by simply asking a question such as, "What did you *think* when you were told you had cancer?"

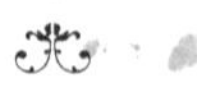

The Existential Aspect of Meaning

The existential component of meaning is concerned with existence—that is, the specifically human mode of being and the meaning of personal existence (Hartman & Zimberoff, 2003, p. 3). It pertains to the drive to find meaning in life and to live a life that has purpose. Frankl (1963, p. 98) described the "will to meaning" as an innate drive to find value in personal existence, especially in the face of suffering. This motivation to find meaning is based on the premise that life is a gift and that its goal is to live it with meaning and authenticity (Hartman & Zimberoff, 2003, p. 5). Thus, the tendency toward acquisition of meaning is driven by the need to have a depth to life beyond merely existing (Yalom, 1980).

A colleague once described a statement on an infant's tombstone that perhaps describes this existential question most simply and poignantly: "It is so soon that I am done for, I wonder what I was begun for." Sources of meaning vary in response to each person's worldview. Meaning can be found by feeling a connectedness with God or a higher being (Halstead & Mickley, 1997); through the arts, family, work, or money; or through other people (Dyson, Cobb, & Formann, 1997). Each person's meaning is specific to him or her. Asking what moves the person, what provides him or her with motivation, and what helps him or her to manage during times of suffering are crucial to understanding that specific worldview. The unique perspective of social work is based on a consideration of the person within this context and understanding what he or she brings to the cancer experience as a starting point to working with the patient. This perspective requires that the various social influences in a person's life be considered, as well as his or her own psychological perspective.

Meaning in the Setting of Cancer

Although people living with cancer can experience suffering (including physical, psychological, and existential distress), they can also experience high levels of meaning (Lethborg, Aranda, & Kissane, 2007). This coexistence of meaning and suffering may seem paradoxical but can be understood as follows: A person experiences an ongoing stressor (cancer) that prompts him or her to find meaning and rationality through the need for a sense of coherence (Antonovsky, 1979) and the will to meaning (Frankl, 1963). Sources of meaning may become more obvious through these processes. The cancer patient can move between meaning, coping, and suffering throughout his or her cancer experience as part of an ongoing process (Lethborg, Aranda, Bloch, & Kissane, 2006).

John, a 30-year-old married father of twin boys, listens to his sons laughing in the garden as he rests in bed after chemotherapy. John feels terrible and as tears come he thinks, "I can't do this—it is killing me to have no energy and to be missing out on life" (suffering). Just then his sister walks into his room with tea and medication to reduce his nausea. She sits next to him and helps him sip his tea. "You know this always perks you up," she says. "Why don't you rest, let the tablets work, and we'll watch television with the boys later?" John takes his medication and falls asleep. On waking, he feels better and more energized (coping). His wife gives him a kiss, helps him up, and walks to where the twins are watching TV. "Daddy!" his 5-year-old son says, "Come and sit here next to us." John sits on the couch, one twin under each arm. He smiles to himself and thinks about how lucky and loved he is (meaning).

The process of moving in and out of suffering, coping, and meaning occurs throughout the cancer experience and often throughout a day. Indeed, in writing about resilience, Deveson (2004, p. 149) asks, "What does matter most to people? Is it not our personal relationships and the meaning we make of our lives?"

Sitting in the room of a busy inner-city hospital where I see patients being treated for cancer and their families, I was listening to Frank, a 55-year-old farmer, talk about his lack of sleep and appetite. His youngest son (Tom, aged 15) was being treated for acute myeloid leukemia and every treatment we offered had failed. Frank was a loving, heartbroken father. His take on life was simple: He loved his family, worked hard on the land, and believed in community. He proudly brought us produce from his farm on the many 4-hour trips back down to "the big smoke" with his beloved son and his quiet, teary wife and hoped for a miracle.

He tells me about the way he cried on the day of his son's birth, because his hand was so tiny it got lost in Frank's big rough palm. He tells me how, since his son's deterioration, he has had a recurrent dream about cradling his son in his arms and pacing through the night hours as he did while his wife recovered from pneumonia for weeks following his son's birth. He makes sure I understand about the exquisite connection he has with his child: "See it's like this: A child is born from your heart, your heart grows to fit each one in and then that is part of who you are. So to lose one, to let one go means that part of your heart is ripped out, broken, and it's a wound that never heals." "I can't seem to stop crying," he laments.

But this statement also indicated Frank's capacity to feel and to understand what brings joy in life, even in the setting of suffering. I thus explored the meaning in Frank's life, and he spoke eloquently about how the sun on the crisp frost across the back paddock that morning had "lifted his spirits" and how much he loved being a father, a husband, and a member of a strong community. The depth of his pain was great, but I could see glimmers of hope.

The presence of meaning in the lives of people with cancer is thus important in both adjusting to their diagnosis and balancing the suffering. Previous work (Lethborg et al., 2007) has indicated that the level of meaning in a cancer patient's life is predictive of adjustment. This study was conducted with adults attending an Australian metropolitan cancer service (n = 100). It explored the associations of suffering (physical and existential distress) and coping (through social support) with psychological distress and global meaning using a battery of instruments. The contributions of suffering and coping to psychological distress and meaning were examined using a variety of statistical methods. Multiple regression analyses were conducted to further examine relative contributions to both psychological distress and global meaning.

This study found that physical and existential distress were positively associated with psychological distress, whereas high social support and personal meaning were related to lower levels. Social support was the strongest correlate of global meaning, whereas high levels of existential distress were related to lower levels. Thus, the factors related to suffering in those living with cancer were found to promote psychological distress, and the reverse was true for global meaning.

Others have found that those who struggle with meaning in the face of cancer can experience regret (Tomer & Eliason, 1996), meaninglessness (Saunders, 1988), and demoralization (Kissane, Clarke, & Street, 2001). This study highlighted that patients with less meaning in life and less perceived social support expressed higher levels of psychological distress. It thus makes clinical sense to use a meaning focus in understanding patients' lived experience and in working therapeutically with them as they adjust to living with a cancer diagnosis (Lethborg, Aranda, & Kissane, 2008). As existential questions arise in the setting of cancer, meaning-focused therapy offers a framework that encourages further exploration of core values and areas of significance in life, thus decreasing the focus on distress that can overwhelm the cancer experience.

From a social work perspective, using meaning in clinical interventions is compatible with the core goal of "starting where a client is at" and working with the client to navigate his or her adjustment to illness. Further social work goals in the cancer setting include encouraging meaning while also recognizing suffering, promoting coherence, and supporting social connections.

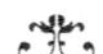

Meaning-Based Therapeutic Goals

Encouraging Meaning and Purpose While Recognizing Suffering

Suffering exposes the limitation of one's existence, bringing about a greater awareness of the meaning in life. Adjusting to a cancer diagnosis can be construed as the struggle to achieve meaning in the face of suffering. For this reason, interventions need to focus on both enhancing meaning and acknowledging suffering. It is also important that the person not be incapacitated by suffering (Younger, 1995) and be able to experience meaning.

Managing John's (the father of twins mentioned previously) nausea and fatigue pharmacologically was imperative. This strategy alone, however, would not have enabled his mood to rise the way it did by coupling medication with love and care from his wife and sister and the joy of being around his sons. In a clinical setting, then, a more holistic focus is achieved by determining what can be done medically and what can be enhanced in relation to meaning in life.

Promoting Coherence

The ability to comprehend the experience of cancer from each person's own world is important for adjustment. Park and Folkman's (1997) development of meaning-based coping theory suggests that processes such as positive reappraisal, finding benefit, revising beliefs, and revising goals are all useful steps toward the promotion of coherence. Often patients are not aware that they are using these processes. As one patient explained, "Well, in the first two years the hope was that I would get to 10 years.... Then, there is hope that is related to my faith—I know I will go somewhere not bad when I die and that I have a presence with me in the meantime." Returning to specific hopes, Alan added, "It is definitely worth being alive. There are still things that I enjoy enormously." Similarly, as Jacinta, a young single mother with advanced cancer, shared, "Every morning I wake up and I'm generally not feeling the best. I don't sleep so well these days and never wake feeling refreshed, and various things ache, and I sigh and think, 'OK girl, pull yourself together, today's another day.' You muster up whatever you have inside you to get you going again and then you face another day!"

Both Alan and Jacinta illustrate how they use cognitive tools to help them adjust to cancer. Having a discussion with them about where these thoughts come from, what makes them choose to focus on the positives and reappraise situations, and how to alter goals to meet the new limitations of their lives can be empowering in the therapeutic setting.

Strengthening Meaning in Relation to Others

The social world provides the context in which meaning and purpose evolve and fundamentally influences a person's outlook and state of mind (Folkman, 1997). Longing for comfort increases in times of distress, and interconnectedness with others is crucial to gaining and sustaining positive emotions (Forbes, 1999).

Human connectedness is central in dealing with suffering (Giese-Davis, Hermanson, Koopman, Weibel, & Spiegel, 2000). Being able to share with and feel connected to others is central to overall improved adjustment. It provides a buffer to suffering and an enhancement to meaning in life. Feeling connected with others has been found to enhance hope (Ballard, Green, McCaa, & Logsdon, 1997), meaning (Thomas & Retsas, 1999), awareness, and appreciation of life (Mahon & Casperson, 1997).

A patient's social world can provide an environment in which he or she can share suffering, process his or her appraisal of cancer, and feel connected to others. Qualitative work has shown that social support is a central influence associated with enhanced meaning and reducing psychological distress among people with advanced cancer (Lethborg et al., 2006). Some withdrawal from others can be a coping mechanism for those facing existential distress, but many "return" to their social world to pursue adjustment. Cobb's review of social support as a moderator of life stress (1976, p. 314) concludes that "we should start now to teach all our patients, both well and sick, how to give and receive social support." This finding confirms the central role of social work in the setting of cancer.

Although some patients may find it important to spend time in solitude, interventions that uphold the cancer patient's social world can be essential to preventing the patient from having to suffer alone. Through the expression of pain with a compassionate other, it is possible to re-engage with life and restore one's sense of significance (Clarke, 2003). The social worker can encourage patients to review their lives with regard to the influence of their relationships to help patients understand their context, their uniqueness, and their significance to others.

Fred mentioned in the first session with the social worker that he could not talk about his family without crying. Eventually, he described an abusive childhood and the healing that happened when he met his wife and created his own family. He spoke with pride about his children's accomplishments and his happy marriage. However, there was incongruity between these statements and the number of hours Fred was working (especially when he admitted he didn't need the money). The gap between what was meaningful (family) and what he was spending his time doing (work) became obvious to Fred over the four sessions he had with the social worker. He reduced his hours and took a holiday with his family.

Meaning-Based Interventions

Although MaP Therapy can use a combination of modalities, the intervention described here is a four-session, individual, face-to-face therapy that uses methods influenced by narrative therapy, meaning-based coping theory, existential therapy, and cognitive therapy. Here the patient is challenged to move beyond insights about meaning in life toward action that will increase this meaning. The therapist begins by asking about the patient's story with a focus on those aspects of the patient's life that have had the most meaning. This process enables the development of a context to understand how the patient makes sense of his or her cancer experience and provides information that the therapist can reflect back to the patient about meaning and purpose. Questions are posed by the therapist to challenge narrative accounts, promote constructive alternatives to the framing of life stories, and direct attention toward positive, meaningful, and purposeful goals.

> *Jai presented a life story to the social worker of broken relationships with women but of great commitment to his three children whom he parented on a half-time basis. He talked about homeschooling one of his sons during a year-long illness but still highlighted his failure to keep a family. The social worker acknowledged his regrets as he faced the end of his life but also asked him to consider an alternative view of himself as someone who has maintained his family in an impressive way.*

Participants in MaP Therapy describe a greater awareness and appreciation of those aspects of their lives that bring them joy and meaning and of the benefits of refocusing their lives around what is important despite their cancer (Lethborg et al., 2012).

> *Karen had ongoing bone pain and was feeling fatigued and demoralized. The social worker asked her to write two lists: one of things she spent most of her time doing and one of things that brought her the most joy. She was then asked to compare them and share her feelings. Karen listed the things she spent the most time doing as medical appointments, cleaning, lying on the couch, and answering telephone calls from well-meaning friends. Her list of what gave her joy in life (in order of importance) included her granddaughter, her two adult children, her sister, and her garden. In working through these lists, it was clear to Karen that she should fill her life with more of the things that had meaning. Of course, this was not a straightforward process—medical appointments were necessary and she was not able to do as much gardening as she used to. She talked to her sister, who offered to accompany her to her appointments just so they could catch up. Her son and daughter planned "Sundays in the garden" each week where they would visit (with her granddaughter) for an hour each Sunday and sit on a rug in her garden. Thus, bringing meaningful things into life enabled Karen's suffering to be balanced, even though it couldn't be eliminated.*

The broad application of these meaning-based processes can be found in a range of practice models throughout Australian social work. Hegarty, Breaden, Swetenham, and Grbich (2010) used a meaning model to understand staff experiences of working with refractory suffering in the palliative setting. Interviews illustrated how palliative care staff used meaning-making and narrative processes to develop their own sense of coherence and to understand their own reactions and their patients' reactions to suffering. Focusing on patients themselves, Pascal and Endacott (2010) described the existential challenges raised by the uncertainty of a cancer diagnosis and survivorship during interviews with 15 patients over a 6-month period. Participants describe uncertainty as a "wake-up call" that prompted positive and negative outcomes. The uncertainty of patients' survival also affected clinicians in ways they had not anticipated.

Meaning-based models are particularly helpful in understanding cultural and spiritual influences. This is illustrated well by McGrath's (2010) innovative model for Aboriginal palliative care service delivery, which prompts the clinician to gain a full understanding of the illness experience by exploring meanings with clients. This allows the clinician to understand beliefs, the role of family, connections with the land, and experiences of service delivery. Although this model was developed for and with Australian Aboriginal people, it can be applied to all types of patients in the setting of illness.

In the same vein, Kwok, Sullivan, and Cant (2006) explored the specific meanings surrounding the breast with 20 Chinese Australian women. Participants' views were found to be important to the way they viewed breast cancer, breast health practices, and breast cancer risk prevention. Such insight provided important information about the development of culturally appropriate health education programs and supportive interventions. For example, cultural information provided a greater influence on women's engagement with prevention services than biomedical information.

Pearls

- Patients and families report high satisfaction with meaning-making approaches.
- Meaning-making approaches support the coexistence of meaning, purpose, and suffering in the cancer illness experience.
- Interventions such as those outlined in MaP Therapy provide structured clinical focus for social workers.

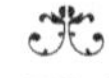

Pitfalls

- The evidence base for meaning-making approaches is drawn from small, qualitative studies. Although these affirm the approach, a stronger evidence base is needed.
- If social workers focus solely on meaning making as an "inner world" experience, the impact of "outer world" experiences can be overlooked.

Meaning-making approaches are increasingly being used by Australian social workers in their interventions with patients and families living with cancer. This chapter has provided an overview of new models such as MaP Therapy, which provide structured clinical interventions in a variety of health contexts. Further research is required to develop a sound evidence base for the efficacy of these interventions.

ADDITIONAL RESOURCES

Clinical Oncology Society of Australia—Social Work: https://www.cosa.org.au/groups/social-work/resources.aspx
National Coalition for Cancer Survivorship—the Cancer Survival Toolbox: http://www.canceradvocacy.org/toolbox/
Oncology Social Work Australia: http://oswa.net.au/

REFERENCES

Antonovsky, A. (1979). *Health, stress, and coping: New perspectives on mental and physical well-being.* San Francisco, CA: Jossey-Bass.

Australian Institute of Health and Welfare (AIHW). (2012). *Cancer.* Canberra, Australia: Author. Retrieved from http://aihw.gov.au/cancer/

Australian Institute of Health and Welfare (AIHW), Cancer Australia (CA), & Australasian Association of Cancer Registries (AACR). (2008). *Cancer survival and prevalence in Australia: Cancers diagnosed from 1982 to 2004.* Cancer Series No. 42. Cat. No. CAN 38. Canberra, Australia: Australian Institute of Health and Welfare.

Ballard, A., Green, T., McCaa, A., & Logsdon, M. C. (1997). A comparison of the level of hope in patients with newly diagnosed and recurrent cancer. *Oncology Nursing Forum, 24,* 899–904.

Clarke, D. (2003). Faith and hope. *Australasian Psychiatry, 11*(2), 164–168.

Cobb, S. (1976). Social support as a moderator of life stress, Psychosomatic Society, Presidential Address-1976. *Psychosomatic Medicine, 38*(5), 300–314.

Deveson, A. (2004). *Resilience.* Sydney, Australia: Allen & Unwin.

Dyson, J., Cobb, M., & Forman, D. (1997). The meaning of spirituality: A literature review. *Journal of Advanced Nursing, 26,* 1183–1188.

Folkman, S. (1997). Positive psychological states and coping with severe stress. *Source Social Science and Medicine, 45*(8), 1207–1221.

Forbes, M. A. R. (1999). Testing a causal model of hope and its antecedents among chronically ill older adults. *Dissertation Abstracts International: Section B: The Sciences and Engineering, 59*(8-B).

Frankl, V. (1963). *Man's search for meaning: An introduction to logotherapy.* New York, NY: Washington Square Press.

Gemmell, K. (2013). *Experiences of older women with ovarian cancer* (Unpublished PhD dissertation). University of Melbourne, Carlton, Australia.

Giese-Davis, J., Hermanson, K., Koopman, C., Weibel, D., & Spiegel, D. (2000). Quality of couples' relationship and adjustment to metastatic breast cancer. *Journal of Family Psychology, 14*(2), 251–266.

Halstead, M., & Mickley, J. (1997). Attempting to unfathom the unfathomable: Descriptive views of spirituality. *Seminars in Oncology Nursing, 13,* 225–230.

Hartman, D., & Zimberoff, M. (2003). The existential approach in heart-centred therapies. *Journal of Heart-Centred Therapies, 6*(1), 3–46.

Hegarty, M., Breaden, K., Swetenham, C., & Grbich, C. (2010). Learning to work with the "unsolvable": Building capacity for working with refractory suffering. *Journal of Palliative Care, 26*(4), 287–294.

Janoff-Bulman, R. (1989). Assumptive worlds and the stress of traumatic events: Applications of the schema construct. *Social Cognition: Special Issue: Stress, Coping, and Social Cognition, 7*(2), 113–136.

Kissane, D., Clarke, D., & Street, A. (2001). Demoralization syndrome—A relevant psychiatric diagnosis for palliative care. *Journal of Palliative Care, 17,* 12–21.

Kwok, C., Sullivan, G., & Cant, R. (2006). The role of culture in breast health practices among Chinese-Australian women. *Patient Education and Counseling, 64*(1–3), 268–276.

Lethborg, C., Aranda, S., Bloch, S., & Kissane, D. (2006). The role of meaning in advanced cancer—Integrating the constructs of assumptive world, sense of coherence and meaning-based coping. *Journal of Psychosocial Oncology, 24,* 27–42.

Lethborg, C., Aranda, S., & Kissane, D. (2007). To what extent does meaning mediate adaptation to cancer? The relationship between physical suffering, meaning in life and connection to others in adjustment to cancer. *Palliative and Supportive Care, 5*(4), 377–388.

Lethborg, C., Aranda, S., & Kissane, D. (2008). Meaning in adjustment to cancer: A model of care. *Palliative and Supportive Care, 6*(1), 61–70.

Lethborg, C., Schofield, P., & Kissane, D. (2012). The patient experience of undertaking Meaning and Purpose "MaP" Therapy in the setting of advanced cancer. *Palliative and Supportive Care, 4*(10), 177–188

Mahon, S. M., & Casperson, D. (1997). Exploring the psychosocial meaning of recurrent cancer: A descriptive study. *Cancer Nursing, 20,* 178–186.

McGrath, P. (2010). The living model: An Australian model for Aboriginal palliative care service delivery with international implications. *Journal of Palliative Care, 26*(1), 59–64.

Park, C., & Folkman, S. (1997). Meaning in the context of stress and coping. *Review of General Psychology, 1*(2), 115–144.

Pascal, J., & Endacott, R. (2010). Ethical and existential challenges associated with a cancer diagnosis. *Journal of Medical Ethics, 36*(5), 279–283.

Saunders, C. (1988). Spiritual pain. *Journal of Palliative Care, 4,* 29–32.

Speck, P., Higginson, I., & Addington-Hall, J. (2004). Spiritual needs in health care. *British Medical Journal, 329,* 123–124.

Thomas, J., & Retsas, A. (1999). Transacting self-preservation: A grounded theory of the spiritual dimensions of people with terminal cancer. *International Journal of Nursing Studies, 36*(3), 191–201.

Tomer, A., & Eliason, G. (1996). Toward a comprehensive model of death anxiety. *Death Studies, 20,* 343–366.

Yalom, I. (1980). *Existential psychotherapy.* New York, NY: Basic Books.

Younger, J. (1995). The alienation of the sufferer. *Advances in Nursing Science, 17*(4), 53–72.

51

Lissa Parsonnet

Schema Therapy With Oncology Patients and Families

Key Concepts

- *To effectively meet the needs of cancer patients, social workers must be well versed in therapeutic models complex enough to address the psychosocial concerns of patients with different needs, across all stages of the disease process.*
- *Schema therapy offers a comprehensive model of assessment and intervention extremely useful in working with the oncology population.*
- *The schema therapy model can be used to inform clinicians' understanding and guide their treatment of a patient's unique responses to a cancer diagnosis and treatment, without offering a full course of schema therapy.*

Cancer has been thought of as "the great equalizer," affecting people regardless of age, gender, socioeconomic status, stage of life, or psychological makeup. Patients come to us with a history of life experiences, an established personality structure, a way of thinking about themselves in the world, and a set of beliefs. Memories that inform their experiences contribute to how they cope with their diagnosis and its treatment. Because of this complexity, oncology social workers need comprehensive therapeutic models that provide insight into a person's response to cancer and offer ways to intervene through the illness process. Schema therapy offers one such framework.

This chapter presents an overview of schema therapy, identifying and explaining the primary early maladaptive schemas likely to present in an oncology setting. Each relevant schema will be described, followed by illustrations of how it can be activated by a cancer diagnosis. Coping strategies for dealing with the schema once activated, as well as therapeutic ways to use this knowledge to help patients cope, will be elaborated.

Nothing prepares a person for a diagnosis of cancer, but many factors may prepare a person for *how he or she will cope with* a cancer diagnosis:

Disease-Related Variables

- Type of cancer
- Stage of illness
- Treatment recommendations and demands
- Treatment side effects
- Prognosis

Sociodemographic Variables

- Age
- Life stage
- Support system
- Access to care
- Financial resources

Individual Psychological Variables

- Individuals' beliefs about themselves, their lives, and their futures

- Coping skills and styles
- Internal strengths and ability to access and utilize internal and external resources
- Past experiences with illness, challenge, and coping

Oncology social work understands individuals within their biopsychosocial environment and the effect of these variables. Schema therapy offers another construct for understanding a person's psychological response to cancer and a way to intervene to promote healthy and effective coping.

Schema therapy, developed by Jeffrey Young and colleagues, is an integrative, unifying theory and treatment designed to address long-standing emotional difficulties with presumed origins in childhood and early adolescence. Schema therapy combines cognitive, behavioral, and Gestalt therapies; attachment and object relations theories; self-psychology; interpersonal neurobiology; and mindfulness with the goal of helping patients meet their core needs in a healthy and adaptive manner through changing maladaptive schemas, coping responses, and modes (Young, Klosko, & Weishaar, 2003). As a needs-based model, schema therapy assumes that difficulties arise when a child's core needs are not met in a healthy, consistent way and that over time, the individual may find or create a supportive environment that provides those needs. For example, an individual whose core need for stability and predictability was not met in childhood may find a highly structured, predictable career that doesn't elicit feelings associated with unmet childhood needs. If his cancer diagnosis takes him out of his career for the duration of chemotherapy and replaces the predictable consistency of his work environment with the unpredictability of a cancer diagnosis and treatment protocol, the individual's unmet needs may resurface, triggering associated schema.

A schema therapy approach is thus very useful in understanding how people respond to their cancer diagnoses and treatment. This approach can help social workers identify and appreciate patients' responses and intervene to meet both the immediate needs that arise at diagnosis and during ensuing treatment and the core unmet needs that a diagnosis and treatment of cancer may reawaken.

The Schema Therapy Model

Early Maladaptive Schemas

Schema therapy focuses on the concept of "early maladaptive schemas," believing that schemas develop early in life to organize and make sense of one's environment. If the environment is not conducive to healthy development and the child's core needs are not met consistently and reliably, the schemas that develop are maladaptive. Early maladaptive schemas are "self-defeating emotional, cognitive and behavioral patterns that begin early in our development and repeat throughout life" (Young et al., 2003, p. 7). Early maladaptive schemas are understood to be:

> A broad, pervasive theme or pattern,
> Composed of memories, feelings, cognitions, and body sensations,
> Regarding oneself and one's relationship with others,
> Developed during childhood or adolescence,
> Elaborated throughout one's lifetime,
> Dysfunctional to a significant degree. (Young et al., 2003, p. 7)

Table 51.1.
Early Maladaptive Schemas

Schema Domain	Early Maladaptive Schemas
Disconnection/ Rejection	Abandonment/Instability Mistrust/Abuse Emotional Deprivation Defectiveness/Shame Social Isolation/Alienation
Impaired Autonomy and Performance	Dependence/Incompetence Vulnerability to Harm Enmeshment/Undeveloped Self Failure Social Isolation/Alienation Dependence/Incompetence
Impaired Limits	Grandiosity/Entitlement Insufficient Self-Control/ Self-Discipline
Other-Directedness	Subjugation Self-Sacrifice Approval/Recognition Seeking
Overvigilance and Inhibition	Emotional Inhibition Unrelenting Standards/ Hypercriticalness Punitiveness

Source: Adapted from Young et al. (2003).

Because these schemas develop early, they are accepted as "truths" by the individual who, rather than questioning the guiding schemas, is likely to distort reality to adhere to them. Some early maladaptive schemas may shape a person's daily life, whereas others may remain dormant unless stimulated by a life experience (Table 51.1). The demands of a cancer diagnosis and its treatment can cause dormant schemas to become active and relevant.

Young and colleagues identified 18 early maladaptive schemas organized into five "schema domains." The schema domains correspond to basic emotional needs of children, including the need for secure attachment, autonomy, freedom to express needs and emotions, spontaneity and play, and realistic limits and self-control. When these needs are not met, children develop self-defeating life patterns.

Schema Therapy With Oncology Patients

A life-threatening illness and the demanding treatment that likely accompanies it may activate schemas that are a part of an individual's daily experience *or* that have been dormant in the absence of environmental triggers. Understanding and appreciating early maladaptive schemas is enormously helpful in interpreting patient responses and providing an effective way to intervene with patients whose responses could undermine treatment efficacy or whose behavior might otherwise be disruptive to the staff, other patients, or their families. It also enables social workers to help patients cope with their physical and emotional realities in ways that meet their needs and are healthy and personally affirming.

In the oncology setting, coping with the demands of a cancer diagnosis and treatment becomes the overarching goal of the schema therapist. Informed by an understanding of the patient's schemas/schema modes, the schema therapist may employ an array of techniques that include cognitive behavioral strategies, imagery techniques, mindfulness training, empathic confrontation, and the therapy relationship to enable the patient to have his or her treatment needs met in a healthy, effective way. These needs may be physical, cognitive, emotional, social, or spiritual.

Although Young and his colleagues have identified 18 early maladaptive schemas within five domains, this chapter addresses those schemas that most often manifest in the treatment of patients with cancer.

Domain of Disconnection and Rejection

Receiving treatment for cancer *requires* patients to interact closely and, in fact, depend on their physicians, nurses, social workers, and other health team members, as well as their family and friends. This presents a unique challenge for patients with disruptions in this domain. "These patients have an expectation that one's needs for security, safety, stability, nurturance, empathy, sharing of feelings, acceptance and respect will not be met in a predictable manner" (Young et al., 2003, p. 14). All of the schemas in this domain are likely to be activated by a cancer diagnosis.

Abandonment/Instability

This schema heightens an individual's perception of instability or unreliability of those he or she relies on for support and connection (Young et al., 2003, p. 14). Patients with this schema are especially likely to struggle with the disruption the illness causes to their interpersonal lives. These responses may be more pronounced during the active treatment and posttreatment phases. Likely triggers for this schema include treatments that require these patients to take leave from their jobs and social milieu, that restrict their ability to maintain a visible presence in school or social or family activities, or that prevent them from being able to predict how they will feel on any given day, making planning impossible. A teaching hospital with rotating physicians is particularly challenging for people who struggle with this schema. These patients are likely to become extremely anxious and perhaps angry if something like a low blood count prevents them from receiving treatment as scheduled. In fact, any *unanticipated* symptom, side effect, test, or procedure may be experienced as instability and lead to responses that appear extreme or disproportional to the situation.

Transitions from one level or modality of care to another may also trigger the abandonment/instability schema. In the posttreatment phase, these patients may have more difficulty than others with the reduced contact with the health care team. The usual waning of support and attention from people in their lives as the illness crisis passes may also elicit feelings of abandonment, as the process of returning to "normal" functioning may provoke feelings of instability.

When the abandonment/instability schema becomes triggered, these patients may be perceived as needy, clingy, or demanding or, depending on their coping style, withdrawn, avoidant, or difficult to engage. An understanding of this schema process enables us to offer personal reassurance of realistic availability. We can try to maintain consistency in staffing as possible (e.g., minimize the number of different chemotherapy nurses). We can provide information in advance about the variables that may disrupt treatment schedules so that, should this occur, it is a *predicted* treatment variable and is less destabilizing. In systems in which physicians rotate through a service, extra efforts could be made to ensure that there is consistency in nursing or social work presence. Families can also be helped to understand that patients may struggle to transition from one phase of treatment to the next and that stability at home can help ease that struggle.

Mistrust/Abuse Schema

Patients with this schema have the expectation that they will be hurt, abused, manipulated, lied to, or otherwise mistreated, either intentionally or through excessive neglect (Young et al., 2003). In the cancer diagnosis phase, these patients may have greater difficulty believing the diagnosis or selecting a physician, because it is difficult for them to trust people, especially when they are feeling vulnerable and dependent. In the active treatment phase, their mistrust of medical institutions, members of the health care team, and the "medical system" may make it particularly difficult for these patients to agree to or comply with treatment. When this schema is triggered, patients may become nonadherent, abrasive, or accusatory. In response, it is easy for the health care team to become defensive and angry, which further provokes the patient. If, rather than viewing these patients as being "difficult" or "paranoid," we can understand that they "are reacting to a set of learned, albeit distorted assumptions about what they can expect from others, the health care team may have an easier time tolerating the mistrust and providing additional information and reassurance to help these patients to feel safe" (Parsonnet & Lethborg, 2011, p. 197).

Emotional Deprivation Schema

This schema leads patients to "expect that their desire for a normal degree of emotional support: nurturing, empathy and protection will not be adequately met by others" (Young et al., 2003, p. 14). These patients may experience intense loneliness and emptiness, as well as feelings of isolation and vulnerability and a sense of being unsafe. Although many patients describe their cancer experience in this way, the experience is intensified when this schema is present. A cancer diagnosis may in itself trigger this schema, as feelings of fear converge with feelings of neediness. During active treatment, even the most emotionally healthy patients may be overwhelmed both by all that they need and by all that they receive from others. Both offers of nurturing and the absence of such offers can activate this schema. In the posttreatment phase, as family and friends return to their own lives and leave the patient (sometimes prematurely) to "return to normal," the patient with an emotional deprivation schema is likely to feel a heightened and at times disruptive sense of deprivation. Throughout the illness process, patients may cope with the activation of this schema in different ways. Some will withdraw to avoid the pain of feeling deprived of the support, nurturing, empathy, and protection they need. In response to their isolating behavior, the health care team may withdraw as well, thinking they are respecting the patient's apparent wishes and boundaries. In this way, the patient's needs are once again not met, and the schema is reinforced. Other patients may respond to this schema by becoming very clingy, dependent, and needy. At first they may get the caring, nurturing responses they need, but it may become difficult for the health care team or for their family and friends to sustain that level of attention. Over time, these patients may appear ungrateful for what they have received and demanding of what they need. The people they are leaning on may feel propelled to withdraw, which will more intensely activate the schema and likely escalate maladaptive behavior in a frantic attempt to get the help they need and avoid the feelings of deprivation that are heightened by the withdrawal of support. If the health care team can understand that patients are responding to what they have learned to expect and how they have learned to respond, they can empathically and sensitively provide both healthy and realistic limits *and* empathy, nurturing, and guidance. As schema therapists, we can also help patients identify behaviors that are schema driven and adopt more adaptive and effective ways of getting their needs met.

Defectiveness/Shame Schema

This schema leads patients to feel and believe that they are "defective, bad, unwanted, inferior or invalid in important respects, or that they would be unlovable to significant others if exposed" (Young et al., 2003, p. 14). Patients with this schema generally can't identify what makes them "defective"; they only know that they are and feel ashamed of their defectiveness. A cancer diagnosis triggers the defectiveness/shame schema by providing a target for the feelings. Patients describe an "I always knew it" response as they are diagnosed with a life-threatening malignancy *growing within them*, which validates their feelings of shame and defect. The use of the term *cancer* in common parlance to represent evil reinforces this feeling. Believing themselves to be defective, they may feel they deserve their diagnosis or may delay diagnosis because they are ashamed to go to a doctor and reveal their defectiveness.

Some cancers present more challenges than others to people with this schema. Cancers with symptoms that include incontinence or impotence may be particularly difficult for people who already struggle with feelings of defectiveness or shame. If this schema is active, patients may sink into depression and passivity, may withdraw to "hide" their shame, or may profess their unworthiness. Observers may find their responses to be melodramatic and self-indulgent and view them as having a "pity party" out of which they must be shaken. These responses further validate the patient's shame and can trigger an abandonment or emotional deprivation schema. Appreciation for the nature and power of this schema can help the medical team respond with compassion and concern rather than with distance or frustration. A social worker versed in schema therapy may intervene with education and cognitive reframing about cancer to dispel the notion that these patients deserve or caused their cancer, and perhaps do imagery with the vulnerable child part of them that was "taught" that they were defective and "should be" ashamed of themselves.

The Social Isolation/Alienation Schema

This schema is characterized by "the feeling that one is isolated from the rest of the world, different from other people, and/or not a part of any group or community" (Young et al., 2003, p. 14). A cancer diagnosis can magnify and give direction to these feelings. Many patients when diagnosed with cancer describe "crossing a line" when they are diagnosed, no longer being one of "us" but becoming one of "them." Patients with this schema may describe never feeling like "one of us" but now feeling even more alien. Such patients may respond to their cancer diagnosis through greater isolation and secrecy, which complicates the necessary integration of the tasks of daily life with the demands of cancer treatment. Recognizing and understanding this, we can introduce these patients to trained volunteers who have been treated for their cancer and encourage and enable participation in targeted support groups. Helpful groups for people with this schema are disease or stage specific and include others in their phase of life. Placing these people in groups of people with diverse cancers, with whom they are unable to relate, reinforces their feeling that they don't fit in anywhere.

Domain of Impaired Autonomy and Performance

These schemas relate to "expectations about oneself and the environment that interfere with one's perceived ability to separate, survive, function independently or perform successfully" (Young et al., 2003, p. 14). Being a patient *requires* that an individual accept help from others and relinquish a degree of autonomy. This dependence may be particularly challenging for patients with schemas in this domain either to accept or to give up when their treatment ends.

Dependence/Incompetence Schema
This schema leads patients to believe that they are "unable to handle their everyday responsibilities in a competent manner, without considerable help from others.... This often presents as helplessness" (Young et al., 2003, p. 15). Patients with this schema will have great difficulty in making the myriad decisions that face cancer patients. Their inability to trust themselves leads them to rely on the health care team to make decisions that may go beyond medical. It also leaves them vulnerable to the influence of others who may be confident but not competent to dictate health-related decisions. These patients may be impacted by the prevalence of treatments claiming miraculous results with little to no empirical testing, especially if these claims are made by people exuding great certainty and confidence or having celebrity status. Although we may not have the time to heal this schema, we can be careful to take the time to help these patients to think through their options, offering ways to think about their choices rather than imposing decisions upon them (though this may be what they ask for). We can also *help these patients discern* the difference between claims that are made with great confidence but possibly little science and those that are empirically based.

The Domain of Other-Directedness

Schemas in this domain relate to "an excessive focus on the desires, feelings and responses of others, at the expense of one's own needs in order to gain love and approval, maintain one's sense of connection, or avoid retaliation." They typically involve "suppression and lack of awareness regarding one's own anger and natural inclinations" (Young et al., 2003, p. 16). In the medical setting, these schemas are often activated when the patient's needs are intense enough that they can't be denied or ignored, and may be particularly intense if their needs conflict with the needs or preferences of others.

Subjugation Schema
This schema involves "excessive surrendering of control to others *because one feels coerced*—submitting in order to avoid anger, retaliation or abandonment." This can appear as the subjugation of needs, preferences, decisions, and desires, or the subjugation of emotions, and is based on the assumption that "one's desires, opinions and feelings are not valid or important to others" (Young et al., 2003, p. 16). Depending on how patients cope with this schema, they can be very easy or very difficult for the health care team. Patients who surrender to this schema surrender all decision making to others. They may be completely compliant with all treatment recommendations and appear excessively flexible and understanding of long wait times, changes in treatment schedules, or tolerating side effects. These patients may be extremely attuned to the thoughts and feelings of others because they have learned to submit to the feelings, needs, and preferences of those around them. This can affect their functioning at all stages of the cancer process. Because they put the perceived needs of others before their own, these patients are in danger of not reporting potentially dangerous symptoms and side effects out of fear of "bothering the doctor" or "disturbing their family." An additional risk is that while subjugating their own needs and preferences, their anger often mounts internally, until it explodes in ways that are disproportional to the situation. This expression frightens the patient and confuses the staff, as it is such an aberration from the patient's usual presentation. It is important to reassure these patients that their questions, concerns, and decisions are truly valued and that their role as a patient includes asking questions and reporting symptoms and concerns. Some patients cope with their subjugation schema by overcompensating, that is, by doing the opposite of what the schema dictates. To avoid feeling controlled by the inclinations of others, these patients may argue with treatment recommendations, object to schedule changes, complain when not being seen on time, and angrily report concerns or symptoms. These patients can present difficulty for the treatment team and lead people to avoid or be curt with them, which reinforces their fears of presenting their needs. If we can identify this as overcompensation for subjugation, we will be able to assure patients that we do respect and value their needs, time, thoughts, feelings, and choices. We can perhaps even guide them toward behavior that will more effectively get their needs met without feeling that people are angry at them and want to avoid or punish them.

Self-Sacrifice Schema
This schema, also under the domain of other-directedness, can appear much the same as the subjugation schema, but its motivation is different. The self-sacrifice schema involves

> *excessive focus on voluntarily meeting the needs of others in daily situations at the expense of one's own gratification. The most common reasons are: to prevent causing pain to others; to avoid guilt from feeling selfish; or to maintain connection with others perceived as needy.... It often leads to a sense that one's own needs are not being adequately met.*
>
> (Young et al., 2003, p. 16)

These may be the patients who bring food to the nursing staff each week or volunteer to drive patients they meet in the waiting room to their next treatment. A danger for these patients, like those with a subjugation schema, is that they won't report symptoms or side effects and may exaggerate how well they are functioning to avoid disappointing or upsetting their doctor or their family. It is often necessary to cross-check their descriptions of how they are feeling and functioning at home with their families to be sure that the health care team is getting an accurate portrayal of their condition. They may also decline offers of help during both the active treatment and the posttreatment phases of illness, which can undermine their treatment, health, and functioning. Again, an understanding of this schema allows us to say something like: "*I understand* that a part of you finds it very difficult to accept help. You are a 'giver' and have never really allowed yourself to receive help in the way you provided it to others—but there may be another part that understands that the only way for you to get through this treatment is to be open to receiving the help that you need. You've given to the people in your life; now they want to give back to you. I urge you to let them. You will benefit from the help, and they may enjoy the feeling of giving to someone who has cared for them so well."

Schema Therapy: Theory, Conceptualization, and Treatment Formulation

The goal of schema therapy is to help patients get their core needs met in a healthy way by eliciting an awareness of the thoughts, feelings, body sensations, and memories that make up the schemas. This awareness and understanding promote the ability to control or modify behavior, maintain healthy environments, increase conscious control over schemas, and weaken the power of the memories, thoughts, feelings, and behaviors that emerge when a schema is evoked. Schema therapy recognizes that individuals' responses to their schemas can create obstacles to getting their core needs met. This cycle serves to reinforce and maintain the distortions that compose the maladaptive schemas. Schemas can be *perpetuated*, that is, reinforced, or *healed*, meaning that *maladaptive coping styles*, including cognitive, affective, and behavioral, are weakened and replaced with healthy, adaptive, and effective ways of coping with stressors and "triggers" (Young et al., 2003, pp. 30–31). Traditionally, schema therapy proceeds from an assessment and education phase to a change phase (Young et al., 2003).

Assessment and Education Phase of Therapy

In this phase, patients are educated about schemas and schema modes and how they can impair functioning, interpersonal relationships, and emotional well-being. An array of inventories may be administered along with assessment interviews and imagery techniques. Once the assessment has been completed, the schema therapist will discuss his or her findings with the patient and they will look together for memories and experiences to support or refute the preliminary assessment. From this, a schema conceptualization and set of goals are constructed. In the oncology setting, social workers may meet patients at different points in the illness process (Young et al., 2003). A full schema assessment and conceptualization may be completed, but more often in oncology settings, assessment is abbreviated and specifically targeted to identify schema activation and responses that are elicited by the diagnosis, treatment, or prognosis and that may interfere with medical decision making, complying with treatment demands, working with the health care team, or coping with disease-related psychosocial stresses.

Change Phase of Therapy

During the change phase of schema therapy, the clinician incorporates cognitive, experiential, and behavioral elements; mindfulness training; empathic confrontation; and the therapy relationships to heal schemas and promote healthy and adaptive efforts to help patients meet their core needs (Young et al., 2003).

Pearls

- Patients come to us with a history of life experiences, an established personality structure, a way of thinking about themselves in the world, and a set of beliefs that affect how they cope with a cancer diagnosis and treatment. Schema therapy offers one approach to intervention that takes full account of this complexity.
- Schema therapy combines cognitive, behavioral, and Gestalt therapies; attachment and object relations theories; self-psychology; interpersonal neurobiology; and mindfulness, with the goal of helping patients to get their core needs met in a healthy and adaptive manner through changing maladaptive schemas and coping responses.

Pitfalls

- Using only one intervention is insufficient for oncology social workers to meet the complex needs of cancer patients and their families across the continuum of care.
- Failing to share a more comprehensive understanding of the patient's responses to cancer and its treatment with the health care team may limit their ability to provide empathic and patient-centered care.

Working with oncology patients offers us the privilege of entering people's lives at a sensitive and critical time. It is incumbent upon us to meet them with not only compassion and respect but also a model of care that enables us to help them effectively navigate the difficult terrain they enter when diagnosed with cancer. Schema therapy offers a rich and inclusive model that enables us to understand their unique responses to their diagnosis, meet them where they are, and guide them through this territory. It also enables us to, by sharing our understanding with the rest of the health care team, prepare the path they travel to be as hospitable as possible.

ADDITIONAL RESOURCES

Arntz, A., & Van Generen, H. (2009). *Schema therapy for borderline personality disorder.* West Sussex, England: Wiley-Blackwell.

Behary, W. T. (2008). *Disarming the narcissist: Surviving and thriving with the self-absorbed.* Oakland, CA: New Harbinger Publications.

International Society of Schema Therapy: http://www.isstonline.com/

Schema Therapy: http://www.schematherapy.com

Young, J. E. (1999). *Cognitive therapy for personality disorders: A schema-focused approach* (Rev. ed.). Sarasota, FL: Professional Resources Press.

Young, J. E., & Klosko, J. S. (1994). *Reinventing your life.* New York, NY: Plume Books.

REFERENCES

Parsonnet, L., & Lethborg, C. (2011). Addressing suffering in palliative care: Two psychotherapeutic models. In T. Altilio and S. Otis-Green (Eds.), *Oxford textbook of palliative social work* (pp. 191–200). New York, NY: Oxford University Press.

Young, J. E., Klosko, J. S., & Weishaar, M. (2003). *Schema therapy: A practitioners' guide.* New York, NY: Guildford Publications.

52

Shlomit Perry

Practice Issues in Social Work and Psychosocial Oncology in Israel

Key Concepts

- *In Israel, oncology social workers constitute the largest group of psychosocial oncology service providers. Their role and function is clearly defined and valued.*
- *Much of what is traditionally taught about the supportive psychotherapies, such as location, time, boundaries, frequency, touching, and denial, need to be altered when working with people with physical illness.*
- *Challenges for psychosocial oncology workers include the reluctance of high-risk populations to use psychosocial interventions and the need to develop a stronger evidence base.*
- *Research is aimed at developing brief psychotherapy models such as CALM, which can be systematically implemented and evaluated with advanced cancer patients, group interventions, supportive therapies, and family conferences that are consistent with the family and community culture of Israel.*

Facing a cancer diagnosis or recurrence, experiencing difficult treatment, and being aware that life may be nearing its end will evoke many different emotions and thoughts in any culture. Even individuals who usually cope well with crises will experience emotions of a previously unknown intensity, which may dominate all aspects of their lives. The individual's ability to cope is influenced by his or her psychological makeup, the availability of support systems, the perception of the disease, and previous experiences of crisis or illness. Individuals with advanced cancer are at increased risk for depression, anxiety, and spiritual distress. These often emerge as a result of the multiple stressors of advanced disease and an individual's strengths and vulnerabilities (Rodin et al., 2009).

Oncology social workers in Israel are trained to manage the stressors of advanced cancer, particularly the relationships between the patient, the family, and external factors. This means developing clinical skills and models of therapy to help reduce psychological distress, anticipate future distress for the patient and his or her family members, support the growth process, and facilitate communication with the attending team.

Helping the client make sense of the experience and find meaning in his or her life with the illness may enhance the depth of the therapeutic relationship and expedite therapeutic processes. This requires clinical and interpersonal skills to develop interventions that can integrate traditional psychological techniques while considering hope, meaning, culture, gender, and age.

Psychosocial oncology (also termed *psychooncology*) is an umbrella term for the various therapeutic interventions undertaken by oncology social workers, as well as other mental health professionals. In Israel, oncology social workers constitute the largest group of psychosocial oncology service providers, although more psychologists have been joining the field. The number of psychiatrists remains low, but there is growing interest in spiritual counselors. The Israel Cancer Association initially seeded several social work positions that are now paid for by hospitals and public health funds. Extensive research and experience have accumulated a large body of knowledge in psychosocial oncology.

Most therapeutic models combine elements of cognitive and existential therapy, brief supportive therapy, crisis intervention, and problem solving. Therapies are provided at various points along the illness trajectory, especially at times of transition in the disease and treatment process (Antoni et al., 2006; Breitbart et al., 2012; Chochinov et al., 2005; Goodwin & Lunenfeld, 2004; Hamama-Raz, Perry, Pat-Horenczyk, Bar-Levav, & Stemmer, 2012; Kissane et al., 2003; Spiegel, Bloom, & Yalom, 1981).

Many of the interventions oncology social workers routinely use appear, at first glance, to be intuitive rather than intentional and structured, which they are. As others have observed, this misunderstanding arises because much of what is traditionally taught about supportive therapy—such as where the client is seen, for how long, how often, the use of touch, and the function of denial—needs to be altered when working with people with physical illness (Lederberg & Holland, 2011). A substantial proportion of oncology social work interventions are supportive, beginning by careful attunement to the problem(s) clients identify as most important and urgent to their ability to cope with the illness and its impact on their lives at this time. Problem solving, practical counseling, and continuity of availability to the patient and family are essential social work interventions in Israel. This chapter focuses particularly on interventions with people with advanced cancer—an acknowledged high-risk population. Some social work approaches and therapeutic challenges will be similar to those experienced by social workers in the United States; others will also reflect Israel's culture and history and its close connection with psychoanalysis and psychotherapeutic models.

The Practice of Oncology Social Work in Israel Today

The Israeli health system is predominantly a public service. Due to the unique circumstances related to the establishment of the state of Israel in 1948, the challenges facing the post-Holocaust society, and the views of the nation's founders, social work formed an integral part of Israel's medical system from its establishment. Over the years, the profession's legal status within the health system was reinforced. The National Health Insurance Law (1995) stated that social work is a mandatory and integral part of the "basket of health services" (Hart, 2001).

Several factors influenced social work's development in Israel. These include the contributions of Lea Baider and Atara Kaplan-DeNour, two members of the founding generation of psychosocial oncologists in Israel. In addition, contributions have been made by the Israel Cancer Association, which has invested extensive resources in funding and training social workers. Currently, all oncology facilities in Israel have a team of social workers. The Davidoff Cancer Center is organized by disease management teams whose core consists of an oncologist, a nurse, and a social worker for each cancer disease area. Israel is a multiethnic society, so hospitals are proactive in hiring social workers from various backgrounds.

The principle guiding the oncology social work model is the continuum of therapies including individual, family, and group, as well as providing ad hoc responses to urgent problems. Social workers try to maintain contact with patients and family members over long periods, reflecting the family and community culture of the country. Oncology social work interventions are usually brief and include aspects of practical problem solving and supportive therapy.

The therapeutic goals of oncology social work are as follows:

- To enable and encourage emotional reflection.
- To support emotional growth, to help the patient find meaning, to set achievable goals, and to assist in the rehabilitation process.
- To address the family unit and needs of its members, particularly the more vulnerable ones (e.g., the patient's children) and to address interpersonal communication and relations.
- To facilitate the relationship and dialogue with the medical staff and to translate medical language into the patient's narrative.
- To assist the patient and family in coping with advanced illness and expected death.
- To help solve day-to-day problems brought about by the illness and treatment.

At the Davidoff Cancer Center, for example, many sessions take place when the patient comes for medical treatment, at the bedside, or in the social worker's office. Sessions may be canceled if the treatment is terminated or if the patient is hospitalized. The course of therapy and counseling is influenced by changing circumstances and cannot always be planned in advance, requiring a large measure of flexibility on the oncology social worker's part. The reactive nature of the therapeutic discourse, especially toward the end of life, is such that the psychotherapeutic language and tradition often seem inadequate and require a new conceptualization.

Social workers also develop and lead group interventions such as those for women recovering from breast cancer and treatment. Research on the outcomes and effectiveness of this group intervention in improving patients' quality of life across the continuum of care is ongoing. Most patients feel confident they can learn to live with early-stage breast cancer. However, the transition back to normative and secure living is often more challenging than they expect. The intervention includes a psychoeducation, resilience-building, and empowerment component; help in maintaining relationships and developing an effective support network; and cognitive behavioral therapy to challenge negative constructs and facilitate behavioral activation. A translated version of the intervention is provided for Arabic-speaking women. The intervention is free and is offered at least 2 months after completion of chemotherapy. All women are invited to participate; about one third of the women treated attend the group (Hamama-Raz et al., 2012).

Social work is required to develop therapeutic interventions consistent with standards in evidence-based medicine while negotiating and often leading complex biopsychosocial negotiations within the multidisciplinary team.

Oncology social work in the Israeli health system addresses four key dimensions:

- Information and access to community support resources including hospital discharge planning.
- The emotional and existential concerns of patient and family regarding the disease.
- Social and interpersonal relationship, collaboration, and negotiation with health providers.
- Raising awareness of the human/psychological dimension and family needs as part of holistic patient treatment and fostering an atmosphere that enables emotional processes to be expressed and processed.

Challenges in Psychosocial Oncology

Efficacy and Effectiveness of Interventions

Relating to current distress screening initiatives, Traeger, Greer, Fernandez-Robles, Temel, and Pirl (2012) suggest that for patients with low anxiety levels, it may be sufficient to provide interventions only at times of acute distress, including the provision of education, information, and liaison with medical/nursing teams. Patients with intermediate to high anxiety levels may require more intensive therapeutic interventions, including cognitive therapy and stress management. However, Coyne, Lepore, and Palmer (2006) found that only a small percentage of patients want to participate in psychosocial interventions. Sollner, Maislinger, Konig, Devries, and Lukas (2004) found that breast cancer patients who screen positive for distress are no more interested in counseling than nondistressed breast cancer patients, with only a minority expressing an interest. A similar finding was reported by Mosher, Champion, and Hanna (2013), who examined families of patients with advanced lung cancer. Their findings indicated a high rate of distress but underuse of professional support services. Baker and colleagues studied the willingness of cancer patients to address their emotional needs. Patients interviewed immediately after diagnosis and before starting treatment regarded their emotional condition as adequate. They appreciated the option to receive help but did not wish to take advantage of it at that stage. However, patients who were already into the routine of treatments were more open to receiving help (Baker et al., 2012).

End of life and death are situations that cannot easily be processed cognitively. During this phase in the disease, patients and family members are confronted with the duality of life and death. The patient is expected, on the one hand, to fully experience life and, on the other, to be rationally involved in the separation processes and make decisions regarding his or her own death. Prognoses provide an inaccurate timeline and, accordingly, it is hard to know when to raise the question of death and final conversations. These findings suggest that synchronizing the timing, location, type, and focus of the intervention to adaptive challenges in relation to the patient's disease and treatment process is required to engage patients in interventions.

Rodin and colleagues assert that there is limited evidence regarding the effectiveness of pharmacological and psychological interventions in reducing anxiety among cancer patients. They suggest that depression and anxiety in cancer patients is a result of an interaction between several stressors. Therefore, interventions such as those used by oncology social workers that address multiple stresses of symptom management, attention to the emotional aspects of patients in context, and help in solving day-to-day problems may prove most effective (Rodin et al., 2007). A distinguishing feature of oncology social work is a particular emphasis on the patient in relation to the family and social circumstances. Thus, family meetings, practical economic advice, and a flexibility of when and where meetings occur characterize the responsive approach of the oncology social worker and distinguish it in large part from the traditional psychotherapy approach. Other social work interventions provided to families of advanced cancer patients include psychoeducation, psychosocial support for the caregiver(s), help with symptom management, sleep promotion, and family meetings (Hudson, Remedios, & Thomas 2010).

Brief Psychotherapy Interventions

To improve the effectiveness of interventions, some research is directed toward studying brief, multifocused, and structured interventions that could be systematically implemented in an anticipatory way. The aim is to educate and assist individuals with critical adaptive challenges in the disease and treatment process that can prevent adverse levels of anxiety and distress in high-risk populations such as advanced cancer patients.

One example of a brief individual therapy for people with advanced cancer is the CALM intervention: Managing Cancer and Living Meaningfully (Halse, Lo, & Rodin, 2010; Lo et al., 2014). CALM attempts to package the contextual system, problem solving, and family interventions with traditional psychodynamic techniques and to apply the resulting composite intervention more systematically with cancer patients so that its effectiveness can be tested. The intervention is proposed to patients with advanced cancer who are seeking discourse about the ways they cope with a life-limiting disease. It is suitable for patients who are willing and able to commit time (three to six 45-minute sessions over 3 months). The themes of the intervention incorporate many of the oncology social work therapeutic goals listed previously. The goal of CALM is to help patients cope with the duality of life and death and the paradox of clinging to life while coping with one's expected death.

CALM Intervention Themes
• *Collaboration and negotiation with health care providers to achieve optimal cancer care and symptom control.* • *Adjustment in sense of self and in spousal, family, and other relationships affected by the disease.* • *Sense of meaning, purpose, and hope.* • *Mortality-related concerns and advance care planning (Halse et al., 2010).*

Supportive Psychotherapy

Supportive therapy is helpful to people who want assistance with problems that arise unexpectedly and demand a flexible response. The skills required include practical problem solving, interpersonal communication, and empathy. Ledberger and Holland (2011) assert that supportive psychotherapy is the single-most important tool for mental health professionals in oncology. The 2007 Institute of Medicine report on psychosocial services to cancer patients, after reviewing numerous studies over 20 years, concluded that a sound evidence base exists to recommend supportive psychotherapy as a valid therapeutic intervention. It is both simple and complex, requiring the highest level of clinical skills while taxing the therapist's emotional capacity. It includes knowing how to clarify and discuss highly charged information and overwhelming emotions, being familiar with medical knowledge, and using psychotherapeutic techniques as needed.

Douglas (2008) argues that in supportive therapy, it is appropriate to help the patient achieve a higher level of self-awareness and insight, but at a timely and appropriate depth. One of the cardinal rules of supportive therapy is "Don't say everything you know, only what will be helpful." The primary goal in supportive therapy is "to build a 'holding environment' to foster the therapeutic alliance and to establish an atmosphere of emotional safety and trust." Hellerstein and colleagues emphasize that supportive therapy relates to the therapeutic alliance as the foundation of therapy, rather than as a vehicle for change. The therapist does not challenge the patient but rather attempts to find ways to reduce anxiety. The therapist strengthens the patient's defenses when these are effective and provides positive feedback to enhance the patient's sense of self-worth and confidence (Hellerstein et al., 1998). Clinicians often feel they are walking a tightrope in this approach and must constantly consider when to intervene, when to reflect, what message to raise, and when to remain silent.

Multidisciplinary Family Meeting

Western attitudes have a major impact on the nature of Israel's medical system: the doctor–patient relationship, emphasis on patient rights and autonomy, and the use of modern drugs. However, Jewish tradition emphasizes the social and ethical role of the family, and therefore, there are often strong competing interests between the paternalistic family and the autonomous individual. The Dying Patient Law in Israel (Steinberg & Sprung, 2006) regards terminal illness as a family process, emphasizing the importance of providing palliative care for the patient and family.

The "family meeting" is an intervention that improves communication among the patient's primary team and the family and may also encourage open dialogue within the family. The family meeting, consistent with the spirit of the Dying Patient Law, is usually coordinated by the oncology social worker. The intervention emphasizes intimate and social relationships and concern for family and the patient. It includes components of providing information, processing information, and offering a safe place for the expression of feelings. This intervention requires knowledge of psychology, family therapy, group dynamics, and problem solving. The family meeting is a brief therapy (sometimes a single meeting) that should provide a safe environment for the expression of strong feelings and a response to practical issues while recognizing limitations of time and resources (Cohen Fineberg & Bauer, 2011; Hannon, O'Reilly, Bennett, Breen, & Lawlor, 2012; Hudson, Quinn, O'Hanlon, & Aranda, 2008; and see Chapter 58 on family conferencing). Clinical guidelines for end-of-life care at the Davidoff Cancer Center place an onus on social workers to develop appropriate skills to run family meetings with the multidisciplinary team.

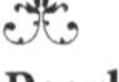

Pearls

- Some social work approaches and therapeutic challenges are similar to those experienced by oncology social workers in the United States; others reflect Israel's culture and history and its close connection with psychoanalysis and psychotherapeutic models.
- Many functions of the brief psychotherapy models being researched incorporate the social work functions of facilitating collaboration with the team, developing the patient's sense of self and sense of meaning of the experience, examining the impact of

the illness on relationships, and defining goals of care and advance care planning.

- Social work leadership in developing crisis intervention models is well developed from the history and experience of this culture and is highly valued.

Pitfalls

- Interventions need to take into account the reluctance of many families in Israel to openly discuss feelings about death, loss, and failure.
- The uncertainties of prognosis in cancer make it difficult to assist patients and families in processing advanced illness phases.

In Israel, social work is the dominant profession in the psychosocial oncology field. The role of the oncology social worker encompasses two key dimensions: responding to practical problems and addressing the emotional world of the patient and family. The CALM model of intervention, supportive therapy, and the family meeting represent a combination of emotional depth and practical concerns. The attempt to adopt an eclectic work routine with a semi-structured therapy at the end of life provides an important opportunity to document the impact of the effectiveness of social work interventions.

Two continuing challenges to oncology social work interventions in Israel include the following:

- Brief psychotherapy interventions such as CALM assume that the verbalization of the experience of disease (e.g., fear of death) in an emotional language will validate and grant meaning to the patient and encourage more informed decision making regarding the use of the remaining time and treatment at the end of life. However, not all patients want insights on their approaching death. Some patients or relatives in Israel become angry when prognosis, stopping treatment, and death are mentioned in therapy sessions. They do not believe it is appropriate or helpful. Even when they are experiencing intense emotional distress, they may not want to discuss their feelings about death, loss, and helplessness.
- Although there is a need for learning better ways to help children of different ages prepare when the death of a parent is imminent, many parents and professionals still believe that children are not able to bear the paradox of life in the shadow of death and should not be informed. They hold these beliefs despite research evidence that shows children benefit from preparation and open communication about the death. A proposed study of the views of children whose parent has advanced cancer was canceled because not one parent agreed to let their child participate in the study.

In Israel, there is recognition and appreciation of the contribution that oncology social work makes in caring for cancer patients. The challenge facing social work is to develop an appropriate arsenal of interventions to meet the needs of different patients and to adapt these models to a complex multidisciplinary system. Ultimately, what is unique and valued about the practice of psychosocial oncology by social workers is the combination of practical counseling, careful attunement to the patient's perspective and urgently felt needs, supportive psychotherapy, interventions to establish appropriate therapeutic goals of care by advocating for the patient, and a timely response to patients' and families' requests for help.

REFERENCES

Antoni, M. H., Wimberly, S. R., Lechner, S. C., Kazi, A., Sifre, T., Urcuyo, K. R., . . . Carver, C. S. (2006). Reduction of cancer-specific thought intrusions and anxiety symptoms with stress management intervention among women undergoing treatment for breast cancer. *American Journal of Psychiatry, 163*, 1791–1797.

Baker, P., Beesley, H., Dinwoodie, R., Fletcher, I., Ablett, J., Holcombe, C., & Salmon, P. (2012). "You're putting thoughts into my head": A qualitative study of the readiness of patients with breast, lung, or prostate cancer to address emotional needs through the first 18 months after diagnosis. *Psycho-Oncology, 22*(6), 1402–1410.

Breitbart, W., Poppito, S., Rosenfeld, B., Vickers, A. J., Li, Y., Abbey, J., . . . Cassileth, B. R. (2012). Pilot randomized controlled trial of individual meaning-centered psychotherapy for patients with advanced cancer. *Journal of Clinical Oncology, 12*, 1304–1309.

Chochinov, H. M., Hack, T., Hassard, T., Kristjanson, J., McClement, S., & Harlos, M. (2005). Dignity therapy: A novel psychotherapeutic intervention for patients near the end of life. *Journal of Clinical Oncology, 23*(24), 5520–5525.

Cohen Fineberg, I., & Bauer, A. (2011). Families and family conferencing. In T. Altilio & S. Otis-Green (Eds.), *Oxford textbook of palliative social work*. New York, NY: Oxford University Press.

Coyne, J., Lepore, S., & Palmer, S. (2006). Efficacy of psychosocial intervention in cancer care: Evidence is weaker than it first looks. *Annals of Behavioral Medicine: A Publication of the Society of Behavioral Medicine, 32*(2), 104–110.

Douglas, J. D. (2008). Teaching supportive psychotherapy to psychiatric residents. *American Journal of Psychiatry, 165*, 445–452.

Goodwin, P. J., & Lunenfeld, S. (2004). Support groups in breast cancer: When a negative result is positive. *Journal of Clinical Oncology, 22*, 4244–4246.

Halse, H., Lo, C., & Rodin, G. (2010). *Managing cancer and living meaningfully (CALM). Treatment manual: An individual psychotherapy for patients with advanced cancer.* Toronto, Ontario, Canada: Princess Margaret Hospital.

Hamama-Raz, Y., Perry, S., Pat-Horenczyk, R., Bar-Levav, R., & Stemmer, S. (2012). Factors affecting participation in group intervention in patients after adjuvant treatment for early-study breast cancer. *Acta Oncologica*, *51*, 208–221.

Hannon, B., O'Reilly, V., Bennett, K., Breen, K., & Lawlor, P. G. (2012). Meeting the family: Measuring effectiveness of family meetings in a specialist inpatient palliative care unit. *Palliative and Supportive Care*, *1*, 43–49.

Hart, J. (2001). Reform of the health care service system in Israel, 1995–2000. *World Hospital Health Services*, *37*, 9–11.

Hellerstein, D. J., Rosental, R. N., Pinsker, H., Samstag, L. W., Muren, J. C., & Winston, A. (1998). A randomized prospective study comparing supportive and dynamic therapies. *Journal of Psychotherapy Practice and Research*, *7*, 261–271.

Hudson, P. L., Quinn, K., O'Hanlon, B., & Aranda, S. (2008). Family meetings in palliative care: Multidisciplinary clinical practice guidelines. *BMC Palliative Care*, *7*, 12.

Hudson, P. L., Remedios, C., & Thomas, K. (2010). A systematic review of psychosocial interventions for family cares of palliative care patients. *BMC Palliative Care*, *9*(1), 17.

Institute of Medicine. (2007). *Cancer care for the whole patient: Meeting psychosocial health needs*. Washington, DC: National Academies Press. Retrieved from http://www.iom.edu/CMS/3809/34252/47228.aspx

Kissane, D. W., Bloch, S., Smith, G. C., Miach, P., Clarke, D. M., Ikin, J., . . . McKenzie D. (2003). Cognitive-existential group psychotherapy for women with primary breast cancer: A randomized controlled trial. *Psycho-Oncology*, *12*, 532–546.

Lederberg, M. S., & Holland, J. C. (2011). Supportive psychotherapy in cancer patients: An essential ingredient of all therapy. In M. Watson & D. Kissane (Eds.), *Handbook of psychotherapy in cancer care*. Hoboken, NJ: Wiley.

Lo, C., Hales, S., Jung, J., Chiu, A., Panday, T., Rydall, A., . . . Rodin, G. (2014). Managing cancer and living meaningfully (CALM): Phase 2 trial of a brief individual psychotherapy for patients with advanced cancer. *Palliative Medicine*, *28*(3), 234–242.

Mosher, C. E., Champion, V. L., & Hanna, N. (2013). Support service use and interest in support services among distress family caregivers of lung cancer patients. *Psycho-Oncology*, *22*(7), 1549–1556.

Rodin, G., Liold, N., Katz, M., Green, E., Mackay, J. A., & Wong, R. K. (2007). The treatment of depression in cancer patients: A systematic review. *Support Care Cancer*, *15*, 123–136.

Rodin, G., Lo, C., Mikulincer, M., Donner, A., Gagliese, L., & Zimmermann, C. (2009). Pathways to distress: The multiple determinants of depression, hopelessness and the desire for hastened death in metastatic cancer patients. *Social Science and Medicine*, *68*, 562–569.

Sollner, W., Maislinger, S., Konig, A., Devries, A., & Lukas, P. (2004). Providing psychosocial support for breast cancer patients based on screening for distress within a consultation-liaison service. *Psycho-Oncology*, *13*, 893–897.

Spiegel, D., Bloom, J. R., & Yalom, I. (1981). Group support for patients with metastatic cancer: A randomized outcome study. *Archives of General Psychiatry*, *38*(5), 527–533.

Steinberg, A., & Sprung, C. L. (2006). The dying patient: New Israeli legislation. *Intensive Care Medicine*, *32*, 1234–1237.

Traeger, L., Greer, J. A., Fernandez-Robles, C., Temel, J. S., & Pirl, W. F. (2012). Evidence-based treatment of anxiety in patients with cancer. *Journal of Clinical Oncology*, *11*, 1197–1205.

53

Cecilia L. W. Chan and Richard R. Dickens

Oncology Social Work Practice in Integrative Medicine

Key Concepts

- *It is common for cancer patients to adopt complementary medicine alongside Western oncological treatments.*
- *Oncology social workers are creatively integrating Eastern and Western psychosocial and spiritual practices to empower cancer patients.*
- *Integrative oncology social work practices involve a holistic perspective of understanding the needs of patients and creative synergy of multimodal interventions, including mind–body techniques of massage, natural remedies, prayers, chanting, religious practice, energy healing, vibration, percussion, and expressive art.*
- *Research on, development of, and training of oncology social workers in integrative medicine in integrative care are discussed.*

Integrative Oncology Social Work Practice

The following case study serves to introduce this chapter, which provides guidance on how integrative medicine can be used to help patients in their journey through oncological and palliative care. In this chapter, we explore various forms of *complementary and alternative medicine* (CAM), including integrative body–mind–spirit (IBMS) approaches that oncology social workers can include in their responses to patients' needs. IBMS techniques include those that focus on the body (e.g., acupressure, hand and ear massage, and breathing exercises), the mind–body (e.g., stress management, relaxation, imagery, self-hypnotic instructions, acupressure, qigong), and the spirit (e.g., mindfulness, meaning making, life review, appreciation, gratitude, and forgiveness).

Mary was 62 years old, a nonsmoker, the mother of two adult children, and wife to Jack when she was diagnosed with Stage 2 lung cancer. With her healthy lifestyle, regular exercise, and positive approach to life, the cancer diagnosis came as a shock. She underwent surgery, followed by chemotherapy. Two years after the end of her treatment, she began losing her sense of balance and fell easily. A computed tomography scan of her brain revealed that a brain tumor was affecting her balance. Mary underwent radiotherapy to control the metastases in her brain. She regained her balance after treatment but understood that she could relapse. A hospital oncology social worker referred the family to a community oncology social worker at a cancer support service.

Mary and Jack came to the cancer support service to seek help on complementary alternative treatments. In the intake interview, Mary and Jack reported high levels of distress and worry about the future. They were overwhelmed by death anxiety and concerned about the cost of targeted therapy, as Mary did not have paid employment and Jack was a self-employed electrician without an insurance policy to cover expensive drugs and treatments for his family members.

The cancer support service offers therapeutic qigong classes, yoga classes, acupuncture and massage services, clinic consultations for traditional Chinese medicine, mindfulness meditation courses, and psychosocial-spiritual counseling groups for patients and family members. Mary and Jack participated in the exercise qigong class for 10 weeks, and both slept better and reported being in a better mood. The couple also joined an integrative body–mind–spirit group for 8 weeks and said that they found the acupressure and massage techniques helpful. Knowing other couples in the group also empowered them in sharing practical tips, recipes, and exercises. One year later, it was discovered that Mary had a further relapse to both of her lungs and her spine. She continued to receive support from Chinese medicine, acupuncture and massage, and counseling and spiritual practice of prayer, as well as energy and hands-on healing. Mary discussed her death preparation with Jack and her children and died peacefully a year later without much discomfort. She lived much longer than expected and enjoyed a good quality of life in her 4 years of life after her cancer diagnosis.

Definition of Complementary and Alternative Medicine

The term *complementary and alternative medicine* (CAM) covers an array of products and services, including alternative medical systems such as acupuncture, Ayurveda, homeopathy, naturopathy, and traditional healing; ideologically based therapies such as chelation-, non-vitamin-, and diet-based approaches; manipulation (e.g., chiropractic and massage); mind–body therapies (e.g., biofeedback and relaxation); and energy-healing therapies. The National Institute of Health (NIH) established an Office of Alternative Medicine (OAM) to develop research and to evaluate complementary therapies, as well as to serve as a clearinghouse for practitioners. Since the establishment of the National Center for Complementary and Alternative Medicine (NCCAM), integrative medicine has been established as a part of training and practice at many prestigious medical schools and institutions. By 1999, two thirds of American medical schools had integrated CAM methods into their curricula. In Germany, the integration of CAM methods into the curriculum for medical students has been required by law since 2003 (Dobos & Tao, 2011) (see Table 53.1).

History and Current State of the Art in Eastern Integrative Practices for Cancer Patients

Traditional Chinese, Indian, Tibetan, and ancient medicine have an established history of Eastern integrative practices for thousands of years. A combination of herbs, shamanism, massage, natural remedies, prayers, chanting, religious practice, and energy healing can be adopted by cancer patients around the world.

Issues of cost also lead to the search for complementary methods by cancer patients. With increasingly sophisticated and expensive treatment modalities, such as targeted and gene therapies, out-of-pocket costs rise rapidly, making it unaffordable for most people, especially when cancer has become a chronic disease requiring continuous intervention for disease control and side effect management (Weil, 2011).

Table 53.1.
Classification of Complementary and Alternative Medicine (CAM) Therapies

Alternative medical systems	**Complete medical systems of theory and practice**: Ayurveda, homeopathy, indigenous healing practices, naturopathy, osteopathy, and traditional Chinese/Indian/Tibetan medicine
Mind–body interventions	**Enhance the mind's capacity to affect bodily functions**: art therapy, behavioral medicine, biofeedback, dance, dream therapy, humor, hypnotherapy, imagery, intuition, meditation, prayer, music/sound therapy, support groups yoga, taiji, qigong, reiki, therapeutic touch, full-spectrum light, electromagnetic field, and transcutaneous electrical nerve stimulation
Biologically based therapies	**Use of substances found in nature**: herbs, aromatherapy, diet, flower essence, nutritional supplements, vitamins, and pharmacological/biological treatments
Manipulative and body-based methods	**Manipulation and/or movement of one or more parts of the body**: acupressure, Alexander technique, chiropractic, craniosacral, Feldenkrasis, massage, osteopathy, reflexology, Rolfing, and Trager method

Note: CAM can be described by the characteristics of being holistic, integrative, naturalistic, relational, and spiritual. These include holistic interventions with attention to the physical body, emotional mind, interpersonal relationships, and harmony with the universe.

Adapted from Barnes et al. (2004).

Evolution and Current State of the Art in Western Integrative Practices for Cancer Patients

Patients suffer various side effects of conventional oncology treatments, such as nausea, fatigue, pain, anxiety, and mental distress. These symptoms are often not satisfactorily relieved or alleviated by conventional medical therapies, and complementary modalities such as acupuncture, mind–body techniques, and massage may relieve symptoms and improve physical and emotional well-being when used in conjunction with mainstream medicine (Dobos & Tao, 2011). Cancer patients have increasingly turned to practitioners of CAM for the management of symptoms and promotion of holistic wellness (Weil, 2011), spending billions of dollars per year out of their own pockets on various CAM therapies (Mumber, 2006).

Integrative Oncology Social Work Practices

Oncology social work gained recognition as a specialization in the early 1970s. Since then, oncology social workers have contributed to addressing the social, emotional, practical, and spiritual needs of patients and family members. Oncology social workers play a pivotal role in helping people successfully navigate their entire illness experience (Lauria & ACS, 2001). Some oncology social workers learn from their patients about how complementary interventions have helped them, which increases social workers' curiosity to learn more on how CAM can be adopted into their own integrated oncology social work practice.

Understanding Integrative Medical Interventions

Provision of integrative health care may be very different between countries, especially among countries that have unique systems of traditional medicines (Robinson, 2011). With increasing globalization, knowledge of the various traditional healing practices are shared in oncology units in major cancer centers around the world. Thus, oncology social workers need to learn about traditional and contemporary medicinal, spiritual, religious, and cultural healing CAM practices across cultures.

Integrative, healing-oriented medicine takes account of the whole person (body, mind, spirit), as well as all aspects of lifestyle, including eating, physical activity, and stress management, and makes use of all appropriate therapies, both conventional and complementary (Weil, 2009). Patients with cancer usually employ CAM to manage their cancer-related symptoms and the side effects following treatments such as surgery, chemotherapy, and radiotherapy (Deng, Cassileth, & Yeung, 2004). Behavioral techniques including breathing, lifestyle management, and exercise associated with lower cost and risk are CAM techniques commonly used during and after conventional cancer treatment.

Understanding Integrative Mind–Body–Spirit Interventions

The IBMS social work model assumes the dynamic balance of and interrelationship among body, mind, and spirit as fundamental to individuals' holistic well-being. *Body* techniques such as movements, acupressure, hand and ear massage, and breathing can facilitate expanding patients' awareness and perspectives, as well as develop a rapid sense of mastery of their physical and emotional well-being (Chan, Ho, Fu, & Chow, 2006; Lee, Ng, Leung, & Chan, 2009). Some "1-second techniques" originating from qigong, taiji, and acupressure in Hong Kong and China were developed by Chan during her work with cancer patients. IBMS intervention helps clients regain a new equilibrium through their self-healing and self-balancing capacities. *Mind–body* techniques of stress management, relaxation, imagery, self-hypnotic instructions, acupressure, and qigong exercise and *spiritual* techniques of mindfulness, meaning making, life review, appreciation, gratitude, and forgiveness are established parts of comprehensive cancer treatment and widely adopted in oncology social work practice in the East (Chan, Ng, Ho, & Chow, 2006; Lee et al., 2009).

Oncology Social Work Practice Through Lifestyle Management

There is a growing body of evidence that lifestyle factors may contribute to prevention and the progress of cancer (Friedenreich & Orenstein, 2002). Comprehensive approaches that involve healthy diet, regular exercise, behavior modification, and stress management may lead to a better prognosis, reduce the risk of recurrence, and improve overall quality of life (Demark-Wahnefried, Campbell, & Hayes, 2012). Many cancer survivors also value having a more active role in their health care and self-care after diagnosis and during and after treatment, including diet and lifestyle changes (Davies, Batehup, & Thomas, 2011). These self-administered health practices can empower self-efficacy and mastery and activate and utilize cancer patients' innate healing power.

Patient Empowerment Interventions

Patient empowerment interventions not only have a positive impact on cancer patients' behavior and mood but also are regarded as a more cost-effective mode of service delivery. Patient empowerment practices can reduce patients' dependency on professional staff, enhance a sense of control over their lives, and help patients develop new meaning out of their suffering.

Qigong and Taiji

Qigong and taiji (also known as chi-gong and tai-chi) are ancient Eastern self-healing mind–body movement exercises combining a set of Eastern philosophies of life of letting go and nonattachment with breathing and imagery (Lee et al., 2009; Manek & Lin, 2012). Qigong aims to facilitate the regulation of the mind, body, and breathing. In a systematic review, qigong was found to be able to improve cancer patients' quality of life (Chan et al., 2012; Lee, Chen, Sancier, & Ernst, 2007). It focuses on the balance between yin and yang, as well as regulating the circulation of qi within the body to maintain the balance of the body, mind, and spirit and achieve optimal health, well-being, and spiritual cultivation. Taiji is also known as "shadow boxing." It consists of slow movements that can foster health and well-being as well.

Exercise and Acupressure Techniques

A systematic review showed that exercising for at least 30 minutes can yield modest positive effects on depressive symptoms, reduce pain and fatigue, and improve quality of life among cancer survivors (Craft, Vaniterson, Helenowski, Rademaker, & Courneya, 2012). Exercise can help to reduce cancer-related fatigue both during and after treatment (Cramp & Daniel, 2008). The types of exercise included in this systematic review include walking, stationary cycling, strength training, resistance training, flexibility training, stretching, yoga, and seated exercises.

Acupressure as a body-nurturing activity enables patients and family members to help themselves. It is based on the meridian theory in traditional Chinese medicine (TCM). The flowing of qi in the meridian network can be regulated by pressing selected acupuncture points using the hands to restore systemic equilibrium and hence the self-healing capacity of the individuals. Chan (2001) selected a few health-promoting acupuncture points that can be learned and mastered by cancer patients through watching a demonstration CD in her patient empowerment book. Due to its nonintrusive and easy-to-learn nature, acupressure has been widely practiced by cancer patients with physical or psychological discomforts (Chan, 2001). Studies show that acupressure is beneficial in the management of chemotherapy-induced nausea and vomiting in breast cancer patients (Chao et al., 2009).

Mindfulness and Meditation

Meditation is a set of self-directed mental practices with roots in Buddhism, Ayurveda, and other ancient contemplative traditions. Practitioners can cultivate their ability to create a mindful existence or meditative state. Mindfulness describes the quality of consciousness as the intentional cultivation of nonjudgmental moment-to-moment awareness through meditation practice (Kabat-zinn, 1990). There are two categories of meditation—one is focused on a specific object such as breathing or sound or thought, the other on mindfulness or insight meditation—that attend to the whole experience in a nonjudgmental and nonattached manner (Biegler, Chaoul, & Cohen, 2009).

Some forms of sitting and walking meditations bring attention to both breathing and clearing the mind. Meditation has been proposed to help improve cancer-related cognitive dysfunction, alleviate other cancer-related sequelae, and improve quality of life as an essential part of survivorship (Biegler et al., 2009). Mindfulness-based stress reduction (MBSR) as supportive therapy has also been widely applied in cancer care and can improve quality of life and mood and reduce distress in cancer patients.

Expressive Art Techniques

Expressive art, also known as creative art, is the use of various artistic expressions, such as painting, drawing, storytelling, dance, music, drama, poetry, percussion, or sand trays, in an integrated manner to foster human growth, development, and healing. Cancer patients often find it hard to express their complex emotions related to the cancer experience. Expressive art can facilitate creative articulation of hidden emotions within a safe environment that helps a patient examine his or her own body, feelings, and thoughts. This process promotes physical, mental, social, and spiritual healing. Expressive art is widely used for patients after diagnosis and during treatment, rehabilitation, recurrence, and palliative care. For patients who cannot themselves create, appreciating works of art or music by others can produce similar benefits (Cassileth & Chwistek, 2005).

A systematic review concluded that art therapy benefits cancer patients in various ways including improving their mental health and their ability to manage a spectrum of treatment-related symptoms and facilitate the process of psychological readjustment to the loss, change, and uncertainty characteristic of cancer survivorship (Geue et al., 2010; Wood, Molassiotis, & Payne, 2011). Many medical centers and cancer programs hold art exhibitions, organize art workshops, or enable expressive art activities for patients because these activities are believed to foster physical, mental, and spiritual healing and to contribute to the well-being of patients and caregivers (Ho, Potash, Fu, Wong, & Chan, 2010).

Research and Development Now and for the Future

Evidence-based practice has become the gold standard in health care for public accountability. Although a wide range of strategies, such as tai chi, qigong, massage, arts therapy, and meditation, have been used by oncology social workers for integrative practice, the evidence of their outcome, impact, efficacy, and cost-effectiveness needs to be collected (Davis, 2009). Thus, social work practitioners must assign time and effort to carefully document, research, and evaluate interventions to provide good-quality evidence of the benefits of psychosocial care in quality of life, treatment outcomes, survival, and quality of death (Chan, Ho, Lee, et al., 2006; Fielding & Chan, 2000; Liu et al., 2008).

Training of Oncology Social Workers in Complementary and Alternative Medicine

Oncology social work has become increasingly complex due to rapid advances in medical interventions from high-tech oncology innovations, including clinical trials, targeted therapy, and a complex array of integrative practices. Advances in biomedicine have been effective in prolonging life for cancer patients, but patients are often expected to manage side effects of complicated treatment regimens on their own. Improvements in symptom management have raised expectations among patients that they will be able to continue to work and maintain their daily routines. This progress has created new challenges to social work practice (Lauria & ACS, 2001).

To date, there has been little focus on integrative health care in social work education, and social work curricula have not typically included coursework that provides information, processes, and strategies to enable social workers to assist clients in decision making regarding integrative health care options. Competent oncology social workers will need skills to guide clients in integrating complementary therapies into their health care plans and to facilitate whole-person healing. Oncology social workers should receive specialized training in integrative oncology care through continuing education, in-service training, academic coursework, and/or field experience in a medical setting.

Pearls

- CAM has been increasingly used by cancer patients as a supplement while receiving conventional treatment. Cancer patients warmly welcome social workers who can empower them with integrative interventions in their path of recovery.
- There is overwhelming evidence on the benefits of exercise in prevention, control, treatment, rehabilitation, and palliative end-of-life interventions for cancer patients. The importance of holistic and creative integration of cultural practices and conventional cognitive behavioral practices into oncology social work has been internationally recognized.
- The beauty of mind–body exercises, especially simple qigong movement and acupressure techniques, is that patients can practice these techniques at home. Oncology social workers can teach clients one or two techniques each time and ask them to practice daily between sessions.

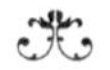

Pitfalls

- Integrative health care models vary from country to country as a result of historical and cultural backgrounds, education available, regulations, standards of practice, and licensing of practitioners.
- There is no standardization of integrative oncology social work practice around the world. Further investment in scientific research and systematic training in integrative oncology social work are urgently needed.
- Despite clinical trials suggesting that integrative oncology social work interventions may be effective in symptom reduction, improved quality of life, relapse prevention, and enhanced immunity, further large-scale rigorously designed and controlled trials are still required.

REFERENCES

Barnes, P. M., Powell-Griner, E., Division of Health Interview Statistics, McFann, K., Nahin, R. L., National Center for Complementary and Alternative Medicine, & National Institutes of Health. (2004). *Complementary and alternative medicine use among adults: United States, 2002*. No. 343. Retrieved from http://nccam.nih.gov/sites/nccam.nih.gov/files/news/camstats/2002/report.pdf

Biegler, K. A., Chaoul, M. A., & Cohen, L. (2009). Cancer, cognitive impairment, and meditation. *Acta Oncology, 48*(1), 18–26.

Cassileth, B. R., & Chwistek, M. (2005). *PDQ integrative oncology: Complementary therapies in cancer care*. New York, NY: BC Decker.

Chan, C. L., Ho, R. T., Fu, W., & Chow, A. Y. (2006). Turning curses into blessings: An Eastern approach to psychosocial oncology. *Journal of Psychosocial Oncology, 24*(4), 15–32.

Chan, C. L., Ho, R. T., Lee, P. W., Cheng, J. Y., Leung, P. P., Foo, W., . . . Spiegel, D. (2006). A randomized controlled trial of psychosocial interventions using the psychophysiological framework for Chinese breast cancer patients. *Journal of Psychosocial Oncology, 24*(1), 3–26.

Chan, C. L., Ng, S. M., Ho, R. T., & Chow, A. Y. (2006). East meets West: Applying Eastern spirituality in clinical practice. *Journal of Clinical Nursing, 15*(7), 822–832.

Chan, C. L. W. (2001). *An Eastern body-mind-spirit approach: A training manual with one-second techniques.* Hong Kong, China: University of Hong Kong. Clips of the techniques can be found on YouTube: http://www.youtube.com/watch?v=VWGLNqpCSLQ

Chan, C. L. W., Wang, C. W., Ho, R. T. H., Ng, S. M., Chan, J. S. M., Ziea, E. T. C., & Wong, V. C. W. (2012). A systematic review of the effectiveness of qigong exercise in supportive cancer care. *Supportive Care in Cancer, 20*(6), 1121–1133.

Chao, L. F., Zhang, A. L., Liu, H. E., Cheng, M. H., Lam, H. B., & Lo, S. K. (2009). The efficacy of acupoint stimulation for the management of therapy-related adverse events in patients with breast cancer: A systematic review. *Breast Cancer Research and Treatment, 118*(2), 255–267.

Craft, L. L., Vaniterson, E. H., Helenowski, I. B., Rademaker, A. W., & Courneya, K. S. (2012). Exercise effects on depressive symptoms in cancer survivors: A systematic review and meta-analysis. *Cancer Epidemiology Biomarkers and Prevention, 21*, 3–19.

Cramp, F., & Daniel, J. (2008). Exercise for the management of cancer-related fatigue in adults. *Cochrane Database of Systematic Reviews*, 2, Art. No.: CD006145. doi:006110.001002/14651858.CD14006145.pub14651852

Davies, N. J., Batehup, L., & Thomas, R. (2011). The role of diet and physical activity in breast, colorectal, and prostate cancer survivorship: A review of the literature. *British Journal Cancer, 8*(105 Suppl. 1), S52–S73.

Davis, C. (2009). *Oncology social work practice in the care of breast and ovarian cancer survivors.* New York, NY: Nova Science.

Demark-Wahnefried, W., Campbell, K. L., & Hayes, S. C. (2012). Weight management and its role in breast cancer rehabilitation. *Cancer, 118*(8 Suppl.), 2277–2287.

Deng, G., Cassileth, B. R., & Yeung, K. S. (2004). Complementary therapies for cancer-related symptoms. *Journal of Supportive Oncology, 2*(5), 419–426.

Dobos, G., & Tao, I. (2011). The model of Western integrative medicine: The role of Chinese medicine. *Chinese Journal of Integrative Medicine, 17*(1), 11–20.

Fielding, R., & Chan, C. L. W. (2000). *Psychosocial oncology and palliative care in Hong Kong: The first decade.* Hong Kong, China: Hong Kong University Press.

Friedenreich, C. M., & Orenstein, M. R. (2002). Physical activity and cancer prevention: Etiologic evidence and biological mechanisms. *Journal of Nutrition, 132*, 3456S–3464S.

Geue, K., Goetze, H., Buttstaedt, M., Kleinert, E., Richter, D., & Singer, S. (2010). An overview of art therapy interventions for cancer patients and the results of research. *Complementary Therapies in Medicine, 18*(3–4), 160–170.

Ho, R. T., Potash, J. S., Fu, W., Wong, K. P., & Chan, C. L. (2010). Changes in breast cancer patients after psychosocial intervention as indicated in drawings. *Psycho-Oncology, 19*, 353–360.

Kabat-zinn, J. (1990). *Full catastrophe living: Using the wisdom of your body and mind to face stress, pain, and illness.* New York, NY: Delta Books.

Lauria, M. M., & American Cancer Society (ACS). (2001). *Social work in oncology: Supporting survivors, families, and caregivers.* Atlanta, GA: American Cancer Society.

Lee, M. S., Chen, K. W., Sancier, K. M., & Ernst, E. (2007). Qigong for cancer treatment: A systematic review of controlled clinical trials. *Acta Oncologica, 46*, 717–722.

Lee, M. Y., Ng, S. M., Leung, P. P. Y., & Chan, C. L. W. (2009). *Integrative body-mind-spirit social work: An empirically based approach to assessment and treatment.* New York, NY: Oxford University Press.

Liu, C. J., Hsiung, P. C., Chang, K. J., Liu, Y. F., Wang, K. C., Hsiao, F. H., . . . Chan, C. L. (2008). A study on the efficacy of body-mind-spirit group therapy for patients with breast cancer. *Journal of Clinical Nursing, 17*, 2539–2549.

Manek, N. J., & Lin, C. (2012). Qigong. In C. S. Yuan, E. J. Bieber, & B. A. Bauer (Ed.), *Traditional Chinese medicine.* London, England: Informa Health care.

Mumber, M. P. (2006). *Integrative oncology: Principles and practice.* London, England: Taylor & Francis.

Robinson, N. (2011). Integrative medicine—traditional Chinese medicine, a model? *Chinese Journal of Integrative Medicine, 17*(1), 21–25.

Weil, A. (2011). The state of the integrative medicine in the U.S. and Western World. *Chinese Journal of Integrative Medicine, 17*(1), 6–10.

Weil, A. T. (2009). Why integrative oncology? In D. I. Abrams & A. T. Weil (Eds.), *Integrative oncology* (pp. 3–14). Oxford, England: Oxford University Press.

Wood, M. J., Molassiotis, A., & Payne, S. (2011). What research evidence is there for the use of art therapy in the management of symptoms in adults with cancer? A systematic review. *Psycho-Oncology, 20*(2), 135–145.

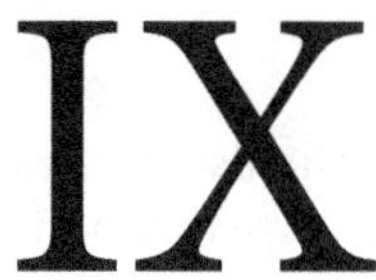

IX Interventions With Families and Caregivers in Oncology

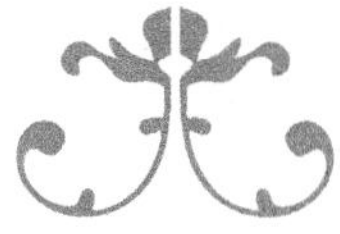

Susan Hedlund

Developing more innovative and effective ways to educate and support family and other informal caregivers has become a priority focus in our current health care system. This is inevitable as increasing numbers of individuals live many years with cancer as a chronic illness, often dealing with multiple treatments and related conditions outside health care institutions. In this section, the authors consider the central roles families and other caregivers play in a cancer patient's diagnosis, treatment, and recovery. Oncology social workers are trained to understand the impact of cancer through a "systems" lens that considers cancer's impact on the patient and on his or her family and support system. This section provides critical perspectives that oncology social workers need to integrate in providing assessment and intervention with patients, couples, families, and their extended support systems.

Susan Hedlund's chapter, "Introduction to Working With Families in Oncology," gives an overview of the issues commonly experienced by the family system including confusion, grief, fear, sadness, hope, and uncertainty as they are challenged to adapt to the changes cancer brings. Also considered are the effects that family history and belief systems, as well as family strengths, capacities, vulnerabilities, and resilience, have on the social work assessment of a family's ability to cope. The children of cancer patients, historically overlooked, are identified as being important in overall family assessment and care. Oncology social workers are the appropriate professionals to address family concerns.

In "Caregivers of Cancer Patients," Ashley Varner defines a cancer caregiver as "anyone who provides physical, emotional, spiritual, financial, or logistical support to a person with cancer" and a primary caregiver as the principal person providing such support. The author also stresses the importance of considering the impact of cancer on the entire social support system when choosing clinical interventions. Varner advocates for education for caregivers and patients about the possible emotional and practical aspects of the role of "cancer caregiver," because this is a crucial aspect of well-being for both. Also stressed is the changing trajectory of the illness, which may require the addition of an expanded support system and technological innovations to assist the primary caregiver over time.

Karen Kayser and Jennifer L. Scott, in "Psychosocial Interventions With Couples Affected by Cancer," remind us that both cancer patients and their spouses/partners experience similar levels of stress when faced with a cancer diagnosis and treatment. They describe a process of interdependence of psychological adjustment, which they call "dyadic coping." The four interventions that have been found to enhance such coping are taught in their Partners in Coping and CanCope programs:

1. Problem-focused strategies to balance work, family, and self-care.
2. Cognitive coping skills.
3. Communicating emotional support.
4. Communicating about end-of-life issues.

These programs are evidence based with practical suggestions designed to be utilized by the oncology social worker in working with couples dealing with cancer.

Betty J. Kramer and Amy Z. Boelk tackle the challenging topic of "Managing Family Conflict: Providing Responsive Family Care at the End of Life." They highlight the challenges that the trajectory of illness and treatment can create with regard to family communication and functioning. They also note that family conflict is not uncommon at the end of life and that a growing body of evidence now exists that helps illuminate its nature, causes, and consequences. Kramer and Boelk encourage oncology and palliative care social workers to understand the many factors that contribute to the development of conflict and to hone their skills in assessment, intervention, and conflict resolution.

Finally, in "Family and Team Conferencing in Oncology," Iris Cohen Fineberg describes how family conferencing and team meetings can assist families in communication, both as a family and with professional caregivers. Fineberg describes group dynamics that occur in both team meetings and conferencing, underscoring how essential these communication tools can be in helping families navigate decision making and ameliorating conflict. She also stresses the essential skills oncology social workers have that position them to lead and provide substantive participation in these forums.

Some interventions for informal caregivers have been studied, but few have been implemented in practice because they are generally not conceptualized and/or structured for the realities of the practice environment. Oncology social workers have the knowledge and skill set to assume leadership in practice and research in this critical area.

54 Introduction to Working With Families in Oncology

Susan Hedlund

Key Concepts

- *Oncology social workers are effective in helping family members adjust to and cope with cancer.*
- *Family history and beliefs about cancer affect family members' ability to be supportive to the person with cancer.*
- *Family strengths, coping abilities, and resilience are important to identify and reinforce as the family adjusts to living with cancer.*
- *Children of cancer patients need oncology social work assessment and support.*

It is well documented how the impact of a cancer diagnosis extends beyond the person with cancer to affect the family and other loved ones. Evidence shows that families play a central role in a cancer patient's diagnosis, treatment, and recovery (Van Campen & Marshall, 2010), and relationships must be reorganized to adjust to the demands of the disease and its treatments. The parents, siblings, partners, and children of the person with cancer experience similar emotions to the patient, including confusion, grief, fear, sadness, hope, and uncertainty, and are additionally challenged to adapt to the myriad changes a cancer diagnosis brings.

For our purposes here, "family" is used to describe the people whom the person with cancer considers to be family and may include people unrelated by marriage or lineage. Thus, family may include same-sex partners, friends, neighbors, and members of their extended support community.

Depending on the patient's age, the type and stage of the disease, and the course of treatment, families may find their lives disrupted and changed, at least temporarily, as they adapt. How *well* a family adapts is largely influenced by family history, previous coping with other traumatic life events, communication patterns, and role allocation. Adaptation will also be influenced by the family's financial stability and the presence or nonexistence of other supportive resources.

Jim and Ellie, married for 12 years, have two children: Ben, 3, and Maddie, 10. The family recently relocated to open a restaurant-supply business. Jim, 38, presented to a local emergency room complaining of back pain. He noted that the pain had existed for several months but, given the long work hours to establish the business, he attributed it to fatigue and stress.

On physical evaluation and testing, he was found to have Stage 4, non-small-cell lung cancer and was prescribed a course of chemotherapy and radiation. Additionally, a referral was made to the oncology social worker to provide psychosocial support and resources to Jim and Ellie. In that initial meeting, the social worker noted that Jim appeared passive and withdrawn, whereas Ellie was demanding and angry and questioned both the diagnosis and the recommended treatment. The social worker arranged a meeting with the couple, the oncologist, and herself in an attempt to give them accurate information and reassurance and to diffuse misunderstanding and anger.

Diagnosis and Course of Illness/Treatment

Studies on family functioning related to disease characteristics (e.g., first diagnosis vs. relapse, time since diagnosis) are lacking (Huizingan, VanderGraaf, & Visser, 2003). How a family adapts to cancer will be influenced by the diagnosis itself, expected treatment plan, and prognosis. If the cancer is considered treatable, the tasks of adjustment will include primary treatment, a restoration to health, survivorship, and possible cure. For cancers not considered curable, for example, most Stage 4 cancers, the family may be challenged to adapt to chronic illness, other treatment options, palliative care, and end of life. As the vignette depicts, being diagnosed with Stage 4 cancer at age 38 is a shocking event likely to be responded to by symptoms of traumatic stress: terror, disbelief, anger, and, often, denial by family members and the patient. Validating the reality of traumatic responses—that it takes time to integrate and adapt to such shocking and life-threatening news—helps families understand and manage these troubling reactions and begin to process the information one step at a time. Rolland (1994) suggests a psychosocial typology matrix, meaning "acute or gradual"; progressive, constant, or relapsing; incapacitating; or fatal. He further maintains that the health care team is challenged to consider the impact of illness on three simultaneous tracts: the developmental age and stage of the patient, the developmental stage of the family, and the developmental stage and expected course of the disease. This perspective is further studied by Veach and Nicholas (1998), who considered combining the clinical course of cancer with stages of family development. How a health care professional assesses the family and determines treatment strategies is influenced by each of these stages.

Depending on the disease stage, course of treatment, and degree of disability, family members may have to provide both physical and psychological care to the person with cancer, which can be taxing for all involved. There are 4.6 million Americans who care for someone with cancer at home (National Alliance for Caregiving, 2009). Family caregivers provide more than half the care needed by patients with cancer, although they often feel unprepared for the role (Blum & Sherman, 2010). Family members may assume the caregiving role with little or no preparation and without considering whether they have enough knowledge, resources, or skills. Additionally, caregiving can have an impact on the caregiver's physical and mental well-being (Given, Wyatt, & Given, 2004).

How families negotiate these role changes depends largely on their ability to communicate openly about the changes, tasks, and needs involved in caring for the patient and the impact on their relationships. Additionally, developing problem-solving skills appears to have an important influence on positive coping. Literature suggests that problem-solving strategies are linked to lower distress levels (Ko et al., 2005; Malcarne, Banthia, Varni, Sadler, & Breenergs, 2002). This has important implications for oncology social workers helping families deal with the stress of cancer.

Ellie and Jim are a young couple simultaneously tasked with creating stability for their young children, maintaining a family business, and developing support systems in a new community. Jim's diagnosis, Stage 4 lung cancer, has an expectation of overall poor survival and his family was challenged to adapt to multiple tasks. Ellie gradually took over those that Jim performed in their family business. Jim stayed at home, and Ellie expected that he would assume the family home functions, including child care, cooking, laundry, grocery shopping, and errands. As Jim became more ill, he was increasingly unable to do so. Ellie's anger escalated.

The children began to show signs of distress. Three-year-old Ben regressed in tasks of language and toilet training and exhibited aggression with playmates. Ten-year-old Maddie began to assume household tasks such as laundry and meal preparation. Her distress was evident in a large chalk drawing on the driveway that said, "Don't worry, Mom and Dad, I will take care of us." In a visit with the social worker, Ellie burst into tears and said, "I guess I thought if we just exchanged roles, everything would be okay. He really is sick, isn't he?"

It was clear that the family was in crisis and needed more assistance to maintain family functioning. Because of the severity of the diagnosis and the family's young age, it is understandable that they could not immediately accept the diagnosis, its life threat, and its impact. Ellie's statement is psychologically diagnostic and poignant: "He really is sick, isn't he?" She acts angry, but she is frightened and sad. Both Jim and Ellie were asked to identify resources that could help, and they suggested that they could accept offers of financial and emotional support from their parents, who lived some distance away. They also remembered a neighbor who had offered to take the children to school. The oncology social worker suggested ways for them to help the children maintain their normal routines as children. For the first time since Jim's diagnosis, Ellie was able to express her fears and sadness openly with Jim and appeared less angry. Jim was able to express his love for Ellie and his sadness about the strain the illness was putting on the family.

The social worker also suggested that the children see the cancer center's child life therapist, and with their permission, a referral was made.

Family History

It is important to assess the family's history to determine what other experiences may affect the adjustment to the cancer diagnosis. Past behavior can guide present appraisals or interpretations of the crisis, the resources available to assist, the roles different family members are expected to assume, and the belief in (or lack of) family strength and resilience.

If there is a previous family history of cancer, what did that involve? Families with previous cancer experiences may or may not have coped well and also may come to the present situation with prevailing beliefs and/or expectations. For example, if the previous cancer experience was many years ago, they may have witnessed family members who experienced pain, nausea, and other symptoms not managed as they would be today. For reassurance, it is important to help the patient and family gain as much information about current treatment courses and the management of symptoms and side effects as possible.

Other aspects of the family history may influence the adaptation to cancer as well. Is the family managing other illnesses concurrently? Is there a history of alcoholism, substance abuse, or violence? How have previous generations adapted to adversity, and what effect did that have on the current family?

The stage of the family life cycle will also influence a family's coping. Young families may be less prepared to cope with the stresses inherent in having cancer, because they have less life experience and may have fewer financial resources. Parents with school-age children and/or adolescents may find it challenging to maintain family organization and stability while also adapting to the cancer diagnosis. Older families may have fewer loved ones living nearby and may be caregivers themselves or may have retired.

Considering the course of treatment alongside the family's developmental stage can provide a framework for understanding what the impact of cancer might be, how the family might cope, and how health care professionals may be of service.

Family Functioning

Functioning in families experiencing cancer has been examined as an indicator of distress in adult family members. Lower levels of psychological distress have been found in families showing high cohesiveness and good conflict-solving skills (Kissane, Block, & Burns, 1994; Kissane et al., 1996). In families where members acted openly, expressed feelings directly, and had good problem-solving skills, there were lower levels of depression and anxiety (Hagedoorn, Buunk, & Kuijer, 2000).

All families, even those appearing chaotic, have a complex structure. A stable structure that promotes "predictability, security, and cohesiveness" is valued by family members (Rait & Lederberg, 1989), and there is a tendency to maintain that homeostasis at any cost. The cancer crisis destabilizes the family so that even the most flexible families may find themselves stressed. A cancer diagnosis may change plans, family members may experience a sense of helplessness and loss of control, and the standard of living may decrease due to the economic burdens from the direct or hidden costs of cancer.

Families who are able to remain flexible often cope remarkably well despite the stress of cancer. However, the process is rarely smooth. The family that is capable of adapting under stress may develop new skills and resources to help them cope amid difficulty. The family's strengths, coping abilities, and resilience will be important to identify and reinforce as the family adjusts to the current situation.

Patterns of Communication

As noted, it is well documented that patterns of communication influence how well a family adapts to cancer in one of its members (Edwards & Clarke, 2004; Wellisch, Mosher, & VanScoy, 1978). Families with more open patterns of communication will be better able to talk about both the emotions and the practical aspects of the cancer experience. Vess, Moreland, and Schwebel (1985) found that while the stage of the family life cycle was important, the clearest finding was the value of open communication between spouses. Effective communication reduces conflict and role strain while promoting cohesion and mutual support (Vess et al., 1985). Many challenges will exist as the family adjusts its roles and expectations during the cancer experience. Is the person with cancer working, and if so, will he or she be able to continue working? Does the family have young or school-aged children requiring supervision and care? Can the person with cancer or a family member take care of the tasks of daily living (food preparation and shopping, laundry, house cleaning, yard maintenance)? Often, couples are challenged to negotiate role changes that include tasks of daily living, patterns of communication, and intimacy.

For families with a history of more strained communication or conflict, cancer adds additional stress where it already exists and may magnify preexisting problems. When conflict exists between family members, it will be more difficult to communicate well about the cancer, provide support, and negotiate changes in family roles. Conflict in the family may further extend to the treatment team. The family may require an oncology social worker to redirect or assist with problem solving.

Meeting with the oncology social worker, Jim and Ellie initially described their relationship as "warm and loving," although both admitted the toll from relocating and starting a family business. Jim worked 6 to 7 days a week, often leaving before the children were awake and returning after they were asleep. All of the home and family tasks fell to Ellie, who appeared tired and frustrated. The oncology social worker noted that Jim seemed to withdraw in the face of Ellie's anger, which appeared to make her more frustrated. "How am I supposed to handle all this?" Ellie inquired. The social worker asked if there were other family members or friends to help. Ellie and Jim indicated that their parents and siblings, while concerned, lived several states away.

The social worker also asked if there were other supports. Ellie indicated that she had attempted to establish membership at a new church but had been unable to attend much. The social worker asked if that could become a source of support for them, and Ellie indicated that she would call the minister to let him know their situation.

Family Beliefs

A family's beliefs about cancer, and the meanings attached to those beliefs, affect how a family may respond to a cancer diagnosis. For example, if the family believes that illness is an emotional weakness, that belief may prevent family members from supporting one another. Some may believe that if the patient is positive and optimistic, the cancer will be cured. If this doesn't happen, it may result in the patient feeling blamed and can place a huge burden on the person with cancer. Unresolved family issues (e.g., blame, shame, guilt) can also strongly affect views of cancer's causes or cure.

Cancer, Culture, and Diversity

The need to shift a treatment approach from patient centered to family focused becomes clearer when seen through the lenses of culture and diversity. Cultural values affect how cancer is viewed, the degree to which we keep information about the illness public or private, and the role of the family in treatment decisions. Health care providers are challenged to educate themselves about differences in language, sexual orientation, and social customs. It is also essential to understand the barriers that can arise when one fails to address cultural beliefs and life experiences when extending outreach services to the underserved.

Assessment should include understanding that cultural factors can play a powerful role in facing serious illness. To provide culturally and linguistically appropriate services, providers should ask patients about their specific beliefs and practices (The Joint Commission, 2010). See Section 7 for further discussion of cultural issues in oncology social work.

The Impact on Family Members

As noted, the stress of cancer on the family unit is not limited to just the patient. Children are sometimes overlooked as the adults attempt to navigate the many challenges of the disease and manage their own distress. The impact of parental cancer on children's mental health has been studied (Grabiak, Bender, & Puskar, 2007; Osborn, 2007). The family, crucial for a child's development, can be either protective or a risk factor and can buffer or exacerbate stress depending on how the family is functioning. Additional risk factors such as parental depression, single parenthood, low income, and the experience of psychosocial adversity in families affected by cancer make children more vulnerable to psychological problems (Rutter, 2005). It has been reported that adolescents facing parental cancer have specific needs that generally are not assessed and that minimal attention is paid to what they experience (Davey, Gulish, Askew, Godette, & Childs, 2005). Adolescents have been reported to be the most negatively affected group when facing early-stage parental cancer (Osborn, 2007). Parental cancer has been associated with less parental availability, or even some parental disengagement, which can hinder adolescent development and adaptation (Folkner & Davey, 2002; Lewis, Casey, Brandt, Shands, & Zahlis, 2006). Coping with cancer and the intensity of treatment requires such demanding and numerous adjustments that parents may overlook and/or not respond to the needs of both young children and adolescents. Social work interventions that consider the impact cancer has on the family system are essential to help parents with cancer recognize the needs of and provide support for their children.

Implications for Practice

Many health care professionals are trained to focus on the individual with cancer and the disease itself. Oncology social workers are trained to understand the impact of cancer through a "systems" lens that considers cancer's impact on the patient and on his or her family and support system. Additionally, issues of culture, socioeconomic status, and access or barriers to resources are among the things considered from a social work perspective.

Greater attention is needed to understand ways to promote family communication and cohesion, as well as to develop programs that attend to children of cancer patients. Family-centered approaches that enhance resilience and adaptation are needed. Using these approaches will enhance both short- and long-term adaptation for patients and their loved ones during and after the cancer experience.

Pearls

- The oncology social worker must advocate for family perspectives and needs to be included in the broad range of support services provided.

- Understanding the developmental level of the family (young, middle aged, older) and characteristics of the disease and treatment process is essential in assessing families' responses to a cancer diagnosis and its treatment, in addition to other psychosocial variables.
- The needs of children and adolescents should be included in interventions and programs for families.

Pitfalls

- The health care professional must be careful about the assumptions made about a patient's "family" (e.g., composition, who is the closest to the patient).
- A health care professional may overlook the belief systems that patients and families hold about cancer based on previous experience or culture.
- Cancer research that looks at family-based interventions across low-income and ethnically diverse groups is needed. Such research would identify ways to prepare family members to support a cancer patient and assist cosurvivors.

The physical and psychological stresses associated with cancer and its treatment can be overwhelming and long lasting. Coping and supportive interventions have long been thought to moderate the stress and assist in adjusting to chronic illness. More research is needed to understand the specific stressors and tasks associated with coping with specific stages of cancer and the impact on the family system. A family's personal and interpersonal resources, how they view their situation, and the ability to develop problem-solving skills will influence the adaptation to cancer and its treatment. Support programs tailored to address the family's needs must continue to be developed to promote resilience and minimize the disruption for all involved while dealing with cancer. Assisting families in adjustment and promoting healthy family functioning will be essential for social workers to continue to address.

ADDITIONAL RESOURCES

American Cancer Society. (2012). *Helping children when a family member has cancer: Dealing with diagnosis*. Retrieved from http://www.cancer.org/acs/groups/cid/documents/webcontent/002601-pdf.pdf

American Society of Clinical Oncology. (2012, April). Talking with your children. Retrieved from http://www.cancer.net/coping-and-emotions/communicating-loved-ones/talking-about-cancer/talking-your-children

Harpham, W. S. (2004). *When a parent has cancer: A guide to caring for your children*. New York, NY: HarperCollins Publishers.

Marshall, C. A. (Ed.). (2010). *Surviving cancer as a family and helping co-survivors thrive*. Westport, CT: Praeger, ABC CLIO.

REFERENCES

Blum, K., & Sherman, D. W. (2010). Understanding the experience of caregivers: A focus on transitions. *Seminars in Oncology Nursing, 26*, 243–258.

Davey, M., Gulish, L., Askew, J., Godette, K., & Childs, N. (2005). Adolescents coping with mom's breast cancer: Developing family intervention programs. *Journal of Marital and Family Therapy, 31*(2), 247–258.

Edwards, B., & Clarke, V. (2004). The psychological impact of a cancer diagnosis on families: The influence of family functioning and patients' illness characteristics on depression and anxiety. *Psycho-Oncology, 13*, 562–576.

Folkner, R. A., & Davey, M. (2002). Children and adolescents of cancer patients: The impact of cancer on the family. *American Journal of Family Therapy, 30*, 63–72.

Given, B., Wyatt, G., & Given, C. (2004). Burden and depression among caregivers of patients with cancer at the end of life. *Oncology Nursing Forum, 31*, 1105–1117.

Grabiak, B. R., Bender, C. M., & Puskar, K. R. (2007). The impact of parental cancer on the adolescent: An analysis of the literature. *Psycho-Oncology, 16*(2), 127–137.

Hagedoorn, M., Buunk, B. P., & Kuijer, R. G. (2000). Couples dealing with cancer: Role and gender differences regarding psychological distress and quality of life. *Psycho-Oncology, 9*, 232–242.

Huizingan, G. A., Van der Graff, W. T. A., & Visser, A. (2003). Psychosocial consequences for children of a parent with cancer: A pilot study. *Cancer Nursing, 26*, 195–202.

The Joint Commission. (2010). *Advancing effective communication, cultural competence and patient-and family-centered care: A roadmap for hospitals*. Retrieved from http://www.jointcommission.org/assets/1/6/aroadmapforhospitalsfinalversion727.pdf

Kissane, D. W., Bloch S., & Burns, W. I. (1994). Perceptions of family functioning and cancer. *Psycho-Oncology, 3*, 259–269.

Kissane, D. W., Bloch, S., Dowe, D. L., Snyder, R. D., Onghena, P., McKenzie, D. P., & Wallace, C. S. (1996). The Melbourne Family Grief Study I: Perceptions of family functioning in bereavement. *American Journal of Psychiatry, 153*, 650–658.

Ko, C. M., Malcarne, V. L., Varni, J. W., Roesch, S. C., Bantia, R., Greengergs, H. L., & Sadler, G. R. (2005). Problem-solving and distress in prostate cancer patients and their spousal caregivers. *Supportive Care in Cancer, 13*(6), 367–364.

Lewis, F. M., Casey, S. M., Brandt, P. A., Shands, M. E., & Zahlis, E. H. (2006). The enhancing connections program: Pilot study of a cognitive-behavioral intervention for mothers and children affected by breast cancer. *Psycho-Oncology, 15*, 486–497.

Malcarne, V. L., Banthia, R., Varni, J. W., Sadler, G. R., & Breenergs, H. L. (2002). Problem-solving skills and emotional distress in spouses of men with prostate cancer. *Journal of Cancer Education, 17*(3), 150–154.

National Alliance for Caregiving. (2009). Caregiving in the United States. Retrieved from http://www.caregiving.org

Osborn, T. (2007). The psychosocial impact of parental cancer on children and adolescents: A systemic review. *Psycho-Oncology, 16*(2), 101–126.

Rait, D. S., & Lederberg, M. (1989). The family of the cancer patient. In J. C. Holland & J. H. Rowland (Eds.), *Handbook of psychooncology: Psychological care of the patient with cancer* (pp. 585–597). New York, NY: Oxford University Press.

Rolland, J. S. (1994). *Families, illness, and disability: An integrative treatment model.* New York, NY: Basic Books.

Rutter, M. (2005). How the environment affects mental health. *British Journal of Psychiatry, 186,* 4–6.

Van Campen, K. S., & Marshall, C. A. (2010). *How families cope with cancer.* Frances McClelland Institute for Children, Youth, and Families. ResearchLink, 2(4). Tucson, AZ: University of Arizona Press.

Veach, T. A., & Nicholas, D. R. (1998). Understanding families of adults with cancer: Combining the clinical course of cancer and stages of family development. *Journal of Counseling and Development, 76,* 144–156.

Vess, J. D., Moreland, J. R., & Schwebel, A. I. (1985). An empirical assessment of the effects of cancer on family functioning. *Journal of Psychosocial Oncology, 11,* 1–17.

Wellisch, D. K., Mosher, M. B., & VanScoy, C. (1978). Management of family emotion stress: Family group therapy in a private oncology practice. *International Journal of Psychotherapy, 28,* 225–231.

55 Caregivers of Cancer Patients

Ashley Varner

Key Concepts

- *A cancer caregiver is anyone who provides physical, emotional, spiritual, financial, or logistical support to a person with cancer. The primary caregiver is the principal person providing such support.*
- *Oncology social workers should consider the impact of cancer on the patient's entire social system when completing assessments and interventions.*
- *Education for caregivers and patients about possible emotional and practical aspects of the role of "cancer caregiver" is crucial to improve well-being.*
- *Cancer caregiver needs and experiences change during the trajectory of the illness, and other caregivers may become involved over time to support the primary caregiver.*
- *Understanding family and cultural narratives about illness can be helpful in working effectively with caregivers and those diagnosed with cancer.*

The Institute of Medicine (2008) report *Cancer Care for the Whole Patient* mandates that health care teams address the social and emotional needs of not only cancer patients but also their *caregivers*. Among team members, addressing the emotional and social needs of informal cancer caregivers has historically been largely the domain of oncology social workers (Lauria, Clark, Hermann, & Stearns, 2001).

Caregivers, also called *cosurvivors, family caregivers, informal caregivers*, and, in the United Kingdom, *carers*, are those who provide physical, emotional, spiritual, financial, or logistical support to a loved one with cancer, with the *primary caregiver* being the principal person providing support. Among cancer caregivers, more than half are the patient's spouse (Mellon, Northouse, & Weiss, 2006), with another estimated 20% being adult children (Mosher & Weiss, 2010). Other caregivers include siblings, friends, neighbors, and work colleagues (Case, 2006). Caregivers may also be school-aged or adolescent children, especially in situations of advanced illness (Charles, Stainton, & Marshal, 2012; Siskowski, 2009; Siskowski, Diac, Connors, & Mize, 2007). Professional caregivers, such as members of the health care team, can be counted among the ranks of caregivers; however, this chapter focuses on informal caregivers.

The needs of cancer caregivers are often overlooked by professionals, friends, and family members (Harding, List, Epiphaniou, & Jones, 2011; O'Mara, 2005). Research indicates that cancer caregivers have a variety of health concerns, including increased incidence of anxiety and depression (Carter & Acton, 2006; Pitceathly, Maguire, Haddad, & Fletcher, 2004), disturbed sleep (Carter & Acton, 2006), and poor health (Borg & Hallberg, 2006), compared to their noncaregiving counterparts. A subgroup of about 20% of cancer caregivers appears to experience high levels of distress in response to cancer (Edwards & Clarke, 2004).

Caregivers face many challenges, including role recognition, role shifts, skill acquisition, multiple time and energy demands, health concerns of their own, and making time to take care of their own needs (Carter & Acton, 2006; Gilbar & Ben-Zur, 2002; Given, Given, Kozachik, & Rawl, 2003; Grimm, Zawacki, Mock, Krumm, & Frink, 2000; Harding et al., 2011). This chapter provides an overview of the experience of cancer caregivers and social work interventions at various points during the trajectory of the illness.

Diagnosis

Whether one is the patient or the caregiver, hearing a diagnosis of cancer is overwhelming. In addition to attending medical appointments and learning to navigate the medical landscape, each caregiver is faced with questions about what the cancer and treatment journey means to him or her. Most caregivers are thrust into their new role with no training or experience (O'Mara, 2005). Yet, one highly experienced hospice social worker also describes how strongly she was affected by her husband's Stage 4 cancer diagnosis, despite her professional experiences (Oliver, 2013, p. 208):

> *Our life has been a fairy tale, a love story, perfect. That is, until one day last fall, when we were hit by a meteor. Our family's world was forever changed as the love of my life was diagnosed with Stage IV terminal cancer. That day marked the beginning of a paralyzing pain and loss that appears in moments throughout each day. At times it takes my breath away and literally I am unsure how to manage the next minute.... The privilege of my background, knowledge, and skill has only heightened my awareness of the tremendous struggles for caregivers and their lack of support across health care settings.*

Many patients and caregivers describe the first weeks after diagnosis as like walking into a tornado. At this early stage, individuals are usually in crisis mode.

Depending on the practice setting, a helpful early intervention with both patients and caregivers is to clarify that an oncology social worker is available to support both patients and caregivers. Those diagnosed with cancer are often just as worried about their loved ones as their loved ones are about them (Segrin & Badger, 2010). Patients will often share how grateful they are to know that someone is available to help.

During the first meeting with the patient and his or her family, it also helpful to validate that cancer is a family illness (Rolland, 1988). The impact of the diagnosis on the family can initially be obscured by the diagnostic tests, education about treatment options, and push for decisions about treatment plans. It is usually helpful at this point to introduce the term *caregiver* and to explain that although the caregiver's roles and responsibilities are certainly different from those of the patient, both have challenges (Gilbar & Ben-Zur, 2002). It can be important to clarify that even if the person with cancer is completely self-sufficient, those who love the patient are still in a caregiver role. The emotional support provided by caregivers is different but just as taxing as physical support (Kim & Schultz, 2008).

Oncology social workers can introduce possible sources of support for caregivers, including reputable websites with information about cancer caregiving, online support groups, and the Family Medical Leave Act. Caregivers often sigh with relief when they hear that feelings of powerlessness and of being overwhelmed are not unique to them and that others have made it through.

In addition to normalizing feelings, completing a psychosocial assessment early in the relationship with a patient is important, and the assessment should include an understanding of the relationship between the caregiver(s) and the person diagnosed with cancer.

Possible Questions for Brief Patient–Caregiver Dyad Psychosocial Assessment

1. *Tell me about your relationship.*
    a. *How long have you known each other?*
    b. *Are you related? If so, how?*
    c. *What are your strengths as a pair?*
2. *Have either of you encountered illness before? Can you tell me a little about that?*
3. *What do each of you find supportive?*
4. *Whom do each of you go to for support?*
5. *What are your biggest concerns at this time? Are you worried about other family members?*
6. *Is there anything else I should know?*
7. *How can I and the medical team best help you?*

This assessment can help the social worker and the patient–caregiver dyad identify coping strategies. In the hectic time of diagnosis and treatment planning when patient–caregiver dyads often feel out of control, oncology social workers can help dyads slow down, interrupt the anxiety/crisis response, and recognize their strengths. Asking both dyad members about other difficult situations with which they have coped and what worked for them at that time can remind them of their coping strengths.

Encouraging the patient and caregiver to think about how they best work together to solve problems is also good practice. Usually at this stage, caregivers feel a strong need to help but are unsure how. Reminding the patient and caregiver that they can decide together how to move through this process often initiates effective communication. For instance, an oncology social worker can suggest that they consider what information each of them wants and the best ways to obtain it. Do they want to attend appointments together? Would it be useful to make a list of their questions before each health care appointment? Would bringing pen and paper or a recorder to each appointment and developing a record-keeping system be useful? Many caregivers find comfort and a sense of agency in having assigned, concrete tasks (Given et al., 2003).

As clinicians, social workers need to clarify with clients at an early meeting how boundaries will be managed with both the patient and caregiver. Explaining what will be noted in the patient's chart and what patients and caregivers can expect with regard to meeting, separately and/or together, is helpful. It is also useful to tell clients what is shared with the medical team, any limits to confidentiality, and how social workers can help the caregiver–patient dyad negotiate the complexities of the health care system.

Initial Treatment

With the beginning of treatment, most caregiver–patient dyads find that the crisis energy of diagnosis begins to dissipate. The crisis response does not persist for more than 6 to 8 weeks (Regehr, 2011), and the routine that usually comes with both radiation and chemotherapy treatment provides a semblance of predictability often missing during the diagnostic process. The beginning of cancer treatment can often be a good time to circle back with caregivers, reinforce their strengths, encourage them to continue to expand their support networks, and ascertain their needs once crisis energy has dissipated.

At this point for some patient–caregiver dyads, information about the spectrum of relational styles can be helpful. Whereas some individuals feel most supported when they are able to talk about or "process" their thoughts and feelings, others are more comfortable with problem solving or "fixing" (Loscalzo, Kim, & Clark, 2010). Many dyads, when this is explained, recognize the differences in their problem-solving styles and are better able to work together.

During the early days of treatment, more than one caregiver has said: "I keep waiting to wake up from this nightmare, but I'm not going to wake up, am I? This is for real." This can be an opportunity to point out caregivers' strengths and also encourage them to calibrate expectations of themselves, their loved one with cancer, and others. It can be helpful to remind caregivers to pace for the marathon of the cancer treatment journey rather than the sprint of crisis management and to learn to say yes when others offer assistance (Gaugler, Eppinger, King, Sandberg, & Regine, 2013).

Treatment brings many practical concerns for both patients and caregivers. If surgery is part of treatment, caregivers are often called upon to change dressings and help monitor healing after discharge. Oncology social workers can help by working with the rest of the medical team to educate caregivers about the care needed and by exploring with caregivers their comfort with providing care at home. Research indicates that education improves the overall well-being of informal caregivers (Creedle et al., 2012). Oncology social workers also have the responsibility to advocate for alternate plans if a caregiver feels unable to provide care at home.

Caregivers also often wonder if they can/should arrange their schedule to accompany their loved one to chemotherapy and/or radiation. This may contribute to worries about paying the expenses of treatment, maintaining health insurance, balancing the demands of work, caring for children and elders, supporting the one with cancer, and so on. Again, it is usually good practice to encourage the caregiver–patient dyad to work together on this issue. Oncology social workers and other team members can provide practical suggestions if time away from other responsibilities such as work or child care is problematic. Using family medical leave, carefully scheduling appointments, prioritizing which appointments to attend, and adjusting expectations may be recommended.

End of Treatment and Long-Term Survivorship

Caregivers experience many of the same conflicting emotions as cancer survivors when treatment ends, including relief, fear of recurrence (Matthews, Baker, & Spillers, 2003), worry (Northouse, 2005), and uncertainty (Kim et al., 2008). However, when treatment is done, informal caregivers are often ready to "get back to normal," whereas survivors may be trying to come to grips with all that has happened during the months of treatment and how their bodies have been altered (Lethborg, Kissane, & Burns, 2003). This difference in focus between survivors and their loved ones can be an additional source of distress (Schnipper, 2006).

Oncology social workers can help during this time by preparing caregiver–patient dyads for the possibility of confusing and conflicting feelings when treatment ends. In the conversation about the end of treatment, one can say something like, "Many patients and caregivers are surprised at the end of treatment by the myriad feelings they have—relief, of course, but also sometimes feeling 'lost' and, sometimes, patients and loved ones experience the end of treatment differently." This type of preparation is helpful to normalize the experience. Both caregivers and patients may also find themselves unprepared for the reality that life after cancer treatment is not the same as life before cancer. Some experts, patients, and caregivers refer to these changes as a "new normal" (Harpham, 1995). Some of these changes can be with priorities, comfort with intimacy, altered energy levels, and other physical changes. Old conflicts between the dyad members may surface. Encouraging communication between patients and caregivers is essential, emphasizing for both that recovery from cancer treatment is not immediate and includes physical, emotional, social, and spiritual aspects (Varner, 2012).

The end of treatment often also brings financial concerns to both patients and caregivers. Health care bills may begin to arrive, or such bills may become more pressing if they have been put aside until treatment is complete. Some caregivers are reluctant to discuss their financial concerns, and oncology social workers can help by providing conversational openings, such as asking if they have questions in this area.

The end of treatment can also be a good time to encourage patients and caregivers to take care of practical items such as living wills and durable powers of attorney for health care if they have not already done so. Furthermore, many caregivers postpone their own medical and dental care while their loved one is undergoing treatment. It's common to hear, "We can only deal with one of us going to the doctor." Caregivers should be encouraged to attend their appointments throughout their loved one's treatment journey, but when treatment is done it is a good time to encourage caregivers to catch up on anything they have postponed.

Cancer Recurrence and Metastatic Disease

Learning that cancer has returned is usually a shock for both patient and caregiver, and it can precipitate an even greater crisis than that of the initial diagnosis. Likewise, hearing at the time of diagnosis that cancer has already become metastatic brings caregivers a different set of stressors. Metastatic or Stage 4 cancer is, with few exceptions, not curable. Caregivers and patients often process this information differently. Sometimes, caregivers are ready to grapple with this, but patients are not. Other times, patients may want to talk about the possibility of death, but caregivers are not ready. Treatment options may be arduous with many side effects and risks. Regardless, a diagnosis of metastatic disease usually means changing gears from an exclusive focus on cure to one that more clearly integrates consideration of quality of life.

During the crisis period just after discovery of metastatic disease, oncology social workers can help caregivers and patients by providing information, reminders about their coping strengths, and a safe space to process feelings. As the intensity of the initial crisis passes, the caregiver–patient dyad may benefit from individual sessions and/or being together in counseling to express complicated feelings and talk about how best to manage their new situation. Meeting both the patient and the caregiver where they are by respecting each one's sense of pacing is especially important at this point.

As noted in other chapters of this book (particularly Chapters 87 and 91), if they have not already done so, this is the time when caregivers and patients should complete any necessary legal business, begin to discuss end-of-life choices, and plan for their family's future. Although it can be difficult to raise these issues, caregivers routinely have them on their mind and are often relieved to have a place to discuss them and then, for some, put them aside and go on with day-to-day living. Oncology social workers can assist caregivers by providing room to think about and discuss what they want and perhaps even role-play conversations with their loved one. Other helpful interventions when cancer recurs include asking caregivers what helped before, encouraging them to explore how these strategies can be employed now, and encouraging caregivers and patients to commit to do something fun at least once a week, either together or apart.

End of Life

Informal cancer caregivers whose loved ones are at the end of life have, as a group, the greatest need for education and physical and emotional support (Harding et al., 2011). Caregivers are typically confronting the emotional challenges of the impending death of their loved one, as well as the challenges of increased physical care. They may also find themselves struggling with conflicting feelings. A caregiver never wants a loved one to die, yet at the same time that caregiver may want the suffering to end. Particularly poignant, caregivers sometimes acknowledge privately that although they do not want their loved one to die, they are not sure how much longer they will be able to provide care. Caregiving at the end of life is never easy.

Oncology social workers can help by introducing possible practical supports such as palliative care, home care, and hospice care early in the journey. Listening can be a potent clinical intervention at this stage. Caregivers often comment, "I can't talk about this with just anybody, but I know I do have to talk about it. This is the hardest thing I've ever done."

Psychoeducation about anticipatory grief and the grieving process is often helpful for caregivers. It gives a name to the experience. It can also be helpful to provide information about what caregivers can expect during the dying process, but again, it is vital to meet caregivers where they are and honor their sense of pacing. Bereavement resources and interventions are crucial and covered elsewhere in this book (see Chapters 74 and 75).

Current health care trends encourage the terminally ill patient to be cared for in the home. Waldrop and Meeker (2011) describe the increasing difficulty caregivers face in providing adequate care in the home at the end of life for individuals who may now present with complex illnesses and symptoms from previous cancer treatments and from their terminal illness. These conditions often result in the need to provide extensive and prolonged personal care that includes feeding, bathing, and toileting, tasks that "force the dissolution of familiar and comfortable social and personal boundaries" (Waldrop & Meeker, 2011, p. 118). These more intensive care needs require social work assessment of caregivers' education, support, resources, needs, and capacities to manage the process and maintain their own health. Spouses may be helped to consider an alternative location for the patient's care to maintain their own health and their ability to relate to the patient as an intimate partner or family member, not solely as a caregiver.

Pearls

- Caregivers are often reluctant to accept attention and support, stating, "My job is to help my loved one." Explaining that by accepting help the caregiver is actually maximizing quality of life for both the patient and the caregiver will often enable him or her to accept support.

- When given time to slow down and a safe space in which to discuss their thoughts, caregivers can almost always articulate what they need. Listening carefully can be a powerful clinical intervention.
- Oncology social workers are human beings, so they inevitably will have their own feelings about the patient, caregiver, and family whose struggle with illness and loss they have come to know so well. Therefore, they may have strong reactions when patients and/or caregivers make choices that they consider ill-advised. Clinical or peer supervision is invaluable to help manage such reactions (see Chapters 96, 99, and 105).

Pitfalls

- Working with both the patient and his or her caregiver can be challenging. It is important to clarify with the patient, caregiver, and medical team what will be shared and with whom. It is also important to develop a protocol for obtaining informed consent to work with caregivers, as they are not the official "patient."
- Particularly with families and caregiver–patient dyads that have more contentious relationships, social workers and other members of the medical care team can easily become triangulated or "split." Educating the medical care team about this possibility and being alert to its development is important.
- It is essential for oncology social workers to intentionally work to create a safe environment for caregivers to share their concerns about caregiving demands and notify the team if the home care or other plan is not advisable.
- Caregivers should be considered and treated as a vital part of the care team.
- Although identifying a primary caregiver is important, other caregivers are likely to become involved over time and with advanced illness, including children and adolescents. Their needs for education, information, and support are often neglected.

Bill is 77 years old, and Ann is 75. They have been married for 55 years. Two days ago, Bill was admitted to the hospital with complaints of increased fatigue; diffuse pain, especially with movement; and a recent fall. Yesterday he was found to have Stage 4 prostate cancer.

As an integral part of the medical care team, the oncology social worker:

- *Met on the first day of the admission with Bill and Ann and explained his role on the team and what Bill and Ann could expect with regard to confidentiality, education, assistance with resources, and assistance at the time of discharge.*
- *Asked Bill and Ann about their relationship, other supports, and their concerns.*
- *Discovered through careful listening during individual meetings with Ann and Bill that both were concerned that Ann would no longer be able to provide all the help for Bill that he needed.*
- *Advocated with the medical care team to discuss all treatment options with the couple including subacute rehabilitation placement, palliative care, and hospice.*
- *Insisted that the discharge plan include sufficient support for the couple given their concerns.*
- *Worked with Ann and Bill to mobilize a support system of other family members, friends, and church members.*

Caregiving is an increasingly important area that requires developing a better understanding of the stresses and strains involved and how the health care team and particularly oncology social workers can inform, educate, and support caregivers more adequately. A variety of developments over the last 20 years have led to increased caregiver strain, including improved survival rates, the aging population, and a shift in cancer care from a primarily inpatient to a primarily outpatient setting. Research on cancer caregiving is increasing. Several interventions have been developed (Bucher et al., 2001; Given et al., 2003; Northouse, 2005), but more translational research is needed. Social workers have the expertise and scope of practice to take leadership in this vital area.

ADDITIONAL RESOURCES

American Cancer Society: http://www.cancer.org/treatment/caregivers/index

Cancer Support Community: http://www.cancersupportcommunity.org

Cancer*Care*: http://www.cancercare.org/tagged/caregiving

National Cancer Institute: http://www.cancer.gov/cancertopics/coping/when-someone-you-love-is-treated/page1

U.S. Department of Labor—Family Medical Leave Act: http://www.dol.gov/whd/fmla/

REFERENCES

Borg, C., & Hallberg, I. R. (2006). Life satisfaction among informal caregivers in comparison with non-caregivers. *Scandinavian Journal of Caring Sciences*, *20*(4), 427–438. doi:10.1111/j.1471-6712.2006.00424.x)

Bucher, J. A., Loscalzo, M., Zabora, J., Houts, P. S., Hooker, C., & BrintzenhofSzoc, K. (2001). Problem-solving cancer care education for patients and caregivers. *Cancer Practice*, *9*(2), 66–70.

Carter, P. A., & Acton, G. J. (2006). Personality and coping: Predictors of depression and sleep problems among caregivers of individuals who have cancer. *Journal of Gerontological Nursing, 32*(2), 45–53.

Case, P. (2006). Social opportunity in the face of cancer: Understanding the burden of the extended caregiver network. *Illness, Crisis, and Loss, 14*(4), 299–318.

Charles, G., Stainton, T., & Marshall, S. (2012). *Young carers in Canada: The hidden costs and benefits of young caregiving.* Ottawa, Canada: Vanier Institute of the Family. Retrieved from http://www.vanierinstitute.ca/include/get.php?nodeid=2036&format=download

Creedle, C., Leak, A., Deal, A. M., Walton, A. M., Talbert, G., Riff, B., & Hornback, A. (2012). The impact of education on caregiver burden on two inpatient oncology units. *Journal of Cancer Education, 27,* 250–256. doi:10.1007/s13187-011-0302-3

Edwards, B., & Clarke, V. (2004). The psychological impact of a cancer diagnosis on families: The influence of family functioning and patients' illness characteristics on depression and anxiety. *Psycho-Oncology, 13*(8), 562–576.

Gaugler, J. E., Eppinger, A., King, J., Sandberg, T., & Regine, W. F. (2013). Coping and its effects on cancer caregiving. *Supportive Care in Cancer, 21,* 385–395. doi:10.1007/s00520-012-1525-5

Gilbar, O., & Ben-Zur, H. (2002). *Cancer and the family caregiver: Distress and coping.* Springfield, IL: Charles C. Thomas Publisher.

Given, B., Given, C. W., Kozachik, S., & Rawl, S. (2003). Family caregiving interventions in cancer care. In C. W. Given, B. Given, V. L. Champion, S. Kozachik, & D. N. DeVoss (Eds.), *Evidence-based cancer care and prevention: Behavioral interventions* (pp. 332–370). New York, NY: Springer Publishing Company.

Grimm, P. M., Zawacki, K. L., Mock, V., Krumm, S., & Frink, B. B. (2000). Caregiver responses and needs: An ambulatory bone marrow transplant model. *Cancer Practice, 8*(3), 120–128.

Harding, R., List, S., Epiphaniou, E., & Jones, H. (2011). How can informal caregivers in cancer and palliative care be supported? An updated systematic literature review of interventions and their effectiveness. *Palliative Medicine, 26*(1), 7–22.

Harpham, W. (1995). *After cancer: A guide to your new life.* New York, NY: Harper Perennial.

Institute of Medicine. (2008). *Cancer care for the whole patient: Meeting psychosocial health needs.* Washington, DC: National Academies Press.

Kim, Y., Kashy, D. A., Wellisch, D. K., Spillers, R. L., Kaw, C. K., & Smith, T. G. (2008). Quality of life of couples dealing with cancer: Dyadic and individual adjustment among breast and prostate cancer survivors and their spousal caregivers. *Annals of Behavioral Medicine, 35*(2), 230–238.

Kim, Y., & Schultz, R. (2008). Family caregivers' strains: Comparative analysis of cancer caregiving with dementia, diabetes, and frail elderly caregiving. *Journal of Aging and Health, 20*(5), 483–503.

Lauria, M. M., Clark, E. J., Hermann, J. F., & Stearns, N. M. (2001). *Social work in oncology: Supporting survivors, families, and caregivers.* Atlanta, GA: American Cancer Society.

Lethborg, C. E., Kissane, D., & Burns, W. I. (2003). "It's not the easy part": The experience of significant others of women with early stage breast cancer, at treatment completion. *Social Work in Health Care, 37*(1), 63–85.

Loscalzo, M., Kim, Y., & Clark, K. L. (2010). Gender and caregiving. In J. C. Holland, W. S. Breitbart, P. B. Jacobsen, M. S. Lederberg, M. J. Loscalzo, & R. McCorkle (Eds.), *Psycho-oncology* (2nd ed., pp. 522–526). New York, NY: Oxford University Press.

Matthews, B. A., Baker, F., & Spillers, R. L. (2003). Family caregivers and indicators of cancer-related distress. *Psychology, Health, and Medicine, 8*(1), 45–56.

Mellon, S., Northouse, L. L., & Weiss, L. K. (2006). A population-based study of the quality of life of cancer survivors and their family caregivers. *Cancer Nursing, 29,* 120–131.

Mosher, C. E., & Weiss, T. R. (2010). Psychosocial research and practice with adult children of cancer patients. In J. C. Holland, W. S. Breitbart, P. B. Jacobsen, M. S. Lederberg, M. J. Loscalzo, & R. McCorkle (Eds.), *Psycho-oncology* (2nd ed., pp. 532–535). New York, NY: Oxford University Press.

Northouse, L. L. (2005). Helping families of patients with cancer. *Oncology Nursing Forum, 32*(4), 743–750.

Oliver, D. (2013). When worlds collide: When research becomes reality. *Journal of Palliative Medicine, 16*(2), 208–210.

O'Mara, A. (2005). Who's taking care of the caregiver? *Journal of Clinical Oncology, 23*(28), 6820–6821.

Pitceathly, C., Maguire, P., Haddad, P., & Fletcher, I. (2004). Prevalence of and markers for affective disorders among cancer patients' caregivers. *Journal of Psychosocial Oncology, 22*(3), 45–68. doi:10.1300/J077v22n03•03

Regehr, C. (2011). Crisis theory and social work treatment. In F. J. Turner (Ed.), *Social work treatment: Interlocking theoretical approaches* (5th ed., pp. 134–143). New York, NY: Oxford University Press.

Rolland, J. S. (1988). A conceptual model of chronic and life-threatening illness and its impact on families. In C. S. Chilman, E. W. Nunnally, & F. M. Cox (Eds.), *Chronic illness and disability* (pp. 17–68). Thousand Oaks, CA: Sage Publications.

Schnipper, H. H. (2006). *After breast cancer: A common-sense guide to life after treatment.* New York, NY: Bantam Books.

Segrin, C., & Badger, T. (2010). Psychological distress in different social network members of breast and prostate cancer survivors. *Research in Nursing and Health, 33*(5), 450–464. doi:10.1002/nur.20394

Siskowski, C., Diac, N., Connors, L., & Mize, N. (2007). Recognition and assessment of caregiving youth, *Hospice and Home Healthcare, 25*(7), 433–438.

Siskowski, C. (2009). Adolescent caregivers. In K. Shifren (Ed.), *How caregiving affects development: Psychological implications for child, adolescent and adult caregivers* (pp. 65–91). Washington, DC: American Psychological Association.

Varner, A. (2012). Co-survivors, family and friends. In K. Miller (Ed.), *Excellent care for cancer survivors: A guide to fully meet their needs in medical offices and in the community* (pp. 155–161). Santa Barbara, CA: Praeger.

Waldrop, D., & Meeker, M. (2011). Crisis in caregiving: When home based end-of-life care is no longer possible. *Journal of Palliative Care, 27*(2), 117–125.

56

Karen Kayser and Jennifer L. Scott

Psychosocial Interventions With Couples Affected by Cancer

Key Concepts

- *Cancer patients and their spouses/partners often experience similar levels of stress when faced with a cancer diagnosis and treatment.*
- *The process of a couple managing stress together is called dyadic coping.*
- *Four interventions are described that have been found to enhance dyadic coping.*

Stress related to a cancer diagnosis and treatment can easily be felt by both the patient and an intimate partner, becoming a shared stress or a "we disease." As the stress is mutually experienced, each individual's response can influence the other person and the relationship as a whole. Hence, an interdependence of psychological adjustment to the illness develops. Cancer patients and partners often report similar reactions to a cancer diagnosis: feelings of hopelessness or depression, anxiety, fear, and uncertainty (Given, Sherwood, & Given, 2009; Meyerowitz & Oh, 2009; Resendes & McCorkle, 2006). The overall psychosocial adjustment to cancer can be similar for husbands and wives (McClure, Nezu, Nezu, O'Hea, & McMahon, 2012; Segrin, Badher, Dorros, Meek, & Lopez, 2007) and may continue throughout the illness trajectory (Northouse, Templin, & Mood, 2001; Song et al., 2011). However, although both the patient and his or her partner may share similar experiences across their cancer journey, they may not always know how to support each other emotionally and in a practical sense.

Just as the negative responses to cancer can be mutually experienced, positive responses can also be shared and contribute to effective coping. Correlations of quality of life (QOL) between prostate cancer patients and partners suggest that patients and partners manage the demands as a team (Song et al., 2011). What differentiates the couples who can transform the experience into positive growth from those who respond with despair, hopelessness, and fear? A simple answer suggests two fundamental requirements: (1) the quality of the couple's relationship before the cancer diagnosis and (2) how the couple copes together as a team.

The overall goal of a couple-based intervention is to enhance dyadic coping, that is, the couple's ability to cope together with the various cancer-related stresses. Dyadic coping is defined as a stress management process whereby partners either ignore or react to each other's stress signals to adapt to the cancer and return to a preillness level of well-being as individuals and as a couple (Bodenmann, 2005). This chapter first presents a framework for assessing dyadic coping and couples' adjustment to cancer and second describes four evidence-based techniques for enhancing couples' coping.

Psychosocial Assessment of Couples

Assessing the Couple's Adjustment to Cancer

During the initial assessment with the couple, the oncology social worker can begin to build an empathic relationship by asking general questions about their lives since the cancer diagnosis. This conversation enables the practitioner to observe how the partners communicate with and support each other emotionally when discussing cancer-related issues. Some partners may respond to each other with physical or verbal comforting (e.g., a hug or soothing words); in others, the partners may seem uncomfortable with the distress signs and may be reluctant to respond. The couple's behaviors help the clinician to generate hypotheses about the partners' strengths and weaknesses in their support of each other. During the assessment interview, each partner/spouse is asked questions and given the opportunity to express individual thoughts and feelings. Also, standardized self-report instruments can be useful tools in assessing close relationships and dyadic coping (see Table 56.1), and a genogram can be drawn with the couple to assess their social support network.

Assessing the Impact of Cancer on the Couple

1. *What is the most important change in your life as a couple since the diagnosis?*
2. *What things are you handling best as a couple?*
3. *What things are you handling less well?*
4. *I would like you to think about how well you, as a couple, are coping with the illness. We will use a scale ranging from 1, indicating poor coping, to 10, indicating very good coping. Before selecting a number, tell me how you would define a number 10. How do you know when you are coping very well? How do you know when you are not—namely, coping at a level of 1? Keeping in mind these end points of the coping scale, rate how well you as a couple are coping with the illness. (Circle their answers on the scale that follows.)*

Patient's Rating

|···|

1 2 3 4 5 6 7 8 9 10

poor *very well*

Partner's Rating

|···|

1 2 3 4 5 6 7 8 9 10

poor *very well*

5. *Is there anything positive for you as a couple that may have resulted from the cancer?*
6. *Have you as a couple experienced any other cancers or similar major illnesses (involving one of you or someone close to you)? If so, how do you think it has affected the way you think about and cope with your (your partner's) cancer? (Probe for whether they feel more or less prepared or more or less fearful.)*
7. *Sometimes people who are faced with a cancer diagnosis are dealing with other challenges in their lives, besides cancer. For some people, cancer is not the major source of stress. Other matters in life may be more demanding or cancer is just an added stress. Tell me, are there any other things you are managing or dealing with in your life? (Probe for other major caregiving roles, extreme financial difficulties, child behavior and parenting problems, or major interpersonal problems.)*

Gene (60 years old) and Marie (58 years old) are an African American couple married for 35 years. Marie was diagnosed with triple negative breast cancer (Stage 3) and was beginning chemotherapy at the time that the social worker met with her. Marie is the recreational director at a local assisted-living facility, and Gene has worked in hotel food service over the past 40 years. They have a son and daughter, both married with young children. The couple was referred to the social worker when Marie expressed concern to the chemotherapy nurse about her husband. She reported that it has not been easy for her husband to talk about his feelings and she didn't know how to interpret his silence. Her husband was willing to meet with the social worker "if it would help Marie."

During the initial appointment, Marie stated that the most stressful changes for her since the diagnosis were the loss of independence and fatigue. She had maintained her full-time work schedule until the side effects of her chemotherapy became so debilitating that she took leave from work. She spent more time at home and needed to rely on her daughter to grocery shop and cook meals. Gene's biggest concern was that Marie would die and he would be left alone. They thought that they were handling the medical decisions and appointments but, emotionally, were not dealing well with the illness. Gene was working overtime to make up for the loss of income from Marie's medical leave. Neither of them could see a "silver lining" in the dark cloud of the cancer.

When the social worker drew a genogram, she noted that Gene's family had cancer in the past. His father had died from lung cancer and he had two maternal aunts who died from breast cancer, as had Marie's grandmother. It was evident that Gene and Marie perceived a cancer diagnosis as life threatening. Although Gene and Marie were close to their daughter, their son had moved to another state and didn't visit often. Marie had an extensive social support network, with most of her six siblings living close by. Gene's network was much smaller, with neither of his two siblings living close to them. Both Gene and Marie were active in their church and socialized with several of the couples from their church community.

Table 56.1.
Standardized Instruments to Measure Relationship Factors

Dimension	Measures	Items	Source
Relationship satisfaction	Abbreviated Dyadic Adjustment Scale (ADAS)	4	Sabourin, Valois, and Lussier (2005)
	Relationship Assessment Scale (RAS)	7	Hendrick (1988)
Dyadic coping	Dyadic Coping Inventory (DCI) (English and German languages)	37	Bodenmann (2007)
Mutuality and emotional support	Mutual Psychological Development Questionnaire (MPDQ)	22	Genero, Miller, Surrey, and Baldwin (1992)
Satisfaction with support	Sarason's Social Support Questionnaire (short form)	6	Rascle, Bruchon-Schweitzer, & Sarason (2005)
Self-neglect and overinvolvement with others	Revised Unmitigated Communion Scale	9	Fritz and Helgeson (1998)
Silencing the self schema in intimate relationships	Silencing the Self Scale	31	Jack and Dill (1992)
Sexual concerns	InSYNC Questionnaire	12	Crowley et al. (n.d.)
Finding meaning or benefit from illness experience	Posttraumatic Growth Inventory	21	Tedeschi and Calhoun (1996)

Interventions to Enhance Couples' Coping With Cancer

In this section, we describe four interventions that focus on enhancing dyadic coping through (1) using problem-focused strategies to balance work, family, and self-care; (2) building cognitive coping skills in managing stressful situations; (3) communicating emotional support; and (4) addressing end-of-life issues. These techniques were derived from our treatment protocols for the Partners in Coping Program (PICP) and CanCOPE.[1]

Intervention 1: Assisting Couples With Work, Family, and Self-Care

When initially confronted with a cancer diagnosis, couples may attempt to carry on their work outside and inside the home as usual. But trying to incorporate numerous medical appointments, time to recover from surgery, and weeks of daily clinical visits can take its toll. Some couples and families automatically redistribute household work and tasks, whereas others make very little accommodation to the new situation. The additional demands that a partner's cancer treatment imposes on a couple's time and resources require collaboration to juggle the competing responsibilities of their relationship, family, and self-care. By collaborating, they can conserve their energy, engage their social support network, and use their time and resources effectively.

The social worker can assist a couple in determining how the work of the family is being shared and, if necessary, how to allocate new roles and responsibilities. It may become impossible for individuals to perform roles important to them. For example, the patient may be unable to work outside the home and find it difficult to keep up with household chores, and the partner may need to work more hours and may not have time to be as involved with child care. Ultimately, the couple will have to restructure how they get their work done.

To accomplish this, the social worker facilitates a discussion with the couple on how they plan to manage work of the family in a way that effectively spreads the tasks around to each member. On a large piece of paper or flipchart, the practitioner draws four columns with the headings "Tasks," "Primary Person" "Helper," and "Ideal." First, the couple generates a list of tasks that they are currently doing to keep the family and household going (e.g., cooking, household cleaning, transportation, repairs, yardwork, arranging social events, etc.); the social worker writes these in the first column. Second, for each task, the couple lists the person who is primarily responsible for the job in the column with the heading "Primary Person." If there is anyone who routinely helps with it, his or her name is written in the third column, "Helper." When the listing of tasks and columns two and three are complete, the couple evaluates the effectiveness and efficiency of the distribution of tasks. Next, they discuss the best way to handle the family tasks and if there is someone else who ideally should be responsible for the task. If disagreements emerge, the social worker helps the couple come to an agreement about what the distribution should ideally be to function most effectively. The clinician helps the couple negotiate differences, think about alternative solutions, and proceed with a problem-solving approach.

Finally, spouses may need to negotiate with their workplaces to free up the time needed to meet the demands of treatment and family work. Hence, the social worker can help them assess options in the workplace, such as paid medical leave, insurance benefits while on leave, family leave, and working at home. Spouses and partners are not always aware of the benefits that are available at the workplace, and these possibilities need to be explored.

Intervention 2: Building Cognitive Coping Skills

How individuals think about the challenges of cancer affects the way they cope with cancer and, ultimately, how they adjust. Negative thoughts of helplessness or blaming oneself can produce high distress in patients and their partners and affect social functioning (Northouse et al., 2001). In contrast, viewing stressful events in a positive way facilitates an acceptance of reality and helps in making meaning of the situation. The outcome is positive emotion and less distress (Folkman & Greer, 2000) and, ultimately, an improved adjustment to cancer (Lepore, Ragan, & Jones, 2000; Stanton, Danoff-Burg, & Huggins, 2002).

Through cognitive therapy techniques, the practitioner can teach couples to develop a shared cognitive approach to coping by fostering and reinforcing adaptive, cognitive coping strategies. This is accomplished through a series of techniques that assist the couple in understanding the stress response process, identifying unhelpful cognitions, challenging the validity of these thoughts, and replacing them with more helpful ones. By implementing the technique of restructuring in the context of a couple's session, the clinician teaches the partners how to support each other as they go through the process of challenging negative and unhelpful thoughts. The ultimate goal is engagement of more adaptive dyadic coping whereby the partners are not only using individual adaptive coping but also reinforcing each other's adaptive coping.

During the third session, the social worker noticed some tension between Gene and Marie. Marie was visibly upset and angry when she reported an incident during the previous week—Gene had forgotten to pick her up from home and she missed a very important follow-up treatment appointment. Marie expressed her anxiety about the appointment and her anger toward Gene's uncaring attitude. Gene sat silently and then proceeded to defend his forgetfulness by blaming her for not reminding him. The social worker did not allow the negative exchange to continue but turned their attention to the role of cognitions in responses to stressful situations. Using the Coping Self-Talk technique, the social worker facilitated Marie in identifying her unhelpful self-talk, such as jumping to conclusions that Gene was "uncaring" and "does not love me," and how these unhelpful thoughts produced a strong response to his behavior. The situation also elicited thoughts that she had about her own inadequacies as a wife (e.g., "I am not a good wife because I am sick all the time") and her increased dependence on others (e.g., "I am a burden on my family"). Gene explained how he had been so involved in work that he had lost sight of the time and forgot that he had to leave early to pick her up. He reassured Marie that his behavior had nothing to do with his care and love for her and had been his fault for not writing the appointment down. He also stated that taking care of her was not a burden but a rewarding experience and a way to reciprocate for all of the things that she had done for him over the years.

Intervention 3: Communicating Support

Enhancing communication between cancer patients and their partners is a critical task for the oncology social worker. A frequent remark made by patients and their partners is the reluctance to talk about the cancer for fear of upsetting the other. A conspiracy of silence persists as each person protects the other from experiencing further distress, getting upset, or burdening them with their own anxieties and fears. In part, this conspiracy continues because there is the uncertainty of knowing what to do or say that would be helpful to the person facing cancer. Even couples with good communication before the cancer may still find it difficult to broach this fear-provoking subject. Yet in our daily lives, verbal and nonverbal communications are the vehicles by which we demonstrate support, care, and concern and manage feelings during stressful situations.

British psychologists Pistrang and Barker (2005) studied the communication of couples coping with breast cancer with a procedure called "tape-assisted recall." The process of spouses communicating emotional support to each other is recorded and then followed by a discussion of what is or is not helpful in dealing with their stress. The process enables partners to explain to each other which communications are especially supportive and which are not helpful at all—thus teaching them how to elicit and respond with support. According to Pistrang and Barker (2005), tape-assisted recall examines partners' process of communication as it unfolds, from moment to moment, and also allows the couple to comment on their moment-by-moment perceptions of and reactions to their communication process. The aim is to determine if there is a matching of support provided by one partner with the perception of support received from the other partner.

Gene and Marie continued to work on their communication. Using the tape-assisted recall, Gene learned that his attempts to "fix" problems were not helpful to Marie. Marie gave him feedback that a more supportive response was to listen to her feelings rather than coming up with a solution for them. In a similar vein, Marie learned that jumping in to take care of Gene and protect him from feeling bad was not acknowledging how he felt and that she needed to allow him the space to express his feelings without being judgmental.

Intervention 4: Addressing End-of-Life Issues With a Couple

As expected, news that cancer has returned or is spreading can trigger a more intense emotional response than that experienced after the initial diagnosis. Many couples feel disappointed and anxious about the prospect of undergoing treatment again. However, when there are no more curative treatments available, the focus turns from curative to palliative or "comfort" care. Couples at this stage report a heightened need for communication, affection, and emotional support from their spouse/partner. In a life-threatening situation, there is a natural desire to seek solace and emotional support in one's close relationships. Nurturing relationships become a high priority, and interpersonal concerns at times exceed disease-related concerns such as pain and symptom management (McLean, Walton, Rodin, Esplen, & Jones, 2011). A cancer patient and his or her partner may want to discuss making funeral arrangements, writing a will, saying good-byes, resolving relationship conflicts, and addressing concerns about how their children will adjust to impending bereavement. These are sensitive and emotional issues that can be difficult to broach and discuss—even with one's intimate partner. Couples who feel particularly anxious about these issues may choose to avoid them; this avoidance may lead to even greater distress during the terminal phase of the illness.

Although the terminal phase of the illness can be emotionally difficult for partners, this degree of difficulty is closely tied to the physical well-being of the patient. As physical functioning declines, caregiver demands increase as the partner takes on more caregiving responsibilities and perhaps a more complex or demanding regimen that needs to be incorporated into household routines.

The objectives of interventions for couples during the end-of-life phase focus on helping them (1) communicate their emotions/feelings and manage any intrusive unhelpful thoughts and (2) keep important activities in their lives for as long as they are physically capable. Mindfulness-based cognitive therapy (MBCT) is a helpful approach in managing intrusive thoughts and feelings. The MBCT approach encourages the person to let his or her fears or worries come and go. Rather than actively trying to change or fight them, a better way to manage them might be to recognize that they are just thoughts, they do not have power, and they do not deserve special attention (Kayser & Scott, 2008).

Helping couples find ways to keep important activities in their lives for as long as they are physically capable is also important at this phase of the cancer journey. The clinician can help them discuss how to pace activities and match their activity to the times of the day when their energy levels are best or when the pain is relatively low. For example, being able to sit at a dinner table to eat may signify to the patient that he or she is still capable of some independence and be a source of self-esteem. For the caregiver, this activity might signify a sense of normality in his or her life, which otherwise feels overwhelmed with unfamiliar routines, such as nursing and caregiving activities. For many couples, planning activities is a balancing act between striving for goals and knowing when to accept that goals are now unattainable. It can be hard to know when to let go of them and move on. Helping couples find this balance is challenging, but one solution is to redefine the scale and scope of the activities that they are striving to maintain.

At their last session, Gene and Marie reviewed their cancer journey and how they had to change as a couple to respond to the various challenges of the treatment. In their first session, they could not identify anything positive about the cancer diagnosis, but now they talked about how coping with cancer together had brought them closer. By trusting each other with their personal vulnerabilities and honest disclosures of feelings, they experienced a deeper level of intimacy and appreciation for each other. The social worker discussed with them their priorities in their relationship and what activities they would like to continue to maintain.

Although Marie's cancer was in remission, she and Gene still had worries of a reoccurrence. The social worker taught them the MBCT technique to deal with their concerns, which emphasizes acceptance that they are normal, not fighting them, and allowing them to come and go. Attending sessions together enabled Gene and Marie to reinforce each other's positive coping skills.

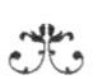

Pearls

- Use an evidence-based protocol to guide your practice. Examples include CanCOPE (Scott, Halford, & Ward, 2004), Partners in Coping (Kayser, Feldman, Borstelmann, & Daniels, 2010), and CanThrive (Baucom et al., 2009).
- Cultural factors, such as beliefs, values, and expectations regarding intimate relationships and gender roles, will influence how couples interact.
- Help spouses/partners accept and relate constructively to each other's different ways of coping.
- Be mindful to address both partners' cognitions about cancer and coping. Some thoughts are deeply held and originate from past life experiences in the family of origin.

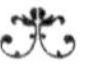

Pitfalls

- Expecting that you can repair a couple's relationship that has long-standing distress and/or disaffection. Referral of couples to an experienced couple's therapist can complement the oncology social worker's work as the couple copes with cancer.
- Assuming that older couples are not amenable or interested in couples work.
- Not offering help to same-sex couples. Gay or lesbian partners of cancer patients often feel excluded by the medical system, yet they play a critically supportive role for cancer patients.

Cancer patients and their intimate partners can mutually experience cancer-related stress so that the cancer becomes a "we stress." However, facing the stress together and coping as a dyad can empower both individuals to transform the difficult challenges into a growth-enhancing journey. Hence, oncology social workers must involve partners in their care plans from diagnosis throughout the disease trajectory. Working with couples can be challenging for the practitioner, but the benefits can be tremendous as two people pull together their resources to deal with the consequences of a potentially life-threatening disease. It is gratifying to the practitioner who witnesses the transformation and growth of the individual partners and the relationship as they learn to cope together with the cancer experience.

NOTE

1. More details about these techniques and other techniques for working with couples can be found in our book, *Helping Couples Cope With Women's Cancers: An Evidence-Based Approach for Practitioners* (Kayser & Scott, 2008).

REFERENCES

Baucom, D. H., Porter, L. S., Kirby, J. S., Gremore, T. M., Wiesenthal, N., Aldridge, W.,... Keefe, F. J. (2009). A couple-based intervention for female breast cancer: Randomized controlled trial, *Psycho-Oncology, 18*(3), 276–283. doi:10.1002/pon.1395

Bodenmann, G. (2005). Dyadic coping and its significance for marital functioning. In T. A. Revenson, K. Kayser, & G. Bodenmann (Eds.), *Couples coping with stress: Emerging perspectives on dyadic coping* (pp. 33–50). Washington, DC: American Psychological Association.

Bodenmann, G. (2007). *Dyadic Coping Inventory (DCI). Test manual*. Bern, Switzerland & Göttingen, Germany: Huber & Hogrefe.

Crowley, S. A., Foley, S. M., Wittmann, D., Jagielski, K., Dunn, R. L., Peterson, K.,... Janz, N. K. (n.d.). *Sexual health concerns among survivors of breast and prostate cancer*. Unpublished paper.

Folkman, S., & Greer, S. (2000). Promoting psychological well-being in the face of serious illness when theory, research, and practice inform each other. *Psycho-Oncology, 9*, 11–19.

Fritz, H. L., & Helgeson, V. S. (1998). Distinctions of unmitigated communion from communion: Self-neglect and overinvolvement with others. *Journal of Personality and Social Psychology, 75*, 121–140.

Genero, N. P., Miller, J. B., Surrey, J., & Baldwin, L. (1992). Measuring perceived mutuality in close relationships: Validation of the mutual psychological development questionnaire. *Journal of Family Psychology, 6*(1), 36–48.

Given, B., Sherwood, P., & Given, C. (2009). Family care during cancer care. In S. Miller (Ed.), *Handbook of cancer control and behavioral science: A resource for researchers, practitioners, and policymakers* (pp. 391–408). Washington, DC: American Psychological Association.

Hendrick, S. S. (1988). A generic measure of relationship satisfaction. *Journal of Marriage and Family, 50*, 93–98.

Jack, D. C., & Dill, D. (1992). The Silencing the Self Scale: Schemas of intimacy associated with depression in women. *Psychology of Women Quarterly, 16*(1), 97–106.

Kayser, K., Feldman, B. N., Borstelmann, N. A., & Daniels, A. (2010). The effects of a randomized couple-based intervention on the quality of life of breast cancer patients and their partners. *Journal of Social Work Research, 34*(1), 20–32.

Kayser, K., & Scott, J. L. (2008). *Helping couples cope with women's cancers: An evidence-based approach for practitioners*. New York, NY: Springer.

Lepore, S. J., Ragan, J. D., & Jones, S. (2000). Talking facilitates cognitive-emotional processes of adaptation to an acute stressor. *Journal of Personality and Social Psychology, 78*(3), 499–508.

McClure, K. S., Nezu, A. M., Nezu, C. M., O'Hea, E. L., & McMahon, C. (2012). Social problem solving and depression in couples coping with caner. *Psycho-Oncology, 21*(1), 11–19. doi:10.1002/pon.1856

McLean, L. M., Walton, T., Rodin, G., Esplen, M. J., & Jones, J. M. (2011). A couple-based intervention for patients and caregivers facing end-stage cancer: Outcomes of a randomized controlled trial. *Psycho-Oncology, 22*(1), 28–38. doi:10.1002/pon.2046

Meyerowitz, B. E., & Oh, S. (2009). Psychosocial response to cancer diagnosis and treatment. In S. Miller (Ed.), *Handbook of cancer control and behavioral science: A resource for researchers, practitioners, and policymakers* (pp. 361–389). Washington, DC: American Psychological Association.

Northouse, L., Templin, T., & Mood, D. (2001). Couples' adjustment to breast disease during the first year following diagnosis. [Research Support, U.S. Gov't, P.H.S.]. *Journal of Behavioral Medicine, 24*(2), 115–136. doi:10.1023/A:1010772913717

Pistrang, N., & Barker, C. (2005). How partners talk in times of stress: A process analysis approach. In T. A. Revenson, K. Kayser, & G. Bodenmann (Eds.), *Couples coping with stress: Emerging perspectives on dyadic coping* (pp. 97–120). Washington, DC: American Psychological Association.

Rascle, N., Bruchon-Schweitzer, M., & Sarason, I. G. (2005). Sarason's social support questionnaire—short form. *Psychological Reports, 97*(1), 195–202.

Resendes, L. A., & McCorkle, R. (2006). Spousal responses to prostate cancer: An integrative review. *Cancer Investigation, 24*(2), 192–198. doi:10.1080/07357900500524652

Sabourin, S., Valois, P., & Lussier, Y. (2005). Development and validation of a brief version of the dyadic adjustment scale with a nonparametric item analysis model. *Psychological Assessment, 17*(1), 15–27.

Scott, J. L., Halford, W. K., & Ward, B. G. (2004). United we stand? The effects of a couple-coping intervention on adjustment to early stage breast or gynecological cancer. *Journal of Consulting and Clinical Psychology, 72*, 1122–1135.

Segrin, C., Badger, T., Dorros, S. M., Meek, P., & Lopez, A. M. (2007). Interdependent anxiety and psychological distress in women with breast cancer and their partners. *Psycho-Oncology, 16*(7), 634–643. doi:10.1002/pon.1111

Song, L., Northouse, L. L., Braun, T. M., Zhang, L., Cimprich, B., Ronis, D. L., & Mood, D. W. (2011). Assessing longitudinal quality of life in prostate cancer patients and their spouses: A multilevel modeling approach, *Quality Life Research, 20*, 371–381. doi:10.1007/s11136-010-9753-y

Stanton, A. L., Danoff-Burg, S., & Huggins, M. E. (2002). The first year after breast cancer diagnosis: Hope and coping strategies as predictors of adjustment. *Psycho-Oncology, 11*(2), 93–102.

Tedeschi, R. G., & Calhoun, L. G. (1996). The posttraumatic growth inventory: Measuring the positive legacy of trauma. *Journal of Traumatic Stress, 9*, 455–471.

57

Betty J. Kramer and Amy Z. Boelk

Managing Family Conflict: Providing Responsive Family Care at the End of Life

Key Concepts

- *A cancer diagnosis and the trajectory of illness and treatment often pose substantial challenges to family communication and functioning.*
- *Family conflict is not uncommon at the end of life, and a growing body of evidence helps illuminate understanding of the nature, causes, and consequences of family conflict.*
- *Oncology and palliative care social workers should seek to understand the myriad factors that contribute to the development of conflict, become skillful at determining when professional intervention is indicated, and utilize and test interventions to prevent, ameliorate, manage, or resolve conflict as appropriate.*

> *It seems that families that are in conflict rise to the top. They are the families that nurses are having the most concerns about and they're getting called there frequently. They're the ones that are going to come to a social worker's attention because they're kind of the "problem children." Usually, a family conflict has been long growing. It is not a new problem, but we need to be able to work within that system.*
>
> —*Hospice social worker*

The effect of a cancer diagnosis on family communication and functioning is striking, with one study indicating that 65% of families living with a lung cancer diagnosis reported communication problems. Communication problems also often increase as cancer progresses (Zhang & Siminoff, 2003), with illness severity being a predictor of higher levels of family strain (Sales, Schulz, & Biegel, 1992). At the end of life, family conflict is not uncommon and has been found among 35% to 57% of families studied (Boelk & Kramer, 2012; Kramer, Kavanaugh, Trentham-Dietz, Walsh, & Yonker, 2010b).

Several trends may contribute to family conflict at the end of life. The increasing emphasis on home care for patients with complex illnesses and high symptom burden has resulted in consistent reports by family caregivers of feeling unprepared for the intense demands associated with caregiving at home and the emotional impact of the dying process (National Alliance for Caregiving, 2003). In addition, smaller family size and geographic dispersion of family members also intensify demands facing family caregivers who may be involved in managing pain and symptoms; coordinating care; personal caregiving, including bathing, feeding, and toileting; and end-of-life decision making while balancing multiple other life responsibilities (Waldrop & Meeker, 2011). Finally, families are forced to navigate health care systems fraught with deficiencies, including poor provider communication, inadequate pain and symptom management, fragmented service delivery, and insufficient training to meet the emotional and support needs of the family caregiver (SUPPORT Principal Investigators, 1995).

Family conflict directly influences patient and caregiver well-being (Tilden, Tolle, Drach, & Perrin, 2004). For example, cancer treatment–related side effects (i.e., nausea) are related to the degree of conflict in the family (Kim & Morrow, 2003). When family relationships are conflicted at the end of life, it is very difficult to feel any sense of ease or peace, and bereaved survivors experience a more complicated grief response (Kramer et al., 2010a). To ensure the provision of good clinical care of patients and families, oncology social workers must understand the factors that contribute to family conflict at the end of life and equip themselves with the knowledge and skills to effectively and compassionately respond to, prevent, ameliorate, or manage conflict. This chapter reviews what we know about the nature, causes, and consequences of family conflict at the end of life and discusses implications for a family-centered approach to conflict prevention and management.

The Nature, Causes, and Consequences of Family Conflict at the End of Life

I worked with a patient in his late 40s who was dying of cancer. He was divorced and living with his brother, and he had custody of a teenage daughter. This family had long-standing conflict.... The brother was a police officer and the patient had ongoing problems with alcohol and drugs. The brother had spent years and years trying to clean the patient up. And now here we are at the end of his life and the brother is trying to care for him and is struggling with "He brought this on himself, but he's my little brother. I love him. How am I going to take care of him? And now I'm telling him what to do again and he's still telling me, 'go beat off.'" And

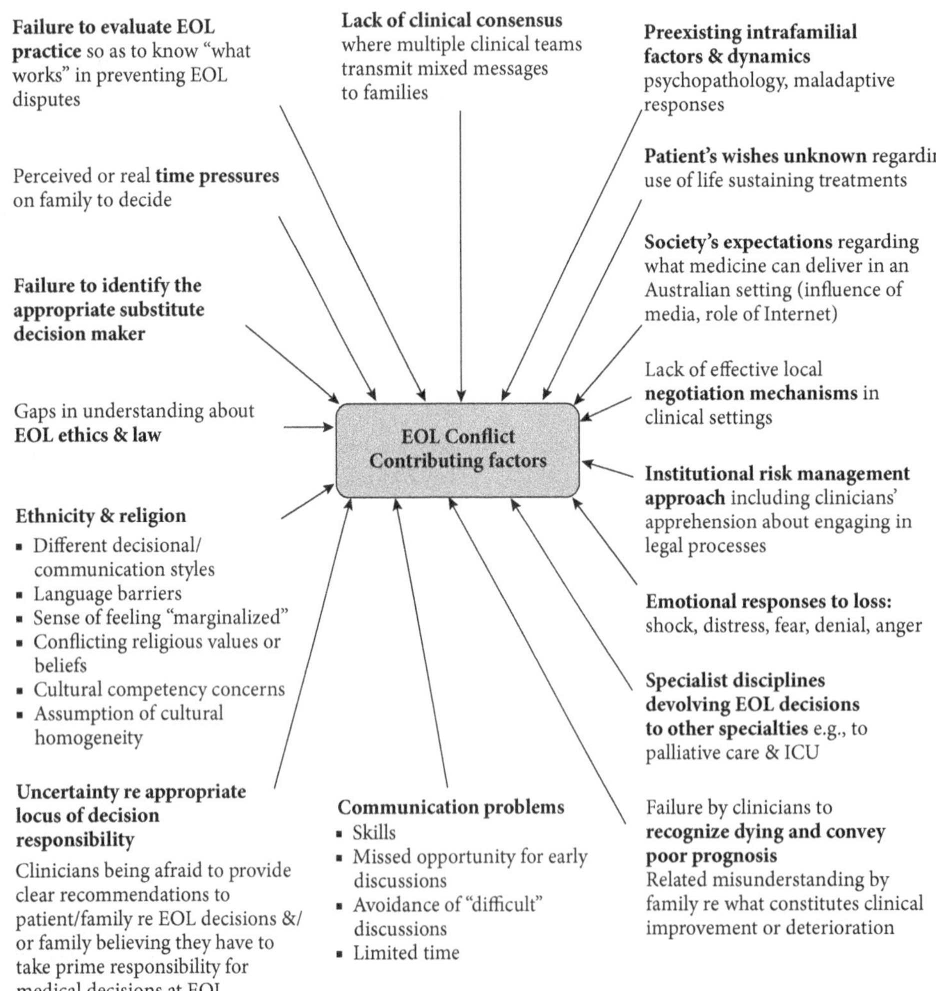

Figure 57.1. Factors Contributing to End-of-Life Conflicts
Reproduced with permission from CRELS Working Group (2010).

> *then there was the dynamic with the daughter, who did not have a great relationship with her dad and did not respect her uncle's authority. So, there were some very tense dynamics that we as a hospice organization had to insert ourselves into and figure it all out in a fairly short amount of time to allow our goal, which was a peaceful death at home.*
>
> *—Hospice social worker*

Concerned with several high-profile court cases illustrating the horrific consequences of family conflict for patients, and wishing to develop consensus on how to provide shared decision making for end-of-life care, a multidisciplinary work group in Australia initiated *Conflict Resolution in End of Life Settings (CRELS)*. This project was developed to illuminate the factors contributing to end-of-life conflicts and develop recommendations for improving decision making in health care settings (CRELS Working Group, 2010). As shown in Figure 57.1, the group identified a broad range of factors outside the family that contribute to end-of-life conflict, including societal expectations and norms, communication problems, failure to evaluate end-of-life practices and recognize dying, preexisting family dynamics, time pressures, cultural issues, and gaps in understanding legal and ethical issues.

A series of studies have illuminated understanding of the nature of, causes of, and contributing factors to end-of-life conflict within the family (Boelk & Kramer, 2012; Kramer et al., 2010b). An explanatory matrix of family conflict that was developed, expanded, and refined in one study (Boelk & Kramer, 2012) is particularly useful for understanding myriad factors that put families most at risk. Figure 57.2 highlights the contextual elements, conditions, contributing factors, and consequences of the phenomenon of family conflict that were identified.

The family context domain provides valuable insights for assessment considerations and identification of families at risk for conflict, and the conditions and contributing factors may be targets for preventive and intervention efforts.

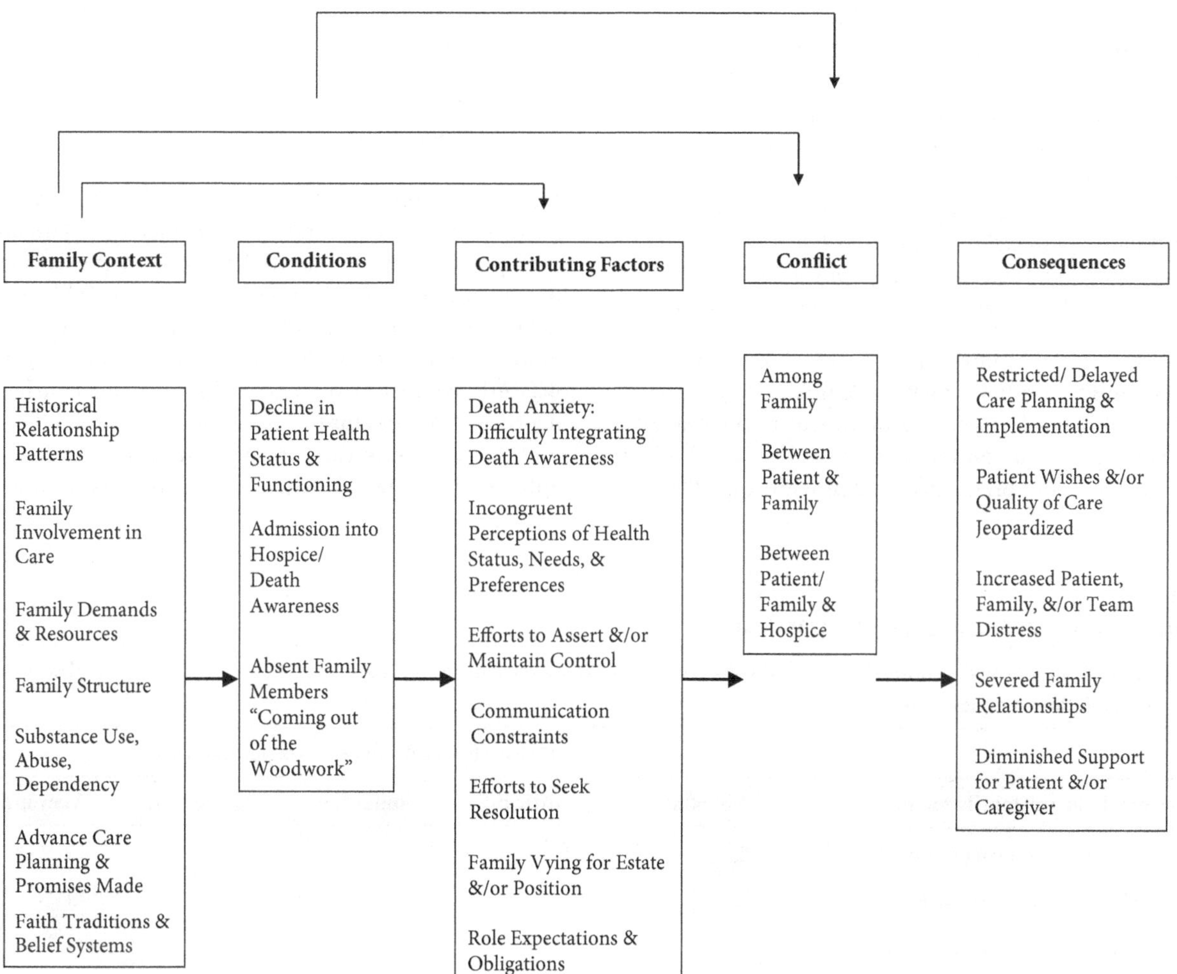

Figure 57.2. Explanatory Matrix of Family Conflict at the End-of-Life
Reproduced with permission from Boelk and Kramer (2012).

Study findings revealed that the nature of conflict reported by family members included a broad spectrum of topics, including caregiving; family roles, responsibilities, and level of involvement; communication; coping; the nature of the patient's condition; program enrollment decisions; where the patient should reside and receive care; finance and estate matters; postdeath decisions; spirituality; and the use of various treatments, procedures, medications, and life-sustaining measures (Boelk & Kramer, 2012). The profoundly negative consequences that may result for the patient, caregiver, and professionals included diminished support, increased stress, and sometimes permanently severed family relationships. Quantitative studies have validated some of these consequences. For example, as mentioned previously, family conflict was a predictor of complicated grief symptoms among bereaved caregivers of persons with lung cancer, diminishing the degree to which professionals felt they were able to successfully address end-of-life needs of low-income elders with advanced chronic disease (Kramer & Yonker, 2011).

Implications for a Family-Centered Approach

> *A complete understanding of the patient's personhood must consider the social network that helps define the patient's core identity.... An ethic of accommodation emphasizes the need to negotiate care plans that do not compromise patients' basic interests but that recognize the capacities and limitations of family members*
>
> *—Levine and Zuckerman (1999, pp. 148–149)*

Professionals often report feeling ill prepared to effectively address family conflict (Back & Arnold, 2005; King & Quill, 2006), identifying it as a detriment to their success in addressing patient and family needs and as a major barrier to talking about preferences and providing quality care (Kayashima & Braun, 2001). How professionals most appropriately address or respond to family conflict at the end of life may be determined by the nature and timing of conflict and the overriding goals of intervention. In some instances, conflict may be anticipated and prevented, whereas in others, existing conflict may actually be resolved. In some situations, conflict may not be amenable to change, and as such, conflict management strategies may be most appropriate.

Conflict Prevention

Professionals may be reluctant to implement measures to prevent conflict due to time constraints, large caseloads, administrative responsibilities, and short lengths of time to serve families in their programs. Given that family conflict is likely to delay care planning, jeopardize care, and require a great deal of attention (Boelk & Kramer, 2012; Kramer, Boelk, & Auer, 2006), integrating preventive efforts may actually save time in the long term and prevent large amounts of distress for patients, family members, and professionals. Four promising strategies relevant to prevention of conflict are highlighted here.

Routine Assessment

Routine screening for family functioning in a variety of health care settings should be considered a standard for good practice and is essential to conflict prevention and management (Boelk & Kramer, 2012; Kissane & Bloch, 2002; Lichtenthal & Kissane, 2008). Many strategies to assess for family conflict exist, which include the explanatory matrix of family conflict at the end of life described earlier that identifies risk areas for the assessment protocol. Likewise, a modified version of the Family Relationships Index (originally developed by Moos & Moos [1981]) has been used to

Table 57.1.
Family Conflict at the End-of-Life (FC-EOL) Scale

As you think about the decisions that you and your family are facing regarding your care (or the care of ________), please answer the following questions:

	Please check one answer box per question				
How much do any family members...	**Not at all**	**A little bit**	**Somewhat**	**Quite a bit**	**Very much**
a. Disagree or argue with one another?	☐	☐	☐	☐	☐
b. Feel resentment toward one another?	☐	☐	☐	☐	☐
c. Feel anger toward one another?	☐	☐	☐	☐	☐
d. Insult or yell at one another?	☐	☐	☐	☐	☐

Developed by Kramer et al. (2006).

Table 57.2.
Family Conference Process Steps

1. **Why are you meeting?**
   Clarify conference goals in your own mind. What do you hope to accomplish?
2. **Where?**
   A room with comfort, privacy, and circular seating.
3. **Who?**
   Patient (if capable of participating); legal decision maker/health care power of attorney; family members; social support; key health care professionals.
4. **Introduction and relationship building**
   - Introduce self and others; review meeting goals; clarify if specific decisions need to be made.
   - Establish ground rules: Each person will have a chance to ask questions and express views; no interruptions; identify legal decision maker; describe importance of supportive decision making.
   - If you are new to the patient/family, spend time seeking to get to know the "person"—ask about hobbies, family, etc.
5. **Determining what the patient/family already knows**
   "Tell me your understanding of the current medical condition." Ask everyone in the room to speak. Also ask about the past 1–6 months—what has changed in terms of functional decline, weight loss, etc.?
6. **Reviewing medical status**
   - Review current status, prognosis, and treatment options.
   - Ask all family members in turn if they have any questions about current status, plan, and prognosis.
   - Defer discussion of decision making until the next step.
   - Respond to emotional reactions.
7. **Family discussion with decisional patient**
   - Ask patient: "What decision(s) are you considering?"
   - Ask each family member: "Do you have questions or concerns about the treatment plan? How can you support the patient?"
8. **Family discussion with nondecisional patient**
   - Ask each family member in turn: "What do you believe the patient would choose if he or she could speak for him- or herself?"
   - Ask each family member: "What do you think should be done?"
   - Ask the family: "Would you like me to leave the room and let you discuss things alone?"
   - If there is consensus, go to 10; if no consensus, go to 9.
9. **When there is no consensus**
   - Re-state goal: "What would the patient say if he or she could speak?"
   - Use time as ally: Schedule a follow-up conference the next day.
   - Try further discussion: "What values is your decision based on? How will the decision affect you and other family members?"
   - Identify other resources: minister/priest; other physicians; ethics committee.
10. **Wrap-up**
    - Summarize consensus, disagreements, decisions, and plan.
    - Caution against unexpected outcomes.
    - Identify family spokesperson for ongoing communication.

Document in the chart who was present, what decisions were made, and the follow-up plan.
From Ambuel and Weissman (2005).

successfully screen at-risk families and to identify those more likely to benefit from intervention, as has the index and scoring rubric found in the text titled *Family Focused Grief Therapy* (Kissane & Bloch, 2002). Here, sample items include "Family members often keep their feelings to themselves," "We fight a lot in our family," and "Family members rarely become openly angry." Additionally, the following open-ended questions might also provide a basis for discussion of conflict: "How are big decisions made in your family?" "Who takes the lead in decision making?" and "We all want what is best for (patient), but it is natural to have some areas of agreement/disagreement as to what should be done. What things do you all agree should be done? Should not be done?" (King & Quill, 2006). Finally, quick assessment tools have also been cited as having the potential to guide meaningful and effective intervention when time is short (Waldrop & Rinfrette, 2009). The Family Conflict at the End of Life (FC-EOL) scale, developed by Kramer in 2006, is one such brief measure found to have strong internal consistency (Kramer et al., 2010a) that could be readily integrated into the assessment protocol (see Table 57.1).

Encourage and Facilitate Advance Planning

Promoting advance care planning may reduce the potential for conflict and stress in families facing difficult decisions at the end of life (Tilden et al., 2004). Rather than rely solely on the completion of documents, social workers should give greater attention to the "emotional preparation of patients and families for future crises" (Perkins, 2007, p. 51). Conversations about care preferences, how caregiving will occur, and the designation of a spokesperson may ward off contributing factors to conflict such as communication constraints, uncertainty about patient wishes and care provision, and family members vying for control. Several models, such as Respecting Choices (see http://www.gundersenhealth.org/respecting-choices), exist to prepare professionals to help families engage in these important conversations.

Facilitate Family Conferences

The use of family conferencing as a preventive and responsive measure to address family conflict has gained recognition (Lichtenthal & Kissane, 2008; Miller, Kretch, & Walsh, 1991) and has a strong evidence base for preventing and managing conflict (CRELS Working Group, 2010). Family conferences must be approached with care, because they can potentially spur conflict due to information gaps, heightened emotions, difficult family or team dynamics, or a strained patient–clinician relationship (Weissman, Quill, & Arnold, 2010). When planned well and handled skillfully, family conferences promote shared decision making, family cohesion and mutual support, open communication, and increased knowledge of the medical situation and its implications (Miller et al., 1991). They also encourage active participation in care planning (Hansen, Cornish, & Kayser, 1998) and provide a mechanism to address issues like advance planning, ethical issues, care goals, pain and symptom management, spirituality, concerns and fears about dying, decisions about life-sustaining measures, and feelings of loss and grief (Miller et al., 1991). Essential resources for conducting family conferences include a research-based theoretical model for family conferencing with families facing life-threatening illness (Fineberg, Kawashima, & Asch, 2011); a step-by step approach for moderating end-of-life conferences, which is provided in Table 57.2 (Ambuel & Weissman, 2005); and clinical practice guidelines for family meetings in palliative care (Hudson, Quinn, O'Hanlon, & Aranda, 2008).

Normalize Illness and Death in Our Society

Generating comfort with issues surrounding death and dying may go a long way in preventing family conflict that occurs as a result of death anxiety, communication constraints, and different ideas about the use of treatments and life-sustaining measures. When health care professionals fuel perceptions that death can be avoided, people are unprepared when contrary situations arise. Efforts aiming to normalize and promote death awareness in our society, coordinate earlier referral to hospice, and address family needs throughout the continuum of care are needed to provide a context in which prevention of family conflict can take place.

Conflict Management and Resolution

> *Family feuds arise when... tension that accompanies unresolved conflicts continues to mount, resulting in a volcano of feeling. This... emotional intensity is so strong that it's palpable. With such a strong feeling of incompleteness comes an urgent need to bring hidden issues to a climax.... When small clashes don't get resolved, and resentments become stronger and more entrenched, the people involved are left with deep emotional wounds that leave them in a state of suspended tension. Lingering hurt or anger has the potential to erupt at any moment, under nearly any circumstance*
>
> —*Heilveil (1998, p. 13)*

Oncology and palliative care social workers are often relied upon to optimize family functioning and manage conflicts that arise at the end of life. Although professional responses to family conflict have been promoted (Back & Arnold, 2005; Levine & Zuckerman, 1999), the efficacy of these approaches remain untested. Practical recommendations for conflict management and resolution put forth for end-of-life professionals (CRELS Working Group, 2010; Holst, Lundgren, Olsen, & Ishøy, 2009; Kendall & Arnold, 2007a, 2007b; Lichtenthal & Kissane, 2008) have utility for social workers in various settings. Table 57.3 highlights Arresødal Hospice's Principles of Management of Intra-Familial Conflicts (Holst et al., 2009), which are consistent with the aforementioned practical recommendations.

"Principled Negotiation," an "interest-based" approach for negotiating agreements, may support the mediation process employed by social workers and is guided by four primary principles: (1) separate the people (i.e., relationship issues) from the problem (i.e., substantive problems), (2) focus on interests, not positions (i.e., the interests both parties may share rather than their differences), (3) invent solutions (i.e., brainstorming), and (4) outline objective criteria (i.e., scientific findings to support course of action, legal precedent, and outside recommendations; Fisher & Ury,

Table 57.3.
Arresødal Hospice's Principles of Management of Intra-Familial Conflicts

Principle	Suggestions
Maintain the palliative perspective	Consider the possibility and implementation of palliative management strategies in certain subtypes of family dysfunction and (if favorable circumstances allow), to extend beyond this, incorporating a more long-term outlook for future rehabilitation of the surviving relatives.
Maintain flexibility	Take into account the strengths, psychological resources, level of intellect, and emotional state of conflicting family members before deciding whether to use interpretive or supportive techniques. Be prepared to reflect on strategies that have not been optimal and modify as necessary.
Maintain neutrality, transparency, and professionalism	Current information for all staff members involved through mono- or multidisciplinary meetings is essential. It is important to handle conflicting family dynamics in an open, transparent, and professional way; not to be unexpectedly absorbed as an active part of the conflict; and avoid covert behaviors. The principle of neutrality applies to this strategy in that involvement in long-term prior conflicts is to be avoided.
Avoid splitting	Avoid, or at least identify and understand, splitting between staff members by recognizing that the families with conflicting dynamics may display completely opposing attitudes within short periods of time, which can be challenging to staff. In the worst-case scenarios, relatives in conflict may project their issues onto others as a way to control fragmented or distressed parts of themselves.
Avoid demonizing	Encourage and enable staff to share awkward, challenging, and/or negative feelings brought on by sudden or inadvertent involvement in conflicting family dynamics.
Set necessary limits	Limits need to be identified and maintained consistently if behaviors of family members threaten the integrity or safety of the patient, other relatives, staff, or the palliative-therapeutic relationship.
Intervention	Encourage staff members to maintain the professional/personal balance through multidisciplinary discussions, counseling, and prompt debriefing.

Reproduced with permission from Holst, Lundgren, Olsen, and Ishøy (2009, p. 40).

1983). This process and supporting principles provide guidance to social workers striving to diffuse family conflict.

Family conferences, previously discussed under "Conflict Prevention," may provide a forum for managing and helping resolve conflicts, and ethics consultations may help address difficult conflicts that revolve around the use of futile medical treatments (Schneiderman et al., 2003). Another promising intervention, the Family Focused Grief Therapy (FFGT) model, is a proactive multisession therapy approach aimed to enhance family functioning in care at the end of life, reduce bereavement morbidity, and promote cohesion, effective communication, and

Table 57.4.
Practical Elements of the Family Focused Grief Therapy Model

- Build rapport with each family member to create a therapeutic alliance.
- Elicit concerns.
- Acknowledge and foster family strengths.
- Focus first on improving teamwork and communication, and then target conflict.
- Remain neutral.
- Reframe by shifting attention away from content of arguments to underlying meaning (i.e., why they feel so heated, what the difference represents).
- Pose questions that invite reflection and curiosity.
- Invite storytelling.
- Generate hypotheses about family dynamics related to cohesiveness, expressiveness, and conflict resolution.
- Summarize hypotheses for consideration and modification.

From Kissane and Bloch (2002).

adaptive resolution of conflict (Kissane & Bloch, 2002). This model may also be viewed as preventive in that families at risk for poor functioning are targeted for intervention; however, conflict management strategies are used over the course of treatment, which may begin during palliative care and continue into bereavement. Table 57.4 summarizes essential practical elements of this model that might be applied across care settings, though clinicians may benefit most from review of the model in its entirety (Kissane & Bloch, 2002).

Family conflict is common at the end of life. Rather than view families in conflict as "problematic," social workers must understand the deep suffering that is likely experienced by those involved. Oncology and palliative care social workers should seek to understand the myriad micro-, mezzo-, and macro-level factors that contribute to the development of conflict; become skillful at determining when professional intervention is or is not indicated; and utilize and test interventions to prevent, ameliorate, manage, or resolve conflict as appropriate. Social workers possess unique foundational skills to work with conflicted families and have opportunities to make distinctive contributions to the advancement of practice in this important yet understudied area. The approaches put forth in this chapter may better equip social workers to respond to family conflict with increasing levels of compassion, wisdom, and confidence.

Pearls

- Implementing preventative measures such as assessment to identify families at risk, facilitating advance care planning conversations, and holding routine family meetings for "at risk" families, may save professionals time and resources in the long run and reduce distress experienced by patients, family members, and professionals.
- Training in basic conflict management strategies may allow the social worker to respond to families in conflict with more skill and confidence.

Pitfalls

- Failing to understand the contextual and contributing factors of family conflict will limit the social worker's capacity to identify families at risk who are in most need of support and intervention.
- Not all conflicts are amenable to change; however, viewing all conflicts as problematic will foster a "hands off" or avoidant approach, when learning, growth, and healing at the end of life may be possible for the patient and family.

REFERENCES

Ambuel, B., & Weissman, D. E. (2005, August). *Fast facts and concepts #16: Moderating an end-of-life family conference* (2nd ed.). Retrieved from http://www.aging.pitt.edu/professionals/resources-polst/Fast-Fact-16-Family-Conf-2005.pdf

Back, A. L., & Arnold, R. M. (2005). Dealing with conflict in caring for the seriously ill: It was just out of the question. *Journal of the American Medical Association*, *293*(11), 1374–1381.

Boelk, A. Z., & Kramer, B. J. (2012). Advancing theory of family conflict at the end of life: A hospice case study. *Journal of Pain and Symptom Management*, *44*, 655–670.

CRELS Working Group. (2010). *Conflict Resolution in End of Life Settings (CRELS)*. North Sydney, NSW, Australia: NSW Department of Health. Retrieved from http://www.health.nsw.gov.au/pubs/2010/pdf/conflict_resolution.pdf

Fineberg, I., Kawashima, M., & Asch, S. M. (2011). Communication with families facing life-threatening illness: A research-based model for family conferences. *Journal of Palliative Medicine*, *14*(4), 421–427.

Fisher, R., & Ury, W. (1983). *Getting to yes: Negotiating agreement without giving in*. New York, NY: Penguin Books. (A useful summary of key points of this book may be found at http://www.colorado.edu/conflict/peace/example/fish7513.htm)

Hansen, P., Cornish, P., & Kayser, K. (1998). Family conferences as forums for decision making in hospital settings. *Social Work in Health Care*, *27*(3), 57–74.

Heilveil, I. (1998). *When families feud: Understanding and resolving family conflicts*. New York, NY: Berkeley Publishing Group.

Holst, L., Lundgren, M., Olsen, L., & Ishøy, T. (2009). Dire deadlines: Coping with dysfunctional family dynamics in an end-of-life care setting. *International Journal of Palliative Nursing*, *15*(1), 34–41.

Hudson, P., Quinn, K., O'Hanlon, B., & Aranda, S. (2008). Family meetings in palliative care: Multidisciplinary clinical practice guidelines. *BioMedicalCentral Journal*, *7*(12). Retrieved from http://www.biomedcentral.com/1472-684X/7/12

Kayashima, R., & Braun, K. L. (2001). Barriers to good end-of-life care: A physician survey. *Hawaii Medical Journal*, *60*, 40–47.

Kendall, A., & Arnold, R. (2007a, July). *Fast facts and concepts #183: Conflict resolution I: Careful communication*. Retrieved from http://www.eperc.mcw.edu/FileLibrary/User/jrehm/fastfactpdfs/Concept183.pdf

Kendall A., & Arnold R. (2007b, July). *Fast facts and concepts #184: Conflict resolution II: Principled negotiation*. Retrieved from http://www.eperc.mcw.edu/FileLibrary/User/jrehm/fastfactpdfs/Concept184.pdf

Kim, Y., & Morrow, G. R. (2003). Changes in family relationships affect the development of chemotherapy-related nausea symptoms. *Supportive Care in Cancer*, *11*(3), 171–177.

King, D. A., & Quill, T. (2006). Working with families in palliative care: One size does not fit all. *Journal of Palliative Medicine*, *9*, 704–715.

Kissane, D. W., & Bloch, S. (2002). *Family focused grief therapy*. New York, NY: Open University Press.

Kramer, B. J., Boelk, A., & Auer, C. (2006). Family conflict at the end-of-life: Lessons learned in a model program for vulnerable older adults. *Journal of Palliative Medicine*, *9*, 791–801.

Kramer, B. J., Kavanaugh, M., Trentham-Dietz, A., Walsh, M., & Yonker, J. A. (2010a). Complicated grief in caregivers of persons with lung cancer: The role of family conflict, intrapsychic strains and hospice utilization. *OMEGA: Journal of Death and Dying*, *62*, 201–220.

Kramer, B. J., Kavanaugh, M., Trentham-Dietz, A., Walsh, M., & Yonker, J. A. (2010b). Predictors of family conflict at the end of life: The experience of spouses and adult children of persons with lung cancer. *Gerontologist*, *50*, 215–225.

Kramer, B. J., & Yonker, J. A. (2011). Perceived success in addressing end-of-life care needs of low-income elders and their families: What's family conflict got to do with it? *Journal of Pain and Symptom Management*, *41*(1), 35–48. doi:10.1016/j.jpainsymman.2010.04.017

Levine, C., & Zuckerman, C. (1999). The trouble with families: Toward an ethic of accommodation. *Annals of Internal Medicine*, *130*(2), 148–152.

Lichtenthal, W. G., & Kissane, D. W. (2008). The management of family conflict in palliative care. *Progress in Palliative Care*, *16*(1), 1–7.

Miller, R., Krech, R., & Walsh, T. (1991). The role of a palliative care service family conference in the management of the patient with advanced cancer. *Palliative Medicine*, *5*(1), 34–39.

Moos, R. H., & Moos, B. S. (1981). *Family Environment Scale manual*. Stanford, CA: Consulting Psychologists Press.

National Alliance for Caregiving. (2003). *Family caregiving and public policy: Principles for change*. Retrieved from http://www.caregiving.org/data/principles04.pdf

Perkins, H. S. (2007). Controlling death: The false promise of advance directives. *Annals of Internal Medicine*, *147*, 51–57.

Sales, E., Schulz, R., & Biegel, D. (1992). Predictors of strain in families of cancer patients: A review of the literature. *Journal of Psychosocial Oncology*, *10*, 1–26.

Schneiderman, L. J., Gilmer, T., Teetzel, H. D., Dugan, D. O., Blustein, J., Cranford, R., . . . & Young, E. W. D. (2003). Effect of ethics consultations on nonbeneficial life-sustaining treatments in the intensive care setting: A randomized controlled trial. *Journal of the American Medical Association*, *290*, 1166–1172.

SUPPORT Principal Investigators. (1995). A controlled trial to improve care for seriously ill hospitalized patients: The Study to Understand Prognoses and Preferences for Outcomes and Risks of Treatments (SUPPORT). *Journal of the American Medical Association*, *274*, 1591–1598.

Tilden, V. P., Tolle, S. W., Drach, L. L., & Perrin, N. A. (2004). Out-of-hospital death: Advance care planning, decedent symptoms, and caregiver burden. *Journal of the American Geriatrics Society*, *52*, 532–539.

Waldrop, D. P., & Meeker, M. (2011). Crisis in caregiving: When home-based end-of-life care is no longer possible. *Journal of Palliative Care*, *27*, 117–125.

Waldrop, D. P., & Rinfrette, E. S. (2009). Can short enrollment be long enough? Comparing the perspectives of hospice professionals and family caregivers. *Palliative & Supportive Care*, *7*(1), 37–47.

Weissman, D. E., Quill, T. E., & Arnold, R. M. (2010, January). *Fast facts and concepts #225: The family meeting: Causes of conflict*. Retrieved from http://www.eperc.mcw.edu/FileLibrary/User/jrehm/fastfactpdfs/Concept225.pdf

Zhang, A. Y., & Siminoff, L. A. (2003). Silence and cancer: Why do families and patients fail to communicate? *Health Communications*, *15*, 415–429.

58

Iris Cohen Fineberg

Family and Team Conferencing in Oncology

Key Concepts

- *Family conferences and team meetings are tools for enhancing communication in oncology care.*
- *Family conferences and team meetings involve groups and group dynamics.*
- *Social workers have competencies in numerous aspects of family conferencing and team meetings, making them well positioned for leadership and/or substantive participation in these forums.*

Family conferences are used in many areas of social work practice, such as pediatric and geriatric care, mental health treatment, oncology, palliative care, and end-of-life care. Much research on family conferences in the medical setting has centered on intensive and palliative care (Curtis et al., 2001; Fineberg, Kawashima, & Asch, 2011; Hudson, Quinn, O'Hanlon, & Aranda, 2008). The discussion in this chapter focuses on oncology practices, which often include palliative and end-of-life care.

Achieving and maintaining excellent communication in oncology care is a continuous goal and a frequent challenge for health care providers (Institute of Medicine, 2008). Oncology social workers bring skills in interpersonal, family, and group processes that can inform and enhance communication within teams and among patients, families, and professional caregivers.

The first portion of this chapter focuses on reasons for and considerations in implementing family conferences in oncology. The second portion of the chapter addresses features and types of team meetings and the roles for social workers.

Family Conferences

Families have always met to exchange information, make decisions, provide support, argue, laugh, and share special moments—typically without the presence of an external person charged with observing or mediating the exchange. Within the setting of oncology care, however, the internal exchanges of families become public and visible to those who are caring for them. In this context, health care providers have the privilege of participating in these exchanges—a privilege that also entails recognizing and honoring the significance of being allowed to witness the workings of the family.

Family conferences, sometimes called family meetings, are meetings involving family members, health care providers, and, when possible, patients (Blacker & Jordan, 2004; Fineberg, 2005). They tend to be planned events rather than spontaneous gatherings and are distinct from the impromptu conversations that occur between people at the bedside, in the clinic, or in the hallway. The reasons for having family conferences are numerous and include the following:

- To provide diagnosis or diagnostic information.
- To discuss treatment options, related care, and care planning.
- To plan for discharge and/or clarify the transition process from hospital to home or other care facility.
- To discuss end-of-life treatment, palliative care, hospice, place of care, and personal care options and support.
- To discuss decision capacity and/or mental health concerns.
- To discuss ethical, psychosocial, cultural, and/or spiritual issues affecting care.
- To discuss family matters, such as the patient's wishes, decision making in the family, differences, and conflicts affecting care (Curtis et al., 2002; Hansen, Cornish, & Kayser, 1998; Hudson, Thomas, Quinn, & Aranda, 2009).

The specific purposes of the meeting affect who should attend, what kinds of information should be presented, and follow-up processes. Family conferences are usually one-time meetings focused on a particular event, decision, or situation. Although they may have a fundamental effect on the functioning of the family in the same way that therapy might, this is not their primary intent.

Conference Participants

The attendees at a family conference are determined by many factors—for example, who initiates the conference, the topic(s) and intent of the meeting, the capacity of the patient to participate (physically, mentally, and emotionally), and the availability of family members and health care providers. The person who initiates the meeting may also have overt and/or covert reasons for the meeting. For example, a physician may want to discuss treatment to confirm plans for intervention (overtly stated reason) and to increase the likelihood of the patient's adherence to the plan (covert reason). Covert reasons are neither inherently positive nor negative, and they are not always recognized, even by the meeting planner. In the end, family conferences often have intended and unintended outcomes.

A discussion of the working definition of *family* is core to thinking about family conferences in oncology. For a full discussion about defining the term, refer to the beginning of this section (Chapter 54). Whenever possible, patients should be asked to provide guidance about whom they want involved in family conferences and care discussions.

Cultural considerations are of great importance in all aspects of patient and family care, including family communication and decision making. Western culture tends to prioritize individual over family decision making, whereas Eastern culture and others more often look to the family and related community network for guidance regarding communication and care decisions. Similarly, professionals need to consider whether and to what extent a patient and family want open communication about the cancer diagnosis and treatment. Despite the great potential of the family conference as a tool in oncology care, it needs to be culturally appropriate. Cultural norms related to nationality or ethnic affiliation should be part of professionals' awareness, but the consideration should not cease there. Families have their own cultural norms that need to be understood; they should not be treated based on assumptions or stereotypes.

The topic and intention of the specific family conference determines which health care providers are involved. Social workers are often the conference organizers, leaders, co-leaders, and meeting participants, but they are not necessarily involved in the meeting (Fineberg, 2010). A physician is often a leader or co-leader of a conference, especially when the focus is on medical information or care decisions. Additional physicians, nurses, and other members of the health care team may be important participants: for example, pastoral or spiritual care providers, psychologists, physical therapists, or respiratory therapists. The proportion of professionals to laypeople should be balanced so that the patient and family are not overwhelmed.

The social work profession is grounded in advocacy and empowerment. As a result, oncology social workers have an important role in attending to conference participants, who may be especially vulnerable or disempowered. Although the determination of who is vulnerable needs to be made on an individual basis, social workers should be particularly aware with regard to specific population groups, such as young children, very elderly people, people with intellectual or other illnesses and disabilities, people with hearing and/or sight impairments, people whose primary language is different from that of the conveners, people from ethnic or cultural minorities, people who have experienced a known trauma that might affect their conference experience, and people who may experience disempowerment due to being lesbian, gay, bisexual, or transsexual. The social worker should not assume that people in these population groups are automatically vulnerable or in need of advocacy, but he or she should pay attention to this possibility. In the case of children and adolescents who are not patients themselves, these young participants should not be viewed as decision makers in the conference but should be nonetheless invited to express their perspectives and considered in conference conduct.

Physical Settings

The number of people who will attend is a primary consideration in choosing a physical setting for a family conference. The outpatient clinic may require the use of an examination or conference room for a meeting, whereas an inpatient meeting may take place in a patient's room, private or shared, especially if the patient has limited mobility. Conference rooms or family lounges are also common locations for family conferences. Conference organizers will want to maximize privacy to encourage open communication. All participants should be able to sit to minimize power imbalances created by some people "standing over" others. Professionals should remember that family conferences held in health care settings bestow a power and culture advantage to the professionals. Thoughtful attention to these dynamics and the impact of the setting on participants is likely to enhance successful communication, as well as the conference process and outcomes.

Conference Structure and Process

The structure of a family conference is determined by the conference goal and the leader's personal preferences. Although it may be tempting to have a step-by-step plan, the "steps" of the conference should not be viewed as linear or rigid. There is a logical order to some elements (e.g., introductions should occur at the beginning), but other components may occur in a different order. More detailed literature on suggested conference components is available (Ambuel, 2000; Fineberg et al., 2011; Hudson et al., 2008), Table 58.1 includes some possible elements.

The process of the family conference is most satisfying to patients and families when they have the opportunity to speak and actively participate (McDonagh et al., 2004). Leaders can promote participation by eliciting reactions and questions, allowing periods of silence to give participants time to digest information and consider responses, demonstrating active listening, and engaging appropriately in the emotional experience of the conference (Fineberg et al., 2011). The process needs to reflect consideration of the cultural factors and participant characteristics previously noted in this chapter.

Lena is a 63-year-old Russian woman who has been newly diagnosed with ovarian cancer. She lives in a suburban area with her second husband and her 31-year-old daughter, who has a developmental delay. The daughter works at a local store during the week but depends on Lena for assistance in managing everyday life. Lena also has a 33-year-old daughter who is married and lives nearby. Lena's husband is older and retired. Lena is the primary earner in the family and is employed as an account specialist in a bank. She has lived in the United States most of her life and has an established social network. She is not particularly religious but identifies herself as Christian.

Lena was diagnosed after experiencing some bleeding, for which she sought immediate medical attention. A preliminary surgery revealed a rare form of ovarian cancer and testing confirmed metastatic disease. Lena's coping style is stoic and pragmatic, focused on decisions that need to be made. She was initially hesitant about sharing the news with her family but realized it would be necessary to involve them. Her older daughter is emotionally close to her mother and feels anxious about the severity of Lena's illness.

Upon learning that her mother would need further treatment, Lena's older daughter contacted the social worker to request resources related to her younger sister's care. The social worker determined that a family conference would be important to identify and address the complex factors involved in treatment planning. After speaking with team members to confirm their availability, the social worker consulted Lena to ensure that her choice of family members would be invited to the meeting. Lena identified herself, her husband, her two daughters, and her son-in-law as desired family participants. Although Lena has siblings, they live many hours away and would not be directly involved in her treatment experience.

In preparation for the conference, the social worker spoke with the gynecologic oncologist and the nurse overseeing Lena's care to determine which other professionals should be involved in the conference, the conference leadership, and a conference agenda. The team had been unaware of Lena's caregiving responsibilities at home. It was agreed that the physician and social worker would co-lead, and that the social worker would start the conference. The social worker gathered information about support services for the younger daughter and alerted the physician that Lena would likely ask about aspects of treatment as they related to her ability to care for her daughter. The social worker informed the team that the younger daughter would be taking part in the meeting; consequently, the team needed to be particularly mindful of the younger daughter's needs, assessing whether participants were using language and conveying ideas in a manner that she could understand. The goals of the conference were to (1) discuss treatment options, (2) identify support resources, and (3) bring Lena and the primary family and professional caregivers to a shared understanding of the concerns, needs, and plans surrounding Lena's care.

The social worker began the family conference by facilitating introductions among the participants and summarizing the reasons for the conference. She invited the participants to comment on the goals for the meeting, and everyone was in agreement. The rest of the meeting was coled collaboratively by the social worker and physician. On a couple of occasions, the social worker assessed the younger daughter's understanding of the meeting and restated medical information provided by the physician using simpler language that enhanced the younger daughter's understanding of the information. The meeting enabled Lena and each of her family members to ask questions about treatment options and their implications for family life, and about the support resources available to them. The social worker had key roles in organizing and leading the conference, observing and listening throughout the meeting, assessing needs, advocating for vulnerable participants, and enhancing communication among the team members, patient, and family.

Table 58.1.
Selected Structural Elements of Family Conferences

Structural Conference Component	Explanation
Preparation	Invite the relevant participants. Coordinate the agenda and plan with conference leaders and key participants. Ensure potentially needed information is gathered (e.g., test results, financial resources, discharge options).
Introductions	Have participants introduce themselves to all conference participants.
Agenda setting	Explicitly state the reasons for the meeting and suggest an order for the discussion.
Patient history	Provide an overview of the illness experience that has brought the patient to this point, noting key points.
Provision of information (diagnosis/prognosis)	Explain diagnosis and/or prognosis with attention to participants' understanding of the information.
Patient/family explanatory models	Elicit patient/family participants' understanding of why/how they think something has occurred.
Care plan/discharge plan	Present options and facilitate decision making for how care will proceed following the conference.
Closing/wrap-up	Summarize key points from the discussion and the agreed-upon conclusion/steps forward.
Follow-up	Document in the medical record the important aspects and outcomes of the family conference. Contact the patient, family, and/or health care professionals following the conference to ensure that agreed-upon steps have been accomplished.

Oncology Social Work in Family Conferencing

Social workers bring a tremendous amount of knowledge and skill to this communication forum, regardless of whether they have a formally recognized role in a particular family conference (Fineberg, 2010). As specialists in psychosocial care, social workers observe and recognize individual reactions, family interactions, and group dynamics. Social workers therefore intervene to clarify communication, facilitate negotiation in decision-making discussions, advocate for participants who may not be fully "heard" in the conference, provide information about financial and community resources, and enhance continuity of care through pre- and postconference contact with conference participants. Box 58.1 includes questions for social workers to use in thinking about their roles in family conferences held in the oncology setting. Family conferences are communication tools that allow a key set of people to, at the same time, hear and exchange information in service of the patient and family. Social workers have much to contribute toward enhancing the patient and family experience through this form of communication.

Team Meetings

Professional team meetings in oncology settings may occur for different purposes, such as patient care, professional education, or case review. In this chapter, the term *team meetings* refers to meetings in which a group of professionals from different disciplines gathers to discuss patient care. Such meetings may be called team meetings, team conferences, case conferences, multidisciplinary team meetings, and interdisciplinary team meetings (McCallin, 2001). Professionals should be aware that physicians may use the term *multidisciplinary* to refer to a mix of physicians from different medical specialties (oncology, infectious disease, pulmonary, etc.), rather than a mix of participants from different professions (social work, nursing, pastoral care, etc.).

Oncology care often involves disease-centered or setting-centered teams of professionals who usually work together, thereby allowing team members to build relationships and develop effective communication patterns. Although some team members may be more transient, such as a medical resident or social work intern, there is often a permanent core group. By contrast, some teams have frequently changing participants or combinations of participants based on their setting and purpose. For example, an oncology clinic may have different team members depending on shift schedules and the availability of participants from various disciplines. Such teams face the challenge of less familiarity among team members and minimal opportunity to identify optimal approaches to collaboration. Although a thorough discussion of teamwork is beyond the scope of this chapter, the following sections focus on team meetings and some aspects of teamwork.

Box 58.1
Questions for Consideration

Preconference

- *Who has requested the family conference and what are the implications?*
- *Is the reason for the conference explicit? If not, how might the social worker enhance clarification?*
- *What is the patient's role in planning the conference, and is it appropriate?*
- *Have all relevant participants been invited?*
- *Has the best available location been arranged?*
- *What topics and challenges might be anticipated?*
- *What information would be helpful to gather and prepare for the conference?*

During the Family Conference

- *Is the agenda for the conference clearly communicated? If not, how might the social worker effectively provide clarification?*
- *Do all participants seem able to participate? If not, how might the social worker assist them?*
- *How effective is communication during the family conference, and how might the social worker enhance it?*
- *Is the conference revealing misinformation that requires correcting?*
- *Are the explanatory models of the patient, family, and professionals congruent? If not, how might any incongruence be mediated?*
- *What can be learned about the patient's/family's/professionals' dynamics?*
- *Has the goal been met? If not, how might it be achieved?*

Postconference

- *Determine what participants concluded from the conference and whether it matches the conclusions stated at the conference.*
- *Determine who from the health care team will document the family conference in the medical record.*
- *How might the social worker build on the work and relationships developed during the conference to enhance the patient/family experience of care?*

Types of Team Collaboration

Different types of team interaction reflect the ways in which team members relate to professional roles. *Multidisciplinary, interdisciplinary,* and *transdisciplinary* are terms used to describe the degree and nature of professional collaborations among team members (Otis-Green & Fineberg, 2010). Most oncology teams self-classify as multidisciplinary or interdisciplinary, although their true form of collaboration may be different (Speck, 2006) (see Table 58.2).

Group, Team, and Disciplinary Dynamics

Although not all groups are teams, all teams are groups. Consequently, teams have group dynamics that affect the processes and outcomes of team meetings. The social forces of such characteristics as age, gender, ethnicity, and profession are all components of group interaction. Setting characteristics, such as the hierarchical structure and physician dominance in medical settings, are part of the team's context (Corless & Nicholas, 2004). Social workers have particular knowledge about groups and group dynamics and are well positioned to observe and recognize patterns in the team's interactions. These observations can help the social worker be an effective team member. In general, however, the power dynamics of the medical setting dictate that physicians dominate and hold leadership roles.

Each profession socializes its members to the expectations and norms of that profession. An understanding of team dynamics requires that professionals recognize these roles (Hall, 2005). For example, physicians are socialized to be the leading voices in the medical setting, to convey information in abbreviated segments, and to identify pathology. By contrast, social workers are socialized to assess context, specifically using the "person in environment" to attend to the "environment" in its fullest sense (Hare, 2004). The social work profession is also oriented toward identifying strengths in, advocating for, and empowering others. Recognizing fundamental differences in professional socialization can help participants understand other professionals' behavior in meetings and provides an opportunity for educating colleagues about each profession's contributions to the meeting.

Role and Contributions of Oncology Social Work

Variability in care settings, team types, team styles, and individuals' influence on team functioning means that there is no single formula for the role of the social worker in the oncology team meeting. The social worker may lead the team meeting in some settings. Social workers offer particular knowledge and understanding about psychosocial aspects of the patient/family experience (Gardner & Werner-Lin, 2012). The social worker may ensure that the meeting includes consideration of known psychosocial information about a patient/family, as well as of the psychosocial implications of decisions and care plans under discussion. As a patient/family advocate, the social worker serves as a patient/family voice in the meeting, providing information that may not be known or prioritized by other team members regarding the strengths, concerns, preferences, and priorities of the patient/family. As a resource specialist, the social worker also brings to the meeting a thorough knowledge of community, state, and federal resources pertinent to the patient/family situation.

Table 58.2.
Types of Team Collaboration

Type of Team	Characteristics of the Team
Multidisciplinary	• Team participants are from different disciplines. • Participants provide discipline-specific patient care independently of other professionals' interventions. • Team participants may exchange information but tend to work in disciplinary "silos."
Interdisciplinary	• Team participants are from different disciplines. • Participants provide their specialized disciplinary care in coordination with other members of the care team. • Coordination among team members aims to provide a cohesive, synchronized care experience for the patient/family.
Transdisciplinary	• Team participants are from different disciplines. • Care focuses on the situation and needs of the patient/family, rather than disciplinary-specific interventions. • Team members develop shared/overlapping knowledge that allows members to be interchangeable regarding some aspects of care. • Although team members overlap in many roles and functions on the team, each discipline is respected and valued for its unique contribution to the team's knowledge and expertise.

Team meetings warrant preparation. The social worker's preparation for the meeting can allow him or her to play a stronger and more influential role. The social worker's anticipation of what might be discussed about each patient/family and what information and resources would be helpful enables the most effective participation. The value of the social worker's involvement is reinforced when needed information is furnished at the time of the meeting.

Pearls

- Social workers educate their colleagues and clients about the roles and strengths of oncology social work by taking the lead in family conference initiation, planning, and implementation.
- Social workers' ability to articulate their role is vital if professional team members are to learn about oncology social work.
- Flexibility is essential in working collaboratively in the oncology setting. Assessment and listening skills are critical in identifying the best strategy and role in working with a particular family and team situation.

Pitfalls

- Social workers should not wait for an invitation to participate or contribute to family conferences and team meetings.
- Information about family conferences and team meetings should be viewed as a guide rather than a prescription for how to practice in these settings.

Family conferences and team meetings are forms of group communication in oncology care. They have great potential for increasing shared and synchronized understanding of patient and family care needs and plans. Social work professionals are well prepared to lead and educate about these forums. Each family conference and team meeting is a unique event and requires individualized attention. However, the core principles and considerations discussed in this chapter can guide social workers in thinking about clinical practices.

ADDITIONAL RESOURCES

Association of Oncology Social Work: http://www.aosw.org
Association of Pediatric Oncology Social Workers: http://www.aposw.org
NCI Cancer Topics: Family Caregivers in Cancer: http://www.cancer.gov/cancertopics/pdq/supportivecare/caregivers/healthprofessional

REFERENCES

Ambuel, B. (2000). Conducting a family conference. *Principles and Practice of Supportive Oncology Updates, 3*(3), 1–12.

Blacker, S., & Jordan, A. R. (2004). Working with families facing life-threatening illness in the medical setting. In J. Berzoff & P. R. Silverman (Eds.), *Living with dying: A handbook for end-of-life healthcare practitioners* (pp. 548–570). New York, NY: Columbia University Press.

Corless, I. B., & Nicholas, P. K. (2004). The interdisciplinary team: An oxymoron? In J. Berzoff & P. R. Silverman (Eds.),

Living with dying: A handbook for end-of-life healthcare practitioners (pp. 161–170). New York, NY: Columbia University Press.

Curtis, J. R., Engelberg, R. A., Wenrich, M. D., Nielsen, E. L., Shannon, S. E., Treece, P. D., . . . Rubenfeld, G. D. (2002). Studying communication about end-of-life care during the ICU family conference: Development of a framework. *Journal of Critical Care, 17*(3), 147–160.

Curtis, J. R., Patrick, D. L., Shannon, S. E., Treece, P. D., Engelberg, R. A., & Rubenfeld, G. D. (2001). The family conference as a focus to improve communication about end-of-life care in the intensive care unit: Opportunities for improvement. *Critical Care Medicine, 29*(2), N26–N33.

Fineberg, I. C. (2005). Preparing professionals for family conferences in palliative care: Evaluation results of an interdisciplinary approach. *Journal of Palliative Medicine, 8*(4), 857–866.

Fineberg, I. C. (2010). Social work perspectives on family communication and family conferences in palliative care. *Progress in Palliative Care, 18*(4), 213–220.

Fineberg, I. C., Kawashima, M., & Asch, S. M. (2011). Communication with families facing life-threatening illness: A research-based model for family conferences. *Journal of Palliative Medicine, 14*(4), 421–427.

Gardner, D. S., & Werner-Lin, A. (2012). Oncology social work. In S. Gehlert & T. Browne (Eds.), *Handbook of health social work* (2nd ed., pp. 498–525). Hoboken, NJ: John Wiley & Sons.

Hall, P. (2005). Interprofessional teamwork: Professional cultures as barriers. *Journal of Interprofessional Care, S1*, 188–196.

Hansen, P., Cornish, P., & Kayser, K. (1998). Family conferences as forums for decision making in hospital settings. *Social Work in Health Care, 27*(3), 57–74.

Hare, I. (2004). Defining social work for the 21st century: The International Federation of Social Workers' revised definition of social work. *International Social Work, 47*(3), 407–424.

Hudson, P., Quinn, K., O'Hanlon, B., & Aranda, S. (2008). Family meetings in palliative care: Multidisciplinary clinical practice guidelines. *BMC Palliative Care, 7*(12). Retrieved from http://www.biomedcentral.com/1472-684X/9/17

Hudson, P., Thomas, T., Quinn, K., & Aranda, S. (2009). Family meetings in palliative care: Are they effective? *Palliative Medicine, 23*, 150–157.

Institute of Medicine. (2008). *Cancer care for the whole patient: Meeting psychosocial health needs*. Washington, DC: National Academies Press.

McCallin, A. (2001). Interdisciplinary practice—a matter of teamwork: An integrated literature review. *Journal of Clinical Nursing, 10*, 419–428.

McDonagh, J. R., Elliott, T. B., Engelberg, R. A., Treece, P. D., Shannon, S. E., Rubenfeld, G. D., . . . Curtis, J. R. (2004). Family satisfaction with family conferences about end-of-life care in the intensive care unit: Increased proportion of family speech is associated with increased satisfaction. *Critical Care Medicine, 32*(7), 1484–1488.

Otis-Green, S., & Fineberg, I. C. (2010). Enhancing team effectiveness. In B. R. Ferrell & N. Coyle (Eds.), *Oxford textbook of palliative nursing* (3rd ed., pp. 1225–1235). New York, NY: Oxford University Press.

Speck, P. (2006). Team or group—spot the difference. In P. Speck (Ed.), *Teamwork in palliative care: Fulfilling or frustrating?* (pp. 7–23). New York, NY: Oxford University Press.

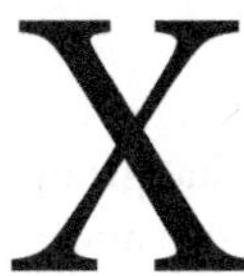

Interventions With Parental Cancer, Dependent Children, and Adolescents

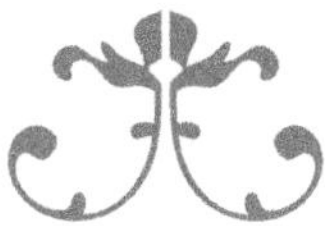

Lynn C. Behar

Parental cancer is a stressful condition for the whole family, and especially troubling to dependent children and adolescents. Parents worry about the best ways to inform their children that will prepare them to cope with changes in the family routines and atmosphere, help them to process their emotions, and enable them to go on with their normal activities and relationships with confidence that they will continue to be loved and cared for. Families need to understand that children generally become more aware of the illness than parents realize and therefore, without open communication, are likely to suffer even greater sadness, anxiety, and fear due to the effect of misunderstanding, misinterpretations, and a sense of isolation.

There is no natural "point of entry" into the medical system at which children can easily be pulled onto the care team. The oncology social worker is the pivotal person on the team to make sure the children are included and offered information and support, and that their parents are provided current knowledge about how best to inform and communicate with children and adolescents around these issues. They should not be the invisible members of the support team, nor left alone with their fears and misunderstandings. In addition, children can provide meaning and strength for parents in fighting the cancer. They are an integral part of the home team and can be a positive force in their parents' care and support.

The chapters in this section focus on three areas for the support of children whose parent has cancer: developmentally informed practice guidelines, issues specific to single-parent families, and use of parallel groups and expressive activities to facilitate communication in this emotionally intense situation.

Grace Christ, a long-established expert with children and parents facing illness and loss, promotes a detailed plan for family consultation services with children and parents when one parent has cancer. Her chapter, "Parental Cancer: Developmentally Informed Practice Guidelines for Family Consultation and Communication," focuses on children's developmental stages throughout the continuum of the parent's cancer experience and provides guidance for parents' competent and effective communication with their children. Christ guides the oncology social worker in a range of specific interventions for practice with parents and children, taking into account the ages of the children and the stage of the family and disease. The goal is to create a platform for open communication, consistent with the family's own communication style, to meet the informational and emotional needs of the children.

In "Single Parents Coping With Cancer and Children," Lynn C. Behar and Frances Marcus Lewis describe the specific challenges and strengths of parents and children living with the cancer of a single parent. These parents cope with cancer alone while shouldering the responsibility of maintaining their children's well-being, often denying their own needs to do so. Children's responses to their parent's cancer vary due to age and developmental level, but in single-parent families, they experience increased anxiety about what will happen to them if the parent dies. Helping single parents engage additional resources and plan for their children's care is a major therapeutic goal. In single-parent situations, children may take on responsibilities for home maintenance, care of siblings, and even their parent's personal care without being given adequate support for these tasks. Conversely, single-parent families often develop resilience because of the need to rely on each other that can be mobilized and supported in the situation of an ill parent.

In "A Parallel Group Program for Parents and Children: Using Expressive Techniques and Activities to Facilitate Communication," Krista Nelson details a parallel group program for children, adolescents, and their parents when dealing with parental cancer. This chapter provides concrete assessment tools, step-by-step strategies, and innovative activities used in these hospital-based family groups. Creative art, play, and other activities help children, adolescents, and parents communicate openly and effectively. Preliminary program evaluation results suggest that group participation reduced children's anxiety about cancer, enhanced coping and communication, and helped family members feel closer to each other.

All families with dependent children dealing with parental cancer should be referred to an oncology social worker who will consider the needs of the whole family. Oncology social work interventions encompass assessment, intervention, interdisciplinary collaboration, and support for the children in the family so they will not be invisible and will have their needs met during their parent's cancer experience.

59

Grace Christ

Parental Cancer: Developmentally Informed Practice Guidelines for Family Consultation and Communication

Key Concepts

- *Family consultation services for families with dependent children in which one parent has cancer are essential social work initiatives. Such programs have multiple components, including individual interviews with children and parents, outreach, parallel groups with children and parents, educational resources, and advocacy with schools and communities.*
- *The oncology social worker needs to consider preexisting family patterns of communication and family members' strengths and limitations in the context of parental cancer. Four such patterns that have been identified by qualitative research are described.*
- *Adaptation issues confronting five different developmental groupings (ages 3 to 5, 6 to 8, 9 to 11, 12 to 14, and 15 to 17) and related practice guidelines for intervening in serious illness should direct intervention.*

Estimates are that 2.85 million dependent children are living with a parent who is a cancer survivor. The estimate is based on the fact that 21% of all patients newly diagnosed with cancer are between 25 and 54 years old, the age range within which many individuals have dependent children (Weaver, Rowland, Alfano, & McNeel, 2010). The whole family experiences disruption and distress when a parent is diagnosed with a serious illness such as cancer. Children are especially affected because of their dependence on the family unit. Multiple studies have reported that children confronting parental cancer experience problems in emotional, social, cognitive, behavioral, and physical areas of functioning (Buchwald, Delmar, & Schantz-Laursen, 2012; Huang, O'Connor, & Lee, 2014; Kennedy & Lloyd-Williams, 2009; Russell & Rauch, 2012; Saldinger, Cain, & Porterfield, 2003; Siegel et al., 1992; Siegel, Karus, & Raveis, 1996; Visser, Huizinga, Van der Graaf, Hoekstra, & Hoekstra-Weebers, 2004).

Parents are especially stressed during their transition to advanced illness (Christ, Siegel, Karus, & Christ, 2005; Siegel, Karus, et al., 1996) and most often request professional help when they perceive the need to inform and prepare their children for their possible or imminent death. A study of 126 children from 88 families in which a parent had advanced illness found that children experienced the highest levels of anxiety and depression during the period of advanced illness. Children's anxiety and depression significantly decreased after the parent's death, indicating that the advanced illness period is one of high distress and provides an opportunity for preventive intervention (Siegel, Karus, et al., 1996).

However, interventions at earlier phases in the continuum of care can also be powerful. They help parents establish a process of effective communication with children consistent with the family style, the children's developmental and communication needs, and the particular phase of the illness (Lewis, Casey, Brandt, Shands, & Zahlis, 2006).

It is important that children and adolescents know that they will have ongoing opportunities for questions, discussion, clarification, and reflection. At the same time, every effort should be made to help them continue with normal life experiences to the greatest extent possible.

A 15-year-old son reflected on his family's communication style over the 8 years of his father's cancer, transplant, and diagnosis of glioblastoma and terminal illness in hospice. What was most important to him was "to be told and to feel like you weren't being left out even if you didn't completely understand what was going on, just to know you were still being informed with everything... you were always in the loop."

(Sheehan et al., 2014, p. 4)

A consultation service that helps families communicate with and support their children during a parent's illness with cancer is an essential oncology social work initiative. Programs need to provide multiple interventions to address the broad range of needs these families have across the continuum of care. This chapter describes the necessary components of a family consultation service, family patterns of communication around serious illness, and developmental characteristics and related practice guidelines for intervening with children and adolescents at different developmental levels. These substantive areas constitute a required knowledge base and skill set for implementing an effective consultation service. Interventions are aimed at improving the competence of parents in providing developmentally appropriate communication and support to their children at different illness transitions.

Family Consultation Service Functions

Family consultation services provide a program that offers multiple ways to meet families' needs, including the following:

- Individual consultation can be provided to families who have urgent needs for help in communicating to and supporting their children through a particular transition in the illness. This includes direct interviews with children and parents, as well as joint sessions.
- Outreach can acquaint families with education and resource information, as well as individual, family, and group support that may be available to them.
- Parallel group programs for parents and children, as described in Chapter 61, provide activities and expressive techniques to facilitate children's ability to normalize, describe, and communicate their reactions. At the same time, a parallel group for parents helps them to understand the role of development in children's reactions and to identify the best ways to provide children with information and support.
- Some cancer centers use the parallel group structure developed by the CLIMB Support Program. This program provides materials and professional training that were developed by the Children's Treehouse Foundation, a nonprofit dedicated to the emotional support of children who have parents with cancer. CLIMB stands for "Children's Lives Include Moments of Bravery" and includes six consecutive 2-hour weekly group meetings. During these meetings, conversation and art are used to help children identify and appropriately express complex feelings. Each child is given his or her own workbook to capture progress that he or she can share with the family at home (Murphy, Gallo-Silver, & Kramer, 2005).
- Quality educational resources and materials for parents and children should be selected and made available to families.
- Counseling resources for children who already show clinical symptoms and behaviors are essential.
- Social work advocacy to schools and community programs can help extend support to children who have a parent with cancer at home.

Multiple research studies have found that the surviving caregiver's parenting competence and communication capacities are critical factors in preventing adverse consequences in children when a parent has a serious illness (Huizinga, van der Graff, Visser, Dijkstra, & Hoestra-Weebers, 2003; Krattenmacher et al., 2012; Osborn, 2007; Raveis & Siegel, 1999; Sandler, Ayers, & Romer, 2002). Parents find it difficult to communicate with their children about the illness throughout the cancer experience. They themselves are emotionally distraught and challenged by new demands on their time and attention. Even previously well-functioning parents, or those that regard their communication as quite direct and honest, can, for a variety of reasons, experience a reluctance to communicate with their children about their illness. They are often unclear about which words and concepts are most helpful for children of different ages during different stages of the illness and treatment. Most of all, they fear interrupting children's day-to-day functioning with the anxiety that such a conversation would evoke. We learned from our previous research that parents are often unaware of how anxious their children already are about information they have overheard and interpreted and misinterpreted on their own because they did not feel they had permission to discuss these concerns with the parent (Christ et al., 2005; Siegel, Raveis, & Karus, 1996). It is enormously relieving to children and adolescents to have their parents discuss the situation, clarify information, and reassure them that they are strong and that ongoing care will be provided.

Parents are often concerned about breaking down in front of their child or that the child will pose questions or issues that will force them to acknowledge the seriousness of the illness before they are ready. They should take the time to prepare themselves with words and concepts for these conversations and be aware of their own emotional capacity and limitations. Children take their cues from parents regarding the acceptability of communication. The parent's approach conveys to the children either that the illness is safe to talk about and that its effects can be mastered or that discussion is prohibited and will upset/overwhelm their parents (Siegel, Raveis, et al., 1996). It is often necessary to have separate communication with children to prepare for an effective family consultation. Separate and joint interviews with both parents and children were integral to the effectiveness of a social work family intervention that was studied at a major cancer center (Christ et al., 2005). Children's groups also provide the words for emotions and enhance their understanding of their reactions within the context of sharing the experiences of other peers. As a result, children gain the confidence and courage to speak more openly with their parents about these issues and share their questions and worries.

Understanding Family Patterns of Communication

The overall goal of education and parental support during a parent's illness is to help parents communicate with their children in ways that mitigate the traumatic and stressful aspects of the illness. They need to talk with their children in ways that help the children accept the reality of the situation but give them the courage, confidence, and guidance to find ways to cope with it while going on with their own lives. Parents need to explain changes in treatments and their impacts on the family functioning and environment, which must be consistent with what children observe. Parents should view this communication as an ongoing process, not a one-time event. There must be opportunities for clarifications, questions, corrections, and changing reflections.

A qualitative descriptive study of 22 families' ways of informing their adolescents about the parent entering hospice described parents' communication efforts as trying to "make it easier for their children to swallow." They wanted to spare children unnecessary worry, burdens, or emotional distress and to "soften the blow." They did this by combining news of the parent's illness with efforts to comfort and reassure children of the love of both parents, providing guarantees that the family would be "okay" and that they would be there for them through it all (Sheehan et al., 2014).

As the parents described discussions during earlier and later phases of the illness, it was observed that families generally had a consistent communication style that they had used throughout the illness (Sheehan et al., 2014). This suggested that understanding the families' usual way of communicating about the illness may be an important starting point for an intervention. How are they talking about the illness in the current situation? What are the strengths and limitations of their approach? What evidence is there of how satisfied or dissatisfied the children are with the communication?

Four distinct family patterns of communication with adolescents were identified, though there may be various others if ongoing treatment is taking place in a cancer center. There may also be differences in how these patterns apply to communication with younger children.

Measured Telling

This approach was described as satisfying to adolescents, who felt they were "kept in the loop" throughout what was often a lengthy cancer illness. These families described themselves as being quite honest and outspoken. Parents generally first took the time to process new information that they received from the hospice or medical staff with each other, and then shared it with other family members and/or other health professionals. They carefully selected the best time for telling their children. They tried to inform the adolescent consistently and described how they utilized the adolescent's responses and the realities of the situation to make adjustments throughout the illness on how much information they provided and in what ways. The following is a practice example of this approach.

The mother of a 14-year-old boy and a 16-year-old girl talked with them after she returned from a visit to the hospice during which she had discussed with her husband what they would tell their children about discontinuing curative treatment after eight years. After seeing that her teens had just watched a movie about cancer, she decided to tell them together about Dad's decision to enter hospice and his terminal condition. They shared the sadness, but also the strength of the mother, their family unit, and their community to support them through this difficult transition and loss.

Skirted Telling: Beating Around the Bush

This approach includes talking with the adolescent about the terminal illness in a more indirect or ambiguous way. Although parents who used this approach didn't hide information, they tried not to use very specific, blunt, or shocking language. Many parents and professionals observe that adolescents will often tell you what they do not want to hear. Parents who used this approach believed they were responding to what their adolescent viewed as a need for distance from the most evocative information. They used a more gradual way of telling to give the children time to integrate and absorb in their own way. Adolescents didn't feel information was being withheld, but that their preferences, emotions, and process were being respected. Some wanted to maintain hope and optimism by, for example, talking about future trips as if the parent were not dying. Parents might say the chemotherapy was not working, but they did not reveal that they had been told that their prognosis was 6 to 8 weeks. Parents and adolescents seemed to be on the "same page" with how information should be communicated. Parents thought they were helping their child to live normally while gradually coming to terms with the impending loss. The practice example below describes an adolescent's gradual acceptance of the patient's terminal condition.

> *I mean, I don't know if I am OK with that (her father dying), but I know that I have to live with it. Um, I haven't decided how I feel about it yet, I am still thinking, like right now, I just, I try to avoid it, and I know a lot of people do like when they find out stuff like that and they try to deny it, I am not denying it, I am just avoiding it and that, that's it. But that is definitely the next thing that I would go to if that didn't work, like avoiding it, like before he was gone, be like, "Hey you know this is what I have always felt about you, and thanks." I haven't done that yet, I don't, I don't want to let go yet, not yet.*
>
> *—14-year-old daughter of ill father*

Matter-of-Fact Telling

This style was described as "having a conversation." It was matter-of-fact, was often unemotional, and focused on practical issues and keeping the adolescent informed of the progress of the disease and prepared for death when it was likely to occur. The parents were explaining symptoms and telling them how the illness would affect their lives in practical and realistic ways rather than eliciting discussion of their grief. The disclosures were straightforward and informative rather than emotional. Some of these situations involved a more fractured, distant, or ambivalent relationship with the ill parent. In other situations, the adolescent had a disability that limited his or her capacity to "feel the gravity" of such situations. The children were sometimes poignantly aware of their inability to deal with intense emotions, and the family respected their limits and did not require them to be involved in caregiving. In other families, poverty and family stressors took precedence over emotional grief work related to the ill parent's death—that is, just managing the day-to-day caring for such an ill parent.

Inconsistent Telling: Not Knowing What Is Going On

The most difficult situation for adolescents seemed to occur in families in which the communication was inconsistent. Adolescents often felt they did not know what was going on. The illness was communicated in varying ways, with a mixture of withholding information, delaying telling, and then telling very directly. In one situation, an older adolescent was given more information than a younger one; anger resulted when the 12-year-old learned that the knowledge of the 2-week prognosis had not been withheld from his 17-year-old brother. The facts seemed to change and there was often confusion and disagreement between parents about the details of the illness. Families in the study who used this kind of communication had special problems that placed them at greater risk for adverse psychological consequences. These problems included severe family conflict, estranged relationship of the surviving parent with the children, and a surviving caregiver who had substance abuse or other mental or physical conditions that caused the adolescents to have little confidence in his or her ability to manage the family after the patient died. These families were viewed as in need of ongoing support.

Such an inconsistent pattern has been seen in other studies in families in which one or both parents struggle with depression. Depression can make parents more fearful of dealing with intense emotions and causes them to vacillate between not revealing information and relating dire information "straight out." Families that are overcome with concurrent stressors, such as other deaths or illnesses in the family and severe economic conditions, can also find it difficult to have discussions that will evoke strong emotions. They fear that they will break down and frighten their children more.

Key Characteristics of Development and Related Practice Guidelines

It is necessary to understand the key characteristics of development for each age grouping and translate them into guidelines for interventions with children and adolescents. The findings presented here were drawn from 126 children and adolescents whose families participated in the parent guidance intervention study previously cited (Christ et al., 2005) and from the consultation model used to assist the widows of firefighters who died on 9/11 (Christ, Kane, & Horsley, 2011). The children in these studies were placed into five age groupings—3 to 5, 6 to 8, 9 to 11, 12 to 14, and 15 to 17—based on similarities of responses to a parent's cancer illness (Christ, 2000).

Children ages 6 to 12 ubiquitously ask three questions about the parent's illness: (1) Did I cause the illness? (2) Is it contagious? and (3) Will my well parent be able to take care of me? Adolescents may also be concerned about what causes this type of illness, whether it is contagious or genetically transmitted, and whether their parent might die.

3- to 5-Year-Old Children: "He Can't Take Care of Me Anymore"

- Separation from a primary caregiver is the greatest source of children's stress in this age grouping. Even very young children can experience night terrors and other more obvious distress responses related to the sudden and frequent removal of a primary caregiver, which can occur when either the ill or well parent is spending time being treated, often in the hospital. After her father's death, 4-year-old Rachel was reflecting on her visits to see him in the hospital. Rather than talking about missing her father, she focused on how much her mother had been away from her during that time and that she had wanted to be with her.

- Children in this age group are easily distressed by the primary caregiver's strong emotional responses—for example, a 3-year-old girl refused to enter her father's hospital room with her mother because the mother and father cried together while she was there. She was frightened. The parents were helped to provide positive activities to which she looked forward to and to realize her inability to share in their intense sadness.
- Because they have no concept of illness (or of death's permanence, believing the parent can return after death), these children are often befuddled by what is occurring, and with the parent's changing capacities due to treatments. They can repeat a memorized script that explains the situation and helps them feel mastery without necessarily understanding it. When 4-year-old Rachel was told that her father would stay with her while her mother went out with a friend, she noticed his difficulty with ambulation and said, "He can't take care of me anymore." Her mother assured her that someone else would be there as well. Repetitive questions are a way for children of this age to master the situation. It can be difficult for adults to keep repeating the answers about the parent's condition (Christ 2000, p. 3).
- Children of this age can accept a competent substitute caregiver if they are prepared ahead of time. They often use play, fantasy, and activities to express their reactions and anxieties: During a father's advanced illness, a 4-year-old expressed anxiety about his obvious frailty (he had lost ambulation) by describing her new imaginary companions who became ill and died and were replaced by bigger and stronger brothers who watched over her and took care of her. Their father taught her and her 7-year-old sister how to make their favorite pancakes and spent hours dragging himself across the floor while creating a stained-glass window for them (Christ, 2000, p. 65).

Guidelines for Practice

- Provide a consistent script about what is happening to the ill parent, those things the child observes, and how people are reacting. The child can memorize and repeat the story without necessarily understanding it, but feels less upset if he or she has something to say.
- Always remember the centrality of separation anxiety for children this young. It is necessary to find ways to cope with separations necessitated by the illness from either the ill or well parent.
- Encourage parents to provide reassurance of the caregivers' strength, capacity, and desire to care for the child.
- Use activities, for example, playing with dolls or puppets, art, or fantasy, to illustrate and concretize the complex events that are occurring in the family. "When 4-year-old Rachel's father died, Mom found a male doll and a box and showed her how a burial worked. 'When is he coming back?' Rachel asked. 'Well, Rachel when people die they don't come back. We remember them and we think about them, but they don't come back.'. . . 'Can Daddy move in the box?' 'When you are dead, you don't move anymore.' 'But when is Daddy coming home?' 'Daddy isn't coming home. He will never come home. We love him and we will miss him, but he can never come home again.' She cried, but then the next day began asking again when her father was coming home" (Christ, 2000, p. 4).
- Seeing the parent having a "good cry" may be frightening rather than cathartic for young children. Normalize intermittent, brief, and intense emotional expression. Allowing them to change the subject and go off to play serve as important safety valves. They are reassured that the parent's emotion is a temporary event and that their caregiver remains strong. "Four-year-old Rachel said to her mother, 'Remember the other day when we were crying together? Two people aren't allowed to cry at the same time. I was crying first.' Mother said she was tempted to say she wouldn't do that again, but thought better of it and said, 'You know, Mommies are allowed to be sad too and they are allowed to cry. I'm strong and I can take care of you, but sometimes I hurt too'" (Christ, 2000, p. 3).
- Establish a consistent time when the child is encouraged to ask questions and share feelings, such as at bedtime.

6- to 8-Year-Old Children: "Dad Won't Let Me Sit on His Lap Now; I Don't Think He Loves Me Anymore"

- Though language skills are more advanced, the presence of both magical and logical thinking causes many logical errors and anxiety through misunderstanding of cause and effect. "A 7-year-old girl reflecting on her mother's advanced illness said, 'If I talked about her illness when she was sick, I thought I might make something bad happen'" (Christ & Christ, 2006, p. 205).
- It is important to realize that children this age cannot retrace ideas to correct erroneous thoughts and may therefore repeat certain fixed ideas in a way that is confusing and frustrating to adults. Once children of this age believe their own view of events, it can be

difficult to alter. "Seven-year-old Katy was told repeatedly that her father was too ill to hold her on his lap, but she maintained the idea that he no longer loved her and was angry" (Christ, 2000, p. 73).

- Children of this age are highly emotional and blame themselves when bad things happen. "Seven-year-old Coleen did not want to visit her mother in the hospital because her school grades had fallen and she feared her mother would be disappointed in her" (Christ, 2000, p. 103).
- Changes in the family environment that occur around illness are especially disturbing to children this age. "Seven-year-old Katy also said: 'Mom and Dad used to go dancing. They don't do that any more, and Mom is angry all the time'" (Christ, 2000, p. 73).
- Self-esteem of children this age is fragile. They are aided by the constant reassurances of parents and teachers, who now have become an important part of their support network. However, they are also sensitive to rejection by peers. An 8-year-old daughter cried because a classmate said, "You can't go to the father–daughter dance because your daddy is dead!"
- Extended separations from the primary caregiver can also be disturbing to children. One mother observed that her young children were relieved when their father died because she had spent so much time with him in the hospital. At least they now had one parent home.
- Children in this age group understand that death is universal and therefore it could happen to them. They become anxious and may fear catastrophe. "An eight-year-old boy whose father was ill, said, 'I began to think maybe grandma and grandpa would die, my mom would also die, and maybe the whole world would end, and nothing would be there'" (Christ & Christ, 2006, p. 203).

Guidelines for Practice

Often children this age are given insufficient information about the parent's illness because of their emotionality. One 8-year-old boy developed elaborate eavesdropping methods, picking up extension phones, and listening through closet walls to conversations. The lack of information was a major source of his distress. They are helped by continuous dialogue and clarification. Repetition is required.

The following types of information are suggested:

- Provide simple, concrete, definitional disease-related information such as the name of the disease and its progress, symptoms, treatments, and causes. Information should be optimistic and hopeful, but not unrealistic, and without great detail. To the question, "Are you going to die?": "Well I hope I'm not going to die, I'm going to do everything I can to not die from this. I'm going to do my very best and get better. The treatments have been effective with others, and the doctors believe they will be with me as well" (McCue, 2011, p. 29).
- Offer a simple explanation of the causal relationship between the patient's behavior and appearance and the symptoms and treatment of the disease.
- If the parent's death becomes imminent, then the child should know that the parent may die and should have the opportunity for final conversations or expressions of love.
- Encourage parents to contain intense emotions.
- Normalize temporary reductions in children's grades for parents, children, and teachers. Enlist help in maintaining developmentally appropriate activities for children.
- Reassure children that the illness is not their fault and that they did not cause it.
- Prepare children to visit with the parent in the hospital, explain what they will be seeing, and leave time for follow-up afterward.
- Separation from the primary caregiver continues to cause distress. Prepare children for medical emergencies that may require parents to leave the house unexpectedly.
- Remind parents of their central role in maintaining self-esteem by providing praise.
- Establish a consistent time when the child is encouraged to ask questions, share feelings, and gain reassurance, such as at bedtime.

9- to 11-Year-Old Children: "Just Give Me the Facts"

- Children of this age can use logical thinking more consistently, understand cause and effect better, and correct previously held erroneous ideas. "A 9-year-old girl described how she was different from her 6-year-old sister. Her parents clarified the fact that she was not responsible for her mother's illness. She believed them, but her sister was not so sure. 'I know it's not my fault, and I couldn't have done nothing to prevent it. It wasn't our fault'" (Christ & Christ, 2006, p. 206).
- This is perhaps the easiest age group for parents to relate to around illness and changes in the family if they are given adequate information and incremental knowledge over time.
- They need detailed, concrete explanations about the parent's illness and course of treatment to understand and feel a sense of control. Unlike adolescents, they cannot draw inferences from limited information. They become frustrated and angry if they are not given sufficient and timely information as they are not able to understand context in the absence of detail. "An 11-year-old boy said, 'I thought it was not cancer just a tumor that Dad had. My mom finally put

it straight to me, but I had to go up to her and ask!'" (Christ & Christ, 2006, p. 206).

- In contrast to younger children, they are able to use compartmentalization and distraction to avoid strong emotions. However, it is normal for them to have outbursts of emotion followed by embarrassment and avoidance.
- Children of this age want to be helpful in caring for an ill parent, and in resource-poor environments they may be the sole caregiver for a seriously ill parent, placing them at risk for a broad range of adverse consequences. For example, they may feel responsible when the parent becomes sicker. They may be stigmatized at school due to their school absences and reduced performance.

Guidelines for Practice

- Give children detailed information when the parent's diagnosis is verified: name of the disease, symptoms, known causes, treatments, and possible side effects. Information should be optimistic and hopeful, but not unrealistic. Respond to the child's observations and specific questions.
- It continues to be important to assure children that it is not their fault.
- Acknowledge that the stresses and uncertainty are difficult for everyone, but emphasize the strength of the family and their ability to manage this.
- Normalize the emotions children have when a parent is ill. Give permission to show feelings, but do not expect them to freely express emotions. Other professional staff are often puzzled by their lack of expressed emotion and are relieved to understand that discussing the facts of the situation is the most frequent mode of coping for these young scientists. They are dealing with their feelings by dealing with the facts.
- Provide reassurance and guidance for them when they become overwhelmed and have outbursts or intense emotion. "A 9-year-old boy ran to his room and closed the door when his mother came home from the hospital after the father died because he did not want to hear the news until he was ready. He indicated later that he was embarrassed by his behavior" (Christ 2000, p. 177).
- Have them attend a physician's visit or treatment session if they are willing or visit the hospital where the patient is staying. Children of this age can benefit from talking with staff members who are caring for their parent, learning about treatments, and becoming familiar with the treatment environment (e.g., the cafeteria or the gift shop). Even adolescents are often not given the opportunity to talk with staff caring for their parent.
- Help the child remain involved in after-school activities, in sports, and with friends. One school accommodated two children whose mother was ill by regularly allowing them to do their homework for an hour in the classroom after school. They would then not be stressed with homework completion when visiting with their mother at home.
- Encourage children's interest in reading or writing about the disease or treatment and discuss their responses.

12- to 14-Year-Old Adolescents—"I Cry in My Room Alone"

- Both abstract and logical thinking are possible for early adolescents, and they are able to take the initiative to obtain information. They may seem to understand the reality of the parent's illness and possible complications, but they lack the experience to know how to deal with it and with the strong emotions it evokes in themselves and others.
- They become emotion avoidant, fearing any public expression of their feelings and often saying, "I cry in my room alone." This may become exaggerated by the stress of the parent's illness. They may avoid discussion of the facts because talking about the situation creates emotional reactions in them and in their parents. This limits their ability to obtain empathic support, which is often very needed by young adolescents.
- Young adolescents are primarily concerned with being accepted by peers. Peers at this age are also limited in their ability to respond appropriately to an emotionally intense situation, so their network of support is more limited than those of older adolescents.
- Requests for increased household assistance may clash with the adolescent's withdrawing from parents, achieving emotional independence, and, most of all, being accepted by peers.
- Adolescents become more egocentric with pubertal changes and may seem callous toward the parent's illness and needs. "One 14-year-old said, 'If he could drive to his chemotherapy, he can drive me to my party tonight.' This exaggerated self-centeredness can sometimes lead to spiraling family conflicts if misunderstood" (Christ, 2001, p. 152).

Guidelines for Practice

- Keep the young adolescent "in the loop" in understanding the parent's diagnosis, treatment, treatment goals, and expectations for recovery. Sometimes they are left out of prognostic information when death is imminent, whereas older adolescents are included. They resent this and it leads to mistrust. Although they may try to avoid information, it should be provided.
- Help parents understand how normal developmental strivings may conflict with the parent's need for

physical help, support, and understanding. Young adolescents are likely feeling more distress than they are able to show or deal with; they withdraw when overwhelmed.

- Provide access to education, information, and discussions with physicians and other staff about the parent's illness.
- Reduce family conflict that may emerge from frustration with their self-focus. Interpret it as a temporary situation that will change over time as they are able to adapt.
- Encourage expression through writing, journaling, music, art, expressive activities, and socializing. These seem to be more accessible ways for them to communicate about highly emotional situations. Individual counseling should also be considered if affective or behavioral symptoms are emerging. Often, parents are shocked by the complexity and depth of the adolescent's written story about the parent's illness, reactions, and relationship; adolescents are often unable to express these feelings verbally.
- Communicate with the adolescent's school about the parent's condition, especially if the illness advances. For example, the school can be helpful in assigning one teacher/counselor to receive information about changes in the illness and distribute it to other teachers. This frees the adolescent from having to tell each teacher individually when he or she is trying to focus on school work. The schools can provide special homework assistance or other accommodations in the classroom.
- Respect the adolescent's need for peer contact.

15- to 17-Year-Old Adolescents: "So Much Has Changed; Nothing Will Ever Be the Same Again"

- Middle adolescents tend to be more constrained in behavior, more understanding of situational demands, more empathic to parent's needs, and more helpful than their younger peers.
- Advanced cognitive abilities that permit a clearer understanding of past, present, and future impacts of the parent's illness and possible loss can lead to intense and sustained anxiety and depression. The intensity of reactions is sometimes more similar to those of adults.
- Their inexperience in managing such intensity, however, can present coping challenges, including high levels of anxiety and depression. Destructive acting-out behaviors should always be assessed.
- The ability to form more intimate individual supportive relationships than younger adolescents gives them a potentially stronger support network of peers that may be less threatened by emotional intensity.
- Online communication with peers can also be helpful for adolescents this age.
- Because they are less ambivalent about independence, middle and older adolescents often distance themselves considerably from family and struggle with how to balance their own desires and needs with those of the family.

Guidelines for Practice

- Facilitate parents' providing honest, open, and detailed information about the disease and treatment process in hopeful ways without being unrealistic. Maintain an ongoing dialogue with the adolescent about the parent's medical condition and provide opportunities for questions and reactions.
- Discuss the ways in which they can be helpful but, to the extent possible, maintain their normal routines with school and family. Recognize their concerns about the impact on their own plans, with which they are preoccupied at this age.
- Clarify the adolescent's support network and make suggestions about groups, online opportunities, or individuals with whom they may discuss their responses. Validate their need for opportunities to express their responses. "Three teens, 13, 15, and 17, reported they were upset with their mother's refusal to allow them to talk with friends about her breast cancer. At earlier stages of her illness, they were okay with the secrecy, but as she was traveling around the country seeking new treatments, they felt they needed to share with friends. The father, a policeman, said he also would be more comfortable explaining some of his absences from work if he could reveal her condition. She agreed. The father went first and reported that his peers were quite supportive and he felt relieved. The 15- and 17-year-old were second to tell peers, and they too reported feeling relieved and supported. Finally, the 13-year-old had the courage to tell her friends and this also went satisfactorily" (Christ, 2000, p. 217).
- Provide opportunities to communicate with physicians and hospital staff when the parent is in the hospital.
- If the adolescent becomes involved in caregiving, a not uncommon situation for adolescents this age, provide education, information, and debriefing opportunities to acknowledge and support their caregiving role. They can be hidden caregivers, overwhelmed and unprepared for that role.
- Help parents recognize the differences in reactions to stress between older adolescents and adults. Older adolescents may experience distress more briefly and desire opportunities for distraction. They may become impatient with the well parent's emotionality, as well as that of the patient.
- Older adolescents may be more emotionally overwhelmed than they appear. Assessing for anxiety,

depression, and potential for destructive acting out should be ongoing.

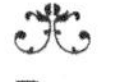

Pearls

- It is important to interview children and adolescents directly, as well as their parents, when consulting about communication with them regarding a parent's illness. Children often withhold their questions and concerns about their parent's condition as they fear upsetting the parent. Parents often believe children know much less than they actually do and they underestimate their anxiety about and misinterpretations of partial information.
- Helping parents with communication early in the parent's cancer illness may assist them in establishing an effective pathway of open communication with their children that is consistent with their family's communication style and meets the informational and emotional needs of children of different ages.
- Parents generally need some time to process their own responses to illness and treatment changes before they share information with their children; therefore, they may not want to engage in such discussions during the diagnostic process. They may also need help with listening and responding to their own reactions and with drawing out their children's concerns.
- Family consultation services require a range of interventions to meet the diverse needs of families across the continuum of care, including individual, family, group, outreach, educational, resource, and school advocacy interventions.

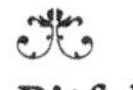

Pitfalls

- Interviewing only the parent with cancer and the well parent when providing consultation about communication with children may limit the effectiveness of the intervention. When possible, the children should also be interviewed individually or in a group.
- Failing to understand developmental variations in processing information, managing emotions, and obtaining support and solace around the parent's diagnosis will limit effectiveness in guiding parent communication.

Oncology social workers have the knowledge, skill, and value set to lead the development of family consultation services in oncology programs across the continuum of care. This is often a signature program for social work that demonstrates oncology social work expertise and ability to access families on these issues. More individuals are living with cancer as a chronic illness over many years. Effective communication with children about the cancer and its impact on their lives is essential to support them through its stressful and successful transitions. More and more parallel group programs with parents and children are using a variety of activities and expressive techniques to engage children in more openly communicating their thoughts and feelings and to show parents how communication with children about cancer's impact can create strong family bonds, reduce anxiety, and improve functioning. Individual consultation will continue to be required when families become overwhelmed with tasks created by the illness and have needs for guidance that are urgent, complex, and specific to them.

REFERENCES

Buchwald, D., Delmar, C., & Schantz-Laursen, B. (2012). How children handle life when their mother or father is seriously ill and dying. *Scandinavian Journal of Caring Sciences, 26*, 228–235.

Christ, G. (2000). *Healing children's grief: Surviving a parent's death from cancer.* New York, NY: Oxford University Press.

Christ, G., & Christ, A. (2006). Current approaches to helping children cope with a parent's terminal illness. *CA: A Cancer Journal for Clinicians, 56*, 197–212.

Christ, G., Kane, D., & Horsley, H. (2011). Grief and terrorism: Toward a family focused intervention. In R. A. Neimeyer, H. Winokuer, D. Harris, & G. Thornton (Eds.), *Grief and bereavement in contemporary society: Bridging research and practice* (pp. 203–223). London, England: Routledge.

Christ, G., Siegel, K., Karus, D., & Christ, A. (2005). Evaluation of an intervention for bereaved children. *Social Work in End-of-Life and Palliative Care, 1*(3), 57–81.

Huang, X., O-Connor, M., & Lee, S. (2014). School-aged and adolescent children's experience when a parent has non-terminal cancer: A systematic review and meta-synthesis of qualitative studies. *Psycho-Oncology, 23*, 493–506.

Huizinga, G. A., van der Graff, W. T., Visser, A., Dijkstra, J. S., & Hoestra-Weebers, J. E. (2003). Psychosocial consequences for children of a parent with cancer. *Cancer Nursing, 26*, 195–202.

Kennedy, V. L., & Lloyd-Williams, M. (2009). How children cope when a parent has advanced cancer. *Psycho-Oncology, 18*, 886–892. doi:10.1002/pon.1455

Krattenmacher, T., Kuhne, F., Ernst, J., Bergelt, C., Romer, G., & Moller, B. (2012). Parental cancer: Factors associated with children's psychosocial adjustment—a systematic review. *Journal of Psychosomatic Research, 72*, 344–356.

Lewis, F., Casey, S., Brandt, P., Shands, M., & Zahlis, E. (2006). The enhancing connections program: Pilot study of a cognitive-behavioral intervention for mothers and children affected by breast cancer. *Psycho-Oncology, 15*, 486–497.

McCue, K. (2011). *How to help children through a parent's serious illness.* New York, NY: St. Martin's Griffin.

Murphy, P., Gallo-Silver, L., & Kramer, S. (2005). Sharing the journey with your child. In P. Van Dernoot (Ed.), *Helping your children cope with cancer.* New York, NY: Hatherleight Press.

Osborn, T. (2007). The psychosocial impact of parental cancer on children and adolescents: A systematic review. *Psycho-Oncology, 16*, 101–126.

Raveis, V. H., & Siegel, K. (1999). Children's psychological distress following the death of a parent. *Journal of Youth and Adolescence, 28*, 165.

Russell, K., & Rauch, P. (2012). Parenting with cancer I: Developmental perspective, communication, and coping. *Advances in Experimental Medicine and Biology, 732*, P141–P149.

Saldinger, A., Cain, A., & Porterfield, K. (2003). Managing traumatic stress in children anticipating parental death. *Psychiatry, 66*(2), 168–181.

Sandler, I. N., Ayers, T. S., & Romer, A. L. (2002). Fostering resilience in families in which a parent has died. *Journal of Palliative Medicine, 5*(6), 945–956.

Sheehan, D., Draucker, C., Christ, G., Mayo, M., Heim, K., & Parish, S. (2014). Telling adolescents a parent is dying. *Journal of Palliative Medicine, 17*(5), 1–9. doi:10.1089/jpm. 2013.0344

Siegel, K., Karus, D., & Raveis, V. H. (1996). Adjustment of children facing the death of a parent due to cancer. *Journal of the American Academy of Child and Adolescent Psychiatry, 35*, 442–450.

Siegel, K., Mesagno, F., Karus, D., Christ, G., Banks, K., & Moynihan, R. (1992). Psychosocial adjustment of children with a terminally ill parent. *Journal of the Academy of Child and Adolescent Psychiatry, 31*, 327–333.

Siegel, K., Raveis, V., & Karus, D. (1996). Pattern of communication with children when a parent has cancer. In L. Baider, C. Cooper, & A. Kaplan De-Nour (Eds.), *Cancer and the family* (pp. 109–128). New York, NY: John Wiley.

Visser, A., Huizinga, G. A., Van der Graaf, W. T. A., Hoekstra, H. J., & Hoekstra-Weebers, J. (2004). The impact of parental cancer on children and the family: A review of the literature. *Cancer Treatment Review, 30*, 683–694.

Weaver, K., Rowland, J., Alfano, C., & McNeel, T. (2010). Parental cancer and the family: A population-based estimate of the number of US cancer survivors residing with their minor children. *Cancer, 116*, 4395–4401.

60

Lynn Behar and Frances Marcus Lewis

Single Parents Coping With Cancer and Children

Key Concepts

- *Single parents have special challenges when diagnosed with cancer and raising children alone.*
- *Single parents diagnosed with cancer should be referred to an oncology social worker for assessment and support.*
- *Children of single parents with cancer have challenges unique to their position in a single-parent family.*
- *Single-parent families develop strengths by learning self-reliance and interdependence.*

Nearly a quarter of U.S. adults living with cancer are raising dependent children (Semple & McCance, 2010; Weaver, Rowland, Alfano, & McNeel, 2010), and approximately 29.5% of them are single parents (U.S. Census Bureau, 2009). Thus, a large number of single-parent families are struggling to access support and necessary services within the health care system. These single-parent families facing parental cancer have the same stressors as two-parent families, but also others unique to their circumstances. This chapter identifies special issues faced by single parents with cancer, describes challenges specific to children and adolescents of single parents who have cancer, indicates strengths that single-parent families develop to deal with difficulties, suggests aspects of family assessment, identifies appropriate interventions, and provides resources for single-parent families.

Who Are Single Parents and What Are Their Challenges?

The majority of single parents started out in committed relationships and did not anticipate raising children alone. The percentage of single-parent homes increased substantially, from 19.5% to 29.5%, between 1980 and 2008 (U.S. Census Bureau, 2012). Experts in the United States have identified several factors connected to the increase in single-parent households: a cultural shift toward greater acceptance of single-parent childrearing (NewsOne, 2011), which includes more single-father homes; expansion of single-parent adoption; and a substantial increase in births to unmarried women (from 18.4% in 1980 to 40.6% in 2008; U.S. Census Bureau, 2009).

Challenges for single parents with cancer involve not only the stresses of coping with the disease itself but also worries about how to get the support they need, their children's well-being and future, and financial concerns. These areas and the challenges for the children themselves are discussed in detail.

What Are the Particular Concerns for Single Parents With Cancer?

Little is written about single parents with cancer, meaning that much has to be extrapolated from literature about two-parent homes. When reviewing this literature, one should always ask, "How would this be different for single parents?" Presumably, in two-parent families, if one partner is diagnosed with cancer, the other partner is available to provide emotional, financial, and household support, including child care. Single parents diagnosed with cancer may not have a co-parent built into their family structure and may find it more difficult to engage someone in that role at such a stressful time. Lewis and Darby (2003) showed that two-parent households provide a protective factor in supportive parenting, which is less likely with single parents.

Whereas all parents worry about the uncertainty of cancer and their children's well-being, single parents agonize from the time of diagnosis about how they will get through it alone and what will happen to their children if they die (Behar, 1999). The few studies of single parents with cancer are mainly limited to single mothers. An overall theme of "getting through it alone" was identified in a descriptive study of single women with breast cancer (Behar, 1999).

All parents living with cancer find talking with their children about the illness to be onerous, but single parents generally have the added difficulty of being alone in such situations. The need to talk to the children about the initial diagnosis, the course of treatment, and the future becomes a burden compounded by this sense of having to do everything alone. Parents often lack the knowledge about cancer, as well as how to give information in a way the children will understand (Elmberger, Bolund, & Lutzen, 2000). Yet they seldom obtain professional help in telling the children about the cancer in an age-appropriate manner (Fitch, Bunston, & Elliot, 1999). Feeling unprepared and lacking skills, parents try to strike the balance between telling their children the truth and protecting them (Elmberger, Bolund, Magnusson, Lutzen, & Andershed, 2008). Parents need support and education to help develop strategies for open communication about their cancer and to reduce isolation and maintain their children's trust (Semple & McCance, 2010). Oncology social workers are specifically trained to assist families in reaching these goals.

A cancer diagnosis and accompanying treatment is emotionally and physically exhausting for the ill parent. On top of this, not being able to perform as a "good parent" can be distressing (Elmberger et al., 2000). Symptoms and treatment-related side effects often disrupt parenting. One study of young mothers with breast cancer found that one in five women with young children skipped potentially lifesaving postsurgery radiation treatment because they needed to take care of their children (Pan, Smith, & Shih, 2013). Hospitalization for treatment or infections is especially problematic for single parents with insufficient external help. Shands, Lewis, and Zahlis (2000) studied mothers with breast cancer and found that the mothers' goal was to maintain the children's lifestyles and maintain a sense of normalcy, even if such goals required that the parent act normal and "strong." When unable to perform perceived important parenting tasks, diagnosed parents felt overwhelming guilt (Elmberger et al., 2008; Semple & McCance, 2010).

In the face of this need to be strong, some single parents are reluctant to ask family members or friends for help because it would be admitting weakness (Elmberger et al., 2000). In one study, even when single mothers could identify people who could help, they were reluctant to ask. They resisted asking for or accepting help they thought they could not "pay back" (Behar, 1999). Although expressing concerns about their children "growing up too soon" (Fitch et al., 1999), mothers eventually found they had to ask their children to take on more responsibilities in the family.

Living with cancer is financially devastating for many people, but for single parents, it can be doubly so in that there is no second income and often limited savings as backup. And the differences between men and women experiencing financial challenges are significant. In the United States, 27% of custodial single mothers and their children live in poverty, in contrast to 12.9% of custodial single fathers (U.S. Census Bureau, 2009). The employment status of single parents is also a factor in financial stress. Although the majority of single parents are gainfully employed (79.2% for custodial mothers and 92% for custodial fathers), only 50% of the mothers and 74% of the fathers work full-time year-round (U.S. Census Bureau, 2009). In addition, the lack of financial support by an absent parent is significant; only 41.2% of custodial parents received the full mandated child support in 2009 (U.S. Census Bureau, 2009). When symptoms or disease progression limit a parent's ability to work, especially the single parent's, financial uncertainties abound, including loss of employer-sponsored medical insurance.

One of the most painful aspects of having cancer is the possibility that parents may not be able to plan for their children's futures and see them grow to maturity. Making arrangements for death is an overwhelming task for single parents, even though they think about the possibility from the time of diagnosis. As much as this planning is considered (most often not with the children), single parents often neglect to prepare adequately. In a retrospective review of single parents who died from cancer, Willis, Peck, Sells, and Rodabaugh (2001) found that only five of the 10 families in their study had developed custody plans that were ultimately successful. In 40% of the cases, the children eventually went to people to whom the deceased parents were opposed. Half of the children had not been told of their custody plans (Willis et al., 2001). When parents were able to make arrangements and talk with their children about who would take over parental responsibility, children felt less frightened. One mother said, "It is better to face it and deal with it—not to be a victim of all your fears. This brought us very close together as a family" (Elmberger et al., 2000, p. 494).

In spite of the problems elucidated previously, many parents realize they have strengths that developed because of the life changes they have undergone in response to their cancer. They value life in a new way (Elmberger et al., 2000). Mothers are found to spend more time with their children, engaging in various activities as part of helping their children cope. Their expressed desire to be strong for their children can be a positive factor (Shands et al., 2000). Others have reported more tolerance and closer bonds with their children (Semple & McCance, 2010). They focus on being more peaceful and patient, living in the moment, doing more with their children in the here and now, and being grateful daily for a life with happiness in it (Elmberger et al., 2008).

What Challenges Do the Children and Adolescents of Single Parents With Cancer Face?

Children vary in their responses to their parent's cancer by virtue of age and level of maturity. Adolescents often find themselves unable to continue with their normal development and take on adult responsibilities. Even very young children will perceive and react to the fear and insecurity of a parent dealing with cancer.

Children of parents with cancer experience many anxieties around their future. Gaining comprehensive insight into these issues is difficult, because most studies have interviewed parents about their children rather than the children themselves. However, some school-age and older children have been study participants. In one retrospective qualitative study of 35 children (ages 11 to 18) 3 to 5 years after their mother was diagnosed with breast cancer, the children identified categories of worry and confusion that they remembered (Zahlis, 2001). In almost every study of children of single parents, children speak of fear that their parent will die (Elmberger et al., 2000; Kristjanson, Chalmers, & Woodgate, 2004; Lewis et al., 2000; Zahlis, 2001). For children living with a single parent, this concern could be extreme. Another worry expressed by children in the Zahlis study was concern about what was happening to their mother during treatment. They also worried about others in the family, which would be intensified for an older child who feels responsible for younger siblings. They worried about money, which is definitely exacerbated in single-parent families. They worried about how to talk to their mothers, and they were afraid to talk to friends for fear they would think them weird or contagious (Zahlis, 2001). They worried about getting cancer themselves. Young children may need extra reassurance and attention; they may display regressive behavior, may revert to bedwetting and the need for transitional objects, and may want to sleep with the parent (Elmberger et al., 2000). They may have more guilt than older children do, thinking they may have caused the cancer (Kristjanson et al., 2004). These responses make it clear that children need ongoing communication and the opportunity to ask questions, talk about feelings, and know they can talk to their parent or others about their experience (Zahlis, 2001). A family-centered oncology social worker provides this direction and support.

In connection with the anxieties just described, children who have a parent with cancer may have a greater risk of experiencing emotional and behavioral problems than is seen in the general population. The results of research studies around these potential problems are mixed but generally indicate that children with an ill parent display more internalizing and externalizing problem behavior than do children with a healthy parent (Sieh, Meijer, Oort, Visser-Meily, & Van der Leij, 2010; Watson et al., 2006). Confounding factors are the nature and severity of the illness and treatment; differences in families' social, cultural, and psychological resources and supports; self-esteem; adjustment in the parent; age and gender of the child (Watson et al., 2006); and whether parents or children report the problems (Thastum et al., 2009). In a seminal study of single mothers with breast cancer, Lewis, Zahlis, Shands, Sinsheimer, and Hammond (1996) illustrate that income may be the causative factor in the relatively lower level of functioning of the children in their study. Even if the risks for children of single parents living with cancer are not statistically higher than for others, the children will have unique needs for support, varying by age and other factors.

What is considered the normal process of young people becoming adults in their own right can be disrupted in families living with a cancer diagnosis. Even though the quality of their relationship with their parent is a major protective factor in psychosocial functioning (Lewis et al., 2000; Lewis & Darby, 2003), separating and individuating are important steps for adolescents, and a parent's cancer may interrupt this process by throwing the adolescent into an unnatural state. Adolescents have reported feeling nervous, with a diminished ability to focus or concentrate. They have described needing to be home because of increased household responsibilities and found they were "thinking about their mothers' cancer and not just about school, friends, and activities" (Clemmons, 2009, p. 573). These adolescents said they sometimes needed to be alone and get away, but they also all expressed an intense desire to be close to their mothers.

Single parents living with cancer may exert unusually heavy demands, unconsciously and unintentionally, that lead these children to take on early adult responsibilities. Adolescents learn that they can be strong for their mothers by handling their own worries quietly or by reaching out to their mothers rather than waiting for their mothers to reach out (Clemmons, 2009). Linked to this strengthened bond and increased maturity are more responsibilities, ranging from house cleaning, caring for younger siblings, cooking, and doing laundry to sometimes even providing financial support (Behar, 1999); and although it is rarely mentioned, many children provide personal care for their parents who are ill (Bauman et al., 2006; Gates & Lackey, 1998). The long-term effects of these increased demands on adolescents, sometimes described as "parentification," remain unclear.

In their position as emerging adults, adolescents believe they should be treated as people who deserve to be kept well informed about their parent's illness, about the feelings and changes they might see or expect from the parent with cancer, and even about what they might feel or expect themselves. Participants in the Kristjanson et al. (2004) study noted that they appreciated recognition of their feelings from people who were straightforward. They valued positive verbal and nonverbal emotional supportive gestures and reported intolerance for insincerity.

What Are the Assessment and Intervention Needs for Single-Parent Families?

The medical system must offer relevant procedures for the family needs of parents diagnosed with cancer, especially single parents. These parents should be referred to a family-centered oncology social worker who takes the lead in assessment of needs. A formalized intake should assess the family system's strengths and needs, identify parenting concerns and children's needs, and determine the availability of support systems (in a genogram prepared for the care team). Children should be assessed separately to identify their own needs for information and support.

Single parents with young children should be offered oncology social work support in regard to parenting issues throughout their cancer trajectory. Family/team conferences should be arranged to provide accurate information, facilitate family communication, and encourage discussion. Oncology social work involvement should focus on family-oriented care, information, and support around communicating with children in developmentally appropriate ways and facilitating information sharing between family members and others. The Parenting Concerns Questionnaire (PCQ) is a useful comprehensive instrument for assessing specific needs of parents with cancer (Muriel et al., 2012). In addition to the work with the parents, children should be provided experiences (hospital/clinic visits) and written information to facilitate understanding of their parent's experience. They should be given the opportunity to express their most frightening visions. Planning for the family's future should be an important part of discussions from the beginning of the team's involvement with the parent, ultimately resulting in a firm legal custody plan for the children. These discussions need to include the children, giving them age-appropriate information.

Evelyn is an African American single mother of 16-year-old Peter, 13-year-old Kathy, and 8-year-old Sally. She has been employed in middle management in a large corporation, making a salary sufficient to support her three children. She has been divorced for 7 years from the children's father, who has been estranged from the family since he moved to Florida with a new wife 6 years ago. He does not provide financial support for his first family.

A year ago, Evelyn was diagnosed with a rare and fast-growing inflammatory breast cancer. Through scans, Evelyn was found to have lymph node involvement plus a small lesion in her lung, equating to a Stage 4 diagnosis. She was told her prognosis for survival for 5 years was low.

Determined to be a survivor, Evelyn underwent aggressive neoadjuvant chemotherapy, during which she was unable to work for 6 months. She then had a modified radical mastectomy and started a 6-week daily radiation protocol. Evelyn's skin became raw, oozing, and painful, and when she saw her oncologist, she said she didn't think she could continue the treatment. Her doctor requested an oncology social work consultation.

The social worker found that Evelyn had been a strong, self-sufficient woman during her treatment period and had not asked for help from people other than her children, not even from her mother and siblings. She belongs to a church but has not told people there of her diagnosis. She had been referred to a breast cancer support group but didn't feel like her cancer was similar to those of other women there, and she found she was not comfortable being the only African American woman, so she quit after a few visits. She recently had to go on disability when her sick leave expired.

The children have had varying reactions to Evelyn's cancer. Peter has become "the little man," having taken a job in a grocery store to help financially. However, his grades have fallen, and he tries to boss his sisters around. Kathy refuses to take orders from Peter. Although her grades have not suffered, Kathy has withdrawn from the family and is out of the house as much as possible. The youngest child, Sally, has regressed, wants to sleep with her mother, and has occasionally wet the bed; she has returned to thumb sucking and bursts into tears over even minor altercations.

Evelyn has some savings but is concerned about finances. She says she has been unwilling to allow herself to think she could die and leave her children, but that the thought has been intruding lately because she feels so ill. The possibility of leaving her children is the worst thing Evelyn can imagine because she can think of no plan for them at this time. She does not want them pulled out of their home, and she does not want her ex-husband raising them.

Oncology Social Work Assessment

Meet with Evelyn to determine support needs, next steps, and goals. Create a genogram to identify possible support people she is willing to access for support when she needs it. Meet with children individually and together.

The following interventions can be planned depending on goals set with Evelyn:

1. *Family meeting with Evelyn and children to help each of them express feelings and concerns. What do the children think is happening?*
2. *Connecting Evelyn and the children to a 24-hour support line and/or online groups for ongoing emotional support.*

3. *Team meeting to discuss roles of individual team members in best supporting this family.*
4. *Spiritual assessment and possible referral to team's spiritual counselor, or perhaps reinvolvement with her church/pastor if Evelyn is open to this.*
5. *Continued assessment of Evelyn's financial situation and the financial resources available to her.*
6. *Continued assessment of options and permanency planning for children. Ensure that Evelyn knows that by not addressing this, her ex-husband will be the legal caregiver of the children if she dies.*
7. *Foremost goal of maintaining hope mixed with planning if Evelyn's health deteriorates.*

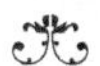

Pearls

- When single parents are diagnosed with cancer, their first concern is their children, with a focus on providing good parenting during their illness and deciding what will happen to the children if they die, although few make firm legal plans for the custody of their children.
- Children and adolescents in single-parent families experience anxieties and worries in addition to those experienced by children of dual-parent families.
- Children and their parents in single-family homes are resilient by virtue of having been single, relying on each other, and working together for family cohesion. Children provide meaning and strength for parents in fighting their illness.

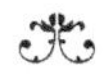

Pitfalls

- Not having a natural point of entry in the medical system for oncology social work involvement in addressing family issues.
- Health care professionals lacking necessary knowledge about the specific needs of single parents.
- Not having a team member whose responsibility it is to ask about the children and the parent's perceived abilities to parent.
- Lack of health care providers' knowledge about how to help people face the issue of custody planning.
- Limited studies on single-parent families and the children in single-parent families—existing study samples are almost all White, middle-class mothers, predominantly with breast cancer.

Single parents and their children have support needs beyond those of dual-parent families. However, the parents may well have strengths that help them face the challenges of being a single parent with cancer that can be explicated and used as part of generating support systems for families. Longitudinal research is needed to follow single parents and their children to identify the range of developmental trajectories experienced and whether some children emerge with new strengths. The results of such studies could be used in developing intervention planning procedures for these vulnerable families.

ADDITIONAL RESOURCES

Single Parenting With Cancer Blogs

Singleton Moms—hope, help and support for single parents with cancer: http://singletonmoms.org

Single Women in Motion (S.W.I.M.) Cancer Foundation—resources and support services for single mothers with cancer: http://www.swimcancerfoundation.org

Parenting With Cancer

About Mothers With Cancer: http://motherswithcancer.wordpress.com/help/

Cancer Support Community: http://www.cancersupportcommunity.org/MainMenu/Family-Friends/Parenting-Through-Cancer.html

Parenting With Cancer: http://parentingwithcancer.com/blog/

Written Material

Ackerman, A., & Ackerman, A. (2002). *Our mom has cancer.* Atlanta, GA: American Cancer Society. Written by two children whose mother is diagnosed with breast cancer.

McCue, K. (1994). *How to help children through a parent's serious illness.* New York, NY: St. Martin's Press.

Ness, P. (2011). *A monster calls.* Somerville, MA: Candlewick Press. A novel about an adolescent whose mother has cancer.

Rauch, P., & Muriel, A. (2005). *Raising an emotionally healthy child when a parent is sick.* New York, NY: McGraw-Hill.

Schlessel Harpham, W. (1997). *When a parent has cancer: A guide to caring for your children.* New York, NY: Harper Collins.

Smith, I. (2000). *Tiny boat at sea: How to help children when a parent has cancer.* Portland, OR: Grief Watch.

When a parent has cancer: How to talk to your kids. A guide for parents with cancer, their families and friends. New South Wales, Australia: Cancer Council. Retrieved from http://www.touro.com/upload/assets/pdfs/cancer_center/whenaparenthascancer.pdf

Multiple books on this website: http://www.touchedbycancer.org/wp-content/uploads/2011/06/Bibliography-When-an-adult-has-cancer-2010.pdf

REFERENCES

Bauman, L. J., Foster, G., Silver, E. J., Berman, R., Gamble, I., & Muchaneta, L. (2006). Children caring for their ill parents with HIV/AIDS. *Vulnerable Children and Youth Studies, 1*(1), 56–70.

Behar, L. C. (1999). Getting through it alone: A descriptive study of the experiences of single mothers with breast cancer and adolescent children. (Doctoral dissertation). University of Washington. *Dissertation Abstracts International, 60*(2000), 3135.

Clemmons, D. A. (2009). The significance of motherhood for adolescents whose mothers have breast cancer. *Oncology Nursing Forum*, *36*(5), 571–577.

Elmberger, E., Bolund, C., & Lutzen, K. (2000). Transforming the exhausting to energizing process of being a good parent in the face of cancer. *Health Care for Women International*, *21*, 485–499.

Elmberger, E., Bolund, C., Magnusson, A., Lutzen, K., & Andershed, B. (2008). Being a mother with cancer: Achieving a balance in the transition process. *Cancer Nursing*, *31*(1), 58–66.

Fitch, M. I., Bunston, T., & Elliot, M. (1999). All in the family: When mom's sick: Changes in a mother's role and in the family after her diagnosis of cancer. *Cancer Nursing*, *22*(1), 58–63.

Gates, M. F., & Lackey, N. R. (1998). Youngsters caring for adults with cancer. *Image: The Journal of Nursing Scholarship*, *30*(1), 11–15. doi:10.1111/1547-5069. 1998.tb01229.x.

Kristjanson, L. J., Chalmers, K. I., & Woodgate, R. (2004). Information and support needs of adolescent children of women with breast cancer. *Oncology Nursing Forum*, *31*(1), 111–119.

Lewis, F. M., Behar, L. C., Anderson, K. A., Shands, M. E., Zahlis, E. H., Darby, E., & Sinsheimer, J. A. (2000). Blowing away the myths of the child's experience with the mother's breast cancer. In L. Baider, C. L. Cooper, & A. Kaplan De-Nour (Eds.), *Cancer and the family* (2nd ed., pp. 201–221). New York, NY: John Wiley & Sons.

Lewis, F. M., & Darby, E. L. (2003). Adolescent adjustment and maternal breast cancer: A test of the "faucet hypothesis." *Journal of Psychosocial Oncology*, *21*(4), 83–106.

Lewis, F. M., Zahlis, E. H., Shands, M. E., Sinsheimer, J. A., & Hammond, M. A. (1996). The functioning of single women with breast cancer and their school-aged children. *Cancer Practice*, *4*(1), 15–24.

Muriel, A. C., Moore, C. W., Baer, L., Park, E. R., Kornblith, A. B., Piri, W., ... Rauch, P. K. (2012). Measuring psychosocial distress and parenting concerns among adults with cancer. *Cancer*, *118*(22), 5671–5678. doi:10/1002/cncr.27572

NewsOne. (2011, April 27). 72 percent of black kids raised by single parent, 25% overall in U.S. Retrieved from http://newsone.com/1195075/children-single-parents-u-s-american/

Pan, I-W., Smith, B. D., & Shih, Y-C. T. (2013). Factors contributing to underuse of radiation among younger women with breast cancer. *Journal of the National Cancer Institute*. Retrieved from http://secure.oxfordjournals.org/our_journals/jnci/press_releases/djt340.pdf

Semple, C. J., & McCance, T. (2010). Parents' experience of cancer who have young children: A literature review. *Cancer Nursing*, *33*(2), 110–118.

Shands, M. E., Lewis, F. M., & Zahlis, E. H. (2000). Mothers' and children's interactions about the mother's breast cancer: An interview study. *Oncology Nursing Forum*, *52*(1), 4399–4402.

Sieh, D. S., Meijer, A. M., Oort, F. H., Visser-Meily, J. M. A., & Van der Leij, D. A. V. (2010). Problem behavior in children of chronically ill parents: A meta-analysis. *Clinical Child and Family Psychology Review*, *13*(4), 384–397. doi:1007/s10567-010-0074-z

Thastum, M., Watson, M., Kienbacher, C., Piha, J., Steck, B., Zachariae, R., ... Romer, G. (2009). Prevalence and predictors of emotional and behavioural functioning of children where a parent has cancer. *Cancer*, *115*(17), 4030–4039. doi:10.1002/cncr.24449

U.S. Census Bureau. (2009). *Custodial mothers and fathers and their child support*. Retrieved from http://www.census.gov/prod/2011pubs/p60-240.pdf

U.S. Census Bureau. (2012). Statistical abstract of the United States. Retrieved from http://www.census.gov/compendia/statab/

Watson, M., St. James-Roberts, I., Ashley, S., Tilney, C., Brougham, B., Edwards, L., ... Romer, G. (2006). Factors associated with emotional and behavioural problems among school age children of breast cancer patients. *British Journal of Cancer*, *94*, 43–50.

Weaver, E. E., Rowland, J. H., Alfano, C. M., & McNeel, T. S. (2010). Parental cancer and the family: A population-based estimate of the number of U.S. cancer survivors residing with their minor children. *Cancer*, *116*(18), 4395–4401. doi:10.1002/cncr.25368

Willis, L., Peck, M., Sells, S., & Rodabaugh, K. H. (2001). Custody planning: A retrospective review of oncology patients who were single parents. *Journal of Pain and Symptom Management*, *21*(5), 380–384.

Zahlis, E. H. (2001). The child's worries about the mother's breast cancer: Sources of distress in school-age children. *Oncology Nursing Forum*, *28*(6), 1019–1025.

61

Krista Nelson

A Parallel Group Program for Parents and Children: Using Expressive Techniques and Activities to Facilitate Communication

Key Concepts

- *Parents diagnosed with cancer want to know how best to mitigate the traumatic aspects of their condition on their children and family.*
- *Parallel group interventions with parents and children have shown a positive impact on children's functioning during bereavement. This model was replicated with parents in a hospital setting during the patient's treatment, for most families when the patient's illness was advanced.*
- *This hospital-based group intervention program used art, play, and other creative activities with young children, adolescents, and families to enhance coping with and communication about the parent's cancer illness.*
- *Knowledge of child development is essential in providing support to parents with cancer.*
- *Oncology social workers are well situated to engage families in interventions and programs that help patients communicate effectively with the children in their lives.*

The National Cancer Institute estimates that 24% of all patients with cancer are parenting a child age 18 or younger (National Cancer Institute, 1992) and that an estimated 562,000 minor children in the United States are living with a parent in the early phases of cancer treatment and recovery (Weaver, Rowland, Alfano, & McNeel, 2010). Therefore, an essential skill for all oncology social workers and those who help with patient navigation is to have an understanding of the impact of a parent's cancer diagnosis and its treatment on their children. Oncology social workers are well aligned by knowledge, skill, and clinical assignment to provide consultation and guidance to families on these issues.

When patients with cancer are parenting younger children and adolescents, preoccupation with how to communicate the diagnosis and how much information to provide is common (Turner, Kelly, Allison, & Wetzig, 2005). These children's stress and their parents' associated stress are often hidden from the medical team (Rait & Lederberg, 1990). But given an opportunity to talk with social workers and other mental health professionals, parents inquire how best to mitigate the traumatic aspects of life-threatening illness on their children and family (Christ, 2000).

New mandates for psychosocial screening and assessment make it possible to identify patients and families that may benefit from individual and group interventions (see Section 4). Parents need early and ongoing information and support throughout the cancer trajectory with techniques and specific examples about how to communicate and cope (Davis Kirsch, Brandt, & Lewis, 2003; Stiffler, Haase, Hosei, & Barada, 2008).

Support groups are a potentially time- and cost-efficient way to effectively engage families of cancer patients, provide them with tools to enhance communication and coping, and help them normalize their feelings. This format also affords peer support and creates opportunities for participants to hear others' helpful experiences. Because children's adaptation to a parent's cancer illness is consistently related to family communication and functioning, a family-oriented approach to support is recommended (Bugge, Helseth, & Darbyshire, 2009; Christ, Siegel, Karus, & Christ, 2005; Raveis & Siegel, 1999; Thastum et al., 2009). This chapter describes a group intervention that has been successfully implemented in

Portland, Oregon, sponsored by Providence Cancer Center with additional community sponsors. This group was established in 2004 and has served over 360 families in 9 years.

Impact of Cancer on Families

Oncology social workers are well situated by their assignment to work with families as the initial contact and resource for younger cancer patients who are also parents. With the 2007 Institute of Medicine report *Cancer Care for the Whole Patient: Meeting Psychosocial Health Needs* (Institute of Medicine, 2007), oncology social workers are positioned to initiate early screening, assessment, information, and referrals to these patients. Open and honest communication tailored to the developmental level of the child and where the patient is along the cancer trajectory is recommended. Appropriate and timely communication can help children understand and cope with a parent's cancer, express their own thoughts and emotions, and build relationships of trust with parents that can mitigate cancer's adverse consequences on their development and functioning.

Parents frequently make the mistake of withholding information in the belief that they are protecting their children from the burden of cancer and treatment and from the threat of loss, thereby normalizing their lives. Perceiving a parent's anxiety about cancer, children may avoid asking questions. Consultation with an oncology social worker can teach the parents the importance of using real words, like *cancer* and *chemotherapy*, and remind them that, unlike for adults, words like *cancer* are not emotionally charged for children. Parents often say the reason for not communicating is to avoid children's questions about a parent's possible death. Social work consultation can provide guidance and support from a knowledgeable professional about how to answer these difficult questions (Barnes et al., 2000; Christ, 2000; Turner et al., 2005).

E-mails From Families After Initial Consult With Oncology Social Worker

"Thanks again for your advice today about how to tell the kids. Shortly after you and I spoke, I talked to the boys and just went for it. When you told me what you thought one of the boys would eventually say to me, I thought . . . yeah, you don't know my boys. They say nothing. But Jonathan said it almost verbatim! He said 'Mom, this is boring. I get it, I know dad is sick. I know he's going to die. I don't need to talk about it, I already know everything.' (And, it was very cute, a couple seconds later he sort of patted my shoulder and validated that he heard my feelings.)"

"One of the big hurdles we had to jump was informing our kids—Tomas (8) and Rosey (5). We can't thank you enough for giving us the verbiage and strength for the conversation. It went better than we could have expected. Thank you so much!!"

Impact on Children

Children want to hear that they are going to be safe, cared for, and loved. Many studies show that open communication within the family may lead to more effective coping for children whose parents have been diagnosed with cancer (Gazendam-Donofrio et al., 2009) and decrease their levels of anxiety (Watson et al., 2006). In one study, children's well-being was found to be particularly affected at diagnosis and when the illness changed/recurred (i.e., times of increasing stress for the patient and family as well; Helseth & Ulfsaet, 2003). This is promising for families because it suggests that by enhancing communication at these times, parents can mitigate the impact of their cancer on their children. Adolescents reported that receiving information regarding diagnosis, treatment, and even prognosis was important to them and that they benefited from understanding normal emotional reactions to this information (Kristjanson, Chalmers, & Woodgate, 2004). Across studies, relationship to the surviving parent or caregiver, effective parenting, and open communication with children are consistently found to have an effect on children's functioning (Osborn, 2007; Visser, Huizinga, van der Fraaf, Hoekstra, & Hoekstra-Weevers, 2004).

Group and Family Intervention

Rationale

This chapter describes a support group intervention used at Providence Cancer Center in Portland, Oregon. Parallel groups for parents/caregivers and children have been found to be an effective format for helping families and children during the bereavement process (Sandler et al., 2003). This current model represents a modification for parents with cancer. The program prioritizes coping, communication, and identification of feelings as the group therapeutic components and curriculum focus.

The family-group intervention provides concrete strategies and activities that are child oriented to enhance communication within the family (Davis Kirsch et al., 2003). The group also offers mutual peer support. The addition of art, play, and other facilitative techniques and activities helps patients express their responses to the situation of the their cancer (Serlin, Classen, Frances, & Angell, 2000). Reflective listening is an essential skill used in the children's groups, and staff and volunteers have been trained in reflective listening techniques.

Program Description

The Providence Family Program Support Group was created to provide education for these parents about ways to communicate, especially at the time of diagnosis and recurrence (Barnes et al., 2000). The group was created for families of patients who are parenting children aged 5 to 18 years. This monthly group is free to participants and open to anyone in the community, regardless of where they seek medical treatment. The group is held in the evening from 6:00 to 8:00 p.m.

Families are provided with a free meal (often pizza) together with other families. At 6:30, the participants (between 40 and 60 family members) are divided into age-specific groups that meet simultaneously. All groups are facilitated by master's degree–trained oncology social workers and supplemented by trained volunteer facilitators. Volunteers have ongoing training in reflective listening techniques and general education on cancer and children provided by Providence Cancer Center. Volunteer and paid staff are e-mailed curriculum and journal articles supporting the group activities before the group meeting.

Individual group structure varies depending on the developmental needs of the group. Groups focus on teaching the parents and children to identify feelings and enhance their coping skills, and parents are also educated about the developmental needs of their children through the cancer trajectory. All groups utilize art as one modality to communicate about the cancer and the effect of that cancer on family functioning. These art projects act as a bridge to communication about cancer in the home setting. Parents are encouraged to share their art projects with their children and use them to model open communication outside the group setting. Creative activities are geared to children aged 5 years and older.

Group Structure

Families referred to the Providence Family Support Group are assessed for communication patterns within the family, special needs of children, and group appropriateness. Initial referrals and phone calls help educate families on how to talk to their children about the cancer. Most families that participate are dealing with advanced cancer. At the time of assessment, group format is discussed and families are informed that deaths are honored in the group setting when one occurs. The group is an open, ongoing format, although group curriculum can be translated into a closed group format. The open group format was chosen to ensure access; that is, timely interventions and support can be offered to families facing cancer, and group members who have participated in the past can return to act as mentors within the group to new families.

Trained volunteer facilitators and staff participate in a prebriefing session for updates of group participants' health and social situations, as well as review of group curriculum. The facilitators mingle with families during meal time and then move to group facilitation in the parallel groups. A standard of using a minimum of two facilitators per group is recommended, with a larger ratio of staff to children in the children's group. After group, facilitators have a chance to debrief the group and assess concerns regarding the participants who require active follow-up.

Children's Group (Ages 5 to 12)

The children's group utilizes art and play to enhance communication and participation. The group begins with an opening circle where rules are reviewed. A talking stick is used so each member can share the specifics of who in his or her family has cancer, the type of cancer if he or she knows it, and his or her age and grade in school. Children are encouraged to think of a fun question to ask each other as they share around the circle. The facilitators then transition to popcorn-type sharing around a specified theme; for example, they might ask the group how they learned the person in their family had cancer or how they know if their parent is mad. Facilitators may also use this circle to teach breathing or relaxation techniques.

Art Session

Children then move to the art room, where participants work in small facilitated groups for continued sharing as they complete the creative art activity for the session. After the children complete their art project, they transition to the play room.

Play Session

The children's play area is divided into low- and high-energy areas. There are a variety of child-driven play activities, with facilitators using reflective play and listening whenever possible. The rooms are set up with varied activities including board games, a medical-play area, soft building blocks, a dollhouse, Legos, dodge ball, Twister, and bowling. This play area offers children an avenue to work through any strong emotions that may have come up in the group.

Closing Session

The children's group closes with the children forming a circle, where they have an opportunity to share the art they created. All groups conclude with participants making a wish for the month by placing a ceramic heart in a bowl as it is passed around the circle. These wishes may be silent or said aloud as the closing ritual.

Teen Group (Ages 13 to 18)

The teen group completes the same creative activity that all family members are doing in their respective groups. The structure of this group is flexible as group attendance fluctuates. After the facilitators introduce the theme and curriculum, they allow time for sharing, mutual support, and silence while the teens work on their project. Background music is played throughout, with teens encouraged to bring music to be played in the room for the group.

Parent Group

The adult participant attendance numbers often justify two adult groups. Supportive education is provided regarding ways to parent through the cancer experience, the impact on the children, and tools for coping. Parents also offer peer support around the difficulties of parenting when they are overwhelmed themselves. Adults also engage in a creative activity, which they are encouraged to share at home when they are asking about their children's activity. The adult group tends to be the most challenging to facilitate due to the parents' stress levels and the multiple demands on their time and energy. Parents are often appreciative of the support they receive from each other but have difficulty focusing on the curriculum, particularly when there has been a death in the group. When a death occurs, hearts are passed around in each group to honor the person who has died and his or her family.

Family Support Group Goals:
• *Peer support* • *Identification of feelings/coping skills* • *Enhanced communication* • *Education on benefits of open communication* • *Reduction of fear and anxiety around talking about cancer*

The closing ritual of the evening brings all family members together to form a circle and allow some of the children to share their art activity. This larger group ends with a closing circle with all participants holding hands and passing a hand squeeze around the circle.

A variation on the parallel group method is used two times a year, usually near or coincident with school vacation breaks. All family members are kept together for the group activity as a family unit for the evening. These meetings use curricula (e.g., drumming circles, wish flags, memory books, and a family coat of arms) that promote family communication and rituals.

Attrition

Our experience has been that patients who participate in this program are dealing with the diagnosis and treatment of a life-threatening illness that affects their family's day-to-day activities. Historically, only 20% to 30% of families with early-stage cancer are in attendance. Typically, these families participate during the active-treatment phase of their cancer but describe how difficult it is to watch other patients "not make it." Families whose loved one's cancer is stable or in remission often transition out of the group, although they are encouraged to connect in other ways as a family. The majority of participants, however, remain connected until the death of the parent, after which they do not return to group. Bereavement follow-up is provided and referrals are made to programs that support child and family bereavement.

E-mail From Surviving Parent
"The girls and I are doing really well. Not to say we don't miss him VERY much, but we are putting our lives back together and starting over. Knowing we weren't alone and going to group was very helpful in helping us have the 'hard' conversations."

Therapeutic Activities

Coping

- Coping Backpack/Coping Boxes is an activity used to help participants identify strategies to cope when feeling overwhelmed. First, the group passes items that symbolize life stressors (e.g., keys, phone, kitchen utensils, pill bottles, picture of kids) in a circle using only one hand. Next, the facilitator sends more items in the opposite direction. When participants end up with multiple items, discussion focuses on how to cope, or different ways to deal with all of the items. The children and teen group may pass balls with their feet as a variation. Family members are encouraged to share where they feel stress in their body and brainstorm ideas of things they can do to feel better. Children and parents identify items and fill a backpack with things that help them cope, such as healthy snacks, games, books, balls, guided imagery CDs, iTunes cards, chalk, bubbles, Frisbees, or journals, or they can write other things on paper that may be helpful to them.
- Journaling is identified as a modality for expression of emotion as coping. Group participants are encouraged to write/draw about big emotions, feelings about the person with cancer, how things have changed in their families, and what is better and worse. Children place sentence starters in a bowl, which group members then pick. Children may be asked to write or draw three things that make them happy, or to identify a favorite place and give details of how it looks and smells. The privacy and benefits of journaling are also described. All group participants then personalize the outside of their journal.
- Play as coping is another theme that is documented in the literature for positive coping in families and child development (Ginsburg, 2007). Examples are decorating paper kites, beach balls, or Frisbees

with memories and activities that help them cope. Families are encouraged to play together with their creation at home.

Communication

Native American talking sticks (used by tribal council members to present their sacred points of view) identify who is speaking in both adult and children's meetings. Everyone is encouraged to listen respectfully to one another's viewpoint. People responsible for holding any type of meeting are required to make their own talking stick, which may be used to teach children, hold council, make decisions regarding disputes, hold powwow gatherings, have storytelling circles, or conduct a ceremony where more than one person will speak. Traditionally, the decorations used on each stick all have meaning. Each talking stick is unique and speaks of the personal medicine of the stick owner. In the Lakotah tradition, for instance, yellow represents knowledge, blue indicates prayer and wisdom, and purple symbolizes healing. Group members are encouraged to decorate their talking stick with colored tape, ribbons, leather rope, feathers, and beads with these ideas in mind. In the parent group, the concept of listening and giving each person an opportunity to share perspectives, as well as identifying barriers to communication, is discussed.

E-mail From Dad With Cancer After Talking Stick Activity
"I wanted to tell you, yesterday I heard the kids fighting and getting louder to make their point heard. I said 'Do you remember what they taught you last night?' They quieted down instantly and ran into another room and respectfully listened to each other. I was shock(ed) and please(d) that the same info was taught in both groups, and it works."

Painting plates is an easy activity that encourages family rituals and togetherness. Between treatment and already hectic lives, many families, for example, do not share meals, which Fulkerson and colleagues suggest improves family cohesiveness and promotes healthy adolescent development (Fulkerson et al., 2006). Facilitators encourage family members to share family rituals or traditions and discuss the value of them. Participants may also share what has changed in these rituals since the person in their family was diagnosed with cancer. One ritual might be that the family comes to group once a month. Family members paint plates with memories of activities done with the person with cancer or things they would like to do. The bridging activity includes encouraging the family to share a meal together on these plates.

Creating coats of arms is an activity that families can complete when group involves families staying together for the evening. Pictures are taken of the family as they enter the room and printed while they eat. Families are then encouraged to use precut symbols, paint, pens, and so on to create their coat of arms. They use colors and symbols to represent their family's identity and what is important to them.

Identification of Feelings

Mask making helps group participants to identify both the feelings they experience on the inside and those that they show to those around them. Participants are encouraged to use colors and lines to represent different feelings, as well as decorative items such as jewels and glitter. Sentence starters may be used in any group's opening circle: "What color might let someone know they are happy?" "What kind of line would you draw to let someone know you are excited? Confused?" Group facilitators are encouraged to describe feelings that they observe in individuals' masks when possible. Parents and children reflect on how the mask's insides and outsides differ and engage in dialogue about all these feelings.

A fear collage can help group participants of all ages externalize their fears and open lines of communication within the family. Recognizing that everyone has fears creates commonality. Family members use images and words in magazines to create their collage. Seeing the same fears on their children's collages helps parents encourage and model coping techniques for the entire family for the fears they can't control (e.g., recurrence or death).

Hope/gratitude flags are a modification of traditional Buddhist prayer flags. This creative activity can be done either in family or in individual group sessions. Participants receive a piece of muslin and fabric markers and then write or draw the things they are hopeful for. Parents additionally receive a colored line long enough to tie everyone's hope flags together. Some families may choose to hang them outside so the wind can carry their hopes and wishes into the heavens.

Funding

The cost for this program is currently under $7,000 for 11 groups a year. Providing food for the groups costs around $350 a month but enables busy families to have one less thing to worry about to get to group on time. The supply budget for the creative activities typically runs under $300 because a similar curriculum has been used for over 8 years. To save money, purchases are made in bulk and some supplies are reused. Staffing costs are covered under the hospital's Cancer Support Services budget with volunteers supplementing staff time. The group is held at the hospital, so space is free. Start-up costs were supported by a $20,000 grant from the hospital foundation to cover the purchase of toys, pillows for opening circle, and other supplies.

Outcomes

Since January 2011, the average group makeup is 16 adults, 6 teens, and 11 children. A program evaluation survey was emailed to 22 families, and 16 families, representing 35 children, responded. Preliminary results show that 100% of parents with cancer who responded to the survey felt that their children had benefited from being around other children with a parent with cancer. Notably, 73% of respondents felt that participating in the group had reduced their children's anxiety about cancer, helped them feel closer as a family, and changed the way they communicated as a family; and 86% of respondents felt that the use of art in the group had helped their family talk about their feelings about cancer. When asked for comments, parents stated, "It's such an incredible and helpful place to be," "The support we received in this group allows us to find safety and love during very challenging times," and "There is grief in not being able to control cancer and the damage it does on everyone. . . . You give us renewed hope in this group."

Tips for Parents

Talking with your children and others about your cancer diagnosis is a process, not a one-time event.

- *Tell your children's teachers and counselors about the cancer diagnosis and update them periodically.*
- *Remind children that they can't catch or cause cancer.*
- *Avoid euphemisms; use real words such as chemotherapy.*
- *Consider the timing when you tell the children about the diagnosis so that there is time afterward to discuss (e.g., not right before bedtime).*
- *Tell siblings about the cancer information together if possible so everyone hears the same thing; more specific knowledge for children of different ages may be given over time as needed or requested.*
- *Set up time for children to ask more questions in a few days, but also encourage them to come to you sooner with questions if they like.*
- *Identify with children other adults they can talk to aside from the parent with cancer.*
- *Maintain routines when possible.*

Pearls

- Staff engagement, committed volunteers, community referrals, and leadership are integral to the success of a family and children parallel group program.
- A broad range of expressive techniques and activities help children and their parents to communicate effectively when a parent has cancer.
- The parallel group structure with parents and children is valuable for children and adolescents in facilitating emotional expression, a sense of normalcy and camaraderie with other children in similar situations, and more open communication within the family.
- Working with parents in group is especially challenging because of the crisis nature of a cancer diagnosis and treatment, particularly when it is in advanced stages. Parents are often emotionally overwhelmed. Yet parental presence supports children's participation, emotional expression, and coping.
- Family support groups are an effective way to engage all members of a family enduring cancer treatment.
- Flexibility in curriculum and group structure to fit the needs of the individuals present will improve participants' experience.

Pitfalls

- Staffing is a challenge because of the unpredictability of the number of group participants from month to month.
- Multiple deaths within the group may have a negative emotional impact on other group members who may be facing their own death, as well as on staff who facilitate the group.
- Family members who survive cancer may need encouragement and acceptance of their need to leave the group when they are coping with day-to-day challenges of returning to normal activities.
- Space may be a limitation to being able to split children into groups that would meet their needs better, for instance, not having the 5- and 12-year-olds together, but having a "middles" group.

A group intervention for families dealing with cancer can facilitate open and honest communication within the family, increase family cohesiveness, and reduce children's and parents' fears and anxieties. The shared knowledge of ways to bridge the gaps in their communication helps ease their fear of causing more pain and harm by openness. Rather, they experience greater strength and confidence that the family unit will endure. The use of creative modalities in parallel groups enhances communication around feelings and coping strategies within the family and encourages ongoing conversations in the home setting.

Acknowledgment

The author acknowledges Katie Hartnett, Jocelyn Libby, A'lee Wardwell, and Mark Weinmeister in the initial and ongoing development of the Providence Cancer Center Family Support Group.

ADDITIONAL RESOURCES

Cancer*Care*: http://www.cancercare.org/publications/49helping_children_understand_cancer_talking_to_your_kids_about_your_diagnosis

Children's Treehouse Foundation: http://www.childrenstreehousefdn.org

Kids Konnected: http://kidskonnected.org/

McCue, K., & Bonn, R. (2011). *How to help children through a parent's serious illness: Supportive, practical advice from a leading child life specialist.* New York, NY: St. Martin's Press.

REFERENCES

Barnes, J., Kroll, L., Burke, O., Lee, J., Jones, A., & Stein, A. (2000). Qualitative interview study of communication between parents and children about maternal breast cancer. *Western Journal of Medicine, 173*(6), 385–389.

Bugge, K. E., Helseth, S., & Darbyshire, P. (2009). Parents' experiences of a family support program when a parent has incurable cancer. *Journal of Clinical Nursing, 18*(24), 3480–3488.

Christ, G., Siegel, K., Karus, D., & Christ, A. (2005). Evaluation of an intervention for bereaved children. *Social Work in End-of-Life and Palliative Care, 1*(3), 57–81.

Christ, G. (2000). *Healing children's grief: Surviving a parent's death from cancer.* New York, NY: Oxford University Press.

Commission on Cancer. (2012). *Cancer program standards 2012: Ensuring patient-centered care.* Chicago, IL: American College of Surgeons.

Davis Kirsch, S. E., Brandt, P., & Lewis, F. (2003). Making the most of the moment: When a child's mother has breast cancer. *Cancer Nursing, 26*(1), 47–54.

Fulkerson, J. A., Story, M., Mellin, A., Leffert, N., Neumark-Sztainer, D., & French, S. A. (2006). Family dinner meal frequency and adolescent development: Relationships with developmental assets and high-risk behaviors. *Journal of Adolescent Health, 39*(3), 337–345.

Gazendam-Donofrio, S., Hoekstra, H., van der Graaf, W., van de Wiel, H., Visser, A., Huizinga, G., & Hoekstra-Weebers, J. (2009). Parent-child communication patterns during the first year after a parent's cancer diagnosis. *Cancer, 115*(18), 4227–4237.

Ginsburg, K. (2007). The importance of play in promoting healthy child development and maintaining strong parent-child bonds. *Pediatrics, 119*(1), 182–191.

Institute of Medicine. (2007). *Cancer care for the whole patient: Meeting psychosocial health needs.* Washington, DC: National Academies Press. Retrieved from http://www.iom.edu/CMS/3809/34252/47228.aspx

Helseth, S., & Ulfsaet, N. (2003). Having a parent with cancer: Coping and quality of life of children during serious illness in the family. *Cancer Nursing, 26*(5), 355–362.

Kristjanson, L. J., Chalmers, K. I., & Woodgate, R. (2004). Information and support needs of adolescent children of women with breast cancer. *Oncology Nursing Forum, 31*(1), 111–119.

National Cancer Institute. (1992). *National health interview survey.* Bethesda, MD: National Cancer Institute, Division of Cancer Control and Population Sciences, Office of Cancer Survivorship.

Osborn, T., (2007). The psychosocial impact of parental cancer on children and adolescents: A systematic review. *Psycho-Oncology, 16*(2), 101–126.

Rait, D., & Lederberg, M. (1990). The family of the cancer patient. In J. Holland & J. Rowland (Eds.), *Handbook of psychooncology* (pp. 585–597). New York, NY: Oxford University Press.

Raveis, V. H., & Siegel, K. (1999). Children's psychological distress following the death of a parent. *Journal of Youth and Adolescence, 28*(2), 165–172.

Sandler, I. N., Ayers, T. S., Wolchik, S. A., Tein, J-Y., Kwok, O-M., Haine, R. A., . . . Griffin, W. A. (2003). The Family Bereavement Program: Efficacy evaluation of a theory-based prevention program for parentally bereaved children and adolescents. *Journal of Consulting and Clinical Psychology, 71*(3), 587–600.

Serlin, I. A., Classen, C., Frances, B., & Angell, K. (2000). Symposium: Support groups for women with breast cancer; traditional and alternative expressive approaches. *The Arts in Psychotherapy, 27*(2), 124–137.

Stiffler, D., Haase, J., Hosei, B., & Barada, B. (2008). Parenting experiences with adolescent daughters when mothers have breast cancer. *Oncology Nursing Forum, 35*(1), 113–120.

Thastum, M., Watson, M., Kienbacker, C., Piha, J., Steck, B., Zachariae, R., . . . Romer, G. (2009). Prevalence and predictors of emotional and behavioural functioning of children where a parent has cancer. *Cancer, 115*(7), 4030–4039.

Turner, J., Kelly, B., Allison, R., & Wetzig, N. (2005). Psychosocial impact of newly diagnosed advanced breast cancer. *Psycho-Oncology, 14*(5), 396–407.

Visser, A., Huizinga, G., van der Fraaf, W., Hoekstra, H., & Hoekstra-Weevers, J. (2004). The impact of parental cancer on children and the family: A review of the literature. *Cancer Treatment Review, 30*, 683–694.

Watson, M., St. James-Roberts, I., Ashley, S., Tilney, C., Brougham, B., Edwards, L., & Romer, G. (2006). Factors associated with emotional and behavioural problems among school age children of breast cancer patients. *British Journal of Cancer, 94*, 43–50.

Weaver, K., Rowland, J., Alfano, C., & McNeel, T. (2010). Parental cancer and the family: A population-based estimate of the number of US cancer survivors with their minor children. *Cancer, 116*(18), 4395–4401.

XI

Pediatrics: Assessment and Interventions With Children and Adolescent Cancer Patients—The Unique Challenges of Pediatric Oncology

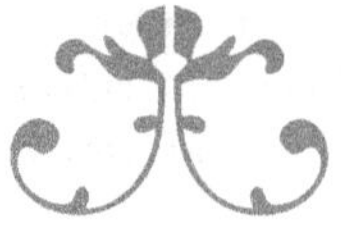

Barbara L. Jones

Childhood cancer is relatively rare as compared to adult cancer, and given advances in treatment, overall 5-year survival rates for childhood cancers are 80% for children diagnosed today (Howlader, Noone, & Krapcho, 2013; Ward, DeSantis, Robbins, Kohler, & Jemal, 2014). In 2014, there will be an estimated 15,780 new cases of cancer and 1,960 deaths from cancer among children and adolescents aged 0 to 19 years. However, childhood cancer is still the second leading cause of death in children aged 5 to 14 years. And there are an estimated 379,000 childhood and adolescent cancer survivors alive in the United States as of 2010 statistics (Ward et al., 2014). Regardless of survival rates, children and their families still face preventable psychosocial and physical suffering (Cullen, 2014; Wolfe et al., 2000). Children, adolescents, and young adult survivors of childhood cancer do experience struggles in peer relationships, identity formation, job and school opportunities, late effects, and fear and risk of recurrence, among other psychosocial challenges (Hudson et al., 2013; Oeffinger et al., 2006). And yet there is growing evidence that children and families who have faced childhood cancer also display tremendous resilience and potentially posttraumatic growth (Jones, Parker-Raley, & Barczyk, 2011; Jones et al., 2010; Phillips & Jones, 2013; Rosenberg, Starks, & Jones, 2014).

In providing pediatric psychosocial care, social workers are at the forefront of many critical issues in patient- and family-centered care. With the passage of the Patient Protection and Affordable Care Act (PPACA), social workers will be even more necessary in the interprofessional and transdisciplinary health care team. The PPACA mandates that behavioral health be an essential covered benefit and specifically highlights the importance of patient-centered medical homes and effective care coordination (Andrews, Darnell, McBride, & Gehlert, 2013). Social workers are uniquely trained as integrated behavioral health specialists who can coordinate care and help the child and family navigate the health care system. Social workers in pediatric oncology can and should be taking the lead in reforming health care given their specific focus on family-centered care, collaboration and coordination, social justice, self-determination, and evidence-based practice. In this section of the *Handbook*, leading pediatric oncology social work clinicians, researchers, and advocates discuss the critical issues in the care of children and adolescents with cancer and their families.

In the first chapter, "Interventions for Children Under Age 15 Living With Cancer," Lori Wiener and Ursula M. Sansom-Daly set the stage for understanding the experience of a cancer diagnosis for children. They identify the key developmental needs for children throughout the illness trajectory and offer suggestions for intervening, supporting, and advocating for them and their families at various stages of care.

In "Interventions for Adolescents Living With Cancer," Rebecca G. Block introduces the reader to the unique developmental and identity challenges for adolescents facing a cancer diagnosis. Adolescence is a time of growing independence and capacity for self-determination and decision making. Block highlights the practical and existential challenges related to a diagnosis of cancer at this time of life, including the importance of self-identity, control over treatment decisions, peer support, and structured conversations about plans. Although adolescents report resilience and stress-related growth, identified risk factors for long-term adaptation have implications for how adolescents are treated, monitored, and supported over time.

Nancy F. Cincotta's chapter, "The Family Experience in Pediatric Oncology," contextualizes the diagnosis of cancer within the family. She clearly demonstrates that family members have unique responses to the child's diagnosis and to each other and how that can influence each person's overall well-being. Using words from families to highlight their perspective, she shows the reader how devastating and potentially life altering a diagnosis of childhood cancer can be for families.

In "Helping Siblings of Pediatric Oncology Patients," Nancy F. Cincotta describes the unique emotional challenges and isolation that siblings of children with cancer experience. She advocates for targeted interventions to help siblings cope with a brother or sister's cancer diagnosis and its impact on the family. She highlights the importance of sibling support groups and professional support to reduce isolation, fear, and confusion in siblings. Using siblings' words, Cincotta also shows evidence of resilience in siblings of children with cancer and specific ways to build on it.

In "Reaching Out to Culturally Diverse Populations in Pediatric Oncology," Nancy Contro and Analisa Trott discuss how an oncology diagnosis can present additional burdens on families that are already marginalized or vulnerable. They show specific ways social workers use their training in understanding issues of justice and cultural competence to assist families and serve as role models for the interdisciplinary team.

Kate Shafer and Constance Connor's chapter, "Pediatric Cancer Survivors," identifies the common psychological and medical late effects for children and adolescents who survive cancer. Given the advances in treatment and the growing number of survivors, this chapter provides a road map for understanding and responding to the long-term psychosocial needs of this population. Specifically, Shafer and Connor highlight some practice exemplars of interventions that have been shown to help survivors in their transition from cancer patient to cancer survivor.

The last chapter in this section, "Pediatric Palliative Care," by Stacy S. Remke, is a guide to providing palliative care in the pediatric setting. Advocating for the introduction of palliative care from the moment of diagnosis, Remke identifies the skills and interventions that may assist children and families in making decisions about care that is not curative. This chapter helps the practitioner think about ways to help families manage and hold uncertainty, make informed decisions that are culturally congruent, communicate with the medical team and with the child, and focus on the quality of life of each child in the context of his or her family. She discusses the importance of intentional collaborative processes with the oncology social worker and the specialist pediatric palliative social worker.

Overall, this section of the *Handbook* discusses critical and cutting-edge practice and research in pediatric oncology for children, adolescents, young adults, and their families. Putting the child and family at the center of care and empowering them to make the best decisions for themselves is a hallmark of social work practice. Pediatric oncology social workers are well trained to be behavioral health specialists, navigators, care coordinators, and passionate clinicians for children and families facing cancer. Social workers also serve an important role as collaborative members and leaders of the interprofessional team, bringing their unique perspective to advocate for the psychosocial needs of the child and family.

REFERENCES

Andrews, C. M., Darnell, J. S., McBride, T. D., & Gehlert, S. (2013). Social work and implementation of the affordable care act. *Health and Social Work, 38*(2), 67–71.

Cullen, J. (2014). Because statistics don't tell the whole story: A call for comprehensive care for children with cancer. *CA: A Cancer Journal for Clinicians, 64*(2), 79–82. doi:10.3322/caac.21215

Howlader, N., Noone, A., & Krapcho, M. (2013). *SEER cancer statistics review, 1975–2010*. Bethesda, MD: National Cancer Institute.

Hudson, M. M., Ness, K. K., Gurney, J. G., Mulrooney, D. A., Chemaitilly, W., & Krull, K. R. (2013). Clinical ascertainment of health outcomes among adults treated for childhood cancer. *Journal of the American Medical Association, 309*(22), 2371–2381.

Jones, B. L., Parker-Raley, J., & Barczyk, A. (2011). Adolescent cancer survivors: Identity paradox and the need to belong. *Qualitative Health Research, 21*(8), 1033–1040. doi:10.1177/1049732311404029

Jones, B. L., Volker, D. L., Vinajeras, Y., Butros, L., Fitchpatrick, C., & Rossetto, K. (2010). The meaning of surviving cancer for Latino adolescents and emerging young adults. *Cancer Nursing, 33*(1), 74.

Oeffinger, K. C., Mertens, A. C., Sklar, C. A., Kawashima, T., Hudson, M. M., & Meadows, A. T. (2006). Chronic health conditions in adult survivors of childhood cancer. *New England Journal of Medicine, 355*(15), 1572–1582. doi:10.1056/NEJMsa060185

Phillips, F., & Jones, B. L. (2013). Understanding the lived experience of Latino adolescent and young adult survivors of childhood cancer. *Journal of Cancer Survivorship*, 1–10. Retrieved from http://www.researchgate.net/publication/257072142_Understanding_the_lived_experience_of_Latino_adolescent_and_young_adult_survivors_of_childhood_cancer

Rosenberg, A., Starks, H., & Jones, B. (2014). "I know it when I see it": The complexities of measuring resilience in pediatric cancer. *Journal of Supportive Care in Cancer, 22*, 2261–2668.

Ward, E., DeSantis, C., Robbins, A., Kohler, B., & Jemal, A. (2014). Childhood and adolescent cancer statistics, 2014. *CA: A Cancer Journal for Clinicians*, *64*(2), 83–103. doi:10.3322/caac.21219

Wolfe, J., Grier, H. E., Klar, N., Levin, S. B., Ellenbogen, J. M., & Salem-Schatz, S. (2000). Symptoms and suffering at the end of life in children with cancer. *New England Journal of Medicine*, *342*(5), 326–333.

62

Lori Wiener and Ursula M. Sansom-Daly

Interventions for Children Under Age 15 Living With Cancer

Key Concepts

- *Each stage of the cancer trajectory has its own unique challenges for all family members.*
- *Child and family coping can be greatly influenced by preexisting risk factors, family structures, socioeconomic factors, and individual and family resilience.*
- *Specific intervention skills are used to assist children and families as they travel through each phase of the illness.*
- *The oncology social worker helps children and families identify both sources of distress and opportunities for resilience as they navigate the cancer experience.*

For all parents, receiving the news that their child has cancer is devastating; even when their child's health has been poor, they are generally unprepared for this diagnosis. The cancer treatment process requires immediate, well-informed, and life-dependent decision-making processes. By assisting parents in navigating the cancer trajectory, social workers can help them obtain a sense of mastery of the disease, treatment, and late effects, facilitating improved quality of life for the child and family over time.

Beyond the parents and the child with cancer, the diagnosis affects a network of family members, friends, and community members. Siblings often feel isolated, have drastically reduced time with their parents, and may struggle with mixed emotions. Grandparents can experience extreme anxiety, helplessness, and a sense of "double grief," fearing not only for their grandchild's health but also for their own child, the parent, as well. Social workers fulfill key roles, including advocating for the child and family among the medical team, helping families understand complex medical information, identifying available resources, teaching coping skills, and promoting resilience. This chapter reviews how social workers can guide the child and family, monitor for depressive and traumatic responses, assess and intervene during family conflict, and promote cohesion and resilience throughout the continuum of cancer care.

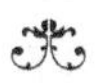

Diagnosis

Skills focus: Provide practical and emotional support in helping parents adjust to new roles. Promote developmentally appropriate discussion around illness and assess the child's understanding. Screen for key psychosocial risk indicators. Coordinate referrals and linkages to other health care professionals. Apply different therapeutic techniques to help families manage the tasks of the new diagnosis.

Understanding and Managing Typical Family Reactions

At diagnosis, families typically experience a range of strong emotions. Guilt and self-blame are almost universal, with parents feeling helpless and unable to protect their child from traumatic and painful medical procedures. As parents begin absorbing distressing information, a sense of disbelief and denial may be a useful short-term coping mechanism. Here, the social worker plays an important role—carefully assessing families' responses to diagnoses, identifying cultural or religious factors and prior experiences with illness or death that might impede or support treatment adherence and coping, and facilitating the medical team's understanding of families' diverse reactions.

Promoting Developmentally Appropriate Communication

Social workers play a critical role in supporting and assisting parents to engage in honest, age-appropriate communication with their child about the diagnosis; saving parents from expending unnecessary energy on maintaining secrecy; giving children an opportunity to ask questions; and providing models of adaptive and proactive coping. However, a desire to "protect" their child may make parents reluctant to initiate this conversation. Because children are sensitive to nonverbal signals from those around them that something is wrong, it is important to inform parents that hiding the diagnosis can in fact increase the child's anxiety, fears, and mistrust of health care providers (Chesler, Paris, & Barbarin, 1986). Children of all ages are capable of understanding illness-related concepts when they receive age-appropriate explanations. Initiating this conversation also allows children the opportunity to build rapport with and a sense of trust in their treatment team, learn effective coping strategies, and actively participate in their own care.

Regardless of age, parents should be encouraged to use language both familiar and meaningful, including references to stories, metaphors, or past experiences unique to the child. For example, a child who plays with toy soldiers may benefit from "little helper soldiers" as an immune system metaphor; other children have found that the video game Pac-Man helps them understand how chemotherapy can destroy cancer cells in their body. Parents typically know what their child will relate to best, and introducing new information using familiar images (e.g., "Remember when I told you about...?") can reduce anxiety. The social worker should always highlight and reinforce parents' existing parenting skills and strengths to illustrate how they can be applied to each new situation.

Establishing a positive, collaborative relationship between the medical team and child is crucial. Children older than 12 or 13 often prefer clinicians to talk directly to them, rather than to their parents. This direct approach may reduce the feeling that the treatment process is happening "to them" without their active participation or assent (Gibson, Aldiss, Horstman, Kumpunen, & Richardson, 2010). With the parents' permission, the social worker can facilitate the inclusion of younger children by asking the extent to which they would like to be included in meetings, how much information they would like to have, how they learn information best (e.g., "Would pictures and diagrams be useful?"), and how they would like to ask questions. Information pace, flow, and delivery should be tailored to a family's reactions, and it is important to repeat information periodically and check understanding as concepts are explained (Levetown, 2008). Avoiding medical jargon and using visual aids to explain concepts to children and their parents can also be helpful, particularly when English is not their primary language (Abbe, Simon, Angiolillo, Ruccione, & Kodish, 2006).

Soon after the diagnosis, when families are still trying to absorb the full implications of a cancer diagnosis, treatment decisions need to be made. This is typically an overwhelming period as parents try to understand complicated information. Reinforcing their competencies and engaging them in an active, collaborative partnership as "experts" on their child's needs is a powerful intervention. Coaching and role-playing can help parents apply preexisting skills to these new parenting challenges and demands. For young children, this will mean ensuring time for play to promote positive age-appropriate coping and development. For children of all ages, allowing some control over certain aspects of treatment (e.g., when and where blood is drawn) can help reduce acute distress (Kazak & Baxt, 2007).

Understanding and Screening for Psychological Risk Factors

Poor parental and family coping when the child's disease is newly diagnosed predicts greater parental distress and poorer coping (Vrijmoet-Wiersma et al., 2008), as well as the child's poorer adjustment over the longer term (Barrera et al., 2003). Therefore, social workers must address potential psychosocial "red flags" at diagnosis while initiating and continuing ongoing monitoring of the family's adjustment. Several validated psychosocial screening tools exist to help social workers assess these domains (Tables 62.1 and 62.2). Validated tools are best viewed as a supplement to ongoing clinical assessment that includes the child's perspective (which these scales do not assess). Repeated, ongoing assessment of the child's and parents' distress can also assist social workers in distinguishing between transient, normative, and clinical-level distress. Asking the child simple, age-appropriate questions such as "What worries you the most right now?" and "What do you hope for now?" can be useful in helping the child express any needs, desires, or distress. Indications of clinical depression, anxiety, posttraumatic stress, or poor coping should prompt further evaluation and treatment. A range of interventions may be appropriate, including cognitive behavioral approaches, family therapy, support groups, or a combination of approaches.

Table 62.1.
Key Issues at Each Stage of the Cancer Trajectory

Aspects to Assess	Clinical Considerations	Interventions
Diagnosis		
• Parents' and child's understanding of diagnosis and treatment options[a]	*Level of education?* *Is English their primary language?* *Amount and type of information family wants?*	• Encourage use of a notebook to record names, questions, and treatment-related details. • Provide/draw visual pictures to explain concepts. • Regularly repeat information and "check in" to gauge understanding.
• Whether child has been told	*Parents' concerns about telling their child? Siblings? Extended family?*	• Discuss pros/cons of honesty and secrecy.
• Parents' sense of competency to disclose	*Do parents have beliefs (personal, cultural, or religious) about disclosing the diagnosis to their child?*	• Model and role-play age-appropriate disclosure techniques. • Explore previous times parents have told their child difficult news and highlight parents' strengths in doing so. • Clarify that the health care providers can help but will not lie.
• Beliefs around the illness cause	*Negative/faulty beliefs as to what caused the cancer?*	• Assess child's thoughts about causality. • Dispel misconceptions. • Normalize parental guilt and self-blame. • Assist parents to reframe these thoughts to a more proactive stance (focusing on what they "can do/ control"). • Facilitate parents meeting other parents to gain peer support.
• Family's prior experiences with illness, cancer, death, or medical trauma	*How did the child come to be diagnosed? Impact on trust in health care providers?* *Parents' expectations about child's prognosis?*	• Provide an opportunity to talk about their experiences with cancer, illness, hospitals, and death. • Normalize concerns and encourage an attitude of hope (e.g., provide cure rates where appropriate). • Consider the Family Illness Beliefs Inventory to identify areas of concern (Kazak et al., 2004).
• Support network	*Adequate family support network?* *Supports nearby?* *Does child need help telling friends or asking for specific support?*	• Assist family to identify unmet needs and sources of support. • Use modeling and role-playing to help parents ask for support through their extended network. • Consider standardized screening, such as the Psychosocial Assessment Tool (Kazak et al., 2001), to assess psychosocial risk.
• Family coping and problem-solving abilities • Educational needs	*Factors that may complicate child's ability to cope?* *Is the child receiving disfiguring surgery, amputation, and/or treatment with physical ramifications?* *Where would schooling best be provided (hospital, home, at school)?*	• Assess child's coping, parent coping, marital/family cohesion. • Help prepare children who will receive disfiguring surgery/amputation: e.g., bibliotherapy, art or music therapy, or writing a letter to their limb that requires amputation. • Consider evidence-based problem-solving intervention (Sahler et al., 2005). • Organize a meeting with the child's class teacher, principal, and other relevant support staff to discuss child's recovery, current abilities, and needs. Include parents in meeting so that both parents and school understand their roles in child's return to school.

(*continued*)

Table 62.1. (Continued)		
Aspects to Assess	Clinical Considerations	Interventions
Treatment Initiation		
• Informed consent and assent	*Have treatment options been discussed with the child, with an opportunity to provide his or her assent?* *Have older children had the opportunity to participate in treatment discussions?*	• Assist parents/child to prepare a list of questions they have about treatment before meeting with the oncologist. • Consider audio-recording the meeting so that information can be reviewed later. • Check with child to ensure that he or she understood the answers given.
• Knowledge about side effects	*Have possible side effects of treatment been explained to the child with an opportunity to ask questions?*	• Ask child what he or she understands about side effects, prognosis, and any concerns. • Discuss potential interventions for side effects "if and when" these come up.
Maintenance/Ongoing Treatment Management		
• Adherence to treatment	*Child's level of adherence? Are parents monitoring and supporting their child's adherence? Do they understand the implications of nonadherence?*	• Assess for parent/child conflict over adherence. • Assist with coping strategies. • Introduce pill box and strategies for adherence. • Consider text reminders.
• Quality of life	*How is the child eating, sleeping, and coping with procedures?* *Is the child engaged in social and fun activities? Accepted and supported by peers?*	• Offer coping techniques: cognitive restructuring, relaxation, practical strategies, seeking social support, expressing feelings • Use distraction techniques for procedural distress.
Relapse		
• Understanding of treatment options	*Do parents understand the pros/cons of the remaining treatment options available?*	• Inquire about expected outcomes and what child understands.
• Expectations regarding treatment outcome	*Do parents understand any changed treatment expectations? Have treatment toxicities been discussed?*	• Make a pro/con sheet for each treatment offered for the family to complete/discuss.
• Family, child, and parent coping	*Is the family able to access the same supports as at diagnosis? How is the child coping? Signs of emotional and physical exhaustion?*	• Reassess coping and adaptation. Teach problem-solving skills and offer child and family counseling. • Educate about the need to conserve emotional/physical energy and self-care.
End of Treatment		
• Psychosocial adjustment to life after treatment	*Has the family planned for life after treatment? Planned an event to mark this milestone?* *Quality of child/family's supports at treatment completion?*	• Suggest planning a coming-off-treatment party or similar event. • Create a "congratulations" certificate for child and family or plan a "graduating from treatment" ceremony with the staff and family. • Discuss child/family's support system and availability of hospital-based psychosocial support after treatment.
• Expectations regarding their return to "normal life"	*Are expectations about the posttreatment period realistic?*	• Discuss child's expectations about getting back to normal. • Organize a team meeting with the family to discuss their transition to off treatment, including medical check-ups, health behaviors, and other psychosocial needs.

(*continued*)

Table 62.1. (Continued)

Aspects to Assess	Clinical Considerations	Interventions
• Need for support in transition back to school	*How much school did the child miss? Will the child be returning to his or her regular class?* *Are cognitive changes evident in the child? Is other assistance, resources, cognitive testing, or support (e.g., letters to teachers/principal, etc.) needed to facilitate a smooth transition back after treatment?*	• Discuss child's schooling situation with parents. Assess change from premorbid functioning, amount of school attended since diagnosis (either home or hospital), and point of school year child will be returning to. • For children with central nervous system tumors, facilitate neurocognitive testing (first year of treatment and then annually with a brief neurocognitive battery—IQ, processing speed, attention/concentration, memory).

[a] Although the table refers to parents, these considerations apply equally to any other primary/legal guardian or caregiver of the child diagnosed with cancer. Similar considerations may also apply to members of the child's extended family.

The Treatment Period

Skills focus: Help prepare the child for cancer treatment and its side effects and the impact those can have on his or her daily life and emotional well-being. Teach the child and parents coping strategies to manage both medical and nonmedical stressors. Assess the family dynamics and enhance the family's and community's strengths that promote growth.

Developmental Interruption

Cancer disrupts the typical avenues of social activity, forcing the child to temporarily relinquish the usual roles of school, peers, and outside activities. Due to the critical importance of social interactions for a child's social development, the child should be encouraged to resume former social activities and roles as soon as medically able. Contact with friends can also be encouraged by planning short visits, telephone calls, or Skype and Facebook encounters, which keep the child connected to a life outside of cancer and medical personnel. Children whose primary disease involves the central nervous system and cognitive impairment tend to be at greatest risk for problems with peers (Vannatta, Gerhardt, Wells, & Noll, 2007); therefore, particular attention should be given to their social relationships and functioning.

At this time, the social worker's role is to help the family attain a new sense of normalcy by re-establishing patterns and routines of daily life disrupted by the cancer diagnosis and treatment. For young children, familiar routines related to bedtime, toileting, feeding, naps, and play are important as each activity creates a sense of control and security. Any difficulty swallowing pills should be noted and addressed by either the social worker or a provider skilled in teaching pill swallowing. If the child expresses anxiety associated with a change in routines, helping the family quickly develop new routines is important. For older children, attention should be paid to re-establishing appropriate household chores and expectations regarding school—whether the school is hospital based, at home, or the school the child attended before the diagnosis. Parents are encouraged to maintain consistent discipline, because parents who become overprotective, overindulgent, or lax in their expectations of ill children often establish a cycle that can result in behavioral problems, a reduced sense of self-worth, or both (Wiener, Alderfer, & Hersh, 2011). In addition, attending to the needs of the patient's siblings is essential because those who recognize disparity between rules and expectations can suffer psychologically.

During active treatment, children must cope with the side effects of treatments, such as fatigue, restricted activity, and changes in physical appearance (e.g., weight loss, alopecia, surgical scars, amputation), along with fears of treatment failure. Most children return to school while still on treatment. Because anxieties, embarrassment, and possible depression can contribute to a child's withdrawal from peers and reluctance to attend school, it is important to differentiate between the expected adjustment trajectory and maladjustment. Establishing a system for early and ongoing communication among the family, school, and medical personnel can help the child remain in school (see Chapter 64).

Adaptation of Child, Parent, and Family

Most children and families adjust well to the distress and disruptions associated with treatment, with improvements in overall psychological well-being following the first year after diagnosis. Specific factors associated with adaptive functioning include open communication within the family about the illness, an attitude of living in the present, lack of other major concurrent stresses (marital, financial, illness of other family members), previous adaptive coping, and availability of a strong support system. Maladaptive coping may include excessive concern about relapse and death; reluctance to allow the child to return to everyday activities; interpersonal strife,

Table 62.2.
Developmental Understanding of Illness and Explanations

Age Range (years)	Understanding of Illness	Ways to Explain Cancer[a]	Causal Aspects
2–5	Magical thinking, limited conception of time, and difficulty differentiating fact from fantasy. Illness may be perceived as being caused by a concrete, random phenomenon (e.g., people get colds from "the sun") or magical causes (e.g., people get colds "when someone else gets near them").	*"Your blood is not working right and we need to fix it." "A lump is growing in your ___ and we need to make it go away."*	• No one knows • Nothing you did • Not contagious
6–10	May range from magical ideas to ideas about *contamination* from outside sources (e.g., people get colds "when outside without a hat") and the *effects* of outside sources (e.g., people get colds by breathing in "bacteria").	*"Our blood is made up of red and white blood cells and platelets."* (Explain function of each.) *"Your body is making too many white cells, which are crowding out the other cells and stopping them from doing their jobs."*	• No one knows • Not something you did • Not punishment for anything • Not something anyone else did
11–14	More capable of understanding complex internal processes and abstract ideas (e.g., people get colds from "viruses"). Adolescents may also conceive of the link between psychological and physical factors and may perceive that psychological events led to their cancer (e.g., "I got cancer because I was too stressed at school").	In addition to previous explanation, adolescents should be given the choice about how much information they would like. *"Young people often tell me that they experience many different side effects. Would you prefer me to tell you about all of these now or would you rather ask me about them as you go along?"* Adolescents may wish to know about late effects they can expect.	• No one knows • Not something you did • Not punishment for anything • Not because you got mad/stressed/had bad thoughts about someone • Not something anyone else did

[a] The italicized scripts are merely suggestions for how to talk about cancer. Social workers should be encouraged to develop their own repertoire of language for discussing cancer with children.

Adapted from Breyer (2009).

emotional distress, and persistent or escalating anxiety or depression; behavioral symptoms in well siblings; difficulties making clinic visits or treatments; reluctance to interact with other patients or families; and ongoing pessimism (Wiener, Alderfer, et al., 2011). Concerned about the potential psychosocial aftereffects of their child's cancer, parents may be hypervigilant about the child's otherwise developmentally normal social interactions (e.g., viewing peer-to-peer banter as teasing or bullying) and exaggerate the degree to which the child shows evidence of social dysfunction (Noll & Bukowski, 2012).

For school-age children exhibiting symptoms of distress (anxiety or withdrawal from friends or activities they once enjoyed), further assessment and initiation of a treatment plan is indicated. This may entail cognitive behavioral approaches, interventions by art or music therapists, support groups, psychotropic medications, or a combination of approaches. Because not all youths benefit from or feel comfortable with "talking" therapies, the social worker may seek training in other techniques to enhance the child's self-understanding and promote his or her coping skills (Pao & Wiener, 2011). Several techniques are described next.

Bibliotherapy

This technique begins with choosing a story to read to a child. The story should include characters whose struggles and triumphs the child can identify with (such as a story about a child with cancer). After reading the story (or taking turns reading pages to each other), the social worker may ask the child to suggest additions or changes in the story. Together, they might write a new story that exemplifies the individual child's struggles and strengths and gives meaning to his or her life. By externalizing a problem and re-creating endings, children can begin to experience a sense of mastery over their circumstances.

Play Therapy

Play is the language and vehicle for a child's expression and a mechanism to promote healing. A variety of play therapy approaches exist to reduce the anxiety and depression critically ill children may experience. The social worker should let the child choose between games, objects, and therapeutic toys. Medical play can be valuable when a child is struggling with specific procedures, such as needle sticks, and can involve alcohol pads, syringes, stethoscopes, or other objects the child can control, such as Play-Doh, bubbles, finger paints, puppets, and sand. Board games such as *ShopTalk* allow the child to share thoughts, worries, hopes, and dreams in a nonthreatening and fun way and can be highly effective in identifying major stressors (Wiener, Battles, Mamalian, & Zadeh, 2011). Maintaining open communication and closeness between the child and parents is essential; consequently, there are times when it is useful to have the parents join the child in playing such games.

Writing Techniques
The use of therapeutic workbooks (e.g., *This Is My World*, Zadeh & Wiener, 2011) allows the child to describe and document his or her experience of living with cancer by completing age-appropriate activities. Even creating a list of feelings or statements written by both the therapist and the child about what activities and feelings were evident that day can be helpful. When a relationship has been established between the child and social worker and the child returns home, a narrative therapy approach of letter writing (postal or e-mail) between sessions also can be used to maintain open communication with the child. Adolescents, particularly, appreciate the opportunity to use writing techniques to counteract their anxiety, sadness, and grief. These techniques can take the form of a personal narrative, song, or poem.

Art and Photography
Art is another creative technique that enables children to express their concerns and externalize their fears and anxieties. Mandalas (circular drawings filled in with the child's emotions identified during a therapeutic session) are especially useful to help a child express feelings too difficult to put into words (Sourkes, 1995; Wiener & Battles, 2002). Photography is another powerful modality to document one's experience living with cancer. Following institutional policies pertaining to confidentiality, the social worker may provide a child with a camera and ask him or her to take pictures that will show others what it is like to be sick, which can provide friends, family, and providers with insights into the child's inner world. Art media can be used as memory-making or legacy-building activities. Worry boxes, art (such as outlining, then painting a parent's and child's hands touching), and family quilts can be potent forms of self-expression and healing.

End of Treatment

Skills focus: Educate families about common psychological reactions to completion of treatment. Help the child and family set realistic goals for the off-treatment time. If needed, educate parents about the common cognitive effects of cancer treatment, the role of neurocognitive testing, and other available rehabilitative resources and supports. Reinforce the importance of attending follow-up appointments in the longer term.

Emotional Reactions to Finishing Treatment

For most children and their families, looking forward to the last day of treatment is a powerful motivator for getting through the arduous treatment period. Although most families experience relief and joy at completing treatment, negative and confusing emotions can also occur (Wakefield, McLoone, Butow, Lenthen, & Cohn, 2010; Wakefield, McLoone, Goodenough, et al., 2010). These include uncertainty and anxiety about recurrence of the cancer or leaving the protective hospital setting; a sense of discomfort at changed priorities, goals, or abilities; and concern about "fitting in" again with peers. Parents may also encounter stress from other areas of life, as old problems that had been put on hold during treatment now return to occupy their time and attention. Normalizing these experiences and helping families to anticipate a realistic recovery time and the return to normal activities can help stave off later confusion, guilt, and excessive frustration. Social workers should monitor families for ongoing (or emerging) clinical depression, anxiety, or posttraumatic stress responses.

Ensuring that the family still feels supported after leaving the hospital environment is also important. After the child's treatment is completed, many parents report feeling alone and "abandoned" by hospital staff and lacking adequate information about posttreatment challenges; yet many hesitate to disturb hospital staff with their concerns out of respect for the other families whose child is still on active treatment (Wakefield, Butow, Fleming, Daniel, & Cohn, 2012). Creating a plan with families for ongoing support in survivorship, such as anticipated future needs (e.g., rehabilitative services for the child) and the process of referring families for services outside of the hospital when more intensive or longer term support is needed, will help ease this transition.

Although most survivors of childhood and adolescent cancer are resilient, research suggests the existence of a small subset of survivors whose distress and difficulty coping can persist for many years after treatment ends (Seitz et al., 2010; Wiener et al., 2006). It is therefore critically important to continue assessing and monitoring levels of distress and functioning of survivors (and families) into long-term survivorship. Furthermore, young adult cancer survivors are more likely than their peers to be financially and emotionally dependent upon their parents. Therefore, social workers need to balance parental involvement in survivors' ongoing care while encouraging age-appropriate autonomy and independence as the survivors begin to take more responsibility for their medical care.

As pediatric survivors become older adolescents and young adults, long-term sequelae of the treatment may emerge and negatively affect their psychosocial well-being. Those sequelae include secondary and recurrent cancers, medical late effects, infertility, sexuality and body issues, and disclosure of the cancer history to romantic partners. Many survivors may benefit from discussing these issues with their social worker or from being connected with other cancer survivors to gain perspective and support from their peers (see Chapter 67).

Recurrent and Progressive Disease

Skills focus: Assess expectations of continued treatment, disease outcome, and the information communicated to the child and siblings. Discuss balancing treatment decisions with quality of life. If no further treatment will be provided, help the child and family plan where and how supportive and palliative care will be provided and how they wish to live for the remainder of the child's life. When appropriate, give the child the opportunity to express his or her thoughts about end-of-life care and wishes for a legacy.

Although more children with cancer are able to remain free of disease, some inevitably experience a relapse or recurrence. With each relapse, cure becomes increasingly unlikely, and for some families, this period can be more devastating than the initial diagnosis. Encouraging the child and family to regain a positive attitude toward treatment is a challenge. As families search for ways to cope with the renewed threat to life and to obtain emotional equilibrium, the social worker's availability is just as critical as at the initial diagnosis.

Most families manage to cope adequately through their child's second round of treatment, but the altered prognosis elicits feelings of sadness and fears of separation and loss. Parents' emotional or physical withdrawal from the child or the child's withdrawal from the family is a maladaptive response that requires immediate intervention. If another remission is achieved, the termination of active treatment often activates a crisis that requires additional education and support as parents worry about repeated relapses and may exhibit tremendous anxiety upon restaging and scan visits. Education about such responses and the initiation of breathing and other relaxation techniques are extremely useful for, and greatly appreciated by, families.

End of Life

Unfortunately, despite scientific advances, approximately 20% of children with cancer will die from their disease. Some undergo several treatment trials after each relapse, whereas others never respond to available therapies. Most parents search desperately for a cure or a treatment that can help prolong the child's life. Once the medical team concludes that comfort is the primary goal of the child's care, critical decisions turn to concerns about where the family would like care to be provided (home or hospital) and whether attempts should be made to revive (resuscitate) the child. The social worker can prepare families for these conversations with the medical team using an approach that elicits the family's prognostic understanding and primary goals. This information can help the clinician integrate the parents' goals and formulate a recommendation regarding the child's resuscitation status and future care options.

A question often arises whether children should participate in end-of-life care and decisions about resuscitation status. The American Academy of Pediatrics, Committee on Bioethics and Committee on Hospital Care (2000) recommends that children who are able to understand should participate in these discussions so that the medical team and the family are able to carry out the child's wishes. To determine whether the child is capable of understanding the options, other factors in addition to the child's age and stage of development must be considered. These factors include the length of time the child has been living with cancer, the number of relapses, experiences with the deaths of fellow patients with the same disease, whether illness or treatment has resulted in cognitive deficits, the family's communication style (e.g., if difficult issues are evaded or the child is provided with limited information), and the child's personality style (e.g., the child prefers the parents to obtain the information and tell the child later).

When it comes to making treatment decisions, some children are heavily influenced by their parents' wishes and the perceived desires of their physicians. The social worker's role is to assess the child's understanding (not assume the child understands or agrees with decisions being made) and then respectfully balance the child's preferences, parents' desires, and physicians' recommendations. This goal can be accomplished by meeting with each party individually, then developing a plan to achieve consensus on these issues. (See the chapters in Section 13 for helpful suggestions pertaining to end-of-life care and bereavement services.)

Pearls

- Stresses families experience over the course of a cancer illness vary greatly and can be traumatic.
- When communication is open, children and families can be creative and resilient in finding solutions to the challenges they face.

Pitfalls

- Failing to obtain the child's perspective on communication and coping can limit the social worker's ability to help the family as a whole adapt.

Many factors, including the child's cognitive and emotional development, family dynamics, coping abilities, and previous experience with illness, influence how children adapt to living with cancer. Social workers are particularly skilled at interventions and strategies aimed at identifying the continuum of coping responses, building on family strengths, assisting families regarding special needs, and enhancing adaptive coping skills that can facilitate both family growth and survival through the crises generated by childhood cancer.

REFERENCES

Abbe, A., Simon, C., Angiolillo, A., Ruccione, K., & Kodish, E. D. (2006). A survey of language barriers from the perspective of pediatric oncologists, interpreters, and parents. *Pediatric Blood and Cancer, 47*, 819–824.

American Academy of Pediatrics, Committee on Bioethics and Committee on Hospital Care. (2000). Palliative care for children. *Pediatrics, 106*(2, Pt. 1), 351–357.

Barrera, M., Wayland, L-A., D'Agostino, N. M., Gibson, J., Weksberg, R., & Malkin, D. (2003). Developmental differences in psychological adjustment and health-related quality of life in pediatric cancer patients. *Children's Health Care, 32*(3), 215–232.

Breyer, J. (2009). Talking to children and adolescents. In L. Wiener, M. Pao, M. E. Kazak, M. J. Kupst, & A. F. Patenaude (Eds.), *Quick reference for pediatric oncology clinicians: The psychiatric and psychological dimensions of pediatric cancer symptom management* (pp. 4–22). Charlottesville, VA: American Psychosocial Oncology Society.

Chesler, M. A., Paris, J., & Barbarin, O. A. (1986). "Telling" the child with cancer: Parental choices to share information with 111 children. *Journal of Pediatric Psychology, 11*(4), 497–516.

Gibson, F., Aldiss, S., Horstman, M., Kumpunen, S., & Richardson, A. (2010). Children and young people's experiences of cancer care: A qualitative research study using participatory methods. *International Journal of Nursing Studies, 47*, 1397–1407.

Kazak, A. E., & Baxt, C. (2007). Families of infants and young children with cancer: A post-traumatic stress framework. *Pediatric Blood and Cancer, 49*, 1109–1113.

Kazak, A. E., McClure, K. S., Alderfer, M. A., Hwang, W-T., Crump, T. A., Le, L. T.,... Rourke, M. T. (2004). Cancer-related parental beliefs: The family illness beliefs inventory (FIBI). *Journal of Pediatric Psychology, 29*(7), 531–542.

Kazak, A. E., Prusak, A., McSherry, M., Simms, S., Beele, D., Rourke, M.,... Lange, B. (2001). The Psychosocial Assessment Tool (PAT)©: Pilot data on a brief screening instrument for identifying high risk families in pediatric oncology. *Families, Systems, and Health, 19*(3), 303–317.

Levetown, M. (2008). Communicating with children and families: From everyday interactions to skill in conveying distressing information. *Pediatrics, 121*(5), e1441–e1460.

Noll, R. B., & Bukowski, W. M. (2012). Commentary: Social competence in children with chronic illness: The devil is in the details. *Journal of Pediatric Psychology, 37*(9), 959–966.

Pao, M., & Wiener, L. (2011). Anxiety and depression. In J. Wolfe, P. Hinds, & B. Sourkes (Eds.), *Textbook of interdisciplinary pediatric palliative care* (pp. 220–238). Philadelphia, PA: Elsevier.

Sahler, O. J. Z., Fairclough, D. L., Phipps, S., Mulhern, R. K., Dolgin, M. J., Noll, R. B.,... Butler, R. W. (2005). Using problem-solving skills training to reduce negative affectivity in mothers of children with newly diagnosed cancer: Report of a multisite randomized trial. *Journal of Consulting and Clinical Psychology, 73*(2), 272–283.

Seitz, D. C. M., Besier, T., Debatin, K-M., Grabow, D., Dieluweit, U., Hinz, A.,... Goldbeck, L. (2010). Posttraumatic stress, depression, and anxiety among adult long-term survivors of cancer in adolescence. *European Journal of Cancer, 46*, 1596–1606.

Sourkes, B. M. (1995). *Armfuls of time*. Pittsburgh, PA: University of Pittsburgh Press.

Vannatta, K., Gerhardt, C. A., Wells, R. J., & Noll, R. B. (2007). Intensity of CNS treatment for pediatric cancer: Prediction of social outcomes in survivors. *Pediatric Blood and Cancer, 49*, 716–722.

Vrijmoet-Wiersma, C. M. J., van Klink, J. M. M., Kolk, A. M., Koopman, H. M., Ball, L. M., & Egeler, R. M. (2008). Assessment of parental psychological stress in pediatric cancer: A review. *Journal of Pediatric Psychology, 33*(7), 694–706.

Wakefield, C. E., Butow, P., Fleming, C. A., Daniel, G., & Cohn, R. J. (2012). Family information needs at childhood cancer treatment completion. *Pediatric Blood and Cancer, 58*(4), 621–626.

Wakefield, C. E., McLoone, J. K., Butow, P., Lenthen, K., & Cohn, R. J. (2010). Parental adjustment to the completion of their child's cancer treatment. *Pediatric Blood and Cancer, 56*(4), 524–531.

Wakefield, C. E., McLoone, J. K., Goodenough, B., Lenthen, K., Cairns, D. R., & Cohn, R. J. (2010). The psychosocial impact of completing childhood cancer treatment: A systematic review of the literature. *Journal of Pediatric Psychology, 35*(3), 262–274.

Wiener, L., Alderfer, M., & Hersh, S. P. (2011). Psychiatric and psychosocial support for child and family. In P. A. Pizzo & D. G. Poplack (Eds.), *Principles and practice of pediatric oncology* (6th ed., pp. 1322–1346). Philadelphia, PA: J. B. Lippincott.

Wiener, L., & Battles, H. B. (2002). Mandalas as a therapeutic technique for HIV infected children and adolescents. *Journal of HIV/AIDS and Social Work, 1*(3), 27–39.

Wiener, L., Battles, H. B., Bernstein, D., Long, L., Mansky, P., & Mackall, C. (2006). Persistent psychological distress in long-term survivors of pediatric sarcoma, *Psycho-Oncology, 15*, 898–910.

Wiener, L., Battles, H. B., Mamalian, C., & Zadeh, S. (2011). *ShopTalk*: A pilot study of the feasibility and utility of a therapeutic board game for children and adolescents living with cancer. *Support Care Cancer, 19*(7), 1049–1054.

Zadeh, S., & Wiener, L. (2011). This is my world (2nd ed.). Bethesda, MD: National Institute of Mental Health.

63

Rebecca G. Block

Interventions for Adolescents Living With Cancer

Key Concepts

- *Adolescents who have cancer are still adolescents and seek ways to meet age-related developmental tasks throughout their cancer journey. Cancer in adolescents must be considered through this developmental lens.*
- *Cancer affects sense of self for adolescents, impacting self-esteem, the developing relationship to their bodies, self-awareness, peer relationships, and plans.*
- *Adolescence is already challenging emotionally; having cancer can compound this normal adolescent turmoil but can also serve as a point of emotional growth.*
- *Adolescents with cancer may face practical and concrete challenges related to diagnosis and the intensity and complexity of treatment.*

Social work with adolescents with cancer requires knowledge of development, psychosocial issues, evidence-informed interventions, and an appreciation of the potential within each adolescent to learn and grow, even with a cancer diagnosis. During this period, the profound social, emotional, and cognitive development and the likelihood of both trauma and growth from the cancer experience drive the need for social work. For an informed fictional narrative description of the adolescent cancer patient's struggle to achieve developmental goals and experiences in the context of treatment and life-threatening disease, read John Green's book *The Fault in Our Stars* (Green, 2012).

This chapter reviews existing knowledge about adolescents with cancer and presents key characteristics, areas of focus, and principles specific to this population. Although adolescents are often included in pediatric oncology studies or in cancer research studies of adolescents and young adults, research focused only on adolescents with cancer is limited, with much of this work on adolescent survivors after treatment. The most relevant literature is discussed here, which includes some adolescent and young adult, pediatric, and survivorship literature. A comprehensive exploration of survivorship is addressed in Chapter 9 in this book. Review articles are cited to provide a broad opportunity for further reading.

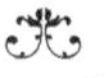

Background

Between 2004 and 2008, approximately 15,500 U.S. adolescents were diagnosed with cancer, with leukemia and lymphoma, cancers of the central nervous system (CNS), malignant bone tumors, soft tissue and Kaposi's sarcomas, germ cell tumors, thyroid cancer, and melanoma of the skin being most common. Incidence and 5-year survival differ by race and ethnicity: Caucasian, non-Hispanics have the highest incidence and greatest 5-year survival rates, whereas American Indian and Alaska Natives have the lowest incidence rates and low 5-year survival rates. African American adolescents have the lowest 5-year survival rates, and those for Hispanics are only slightly better (Surveillance, Epidemiology, and End Results, 2009). The differences in survival rates infer disparities in timely diagnosis, appropriate and accessible treatment, and supportive care.

Multiple developmental theories outline the tasks, challenges, and benchmarks for the social-emotional development of adolescents centered on identity development, relationship building, and autonomy and independence. To reach these developmental targets, adolescents shift the focus of attachments from parents to friends and romantic partnerships, consider themselves in relation to others and to the world, have increased awareness of their bodies, and plan for the future with preliminary envisioning of a future self (Christie & Viner, 2005; Erikson, 1963; Suris, Michaud, & Viner, 2004). Interactions and experiences are the vehicles for developmental progress; frequent hospitalizations, feeling ill, and being isolated to protect a compromised immune system minimize and change the frequency, quality, and nature of interactions (Suris et al., 2004).

Levels of anxiety and depression in adolescents with cancer compared to healthy peers have been measured in multiple studies with mixed results. Data demonstrate higher levels of anxiety and depression in adolescents with cancer (Jorngarden, Mattsson, & von Essen, 2007), with health-related quality of life for adolescents on treatment lower compared to posttreatment survivors and healthy peers (Abrams, Hazen, & Penson, 2007; Wu, Sheen, Shu, Chang, & Hsiao, 2012). Changes in anxiety, depression, and quality of life have been attributed to posttraumatic growth by some and to response shift by others (Barakat, Alderfer, & Kazak, 2006; Jorngarden et al., 2007; see Chapter 48).

Health-harming and health-promoting or heath-protective behaviors are important to consider when discussing the psychosocial state of adolescents with cancer. Health-harming behaviors include smoking, using alcohol and other drugs, and engaging in risky sexual behaviors, whereas health-promoting behaviors include balanced diet and regular physical activity. Although healthy adolescents also engage in these behaviors, the adverse consequences in adolescents who are being treated or have been treated for cancer may be greater (Carpentier, Mullins, Elkin, & Wolfe-Christensen, 2008).

Adolescents with cancer identify social support, being optimistic about recovery, and seeking normalcy as effective coping skills (Kyngas et al., 2001) and include parents and peers as sources of support. An adolescent with cancer seeking support from parents may experience increased dependence due to the physical and emotional challenges of cancer (Abrams et al., 2007; Ritchie, 2001); although parental support helps with coping, overdependence on one's parents may have adverse effects on development, especially if the parent is unable to encourage independent behaviors when the adolescent is able to function more independently. Understanding their disease and treatment and being active in their treatment and recovery increase adolescents' confidence that they will get well (Kyngas et al., 2001), but unmet informational needs are frequently reported (Dyson, Thompson, Palmer, Thomas, & Schofield, 2012).

The health care system can also present barriers (Bellizzi et al., 2012). Cancer may not be suspected in youths and therefore may lead to misdiagnosis, which delays the accurate cancer diagnosis (Bleyer, Budd, & Montello, 2006; National Cancer Institute and Lance Armstrong Foundation, 2006). Adolescents may also not receive the necessary referrals to specialists and diagnostic testing in a timely manner. Once diagnosed, adolescents may be treated on the pediatric or adult side of a cancer center, a children's hospital, or a community clinic. Medical care, supportive care, access to clinical trials, and the caregiving environment within each setting may be drastically different. Adolescents may feel isolated in the pediatric setting with playrooms full of toys and rooms decorated with animals and cartoon characters. Conversely, in more adult settings, they can also feel isolated by the lack of common areas and special activities geared toward their age group and knowing that they are missing shared activities with their friends (Zebrack & Isaacson, 2012). Some cancer centers are working to improve services and care delivery to adolescents by offering adolescent or young adult lounges, evening activities, additional visiting hours for peers, and specific supportive care services for adolescents (Abrams et al., 2007).

Adolescents receiving pediatric care must later transition to adult care. The timing for this transition may depend on diagnosis and prognosis, policies of the treating facility, and patient and family preferences (Freyer, 2010). Adolescents must also at some point become more responsible for their health and health care and face the challenges of navigating the adult health care system and health insurance (National Cancer Institute and Lance Armstrong Foundation, 2006). Adolescents' lack of knowledge and experience is a problem in an adult system that does not as readily interact with families and expects adolescents to understand and manage their treatment in a more adult manner than may be possible given their age and experience level.

A 17-year-old adolescent football player was called in for an appointment at the cancer center that had completed diagnostic testing regarding his leg pain. Without informing his parents, the adolescent came to the appointment by himself. During that interview, he was told he would need an amputation and chemotherapy and that his planned career in football was over. Seven years later during a research follow-up interview, he recalled still feeling traumatized and having flashbacks and intense anxiety about that conversation that took place with no family present.

Most of the published literature on adolescents with cancer describes the psychosocial challenges adolescents face, and publications make recommendations for interventions that promote health-protective behaviors (Carpentier et al., 2008) or engage family members and peers (Abrams et al., 2007). Two review articles describe promising practices in support groups, camps, retreats, and individual and family interventions (Seitz, Besier, & Goldbeck, 2009; Treadgold & Kuperberg, 2010).

Guidelines and recommendations for care and delivery of care to adolescents and young adults with cancer highlight the cancer burdens that are unique to young people and are specifically relevant to adolescents (National Comprehensive Cancer Network, 2012; Teenage Cancer Trust, 2012; Thomas, Seymour, O'Brien, Sawyer, & Ashley, 2006; Zebrack, Mathews-Bradshaw, & Siegel, 2010). Common to each set of recommendations and guidelines are the need for psychosocial assessment and psychosocial support, practical and concrete needs of survivors and their families, and the financial burden of cancer in the United States.

Four Key Concepts

1. *Cancer in adolescents must be considered through a developmental lens.*
2. *Cancer affects sense of self for adolescents, affecting self-esteem, the developing relationship to their bodies, self-awareness, and plans for the future.*
3. *Adolescence is already challenging emotionally, and having cancer can both compound this and serve as a point of emotional growth.*
4. *Adolescents with cancer may face practical and concrete challenges related to their diagnosis and treatment.*

Discussion of Key Concepts

A Developmental Lens

Identity Development Through Activities

Identity development takes place in adolescence through experiences: trying on different identities, activities, and interests; practicing skills; and testing abilities and desires (Christie & Viner, 2005; Erikson, 1963; Suris et al., 2004). Adolescents with cancer have different experiences and opportunities compared to healthy peers (Suris et al., 2004) and may have experiences that older adults have and that peers may never have, such as facing mortality, diminished function, long-term health problems, and the need to maintain health insurance (Abrams et al., 2007). This often leaves survivors wise and mature beyond their years in relation to dealing with adversity, but it may also leave them socially and developmentally delayed in some ways due to the lack of normative experiences (Lockhart, 2006).

Adolescents with cancer report being removed from a "normal adolescence" (Abrams et al., 2007), in contrast to peers who are experiencing increasing levels of autonomy and independence from parents and spending more time with peers (Jones, 2008). Many feel that they miss out on regular teenage activities, such as school dances and plays, sports, dating, jobs, and family vacations (Pini, Hugh-Jones, & Gardner, 2012).

Development of Satisfying Relationships

Personal relationships are also an important part of adolescence because they are a training ground for both identity development and future relationships (Christie & Viner, 2005). Cancer changes the dynamics of existing relationships, colors the development of new relationships, and may cause the beginning or end of relationships (Suris et al., 2004). Many adolescents with cancer talk about increased value on family and family relationships. Some report preferring to spend time with family over friends, whereas others seek the peer connections they feel they have been missing out on (Evan & Zeltzer, 2006).

Although adolescents with cancer may feel disconnected from peers, there is a level of intensity and emotional intimacy that develops in relationships for adolescents with cancer. They come to expect this level of depth in relationships and may be dissatisfied with the more superficial relationships of their same-aged peers (Green, 2012; Thaler-DeMers, 2001). Many adolescents find they have two groups of friends—cancer friends and noncancer friends (Abrams et al., 2007). During treatment, fellow patients and survivors may be the primary friend group, which may or may not change after treatment. Developing ways to maintain different kinds of relationships with varying levels of intimacy and intensity is important for healthy development and becomes another area of social work focus (Decker, 2007).

Disclosure of Cancer Illness

The prospect of developing new relationships during or following treatment raises questions about disclosure, which may be challenging for adolescents (Hilton, Emslie, Hunt, Chapple, & Ziebland, 2009; Servitzoglou, Papadatou, T siantis, & Vasilatou-Kosmidis, 2008). Disclosure is often most difficult in dating or potential dating relationships (Servitzoglou et al., 2008). A cancer diagnosis or associated health problems such as infertility from treatment may leave adolescents feeling uninterested in or unworthy of dating or being in an intimate relationship (Crawshaw & Sloper, 2010; Quinn, Murphy, Wang, Sawczyn, & Knapp, 2013). This feeling may decrease over time, but it negatively affects emotional well-being and social-emotional development because dating is an important experience in social development.

Adolescents with cancer also face the challenge of multiple identities, including a patient and survivor identity (Jones, Parker-Raley, & Barczyk, 2011). Struggles with identity increase feelings of isolation, as well as the possibility of engaging in high-risk behaviors (Cantrell & Conte, 2009; Jones et al., 2011). Social workers are well placed to support identity development by normalizing the experiences adolescents are having and finding opportunities for them to spend time with both patient and nonpatient peers, have new experiences, and try new things. It is important to provide information to adolescents in a way that they can process and use to become increasingly active in decision making (Abrams et al., 2007). Both the American Academy of Pediatrics and the Children's Oncology Group have guidelines for assent and clinical trial enrollment, respectively. Neither address participation in decision making as a developmental milestone for adolescents.

Cancer as a Source of Growth and Inspiration
Cancer can become a source of growth and inspiration, as well as an assault on development, underscoring the importance of interventions focusing on stress-related growth and building resilience. Life is dynamic for adolescents, which becomes a great asset in managing a cancer diagnosis (Kyngas et al., 2001; Stegenga & Ward-Smith, 2009). Although adherence can be challenging, when given the information they need and want, adolescents can be active participants in their treatment and find points for growth within their cancer experience (Butow et al., 2010). Social workers must recognize the balance between barriers to development and areas of potential growth to honor the struggle and facilitate increasing self-esteem, building resilience, and promoting emotional well-being.

Sense of Self

Adolescents have a sense of self that is physical, emotional, and existential. A diagnosis of cancer, subsequent medical treatment, late effects, and emotional reactions challenge the development of a positive sense of self (Arnett, 2001; Ritchie, 2001). Adolescents may feel their body has betrayed them. Changes such as weight gain or loss, scars, or hair or limb loss can leave adolescents feeling unrecognizable to themselves, making it difficult to develop a healthy relationship with their body (Fan & Eiser, 2009). Adolescence is also a time for existential questioning, which is part of the process of developing a sense of self. Religious beliefs and spiritual practices serve as sources of support for some adolescents with cancer, whereas others feel betrayed by their previously held beliefs of what they can expect and what is fair (Hendricks-Ferguson, 2006).

Interventions focus on supporting a positive sense of self in adolescents by emphasizing the importance of having a relationship with oneself that encompasses the physical, emotional, and existential or spiritual self. The ability to envision a future self is also a helpful area for social workers to explore with adolescents with cancer.

Emotional Challenges and Growth

Adolescence is full of many changes, first-time experiences, new expectations, and endings, all of which can be highly emotional (Arnett, 2001). Cancer influences how adolescents experience their emotions, amplifies emotions, and may lead to feelings of fear, anger, anxiety, disappointment, or sadness (Wicks & Mitchell, 2010). Adolescents express and respond to difficult and intense emotions differently (Kyngas et al., 2001; Wu et al., 2012). Some turn their cancer experience into a source of strength, whereas others may hide from it. Some adolescents become outspoken and strong self-advocates, whereas others lash out in anger. Adolescents with cancer may experience elevated levels of depression, anxiety, and distress at diagnosis and during treatment (Jorngarden et al., 2007); some adolescents turn these feelings into a drive to survive, but others develop depression or anxiety disorders and struggle emotionally into long-term survivorship (Dieluweit et al., 2010).

Risk factors for increased anxiety and depression and decreased quality of life in adolescent cancer survivors include the following:

- Treatment intensity experienced as painful, traumatic, and extended
- Poor prognosis
- The severing of familial, school, and social ties during extended treatment
- Lack of social support and sense of isolation after treatment
- Lack of satisfaction of informational needs (Wiener et al., 2006)

Worry associated with missed school and activities, prognosis, and physical changes and symptoms are associated with increased levels of distress (Hedstrom, Ljungman, & von Essen, 2005). Cancer types, level of uncertainty about prognosis, parental coping, and preexisting social or emotional problems have also been associated with outcomes in larger pediatric samples (Abrams et al., 2007).

Adolescents may have previously felt a sense of mastery in managing their emotions and have a limited set of coping skills. A cancer diagnosis and cancer treatment can challenge both this sense of mastery and effective coping. The coping skills that adolescents found helpful when a relationship ended may fail them when faced with the fear of death, limb loss, the inability to have biological children, or the lifelong management of health challenges. Social work interventions focus on teaching coping skills and reminding adolescents of both their inherent ability to cope and their potential to learn new ways of coping.

Viewing adolescents with cancer as full of potential allows for leveraging emotionally difficult times as opportunities for growth. Some adolescents report finding meaning in their diagnosis and learning what they truly value, allowing their experiences with cancer to inform their behaviors and their perspectives (Barakat et al., 2006; Wu et al., 2012). Others may have a harder time seeing their cancer experience as a learning experience (Wu et al., 2012). Picking up on small things they see as positive that have come out of their cancer experience and encouraging exploration of those identified experiences can be helpful. Cancer can both be very challenging and reveal meaning at the same time. The social worker must hold that dual focus to effectively promote emotional well-being and growth in the midst of the trauma that a cancer diagnosis can cause.

Key Areas of Focus for Adolescent Oncology Social Workers
• *Facilitate experiences and interactions to promote getting to know and developing relationships with oneself and with a variety of other people.* • *Recognize and honor the dichotomies of cancer and cancer treatment—difficult and provides opportunities for growth; causes loss which leads to grief and creates space for opportunities and hope; painful and value-clarifying.* • *Connect adolescents and families with needed services and advocate for relevant and responsive delivery of services.* • *Educate adolescents, families, and health care professionals about psychosocial and developmental challenges that cancer raises.* • *Work with health care professionals to increase effective communication, compliance, and adherence in adolescents with cancer.*

Practical and Concrete Challenges

A cancer diagnosis and subsequent treatment require adolescents to interface with medical institutions and health care professionals, and often raise challenges with concrete issues such as housing, finances, health insurance, education, and employment (Keegan et al., 2012; Stinson et al., 2012; Zebrack, Bleyer, Albritton, Medearis, & Tang, 2006). A cancer diagnosis may also introduce or exacerbate financial stresses for the adolescent or the whole family (Zebrack et al., 2006). Loss of income for the adolescent or parents or treatment costs in excess of insurance coverage may create additional financial strain. Some adolescents may not be living in a housing situation that is healthy or conducive to their health care needs, such as with many peers or without a clean, safe space of their own. Few adolescents have spent much time thinking about health insurance until they are diagnosed with cancer. During or upon completion of treatment, adolescents realize that, as a cancer survivor, they need health insurance and that it may be expensive, difficult to maintain, or insufficient in covering their health care needs.

Most adolescents have had little experience with medical care, which changes with a cancer diagnosis. They are also confronted with the limitations of their physical bodies at a time in their lives when most adolescents maintain a sense of immortality and indestructibility (Arnett, 2001), and the process of diagnosis and treatment can challenge their modesty.

Many adolescents are treated by pediatricians who rely on parental reporting and decision making to guide treatment. Older adolescents treated by adult health care professionals may be asked to make decisions they do not feel equipped to make or be presented information in a way they do not understand. Either treatment setting can be confusing and challenging if it is not equipped for adolescents and the health care professionals do not understand how best to communicate with and subsequently treat adolescents (Bleyer, 2007).

One of the most common practical challenges faced by adolescents with cancer is interruption of education and/or employment (Pini et al., 2012). Educational disruption may mean delaying high school graduation, entering a GED program, deferring college entrance, attending a community college instead of a 4-year university, or taking a leave of absence. Adolescents with cancer may lose their jobs, have to select a new career path, be passed over for a promotion, or leave the workforce permanently. This would be challenging at any age but is especially difficult at this time of transition from childhood to adulthood based on the symbolism of education and employment as markers of adulthood (Arnett, 2001).

Social workers are called on as brokers and advocates to connect adolescents and their families with resources, information, and referrals specific to their needs. Some agencies or resources may not have experience working with cancer survivors, and others may not be used to serving adolescents. A social worker's advocacy skills become very important in helping these organizations serve this population appropriately and supporting the adolescent through potentially bumpy service provision.

Pearls

- Experience drives development. This means that adolescents need to have experiences to progress developmentally.
- Relationships are context for experiences and are experiences themselves.
- Most adolescents have not interfaced with the medical system much.
- Adolescents have great potential to adapt.

Pitfalls

- Adolescents are often left out of conversations or not provided complete information.
- Decisions may be made without discussing with the adolescent or asking for their input, or even without their knowledge. This exclusion may be based on the assumptions that they would not understand, are too emotional, and cannot handle the information or that it is too scary for them.
- The emotionality of adolescents can also lead to assumptions about their hopes, fears, and desires.

Adults often assign their own fears and expectations to adolescents and may fail to recognize or acknowledge adolescents' own fears and expectations. Social workers have the opportunity to listen to adolescents' hopes, fears, and desires and assist other adults in doing the same.

- Existential struggles and the ability to find meaning and growth in the challenges of cancer may be underestimated or overlooked by adults despite their prominent role for adolescents. Assumptions are often made about the spiritual life of adolescents—that theirs is identical to that of the parents or that they lack an existential understanding or the ability to make meaning of difficult experiences. Again, the social worker becomes a steward and role model of communication. The social worker may also serve as a broker to connect adolescents with needed supports.

Adolescents diagnosed with cancer are still adolescents and need help to creatively find ways to fulfill developmental tasks while confronting a life-threatening diagnosis and often long periods of intense, painful, and disfiguring treatment. Some evidence suggests that these treatments can remain intrusive traumatic memories that cause avoidant behaviors. The ruptures in home, school, and peer activities are difficult for them, and they face readjusting to work and school after treatment and locating satisfying employment.

REFERENCES

Abrams, A. N., Hazen, E. P., & Penson, R. T. (2007). Psychosocial issues in adolescents with cancer. *Cancer Treatment Reviews, 33*(7), 622–630.

Arnett, J. J. (2001). Conceptions of the transition to adulthood from adolescence through midlife. *Journal of Adult Development, 8*, 133–143.

Barakat, L. P., Alderfer, M. A., & Kazak, A. E. (2006). Posttraumatic growth in adolescent survivors of cancer and their mothers and fathers. *Journal of Pediatric Psychology, 31*, 413–419.

Bellizzi, K. M., Smith, A., Schmidt, S., Keegan, T. H. M., Zebrack, B., Lynch, C. F.,... Adolescent and Young Adult Health Outcomes and Patient Experience (AYA HOPE) Study Collaborative Group. (2012). Positive and negative psychosocial impact of being diagnosed with cancer as an adolescent or young adult. *Cancer, 118*(20), 5155–5162. doi:10.1002/cncr.27512

Bleyer, A. (2007). Adolescent and young adult (AYA) oncology: The first A. *Pediatric Hematology-Oncology, 24*, 325–336.

Bleyer, A., Budd, T., & Montello, M. (2006). Adolescents and young adults with cancer: The scope of the problem and the criticality of clinical trials. *Cancer, 107*(S7), 1645–1655.

Butow, P., Palmer, S., Pai, A., Goodenough, B., Luckett, T., & King, M. (2010). Review of adherence-related issues in adolescents and young adults with cancer. *Journal of Clinical Oncology, 28*, 4800–4809.

Cantrell, M. A., & Conte, T. M. (2009). Between being cured and being healed: The paradox of childhood cancer survivorship. *Qualitative Health Research, 19*, 312–322.

Carpentier, M. Y., Mullins, L. L., Elkin, T. D., & Wolfe-Christensen, C. (2008). Predictors of health-harming and health-protective behaviors in adolescents with cancer. *Pediatric Blood and Cancer, 51*, 525–530. doi:10.1002/pbc.21605

Christie, D., & Viner, R. M. (2005). ABC of adolescence: Adolescent development. *British Medical Journal, 330*, 301–304.

Crawshaw, M. A., & Sloper, P. (2010). "Swimming against the tide"—the influence of fertility matters on the transition to adulthood or survivorship following adolescent cancer. *European Journal of Cancer Care, 19*(5), 610–620.

Decker, C. L. (2007). Social support and adolescent cancer survivors: A review of the literature. *Psycho-Oncology, 16*, 1–11. doi:10.1002/pon.1073

Dieluweit, U., Debatin, K. M., Grabow, D., Kaatsch, P., Peter, R., Seitz, D. C. M., & Goldbeck, L. (2010). Social outcomes of long-term survivors of adolescent cancer. *Psycho-Oncology, 19*(12), 1277–1284.

Dyson, G. J., Thompson, K., Palmer, S., Thomas, D. M., & Schofield, P. (2012). The relationship between unmet needs and distress amongst young people with cancer. *Supportive Care in Cancer, 20*, 75–85.

Erikson, E. (1963). *Childhood and society* (2nd ed.). New York, NY: W. W. Norton.

Evan, E. E., & Zeltzer, L. K. (2006). Psychosocial dimensions of cancer in adolescents and young adults. *Cancer, 107*, 1663–1671. doi:10.1002/cncr.22107

Fan, S., & Eiser, C. (2009). Body image of children and adolescents with cancer: A systematic review. *Body Image, 6*, 247–256.

Freyer, D. R. (2010). Transition of care for young adult survivors of childhood and adolescent cancer: Rationale and approaches. *Journal of Clinical Oncology, 28*, 4810–4818.

Green, J. (2012). *The fault in our stars*. New York, NY: Dutton.

Hedstrom, M., Ljungman, G., & von Essen, L. (2005). Perceptions of distress among adolescents recently diagnosed with cancer. *Journal of Pediatric Hematology/Oncology, 27*, 15–22.

Hendricks-Ferguson, V. (2006). Relationships of age and gender to hope and spiritual well-being among adolescents with cancer. *Journal of Pediatric Oncology Nursing, 23*, 189–199.

Hilton, S., Emslie, C., Hunt, K., Chapple, A., & Ziebland, S. (2009). Disclosing a cancer diagnosis to friends and family: A gendered analysis of young men's and women's experiences. *Qualitative Health Research, 19*, 744–754. doi:10.1177/1049732309334737

Jones, B. L. (2008). Promoting healthy development among survivors of adolescent cancer. *Family and Community Health, 31*, S61–S70. doi:10.1097/01.FCH.0000304019.98007.ae] PMID:18091144

Jones, B. L., Parker-Raley, J., & Barczyk, A. (2011). Adolescent cancer survivors: Identity paradox and the need to belong, *Qualitative Health Research, 21*(8), 1033–1040.

Jorngarden, A., Mattsson, E., & von Essen, L. (2007). Health-related quality of life, anxiety, and depression among adolescents and young adults with cancer: A prospective longitudinal study. *European Journal of Cancer, 43*, 1952–1958. PMID:17624761

Keegan, T. H., Lichtensztain, D. Y., Kato, I., Kent, E. E., Wu, X. C., West, M. M.,... AYA HOPE Study Collaborative Group. (2012). Unmet adolescent and young adult cancer survivors information and service needs: A population-based cancer registry study. *Journal of Cancer Survivorship, 6*, 239–250.

Kyngas, H., Mikkonen, R., Nousiainen, E. M., Rytilahti, M., Seppanen, P., Vaattovaara, R., & Jamsa, T. (2001). Coping with the onset of cancer: Coping strategies and resources of young people with cancer. *European Journal of Cancer Care, 10*, 6–11. doi:10.1046/j.1365-2354.2001.00243.x

Lockhart, S. K. (2006, June 10). *Childhood cancer therapy: Current state of the art. ABCs of childhood cancer.* Paper presented at Texas Medical Association, Physician's Oncology Education Program, Austin, TX.

National Cancer Institute and Lance Armstrong Foundation. (2006). Closing the gap: Research and care imperatives for adolescents and young adults with cancer: Report of the Adolescent and Young Adult Oncology Progress Review Group. NIH Pub. No. 06-6067. Bethesda, MD: National Cancer Institute; Austin, TX: Lance Armstrong Foundation.

National Comprehensive Cancer Network. (2012). *Clinical practice guidelines in oncology: Adolescent and young adult oncology* (Version 1.2012). Fort Washington, PA: Author.

Pini, S., Hugh-Jones, S., & Gardner, P. H. (2012). What effect does a cancer diagnosis have on the educational engagement and school life of teenagers? A systematic review. *Psycho-Oncology, 21*, 685–694. doi:10.1002/pon.2082

Quinn, G. P, Murphy, D., Wang, H., Sawczyn, K. K., & Knapp, C. (2013). Having cancer does not change wanting a baby: Healthy adolescent girls' perceptions of cancer-related infertility. *Journal of Adolescent Health, 52*(2), 164–169.

Ritchie, M. A. (2001). Self-esteem and hopefulness in adolescents with cancer. *Journal of Pediatric Nursing, 16*, 35–42.

Seitz, D. C. M., Besier, T., & Goldbeck, L. (2009). Psychosocial interventions for adolescent cancer patients: A systematic review of the literature. *Psycho-Oncology, 18*, 683–690. doi:10.1002/pon.1473

Servitzoglou, M., Papadatou, D., Tsiantis, I., & Vasilatou-Kosmidis, H. (2008). Psychosocial functioning of young adolescent and adult survivors of childhood cancer. *Support Care Cancer, 16*, 29–36. doi:10.1007/s00520-007-0278-z

Stegenga, K., & Ward-Smith, M. (2009). On receiving the diagnosis of cancer: The adolescent perspective. *Journal of Pediatric Oncology Nursing, 26*, 75–80.

Stinson, J. N., Sung, L., Gupta, A., White, M. E., Jibb, L. A., Dettmer, E., & Baker, N. (2012). Disease self-management needs of adolescents with cancer: Perspectives of adolescents with cancer and their parents and healthcare providers. *Journal of Cancer Survivorship, 6*, 278–286.

Suris, J. C., Michaud, P. A., & Viner, R. M. (2004). The adolescent with a chronic condition. Part I: Developmental issues. *Archives of Disease in Childhood, 89*, 938–942.

Surveillance, Epidemiology, and End Results. (2009). Surveillance, Epidemiology, and End Results (SEER) program. Retrieved from http://seer.cancer.gov

Teenage Cancer Trust. (2012). *A blueprint of care for teenagers and young adults with cancer.* Retrieved from http://www.teenagecancertrust.org/workspace/documents/Blueprint-of-care.pdf

Thaler-DeMers, D. (2001). Intimacy issues: Sexuality, fertility, and relationships. *Seminars in Oncology Nursing, 17*, 255–262.

Thomas, D. M., Seymour, J. F., O'Brien, T., Sawyer, S. M., & Ashley, D. M. (2006). Adolescent and young adult cancer: A revolution in evolution? *Internal Medicine Journal, 36*, 302–307. doi:10.1111/j.1445-5994.2006.01062.x

Treadgold, C. L., & Kuperberg, A. (2010). Been there, done that, wrote the blog: The choices and challenges of supporting adolescents and young adults with cancer. *Journal of Clinical Oncology, 28*, 4842–4849.

Wicks, L., & Mitchell, A. (2010). The adolescent cancer experience: Loss of control and benefit finding. *European Journal of Cancer Care, 19*, 778–785.

Wiener, L., Battles, H., Bernstein, D., Long, L., Derdak, J., Mackall, C., & Mansky, P. (2006). Persistent psychological distress in long-term survivors of pediatric sarcoma: The experience at a single institution. *Psycho-Oncology, 15*, 898–910.

Wu, L. M., Sheen, J. M., Shu, H. L., Chang, S. C., & Hsiao, C. C. (2012). Predictors of anxiety and resilience in adolescents undergoing cancer treatment. *Journal of Advanced Nursing, 69*(1),158–166. doi:10.1111/j.1365-2648.2012.06003.x

Zebrack, B., Bleyer, A., Albritton, K., Medearis, S., & Tang, J. (2006). Assessing the health care needs of adolescent and young adult cancer patients and survivors. *Cancer, 107*, 2915–2923. doi:10.1002/cncr.22338

Zebrack, B., & Isaacson, S. (2012). Psychosocial care of adolescent and young adult patients with cancer and survivors. *Journal of Clinical Oncology, 30*, 1221–1226.

Zebrack, B., Mathews-Bradshaw, B., & Siegel, S. (2010). Quality cancer care for adolescents and young adults: A position statement. *Journal of Clinical Oncology, 28*, 4862–4867.

64

Nancy F. Cincotta

The Family Experience in Pediatric Oncology

Your child doesn't get cancer; your family gets cancer. It is not some isolated thing, but something that forever shapes your family. It makes you appreciate a healthy child in a way that I could never understand before.

—*Mother of a child with leukemia*

I wouldn't give it up for the world. If a genie popped out of a lamp tomorrow morning and told me, "I can put you back . . . before you ever even started going to Boston, before anything was wrong, and I can make it so that it doesn't happen," I'd tell him no. I'd tell him, "Get back in your lamp."

—*24-year-old lymphoma survivor*

Don't be scared that you have cancer; be proud that you have it. It's almost like getting struck by lightning. It means you can win the lottery.

—*8-year-old melanoma survivor*

Key Concepts

- *The diagnosis of childhood cancer is a family diagnosis, because it has an impact on the entire family system.*
- *When a child is diagnosed with cancer, family life changes in two dimensions—the present and the future.*
- *Stages of development of the children and of the family influence the process for the family and the psychosocial work.*
- *The practical and emotional needs and resources of each family member play a role in assessment and intervention.*
- *The needs of siblings of children with cancer require unique understanding at diagnosis and throughout the course of illness.*

Although adults interact and understand themselves in many different societal contexts, the primary influence on children is the family. Family life itself is all-consuming during the decades when families are raising children, and families work diligently to maintain stability and integrity during this time. When a child is diagnosed with cancer, the homeostasis of family life is changed, altering the family's energy, focus, and mission. Even in an era of greater treatment success rates, childhood cancer imposes a threat to one of the weakest members of the family system and introduces vulnerability into the whole system. Everyone is affected. Because childhood cancer is a family affair, psychosocial interventions are best conceived within the context of the developmental levels of the children involved and with consideration of the family's developmental stage.

Impact on the Family

It magnified everything that we had before, good and bad things. We learned to be more patient and forgiving. We became more thoughtful about our own and other people's feelings and limitations.

—*Parent of a child with Ewing sarcoma*

As treatment is initiated, the "new normal" (Woodgate, 2006) begins to emerge. New goals and aspirations become ensconced in an old framework, an interesting dichotomy between what was then and what is now. The rhythm of family life needs to be readjusted to fit within the context of cancer, and it becomes apparent that the response is embedded in the soul of the family. Parental language frequently uses the first person plural—when "we" go to treatment, when "we" have surgery, when "we" were in the hospital—that indicates how actions, decisions, and emotions are intermingled among parents and children and how each family member is both wounded by and connected to the childhood cancer process.

Parents rarely anticipate the strength and endurance they will have when their child is diagnosed. Once it has happened, however, the ability of family members to regroup and continue to function speaks to the intrinsic strength and survival instinct of the children with cancer and each of their family members (Rosenberg, Baker, Syrjala, Back, & Wolfe, 2013). Childhood cancer teaches parents to stand up and advocate both for themselves and their children's needs. Over 600 parents of children with cancer are asked annually, "What have you learned about yourself since your child's diagnosis?" The overwhelming majority say they learned that they are stronger and more capable than they ever thought they could be.[1]

The following five themes emerged from a qualitative study of the experiences of children with cancer and their parents: the experience of illness, the upside of being sick, refocusing on what is important, acquiring a new perspective, and the experience of returning to well-being (Griffiths, Schweitzer, & Yates, 2011).

The following recommendations help ease the burden and mitigate against some of the overwhelming features of the childhood cancer experience: promote carefully thought out presentations of medical information by health care personnel (Mack, Wolfe, Grier, Cleary, & Weeks, 2006), enable resilience (Rosenberg et al., 2013), embrace hope, create memories (Cincotta, 2011), provide support, help families engage their own support systems, and introduce families to others facing the same issues.

Family Development

We as a family have learned that we are stronger than we think, that in the face of adversity we pull together and support each other through thick and thin. Everyone possesses an inner strength that we don't realize we have, until we have to use it.

—Mother of a child with neuroblastoma

The journeys traveled by families affected by childhood cancer are filled with essential partnerships and shared responsibilities for completing the physical and emotional tasks of the household, coupled with illness-related tasks. Families, like children, have different stages of development. "Newly formed" families with young, recently married parents early in their careers have very different emotional and financial needs when their child is diagnosed with cancer than those who have been together for many years, have older children, and are well established professionally.

Families require strategies for coping that sustain them from diagnosis through the various components of treatment. Just when a family gets into the rhythm of one phase, the rhythm changes; the paradigm for coping, however, can be applied to the next situation. Strengths acquired during the initial diagnosis can be built upon for each new phase of treatment.

Situations That Can Complicate Family Dynamics

- *A parent or another child in the family also has a life-threatening illness.*
- *A mother is pregnant.*
- *Family members do not agree on treatment.*
- *The family has limited social support.*
- *Any family member has a mental health diagnosis.*
- *Financial needs exceed all other needs.*

Families begin to develop differently after diagnosis, subtly or dramatically altering their course as a unit and individually. To say a child's cancer diagnosis affects everyone in the family is not to say that each person's experience is the same. The number and ages of children, the financial needs and work structure of the family members, and the resilience of parents are all pivotal determinants of the ways in which a family copes. Some families, particularly young families, may have little flexibility in their emotional, financial, and interpersonal resources. The crisis of their child's illness may be the first that these parents encounter. The skills for dealing with such a crisis may have to be learned "on the job" during treatment. Parents of teenagers are more seasoned in their parental roles than parents of newborns. Even though parenting an adolescent with cancer is not easy, it is accompanied by at least a dozen years of childrearing experience.

Questions to Consider

- *At what stage in life is the family?*
- *Is this the first child, or the youngest child?*
- *Are the parents new to parenting?*
- *What is the family's past experience with cancer?*
- *What is the emotional climate of the family?*
- *Is the family environment comfortable and conducive to care and support?*
- *What enables them to cope as a family?*
- *What disables them?*

Child Development

When an eight-year-old boy went to the mall after his arm had been amputated, his family was worried about how people would react. He was worried that people would notice that he was bald.

When a child got tired of telling people the story of her amputation, she began telling people that "The lion at the zoo bit my arm off."

Children are children first. Their experience of cancer varies considerably as they respond in a multitude of ways to stressful stimuli (Griffiths et al., 2011). A traumatic back-to-school experience for one—the child who does not want anyone to see him with no hair—could be a source of pride for another—the child who has other children sign his head.

Cancer treatment protocols can span many years, and children with cancer and their siblings continue to develop throughout this time, development that is not linear or arrested. Children can react to diagnosis and treatment in various ways; developmental levels and how a child responds to the rigors of diagnosis and treatment will affect the entire family fabric. Limited comprehension of cancer and its treatment can impede coping and compliance. Open communication in an age-appropriate fashion creates an environment that fosters trust and growth.

Techniques That Help a Family to Help Young Children
• *The use of metaphors about cancer* • *Playing out medical details to enhance comprehension and mastery* • *Age-appropriate educational games and toys* • *Psychoeducational approaches, teaching tools, and books* • *Assessing mastery of the medical situation, enabling comprehension, and facilitating coping*

Conversations about cancer and its treatment seem difficult at first, but communication becomes much more comfortable within a structure that facilitates discussion (Young, Dixon-Woods, Windridge, & Heney, 2003). The dialogue with a 4-year-old child will be different from one with a 13-year-old. A 3-year-old needs to be informed in an age-appropriate way; an 8-year-old needs to assent to and understand what is happening more concretely; an 18-year-old needs to consent to care. Medical decisions are often made for the child or in partnership with the child. Given the many layers of decision making and the speed with which the acclimation to information needs to occur, parents will need to make the best decisions they can with the information they have assimilated (Holm, Patterson, & Gurney, 2003).

Children must be educated in an ongoing way about the illness and its treatment, in concert with their cognitive and emotional growth. As children and teens get older, explanations should parallel their greater cognition, clarify any misperceptions they might have, and allow them the opportunity to gain greater expertise about the illness, its treatment, and the journey forward.

I had a horrible attitude as a kid. I hated everyone. I swore at teachers.... After I was sick, I met a lot of amazing people and it just... really changed my outlook on the world. I don't see the glass half empty or half full; it's a glass of water. You can take a sip or you can let it sit there. I'm going to experience every last thing I can, in whatever years I have left on this earth, and I don't think I would think that way if I had never been sick.

—Young adult survivor of lymphoma as an adolescent

Siblings: Who Tucks in Whom at Night?

It was the first time that I walked to school without my mother.

—7-year-old sibling of a child with leukemia

There is an appropriate outpouring of concern when a child is diagnosed with cancer. However, *all* children in the family are at risk and vulnerable at this time. Parents may need assistance in recognizing the needs of siblings (see Chapter 65). Children with cancer can mature beyond their developmental ages and are often described by their parents as being wise beyond their years. It is not uncommon for a parent to say, "I am glad that it was this child who got cancer, because my other child would not have been able to tolerate it."

Grandparents

My son and daughter-in-law are very responsible and can handle any situation on their own and need support for their decisions. It wasn't easy for me (a "take charge" person) to sit back and just be there for them as they needed me.

—Grandparent of a child with leukemia

Grandparents are often called upon to be caregivers to the siblings of the child with cancer (Flury, Caflisch, Ullmann-Bremi, & Spichiger, 2011). One of the complexities for grandparents is "double exposure"—feeling both their own pain as it relates to their grandchild's illness and the pain for their own children's experience. Although grandparents can be invaluable in some families, their caregiver burden is less recognized. A grandparent's inability to be helpful can sometimes be related to earlier issues in the grandparent–parent relationship or can cause new problems. Either way, the potential complexity and significance of these relationships cannot go unnoticed.

Socialization and Friendship

Cancer can have major implications for the social lives of children and adolescents, altering many friendships. It can change the course of a child's life by preventing the achievement of milestones in parallel with his or her peers; friendships may not be the primary focus. Katz, Leary, Breiger, and Friedman (2011) found that survivors of acute lymphoblastic leukemia had compromised relationships with their best friends. Children with brain tumors may also be isolated by physical and neurocognitive differences (Sands & Pasichow, 2009). Childhood cancer survivors invariably become accustomed to connections with a more adult cohort of medical professionals, parents, and teachers, which may impose barriers to ongoing friendships and re-entry to school.

After living through the cancer experience, children and their parents may think differently about friends and socializing. Adolescent cancer survivors are very aware of life's fragility. For example, when they reconnect with peers, they may not enjoy all of the same activities that a healthy teen does.

Siblings impacted by childhood cancer may have less time, energy, or contact with friends. Their availability to friends or activities is affected by where and with whom they are living. Friends or their friends' parents may not always understand the diagnosis or may have anxiety about the condition and its treatment, which can impede friendships. Sometimes, the child with cancer may become reliant on a sibling and sibling's friends for socialization.

The childhood cancer experience can frequently cause parents to reassess those in their lives, as they begin to understand who has been available to them and who has not. It is one of the few times in life that forces an active evaluation of the people in a family's support system. The diagnosis of cancer provides a catalyst for such scrutiny, testing the meanings of friendship. It is helpful to afford parents an opportunity to recognize the reality that they themselves have been changed by this experience, and that they too play a role in reaching out for or limiting help from others. Family and friends who persevere and strangers who come forward to assist form a new, more refined, more resilient support network.

One of the strongest components of friendship that emerges is the bond that family members create with other families of children with cancer. These connections often enable children and adults to endure treatment and life after treatment and foster a shared understanding that each family is not alone in the childhood cancer journey.

> *Meeting other families going through the same thing, gave me hope that we could make it through this.... When I'm having a bad day or struggling with something to do with her illness, I know that I have so many people that understand that will talk me through it.*
>
> —*Mother of a child with a brain tumor*

Employment and Parenting

Management of childhood cancer truly requires negotiation among family members. The relationship between parents will be impacted as responsibilities and priorities change after diagnosis. One parent will often stay at the hospital while the other takes prime responsibility for managing the home. Family roles are affected by the medical needs of the child with cancer, which parent is best able to comfort the child during treatment, which parent is most comfortable navigating the medical world, the number of other children, and the workload of the employed members of the family.

Illness often potentiates "traditional" gender roles for parents. The "cancer mom" is a well-recognized role in the pediatric cancer community. Clarke, McCarthy, Downie, Ashley, and Anderson (2009) conducted an extensive review of the literature on gender differences in parental responses to childhood cancer. They found that mothers were more likely to give up work and felt more effective with medical caregiving, whereas fathers reported feeling more financially involved.

Employment is a complex part of the formula, and a child's cancer affects parental careers. The person who remains employed may feel the burden of responsibility for maintaining the family's financial stability and medical insurance. Parents' perceptions of work will be affected by how employers react to the diagnosis and the child's treatment. Fathers in support groups often report that their drive at work is diminished. Opportunities for alternative employment may have to be foregone because of insurance considerations, which can lead to dissatisfaction in the workplace.

Working parents are less available during treatment, which can lead to a different rapport with treatment staff. Jones, Pelletier, Decker, Barczyk, and Dungan (2010) conducted an analysis of the literature concerning fathers of children with cancer and emphasized the need for enhanced psychosocial programming for fathers. Given their roles in society, fathers often neither seek nor receive as much emotional support as mothers during treatment, yet their voices and needs equal those of their spouses.

It may sometimes be necessary for a father to stay home to manage a job, the household, and the children at home while a mother goes to another city with a child for bone marrow transplantation or other specialty care. Bonds and alliances in families may shift during these periods. The person who stays at home benefits by providing stability in the household and forging closer bonds with the children who remain behind.

The person who was the primary caretaker for the child may find him- or herself in an existential life crisis after treatment is finished. He or she may experience confusion between the relief associated with the completion of treatment and the sense of isolation, loss of focus, and loss of support from the treatment center.

Despite the challenges, families of children with cancer often report posttraumatic growth (Barakat, Alderfer, & Kazak, 2006) and positive changes in their relationships (Barbarin, Hughes, & Chesler, 1985), thereby attesting to the resilience of families in the face of adversity.

> *When my mother came home, she expected that everything would go back to pre-transplant life. There was no way that was going to happen.*
>
> *—Sibling whose sister and mother went to bone marrow transplant*

Transitioning Off Treatment

Adjusting to cancer throughout the many stages of treatment, readjusting when the cancer experience is over, balancing everything, and returning to a "changed ordinary life" (Björk, Nordström, Wiebe, & Hallström, 2011) can be stressful. The medical and psychosocial complexities associated with treatment increase along with the longevity of children with cancer. Each treatment modality is accompanied by possible side effects and implications. Parents and other family members may be protective of the child with cancer throughout the child's life, which will impact family dynamics. Some childhood cancer survivors will be quite independent, whereas others will always need the support of their families for enduring illness- and treatment-related burdens. Children who have been treated with certain leukemia protocols may exhibit a range of cognitive and behavioral issues, frailty, early aging (Ness et al., 2013), and other malignancies. Adults who have survived childhood cancer treatment need to know specific details of their treatment to understand the potential medical issues they face. Many of the services available to families end with treatment. As a result, children and their families can feel, "We were only important because of the cancer."

The Internet

Thirty years ago, mothers in parents' groups would talk about feeling isolated and needing their husbands to talk more, cry more, and be more connected around their child's illness. Currently, fathers in groups talk about mothers staying up late, always being on the Internet, and being connected to so many families that it depletes the emotional energy they need to focus on their own family.

The Internet has changed many things, including family communication. More knowledge is available very quickly. From the very beginning, people do not feel alone. Access to information and social media, including CaringBridge sites and Facebook, have made the journey of childhood cancer different. Informational and emotional support are effectively provided by family members connecting with each other through online support groups (Coulson & Greenwood, 2012).

The Internet benefits people who live far from one another, those who find themselves alone in the middle of the night, and those who would be reluctant to join in-person support groups. A new task has emerged: Assess what you are reading, synthesize immense amounts of data, and decide when to stop reading. For many, however, the benefits of face-to-face contact and the feelings of hope engendered by those connections are unequaled. Family members, particularly children, should not learn about changes in a child's clinical status "online."

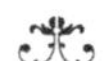

Pearls

- Family-focused care is of paramount importance in the approach to childhood cancers.
- Recognize that family communication is always influenced by families' fear of alienating the medical and nursing staff in ways that will adversely affect their child's care.
- Engage and educate both parents to support that dyadic relationship throughout the treatment process.
- Encourage family members to utilize concrete and emotional resources that have helped them cope previously.
- Refer families to organizations that provide specific services that your organization does not. Be aware of the many online services that provide information and resources.
- Be mindful of the financial burden imposed by childhood cancer.
- Promote communication around family needs with other professionals; advocate for family-centered care (e.g., sibling visitation policies).
- Help families compartmentalize components of treatment—e.g., "What do I need to do for chemo this week?" not "What will happen in 7 months?"
- Assist parents in living and creating joyful experiences for their family while going through treatment. Refer to programs that enable the family to regroup, reconnect, and have fun together.

- Foster hope. Help family members live in the present and anticipate the future.
- Allow for opportunities to talk about the experience while it is happening and after it is over.

Pitfalls

- Disregarding parents' opinions concerning their child's medical issues.
- Suggesting that families "keep everything normal." Life is not and will not be normal after a child is diagnosed with cancer. The realistic approach is to accept that things will be different but that things can still be all right.
- Not recognizing that a family needs help because they are not asking for it. Many families need "help with help," both asking for and accepting it.
- Allowing the Health Insurance Portability and Accountability Act (HIPAA) to impede support instead of safeguarding privacy, its original intent. Oncology programs have long been the leaders in providing support to patients. Some of the strongest connections that will be made in life are the ones among families who experience treatment together.
- Being naïve to developmental considerations. Children may have irrational fears or misperceptions based on their comprehension. "Understanding what is understood" is an important technique in helping family members of all ages.
- Focusing solely on the child with cancer or focusing solely on the parents.
- Inadequate reaching out to fathers to provide information and support.

> *Hope played an enormous role in my (our) life. One thing that I promised myself that I would never do was to lose sight of the light at the end of the tunnel. Some days it seemed like only a pinprick of light, but it represented a ray of hope nonetheless.*
>
> *—Father of a child with acute myelogenous leukemia*

Hope is, and remains, a strong concept in the work with children facing cancer and their families. The landscape is promising, and advances in childhood cancer have brought hope for a healthy future within our grasp. This does not change the reality that children still die from cancer, and that survivors and their family members may experience lifelong effects from treatment. Living with the challenges presented by childhood cancer takes fortitude and a rational, realistic approach to life. Ringnér, Jansson, and Graneheim (2011) interviewed parents of children with cancer to assess their experiences with acquiring information regarding the illness. They abstracted several themes: feeling acknowledged as a person of significance, feeling safe and secure in spite of uncertainty, having one's hopes supported, and getting relief from other families' experiences.

A social worker's past experience is invaluable to families facing childhood cancer. The experienced pediatric oncology social worker has the unique ability to bring the knowledge and wisdom gained from the many families he or she has previously worked with to each new family. Trust is enabled once a family understands that the social worker has not lived through the actual experience but has been connected with many others who have traveled the road. One of the greatest achievements a social worker can accomplish is to facilitate support among families in the same situation. Once families find each other, their mutual impact can be monumental.

Although no one would choose a cancer diagnosis, family members frequently say that they prefer who they are now, compared with who they were before treatment. There is a sense of pride in the accomplishment of taking on cancer. There is also a sense of privilege of working with this population, both for the families of children who survive and those who do not.

Strategies for Helping Families

- Educate families regarding the need to "grow" information about the illness and its treatment as children get older. Their developmental levels will determine what constitutes appropriate information.
- Afford family members program resources and ideas to help them create joyful and hopeful times, thus promoting the evolution of positive memories (Cincotta, 2001).
- Create a space for discussion about family size at an appropriate time. If a first child is diagnosed with cancer, it may influence parents' choices about having other children. Introduce parents to others who have been challenged by similar issues.
- Educate families to the reality that some treatment protocols will have late effects that may create behavioral or cognitive issues for the child. Some families try to hide issues that emerge, fearing them to be the result of their parenting.
- Allow families an opportunity to talk as a family unit about the impact that treatment has had on them and their outlook on life. It affords family members a time for reflection and sense of mastery over the cancer experience.
- Encourage parents to create opportunities for siblings to have alone time with them, and to bring them into the dialogue about the illness. Siblings need to hear that they are loved and cared for, that "We are all in this together and would do the same thing for you."

- All children in a family may remember things differently and may have confusing memories based on their age and emotional state. It can be helpful to revisit components of the medical experience as children get older to help them understand and process the experience.

NOTE

1. Generated from ongoing work with parents of children with cancer in the context of a family retreat program at Camp Sunshine at Sebago Lake, Casco, Maine.

ADDITIONAL RESOURCES

Camp Sunshine at Sebago Lake: A retreat program for the entire family when a child is diagnosed with cancer. It offers year-round programming and facilitates networking and group opportunities for adults and children: http://www.campsunshine.org

CancerCare: Nationwide, supportive services for any family member affected by cancer: http://www.cancercare.org

CaringBridge: Provides online sites allowing families to keep families and friends updated, keep a journal of the illness experiences, and access help when needed: http://www.caringbridge.org

Chai Lifeline: Support and community services for Jewish children with cancer and their families: http://www.chailife.org

Children's Oncology Group: A National Cancer Institute–supported clinical trials group. It is the world's largest organization devoted exclusively to childhood and adolescent cancer research: http://www.childrensoncologygroup.org

CureSearch for Children's Cancer: Funds and supports children's cancer research and provides information and resources to all those affected by children's cancer: http://www.curesearch.org

Leukemia & Lymphoma Society: Provides support groups, financial resources, and back-to-school programs for children and their families: http://www.lls.org

Make-a-Wish: Provides wishes for children diagnosed with cancer. It includes family members in the wish: http://www.makeawish.org

Team Impact: Enables college sports teams to adopt children with cancer and their families and provide a supportive team membership experience: http://www.teamimpact.org

Online Support Groups for Parents of Children with Cancer

American Childhood Cancer Foundation: http://www.acco.org/Information/Support/OnlineSupportGroups.aspx

Association of Cancer Online Resources: http://www.acor.org

Children's Brain Tumor Foundation: http://www.cbtf.org/

Ped-Onc Resource Center: http://www.ped-onc.org/cfissues/maillist.html

Stupid Cancer: The Voice of Young Adult Cancer: http://www.stupidcancer.org/directories/yaorgs.shtml

REFERENCES

Barakat, L. P., Alderfer, M. A., & Kazak, A. E. (2006). Posttraumatic growth in adolescent survivors of cancer and their mothers and fathers. *Journal of Pediatric Psychology, 31*(4), 413–419. doi:10.1093/jpepsy/jsj058

Barbarin, O. A., Hughes, D., & Chesler, M. A. (1985). Stress, coping, and marital functioning among parents of children with cancer. *Journal of Marriage and the Family, 47*(2), 473–480. doi:10.2307/352146

Björk, M., Nordström, B., Wiebe, T., & Hallström, I. (2011). Returning to a changed ordinary life: Families' lived experience after completing a child's cancer treatment. *European Journal of Cancer Care, 20*(2), 163–169. doi:10.1111/j.1365-2354.2009.01159.x

Cincotta, N. F. (2001). Special programs for children with cancer and their families. In M. M. Lauria, E. J. Clarke, & N. M. Stearns (Eds.), *Social work in oncology: Supporting survivors, families, and caregivers* (pp. 169–192). Atlanta, GA: American Cancer Society.

Cincotta, N. F. (2011). Bereavement in the beginning phase of life: Grief in children and their families. In T. Altilio & S. Otis-Green (Eds.), *Oxford textbook of palliative social work* (pp. 305–317). New York, NY: Oxford University Press.

Clarke, N. E., McCarthy, M. C., Downie, P., Ashley, D. M., & Anderson, V. A. (2009). Gender differences in the psychosocial experience of parents of children with cancer: A review of the literature. *Psycho-Oncology, 18*(9), 907–915. doi:10.1002/pon.1515

Coulson, N. S., & Greenwood, N. (2012). Families affected by childhood cancer: An analysis of the provision of social support within online support groups. *Child Care Health and Development, 38*(6), 870–877. doi:10.1111/j.1365-2214.2011.01316.x

Flury, M., Caflisch, U., Ullmann-Bremi, A., & Spichiger, E. (2011). Experiences of parents with caring for their child after a cancer diagnosis. *Journal of Pediatric Oncology Nursing, 28*(3), 143–153. doi:10.1177/1043454210378015

Griffiths, M., Schweitzer, R., & Yates, P. (2011). Childhood experiences of cancer: An interpretative phenomenological analysis approach. *Journal of Pediatric Oncology Nursing, 28*(2), 83–92. doi:10.1177/1043454210377902

Holm, K. E., Patterson, J. M., & Gurney, J. G. (2003). Parental involvement and family-centered care in the diagnostic and treatment phases of childhood cancer: Results from a qualitative study. *Journal of Pediatric Oncology Nursing, 20*(6), 301–313. doi:10.1177/1043454203254984

Jones, B. L., Pelletier, W., Decker, C., Barczyk, A., & Dungan, S. S. (2010). Fathers of children with cancer: A descriptive synthesis of the literature. *Social Work in Health Care, 49*(5). doi:10.1080/00981380903539723

Katz, L. F., Leary, A., Breiger, D., & Friedman, D. (2011). Pediatric cancer and the quality of children's dyadic peer interactions. *Journal of Pediatric Psychology, 36*(2), 237–247. doi:10.1093/jpepsy/jsq050

Mack, J. W., Wolfe, J., Grier, H. E., Cleary, P. D., & Weeks, J. C. (2006). Communication about prognosis between parents and physicians of children with cancer: Parent preferences and the impact of prognostic information. *Journal of Clinical Oncology, 24*(33), 5265–5270. doi:10.1200/jco.2006.06.5326

Ness, K. K., Krull, K. R., Jones, K. E., Mulrooney, D. A., Armstrong, G. T., Green, D. M., . . . Hudson, M. M. (2013).

Physiologic frailty as a sign of accelerated aging among adult survivors of childhood cancer: A report from the St. Jude lifetime cohort study. *Journal of Clinical Oncology, 31*(36), 4496–4503. doi:10.1200/JCO.2013.52.2268

Ringnér, A., Jansson, L., & Graneheim, U. H. (2011). Parental experiences of information within pediatric oncology. *Journal of Pediatric Oncology Nursing, 28*(4), 244–251. doi:10.1177/1043454211409587

Rosenberg, A. R., Baker, K. S., Syrjala, K. L., Back, A. L., & Wolfe, J. (2013). Promoting resilience among parents and caregivers of children with cancer. *Journal of Palliative Medicine, 16*(6), 645–652. doi:10.1089/jpm.2012.0494

Sands, S. A., & Pasichow, K. P. (2009). Psychological and social impact of being a brain tumor survivor. In S. Goldman & C. D. Turner (Eds.), *Late effects of treatment for brain tumors* (pp. 297–307). New York, NY: Springer.

Woodgate, R. L. (2006). Life is never the same: Childhood cancer narratives. *European Journal of Cancer Care, 15*(1), 8–18. doi:10.1111/j.1365-2354.2005.00614.x

Young, B., Dixon-Woods, M., Windridge, K. C., & Heney, D. (2003). Managing communication with young people who have a potentially life threatening chronic illness: Qualitative study of patients and parents. *British Medical Journal, 326*(7384), 305–308B. doi:10.1136/bmj.326.7384.305

65

Nancy F. Cincotta

Helping Siblings of Pediatric Cancer Patients

The mother of a baby with cancer described how the baby's twin stayed in the crib with her twin and held her hand throughout her course of chemotherapy.[1]

Key Concepts

- *Siblings of children with cancer encounter many emotional challenges, some of which can be minimized with open communication.*
- *Age-appropriate information and discussion enhance siblings' abilities to cope.*
- *Parents who are managing the medical protocols for their children with cancer can benefit from guidance in understanding the unique emotional sequelae that their children without cancer experience.*
- *Sibling support groups empower siblings, enable siblings to feel less isolated, and are an effective modality in helping children and teens cope with the cancer experience.*

In a particularly complicated sibling support group, I found myself with a cohort of children focused on how much less their parents cared about them than they did their siblings with cancer. Although I used every technique imaginable, I was unable to engage them in moving forward from this concept. Finally, I asked the group, "If you had cancer, do you think your parents would care about you as much as your sibling?" After a period of silence, one of the girls said, "No, because then I would be the second child in the family with cancer and it wouldn't be a big deal."

The Context of Being a Sibling

Childhood cancer impacts the entire family and has implications for each member. Siblings can experience feelings of confusion, loss, anxiety, and sadness in the days that follow the diagnosis. Sibling rivalry does not suddenly emerge from the childhood cancer experience and cannot be expected to disappear when a sibling is diagnosed with cancer.

The siblings of young children have been their playmates and confidants. They are the people whom they argue with *and* defend the most. If they don't live in the same room, they frequently live next door. They go on family vacations together, are together for holidays, borrow clothing, and share toys and secrets—even if they are competitive or at times antagonistic. They may break each other's things or fight unrelentingly, but there is solace in knowing that siblings will always be there for the next fight. For most individuals, the relationships with their siblings will be longer lived than those with their parents, spouses, or other relatives (Cincotta, 2011).

Diagnosis

When a brother or sister is diagnosed with cancer, the private sibling world is challenged. Suddenly siblings no longer share every experience. The patterns and routines that frame a sibling's world are shaken, and the sibling journey has no road map. There is not enough time to discern what is happening in the family as its priorities change suddenly and dramatically.

Siblings may start to feel distressed shortly after diagnosis, as they are not often present during all steps of the initial evaluation and subsequent treatment (Lähteenmäki, Sjöblom, Korhonen, & Salmi, 2004; Murray, 2000). Appropriately, the amount of attention a child with cancer gets in the treatment center is remarkable; even at the best of institutions, however, the attention a sibling gets is limited (Mitchell, Clarke, & Sloper, 2005).

At certain ages, children have no external world apart from the one they share with their family, and children are completely dependent on their family. Siblings of children with cancer tend to experience more anxiety, psychological distress, problems in school, and other maladaptive behaviors, along with feelings of separation anxiety and sadness, than others their age as a result of the postdiagnosis changes in the family routine and pattern of support from parents (Alderfer et al. 2010; Lähteenmäki et al., 2004). The sibling is often the person with the least control. Suddenly, everything is different, and the primary focus of the household shifts to the needs of the child with cancer. The developmental stage of siblings at the time of diagnosis and the evolution they undergo during treatment influence their interpretation, acceptance, emotional growth, and stability. Changing medical situations and comprehension require an ongoing informational dialogue with siblings that should be based on an understanding of developmental theory (Murray, 2000).

I was left with anyone they could find at the time.
—9-year-old sibling of a child with cancer

When treatment begins, parents ideally create a plan for the children without cancer, often designating a primary person to be in charge of their care in the parents' absence. Care of healthy siblings is often taken over by grandparents, other relatives, or friends (Flury, Caflisch, Ullmann-Bremi, & Spichiger, 2011). Although it is optimal to have consistent alternate caregivers, it does not compensate for the time the family would have shared. Changes in the living situation can create a sense of unrest and uneasiness for siblings. Mothers are generally in the hospital tending to the patient's needs, and fathers often divide their time between work, home, and hospital (Jones, Pelletier, Decker, Barczyk, & Dungan, 2010). Being displaced can leave siblings feeling angry, resentful, unloved, and unlovable.

The Career of a Cancer Sibling

Advice for Parents From Siblings of Children With Brain Tumors

- *Treat us a little more fairly. Don't just give everything to our sibling.*
- *Do not yell at my sister. Life would be a lot easier if you didn't yell.*
- *Try to have equal time with each kid, so the sibling feels equally important as the child with the brain tumor.*
- *Don't always listen to the doctor. Sometimes the doctor says that my brother can't do something, but he can. Just let him try.*
- *Try not to be so protective.*
- *Trust the sibling; allow him to be helpful.*
- *Don't care more about my sister than me.*
- *Sometimes we (sibs) feel unappreciated. Appreciate us.*
- *When a sibling gets an injury, it should be just as important.*
- *Getting a flu shot is a big deal for the sibling, because he is not used to getting shots.*

The ambiguity of being a sibling of a child with cancer and the shifts in caregiving and available support place them in a vulnerable position negotiating the emotional complexities of their sibling's cancer treatment. Some siblings become more mature and committed to the care of family members as a result of the experience (Chesler, Allswede, & Barbarin, 1991). Siblings also speak of being proud of their brothers and sisters. Siblings often report feeling guilty that something they did or said gave their sibling cancer, or because it was their sibling who got sick and not them. The older ones in particular may feel guilty that they could not prevent their sibling from getting cancer. Siblings are protective and worry about their siblings, their parents, and themselves. And yet siblings also feel vulnerable (Cincotta, 2004).

Who will take care of me if I get sick? What would it be like if I got cancer?
—Sibling of a child with a brain tumor

Siblings are less likely to externalize the problems they are having because they fear confrontation with family members and that their problems are unimportant (Cordaro, Veneroni, Massimino, & Clerici, 2012). Cohen, Friedrich, Jaworski, Copeland, and Pendergrass (1994) found that siblings of children with cancer in families with high levels of cohesion and adaptability tended to adjust better to a life with cancer because they communicated more openly. In a longitudinal study, Houtzager and colleagues (2004) found that family adaptability may be effective as an initial strategy but might hamper sibling adjustment if the cancer process continues over a longer period of time.

Information for Siblings

I would tell parents to talk to their children, to tell them what is going on. It is all very confusing this way.
—9-year-old sibling of a child with cancer

Siblings want to understand what is taking place and how they might help (Spinetta et al., 1999). O'Shea, Shea, Robert, and Cavanaugh (2012) surveyed pediatric oncology nurses regarding the needs of siblings of children with cancer. They concluded that siblings need ongoing attention and support from other family members. Taking the time to explain the illness and its treatment to a sibling helps reduce anxiety but may not always be enough (Hamama, Ronen, & Rahav, 2008; Houtzager, Grootenhuis, & Last, 2001). Peer support groups and relationships with peers that allow siblings to voice their concerns are great tools to enhance coping (Barrera, Chung, Greenberg, & Fleming, 2002; Heiney, Goon-Johnson, Ettinger, & Ettinger, 1990; Prchal & Landolt, 2012; Sidhu, Passmore, & Baker, 2006). Summer camp programs in particular give siblings the opportunity to feel that they are part of a community, boost self-esteem, and provide connections with other children and adolescents in similar situations (Creed, Ruffin, & Ward, 2001; Hancock, 2011).

The period of initial diagnosis and treatment can be overwhelming. Because most families have not had prior experience with this situation, they can benefit from the support of a professional, such as a social worker, who is familiar with the dynamics of this situation.

In addition to what they are told and what they surmise, children gather information from what they see and overhear. They observe things others may not see, both because of their closeness with the sibling and because of the distance imposed by the illness. If a child has been separated from his or her sibling for a period of time, the child may perceive and be fearful of changes in his or her sibling (Wakefield, McLoone, Butow, Lenthen, & Cohn, 2013). What siblings know, what they hear, and what they are willing to share with parents are all different aspects of their experience. Siblings consistently express their appreciation of all that their parents have to do because of their brother or sister's illness. They do not want to worry them with their own feelings, problems, or failures.

Family Challenges

Families facing a pediatric oncology diagnosis tend to be overwhelmed and focused on issues faced by the patient, suppressing the needs of other family members to survive. Stepping up to the level of knowledge needed to be a "cancer mom" (or dad) and feeling competent may seem like an insurmountable task. It may be difficult to hear that their children without cancer are also having problems. The personal coping methods employed by parents and the early medical information they provide to their children are important determinants of how well siblings cope (Carpenter & LeVant, 1994). Educating and enabling parents to understand and help their children who do not have cancer empowers them.

Often parents try to do all that they can to keep their other children's lives and schedules as normal as possible. Achieving such a goal would require siblings to remain behind when their brother or sister goes to the hospital. Alternatively, siblings would have to abandon routine activities to always be with the family at the hospital. Keeping siblings out of the medical environment or having them miss their activities creates a "disconnect" in their lives. The reality is that the situation is not normal and it is necessary to find a new balance.

If there is a choice between leaving siblings with alternate caregivers and taking them to the hospital, the siblings should optimally make the decision. If this is not feasible, it is helpful for parents to indicate that they wish they could give the child another option. These discussions allow siblings to feel connected to the family process. Even the most thoroughly thought out plan will not satisfy a sibling's intrinsic need to have the family be the same as it was before diagnosis.

Children with cancer are often the recipients of "things," most notably toys and stuffed animals, and are the beneficiaries of wish programs. The sibling observes this outpouring of affection and can feel inferior, less loved, and left out. There are many practical solutions to this problem: Inform people that it is optimal to bring small gifts for all the children, ask them to bring things everyone can enjoy, move the focus away from gifts, or present a "family focus" on gifts.

Family alliances and dynamics may change, depending on who is at home, who is at the hospital, and which parent is with which child. The relationship between siblings is likely to shift during treatment. Secrets that might have been shared with the sibling who is ill may now be shared with another sibling or a parent. As one child becomes worried about the other's health, or as siblings become less available to each other, the balance changes. Families may experience a paradigm shift in roles among members, which adds to feelings of confusion during the treatment period.

Sibling Wisdom

> *When children are asked to provide one word describing what it is like to be the sibling of a child with cancer, the words speak for themselves. One group's response was: difficult; alone; hard; empty; conflicted; life-changing; confused; changed; ignored; unique.*
>
> *—Sibling bereavement group, Camp Sunshine at Sebago Lake*

The end of treatment for the child with cancer can have an impact on healthy siblings. Despite being happy that treatment is over, siblings may feel as if they do not have enough information about the future. They may remain concerned about what caused the illness and question whether they are at risk for being diagnosed with cancer (Wakefield, Butow, Fleming, Daniel, & Cohn, 2012). The end of treatment can make siblings miss the support they found at the hospital (Björk, Nordström, Wiebe, & Hallström, 2011); this feeling of loss disappears as siblings experience greater parental presence at home.

Fifteen years after her sister was diagnosed with leukemia, an older sibling ended up in the emergency room. She called her mother and clearly stated that she did not need her to come, because she was with her friends and she was fine. When her mother arrived at the emergency room shortly thereafter, the woman realized for the first time that her mother would really be there for her.

Children frequently state that they believe a parent cares more about the sibling with cancer. Even after treatment, the child with cancer often continues to be a "star," which presents ongoing challenges in many families. As families regain homeostasis after treatment, there is time to discuss and process past experiences. Children tend to adjust better and their level of anxiety lessens once their sibling's treatment is over (Buchbinder, Casillas, & Zeltzer, 2011) (see Table 65.1).

Sibling Feelings and Concerns

> *We feel alone, scared, sad, jealous, angry, guilty, and so much more. All of these feelings constantly contradict each other and battle in our heads.... How could you ever be angry with your sick sibling? How dare you feel jealous? She deserves those toys; don't you know what she's going through?*
>
> *—17-year-old sister of a child with a brain tumor*

Table 65.1.
Sibling Issues and Recommendations

Sibling Issues	Sibling Dialogue and Recommendations
1. Misperceptions of facts and feelings • Never told facts • Told facts, but did not understand them • Misinterpret the situation, believing it is something it is not • Misperceive their significance in the family • Perceptions of no longer being loved, not being loved enough, or being left out	*They said they were going to have his blood taken. I thought they were going to take all of his blood out.* *The child life specialist said I was going to be the bow and arrow donor, but I don't have a bow and arrow.* • Envision words and their various meanings and how they can be confusing to children. • Education in an age-appropriate way is the best ammunition against misperceptions and the attendant feelings. • Understand developmental level—it influences comprehension and coping.
2. Jealousy • Preexisting rivalries, competitive feelings with sibling (exacerbated or affirmed) • New competitive feelings after the diagnosis • Jealous of love, attention, activities • Jealous of time sibling spends with parents/special relationships • Perception that sibling is preferred	*I wish I had cancer.* *My brother got too many popsicles.* *She is always treated like she is special.* • Jealousy can be magnified by the cancer experience. Parents can monitor and regulate gift giving, time, affection, and misperceptions.
3. Exhibiting/expressing anger • Manifestation of another emotion: easier to feel anger than sadness • Perceive the world to be unfair • Anger at what the situation imposes on them: losses, additional responsibilities, separation from family • Anger at parents/siblings • Anger at cancer	*She still gets all the attention.* *He could do no wrong; we had more responsibility than he did.* *Whenever he had a problem, mom responded right away.* *My mother always told me to hold on or wait till she was done tending to him.* • Think about outlets and activities to assist in the understanding and management of anger. Help siblings to understand the ill child's needs and to think through and redirect their anger.
4. Loneliness and abandonment *Physical* • Being left alone abruptly • Separated from sibling, from parents • Not included in cancer-related or hospital activities • Missing normal family activities • Longing for nuclear family members when with other family or friends	*I got left out a lot.* *We were kind of left behind.* *People always ask how he is doing. No one realized I was coming home to nothing every day.* *I was supposed to go to Disney World with my mom, but she took her.* • Allow siblings to accompany patient or visit during treatment. • Initiate projects that foster regular communication—e.g., diary between parent and child with daily entries to each other.

Table 65.1. (Continued)	
Sibling Issues	**Sibling Dialogue and Recommendations**
Emotional • Feelings of being forgotten • Living a different life experience • Longing for life as it was before cancer • Family members may be present physically but absent emotionally • Not fitting in where they are *Existential* • Sense of isolation • Where do I belong? • Feeling abandoned	• Brainstorm ways in which the sibling can remain part of the family or connections can be intensified during inpatient stays. • Clarify reasons for separations. • Assure siblings that they have not been abandoned, regardless of their feelings. • Encourage opportunities for parents and siblings to be alone with each other.
5. Guilt • At not being the one who is ill • At feeling responsible for or not having been able to prevent the illness • At feeling jealous or angry • Can exist on several levels and is often left unspoken	*It should have been me.* *It was because I said I wished she were dead.* *I am the older sister. I should have been able to protect her.* *This should have happened to me.* • Engage in dialogue to acknowledge and normalize feelings of guilt. • Educate the sibling with an age-appropriate explanation of the illness and mitigate blame: "Nothing you did or said caused this."
6. Sadness/depression • Disappointment • Hopelessness • Helplessness • Self-esteem, self-worth • Loss • Not feeling understood • Sleep issues	*Everyone in the house is acting differently.* *When my mother came back, her mind was away.* • Create opportunities for success, fun, and connection. • Create a "cancer-free" zone, where everything except cancer matters. • Refer to cancer-based family programs.
7. Anxiety/fear/worry • About illness in general • About "catching" the illness • About death • For sibling • For oneself • For other siblings without cancer • About who will help them with life changes • About new routines and about the future	*I cried about him. I thought he was going to die.* *Even though he gets all the attention, I do not want him to die.* *I cried every night.* • Parents generally serve as a buffer to overwhelming emotions for their children. Resources and discussions to support children with their feelings need to be provided. • Give permission to talk.
8. Confusion and uncertainty • Homeostasis changes quickly • Feeling lost, situation unlike any other the child has had to deal with • Not being told details • Not understanding details • Inability to focus • Inability to process things with parents	*My mother left in a hurry, was gone for a long time, and came back a different person.* • Assess whether these feelings are present, understand why, and address the issues. • Present ideas of certainty, talk about the treatment plan and schedules, and anticipate issues relevant to the sibling.

(*continued*)

Table 65.1. (Continued)

Sibling Issues	Sibling Dialogue and Recommendations
9. Developmental issues	
• Acting out	*I didn't tell them I was cutting school, and they didn't notice.*
• Attention seeking	*I never really fit in with my peers, because they didn't understand my brother's illness.*
• Peer problems	*I did not want to tell them I was having problems at school; they had too much to worry about.*
• Poor academic performance	*My other daughter had learning issues. We had no idea.*
• Physical illness (real and somaticized)	• School personnel need to be aware of the situation and should keep parents informed of any concerns.
• Unattended academic, physical, and social issues	• Behavioral problems in siblings may be indicative of problems in coping with the diagnosis.
• Family expectations of responsibility (for self or sibling) may exceed their ability	
• Parentified child	
10. Compassion/growth	
• The need to help	*I try to help in any way I can.*
• The desire to take care of family members	*I wanted to be the donor, but they said that I could not do it.*
• Feeling protective	• Work with siblings to develop a unique and helpful role during the treatment period.
• Feeling proud	• Create opportunities to stimulate emotional growth and develop compassion (e.g., volunteer opportunities and family programs).
• Opportunities for growth	
• Maturity and understanding	
• Concern for parents	

Sibling Perspectives

I was sent to detention 17 times and my parents never knew. I wanted to hurt people, because I wanted them to understand how much my sister hurt.

—*Cincotta (2011)*

Siblings live their lives feeling forgotten about.... Just knowing that there is a group specifically for YOU makes you feel like people really do care, that you're not just ignored and in the way.... The sibling journey is so complicated and challenging, but most people don't realize that.

That is why sibling programs are so important, because they give siblings a chance to talk to other siblings. When they talk about everything they've been feeling and thinking, they realize that everyone is saying just about the same things. They are not alone. They are not wrong to feel certain ways. It is what it is and it's ok because it is normal.... Sibling programs allow siblings to get everything off their chests without worrying about being judged or feeling isolated with their radical feelings, because they are in fact not radical whatsoever.

—*17-year-old sister of a child with astrocytoma*

Special Circumstance: Siblings as Bone Marrow Donors

A teenager wanted to see the bone marrow cells that he was donating for his sister's transplant; it became quite an ordeal for him to get to see them. In the end, 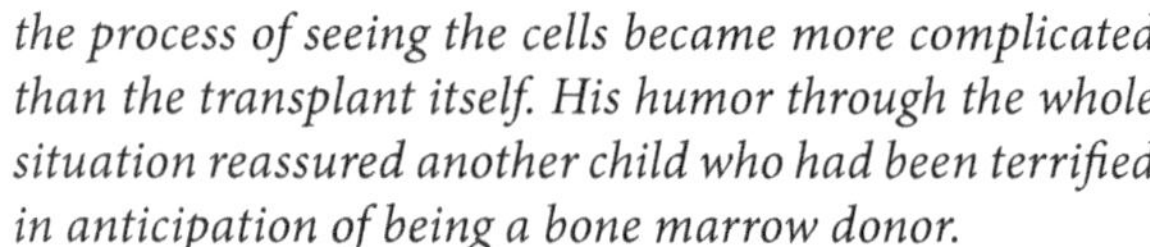
the process of seeing the cells became more complicated than the transplant itself. His humor through the whole situation reassured another child who had been terrified in anticipation of being a bone marrow donor.

—*Regarding the adolescent brother of a child with Fanconi anemia*

Bone marrow and hematopoietic stem cell transplants can leave lasting effects on both the patient and sibling donor. MacLeod, Whitsett, Mash, and Pelletier (2003) found both positive and negative effects on sibling donors. Some reported positive effects of successful sibling donation were a closer relationship with the patient, a decreased sense of helplessness, and an increase in sibling donor self-esteem. Sibling donors also felt more included in the family and in the decision-making process for the patient's treatment (MacLeod et al., 2003). Anger, guilt, and shame are among the lasting negative psychological effects of unsuccessful sibling donations. In another study, sibling donors were reported to have higher self-reported levels of anxiety and lower self-esteem compared to nondonor siblings (Packman et al., 1997). Many sibling donors have felt as if they had no choice in the matter, due either to their personal beliefs or to family pressures (MacLeod et al., 2003). Although sibling donors admit that they would have gone through with the donation either way, many felt unprepared because they did not understand the procedure and its complications.

Interventions for Families

Children with cancer and their siblings often know much more than the adults around them perceive (Cincotta, 1993).

It is important to provide creative opportunities that identify and acknowledge siblings' feelings and offer activities that allow for expression of those feelings and enable positive coping strategies. Such experiences provide children and adolescents with a structure within which they can begin to piece the sibling experience together. Therapeutic activities can often address a child's identified emotional needs and find an actual or metaphorical way to manage issues. For instance, helping a child who is feeling lost with an activity that will help him or her feel grounded (e.g., drawing a picture weekly, and then at the end making his or her own book about what his or her time was like when the sibling was on treatment) will help the child gain control and mastery of the situation.

Communicate: Create Room for Dialogue

We are all in this together. ←→ *We will get through it together.*
We love you. ←→ *We love you as much as we love your sibling.*
We did not want this to happen. ←→ *We would take care of you in the same way if something happened to you.*

- Acknowledge feelings and the impact on the family.
- Acknowledge losses because of the sibling's cancer (e.g., having one's mother miss his or her school play, being isolated when one has chicken pox).
- Acknowledge gains (e.g., special opportunities, personal growth).

Process: The Treatment Experience

- Bring siblings to the place where the child is receiving or has received treatment, so they can be connected to the actual experience.
- Talk about the illness:

  What is the one question you would like answered?
  What do you remember from the night your brother got sick?
  What do you understand about leukemia?

- Talk about the sibling's experience:

  What is it like being home?
  What is the hardest part?
  What is the best part?
  What has changed for you?

One goal is to help siblings have a realistic view of the situation so that it does not seem too frightening or glamorous. Sometimes it is the small things—for example, nighttime rituals or the ways in which parents connect with children—that provide children with the psychic energy to move from one experience to the next. Parents provide support and stability for children; siblings long for parental attention to help them cope with this journey.

Empower: Give Siblings a Voice

- Provide siblings with an opportunity to take charge of something.
- Find them a support group, either with other siblings of children with cancer or with siblings of children with any illness who are facing similar challenges.

Inform: Education and Support

- Seek and utilize existing resources: sibling support groups, sibling camps, hospital-based sibling days.
- Afford the sibling an opportunity to meet with an oncology professional.
- Seek individual counseling for needs that emerge that are unable to be met by a parent or a sibling program.
- Age-appropriate intervention is effective if the child can integrate the information. Ask children to explain what they understand to assess their comprehension.

The Magic of Sibling Support Groups

Sobbing throughout the discussion, a child remained insistent that her parents preferred her sister. She woefully spoke of her life being ruined by her sister's illness, and her guilt for having such feelings.

—Regarding a 12-year-old sibling of a child with osteosarcoma

Being in the presence of other siblings provides a sense of community. Sibling programs acknowledge the uniqueness of the sibling role and give it prominence. It is not the frequency of support groups that matters; it is the content and the concept of groups. Many different group styles can be effective: one session, short-term or monthly groups, or camp programs.

Camp Sunshine at Sebago Lake has been able to foster opportunities for siblings. Within this framework, children with cancer and their siblings become connected to other children with cancer and the siblings of those children. This environment creates a natural opportunity for sibling support groups.

The insight of these groups of children is unequaled. Group attendance varies, with as many as 26 children in attendance. Some children come to the group just once, and others attend multiple times in various trips to the program. The group also exists as a one-time intervention. Anyone who participates can feel that he or she has ownership of the process. The sibling group has its own legacy and themes that carry over; the content is universal.

Sibling Voice: A Sibling's Explanation of the Sibling Support Group

As for me, sibling groups have made me realize that I am not alone. Before I went to a sibling group, I had a lot of confusing feelings all balled up inside of me. I thought they were "wrong" and I was a horrible sister for feeling as I did. I couldn't tell people, because they wouldn't understand. Anytime I even just complained about my sister being annoying, my friends would respond with, "But she's been through so much, how could you say that?" or something like that and I couldn't imagine admitting my true feelings of jealousy and anger. However, I was jealous and I was angry.

My sister got special treatment and of course I knew she deserved it, because of what she had to go through, but that didn't mean I didn't feel ignored and less cared about. Then I would want to take back those feelings and I'd feel guilty forever for feeling jealous. It was a mess and more than my brain could handle. Sibling programs have allowed me to talk about my feelings with people who not only don't judge me, but also feel the same way.

I remember my first sibling group when we all just broke down crying while talking about everything. Those tears were a combination mainly of all the feelings kept in for so long, but also of the relief of knowing that we were not alone. We were not bad people. We were just siblings of cancer patients and no one else would ever really understand, but that was ok because we had each other.... I know I'm not alone. We support each other and it is the sibling programs that brought us together.

—17-year-old sister of a child with a brain tumor

Sibling support groups illuminate what children and adolescents are thinking and the range of emotions they are experiencing. The themes in sibling groups range from the heartfelt fear that a sibling will die to the guilt experienced when feeling angry with a sibling for garnering family attention. The groups serve as an excellent mediator of sibling emotions. Knowledge of what other siblings experience normalizes each child's sibling narrative.

Something transformative occurs the first time siblings hear another child in a group express the same feelings that they are experiencing. Sibling groups create an effective community of like-minded people on the same path. Things that seemed personal and painful emerge as universal and comfortable.

Sibling Support Groups

- *Allow siblings to voice their feelings.*
- *Engender a built-in message: Siblings are important because a program has been created for them.*
- *Allow siblings to identify with others who raise pertinent issues without having to raise the issues themselves.*
- *Provide intrinsic support and comfort.*
- *Minimize isolation, affording each member a cohort of individuals with similar thoughts.*
- *Create a sense of community that is unequaled.*
- *Provide a "normalizing" experience simply through participation.*
- *Provide a cross-generational discourse about a range of emotions. Regardless of siblings' age at the time of the group, they can connect to children who are either the same age now, the age that they were when their sibling was diagnosed, or at a stage that they are anticipating (e.g., going to college).*
- *Provide an outlet for the appreciation of the journey of their siblings with cancer.*
- *Serve as a vehicle to educate parents about the needs of siblings.*

Strategies to Help Siblings With the Emotional Journey

- Afford siblings the chance to ask questions.
- Understand that there may be misperceptions.
- Interject knowledge of sibling issues—for example, the feeling of being forgotten.
- Raise confusing sibling issues.
- Clarify information with age-appropriate language and explanations.
- Ask questions to assess whether the provided information is understood.
- Acknowledge and address painful experiences.
- Create age-appropriate activities to deal with sibling issues.
- Anticipate potential challenges and create memorable opportunities for positive experiences and memory making.
- Provide opportunities for interactions with other siblings of children with cancer.
- Create and maintain a routine to encourage normalcy.
- Create an environment that fosters communication.

Strategies to Help Families With the Emotional Journey of Siblings

- Encourage family communication. Start the dialogue.
- Provide age-appropriate information and explanations.
- Recognize the magnitude of feelings.
- Listen, no matter how painful.
- Help siblings discern what they feel, even if it is not what you want to hear.
- Childhood cancer is a family affair. Make it a family affair—maximize family involvement.
- Universalize and acknowledge feelings.
- Create alone time with siblings; time is important.
- Create special family activities everyone can participate in (e.g., game night).
- Reiterate the messages of caring and concern for the sibling.

- Reiterate that parents should remind siblings regularly that they are in the parents' thoughts, important to the parents, and missed when the parents must be apart from them.
- Maintain an open family dialogue with siblings; siblings hate to learn what is happening in their families on social media.
- Discuss decisions that affect the whole family.
- Work with all children about "roles" during treatment.
- Bring siblings to the hospital to familiarize them with their sibling's new world.
- Prepare siblings for what is going to be happening with their sibling's care.
- Give siblings choices about subsequent visits.
- Find avenues to introduce siblings to other siblings of children with cancer.

Siblings often have much more autonomy than they did before their sibling's diagnosis, leading to more independence and self-reliance. Research about siblings varies, depending on whose voice is being studied and when. A study examining parental perspectives noted that siblings' understanding of the situation and degree of change in daily routine did not appear to affect their adjustment (Cordaro et al., 2012). However, studies focused primarily on the sibling's perspective have noted that anxiety may be reduced by explaining to siblings what is going on and decreasing the amount of disruption in their lives (Alderfer et al., 2010; Hamama et al., 2008). Additional research exploring sibling voices, their needs, and how they are affected at different ages could influence the sibling experience at a programmatic level.

Long, Marsland, and Alderfer (2013) analyzed cumulative family risk and found that distress in a population of 209 siblings of children with cancer was correlated with self-reported measures of disturbed family functioning and parenting, but not by parent-reported measures. They also found that most siblings did not report clinical depression or anxiety. However, 62% evidenced moderate/severe posttraumatic stress symptoms and 25% met posttraumatic stress disorder criteria—rates higher than those reported for pediatric cancer survivors themselves.

Siblings recount missed birthday parties, holidays spent in the hospital, and sadness. The complexity of what it is like to be a sibling of a child with cancer comes with an outpouring of concern, a sense of growth, ambivalence, and a feeling of being wounded on an existential level.

> *They see the patient suffering physically and feel bad for them. They can easily SEE their struggles. As siblings, we go through just as hard a journey but it is internal, more of an emotional journey. I like to call it the undiagnosed disease.*
>
> *—17-year-old sibling of a child with a brain tumor*

Children with cancer are often applauded for their strength and resilience. It is understandable that they be afforded a certain amount of privilege when they are fighting for their lives. The journey is also burdensome for siblings, who sit by and watch or who are unintentionally overlooked. Siblings must be afforded similar privileges within the emotional realm of family life and the fact acknowledged that the childhood cancer journey may not be any easier for them than it is for the child with cancer.

Pearls

- Do not forget siblings. Perceive their needs to be similarly important to those of the child with cancer.
- Provide siblings with timely, age-appropriate information and dialogues about their sibling's illness.
- Recognize that siblings' ages, the number of children in the family, and birth order will have an impact on each child's experience.
- Create activities that allow for separate time for all children in the family.
- Foster the expression of feelings and concerns. Acknowledge and support such feelings.
- Maintain family integrity; prioritize family business.
- Treat most days as family days and make them important.
- Do not inform outsiders before informing insiders. Children should not learn things about their families on any form of social media (Facebook, CaringBridge, blogs) or from teachers or anyone else at school.
- Encourage family and friends to ask about all the children in the family.

Pitfalls

- Assuming siblings are at the same level of comprehension as other family members and not offering explanations befitting their cognitive and emotional capability.
- Believing that siblings are okay because they don't have cancer.
- Equating physical and emotional health.
- Excluding siblings from visiting, special programs, or activities.
- Burdening siblings with too much information and responsibility.
- Underestimating how the cancer experience has changed a sibling's life.

NOTE

1. Dialogue for this chapter was generated from the ongoing work with siblings in the context of a family program at Camp Sunshine at Sebago Lake, Casco, Maine, where sibling voices are loud and demand to be heard.

ADDITIONAL RESOURCES

Organizations

Camp Sunshine at Sebago Lake: Provides retreat programs for children with cancer and their families, creating a natural opportunity for support groups for siblings: http://www.campsunshine.org

KIDSCOPE: A nonprofit organization that aims to help children and families cope with having a family member with cancer. The organization's resources allow children to get a better understanding of cancer from their point of view: http://www.kidscope.org

Siblings Information Network: (860) 344-7500 (U.S.)

Sibshops Sibling Support Project: Provides interactive workshops for siblings of children with special needs. The workshops focus on peer support and celebrate the contributions of brothers and sisters: http://www.siblingsupport.org

Starbright World: Part of the Starlight Children's Foundation. It is an online social network for teens with chronic and life-threatening illnesses and their siblings: http://www.starbrightworld.org

SuperSibs!: Provides personalized, age-appropriate resources and teaching tools for siblings (aged 4 to 18 years) of children with cancer, their families, and professionals: http://www.supersibs.org

Workbooks and Brochures

CancerCare. *Helping the sibling of the child with cancer.* Retrieved from http://www.cancercare.org/publications/50-helping_the_ siblings_of_the_child_with_cancer

National Cancer Institute. *When your brother or sister has cancer: A guide for teens. Parent guide.* http://www.cancer.gov/cancertopics/coping/when-your- sibling-has-cancer

SuperSibs! Tips for parents. Retrieved from http://www.supersibs.org/gethelp/parents-guardians/tips-for-parents/

Weiner, L. (2006). *Brothers and sisters together: A workbook for siblings of siblings who are sick.* Retrieved from http://www.cc.nih.gov/ccc/patient_education/pepubs/siblings_workbook.pdf

Books

Apel, M. A. (2001). *Coping with leukemia.* New York, NY: Rosen.

- Has a chapter for teenage siblings and discussion of the emotional side of living with cancer.

Peterkin, A. (1992). *What about me? When brothers and sisters get sick.* New York, NY: Magination Press.

- The story deals with the many complicated feelings that siblings experience and provides parents and their well children an opportunity to take some time out for one another and to forge a renewed sense of family.

Sonnenblick, J. (2006). *Drums, girls, and dangerous pie.* New York, NY: Scholastic Press.

- This book presents a realistic portrayal of the life of a sibling whose brother is diagnosed with cancer.

Williams, L. (2012). *Forgotten.* CreateSpace Independent Publishing Platform.

- This story portrays the journey of a sibling of a cancer patient.

Wozanick, L. A. (2002). *Living with childhood cancer: A practical guide to help families cope.* Washington, DC: American Psychological Association.

REFERENCES

Alderfer, M., Long, K., Lown, E., Marsland, A., Ostrowski, N., Hock, J., & Ewing, L. (2010). Psychosocial adjustment of siblings of children with cancer: A systematic review. *Psycho-Oncology, 19*(8), 789–805.

Barrera, M., Chung, J. Y. Y., Greenberg, M., & Fleming, C. (2002). Preliminary investigation of a group intervention for siblings of pediatric cancer patients. *Children's Health Care, 31*(2), 131–142. doi:10.1207/s15326888chc3102_4

Björk, M., Nordström, B., Wiebe, T., & Hallström, I. (2011). Returning to a changed ordinary life—families' lived experience after completing a child's cancer treatment. *European Journal of Cancer Care, 20*(2), 163–169. doi:10.1111/j.1365-2354.2009.01159.x

Buchbinder, D., Casillas, J., & Zeltzer, L. (2011). Meeting the psychosocial needs of sibling survivors: A family systems approach. *Journal of Pediatric Oncology Nursing, 28*(3), 123–136. doi:10.1177/1043454210384601

Carpenter, P. J., & LeVant, C. S. (1994). Sibling adaptation to the family crisis of childhood cancer. In D. J. Bearison & R. K. Mulhern (Eds.), *Pediatric psychooncology: Psychological perspectives on children with cancer* (pp. 122–142). New York, NY: Oxford University Press.

Chesler, M. A., Allswede, J., & Barbarin, O. O. (1991). Voices from the margin of the family siblings of children with cancer. *Journal of Psychosocial Oncology, 9*(4), 19–42.

Cincotta, N. F. (1993). Psychosocial issues in the world of children with cancer. *Cancer, 71*(10), 3251–3260. doi:10.1002/1097-0142(19930515)71:10+<3251::aid-cncr2820711718>3.0.co;2-d

Cincotta, N. F. (2004). The end of life at the beginning of life: Working with dying children and their families. In J. Berzoff & P. R. Silverman (Eds.), *Living with dying* (pp. 318–347). New York, NY: Columbia University Press.

Cincotta, N. F. (2011). Bereavement in the beginning phase of life: Grief in children and their families. In T. Altilio & S. Otis-Green (Eds.), *Oxford textbook of palliative social work* (pp. 305–317). New York, NY: Oxford University Press.

Cohen, D. S., Friedrich, W. N., Jaworski, T. M., Copeland, D., & Pendergrass, T. (1994). Pediatric cancer—predicting sibling adjustment. *Journal of Clinical Psychology, 50*(3), 303–319.

Cordaro, G., Veneroni, L., Massimino, M., & Clerici, C. A. (2012). Assessing psychological adjustment in siblings of children with cancer. *Cancer Nursing, 35*(1), E42–E48. doi:10.1097/NCC.0b013e3182182869

Creed, J., Ruffin, J. E., & Ward, M. (2001). A weekend camp for bereaved siblings. *Cancer Practice, 9*(4), 176–182. doi:10.1046/j.1523-5394.2001.94005.x

Flury, M., Caflisch, U., Ullmann-Bremi, A., & Spichiger, E. (2011). Experiences of parents with caring for their child after a cancer diagnosis. *Journal of Pediatric Oncology Nursing, 28*(3), 143–153. doi:10.1177/1043454210378015

Hamama, L., Ronen, T., & Rahav, G. (2008). Self-control, self-efficacy, role overload, and stress responses among siblings of children with cancer. *Health and Social Work, 33*(2), 121–132.

Hancock, L. (2011). The camp experience for siblings of pediatric cancer patients. *Journal of Pediatric Oncology Nursing, 28*(3), 137–142. doi:10.1177/1043454211408102

Heiney, S. P., Goon-Johnson, K., Ettinger, R. S., & Ettinger, S. (1990). The effects of group therapy on siblings of pediatric oncology patients. *Journal of Pediatric Oncology Nursing, 7*(3), 95–100. doi:10.1177/104345429000700303

Houtzager, B. A., Grootenhuis, M. A., & Last, B. F. (2001). Supportive groups for siblings of pediatric oncology patients: Impact on anxiety. *Psycho-Oncology, 10*(4), 315–324. doi:10.1002/pon.528

Houtzager, B. A., Oort, F. J., Hoekstra-Weebers, J., Caron, H. N., Grootenhuis, M. A., & Last, B. F. (2004). Coping and family functioning predict longitudinal psychological adaptation of siblings of childhood cancer patients. *Journal of Pediatric Psychology, 29*(8), 591–605. doi:10.1093/jpepsy/jsh061

Jones, B. L., Pelletier, W., Decker, C., Barczyk, A., & Dungan, S. S. (2010). Fathers of children with cancer: A descriptive synthesis of the literature. *Social Work in Health Care, 49*(5), 458–493. doi:10.1080/00981380903539723

Lähteenmäki, P. M., Sjöblom, J., Korhonen, T., & Salmi, T. T. (2004). The siblings of childhood cancer patients need early support: A follow up study over the first year. *Archives of Disease in Childhood, 89*(11), 1008–1013. doi:10.1136/adc.2002.012088

Long, K. A., Marsland, A. L., & Alderfer, M. A. (2013). Cumulative family risk predicts sibling adjustment to childhood cancer. *Cancer, 119*(13), 2503–2510. doi:10.1002/cncr.28077

MacLeod, K. D., Whitsett, S. F., Mash, E. J., & Pelletier, W. (2003). Pediatric sibling donors of successful and unsuccessful hematopoietic stem cell transplants (HSCT): A qualitative study of their psychosocial experience. *Journal of Pediatric Psychology, 28*(4), 223–231. doi:10.1093/jpepsy/jsg010

Mitchell, W., Clarke, S., & Sloper, P. (2005). Survey of psychosocial support provided by UK paediatric oncology centres. *Archives of Disease in Childhood, 90*(8), 796–800. doi:10.1136/adc.2004.065177

Murray, J. S. (2000). Understanding sibling adaptation to childhood cancer. *Issues in Comprehensive Pediatric Nursing, 23*(1), 39–47. doi:10.1080/014608600265200

O'Shea, E. R., Shea, J., Robert, T., & Cavanaugh, C. (2012). The needs of siblings of children with cancer: A nursing perspective. *Journal of Pediatric Oncology Nursing, 29*(4), 221–231. doi:10.1177/1043454212451365

Packman, W. L., Crittenden, M. R., Fischer, J. B. R., Schaeffer, E., Bongar, B., & Cowan, M. J. (1997). Siblings' perceptions of the bone marrow transplantation process. *Journal of Psychosocial Oncology, 15*(3–4), 81–105.

Prchal, A., & Landolt, M. A. (2012). How siblings of pediatric cancer patients experience the first time after diagnosis: A qualitative study. *Cancer Nursing, 35*(2), 133–140. doi:10.1097/NCC.0b013e31821e0c59

Sidhu, R., Passmore, A., & Baker, D. (2006). The effectiveness of a peer support camp for siblings of children with cancer. *Pediatric Blood and Cancer, 47*(5), 580–588. doi:10.1002/pbc.20653

Spinetta, J. J., Jankovic, M., Eden, T., Green, D., Martins, A. G., Wandzura, C., . . . Masera, G. (1999). Guidelines for assistance to siblings of children with cancer: Report of the SIOP Working Committee on Psychosocial Issues in Pediatric Oncology. *Medical and Pediatric Oncology, 33*(4), 395–398. doi:10.1002/(sici)1096-911x(199910)33:4<395::aid-mpo9>3.0.co;2-s

Wakefield, C. E., Butow, P., Fleming, C. A. K., Daniel, G., & Cohn, R. J. (2012). Family information needs at childhood cancer treatment completion. *Pediatric Blood and Cancer, 58*(4), 621–626. doi:10.1002/pbc.23316

Wakefield, C. E., McLoone, J., Butow, P., Lenthen, K., & Cohn, R. J. (2013). Support after the completion of cancer treatment: Perspectives of Australian adolescents and their families. *European Journal of Cancer Care, 22*(4), 530–539. doi:10.1111/ecc.12059

66

Nancy Contro and Analisa Trott

Reaching Out to Culturally Diverse Populations in Pediatric Oncology

Key Concepts

- *An oncology diagnosis in a child disrupts the equilibrium of the entire family, leaving already-vulnerable families at higher risk for adverse consequences.*
- *A thorough assessment is an important social work tool and forms the foundation of a therapeutic alliance.*
- *The social work role of "navigator" is crucial to helping guide the family and team through complex situations.*
- *The social worker serves as a model for the team by demonstrating respect for family values and beliefs, even when they may not be shared by the care providers.*

A child's oncology diagnosis is a devastating event for the entire family, as day-to-day routines are disrupted, family relationships are strained, and families are required to master an often unfamiliar and overwhelming medical system (Contro, Larson, Scofield, Sourkes, & Cohen, 2002; Suzuki & Kato, 2003). New stressors may vary depending on the specific child's treatment or outcome and can be intense, emotionally depleting, and long lasting. Furthermore, these stressors can impact employment, relationships, and financial stability (Kuspt & Schulman, 1988; Sloper, 2000). Even the most stable families often have difficulty regaining equilibrium; families who are already vulnerable due to such issues as immigration, poverty, mental health struggles, or lack of language and literacy skills are immediately at higher risk for adverse consequences (Contro et al., 2002; Kuspt & Schulman, 1988; Pergert, Ekblad, Enskar, & Bjork, 2007). In a pediatric oncology setting, social workers play a critical role in creating the best possible path for all families, but the importance of this role intensifies when working with particularly vulnerable families who are easily misunderstood and at risk for possible medical compliance challenges.

The Social Work Role: Where Do We Start?

Effective social work interventions in a medical setting begin with a thorough initial assessment, which means taking the time to learn about and understand the family. This process helps demonstrate a true interest and sense of compassion, forming the beginning of a therapeutic relationship. When done well, it can provide the foundation from which a caring professional can help guide a family on an unimaginable, complex journey through their child's illness and cure or through death and bereavement. The first task of the assessment is to define the family, because the composition of families has changed dramatically (Goldman, Hain, & Liben, 2012). The American Academy of Pediatrics Task Force on the Family states that "not only is there tremendous variety in the composition of families, there is also great variation in racial and ethnic heritage, religious practices and communication and life styles" (Schor, 2003). Understanding and acknowledging that this variety exists opens the door for the development of an appreciation of the many different families a social work clinician will encounter.

As previously stated, the importance of the initial assessment is heightened when working with families who are culturally diverse, individuals with mental health problems, or individuals who in general are less connected to "mainstream" society and who have greater potential for being misunderstood and alienated from the medical system. When working with vulnerable and marginalized populations, the assessment of risk must remain at the forefront of the social worker's thinking. Families with difficulties such as prior mental health diagnoses, substance abuse, substantial history of loss or trauma, suicidality, extreme poverty, family violence, traumatic immigration histories, or concern with immigration status require special vigilance by the social worker. The initial assessment is just a starting place.

Pediatric oncology is both an intense and a rewarding area of social work. It is also fraught with the potential to spark personal reactions and feelings in the clinician. Complex families tend to create higher demands on staff that, in turn, can lead to resentment and less willingness to spend the time and energy required to provide care for the child (Klassen, Gulati, & Dix, 2012; Pergert et al., 2007; Suzuki & Kato, 2003). When team members encounter such problems as communication difficulties, angry family members, misunderstanding of cultural perspectives, and unfamiliar or strained family systems, biases can occur that detract from optimal patient care. In these circumstances, the social worker's role is most clearly to act as a "navigator" to build a bridge of mutual understanding, respect, and trust between the family and the medical team (Jones, 2006).

The social worker can help bring the voice of the family forward, to underscore their strengths, and to plan for challenges. By developing a thorough understanding of the family and what they bring to the table, the social worker can guide the team to help develop strategies that will avert crises. For example, early recognition of vulnerable families' multiple needs can help the team provide information and resources in a timely manner and often avoid surprises that may upset family and team members alike.

Many families who are not primarily English speaking have reported mild to severe consequences in their child's medical care as a result of miscommunications with staff (Contro et al., 2002; Flores, 2005; Wiener, Mcconnell, Latella, & Ludi, 2013). Immigrant families have also reported feelings of discrimination based on outward appearances, limited language proficiency, and socioeconomic status. It is important to families caring for ill children to believe they have done everything possible to help their children. Being unable to communicate with care providers or feeling criticized can negatively impact families' feeling of competence and increase feelings of helplessness and hopelessness (Davies, Larson, Contro, & Cabrera, 2011). Care providers, in turn, report frustration over being unable to communicate effectively with families who do not speak their language and even report feeling resentful toward families due to the strain it puts on them (Pergert, Ekblad, Enskar, & Bjork, 2008). Social workers can immediately identify the need for help with language barriers and remind staff to make every effort to communicate with the family. Bringing in professional interpreters rather than relying on family members to serve as interpreters is instrumental in establishing clear communication. Use of family members to transmit medical information often puts further strain on the family, especially when children must interpret for their parents (Jones, 2005).

Immigrant children have often experienced traumas either in their home country or during the immigration process. They may be reluctant to trust and acutely aware of past losses while dealing with grief and loss issues having to do with leaving their home country. Sometimes, key family members may have even been left behind. Each of these situations requires recognition and careful consideration when developing a treatment plan, and not establishing a trusting relationship can cause these issues to be missed. Again, the social worker acts as a conduit of information about both the psychological makeup of the child and the important history that shapes the responses of the child and family in the medical setting (Contro, Davies, Larson, & Sourkes, 2010; Contro et al., 2002; Davies et al., 2011). Cross-generational issues can also impact the child. Care must be taken not to inadvertently increase conflict or emotional distance between the child and the family when the child is more acculturated than the parents.

Remembering What Is Important: The Child's World

Respecting the role of parents or caretakers goes a long way toward building rapport. It also helps the child, because most often the health and well-being of the child is directly connected to the health and well-being of the family (Kazak et al., 2011). Acknowledging the special role of parents and their relationship with their children also helps solidify their place within the care team. The social worker can serve as a model for other team members by demonstrating respect for family values, cultural mores, and tolerance for beliefs that might be difficult to understand. Remembering that the child's world revolves around his or her family—however it is defined—can serve as the mantra to guide the medical team as they reach out to diverse and marginalized families.

Case Examples

Jose's Story

Jose is a 2-year-old Mexican American boy who was diagnosed with acute lymphoblastic leukemia in his home community and referred to the children's hospital 150 miles from his home. He lives in a rural farming community with his mother, father, and 1-year-old brother. Jose's parents were born in a remote area of Mexico and speak Mixteco, a less common dialect of Spanish. They are undocumented and have lived in the United States since 2008. Their experience crossing the border was traumatic, dangerous, and costly. They used their savings to pay a "coyote" to sneak them across the border from Mexico to the United States. The parents have two older sons, ages 13 and 6, whom they left in the care of the children's grandmother in Mexico. The family could not afford to bring the children to the United States and hope to reunite with their older children when they have the funds to do so. Both parents have no formal education and are illiterate. The parents speak only basic conversational Spanish but declined a Mixteco interpreter for communication at the hospital, preferring to have an interpreter who spoke Spanish. Both parents are employed as farm workers. They pick fruit 7 days a week, 11 hours a day during the season. Since Jose's diagnosis, his mother has not worked to remain at the bedside of her child. The parents do not own a car, nor do they have alternative transportation to the hospital. Consequently, to be close to the hospital, Jose and his mother stayed at the local Ronald McDonald House during the initial phases of treatment even though the separation from the rest of the family was very difficult. Jose's father continued working and with the help of neighbors cared for the 1-year-old sibling.

Jose quickly engaged with the staff and immediately demonstrated his good nature and resilience. His initial admission was difficult for the medical team, because they had to spend many hours with Jose's mother to teach her about his illness and the necessary care. They were often frustrated by and concerned about the mother's lack of education and her seeming inability to grasp even elementary medical concepts. They commented that they had to repeat information many times and break it down into the simplest terms for her to understand. The staff expressed frustration over the amount of time they had to spend teaching Jose's mother basic information. Due to Jose's father's need to continue working, his mother was alone for most of the discussions with the medical team. The medical team offered to provide medical updates to the father by phone. However, the father primarily received updates from the mother. The social worker kept the father involved as much as possible, including meeting with him on the rare occasions that he was able to come to the hospital and speaking with him by phone when he was able. She relayed to the team her assessment that he was a dedicated father who was trying his best to care for his family.

Given the family's meager income and the mother's inability to work, the family was unable to save money for the rainy season when work is limited. Jose's mother reluctantly revealed to the social worker her fears regarding their ability to manage expenses when work was no longer available. Due to the family's documentation status, they were not eligible for many public resources. However, the social worker helped them secure some oncology funds and informed the parents about government assistance available for their son, who was a U.S. citizen. Jose's parents expressed fear that applying for resources would limit their ability to apply for documentation at a later time. The parents also feared that the financial aid Jose received now would limit his ability to find work as an adult or would require him to return payment after he turned 18. After much discussion, the family was able to secure and accept some limited financial support.

The nursing staff worked extensively with Jose's mother to prepare her for discharge to the Ronald McDonald House and the eventual care of her son at home. The social worker was able to help staff think creatively about ways to help the family, which had few educational and financial resources. Jose's parents and the nursing staff created a color-coded system for medications that helped enable the mother to adequately care for her child as an outpatient. Much of this system required memorization for the mother, but she worked diligently to master it.

Once Jose became an outpatient, the social worker continued to assess the mother's coping with Jose's care. As the social worker witnessed how the outpatient staff struggled to communicate with the mother about the intricacies of his care and changes in medication, she was able to provide support to the mother and education to the staff about the mother's areas of concern. For instance, she learned that Jose's mother did not understand that certain medications she had received required refrigeration and also that the mother's color-coded chart used a depiction of an analog clock to indicate the time medication should be given, but the mother wore a digital watch and did not know how to read an analog clock, a fact she was initially embarrassed to admit to staff.

Jose's mother then revealed that she felt that Jose's father did not visit because he was afraid of the strange hospital environment. The social worker arranged transportation through a community agency for Jose's father and brother. The family stayed together for several nights at the Ronald McDonald House. The social worker met with the parents and at the mother's urging the father talked about his fears regarding Jose's future. The family then also explored their feelings of loss related to leaving their other children in Mexico and their fears that they would lose Jose as well. Jose's father attended a care conference where he received direct information from the medical team. The father's presence and participation was a critical step in preparing the family for the son's discharge. It also allowed the father to begin to regain his place in the family and have input into Jose's care. Jose returned home and the family continues to struggle to meet their basic needs.

Implications

- It is relatively common for immigrant parents to leave other children in their country of origin until they have the funds to send for them. After basic needs were addressed and rapport was built with this family, the social worker was able to explore the loss of homeland and separation of family, which played heavily into their fears of losing Jose as well.

- The social worker was the only member of Jose's primary team who followed the family from their inpatient to outpatient status. This was advantageous to the family because they had an advocate that had witnessed and supported them in both settings.
- The social worker observed frequent occasions when the parents were too fearful to advocate for themselves due to lack of understanding about resources or their legal rights. The social worker assisted in educating the parents about resources available to them and connecting them with free legal counsel. Addressing the family's immediate financial stressors helped establish rapid rapport with the family. The parents began trusting the social worker, allowing for more open disclosure.
- The social worker continually assessed the mother's comfort and transition to the hospital environment. By supporting the mother through each new experience, the social worker was able to provide support and encourage the development of skills she needed to handle the daunting task of caring for her sick child.
- The social worker advocated for the mother by educating staff about the family's vast cultural adjustment to life in the hospital and requested a nursing assistant's help in sitting at the bedside with Jose when possible, thereby allowing the mother to leave for the kitchen, cafeteria, and laundry.
- Because of the social worker's extensive work with the mother, she was able to challenge staff rumors and help them better understand the mother's behavior. By encouraging them to think creatively about helping the family and pointing out the mother's strengths, she was able to facilitate a more productive relationship that in the end benefited Jose.

Habibah's Story

Habibah was diagnosed with alveolar rhabdomyosarcoma at age 16. At that time, she lived with her mother, father, and 12-year-old brother. She also had a 28-year-old sister who lived outside of the home but was a strong support to the family throughout her illness. Habibah was 18 years old when she died, had graduated from high school, and was awaiting her first semester of college at a prestigious university.

Habibah's parents were from Iran and moved to the United States before the birth of their three children. The family, particularly the parents, identified strongly with their Iranian culture; however, they stated that they were not religious. Habibah was a high-achieving student and involved in many scholastic clubs and extracurricular activities. She was a bright, outgoing, and personable young woman who often showed glimmers of a well-developed sense of humor. Habibah's family had some local family support, but most of their extended family resided in Europe and Iran. Both parents spoke English; however, during medical team conferences, the mother would often speak with the father and brother-in-law in Farsi and rarely stated anything directly to the medical team.

Since the time of Habibah's diagnosis, the family had expressed a clear preference for how information should be disseminated. Habibah stated that she did not wish to know any details about her disease or care and wished to rely on her family to inform her of pertinent information as issues arose. Her family believed that this approach would strengthen Habibah's ability to cope with her illness and treatment. Habibah's family made it clear that to protect her, they would provide only minimal information to Habibah about her disease and prognosis. Furthermore, Habibah's father requested that all important information be given to him directly and he would then relay information to his wife and older daughter as he felt necessary. Immediately, the medical team felt conflicted with this approach and stated that they would like Habibah to assent to treatment and also felt compelled to share information with the mother. Trust between Habibah's family and the medical team was tenuous, and her father expressed fear to the social worker that their wishes would not be respected. With deliberate attention to the father and then with his agreement, the social worker spent individual time with each family member. She established a therapeutic alliance with the family by developing an understanding of their cultural mores and demonstrating respect for their choices. In turn, she reassured the medical staff that she would work with them and the family to find an avenue of communication with which both parties were comfortable.

During the initial phases of treatment, the social worker let the family guide their conversations. Much of the early discussions centered on family, school, and Habibah's interests. Eventually, the social worker explored how the family felt about being at the hospital and what they would find helpful while Habibah was an inpatient, all the while taking care not to press about specific disease-related topics. Once the family understood the social worker's advocacy role, they began to feel more comfortable sharing their wishes and concerns. Through repeated meetings, the social worker established a deeper understanding of the family's cultural perspective, verbalized her respect for the family's wishes, and helped communicate those wishes to the larger hospital team. The social worker also offered to speak with Habibah individually for support while making sure she acknowledged the strength and support her family offered her. The social worker requested that the parents let her know when Habibah or the family would feel comfortable with this plan, ultimately allowing them to feel in control of the therapeutic relationship.

The social worker continually assessed and validated the family's wishes and concerns and, at the same time, educated them about the hospital system. Once the parents trusted her, they invited the social worker to meet with Habibah individually to assess her wishes and coping.

Immediately, the social worker saw the delicate situation Habibah was balancing between respecting her parents and their cultural mores while trying to figure out how to assert her own beliefs. In addition, given her developmental stage, she vacillated between wanting independence and fear of standing on her own. The social worker also attended all conferences with the family and medical team to understand what information was provided and to be able to assess each family member's understanding of information as it was disseminated to them by Habibah's father. She consistently communicated her assessments to the medical team, which alleviated much of their concern about what type of information, if any, was transmitted to Habibah and her mother. The social worker educated the staff about the different emotional/developmental tasks Habibah was negotiating and encouraged them to allow her to have the autonomy she needed in this process. The social worker's cycle of assessment, reassessment, communication between the family and medical team, and assisting the staff in understanding the family was a constant and fluid process.

The ongoing and consistent relationship with the social worker paved the way for future admissions, which allowed for better observance of the family's cultural wishes and needs. Although the team continued to struggle with the family's communication style, they relied on the social worker to guide these interactions. The primary medical team developed an understanding of the family and a solid rapport with them. However, every admission brought cultural issues to the forefront, and the family continued to be fearful that new team members would not respect their wishes. Working within the context of an academic institution where trainees constantly rotated in and out of the care team was especially challenging for this family. There were times when staff who were unfamiliar with the family provided bedside medical updates without the father present. Habibah and her parents expressed their anxiety to the social worker about these occurrences and frustration that the medical team did not respect their wishes.

Habibah started experiencing back pain 3 months after completing her chemotherapy treatment. Scans revealed metastatic disease in her spine and brain. At the time of the recurrence of her disease, Habibah was 18. However, she did not have an advanced directive and was now legally able to consent for all medical care despite her parents' wishes to keep her sheltered. How to handle these new legal and ethical was the subject of much team discussion.

Habibah's preference was to be in the hospital as little as possible. This was a fact she had made clear to her parents and her medical team from the beginning. However, as her disease progressed, so did her pain and discomfort. Her parents no longer felt comfortable caring for her at home and came back to the hospital for inpatient pain management. Habibah's parents did not want any information provided to her directly because they feared that the team would talk about dying. The medical team felt uncomfortable with this decision because Habibah was 18 and the conflict regarding the team giving prognostic information to Habibah came to a head. Habibah's father suggested that the social worker facilitate conversations between him and the medical team regarding his wishes and the team's legal and ethical obligations. He also allowed the social worker to talk with Habibah about her wishes for information. Habibah stated that she wanted control over her pain management but did not want additional medical information. The social worker guided Habibah through the advanced directive process and focused the reasoning for the document on her specific wishes for limited information and her current age, rather than her immediate decline of health and impending death.

Close to the time of Habibah's death, her parents and older sister were at her bedside and requested that the social worker join them. Habibah died about an hour later.

Due to the family's wish to limit information given to Habibah's 12-year-old brother, he was frequently kept away from the hospital. At the time of Habibah's death, her younger brother was in the family lounge area at the hospital with extended relatives. Per his parent's wishes, he was brought home by extended relatives and was not informed of Habibah death until the following day. The social worker met with the parents to discuss this wish and the family shared that they wanted time to process their thoughts and give their son the news away from the hospital. The family wanted to have Habibah's arrangements made promptly, and the social worker assisted in facilitating a mortuary to pick up the patient on the evening of her death. The family expressed relief in knowing that these arrangements were made the same night of Habibah's death because they knew how much Habibah disliked being at the hospital. They felt that in doing this, they were continuing to honor their beloved daughter's wishes. The social worker contacted the family a few weeks after Habibah's death and offered to meet with her younger brother and parents. The father agreed and said he would contact her when the time was right.

Implications

- Through patience and slow methodical investigation, the social worker was able to form an alliance with this family that strengthened throughout the treatment process. Her ability to develop a true understanding of the wishes of each family member and to translate those to the team avoided many conflicts and misunderstandings.
- By dispelling rumors and quieting staff judgments with education about the family, the social worker was able to eventually help the team and the family reach a middle ground regarding many difficult decisions.
- Because the patient was an adolescent and born in America, she faced the challenges both of fitting into two cultures and of negotiating the transition from adolescence to adulthood. These factors complicated her need and desire for information and control over

her care. Habibah chose to assert her control by focusing on pain management while letting her parents manage the information about her poor prognosis. The social worker accommodated this compromise by reframing the advance directive in a way the family could tolerate.

- The team averted the conflict that would have arisen if they had pushed forward with their desire to provide information to Habibah and looked to her for decisions about her impending death. To challenge the family system at this delicate time would have created a crisis that would have drawn attention from the family being totally emotionally present during the dying process.
- Valuing, instead of judging, what the family brought to the table and their understanding of their daughter proved to be an invaluable tool in working effectively with them throughout the illness.
- In this situation, the social worker played a crucial role as negotiator, therapist, educator, and advocate.

Pearls

- When working with vulnerable and/or marginalized populations, the social worker often has to use creative interventions to establish trust and advocate for the family.
- Remember what's important: The well-being of the child is directly connected to the well-being of the family—let this concept guide the work.
- Always ask, never assume: Understanding complex families is achieved through patient, ongoing inquiry about family values, cultural/spiritual mores, beliefs, and practices.

Pitfalls

- The emotional nature of working in oncology with children and their families facing life-threatening conditions can lead to complex feelings within the social work clinician and can interfere with clinical judgment if not recognized and addressed.

Working in pediatric oncology is demanding and complex work. When done well, this work is extremely rewarding and leads to optimal care of patients and their families. The social work role with vulnerable families is especially important because these families are often at risk of being misunderstood and marginalized in complex medical systems. Taking the time to truly understand the family, educate the staff about family and social dynamics, and create a respectful environment is critical to providing the best possible care for the child.

REFERENCES

Contro, N., Davies, B., Larson, J., & Sourkes, B. (2010). Away from home: Experiences of Mexican American families in pediatric palliative care. *Journal of Social Work in End-of-Life and Palliative Care*, *6*(3–4), 185–204.

Contro, N., Larson, J., Scofield, S., Sourkes, B., & Cohen, H. (2002). Family perspectives on pediatric palliative care. *Archives of Adolescent Medicine*, *156*(1), 14–19.

Davies, B., Larson, J., Contro, N., & Cabrera A. (2011). Perceptions of discrimination among Mexican American families of seriously ill children. *Journal of Palliative Medicine*, *14*(1), 71–76.

Flores, G. (2005). The impact of medical interpreter services on the quality of health care: A systematic review. *Medical Care Research and Review*, *62*(3), 255–299.

Goldman, A., Hain, R., & Liben, S. (Eds.). (2012). *Oxford textbook of palliative care for children*. New York, NY: Oxford University Press.

Jones, B. (2005). Pediatric palliative and end-of-life care: The role of social work in pediatric oncology. *Journal of Social Work in End-of-Life and Palliative Care*, *1*(4), 35–61.

Jones, B. (2006). Companionship, control and compassion: A social work perspective on the needs of children with cancer and their families at the end of life. *Journal of Palliative Medicine*, *9*(3), 774–788.

Kazak, A., Barakat, L., Hwang, W., Ditaranto, S., Biros, D., Beele, D., . . . Reilly, A. (2011). Association of psychological risk screening in pediatric cancer with psychological services provided. *Psycho-Oncology*, *20*(7), 715–723.

Klassen, A., Gulati, S., & Dix, D. (2012). Health care providers' perspectives about working with parents of children with cancer: A qualitative study. *Journal of Pediatric Oncology Nursing*, *29*(2), 92–97.

Kuspt, M., & Schulman, J. (1988). Long-term coping with pediatric leukemia: A six-year follow-up study. *Journal of Pediatric Psychology*, *13*(1), 7–22.

Pergert, P., Ekblad, S., Enskar, K., & Bjork, O. (2007). Obstacles to transcultural caring relationships: Experiences of health care staff in pediatric oncology. *Journal of Pediatric Oncology Nursing*, *24*(6), 314–328.

Pergert, P., Ekblad, S., Enskar, K., & Bjork, O. (2008). Protecting professional composure in transcultural pediatric nursing. *Qualitative Health Research*, *18*(5), 647–657.

Schor, E. (2003). Family pediatrics: Report of the task force on the family. *Pediatrics*, *111*(6), 1541–1571.

Sloper, P. (2000). Predictors of distress in parents of children with cancer: A prospective study. *Journal of Pediatric Psychology*, *25*(2), 79–91.

Suzuki, L., & Kato, P. (2003). Psychosocial support for patients in pediatric oncology: The influences of parents, schools, peers, and technology. *Journal of Pediatric Oncology Nursing*, *20*(4), 159–174.

Wiener, L., McConnell, D., Latella, L., & Ludi, E. (2013). Cultural and religious considerations in pediatric palliative care. *Palliative and Supportive Care*, *11*(1), 47–67.

67 Pediatric Cancer Survivors

Kate Shafer and Constance Connor

Key Concepts

- *Research has led to increasing numbers of childhood cancer survivors living into adulthood.*
- *Childhood cancer survivors face medical and psychosocial late effects of their cancer and treatment.*
- *Knowledge of childhood cancer survivorship is essential for meeting the long-term psychosocial needs of this growing population.*

Individuals and organizations define the term *cancer survivor* differently. The traditional survivor benchmark of 5 years from the date of diagnosis has limitations because most childhood cancer survivors live many decades beyond this. The 2003 Institute of Medicine report "Childhood Cancer Survivorship: Improving Care and Quality of Life" includes the following definition in the summary: "An individual is considered a cancer survivor from the time of diagnosis, through the balance of his or her life" (p. 2). Because the period from diagnosis through active treatment is addressed elsewhere in this book, for this chapter we define childhood cancer survivors as "individuals who have no evidence of disease, two years from the completion of planned therapy" (American Society of Clinical Oncology, 2013; G. H. Reaman, MD, personal communication, August 2012). As one 18-year-old amputee and survivor of osteosarcoma who responded to a questionnaire we handed out at a conference explained, "To me, survivorship simply means that I have had cancer, underwent treatment, and am now cancer free, both physically and mentally. The physical aspect is obvious, free of cancer. The mental aspect is coming out of the experience, and with a positive attitude."

For many years, pediatric cancer treatments underestimated the challenges of a child's psychological and social adaptation to the disease and treatment. After a research interview, one 15-year-old 5-year survivor of osteosarcoma asked, "What took you so long to get to me? It took five years for someone to ask how I was managing my life after treatment."

This chapter examines the long-term medical impacts and psychosocial needs of a growing population of survivors of childhood cancer and presents specific suggestions for assessment at critical points of transition and two novel approaches to addressing survivors' needs.

Childhood Cancer Research

The relatively small number of children diagnosed with cancer, approximately 12,500 each year, means that no single institution is able to accrue enough patients with the same diagnosis to do meaningful research. The Children's Oncology Group (COG, 2007) was formed in 2000 to conduct multi-institution, cooperative clinical trials research in more than 200 member institutions. "More than any other factor, clinical research of this type has been responsible for dramatic improvements in survival rates of children with cancer. Cure rates have improved from less than 10%—when the cooperative groups were founded—to nearly 80% at present" (O'Leary, Krailo, Anderson, & Reaman, 2008, p. 485).

Today, in the United States, there are more than 328,000 cancer survivors who were diagnosed under the age of 21, and approximately 80% of children diagnosed with cancer survive at least 5 years from diagnosis (National Cancer Institute, 2012). The long-term medical and psychosocial impact of surviving childhood cancer is an increasingly important area of interest and one in which social workers play a critical role.

Survivorship in Childhood Cancer

For most children diagnosed with cancer, the end of treatment is often just the beginning of a lifetime of chronic illness and psychosocial challenge. As more children with cancer survive into their adult years, social workers need to understand the biopsychosocial long-term and medical late effects of treatment impacting quality of life:

- Long-term effects: develop during treatment and remain following the end of treatment; may resolve after a period of time or may become chronic problems
- Late effects: health problems that arise months or years after treatment has ended (National Cancer Institute, 2012)

Much of what we know about the long-term health consequences of childhood cancer and treatment comes from the Childhood Cancer Survivor Study (CCSS, available from St. Jude Children's Research Hospital, n.d.). The CCSS is a retrospective study that includes 20,000 childhood cancer survivors diagnosed between 1970 and 1986 and a comparison group of survivors' healthy siblings. A second cohort of survivors treated between 1987 and 1999 is being recruited.

A 2006 comprehensive analysis of medical late effects of survivorship reported on 10,397 survivors. Long-term survivors are more likely to have diminished health status and to die prematurely than are adults never diagnosed with childhood cancer. In survey data, 137 health conditions were reported within vision and eye, hearing, speech, cardiovascular, pulmonary, gastrointestinal, musculoskeletal, neurological, endocrine, and secondary malignancies categories (Oeffinger et al., 2006).

Psychological and Psychosocial Long-Term Outcomes

Pediatric cancer has long been considered a highly stressful and traumatic experience for children and their families because of its invasive procedures, painful treatments, and disruption of family life and social and educational activities, "all of which occur in the context of a significant threat to their survival" (Phipps, 2007, p. 1055). Clinicians have expected an increased frequency of adjustment difficulties and emotional distress in children undergoing treatment and who have survived cancer. Phipps describes in a selective review of the literature the "adaptive style paradigm" as a framework for understanding "the positive adjustment of children with cancer" (Phipps, 2007, p. 1055). Available data supports the view that children with cancer can be exceptionally well adjusted and resilient.

Research into psychosocial outcomes in adult survivors of childhood cancer offers a mixed picture of the long-term adjustment, psychological distress, and health-related quality of life. Within the CCSS cohort, survivors report higher levels of global distress than their siblings. However, compared with population norms, both survivors and siblings report lower levels of distress. Studies do reveal subgroups at greater risk for negative psychosocial outcomes including female gender, treatment for central nervous system tumors, treatment resulting in neurocognitive or neurosensory deficit, and amputation (Zebrack et al., 2007; Zeltzer et al., 2008). High levels of persistent psychological distress have also been found in young adult survivors of pediatric sarcomas, especially males, long after completion of therapy (Weiner et al., 2006). Kazak and colleagues have described higher rates of posttraumatic stress symptoms (PTSSs) and posttraumatic stress disorder (PTSD) in young adult survivors as compared to younger cohorts (Kazak et al., 2004). Additional psychosocial outcomes for survivors include lower educational attainment, being unemployed or underemployed, having lower household income, and being less likely to achieve independent living or be in a long-term relationship (Dowling et al., 2010; Ellenberg et al., 2009; Gurney et al., 2009; Kunin-Batson et al., 2011; Zebrack et al., 2007; Zeltzer et al., 2008).

Survivorship Care: Implications for Social Work

Survivorship includes many phases in the cancer journey and along the spectrum of human development, from active treatment to long-term follow-up and from pediatric to adult health care. The concept of survivor-specific, long-term follow-up care was first described in 1986 by Meadows and Hobbie. The COG has published *Establishing and Enhancing Services for Childhood Cancer Survivors: Long-Term Follow-Up Program Resource Guide*, which establishes criteria for comprehensive, multidisciplinary survivorship care (COG, 2007). In addition to medical late effects, one of the purposes of long-term follow-up is to assess survivor quality of life.

There is no unifying theoretical framework or single model of intervention for social work in survivorship. As part of a multidisciplinary team, social workers play a key role in addressing psychosocial concerns, identifying areas of functioning where cancer treatment may have had both negative and positive impacts, and connecting survivors and families with resources in the community to ameliorate problems and optimize functioning. Social workers are educators, advocates, and counselors in survivorship. As in all oncology care, times of change or transition in cancer or its treatment, or any new life challenges that are heightened by cancer and its residuals, evoke anxiety and require periods of adjustment for the patient and family (Keene, Hobbie, & Ruccione, 2012).

Transition From Active Treatment to Long-Term Follow-Up

The end of active treatment and transition to long-term, follow-up status, although cause for celebration, can also be a time of anxiety for parents who have adapted to the heavy demand of being a "cancer family." As visits to the clinic become less frequent, parents experience the loss of relationships with medical staff and lose the reassurance of frequent exams and laboratory and other tests that affirm their child's survival. Relationships with other families whose children are still in active treatment diminish, and supportive neighbors, extended family, and the school community move on while the survivor may continue to have multiple care needs. Survivors will continue to be followed for years for signs of recurrence, but as the likelihood of relapse diminishes, care shifts to monitoring for medical and neurocognitive late effects and focusing on personal adjustment, school performance, vocational planning, relationships, and other quality-of-life concerns. Findings related to the long-term psychosocial impact on parents of having a child diagnosed with cancer are mixed. Some studies have found that parents describe permanently changed lives and distress that persists long after the end of treatment, as well as high rates of PTSSs and PTSD related to memories of treatment, fear of recurrence, loss of control, worry about late effects, and uncertainty about the future of their survivor child (Bruce, 2006; Kazak et al., 2004; Van Dongen-Melman, Van Zuuren, & Verhulst, 1998). Other studies suggest that high levels of parental distress evident at the time of diagnosis decrease over time (Kazak, 2005; Steele, Long, Reddy, Luhr, & Phipps, 2003). Maurice-Stam, Oort, Last, and Grootenhuis (2008) studied emotional functioning of parents of children with cancer for the first 5 years following the end of treatment and found high levels of parental distress in the first 2 months following transition from active treatment to survivorship. However, distress and feelings of uncertainty and helplessness returned to normal levels within 2 years following the end of treatment.

During the period of transition and throughout long-term follow-up, areas for continued social work assessment and intervention include:

For Parent/Family

- Anxiety, depression, and/or PTSSs related to the child's cancer
- Understanding late effects and the importance and schedule of continued surveillance
- Financial need, health insurance, public benefits
- Impact on siblings

For Survivors

- Academic status, need for neuropsychological testing, IEP, and 504 plans
- College, career, or vocational planning
- Risk-taking behavior (smoking, drinking, and drug use)
- Psychosexual development, dating, and sexual activity
- Social adjustment including friendships, activities, and behavioral concerns
- Anxiety, depression, and/or PTSSs
- Healthy behaviors such as diet, exercise, use of sunscreen, and sleep hygiene

Transition From Pediatric to Adult Health Care

Transition is more than just the transfer of care from one system to another. As the mother of one young adult survivor of acute lymphoblastic leukemia (ALL) explained about the time of her daughter's first adult clinic visit, "I was a mess in the waiting room holding back and letting her move on. Our parenting style has always had a child have ownership of decisions. So it seemed right to let her go .... I didn't realize how emotional it would be for me. Ah life!!! I get the Emmy Award for not letting her know!!!!"

As the number of survivors continues to grow, there is a need for them to transition from the pediatric health care setting to adult health care. For childhood cancer survivors, the transition can be laden with extra concern on the part of parents and difficulty letting go due to years of close monitoring of their child's illness and health and mutual dependence. Leaving the familiar, family-focused, and lifesaving setting of the pediatric oncology service can be a psychologically complex process for all parties. For young adult survivors, it means assuming responsibility for one's own health care and decision making, finding and keeping health insurance, and becoming one's own advocate.

Depending on the age at diagnosis, many pediatric survivors will have few memories of their diagnosis and time spent in treatment, especially if diagnosed in infancy or as a toddler. As one 19-year-old hepatoblastoma survivor diagnosed at age 2½ explained, "Beyond the playroom and the rides on my IV pole, I remember very little about being in the hospital when I was three. The rest of the 'memories' I have are mostly constructed, pieced together during the once-a-year journeys back to Children's Hospital of Philadelphia."

Although the experience of their child's life-threatening illness was likely traumatic for the parents, the history as told by the parent may be greatly sanitized and the survivor may have little knowledge of his or her cancer and potential for late effects. The mother of a young adult ALL survivor anticipating transition described it as "a tough one for me, in our case our son was only two and a half years old at the time of diagnosis, so I took care of everything. Now that he's an adult, he is still very dependent on me for his medical needs. We are working on getting him more aware of his medical needs."

Recommendations regarding transition include several years of planning before transition with flexibility related to developmental readiness, a gradual shift of health care responsibility from parent to patient, illness-specific education, and self-advocacy skills (American Academy of Pediatrics, American Academy of Family Physicians, & American College of Physicians, 2002, 2011; White, McManus, McAllister, & Cooley, 2012). During this time, social workers can assess transition readiness, educate survivors where there may be knowledge or resource deficits, and work with parents to identify barriers, lessen anxiety, and become partners in their young adult survivor's long-term health. Transition readiness assessment includes the following:

- Knowledge of diagnosis and treatment
- Knowledge of potential late effects and surveillance recommendations
- Awareness of health insurance status
- Identification of primary health care setting with providers who are knowledgeable of the late effects of childhood cancer
- Ability to make and keep appointments, fill prescriptions, and follow health care recommendations

Adult survivors continue to need long-term follow-up care for their lifetime. Despite this need, in 2006, only 20% of survivors were seen in specialized long-term follow-up clinics, and the percentage drops the more time passes since the end of treatment (Oeffinger et al., 2006). Social workers play a role in helping adult survivors meet the challenges of known late effects and the uncertainty about future late effects, including secondary malignancies and other chronic health conditions that may be disabling. Social workers may also be instrumental in helping survivors achieve adult milestones in employment; obtain and maintain insurance; apply to college or vocational school, including scholarships and accommodations; and establish peer relationships and social connections.

Two Novel Social Work Interventions With Survivors of Childhood Cancer

Heads Up: A Social Skill Development Group for Young Adult Brain Tumor Survivors

Survivors of brain tumors have been identified as a subgroup at increased risk for negative long-term outcomes resulting from their cancer and treatment (Ellenberg et al., 2009; Schulte & Barrera, 2010). Practice observation in a long-term follow-up clinic for survivors confirms that because of physical, neurosensory, and neurocognitive differences, many brain tumor survivors are socially isolated and lack a peer group. This is especially the case following completion of high school, when there are fewer opportunities to interact with same-age peers. Many survivors continue to live with and are dependent on parents. There are few programs in place to address the social limitations and needs of this young adult group. Social skills training is an evidence-informed behavioral therapy modality used in autism spectrum disorder, attention deficit hyperactivity disorder, acquired brain injury, and developmental disabilities (Laugeson, Frankel, Gantman, Dillon, & Mogil, 2012). This modality has been used with young brain tumor survivors (Barrera & Schulte, 2009).

Heads Up is for brain tumor survivors aged 18 and over and consists of monthly 2-hour meetings cofacilitated by two clinical social workers. Meetings follow an activity-based observation–response–practice format with skills focused on social initiation and friendship, cooperation and team building, empathy, confidence building, and social problem solving. A photography component incorporated into each meeting gives group members the opportunity to use an art form to identify personal strengths and challenges, express feelings, explore career options and obstacles, expand social engagement, and support and identify with peers.

Incidence of Chronic Health Conditions in Survivors of Childhood Cancer	
62.3%	*Reported having at least one chronic health condition*
27.5%	*Reporting a severe or life-threatening condition*
37.6%	*Reported having two or more health conditions*
23.8%	*Reported having three or more health conditions*

I'm Cured... Now What? A Conference for Teen and Young Adult Survivors of Childhood Cancer

Given the known health outcomes and late effects, adolescent and young adult survivors of childhood cancer must be aware of treatment-related health risks. In a study of survivors' knowledge of past diagnosis and treatment, only 72% accurately reported their diagnosis with precision; 19% were accurate but not precise. Many survivors interviewed were unable to name important elements of their treatment (e.g., whether they received radiation and to what specific site). None of the study participants could provide an accurate detailed summary of all their therapy. This was even true of those who had attended long-term follow-up programs (Kadan-Lottick et al., 2002). All of these issues have implications for long-term health risks, especially as young adult survivors move away from parents and assume responsibility for their own health. A specific recommendation of the 2003 Institute of Medicine report on childhood cancer survivorship is to "improve awareness of late effects and their implications for long-term health for childhood cancer and their families" (p. 197).

Annually, since 2006, Life with Cancer has addressed this recommendation by hosting the "I'm Cured... Now What? Conference for Teen and Young Adult Survivors of Childhood Cancer." Originally funded by the National Children's Cancer Society and organized and led by a pediatric oncology social worker, the specific conference objectives have included the following:

- Educating survivors and parents about late effects
- Educating survivors and parents on how to minimize risks
- Promoting a healthy lifestyle after treatment
- Empowering survivors to take charge of their own health

In addition to providing risk-specific information on late effects, topics have included college and career planning, sexuality, fertility, insurance and legal issues, dating and disclosure, psychological implications, and nutrition, with hands-on opportunities to experience different forms of exercise (e.g., Zumba, kickboxing, Pilates, yoga, weight training) and complementary therapies (e.g., Reiki, massage, music and art therapy). The all-day, multi-institutionally supported educational event has reached hundreds of survivors and parents, providing a valuable opportunity to meet and network with others, including medical experts from long-term follow-up programs and childhood cancer organizations (Sadak, Connor, & Deluca, 2013). The most important innovative incentive to attract and engage survivors who might not otherwise attend has been the awarding of several $1,000 scholarships for college, vocational, or graduate school at each conference. Since 2006, more than $100,000 in scholarships has been awarded with funds provided by local childhood cancer organizations. Evaluation of the program has demonstrated the effectiveness of these events in increasing knowledge about late effects and the need for a healthy diet, physical exercise, and stress reduction to keep healthy (Connor, DeLuca & Sadak, 2010) and improving group knowledge and practice about nutrition and fitness after 6 months (Sadak, Deluca, Connor, & Bolte, 2012).

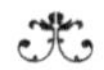

Pearls

- Social workers play an integral role in the psychosocial care of pediatric, adolescent, and young adult survivors of childhood cancer. This includes resource referrals; vocational and educational planning; assessing relationships with peers, partners, parents, and siblings; and addressing sexuality and fertility concerns, risk-taking behavior, substance abuse, emotional status, and the presence of PTSD/PTSS in survivors and family members.
- Social workers are uniquely qualified in developing and conducting innovative and effective programs to address survivors' therapeutic, social, and educational needs.
- Social workers contribute to the body of knowledge and research in childhood cancer survivorship.

Pitfalls

- There is wide variation in availability of survivorship clinics and programs, especially for young adult survivors.
- Social workers may have limited time and resources to devote to survivorship issues.
- Social workers are often confronted by barriers to obtaining financial resources, support programs, and services in the community for survivors.

Childhood cancer survivors are a growing and aging population. They are at risk for known medical and psychosocial late effects of their cancer and treatment. Some of these effects may not be apparent for many years following the completion of treatment. Survivors benefit from developmentally appropriate long-term follow-up throughout their lifetimes for surveillance and early intervention for new late effects. The following advice from an 18-year-old amputee and survivor of osteosarcoma illustrates the importance of psychosocial support:

> *Do not see cancer as a giant road block in the path of your future; use it as a stepping stone towards building your future. Always keep in mind that, no matter how bad things might look today, it doesn't hurt to believe in tomorrow. Tomorrow will always be better, even just by a little bit, because you are not alone, you are surrounded by those who love you and will do anything to get you through.*

ADDITIONAL RESOURCES

Association of Pediatric Oncology Social Workers Special Interest Group on Survivorship assessment guidelines: http://www.aposw.org

Social skills activity manual: http://www.dannypettry.com

REFERENCES

American Academy of Pediatrics, American Academy of Family Physicians, & American College of Physicians-American Society of Internal Medicine. (2002). A consensus statement on health care transitions for young adults with special health care needs. *Pediatrics, 110*(6, Pt. 2), 1304–1306.

American Academy of Pediatrics, American Academy of Family Physicians, & College of Physicians. (2011). Clinical report—Supporting the health care transition from adolescence to adulthood in the medical home. *Pediatrics, 128*, 182–200. doi:10.1542/peds.2011-0969

American Society of Clinical Oncology. (2013). About survivorship. Retrieved from http://www.cancer.net/survivorship/about-survivorship

Barrera, M., & Schulte, F. (2009). A group social skills intervention program for survivors of childhood brain tumors. *Journal of Pediatric Psychology, 34*, 1108–1118. doi:10.1093/jpepsy/jsp018

Bruce, M. (2006). A systematic and conceptual review of posttraumatic stress in childhood cancer survivors and their parents. *Clinical Psychology Review, 26*(3), 233–256. doi:10.1016/j.cpr.2005.10.002

Children's Oncology Group (COG). (2007). *Establishing and enhancing services for childhood cancer survivors: Long-term follow-up program resource guide*. Duarte, CA: Author. Retrieved from http://www.survivorshipguidelines.org/pdf/LTFUResourceGuide.pdf

Connor, C., DeLuca, H., & Sadak, K., (2010, June 11–12). *Outcomes of an educational conference series for adolescent and young adult survivors of childhood cancer.* Abstract #68. Poster presentation, 11th International Conference on Long-Term Complications of Treatment of Children and Adolescents for Cancer, Williamsburg, VA.

Dowling, E., Yabroff, K. R., Mariotto, A., McNeel, T., Zeruto, C., & Buckman, D. (2010). Burden of illness in adult survivors of childhood cancer: Findings from a population-based national sample. *Cancer, 116*(15), 3712–3721. doi:10.1002/cncr.25141

Ellenberg, L., Liu, Q., Gioia, G., Yasui, Y., Packer, R. J., Mertens, A.,... Zeltzer, L. (2009). Neurocognitive status in long-term survivors of childhood CNS malignancies: A report from the Childhood Cancer Survivor Study. *Neuropsychology, 23*, 705–717. doi:10.1037a0016674

Gurney, J. G., Krull, K. R., Kaden-Lottick, N., Nicholson, H. S., Nathan, P. C., Zebrack, B.,... Ness, K. (2009). Social outcomes in the childhood cancer survivor study cohort. *Journal of Clinical Oncology, 27*(14), 2390–2395. doi:10.1200/JCO.2008.21.1458

Institute of Medicine. (2003). Childhood cancer survivorship: Improving care and quality of life. Retrieved from http://www.iom.edu/Reports/2003/Childhood-Cancer-Survivorship-Improving-Care-and-Quality-of-Life.aspx

Kadan-Lottick, N. S., Robison, L. L., Gurney, J. G., Neglia, J. P., Yasui, Y., Hayashi. R.,... Mertens, A. C. (2002). Childhood cancer survivors' knowledge about their past diagnosis and treatment: Childhood cancer survivor study. *Journal of the American Medical Association, 28*(14), 1832–1839.

Kazak, A., Alderfer, M., Rourke, M., Simms, S., Streisand, R., & Grossman, J. (2004). Posttraumatic stress disorder (PTSD) and posttraumatic stress symptoms (PTSS) in families of adolescent childhood cancer survivors. *Journal of Pediatric Psychology, 29*(3), 211–219. doi:10.1093/jpepsy/jsh022

Kazak, A. E. (2005). Evidence-based interventions for survivors of childhood cancer and their families. *Journal of Pediatric Psychology, 30*(1), 29–39. doi:10.1093/jpepsy/jsi013

Keene, N., Hobbie, W., & Ruccione, K. (2012). *Childhood cancer survivors: A practical guide to your future* (3rd ed.). Sebastapol, CA: O'Reilly Media.

Kunin-Batson, A., Kadan-Lottick, N., Zhu, L., Cox, C., Bordes-Edgar, V., Srivastava, D. K.,... Krull, K. R. (2011). Predictors of independent living status in adult survivors of childhood cancer: A report from the Childhood Cancer Survivor Study. *Pediatric Blood and Cancer, 57*(7), 1197–1203. doi:10.1002/pbc.22982

Laugeson, E., Frankel, F., Gantman, A., Dillon, A., & Mogil, C. (2012). Evidence-based social skills training for adolescents with autism spectrum disorders: The UCLA PEERS program. *Journal of Autism and Developmental Disorders, 42*(6), 1025–1036. doi:10.1007/s10803-011-1339-1

Maurice-Stam, H., Oort, F. J., Last, B., & Grootenhuis, M. A. (2008). Emotional functioning of parents of children with cancer: The first five years of continuous remission after the end of treatment. *Psycho-Oncology, 17*, 448–459. doi:10.1002/pon.1260

Meadows, A. T., & Hobbie, W. L. (1986). The medical consequences of cure. *Cancer, 58*, 524–528.

National Cancer Institute. (2012). Childhood cancer survivor study: An overview. Retrieved from http://www.cancer.gov/cancertopics/coping/ccss/

Oeffinger, K., Mertens, A., Sklar, C., Kawashima, M. S., Hudson, M. D., Meadows, A. T.,... Robison, L. L. (2006). Chronic health conditions in adult survivors of childhood cancer. *New England Journal of Medicine, 355*, 1572–1582.

O'Leary, M., Krailo, M., Anderson, J. R., & Reaman, G. H. (2008). Progress in childhood cancer: 50 years of research collaboration, a report from the Children's Oncology Group. *Seminars in Oncology, 35*(5), 484–493. doi:10.1053/j.seminoncol.2008.07.008

Phipps, S. (2007). Adaptive style in children with cancer: Implications for a positive psychology approach. *Journal of Pediatric Psychology, 32*(9), 1055–1066. doi:10.1093/jpepsy/jsm060

Sadak, K., Connor, C., & Deluca, H. (2013). Innovative educational approaches to engage and empower the adolescent and young adult childhood cancer survivor. *Pediatric Blood and Cancer, 60*, 1919–1921. doi:10.1002/pbc.24635

Sadak, K., Deluca, H., Connor, C., & Bolte, S. (2012, June 8–9). *Longitudinal program evaluation of an educational intervention for adolescent and young adult survivors of childhood cancer.* Abstract #88. 12th International Conference on Long-Term Complications of Treatment of Children and Adolescents for Cancer, Williamsburg, VA.

Schulte, F., & Barrera, M. (2010). Social competence in childhood brain tumor survivors: A comprehensive review. *Support Care Cancer, 18*, 1499–1513.

Steele, R. G., Long, A., Reddy, K. A., Luhr, M., & Phipps, S. (2003). Changes in maternal distress and child-rearing strategies across treatment for pediatric cancer. *Journal of Pediatric Psychology, 28*(7), 447–452. doi:10.1093/jpepsy/jsg035

St. Jude Children's Research Hospital. (n.d.). Childhood cancer survivor study. Retrieved from http://ccss.stjude.org/

Van Dongen-Melman, J. E. W., Van Zuuren, F., & Verhulst, F. (1998). Experiences of parents of childhood cancer survivors: a qualitative analysis. *Patient Education and Counseling, 34*(3), 185–200. doi:10.1016/S0738-3991(98)00031-7

Weiner, L., Battles, H., Bernstein, D., Long, L., Derdak, J., Mackall, C., & Lansky, P. (2006). Persistent psychological distress in long-term survivors of pediatric sarcoma: The experience at a single institution. *Psycho-Oncology, 15*, 898–910. doi:10.1002/pon.1024

White, P. H., McManus, M. A., McAllister, J. W., & Cooley, C. (2012). A primary care quality improvement approach to health care transition. *Pediatric Annals, 41*(5), 1–7. doi:10.3928/00904481-20120426-e-7

Zebrack, B. J., Zevon, M. A., Turk, N., Nagarajan, R., Whitton, J., Robison, L. L., & Zeltzer, L. K. (2007). Psychological distress in long-term survivors of solid tumors diagnosed in childhood: A report from the Childhood Cancer Survivor Study. *Pediatric Blood and Cancer, 49*, 47–51. doi:10.1002/pbc.20914

Zeltzer, L. K., Lu, Q., Leisenring, W., Reklitis, C., Armstrong, G., Mertens, A. C., . . . & Ness, K. K. (2008). Psychosocial outcomes and health-related quality of life in adult childhood cancer survivors: A report from the Childhood Cancer Survivor Study. *Cancer Epidemiology Biomarkers and Prevention, 17*(435), 1–7. doi:10.1158/1055-9965.EPI-07-2541

68

Stacy S. Remke

Pediatric Palliative Care

Key Concepts

- *A child diagnosed with cancer requires medical and psychosocial care over time. Anticipatory guidance and focused, individualized, and coordinated interventions are key.*
- *Social work practitioners from oncology services and palliative care services each have distinct, complementary, and overlapping skill sets that, when well coordinated, are most helpful to families. Distinctions between "primary oncology" and "specialty" palliative care social work practice are discussed.*
- *Well-coordinated and intentional social work collaboration can provide seamless care and patient navigation when children require simultaneous treatment from several services.*
- *Families are chronically stressed, if not overwhelmed, and need social work involvement to minimize the burdens of the disease process.*
- *Palliative care is recommended all along the illness trajectory from the point of diagnosis through cure or death.*

Advances in oncology treatment for children have made remarkable strides in recent decades, with National Cancer Institute statistics reporting on long-term remission rates increasing from 58% in 1975 to almost 80% in 2003 (National Cancer Institute, 2008). These improvements can be attributed to many factors, including better therapies and earlier detection. Cancer, however, remains the leading disease-related cause of death in children (Lafond, Rood, Jacobs, & Reaman, 2011).

Childhood cancer disrupts family life, with its rigorous treatments, unpredictable setbacks, demanding schedules, repeated invasive procedures, and symptoms and therapies that are burdensome to the child. For too many, progressive disease, relapses, and complications of treatment require additional remobilization for prolonged coping when the family resources have already become depleted. Therapy is rigorous and exhausting, and when therapy is unsuccessful and death cannot be prevented, the impact is even greater, having important ramifications for long-term family functioning, grief reactions, and resolution of the loss.

All of this has led to a growing awareness of the importance of providing palliative care alongside cure-oriented therapies. The contributions of social work to "primary palliative care" are provided throughout the illness trajectory by the oncology team, often by the pediatric oncology social worker. At the specialty level, services are provided by the pediatric palliative social worker. Beginning in the diagnostic and early treatment phases, care goals for the patient and family should be clearly outlined and addressed, including managing distress, pain, and discomfort; the importance of open communication between the patient, family, and treatment team; weighing burdens and benefits of recommended treatments; and caring for the needs of the patient and family as a whole—needs that may be informational, educational, psychological, social, emotional, economic, cultural, spiritual, or practical.

This chapter reviews the palliative role of the oncology social worker on the treatment team, as well as the palliative social work specialist on the palliative care team. Strategies for enhancing the provision of palliative care to children and families through social work intervention are described. Recommendations for collaborative practice between the oncology social worker and the palliative social worker that consider the needs and preferences of families and those of the treating services are described.

Pediatric Oncology Social Work

Families of a child diagnosed with cancer are as varied and diverse as the general population. Their needs range from adapting to the illness, treatment, and system of care delivery to managing increasing financial burdens, potential traumatic events related to disease and treatment, school and work coordination, emotional and spiritual coping, and the routine demands of family life.

An individualized psychosocial assessment for families is recommended so interventions and support can be tailored to family needs (Kazak et al., 2003; Kazak et al., 2007). Early assessment also allows for identification of family and patient communication style, strengths, and vulnerabilities. Given that all families in pediatric oncology are highly stressed, the need to provide a standardized form of triage to direct resources to those with the greatest need while also providing adequate support to all patients and families is widely acknowledged to be a challenge to teams in general, and to social workers in particular.

Many children with cancer and their families will experience potentially traumatic events during their illness and treatment and are at risk for posttraumatic stress (Kazak et al., 2006). Families have indicated that consistent relationships with health care team members reduce their stress (Contro, Larson, Scofield, Sourkes, & Cohen, 2004), because they are not emotionally or psychologically available to engage new people in complex or intimate discussions at the very last stage of their child's life (Contro, Larson, Scofield, Sourkes, & Cohen, 2002; Contro et al., 2004; Kazak, Simms, & Rourke, 2002). Models of psychosocial care all include efforts to normalize experiences, provide anticipatory guidance, and empower family coping (Contro et al., 2002; Kazak et al., 2007).

In pediatric oncology in particular, clear communication with families, sensitive and skillfully facilitated "difficult conversations" or breaking of bad news, and caring attitudes of the professionals toward the child and family are associated with higher satisfaction with care during the patient's terminal illness process (Contro et al., 2004; Feudtner, 2007; Wolfe et al., 2000). These practices also impact the family's bereavement after the patient's death (Contro et al., 2004; Robert et al., 2012). The difficulty that pediatric oncologists have in managing transitions from active treatment to end-of-life care has been described by oncologists themselves (Hilden et al., 2001). Oncology teams that have cared for children in intense circumstances over time develop strong bonds with them and their families, and these can influence judgments about communicating transition to end of life and in discussing options (Lafond et al., 2011).

Given their expertise with systems, groups, and communication, social workers often emerge as leaders and facilitators of team dynamics within both pediatric oncology teams (Jones, 2005) and pediatric palliative care teams (Jones, Remke, & Phillips, 2011; Remke & Schermer, 2012). The role of the social worker as an important member of the interdisciplinary team has also been described (Jones, 2005; Jones et al., 2011; Meier & Beresford, 2008).

Oncology Social Workers as Palliative Care Specialists

As pediatric palliative care programs have been established and palliative care has emerged as a specialty, pediatric palliative social work has also developed as a specialty with credentials now available to designate the expertise of the hospice and palliative care social worker.

As these social work specialists emerge, it is important to develop a clearer understanding and respect for their distinct roles and skills to implement effective collaborative practice. Without this, role unclarity and conflict may confuse patients and families and limit social work's effectiveness in working with the interdisciplinary team.

Social Workers on Pediatric Palliative Care Teams

In pediatrics, the goal is to support growth and development and to treat disease. However, some diagnoses—osteosarcoma, Stage 4, or multiply relapsed cancers—carry greater risk for morbidity and/or death than others. Risks of treatment failure here are particularly high, and the treatment options may pose complex decision-making challenges and quality-of-life considerations, often simultaneously, for the patient and family.

Based on the hospice philosophy, palliative care focuses on comfort, quality of life, and the development of goals for care to drive interventions, making the situations mentioned previously particularly appropriate for palliative care. However, palliative care is often confused with hospice or end-of-life care for patients and families, and as a consequence, providers may be reluctant to refer, fearing they will appear to be "giving up" on their patients and families who they feel are "not there yet." Likewise, families are loath to "give up" on their children and are reluctant to access hospice care at any stage as a result.

Even though they may not prevent death, many medical interventions (e.g., medical nutrition and hydration, mechanical ventilation) are palliative in nature and as such, palliative care provided alongside active, cure-oriented therapies has emerged as a preferred model for supportive care.

Social workers on pediatric palliative care teams may provide assessment to the patient and family and/or consult and collaborate on interventions with the primary care team as needed. Specific activities are often determined by the assessment, which should include an understanding of how the primary oncology team is operating, their relationships with the child and family, and challenges they have encountered. In addition, the assessment can provide a fresh perspective of the family and often help illuminate misunderstandings, biases, and conflicts that may have inadvertently developed during treatment thus far.

The palliative care social worker has the responsibility for seeking out the primary oncology social worker and asking about his or her perspective on the case and then developing a way to approach this family and bridge the oncology and palliative care team. The first questions should include: "How can we help you?" and "What are you struggling with or most concerned about in this case?"

Managing Uncertainty

Oncology treatment is, of course, focused on cure whenever possible. In many circumstances, children with cancer are at high risk for eventual death, though periods of remission and relative stability may occur (Lafond et al., 2011). As options for cure decrease, some therapies are of uncertain benefit, for instance, Phase 1 trials whose purpose is for ascertaining drug toxicity. In other situations, major surgery may buy more time for the child or adolescent patient but create new risks and burdens.

Such situations pose complex dilemmas and require ethical decisions to be made based on various factors and considerations. Informed consent for the family, and for the child according to his or her capacity, is critical, as is a clear understanding of the alternatives and their potential consequences. Social workers are routinely engaged in such discussions, helping facilitate communication, seeking resolution of conflicts, and providing emotional support. Likewise, social workers on oncology teams may understand when a child's situation is evolving from more standard care into more complex or uncertain circumstances. They can help prepare families for this potentiality and mobilize the team to discuss options, plan sensitive communication, and develop support strategies for the patient and family.

Seventeen-year-old Josh had exhausted known treatment options for his Stage 4, multiply relapsed cancer diagnosis. He asked his doctor if there was anything else they could try. His doctor described some Phase 1 research trials that Josh might be eligible to participate in but also stated his concern that they might not help. After the doctor left the meeting, the oncology social worker talked further with Josh and his parents about their hopes for a cure. Josh talked about his desire to finish the school year and attend college; his parents talked about wanting to help him be as pain free as possible so he could enjoy himself with friends and family after almost 3 years of tough treatment.

The next time the family and social worker met with the doctor, the social worker referred to this earlier conversation and asked the doctor to explain how participation in a Phase 1 trial might affect those goals and to explain in more detail what the purposes of these trials are. Before this, the doctor and social worker had agreed on what information they felt would be helpful to offer the family. After the doctor explained that Phase 1 trials were designed to identify toxicity of new potential therapies and that curative intent was not the purpose, Josh and his family indicated that they were unsure about proceeding. They discussed which side effects Josh had greatest difficulty with and also what hopes he had for living as long as possible. Josh also shared that he hoped his experiences might aid science in helping others in the future. The doctor listened to their concerns, and the social worker offered supportive encouragement. The doctor said he would look for those trials that were most likely to offer meaningful results while minimizing side effects to allow Josh and his family to make an informed decision. The doctor also reiterated that Josh could change his mind at any time and that the team would always do their best to keep Josh as comfortable and as active as possible.

As Josh's case illustrates, the best plans emerge through a series of complicated discussions. Facts and beliefs become apparent through conversations facilitated in an atmosphere of openness and trust. Informed consent is only truly obtained when the patient and family understand not only their choices but also the likely consequences of them. Providers are reassured that decisions are best when full airing of concerns have taken place. Such discussions require comfort with conflict and silences, as well as skills in eliciting concerns. One study suggests that the involvement of a social worker in care can increase the family's understanding and acceptance of difficult news (Wolfe et al., 2000).

Although teams hope to be proactive and plan with families, there are times when families identify concerns before their providers do. One study found that 51% of parents reported that their understanding that their child was in a dying process came from dreams, "feelings," or other perceptions rather than conversations with health care providers (Wolfe et al., 2000).

Families may wonder when "enough is enough" or whether changes mean death is certain, but they may not express these concerns to their oncologist or team for fear of appearing to "give up" on their child. The silence that can evolve from good intentions can unintentionally leave the child and family dealing with these vital concerns in isolation. Even when it is not clear what families understand about their child's prognosis, a discussion with the palliative care team may allow an opportunity for the airing of questions and perceptions.

Three-year-old Alicia has been awaiting authorization for a bone marrow transplant (BMT) recommended as the last option for cure-oriented therapy. She has experienced a series of infections and setbacks requiring multiple needle insertions and invasive therapies. Her intensive care doctor is concerned about multiple organ failure and questions whether she would survive BMT in her weakened state, but her oncologist hopes to keep her stable until the BMT can be obtained. The oncology social worker is unaware of these latest developments, which occurred during the child's intensive care unit stay. A referral to the palliative care team (PCT) has been made, with the referring doctor saying to the team: "Just come by to meet them. They are in denial, and not ready at all for the kinds of decisions we might need to face, but let's get you involved now so they can get to know your team."

The PCT social worker and physician met the family and described what the PCT does. The bereft father asked, "When is enough enough? I can't stand to see my baby suffer like this." The mother also began to cry and nodded her head. She said, "I was up all night, wondering if we are doing the right thing, making her go through all this.... If I ask God to take her, am I a bad mother?"

The PCT talked with the parents, reassuring them that their concerns and feelings were loving and appropriate, and invited them to share more about their experiences and goals for her care. In the process of this discussion, the parents acknowledged they had been afraid to discuss these feelings and questions with their usual team because they valued their team so much, didn't want them to think they had failed, and didn't want them to think they were bad parents or giving up on their child. The PCT arranged a second meeting with the PCT, oncology team doctor, primary nurse, social worker, and family so they could address these concerns and define goals for care going forward. The oncology team was relieved that the family seemed to understand what was going on with their daughter.

As Alicia's case illustrates, good reasons exist for more than one social worker to be involved in a case during difficult transitions in the disease and treatment process. Sometimes, the complexity and intensity of the situation may require more intervention than one social worker can hope to manage. Additionally, as members of different teams, social workers are party to different discussions and planning efforts. Collaboration can therefore lead to better communication and coordination of care. Different relationships may allow family members to explore sensitive topics without fear of alienating those they rely on to care for their child. Relative comfort with difficult topics may allow a practitioner to wade more easily into such difficult discussions as planning for death or making hard decisions about whether to proceed with cancer-directed therapy after multiple relapses. Both oncology and palliative social work specialists are likely to have experience with these concerns.

As with any other specialty practice area, the more one does something, the better one becomes at it. This is true for both oncology social work experts and palliative care social work experts. Sometimes, there may be a strategy involved in creating multiple relationships with families. "Good cop, bad cop" interventions may be needed, or the complexity and intensity of the situation may require more intervention than one social worker can hope to manage.

Competing demands of other patients and families may require additional resources for the most seriously ill. Different relationships create different possibilities for sharing and communication. The potential overlap in roles can be addressed directly with families by describing the different roles and ensuring them that they can choose to discuss whatever they need to with either social worker, and the social workers can take responsibility for coordination. Reassurances can be made that roles will not be replaced. This is usually not a problem for families, who more often appreciate the options and efforts to reduce their stress.

Tim's oncology social worker was Sandy, and his palliative care team social worker was Jeff. Both social workers have had extensive conversations with Tim and his family in their separate teams' work and feel they have good relationships with the family. When Sandy took a 2-week vacation, she asked Jeff to follow the family because he was already well known to them and the plan for Sandy's time off involved three separate social workers covering her shifts, and she wanted to spare Tim's family the potential stress of having to explain their situation to strangers who would have no ongoing involvement in Tim's treatment once Sandy had returned. Jeff would be informed of changes and needs from the perspective of the palliative care team, so greater continuity could be achieved. Jeff was happy to cover, and Tim's family was glad to know that if they needed anything, a familiar person was available to help them at this critical time in their child's treatment.

Although the job descriptions of the oncology social worker and the palliative care social worker may be similar, sometimes it is the depth of coverage possible with collaboration that is the important consideration. Strategic collaboration can enhance care and create a seamless system for intervention over time that a single practitioner cannot hope to guarantee.

There are also health care politics that may become barriers to certain topics being broached by the oncology social worker. Teams are diverse, and many have evolved respectful and effective transdisciplinary processes, whereas others remain hierarchical and staunchly physician led, as in the traditional medical model. It is important for social workers to understand the culture of the medical system in which they work and be strategic advocates for child and family needs, using the array of resources at their disposal.

Louise was the oncology social worker for 12-year-old Lisa, who was being treated for serious complications of her second relapse of acute myelogenous leukemia (AML). Tracey was the palliative care team social worker. The PCT was also following Lisa and her family and was in a team rounds discussion of patients seen by both services. Louise mentioned that Lisa was asking everyone if she was going to die. Louise described this as a symptom of her heightened anxiety related to another unexpected hospitalization. The team discussed child life services providing training for relaxation and mental imagery in an effort to help her relax. Tracey mentioned that the PCT had been discussing how to treat her likely escalating physical symptoms given that her condition was deteriorating so quickly and she was unlikely to survive the relapse. They began to identify end-of-life care options. Tracey added that Lisa's mom understood that the options were now limited and was mostly concerned about keeping Lisa comfortable. This was not a viewpoint that Louise had heard the oncologists discuss as they had been focused on identifying next steps in cancer-directed therapy. Louise asked the oncologist who was present at the rounds to comment on whether he felt it was likely that a treatment would be found that offered hope for cure. The physician stated that they would keep trying but doubted a cure was likely. He went on to say that they dreaded breaking this news to Lisa's mom.

After this discussion, Louise changed her approach with the family and recommended meeting with Lisa and her family to begin the process of helping Lisa address her realistic fear of dying. She convened a meeting of Lisa's PCT to discuss how to respond to her questions and how to help her with her anxiety. Louise and Tracey met to discuss how to support Lisa and her mom through this difficult transition and how to engage the broader team, including oncology and palliative care, so that everyone could get on the same page with recommendations and discussions. Louise and Tracey also discussed ways they could support the team with these difficult conversations and decision-making challenges. They acknowledged that everyone was very disappointed that this was happening to Lisa and her family but that they wanted to do the best they could to ease their way. Louise and Tracey made a plan to meet with Lisa's mother to talk about options for comfort and how to accommodate Lisa's preference for being at home as much as possible.

As Lisa's case illustrates, social workers as members of their respective teams are party to different conversations and planning efforts based on their team's perspective and focus. Louise reacted to new information by demonstrating leadership as she had important discussions and advocated for new directions for intervention. By collaborating, sharing information, and engaging in focused discussions with key stakeholders, social workers can help ensure that families have the information they need to make the best decisions for their child. Social workers can be realistic about the complexity of the health care system and the personalities, strengths, and challenges involved, thereby helping to empower access, self-determination, and family-centered care practices.

Pearls

- Understand that social workers specializing in oncology and palliative care can collaborate effectively.
- Model communication and care coordination among the teams of providers and the family.
- Plan for anticipated needs over the long course of therapy.
- Identify tasks and needs and discuss who will address each. Take the time to communicate and coordinate.

Pitfalls

- Making assumptions about patient and family needs, and who is doing what.
- Avoiding involvement in a case because someone said, "They already have a social worker."
- Failing to look at needs over time and not planning ahead.
- Failing to communicate fully and often to coordinate social work involvement between the palliative and oncology teams.
- Failing to recognize the depth, breadth, and value of the oncology social worker's palliative skills.

The core skills, attitudes, and knowledge that social workers bring to their practice can make the critical difference for children with cancer and their families as they navigate the complex world of disease, treatment, and its aftermath. Through advocating for family needs and preferences and empowering choices, social workers facilitate the coping and survival of these children and their families in ways that have a long-term impact. The minimization of potentially traumatic events, advocacy for family partnership, and provision of diverse interventions for the enhancement of coping all work to reduce the suffering and hardship that can occur when a child or adolescent in a family has cancer.

In those situations when death cannot be avoided, collaboration between palliative care and oncology social workers ensures seamless care of children and their families and access to all needed resources at this critical transition. By understanding each other's roles and responsibilities, as well as the opportunities that each brings to the table, oncology social workers and palliative care social workers can enhance systemic efforts for family-centered, strengths-based care practices that empower families, support colleagues, and, perhaps most importantly, lessen suffering.

REFERENCES

Contro, N., Larson, J., Scofield, S., Sourkes, B., & Cohen, H. J. (2002). Family perspectives on the quality of pediatric palliative care. *Archives of Pediatric and Adolescent Medicine, 156*, 14–19.

Contro, N., Larson, J., Scofield, S., Sourkes, B., & Cohen, H. J. (2004). Hospital staff and family perspectives regarding the quality of pediatric palliative care. *Pediatrics, 114*(5), 1248–1252.

Feudtner, C. (2007). Collaborative communication in pediatric palliative care: A foundation for problem-solving and decision making. *Pediatric Clinics of North America, 54*, 583–607.

Hilden, J., Emanuel, E., Fairclough, D. L., Link, M. P., Foley, K. M., ... Mayer, R. J. (2001). Attitudes and practices among pediatric oncologists regarding end-of-life care: Results of the 1998 American Society of Clinical Oncology study. *Journal of the Study of Clinical Oncology, 19*, 205–212.

Jones, B. (2005). Pediatric palliative and end-of-life care: The role of social work in pediatric oncology. *Journal of Social Work in End-of-Life and Palliative Care, 1*(4), 35–62.

Jones, B. L., Remke, S. S., & Phillips, F. (2011). Social work in pediatric palliative care. In T. Altilio & S. Otis-Green (Eds.), *Oxford textbook of palliative social work* (pp. 387–396). New York, NY: Oxford University Press.

Kazak, A. E., Cant, C., Jensen, M. M., McSherry, M., Rourke, M. T., Hwang, W. T., ... Lange, B. (2003). Identifying psychosocial risk indicative of subsequent resource use in families of newly diagnosed pediatric oncology patients. *Journal of Clinical Oncology, 21*, 3220–3225.

Kazak, A. E., Kassam-Adams, N., Schneider, S., Zelikovsky, N., Alderfer, M. A., & Rourke, M. (2006). An integrative model of pediatric medical traumatic stress. *Journal of Pediatric Psychology, 31*(4), 343–355.

Kazak, A. E., Rourke, M. T., Alderfer, M. A., Pai, A., Reilly, A. F., & Meadows, A. T. (2007). Evidence-based assessment, intervention, and psychosocial care in pediatric oncology: A blueprint for comprehensive services across treatment. *Journal of Pediatric Psychology, 32*(9), 1099–1110.

Kazak, A. E., Simms, S., & Rourke, M. T. (2002). Family systems practice in pediatric oncology. *Journal of Pediatric Psychology, 27*(2), 133–143.

Lafond, D. A., Rood, B. R., Jacobs, S. S., & Reaman, G. H. (2011). Integration of therapeutic and palliative care in pediatric oncology. In J. Wolfe, P. Hinds, & B. Sourkes (Eds.), *Textbook of interdisciplinary pediatric palliative care* (pp. 460–469). Philadelphia, PA: Elsevier Saunders.

Meier, D., & Beresford, L. (2008). The palliative care team. *Journal of Palliative Medicine, 11*(5), 677–681.

National Cancer Institute. (2008). Childhood cancers. Retrieved from www.cancer.gov/cancertopics/factsheet/Sites-Types/childhood

Remke, S. S., & Schermer, M. M. (2012). Team collaboration in pediatric palliative care. *Journal of Social Work in End-of-Life and Palliative Care, 8*(4), 286–296.

Robert, R., Zhukovsky, D. S., Mauricio, R., Gilmore, K., Morrison, S., & Palos, G. R. (2012). Bereaved parents' perspectives on pediatric palliative care. *Journal of Social Work in End-of-Life and Palliative Care, 8*(4), 316–338.

Wolfe, J., Klar, N., Holcomb, E. G., Duncan, J., Salem-Schatz, S., Emanuel, E., & Weeks, J. C. (2000). Understanding of prognosis among parents whose child died of cancer: Impact on treatment goals and integration of palliative care. *Journal of the American Medical Association, 284*(19), 2469.

XII

Impact of a Cancer Diagnosis Across the Adult Life Span

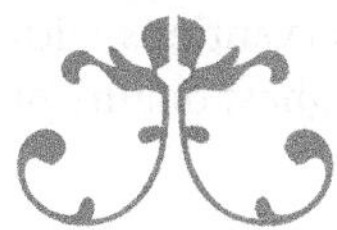

Tara Schapmire

At different phases of adult development, there are specific medical and psychosocial challenges for both patients and their families living with cancer. This section explores the variations in how cancer impacts adults in three different age groupings: young adults (20 to 39 years), middle-aged adults (40 to 64 years), and older adults (65 and older).

In "Young Adults (20 to 39) With Cancer," Sage Bolte reminds us that although the rate of increase in long-term survivorship in young adults is not as high as it is in older and pediatric age groups, many young adults are living longer with their disease controlled or cured than has occurred in previous decades. A cancer diagnosis and/or treatment in young adults may cause an interruption to the normative development of identity, autonomy, the search for a worldview and spiritual exploration, interpersonal functioning, and sexual health. Young adults with cancer are at risk for high levels of psychological distress, including anxiety and depression, which may lead to functional impairments. Serious illnesses of any kind are not expected or normative in this age group. Many have difficulty adhering to the complex treatment plans that a cancer diagnosis may involve. Interventions require effective engagement with the young adult patient and his or her family, anticipation of developmental needs and mental health challenges, and provision of a survivorship care plan that supports adherence and surveillance and ensures accessible psychosocial supports and resources over time.

In "Parents of Younger Adults With Cancer," Susan Hedlund advocates for expanded recognition of the support needs of parents of older adolescents and younger adults with cancer. They experience their own fears and losses as they return to more intense parenting at a time when they are ready to release their child into adulthood and independence. Hedlund describes knowledge and skills oncology social workers can use to help patients and families understand both developmental and disease-related needs, negotiate relational boundaries, determine how and when to offer help, support treatment adherence, learn gratifying ways to interact with each other, obtain up-to-date disease and treatment information, and effectively communicate with members of the health care team.

In "Cancer and Middle-Aged Adults (40 to 64)," Cindy Davis and Connie Rust describe this period of life as a time when individuals have many family, work, and social responsibilities and activities. Interruptions in these activities can be practically and emotionally challenging because they represent primary areas of identity, achievement, life satisfaction, and economic capacity. Oncology social workers normalize patient and family reactions to these losses and help them explore employment rights, medical coverage options, and financial and other resource supports. Family members of middle-aged adults also need support to provide caregiving tasks for the patient and to realign and reassign family roles, responsibilities, and resources as required.

In "Cancer and Older Adults (65 Plus)," Tara Schapmire and Anna Faul suggest interventions for oncology social workers who work with this age group that is most impacted by cancer. The risk of developing cancer nearly doubles after the age of 70 (American Cancer Society, 2012). They describe the common developmentally related issues for older adults using a modified model of Maslow's hierarchy of needs. It provides a useful framework to organize and prioritize assessment and interventions for their often complex needs. These include (1) physiological needs related to comorbidities, symptom management, and increased functional impairment and disability; (2) safety needs related to internal psychological problems such as depression and/or optimism, as well as external resource needs; (3) love and belonging needs created by a more limited network of family and friends who are accessible; (4) self-esteem needs related to a lack of self-efficacy and a need to restore self-enhancing cognitions; and (5) self-actualization needs that are helped by a process of life affirmation and transcendence.

In "Working With Families of Older Adults With Cancer," Daniel S. Gardner reviews the rapidly expanding literature on the needs of families caring for the growing population of older adults diagnosed and living with cancer, as well as the evidence-based interventions that may help them. He confronts the fact that spouses and adult children—typically wives and daughters, who most often assume primary caregiving responsibilities for older family members—are largely unreimbursed for their efforts. They help older people cope with cancer and treatment, avoid unnecessary hospitalizations, and live independently in the community. Many promising interventions for family caregivers of older adults are being evaluated by oncology social workers and nurses, such as telehealth and Web-based groups aimed to reduce symptom burden and social isolation, as well as home-based exercise and nutrition interventions that help improve functioning, prevent falls, and reduce readmissions.

Oncology social workers are critical in the provision of high-quality, developmentally informed, and family-centered interdisciplinary biopsychosocial care to adult patients and their families across the continuum of care. Knowledge of normative reactions at different phases in the adult life span facilitates more focused and informative assessments and the development of more targeted and effective interventions to meet their needs. Appropriately disseminated, it also enhances interdisciplinary understanding of the variations in patients' responses. True family-centered, interdisciplinary practice is recommended as a guiding framework for all interventions with adults with cancer in order to achieve the highest quality of patient- and family-centered care.

REFERENCE

American Cancer Society. (2012). *Cancer facts and figures 2012*. Atlanta, GA: Author.

69 Sage Bolte

Young Adults (20 to 39) with Cancer

Key Concepts

- *Although the rate of survivorship in young adults is not as high as in other populations, many are living longer with or surviving cancer.*
- *A cancer diagnosis and/or treatments in young adults may cause an interruption to the normative issues of identity development, autonomy, the search for a worldview and spiritual exploration, interpersonal functioning, sexual health, and expression of sexual orientation.*
- *Young adults with cancer have a greater risk of mental health conditions than older cancer patients.*
- *Interventions require effective engagement with the young adult patient and his or her family, anticipation of developmental and mental health challenges, and provision of a survivorship care plan that supports adherence and surveillance and ensures accessible individual, group, and resource interventions.*

"I thought I was just stressed out," reported "Anna" as she described her disbelief upon learning she had colon cancer. Reflecting upon the earlier, ignored symptoms, she said, "I thought I wasn't getting enough sleep, was working too much, and wasn't eating and drinking well. I never in a million years thought it was cancer."

At age 28, Anna is facing issues that many under age 60 have not yet had to confront, including the possible loss of fertility, body image changes, interruption in career plans, and challenges within her social life, to name a few. Anna is faced with the sheer reality that she is "vulnerable and not invincible," and her story is not uncommon. She is one of the more than 70,000 young adults each year who experience shock and disbelief over a cancer diagnosis.

Unfortunately, young adults' survivorship rates are not increasing at the same rate as those of their older and younger counterparts. However, issues of survivorship (both for those living with advanced disease and those who have completed treatment) and other biopsychosocial-spiritual factors in this population present an opportunity for oncology social workers to make a difference. Although much of the data on young adults have examined those diagnosed between the ages of 15 and 39, this chapter will focus on the biopsychosocial-spiritual needs of, and interventions for, those diagnosed between the ages of 18 and 39.

Review of Literature

Facts and Figures

Over 70,000 young adults between the ages of 18 and 39 are diagnosed with cancer in the United States each year. They are eight times more likely to be diagnosed with cancer than their younger counterparts and have lower survivorship rates (Bleyer, O'Leary, Barr, & Ries, 2006). Still, long-term cancer survivorship is on the rise, and greater than 60% of adult oncology patients are expected to live 5 or more years after diagnosis (American Cancer Society, 2012). And although young adults' survivorship rates are not increasing at the same speed, many are living longer with or surviving cancer. As a result, the biopsychosocial-spiritual long-term and late effects of treatment are now beginning to be recognized in young adult cancer survivors. The National Cancer Institute (NCI) reports late effects as health problems that appear months to years after cancer treatments are completed. They can include both physical and mental effects, as well as secondary cancers (NCI, n.d.). Late effects, such as heart problems or heart failure, hearing changes/loss, chronic fatigue, early menopause, infertility, increased risk of osteoporosis, cognitive impairments, and secondary cancers, have been identified in adolescent and young adult cancer survivors (AYAOPRG, 2006; Evan, Kaufman, Cook, & Zeltzer, 2006; Zebrack, Bleyer, Albritton, Medearis, & Tang, 2006). Psychosocial-spiritual late effects have been mostly explored in the middle-adult population, with limited literature about young adults' psychosocial-spiritual long-term well-being. However, changes in perceptions of body image and self-esteem, relationship and social development issues, employment and insurance challenges, and issues around ongoing communication with medical professionals and the community have been identified (Elad, Yagil, Cohen, & Meller, 2003; Evan & Zeltzer, 2006; Zebrack et al., 2006).

The distribution of cancer diagnoses faced by young adults differs from that of the pediatric and adult oncology populations. Hodgkin and non-Hodgkin lymphoma, melanoma, testicular cancer, female genital tract malignancies, thyroid cancer, soft tissue and bone sarcomas, leukemia, brain and spinal cord tumors, breast cancer, and nongonadal germ cell tumors account for 95% of all young adult cancers (Hayes-Lattin, 2013; Soliman & Agresta, 2008).

Unique Factors and Specific Issues in Young Adults

Developmental Milestones

All persons come to the cancer experience with their own biopsychosocial-spiritual histories and interpersonal resources, which directly and indirectly influence the way they make sense of and cope with a diagnosis. Young adulthood is typically a time of major changes, stress, and exploration that can confound a young adult cancer survivor's developmental experience (Bolte, 2010; Bolte & Zebrack, 2008; Zebrack, 2008). Additionally, young adults are also managing "the delicate interplay of physical, psychological, and interpersonal factors... [and] must tackle normative development issues and treatment-related challenges" (Olivo & Woolverton, 2001, p. 172). A cancer diagnosis and/or the ensuing treatments may cause interruption to the normative developmental issues of identity development, autonomy, the search for a worldview and spiritual exploration, interpersonal functioning, sexual health, and the exploration of sexual orientation (Bolte, 2010; Olivo & Woolverton, 2001; Roberts, Turney, & Knowles, 1998; Stern, Norman, & Zevon, 1993; Zebrack, 2008).

Psychosocial-Spiritual Adjustments

Young adults face multiple psychosocial adjustments, growths, and challenges, such as separating and developing independence, building relationships, starting a career, and so on. Johnson reports that young adults have an

> *increased risk of suicidal thoughts and a higher risk of depression related to chronic health conditions that affect quality of life. About 16% of young adult survivors face post-traumatic stress disorder. Treatment and subsequent chemobrain—attention and cognitive function declines—affect reentry into social circles, school and/or the workforce.*
>
> —*Johnson, 2012, para. 7*

Costanzo, Ryff, and Singer (2009) reported that mental health, mood, and psychological well-being issues, along with pre- to postdiagnostic increases in mental health symptoms, were higher and more evident in younger cancer survivors. Young adults may "also have greater demands in the areas of work or parenting and fewer coping resources, which make contending with cancer particularly stressful" (Costanzo et al., 2009, p. 147). Imagine the challenges that a young adult may face if he or she has to drop out of school and return home to receive the appropriate treatments and caregiving. In addition to isolating him or her from peers, this decision would delay short- and long-term goals. A regression in developing autonomy may also occur secondary to the need to once again be dependent upon the care of a parent/family member. Additionally, the parent(s) may begin to treat the young adult as a young child, creating greater dependence and possible animosity.

One must also recognize that young adults may have begun to develop their own spirituality, in addition to the normal development of interpersonal and social relationships. As mentioned in other chapters, "spirituality" is a broad term and could mean anything from the belief in a higher power to the connection with nature to the meaning and purpose one derives from being with his or her family. One young man told me, "I am so tired of my family and friends challenging my belief in God. Who cares if I believe that a miracle is possible? Who cares if my belief has grown since I was diagnosed? . . . Why does it matter to them? . . . Don't you think they should just be supportive?"

The search for meaning (i.e., how one makes sense of a cancer diagnosis and all of its implications) is an important part of any psychosocial-spiritual assessment. This may be especially true for the young adult who is just exploring a new faith or spirituality. On the one hand, his or her spiritual self may be fragile and shatter from the many challenges and even joys that can occur after a diagnosis. On the other hand, his or her spiritual self might be strengthened and be a strong resource during the ups and downs of survivorship. One of our roles as oncology social workers is to offer the young adult permission to "be with and sit with" his or her spiritual self and to encourage its growth as a resource during and after treatments. Sometimes, the conversation may be started by simply posing a question, such as "When someone is diagnosed with cancer, it often raises a lot of questions, some of which you may or may not be able to answer. Some may believe that there is a reason or purpose for their diagnosis. Others may believe that there was just a cell that went rogue and now they have cancer. How are you making sense of or meaning out of your diagnosis?" Or it may be simpler, such as "What gets you up in the morning?" I once asked this of a young adult and she jokingly said, "my nausea." We both laughed and it segued into an easy conversation about how frustrating it can be to manage all the side effects and what resources she enlisted to find strength, including the belief in a higher power.

Relationships and Sense of Self

Interpersonal relationships and the development of close and intimate relationships, including spiritual relationships, are critical to the young adult's development of a sense of self and support resources. Young adult patients often report sentiments such as "My friends just don't get it" or "They've completely disappeared" or "They ignore the cancer, don't even talk about it, and want me to be the same person I was." Not being understood by their peers (and family members) may increase social isolation and influence whether they participate in normal and age-appropriate activities, such as sexual experimentation/exploration, living independently, exploring various career options, and developing or deepening intimacy (Bolte, 2010). Young adulthood is a "time of increased vulnerability and stress" (Zebrack, 2008, p. 1353), which could present these survivors with major developmental milestone challenges beyond those faced by their peers (Bolte, 2010; Evan et al., 2006; Lock, 1998; Zebrack, 2008).

The alienation from peers might also negatively contribute to the way a young adult views him- or herself. Alienation might include relationships that have been challenged or changed while the young adult is in treatment, but might also include the alienation he or she might unintentionally create after treatment when meeting new people or reintegrating into life. This isolation may be created by the fear of how people will react to his or her cancer story, not knowing what to say or how to tell the story, having lower self-esteem, or having physical effects that keep him or her from being able to engage in some common peer activities. This might be especially true for the young adult with advanced disease or one who has several long-term effects that continue to impact day-to-day living (e.g., chronic pain, fatigue, graft-versus-host disease).

Clinical interventions grounded in social work practice theories will assist in increasing young adult patients' (and loved ones') abilities to cope with the challenges and changes they face. Young adults need to be provided with a place to talk about their thoughts and feelings of isolation, frustration, gratitude, fears, hopes, and so on. It is also important to normalize and validate their experiences with statements such as "Many of my young adult patients report similar experiences, hopes, and frustrations, and often find it helpful to connect to other peers who 'get it.'" The social worker should connect them and their loved ones to a face-to-face support group, an online support group, a peer-to-peer matching organization, other support resources offered locally or nationally, or additional counseling if long-term therapeutic interventions are needed (see Additional Resources and the end of this chapter).

One 19-year-old survivor of non-Hodgkin lymphoma reported in research conducted by Olivo and Woolverton (2001):

> *My last chemo did not mark the end of my medical problems. . . . After the treatment was over, my counts stayed suppressed for months. I was tired all the time and short of breath. Before my diagnosis, I was hoping to be a ballplayer. For a long time afterwards, sports were impossible for me to do. Now I still feel like I'm a little old man or something. And who knows what will go wrong in the future? (p. 174)*

In addition to muddling through the management of long-term effects of the illness, this young adult also saw himself as an "old man." Negative thoughts about oneself may lead to a decrease in self-esteem, sexual esteem, and a willingness to share or make oneself emotionally vulnerable in dating situations. How a young adult views his or her physical self typically affects self-esteem or a sense of liking oneself (Magill & Hurlbut, 1986). While exploring adolescent cancer survivors' body image and social adjustment, Pendley, Dahlquist, and Dreyer (1997) realized that cancer survivors did not differ from their healthy peers in social anxiety, loneliness, or composite body image scores. However, the survivors who were further out from treatment reported higher social anxiety, lower feelings of self-worth, and a greater negative body image. Interestingly, the survivors' ratings of their attractiveness were not any lower than those of their peers. These findings suggest that body image concerns and social anxiety may not develop in younger patients until years after finishing treatment, secondary to the various interruptions to "normal" developmental experiences. The same may be true for young adults, because their developmental norms and milestones may be rudely interrupted with treatment, side effects, and life changes forced by their diagnosis. The role of the oncology social worker is critical in assessing, identifying, and treating young adult cancer survivors' various biopsychosocial-spiritual issues (Bolte, 2010).

A single young adult may face relationship difficulties, but the young adult who has a partner needs to acknowledge the very real challenges that affect the partner. Although the issues of young partners may not be that different from those of their older cohorts, it is important to recognize that they may experience these issues differently. Young partners may have wanted children and are now faced with the very real possibility that the partner may not be able to conceive or bear a child. The couple may not have been prepared to face the financial burdens and demands of treatment and caregiving. Additionally, the reality of needing to plan for long-term effects may be lost to the more immediate threat of the mother-in-law who moves into their one-bedroom apartment to help take care of her son. The partner may be bothered by thoughts or questions—for example, "This isn't what I signed up for"; "I'm not sure I can live the rest of my life and not have children"; or "I don't feel like I have a say in any of this and that your parents are the ones making the decisions that impact us." Although these issues are not unique, the experiences of a couple in their early 30s will be very different from those of a couple in their 60s.

Insurance, Financial, and Medical Needs

Even with changes in health care policy, the young adult population is one of the most under- and uninsured populations in the United States. A variety of factors may be causing the lack or absence of coverage: being in between insurance plans because of a leave from college or a job change; aging out of parental insurance plans; opting out of coverage to save money; and finding it difficult to find affordable insurance because of previous illnesses, such as childhood cancer. Lack of adequate medical insurance makes it more challenging to obtain treatment and adds to higher death rates (Johnson, 2012). Fewer financial resources often result in a late diagnosis, decreased access to clinical trials, and poor follow-up care. With the Affordable Health Care Act, some of these expenses may be alleviated; however, expenses such as rent, utilities, medical bills, and private insurance plans may continue to impede treatment.

Seeking employment both during and after a cancer diagnosis can be problematic. Many young adults experience concerns about how to explain the gap in employment while they were undergoing treatment, whether they have to disclose their cancer history to current or future employers, and fears of "being stuck" in a current job because they need the insurance coverage. Organizations such as Cancer and Careers, Patient Advocate Foundation, and Cancer Legal Resource Center were created to help people identify ways to advocate for their rights to coverage, as well as reintegrate into the workforce during and after a cancer diagnosis. Young adults need help to identify professionals who are experts in finances and appealing denials of coverage and knowledgeable about patients' legal rights.

Survivorship Issues

Issues of survivorship (i.e., after treatment has finished or for someone who is living with advanced disease) have been mentioned throughout this book. The following section will briefly highlight areas of highest biopsychosocial-spiritual risk for young adults and include guides for assessment and intervention.

Posttraumatic Stress Disorder and Distress Risks

There is limited research on posttraumatic stress disorder (PTSD) among those diagnosed with cancer between the ages of 18 and 40. There are, however, growing data on PTSD in those who were diagnosed with cancer as children or in adulthood; these data may contribute to our understanding of the young adult's experience. Some studies have indicated that younger age, lower income, and less education are risk factors for PTSD (Cordova, Studts, Hann, Jacobsen, & Andrykowski, 2000; Rourke, Hobbie, Schwartz, & Kazak, 2007). The NCI's Physician Data Query (PDQ) on "Post-Traumatic Stress Disorder" (2013) reports that several variables have been shown to predict PTSD in survivors: more advanced disease, a longer hospital stay, and duration and intensity of treatment (as opposed to time since treatment; Weiner et al., 2006).

Oncology social workers need to be aware of risk factors and warning signs to appropriately address traumatic reminders that produce symptoms of unhelpful avoidance of positive activities and experiences, isolation, hyperarousal, or heightened anxiety, and emotional states that impede sleep, work, and productive activities. Interventions such as relaxation, desensitization, and other cognitive behavioral interventions and medications have been effective.

Long-Term Effects and Secondary Risks

Long-term and/or late effects of treatments are just beginning to be identified as numbers of survivors increase. Late effects, such as cardiovascular symptoms, fatigue, pain, and neurocognitive effects ("chemobrain"), continue to interfere with quality of life long after treatments are complete (Tai et al., 2012). A few of these long-term and/or late effects are discussed here.

Infertility

Infertility affects both male and female cancer patients during their reproductive years (up to age 45) and is a common side effect of chemotherapies (especially alkylating or platinum-based treatments), surgery, and radiation.

Knowledge about infertility and options for fertility preservation are still poorly shared with cancer patients before the start of treatment, with physicians citing lack of time, lack of knowledge, and low comfort levels with these discussions (Johnson & Kroon, 2013). The loss associated with infertility is very real, and preservation options should be presented to patients when they are diagnosed. Providing resources *before* treatments affords the patient some sense of control over decisions about fertility preservation and may decrease distress (see LIVE**STRONG**, n.d., for additional information). Patients may be helped by resources such as Fertile Hope or by utilizing the iSaveFertility app to obtain support and information on fertility preservation options. It is critical to provide resources and information to all patients, regardless of age, gender, and relationship status.

Hormonal Changes

A change in hormones is not uncommon, especially in young adults who have had high-dose chemotherapy, radiation to the gonads or pelvic region, removal of the ovaries, and/or stem cell or bone marrow transplants. Young women may be put into an early or medically induced menopause. Side effects such as hot flashes, weight gain, mood fluctuations, skin changes, vaginal dryness, and changes in vaginal integrity, including atrophy and stenosis, are possible (see Chapter 34). Hormone changes in young survivors can also affect mood, weight gain, memory loss, and a decrease in sex drive. All of these changes are contrary to the desires of most young adults (e.g., healthy sex drive, healthy weight, energy, and a strong memory needed for school, dating, and a career).

Adherence: Keeping Young Adults Engaged

Adherence can be challenging for young adults because they face so many common environmental/social challenges. Young adults are quite often transient, experience multiple life changes, and may have a variety of caregivers involved in their care during treatment (rather than one designated caregiver). These caregivers may or may not be involved in the young adult's aftercare or long-term follow-up. The inherent nature of being a young adult with its accompanying life changes makes it challenging for medical staff to keep in touch with patients once they have completed treatment. Keeping a point of contact (e.g., parent or family member whose residence will most likely stay the same) may assist the team in reaching the patient for needed follow-up procedures. Adherence to follow-up treatments and protocols may also be improved by having a survivorship care plan in place at the beginning and upon completion of treatment. The survivorship care plan should include the following minimum elements:

- A brief history of diagnosis and treatments received
- Follow-up treatment recommendations
- Dates of scheduled appointments
- Contact information for both the young adult and any health care provider to whom he or she may transfer care

This information should be placed in a designated survivorship care plan folder, put on a USB drive, and/or sent to the patient via e-mail to reduce chances of loss. Another way to increase adherence is to send e-mail and/or text reminders through the hospital system about important follow-up procedures or appointments. Finding effective ways of communication is as critical to success in working with the young adult population as it is with their older and younger counterparts.

Quick Tips on What Young Adults Want/Need From Oncology Social Workers

- *Young adults want information on disease, treatments, and what to expect before, during, and after treatment.*
- *Speak their language; do not use medical jargon.*
- *Find creative ways to communicate with young adults:*
  - *Provide multiple ways to access information on disease and treatment: websites, e-mail contacts, books, blogs, peer support/referral.*
  - *Find alternative modes of communication (e.g., social media, texting, treatment or side effect reporting apps) to keep them engaged.*
  - *Provide them with e-mail/text points of contact to your team (if appropriate), but be clear about expectations for returning e-mail and response time.*
  - *Utilize social networking for your institution and possibly a separate platform just for young adults.*
  - *If you have the option and team members feel comfortable giving out their cell phone number, text patients to remind them of treatment times, symptoms/side effects they should be alert to, and so on. Although you need to set clear boundaries on the use of texting and its purpose, it can be a good resource.*
- *Be aware of treatment time to improve compliance (e.g., it's probably best not to schedule a 9:00 a.m. treatment time for a 20-year-old college student unless he or she requests it).*
- *Connect them with peers who "get it," either through peer support networks such as Imerman Angels or through a buddy-matching system in your hospital system.*
- *Start a young adult group or refer to a young adult group (ages 18 to 40). It helps if you can find one or two young adults who are willing to be group "champions" and reach out to the other survivors. Or start a local social media page (e.g., Facebook) for local young adult survivors so they can virtually connect.*
- *Host a meeting once or twice a month at a restaurant, community center, campus, or other location outside the hospital.*
- *Acknowledge the emotional and physical implications of "life getting turned upside down."*

- *Assess psychosocial-spiritual well-being at regular intervals or as indicated.*
- *Normalize the emotional, mental, and spiritual challenges that young adults face.*
- *Develop a treatment plan to address these concerns and make referrals to appropriate internal or external resources for further support and psychiatric evaluation if needed.*
- *Have a list of community resources and professionals that are comfortable working with the young adult survivor population:*
    - *Gynecologists/endocrinologists/urologists/psychiatrists*
    - *Counselors/therapists*
    - *Websites and resources both local and national*
    - *Survivorship care plan(s)*

Pearls

- The diagnosis of cancer in early adulthood is untimely and challenges developmental progression, adaptation, and self-esteem in ways that require making group, individual, and programmatic interventions readily accessible to ensure physical and psychosocial recovery over the short and long term.
- Young adults with cancer experience higher risks of mental health symptoms, including anxiety, depression, PTSD, and suicidal thinking, than do older cancer patients. These symptoms in younger adults appear to be related to advanced disease, longer hospital stay, duration/intensity of treatment, lower income, and less education.

Pitfalls

- Failing to effectively engage and follow up with young adult cancer patients and their families with appropriate and accessible individual and group interventions, resources, and referrals may limit their long-term adaptation.
- The initiation of timely interventions may be limited if one underestimates the intensity of reactions and challenges to functioning of young adults diagnosed with cancer and undergoing treatment over the long term.

Young adults diagnosed with cancer between the ages of 18 and 39 have unique and specific biopsychosocial-spiritual issues that can impact diagnosis, treatment, and follow-up care. More young adults are being diagnosed with cancer and general survivorship rates are rising. As a result, health care providers are encouraged to stop, think, and evaluate best practices for treating and providing follow-up care to the young adult population. Oncology social workers can help care for young adults and enhance their quality of life by providing relevant information and resources (see Additional Resources), education, counseling support, and advocacy.

ADDITIONAL RESOURCES

Cancer*Care*: http://www.cancercare.org/tagged/young_adults
Fertile HOPE: http://www.fertilehope.org
Imerman Angels: http://www.imermanangels.org/
Lance Armstrong Foundation, LIVE**STRONG**: http://www.livestrong.org/
Leukemia Lymphoma Society online professionally moderated chat, YA Connect: http://www.lls.org/diseaseinformation/managingyourcancer/newlydiagnosed/teensyoungadults/
Outdoor adventures for young adults: https://firstdescents.org/ and http://www.athletes4cancer.org/
Planet Cancer: http://myplanet.planetcancer.org/
Stupid Cancer: http://www.stupidcancer.org
Young Survival Coalition (for women with a breast cancer diagnosis): http://www.youngsurvival.org

Advocacy Resources

Employment issues: http://www.CancerandCareers.org
Financial resources: http://www.thesamfund.org
Insurance and healthcare access: http://www.Patientadvocate.org
iTunes app: iSaveFertility (free from iTunes store)
Legal rights: http://www.disabilityrightslegalcenter.org/cancer-legal-resource-center

Books

Rosenthal, K. (2009). *Everything changes: The insiders' guide to cancer in your 20's and 30's.* Hoboken, NJ: Wiley.
Schultz-Adams, H. (2010). *Planet cancer: The frequently bizarre, yet always informative thoughts of your fellow natives.* Guilford, CT: Lyons Press.

REFERENCES

American Cancer Society. (2012). *Cancer facts & figures 2012.* Atlanta, GA: Author.

Adolescent and Young Adult Oncology Progress Review Group (AYAOPRG). (2006). *Closing the gap: Research and care imperatives for adolescents and young adults with cancer.* Report of the Adolescent and Young Adult Oncology Progress Review Group. Retrieved from http://planning.cancer.gov/library/AYAO_PRG_Report_2006_FINAL.pdf

Bleyer, A., O'Leary, M., Barr, R., & Ries, L. A. G. (Eds.). (2006). *Cancer epidemiology in older adolescents and young adults 15 to 29 years of age, including SEER incidence and survival: 1975–2000* (p. 179). Retrieved from http://seer.cancer.gov/archive/publications/aya/aya_mono_complete.pdf

Bolte, S. (2010). *The impact of cancer and its treatments on the sexual self of young adult cancer survivors as compared to their healthy peers.* Retrieved from Washington Research Library Consortium, http://hdl.handle.net/1961/9180

Bolte, S., & Zebrack, B. (2008). Sexual issues in special populations: Adolescents and young adults. *Seminars in Oncology Nursing, 24*(2), 115–119.

Cordova, M. J., Studts, J. L., Hann, D. M., Jacobsen, P. B., & Andrykowski, M. A. (2000). Symptom structure of PTSD following breast cancer. *Journal of Traumatic Stress, 13*, 301–319.

Costanzo, E., Ryff, C., & Singer, B. (2009). Psychosocial adjustment among cancer survivors: Findings from a national survey of health and well-being. *Healthy Psychology, 26*(2), 147–156.

Elad, P., Yagil, Y., Cohen, L., & Meller, I. (2003). A jeep trip with young adult cancer survivors. *Supportive Care in Cancer, 11*(4), 201–206.

Evan, E., & Zeltzer, L. (2006). Psychosocial dimensions of cancer in adolescents and young adults. *Cancer, 107*(7), 1663–1671.

Evan, E., Kaufman, M., Cook, A., & Zeltzer, L. (2006). Sexual health and self-esteem in adolescents and young adults with cancer. *Cancer, 107*(7), 1672–1679.

Hayes-Lattin, B. (2013). Graphs created from SEER data US incidences of cancer ages 15–39, sorted by gender. Retrieved from http://www.iom.edu/Reports/2013/Identifying-and-Addressing-the-Needs-of-Adolescents-and-Young-Adults-with-Cancer.aspx

Johnson, R. (2012). Issues facing young adult cancer survivors: Frequently asked questions. Fred Hutchinson Research Cancer Center. Retrieved from http://www.fhcrc.org/en/treatment/survivorship/survival-strategies/young-adult-survivors.html

Johnson, R. H., & Kroon, L. (2013). Optimizing fertility preservation practices for adolescents and young adult cancer patients. *Journal of the National Comprehensive Cancer Network, 11*(1), 71–77.

LIVE**STRONG**. (n.d.). Fertile hope. Retrieved from http://www.fertilehope.org/healthcare-professionals/index.cfm

Lock, J. (1998). Psychosexual development in adolescents with chronic illness. *Psychosomatics, 39*, 340–349.

Magill, J., & Hurlbut, N. (1986). The self-esteem of adolescents with cerebral palsy. *American Journal of Occupational Therapy, 40*, 402–407.

National Cancer Institute. (2013). Post-traumatic stress disorder: PDQ®. Bethesda, MD: Author. Retrieved from http://www.cancer.gov/cancertopics/pdq/supportivecare/post-traumatic-stress/Patient/page1

National Cancer Institute. (n.d.). *NCI dictionary of cancer terms*. Retrieved from http://www.cancer.gov/dictionary/

Olivo, E., & Woolverton, K. (2001). Surviving childhood cancer: Disruptions in the developmental building blocks of sexuality. *Journal of Sex Education and Therapy, 26*(3), 172–181.

Pendley, J. S., Dahlquist, L., & Dreyer, Z. (1997). Body image and psychosocial adjustment in adolescent cancer survivors. *Journal of Pediatric Psychology, 22*(1), 29–43.

Roberts, C. S., Turney, M. E., & Knowles, A. M. (1998). Psychosocial issues of adolescents with cancer. *Social Work in Health Care, 27*, 3–18.

Rourke, M. T., Hobbie, W. L., Schwartz, L., & Kazak, A. E. (2007). Posttraumatic stress disorder (PTSD) in young adult survivors of childhood cancer. *Pediatric Blood and Cancer, 49*, 177–182.

Soliman, H., & Agresta, S. V. (2008). Current issues in adolescent and young adult cancer survivorship. *Cancer Control, 15*(1), 55–62.

Stern, M., Norman, S., & Zevon, M. (1993). Adolescents with cancer: Self-image and perceived social support as indexes of adaptation. *Journal of Adolescent Research, 8*, 124–142.

Tai, E., Buchanan, N., Townsend, J., Fairley, T., Moore, A., & Richardson, L. C. (2012). Health status of adolescent and young adult cancer survivors. *Cancer, 118*(19), 4884–4891. doi:10.1002/cncr.27445

Weiner, L., Battles, H., Bernstein, D., Long, L., Derdak, J., Mackall, C., & Lansky, P. (2006). Persistent psychological distress in long term survivors of pediatric sarcoma: The experience at a single institution. *Psycho-Oncology, 15*, 898–910. doi:10.1002/pon.1024

Zebrack, B. (2008). Information and service needs for young adult cancer patients. *Supportive Care in Cancer, 16*, 1353–1360.

Zebrack, B., Bleyer, A., Albritton, K., Medearis, S., & Tang, J. (2006). Assessing the health care needs of adolescent and young adult cancer patients and survivors. *Cancer, 107*(12), 2915–2923.

70 Parents of Younger Adults With Cancer

Susan Hedlund

Key Concepts

- *Older adolescents and young adults experience developmental disruptions after a cancer diagnosis.*
- *Parents of older adolescents and younger adults with cancer experience their own losses as they return to more intense parenting at a time when they are ready to release their child into adulthood and independence.*
- *Oncology social workers can help parents determine how and when to offer help and help patients and families negotiate relational boundaries, learn effective ways to interact with each other, obtain up-to-date disease and treatment information, and communicate with members of the health care team.*

Each year, more than 70,000 young adults are diagnosed with cancer in the United States. A cancer diagnosis between the ages of 15 and 40 is nearly eight times more common than a diagnosis during the first 15 years of life. Young adults encounter an unequal burden of cancer in spite of advances in treatment, detection, and prevention (Bleyer, O'Leary, Barr, & Ries, 2006; Bleyer, Viny, & Barrm, 2006). Although survival rates are improving for both younger and older patients, the rates for older adolescents and younger adults have not improved and the gap is worsening. Today, cancer is the leading disease killer among 20- to 39-year-olds (Bleyer, Viny, et al., 2006).

What We Have Learned So Far

Some of the contextual issues contributing to the lack of improvement in cancer survival in the older adolescent and younger adult population include delays in cancer recognition and diagnosis, lack of adequate health insurance during all phases of diagnosis and treatment, lack of clinical trial participation, biological differences in both the disease and the patient with the disease at this age, and the availability of treatments that are tailored to the biological differences of the older adolescent and younger adult populations. Quality of survival both during and after treatment is a critical issue for older adolescents and young adults. The effects and side effects of treatment are harder for them to cope with. The disease and treatment may compromise or delay independent functioning, career advancement, and fulfillment of family responsibilities, major goals for young adults (Bleyer, Viny, et al., 2006). These issues also affect the parents of adolescents and young adults with cancer. For example, a diagnosis delay may impact an overall prognosis and survival rate, which in turn will have an effect for parents if the young adult has advanced disease at diagnosis. Lack of health insurance may create a financial burden on the family as a whole and is also a worry for parents, as is the uncertainty of treatment, including clinical trial participation.

The literature is sparse concerning the impact on parents and families when an older adolescent or young adult is diagnosed with cancer (Carey, Clinton-McHarg, Sanson-Fisher, &

Shakeshaft, 2012). However, increasingly, the uniqueness of the physical, emotional, and social impact of cancer in this age group is recognized as challenging to families and health care providers. This chapter focuses on the unique issues experienced by the parents of older adolescents and young adults with cancer and how families can be helped to provide support to the patient under these circumstances. Details specific to these patients themselves are covered elsewhere in this *Handbook* (Chapter 69).

Developmental Interruption for Young Adults

When an adolescent or young adult is diagnosed with cancer, their life is disrupted developmentally. For adolescents, the attempt to establish identity can be eclipsed by becoming a cancer patient. Attempts to separate from one's family is virtually impossible if the adolescent is forced to become more dependent on them and is increasingly disconnected from peers as a result of hospitalization, treatment, and being "different" from peers.

For young adults, cancer may disrupt college and/or employment and may force their return to the family home at precisely the time they are trying to establish a life apart from the family. Again, a "disconnect" from peers often occurs as a result, because of both the interruption of plans and the difficulty of fitting in with peers. Some young adults describe feeling "old too soon" and may feel a sense of injustice and anger at being "different." This also has an impact on parents, described next.

Impact on Parents

Family Development Interruption

In families with older adolescents and young adults with cancer, family development is interrupted. In one- or two-parent families, parents' dreams about life without children at home may need to be postponed, when the change in their own independence has only just been reclaimed. The family must reorganize around the demands of treatment. With an adolescent, the parents return to a state of vigilance more common with younger children. The young adult may return to live in the parent's home and both the child and the parents confront new issues of connection versus independence. All these issues exist whether the parents are heterosexual, gay, or lesbian. For single parents, the financial impact and the emotional burden may result in greater isolation from supports. The need for support from family, friends, and professionals in all of these situations cannot be overemphasized.

Carter and McGoldrick (1989) were among the first to describe stages of the family life cycle and note that the stage of "families with adolescents" requires increased flexibility of family boundaries that accommodate children's greater independence, along with parents' refocus on midlife marital and career issues. The stage they describe as "launching children and moving on" entails the acceptance of a multitude of exits from and entries into the family. These transitions are disrupted if an adolescent or young adult is diagnosed with cancer. The "launching" that Carter and McGoldrick described may be reversed with the young adult returning home and/or experiencing a greater level of dependency that is challenging to both the patient and the parents.

Helping Without Unnecessarily Limiting Autonomy

Parents must juggle their own fears and desires to "protect" their older adolescent or young adult with the need to allow the child autonomy in this experience. Zebrack, Mills, and Weitzman (2007) acknowledge the understandable difficulty parents have "letting go" while remaining involved in the cancer experience. Parents must constantly consider their adolescent/young adult's quality of life, both in terms of medical management of the disease and normative developmental tasks. Often one must be sacrificed for the other (Rolland, 1994).

Overprotection of the older adolescent/young adult may be met with resistance or with a return to passive dependency. One young patient, following an arm amputation as a result of a sarcoma, said, "My mom wants to cut up my pizza and feed it to me! I ate pizza one-handed before my surgery. It is maddening. I know she is worried but it makes me feel even more helpless" (personal communication, June 22, 2008). One mother expressed that over time she had learned to sit back and wait until it became clear whether her young adult son with cancer needed help. She said, "I needed to trust that we had raised him well enough that he would tell us when he needed our help. It took a lot of self-restraint on my part, however" (personal communication, May 3, 2012). Many parents have described the optimal approach as moving in with direct assistance when the patient's treatment or condition requires it, but standing back and allowing the young adult to normalize when the "crisis" is passed.

Financial Strain

Considerable financial strain exists for parents who need to assume economic responsibility for their child's needs, particularly if the child lacks health insurance. Some parents assume second mortgages or cash out savings to cover the costs of necessary treatment and support. The family's competing financial demands may also include the costs of education for other siblings at the same time, and thus parents may be faced with difficult decisions and financial reprioritizing within the family (Grinyer & Thomas, 2001).

Long-Term Worries

Additionally, long-term worries continue for parents, even when treatment is complete. One parent said, "Even though Jamie has finished chemo and is cancer free right now, I don't think I will ever be free of the fear that it will return. Any little complaint and my mind immediately goes to that direction" (Care Pages [see Additional Resources at the end of the chapter]). For others, the consequence of treatment results in further medical issues: "It has been a very long road through treatment and a bone marrow transplant with two life-threatening scares. He is now 20 and is facing a heart transplant due to the damage of chemotherapy. So our fight continues" (Care Pages).

Parents experience a possible threat to their dreams of their young adult's capacities and functioning beyond their own lives, with feelings of disappointment and sadness. Some young adults describe needing to distance themselves from parents to avoid seeing this sadness in their eyes. They often find satisfaction, distraction, and pleasure in pursuing developmentally normative tasks, connecting with peers, working, and completing an education.

Impact on Siblings

Another aspect for parents is the impact of the young adult's illness on siblings and the challenge for parents to juggle the needs of the entire family. Siblings of adolescents or young adults with cancer, not unlike the siblings of young children with cancer, may find that their own needs are postponed (i.e., placed on the "back burner") as a result of the urgency of the sick sibling's situation. It is not uncommon for siblings to feel like forgotten family members. Brothers or sisters may feel resentment about the family interruption or may feel some degree of guilt for their own health. Some siblings respond by assuming parental responsibilities, or they may attempt to become "perfect" to reduce their parents' anxiety and worry. In other families, the healthy brother or sister may gradually withdraw, spending more time away from home and the family. Parents preoccupied with worry about the sick child may or may not notice changing behaviors of the siblings. Attention to the impact of the adolescent/young adult's illness on the entire family system is imperative to prevent deterioration of the family unit.

Impact on Parents' Relationship to Each Other

The impact of a child's illness on a parental couple is never easy. Some couples may emerge strengthened as a result of the family crisis and find a fortified bond as they focus on the goal of healing the sick child. For couples who may have already had a strained relationship or who may no longer be together, the impact of an adolescent or young adult's illness may add to what was already a difficult relationship. Previous strain or conflict within their relationship may become displaced by focus on the ill child, which increases family dysfunction. In such cases, an oncology social worker can function as a mediator to help negotiate decision making in important areas of treatment, the child's autonomy, and family roles.

Jessica, 24, had completed her master's degree in communication; had a new, well-paying job; and had relocated to a different city to work in the broadcast business. She was at the "top of her game" when she was diagnosed with Hodgkin lymphoma. The rigors and side effects of treatment were enough that she had to quit her job. Her payments to maintain her health insurance took all of her savings. She felt her only option was to move back in with her parents. Although grateful to have her near and to be able to support her during treatment, Jessica's parents, whose marriage was just beginning to reconnect after years of emotional distance, felt the stress of having the healing process for the marriage disrupted. At the same time, they were worried about Jessica's continued health.

Jessica, who had left her new job and new friends behind, attempted to reconnect with her hometown friends. Most of them were married, having children, and moving on. "I have absolutely nothing in common with them. No one can handle talking about cancer, and I can't relate to them," Jessica said. Both Jessica and her parents felt lost and unsure of how to plan for the next chapter in their lives.

The family was referred to an oncology social worker in the cancer center in the community where they lived. After evaluation and assessment of the current stressors for Jessica and her family, Jessica was encouraged to attend a support group for adolescents and young adults that met twice a month at the cancer center. There she met other young men and women who were in similar circumstances, with similar concerns. After attending the group several times, Jessica reported feeling less alone and feeling understood by this new group of peers.

Jessica's parents were encouraged to see a social worker who specialized in marital therapy to help them continue rebuilding their marriage and develop new communication skills and mutual support. The social worker also encourage them to make time for themselves as a couple as part of this process while remaining supportive of their daughter.

Parent Involvement in Decision Making

In addition to the aforementioned needs and concerns, issues regarding involvement in medical decision making become complex when the patient is an older adolescent or young adult. The question of "Who owns the knowledge?"

has been posed by Grinyer (2002). Young adults are legally entitled to be the recipient of medical information and may or may not choose to share this information with their parents. Grinyer reports that mothers, in particular, feel excluded when asked to stay in the waiting room (Grinyer, 2002). Although the need for independence among young adults is understandable, when the diagnosis is or may be cancer related, exclusion can be particularly difficult for parents. Such a situation will almost certainly result in parental reinvolvement, or at least an attempt at reinvolvement, with health-related decisions.

Parents' concerns may be seen as interference and a source of irritation by young adults and the health care team. Young adults may struggle to take their parents' concerns seriously when the parents worry that something is wrong. Parents worry that their child lacks the experience to know whether he or she is receiving good medical care. And indeed, most young adults have had no training in communicating with doctors or health professionals, providing information, and negotiating health care systems. Some parents have reported confusion whether to view their young adult children as adults or children, and they observe that medical professionals sometimes seem equally confused (Grinyer, 2002). The reality is that oscillation between the two approaches is often required. Medical professionals' strict adherence to confidentiality standards may further exclude parents and not be easily understood by families.

Although parents may not be included in decision making, they are often left to pick up the pieces in the aftermath of their young adult child's decisions. A skilled oncology social worker can help parents educate their young adult child about ways to communicate with health professionals and negotiate with their child around what are perceived as boundary violations by either the parent or the young adult.

Young, Married Adults

Young adults who are married face additional challenges as they negotiate the dynamics of treatment, a relatively new marriage, and relationships with their spouse, parents, and extended family and sometimes young children of their own. If the relationships are relatively open and mutually respectful, the role of the spouse and the role of the parents can be integrated as they take turns offering support and involvement with the young adult patient. If, however, the new spouse has not yet established his or her relationship with the patient's parents, it can be challenging to determine what boundaries should and do exist. Unfortunately, there may be times when the newer spouse feels shut out by the parents who are trying to support and protect the patient, and/or the parents may resent the role and decision-making involvement that the newer spouse has with the patient. Again, the family can be helped by acknowledging these stresses and related emotions and finding ways to negotiate roles, boundaries, and relationships that support the young adult and his or her own family during the cancer experience.

Implications for Practice

Because this is a relatively new area of study of psychosocial oncology practice, much more needs to be understood in terms of the clinical ramifications and practice approaches that may be most helpful to adolescents and young adults with cancer and their parents and families. What is clear is that cancer at this life stage is perceived as profoundly unfair and imposes developmental interruptions for all involved. Specific interventions should focus on determining appropriate levels of direct assistance when needed and standing back to permit autonomy and developmental normalcy when the demands of the cancer diagnosis and treatment in an adolescent or young adult permit.

Emerging literature suggests that adolescents and young adults long for affiliation with like-affected peers; thus, activities such as young survivor support groups, social events, and camp/retreat offerings provide patients an opportunity to affiliate with those in their own age groups who have had similar experiences. Age-appropriate information, counseling, being responsible for one's own health care decision making, and peer support are paramount (Zebrack et al., 2007). Information about fertility sparing and options are additionally important. The supportive care needs for this population exist along a continuum. In their study of health care needs of young adult cancer patients and survivors, Zebrack and colleagues (2007) found that the young adult patients' highest priorities were for the availability of state-of-the-art treatments and health care providers skilled in treating young adults. These authors also found that the role of family and friends was paramount. Of note, it was acknowledged that further into the survivorship period, these young adults found benefit in meeting other young cancer survivors. This is consistent with theories of identity development that find that older adolescents and young adults define themselves through social interaction with groups and peers (Seifert, Hoffnung, & Hoffnung, 2000).

Supportive Care Needs

Although the illness of a child can challenge even emotionally healthy couples, open and direct communication continues to be an essential component of coping well with the illness of a family member. The more clearly the parental unit can communicate with one another, the stronger the family unit will be as a result. Parents may need assistance in learning to communicate with one another and with all of their children about difficult topics. Meeting with the oncology social worker and the health care team, as well as attending a parent support group, may help them balance the tension between "holding on" and "letting go" when an adolescent or young adult is ill. Parents especially need to understand the developmental challenges the illness creates for everyone in the family. These include the challenges to build a new sense of normalcy for both the individual and the family as a system. They need to learn to make room for the demands of the disease while also maintaining other family functions such as laughter, fun, family roles, and other experiences.

For the young adult with cancer, in addition to peer affiliation, it will be important to balance the challenges that seem developmentally "out of order" with some normal hopes and dreams for this stage in life. Such themes include facing death, serious illness, and the loss of dreams at a time when they should be feeling invincible and able to pursue their own identity. For parents of young adults with cancer, it is important to support them as they deal both with the illness of their young adult child and with the disruption of their child's normal developmental transitions as well.

Pearls

- The needs of older adolescents and young adults with cancer should be recognized as different from the needs of either younger children or older adults with cancer.
- Parents of adolescents and young adults require guidance in balancing their need to protect and support their child while also making room for the child's autonomy and continued developmental progression.
- Addressing the unique challenges of the parents of this population is essential for the well-being of both the patient and the parents.

Pitfalls

- Many cancer treatment centers do not have specific programs for older adolescents and young adults dealing with cancer.
- The impact of family functioning on the adolescent or young adult is often underestimated and therefore is not assessed or integrated into care.
- Families of adolescents and young adults are often assumed to be similar to families of young children and adult patients. They are not.

Additional study is needed to develop best practices for helping the parents of this population. The entire family system is affected when an adolescent or young adult is diagnosed with cancer. Efforts are essential that help families obtain up-to-date information and support to provide the care that is needed while they encourage the young adult's autonomy and experiences that promote developmental progression whenever that is possible. The goal is to navigate developmental interruptions in a way that mitigates the negative impact for both patients and parents and leads to greater mutual understanding, positive interactions, and a sense of satisfaction and fulfillment in traveling this journey together.

ADDITIONAL RESOURCES

Websites

Care Pages: http://www.carepages.com/forums/parenting/topics/22-parents-of-young-adults-withcancer

Ulman Cancer Fund for Young Adults: http://ulmanfund.org/

Books

Green, J. (2012). *The fault in our stars*. New York, NY: Button Books.

Zammett, E. (2005). *My (so-called) normal life: How I learned to balance love, work, family, friends... and cancer at 23*. New York, NY: Overlook Duckworth.

REFERENCES

Bleyer, A., O'Leary, M., Barr, R., & Ries, L. A. G. (Eds.). (2006). *Cancer epidemiology in older adolescents and young adults 15–29 years of age, including SEER incidence and survival, 1975–2000*. National Cancer Institute, NIH Pub. No. 06-5767. Bethesda, MD: National Cancer Institute.

Bleyer, A., Viny, A., & Barrm, R. D. (2006). *Cancer epidemiology in older adolescents and young adults 15–29 years*. Bethesda, MD: National Cancer Institute.

Carey, M., Clinton-McHarg, T., Sanson-Fisher, R., & Shakeshaft, A. (2012). Development of cancer needs questionnaire for parents and carers of adolescents and young adults with cancer. *Supportive Care in Cancer, 20*, 991–1010.

Carter, E. A., & McGoldrick, M. (Eds.). (1989). *The changing family life cycle: A framework for family therapy* (2nd ed.). Boston, MA: Allyn & Bacon.

Grinyer, A. (2002). *Cancer in young adults through parents' eyes*. Philadelphia, PA: Open University Press.

Grinyer, A., & Thomas, C. (2001). Young adults with cancer: The effect of the illness on parents and families. *International Journal of Palliative Nursing, 7*(4), 164–170.

Rolland, J. S. (1994). *Families, illness, and disability: An integrative treatment model*. New York, NY: Basic Books.

Seifert, K. L., Hoffnung, R. J., & Hoffnung, M. (2000). *Lifespan development* (2nd ed.). Boston, MA: Houghton Mifflin.

Zebrack, B. J., Mills, J., & Weitsman, T. S. (2007). Health and supportive needs of young adult cancer patients and survivors. *Journal of Cancer Survivorship, 1*, 137–145.

71 Cancer and Middle-Aged Adults (40 to 64)

Cindy Davis and Connie Rust

The social worker approached me and asked, "Anything you want me to do for you?" Yes . . . pay bills, help me talk to the doctor, fix my insurance problems, rent? Well, she just wanted to talk about my problems NOT solve them, so I didn't call her anymore.
—*Personal communication (2011)*

Key Concepts

- *In the middle-adult stage of life, people with cancer generally juggle many roles and responsibilities.*
- *Middle adulthood is often a time when people are at the peak of their career, may be raising children, and perceive themselves as strong and able to sustain a high level of activity. Cancer is not anticipated.*
- *Middle adults often have healthy parents and a cancer diagnosis seems "out of order" for both them and their parents.*
- *Cancer has an impact on their work life. People with cancer need to understand their legal rights, financial responsibilities, and medical coverage options.*
- *Partners and families of cancer patients and survivors have many needs and fears as they move into the caregiver role. Over time, the family role, social relationships, and work life of the middle adult may change considerably from what he or she had expected, requiring the development of a new normal lifestyle. The middle adult needs to know how to find necessary resources and support.*

People diagnosed with cancer in the middle-adult phase of life face multiple issues. These years are often the busiest of a person's life. Middle adults may be providing care to children and aging parents and required to multitask to meet the needs of others at work as well. Erikson's theory of psychosocial development characterizes middle adulthood as the building of one's life with a focus on career and family, with success often perceived as being actively involved in one's home and community. Inability to attain or maintain this involvement often results in feeling unproductive and unsuccessful (Erikson, 1994).

This chapter addresses normative issues faced by cancer patients who are middle adults, including financial issues, health literacy, role changes, and relationships.

Work/Financial Issues

Cancer commonly disrupts the career focus of middle-aged adults as they experience the primary working years of their lives. Although work is central to financial security and survival, the importance of work is more than financial security. A systematic review of the literature found that for middle adults with cancer, "work" forms a central basis for self-identity and self-esteem, provides financial security, forms and maintains social relationships, and represents an individual's abilities, talents, and health (Wells et al., 2013). The survivor's ability to work is affected during both the treatment and the recovery phase because survivors can face work limitations for years after diagnosis.

Individuals diagnosed with cancer may grapple with considerable financial hardships and resulting barriers to quality health care. According to a report by the American Cancer Society (2014), cancer is the most costly illness in the United States, exceeding $216 billion in 2009, including $86.6 billion in direct medical costs. Those who depend on their jobs for survival are the people most likely to lose their jobs because of cancer due to the lack of job security and the inability to take extended leave from work for medical reasons. These same people typically do not have the resources to pursue their employment rights through the legal system.

> *I was still an employee, and when the doctor turned me loose to go back to work, that's when they wouldn't let me come back. I worked for 17 years... worked hard; worked smarter.... They wouldn't let me come back.*
> —*personal communication, 2011*

Among people with health insurance, many have inadequate coverage for a cancer diagnosis and are at risk of a health-related financial burden. This risk is exponentially greater for individuals without insurance. The impact of health insurance status on access to quality care, and the disproportionate out-of-pocket expenses low-income families bear, has been "business as usual" for too long. Direct, nonmedical expenses for treatment create further financial burden. These expenses, which include child care, housekeeping, home care, wigs, prostheses, over-the-counter medications, and travel expenses, are rarely covered, even for those with health insurance or access to health care.

Oncology social workers have a key role to play in educating cancer patients and their families about their rights as cancer survivors. Advocacy skills are essential to empower cancer patients to stand up for their rights within their work settings. It is important to provide resources on this topic (Gregg, 2009; Hamilton, Stewart, Crandell, & Lynn, 2009; Yoo, Levine, Aviv, Ewing, & Au, 2010; see also Section 15).

Health Literacy

Middle adults may be hesitant to admit they do not understand the information given during diagnosis, treatment, and posttreatment survivorship because they may expect to have the same level of understanding of medical terminology and process as they have in their professional or family life. However, the information today in cancer diagnosis and treatment is often highly complex, ambiguous, and difficult to understand for most adults. Health literacy is defined as "the degree to which individuals have the capacity to obtain, process, and understand basic health information and services needed to make appropriate health decisions" (USDHHS, 2014, p. 1). Results from the 2003 National Assessment of Adult Literacy reveal that only 12% of the American population has proficient health literacy (Kutner, Greenberg, Jin, & Paulsen, 2006). Health literacy is a critical factor in patient–provider communication, positive health outcomes, and provision of optimum health care (Jeppesen, Coyle, & Miser, 2009; Williams, Davis, Parker, & Weiss, 2002). Individuals with low health literacy generally have poor health (Baker et al, 2002) and associated stigma or shame (Baker et al., 1996). Additionally, there is a relationship between health literacy and medication adherence (Juzych et al., 2008; Kalichman et al., 2008).

Oncology social workers can effectively identify and screen for each individual's health literacy and provide the appropriate resources that will address informational needs at all levels of literacy (Marcus, 2006). For example, within a collaborative structure, social workers and pharmacists have an opportunity to work together to screen for health literacy, provide education about proper medication usage, and identify barriers to proper medication use (see Chapter 30).

Family/Roles

Cancer interrupts life and disrupts the many roles filled by middle adults, such as worker, spouse/partner, parent, and caregiver of aging parents. Inevitably, relationships will change when one partner or family member becomes ill. For the patient, feelings of guilt and inadequacy about his or her perceived change in ability can be overwhelming.

> *My husband didn't understand why I couldn't get things done at home. I didn't have much support at home.*
> —*personal communication, 2011*

It is important for the oncology social worker to assist survivors and their family members to develop strategies to deal with the demands of middle-adulthood roles. Parents often want to protect their families by keeping the routine as "normal" as possible, especially for their children. However, this is often emotionally and physically draining for the person who has cancer. It is necessary to develop a realistic plan with parents to meet both the needs of their children and families and their need to take care of themselves.

> *It's actually the family who suffers because there is nobody to help them through the process. I have my medical team, but my family had no one.*
> —*personal communication, 2011*

Due to the increasingly chronic nature of cancer, the demands of this disease continue long past the acute treatment phase. Partners and families may expect the cancer survivor to "return to normal" once treatment is completed; it can, therefore, be difficult to deal with the long-term impact of cancer and to define what a "new normal" might be (Davis, 2009). The partners of cancer patients may move into a caregiving role that requires them to leave a job or take a different one that permits more flexibility or accessibility. The patient may need to change careers, develop a new career, or take an early retirement, which family must find a way to support. One of the most poignant and sad situations in middle life is when cancer makes it impossible for patients and their families to experience a planned retirement, pleasant leisure activities, and time to enjoy personal relationships after years of hard work and family caregiving.

The National Cancer Institute defines a "caregiver" as a family member or friend who helps a loved one manage cancer treatment in ways ranging from day-to-day activities to doctor visits to medical care options (NCI, 2005). Being a caregiver is challenging, with high emotional, mental, and physical demands, and caregivers are often called upon to negotiate a difficult health system, advocate for services, haggle with insurance companies, and/or manage the household and children (Kim, Baker, Spillers, & Wellisch, 2006). Additionally, the emotional strain of renegotiating roles within the relationship to the patient and the family is burdensome. This can be especially difficult for men not typically socialized into the caregiving role.

Literally hundreds of articles have documented the stressful physical, social, and psychological impact of family caregiving for cancer patients (Stenberg, Ruland, & Miaskowski, 2010). A study even found an increased risk of hospitalization for severe depression for male partners of women with breast cancer (Nakaya et al., 2010). In addition, although research on caregiver interventions finds them effective, very few interventions have been implemented in practice, because they were not initially designed for the realities and cost restrictions of practice settings (Northouse, Williams, Given, & McCorkle, 2012).

> *I think there should be a plan, just like there are therapies for domestic abuse families and therapies for abused children, there should be therapy that would teach the family what a person with cancer is like and how they feel.*
>
> —*personal communication, 2011*

There is no question that a cancer diagnosis during middle adulthood tests relationships. It is not unusual for cancer to precipitate divorce or separation; however, a large randomized study on a Danish sample found that cancer survivors were not at a *greater* risk for divorce than the general population, with the exception of survivors of cervical cancer (Carlsen, Oksbjerg, Frederiksen, Diderichsen, & Johansen, 2007). Most relationships in middle adults that are stable before a cancer diagnosis remain intact after surgery and treatment (Y-ME, 2006).

Trust, honesty, and communication are necessary for maintaining satisfying intimate relationships in general, but perhaps even more so if one of the partners has cancer (Bolte, 2007). Strong relationship ties increase the likelihood of emotional thriving in a crisis such as cancer (Cancer*Care*, 2007). How cancer patients and families cope with the experience of cancer can directly influence perceived levels of hope and suffering (Langhorne, Fulton, & Otto, 2007). Because the emotional, physical, spiritual, and relational challenges confronting a patient diagnosed with cancer and his or her family vary across the cancer continuum, it is helpful to discuss potential changes and coping strategies with the cancer patient's partner, children, and other supports during the stages of diagnosis, treatment, and survival or end of life (Y-ME, 2006).

Partners are frequently anxious about the future and potential loss of their loved one. They may confront their own mortality for the first time. Common reactions include fear, anger, denial, and a sense of betrayal. The patient and family member may also be concerned about existential issues. For example, they may perceive illness at such an important time of responsibility in the individual's life as a punishment or abandonment by God and therefore feel worry about their eternal future rather than comfort from their spirituality (Koenig, 2002). Thus, different spiritual interpretations can have different outcomes for psychological health. Family members may disagree about the role of spirituality in the illness trajectory, creating stress within the family system (Edmondson, Park, Blank, Fenster, & Mills, 2008; Wolf & Stevens, 2001; see also Chapter 46).

Another typical feeling experienced by partners of middle-aged adults with cancer is guilt. Partners may personally experience intense emotional turmoil, yet know their significant other, whom they have been used to relying on for emotional support, is already burdened with the news of his or her cancer diagnosis and an arduous treatment process. Therefore, partners' feelings may go unaddressed. The partner and family must receive permission to acknowledge their own needs and fears. The unmet psychosocial needs of partners can sometimes continue to affect relationships into long-term survivorship (Hodgkinson, Butow, Hobbs, & Wain, 2007).

Partners may also need to adapt to the changes in sexuality and intimacy that threaten the loss of established patterns of relating. The literature reports that 30% to 90% of cancer patients and survivors find treatment alters or disrupts intimacy. The most common changes experienced are decreased libido, pain with penetration for women, and erectile dysfunction in men (Roth, Carter, & Nelson, 2010). Oncology social workers assess for these issues and offer resources for help (see Sections 1 and 6, and Chapter 13).

Stella is a 58-year-old Hispanic woman who was diagnosed with breast cancer 4 years ago. Stella worked in a factory before having cancer, but she had to quit her job during her cancer treatment. She is currently unemployed. Upon diagnosis, she had a lumpectomy, chemotherapy, and radiation. She is in her second year of taking tamoxifen orally. In addition, she takes eight medications for other health issues, which include diabetes, hypertension, and asthma. Stella has four children and is the primary caretaker of her two grandchildren. Her insurance is through state health care coverage, which pays for only five of her medications. She often does not have transportation to doctor appointments and the pharmacy. She receives diabetes counseling at the clinic where she is treated but has difficulty understanding her rigid schedule of blood glucose monitoring and insulin injections. The oncology clinic has a nurse practitioner and social worker on staff to monitor progress with her breast cancer survival, but Stella does not want to "bother them" with questions about treatment and coping. Her retail pharmacist explained her medications to her when she first had them filled, but she cannot remember the oral instructions and has difficulty reading the prescription labels and patient leaflets. Stella comments that she only takes her oral medications when she is feeling run down to make them last longer.

Stella's situation demonstrates the multiple issues that arise for underserved cancer survivors with limited health literacy as they navigate the health care system, which can lead to distress for the patient. After the pharmacist informed the oncology social worker of Stella's hesitance to "bother" her, the social worker reached out to Stella and told her about a study she was running with her oncology social work colleagues at a local university. The study offered group psychosocial skills training to help her gain the tools needed to communicate with providers, retrieve information, stand up for her rights, and increase understanding of medication usage and access to resources to obtain medications. She agreed to participate, and at the end of the 7 weeks of training, Stella reported increased self-confidence and efficacy in being able to handle the psychosocial issues of her health and well-being.

Oncology social workers address the emotional concerns and practical needs of family members of middle-aged patients, which can be as challenging as those of older and younger adult patients. Families and partners often lack the skills and resources necessary to deal with their own intense emotions. It is important to normalize their reactions and connect them with resources to deal with their own issues. A diagnosis of cancer in midlife, often with patients who have work and family responsibilities and involvement, is a life-changing experience. Partners and family members need time and their own safe space to deal with these changes. They often think they have to be "strong" for the cancer survivor. The oncology social worker engages partners and family members around their own experiences, and many organizations provide support groups or services for loved ones of cancer survivors. Research also suggests male caregivers may be more comfortable sharing their feelings in a men-only forum or group (Borstelmann & Cope, 2008). It is important to refer all of those affected by cancer to resources that can address their individual struggles and meet their needs.

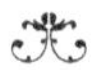

Pearls

- Middle-adult cancer survivors are in a period of life when they are faced with high demands on their time and competence at work and within the family.
- Financial issues are a great source of stress to middle-adult cancer survivors, especially those who are underserved.
- It is important to recognize hidden problems with health literacy in middle-aged adults, normalize them as expected with a complex health condition, and provide educational resources, perhaps in collaboration with other health care personnel.
- Spiritual belief needs recognition as a viable coping skill with some middle adults. Family and social issues can be major concerns in the life of the middle-adult cancer survivor and should be a priority in assessment and intervention.

Pitfalls

- Health care professionals should not underestimate the role of work and employment on a patient's identity and self-esteem, in addition to the financial concerns.
- Oncology social workers should not assume that patients, partners, families, or friends are a source of support. Rather, the patient's support network may be a burden on the patient.
- Cancer can become a chronic disease, and families are often unprepared for the long-term implications of cancer on the survivor. Social workers need to educate, prepare, and support the families of middle-aged adults across the continuum of care, especially as survivors and their families transition from acute treatment to either survivorship or end-of-life concerns.

Middle-adult cancer patients are parents, children, spouses, partners, employers, employees, and community members. However singular they may feel, more often than not, one diagnosis of cancer can affect entire groups of people. Survivors can have an impact on those around them and, in turn, can be impacted by them. This chapter has broadly addressed some of the main issues faced by patients in the middle-adult age group. Oncology social workers have an invaluable role in these people's lives to both support and empower them to achieve optimum survivorship.

Learning Exercises

Learning Activity 1

Brainstorm a list of five to 10 roles that a person might have at age 50. How would these roles be impacted by a diagnosis of cancer? How might an oncology social worker intervene to assist this patient? What resources would he or she need to cope with a diagnosis and long-term effects of cancer?

Learning Activity 2

Imagine you are working with the partner of a cancer patient. The partner reports feeling intense emotions such as fear, anger, denial, and guilt. Develop an intervention to help the partner. Make sure to include referrals and options. How might this intervention differ for a male partner versus a female partner?

Learning Activity 3

It is important for a cancer patient and his or her supports to have good health literacy so that they can better understand and comply with treatment. How might you, as an oncology social worker, screen for health literacy? What can you do to improve a patient's health literacy?

ADDITIONAL RESOURCES

Websites

National Cancer Institute Cancer Information Services: http://www.cancer.gov
National Coalition for Cancer Survivorship: http://www.canceradvocacy.org
OncoChat: http://www.oncochat.org
Young Survival Coalition: http://www.youngsurvival.org

Books

Babcock, E. N. (1997). *When life becomes precious: A guide for loved ones and friends of cancer patients.* New York, NY: Bantam.

National Cancer Institute. (2012). *Taking time: Support for people with cancer and the people who care about them.* Retrieved from http://www.cancer.gov/cancertopics/takingtime/page1

REFERENCES

American Cancer Society. (2014). *Cancer facts and figures 2014.* Atlanta, GA: Author.

Baker, D. W., Gazmararian, J. A., Williams, M. V., Scott, T., Parker, R. M., Green, D., . . . Peel, J. (2002). Functional health literacy and the risk of hospital admission among Medicare managed care enrollees. *American Journal of Public Health, 92*(8), 1278–1283.

Baker, D. W., Parker, M. R., Williams, M. V., Ptikin, K., Parikh, N. S., Coates, W., & Imara, M. (1996). The health care experience of patients with low literacy. *Archives of Family Medicine, 5*(6), 329–334.

Bolte, S. (2007). Sexuality, intimacy, and cancer. *Life With Cancer.* Life with Cancer Patient and Partner Education Newsletter, Spring.

Borstelmann, N. A., & Cope, R. S. (2008, May). *Current issues and ideas about men as caregivers.* Paper presented at the 24th Annual Conference of the Association of Oncology Social Work, Louisville, KY.

Cancer*Care*. (2007). *What can I say to a newly diagnosed loved one?* New York, NY: Author.

Carlsen, K., Oksbjerg, D., Frederiksen, K., Diderichsen, F., & Johansen, C. (2007). Are cancer survivors at an increased risk for divorce? A Danish cohort study. *European Journal of Cancer, 43*(14), 2093–2099.

Davis, C. (2009). *Oncology social work practice in the care of breast and ovarian cancer survivors.* New York, NY: Nova Science Publishers.

Edmondson, D., Park, C. L., Blank, T. O., Fenster, J. R., & Mills, M. A. (2008). Deconstructing spiritual well-being: Existential well-being and HRQOL in cancer survivors. *Psycho-Oncology, 17*(2), 161–169.

Erikson, E. (1994). *Identity and the life cycle.* London, England: W. W. Norton & Company.

Gregg, G. (2009). Psychosocial issues facing African and African American women diagnosed with breast cancer. *Social Work in Public Health, 24*(1–2), 100–116.

Hamilton, J. B., Stewart, B. J., Crandell, J. L., & Lynn, M. R. (2009). Development of the Ways of Helping questionnaire: A measure of preferred coping strategies for older African American cancer survivors. *Research in Nursing Health, 32*(3), 243–259.

Hodgkinson, K., Butow, P., Hobbs, K. M., & Wain, G. (2007). After cancer: The unmet supportive care needs of survivors and their partners. *Journal of Psychosocial Oncology, 25*(4), 89–104.

Jeppesen, K. M., Coyle, J. D., & Miser, W. F. (2009). Screening questions to predict limited health literacy: A cross-sectional study of patients with diabetes mellitus. *Annals of Family Medicine, 7*(1), 24–31.

Juzych, M. S., Randhawa, S., Shukairy, A., Kaushal, P., Gupta, A., & Shalauta, N. (2008). Functional health literacy in patients with glaucoma in urban settings. *Archives of Ophthalmology, 126*(5), 718–724.

Kalichman, S. C., Pope, H., White, D., Cherry, C., Amaral, C. M., Swetzes, C., . . . Kalichman, M. O. (2008). Association between health literacy and HIV treatment adherence: Further evidence from objectively measured medication adherence. *Journal of International Association of Physicians AIDS Care, 7*(6), 317–323.

Kim, Y., Baker, F., Spillers, R. L., & Wellisch, D. K. (2006). Psychological adjustment of cancer caregivers with multiple roles. *Psycho-Oncology, 15*, 795–804.

Koenig, H. (2002). A commentary: The role of religion and spirituality at the end of life. *The Gerontologist, 42*, 24–25.

Kutner, M., Greenberg, E., Jin, Y., & Paulsen, C. (2006). *The health literacy of America's adults: Results from the 2003 National Assessment of Adult Literacy* (NCES 2006-483). U.S. Department of Education. Washington, DC: National Center for Education Statistics.

Langhorne, M. E., Fulton, J. S., & Otto, S. E. (2007). *Oncology nursing* (5th ed.). St. Louis, MO: Mosby Elsevier.

Marcus, E. (2006). The silent epidemic-the health effects of illiteracy. *New England Journal of Medicine, 355*(4), 339–341.

Nakaya, N., Saito-Nakaya, K., Bidstrup, P., Dalton, S., Frederiksen, K., Steding-Jessen, M., . . . Johanasen, C. (2010). Increased risk of severe depression in male partners of women with breast cancer. *Cancer, 116*, 5527–5534.

National Cancer Institute (NCI). (2005). *Facing forward: When someone you love has completed cancer treatment.* Bethesda, MD: Author.

Northouse, L., Williams, A., Given, B., & McCorkle, R. (2012). Psychosocial care for family caregivers of patients with cancer. *Journal of Clinical Oncology, 30*(11), 1227–1234.

Roth, A. J., Carter, J., & Nelson, C. J. (2010). Sexuality after cancer. In W. S. Breitbart (Ed.), *Psycho-oncology* (pp. 245–250). New York, NY: Oxford University Press.

Stenberg, U., Ruland, C., & Miaskowski, C. (2010). Review of the literature on the effects of caring for a patient with cancer. *Psycho-Oncology, 19*, 1013–1025.

U.S. Department of Health and Human Services (USDHHS). (2014). Quick guide to health literacy: Fact sheet. Retrieved from http://www.health.gov/communication/literacy/quickguide/factsbasic.htm

Wells, M., Williams, B., Firnigl, D. Lang, H., Coyle, J., Kroll, T., & MacGillivray, S. (2013). Supporting "work-related goals" rather than "return to work" after cancer? A systematic review and meta-synthesis of 25 qualitative studies. *Psycho-Oncology*, 22(6), 1208–1219.

Williams, M. V., Davis, T., Parker, R. M., & Weiss, B. D. (2002). The role of health literacy in patient-physician communication. *Family Medicine, 34*(5), 383–389.

Wolf, C. T., & Stevens, P. (2001). Integrating religion and spirituality in marriage and family counseling. *Counseling and Values, 46*, 66–75.

Y-ME National Breast Cancer Organization (Y-ME). (2006). *When the woman you love has breast cancer.* Chicago, IL: Author.

Yoo, G. J., Levine, E. G., Aviv, C., Ewing, C., & Au, A. (2010). Older women, breast cancer, and social support. *Supportive Care in Cancer, 18*(12), 1521–1530.

72

Tara Schapmire and Anna Faul

Cancer and Older Adults (65 Plus)

Key Concepts

- *Seventy percent of all cancers are diagnosed among people over age 65, yet research on what psychosocial interventions work best with this group is limited.*
- *A developmental, life course approach is helpful in understanding people's patterns of aging and their reactions to major life events such as a cancer diagnosis.*
- *Maslow's hierarchy of needs is a useful framework to understand how to assess and plan interventions for the needs of older adults based on their developmental level and their cancer and its treatment.*

Age is a primary risk factor for most cancers, with about 70% of all cancers diagnosed among people aged 65 or older (Blank, 2012). In the United States, the most common cancers in this age group are breast cancer (women) and prostate cancer (men); for both older women and men, lung and colorectal cancers are also very common (ACS, 2012). Because older adults make up most of those affected by this disease, understanding their psychosocial adjustment needs is vitally important.

Unique considerations exist in providing appropriate care and treatment to older adults with cancer because they may have different treatment goals or preferences than younger adults (IOM, 2013). Although it is not possible to cover extensive and varying needs of individuals affected by cancer in the 65-and-older range, this chapter introduces the most common issues and challenges among them using a life course approach. This chapter also introduces the usefulness of Maslow's hierarchy in assessing and intervening at the appropriate developmental stage for older adults affected by cancer.

A Framework for Assessment and Intervention of Older Adults With Cancer

Cancer and its associated stressors and demands on resources can interrupt or delay the activities typically engaged in during older adulthood; for example, older adults might face "unplanned retirement, limitations in grand-parenting abilities, inability to act as caregivers to others in the family, or limitations in their ability to work" (IOM, 2008, p. 32). Oncology social workers are called upon in a variety of settings to assess, intervene with, and support older adults affected by cancer. In often-brief encounters, it can be helpful to use organizing frameworks to begin the work with clients where they are—a basic tenet of social work.

Maslow's hierarchy of needs (Maslow, 1970) is a useful framework to understand how oncology social workers should assess and plan such interventions. Fundamental to Maslow's theory of motivation is that human needs are hierarchical—unfulfilled lower needs dominate one's thinking, actions, and being until satisfied. When lower needs are fulfilled, next levels surface and can be addressed. When basic needs are satisfied, human beings then tend to pursue

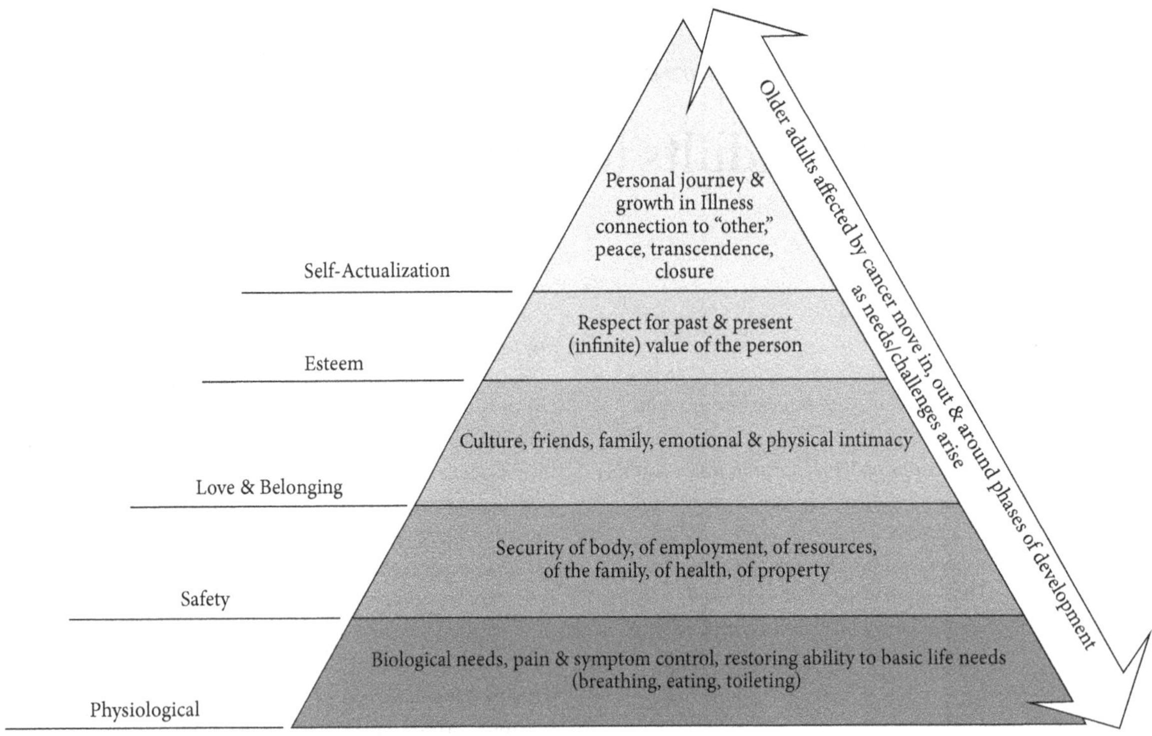

Figure 72.1. Maslow's Hierarchy Adapted to Oncology Social Work with Older Adults
Adapted from Zalenski and Raspa (2006).

the higher needs of self-actualization. Zalenski and Raspa (2006) and Wood-Mintz (2013) applied Maslow's hierarchy to create frameworks for achieving human potential in hospice and end-of-life care (Figure 72.1). Oncology social workers know that those affected by cancer may move around, forward, and backward on the hierarchy at different points in the cancer trajectory depending on their physical, emotional, social, and spiritual challenges. Although there may not be time to help older adults affected by cancer to advance through all the levels in the adapted hierarchy, it can be used to analyze the current level of their needs and then intervene to achieve a sense of completion and closure of tasks in that specific area (Wood-Mintz, 2013).

Physiological Needs of Older Adults

A vitally important need of all cancer patients is the effective management of the body's biological and physiological reactions. These reactions are many times more severe, because comorbidities, such as lung disease, heart disease, arthritis, incontinence, frequent pain, and obesity, are more prevalent in older adult cancer survivors (Avis & Deimling, 2008). Older adults with cancer may have increased functional impairment and disability related to cancer or comorbid conditions (IOM, 2008), and greater amounts of comorbid conditions and pain have been consistently linked with poorer psychosocial adjustment in cancer patients (Spiegel & Giese-Davis, 2003). Comorbid conditions may also result in overuse of medication. Older people with cancer are more vulnerable to adverse drug events, which can lead to polypharmacy when they are misinterpreted as a new medical condition (Given & Given, 2010).

Asking cancer patients how they rate their own health may provide indications of how they are framing their experience. Perceived health is an important personal resource that compares favorably to more objective measures of physical health (Fisher, Faul, Weir, & Wallace, 2005). Among cancer patients, it has been found to be a predictor of survival (Osoba, 2007), as well as a risk factor for distress (Schnoll & Harlow, 2001). Table 72.1 highlights important areas of assessment and intervention within each developmental area. Potential interventions in the physiological phase include careful identification of the patient's comorbidities and their treatments, which can be transmitted to interdisciplinary team members. In addition, education can be provided around common physical responses to cancer (i.e., what can be expected in terms of biological and care needs). Integrating communication and support of the caregiver, advocating for the patient with the health care team, and making the necessary connections among multiple care providers to ensure adequate care coordination are critical interventions for older adult cancer patients. Cognitive behavioral techniques can also be taught to the patient and caregiver to address some physical symptom distress (e.g., distraction, relaxation, and guided imagery).

Table 72.1.
Developmental Tasks and Appropriate Areas of Oncology Social Work Assessment and Intervention

Developmental Task	Aspects of Oncology Social Work Assessment	Oncology Social Work Intervention Skills[a]
Self-Actualization	• Religious and spiritual values and expectations associated with illness and end of life • Emotional issues, including cognitive and emotional integration of diagnosis and prognosis, emotional coping, death anxiety, adaptive and maladaptive denial, and grief-related issues	• Assessment, exploration, clarification, referrals, and reframing of hope • Assisting with life review, memory making, and legacy building • Supportive listening • Cognitive behavioral and integrative interventions to facilitate adaptation and enhance coping • Individual and group supportive counseling and integrative therapies • Family counseling and therapy • Clinical interventions related to meaning making, transcendence, grief, and bereavement
Esteem	• Sources of joy, pride, happiness, and belonging	• Life review • Enhancing communication between patient/family and health care team to maximize effective and compassionate care that promotes dignity and self-worth
Love and Belonging	• Family (and other relationships) dynamics and supports • Cultural expectations, preferences, and health beliefs and values related to issues such as truth telling, advanced care planning, perception of illness, and prognosis	• Effective organization, leadership, and/or participation in family meetings or family/team meetings, group psychotherapy, counseling, and psychoeducational interventions • Conflict resolution, including facilitating communication and addressing intergenerational conflict and family stresses • Delivery of culturally sensitive services • Enhancing communication to maximize effective and compassionate care • Connecting clients with others of their culture and background • Effective communication with those of various cultures • Advocacy
Safety	• Screening for mental, emotional, and behavioral disorders • Impact of illness • Safety issues • Functional and environmental issues • Financial situation • Health insurance • Potential barriers and risk factors that may impede the care plan • Educational needs • Other unmet needs, and resources and supports to address them	• Cognitive behavioral and integrative interventions to facilitate adaptation, enhance coping, and manage distress • Environmental interventions such as arranging for equipment and altering or personalizing the physical environment. • Educational interventions including information related to illness, pain, and symptom management, and insurance and financial issues • Case management interventions including referrals, assistance with navigation, and facilitation of continuity of care • Risk management • Crisis intervention
Physiological	• Symptom management experience • Unmet needs	• Case management interventions including referrals, assistance with navigation and care coordination, and facilitation of continuity of care • Risk management • Crisis intervention • Cognitive behavioral and integrative interventions to facilitate adaptation, enhance coping, manage distress, pain, and symptoms

[a] Adapted from Gwyther et al. (2005).

Safety Needs of Older Adults

Safety of body and health, of family, and of socioeconomic resources may be a developmental area most familiar to oncology social workers. Assessment of internal (personal) and external (social) barriers that impede care, and resources that promote successful adaptation and safety, are important oncology social work skills.

Depression is one of the most frequent causes of emotional distress in older adults and is one of five top concerns the elderly face (Morley, 2004). Depression among those with cancer increases with disease severity and symptoms such as pain and fatigue (Spiegel & Giese-Davis, 2003). General depressive conditions are leading causes of functional disability and potent risk factors for mortality from general medical conditions and for suicide in elderly persons (Lyness, 2004). Anxiety is also an important concern, because older adult long-term survivors have been found to worry about recurrence, about a second cancer, and that the symptoms they experience may be from cancer (Deimling, Bowman, Sterns, Wagner, & Kahana, 2006).

The oncology social worker should determine how the cancer diagnosis fits within the life course trajectory. If a person has learned over the life span to deal effectively with illness and take an active role in managing physical health, this can be seen as an important internal resource. A history of distress has been established in the literature as a clear predictor of higher distress after cancer (Alfano & Rowland, 2009). Having more experience with negative life events may mitigate the impact of cancer and may even serve as a resource for older individuals (Blank & Bellizzi, 2008). However, it can also reflect multiple and cumulative stresses that create greater vulnerability.

Dispositional optimism—a tendency to expect positive outcomes—predicts lower symptoms of depression in cancer patients consistently across the disease trajectory (Meyerowitz & Oh, 2009). However, increased age has been associated with lower use of all forms of coping among long-term cancer survivors (Deimling et al., 2006).

Socioeconomic barriers, for example, lack of financial resources and lack of, loss of, or changes in health insurance, may result in difficulties adjusting to the cancer diagnosis. Involuntary job loss has been linked to depression in older adults (Gallo et al., 2006). Health insurance can improve health, especially for older adults as they become eligible for Medicare (McWilliams, Meara, Zaslavsky, & Ayanian, 2007). Under- and uninsured patients receive delayed or no treatment, are unable to obtain needed prescriptions, and have worse outcomes of medical treatment (IOM, 2002, 2008). Lower levels of income have been associated with greater psychosocial distress (Schnoll & Harlow, 2001), disability, illness, and death (IOM, 2008). Loss in wealth resources associated with cancer, including high costs of medical treatment, drugs, and medical supplies, may increase distress (Head & Faul, 2008; IOM, 2008). Recommended interventions include crisis intervention, education, supportive counseling, case management, and linking with external resources (Table 72.1).

Love and Belonging Needs of Older Adults

Relationships with others and with the world can both control and support an individual's behavior and adjustment, with social support being an obvious element of love and belonging. Competition among the different roles facing a spouse or caregiver of an older adult with cancer might change the impact of the cancer on that survivor, especially if the spouse or caregiver is a primary social support who now needs to be a caregiver as well. Social support has been studied extensively as a resource for cancer patients and is consistently associated with better adjustment (Meyerowitz & Oh, 2009). This external resource reduces an individual's vulnerability during times of stress (Hobfoll, 2002) and has helped explain distinct trajectories of distress among those affected by cancer (Helgeson, Snyder, & Seltman, 2004).

Marital status is another important aspect of social support. Loss of a spouse is a primary risk factor for depression in older adults (Given & Given, 2010). Interventions related to needs for love and belonging include supporting older adults' cultural expectations, beliefs, and differences, including awareness of personal and societal biases, "isms," and phobias that may make it difficult to maintain positive and supportive relationships.

Social work assessments should explore family dynamics and support systems, cultural expectations, beliefs, and goals. Interventions include delivery of culturally appropriate services and counseling, communication facilitation, family meetings, and conflict resolution (Table 72.1).

Esteem Needs of Older Adults

Maslow (1970) identified two levels of esteem. *Lower esteem* is seen as the need for respect from others, recognition, reputation, and status. *Higher esteem* is when people want to feel good about themselves, valuable, confident, independent, and free. Self-esteem is an important personal resource that facilitates coping; negative self-esteem has been linked to depressive symptoms in cancer patients, as well as decreased social support. Self-enhancing cognitions protect cancer patients against threats to their self-esteem and social support structures (Schroevers, Ranchor, & Sanderman, 2003).

Addressing esteem needs for older adults involves supporting environmental mastery and societal recognition and encouraging choices that set the context and direction of their lives. Understanding the concepts of Bandura's (1997) self-efficacy (sense of personal competence) and efficacy expectation (expectation that one can personally accomplish a goal) is vital to supporting the personal power an older adult has to establish and achieve realistic goals.

Assessment should also address the older adult's source of joy, pride, happiness, and belonging (Table 72.1). Interventions such as life review—to help cancer patients realize what gave them joy and pride in their lives—may enhance their sense of happiness and self-esteem. Guiding older adults through enhanced communication with others may also help them maintain a sense of self, participate in their own health care decisions and planning, and feel valued. Oncology social workers can also support family members by helping them be involved in constructive ways.

Self-Actualization Needs of Older Adults

Maslow posits that by completing tasks in the first four areas, self-actualization within illness can be reached (1970). Positive self-esteem is seen as a powerful foundation for self-actualization. To reach self-actualization within a cancer diagnosis means to see the cancer experience as a chance for growth, to enjoy what life brings, and to find peace at the end of a life well lived.

To reach self-actualization within later life after a cancer diagnosis, the process of transcendence is seen as an important developmental task. In completing this task, the older adult shifts his or her perspective "from a rational, materialistic view to a wider world view, characterized by broadened personal boundaries within interpersonal, intrapersonal, transpersonal, and temporal dimensions" (McCarthy & Bockweg, 2013, p. 88). The outcomes of transcendence are seen as a sense of meaning in life, well-being, and life satisfaction.

The hospice philosophy of life affirmation supports self-actualization. Allowing older adults to reflect on what brings meaning and purpose to their lives—while encouraging caregivers and family members to allow space and time to listen—may let them transcend loss and incorporate their illness and/or death story into their life story. The oncology social work assessment should address the older adult's religious and spiritual values and expectations associated with illness and end of life, as well as cognitive and emotional integration of diagnosis and prognosis, emotional coping, death anxiety, denial (adaptive and maladaptive), and grief. Interventions such as life review, memory making, legacy building, and supportive listening can develop self-actualization (Table 72.1).

Pearls

- Maslow's hierarchy of needs provides a framework for oncology social workers to determine the most important areas of focus for older adults affected by cancer.
- Although older adults may move around on the hierarchy depending on specific demands of the illness at any given time, in general, lower needs/tasks related to physical needs and safety may need to be satisfied first, before higher needs related to love and belonging, esteem, and self-actualization can be addressed.
- The adapted Maslow's hierarchy can be used to identify the current developmentally shaped tasks and intervene to achieve a sense of completion and closure in that stage.

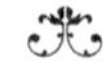

Pitfalls

- Oncology social workers may not be able to spend enough time with older adults to help them complete every task associated with their illness.
- Oncology social workers should not focus on tasks related to higher needs on Maslow's hierarchy if lower needs are not fulfilled—for example, focusing on transcendence when basic symptom management has not been accomplished—unless directed by patient wishes.

Joyce, a 72-year-old African American woman, was happily remarried, retired, and planning the wedding of her 30-year-old son and the arrival of her first grandchild when she was diagnosed with a recurrent Stage 4 breast cancer after 20 years in remission. In previous clinic visits, the social worker learned that Joyce had survived a divorce and remarriage during middle adulthood and had her first and only child at age 42 after many miscarriages. She had a strong faith in God and a tremendous amount of psychosocial and spiritual support from her church and family. They had previously worked together on clarifying her goals of care, which had allowed her to make the decision to refuse aggressive, life-prolonging treatments and elect palliative care. In a later clinic appointment with the social worker, Joyce explained she hoped to "make sense" of her cancer experience and expressed some frustration with family members and friends being unable to help her with this due to their own grief about her illness. The social worker offered to work with her on ways to talk with her loved ones and encouraged her to consider joining the clinic support group for women living with advanced breast cancer, where she might meet others who would understand her experiences. She agreed to both group and individual sessions with the social worker, who introduced meaning-making and life review interventions to help her place the fact of her dying into the context of her life. Although she sought out the support group for philosophical/existential support, in many ways Joyce became the philosopher of the group. Her strength, drawn from many difficult life experiences, combined with her natural grace cultivated interdependence with the other women who journeyed with her through their cancer experience, creating a very special sense of community. Joyce was very focused on her legacy; she had "put all of her affairs in order," yet she realized that she very much wanted to plan her own funeral. The social worker devoted one group session to funeral planning for her and the other women, and they left with an outline of what their service might look like. At a later support group session, Joyce brought a complete plan for her funeral service to share with the group; she shared some poems she had written and photographs she had taken and even played some of the music she had selected, in a sense practicing her funeral with the other women and allowing her to complete the important legacy task she desired.

In summary, this chapter presented the most common issues and challenges among older adults affected by cancer using a life course approach and a framework for assessing and addressing them. Our evidence-based knowledge of psychosocial interventions for older adults affected by cancer is limited but emerging. Oncology social workers should stay abreast of relevant national policy initiatives that affect those with whom they work. The latest report of the IOM (2013) on quality cancer care calls for an increase in evidence-based cancer care for older adults and individuals with comorbid conditions. Specifically, the IOM suggests that funding agencies mandate that researchers include a plan of study that mirrors the age distribution and health-risk profile of patients with the disease. Oncology social workers can use this and other resources (listed in Additional Resources) to effect change in their institutions and improve quality for those with whom they work.

ADDITIONAL RESOURCES

Cancer in Older Adults: http://www.cancer.net/coping/age-specific-information/cancer-older-adults

Cancer Facts for People Over 50: http://www.nia.nih.gov/health/publication/cancer-facts-people-over-50

Geriatric Mental Health Foundation's Guide to Mental Wellness in Older Age: Recognizing and Overcoming Depression: http://www.gmhfonline.org/gmhf/consumer/depression_toolkit.html

The Institute of Medicine Report: *Delivering High-Quality Cancer Care: Charting a New Course for a System in Crisis*: http://www.nap.edu/catalog.php?record_id=18359

National Coalition for Cancer Survivorship's Cancer Survival Toolbox Topics of Older Persons: http://www.canceradvocacy.org/resources/cancer-survival-toolbox/special-topics/topics-for-older-persons/

REFERENCES

Alfano, C. M., & Rowland, J. H. (2009). The experience of survival for patients: Psychosocial adjustment. In S. M. Miller, D. J. Bowen, R. T. Croyle, & J. H. Rowland (Eds.), *Handbook of cancer control and behavioral science* (pp. 413–430). Washington, DC: American Psychological Association.

American Cancer Society (ACS). (2012). *Cancer facts & figures 2012*. Retrieved from http://www.cancer.org/acs/groups/content/@epidemiologysurveilance/documents/document/acspc-031941.pdf

Avis, N. E., & Deimling, G. T. (2008). Cancer survivorship and aging. *Cancer, 113*(S12), 3519–3529. doi:10.1002/cncr.23941

Bandura, A. (1997). *Self-efficacy: The exercise of control*. New York, NY: W. H. Freeman and Company.

Blank, T. O. (2012). Theoretical perspectives from gerontology and lifespan development. In K. M. Bellizzi & M. A. Gosney (Eds.), *Cancer and aging handbook: Research and practice*. Hoboken, NJ: Wiley-Blackwell.

Blank, T. O., & Bellizzi, K. M. (2008). A gerontologic perspective on cancer and aging. *Cancer, 112*(11 Suppl.), 2569–2576.

Deimling, G. T., Bowman, K. F., Sterns, S., Wagner, L. J., & Kahana, B. (2006). Cancer-related health worries and psychological distress among older adult, long-term cancer survivors. *Psycho-Oncology, 15*(4), 306–320.

Fisher, G. G., Faul, J. D., Weir, D. R., & Wallace, R. B. (2005). *Documentation of chronic disease measures in the Health and Retirement Study (HRS/AHEAD)*. Ann Arbor, MI: University of Michigan.

Gallo, W. T., Bradley, E. H., Dubin, J. A., Jones, R. N., Falba, T. A., Hsun-Mei, T., & Stanislav, V. K. (2006). The persistence of depressive symptoms in older workers who experience involuntary job loss: Results from the Health and Retirement Survey. *Journals of Gerontology, Series B: Psychological Sciences & Social Sciences, 61B*(4), S221–S228.

Given, B. A., & Given, C. W. (2010). The older patient. In J. C. Holland, W. S. Breitbart, P. B. Jacobsen, M. S. Lederberg, M. J. Loscalzo, & R. McCorkle (Eds.), *Psycho-oncology* (2nd ed., pp. 491–496). New York, NY: Oxford University Press.

Gwyther, L. P., Altilio, T., Blacker, S., Christ, G., Csikai, E. L., Hooyman, N.,... Howe, J. (2005). Social work competencies in palliative and end-of-life care. *Journal of Social Work in End-of-Life & Palliative Care, 1*(1), 87–120. doi:10.1300/J457v01n01_06

Head, B. A., & Faul, A. C. (2008). Development and validation of a scale to measure socioeconomic well-being in persons with cancer. *Journal of Supportive Oncology, 6*(4), 183–192.

Helgeson, V. S., Snyder, P., & Seltman, H. (2004). Psychological and physical adjustment to breast cancer over 4 years: Identifying distinct trajectories of change. *Health Psychology, 23*(1), 3–15.

Hobfoll, S. E. (2002). Social and psychological resources and adaptation. *Review of General Psychology, 6*(4), 307–324.

Institute of Medicine (IOM). (2002). *Care without coverage: Too little, too late*. Washington, DC: National Academies Press.

Institute of Medicine (IOM). (2008). *Cancer care for the whole patient: Meeting psychosocial health needs*. Washington, DC: National Academies Press.

Institute of Medicine (IOM). (2013). *Delivering high-quality cancer care: Charting a new course for a system in crisis*. Washington, DC: National Academies Press.

Lyness, J. M. (2004). Treatment of depressive conditions in later life: Real-world light for dark (or dim) tunnels. *JAMA: Journal of the American Medical Association, 291*(13), 1626–1628.

Maslow, A. (1970). *Motivation and personality* (2nd ed.). New York, NY: Harper and Row.

McCarthy, V. L., & Bockweg, A. (2013). The role of transcendence in a holistic view of successful aging: A concept analysis and model of transcendence in maturation and aging. *Journal of Holistic Nursing*, *31*(2), 84–92. doi:http://dx.doi.org/10.1177/0898010112463492

McWilliams, J. M., Meara, E., Zaslavsky, A. M., & Ayanian, J. Z. (2007). Health of previously uninsured adults after acquiring Medicare coverage. *JAMA: Journal of the American Medical Association*, *298*(24), 2886–2894.

Meyerowitz, B. E., & Oh, S. (2009). Psychosocial response to cancer diagnosis and treatment. In S. M. Miller, D. J. Bowen, R. T. Croyle, & J. H. Rowland (Eds.), *Handbook of cancer control and behavioral science: A resource for researchers, practitioners, and policymakers* (pp. 361–377). Washington, DC: American Psychological Association.

Morley, J. E. (2004). The top 10 hot topics in aging. *Journals of Gerontology, Series A: Biological Sciences and Medical Sciences*, *59*(1), 24–33.

Osoba, D. (2007). Translating the science of patient-reported outcomes assessment into clinical practice. *Journal of the National Cancer Institute Monographs*, *37*(37), 5–11.

Schnoll, R. A., & Harlow, L. L. (2001). Using disease-related and demographic variables to form cancer-distress risk groups. *Journal of Behavioral Medicine*, *24*(1), 57–74. doi:http://dx.doi.org/10.1023/A:1005686404723

Schroevers, M. J., Ranchor, A. V., & Sanderman, R. (2003). The role of social support and self-esteem in the presence and course of depressive symptoms: A comparison of cancer patients and individuals from the general population. *Social Science and Medicine*, *57*, 375–385.

Spiegel, D., & Giese-Davis, J. (2003). Depression and cancer: Mechanisms and disease progression. *Biological Psychiatry*, *54*(3), 269–282. doi:http://dx.doi.org/10.1016/S0006-3223%2803%2900566-3

Wood-Mintz, J. (2013, March). *Dying as a developmental task: Using Maslow to guide social work intervention in end-of-life-care*. Paper presented at the 2013 Social Work Hospice & Palliative Care Network General Assembly, New Orleans, LA.

Zalenski, R. J., & Raspa, R. (2006). Maslow's hierarchy of needs: A framework for achieving human potential in hospice. *Journal of Palliative Medicine*, *9*(5), 1120–1127.

73 Working With Families of Older Adults With Cancer

Daniel S. Gardner

Key Concepts

- *Due to an aging population, increased longevity, and declining cancer mortality, the prevalence of older adults with cancer is rising.*
- *Older adults often have multiple chronic conditions and functional limitations, which can complicate cancer diagnosis, treatment, and recovery.*
- *Older adults may also have considerable experience in coping with illness that should be acknowledged and supported in their cancer treatment and care.*
- *Family-centered interventions help caregivers cope with cancer, remain engaged in patient care, and minimize burden.*
- *Essential competencies for oncology social workers working with older adults include comprehensive geriatric assessment and family-centered and interdisciplinary care.*

Cancer is increasingly a disease of later life. An estimated 66% of new malignancies are diagnosed in people 60 years of age or older (CDC, 2011), and the risk of developing cancer nearly doubles after the age of 70 (ACS, 2012). As life expectancies grow and cancer mortality rates decline over the next several decades, the prevalence of cancer among older adults is expected to increase dramatically (Hurria & Balducci, 2009).

Living with cancer poses distinct challenges for older patients, their families, and providers. Age-related physical, emotional, and psychosocial changes affect the ways in which older adults experience cancer and its treatment (Balducci & Ershler, 2005; Hurria et al., 2012). Despite the disproportionate cancer burden in later life, older adults are underrepresented in the clinical trials that guide the development of evidence-based treatment protocols (Hurria et al., 2012). Relatively little is known about how older cancer patients respond to treatments tested in younger adults, their supportive care needs, or the needs of their family caregivers. There is a growing interest in understanding and addressing the biopsychosocial concerns of aging patients and their families (Given & Given, 2009; Hodges, Humphris, & MacFarlane, 2005; and see Chapters 72 and 73). This chapter explores the individual and familial challenges of coping with cancer in later life and the role of social workers in meeting these needs.

Cancer and the Aging Family

Ada is a 72-year-old Jewish woman who was diagnosed last year with non-Hodgkin lymphoma. She has a history of cardiovascular disease and diabetes and has been undergoing a mild course of treatment modified from the standardized guidelines. She had been tolerating the treatment well but has had some trouble regulating her blood sugar and is often short of breath with fatigue and muscle weakness. Ada was hospitalized last week to stabilize her insulin dosage.

Ada lives alone in an apartment on the third floor of a walk-up building, which has become increasingly difficult for her to manage. She identifies her 46-year-old daughter—who lives with her partner and stepchild about 2 hours away by car—as her primary caregiver. Ada was to be discharged to a short-term inpatient rehabilitation facility, but she refuses, stating repeatedly that she wants to go home. When the social worker meets with her alone, she admits that she is concerned that if she is not discharged to home, she will "end up rotting in a nursing home." The social worker convinces Ada to share her concerns with her daughter, who assures her she is committed to doing whatever she can to ensure Ada can remain in her own apartment as long as she can manage. Ada agrees to a transfer to the rehabilitation facility to receive physical therapy and regain the strength she needs to negotiate the stairs and return home.

As Ada's story demonstrates, older cancer patients often experience lasting physical, functional, and psychological effects from cancer and its treatment, and they are less likely to recover prior functioning than younger patients (Hurria & Balducci, 2009; Repetto, 2003). Older adults develop functional limitations, often with complex home care needs, and may require daily assistance to function independently (Hurria et al., 2012). Greater treatment complications and comorbid illnesses (e.g., diabetes, cardiovascular disease, osteoarthritis, and dementia) ultimately result in poorer prognoses than those for younger patients (Balducci & Ershler, 2005; Marengoni, Rizzuto, Wang, Winblad, & Fratiglioni, 2009; and see Chapter 31). Older adults also take more prescribed medications or misuse medications (Fulton & Riley Allen, 2005), leading to adverse drug reactions, confusion, mobility limitations, and frequent hospitalizations (Maggiore, Gross, & Hurria, 2010).

The complex care needs and functional limitations often increase the burden of cancer on older adults and their families (Kotkamp-Mothes, Slawinsky, Hindermann, & Strauss, 2005; Weitzner, Haley, & Chen, 2000). Identifying and helping access existing strengths and resources is an essential skill for oncology social workers who work with older cancer patients and family caregivers (Gardner & Werner-Lin, 2011).

Families in Later Life

Families with aging parents and adult children often draw on established relationships and deeply ingrained patterns of interaction. Living with cancer upends familiar roles, boundaries, communication, and emotional processes and requires family members to assume new functions and cope with crises (Wellisch & Kissane, 2013). Families often struggle to re-establish preillness homeostasis (Patterson, 2002) or to construct an adaptive "new normal" (Walsh, 2006).

Later-life families cope with distinct developmental challenges (e.g., adult children forming and re-forming their own families, mobility and increased physical and emotional distance, divorce, retirement, widowhood, and children assuming financial and caregiving responsibilities for their parents), raising issues of loss and ambivalence (Pillemer et al., 2007). Maintaining continuity and connection can be particularly challenging. Adult children may not be ready to manage their aging parents' increasing care needs, and older adults may be reluctant to sacrifice their autonomy and self-determination. The costs of care may also become burdensome as they extend over several years. Oncology social workers help families acknowledge shared losses, communicate openly about family changes, negotiate new roles, and develop adaptive family narratives (Gardner & Werner-Lin, 2011; Walsh, 2006).

Family Caregiving

Spouses and adult children—typically, wives and daughters—most often assume primary caregiving responsibilities for older family members (Rabow, Hauser, & Adams, 2004; Weitzner et al., 2000). This largely unreimbursed effort is critical to helping older people cope with cancer and treatment, avoid unnecessary hospitalizations, and live independently in the community (Charles & Sevak, 2005; Haley, 2003).

Family caregivers frequently experience emotional, physical, and financial strains and report levels of distress as high as or higher than the patients themselves (Haley, 2003; Hodges et al., 2005). Caregivers are at greater risk for depression, anxiety, chronic fatigue, obesity, and heart disease (Kurtz, Kurtz, Given, & Given, 2004; Raveis, Karus, & Pretter, 2004). Common stressors of family caregiving include role strain due to competing demands (Haley, 2003), family discord (Manne, 1998; Nijboer et al., 2000), isolation, and neglect of one's own health (Kim & Given, 2008; Northouse, 2005). Caregiving, however, can increase one's sense of self-worth and mastery, enhance emotional closeness among family members, and improve mood (Kim, Schulz, & Carver, 2007; Nijboer et al., 2000).

Family Communication and Decision Making

Older cancer patients and their families face decisions about all aspects of the patient's care, before and across the illness trajectory (Csikai, 2009). These include the decision to seek treatment, choice of provider, ongoing treatment decisions, and choice of care settings (e.g., home, nursing home, hospice residence). Inherent to these tasks is communication about topics not previously broached, which can trigger family conflicts (Csikai, 2009; Kramer, Boelk, & Auer, 2006).

Communication and decision making in later life is generally consistent with long-standing familial patterns (Wellisch & Kissane, 2013). Structural and power dynamics shift after adult children mature, making direct communication and conflict resolution more difficult. Kramer et al. (2006) found that past conflict, a closed communication style, and the perception that one family member is taking undue control can lead to family conflict at the end of life.

Ted Wilson is a 68-year-old African American man with metastatic prostate cancer. Ted, a retired electrical engineer, lives with his wife, Alva, of 41 years. He has been in relatively good health until now. They exercise daily and enjoy traveling several times a year. He has thus far experienced little pain or discomfort and feels confident that—despite a poor prognosis—his treatment is working and he will "beat this thing."

Despite Ted's insistence that he doesn't want to "burden" his family, the Wilsons have actively worked together to help him manage the demands of his illness and treatment. Alva has taken time off from her job as a school administrator to accompany Ted to his medical appointments, participating in most of his conversations with his providers. Their only child, James, a 38-year-old pharmacist, lives with his wife and children in another state but checks in daily by phone. James has only been able to visit twice since Ted's diagnosis due to his responsibilities at work and to his family.

The Wilsons have not talked about Ted's care preferences or about what he wants to do if the treatment is ineffective. Alva and James both acknowledge to their social worker that they expect Ted's health to decline soon, but they respect Ted's optimism and resolve and don't want to "take away his hope." Ted shared with his nurse that he does not want extraordinary measures but has not talked with the family explicitly, identified a health care proxy, or documented any of his advance directives. After speaking with each family member, the social worker plans a family conference call to help the family begin to communicate about Ted's preferences and make decisions about his future care.

Advanced care planning presents additional challenges for families of older patients who are dying and for the providers who facilitate the process. As is the case with the Wilsons, many families avoid communicating about the patient's concerns and preferences until the last minute, when their time and capacity for decision making are limited and emotions are high (Waldrop, Kramer, Skretny, Milch, & Finn, 2005). When older parents are seriously ill, issues of inheritance and long-standing family rivalries or secrets may create additional barriers. Reluctance to talk about the decline and ultimate death of an older family member may emanate from cultural or spiritual beliefs that preclude talking about death or from a fear of "giving up hope." Such a discussion can be documented using state-approved documents such as the MOLST (Medical Orders for Life Sustaining Treatment) form (Csikai, 2009; Waldrop et al., 2005). Oncology social workers bring an understanding of family dynamics and communication to facilitating family conversations about everyone's concerns, values, needs, and hopes (Black, 2005; Fineberg, 2010).

Social Isolation and the Lack of Family Supports

Many older Americans in our increasingly mobile society live alone or lack the social supports necessary to manage chronic conditions, perform activities of daily living, or live independently (Victor, Scambler, Bond, & Bowling, 2000) and have a greater risk for illness, economic insecurity and hunger, unnecessary hospitalization, and mortality (Lyyra & Heikkinen, 2006; Murphy et al., 2008). Women with low levels of social integration before diagnosis of breast cancer had a 66% increased risk of all-cause mortality and a twofold increased risk of cancer mortality (Kroenke, Kubzansky, Schernhammer, Holmes, & Kawachi, 2006). After functional and cognitive impairment, living alone is one of the highest risk factors for nursing home placement (Gaugler, Duval, Anderson, & Kane, 2007).

Comprehensive Geriatric Assessment

Effective biopsychosocial care of older adults begins with multidimensional assessment of the individual's health, physical reserve, and functional status, including cognitive, behavioral, emotional, spiritual, and social functioning (Adler & Page, 2007; Extermann & Hurria, 2007). Comprehensive geriatric assessment gives providers a clearer view of the coming challenges and existing strengths (Hurria & Balducci, 2009). It also helps screen for developing physical and psychological comorbidities in nearly three quarters of older patients (Puts et al., 2012; Chapter 31).

Comprehensive assessment includes examining the family's living situation, functioning, history, processes, and illness beliefs. Oncology social workers should attempt to assess all family members' perceived burden, level of self-care, and quality of life (Kim & Given, 2008). Understanding social and financial family resources and openness to outside assistance maximizes engagement (Francoeur, 2001; Walsh, 2006). Such assessment and involvement allow the team to practice "family-centered care."

Family-Centered Practice

Oncology social workers help families adapt to changing roles and responsibilities, improve family problem solving and decision making, and help family members communicate more effectively with each other and with the health care team about patients' needs and preferences (Gardner & Werner-Lin, 2011; Wellisch & Kissane, 2013). Family conferences and family psychoeducation are evidence-based practices that reduce caregiver burden and depression, improve caregiver well-being, and promote self-efficacy in caring for older patients (Fineberg, 2010; Northouse, Katapodi, Song, Zhang, & Mood, 2010; Sörensen, Pinquart, & Duberstein, 2002).

Family caregivers consistently report a desire for more timely and accurate information about the patient's changing medical status (Given, Given, & Kozachick, 2001). Oncology social workers advocate for the needs of the patient and his or her family and help enhance communication between patients, family members, and care providers. Social workers also empower families to formulate and ask questions of their medical providers and access reliable resources online and in the community (AOSW, 2012; Blum, Clark, & Marcusen, 2001).

Interdisciplinary Collaboration

Research in geriatric oncology strongly supports the efficacy of coordinated and collaborative interdisciplinary team care to provide effective biopsychosocial care of seriously ill older adults and their families (Adler & Page, 2007; Mion, Odegard, Resnick, & Segal-Galan, 2006). Interdisciplinary care (including physicians, nurses, social workers, and professionals in rehabilitation medicine, nutrition, and mental health) is associated with improved health and psychological well-being, increased social integration, and reduced hospitalization in chronically ill older adults (Mukamel et al., 2006; Sommers, Marton, Barbaccia, & Randolph, 2000).

Evidence-Based Interventions

The literature on evidence-based, supportive interventions for older cancer patients and their families is still emerging. Most evaluated interventions are group programs for breast cancer patients and their spouses (Fisher & Weihs, 2000; Sörensen et al., 2002). Effective group interventions include psychoeducation, mutual aid, and cognitive behavioral approaches that increase patients' and families' sense of control and improve patients' and caregivers' well-being (Maramaldi, Dungan, & Poorvu, 2008). Chronic illness self-management and medication management programs have been found to increase medical understanding, engage patients and families in the patient's care, and reduce unnecessary hospitalizations (McCorkle et al., 2011). Interventions increase knowledge and self-efficacy, reduce caregiver burden, and increase well-being among family caregivers (Sörensen et al., 2002).

Promising interventions that are currently being evaluated by oncology social workers and nurses include telehealth and web-based groups designed to reduce symptom burden and social isolation for homebound elders (Glueckauf & Ketterson, 2004; Head et al., 2011) and home-based exercise and nutrition interventions that aim to improve functioning, prevent falls, and reduce readmissions for older patients after discharge (Snyder et al., 2009). There is some evidence that case management, care coordination, and family conferences help older patients and their families navigate complex systems, access and utilize appropriate resources, and reduce polypharmacy among frail elders (Balducci, Goetz-Parten, & Steinman, 2013; Fineberg, 2010). Screening and assessment interventions, such as ongoing, regular comprehensive geriatric assessment, have demonstrated some success to reduce morbidity and maintain quality of life in older breast cancer patients (Extermann et al., 2004).

Pearls

- Older adults have a higher risk for cancer and other diseases that may affect cancer treatment, care, and recovery.
- Treatment decisions should be made based on the older adults' physical condition and functional abilities, not on the person's age.
- Managing the multiple comorbidities and identifying capable and affordable caregiving are emerging challenges for managing the care of the older cancer patient.
- Building on strengths and resilience of identified, previous coping experiences of older adults and their families is critical to effective interventions.

Pitfalls

- Failing to conduct a comprehensive geriatric assessment of the older adult with a diagnosis of cancer to determine treatment and care plan.
- Inadequate training in interdisciplinary care of older adults, family-centered practice, and support for caregivers.
- Oncology social workers need expertise in evidence-based interventions such as family conferences and telehealth that support older patients and their families and may improve access to care.

Oncology social workers are critical to the provision of high-quality, family-centered biopsychosocial care to older cancer patients and their families through the illness trajectory, across institutional and community-based systems, and on micro and macro levels. Oncology social workers help patients and families cope with the illness and treatment, navigate complex health and social support systems, access needed services and resources, communicate more openly with each other and with care providers, and make informed decisions about all aspects of patient care. Our commitment to cultural proficiency and social justice promotes sensitivity to the needs of underserved patients and families and guides our ongoing efforts to reduce inequalities (Association of Oncology Social Work, 2012).

ADDITIONAL RESOURCES

Morrison, R. S., Meier, D., & Capello, C. (Eds.). (2003). *Geriatric palliative care*. New York, NY: Oxford University Press.

Shapiro, G., & Browner, I. (2010). *Johns Hopkins patients' guide to cancer in older adults*. Boston, MA: Jones & Bartlett Learning.

REFERENCES

Adler, N., & Page, A. (Eds.). (2007). *Cancer care for the whole patient: Meeting psychosocial needs*. Washington, DC: National Academies Press.

American Cancer Society (ACS). (2012). *Cancer facts and figures: 2013*. Atlanta, GA: Author. Retrieved from http://www.cancer.org/acs/groups/content/@epidemiologysurveilance/documents/document/acspc-036845.pdf

Association of Oncology Social Work (AOSW). (2012). *AOSW oncology social work standards of practice*. Retrieved from http://www.aosw.org/iMIS201/AOSWMain/professionals/standards-of-practice/AOSWMain/Professional-Development/standards-of-practice.aspx?hkey=51fda308-28bd-48b0-8a75-a17d01251b5e

Balducci, L., & Ershler, W. (2005). Cancer and ageing: A nexus at several levels. *Nature Reviews: Cancer*, *5*(8), 655–662.

Balducci, L., Goetz-Parten, D., & Steinman, M. (2013). Polypharmacy and the management of the older cancer patient. *Annals of Oncology*, *24*(Suppl. 7), 36–40.

Black, K. (2005). Advance directive communication practices: Social workers' contributions to the interdisciplinary health care team. *Social Work in Health Care*, *40*(3), 39–55.

Blum, D., Clark, E., & Marcusen, C. (2001). Oncology social work in the 21st century. In M. M. Lauria, E. J. Clark, J. F. Hermann, and N. M. Stearns (Eds.), *Social work in oncology: Supporting survivors, families, and caregivers* (pp. 45–71). Atlanta, GA: American Cancer Society.

Centers for Disease Control and Prevention (CDC). (2011). U.S. Cancer Statistics: 1999–2009 Incidence. *WONDER Online Database*. Retrieved from http://wonder.cdc.gov/cancer-v2009.html

Charles, K., & Sevak, P. (2005). Can family caregiving substitute for nursing home care? *Journal of Health Economics*, *24*(6), 1174–1190.

Csikai, E. (2009). Communication related to end-of-life care and decisions. In J. Werth & D. Blevins (Eds.), *Decision making near the end of life* (pp. 169–188). New York, NY: Routledge.

Extermann, M., & Hurria, A. (2007). Comprehensive geriatric assessment for older patients with cancer. *Journal of Clinical Oncology*, *25*(14), 1824–1831.

Extermann, M., Meyer, J., McGinnis, M., Crocker, T. T., Corcoran, M. B., Yoder, J., ... Balducci, L. (2004). A comprehensive geriatric intervention detects multiple problems in older breast cancer patients. *Critical Reviews in Oncology/Hematology*, *49*(1), 69–75.

Fineberg, I. C. (2010). Social work perspectives on family communication and family conferences in palliative care. *Progress in Palliative Care*, *18*(4), 213–220.

Fisher, L., & Weihs, K. (2000). Can addressing family relationships improve outcomes in chronic disease? *Journal of Family Practice*, *49*(6), 561–566.

Francoeur, R. (2001). Reformulating financial problems and interventions to improve psychosocial and functional outcomes in cancer patients and their families. *Journal of Psychosocial Oncology*, *19*(1), 1–20.

Fulton, M., & Riley Allen, E. (2005). Polypharmacy in the elderly: A literature review. *Journal of the American Academy of Nurse Practitioners*, *17*(4), 123–132.

Gardner, D., & Werner-Lin, A. (2011). Oncology social work. In S. Gehlert & T. Browne (Eds.), *Handbook of health social work* (2nd ed., pp. 498–525). Hoboken, NJ: John Wiley & Sons.

Gaugler, J., Duval, S., Anderson, K., & Kane, R. L. (2007). Predicting nursing home admission in the US: A meta-analysis. *BMC Geriatrics*, *7*(1), 13.

Given, B., Given, C., & Kozachick, S. (2001). Family support in advanced cancer. *CA: A Cancer Journal for Clinicians*, *51*(4), 213–231.

Given, B., & Given, C. W. (2009). Cancer treatment in older adults: Implications for psychosocial research. *Journal of the American Geriatrics Society*, *57*(2), 283–285.

Glueckauf, R., & Ketterson, T. (2004). Telehealth interventions for individuals with chronic illness: Research review and implications for practice. *Professional Psychology: Research and Practice*, *35*(6), 615–627.

Haley, W. (2003). The costs of family caregiving: Implications for geriatric oncology. *Critical Reviews in Oncology/Hematology*, *48*(2), 151–158.

Head, B., Keeney, C., Studts, J., Khayat, M., Bumpous, J., & Pfeifer, M. (2011). Feasibility and acceptance of a telehealth intervention to promote symptom management during treatment for head and neck cancer. *Journal of Supportive Oncology*, *9*(1), 1–11.

Hodges, L., Humphris, G., & Macfarlane, G. (2005). A meta-analytic investigation of the relationship between the psychological distress of cancer patients and their careers. *Social Science and Medicine*, *60*(1), 1–12.

Hurria, A., & Balducci, L. (Eds.). (2009). *Geriatric oncology: Treatment, assessment, and management*. New York, NY: Springer Publications.

Hurria, A., Browner, I., Cohen, H., Denlinger, C., Extermann, M., Ganti, A., ... Wildes, T. (2012). Senior adult oncology. *Journal of the National Comprehensive Cancer Network*, *10*(2), 162–209.

Kim, Y., & Given, B. (2008). Quality of life of family caregivers of cancer survivors. *Cancer*, *112*(S11), 2556–2568.

Kim, Y., Schulz, R., & Carver, C. (2007). Benefit finding in the cancer caregiving experience. *Psychosomatic Medicine*, *69*(3), 283–291.

Kotkamp-Mothes, N., Slawinsky, D., Hindermann, S., & Strauss, B. (2005). Coping and psychological well-being in families of elderly cancer patients. *Critical Reviews in Oncology/Hematology*, *55*(3), 213.

Kramer, B. J., Boelk, A., & Auer, C. (2006). Family conflict at the end of life: Lessons learned in a model program for vulnerable older adults. *Journal of Palliative Care*, *9*(3), 791–801.

Kroenke, C., Kubzansky, L., Schernhammer, E., Holmes, M., & Kawachi, I. (2006). Social networks, social support, and survival after breast cancer diagnosis. *Journal of Clinical Oncology*, *24*(7), 1105–1111.

Kurtz, M., Kurtz, J., Given, C., & Given, B. (2004). Depression and physical health among family caregivers of geriatric patients with cancer—A longitudinal view. *Medical Science Monitor: International Medical Journal of Experimental and Clinical Research*, *10*(8), CR447.

Lyyra, T., & Heikkinen, R. (2006). Perceived social support and mortality in older people. *Journals of Gerontology*, *61B*, S147–S153.

Maggiore, R., Gross, C., & Hurria, A. (2010). Polypharmacy in older adults with cancer. *The Oncologist*, *15*(5), 507–522.

Manne, S. (1998). Cancer in the marital context: A review of the literature. *Cancer Investigation*, *16*(3), 188–202.

Maramaldi, P., Dungan, S., & Poorvu, N. (2008). Cancer treatments. *Journal of Gerontological Social Work*, *50*(S1), 45–77.

Marengoni, A., Rizzuto, D., Wang, H., Winblad, B., & Fratiglioni, L. (2009). Patterns of chronic multimorbidity in the elderly population. *Journal of the American Geriatrics Society*, *57*(2), 225–230.

McCorkle, R., Ercolano, E., Lazenby, M., Schulman-Green, D., Schilling, L. S., Lorig, K., & Wagner, E. H. (2011). Self-management: Enabling and empowering patients living with cancer as a chronic illness. *CA: A Cancer Journal for Clinicians*, *61*(1), 50–62.

Mion, L., Odegard, P., Resnick, B., & Segal-Galan, F. (2006). Geriatrics Interdisciplinary Advisory Group AGS: Interdisciplinary care for older adults with complex needs: American Geriatrics Society position statement. *Journal of the American Geriatrics Society*, *54*, 849–852.

Mukamel, D., Temkin-Greener, H., Delavan, R., Peterson, D., Gross, D., Kunitz, S., & Williams, T. (2006). Team performance and risk-adjusted health outcomes in the program of all-inclusive care for the elderly (PACE). *The Gerontologist*, *46*(2), 227–237.

Murphy, B., Elliott, P., Le Grande, M., Higgins, R., Ernest, C., Goble, A., Tatoulis, J., & Worcester, M. (2008). Living alone predicts 30-day hospital readmission after coronary artery bypass graft surgery. *European Journal of Cardiovascular Prevention and Rehabilitation*, *15*, 210–215.

Nijboer, C., Triemstra, M., Tempelaar, R., Mulder, M., Sanderman, R., & van den Bos, G. A. (2000). Patterns of caregiver experiences among partners of cancer patients. *The Gerontologist*, *40*(6), 738–746.

Northouse, L. (2005). Helping families of patients with cancer. *Oncology Nursing Forum*, *32*(4), 743–750.

Northouse, L., Katapodi, M., Song, L., Zhang, L., & Mood, D. (2010). Interventions with family caregivers of cancer patients: Meta-analysis of randomized trials. *CA: A Cancer Journal for Clinicians*, *60*(5), 317–339.

Patterson, J. (2002). Integrating family resilience and family stress theory. *Journal of Marriage and Family*, *64*(2), 349–360.

Pillemer, K., Suitor, J., Mock, S. E., Sabir, M., Pardo, T., & Sechrist, J. (2007). Capturing the complexity of intergenerational relations: Exploring ambivalence within later-life families. *Journal of Social Issues*, *63*(4), 775–791.

Puts, M., Hardt, J., Monette, J., Girre, V., Springall, E., & Alibhai, S. (2012). Use of geriatric assessment for older adults in the oncology setting: A systematic review. *Journal of the National Cancer Institute*, *104*(15), 1134–1164.

Rabow, M., Hauser, J., & Adams, J. (2004). Supporting family caregivers at the end of life: "They don't know what they don't know." *JAMA: Journal of the American Medical Association*, *291*(4), 483–491.

Raveis, V., Karus, D., & Pretter, S. (2004). Impact of cancer caregiving over the disease course: Depressive distress in adult daughters. *Psycho-Oncology*, *13*, S47.

Repetto, L. (2003). Greater risks of chemotherapy toxicity in elderly patients with cancer. *Journal of Supportive Oncology*, *1*(4 Suppl. 2), 18–24.

Snyder, D. C., Morey, M. C., Sloane, R., Stull, V., Cohen, H. J., Peterson, B., . . . Demark-Wahnefried, W. (2009). Reach out to ENhancE Wellness in Older Cancer Survivors (RENEW): Design, methods and recruitment challenges of a home-based exercise and diet intervention to improve physical function among long-term survivors of breast, prostate, and colorectal cancer. *Psycho-Oncology*, *18*(4), 429–439.

Sommers, L., Marton, K., Barbaccia, J., & Randolph, J. (2000). Physician, nurse, and social worker collaboration in primary care for chronically ill seniors. *Archives of Internal Medicine*, *160*, 1825–1833.

Sörensen, S., Pinquart, M., & Duberstein, P. (2002). How effective are interventions with caregivers? An updated meta-analysis. *The Gerontologist*, *42*(3), 356–372.

Victor, C., Scambler, S., Bond, J., & Bowling, A. (2000). Being alone in later life: Loneliness, social isolation, and living alone. *Reviews in Clinical Gerontology*, *10*(4), 407–417.

Waldrop, D., Kramer, B. J., Skretny, J., Milch, R., & Finn, W. (2005). Final transitions: Family caregiving at the end of life. *Journal of Palliative Medicine*, *8*(3), 623–638.

Walsh, F. (2006). *Strengthening family resilience* (2nd ed.). New York, NY: Guilford Press.

Weitzner, M., Haley, W., & Chen, H. (2000). The family caregiver of the older cancer patient. *Hematology/Oncology Clinics of North America*, *14*(1), 269–281.

Wellisch, D., & Kissane, D. (2013). Family issues and palliative care. In H. Chochinov & W. Breitbart (Eds.), *Handbook of psychiatry in palliative medicine* (2nd ed., pp. 220–235). New York, NY: Oxford University Press.

XIII

Loss, Grief, and Bereavement

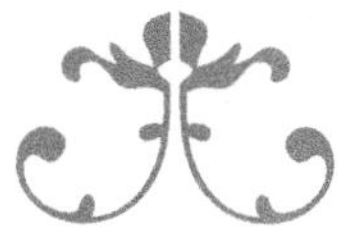

Mary Sormanti

Given the life-altering and life-threatening potential of serious illness, stress and change are inevitable components of the illness experience for everyone affected—even when treatment is successful. For this reason, oncology social workers are always attuned to the many and varied losses that can accompany the diagnosis and treatment of cancer and the understandable grief people face in their wake. Even in the current context of medical and technological advances so great that long-term survival is now common with numerous types of cancer, the disease is fatal for many individuals, leaving that many more family members and friends to grieve these deaths. In this section, authors turn their attention to some of the unique losses and grief associated with the death of a loved one to cancer, as well as related interventions. Although proportionally this subgroup is much smaller than it once was, addressing their needs remains an important goal for oncology social workers. Moreover, because conversations about dying and death are still considered sources of considerable distress and anxiety by much of the lay public, and thus avoided, a focus on bereavement is especially critical.

In the opening chapter, "Understanding Bereavement: How Theory, Research, and Practice Inform What We Do," Mary Sormanti provides an overview of prominent theories that have guided the profession's understanding of bereavement and empirical findings that have supported or contradicted them. The chapter highlights the variations and complexities of grief responses, including current conceptualizations about what is normative and the contextual factors understood to be correlated with better or poorer adjustment to bereavement for some samples. Also included are highlighted findings from the steadily growing literature on bereavement interventions and suggested readings about interventions that are likely to be especially relevant to oncology social workers.

Two of the remaining five chapters in this section address the bereavement experiences of specific populations. In "Spousal/Intimate Partner Loss and Bereavement," Deborah Carr offers a comprehensive overview of the psychosocial context and outcomes of widowhood. She reminds readers that widowhood is not simply a potentially tragic event but rather an adjustment process shaped by a range of risk and protective factors, which she describes and groups into easily understood categories, including the nature of the marital relationship and co-occurring losses and stressors. Of particular relevance to oncology social workers is the author's synthesis of research findings, which demonstrates that certain factors related to the context of a spouse's death (e.g., surviving spouse's perception that quality of health care provided to the deceased was poor) affect bereavement outcomes.

In "Mourning the Death of a Child," Nancy F. Cincotta builds upon her general chapter on working with families of pediatric cancer patients (see Chapter 64) to address the issues faced by those who experience the death of a son, daughter, brother, or sister to cancer. Integrating findings from her own hospital- and community-based work with bereaved parents and siblings, Cincotta provides an intimate look into the thoughts, feelings, and behavioral responses of this distinctive subset of the bereaved and does so within a framework that highlights critical moments (e.g., the moment of death, the funeral) in what she calls the "bereavement journey." In addition to pearls and pitfalls, her chapter includes a succinct set of helpful hints that will be useful to even seasoned professionals.

Completing the section are two chapters dedicated to specific types of interventions with the bereaved. In "Developing Culturally Informed Research on Bereavement Interventions," Amy Yin Man Chow underscores the need for more sensitive and systematic ways of defining the psychosocial experience of bereavement in various cultural contexts and developing and testing interventions tailored to these experiences. She describes one such study, which featured careful adaptation of the content, structure, and format of an intervention to fit into the cultural context of widows based in Hong Kong. Chow's preliminary findings not only demonstrate improvements in widows' coping but also highlight the importance and feasibility of translating interventions to better reflect and serve different target populations.

Finally, in "Leading Bereavement Groups," Richard T. Hara and Rachel Odo provide a concise overview of the history and rationale for this important modality and details about the structural components and procedures for planning and implementing a bereavement group in the context of a cancer-related death. Highlights of the chapter include practical wisdom about such challenging issues as determining which individuals are likely to benefit from and contribute to a successful group experience, addressing participants' unhelpful comparisons with one another's losses and grief experiences, and balancing attention to participants' grief and to their efforts to continue living in their loved one's absence.

74 Understanding Bereavement: How Theory, Research, and Practice Inform What We Do

Mary Sormanti

Key Concepts

- *The field of bereavement studies has grown steadily over the past several decades and offers oncology social workers a rich and useful body of theoretical and empirical information.*
- *Within the broad and diverse scope of known grief reactions to the death of a loved one, mounting evidence suggests that certain reactions that remain highly intense for more than 12 months may be maladaptive;* complicated grief *and* prolonged grief disorder *are several of the proposed terminologies for such presentations.*
- *Many variables affect an individual's experience of bereavement; ongoing research will further contribute to a developing understanding of what contributes to better or poorer adjustment.*

Although the human experience of bereavement has a long and uninterrupted history, conceptual frameworks and theories about its mechanisms, mediators and moderators of risk and resilience, and outcomes have changed considerably over time. Throughout the 20th century, the work of prominent professionals such as Sigmund Freud, Eric Lindemann, John Bowlby, and Elizabeth Kübler-Ross brought increasing, systematic attention to the circumstances and needs of people suffering in the wake of great loss and stimulated development of specialized services aimed at mitigating its negative consequences. In the past several decades particularly, knowledge and intervention development, implementation, and evaluation efforts in bereavement have burgeoned, resulting in a rich, sometimes dizzying array of ideas, theories, and practices for contemporary professionals—and laypersons—to draw upon. This chapter provides an overview of theoretical and empirical contributions to the field of grief studies and suggests ways oncology social workers might utilize and contribute to this knowledge base.

Prevailing Wisdom

With the works of pioneering scholars as a respected foundation (e.g., Bowlby's general attachment theory of loss, Kübler-Ross's stage theory of adjustment to one's own impending death), a steady procession of practitioners and researchers have since introduced new perspectives, questions, and data that have challenged, confirmed, extended, and replaced various pieces of the dynamic and expansive literature on loss and grief. Although many questions remain unanswered (indeed, some are not yet formulated), there is growing professional consensus regarding some fundamental, interrelated issues surrounding the grief of adults during bereavement, including (1) differential features, (2) related contextual factors, and (3) recommendations for professional intervention.

Defining Features of Bereavement-Related Grief

Within its overarching universality, grief is profoundly idiosyncratic. There are not only many and varied types of loss experiences but also a vast array of diverse individuals living in diverse contexts, responding to them (i.e., grieving) in assorted ways. Not surprisingly, a single definitive archetype of grief has not emerged. Instead, guided by social, cultural, historical, and biological forces, grief experiences have been scrutinized and categorized on a continuum of health and pathology alongside every other knowable human behavior. Nevertheless, grief is commonly characterized by some combination of emotional, physical, behavioral, relational, and spiritual changes. Although deep sadness is perhaps the most recognized and anticipated feature of grief, numerous other distressing emotions, cognitions, and behavioral responses (e.g., fear, anger, confusion, guilt, intrusive thoughts about the deceased, avoidance of reminders about the deceased) are also commonly experienced by people enduring the death of an important attachment figure.

Many studies have documented a wide range of grief's psychosocial morbidities. Among samples of people whose loved ones died of cancer, these include elevated rates of anxiety, depression, psychological distress, and poor quality of life (Caserta, Utz, & Lund, 2013; Rosenberg, Baker, Syrjala, & Wolfe, 2012). Bereavement is also associated with concurrent physiological changes. Some of these, for example, fatigue, shortness of breath, headache, and chest tightness, which also occur commonly in the wake of other stressful life events, are broadly regarded as manifestations of the "human stress response" (see Everly & Lating, 2013, for a useful overview). Although these physiological responses are often relatively mild and require minimal medical intervention, for some they may be associated with heightened risk for serious health problems (e.g., cardiovascular disease) and death (Buckley et al., 2012). Among adults bereaved as a result of cancer, researchers have noted increased risk for chronic pain (Ásgeirsdóttir, Valdimarsdóttir, Fürst, Steineck, & Hauksdóttir, 2013) and sleep disturbances (Valdimarsdottir, Helgason, Fürst, Adolfsson, & Steineck, 2003). The nature of these associations (i.e., the occurrence and relevance of potential mediators) is not sufficiently understood, however. Efforts to address this notable gap in the current literature are underway. For example, researchers determined that the somatic grief symptoms experienced by a sample of bereaved adults were mediated by anxiety rather than a direct consequence of their bereavement (Konkolÿ Thege, Pilling, Cserháti, & Kopp, 2012).

Despite these and other associated challenges, professionals generally agree that most people grieving the death of a loved one will adjust well to that loss without the need for professional help. Longitudinal data suggest that even some of the most distressing experiences that accompany grief (e.g., shock, deep yearning for the deceased, profound sadness) decline in intensity for most people across a 22-month follow-up period (Maciejewski, Zhang, Block, & Prigerson, 2007). According to the U.S. Department of Health and Human Services, "grief lasts as long as it takes you to accept and learn to live with your loss. For some people, grief lasts a few months. For others, grieving may take years" (Substance Abuse and Mental Health Services Administration, 2001. p. 1).

Other Notable Variations of Grief

A comprehensive understanding of grief is not limited to information about features commonly highlighted in the literature or reflective of many grievers (e.g., those who adapt well without professional intervention). Rather, it also includes information about characteristics and experiences of grief that are less frequently observed or documented, as well as those associated with smaller or marginalized subgroups of the bereaved. For example, although the relevance of culture is referred to with increasing frequency in the professional grief literature, culturally specific frameworks and interventions are a very small segment thereof (Hooyman & Kramer, 2006; Vazquez & Rosa, 2011). Also, although not the leading focus in either academic scholarship or popular books and media, bereavement may include responses not typically associated with distress such as relief, pride, peacefulness, satisfaction, and gratitude. Such responses occur in the context of oncology as well. For example, it is not uncommon for bereaved survivors to experience declines in levels of distress after the death of a loved one who has endured an extended period of illness and its many associated treatment demands and side effects (Waldrop, 2007). Some family members of cancer patients who had endured episodes of delirium during the last 2 weeks reported positive emotions such as relief and happiness that their loved one did not appear to be in pain during the episodes (Namba et al., 2007).

Similarly, oncology social workers know from their clinical experiences that family and friends can and will laugh and smile while sharing a funny anecdote about a deceased loved one, feel satisfaction or pride with their own caregiving efforts, and even feel happiness when others remember their loved one's unique qualities. In a study of more than 500 family caregivers of individuals with terminal cancer, a large majority reported positive consequences of their caregiving experiences (Kang et al., 2013). Other studies have documented a variety of reported positive aspects of caregiving provided by one spouse for another with cancer (Li & Loke, 2013).

Finally, it is also important to acknowledge that some bereaved individuals experience grief that falls on either side of what most professionals would describe as a wide continuum of adaptive responses. Individuals who experience very few signs of emotional distress and only in the period soon after the loss could be construed (Mancini, Robinaugh, Shear, & Bonanno, 2009) as being closer to one end of this continuum. Although this pattern of grief was once thought to be atypical and pathological, current research refutes these assumptions; consistent minimal distress following the death of a loved one is not only a relatively commonplace response but also can be adaptive (Mancini & Bonanno, 2011). For example, individuals frequently experience relief that a loved individual is free of pain, discomfort, or disability. The relationship to the deceased may have been ambivalent, negative, or quite limited, even though there was a formal family relationship, and therefore the loss evokes minimal distress.

Alternatively, individuals who experience unremitting intense grief for extended periods make up a smaller segment of the bereaved whose responses are considered to be maladaptive or pathological. The grief responses of this group have been categorized by some as "prolonged grief disorder" and others as "complicated grief." They reflect difficulties in intensity or duration that extend beyond those viewed as normative (Mancini, Griffin, & Bonanno, 2012; M. K. Shear, Ghesquiere, & Glickman, 2013). Both terms now have considerable empirical evidence of validity. Before current information and perspectives are described about the proposed subset of grief they reflect, a brief overview of several major paradigms regarding the course of grief and adjustment to it provides a useful context for understanding their development.

Course and Adjustment

Throughout much of the 20th century, Western theories and perspectives highlighted stages or phases of grief and related psychological and behavioral tasks deemed essential for healthy adaptation. Prominent among these were beliefs that the bereaved must release their emotional attachment to a deceased loved one and actively grapple with thoughts, feelings, and memories related to a loved one's death (i.e., "grief work"). Over time, as the knowledge base and its contributors shifted and expanded, even these well-established perspectives were challenged and newer paradigms emerged. Given their contributions to the field of grief studies, two of these—the "continuing bonds" framework popularized by Klass, Silverman, and Nickman (1996) and the Dual Process Model proposed by M. S. Stroebe and Schut (1999)—merit attention.

The Continuing Bonds Framework

More than 20 years ago, M. Stroebe, Gergen, Gergen, and Stroebe (1992) scrutinized the assumption that healthy adjustment to bereavement could be achieved only if attachments to the deceased person were relinquished (called the "breaking bonds" perspective). This point of view, they argued, was culturally biased and pathologized grief reactions (e.g., frequent visitations to gravesites, talking with the dead) that, in some situations and settings, are considered appropriate and sensible. They believed the breaking bonds perspective failed to offer a comprehensive understanding of bereavement. In response, they initiated research to explore the sociocultural context of bereavement and called upon others to do the same. As a result, an exciting and rich body of work examining sociocultural variables and a new framework called the "continuing bonds" perspective emerged.

Rather than automatically and uniformly pathologizing survivors' desires and attempts to stay connected with deceased loved ones, the continuing bonds perspective suggested that interacting with the dead was not only common but also quite possibly healthy (Silverman & Klass, 1996). Perhaps not surprisingly, given the field's push to expand its knowledge base, the continuing bonds perspective was quickly integrated into both professional and popular literature. Although this new paradigm invited an expanded definition of healthy adjustment to bereavement and reinvigorated scholarship in the field, it may also have had an unintended downside: Some misinterpreted the framework as an assertion that continuing bonds led to healthy adjustment to the death of a loved one, what Klass (2006) called the "causality thesis." Subsequent investigations of the associations between continuing bonds and adjustment have yielded equivocal data, and various findings suggest that ongoing connections with a deceased loved one facilitate, hinder, or demonstrate no relationship to the survivor's adjustment to bereavement (M. S. Stroebe & Schut, 2005). Klass (2006) argued that these disparate results reflected a too-narrow analytic frame and encouraged the field to explore more substantive complexities of bereavement, including ways social, political, and cultural variables may shape it.

The Dual Process Model

The Dual Process Model (DPM) of grief, developed by M. S. Stroebe and Schut (1999), also emerged through research that challenged prevailing assumptions. According to the DPM, bereaved individuals face two distinct areas of challenge: (1) separating from the person who has died and (2) building a new life and identity in that person's physical absence. In contrast to the widely accepted assertion that repeated, active, and direct attention to the loss is necessary for healthy adaptation, the DPM conceptualized grief as a process involving both confrontation and avoidance of painful cognitive and emotional aspects of loss. Rather than a completion of tasks proposed by previous theorists, adaption to grief results from a dynamic "oscillation" between attending to both the loss ("loss-oriented coping") and the resumption of life in its wake ("restoration-oriented coping"). Coping efforts once considered extreme or even abnormal (e.g., maintaining an emotional connection to the deceased, resuming one's life, and feeling okay or even happy at times) were reframed as potentially reasonable and useful.

Loss-oriented coping efforts include crying, yearning, ruminating about the deceased and times spent with him or her, and retelling the circumstances surrounding the death. Restoration-oriented processes center on the development of a new life and identity in the wake of the loved one's death; related activities include efforts to manage the "secondary consequences" associated with a loved one's death such as taking over tasks and responsibilities the deceased used to manage, navigating social relationships and interactions as a person now seen as different than before his or her loved one's death, and engaging in pleasurable and otherwise meaningful activities that serve as distractions from grief. Although both processes occur during bereavement, M. S. Stroebe and Schut (2010) suggest loss-oriented coping is likely to be more prominent earlier in bereavement, whereas restoration-oriented coping is likely to become more central later.

Regardless of an individual's balance between the two processes, the DPM's broader conceptualization of adaptation to bereavement addressed several noted gaps in earlier grief theories and was well received by experts. Subsequent research has provided validation for the model's primary concepts (loss-oriented coping, restoration-oriented coping, oscillation). Richardson (2006) found that women and men engaged in both loss- and restoration-oriented coping activities at 6 and 18 months and 4 years after the death of a spouse. Similarly, Caserta and Lund (2007) found evidence of engagement in loss- and restoration-oriented activities among women and men during the earlier (average 3.5 months postdeath) and later (average 13 months postdeath) periods of spousal bereavement. Further testing and evaluation, including with other subgroups of the bereaved (e.g., youth), may guide elaboration and revision of the DPM.

Prolonged Grief Disorder and Complicated Grief

Prevalence estimates of grief that falls outside current conceptualizations of what is considered normative for bereavement vary by study sample and defining criteria (e.g., complicated grief, prolonged grief disorder). Estimates range from just under 4% of a population-based sample (Kersting, Brähler, Glaesmer, & Wagner, 2011) to 19% of a sample of bereaved young adults (Herberman Mash, Fullerton, & Ursano, 2013) to more than 75% of adults who experienced the death of a child to suicide or accident (K. Dyregrov, Nordanger, & Dyregrov, 2003). In one study, more than 40% of adults grieving the death of a family member to suicide met criteria for complicated grief, with closely related survivors experiencing nearly twice the level of complicated grief as distantly related survivors (Mitchell, Kim, Prigerson, & Mortimer-Stephens, 2004). In another study, 20% of bereaved adults grieving the death of a relative who had suffered with dementia and for whom they had been the caregiver demonstrated complicated grief (Schulz, Boerner, Shear, Zhang, & Gitlin, 2006). And in yet another, 14% of adults who had experienced the death of a family member to genocide decades earlier continued to meet criteria for complicated grief (Stammel et al., 2013).

The common features of grief noted in these small subgroups of the bereaved are similar to those characteristic for many during the immediate, short-term aftermath of a meaningful loss (e.g., emotional and cognitive distress, yearning for the deceased, preoccupation with the deceased or circumstances of the death, excessive avoidance of reminders of the deceased; Kacel, Gao, & Prigerson, 2011; Lobb et al., 2010; M. K. Shear, 2012), with identified variations in their intensity, duration, and quality (M. Stroebe, Schut, & van den Bout, 2013). M. K. Shear et al. (2013), for example, refer to this cluster of symptoms as "prolonged acute grief," which they believe reflects a distinct mental health disorder. Others, including Wakefield (2013), assert that categorizing certain grief presentations (e.g., intense yearning) as pathological—rather than extremes on a broader continuum of normalcy—may be an artifact of current researchers' underestimations of the intensity and duration of normative grief.

Professional discourse about whether and how to delineate variations of grief has steadily increased over the past 20 years. Some of the previously noted manifestations of complicated grief resemble those associated with major depressive disorder (and posttraumatic stress reaction, to a lesser extent). To what extent these constructs overlap has been an important area of investigation that remains unresolved (Schaal, 2013). Other key aspects of this discourse include concerns about the potential for misdiagnosis, applicability to all subgroups of the bereaved (e.g., those with intellectual disabilities, bereaved parents), and negative ramifications of the medicalization of grief (Parkes, 2007; Thieleman & Cacciatore, 2014; Wakefield, 2013). Ongoing deliberation about these and other emergent issues is partially reflected in the diagnostic criteria and related descriptive text of disorders included in various iterations of the American Psychiatric Association's *Diagnostic and Statistical Manual of Mental Disorders* (DSM).

Although several proposals to include complicated grief as a diagnostic entry in the DSM have been reviewed by the respective task forces and work groups associated with every revision process, they have not been accepted to date. The *DSM-5* (APA, 2013) does include a description and explicit criteria for "persistent complex bereavement disorder" in its section devoted to conditions for further study.

Differentiating Grief and Major Depressive Disorder: Removing the Bereavement Exclusion in *DSM-5*

Also noteworthy in the *DSM-5* is the removal of an exclusion criterion for major depressive disorder (i.e., the "bereavement exclusion"), which had been in place since the 1980 publication of the *DSM-3*. At its simplest level, this criterion precluded a diagnosis of major depressive disorder if an individual's symptoms began within 2 months of a loved one's death. This relegated bereavement as the only stressful life event that excluded the diagnosis of major depressive disorder (Zisook & Kendler, 2007). Removal of the "bereavement exclusion" reverses this; according to the *DSM-5*, major depressive disorder can occur (and be diagnosed) within the context of bereavement. According to the best research available, any very stressful life event such as going through a divorce, being diagnosed with a fatal medical condition, becoming disabled, or facing financial ruin, as well as confronting the death of an important individual in one's life, can trigger a serious major depressive episode in a vulnerable person (Iglewicz, Seay, Zetumer, & Zisook, 2013).

As was the case before this controversial decision, professional opinions are mixed. According to Iglewicz and colleagues (2013), feared consequences of its removal have not materialized; rather, the *DSM-5* thoughtfully elucidates the boundaries and distinctions between bereavement and major depression (e.g., dysphoria may be evident in both, yet during the former tends to decrease in intensity fairly quickly and is associated with thoughts of the deceased, whereas in the latter it is far more persistent and generalized) and does not pathologize the former. Critics, however, assert that the bereavement exclusion represents a Western cultural tendency to medicalize psychosocial stressors and increase use of pharmacotherapy (Searight, 2014).

Ongoing attention to the *DSM-5* implementation processes and outcomes (e.g., population-based rates of diagnoses) will either substantiate or challenge this early assertion. Similarly, although some scholars are hopeful that research aimed at testing the validity of the *DSM-5* proposed criteria for "complex persistent grief disorder" may bring the field closer to consensus about the complex nature of grief (M. K. Shear et al., 2013), additional research will be an important factor in determining whether it will be included as a psychiatric condition in a future edition of the *DSM*. As suggested by M. Stroebe et al. (2013), who believe an interdisciplinary approach is required to advance the field of grief studies, "it is necessary not only to listen to researchers in order to build on our [complicated grief] knowledge base, but to listen to clinicians as well, and to try to understand what they are in fact doing and then unravel what it is that makes their techniques effective" (p. 311). Given the nature and volume of their practice, oncology social workers have important knowledge to contribute to this critical undertaking; their understanding of the many nuances of bereavement and interventions facilitating adjustment to it can meaningfully inform all phases of a research study.

Contextual Issues Pertinent to Bereavement-Related Grief

An evolving framework of categorized risk and protective factors associated with bereavement outcomes has been proposed by eminent scholars who have contributed to and reviewed related research from across the world (see Burke & Neimeyer, 2013; M. S. Stroebe, Schut, & Stroebe, 2007). For example, considerable research has explored the role of attachment style in bereavement, much of it suggesting that individuals with secure attachments to loved ones who have died may experience less severe symptoms of grief than those with anxious or avoidant attachments (Stroebe, Schut, & Stroebe, 2007; Wijngaards-de Meij et al., 2007). The relevance of available resources and supports during bereavement has also been an area of research focus. In one such investigation, among a national sample of bereaved parents whose children died of cancer, those who reported having access to psychological support from their child's health care team during the child's illness and an opportunity to talk about their child's condition with attending medical staff during the child's last month of life were more likely to have worked through their grief by 4 to 9 years (Kreicbergs, Lannen, Onelov, & Wolfe, 2007). Some research suggests that support from family and friends neither buffers the impact of bereavement nor facilitates one's recovery from it (W. Stroebe, Zech, Stroebe, & Abakoumkin, 2005). Still other research has found linkages between development of complicated grief and certain contextual variables including type of death, time since death, and relationship to the deceased (Newson, Boelen, Hek, Hofman, & Tiemeier, 2011) and age and physical health of the bereaved at the time of a loved one's death (Utz, Caserta, & Lund, 2012).

Taken together, these data underscore both the variations and complexities of grief responses and the need for ongoing knowledge development. Because the extant research is neither exhaustive nor definitive, categories (e.g., intrapersonal, situational and loss specific, social) and variables within the framework may warrant modification as new findings emerge. Additional research, for example, may either confirm the concept of complicated grief and further elucidate what contributes to its emergence as a distinctive variant of grief or indicate a required shift in areas of professional attention. New research may also facilitate even broader and more realistic conceptualizations and expectations about what is normative. Knowing which variables are currently understood to be correlated with better or poorer adjustment to bereavement for some samples may help oncology social workers decide where and what types of their services are most likely to be needed and effective.

Bereavement Interventions

Given the multiple losses associated with a diagnosis and treatment of cancer (e.g., health, sense of self and security, functioning, quality of life), provision of therapeutic interventions to grieving individuals is a cornerstone of oncology social work. Moreover, despite improved survival rates for many types of cancer (albeit within the harsh reality of health disparities), some people die as a result of cancer, leaving even more surviving loved ones to face the loss many consider to be the most challenging. Oncology social workers are uniquely prepared to intervene with people grieving the death of a loved one to cancer; they have a great range of clinical approaches, procedures, and techniques to offer in multiple modalities (e.g., individual, family, group) and service settings (e.g., hospital, community program, long-term care facility). This knowledge base and skill set is also meaningfully applicable to work with bereaved individuals whose loved ones died under a variety of different circumstances (e.g., accident, homicide, other illnesses, war). Perhaps even more important, experienced oncology social workers may be especially well prepared to identify and intervene on behalf of people affected by grief resulting from nondeath losses (e.g., divorce, mental illness, forced migration, aging, substance abuse, disability, partner and family violence, foster care, geographic relocation, incarceration), which frequently bring people to the attention of social workers and other human service professionals (Walsh, 2012).

Within the expanding field of grief studies, the literature about bereavement interventions has also grown. Contributions have begun to address some of its noted long-standing gaps, including (1) insufficiently detailed descriptions about the intervention processes and dynamics used routinely in practice settings, (2) sparse and inconclusive data about the effectiveness of bereavement interventions (Currier, Neimeyer, & Berman, 2008; Larson & Hoyt, 2007), and (3) too little collaboration among clinicians and researchers (Ayers, Condo, & Sandler, 2011). Noteworthy among these are edited collections by M. Stroebe et al. (2013), Wimpenny and Costello (2012), Neimeyer (2012), Neimeyer, Harris, Winokuer, and Thornton (2011), and Parkes and Prigerson (2010). Although each of these publications includes some attention to oncology (e.g., as a context for grief or related interventions), the bereavement needs of those who lose a loved one to cancer remain understudied (Kim, Lucette, & Loscalzo, 2013). Furthermore, although each of these publications includes chapters authored or coauthored by social workers, none uses a social work lens as either an organizing framework or prominent focus. Many books, including the *Oxford Textbook of Palliative Social Work* (Altilio & Otis-Green, 2011), *Living Through Loss: Interventions Across the Life Span* (Hooyman & Kramer, 2006), and *Grief and Loss: Theories and Skills for the Helping Professions* (Walsh, 2012), have been authored by social workers; grounded in the profession's values and aims, they provide a rich integration of theory, practice, and research about loss and grief that can guide social work practice with those bereaved as a result of cancer.

Social workers use a wide variety of approaches and techniques in their work with and on behalf of those who are grieving. Popular techniques and approaches have been organized conceptually in many ways, including by intended aim (e.g., acceptance, meaning reconstruction), cause of loved one's death (e.g., suicide, disease, sudden, expected), specific population (e.g., widows, parents, youth), prevention level (e.g., universal, selective, indicated), assessed need (e.g., information, emotional expression, mutual aid, cognitive restructuring), service setting (e.g., hospital), theoretical orientation (e.g., psychodynamic, cognitive), and required knowledge and skills for implementation. Ideally, intervention choice reflects careful consideration of these factors and empirical data about effectiveness and cultural relevance. Knight and Gitterman (2013), for example, assert that group work, which many social workers are trained to implement, has distinct advantages for bereaved individuals yet is underutilized.

Pearls

- Grief is a natural distress response to loss characterized by a broad array of reactions that vary in intensity and duration yet gradually diminish over a period of weeks to months. Grief characterized by consistently high intensity for at least 1 year is considered by many to be pathological.
- It is important to conduct a thorough assessment of the multilayered impact of bereavement (e.g., emotional, relational, cognitive, physical) and pay particular attention to those individuals identified as "high risk" (e.g., those with preexisting mental health conditions; those confronting traumatic, multiple, and cumulative losses; and those exhibiting symptoms of major depressive disorder).
- If complicated grief is identified, this determination should be shared with the individual along with referral for more intensive therapy (see M. K. Shear, 2012).
- Psychoeducation about the broad manifestations of uncomplicated grief is a critical intervention approach. This information encourages individuals to join with the social worker in determining whether and how their own responses compare to the "norm" and may provide an immediate sense of relief to the many whose distressing thoughts, feelings, and behaviors are not pathological.
- If a bereaved individual expresses interest in group-based intervention, consider referral to a time-limited group aimed at providing education and support to individuals experiencing a similar loss. It is widely believed that such homogeneity in a group setting will increase its effectiveness (Schneider, 2006) and may reduce social isolation.

Pitfalls

- Additional empirical studies of grief reactions in children are needed to determine how they develop over time and whether some may be "complicated" (see A. Dyregrov & Dyregrov, 2013).

- Additional research investigating the relevance of both currently accepted constructs of uncomplicated and complicated grief in diverse cultural groups and culturally determined aspects of grief is warranted.

Scholarship reflects thoughtful attention to the methodological and conceptual problems of earlier studies. As a result, a more robust and coordinated body of research is emerging, and with it, an increased likelihood that firmer conclusions can be drawn from the findings (e.g., which subgroups of bereaved might benefit from which types of interventions, at which points during bereavement). An intervention developed specifically for individuals exhibiting symptoms of complicated grief has demonstrated effectiveness for that group (K. Shear, Frank, Houck, & Reynolds, 2005). Internet-based (Wagner & Maercker, 2008) and family-focused (Kissane & Hooghe, 2011) intervention models have yielded promising results as well, although not enough to qualify them as efficacious for the treatment of complicated grief (Mancini, Griffin, et al., 2012).

REFERENCES

Altilio, T., & Otis-Green, S. (Eds.). (2011). *Oxford textbook of palliative social work*. New York, NY: Oxford University Press.

American Psychiatric Association (APA). (2013). *Diagnostic and statistical manual of mental disorders* (5th ed.). Arlington, VA: American Psychiatric Publishing.

Ásgeirsdóttir, H. G., Valdimarsdóttir, U., Fürst, C. J., Steineck, G., & Hauksdóttir, A. (2013). Low preparedness before the loss of a wife to cancer and the widower's chronic pain 4–5 years later—A population-based study. *Psycho-Oncology, 22*(12), 2763–2770.

Ayers, T. S., Condo, C. C., & Sandler, I. N. (2011). Bridging the gap: Translating a research-based program into an agency-based service for bereaved children and families. In R. A. Neimeyer, D. L. Harris, H. R. Winokuer, & G. F. Thornton (Eds.), *Grief and bereavement in contemporary society: Bridging research and practice* (pp. 117–135). New York, NY: Routledge.

Buckley, T., Sunari, D., Marshall, A., Bartrop, R., McKinley, S., & Tofler, G. (2012). Physiological correlates of bereavement and the impact of bereavement interventions. *Dialogues in Clinical Neuroscience, 14*(2), 129–139.

Burke, L. A., & Neimeyer, R. A. (2013). Prospective risk factors for complicated grief. In M. Stroebe, H. Schut, & J. van den Bout (Eds.), *Complicated grief: Scientific foundations for health care professionals* (pp. 145–161). New York, NY: Routledge.

Caserta, M. S., & Lund, D. A. (2007). Towards the development of an inventory of daily widowed life (IDWL): Guided by the dual process model of coping with bereavement. *Death Studies, 31*, 505–535.

Caserta, M. S., Utz, R. L., & Lund, D. A. (2013). Spousal bereavement following cancer death. *Illness, Crisis, and Loss, 21*(3), 185–202.

Currier, J. A., Neimeyer, R. A., & Berman, J. S. (2008). The effectiveness of psychotherapeutic interventions for bereaved persons: A comprehensive quantitative review. *Psychological Bulletin, 134*(5), 648–661.

Dyregrov, A., & Dyregrov, K. (2013). Complicated grief in children: The perspectives of experienced professionals. *OMEGA—Journal of Death and Dying, 67*(3), 291–303.

Dyregrov, K., Nordanger, D., & Dyregrov, A. (2003). Predictors of psychosocial distress after suicide, SIDS, and accidents. *Death Studies, 27*(2), 143–165.

Everly Jr., G. S., & Lating, J. M. (2013). The anatomy and physiology of the human stress response. In G. S. Everly & J. M. Lating (Eds.), *A clinical guide to the treatment of the human stress response* (pp. 17–51). New York, NY: Springer.

Herberman Mash, H. B., Fullerton, C. S., & Ursano, R. J. (2013). Complicated grief and bereavement in young adults following close friend and sibling loss. *Depression and Anxiety, 30*(12), 1202–1210

Hooyman, N. R., & Kramer, B. J. (2006). *Living through loss: Interventions across the life span*. New York, NY: Columbia University Press.

Iglewicz, A., Seay, K., Zetumer, S., & Zisook, S. (2013). The removal of the bereavement exclusion in the *DSM5*: Exploring the evidence. *Current Psychiatry Reports, 15*(11), 1–9.

Kacel, E., Gao, X., & Prigerson, H. G. (2011). Understanding bereavement: What every oncology practitioner should know. *Journal of Supportive Oncology, 9*(5), 172–180.

Kang, J., Shin, D. W., Choi, J. E., Sanjo, M., Yoon, S. J., Kim, H. K., ... Yoon, W. H. (2013). Factors associated with positive consequences of serving as a family caregiver for a terminal cancer patient. *Psycho-Oncology, 22*(3), 564–571.

Kersting, A., Brähler, E., Glaesmer, H., & Wagner, B. (2011). Prevalence of complicated grief in a representative population-based sample. *Journal of Affective Disorders, 131*(1), 339–343.

Kim, Y., Lucette, A., & Loscalzo, M. (2013). Bereavement needs of adults, children, and families after cancer. *The Cancer Journal, 19*(5), 444–457.

Kissane, D. W., & Hooghe, A. (2011). Family therapy for the bereaved. In R. A. Neimeyer, D. L. Harris, H. R. Winokuer, & G. F. Thornton (Eds.), *Grief and bereavement in contemporary society: Bridging research and practice* (pp. 287–302). New York, NY: Routledge.

Klass, D. (2006). Continuing conversation about continuing bonds. *Death Studies, 30*(9), 843–858.

Klass, D., Silverman, P. R., & Nickman, S. L. (1996). *Continuing bonds: New understandings of grief.* Washington, DC: Taylor & Francis.

Knight, C., & Gitterman, A. (2013). Group work with bereaved individuals: The power of mutual aid. *Social Work, 59*(1), 5–12.

Konkolÿ Thege, B., Pilling, J., Cserháti, Z., & Kopp, M. S. (2012). Mediators between bereavement and somatic symptoms. *BMC Family Practice, 13*, 59.

Kreicbergs, U. C., Lannen, P., Onelov, E., & Wolfe, J. (2007). Parental grief after losing a child to cancer: Impact of professional and social support on long-term outcomes. *Journal of Clinical Oncology, 25*(22), 3307–3312.

Larson, D. G., & Hoyt, W. T. (2007). What has become of grief counseling? An evaluation of the empirical foundations of the new pessimism. *Professional Psychology: Research and Practice, 38*(4), 347–355.

Li, Q., & Loke, A. Y. (2013). The positive aspects of caregiving for cancer patients: A critical review of the literature and directions for future research. *Psycho-Oncology, 22*(11), 2399–2407.

Lobb, E. A., Kristjanson, L. J., Aoun, S. M., Monterosso, L., Halkett, G. K., & Davies, A. (2010). Predictors of complicated grief: A systematic review of empirical studies. *Death Studies, 34*(8), 673–698.

Maciejewski, P. K., Zhang, B., Block, S. D., & Prigerson, H. G. (2007). An empirical examination of the stage theory of grief. *Journal of the American Medical Association 297*(7), 716–723.

Mancini, A. D., & Bonanno, G. A. (2011). Loss and grief: The role of individual differences. In S. M. Southwick, B. T. Litz, D. Charney, & M. J. Friedman (Eds.), *Resilience and mental health: Challenges across the lifespan* (pp. 189–199). New York, NY: Cambridge University Press.

Mancini, A. D., Griffin, P., & Bonanno, G. A. (2012). Recent trends in the treatment of prolonged grief. *Current Opinion in Psychiatry, 25*(1), 46–51.

Mancini, A. D., Robinaugh, D., Shear, K., & Bonanno, G. A. (2009). Does attachment avoidance help people cope with loss? The moderating effects of relationship quality. *Journal of Clinical Psychology, 65*, 1–10.

Mitchell, A. M., Kim, Y., Prigerson, H. G., & Mortimer-Stephens, M. (2004). Complicated grief in survivors of suicide. *Crisis: The Journal of Crisis Intervention and Suicide Prevention, 25*(1), 12–18.

Namba, M., Morita, T., Imura, C., Kiyohara, E., Ishikawa, S., & Hirai, K. (2007). Terminal delirium: Families' experience. *Palliative Medicine, 21*(7), 587–594.

Neimeyer, R. A. (Ed.). (2012). *Techniques of grief therapy: Creative practices for counseling the bereaved.* New York, NY: Routledge.

Neimeyer, R. A., Harris, D. L., Winokuer, H. R., & Thornton, G. F. (Eds.). (2011). *Grief and bereavement in contemporary society: Bridging research and practice.* New York, NY: Routledge.

Newson, R. S., Boelen, P. A., Hek, K., Hofman, A., & Tiemeier, H. (2011). The prevalence and characteristics of complicated grief in older adults. *Journal of Affective Disorders, 132*(1), 231–238.

Parkes, C. M. (2007). Dangerous words. *Bereavement Care, 26*(2), 23–25.

Parkes, C. M., & Prigerson, H. G. (2010). *Bereavement: Studies of grief in adult life.* New York, NY: Routledge.

Richardson, V. E. (2006). A dual process model of grief counseling: Findings from the changing lives of older couples (CLOC) study. *Journal of Gerontological Social Work, 48*(3–4), 311–329.

Rosenberg, A. R., Baker, K. S., Syrjala, K., & Wolfe, J. (2012). Systematic review of psychosocial morbidities among bereaved parents of children with cancer. *Pediatric Blood and Cancer, 58*(4), 503–512.

Schaal, S. (2013). Is prolonged grief distinct from depression? *Journal of Loss and Trauma: International Perspectives on Stress and Coping.* doi:10.1080/15325024.2013.822196

Schulz, R., Boerner, K., Shear, K., Zhang, S., & Gitlin, L. N. (2006). Predictors of complicated grief among dementia caregivers: A prospective study of bereavement. *American Journal of Geriatric Psychiatry, 14*(8), 650–658.

Searight, H. R. (2014). Expanding the boundaries of major depressive disorder in DSM-5: The removal of the bereavement exclusion. *Open Journal of Depression, 3*(1), 9–12. doi:10.4236/ojd.2014.31004

Shear, K., Frank, E., Houck, P. R., & Reynolds, C. F. (2005). Treatment of complicated grief: A randomized controlled trial. *Journal of the American Medical Association, 293*(21), 2601–2608.

Shear, M. K. (2012). Getting straight about grief. *Depression and Anxiety, 29*(6), 461–464.

Shear, M. K., Ghesquiere, A., & Glickman, K. (2013). Bereavement and complicated grief. *Current Psychiatry Reports, 15*(11), 1–7.

Silverman, P. R., & Klass, D. (1996). Introduction: What's the problem? In D. Klass, P. R. Silverman, & S. L. Nickman (Eds.), *Continuing bonds: New understandings of grief* (pp. 3–27). Washington, DC: Taylor & Francis.

Stammel, N., Heeke, C., Bockers, E., Chhim, S., Taing, S., Wagner, B., & Knaevelsrud, C. (2013). Prolonged grief disorder three decades post loss in survivors of the Khmer Rouge regime in Cambodia. *Journal of Affective Disorders, 144*(1), 87–93.

Stroebe, M., Gergen, M., Gergen, K., & Stroebe, W. (1992). Broken hearts: Love and death in historical perspective. *American Psychologist, 47*, 1205–1212.

Stroebe, M., Schut, H., & van den Bout, J. (Eds.). (2013). *Complicated grief: Scientific foundations for health care professionals.* New York, NY: Routledge.

Stroebe, M. S., & Schut, H. (1999). The Dual Process Model of coping with bereavement: Rationale and description. *Death Studies, 23*, 197–224.

Stroebe, M. S., & Schut, H. (2005). To continue or relinquish bonds: A review of consequences for the bereaved. *Death Studies, 29*(6), 477–494.

Stroebe, M. S., & Schut, H. (2010). The dual process model of coping with bereavement: A decade on. *OMEGA—Journal of Death and Dying, 61*(4), 273–289.

Stroebe, M. S., Schut, H., & Stroebe, W. (2007). Health outcomes of bereavement. *Lancet, 370*, 1960–1973.

Stroebe, W., Zech, E., Stroebe, M. S., & Abakoumkin, G. (2005). Does social support help in bereavement? *Journal of Social and Clinical Psychology, 24*(7), 1030–1050.

Substance Abuse and Mental Health Services Administration. (2001). *How to deal with grief.* HHS Publication No. KEN-01-0104. Retrieved from http://www.samhsa.gov/MentalHealth/Anxiety_Grief.pdf

Thieleman, K., & Cacciatore, J. (2014). When a child dies: A critical analysis of grief-related controversies in *DSM-5*. *Research on Social Work Practice, 24*(1), 114–122.

Utz, R. L., Caserta, M., & Lund, D. (2012). Grief, depressive symptoms, and physical health among recently bereaved spouses. *The Gerontologist, 52*(4), 460–471.

Valdimarsdottir, U., Helgason, A. R., Fürst, C. J., Adolfsson, J., & Steineck, G. (2003). Long-term effects of widowhood after terminal cancer: A Swedish nationwide follow-up. *Scandinavian Journal of Public Health, 31*(1), 31–36.

Vazquez, C. I., & Rosa, D. (2011). *Grief therapy with Latinos: Integrating culture for clinicians.* New York, NY: Springer Publishing Company.

Wagner, B., & Maercker, A. (2008). An Internet-based cognitive-behavioral intervention for complicated grief: A pilot study. *Giornale Italiano di Medicina del Lavoro ed Ergonomia, 30*, B47–B53.

Wakefield, J. C. (2013). Is prolonged/complicated grief a disorder? In M. Stroebe, H. Schut, & J. van den Bout (Eds.), *Complicated grief: Scientific foundations for health care professionals* (pp. 99–114). New York, NY: Routledge.

Waldrop, D. P. (2007). Caregiver grief in terminal illness and bereavement: A mixed-methods study. *Health and Social Work*, *32*(3), 197–206.

Walsh, K. (2012). *Grief and loss: Theories and skills for the helping professions*. Upper Saddle River, NJ: Pearson.

Wijngaards-de Meij, L., Stroebe, M., Schut, H., Stroebe, W., van den Bout, J., van der Heijden, P. G., & Dijkstra, I. (2007). Patterns of attachment and parents' adjustment to the death of their child. *Personality and Social Psychology Bulletin*, *33*(4), 537–548.

Wimpenny, P., & Costello, J. F. (Eds.). (2012). *Grief, loss, and bereavement: Evidence and practice for health and social care practitioners*. New York, NY: Routledge.

Zisook, S., & Kendler, K. S. (2007). Is bereavement-related depression different than non-bereavement-related depression? *Psychological Medicine*, *37*(6), 779–794.

75 Deborah Carr

Spousal/Intimate Partner Loss and Bereavement

Key Concepts

- *Spousal loss can occur at any age, yet, in the United States and most advanced nations today, it is a transition overwhelmingly experienced by persons aged 65 and older. Widowhood/widowerhood is the loss of one's husband, wife, or romantic partner through death.*
- *Bereavement is the objective condition of having lost someone meaningful through death.*
- *Complicated grief is a period of at least 6 months immediately following the death of a loved one, marked by prolonged acute grief symptoms and an unsuccessful struggle to rebuild one's life without the decedent. It affects roughly 10% of bereaved persons.*
- *Death context affects the grieving process and includes characteristics of the dying process and death, including location, cause of death, symptoms, duration of illness, pain, and intensity of caregiving.*
- *Caregiving is the process of providing direct physical, emotional, or instrumental care to a person with a physical or mental health condition and may involve basic care or complex personal and nursing care tasks.*
- *Widow(er)s' psychological adjustment varies based on the nature of the relationship lost.*
- *Tailored interventions that take into account heterogeneity in the widow(er)'s experience are more effective than a "one size fits all" approach.*

Spousal bereavement, or the death of one's husband, wife, or long-term romantic partner, is considered one of life's most stressful events (Carr & Jeffreys, 2011). Today, death in the United States and other wealthy nations typically occurs in later life following a long period of chronic illness, such as cancer. Consequently, widowhood is a stressor that overwhelmingly befalls older adults and, given that men have higher mortality rates than women and typically die before their spouse, creates a context where widowhood is largely an older women's problem (Miniño & Murphy, 2012).

Following the death of their spouse, most older adults experience a period of at least 2 weeks marked by sadness, depressive symptoms, and anxiety; a much smaller proportion experience more persistent or serious symptoms including complicated grief, major depression, physical health declines, or death (e.g., Utz, Caserta, & Lund, 2012). Given this wide variation in bereaved spouses' response to loss, researchers have focused on identifying specific characteristics of the late marriage, the survivor, and the death context that contribute to widow(er)'s adjustment.

This chapter (1) summarizes data on the demography of spousal bereavement in the United States today; (2) describes aspects of the late marriage (e.g., marital quality), death context (e.g., cause of death, caregiving, prolongation, quality of care), and co-occurring stressors (e.g., financial strains) that contribute to bereaved spouse well-being; and (3) suggests practices for social work professionals who work with newly and longer-bereaved spouses. Tailored interventions that take into account heterogeneity in the widow(er)'s experience are more effective than a one-size-fits-all approach.

Background: What We Have Learned So Far

The Demography of Spousal Bereavement

Spousal loss can occur at any age, yet, in the United States and most wealthy nations today, it is a transition overwhelmingly experienced by persons aged 65 and older. Of the roughly 900,000 persons widowed annually in the United States, nearly three quarters fall into this age category (FIFARS, 2012). And because life expectancy is roughly 79 years for men and 84 years for women, women are much more likely than men to become widowed (Miniño & Murphy, 2012).

Among persons aged 65 to 74, 26.3% of women but just 7.3% of men are widowed; at ages 75 and older, these percentages jump to 58.2% of women and 20.5% of men (Figure 75.1). This stark gender gap also reflects that widowers are far more likely than widows to remarry and thus may "exit" the widowed category. Widows are less likely than widowers to remarry because of a dearth of potential partners, because for persons aged 65 and older in the United States, the sex ratio is 1.5 women per every one man, and by age 85, this ratio is more than three women per every man. As a result, few widows have the opportunity to remarry even if they would like to do so. Additionally, cultural norms encourage men to marry women younger than themselves, so widowed men may opt to remarry a younger woman, whereas older widows do not typically have that option (FIFARS, 2012). Qualitative interviews also show that women who were caregivers to dying husbands, especially those dying from prolonged, distressing, and treatment-intensive illness such as cancer, are reluctant to remarry again and possibly relive the stressful role of caregiver (Bennett, Hughes, & Smith, 2003).

Far less is known about the number of bereaved persons following a long-term same-sex relationship. According to data from the 2010 U.S. census, there are currently 605,000 same-sex households in the United States, 27% of whom identify as married. The average age of the partners in same-sex households is 48 years old; roughly 13% are 65 or older, and 17% are between 55 and 64 years (Lofquist, 2011). Thus, many older gay and lesbian persons are at risk of losing a partner. As we discuss later in this chapter, gay and lesbian couples both face distinctive obstacles and have access to different resources than do straight couples as they cope with the loss of these relationships.

Historically, spousal or partner loss has been characterized as an *event* that occurs upon the death of one's spouse; however, contemporary late-life widowhood is best conceptualized as a *process*. Most older adults die as a result of chronic diseases that can persist for months and even years, requiring care from a personal caregiver (FIFARS, 2012). The four leading causes of death among older adults in the United States today—heart disease, cancer, cerebrovascular disease, and chronic obstructive pulmonary disorder—account for nearly two thirds of all deaths in this age group. Cancer accounts for 22% of these deaths and one third of all deaths among those aged 55 to 64; thus, most older adults become widowed after at least one spell of caregiving for an ailing spouse. In the case of chronic illness, such as most cancers, spousal caregiving may last for months or even years before death (Kim, 2013). The conditions leading up to and surrounding a spouse's death shape bereavement experiences and are an important consideration when developing interventions.

Adjusting to Spousal Loss: Risk and Protective Factors

Older adults vary widely in their psychological adjustment to the loss of a spouse or partner. Most have some symptoms of depression and anxiety during the first 3 to 6 months

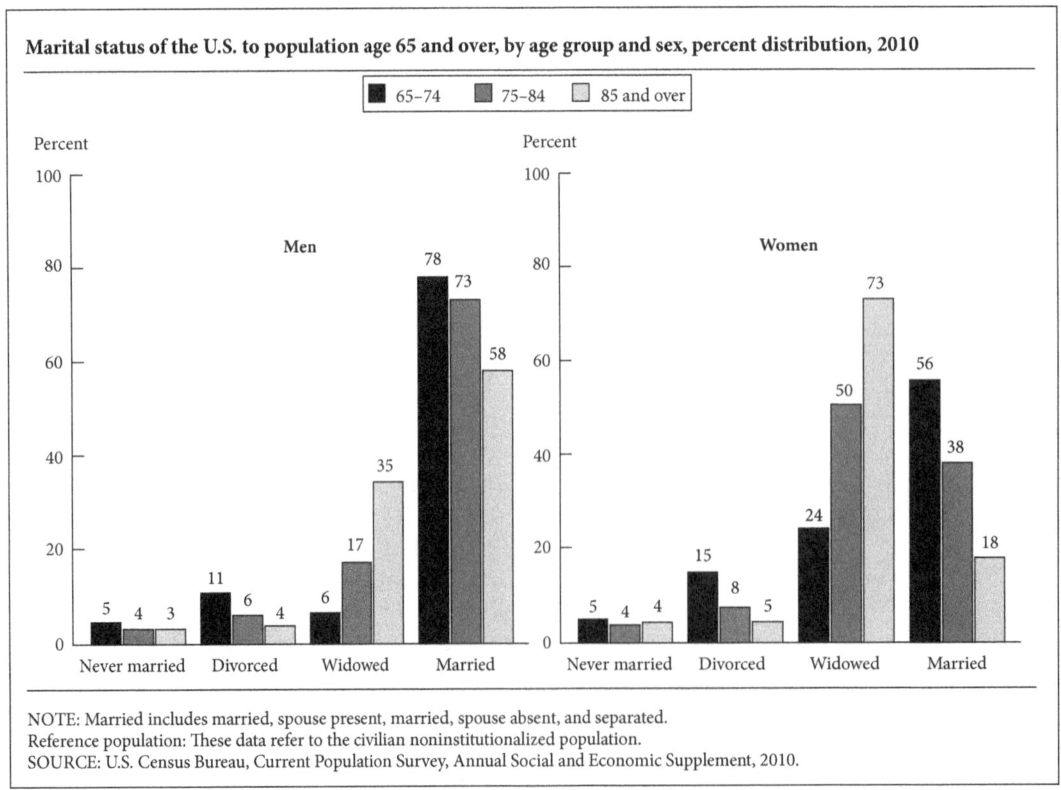

Figure 75.1. Proportion of Older Adults Who Are Widowed, Married, Divorced, or Never Married in the United States (2010)

following loss, although a sizeable minority may experience severe and persistent symptoms, including complicated grief. Complicated grief is diagnosed when an individual's ability to resume normal activities and responsibilities is continually disrupted beyond 6 months of bereavement (Prigerson, Vanderwerker, & Maciejewski, 2008). Myriad biological, psychological, social, and economic factors affect one's adjustment. I focus here on three influences that studies identify as both particularly important and potentially modifiable: the nature of the marital relationship, the death context, and co-occurring losses and stressors.

Nature of the Marriage or Romantic Relationship

Widow(er)s' psychological adjustment varies based on the nature of the relationship lost. Early writings, based on the psychoanalytic tradition, proposed that bereaved persons with troubled marriages find it hard to let go of their deceased spouses, yet also feel angry at the deceased for abandoning them and as a result are most likely to suffer heightened and pathological grief (Parkes & Weiss, 1983). However, contemporary longitudinal studies reveal different findings; older persons whose marriages were marked by high levels of warmth and dependence and low levels of conflict experience elevated grief symptoms within the first 6 months after loss because they yearned most strongly for their spouses (Carr, House, Wortman, Nesse, & Kessler, 2001).

Persons with marriages marked by high levels of warmth and low levels of conflict may suffer a greater sense of sadness within the earlier months of loss, yet their strong emotional ties to the late spouse may prove protective in the longer term. They may be able to draw strength from continuing bonds with the decedent. Early theories about grief held that bereaved persons needed to "relinquish" their emotional ties to the deceased and "get on" with their lives; current research, however, suggests that maintaining a psychological tie to the deceased is an integral part of adaptation (Field, 2008). For instance, bereaved persons may think about what their late spouse might have done when faced with a difficult decision. Others may keep alive their spouse's legacy by recognizing the continuing positive influence the deceased has on their lives. In this way, the warmth and closeness of the relationship may continue to be protective and affirming to the bereaved spouse (Root & Exline, 2013).

Given the complex ways in which cancer shapes marital relations, understanding the ways marital quality affects adjustment to the death of one's partner is particularly important for oncology social workers. Although research is equivocal, most studies find that a cancer diagnosis does not have either uniformly positive or negative implications for marital quality (Hagedoorn, Sanderman, Bolks, Tuinstra, & Coyne, 2008). Rather, the impact of cancer on marital relations is closely tied to the nature of one's marital relationship before the ill partner received a cancer diagnosis (Manne & Badr, 2008). A strong relationship may be a source of solace and support during times of distressing treatments and symptoms; for example, nearly half of women with breast cancer report that the cancer brought them closer to their spouse (Dorval et al., 2005). Conversely, a strained marriage marked by low levels of commitment may not survive the threats and changes imposed by a cancer diagnosis (Glantz et al., 2009). Thus, practitioners working with bereaved spouses of deceased cancer patients need to consider the history and nature of the marital relationship before loss when developing interventions and therapies.

Nature of the Death

Adjustment to spousal loss also is affected by the timing and nature of the death. In general, anticipated deaths tend to be less distressing than unanticipated ones (Carr et al., 2001). The knowledge that one's partner is going to die in the imminent future provides the couple with time to address unresolved emotional, financial, and practical issues. This preparation is believed to enable a smoother transition to widowhood (Carr, 2012). However, for older persons, "anticipated" spousal death often is accompanied by long-term illness, suffering, intensive caregiving, and neglect of one's own health concerns, thus taking a toll on the survivor's well-being (Carr et al., 2001).

Family caregivers—who currently number more than 50 million in the United States alone—experience a range of financial, psychological, and spiritual needs associated with the demands of their caregiving role and often require assistance before the death of their spouse (Family Caregiver Alliance, 2005). Caregivers may benefit from a range of services, including assistance with administering physical care, meal preparation, transporting the patient to treatment, and picking up prescriptions; spiritual support to make sense of the illness and death; and counseling to manage feelings of distress associated with caregiving burden and impending death (National Cancer Institute, 2013).

Caregiver distress levels vary based on the perceived difficulty of the care; those who reported high levels of physical, emotional, or financial strain due specifically to their caregiving responsibilities often show elevated physical and mental health symptoms after the loss (Kim & Schulz, 2008). Caregiving strains may be especially distressing in the days and weeks leading up to the death. In particular, those who provide complex illness-related tasks at home in addition to personal care (e.g., feeding, bathing, and toileting) may experience a crisis in caregiving that requires assistance or relocation of the patient outside the home (Waldrop & Meeker, 2011). Managing ventilators and feeding tubes, tending to pressure sores, and administrating medications are also linked to elevated symptoms of distress among family caregivers (Moorman & Macdonald, 2013).

Emerging research also suggests that caregivers may experience improved psychological well-being following the death of a spouse, perhaps because they are relieved of stressful caregiving duties, are no longer witnessing their loved one suffer, or feel a sense of satisfaction, meaning, and accomplishment from caring for their loved one in his or her final days (Schulz, Boerner, & Hebert, 2008). Practitioners should assess for strains and rewards of caregiving.

Quality of care and place of death also affect the bereavement experience. Older adults who believe their loved one was in pain or received problematic medical care at the end of life report greater postloss anxiety and anger than those whose loved one had a "good death" (Carr, 2003). Use of hospice or palliative care services at the end of life is associated with better bereavement outcomes (Christakis & Iwashyna, 2003). Site of care also matters. Teno et al. (2004) found that family members of recent decedents who received at-home hospice services were more likely than those who died at hospitals or nursing homes to say their loved one received high-quality care and was treated with respect and dignity at the end of life, and that they and the patient received adequate emotional support. However, most Americans currently die in institutions (FIFARS, 2010). The past decade has documented increases in the number of cancer patients who use hospice services, including in-home hospice. Still, fully one third of cancer patients spend their final days in hospitals and intensive-care units, and just over one half use hospice during their final month (Goodman et al., 2010). These patterns carry implications for survivors' well-being.

Other Losses and Stressors

Researchers agree that the psychological consequences of any one stressor may be amplified when experienced in conjunction with other losses or strains. For older bereaved persons, the death of a spouse is almost always accompanied by other stressors, including financial strain; retirement and relocation; compromised health and mobility; decline or loss of sensory functions, including vision and hearing; and even the loss of daily routines that gave one's life order and meaning (Carr & Jeffreys, 2011). In general, partner loss often sets off a chain of "secondary stressors," or stressors that result from the loss of a partner, that in turn may compromise one's emotional and physical well-being. For widowers from older, more traditionally gendered generations, the loss of a confidante, helpmate, and caregiver may be particularly harmful, whereas for widows, financial difficulties often are a source of distress.

The well-documented effects of widowhood on mortality risk, disability and functional limitations, and depressive symptoms are consistently larger for men than women (e.g., Lee & DeMaris, 2007). Although lore suggests that emotionally devastated widowers may "die of a broken heart" shortly after their wives die, research shows the loss of a helpmate and caretaker is really the culprit. Wives monitor their husbands' diets, remind them to take daily medications, and urge them to give up vices like smoking and drinking (August & Sorkin, 2010). Widowers are more likely than married men to die of accidents, alcohol-related deaths, lung cancer, and chronic ischemic heart disease during the first 6 months after their loss, but not from causes less closely linked to health behaviors (Moon, Kondo, Glymour, & Subramanian, 2011; Shor et al., 2012).

Widows, by contrast, often experience declines in their economic well-being, which may trigger anxiety and distress (Stroebe, Folkman, Hansson, & Schut, 2006). Widows experience serious declines in income from all sources, ranging from earned income to pensions to Social Security (Gillen & Kim, 2009). Costs associated with burial, funeral, long-term and medical care, or estate-related legal proceedings can devastate the fixed income of older adults. Because current cohorts of older women typically tended to childrearing and family responsibilities during their younger years, they have had fewer years of paid work experience and lower earnings than their male peers, on average. Older widows who try to re-enter the labor force also may face age discrimination. Younger widows, especially those charged with intensive caregiving, may have exited the labor market during a spouse's illness. Each of these strains may compound the emotional pain and cognitive disruption triggered by spousal loss.

Although gender differences have been widely investigated, relatively little is known about whether gay men and lesbians adjust differently than straight men and women to the loss of their long-term life partners. However, mounting research suggests that older gay men and lesbians may face both distinct challenges and advantages as they cope with loss. The stressors associated with loss may be particularly acute for gay men and lesbians, who may experience institutional and interpersonal discrimination due to their sexual orientation (Meyer, 2003). They may encounter conflict with their deceased partner's family, particularly with respect to the dispersion of personal possessions following death. Legal rights extended to heterosexual married couples have not typically been available for same-sex couples, including the opportunity to make health care and end-of-life decisions for ill partners. Bereaved same-sex partners may not receive sufficient emotional support upon loss because the end of their relationships is not recognized or acknowledged in the wider community (Green & Grant, 2008). The increasing legalization of marriage for same-sex individuals may gradually alleviate some of these stresses.

However, gay men and lesbians also have resources that may enable successful adjustment to partner loss. They have often created their own support networks of friends and selected family members. They also may be more likely than their heterosexual peers to enact flexible gender roles throughout the life course. Because they are not bound to traditional gender-typed family roles, they may be better prepared to manage the daily challenges and responsibilities faced by the newly bereaved (Almack, Seymour, & Bellamy, 2010).

Pearls

- Most widows and widowers are able to begin rebuilding their lives with reduced or less frequent intense grief symptoms about 6 months after the death of a spouse.

- Those whose strong grief symptoms continue and who are unable to begin rebuilding their lives are likely to benefit from more intense psychosocial counseling.
- Sources of stress are quite varied and can include anger about the context of the death, worry over the patient's care, financial challenges, and physical problems, including caregiver exhaustion and the need for relocation.
- Bereaved individuals may need interventions to help them rebuild their support networks, implement their stated goals for themselves, and regain a sense of agency about moving forward (Martell, Dimidjian, & Herman-Dunn, 2010).

Pitfalls

- Not intervening with, assessing, or referring bereaved individuals expressing intense depression and other psychological symptoms.
- Not making bereavement services accessible to bereaved individuals either in the hospital or community.

Contemporary research on spousal bereavement demonstrates that the extent to which widow(er)s mourn following their loss varies widely based on the nature of their marriage, the death context (including caregiving demands), and the postloss financial and lifestyle strains that may arise. Practitioners working with bereaved survivors of cancer patients need to consider this heterogeneity when developing interventions and therapies. The research reviewed in this chapter suggests three key messages for practitioners.

First, a one-size-fits-all model will not be effective in working with the bereaved. Most bereaved spouses experience short-term symptoms of sadness and loneliness and return to normal levels of psychological functioning within 6 months, even in the absence of psychological intervention. More-intensive interventions may be prioritized for those with the most serious symptoms (Bonanno & Lilienfeld, 2008).

Second, those who faced the greatest adversities either preceding or following the loss may be at highest risk of poor adjustment. For example, those with historically strained family relations or who have suffered economic disadvantage throughout their lives may have fewer resources to cope with the death of a spouse. As such, general interventions (bereavement groups or brief counseling) may be helpful but are insufficient for the most distressed individuals. Randomized controlled trials of therapeutic interventions with cancer patients' families both during the dying process and after the loss have been far more effective with functional rather than dysfunctional families; the latter require long-term and more intensive services (Kissane & Hooghe, 2011).

Third, perceptions of the death's context are linked to survivor adjustment. In particular, widow(er)s who view the death as unfair tend to report more symptoms of anger and intrusive thoughts than other bereaved persons (Carr, 2009). These symptoms are particularly distressing; intrusive thoughts may disrupt sleep and regular daily activities, whereas anger often places a barrier between the bereaved and those who would like to provide support. In cases where the surviving spouse viewed others as partly responsible for the death—whether health care professionals providing poor quality care or family members not providing appropriate home-based care—anger symptoms tend to be most severe (Carr, 2009). In such cases, therapists working with bereaved spouses may need to move beyond concrete facts regarding the death and instead focus on the widow(er)'s perceptions of conflicts and inequities during the dying and caregiving process (Kissane & Hooghe, 2011). Helping the bereaved make sense of and accept the death context may facilitate adjustment.

Although research delineates ways the death context shapes spousal bereavement, important questions remain unanswered. I know of no studies that explore the distinctive ways particular cancer deaths are grieved. For example, pancreatic cancer deaths typically occur much more suddenly and rapidly than lung cancer deaths, although the latter may entail more physically difficult and emotionally depleting caregiving demands. Furthermore, little is known about the ways specific combinations of illness and symptoms, such as cancer and dementia, affect the marital relation during the couples' final days, and consequently the survivor's adjustment to loss. Answers to these questions may help practitioners develop more effective and targeted interventions to protect family caregivers and ultimately widow(er)s.

ADDITIONAL RESOURCES

American Association of Retired Persons: Modern Hospice Care: http://www.aarp.org/relationships/caregiving/info-09-2011/modern-hospice-care.html

American Cancer Society: Coping with the Loss of a Loved One: http://www.cancer.org/treatment/treatmentsandsideeffects/emotionalsideeffects/griefandloss/coping-with-the-loss-of-a-loved-one-toc

Stanford Cancer Center: The Experience of Grief: http://cancer.stanford.edu/information/coping/grief.html

REFERENCES

Almack, K., Seymour, J., & Bellamy, G. (2010). Exploring the impact of sexual orientation on experiences and concerns about end of life care and on bereavement for lesbian, gay, and bisexual older people. *Sociology, 44*(5), 908–924.

August, K. J., & Sorkin, D. H. (2010). Marital status and gender differences in managing a chronic illness: The function of health-related social control. *Social Science and Medicine, 71*(10), 1831–1838.

Bennett, K. M., Hughes, G. M., & Smith, P. T. (2003). "I think a woman can take it": Widowed men's views and experiences of gender differences in bereavement. *Ageing International, 28*(4), 408–424

Bonanno, G. A., & Lilienfeld, S. O. (2008). Let's be realistic: When grief counseling is effective and when it's not. *Professional Psychology: Research and Practice, 39*, 377–380.

Carr, D. (2003). A good death for whom? Quality of spouse's death and psychological distress among older widowed persons. *Journal of Health and Social Behavior, 44*, 215–232.

Carr, D. (2009). Who's to blame? Perceived responsibility for spouse's death and psychological distress among older widowed persons. *Journal of Health and Social Behavior, 50*, 359–375.

Carr, D. (2012). Death and dying in the contemporary United States: What are the psychological implications of anticipated death? *Social and Personality Psychology Compass, 6*(2), 184–195.

Carr, D., House, J. S., Wortman, C. B., Nesse, R. M., & Kessler, R. C. (2001). Psychological adjustment to sudden and anticipated spousal death among the older widowed. *Journal of Gerontology Series B: Psychological Sciences and Social Sciences, 56*, S237–S248.

Carr, D., & Jeffreys, J. S. (2011). Spousal bereavement in later life. In R. A. Neimeyer, D. L. Harris, H. R. Winokur, & G. F. Thornton (Eds.), *Grief and bereavement in contemporary society: Bridging research and practice* (pp. 81–92). New York, NY: Routledge.

Christakis, N. A., & Iwashyna, T. J. (2003). The health impact on families of health care: A matched cohort study of hospice use by decedents and mortality outcomes in surviving, widowed spouses. *Social Science and Medicine, 57*, 465–475.

Dorval, M., Guay, S., Mondor, M., Mâsse, B., Falardeau, M., Robidoux, A., . . . Maunsell, E. (2005). Couples who get closer after breast cancer: Frequency and predictors in a prospective investigation. *Journal of Clinical Oncology, 23*, 3588–3596.

Family Caregiver Alliance. (2005). Selected long-term care statistics. Retrieved from https://caregiver.org/selected-long-term-care-statistics

Federal Interagency Forum on Aging-Related Statistics (FIFARS). (2012). *Older Americans 2012: Key indicators of well-being.* Washington, DC: U.S. Government Printing Office.

Field, N. P. (2008). Whether to relinquish or maintain a bond with the deceased. In M. Stroebe, R. O. Hansson, H. Schut, & W. Stroebe (Eds.), *Handbook of bereavement research and practice: 21st-century perspectives* (pp. 133–162). Washington, DC: American Psychological Association Press.

Gillen, M., & Kim, H. (2009). Older women and poverty transition: Consequences of income source changes from widowhood. *Journal of Applied Gerontology, 28*(3), 320–341.

Glantz, M. J., Chamberlain, M. C., Liu, Q., Hsieh, C. C., Edwards, K. R., Van Horn, A., & Recht, L. (2009). Gender disparity in the rate of partner abandonment in patients with serious medical illness. *Cancer, 115*(22), 5237–5242.

Goodman, D. C., Fischer, E. S., Chang, C., Morden, N. E., Jacobson, J. O., Murray, K., & Miesfeldt, S. (2010). *Quality of end-of-life cancer care for Medicare beneficiaries: Regional and hospital-specific analyses.* Hanover, NH: Dartmouth Institute for Health Policy & Clinical Practice.

Green, L., & Grant, V. (2008). "Gagged grief and beleaguered bereavements?" An analysis of multidisciplinary theory and research relating to same sex partnership bereavement. *Sexualities, 11*(3), 275–300.

Hagedoorn, M., Sanderman, R., Bolks, H. N., Tuinstra, J., & Coyne, C. C. (2008). Distress in couples coping with cancer: A meta-analysis and critical review of role and gender effects. *Psychological Bulletin, 134*, 1–30.

Kim, Y. (2013). Cancer caregivership. In B. I. Carr & J. Steel (Eds.), *Psychological aspects of cancer* (pp. 213–220). New York, NY: Springer.

Kim, Y., & Schulz, R. (2008). Family caregivers' strains: Comparative analysis of cancer caregiving with dementia, diabetes, and frail elderly caregiving. *Journal of Aging and Health, 20*, 483–503.

Kissane, D. W., & Hooghe, A. (2011). Family therapy for the bereaved. In R. A. Neimeyer, D. L. Harris, H. R. Winokur, & G. F. Thornton (Eds.), *Grief and bereavement in contemporary society: Bridging research and practice* (pp. 287–302). New York, NY: Routledge.

Lee, G. R., & DeMaris, A. (2007). Widowhood, gender, and depression: A longitudinal analysis. *Research on Aging, 29*, 56–72.

Lofquist, D. (2011). *Same-sex couple households: American Community Survey briefs.* Washington, DC: U.S. Census Bureau. Retrieved from http://www.census.gov/prod/2011pubs/acsbr10-03.pdf

Manne, S., & Badr, H. (2008, April). Intimacy and relationship processes in couples' psychosocial adaptation to cancer. In *Cancer survivorship: Embracing the future* (pp. 2541–2555). Washington, DC: American Cancer Society.

Martell, C., Dimidjian, S., & Herman-Dunn, R. (2010). *Behavioral activation for depression.* New York, NY: Guilford Press.

Meyer, I. H. (2003). Prejudice, social stress, and mental health in lesbian, gay, and bisexual populations: Conceptual issues and research evidence. *Psychological Bulletin, 129*(5), 674–697.

Miniño, A. M., & Murphy, S. L. (2012). *Death in the United States, 2010.* NCHS data brief, no. 99. Hyattsville, MD: National Center for Health Statistics.

Moon, J. R., Kondo, N., Glymour, M. M., & Subramanian, S. V. (2011). Widowhood and mortality: A meta-analysis. *PLoS ONE, 6*(8), e23465. doi:10.1371/journal.pone.0023465

Moorman, S. M., & Macdonald, C. (2013). Medically complex home care and caregiver strain. *The Gerontologist, 53*(3), 407–417.

National Cancer Institute. (2013). Coping with cancer: supportive and palliative care. Retrieved from http://www.cancer.gov/cancertopics/coping/familyfriends

Parkes, C. M., & Weiss, R. S. (1983). *Recovery from bereavement.* New York, NY: Basic.

Prigerson, H. G., Vanderwerker, L. C., & Maciejewski, P. K. (2008). A case for inclusion of prolonged grief disorder in DSM-V. In M. Stroebe, R. O. Hansson, H. Schut, & W. Stroebe (Eds.), *Handbook of bereavement research and practice: 21st-century perspectives* (pp. 165–186). Washington, DC: American Psychological Association Press.

Root, B. L., & Exline, J. J. (2013). The role of continuing bonds in coping with grief: Overview and future directions. *Death Studies, 38*(1–5), 1–8. doi:10.1080/07481187.2012.712608

Schulz, R., Boerner, K., & Hebert, R. S. (2008). Caregiving and bereavement. In M. Stroebe, R. O. Hansson, H. Schut, & W.

Stroebe (Eds.), *Handbook of bereavement research and practice: 21st-century perspectives* (pp. 265–286). Washington, DC: American Psychological Association Press.
Shor, E., Roelfs, D. J., Curreli, M., Clemow, L., Burg, M. M., & Schwartz, J. (2012). Widowhood and mortality: A meta-analysis and meta-regression. *Demography, 49*, 575–606.
Stroebe, M. S., Folkman, S., Hansson, R. O., & Schut, H. (2006). The prediction of bereavement outcome: Development of an integrative risk factor framework. *Social Science and Medicine, 63*(9), 2440–2451.
Teno, J. M., Clarridge, B. R., Casey, V., Welch, L. C., Wetle, T., Shield, R., & Mor, V. (2004). Family perspectives on end-of-life care at the last place of care. *Journal of the American Medical Association, 291*, 88–93.
Utz, R. L., Caserta, M., & Lund, D. (2012). Grief, depressive symptoms, and physical health among recently bereaved spouses. *The Gerontologist, 52*(4), 460–471.
Waldrop, D., & Meeker, M. (2011). Crisis in caregiving: When home-based end-of-life care is no longer possible. *Journal of Palliative Care, 27*(2), 117–125.

76 Mourning the Death of a Child

Nancy F. Cincotta

What do you pray for? "Gratitude for peace—assurance that our children knew that death was a gate, not a blind wall."

—Mother of two children who died of Fanconi anemia

Key Concepts

- *The death of a child is a most, if not the most, difficult loss for a family to face.*
- *Parents mourn the death of a child throughout their lifetimes, with secondary losses anticipated at each life stage the child would have encountered, and during milestones of the child's peers and family members.*
- *Bereaved siblings carry a unique burden: their own grief within the context of their parents' grief.*
- *The moment of a child's death, and the periods shortly before and after, impact a parent's grief and memories of the child's life.*
- *Deceased children live on through family members' and friends' references to them.*

Anticipating the Loss

It is difficult for parents to envision the death of their child of any age. For those whose children face a prolonged illness, the prospect of death may be present long before it occurs. What a family can prepare for varies with the illness and the personality of its members. For some, open discussion about death, funerals, and the afterlife becomes part of the daily routine. For others, "the death dialogue" may be alluded to but is not a dominant feature. For still others, such thinking is emotionally intolerable.[1]

Some family members are able to contemplate the idea of their child's death. Other families choose to remain in a "curative" mode, working with the medical team to keep the child on active treatment until the last possible hope is diminished. There is no single way to gracefully approach the death of a child. Family culture around death needs to be supported and plays a determining role in the social work intervention at the time of death and during bereavement.

Parents' ability to absorb information about their child's incurable illness can be enhanced when presented in advance and at an appropriate time (Lannen et al., 2010). Those who can process this information have the opportunity to influence their child's last days and in turn their family's grief response.

Parents are their children's natural caregivers and are virtually always in that role at the end of their child's life. The days and weeks leading up to a child's death are filled with the last acts of parenting. Because all parents wish to protect their child, they can experience a prevailing sense of failure as the death approaches and in the weeks and months after.

Rituals (e.g., legacy building; Foster et al., 2009) conceived while a child is dying or soon after death can serve as steps in the bereavement journey, paralleling a deceased child's interests and development, thus enabling family members to do something conceptually for, with, or in honor of their child.

During treatment, parents come to know other families of children with cancer and often form life-saving bonds with them. The losses of these children also have a considerable impact on families.

The Moment a Child Dies

The moment when a child dies is a meaningful time in the life of a family. When, where, and how it happens and who is present are factors in the family legacy. Regardless of how much the moment is expected, death can be controlled only rarely.

Dying children often voice their fear of dying alone and their desire for parents to be with them; parents want and need to be present. Witnessing the moment of someone's death, not the least one's own child or sibling, can be visually and emotionally overwhelming. Someone with a calm composure who knows the practical information specific to the situation can provide guidance and make an "intolerable" situation more tolerable. Not being with a child at his or her moment of death presents its own burden. Over time, most parents can accept the reality of the logistics that may have prevented them from being there, but initially it produces strong regret.

The role and whereabouts of siblings at the time of death are also important. Surviving children need help understanding and making peace with their sibling's death and their parents' grief. A surviving child may wonder, "Will my parents be okay?" "Will they be able to take care of me?" "Would they experience the same level of emotion if I had died?" Parents seeming "out of control" can be unnerving for a surviving child. It is essential to have a family member or close family friend available during these moments, particularly one attuned to and attending to the needs of siblings.

The child's final exit from the hospital or home has enduring significance, because those present will have those images embedded in their minds forever.

> *The moment a child dies is a private one. When it happens in a public setting, it already defies that sense of privacy.... When the child dies in the hospital, the family leaves the body. When the child dies at home, the body leaves the family.*
>
> —*Cincotta, 2004, p. 329*

These represent two very different emotional trajectories.

Before the birth of a child, people leave their house knowing they will return with their child. When a child is dying, parents know a time will come when their child will never again return home. For parents, the story of that child's birth is now accompanied by the story of his or her death. Recounting the details of both moments enables parents to endure a child's death. Finding people with whom they can share these stories is invaluable to their grieving process.

Helping a Family at the Moment of the Child's Death

- *Prepare in advance of the death, whenever possible.*
- *Provide sibling support and education about the impending death experience.*
- *Provide information on the care of a child's body:*
  - *What can be expected (breathing, noises, bodily functions)?*
  - *Who will be involved?*
  - *What actions need to be taken?*
  - *Who can do what (staff and family members)?*
- *Discuss how long the family may stay once the child dies.*
- *Discuss how family members can prepare to leave the child:*
  - *How do you help family members say goodbye (develop a ritual, light a candle, send a message with the child)?*
- *Explain the exit plan for the body:*
  - *Where does it go, how, and with whom?*
- *Discuss an autopsy and its emotional and medical implications.*
- *Prepare for what to expect when the family returns home without the child.*
- *Provide resources and information about the weeks and months ahead.*

The Funeral as a Step in the Bereavement Journey

A mother went from the transplant unit to the funeral parlor during her son's bone marrow transplant. Although her child seemed to be doing fine, she knew in her heart what the outcome would be and believed she had to take care of those details to be emotionally available to her son. Every parent has an instilled sense of responsibility: You help your child through transitions, whether to high school or from life.

Planning for a funeral begins the process of actualizing that a child is dying or has died. In one instance, a mother and child picked out the dress in which the child would be buried. Although hospital staff thought it was unusual, this dyad felt a strong sense of partnership in the task. Some dying children find solace in determining the clothing, the music, the readings, and whom they would like to speak at their funerals. Children, teens, and parents may not always be on the same page about these issues, and sometimes children need to take the lead.

> *I will send you all a postcard from Heaven.*
>
> —*A dying teenager with osteosarcoma*

The funeral serves as an oasis of support—a buffer between the world of illness and a world without the child. The enormous sense of grief on that day can feel too difficult to contain. The visual experience of a child's funeral serves as a reminder that it is different when a child dies: a smaller coffin, toys and stuffed animals in the casket, balloons, younger mourners in attendance, and a higher volume of attendees.

The Internet has changed the processes of grief and mourning. When a child died in Missouri, the family chose to have the funeral streamed live, allowing people around the world to be "present." Attending a funeral alone, in your home, or at your desk at work is a very different experience. The faces of mourning and grief continue to evolve as society evolves.

Issues for Parents

It was a privilege to be able to usher my child out of life, the way I had ushered him in.

—Mother of two children who died and who then became a physician

Society recognizes losses and names the people who experience them, such as widow, widower, and orphan (Maklodes, 2012). There is no specific name for a parent who loses a child. Bereaved parents struggle within themselves to determine who they are in the world while simultaneously struggling with a perception of not being understood in society. If losing a child could be talked about openly, named, and accepted in a more global way, perhaps the bereavement journey for parents might be less burdensome.

Unique Considerations Regarding the Loss of a Child

- *The role of the child in the family*
- *Family constellation—i.e., the number of siblings and their ages*
- *The role of the child in the community*
- *The length of the illness; life before the illness*
- *Preparation in advance of the death; anticipatory grief*
- *The parents' relationships with careers or employment*
- *Internal support:*
    - *Support system within the nuclear and extended family*
    - *Strength of the family members*
- *External support:*
    - *Connections with other families of children with cancer and bereaved families*
    - *Support systems in the community*
    - *Religious and spiritual affiliations*
- *The nature of the death experience*
- *The child's last wishes*
- *Death of more than one child—i.e., another living child with the same illness*
- *The role of mental illness in the family:*
    - *Family members with preexisting conditions who may require clinical intervention at the time of death and afterward*
    - *Suicidal ideation in a parent or teenager (and access to the child's medications at the end of life)*

Although the family may have a great deal of support after a child dies, there is ultimately a time when each individual will experience alone the emotion imposed by the bereavement journey. Learning how to live without a child is a grueling experience that almost always begins with a sense of shock, even if the death was anticipated.

The loss of a child leaves the impression of a life that was incomplete. When an infant dies, there will always be the question of who the baby would have grown up to be, sadness that is coupled with a loss of innocence and potential (Cincotta, 1989). The loss of a child is concentrated on the child's identity and on the stage of the child's development (e.g., a first grader). Additionally, a component of the mourners' personal identities is lost when a child dies (e.g., mother, aunt).

Grief is at times unbearable; life without the child is insufferable. It is a loss that is so profound that it can feel too overwhelming to manage. Although the emotional pain dissipates, some parents feel that letting go of the pain means letting go of the child. There can also be a sense that experiencing joy would be disloyal to the child who died. When the child is no longer present to hold on to, family members may feel that holding on to these emotions is all they have left.

The loneliness is like a veil over my heart.

—Mother 3 years after the death of her son

The bereavement journey after the loss of a child is so complex that it is not uncommon for a parent to feel lost and without purpose. Feelings of isolation, depression, loneliness, anger, and guilt abound. Certain predeath experiences, such as bone marrow transplantation, may lead to greater symptomatology after the death (Jalmsell, Onelöv, Steineck, Henter, & Kreicbergs, 2011). Survival strategies begin with learning to live with and through the painful emotions and then learning to compartmentalize the grief by ultimately managing the loss while not forgetting the child.

Forward-looking losses related to the child make the process of grieving the loss of a child unique. As time passes, the child's friends and peers move on with their lives. Their achievements represent experiences lost to the bereaved family and comprise components of "new grief" or what some have defined as "regrief." There is a sense of loss when the annual family holiday card is sent. There is a sense of loss when a sibling gets married. Everywhere the child should have been and everything the child might have done provoke a sense of longing. These subsequent emotional losses are difficult to understand during the earlier phase of grief, because the impact of the initial loss is so pervasive. Yet they all encompass part of a "cumulative grief exposure" that began with the loss of the child. Adjusting to subsequent losses may get easier, but the journey is never easy.

At first, grieving over the loss of your child is like having a radio blaring. Gradually the radio gets turned down. Ultimately the radio remains on, but in the background. It never gets completely turned off.

—*Mother 5 years after the loss of her child*

Grief: Time and Relationships

I felt as though I left my child out in the cold and the rain. I could not sleep.

—*Bereaved mother after a storm following her child's burial*

In early bereavement, parents often continue to employ active parenting paradigms when they think of their deceased child (e.g., feeding, clothing, protection from the elements). A child's presence can still be felt physically after death (e.g., clothing continues to smell like the child and the child is easily envisioned). These feelings may be confusing, sad, and frightening, but they can also be comforting. When the feelings are palpable, it is difficult to concentrate and sleeping may become problematic (Lannen, Wolfe, Prigerson, Onelöv, & Kreicbergs, 2008). When sleep does come, parents often wish to dream about their child. This conscious desire serves as an impediment to such dreams. Feelings of still being entrenched in the medical regimen can prevail when waking, even though the child is no longer alive.

I would wake up afraid every day afraid about what had to be done medically. It took a long time to realize I did not have to be afraid any more.

—*Bereaved mother whose child was on treatment for 7 years*

At the beginning, most parents cannot talk without crying. Talking is possible, but not necessarily comfortable within 6 weeks to 2 months. Many bereaved parents can begin to talk without being completely overwhelmed several months after the loss. As time passes, mundane meetings at the supermarket become less threatening. Finally, for most, there is a time when the good memories can be recalled without always focusing on the illness and death. Ultimately, the essence of the child can be embraced and memories pre-dating the illness return even though the sadness will remain.

In the months after the death, the focus is often on what was happening "at this time last year." It can be helpful for families to chronicle these memories. By the 1-year anniversary, those in the outside world think differently about bereaved families than they did in the earlier months. There may be an expectation that grieving should be over and that life should go on. Often, however, it is not until the second year that the reality hits many parents. It is almost as though the loss of the child is just becoming real.

Father: It is surprising that it is still so hard.
Mother: I have resigned myself to believing that it is just never going to feel any better.

—*Bereaved parents 3 years after the death of their child with leukemia*

I am 3 years out from my son's death and continue to reflect on how lonely grief is.

—*Father of a 7-year-old who died of a brain tumor*

A study in Sweden that followed bereaved parents of children who had died of cancer in a 6-year period found an increase in anxiety and depression in years 4 to 6, and then a return to normal functioning in years 7 to 9 (Kreicbergs, Valdimarsdottir, Onelöv, Henter, & Steineck, 2004). The return to normal functioning is encouraging, but the 7-year timeframe is a bit unsettling.

Parents represent the embodiment of their child after his or her death, as well as all the remaining "things" that represent the child. Frequently parents will ask, "What should I do with my child's clothing?" Creative interventions can be designed in response to this clinical issue. A quilting program, for example, which gives parents the opportunity to create something new out of their deceased children's clothing, provides an opportunity to process the experience and work through the grief.

Concrete and Existential Questions Bereaved Parents Face

Finding meaning and peace in life after the death of a child can pose an existential challenge. Parents have to face the following questions:

- *What do you tell people you encounter about your deceased child and when?*
  I determine whether I am going to get to know someone better, depending on how they react to the information.
- *How do you answer, "How many children do you have?"*
  If I say two and not three, I feel like I am denying the life of my third child. If I say three, I feel like I have to explain what happened.
- *If you have one child…*
  My only child has died. Am I still a parent?
- *How does the single parent of one deceased child redefine family?*
- *How do you connect in life with people who truly do not understand the experience?*

- *How do you make peace in a world where unknowing individuals will judge you if you want to have another child—perhaps seeing you as having a "replacement" child?*
- *How do you find meaning in life?*
- *How do you get up every day and face a world with your child not in it?*

Complicated Grief

Is parental grief always complicated (Thieleman & Cacciatore, 2014)? What is the normal course of grief after a child dies? Prolonged and persistent symptoms are indicators of a more complicated grief reaction.

Symptoms of Complicated Grief
• *Unmet needs of children in the family*
• *Depression*
• *Suicidal ideation*
• *Extreme isolation*
• *Obsession with the deceased child*
• *Severe memory loss*
• *Inability to work*
• *Lack of connection with anything/anyone*
• *Inability to speak without crying*
• *Extreme irritability*

Hopes of Bereaved Parents

- *To see my other daughter grow up, graduate, marry, have children, and outlive her parents.*
- *I hope our family can be whole again.*
- *I hope for the chance of giving birth to more kids.*
- *To be a good father—nothing else really matters right now.*
- *I hope to find a new purpose in life; a more fulfilling employment opportunity.*
- *I hope that my kids can adapt and overcome the tragedy that our family has been through and become stronger people for it.*
- *To be open to the needs of others and to accept the help of others.*
- *I hope to find peace and a balance between the sad memories and the happy ones.*
- *I hope to love more, appreciate more, and remember the very happy moments I had with my daughter.*

Family dynamics, the emotional rhythms, routines, and balance of a family's energy, change after a child dies (Gilmer et al., 2012; Rando, 1986). Mothers who were the primary caregivers often continue to take care of family matters, with fathers frequently maintaining employment (Alam, Barrera, D'Agostino, Nicholas, & Schneiderman, 2012). Fathers often talk about losing their work drive and focus, wanting to find more fulfilling work.[2] On the one hand, that couples rarely grieve in the same way at the same time can cause conflict; on the other hand, the household would likely be immobilized if they actually did grieve in the same way at the same time. Grandparents live with their own sense of loss about their grandchildren but also experience the pain that the loss brings to their own child.

Ongoing Connections

That feeling of being robbed never lets up.
—Mother of a boy who died of neuroblastoma

The love for one's children and the expectations for their lives are never ending, and the connections after death are the same. Research about continuing bonds with children suggests that these ongoing connections are a regular component of grief and adaptation for both parents and siblings after the loss of a child. Parents often engage in purposeful acts to affirm the connection (Foster et al., 2011). Ongoing bonds with the deceased child through dreams can be comforting, but intrusive connections may be indicative of greater distress (Field et al., 2013). Siblings, who often feel that they have lost their best friend or, if it was an older sibling, "their protector," will frequently use their deceased brother or sister "referentially" throughout life (Hogan & Balk, 1990). Continuing bonds may not emerge immediately for all siblings (Packman, Horsley, Davies, & Kramer, 2006).

Families often perceive that they see medical staff more than they see their own families, and after their child dies, they lose the staff as well. Honest, simple, meaningful gestures have a great impact after a child dies. A visit from the treatment team to help assess how a family is doing, to answer questions, and to re-establish connections could be vital to a family's coping (Welch et al., 2012). Rituals are very important to families, and a child being remembered is of the utmost importance. Remembrance services and contact on the anniversary of the child's death or birthday are important markers on the bereavement journey.

A Family Model of Grief Work

A child's death is a family matter that affects every family member on multiple levels. The needs of the family system can best be met by an intervention that can provide support, education, and insight to nuclear family members. The environment of a bereavement family retreat (Cincotta, 2004) creates a parallel process for children and parents and encourages dialogue between and among parents and children.

Bereavement family retreats help family members of all ages understand the more global bereavement journey, appreciate the future, reconnect with each other, and create new memories and relationships (Cincotta, 2011). They give family members permission to have fun and experience growth in the absence of the deceased child. The bereavement retreat model is an effective intervention, because it affords everyone in the family, regardless of age, an opportunity to be proactive about "healing." It gives each member a chance to deal with the loss alone, in a group, and within the context of one's own family. It is a shared experience that creates a synergy within the family system that cannot be achieved in work with individuals or individual families.

Engaging bereaved siblings as teachers, and as a panel talking to parents, allows parents to hear what other bereaved children have to say. Such forums penetrate emotional barriers and enable parents to identify with their own children. This method exposes parents to issues that their surviving children may be experiencing and promotes emotional growth.

Group work with bereaved parents or siblings at different stages of grief is a unique modality that can be invaluable in helping them to understand where they are in their bereavement journey (Cincotta, 2011). Bereavement groups create connections among families that have experienced loss and help them understand and normalize what they are experiencing. Profound parental grief can be immobilizing and can leave the griever "feeling crazy." Inclusion of newer bereaved family members allows older group members to see how they have grown; families who are further along in their grief process afford newer members the possibility of hope for the road ahead.

After everything a family goes through when a child dies, the question arises, "If you knew this was going to be the outcome, would you still have had this child?" The answer is always yes.[3]

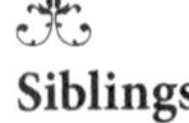

Siblings

I did not die.

—Message for parents from a bereaved sister in a sibling support group, 35 years ago

When a sibling dies, the world changes. Sibling relationships are among the closest experienced in early life, depending on the age differential. Unless you are an only child, who you are is often defined in relationship to siblings: you are the oldest, the youngest, or the middle child. The death of a sibling challenges perceived birth order roles and responsibilities. Those who had only one other sibling now find themselves alone with their parents. Each change is fraught with different feelings and expectations that lead to stresses. Children and teens also face a range of existential issues, perhaps for the first time in their lives: Am I still a sister? Am I the oldest child now? Do I need to take over my sibling's responsibilities? Am I going to die too?

It can be difficult to formulate the best treatment plan for a child who has lost a sibling, because the child is but one of many people in the family experiencing a loss. The death of a child also has a dramatic impact on siblings, because they have borne witness to their parents' reactions, thus making it a "double loss" (Horsley & Patterson, 2006). It is revealing for a child to see his or her parents manage the illness and then suffer the death of their sibling.

The end of life becomes a crisis for everyone in the household, during which the needs of the dying child are paramount. The sibling who is already feeling lost and sad is unprepared for the magnitude of parental grief. Parents, who are the primary caretakers of all the children, may become more physically present yet somewhat emotionally absent during the initial period after their child's death. They are often struggling to manage their own grief responses.

Witnessing the enormity of parental grief can leave children with a sense of just how important their sibling was to their parents. On the one hand, at this vulnerable time, it may be difficult for a child to imagine that their parents could care as much about them in the dramatic way they cared about their sibling, which creates a perceived void for the sibling. On the other hand, bereaved siblings do not want to further burden their parents. A sibling's greatest grief responses may not become apparent until the adults in the household are emotionally available to hearing them. When a child dies, parents may need help in understanding what kind of support their other children need.

After a child dies, a parent may take a leave of absence from work. Yet it is expected that a sibling will return to school shortly after the funeral and go on as usual. The journey forward for bereaved siblings can be lonely and complicated. Depending on their age, they often grow up quickly during their sibling's illness and learn to become more independent. It can then be difficult for them to reconnect with a parent during the mourning phase. What do you begin to tell your parents after you have already distanced yourself from them? How do you rely on them if you feel that they may not be strong enough to be available to you? How do you learn how to deal with your own grief?

It is easy for bereaved siblings to feel that they are the only ones who have lost a brother or sister. Retreats and group programs only for bereaved siblings quickly enable them to move beyond that initial feeling of isolation. They create a natural peer group for children and teens and provide a forum for easy dialogue and understanding. Bereaved siblings, like bereaved parents, are tremendous assets to one another.

Voices of Bereaved Teen Siblings: How to Deal With the Loss of a Sibling

- *Writing helps a lot, whether it's on your own or assigned writing.*
  - *It helps to think about deep stuff and get it all out.*
  - *Writing brings up things you haven't thought about before.*
  - *Write things down that you're afraid of forgetting so they're always there.*
- *Do physical activities like contact sports.*
- *Do things that make you happy and that work best for you—however you want to grieve. Find a way to express what you are feeling and remember good memories.*
- *It helps to have a friend who remembers the sibling; someone to talk to about when the sibling was there.*
- *Create new traditions to keep their spirit alive.*
- *Do things that come to you naturally the most.*
- *Fund-raise to give back and keep the memory alive.*
- *People say there are steps, but just find something that helps you remember in a positive light—drawing, giving back.*
- *Look at pictures and celebrate their life. Sad things do come up, but continue celebrating their life.*
- *Talk about it. When your friends ask, don't be afraid to talk about it.*
- *Find grief groups.*
- *Never forget—hold on to the memories you have.*
- *Grieve at your own pace—when you are ready to take the next step, you will know. You can't force it.*
- *Family and religion provide a lot of strength.*
- *You're going to grieve for your whole life, but the grief changes and you start to miss what could have been.*
- *Do your own thing—go at your own pace with grieving.*
- *Do things to remember your sibling.*
- *"Forget the regret and celebrate." It's easier to celebrate the milestones. Don't regret things.*
- *Don't overthink what you could have done, because you can't change anything. It doesn't help.*
- *Watch videos on milestones, remember, and talk about him or her.*

Professional Practice Guidelines for Working With Bereaved Families

Little in life prepares social workers for being present when a child has died. Preparing oneself for such moments and speaking with other professionals who have shared that experience make sense. Thinking this through will allow a social worker to be more present when the situation arises. It is normal for everyone to experience emotional reactions when a child dies. If a professional is excessively emotional with a grieving family, however, he or she can overstep a boundary in the family's bereavement journey and offer little solace.

Family members will ask social workers if they should bring children to the funeral and whether they should let them see the body. Help family members recognize that children, siblings, cousins, and friends need to be part of the rituals so that they feel included. Children's time in the presence of the deceased should be supervised and limited to mitigate against a feeling of being overwhelmed.

Once a child has died, even seasoned professionals may feel apprehensive about calling a family. Bereaved parents need professionals to reach out to them. Asking for help when newly bereaved is difficult for most people, so establishing a pattern of calling bereaved families can have a positive impact for both the family and the professional. It allows everyone involved to control and segment their emotions, thereby enabling healing. Periodic contact allows families to gradually deal with their new relationship with the medical team and affords them an opportunity to process the illness and death experience.

Future Research Directions

There are many areas for potential study in gaining a more comprehensive understanding of mourning the loss of a child: grief through the eyes of children and teens; the scope of pathological grief in families who have lost a child, as well as its definition and treatment possibilities; a child's death as a catalyst for posttraumatic stress and posttraumatic growth; a longitudinal prospective design (Kim, Lucette, & Loscalzo, 2013) for parental grief; a developmental approach in a study of sibling grief in children and teens; and a design using both the age and number of years since death as parameters for adult survivors of childhood bereavement.

Time changes the experience of grief over the loss of a child; grief does not go away, but it does become different. The transitioning phases of grief and ever-changing emotional triggers along the bereavement journey influence the need for varying types of services at different times. Education to understand the process, the chance to meet people in similar situations, and the availability of resources for short-term and ongoing groups, retreats, and online support (Coulson & Greenwood, 2012) or episodic interventions can lessen the burden by affording individuals the opportunity to understand the bereavement course so they do not have to be afraid or overwhelmed by it. Grief is a normal process for most people and can be approached as such.

Many parents become less afraid to die after experiencing the death of their child, both because they witnessed how their child approached death and because they may feel that they will reconnect with their child after death. Alleviating the fear of death is a remarkable final gift from a child.

Pearls

- Bereaved adults and children need the opportunity to tell the story of the loss in their own words, at their own time:
    - Be present with the loss; be willing to listen.
    - Support individualized ways of coping.
- Resource lists of bereavement services focused on child loss are helpful.
- Help families think of activities that might be helpful in dealing with the loss:
    - Aid families in preserving and chronicling memories through a variety of expressive media.
    - Aid in exploring and creating ideas for family rituals.
- Use the child's name in discussions and creative exercises. Family members find it helpful to hear others say the child's name.
- Help prepare people for things they might feel or think so they can recognize what is to be expected and do not feel like they are crazy—that is, demystify grief.
- Provide parents with tools to answer questions for surviving children in an age-appropriate manner and advise them to revisit the conversation as children develop.
- Connect bereaved parents, children, and teens with other bereaved parents, children, and teens.

Pitfalls With Children/Siblings

- Perceiving that children grieve in the same was as adults, overlooking developmental issues, and making assumptions about a child's grief.
- Not recognizing the significance of the loss to a child because everything seems to be fine.
- Not understanding that the meaning and understanding of the loss will change and need to be addressed again at subsequent stages of development.
- Not seeing the significance of how the child's place in the family changes when a sibling dies.
- Assessing the needs of children exclusively through the lens of adult experiences.

Pitfalls With Adults/Parents

- Minimizing the tremendous and indescribable loss of a child.
- Saying "I know how you feel"—unless you actually have experienced the death of a child.
- Presuming that time is the curative feature rather than seeing bereavement as a process. Some people begin to work through the loss before the child dies and others do it much later (one mother did not open an invitation to an annual memorial service until the ninth year).
- Believing that mourning the loss of a child is uniform.
- Referring to a group program in the first 6 weeks after the loss when there is too much personal pain for the group to be helpful to the parents or for the parents to be helped by other group members.
- Cutting off communication with the family at the time of death: Families feel they lose the child, the community, and the professionals.

NOTES

1. Information in this chapter is generated from ongoing work with parents of children with cancer in the context of a family retreat program at Camp Sunshine at Sebago Lake, Casco, Maine.
2. Content derived from support groups for bereaved fathers at Camp Sunshine at Sebago Lake.
3. This consistently emerges as a question in the bereavement groups at Camp Sunshine at Sebago Lake.

ADDITIONAL RESOURCES

Bereavement Centers (Local/National)

Association for Death Education and Counseling, The Thanatology Association (ADEC): http://www.adec.org

Bereaved Parents of the USA: http://www.bereavedparentsusa.org/

Camp Sunshine at Sebago Lake: http://www.campsunshine.org

Compassionate Friends: http://www.compassionatefriends.org/home.aspx

MISS Foundation: A Community of Compassion and Hope for Grieving Families: http://www.missfoundation.org/

Open to Hope: Finding Hope After Loss: http://www.opentohope.com

Grieving Children

A Caring Hand: The Billy Esposito Bereavement Center: http://acaringhand.org

Camp Erin (The Moyer Foundation): http://www.moyerfoundation.org/programs/camperin.aspx

Comfort Zone Camp: http://www.comfortzonecamp.org/

The Dougy Center: The National Center for Grieving Children & Families: http://www.dougy.org/

KidsAid: http://www.kidsaid.com

A Little HOPE: The National Foundation for Grieving Children, Teens, and Families: http://www.alittlehope.org/contact/default.aspx

National Alliance for Grieving Children: http://childrengrieve.org/

New York Life Foundation Childhood Bereavement Initiative: http://www.newyorklife.com/achildingrief

Twinless Twins Support Group International: http://www.twinlesstwins.org

REFERENCES

Alam, R., Barrera, M., D'Agostino, N., Nicholas, D. B., & Schneiderman, G. (2012). Bereavement experiences of mothers and fathers over time after the death of a child due to cancer. *Death Studies*, *36*(1), 1–22. doi:10.1080/07481187.2011.553312

Cincotta, N. F. (1989). Quality of life—a family decision. In J. van Eys (Ed.), *Cancer in the very young* (pp. 63–73). Springfield, IL: Charles C. Thomas.

Cincotta, N. F. (2004). The end of life at the beginning of life: Working with dying children and their families. In J. Berzoff & P. R. Silverman (Eds.), *Living with dying* (pp. 318–347). New York, NY: Columbia University Press.

Cincotta, N. F. (2011). Bereavement in the beginning phase of life: Grief in children and their families. In T. Altilio & S. Otis-Green (Eds.), *Oxford textbook of palliative social work* (pp. 305–317). New York, NY: Oxford University Press.

Coulson, N. S., & Greenwood, N. (2012). Families affected by childhood cancer: An analysis of the provision of social support within online support groups. *Child Care Health and Development*, *38*(6), 870–877. doi:10.1111/j.1365-2214.2011.01316.x

Field, N. P., Packman, W., Ronen, R., Pries, A., Davies, B., & Kramer, R. (2013). Type of continuing bonds expression and its comforting versus distressing nature: Implications for adjustment among bereaved mothers. *Death Studies*, *37*(10), 889–912. doi:10.1080/07481187.2012.692458

Foster, T. L., Gilmer, M. J., Davies, B., Barrera, M., Fairclough, D., Vannatta, K., & Gerhardt, C. A. (2009). Bereaved parents' and siblings' reports of legacies created by children with cancer. *Journal of Pediatric Oncology Nursing*, *26*, 369–376. doi:10.1177/1043454209340322

Foster, T. L., Gilmer, M. J., Davies, B., Dietrich, M. S., Barrera, M., Fairclough, D. L., ... Gerhardt, C. A. (2011). Comparison of continuing bonds reported by parents and siblings after a child's death from cancer. *Death Studies*, *35*(5), 420–440. doi:10.1080/07481187.2011.553308

Gilmer, M. J., Foster, T. L., Vannatta, K., Barrera, M., Davies, B., Dietrich, M. S., ... Gerhardt, C. A. (2012). Changes in parents after the death of a child from cancer. *Journal of Pain and Symptom Management*, *44*(4), 572–582. doi:10.1016/j.jpainsymman.2011.10.017

Hogan, N. S., & Balk, D. E. (1990). Adolescent reactions to sibling death—perceptions of mothers, fathers, and teenagers. *Nursing Research*, *39*(2), 103–106.

Horsley, H., & Patterson, T. (2006). The effects of a parent guidance intervention on communication among adolescents who have experienced the sudden death of a sibling. *American Journal of Family Therapy*, *34*(2), 119–137. doi:10.1080/01926180500301519

Jalmsell, L., Onelöv, E., Steineck, G., Henter, J.-I., & Kreicbergs, U. (2011). Hematopoietic stem cell transplantation in children with cancer and the risk of long-term psychological morbidity in the bereaved parents. *Bone Marrow Transplantation*, *6*, 1063–1070. doi:10.1038/bmt.2010.287

Kim, Y., Lucette, A., & Loscalzo, M. (2013). Bereavement needs of adults, children, and families after cancer. *Cancer Journal*, *19*(5), 444–457.

Kreicbergs, U., Valdimarsdottir, U., Onelöv, E., Henter, J. I., & Steineck, G. (2004). Anxiety and depression in parents 4-9 years after the loss of a child owing to a malignancy: A population-based follow-up. *Psychological Medicine*, *34*(8), 1431–1441.

Lannen, P., Wolfe, J., Mack, J., Onelöv, E., Nyberg, U., & Kreicbergs, U. (2010). Absorbing information about a child's incurable cancer. *Oncology*, *78*(3–4), 259–266. doi:10.1159/000315732

Lannen, P. K., Wolfe, J., Prigerson, H. G., Onelöv, E., & Kreicbergs, U. C. (2008). Unresolved grief in a national sample of bereaved parents: Impaired mental and physical health 4 to 9 years later. *Journal of Clinical Oncology*, *26*(36), 5870–5876. doi:10.1200/jco.2007.14.6738

Maklodes. (2012). Writer's block: Term for a parent whose kids died (reverse of "orphan," basically). Retrieved from http://tvtropes.org/pmwiki/posts.php?discussion=13269286550A94000100&page=0

Packman, W., Horsley, H., Davies, B., & Kramer, R. (2006). Sibling bereavement and continuing bonds. *Death Studies*, *30*(9), 817–841. doi:10.1080/07481180600886603

Rando, T. (1986). The unique issues and impact of the death of a child. In T. Rando (Ed.), *Parental loss of a child* (pp. 5–44). Champaign, IL: Research Press.

Thieleman, K., & Cacciatore, J. (2014). When a child dies: A critical analysis of grief-related controversies in DSM-5. *Research on Social Work Practice*, *24*(1), 114–122. doi:10.1177/1049731512474695

Welch, J. G., Mannix, M. M., Boergers, J., Jelalian, E., Barbosa, F., Fujii-Rios, H., & Forman, E. N. (2012). Parental interest in a bereavement support visit when a child dies from cancer. *Omega—Journal of Death and Dying*, *65*(4), 335–346. doi:10.2190/OM.65.4.f

77

Amy Yin Man Chow

Developing Culturally Informed Research on Bereavement Interventions

Key Concepts

- *Bereavement care is an integral part of palliative care in oncology.*
- *Though many individuals request bereavement services and report being helped by them, determining their effectiveness is difficult.*
- *Theory-driven and evidence-based bereavement interventions targeted for at-risk populations need to be developed. The group intervention described in this chapter is an exemplar.*
- *Adaptation of bereavement interventions developed in a cultural context other than the one in which implementation will occur requires language translation and refinement of concepts and words. Inclusion of cultural components relevant to the audience may increase the effectiveness of the original intervention model.*

Bereavement, especially the death of one's husband, wife, or long-term romantic partner, is considered one of the most stressful life events (Carr & Jeffreys, 2011). The proportions of widowed older adults in the United Kingdom, the United States, and Hong Kong are 29.54%, 27.3%, and 31.35%, respectively (Hong Kong, Census and Statistics Department, 2012; Office for National Statistics [England and Wales], 2010; U.S. Census Bureau, 2012). In a review of health outcomes of bereavement, Stroebe, Schut, and Stroebe (2007) found bereavement is consistently related to increased risk of mortality and physical and psychiatric morbidity, including headaches, nonspecific pain, loss of appetite, and sleep disturbances. Christakis and Allison (2006) also found an increased risk of mortality for older adults when their spouse was hospitalized. Increases in symptoms of depression and anxiety are commonly reported among spousally bereaved persons (Stroebe, Hansson, Stroebe, & Schut, 2001). Their poor health outcomes might be related to diminished self-care abilities and motivation. Stroebe and colleagues (2001) found that bereaved individuals had more medical consultations, consumed more medication, and had a higher hospitalization rate. Furthermore, among those assessed to have problems in adjusting to grief, utilization of mental health services was low. The majority did not seek help (Lichtenthal et al., 2011).

In the few longitudinal studies of widowed older adults, Bonanno, Wortman, and Nesse (2004) identified five bereavement patterns: chronic grief, chronic depression, common grief, improved depression, and resilient adaptation. Overall, 8% were chronically depressed and 16% had chronic grief. The large percentage of those who demonstrated resilience may overshadow the distress faced by those with chronic depression and chronic grief, leaving the impression that time heals all bereaved individuals. Importantly, there is a heterogeneity of bereavement reactions among widowed older adults. Roughly a quarter of the widowed older population experience clinically significant ongoing distress in adapting to the death of a spouse.

The Challenge: Determining Effectiveness of Bereavement Interventions

Different interventions for easing the adverse consequences of bereavement have been developed. However, such interventions vary greatly in focus, content, and availability. They range from sending a condolence card to intensive psychotherapy and include individual, group, and family approaches. When meta-analyses include this broad range of interventions, modest effectiveness is found (Jordon & Neimeyer, 2003). Neimeyer and Currier (2009) suggest this conclusion is oversimplified. Their analysis studied multiple modalities and both universal bereavement interventions and those interventions targeted for more distressed individuals. Bereavement interventions with more distressed individuals do show greater effectiveness. Thus, there is an increasing need for well-defined bereavement interventions that are theory driven and vigorously examined.

The Dual Process Model of Coping With Bereavement

Among the leading theoretical models of bereavement, the Dual Process Model (DPM) has considerable research support (Stroebe & Schut, 1999). The DPM consists of three elements: loss-oriented (LO) coping, restoration-oriented (RO) coping, and oscillation between loss and restoration coping. One the one hand, LO coping focuses on dealing with the loss experience. It involves grief work and, more generally, appraising and processing different aspects of the loss experience, including painful intrusion of grief. On the other hand, RO coping addresses life changes that may arise from bereavement, including adjustment to new roles, identities, relationships, and experiences. This coping focuses on adaptation to life without the day-to-day presence of the deceased. Oscillation refers to the inevitable alternation between LO and RO coping processes. This ability to move back and forth between these two modes of coping throughout the

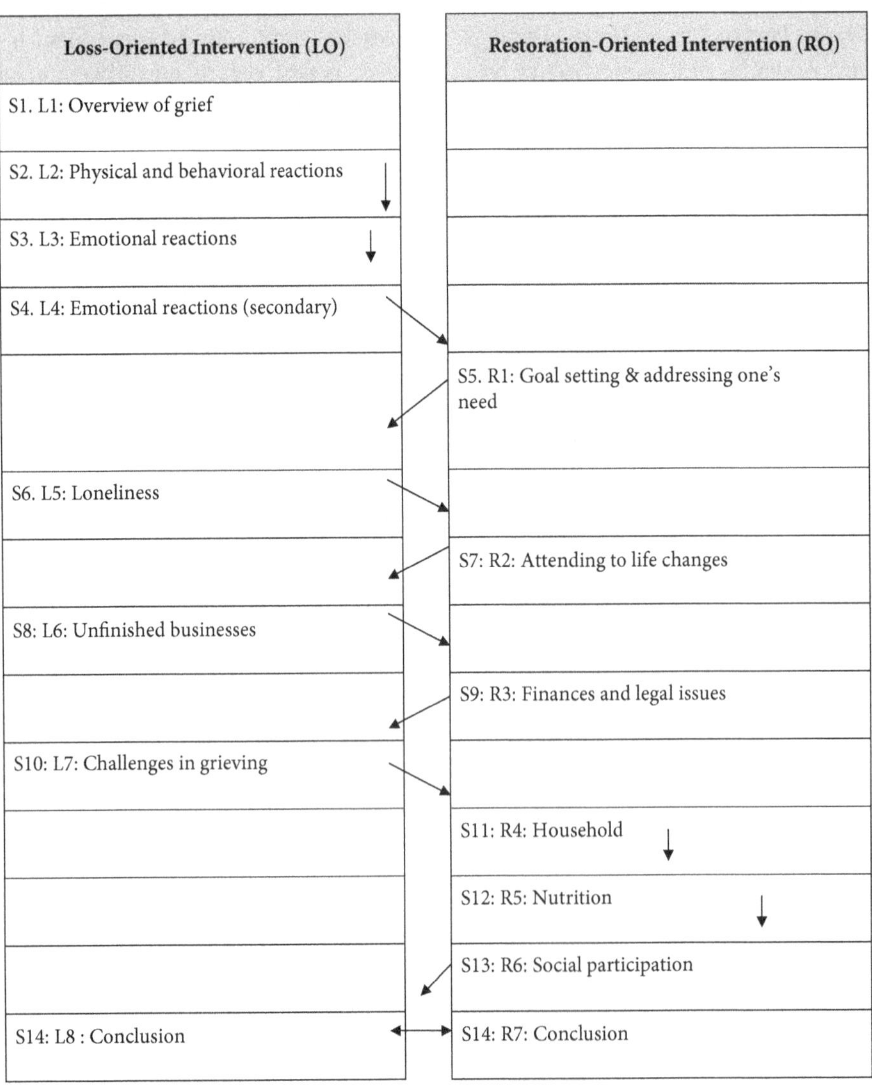

Figure 77.1. The 14-Session Dual Process Model–Based Intervention Model for Bereaved Persons in the United States

bereavement process is expected to predict better mental and physical health outcomes (Stroebe & Schut, 2010).

The Dual Process Model of Bereavement Intervention

Using Stroebe and Schut's DPM as a framework, Lund and Caserta introduced an intervention called Living After Loss (Lund, Caserta, de Vries, & Wright, 2004; Lund, Caserta, Utz, & de Vries, 2010), which has been shown to help widowed older persons adjust to life without a spouse. Unlike traditional bereavement interventions that focus on loss-oriented coping, this intervention aims to provide equal emphasis to restoration-oriented coping and the oscillation between the two foci. Living After Loss consists of eight to 15 group sessions for recently widowed older adults. Weekly 90-minute sessions cover a range of topics (see Figure 77.1). Seven of these topics are focused on loss-orientated coping, including reactions to grief, daily functioning challenges, loneliness, unfinished conversations and interactions, and grieving processes and rituals. Another seven are focused on restoration-orientated coping, including goal setting, self-care, health care, financial and legal issues, household and vehicle responsibilities, nutrition, social relationships, and rediscovering sources of joy. Sequencing of the weekly sessions resembles the oscillation inherent in bereavement and is a unique feature of the approach. The first four sessions focus on LO coping, the next six sessions focus on both LO and RO topics, and the last four sessions focus on RO coping. Group facilitators are guided by an intervention protocol.

The Experiment: Illustration of Emotional Single-Leg Stance Intervention

With consent from its developers, the author adapted Living After Loss for use with Chinese, older, widowed persons in Hong Kong. The adaptation process included literal translation of intervention materials and translation of the model's overall conceptualization. Consideration of several key questions was essential to this process.

Focus Group With Clinicians Recommends Adaptations of Intervention

A focus group of five clinicians who had been working with bereaved persons in the fields of social work, counseling, and nursing for at least 5 years addressed the following questions: (1) Is a 14-session intervention acceptable to potential Chinese participants? (2) Are the topics relevant to the cultural context of Chinese widows? and (3) Are any unique features of a Chinese context absent in this model? Their responses included important suggestions for changes in both intervention structure and content.

Structure of the Intervention

Participants reported that most groups for Chinese, bereaved older adults ranged from four to eight sessions in length. They believed the level of commitment required for participation in a 14-session group might reduce participant motivation. They thought eight sessions should be the maximum and discussed two related problems. First, because the original model opens with four sessions of LO coping followed by six alternating sessions of LO and RO coping, and finally four sessions of RO coping, an eight-session intervention following this pattern would result in few experiences of oscillation. Focus group participants were concerned this would reduce the intervention's effectiveness. To address this concern, they suggested incorporating intrasession oscillation instead of intersession oscillation. This creative adaptation would increase the experience of oscillations even with a reduced number of group sessions.

Second, although focus group participants agreed the suggested LO topics would offer a good platform for bereaved Chinese persons to examine their grief reactions (noting that loneliness, unfinished business, and conversations were commonly shared among Chinese bereaved persons), they did not think the suggested RO topics were common concerns among older bereaved Chinese persons. For example, because they believe the deceased's estate will be inherited by their delegates, Chinese elders tend to settle financial arrangements well before the death. Similarly, house size in Hong Kong is much smaller than in the United States, and healthy older adults are often able to manage household chores, whereas those who are not healthy can easily access community home-help services.

Group participants also proposed additional RO topics identified from their clinical work, including Chinese health and dietary concepts and re-establishing satisfying friendships. Because bereaved Chinese spouses do not want to burden the younger generation, they strive to maintain their physical health and are very interested in physical exercises and diets. Relating to others as a single person is another common concern among older Chinese widows. Many experience the care and concern of family members as stressful when they feel that it undermines their autonomy. Many feel married friends cannot understand what they are going through. Many others are sensitive to the possibility that their friendliness to others may be misperceived as attempts to seek a replacement spouse. Therefore, although building a network of reciprocal support was a topic in the original model, focus group participants believed the particular challenge of role redefinition for Chinese widows required special consideration.

Finally, focus group participants suggested that the adapted intervention include activity-based content because Chinese elders are accustomed to learning through practice. They proposed including a commonly used ritual of setting birds or fish free as a symbol of letting go and re-establishing a new connection with the deceased (Chow & Chan, 2006). In addition, for the transfer of knowledge and skills related to dietary concerns, participants proposed inclusion of a cooking session that would offer bereaved persons a chance to design a healthy recipe and prepare a meal accordingly. In Chinese culture, the anniversary of the death is an important day that includes family gathering to memorialize the deceased. Chinese older adults have additional stress in their planning for this special event as they experience surges of emotion in anticipation of the anniversary. Heightened reactions were found 2 months before the first and second anniversaries of the death in a study with Chinese bereaved persons in Hong Kong (Chow, 2010). Coping strategies for preparing for anniversaries were therefore included in the educational component of the intervention related to grief reactions.

The Emotional Single-Leg Stance

Based on the findings of the focus group, the 14-session Living After Loss was changed into an 8-session group renamed Emotional Single-Leg Stance (單腳踏實地; Figure 77.2) because Chinese persons do not like explicit use of the words *death* or *loss* (Chow & Chan, 2006).

Pilot of Bereavement Group Intervention

Four pilot groups were offered in 2010. Widowed adults aged 65 or older whose spouses died 3 months to 2 years before the start of the group were invited to participate. Other inclusion criteria included having had substantial contact with the spouse before the death (i.e., at least 3 days each week in the prior year) and willingness to join the group. Exclusion criteria included the death of another close family member within 2 years of the group, remarriage, prior attendance in any form of bereavement support group, residence in a long-term care facility, history of psychiatric treatment (other than for reactive depression) before the spouse's death, or impaired mental functioning that prevented completion of study questionnaires. Forty-six individuals participated in the pilot.

Participant Demographics

Participants' ages ranged from 63 to 89 (mean = 76.5; *SD* = 6.80). Time since spouse's death ranged from 1 to 77 months (mean = 15.24; *SD* = 16.56). More than 50% of the participants reported chronic illness as the spouse's cause of death; 35% reported acute illness. About half of the participants received some elementary school education or less; 32.5% reported having received no formal education. Sixty-five percent were living alone at the time of group participation; 25% were living with their children.

Measures

Participants (n = 41) completed pre- and postintervention measures and interview questions regarding their emotional

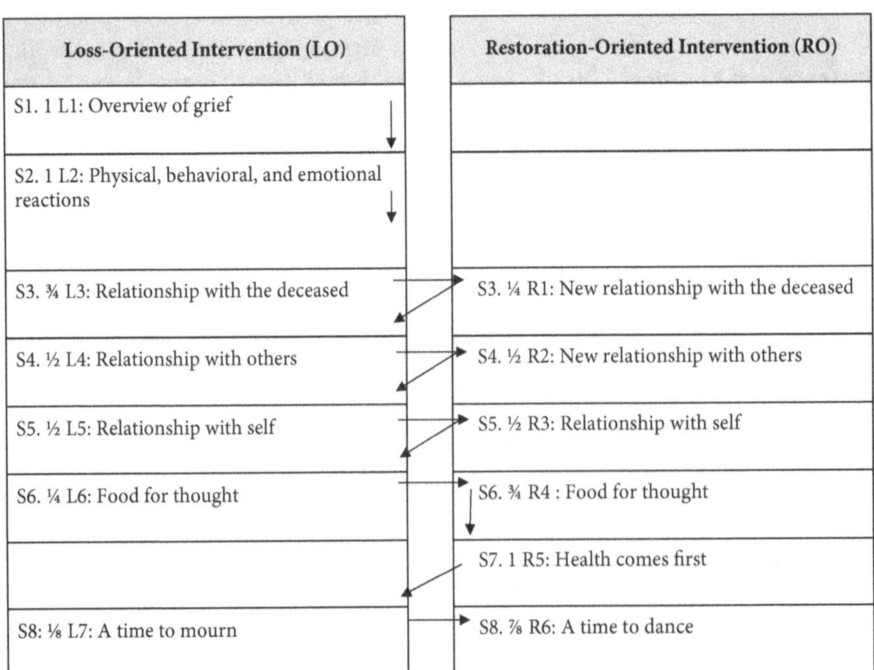

Figure 77.2. The Eight-Session Dual Process Model–Based Intervention Model for Chinese Bereaved Persons

state, grief reactions, and coping. Over 80% of the participants attended all eight sessions. Measures included the Inventory of Daily Widowed Life (Caserta & Lund, 2007), Dual Coping Inventory (Meij et al., 2008), Hospital Anxiety and Depression Scale (C. M. Leung, Wing, Kwong, Lo, & Shum, 1999), Chinese Geriatric Depression Scale (Lee, Chiu, Kwok, Leung, & Kwong, 1993), Chinese Inventory of Complicated Grief (Prigerson et al., 1995), De Jong Gierveld Loneliness Scale (G. T. Y. Leung, De Jong Gierveld, & Lam, 2008), and Inventory of Social Support (Hogan & Schmidt, 2002).

Preliminary Findings

Changes in functioning were in the expected direction: reductions in loss-oriented coping, anxiety, and emotional loneliness and complicated grief reactions, and increases in restoration-oriented coping and social support. Changes in restoration-oriented coping and emotional loneliness demonstrated statistical significance. A summary of means and standard deviations based on original scoring is shown in Table 77.1.

During their postgroup interviews, some group participants felt happier because the group helped them to accept the loss and adjust to their new lives. Many said the act of going out to meet with the group was in itself a positive turning point in their grief. Regarding group content, some participants said they loved the session during which they made a frame for their favorite photo with the deceased; many said the session related to maintaining their health was useful. Some participants expressed a desire for ongoing monthly meetings. One participant suggested periodic follow-up meetings where participants could prepare nutritional meals together.

Pearls

- Theory-driven intervention models are needed for specific target populations of bereaved individuals.
- When adopting bereavement interventions developed in another cultural context, one must give consideration to translation and refinement of concepts and words. Unique cultural components can be added to the original intervention model.
- Bereavement intervention should be not be restricted to loss-oriented coping. Over time, restoration-focused coping becomes equally important. The facilitation of oscillations between these two foci appears to be helpful.

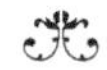

Pitfalls

- Cultural adaptations of effective research interventions may facilitate participation but limit meaningful comparisons of the interventions.

Widowhood is common in older populations. Most individuals can come to terms with the health and emotional consequences of loss and return to preloss levels of

Table 77.1.
Summary of Means and Standard Deviations for All Variables in Pretest (T_1) and Posttest (T_2)

	T_1		T_2		
Variable	*M*	*SD*	*M*	*SD*	*t*
Inventory of Daily Widowed Life (Loss Orientation)	25.60	7.54	26.02	6.94	−0.338
Inventory of Daily Widowed Life (Restoration Orientation)	**24.28**	**5.13**	**26.65**	**5.95**	**−2.509***
Dual Coping Inventory (Loss Orientation)	3.23	1.26	3.02	1.05	1.114
Dual Coping Inventory (Restoration Orientation)	**3.37**	**0.94**	**3.90**	**0.92**	**−2.878***
Chinese Geriatric Depression Scale	6.48	4.05	6.63	4.25	−0.277
Anxiety Subscale	5.15	3.80	5.00	5.62	0.163
Emotional Loneliness	**6.45**	**1.99**	**5.30**	**1.87**	**3.172***
Social Loneliness	5.20	1.99	5.47	2.32	−0.719
Inventory of Complicated Grief	23.45	14.83	19.18	11.56	1.926
Inventory of Social Support	16.93	5.20	17.43	4.55	−0.555

*$p \leq .05$.

functioning within a few months without formal intervention. Yet studies consistently show that some older adults experience a broad range of adverse consequences. The level of effectiveness of psychosocial interventions for bereaved persons varies across studies and reflects the current diversity of intervention type and target population. There is a call for more sensitive and systematic ways of defining the psychosocial experience of bereavement and more vigorous empirical evaluation of related interventions. Living After Loss, which was informed by the Dual Process Model of coping, has helped widowed older persons cope with loss (Lund et al., 2010). An adaptation of this intervention was piloted in Hong Kong after undergoing robust processes of translation and refinement to fit into that cultural context. With the input of focus group participants who were experienced practitioners, the content, structure, and format of the original intervention model were amended. Preliminary findings, including improvement in restoration-oriented coping and emotional loneliness among participants, suggest this eight-session group deserves further testing. Because this was a pilot study, there are limitations that must be taken into account when interpreting the findings. A relatively small sample was used. Thus, caution must be taken when generalizing the findings to other populations. The reported outcome changes might also be an artifact of natural recovery over time. Thus, a potential threat to the internal validity of this study was the absence of a comparison or control group. A study with a larger sample and development of a randomized controlled trial are next steps for addressing these potential threats.

ADDITIONAL RESOURCES

Books and Articles

Chan, C. L. W., & Chow, A. Y. M. (2006). *Death, dying, and bereavement: The Hong Kong Chinese experience.* Hong Kong, China: Hong Kong University Press.

Chow, A. Y. M. (2010). The role of hope in bereavement for Chinese people in Hong Kong. *Death Studies, 34*(4), 330–350.

Stroebe, M. S., Hansson, R. O., Schut, H., & Stroebe, W. (2008). *Handbook of bereavement research and practice: Advances in theory and intervention.* Washington, DC: American Psychological Association.

Stroebe, M. S., Hansson, R. O., Stroebe, W., & Schut, H. (2001). *Handbook of bereavement research: Consequences, coping, and care.* Washington, DC: American Psychological Association.

Websites

Association of Death Education and Counseling: http://www.adec.org

Association of Oncology Social Work: http://aosw.org/

National Institute for Health and Clinical Excellence: http://www.nice.org.uk/

REFERENCES

Bonanno, G. A., Wortman, C. B., & Nesse, R. M. (2004). Prospective patterns of resilience and maladjustment during widowhood. *Psychology and Aging, 19*(2), 260–271.

Carr, D., & Jeffreys, J. S. (2011). Spousal bereavement in later life. In R. A. Neimeyer, D. L. Harris, H. R. Winokur, & G. F. Thornton (Eds.), *Grief and bereavement in contemporary society: Bridging research and practice* (pp. 81–92). New York, NY: Routledge.

Caserta, M. S., & Lund, D. A. (2007). Towards the development of an inventory of daily widowed life (IDWL): Guided by the dual process model of coping with bereavement. *Death Studies, 31*, 505–535.

Chow, A. Y. M. (2010). Anticipatory anniversary bereavement effects and bereavement: Development of an integrated explanatory model. *Journal of Loss and Trauma, 15*(1), 54–68.

Chow, A. Y. M., & Chan, C. L. W. (2006). Bereavement care in Hong Kong: Past, present and future. In C. L. W. Chan & A. Y. M. Chow (Eds.), *Death, dying and bereavement: A Hong Kong Chinese experience* (pp. 253–260). Hong Kong, China: Hong Kong University Press.

Christakis, N., & Allison, P. (2006). Mortality after the hospitalization of a spouse. *New England Journal of Medicine, 354*, 719–730.

Hogan, N. S., & Schmidt, L. A. (2002). Testing the grief to personal growth model using structural equation modeling. *Death Studies, 26*, 615–634.

Hong Kong, Census and Statistics Department. (2012). Usual residents by sex, age and marital status, 2011. Retrieved from http://www.census2011.gov.hk/en/main-table/F104.html

Jordon, J. R., & Neimeyer, R. A. (2003). Does grief counseling work? *Death Studies, 27*, 765–786.

Lee, H. B., Chiu, H. F. K., Kwok, W. Y., Leung, C. M., & Kwong, P. K. (1993). Chinese elderly and the GDS short form: A preliminary study. *Clinical Gerontologist, 14*(2), 37–42.

Leung, C. M., Wing, Y. K., Kwong, P. K., Lo, A., & Shum, K. (1999). Validation of the Chinese-Cantonese version of the Hospital Anxiety and Depression Scale and comparison with the Hamilton Rating Scale of Depression. *Acta Psychiatrica Scandinavica, 100*(6), 456–461.

Leung, G. T. Y., De Jong Gierveld, J., & Lam, L. C. W. (2008). Validation of the Chinese translation of the 6-item De Jong Gierveld Loneliness Scale in elderly Chinese. *International Psychogeriatrics, 20*(6), 1262–1272.

Lichtenthal, W. G., Nilsson, M., Kissane, D. W., Breitbart, W., Kacel, E., Jones, E. C., & Prigerson, H. G. (2011). Underutilization of mental health services among bereaved caregivers with prolonged grief disorder. *Psychiatric Services, 62*(10), 1225–1229.

Lund, D. A., Caserta, M. S., de Vries, B., & Wright, S. (2004). Restoration after bereavement. *Generations Reviews, 14*(4), 9–15.

Lund, D. A., Caserta, M. S., Utz, R., & de Vries, B. (2010). Experiences and early coping of bereaved spouses/partners in an intervention based on the Dual Process Model (DPM). *Omega, 61*(4), 291–313.

Meij, L. W., Stroebe, M. S., Schut, H., Stroebe, W., van den Bout, J., van der Heijden, P. G. M., & Dijkstra, I. (2008). Parents grieving the loss of their child: Interdependence in coping. *British Journal of Clinical Psychology, 47*(1), 31–42.

Neimeyer, R. A., & Currier, J. M. (2009). Grief therapy: Evidence of efficacy and emerging directions. *Current Directions in Psychological Science, 18*(6), 352–356.

Office for National Statistics [England and Wales]. (2010). Marital status population projections for England & Wales, 2008-based marital status projections. Retrieved from http://www.ons.gov.uk/ons/rel/npp/marital-status-population-projections-for-england---wales/2008-based-marital-status-projections/index.html

Prigerson, H. G., Maciejewski, P. K., Reynolds, C. F., Bierhals, A. J., Newsom, J. T., Fasiczka, A., . . . Miller, M. (1995). Inventory of Complicated Grief: A scale to measure maladaptive symptoms of loss. Psychiatry Research, 59(1–2), 65–79. doi:10.1016/0165-1781(95)02757-2

Stroebe, M. S., Hansson, R. O., Stroebe, W., & Schut, H. (2001). Introduction: Concepts and issues in contemporary research on bereavement. In M. S. Stroebe, R. O. Hansson, W. Stroebe, & H. Schut (Eds.), *Handbook of bereavement: Consequences, coping, and care* (pp. 3–22). Washington, DC: American Psychological Association.

Stroebe, M. S., & Schut, H. (1999). The Dual Process Model of coping with bereavement: Rationale and description. *Death Studies, 23*(3), 197–224.

Stroebe, M. S., & Schut, H. (2010). The dual process model of coping with bereavement: A decade on. *Omega, 61*(4), 273–289.

Stroebe, M. S., Schut, H., & Stroebe, W. (2007). Health outcomes of bereavement, *Lancet, 370*, 1960–1937.

U.S. Census Bureau. (2012). The older population in United States: 2011 marital status. Retrieved from http://www.census.gov/population/age/data/2011.html

78 Leading Bereavement Groups

Richard T. Hara and Rachel Odo

Key Concepts

- *The group modality is a powerful tool for addressing the needs of many bereaved persons and provides an opportunity to assess for higher-risk individuals in need of additional services.*
- *Group planning requires attention to the group's form, function, and composition.*
- *Group facilitation requires knowledge about the bereavement process and basic group dynamics, as well as skills for encouraging discussion and responding to highly emotional content.*
- *Group facilitation also requires knowledge and skills to identify and respond to complicated grief when exhibited by a participant.*

The death of a loved one can be an isolating experience. In some respects, this isolation is necessary; a bereaved person needs time and space to adjust to the absence of a loved one and the many ensuing changes. This "grief work" enables "moving on" and the development of a satisfying life without the daily presence of the one who has died. However, extreme and prolonged isolation can undermine the establishment of new norms for daily life. Because there is no standardized cultural script for grieving and healing, many people who lose a loved one to cancer can benefit from the support of peers and professionals as they navigate this process. Bereavement groups are recognized as a way to promote coping after the loss of a loved one through education and support. Groups also provide oncology social workers an opportunity for extended assessment of an individual's grief responses. This chapter explores the rationale for offering group-based services to families of oncology patients who have died and reviews major issues pertaining to their development, implementation, and evaluation.

History and Rationale

> *It seems strange that I am an "old-timer" in this group now. When I found this group, some of the old timers shared a lot of information and experience which was really helpful. I am quite willing to take on the same role now.*
>
> —*Melissa, 52*

> *Grief, it seems, is a consequence of love. You cannot have one without the other.*
>
> —*Parkes (2011, p. 3)*

Support groups for the bereaved can serve a common-sense purpose, traceable to the first widow-to-widow support groups of the 1970s (Van der Houwen, Stroebe, Schut, Stroebe, & van den Bout, 2010). Peer-to-peer groups encourage dialogue about coping with loss and normalize the bereavement experience by involving peers as mentors. Those who seek bereavement groups, however, may have varying needs and hopes for this type of support. Some attend a bereavement group primarily for information and general support. They want to learn about the expected course of grief and how others are managing similar losses; they hope this knowledge will yield new insight into their own grief and ideas for coping with its pain and creating a new life and sense of themselves without the person who died. Others seek a bereavement group because they have been struggling with overwhelming symptoms of acute grief for an extended time. They believe they can't "get over it" in the way they believe they should and are disturbed by the negative impact this grief is having on their current functioning and relationships.

Though the debate about empirical support for bereavement interventions is ongoing, bereavement group members report a strong, positive effect from both the psychoeducational aspects of groups and the sense of a safe haven for emotional expression. Some studies have shown benefits of bereavement interventions for those mourners who show unremitting or increasing levels of distress over time (Jordan & Neimeyer, 2003) and for those who are self-referred (Schut, Stroebe, van den Bout, & Terheggen, 2001).

Sormanti's chapter in this section (Chapter 74) summarizes the historical development of theoretical models attempting to describe the bereavement process and identify "high risk" mourners. Although most models have advanced our knowledge, misunderstandings have also emerged. For example, some are concerned that the current emphasis on distinctions between typical and complicated grief may encourage practitioners to automatically view grief as a problem to be treated rather than the natural process it is for many. In planning and conducting bereavement groups, it is important to convey the field's belief that for most people, grieving is a normal process akin to the physical healing that occurs after a wound (Shear et al., 2011).

Bereavement Group Structure and Process

The following sections address key issues in group structure and process as they relate to the bereaved. The first section explores critical decisions regarding group form and function. The second section offers clinical strategies for safe and effective group facilitation.

Planning a Bereavement Group

> *This is a group for people who have lost a loved one to cancer, and that gives you all a bit of common ground, but, it is a "mixed" group in the sense that you are all from diverse backgrounds and places—you come with your own values, beliefs, lifestyles, priorities, interests, passions and concerns that will influence your unique experience of the loss.*
>
> —*Group leader opening statement*

Ideally, social workers facilitating bereavement groups have specialized group skills and expertise in grief work. However, most social workers face numerous constraints, including limited access to advanced training in groups and limited information on adapting interventions to account for variations in age, gender, and culture. Agency mission and mandate also influence the types and structure of groups offered.

Determining the purpose of an intervention is central to social work practice in all modalities. Bereavement group facilitators must decide whether they will provide primarily supportive interventions (e.g., psychoeducation, establishment of a safe space for emotional expression), and refer those who need additional help with cognitive and behavior change to individual counseling, or employ some combination of supportive and change-based approaches. Once this is determined, the facilitator can begin screening potential participants. Numerous assessment criteria guide a social worker's decision to recommend for or against group participation. Two of the most important include (1) an individual's ability to meaningfully articulate and reflect upon his or her own and others' grief experiences and (2) an individual's overall mental health. Some individuals who experience considerable anxiety about their loss or have specific problems for which they need immediate help may be unable to participate in the exchange of ideas and experiences characteristic of support groups. Additionally, individuals who demonstrate symptoms of major depression, suicidal thinking, anxiety, or substance abuse may require individual treatment to address these issues and may also be at heightened risk for complicated grief. The decision to "screen out" is based primarily on the social worker's assessment of a person's anxiety level and ability to relate to others in the context of a group setting. The social worker's determination that another intervention modality (or type of group) would be a better match at this time should be conveyed sensitively. The social worker should be prepared to provide the individual with referrals to other services. Alternatively, consideration should be given to the possibility of the individual engaging in both individual and group counseling in parallel or considering group after a period of individual counseling.

Group Type

Depending on the resources and limitations of the work setting, social workers may offer a range of group types (Lorenz, 1998). Bereavement groups generally have an emphasis on five primary objectives: support, education, growth, socialization, and self-help (Toseland & Rivas, 2012, p. 20). A smaller subset of the bereaved, whose grief becomes complicated, will require interventions that identify personality and coping factors causing them to stall in acute grief (Stroebe, Hansson, Schut, & Stroebe, 2008). Leaders must be prepared to incorporate more intensive ego-modifying interventions with this population or refer them for additional individual counseling (Piper, Ogrodniczuk, Joyce, & Weideman, 2011).

Group Leadership

Peer mentorship versus professional facilitation is a consideration at times in group planning. Groups designed to be purely support oriented may be successfully facilitated by peers with close supervision from a social worker who monitors the accuracy of information being provided. The competencies and training needs of peer group leaders and the process of supervision continue to be debated. Professional facilitation provides greater flexibility and range in design, treatment goal setting, and potential follow-up with individual members.

Group Structure

Grief is shaped by numerous variables, including characteristics of the bereaved individual (age, gender, sociocultural background, and strengths and vulnerabilities), the type of loss (death of partner, parent, child, sibling, or friend), and length of bereavement. In general, greater homogeneity across these variables encourages greater group identification and cohesion (Walter, 2005; Werner-Lin & Blank, 2009). However, because they all share a common issue of loss, these differences are not necessarily determinative and may be unavoidable due to the limited number of groups available.

Factors most frequently cited as benefiting from specialized groups include the following:

- Young widows often describe feeling distressed in a group of older adult widows as the age differences confront them with the reality of the untimeliness of their loss and the vastly different life challenges they face in single parenting and career development.
- Death of a child, atypical in our culture, is helped by sharing with other parents who have lost a child.
- Loss of a sibling may be helped by meeting with other siblings whose loss is often unrecognized in our culture.

Length of bereavement is another criterion considered in group composition. Some groups separate those bereaved up to 2 years from those bereaved for more than 2 years, because the latter may be experiencing prolonged acute grief. Some studies have also suggested that interventions are more effective when delivered in the 6- to 18-month period following a loss (Jordan & Neimeyer, 2003).

Time-Limited and Open-Ended Groups

Supportive groups can be open and ongoing, meeting monthly or biweekly. More therapeutic groups focusing on cognitive and behavior change are generally closed and time limited: 8 to 12 weeks is typical (Breitbart & Applebaum, 2011). Consideration should also be given to the issue of member participation in successive group series.

Clinical Challenges

Even in well-planned, homogenous groups, there will be differences among members. Incorporating a variety of supportive and therapeutic principles and approaches makes it possible to accommodate the diversity that most group leaders will encounter. Members may make comparisons between and among themselves and their losses. Leaders can use these comparisons to foster or deepen insight about factors that influence the variations in grief experience. For example, the nature, quality, and context of the relationship to the person who died; the type of loss; previous experiences of loss in one's life; and concurrent stresses or other losses in one's present life are factors that shape the specific individual's grief experience.

In her 2007 book *The Year of Magical Thinking*, Joan Didion described her intense grief over the death of her husband with whom she shared a writing career, as well as parenting of an adopted child. Her grief, however, was compounded by her daughter's sudden diagnosis with a life-threatening illness, an illness that her daughter struggled with and ultimately died of 2 years after Didion's husband's death. Didion's husband had had cardiac illness for many years and his death was to some extent expected medically, but her grief was clearly extended due to the compounding effect of the illness and death of two close family members in a short period of time.

Groups that bring together "veterans" with "newbies" can be a source of hope to both. Those who have been managing their grief longer can show the more newly bereaved, and remind themselves, how things can improve with time. They simultaneously benefit from the feeling of purpose and meaning that results from fulfilling a "helper" role.

The expression of cultural and religious beliefs is common in bereavement groups. Although this can facilitate connections among members who share similar beliefs, it may also provoke group conflict. Leaders must be comfortable establishing a group norm wherein personal religious, spiritual, and cultural beliefs can be readily shared even as the diversity among members (including those who identify as agnostic or atheistic and those who choose not to share their beliefs) is respected. Proselytizing in any form, however subtle, must be quickly and sensitively handled so that all members feel welcome in the space.

During a group session, a member may express suicidal ideation or longing to be with the deceased. In this situation, facilitators should respond at both the individual and group level. An assessment for suicide is conducted separately from the group setting. A statement that acknowledges the seriousness of the concern should also be made to the entire group. Doing so opens the door to an exploration of these and other intense feelings and affords all group members an opportunity to voice previously feared or "taboo" topics, such as thoughts about one's own death. The facilitator conveys reassurance that the group will remain a safe place by offering a private assessment of individuals who are troubled by thoughts of suicide while encouraging the group to discuss many thoughts about death that do emerge when a family member or friend has died. Group leaders must be comfortable managing these and other competing issues that arise at critical junctures during the group's development and process.

Leading a Bereavement Group

The bereaved engage in intense emotional and psychological work in the group as they describe the painful feelings of loss, acknowledge the complexity and meaning of their unique loss, seek acceptance of that reality, and begin to create a psychological space for the lost loved one in their minds and lives going forward. At the same time, restoration of their lives without the lost loved one begins immediately in small ways, fulfilling tasks left for them such as finances, work, or caregiving. Reconstitution of their lives and their identities without the person who died becomes an increasing focus of coping over time. "Going on" itself is often a more emotional and difficult process than bereaved individuals anticipate. Bereavement groups aim to normalize this process of oscillation between grief-focused and restoration-focused preoccupation and coping (Stroebe et al., 2008).

Beginning the Group

Clinicians engage members by fostering positive feelings about the clinician and the group as a healing community. Members commit to the group process as they experience normalization of their grief, mutual support, and opportunities to build new relationships while mourning. Articulating group purpose, establishing norms, affirming confidentiality, connecting members with each other's experience, and dealing with early conflict set a therapeutic tone and create the foundation for open expression of thoughts and feelings (Schneider, 2006). Discussions of extra-group contact should be part of this initial phase. For groups that stress socialization, encouraging outside contact may be beneficial but may also lead to the blurring of boundaries and the creation of cliques (Caserta & Lund, 1996). Clinicians should be prepared to manage this potential complication as the group progresses:

> *Ann, Marsha, Sue, and Lynn developed a natural and supportive friendship early in their bereavement group. They spoke frequently by phone and began meeting outside of the group socially. Within the group setting, their private jokes and shared intimacies created a "group within the group" where they quickly became the most vocal members, leaving others feeling excluded and voiceless. Respecting the value and meaning of these emerging friendships while reiterating the importance of maintaining the group norms established at the outset, particularly the issue of confidentiality and not discussing members outside of the group, became a crucial aspect of the leader's role at this point in the process. In addition, consistent efforts to engage members outside of the "clique" paved the way for greater group cohesion overall. As one member wrote in her evaluation at the end of the session, "At first, I didn't feel like I really belonged, maybe I didn't even want to belong. There were only three or four people really talking. I think it got better when everyone else started talking, too, then I felt like I could say what I was thinking."*

Working as a Group

Sharing feelings, problem-solving, exchanging support, challenging one another to meet individual goals in a supportive community constitutes the heart of group work (Sutton & Liechty, 2004). These techniques work well in bereavement groups. "Storytelling" becomes a powerful way to express and process painful emotions and examine spiritual or existential concerns. The use of group rituals and expressive/creative techniques is also consistent with current theoretical conceptions and empirical knowledge. As members begin to process the painful memories associated with a loved one's illness and the dying process itself, there is the opportunity to create a "memory box." Members might be encouraged to spend part of a session decorating a box and writing down each painful memory on a slip of paper. When everyone has finished, those who wish can read their slips aloud to the group as each member places the slips into his or her box. The boxes are closed and members are invited to think about what they will do with their box. Discussion about whether they will keep the boxes to look through again (as they continue to process these painful memories) or put them away, bury them (as members often choose), or otherwise dispose of them (several members have chosen to burn their boxes or to throw them into the ocean) can open the group to considerations of the process of working through and letting go of the painful memories associated with illness and loss.

A similar exercise can also be done as a memory box that is decorated in the group and used to gather the good memories, once again, written on slips of paper during the group, along with small mementos or photos that members bring in. Members may share some of their memories, and discussion can also be focused on where these boxes will be kept and the meaning of cherishing memories throughout one's life. Issues of comfort with readiness to begin "remembering" and the place of "remembering" as a cornerstone for "moving on" can be highlighted. Clinicians also report using journaling, life review, eulogy and epitaph writing, imaginary dialogue, relaxation, and thought diaries (Currier, Holland, & Neimeyer, 2008) in bereavement groups.

Several issues are commonly explored in bereavement groups. Clinicians choose either to elicit specific discussions about these issues or to draw attention to them as they arise in the natural course of discussion:

- Length and nature of the grieving process
- Distinctions between sorrow and depression
- Faith and belief systems
- Changes in existing relationships and development of new relationships
- Ambivalence/uncertainty/guilt/sadness about "moving on"

Some topics that may facilitate the work of the group include the following:

- "Telling the story" of the death
- Secondary losses associated with a loved one's death
- Changes in roles and identity
- Existential issues related to the confrontation of mortality
- How to manage anniversaries and holidays
- Mourning rituals

Topics that encourage members to look to the future may be most effectively raised in the middle to later stages of a time-limited group. These include developing new relationships and life skills and testing new strategies for coping with difficult feelings (Gauthier & Gagliese, 2012; Schneider, 2006). The midstage of the bereavement group process emphasizes the creation of a safe space in which members can express feelings and give and receive support. Clinicians should strive for a balanced expression of negative emotions with a complementary restorative focus so that members can freely acknowledge the pain of loss while reaffirming their strengths, social resources, and personal experiences of healing and growth.

Ending the Group

Successful clinical management of the termination phase of a bereavement group is critical. Through an exploration of members' thoughts and feelings about the ending of the group, clinicians exploit a parallel process in which members gain insight about their reactions to other types of loss and the importance of finding ways to cope with all kinds of transitions as they adapt to the death of their loved one. Reflecting on the growth that has occurred during the group and the growth that is anticipated as members transition to life beyond the group provides a powerful model for ongoing adjustment to bereavement.

> *This has been an incredible group. It is truly something to think about how we started as strangers but have come together with such openness and generosity of spirit. Changes of all kinds, even the most positive transitions, can be challenging, but endings like this ending of our group, can be particularly difficult. They can bring up some of the same feelings of loss and grief that brought you here originally. But, they can also be a powerful and healing opportunity. We have a chance tonight to share some personal reflections on the group experience, to think back and remember how things were when we first met, to consider the changes that have already come about and the ones that are just beginning, to consider the strengths that have been uncovered and where this journey may take you going forward.*
>
> —*Sam, 68*

> *Although members may create lasting bonds with one another, as with any loss, the ending of the group as an entity must be acknowledged.*
>
> *Just wanted to say thank you all for sharing stories and pains and successes... Each one gives me validation for some feeling deep inside.*
>
> —*Sam, 68*

Evaluation

Group evaluation is a meaningful component of termination and postgroup follow-up. Although most research on support groups relies on scientifically validated assessment tools to examine changes in members' emotional distress and mood (Maruyama & Atencio, 2008), attention to other outcomes and use of other measures may provide a fuller picture of the impact of a group.

Pearls

- Determination of primary purpose is essential to planning and implementing a bereavement group.
- Group leaders should determine whether the needs of individual members can be addressed within the group and be prepared to transition members to other forms of support, such as individual counseling, when need exceeds the group's focus.
- Group process, particularly the formation of bonds between members and the management of their termination within the group, is a powerful means for members to experience their loss as manageable.

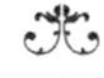

Pitfalls

- Ineffective management of group content and process may interfere with development of group cohesion. For example, rather than simply shutting down group conflict, group leaders must be prepared to hold and reshape the anger and aggressive responses that can be a part of some members' grief process.
- A focus on expression of negative emotions, without recognition of member strengths, growth, and positive emotions related to recovery from loss, can be demoralizing for group members and impede their agency to move forward.

> *What often causes so much pain is trying to hold onto "what was," the sooner we can accept "what is," the more we can appreciate what is, what is left and live more fully in the moment.*
>
> —*Laura, 45*

Social workers facilitating groups for the bereaved face many challenges. In medical settings, these may include institutional resistance to acknowledging death and dying. The bereaved may also be reluctant to return to the place where a loved one was treated or died. In community-based agencies, screening for psychiatric comorbidities and other issues that may complicate a potential member's grief and recruiting enough members to create a group can be challenging. Regardless of work setting, clinicians are affected by the pain and suffering of their clients. Even experienced social workers must monitor countertransference to ensure they are not using the group process to address their own needs, as well as to prevent burnout. Further study is needed to enhance our understanding of best practices with the bereaved. Nevertheless, bereavement groups remain a powerful modality for healing. The "mainstream model" of group support, which draws upon clients' strengths to promote healing, is well suited for use in hospital or community-based agency settings.

ADDITIONAL RESOURCES

WEBSITES

Association of Death Education and Counseling: http://www.adec.org

Cancer Support Community: http://www.cancersupportcommunity.org/

Cancer*Care*: http://www.cancercare.org

Compassionate Friends: http://compassionatefriends.org

Hospice Foundation of America: http://www.hospicefoundation.org

Books

Neimeyer, R. (2006). *Lessons of loss: A guide to coping.* Memphis, TN: Center for the Study of Loss and Transition.

Rando, T. (1991). *How to go on living when someone you love dies.* New York, NY: Bantam Books.

REFERENCES

Breitbart, W., & Applebaum, A. (2011). Meaning-centered group psychotherapy. In M. Watson & D. W. Kissane (Eds.), *Handbook of psychotherapy in cancer care* (pp. 137–147). Chichester, England: Wiley.

Caserta, M., & Lund, D. (1996). Beyond bereavement support group meetings: Exploring outside social contacts among the members. *Death Studies*, *20*, 537–556.

Currier, J., Holland, J., & Neimeyer, R. (2008). Making sense of loss: A content analysis of end-of-life practitioners' therapeutic approaches. *Omega*, *57*, 121–141.

Didion, J. (2007). *The year of magical thinking.* New York, NY: Vintage Press.

Gauthier, L., & Gagliese, L. (2012). Bereavement interventions, end-of-life cancer care, and spousal well-being: A systematic review. *Clinical Psychology: Science and Practice*, *19*, 72–92.

Jordan, J., & Neimeyer, R. (2003). Does grief counseling work? *Death Studies*, *27*, 765–786.

Lorenz, L. (1998). Selecting and implementing support groups for bereaved adults. *Cancer Practice*, *6*, 161–166.

Maruyama, N., & Atencio, C. (2008). Evaluating a bereavement support group. *Palliative and Supportive Care*, *6*, 43–49.

Parkes, C. M. (2011). Introduction: The historical landscape of loss: Development of bereavement studies. In R. Neimeyer, D. Harris, H. Winokur, & G. Thornton (Eds.), *Grief and bereavement in contemporary society: Bridging research and practice* (pp. 1–5). New York, NY: Routledge.

Piper, W. E., Ogrodniczuk, J. S., Joyce, A. S., & Weideman, R. (2011). *Short-term group therapies for complicated grief: Two research-based models.* Washington, DC: American Psychological Association.

Schneider, R. (2006). Group bereavement support for spouses who are grieving the loss of a partner to cancer. *Social Work With Groups*, *29*, 259–278.

Schut, H., Stroebe, M., van den Bout, J., & Terheggen, M. (2001). The efficacy of bereavement interventions: Determining who benefits. In M. Stroebe, R. Hansson, W. Stroebe, & H. Schut (Eds.), *Handbook of bereavement research: Consequences, coping, and care* (pp. 705–737). Washington, DC: American Psychological Association.

Shear, M. K., Simon, N., Wall, M., Zisook, S., Neimeyer, R., Duan, N., . . . Keshaviah, A. (2011). Complicated grief and related bereavement issues for DSM-5. *Depression and Anxiety*, *28*, 103–117.

Stroebe, M., Hansson, R., Schut, H., & Stroebe, W. (2008). *Handbook of bereavement research and practice: Advances in theory and intervention.* Washington, DC: American Psychological Association.

Sutton, A., & Liechty, D. (2004). Clinical practice with groups in end-of-life care. In J. Berzoff & P. Silverman (Eds.), *Living with dying: A handbook for end-of-life healthcare practitioners* (pp. 508–534). New York, NY: Columbia University Press.

Toseland, R., & Rivas, R. (2012). *An introduction to group work practice.* Boston, MA: Allyn & Bacon.

Van der Houwen, K., Stroebe, M., Schut, H., Stroebe, W., & van den Bout, J. (2010). Online mutual support in bereavement: An empirical examination. *Computers in Human Behavior*, *26*, 1519–1525.

Walter, C. (2005). Support groups for widows and widowers. In G. Greif & P. Ephross (Eds.), *Group work with populations at risk* (2nd ed., pp. 109–125). Oxford, England: Oxford University Press.

Werner-Lin, A., & Biank, N. (2009). Along the cancer continuum: Integrating therapeutic support and bereavement groups for children and teens of terminally ill cancer patients. *Journal of Family Social Work*, *12*, 359–370.

XIV

Patient- and Family-Centered Care

Social Work Role and Organizational Models for Psychosocial Services

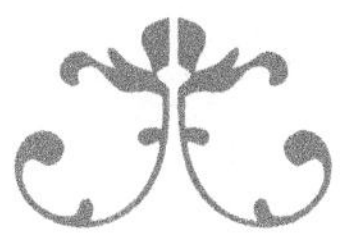

Nancy W. Newman

This section provides a broad overview of patient- and family-centered care, including its congruence with social work values and training; the methods of and mutual benefits derived from partnering with patients and families; how patient-centered communication and patient engagement directly relate to successful outcomes; organizational service models to meet the range of social, emotional, spiritual, and educational needs of cancer patients and their loved ones; and opportunities to extend and enrich services through leadership of volunteer programs.

In "Patient- and Family-Centered Care: A National Mandate and Social Work Goal," Nancy W. Newman and Cynthia Medeiros define patient- and family-centered care, offer its historical perspective, and emphasize how social work training and professional ethos position individuals in the field to substantially contribute to a health care environment that embodies the principles and core concepts of this approach.

In "Integrated Interdisciplinary Staff Leadership Model of Patient-Centered Care," Mathew Loscalzo, Karen Clark, and Barry D. Bultz describe how the combination of psychosocial, spiritual, palliative care, support, and educational services succeeds under the direction of social work leadership and shared accountability among team members across disciplines. Included are the elements required at all levels to develop and sustain an innovative supportive care medical service in an oncology setting, and how partnering with patients and families in the planning and evaluation of services contributed to their success.

In "Directing Stand-Alone Social Work Department Models," Margaret Weld Meyer and Wendy J. Evans, two social workers from one of the oldest and most successful stand-alone U.S. oncology social work departments, provide valuable direction and keys to their success with this model, both organizationally and in clinical care delivery. The chapter emphasizes the importance of partnering with patients and families as a starting point for gathering data to support the value of a stand-alone social work department. In addition, alignment with the institutional mission and goals, professionalism, communication, and visibility are used to enhance respect for the role of social workers within the oncology setting and promote the institutional understanding of the need for and value of social work in patient care.

In "Creating Innovative Cancer Support Programs in Community Cancer Centers," Alison Mayer Sachs and Kerry Irish provide readers with the nuts and bolts of designing, developing, and implementing support programs in hospital-based or community cancer center settings. Needs assessments, inventive ways to approach and gain support from administrators and key stakeholders, the process of cultivating donors, and the creation of productive collaborations are described as imperative in planning and implementing or expanding innovative cancer support programs.

In "Managing Volunteer Services in Oncology," Catherine Credeur and Christine Healy focus on engaging current and former cancer patients and their families as collaborative partners to extend service delivery and improve patients' experiences. This chapter emphasizes how oncology social workers use their clinical, administrative, and community organization skills when leading or supporting a volunteer program, especially one that includes patient and family advisers.

79

Nancy W. Newman and Cynthia Medeiros

Patient- and Family-Centered Care: A National Mandate and Social Work Goal

Key Concepts

- *This chapter outlines the core concepts regarding patient- and family-centered care.*
- *It discusses the congruence of social work's mission, values, purpose, and objectives with this model of care.*
- *Social work has a role at the clinical, administrative, and policy levels in advancing the practice of patient- and family-centered care in institutions and in health care.*

Patient- and family-centered care emphasizes collaboration with patients and families of all ages, at all levels of care, and in all health care settings. It further acknowledges that families, however defined, are essential to patients' health and well-being and are allies for quality and safety within the health care system (Conway et al., 2006). The patient- and family-centered care approach includes equitable, coordinated, and integrated culturally competent care; timely, candid, and useful information; communication and education; individualized care; physical comfort; emotional support; involvement of family and friends; shared decision making; and collaboration with patients and families in the planning, delivery, and evaluation of care. Through their training and professional values, oncology social workers can contribute substantially to the development of a health care environment that embodies these core concepts of the patient- and family-centered model of care. (See the appendix for the Association of Oncology Social Work's *Standards of Practice in Oncology Social Work* [AOSW, 2012].)

Precedents Leading to a Patient- and Family-Centered Model of Care

Although patient- and family-centered care has historical roots in 1960s maternal and child health, it was not until 2001, when the Institute of Medicine's (IOM) Committee on Quality of Health Care in America published its landmark report, *Crossing the Quality Chasm: A New Health System for the 21st Century*, that national momentum fueled advances in the practice of patient- and family-centered care and transformed health care. With the vision of moving health care from where it was to where it should be, the IOM committee addressed key dimensions and proposed six aims for improvement that would result in a safer and more reliable, responsive, integrated, and available patient experience. One aim integral to all others—patient-centered care—"encompasses qualities of compassion, empathy, and responsiveness to the needs, values, and expressed preferences of the individual patient" (IOM, Committee on Quality of Health Care in America, 2001, p. 48). The American Hospital Association (2004), together with the Institute for Family-Centered Care (now the Institute for Patient- and Family-Centered Care), developed tools that define patient- and family-centered care and how leaders, trustees, and senior executives can foster this approach to care.

Six Aims for Improving the 21st-Century Health Care System in America

To improve today's health care, key dimensions need to be addressed. Health care should be:

Safe: *Avoid injuries to patients from care intended to help them.*

Effective: *Provide services based on scientific knowledge to all who could benefit and refrain from providing services to those not likely to benefit.*

Patient Centered: *Provide care that is respectful of and responsive to individual patients' preferences, needs, and values and ensure that patients' values guide all clinical decisions.*

Timely: *Reduce waits and sometimes harmful delays for those who receive care and those who give care.*

Efficient: *Avoid waste, including waste of equipment, supplies, ideas, and energy.*

Equitable: *Provide care that does not vary in quality because of personal characteristics, such as gender, ethnicity, geographic location, and socioeconomic status.*

Source: Institute of Medicine (2001, pp. 5–6).

In patient- and family-centered care, the paradigm shifts from doing things *to* and *for* patients and their families to working *with* them, both clinically and administratively; in some settings, the adopted motto "Nothing about me without me" signifies this commitment.

In addition to improving the patient and family's experience, a growing body of evidence shows that developing patient partnerships is linked to improved health outcomes. For example, evidence shows that patients who are more involved in their care are better able to manage complex chronic conditions, seek appropriate assistance, experience less anxiety and stress, and have shorter hospital stays (Balik, Conway, Zipperer, & Watson, 2011).

The National Cancer Institute (Epstein & Street, 2007), in its publication *Patient-Centered Communication in Cancer Care: Promoting Healing and Reducing Suffering*, acknowledged the growing recognition that an interdisciplinary approach to cancer prevention and control should incorporate patient-centered communication to maximize the benefits of current diagnosis and treatment discoveries, especially in the emerging era of personalized medicine (Epstein & Street, 2007). The authors described patient-centered care as a process composed of essential interrelated elements and interactions that enhance communication and lead to improved health outcomes.

In 2010, The Joint Commission released new standards and revised existing standards to incorporate patient-centered care and, soon after (The Joint Commission, 2010, 2011), published two educational monographs, one addressing effective communication, cultural competence, and patient- and family-centered care, and the other, funded by the Commonwealth Fund and California Endowment, addressing the same issues for the lesbian, gay, bisexual, and transgender community. These monographs were designed to inspire hospitals to go above and beyond what is required in the standards and adopt practices promoting better communication and patient- and family-centered care.

The importance of patient- and family-centered care was further promoted through the Patient Protection and Affordable Care Act of 2010, designed to improve access to affordable, high-quality health care. Because an essential element in achieving this goal was to learn from patients' experiences, the act called for the creation of the Patient-Centered Outcome Research Institute, which requires patient and consumer advocates to be involved as advisers in establishing research priorities and providing oversight of clinical trials (Johnson & Abraham, 2012). In addition, the act called for the creation of affordable care organizations, networks of hospitals, physicians, and other health care providers who deliver coordinated and high-quality care to Medicare patients. Each affordable care organization was mandated to include a beneficiary and a consumer advocate on its governing body.

Several interchangeable terms are used in health care to describe patient- and family-centered care: *patient-centered care, patient-centric care, family-centered care, personalized care*, and *person-directed care*, whereas *personal* and *public engagement* are used outside of health care and *resident-centered care* is used in the long-term care industry. In the oncology field, *patient- and family-centered care* is sometimes called the humanistic side of personalized cancer care. The term *patient engagement* describes the patient–provider partnership in health reform legislation. Regardless of the terminology used, a patient- and family-centered organizational culture is characterized by the partnership between health care professionals and the individuals and families they serve and by its core values and attitudes.

Definition: *Patient- and family-centered care is an innovative approach to the planning, delivery, and evaluation of health care that is grounded in mutually beneficial partnerships among health care providers, patients, and families. Patient- and family-centered care applies to patients of all ages and can be practiced in any health care setting.*

Core Concepts: *Patient- and family-centered care is guided by four core concepts:*

1. *Dignity and respect: Health care practitioners listen to and honor the perspectives and choices of patients and families. The knowledge, values, beliefs, and cultural backgrounds of*

patients and their families are incorporated into the planning and delivery of care.

2. *Information sharing: Health care practitioners communicate and share complete and unbiased information with patients and families in ways that are affirming and useful. To participate effectively in care and decision making, patients and families receive timely, complete, and accurate information.*
3. *Participation: Patients and families are encouraged and supported in participating in care and decision making at the level they choose.*
4. *Collaboration: Patients, families, health care practitioners, and hospital leaders collaborate in the development, implementation, and evaluation of policies and programs; in the design of health care facilities; in professional education; and in the delivery of care.*

Source: Johnson et al. (2008, p. vi).

Oncology Social Work and Patient- and Family-Centered Care

Social work is guided by the following set of values that directly align with the core concepts of patient- and family-centered care (Hepworth, Rooney, Rooney, Strom-Gottfried, & Larson, 2013, p. 7):

- Social workers' professional relationships are built on regard for individual worth and dignity and advanced by mutual participation, acceptance, confidentiality, and honesty.
- Social workers respect the individual's right to make independent decisions and to participate actively in the helping process.
- Social workers are committed to assisting client systems to obtain needed resources.
- Social workers strive to make social institutions more humane and responsive to human needs.

Social workers demonstrate respect for and acceptance of the unique characteristics of diverse populations. As a profession, social work has embodied many core concepts of patient- and family-centered care throughout its history. Social transformation is the primary goal of community organization, an approach in which participants "develop their own solutions, advance their own needs, or build capacity" in partnerships with private or governmental agencies (Hepworth et al., 2013, p. 454). This social work role and partnership with community residents mirror the partnership that social workers and other health care providers have with patients and families in the transformation of health care.

The National Association of Social Work (NASW) standards of practice also focus on the professional roles of empowerment and advocacy, noting that "social workers have a responsibility to advocate for the needs and interests of clients in health care, including advocating for larger system change to improve access to care and improve delivery of services" (2005, p. 24). By embracing the patient- and family-centered approach to care, social workers and other health care providers, in partnership with patients and families, create a health care environment that leads to the best outcomes and enhances quality and safety.

Clinical Level of Care

Oncology social workers provide patient- and family-centered care at the clinical level by using a psychosocial assessment to better understand patients' unique values, beliefs, and backgrounds; using a strengths-based approach; being committed to the patient's right to self-determination; believing that the patient is the source of control; understanding and paying attention to the role of family, however defined by the patient; empowering the patient through education and facilitation of information; and working in partnership with the patient and family in the development and implementation of a mutually agreed-upon plan of care. In addition, the social worker is not only an advocate for the patient and family when barriers to care or services occur but also a positive influence on the team's approach to provision of culturally competent patient- and family-centered care.

Oncology social workers are professionally equipped to help cancer centers and programs become more patient and family centered in their philosophy, practices, policies, procedures, and environment. Having a systems approach, understanding organizational dynamics, possessing astute assessment skills, and being engaged with patients and families, oncology social workers can lead this effort.

Administrative Level of Care

Oncology social work managers and administrators are at a level in the organization that provides them access to other managers and senior leaders. As a result, they are able to educate their colleagues about the core concepts of the patient- and family-centered approach to care, the importance of the approach, and its mutual benefits to the patients and the institution in the areas of safety, quality of care, and patient satisfaction.

A basic premise of social work practice is the centrality of the relationship—indeed, a partnership—built between patient and clinician. Organizational resistance to developing patient and family advisory programs and councils often stems from a misunderstanding of this relationship. Advisers are not there to impose their will. Rather, their role is to share their views and experiences as consumers and to work side by side with staff to design and evaluate services, programs, policies, procedures, and the environment of care.

Social Work Roles in the Advancement of Patient- and Family-Centered Care

- *Facilitate administrative understanding and commitment to the core concepts of patient- and family-centered care.*
- *Propose, plan, and implement patient and family advisory councils.*
- *Help staff understand the roles of advisers on committees.*
- *Oversee and coordinate the operations of patient and family advisory programs and councils.*
- *Ensure follow-through in the organization regarding issues brought forth by the council or other patient and family advisers.*
- *Ensure the goals of the patient and family advisory program are in alignment with the goals of the institution to maximize meaningful collaborative work and achieve organizational successes.*
- *Partner with advisers to recruit, interview, orient, and support new patient and family advisers.*
- *Ensure that advisers are integrated into key quality, safety, service, and process improvement committees and work groups throughout the organization.*
- *Ensure that policies and procedures reflect The Joint Commission's Patient- and Family-Centered Care Standards and those from other regulatory bodies.*
- *Partner with advisers to train and educate staff and faculty about patient- and family-centered care.*
- *Partner with patient and family advisers in the development and management of peer support and visitor programs (see Chapter 83).*

Social workers also can have some resistance to patient- and family-centered care because of concerns about boundaries in the clinical relationship. As they work alongside patients and families as advisers, many social workers worry about how they can continue to provide clinical care when needed.

When an Adviser Is *Your* Patient

Lenny was a member of Dana-Farber Cancer Institute's Patient and Family Advisory Council, which the director of patient and family support services was responsible for developing. He was also a patient to whom the director provided clinical care.

Lenny was a strong voice for the development of an integrative therapies program at the institute. Building such a program subsequently became a major goal of the council, with Lenny taking the lead. Lenny and the director met together frequently to develop a model for an integrated therapies program. Together, they formed a planning committee and served as its cochairs. With the planning committee, they developed the clinical and business case for this program and presented the case to clinical and administrative leadership. They strategized together regarding how to deal with organizational resistance to such an untraditional program in a highly traditional, evidence-based research institution. They spent many hours working with committee members and institutional staff to break down the barriers against establishing the program. Because of the strong support of the council and the work of the Complementary Therapies Planning Committee, their efforts were successful, and the Leonard P. Zakim Center for Integrative Therapies is now one of Dana-Farber's premiere programs. Throughout the planning for this program, Lenny and the director worked as "business" partners.

During all this work, however, the director was fully aware that she had a clinical role with Lenny and his wife. In the year before the Zakim Center opened, Lenny's clinical condition began to deteriorate. The director, in her clinical role, often met with Lenny and his wife to provide support during his physician and treatment visits. The discussions were not about the Zakim Center; they were about his cancer and concerns about his clinical condition. The day before Lenny's death, the director was with him in the clinic, and she, the rest of the clinical team, and his family and friends were with him when he died the following evening. In the year that followed his death, she continued to be available to his family as needed and to work with the council and the institute in creating and administering the Zakim Center. The work she and Lenny did together for the center was for patients and families; the work they did together clinically was for Lenny and his family.

The inclusion of social work in the development of an integrative approach to cancer care at Dana-Farber Cancer Institute and other oncology programs also demonstrates the contribution that oncology social work can bring to the provision of culturally responsive care. There continues to be great disparity in the delivery of health care to people of diverse cultures and ethnic backgrounds. NASW's *Code of Ethics* (2008) requires social workers to understand cultures, recognize their strengths, and deliver services that are sensitive to them. Recruiting advisers who reflect different cultures and ethnic backgrounds provides the vehicle to understanding and developing treatment programs and services that are responsive to their needs and are nondiscriminatory. Because health disparities in cancer care are a serious problem that affects clinical outcomes, the involvement of advisers from diverse groups is key to overcoming barriers to the accrual of members of minority groups for clinical trials. Patient advisers can also be extremely valuable in community benefit programs and community outreach efforts. Oncology social workers who participate in these areas are instrumental to incorporating advisers into these efforts.

Policy Level of Care

In their roles as advocates for patients and families and as champions of patient- and family-centered care, oncology social workers can play a pivotal role at the environmental level. The voice of the patient and family needs to be heard by all who are developing health care policies and programs. Oncology social workers need to be aware of health care legislation at the state and national levels that directly affects consumers, and they can work with patient and family advisers to become spokespersons for social change. Early in 2000, patient and family advisers from Dana-Farber, Brigham and Women's Hospital, and Massachusetts General Hospital worked with administrators from those organizations and state legislators to pass the Massachusetts Pediatric Palliative Care Bill, which provides for the creation and funding of the Pediatric Palliative Care Network. This network provides comprehensive direct and consultative community-based pediatric palliative services that include pain and symptom management, case management and assessment, social services, counseling and bereavement services, volunteer support services, respite services, and complementary services (Bona, Bates, & Wolfe, 2011). Advisers and staff alike testified before the Massachusetts legislature on the network's behalf. Their testimonies were instrumental in the bill's passage.

Examples of Organizational Best Practices in Patient- and Family-Centered Care

- *Patients and families are viewed as essential members of the health care team.*
- *Patients and families are active participants in the planning of, decisions about, and management of the patient's health care.*
- *Families are no longer viewed as visitors, and the family's presence and participation are welcomed and encouraged.*
- *Family is defined as anyone the patient considers family, whether or not the individual is related by blood or marriage.*
- *Information is timely and useful and meets the communication and language needs of the patient and family.*
- *Patient resource centers, patient and family orientation sessions, and patient portals are available for information and navigation.*
- *Reports of nurses' shift changes are at the patient's bedside and include the patient and family in the discussion.*
- *Interdisciplinary rounds include the participation of the patient and family, depending on the patient's preference.*
- *Health care providers help patients and families anticipate what to expect from procedures and treatments and narrate the care as it is happening to reduce their anxiety.*
- *A patient and family council exists that is composed of patient and family advisers, clinicians, and administrators.*
- *Patient and family advisers are integrated into organizational committees and quality initiatives.*
- *Patient and family advisers work in partnership with staff to provide informational, wellness, and supportive services to patients and families.*
- *Patient and family advisers partner with staff to educate health care providers, staff, and medical trainees.*
- *Patient and family advisers work in partnership with staff in legislative efforts for the institution.*

Source: Johnson, Abraham, and Shelton (2009).

Development of a Patient and Family Advisory Program at Moffitt Cancer Center

In late 2004, inspired by Dana-Farber's Patient and Family Advisory Program, the director of Patient Support and Advocacy, an oncology social work administrator at Moffitt Cancer Center in Tampa, Florida, developed a proposal to implement a similar program with the overall goal of ensuring patient safety and high-quality care through collaboration.

In May 2005, the director of Patient Support and Advocacy chaired a steering committee composed of patients, family members, staff, and faculty that was formed to develop a Patient and Family Advisory Program with four components: (1) a Patient and Family Advisory Council composed of patient and family advisers, clinicians, and administrators; (2) the advisory council's committees; (3) patient and family advisers who were integrated into cancer center committees; and (4) a patient and family newsletter called PARTNERS. The program's mission statement, goals, and bylaws were created within the first 3 months.

In August 2005, two patients in active treatment were elected as the first cochairs of the Patient and Family Advisory Council. All patient and family advisers became formal Moffitt volunteers to ensure they were appropriately oriented to the cancer center and complied with the Health Insurance Portability and Accountability Act (HIPAA).

While the council's infrastructure was being developed, the director of Patient Support and Advocacy, in partnership with the patient and family advisers, worked on building a culture of organizational partnership with patients and families. An assessment of the organization's readiness was performed, buy-in from the executive leadership and the medical staff's commitment to the program was obtained, organizational education was provided to staff and faculty, and three council members received intensive training on patient- and family-centered care from the Institute for Patient- and Family-Centered Care. The director's challenge was to obtain the organization's understanding and acceptance of a new paradigm: working side by side with patients and family members on an administrative level (e.g., planning, evaluating, advising, problem solving, and decision making), in addition to the clinical collaboration that had been an ingrained part of the culture at Moffitt Cancer Center since its inception.

In September 2005, the Patient and Family Advisory Council's cochairs led a strategic planning exercise that resulted in a focus on the following specific goals for the next 12 months: (1) promote integration, (2) enhance communication, (3) improve navigation through the system, and (4) improve patient safety and delivery of care. Each year, the council reviews the organization's strategic initiatives, many of which the patient and family advisers have been involved in developing, and generates a plan that is aligned with the organization's goals to help the center achieve success.

In January 2006, the advisers were integrated into 11 high-level committees dedicated to organizational and process improvement, allowing for new ideas and fresh perspectives. The primary topics considered by all 11 committees included, but were not limited to, quality, safety, and patient satisfaction. The director, in partnership with the council's patient cochairs, obtained approval to have advisers on the committees and prepared both the committee chairs and the advisers for the collaborative work in which they would be involved.

A small sample of the Patient and Family Advisory Program's accomplishments over time appears here:

- *The program's advisers participated in planning all the center's new buildings and the renovations of its already-existing buildings.*
- *The Patient and Family Advisory Council provided input into the facility's new navigation features, such as maps and signage.*
- *The council provided input regarding the following programs and initiatives: Total Cancer Care Toolkits, a culturally sensitive care-at-the-bedside initiative, a "Team Up" website, menus served in the cafeteria, the Patient Library's and Welcome Center's programming, the Patient Portal, a Survivorship Program, and patient distress screening.*
- *The patient advisers participated in training fourth-year medical students on how to break bad news to patients and their families.*
- *The director and the patient advisers produced a video about patient- and family-centered care to be shown during the general orientation of staff and faculty.*
- *A collaborative group of staff and patient and family advisers developed a peer visitor program that integrates advisers into the inpatient units and clinics, where they work directly with staff, patients, and families to provide welcoming, supportive, and educational services.*
- *A collaborative group of staff and patient advisers designed and implemented a Patient and Family Orientation program.*
- *The staff and family advisers created additional resources and programming specifically for caregivers.*

By embracing patient- and family-centered care, the benefits of these accomplishments to both Moffitt and the patients and family members have been vast. The ability to address old problems with new ideas from the very people who receive the care has made a big difference in patient care, service delivery, and patient safety.

The oncology social worker's leadership role in the example described in the box is multifaceted and requires the use of a wide range of professional skills. Moffitt Cancer Center's director of patient support and advocacy not only relied on the values, beliefs, and skills learned from her professional education and experience but also obtained further training on patient- and family-centered care from the Institute for Patient- and Family-Centered Care, a nonprofit national organization dedicated to providing essential leadership in advancing the practice (http://www.ipfcc.org).

According to the Planetree and Picker Institute (2008, p. 20):

> *Patient-centered care is about engaging the hearts and minds of those you work with and those you care for. It is about reconnecting staff with their passion for serving others. It is about examining all aspects of the patient experience and considering them from the perspective of patients versus the convenience of providers. Ultimately, it is about a collective commitment to a set of beliefs about the way patients will be cared for, how families will be treated, how leadership will support staff, and how staff will nurture each other and themselves.*

Although the quotation describes patient-centered care, it could also describe aspects of social work practice. Social workers strive to understand from where the client is coming and to use that understanding to develop, with the client, an appropriate treatment plan. The client could be the patient or the patient's family, the treatment team, the other health care providers, the program, or the host facility. Before patient- and family-centered care, facilities strived to provide "patient-focused" care. Although the focus was the patient and the family, the key ingredients—the patient and the family—were not included.

Health care is now challenged to work *with* the patient and family—not *for* them—and social work, by its very nature, can be a central player in this model. Social work has historically advocated *for* the client—for access to care and services, a more humanistic approach, patient rights, and more. Now it is called on to advocate *with* the client to address and improve all aspects of the health care delivery system and ultimately the patient experience.

Pearls

- Patient- and family-centered care places an emphasis on collaborating with patients and families of all ages, at all levels of care, and in all health care settings.
- Evidence shows that patients who are more involved in their care are better able to manage complex chronic conditions, seek appropriate assistance, experience less anxiety and stress, and have shorter hospital stays.
- Patient- and family-centered care shifts the paradigm from doing things *to* and *for* patients to working *with* them both clinically and administratively.

Pitfalls

- Patient- and family-centered care *must* be embraced by the highest level of the organization for the model to succeed.

- Staff must be fully educated regarding the concepts of patient- and family-centered care and the role of patient and family advisers.
- Patient and family advisers need to be involved from the beginning of a project so the patient's perspective is at the table from the outset.
- Advisers need to be carefully chosen, oriented, and supported.
- Advisers are to be seen as integral partners with staff in developing a patient- and family-centered program and improvement efforts, not as "window dressing."

REFERENCES

American Hospital Association. (2004). *Strategies for leadership: Patient- and family-centered care*. Chicago, IL: American Hospital Association, Institute for Family-Centered Care. Retrieved from http://www.aha.org/advocacy-issues/quality/strategies-patientcentered.shtml

Association of Oncology Social Work. (2012). *Standards of practice in oncology social work*. Philadelphia, PA: Author.

Balik, B., Conway, J., Zipperer, L., & Watson, J. (2011). *Achieving an exceptional patient and family experience of inpatient hospital care. IHI innovation series white paper*. Cambridge, MA: Institute for Healthcare Improvement. Retrieved from http://www.IHI.org

Bona, K., Bates, J., & Wolfe, J. (2011). Massachusetts' pediatric palliative care network: Successful implementation of a novel state-funded pediatric palliative care program. *Journal of Palliative Medicine*, *14*(11), 1217–1223.

Conway, J., Johnson, B., Edgman-Levitan, S., Schlucter, J., Ford, D., Sodomka, P., & Simmons, L. (2006). *Partnering with patients and families to design a patient- and family-centered health care system: A roadmap for the future—A work in progress*. Bethesda, MD: Institute for Family-Centered Care. Retrieved from http://www.familycenteredcare.org/pdf/Roadmap.pdf

Epstein, R., & Street, R., Jr. (2007). *Patient-centered communication in cancer care: Promoting healing and reducing suffering*. Bethesda, MD: National Cancer Institute.

Hepworth, D., Rooney, R., Rooney, G., Strom-Gottfried, K., & Larson, J. (2013). *Direct social work practice: Theory and skills* (9th ed.). Belmont, CA: Brooks/Cole.

Institute of Medicine, Committee on Quality of Health Care in America. (2001). *Crossing the quality chasm: A new health system for the 21st century*. Washington, DC: National Academy Press.

Johnson, B., & Abraham, M. (2012). *Partnering with patients, residents, and families: A resource for leaders of hospitals, ambulatory care settings, and long-term care communities*. Bethesda, MD: Institute for Patient- and Family-Centered Care.

Johnson, B., Abraham, M., Conway, J., Simmons, L., Edgman-Levitan, S., Sodomka, P., . . . & Ford, D. (2008). *Partnering with patients and families to design a patient- and family-centered health care system: Recommendations and promising practices*. Bethesda, MD: Institute for Family-Centered Care. Retrieved from http://www.ipfcc.org/pdf/PartneringwithPatientsandFamilies.pdf

Johnson, B., Abraham, M., & Shelton, T. (2009). Patient- and family-centered care: Partnerships for quality and safety. *North Carolina Medical Journal*, *70*(2), 125–130.

The Joint Commission. (2010). *The Joint Commission: Advancing effective communication, cultural competence, and patient- and family-centered care: A roadmap for hospitals*. Oakbrook Terrace, IL: Author.

The Joint Commission. (2011). *The Joint Commission: Advancing effective communication, cultural competence and patient- and family-centered care for the lesbian, gay, bisexual, and transgender (LGBT) community: A field guide*. Oakbrook Terrace, IL: Author.

National Association of Social Workers (NASW). (2005). *Standards for social work practice in health care*. Washington, DC: Author.

National Association of Social Workers. (2008). *Code of ethics*. Washington, DC: Author.

Planetree and Picker Institute. (2008). *Patient-centered care improvement guide*. Camden, ME: Author.

80

Matthew Loscalzo, Karen Clark, and Barry D. Bultz

Integrated Interdisciplinary Staff Leadership Model of Patient-Centered Care

Key Concepts

- *This chapter discusses the current state and future of supportive care programs.*
- *Essential elements of successful patient- and family-centered initiatives are explained.*
- *Successful strategies for interdisciplinary integration are discussed.*

Social workers play an essential role on today's cancer care teams, and their influence and leadership will determine the future of oncology supportive care. Further, because of recent initiatives toward more patient-centered and cost-effective care, social work (as part of the larger supportive care network) has never been in a better position to bring similar initiatives into the health care setting and, at the same time, thrive as a professional discipline. As compassionate experts, social workers have the capacity to play a leadership role in this change process, and by directing the flow of change, they will have the opportunity to do the serious and meaningful work they are capable of doing. But social workers cannot do this on their own—without teamwork and real relationship building that includes all of the stakeholders, including patients and family members, patient- and family-centered care will join the pile-up of other empty catchphrases like reengineering, rightsizing, and so forth. We all need to make the transformation real and not wait. In this chapter, we describe some key elements for building successful patient- and family-centered initiatives in which social workers are an integral part of the team, there is a partnership with patients and families, and there is the necessary leadership at all levels. The authors represent separate but overlapping training and expertise but all with a history of creating model programs (Bultz, Loscalzo, & Clark, 2012; Loscalzo & Von Gunten, 2009).

Supportive Care Programs: Current and Future

Because of a push toward effective, equitable, and safe patient-centered health care (Institute of Medicine, 2011, pp. 5–6), social work, as part of the larger supportive care movement, has the opportunity to bring its humanistic values to the health care setting and thrive as a professional discipline. However, as hospitals continue work on these initiatives, they are also faced with a rapidly evolving health care system that is, at present and by most standards, financially untenable. What is clear is that to survive the current shift in how health care is organized and provided, the care system will have to emphasize cost and efficiency by encouraging and incentivizing patients and families to

Table 80.1.
Patient- and Family-Centered Care Definition and Core Concepts

Definition

Patient- and family-centered care is an innovative approach to the planning, delivery, and evaluation of health care that is grounded in mutually beneficial partnerships among health care providers, patients, and families. Patient- and family-centered care applies to patients of all ages, and it may be practiced in any health care setting.

Core Concepts

Patient- and family-centered care is guided by the following four concepts:

Dignity and respect. Health care practitioners listen to and honor patient and family perspectives and choices. Patient and family knowledge, values, beliefs, and cultural backgrounds are incorporated into the planning and delivery of care.

Information sharing. Health care practitioners communicate and share complete and unbiased information with patients and families in ways that are affirming and useful. Patients and families receive timely, complete, and accurate information to effectively participate in care and decision making.

Participation. Patients and families are encouraged and supported in participating in care and decision making at the level they choose.

Collaboration. Patients, families, health care practitioners, and hospital leaders collaborate in policy and program development, implementation, and evaluation; in health care facility design; and in professional education, as well as in the delivery of care.

become active participants in their own well-being through a patient- and family-centered care approach.

In this approach, patients and family members work together with health care providers in the planning, implementation, and evaluation of care and processes (Johnson et al., 2008). This mutually beneficial work reduces waste, increases efficiency, and improves quality, safety, and patient satisfaction. Table 80.1 includes the definition and core concepts involved in patient- and family-centered care.

When serious life-threatening illness is present, patients and families have heightened expectations about what they want and need from hospitals and cancer centers. The breadth of social work services in health care, especially in hospitals, creates opportunities to address these patient and family needs, including psychological, social, physical, existential/spiritual, and practical problems (clearly, these may be important to all people, but serious illness amplifies these issues for those confronting the challenges of daily living with advanced illness).

It is not possible to predict the future, but some clear and unambiguous trends are hard to ignore. Cancer is still an illness mostly of the elderly (Ries et al., 2003), and the number of older persons in North America will have a dramatic impact on the number of people with cancer and their (mostly) elderly caregivers, although the number of people cured of and living with cancer will also increase. In addition, the 2010 Patient Protection and Affordable Care Act (PPACA) will bring many more formerly underinsured and uninsured individuals into the health care market and into the hospital. This population will have more supportive care needs than the former well-insured groups, and all of these patients and their caregivers will have heightened (some unrealistic) expectations of the health care system. There can be no doubt that patient- and family-centered care, supported by performance outcomes (not just satisfaction), will be an essential element to any plan. Cost, too, will be a major driver of health care policy, much more than it is today. Better supportive care services will be seen as not only better care but also less expensive care.

Biopsychosocial Screening for Distress

Biopsychosocial screening for distress, as pioneered by the authors and others, is inexorably linked to patient- and family-centered care, new technologies, cost containment, and highly tailored triage and follow-up systems.

One of the key benefits supportive care brings to the institution is biopsychosocial screening for distress. SupportScreen, a touch-screen program, has been introduced throughout the City of Hope hospital as a clinical tool for patient satisfaction and research (Loscalzo et al., 2010). The authors have published several papers on the benefits and implementation of screening (Chapters 18 and 19). Although external to the scope of this chapter, it is important to note that wherever the authors have implemented screening, there has been robust growth in the hiring of new staff, at all levels. Social work, in particular, has already gained much as a profession and can enhance this opportunity by building on the existing leadership role in screening. Jim Zabora, a social worker by training, played a major role in the creation of a screening program for use with cancer patients and published papers that are highly influential in psychosocial oncology, and now there are also others (Carlson, Groff, Maciejewski, &

Bultz, 2010; Jacobsen, Holland, & Steensma, 2012; Loscalzo & Clark, 2007; Loscalzo, Bultz, & Jacobsen, 2010; Zabora et al., 2001).

Essential Partnerships

In 2007, philanthropists Sheri and Les Biller, after meeting with the leaders of several major National Cancer Institute–designated comprehensive cancer centers in the United States, partnered with City of Hope to create a model patient- and family-centered program. Their shared humanistic values, vision of philanthropic support combined with hospital funding, and courage to expect, at a minimum, that an integrated interdisciplinary program be developed and implemented were groundbreaking. The goal was to reformulate the conventional, so-called collaborative model of supportive care services to patients and families. The program today consists of approximately 80 colleagues and includes a large and centrally located, fully staffed patient and family resource center (The Sheri & Les Biller Patient and Family Resource Center within the Department of Supportive Care Medicine); a pain and palliative care team; psychiatrists; psychologists; social workers; spiritual care workers; patient, family, and community education; child life specialists; navigators; a positive image center; program evaluators; a volunteer program; an information technology team; and assigned liaisons from both development and marketing.

Team members come from diverse backgrounds in training and hold varying perspectives, but the vision of being the "best program of supportive care services in the world" unites them. The team is committed to creating programs in a manner that realistically and honestly focuses on how patients and families engage the health care system by engaging patients and families in the program development process. Program founders recognized early on that to attain these lofty goals, all colleagues had to feel ownership of and be actively involved in the transformation. Achieving the program's vision also required an unrelenting commitment within the team to care for and about each other at least as well as they treated patients and their families.

Leadership: Values

Leadership in a hierarchical model has often involved the assignment of a single leader who directs and leads other members of a department or program. This model of leadership has always been based on assigned authority. However, some may say that most societies have never been as democratic or tolerant as they are now and, in general, that women tend to have a more relational and interactive leadership style than men, who are inclined to be more individualistic and hierarchical. Health care is increasingly dominated by women, and this influence is expected to result in a greater sense of interdependence and democracy within defined in-groups.

Ultimately, leaders' primary role is to anticipate, prepare for, and maximize the benefits of change. Effective leadership is based on confidence in that leader's intentions, competence, and ability to benefit the group as a whole and, to varying degrees, each individual. The glue that holds together any group is the explicit and implicit values they share based on mutual and self-interest. In health care, caring for patients is usually the explicit value, with personal meaning, status, and money being implicit. The mission statement is an effort to articulate all of the major values, implicit and explicit, and to integrate them in a way members of the department can embrace.

Leadership: Vision and Mission Statements

Although the vision statement may come from one or more leaders of the host institution, professional discipline, and department, it is incumbent upon the leaders to engage most members of the department in pursuit of this aspirational (but never fully achieved) goal. The mission statement can be short or long, but it is usually the "how to the what" aspired to in the vision statement. For example, the vision statement of the Department of Supportive Care Medicine at City of Hope is to be the "best program of supportive care services in the world." This aspirational statement is meant to drive every interaction that colleagues have with patients, families, and each other. Clearly, this general statement lacks the specificity of the mission statement. But the vision statement is a foundational touchstone for all the department does. The mission statement for the department was developed and fine-tuned over a series of months by the entire staff. The present mission statement is:

> *We are an integrated, interdisciplinary team of compassionate experts who provide patient- and family-centered care, develop and lead innovative, evidence-based programs that improve health outcomes, financial metrics, and best practices, and support the work of doctors, nurses, and other staff at City of Hope. We utilize a staff leadership model that maximizes the influence and creativity of all staff members. We see every interaction as having the potential to enrich lives.*

Leading by Learning and Inspiration

Leadership based solely on status, charisma, or threat is a short-term and overused strategy with limited application to the zeitgeist in which health care is evolving. We propose that

Table 80.2.
Recommended Components to Be Included in an Integrated Interdisciplinary Department of Patient-Centered Care

Patient and family program and services evaluation (beyond satisfaction)
Patient and family advisory board that meets at least monthly, and patient and family advisers integrated into committees
Development and acceptance of the content of the Department New Employee Orientation Guide
Yearly anonymous departmental staff satisfaction surveys (shared openly unedited)
Yearly retreats organized and led by the staff resulting in measureable and clearly identified goals for the next year
Staff-led work teams created to achieve the goals from the retreat
Group process, leadership, and project management training for the cochairs of the work teams
Request for proposal opportunities for staff who prefer to focus on clearly defined projects
Topics placed in an anonymous suggestion box that gets preference for the next department-wide meeting for open discussion
Biweekly department-wide leadership meetings (90%–95% staff led, with a standing agenda item of open discussion)
Voluntary ongoing special leadership and communication skills-based trainings by external experts
Twice-yearly evaluation with clearly identifiable performance goals and timelines

our concept of Leading by Learning and Inspiration inevitably leads to a staff leadership model in any circumstance where there are shared values and participation is perceived to be voluntary. Leading by Learning and Inspiration is more of a philosophy (although specific interventions will be listed later) in which the inherent value and creativity of colleagues at all levels of functioning are maximized by continually creating realistic opportunities, in multiple modalities, to learn how to get the very best out of each other. Within this model, leadership is a shared experience with every member of the department, and it is important, outside of the department, to make open, honest, frank, and constructive recommendations on how to be the best program of supportive care services in the world. Staff leadership is based on every team member taking responsibility for his or her own functions while teaching others how to get the best out of them

Table 80.3.
Patient- and Family-Centered Tailored Social Work Interventions Linked to the Action Plan

Patient/Family	Physician and Staff	Institution
• Advocacy • Cognitive behavioral therapy • Consultations • Counseling • Individual, couple, family, and group interventions • Integrative therapies • Patient and family education • Problem-solving therapies • Resource support (transportation, child care, etc.) • School reintegration • Tailored information and referral • Side effect management • Stress management skills • Symptom management • Working in partnership with patient and family advisers in the planning, evaluation, and delivery of care	• Care management strategies for complex situations • Communication to primary team about physical, cognitive, or behavioral symptoms and how treatment plan will be carried out • Consultations to subspecialists and tailored resources • Professional education • Symptom management • Treatment planning with primary team	• Professional education • Service revenue • Coordination of management across the institution • Meeting of regulatory reporting standards • Organization and support of Patient and Family Advisory Programs/ Councils • Leading of efforts to advance the practice of patient- and family-centered care

Table 80.4.
Benefits to Patients/Families, Physician and Staff, and the Institution

Patient/Family	Physician and Staff	Institution
• Increased sense of control and predictability • Increased communication about health system to enhance trust and teamwork • Adaptive patient and family functioning and partnership in care • Organization of conflicted families to make coordinated and appropriate decisions • Enhanced outcomes via adherence to medical care; decreased physical and emotional symptoms; decreased substance abuse; compliance with medication appointments • Enhanced coping, emotional regulation, problem-solving skills • Improved patient hospital experience • Improved family bereavement outcomes • Increased longevity of life (extension of survival time)	• Having a team to manage complex situations—situations physicians do not have time or training to deal with—which provides increased sense of control and predictability • Satisfaction of providing appropriate and efficient medical care • Enhanced team communication • Enhanced clinical operations • Increased teamwork and satisfaction • Increased patient satisfaction and gratitude, creating a calmer work environment • Decreased patient no-shows • Seeing more patients and raising more revenue; increased patient volumes • Staff retention	• Enhanced patient safety • Reduced expenses • Increased revenues • Enhanced employee benefits • Meeting/exceeding of community standards • Positive community benefit • Model of innovation and excellence

as colleagues. At a minimum, team members are expected, with pure and generous hearts, to make suggestions to their colleagues about how to get superior results. The staff leadership model does not ask colleagues to take on duties they are not trained for or sanctioned to perform. But there is an active and relentless pursuit of input, wisdom, creativity, and investment by all members of the team to practice at the top of their license and their training. The extension of boundaries and incessant building of bridges both within and outside of the department is an essential element of the Leading by Learning and Inspiration model.

Successful Strategies for Interdisciplinary Integration

Supportive care services, whether psychosocial or palliative in nature, are ensconced in medical care overall but are necessary in the cancer setting. We believe that palliative care does provide a realistic model of interdisciplinary integration that centers care around the needs of patients and families and that is by definition team based (Loscalzo & Von Gunten, 2009). In fact, the present health care system (in almost all institutions, especially in the largest and most renowned) is a collaborative model (at best) based on personal communication abilities, familiar relationships, and often outdated technologies. In system-centric care, the focus of care is based on the needs of the institution and professionals providing the services and not those of patients and families, who may have limited experience with serious illness.

Communication

The most commonly asked question we receive from other institutions is: "How do you do it?" "How did you get there?" In general, the most important influence has been the relentless pursuit of open and honest communication, from the first day of hire, while holding true to the value that all programs must be seen from the patient's and family member's point of view. Once the team buys into this value, there are some inevitabilities that flow from this precept. Table 80.2 displays several of the recommended components that make up an integrated interdisciplinary department that is patient- and family-centered in its approach.

Defining Social Work Value

Social workers are masters at advocating and communicating patients' interests and needs at a clinical and community level. As with most other health care professionals, however, social workers are not adequately trained in knowing how to communicate with others about what they do, what they accomplish, and, most of all, the multilevel value they provide. Although most professionals have clearly defined roles (e.g., physician or nurse), social workers' role can, at times, be too nebulous for others to comprehend. When this happens, others can feel frustrated with or insecure about social workers and what they can expect of them. Social workers must develop a comfortable language that they can use to define, explain, and internalize what patients, families, their colleagues, and the institution can expect them to do. In the Department of Supportive Care Medicine, we have created a road map, as shown in Tables 80.3 and 80.4, to help social workers and others describe in focused and tailored language what they do and their inherent benefits at multiple levels. An example of this kind of statement is: "Hello, my name is X. I provide for the psychological, social, emotional, and practical needs of cancer patients and their families. Can you please tell me your understanding of your present medical situation?" Knowing and internalizing this information is of great benefit to others but also to social workers as they define, refine, and evolve into the professional they want to be. The influence and leadership that social workers will assume in creating the future of supportive care in cancer is one they will determine.

Looking Forward

Empirical data will be used to support health-related resource expenditures, new information technologies will increase efficiency, community-based medical care will be highly emphasized, and wherever possible, practical and political redundancies will be removed. Of specific significance are the many new patient populations that will be better served by the upholding of the PPACA in the United States and the designation of distress as the 6th vital sign in Canada (Bultz et al., 2011). (See Chapter 18 for a discussion of distress screening as the 6th vital sign.) Both of these important advances in humanistic care will lead to a greater emphasis on problem identification, assessment, and the implementation of supportive care interventions into cancer care. The extensive body of data published by the authors and others relating to the unmet needs of patients and families strongly supports the need for these services as the new standard of cancer care (Bultz & Johansen, 2010; Institute of Medicine, 2008, 2011; Loscalzo & Clark, 2007). In a patient- and family-centered care organization, a range of clinical, supportive, healing, education, and navigation services are made available to patients and families. In this model of care, choice and flexibility are emphasized, allowing the individual's unique needs to be addressed. Social work and interdisciplinary supportive care programs are positioned to contribute to such an environment.

REFERENCES

Bultz, B. D., & Johansen, C. (2010). Call for papers: Special issue of *Psycho-Oncology* on screening for distress, from research to practice. *Psycho-Oncology, 19*, 113.

Bultz, B. D., Groff, S. L., Fitch, M., Blasis, C., Howes, J., Levy, K., & Mayer, C. (2011). Implementing screening for distress, the 6th vital sign: A Canadian strategy for changing practice. *Psycho-Oncology, 20*, 463–469.

Bultz, B. D., Loscalzo, M. J., & Clark, K. L. (2012). Screening for distress, the 6th vital sign, as the connective tissue of health care systems: A roadmap to integrated interdisciplinary person-centered care. In L. Grassi & M. Riba (Eds.), *Clinical psycho-oncology: An international perspective* (pp. 83–96). West Sussex, England: John Wiley & Sons.

Carlson, L. E., Groff, S. L., Maciejewski, O., & Bultz, B. D. (2010). Screening for distress in lung and breast cancer outpatients: A randomized controlled trial. *Journal of Clinical Oncology, 28*, 4884–4891.

Institute of Medicine. (2008). *Cancer care for the whole patient: Meeting psychosocial health needs*. Washington, DC: National Academies Press.

Institute of Medicine. (2011). *Patient-centered cancer treatment planning: Improving the quality of oncology care: Workshop summary*. Washington, DC: National Academies Press.

Jacobsen, P. B., Holland, J. C., & Steensma, D. P. (2012). Caring for the whole patient: The science of psychosocial care. *Journal of Clinical Oncology, 30*, 1151–1153.

Johnson, B., Abraham, M., Conway, J., Simmons, L., Edgman-Levitan, S., Sodomka, P., . . . Ford, D. (2008). *Partnering with patients and families to design a patient-and family-centered health care system*. Bethesda, MD: Institute for Family-Centered Care.

Loscalzo, M. J., & Clark, K. L. (2007). Problem-related distress in cancer patients drives requests for help: A prospective study. *Oncology, 21*, 1133–1138.

Loscalzo, M. J., & Von Gunten, C. F. (2009). Interdisciplinary teamwork in palliative care: Compassionate expertise for serious complex illness. In H. M. Chochinov & W. S. Breitbart (Eds.), *Handbook of psychiatry in palliative medicine* (2nd ed.). New York, NY: Oxford University Press.

Loscalzo, M. J., Bultz, B. D., & Jacobsen, P. B. (2010). Building psychosocial programs: A roadmap to excellence. In J. C. Holland, W. S. Breitbart, P. B. Jacobsen, M. S. Lederberg, M. J. Loscalzo, & R. McCorkle (Eds.), *Psycho-oncology* (2nd ed., pp. 569–574). New York, NY: Oxford University Press.

Loscalzo, M. J., Clark, K., Dillehunt, J., Rinehart, R., Strowbridge, R., & Smith, D. (2010). SupportScreen: A model for improving patient outcomes at your fingertips. *Journal of the National Comprehensive Cancer Network, 8*, 496–504.

Patient Protection and Affordable Care Act, Pub. L. No. 111–148, §2702, 124 Stat. 119, 318–319 (2010).

Ries, L. A., Eisner, M. P., Kosary, C. L., Hankey, B. F., Miller, B. A., & Clegg, L. (Eds.). (2003). *SEER cancer statistics review, 1975–2000*. Bethesda, MD: National Cancer Institute.

Zabora, J., BrintzenhofeSzoc, K., Jacobsen, P., Curbow, B., Piantadosi, S., Hooker, C., . . . Derogatis, L. (2001). A new psychosocial screening instrument for use with cancer patients. *Psychosomatics, 42*, 241–246.

81

Margaret Weld Meyer and Wendy J. Evans

Directing Stand-Alone Social Work Department Models

Key Concepts

- *This chapter discusses designing a stand-alone department of social work based on a clearly defined mission and vision.*
- *Departmental strength can be ensured through staff excellence.*
- *Improved quality of data and staff training will ensure the delivery of best practices in the field.*
- *A visible institutional presence can be maintained through patient care delivery and marketing techniques.*

The value of a stand-alone model of a social work department cannot be overemphasized, particularly in an oncology setting. Before the mid-1990s, stand-alone social work departments were plentiful; however, in the 1990s, hospital systems began to reorganize to contain costs. Decentralization became the norm and stand-alone social work departments became the exception.

This chapter presents a particular model of a stand-alone social work department and discusses how that model can be replicated in other oncology settings. It focuses on the foundation of the department, the organizational structure, the importance of a shared mission and vision, the choice of staff members with a passion for medical social work in an oncology setting, and ways of engaging the staff through supervision and continuing education. The chapter also discusses the importance of a strong partnership with patients and families in the process of delivering care. Finally, the chapter discusses the need for social work to be visible within the larger organization by educating the medical teams and creating strong partnerships with patients and families to promote social work's role within the organization.

Evolution of Social Work Departments in Hospitals

Historically, the introduction of social workers into the acute care setting created a new dimension of health care within the person-in-environment framework. Social workers were called on to improve overall outcomes by conducting patient and familial psychosocial assessments outside the immediate medical complaint and to help patients create a plan that integrates medical care, community interventions, and mental and emotional support to improve the patient's overall health and well-being (Judd & Sheffield, 2009). As the profession expanded, departments of social work emerged to meet the ongoing nonmedical demands of the patient population.

In the mid-1990s, hospital systems began to look at cost containment and initiated a model of reorganization called *reengineering*. The focus was on non-revenue-generating departments. Decentralization and cross-training became more standard, and case management and care management departments appeared. A popular model included both nurse case managers and social workers. In this model, social workers were trained to provide case management services focused more directly on discharge planning and insurance review. However, nurse case managers and social workers trained in the same skill sets created role confusion. Although the goal also was to address the patient's psychosocial needs, this component of care became increasingly more difficult to incorporate with the demands of discharge planning (Berger, Robbins, Lewis, Mizrahi, & Fleit, 2003; Judd & Sheffield, 2009; Neuman, 2003).

The decentralized model is still popular in the general medical acute care setting. However, the oncology setting in particular lends itself to a stand-alone social work department model because of the ongoing and often life-threatening nature of the cancer experience, which creates a heightened need for psychosocial care.

The Foundation of a Stand-Alone Department

The foundation of a stand-alone social work department begins with a solid mission and vision that align with the organization's mission and vision; strategic management, administrative leadership and support, staffing, and continued quality assurance and improvement are imperative.

Strategic Management

Strategic management focuses on what we do, why we do it, for whom we do it, and how we can be the best at what we do. It begins with the department's mission, which can be viewed as the aim of the department, similar to the aim of an organization:

> *A written declaration of an organization's core purpose and focus that normally remains unchanged over time. Properly crafted mission statements (1) serve as filters to separate what is important from what is not, (2) clearly state which markets will be served and how, and (3) communicate a sense of intended direction to the entire organization.*
>
> —*Business Dictionary, 2012*

To create a solid mission for a stand-alone social work department, it is important to look at the organization's overall mission and explore where the department fits into and enhances that mission. For example, if the organization's mission is to eliminate cancer with a focus on patient care, research, and teaching, the department's mission must be to define its own purpose within that context. A social work department's mission should focus on the biopsychosocial well-being of the patients and families. To test the effectiveness of a mission statement, ask yourself, "Could the organization achieve its mission if we did not achieve ours?" If your answer is yes, reconsider your mission statement. Social work should be integral to the organization's success.

The mission is the aim of the department, whereas its vision is the hope for the future. "A mission is different from a vision in that the former is the cause and the latter is the effect; a mission is something to be accomplished whereas a vision is something to be pursued for that accomplishment" (*Business Dictionary*, 2012). A stand-alone department's vision focuses on what the department would be at its absolute best. The department's mission and vision should align not only with the organization's mission and vision but also with the Association of Oncology Social Work's *Standards of Practice in Oncology Social Work* (AOSW, 2012) and National Association of Social Workers' *Code of Ethics* (NASW, 2008).

Quality Assurance and Improvement

Once a department establishes a solid mission and vision, its effectiveness must be challenged through continuous quality assurance and efforts to improve. How does the department know it is doing a good job? How does the department know it has allocated its resources appropriately?

Quality assurance refers to what measures a department uses to ensure that its goals are being achieved. Before engaging in quality assurance, a department must explore its key services. If a key service is patient care, the measure will focus on how this is evidenced and what measures the department uses to ascertain its skill. To make patient care easier to measure, it must be broken down into smaller, more manageable components, such as response time to referrals and average number of patient contacts per social worker.

Once the department identifies its key services, it is important to benchmark these services against those of other organizations and departments, ideally, an organization similar in size and type. When that is not possible, an alternative would be to find an organization with similar components from which the department can extrapolate data for a benchmark. The search also may include looking at processes in industries unrelated to health care.

Another opportunity to engage in quality assurance is to solicit feedback from patients and families. From this and benchmarking data, the department can determine areas for improvement and set goals. As Studer (2003, p. 63) has pointed out, "when clear goals are combined with consistent measurement and aligned behaviors, results start to come." Clear goals combined with consistent measurement lead to evidence-based practice, which has emerged as an important component of clinical social work practice. For a stand-alone social work department, evidence-based practice leads to the ability to engage in research, an area in which social work as a profession has traditionally been weak. Improvement goals can lead to research projects that validate one's practice and have a positive effect not only on the individual department but also on departments in other organizations and on the medical social work profession as a whole. A strength of a stand-alone department is the ability to measure purely on the basis of social work practices.

Administrative Supports

Support from the institution's administrative leaders and strong leadership within the social work department are imperative for a stand-alone social work department to be successful. Collins (2001) studied a set of the highest performing companies to explore what made them great. Concerning leadership, the team found a hierarchy consisting of five levels of executive capabilities, with Level 5 being the highest. They defined Level 5 as leadership that "builds enduring greatness through a paradoxical blend of personal humility and professional will.... [Level 5 leaders] channel their ego needs away from themselves and into the larger goal of building a great company" (pp. 20, 21). Translating these skills to a successful stand-alone social work department necessitates exploring the institution's needs and ensuring that those needs are being met to maintain the administration's support and to further the mission of both the institution and the department. Remember that the institution's mission is dependent on the social work department achieving its mission.

One component of meeting the institution's needs is fiscal value. A stand-alone social work department must be able to demonstrate what the institution is gaining by investing in the department. Because social work is typically a non-revenue-generating profession within health care systems, it is important to speak to the department's cost-effectiveness. Although the department does not bring funds into its organization, it does reduce institutional expenses.

How Social Workers in a Stand-Alone Social Work Department Can Enhance the Institution's Financial Situation

Social workers in stand-alone departments can contribute to the financial status of their institution by:

- *Obtaining payments for health care expenses through referrals to state and federal programs, such as Medicaid and Medicare, and to community programs for assistance with pharmaceutical costs.*
- *Facilitating discharge planning for patients with complex medical and living situations.*
- *Providing resources that reduce barriers to patient care and by engaging in counseling techniques that enhance patient outcomes.*
- *Devoting social work time to addressing patients' psychosocial problems, rather than leaving those problems to practitioners in other disciplines, who may lack the training, the experience, or even the desire to engage in such activities.*

In conjunction with fiscal value, social work contributes to patient satisfaction. Many larger institutions participate in national patient satisfaction databases. Often, these databases are not specific to the services offered by clinical social workers; thus, other means of capturing social work's impact on patient satisfaction are required. Surveys of individual patients are one option for gathering this vital information.

A related responsibility is the concept of managing growth. For instance, as baby boomers age, the number of newly diagnosed patients increases and the demand for oncology and social work services grows alongside that number. Limited hospital economies, however, make it unrealistic to anticipate large increases in social work staffing. Therefore, it is imperative for the leaders of stand-alone social work departments not only to manage growth but also to be able to show how they are managing that growth. Appropriate techniques for managing growth include exploring creative ways to meet the growing needs of disparate populations, such as medical and administrative staff and patients and families, and advocating for growth of the department when necessary.

Staffing

Because social work practice in the oncology setting is fast-paced and requires a balanced knowledge of both resource linkage and clinical counseling, hiring people with the necessary skill set and work ethic is crucial to success. Social workers are educationally prepared with a unique set of skills that differ from those of other mental health professionals. Obtaining the best incoming staff members requires high hiring standards in addition to state certification or licensure. Additionally, new employees must understand the department's mission and how their role supports that mission.

In most health care settings, it is difficult to staff to an ideal ratio. The National Comprehensive Cancer Network (2011) created a distress thermometer that measures patients' distress on a scale of 0 to 10: "Scores of four or higher suggest a level of distress that has clinical significance." Up to 46.5% of new outpatients and 30.4% of returning outpatients may have a score of 4 or higher on the distress scale (Meyer, 2013). Ensuring that the right number of social workers is available to meet the patient need can be a challenge and calls for the creative use and distribution of a stand-alone social work department's greatest resource: staff. According to Collins, maximizing resources requires "getting the right people on the bus. . . . The right people don't need to be tightly managed or fired up: they will be self-motivated by the inner drive to produce the best results and to be part of creating something great" (2001, p. 42). To get the right people on the bus and provide an environment that consistently challenges staff toward growth and creativity, there first must be an organizational structure that promotes growth and creativity, which returns us to the subject of leadership. In a stand-alone social work department, having a social worker as the leader is crucial because sharing the same values, ethics, and professional skills creates a cohesive department. In addition, strong supervisory leadership is required to provide staff with clinical and administrative leadership and to challenge staff to explore the needs of patients and families, recognize gaps in services, and identify positive and creative ways to meet these various needs.

The social work department's organizational structure can increase employee engagement, an important aspect of excellent patient care. Furthermore, the opportunities for professional growth enhance not only the staff's clinical skills but also their engagement in the work. Creating a venue for staff to obtain clinical supervision toward their clinical licensure, providing funds and/or allowing staff time to attend professional conferences and workshops, and using staff involvement to create a robust clinical staff development program are excellent ways of creating a strong, invested, clinically sound social work department.

Ensuring professional growth and program development within the department is in line with the needs of the institution and its primary stakeholders: It is important to partner with patients and families in the process of delivery of care. The process of program development and implementation driven by patients and families ensures that the programs specifically meet the needs of the patients and families they are designed to serve. In addition, the nature of patient- and family-driven programs encourages support that further promotes a positive outcome.

Recipients of Social Work Services

In an oncology setting, patients and their caregivers are the primary, but not sole, focus of social work services. Medical teams, other departments within the institution, and professional community organizations are also recipients of the social work department's attention. To carry out this complex work successfully, a two-pronged approach of working within the medical model while also ensuring a patient- and family-centered approach to care is required. Consequently, social workers are often called on to bring both perspectives together and strike an optimal balance between the two.

Patients and Families

In the oncology setting, social work is known as the discipline that assesses both patients and family members from the biopsychosocial standpoint. To be successful in this, the social worker must partner with the patient and family to explore positive ways of increasing their ability to cope, improving their adjustment to diagnosis, and helping them navigate the grief and loss processes.

A stand-alone social work department is based on united values that foster the growth and development of psychosocial programs designed to meet the identified needs of patients and families. Some programs that have proved to be helpful include those that increase communication between children and parents when a parent has cancer, memorial services intended to meet the emotional needs of bereaved family members, a legacy program designed to help patients connect and share special memories with family members, and a brochure and video targeted specifically toward potential victims of intimate partner violence who are also cancer patients.

Advance care planning is another growing area where partnering with and exploring the needs and wishes of patients and families is of vital importance. Advance care planning differs from completing advance directive documents. According to Weiner and Cole (2004, p. 818):

> *Advance care planning is a process of recurring clinician-patient-family communication that includes: (1) individualized delivery of medical information; (2) utilization of a shared decision-making paradigm; (3) focus on multiple and evolving treatment decisions across the entire trajectory of a life-limiting illness; and (4) clarification of the patient's future treatment preferences.*

Physicians often have a difficult time initiating these conversations, and patients and families have said that, in this area, they feel health care is lacking. Social workers can play an integral role in creating and modeling conversations about advance care planning. These conversations can begin early in the patient's health care trajectory, facilitate communication between family members, and, at times, be a natural lead-in to legacy work with the patient and family. Social work clinicians in a stand-alone department need to take a leadership role in advocating for and educating with regard to advance care planning.

It is important to pick a key service and learn to perform it well. When all social workers in the department do this, the department is ready to branch out and expand to other services. Because opportunities for programmatic growth will inevitably arise in the institution, the leader of the department must seize those opportunities to enhance services offered to patients and their families.

The Medical Team

As a member of the medical team, the social worker can play a variety of roles, such as advocate, educator, modeler, facilitator, and spokesperson. In the role of educator, for example, the social worker's job is to educate the team about how the social worker can be helpful to them in difficult situations and make their jobs easier. This can be done in a variety of ways, such as offering to sit with a physician while discussing hospice care with a patient and family, helping a patient write down questions for the medical team, helping the medical team understand patients' wishes, and working to reduce psychosocial barriers to care. In addition, social workers are able to triage to other mental health programs within the institution to ensure that patients receive the right level and right kind of care at the right time.

The social worker has a unique opportunity to build his or her practice within the medical team and assume a leadership role in the psychosocial care and well-being of patients and families. In this way, the social worker enables the physicians to focus on the medical aspects of the patient's care, trusting the social worker to offer any relevant information that will help provide the patient with the best possible holistic care.

Visibility

A stand-alone social work department has a visibility advantage because the department as a whole can take ownership of institutional programs that originate in the department and use its social work staff to implement and manage the programs. The challenge for social work is the continuous education needed to communicate the value of those programs to patient care. Using the patient- and family-centered approach to care can help greatly here. The more invested the patients and families are in the programs, the more they demonstrate the programs' effectiveness within the institution.

Social Work Presence

Creating a social work presence in the medical team involves demonstrating the value of the profession's interventions to the team through constant communication and education.

Establishing a Social Work Presence in the Medical Team

To create a presence in the medical team, the social worker must demonstrate the value of social work intervention through constant communication and education. Social workers can accomplish this value in three important ways:

- *Exercise their unique ability to build a practice within the oncology setting. Social workers analyze the specific setting, type of cancer, treatments, needs of the patient population served, and personalities of the unit and medical and nursing teams involved.*
- *Maintain good documentation in clinical charts.*
- *Make them readily available to respond to team members' requests and to close the loop by providing verbal feedback regarding the outcomes of previous interventions.*

Marketing

Social work marketing can help maintain a visible institutional presence, expanding beyond the promotion of an individual clinician's practice as a member of a medical team to include education and promotion of services on a wider institutional level. This expansion effort can include such activities as displaying social work posters during Social Work Month and speaking at institutional meetings on social work–related issues.

In institutions with a social media presence, the social work department can submit articles and blogs that provide patients with information and education. This information should promote the department's key services and be of interest to its customers: the patients, caregivers, and the medical team. Topics can cover a range of psychosocial issues, such as advance care planning, intimate partner violence, how to reduce depression during the holidays, training around legacy building, how to talk to children about cancer, stress-reducing techniques, and support services, to name a few.

Professional Communications Oncology Social Workers Rely on as Members of the Medical Team

Professional social work communications are primarily of three types: hand-off, written, and verbal.

- *Hand-off communication refers to information shared between the social worker and other members of the medical team during the normal give and take that occurs as patients move through the continuum of care.*
- *Written communication refers to documentation in a patient's chart that provides other members of the team with the results of the social worker's assessments and interventions.*
- *Verbal communication refers to direct contact with other team members to impart specific information about a patient or family.*

In each form, the social worker must ensure the professionalism of communications, addressing clinical psychosocial aspects of the patient and family, identifying patient and family goals, and implementing social work interventions used to help them meet those goals. The communication also should include plans for next steps. Because social workers represent the only discipline that focuses on the patient's entire psychosocial system, they are uniquely qualified to bring each psychosocial aspect of care into a coordinated intervention that optimizes the process of care for the patient and family.

Growth

When social workers practice in a stand-alone department, it is important to continue growing in all aspects of psychosocial care while staying current concerning cancer care trends. To that end, continuing education is essential, calling on the skills already present in the department and on information from professionals outside the department. In addition, supporting the professional staffs' membership in national organizations and attendance at national conferences exposes them to best practices conducted in similar facilities. Such activities reenergize the professionals, who bring back to their home institution ideas for implementation and innovation, resulting in improved patient care.

Research also promotes growth within a social work department. Exploring research possibilities, engaging in research, and then publishing the results not only provide for growth within the department but also contribute to the growth of professionals within the larger community. As the world changes, so do the needs within the population, which includes, for example, increasing cultural and religious pluralism that must be accommodated in cancer treatment. In partnership with patients and families, social workers who engage in research can explore positive ways to meet patients' and families' needs by relying on empirical data, rather than on speculation.

Professional Visibility

The term *professional visibility* means seeking to educate other professionals on the unique aspects of oncology social work, and it can be accomplished in a variety of ways. Sharing best practices at conferences specifically for social workers in health care, oncology, and mental health provides education to other professionals while promoting professional visibility. In addition, creating avenues for presenting at conferences outside the social work profession creates another level of professional visibility. Social workers have a unique perspective, the sharing of which can enrich the knowledge and skills of other disciplines.

Supporting research and publishing enhances staff members' professional visibility, promotes growth within the department, and supports an evidence-based practice while offering the ability to educate others about the unique role that oncology social workers play in the care of oncology patients and families.

Finally, the term *community visibility* means that oncology social workers can educate the lay community through outreach, networking, and sharing of knowledge. It is important for oncology social workers to understand the impact of health care laws specifically on the cancer population, to explore what that impact means to the patients served, and then to educate others about the best ways to continue meeting the unique needs of cancer patients and families within the ever-changing health care environment.

Pearls

- Professionalism, communication, and visibility can enhance respect for the role of social work within the oncology setting and promote the institutional understanding of the need for and value of social work to patient care.
- Teaching oncology social workers to build a successful practice within their setting may be the single most important selling point on the value of psychosocial interventions for cancer patients and families.

Pitfalls

- Because most social work departments are not revenue generators, extra effort is required to communicate a stand-alone department's value to the larger institution.
- It can be difficult for social workers to build successful practices without a strong departmental supervisory structure, and it may be difficult to create avenues for continuing education, professional visibility, and community visibility without adequate funding.

A stand-alone social work department is vitally important in an oncology setting. Using specific strategic skills and partnering with patients and families can provide an excellent starting point for gathering evidence-based data supporting the value of a stand-alone social work department. It is important to remember that institutions want to provide the best in patient care, and it is the job of the social work department to demonstrate its value by promoting evidence-based care, actively communicating the care provided, and consistently educating others about the role of social work in the care of cancer patients and families.

REFERENCES

Association of Oncology Social Work. (2012). *Standards of practice in oncology social work.* http://www.aosw.org/iMIS201/AOSWMain/professionals/standards-of-practice/AOSWMain/Professional-Development/standards-of-practice.aspx?hkey=51fda308-28bd-48b0-8a75-a17d01251b5e

Berger, C., Robbins, C., Lewis, M., Mizrahi, T., & Fleit, S. (2003). The impact of organizational change on social work staffing in a hospital setting: A national, longitudinal study of social work in hospitals. *Social Work in Health Care, 37*(1), 1–18.

Business dictionary. (2012). Mission statement. Retrieved from http://www.businessdictionary.com/definition/mission-statement.html

Collins, J. (2001). *Good to great.* New York, NY: HarperCollins.

Judd, R., & Sheffield, S. (2009). Hospital social work: Contemporary roles and professional activities. *Social Work in Health Care*, *49*, 856–871.

Meyer, M. W. (2013, June). *A work in progress: Best practices and barriers in implementing distress screening on a large institutional level.* Paper presented at the American College of Surgeons' Commission on Cancer Survey Savvy Conference, Chicago, IL.

National Association of Social Workers. (2008). *Code of ethics.* Retrieved from https://www.socialworkers.org/pubs/code/code.asp

National Comprehensive Cancer Network. (2011). *NCCN guidelines for supportive care: Adult cancer pain guidelines.* Retrieved from http://www.nccn.org/professionals/physician_gls/f_guidelines.asp

Neuman, K. (2003). The effect of organizational reengineering on job satisfaction for staff in hospital social work departments. *Social Work in Health Care*, *36*(4), 19–33.

Studer, Q. (2003). *Hardwiring excellence: Purpose, worthwhile work, making a difference.* Gulf Breeze, FL: Fire Starter Publishing.

Weiner, J., & Cole, S. (2004). Three principles to improving clinician communication for advance care planning: Overcoming emotional, cognitive, and skill barriers. *Journal of Palliative Medicine*, *7*(6), 817–829.

82

Alison Mayer Sachs and Kerry Irish

Creating Innovative Cancer Support Programs in Community Cancer Centers

Key Concepts

- *Collect and evaluate data from patient and community needs assessments. These will demonstrate the need for the creation or expansion of cancer support service programs within a broader cancer program and guide the development of the program's mission, vision, and goals.*
- *Identify key stakeholders and create a plan to achieve institutional and community support.*
- *Create and implement an effective strategic plan for the cancer support program.*
- *Identify potential partners who can contribute knowledge, support, and resources to ensure the program's success.*
- *Use the core concepts of patient- and family-centered care to establish a Patient and Family Advisory Council.*
- *Collaborate with a variety of national cancer organizations to bring existing patient education and support programs into a comprehensive cancer support program.*

Growing acceptance of the need for the professional provision of cancer support/psychosocial services was validated by the 2008 Institute of Medicine report *Cancer Care for the Whole Patient: Meeting Psychosocial Healthcare Needs*. Additionally, the Commission on Cancer has refined its accreditation standards to include requiring programs "to develop and implement a process to integrate and monitor on site psychosocial distress screening and referral for the provision of psychosocial care" (American College of Surgeons Commission on Cancer, 2012, p. 77) by 2015 to achieve or maintain accreditation.

Although a search of the literature shows much reporting on the critical need for psychosocial care in the cancer center setting and information on the development of site-specific and specialty support programs (e.g., breast cancer support or patient navigator), there appears to be a lack of literature addressing the "nuts and bolts" of actually designing, developing, and implementing such programs.

This chapter shares information on how to (1) build a cancer support program within a hospital-based or community cancer center setting and (2) broaden existing programs. Oncology social workers, the "leading experts in providing psychosocial care to people affected by cancer and their families" (Association of Oncology Social Work [AOSW], 2012), are the ideal visionaries to develop, lead, and staff such programs.

Needs Assessment

Any effective new program or practice approach must have as its genesis a clear understanding of what the needs are and how they might best be met. The essential first step of the planning process is to conduct a meaningful needs assessment. Meenaghan, Kilty, and McNutt, as cited in Dudley (2014), identify key social and political factors that may influence the development and implementation of a needs assessment and recommend that evaluators and stakeholders be fully cognizant of the people and groups involved in each of the following activities:

- Who chooses what problems are to be examined?
- Who identifies what information is collected and why?

- Who analyzes and interprets the information that is collected?
- Who controls access to dissemination of the information collected? (Dudley 2014, p. 115)

Needs assessment activities are "critical to the shape that a needs assessment will take, to how the data will be analyzed, to the results that will be emphasized and ignored, to who will have access to the results, and to how the results will be disseminated" (Dudley, 2014, p. 115). Identifying and involving stakeholders as early as possible in this process is crucial. For cancer support programs, stakeholders may include people with cancer, their family members, oncologists, oncology nurses, oncology social workers, community members, hospital or program administrators, public health advocates, and persons of means and influence. Involving a sufficient number and variety of potential stakeholders in the assessment process will enhance the likelihood of ongoing support and commitment to both the program and the client group being served. Finding and/or creating the appropriate needs assessment tool can be challenging. Partnering with researchers in the field of psychosocial oncology to identify and/or create valid needs assessment instruments is recommended.

It is important not to overlook existing sources of data, such as patient needs and satisfaction survey results. Many cancer centers are already measuring psychosocial distress and incorporating questions regarding problems that contribute to patient distress, from concrete to existential needs, relating to the person's adjustment to his or her diagnosis. Working with a researcher to catalog and analyze this data is likely to yield very useful information regarding the needs of cancer patients along the continuum of their care.

Needs assessments may be conducted by self-report, interviews, or focus groups. Holding open community forums and public meetings to solicit input and support from the broader community is one way to gather information. For a comprehensive needs assessment, the oncology social worker should consider advocating for and assisting in the development of a Patient and Family Advisory Council. Such a council ensures that the needs assessment includes the voices of the patients and families the programs will serve and helps develop culturally sensitive and appropriate programs for all (Johnson, Abraham, & Shelton, 2009). Using at least two different formats to measure needs may yield the most helpful results.

Numerous authors (e.g., Axford, 2010; Dudley, 2014) point out that a primary purpose of a needs assessment is to explore whether a new program is needed and will be utilized. Therefore, key questions in a needs assessment may include whether there are enough prospective clients to warrant a new initiative/program, what barriers might exist that would prevent people from accessing the program or services, and when and where a program might best be accessed. With these key questions, it becomes clear that the inclusion of patients and families in an advisory capacity adds much-needed input to a comprehensive needs assessment.

Strategic Planning

Once the needs assessment process has been completed, the next step is to develop an effective strategic plan for meeting those needs. In an era of increasing demand for accountability and relevance, an effective strategic plan gives programs and institutions a distinct advantage in applying for funding and in marketing the program to internal and external customers. Most important, the strategic plan provides a road map for the staff members delivering the services.

Strategic plans typically include five components: a vision, a mission, objectives, strategies, and action plans (Negy & Fawcett, 2012).

- *Vision statements* communicate, concisely, the beliefs and governing principles of a program or organization.
- *Mission statements* describe what a program intends to accomplish and why. Mission statements are similar to vision statements but are more concrete and action oriented.
- *Objectives* refer to specific measurable results for the program's broad goals. An organization's objectives state what it will accomplish and by when.
- *Strategies* describe how the program will reach its objectives. Strategies range from the very broad, which may encompass people and resources from many different sectors, to the very specific, which pinpoint carefully defined areas.
- *Action plans* describe in great detail "exactly how strategies will be implemented to accomplish the objectives developed earlier in the process." Action plans refer to both the needs being met and the specific actions necessary to meet those needs.

Obtaining Institutional and Community Support

If one works in a health care setting, it is important to remember that health care culture is generally highly risk averse, with multiple safeguards in place to ensure patient safety. Adding services often requires developing new policies and procedures, obtaining approval from relevant institutional committees or boards, and eliciting support, approval, and any necessary funding from the administration.

When proposing a new program to the cancer care team and administrators, the program planner, as the team expert in psychosocial care, will have to support the need for such programming by highlighting best practice standards in the field. The program planner should be prepared to discuss funding options for the program, which

Sample Action Plan Excerpt					
Action Step	**Person(s) Responsible**	**Date to Be Completed**	**Resources Required**	**Potential Barriers or Resistance**	**Collaborators**
Establish a meeting schedule and location	Group facilitator and meeting room scheduler	December 1, 2012	Meeting room, food, drinks, educational material	Meeting rooms at center are in high demand (may need to meet off-site)	Cancer center director

may include grants through foundations or industry partners, such as pharmaceutical companies; donations, whether monetary or in-kind; or fee for service. The program planner may also wish to emphasize patient support programs as "gateway services" that support the institution as a whole. Health care marketing specialists suggest that organizations offer support groups and other psychosocial services as viable means for attracting new patients (Whaley, 2010).

As noted earlier, identifying and involving stakeholders as early as possible in the program planning process is crucial. If the planner has already obtained buy-in from cancer program staff by the time he or she must present the proposal to administration, he or she can recruit a "champion for the cause" among staff who may hold some influence with administration (e.g., the chief of oncology). The final three building blocks to establishing a meaningful cancer support program are *collaboration* with national nonprofit cancer organizations in providing educational materials, *evaluation* of these programs once they are offered, and identification of potential funding sources to cover costs most often not placed in operating budgets.

Collaboration

Collaboration starts with identifying partners who can contribute knowledge, support, and resources to help lead the success of a program. Recognizing these partnerships and collaborative opportunities allows for a greater identification of where to seek information and how best to bring that information to the community or patient population served. Another key opportunity for the establishment of a Patient and Family Advisory Council occurs when identifying stakeholders and seeking collaborative partners. Such a council will provide valuable input in the design, implementation, and evaluation of cancer support programs.

In oncology, there are many such opportunities for collaboration and partnership and a wealth of free or low-cost patient educational materials available. National nonprofits such as Cancer*Care*, Leukemia & Lymphoma Society, American Cancer Society (ACS), and Cancer Support Community (CSC) have materials, resources, and websites that offer education, support, guidance, and sometimes financial resources.

Hospital-based cancer centers have an ideal opportunity to work with existing hospital departments and programs by collaborating to offer patient-focused education, community outreach, and program implementation. Leveraging available staff by identifying those interested in providing community lectures and/or attending community health fairs allows expansion of community outreach, provides marketing opportunities, and may identify an administrative, physician, or nurse champion.

Another option is to partner with a national cancer nonprofit to offer what is often called a "program in a box," a program that comes ready to use and contains all or some of the materials needed to offer a support group or an educational lecture. Organizations known to offer these programs are the Leukemia & Lymphoma Society, International Myeloma Foundation, and CSC. Last, an excellent example of a way to broaden programs offered when faced with limited staff availability is to host teleconferences. Cancer*Care* is internationally known for its Cancer*Care* Connect Education Workshops. These live, interactive, telephone teleconferences offer numerous opportunities to broaden the offerings in a cancer support program by bringing educational programs to your community that require little planning or implementation on the part of the oncology social worker. The time required is minimal, consisting of registering online for one or more teleconferences, advertising (fliers, calendars, and so on), and sitting in with attendees for 1 hour.

Within an institution, collaboration with foundation and public relations staff provides maximum benefit through fund-raising and marketing opportunities, with minimum use of social work hours. Using a collaborative care model in the planning, development, and implementation of a cancer support program can help lower costs while maximizing numbers of patients reached. The marketing of programs drives greater attendance, resulting in greater adherence to treatment protocols and enhancing communication between patients and their health care team. The opportunity exists, by working collaboratively, to relieve some of the pressure on the health care team of private community or hospital-based oncology practices.

Evaluation

Program *evaluation* is "the systematic collection of information about the activities, characteristics, and outcomes of programs to make judgments about the program, improve program effectiveness, and/or inform decisions about future program development" (Centers for Disease Control [CDC], 2010, p. 6). There are several types of program evaluations that alone or in combination can be used to evaluate cancer support program offerings (CDC, 2010, p. 9):

- *Formative evaluation* refers to assessments conducted to inform the development of a program.
- *Process or implementation evaluation* is conducted to assess whether a program has been implemented as intended, and why or why not.
- *Outcome or effectiveness evaluation* is conducted to assess whether a program is making progress on the intended short-term, intermediate, or long-term outcomes.
- *Comprehensive evaluation* is a term that is sometimes used to refer to the assessment of a program's implementation and effectiveness.
- *Efficiency evaluation* is conducted to assess whether program activities are being produced with efficient use of resources, including staff time and funding dollars.
- *Cost-effectiveness evaluation* is conducted to assess whether the benefits of a program sufficiently exceed the cost of producing them.
- *Attribution evaluation* is conducted to assess whether the outcomes being produced can be shown to be related to the program, as opposed to other factors or initiatives that may be occurring at the same time.

Evaluation can be an important strategic tool for measuring the extent to and ways in which a program or initiative's goals are being met and how the program or initiative might be contributing to the organization's mission. "The findings of a carefully planned evaluation can then be used to refine the program's strategy, design, and/or implementation, as well as to inform others about the lessons learned, progress, and impact of the program" (Presskill & Jones, 2009, p. 3). In its simplest form, an evaluation of a cancer support program asks good questions that result in useful, credible, and relevant answers to help determine whether the program is meeting the needs of the community it serves, achieving established goals, and using the funds available to best ensure the continuation of the program.

Identifying Potential Funding Sources

Funding for cancer support programs can come from a variety of sources: philanthropy, grants (national/local), cost sharing, fund-raising by the development or foundation office, and institution/department operating budgets.

Philanthropy

Cultivating donors is not something most oncology social workers find in their job descriptions, but cultivating donors is everyone's job. These occasions often present themselves not as "major gift" donation opportunities but as small tokens of appreciation for the care received. Grateful patients are often an overlooked resource for funding cancer support programs. Being able to capitalize on a patient or loved one's statement "I don't know how to thank you" or "How can I repay you for all you've done?" can lead to a one-time gift that might cover the cost of food for a support group or even a larger gift that underwrites an educational program. The Philanthropy Leadership Council's Survey of Hospitals' Largest Gifts states that a sizable percentage of an institution's donors gave to that particular institution out of gratitude for care that they or a family member received for a "life-threatening condition" (Advisory Board Company, 2011). Responding to "What can I do to thank you?" with a list of programs that need funding is an appropriate way of cultivating a donor. By partnering with the institution's foundation/development office and successfully facilitating donations from grateful patients, oncology social workers have the opportunity to not only raise funds for support programs but also place themselves in a "front and center" position with foundation/development office staff should they be looking for places to best allocate donations.

Grants

Grants can range from large, covering entire program costs, to small, covering one aspect or part of a larger program. Funding from diagnosis-specific, nonprofit organizations such as the Leukemia & Lymphoma Society might be available to cover the costs of a group facilitator or food for a support group, and other organizations such as the ACS might provide funding to cover the costs of a navigator position to provide direct services to patients. Many institutions have grant writers, often within their development or foundation office. Grants can be written in partnership with local nonprofit organizations that are also providing support for cancer patients and their loved ones. Another partnering opportunity might exist in sharing the costs of certain programs. Seeking to share costs and alliances with local nonprofits can provide support and free up budgeted dollars for use elsewhere in your program. Identification of these natural partners in promoting quality cancer care "represents a new wave and new opportunities not only for social work practice but also for delivery of services to a larger and broader constituency" (AOSW, 2006). Social workers must be careful, however, not to be seen as "poaching" potential donors from their nonprofit partners.

Institutional Funding

The ideal funding scenario is one in which your institution funds the program partially or in its entirety. High patient satisfaction scores are anticipated when cancer support services are built around a community needs assessment with stakeholder buy-in, producing valuable evaluations to determine if goals have been met and identifying needed changes and ideas for future programming. From an institutional standpoint, being able to focus on the importance of patient satisfaction scores provides opportunities to network and partner with organizational leaders. In seeking funding within an institutional setting, the oncology social worker charged with the task of developing cancer support programs must be able to explain clearly how support programs can provide a return on investment. As Nancy Vesell explains, "Once a patient has had a good experience, hopefully [the service] will serve as a point of entry for other services. Bring people into the service delivery system and, hopefully they will come back for more" (Vesell, n.d.). Having done homework as to what one's community needs, oncology social workers can approach administrators with examples of how cancer support programs not only bolster marketing but also help drive "downstream revenue" by offering community outreach and screening programs that may lead to the use of hospital services such as diagnostics and treatments (Sein, 2009).

In summary, collaboration, partnering and finding funding opportunities for continuation of programs, and program building are all within the scope of practice of an oncology social worker in the design, development, implementation, and sustaining of a cancer support program.

Pearls

- Any effective new program or practice approach must have as its genesis a clear understanding of what the needs are and how they might best be met.
- Involving a sufficient number and variety of potential stakeholders in the assessment process will enhance the likelihood of ongoing support and commitment to both the program and the client group being served.
- Developing a Patient and Family Advisory Council in all phases of program development recognizes the importance of patient- and family-centered care.
- Cultivating donors provides numerous opportunities to raise funds for cancer support programs. Grateful patients are often an overlooked resource for funding cancer support programs.
- Seeking to share costs and alliances with local nonprofits can provide support and free up budgeted dollars to be used elsewhere in your program.
- When seeking institutional funding, the oncology social worker must explain clearly how these programs can provide a return on investment by providing downstream revenue.

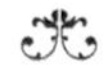

Pitfalls

- All programs will encounter obstacles. Some portions of a program will be easier to institute, whereas others may have to be shelved, if only temporarily.
- Limited staffing is often a roadblock to the building or expansion of cancer support programs.
- Obtaining administrative support requires the oncology social worker to consider the various opportunities that exist within the workplace and to find time to make oneself visible to the key decision makers.
- Finding viable collaborative opportunities, such as being included in departmental operational budget planning, for covering programmatic costs presents unique challenges.

As the demand for psychosocial services increases and provision of these services is required for accreditation for certain cancer centers, the door opens for oncology social workers to take the lead in the planning and implementation of a cancer support program. The size and scope of services offered will be based on institutional support, staffing availability, and financial realities. It is the responsibility of oncology social workers to become active participants in research in and the development of best practices in the creation and implementation of innovative cancer support programs. Opportunities for oncology social workers to partner with their research colleagues can be found within their professional organizations and nonprofits.

REFERENCES

Advisory Board Company. (2011). *Connecting through care: Best practices in grateful patient fundraising.* Retrieved from http://www.advisory.com/research/philanthropy-leadership-council/studies/2007/connecting-through-care

American College of Surgeons, Commission on Cancer. (2012). Cancer program standards 2012: Ensuring patient-centered care, v.1.2.1. Chicago, IL: American College of Surgeons.

Association of Oncology Social Work. (2006). *AOSW member survey report.* Retrieved from http://www.aosw.org/iMIS201/AOSWMain/pdfs/aosw-public-docs/MemberSurvey4.pdf

Association of Oncology Social Work. (2012). *Standards of practice in oncology social work*. Retrieved from http://www.aosw.org/iMIS201/AOSWMain/professionals/standards-of-practice/AOSWMain/Professional-Development/standards-of-practice.aspx?hkey=51fda308-28bd-48b0-8a75-a17d01251b5e

Axford, N. (2010). Conducting needs assessments in children's services. *British Journal of Social Work*, *40*(1), 4–25. doi:10.1093/bjsw/bcn103

Centers for Disease Control and Prevention (CDC). (2010). *Comprehensive cancer control branch toolkit*. Retrieved from http://www.cdc.gov/cancer/ncccp/pdf/CCC_Program_Evaluation_Toolkit.pdf

Dudley, J. R. (2014). *Social work evaluation: Enhancing what we do* (2nd ed.). Chicago, IL: Lyceum Books.

Institute of Medicine. (2008). *Cancer care for the whole patient: Meeting psychosocial health needs*. Washington, DC: National Academies Press.

Johnson, B., Abraham, M., & Shelton, T. (2009). Patient- and family-centered care. *North Carolina Medical Journal*, *70*(2), 125–130.

Negy, J., & Fawcett, S. B. (2012). Developing a strategic plan. In B. Berkowitz & J. Schultz (Eds.), *The community tool box*. Lawrence, KS: University of Kansas Press.

Presskill, H., & Jones, N. (2009). *A practical guide for engaging stakeholders in developing evaluation questions*. Robert Woods Johnson Foundation. Retrieved from http://www.rwjf.org/content/dam/web-assets/2009/01/a-practical-guide-for-engaging-stakeholders-in-developing-evalua

Sein, E. (2009, July 24). *Nurse navigators program and evaluation methods*. Fox Chase Cancer Center Partners. Retrieved from http://pubweb.fccc.edu/panavnet/wp-content/uploads/2010/10/Evaluation-of-Patient-Navigation.pdf

Vesell, N. (n.d.). Some services are small but mighty. Strategic Health Care Communications. Retrieved from http://strategichealthcare.com/pubs/shcm/f1_SmallButMighty.php

Whaley, M. P. (2010, February 10). 50 ways to attract new patients to your practice [Web log post]. *Manage my practice*. Retrieved from http://www.managemypractice.com/50-ways-to-attract-new-patients-to-your-practice/

83

Catherine Credeur and Christine Healy

Managing Volunteer Services in Oncology

Key Concepts

- *Meaningful collaboration with patients and family members by professional staff is necessary for effective patient- and family-centered care.*
- *Recruitment of current and former patients and caregivers in volunteer roles requires specific criteria for selection and programs for orientation, training, and nurturing of these volunteers.*
- *Volunteers can have roles in patient care and nonpatient care activities within the hospital.*
- *An effective collaboration between social worker and volunteer can extend social work services.*
- *The impact of the dual roles of the patient who is also a volunteer must be recognized and clarified in training and supervisory activities.*

Patient- and family-centered care has become a valued and recognized approach to improving safety, quality, and patient satisfaction in oncology and other health care settings. This chapter focuses on engaging current and former cancer patients and their family members as collaborative partners in the planning, delivery, and evaluation of care to extend service delivery and improve patients' experiences. Oncology social workers use their clinical, administrative, and community organization skills when leading or supporting a volunteer program.

A successful program requires a thoughtful and systematic approach to the selection, training, supervision, and support of volunteers. Collaboration with patient and family volunteers is also key to meaningful social work practice. Some oncology social workers have a full-time role in volunteer management, whereas for others, management of volunteers may be only one of many areas of responsibility.

The chapter also focuses on integrating volunteer management into multiple areas of responsibility. Particular attention is paid to the duality of relationships and roles when a patient or family member becomes a volunteer within his or her present or former treatment or support setting.

Oncology social workers benefit from managing volunteers. Often, patient and family volunteers (also called patient and family advisers) are motivated to "give back" to the organization that provided medical care to them or their loved ones. At times, these volunteers are still struggling with the meaning or ongoing consequences of the disease and treatment. Supporting patients and caregivers in this volunteer work can provide satisfaction for staff members who see these volunteers move from the crisis of a cancer diagnosis to a more stable point in life. Management of volunteers can provide oncology social workers with an opportunity to develop supervisory skills and experience. Both the intrinsic and career path benefits are valid reasons for oncology social workers to understand that volunteer management is a natural extension of their existing skill sets. Though the chapter focuses on the management of volunteers who have personal experience with cancer, many of the concepts and approaches discussed also apply to more general volunteer programs.

Hospital Volunteer Programs

From the start, staff members developing an effective hospital volunteer program should establish clear expectations and select potential volunteers according to criteria similar to those used to hire permanent staff members. The primary goal is to orient, train, and nurture volunteers effectively to ensure the program's success, as well as to retain skilled volunteers (Forsyth, cited in Skoglund, 2006). Secondarily, if the volunteer is a patient or family member, it is important to understand where that person is on the cancer journey and to find the right fit for a successful experience.

Steps Needed to Obtain Effective Volunteers

Application and Selection

A key component of screening for and matching potential volunteers with an appropriate role is an assessment of their motivation and interests. An oncology social worker's direct practice assessment skills—the ability to explore, clarify, connect, and follow through to a satisfactory result—translates from the patient population to the volunteer pool.

Training

The standard components of volunteer training should include the organization's mission and values, its niche within the community, and the processes required to protect patient or client confidentiality and safety. A volunteer's need for individualized training will vary, depending on the assigned role and his or her previous work and life experiences.

Age-appropriate teaching styles need to be adapted for child, adolescent, and adult volunteers. Training methods that include a balance of visual, tactile, and auditory learning, as well as modeling or return demonstrations, are appropriate when preparing volunteers in a group setting (Haski-Leventhal & Cnaan, 2009).

Roles in Patient Care

Roles in patient care may include hospitality, transport support, peer support, management of resources (e.g., a library for patients or a wig or scarf boutique), or recreational outlets. Volunteers in pediatric settings may assist with play therapy or teaching, educational tutoring, parental support, and other activities to create a child- or teen-friendly environment. Volunteers also may help implement family support programs to address the needs of children when a family member has cancer. Patient care volunteers need to be carefully matched according to their interest in and sensitivity to a patient or family's needs, as well as for such considerations as infection control.

Roles in Nonpatient Care Activities

When volunteers work in areas other than direct patient care, staff needs to pay particular attention to issues of emotional reward for the volunteers and a sense of connectedness to the organization's mission. For example, volunteers may work on creating a welcoming and safe environment for patients or families as members of an environment-of-care committee, help with fund-raising and public relations, or provide community education about cancer prevention and early detection. Involvement on quality committees or other improvement teams can be highly rewarding for the patient or family adviser and helpful to the organization. An important role for the social worker is to prepare advisers for meaningful committee work by reviewing the committee's purpose and background with them. It also is the social worker's role to help the committee chair understand the volunteer's role and to foster the chair's acceptance and the volunteer's active involvement.

Collaboration or Partnership With the Social Worker

Volunteers working in partnership with the oncology social worker in a clinical setting have an opportunity to reach more patients and families, provide them with additional support, and identify those who need information or formal social work services. This partnership is helpful to the patient population and the social worker and gives the volunteer a sense of reward and meaning. A volunteer providing peer support may receive referrals from the social worker or communicate with the social worker about a patient's situation. Peer supporters may perceive needs that should be reported to the social worker for professional evaluation and treatment. Additionally, peer supporters can encourage patients to attend support groups or other services led by social workers and can orient current patients to the wide range of services available in the cancer setting.

Evaluation

It is essential to evaluate volunteers regarding their adherence to organizational norms and safety and confidentiality requirements (Brown, 2007). Although confronting a volunteer who exhibits nonconstructive behavior may be challenging, it is necessary and may ultimately serve to sustain a strong volunteer and help a struggling one find a better fit for his or her interests.

Patient and Family Adviser Volunteer Programs

As a patient or family adviser, volunteers have had a personal experience with cancer, either personally or with a loved one. They often want to give back, not only in gratitude but also to help improve the system for the next patient. They are encouraged to communicate their experiences in a way that helps everyone—patients, families, and staff—and, ultimately, facilitates their own healing.

In the oncology setting, advisers listen to and share stories with other patients and families, which allows them to relate on a unique and personal level. They are able to provide patients and families with information and valuable resources from a consumer's perspective. Furthermore, by serving on councils and committees, they are able to share a patient or family's perspective to administrators and clinical staff. Finally, advisers can help patients and families feel less alone and that the institution cares about them on a personal level.

The oncology social worker is instrumental in the training and support of these advisers. Because the advisers are patients or caregivers themselves, they must learn how to balance their dual role as volunteer and patient or caregiver. Including the advisers' perspective as consumers helps the organization provide comprehensive care and meet the needs of both patients and families. The oncology social worker's consistent support and supervision also serve to retain the volunteer advisers. Advisers feel competent and effective when they receive feedback and know they are supported when they run into challenging situations. Advisers and the oncology social worker learn from each other in group meetings where experiences, strategies, and challenges are shared.

Use of a Patient Services Checklist in an Oncology Outpatient Clinic

The box that follows describes the results of a collaboration between an oncology social worker and patient advisers in the gastroenterology department's outpatient clinic at the Moffitt center. The department staff, with feedback from patient advisers, determined that clinic patients lacked access to psychosocial resources and social work services. A committee composed of patient advisers, clinic staff, and patient education specialists subsequently developed this checklist to track patients' awareness, participation, and interest in a variety of service areas. The patient advisers administered the checklist to patients and family members in the waiting room, using the opportunity to connect with them on a peer level and to understand the patients' experiences better. The advisers then shared their encounters with the social worker, who assessed the need for intervention.

We Are Here to Help in the GI Clinic

Cancer Information and Support Services Checklist

Name: ______________ *Date of Birth:* ______________

Phone #: ______________ *Date:* ______________

	Aware of Service	**Have Participated** **Satisfaction Rating 1–5** ***(5 being highest)***	**Interested in Service**
Please check as appropriate:			
Patient Education/Orientation			
Patient & Family Orientation	________	________	________
Patient Library and Welcome Center	________	________	________
Daily Meet the Experts in Library	________	________	________
Cancer Answers	________	________	________
Online Cancer Resources	________	________	________
Cancer Prevention Information	________	________	________
Language Assistance	________	________	________
Help With Forms	________	________	________
Diagnosis/Treatment Information	________	________	________
Wellness			
Cancer Screening	________	________	________
Genetic Testing	________	________	________
Massage (free if inpatient)	________	________	________
Yoga	________	________	________
Meditation	________	________	________
Arts in Medicine Studio	________	________	________
Tobacco Treatment Program	________	________	________
Nutrition Care	________	________	________
Rehabilitation Services	________	________	________
Patient/Family Hospitality Coffees	________	________	________
Care Planning			
Fertility Preservation Counseling	________	________	________
Clinical Trials	________	________	________

Advance Directives/Living Wills	______	______	______
Preparing for Hospitalization	______	______	______
Pain Management	______	______	______
Home Care or Hospice	______	______	______
Nursing Home	______	______	______
Support and Resources			
Talking to Your Child About Cancer	______	______	______
Support Groups	______	______	______
Counseling	______	______	______
Caregiver Support/Resources	______	______	______
Spiritual Care	______	______	______
Financial Assistance Resources	______	______	______
Prescription Assistance	______	______	______
Transportation	______	______	______
Lodging	______	______	______
Hope Lodge	______	______	______
Help With Disability Forms	______	______	______
Community Resources	______	______	______
Being a Patient or Family Volunteer	______	______	______
Expressing Concerns or Compliments	______	______	______
Adolescent and Young Adult (AYA) Program (Ages 15–39)	______	______	______

MOFFITT CANCER CENTER

H. LEE MOFFITT CANCER CENTER & RESEARCH INSTITUTE, AN NCI COMPREHENSIVE CANCER CENTER—TAMPA, FL. 1-888-MOFFITT

Models for the Organizational Structure of Volunteer Programs

Physical Location

In some treatment or support programs, volunteers are recruited, trained, and managed within an institution's volunteer department. Because social work professionals have translatable skills in blending personnel management, public relations, and systems orientation, the oncology social worker may be the primary volunteer coordinator.

In other programs, the oncology social worker will be the liaison between oncology departments and volunteers. Some volunteers function in general roles (e.g., clerical or transportation) and are able to be supervised or managed by the volunteer department regardless of unit location. However, volunteers working more directly in oncology-focused care (e.g., peer support or fitting or demonstrating wigs) have more exposure to patients. Thus, they have more need for unit-specific orientation, training, and emotional support as they become emotionally attached to patients.

Basic Requirements for Volunteers

In many health care settings, a volunteer must follow hospital policies and procedures regarding infection control, hand hygiene, emergency codes, and other issues relevant to the area of volunteer service. After the initial interview, an application and background and reference checks often set the process in motion, followed by health screenings (tuberculosis and flu shots), orientations, compliance with the Health Insurance Portability and Accountability Act (HIPAA), and mandatory education (a separate step in the regulatory standards). Although this initial process can be time consuming, it helps to screen out potential volunteers unsure of their motivation or unable to meet the time commitment.

Criteria for Acceptance Into the Program

When a patient will be ready to volunteer after his or her own illness is an important question to consider. Some volunteer programs suggest waiting for a patient to be out of treatment for at least 1 year so the patient and family have time to process their experience and care for their own immediate physical and emotional needs. Later, they will be able to share their perspective as peer support volunteers.

In a patient- and family-centered care setting, including patient or caregiver advisers who remain active within the health care system is vital so that staff receives current and relevant feedback about processes, safety concerns, and quality issues. Thus, the oncology social worker must be able to assess the potential vulnerabilities and strengths of patient advisers concerning balancing this dual role. That assessment gives the social worker an opportunity to determine whether patients and caregivers are ready for the volunteer role of adviser and to help them integrate their survivorship experience into their personal lives.

A minimum time commitment should be clarified with a volunteer at the outset. This commitment may vary by the patient volunteer's role, treatment, and general health status. Although a potential volunteer will move from the role of patient to that of volunteer adviser, he or she will continue to wear two hats. For some patients, this dual role will be straightforward; however, the role will create some challenges. Some programs offer volunteers an informal meeting after their initial 3 months to ensure that both parties are satisfied with the relationship.

Criteria for Selection

Source of Referral

Some prospective volunteers are selected by the volunteer department and referred directly to the oncology department. A volunteer may have mentioned a personal experience with oncology care, suggesting that he or she would be a good fit with that department. Perhaps the department has a project of special interest to the volunteer. When the volunteer is not familiar to the cancer program's staff, it is important to ensure that the volunteer has an accurate understanding of the cancer program's needs and use of volunteers. The social worker is often the key facilitator of this unit-specific orientation.

To partner with and support the range of patients served in a hospital setting, the pool of patient volunteers must mirror the age, gender, race, ethnicity, and educational and professional backgrounds of the patient population. A volunteer's diagnosis and treatment modalities become more relevant in peer support programs.

Qualities Needed by Patient and Family Advisers

When selecting patient and family advisers, look for individuals who can do the following:

- *Show concern for more than one issue or agenda.*
- *Listen well.*
- *Respect the perspectives of others.*
- *Speak comfortably and candidly in a group.*
- *Interact well with many different kinds of people.*
- *Work in partnerships with others.*
- *Share insights and information about their experiences in ways that will benefit others.*
- *See beyond their own personal experiences.*

Source: Adapted from the American Hospital Association (2004)

Motivation for Becoming a Volunteer Adviser

The oncology social worker has the ability to determine the strengths and weaknesses of potential advisers and their motivations for becoming a volunteer. For some patients, volunteering in a familiar setting is a "stepping stone" or "safe haven." The prospect of returning to the "real world" with its many expectations may be a daunting challenge. Such patients give the oncology social worker the opportunity to support them in their transition—this can be a win-win situation for patients as they help others while helping themselves on the cancer trajectory (Cohen & Numa, 2011).

Retention of Volunteers Through Nurturing

Compassion fatigue is a complex notion that is difficult for volunteer advisers to acknowledge. When they arrive at the setting for the first time, they may feel as though they have an unending reserve of energy. After a few hours, however, they may feel empty, having witnessed the pain of others (Worthington, 2008).

Because volunteer advisers may experience the same stresses that oncology social workers experience, they, like everyone else involved in oncology care, need an occasional period of renewal and replenishment. They must be encouraged often to develop their own rituals for winding down. The perspectives and boundaries of social work can not only help them process their experiences and the meaning of those experiences in their lives (Cohen & Numa, 2011) but also give them opportunities to observe the oncology social worker modeling self-care. Monthly meetings provide opportunities for advisers to share their experiences and provide support to one another. As Cohen and Numa (2011, p. 70) pointed out, oncology social workers who facilitate these meetings "provide opportunities for social support, sharing of emotions, and cognitive and emotional processing of the experience and its meanings."

Orientation and training of volunteers take time, and thus it is important for the social worker to have administrative support for the time required to manage and nurture the volunteers. This is especially important when volunteer management is only one of many roles the oncology social worker must juggle in addition to the responsibilities of a dedicated staff position. After this initial oncology social work investment, some volunteer advisers can function independently, consulting with the oncology social worker as needed. Other volunteers need more frequent contact and ongoing support from their social work supervisor.

Assignment of Roles

Assessment of Right Fit for Mutual Benefit and Success

Volunteers who feel happy, appreciated, and productive are community assets for a cancer program and can greatly expand the staff's efforts. Because social workers are often engaged in the program's activities, they tend to have opportunities not only for hands-on assessment of the volunteers but also for direct modeling for the volunteers. The social worker who takes the time to check in with a new volunteer on his or her first day on duty and then several times during the orientation period supports a relationship that is open for the volunteer's questions and need for redirection.

Renegotiation of Roles

Although social workers operating according to the strengths- based model tend to presume that all individuals have value to offer an organization, there inevitably are times when a volunteer's performance does not fit the organization's goals or needs. However, starting in that affirming environment generally makes it easier for volunteers to feel appreciated even when the supervisor needs to make changes in their work assignment (Hustinx & Handy, 2009; Kummerfeldt, 2011). It is important to remind oneself that volunteers are working voluntarily. Therefore, staff needs to be reminded to affirm what volunteers bring to the program and to recognize their need for gratification and replenishment in relation to their work (Skoglund, 2006). Volunteer roles also may need to be renegotiated to accommodate the volunteer's personal schedule and needs.

Ethical Issues: Dual Roles

Some cancer programs use volunteers who formerly received active care under one of those programs. Programs based on the patient- and family-centered model of care will use patients and caregivers who are still actively engaged in the patient's treatment. Given that a dual relationship is almost inevitable, and in some ways perhaps preferable, how do oncology social workers support an ethical transition in the structure of the patient or family relationship with the organization? The oncology professional who returns to the work environment after receiving cancer treatment provides a model for how patient-volunteers can be integrated into the treatment setting. The program's culture and policies need to support the returning professional's adequate self-care for physical needs, emotional reflection, and shifting roles or duties. However, just as the dual perspective of our colleagues as oncology professionals and now cancer survivors is valuable in the culture of our workplace, the dual perspective of our patient-volunteers enriches the patient-centered culture of those who provide treatment.

Social work practitioners are challenged to refer to the following directive in the National Association of Social Workers' *Code of Ethics* (2008, 1.06[c]): "In instances when dual or multiple relationships are unavoidable, social workers should take steps to protect clients and are responsible for setting clear, appropriate, and culturally sensitive boundaries." Oncology social workers start that process by recruiting patient-survivors and caregiver-cosurvivors into volunteer roles. This prompts many questions. For example, do our current or former patients and caregivers truly feel free to volunteer in the capacity and timing that fit their needs? Are they clear about their motivation for volunteering?

As we prepare to orient new volunteers, additional questions arise. Does our volunteer training include information about self-care? Do we recognize the survivor's guilt that may be triggered when survivor volunteers encounter current patients who are struggling physically, emotionally, or financially (Street, Love, & Blackford, 2005)? Do our periodic training sessions and informal assessments allow volunteers to explore and manage these concerns at any point during their volunteer service (Skoglund, 2006)? Do we provide an appropriate therapeutic venue and give volunteers permission to work through feelings that may arise as they work in the cancer program, recognizing that volunteers need to return to the role of patient (Moreno- Jiménez & Villodres, 2010)? Do we acknowledge the strengths of our volunteer colleagues or do we continue to "protect" them as we would a newly diagnosed patient?

There is no one-size-fits-all answer to such questions. Rather, oncology social workers are encouraged to be attuned to the reality of a dual relationship and always keep patient-volunteers' well-being at the top of their priority list. Oncology social workers need to explore these issues with prospective volunteers and encourage limits that place the patient's or family's needs before the volunteer's needs. Because our interdisciplinary colleagues may not have training that places as much emphasis on dual relationships, social workers need to educate teams on the benefits and risks for our patients and families of volunteering within their treatment program.

Pearls

- Social work professionals have translatable skills in blending personnel management, public relations, and systems orientation that equip them well in the role of volunteer coordinator, especially with those volunteers working in patient care areas and related activities.
- Careful selection (with criteria similar to those used for hiring staff), orientation, training, and ongoing support are required for an effective collaboration between professional staff and patient and family volunteers.
- An effective collaboration between social workers and volunteers can extend social work services and make them more accessible.

Pitfalls

- Staff needs to be reminded to affirm what volunteers bring to the program and to recognize their need for gratification and replenishment in relation to their work.
- Failing to recognize and address the challenges inherent in the dual roles of the volunteer as patient and volunteer will limit volunteers' effectiveness in the collaboration with the hospital.

The oncology social worker's skills in navigation, negotiation, and education can help strike a balance between valuing patient or family volunteers and supporting the needs of those volunteers as current patients or cancer survivors or their loved ones. The social worker's role is to connect the medical system and the patient's or family's needs and perspectives. The social worker has an ethical responsibility to balance the needs of the employer and the needs of the patient and family volunteers. Advocacy and leadership blend the needs of patients and families and our medical model–focused colleagues into a care team that not only expands the oncology social work role but also promotes a partnership for improving the quality and safety of patient care and patients' satisfaction.

REFERENCES

American Hospital Association. (2004) *Strategies for leadership: Patient- and family-centered care.* Chicago, IL: American Hospital Association, Institute for Family-Centered Care. Retrieved from http://www.aha.org/advocacy-issues/quality/strategies-patientcentered.shtml

Brown, W. A. (2007). Board development practices and competent board members: Implications for performance. *Nonprofit Management and Leadership, 17*(3), 301–317.

Cohen, M., & Numa, M. (2011). Post-traumatic growth in breast cancer survivors: A comparison of volunteers and non-volunteers. *Psycho-Oncology, 20*(1), 69–76.

Haski-Leventhal, D., & Cnaan, R. A. (2009). Group processes and volunteering: Using groups to enhance volunteerism. *Administration in Social Work, 33*(1), 61–80.

Hustinx, L., & Handy, F. (2009). Where do I belong? Volunteer attachment in a complex organization. *Administration in Social Work, 33*(2), 202–220.

Kummerfeldt, V. D. (2011). *Human resource management strategies for volunteers: A study of job satisfaction, performance, and retention in a nonprofit organization* (Doctoral dissertation). Available from ProQuest Dissertations and Theses. (72-062)

Moreno-Jiménez, M., & Villodres, M. (2010). Prediction of burnout in volunteers. *Journal of Applied Social Psychology, 40*(7), 1798–1818.

National Association of Social Workers. (2008). *Code of ethics.* Washington, DC: Author.

Skoglund, A. (2006). Do not forget about your volunteers: A qualitative analysis of factors influencing volunteer turnover. *Health and Social Work, 31*(3), 217–220.

Street, A., Love, A., & Blackford, J. (2005). Managing family centered palliative care in aged and acute settings. *Nursing and Health Sciences, 7*(1), 45–55.

Worthington, D. L. (2008). Communication skills training in a hospice volunteer training program. *Journal of Social Work in End-of-Life and Palliative Care, 4*(1), 17–37.

XV

Bioethical and Policy Issues in Oncology Social Work

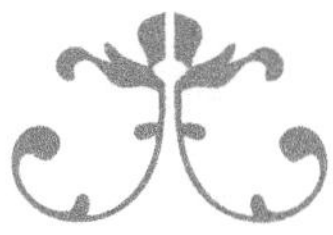

Gary L. Stein

Access to cancer care or related clinical research is dependent on ever-evolving legal, policy, and ethical standards. This section considers critical policy and ethical issues associated with oncology practice today—the ethical principles governing the provision of care and related concerns, the opportunities and challenges to expanded access to care through health care reform, and governmental policies that create barriers to obtaining effective pain management. Social workers need to be apprised of developments in each of these arenas to be effective providers and coordinators of psychosocial care.

Health care reform, as advanced by the Patient Protection and Affordable Care Act (PPACA), is the first nationwide attempt to achieve universal health insurance coverage for all U.S. citizens. In "Historic and Current Perspectives on Health Care Reform," Gunnar Almgren analyzes the history and issues presented by the PPACA, most important of which is to require coverage for all Americans, whether through the workplace or individual coverage, and to provide for individual subsidies and the expansion of Medicaid to ensure access to insurance among lower income populations. These policy changes create challenges for social workers, who will need to become educated on the health exchanges being developed by the states and the federal government and on the expansion of Medicaid to previously ineligible low-income communities. Social workers will need to demonstrate measurable value added to the health care team to ensure their ongoing recognition as care coordinators and psychosocial providers in the new accountable care organizations that will be responsible for patient care.

The interdisciplinary field of bioethics has generated guidelines for analyzing difficult dilemmas in the care of patients with cancer and other serious conditions. Among its great achievements is the consensus to empower patients to make important medical decisions and control their care. Gary L. Stein and Jeanne Kerwin, in "Bioethical Issues in Oncology and the Social Work Response," present a review of the basic ethical principles that support patient care: the rights of patients to autonomy and self-determination, the requirements that health care professionals advance patients' best interests through beneficence and nonmaleficence, and societal expectations of distributive justice, or fairness. Social workers advance these principles by bringing their psychosocial expertise to oncology and palliative care teams by acting as liaisons between the patient/family, the treating physician, and other services; mediating disagreements among patients, their families, and other team members; and advocating on behalf of patient/family interests during team deliberations and ethics consultation.

Research has documented the significant unaddressed pain experienced by patients with cancer and other serious medical conditions and the need for effective pain management. Although hospice and palliative care specialists from all disciplines have promoted pain and symptom management as a primary focus for cancer care, legislation and regulations have occasionally presented barriers to obtaining appropriate pain care. Additional challenges are presented by societal stigma surrounding the use of narcotic drugs, as well as cases of abuse and diversion of both illicit and prescribed drugs. In "Improving Pain Care Policy: Implications for Social Work Advocacy," Mary Beth Morrissey explores the state, national, and international dimensions of pain control policy. She promotes a leadership role for social work in advocating for improved access to pain care, addressing health disparities and treatment inequalities, advancing professional education, and integrating psychosocial perspectives as key dimensions of the pain experience.

84 Historic and Current Perspectives on Health Care Reform

Gunnar Almgren

Key Concepts

- *Passed into law in 2010, the Patient Protection and Affordable Care Act (PPACA) is the first federal legislation in history intended to achieve universal health insurance coverage for all U.S. citizens.*
- *The PPACA package seeks to expand health insurance coverage to 93% of the national population while controlling rising health care costs and improving the health care delivery system.*
- *The PPACA is a centrist approach to the expansion of health insurance coverage in that it seeks to achieve its ends through the preservation of the mixed public and private system of health care finance.*
- *The PPACA strategy for expanded insurance coverage includes insurance market reform, insurance purchase mandates and subsidies, and expansion of public health care entitlement programs.*
- *Although the PPACA's prospects for implementation are at best uncertain, comprehensive health care reform that leads to universal health care entitlement is inevitable for compelling economic reasons.*

The premise of this chapter is that a sophisticated grasp of the historic and contemporary context of health care reform and the current status of policy aimed at achieving that end are essential to informed clinical practice and policy advocacy. The chapter begins with an overview of the historic, social, and political contexts of health care system reform and the most recent effort to extend health insurance coverage to all Americans, the Patient Protection and Affordable Care Act (P.L. 111–148). The chapter then provides a review of the factors that explain President Barack Obama's unprecedented success in getting comprehensive health care reform legislation through Congress and signed into law. After reviewing the main policy aims and basic provisions of the Patient Protection and Affordable Care Act, the chapter concludes with an analysis of its prospects for implementation and the reasons that comprehensive health care reform that provides a universal entitlement to basic health care is ultimately inevitable, regardless of the fate of the Patient Protection and Affordable Care Act.

The Historic, Social, and Political Contexts of Health Care Reform

When President Barack Obama signed the Patient Protection and Affordable Care Act (PPACA) into law in March 2010, a century had passed since the first presidential administration advocated some form of universal health insurance coverage. In 1912, President Theodore Roosevelt advocated a federal policy of universal health insurance coverage as part of his Progressive party platform. Despite Roosevelt's failed bid at re-election, his opponent, Woodrow Wilson, promoted Roosevelt's policy of universal health insurance coverage when he was elected president. Universal health insurance coverage has re-emerged as a policy goal of most presidential administrations since Theodore Roosevelt, including that of Republican president Richard Nixon. The Obama administration was the first to enact legislation designed to accomplish universal health insurance coverage for all American citizens.[1]

Despite the fact that Obama was elected to the presidency by a large margin on a platform that promised aggressive advocacy of universal health insurance coverage for all

Americans, the future of the PPACA is in serious jeopardy. This is partly due to both vitriolic partisan politics and the resurgence of historical obstacles that have defeated prior efforts to achieve this central policy goal of the social work profession. This leaves us to contemplate what continues to be an enduring paradox in American health care politics and policy: the failure to achieve a national policy of universal health insurance coverage despite decades of support for the idea from most Americans (Almgren, 2013, 2006; Roberts, 2010). Without delving into all the complexities of this paradoxical disconnect between public preferences and national policy, it is safe to say that opposition from powerful stakeholder groups invested in a market-based approach to health care during critical historical junctures has been central to the failure of the United States to achieve universal health care coverage.[2]

The PPACA: Political Context and Basic Provisions

The Political Context of the PPACA's Legislative Success

A full analysis of the PPACA's successful journey to presidential signature is beyond the scope of this brief chapter. However, the PPACA's legislative success can largely be attributed to the timely convergence of four factors: a clear electoral mandate, political control of both chambers of Congress, the devolution of employment-based health insurance, and the ability of a politically adroit president to split crucial stakeholder opposition.

Basic Provisions of the PPACA

General Overview

The PPACA (P.L. 111-148) was signed into law by President Barack Obama on March 23, 2010, followed by his signing of the Health Care and Education Reconciliation Act (P.L. 111-152) 1 week later. Together, both pieces of legislation compose the legislative framework of the PPACA, a comprehensive health care reform package that seeks to expand health insurance coverage to 93% of the national population,[3] control rising health care costs, and improve the health care delivery system. The structure of the PPACA is essentially consistent with the approach to health care reform advocated in Obama's 2008 presidential campaign platform—that is, the PPACA seeks to expand health insurance to *near*-universal coverage through a combination of regulatory insurance market reforms, insurance purchase mandates for individuals and employers, and expansions of public entitlement programs.

It is notable that over 23 million U.S. residents will remain uninsured (CMS, 2010) even if the PPACA is fully implemented as Congress intended. In large part, this is because the PPACA excludes undocumented immigrants from health insurance coverage, through either private insurance market regulations or public entitlement programs. Although the exclusion of undocumented immigrants from health insurance coverage is prevalent among countries that are credited with providing "universal insurance coverage," the U.S. economy is dependent on both the labor and taxes of undocumented workers.

There are other, more fundamental approaches to health care reform, in particular some form of a single-payer social insurance fund that would entail universal enrollment of all U.S. citizens and legal residents. In contrast, the PPACA is a middle-ground approach that leaves the employment-based system of private health insurance intact while expanding both health insurance purchase subsidies to low-income households and public entitlement programs. The PPACA also imposes consumer-oriented health insurance market reforms but favors the expansion of commercial health insurance enrollment over publicly funded health insurance. The PPACA imposes some direct cost reductions on health care providers and eliminates a few inherently inflationary provider practices. Its central strategy for reducing the unsustainable growth in national health care expenditures is the fostering of cost-effective approaches to health care through a combination of funding resources for the development of innovative practice models and financial incentives for cost-efficient provider organizations. Finally, the PPACA's implementation strategy is incremental. Although most provisions are scheduled to be implemented by the end of 2014, specific regulatory and entitlement provisions are phased in over a period of 8 years (2010–2018).

The PPACA is among the most complex packages of legislation ever promulgated by the federal government. It seeks to expand health insurance enrollment to over 90% of the nation's population, increase health care quality, and "bend the curve" of ever-rising health care costs, while at the same time leaving an extremely complex mixed private/public model of health care financing intact. Due to this complexity, this chapter summarizes only the PPACA's three major components will be summarized in this chapter: insurance market reform, coverage expansion, and health care system delivery reform.

Insurance Market Reforms

The PPACA has provisions that address the following seven major reforms of the nation's private health insurance market:[4]

1. Elimination of lifetime limits on coverage for health care expenditures (effective 2014).
2. Elimination of "preexisting conditions" clauses that exclude ill or disabled persons from insurance eligibility (effective 6 months following enactment for children and effective 2014 for adults).
3. Limits on out-of-pocket expense requirements for all insurance plans (effective 2014).
4. An 80% limit on the proportion of insurance premium costs that originate from administrative costs and profits (effective 2011).

5. Requirement that all but very small (less than 50 full-time equivalent) employers provide employees with health insurance and that individuals who are not eligible for employer insurance purchase health insurance. These mandates are facilitated by tax penalties for enforcement and subsidies to support the affordability of health insurance (effective 2014).
6. Definition and requirement of a basic minimum benefit package for individual and group health insurance plans (effective 2014).
7. Creation of health insurance cooperatives and insurance exchanges at the state level to enhance the health insurance purchasing power of smaller employers and individuals (phased in between 2011 and 2017).

Collectively, these seven reforms of the nation's private health insurance market represent very fundamental changes that, if fully implemented, might:

- Help tip the balance in favor of the purchasers and consumers of health insurance over the financial interests of the insurance industry.
- Restore, at least to a large extent, the private insurance industry to its original societal purpose: the promotion of access to health care and the protection of households from medical bankruptcy.
- Facilitate the affordability of health insurance to small employers and middle- to low-income Americans.
- Make it far more possible for millions of sick and disabled persons to acquire affordable health insurance.[5]

Health Insurance Coverage Expansion

The term *health insurance coverage* is used broadly in the discussion that follows to extend to public health care entitlement programs such as Medicaid, as well as to private health insurance. For purposes of simplicity, having "health insurance coverage" means a person can walk into a clinic or hospital and present a plastic coverage card from a public or private health care plan that affords access to necessary care. When the PPACA was signed into law in 2010, about 50 million persons in the United States lacked such a coverage card, and although it is disproportionately representative of the low income and poor, this group has increasingly included the middle class. When the PPACA is fully implemented in 2019, the numbers of uninsured are predicted to be reduced (in proportional terms) to 21 million.[6] Although this leaves about 7% of U.S. citizens uninsured, it brings the United States into alignment with the Organization for Economic Co-operation and Development (OECD) general standard of universal health insurance coverage for citizens and legal residents (Wendt, 2009). This approximation of universal health insurance coverage is achieved through three main PPACA policy strategies:[7]

- Various income-based subsidies to individuals and employers for the purchase of health insurance, along with employer and individual insurance coverage mandates (as previously discussed).
- Expansion of mandatory Medicaid eligibility criteria to reach low-income individuals and families, supported by increased federal subsidies to states for newly eligible Medicaid enrollees.
- Promotion of state-level "basic health plan" options, meaning public health plan options for legal state residents who have incomes between 133% and 200% of the federal poverty line.

There are other important but relatively easily implemented measures for increasing coverage, such as requiring that all individual and group plans extend the maximum age of coverage for adult children up to age 26; this provision became effective in 2010. The coverage expansion strategies embedded in the PPACA can be thought of as a combination of a "carrot and stick" approach to private insurance purchasers and an expansion of public programs to the poor and low-income uninsured. The PPACA also permits states wide latitude in the tailoring of their publicly funded health care coverage programs to local economic conditions and policy preferences, thus seeking to expand health insurance coverage within a federalist policy framework.

Health Care Delivery System Reforms

A primary impediment to universal health insurance coverage is that the U.S. health care system is the most expensive in the world. In fact, politicians from both the Left and the Right agree that publicly financed health care entitlements are unsustainable without some fundamental reforms of the health care delivery system. Despite being the most technologically sophisticated health care system in the world, the U.S. health care system also has deeply embedded quality problems, such as unacceptable rates of iatrogenic infections in hospitalized patients (IOM, 2000). These deficits are products of two interrelated aspects of the health care delivery system: fragmentation of patient care and provider incentives that reward higher levels of health care utilization rather than better patient outcomes (Almgren, 2013). The health care delivery system reform components of the PPACA that address these fundamental problems include the following:[8]

- Heavy investment in preventive health services.
- Increased investment and payment incentives in primary care.
- Investment in innovative approaches to manage chronic disease.
- Payment mechanisms that reward cost-effective clinical care.
- Identification and elimination of inflationary provider incentives (such as proprietary doctor-owned hospitals).

Prospects for the PPACA and Fundamental Health Care System Reform

Political Prospects for the PPACA

The first crucial obstacle that the PPACA needed to surmount was the multiple challenges to its constitutionality, in particular, the mandate requiring that individuals carry health insurance.[9] In a mixed decision that surprised legal experts from across the political spectrum, the U.S. Supreme Court ruled in favor of the PPACA's individual mandate in late June 2012, while rejecting the constitutionality of the provision that *required* states to expand Medicaid eligibility. Although the ruling regarding Medicaid will undermine the ability of the PPACA to expand Medicaid coverage to the uninsured in politically conservative states (Almgren, 2013), the Supreme Court's rulings represented a resounding victory for the proponents of the PPACA and advocates of a strong federal role in the financing of health care.

The second crucial obstacle to the PPACA's survival was the November 2012 national elections. Republicans had vowed to repeal the PPACA and would have been able to do so if the November 2012 elections had granted the party either the Senate or the White House. With Obama's election to a second term and a net increase in the Democratic Party majority in the U.S. Senate, even most conservatives concede that the PPACA is now the law of the land.

Progress Toward Implementation

The most crucial data on the PPACA's successful implementation will be gathered in 2014. By the end of 2014, we will have clear evidence on several crucial prognostic indicators:

- Extent to which the relatively healthy and uninsured enroll in health plans in response to the PPACA's incentives and penalties. Ultimately, this trend is crucial to both the affordability of health insurance for those newly insured that are sicker, older, and of lower income and the long-term viability of new insurance rules (effective 2014) eliminating preexisting condition coverage exclusions for persons of all ages.
- Extent to which those eligible have enrolled in states that have chosen to take advantage of the PPACA's provisions to expand Medicaid enrollment.
- Progress toward implementation and successful operation of health insurance exchanges in all states.
- The extent to which the newly insured are able to connect with health care providers essential to their health care needs, primary providers in particular.

As of the final months of 2013, we can at least observe this much about the PPACA's progress toward implementation and its prospects for the achievement of some of its central policy aims:

Reduction of the Population of Uninsured Through the Expansion of Medicaid Eligibility

Because the U.S. Supreme Court precluded the PPACA from mandating that states expand their Medicaid enrollment to include low-wage workers and their families, several politically conservative states have rejected Medicaid expansion despite the availability of federal funds. As of July 1, 2013, there were 30 state governors voicing support for Medicaid expansion, 15 state governors voicing opposition to Medicaid expansion, and the remainder undecided. As the PPACA has garnered more public support, however, even some very conservative governors have changed their position toward Medicaid expansion (Kaiser Family Foundation, 2013a). There is concern that safety-net hospitals and the poor who depend on them for care will be placed in even greater jeopardy in those conservative states that continue to reject funds for Medicaid expansion as the PPACA phases out the federal subsidies to safety-net providers that expanded Medicaid enrollment was intended to offset (Spoerl, 2013).

Creation of State Health Insurance Exchanges

As discussed previously, a key component of the PPACA's health insurance market reform strategy is the development of health insurance co-ops and insurance exchanges to enhance the purchasing power of smaller employers and individuals and to facilitate the enrollment of many of the uninsured into subsidized health insurance plans. States could either use federal funds to develop their own health insurance exchanges or cede this authority to the federal government. As the PPACA target date for health insurance exchanges to be operating in all states approached in 2014, the government agency charged with the task of monitoring the implementation of the PPACA (the Government Accountability Office, or GAO) and the agency responsible for its implementation (the Centers for Medicare and Medicaid Services, or CMS) were in sharp disagreement on the status of progress toward implementation. The GAO adopted the more pessimistic view that the CMS would have a very difficult time achieving operational health insurance exchanges in all of the 34 states that had ceded that task to the federal government (Monegain, 2013; GOA, 2013). Although it is likely that the PPACA's health insurance exchange component will be broadly implemented by the end of 2014, it is unlikely to achieve its policy aim of enrolling 22 million Americans into insurance coverage by the target year of 2016. Even given a slower than desired pace of health insurance exchange implementation, the enrollment of millions of heretofore uninsured Americans into insurance plans that are both more affordable and comprehensive will be a massive health care reform achievement.

The Development of Accountable Care Organizations

The central component of the PPACA's health care system delivery reforms is the development of accountable care organizations (ACOs), that is, organizations composed of doctors, hospitals, and other providers representing the full continuum of care for chronic illness that are rewarded financially for integrated and cost-efficient care. As of 2013, there were 32 hospital systems nationwide that developed model ACO provider structures that will be reimbursed on a "pay for performance" basis by Medicare in accordance with preestablished quality-of-care benchmarks (Kaiser Family Foundation, 2013b). As noted by health care policy scholar Erin Bartolini, the ACOs' global budgeting structure permits providers to shift their focus from volume and intensity of service to a broader, more comprehensive view of health. This new focus allows providers to invest in innovations and services that were not financially viable under the traditional pre-PPACA financing mechanism, such as prevention and wellness, chronic disease management, and behavioral and mental health interventions (Bartolini, 2013, p. 1). As ACOs continue their rapid transformation of the health care industry, there are enormous opportunities for the specific competencies of social workers, but only if social workers invest their professional energies in those particular activities and methodologies that yield measurable added value to patient care outcomes. This *added value to outcome* criterion will determine which professions and practitioners will be winners (or losers) as ACOs become the health care industry standard.

Prospects for Fundamental Health Care Reform (With or Without the PPACA)

Four factors suggest that fundamental health care system reform that ultimately leads to universal health insurance coverage is politically inevitable, regardless of the PPACA's ultimate fate. It is notable that these four factors reflect economic realities independent of the ideological preferences of whichever political party may shape national health care policy over the next several years.

The Unsustainable Pace of Health Care Inflation

The mixed public and private approach to the financing and delivery of health care in America is rife with incentives that drive up the cost of care while yielding very limited benefits to the overall health of the national population. At this point, nearly 18% of the nation's gross domestic product (GDP) is devoted to health care, a figure that is projected to grow to 20% by the end of the decade, even with the implementation of many of the PPACA cost containment provisions (Keehan et al., 2012). At this level of national expenditure on health care, the United States will be unable make the other kinds of investments that are essential to global competitiveness. Three decades of incremental health care reform have demonstrated that such measures are insufficient to restrain health care inflation, thus making fundamental reforms in both health care delivery and financing inevitable.

The Impending Collapse of the Medicare Hospital Insurance Trust Fund

Even if the Medicare cost-saving provisions of the PPACA are fully implemented, the Medicare Hospital Insurance Trust Fund (Medicare Part A) is projected to become insolvent by the year 2024. It will collapse even sooner—perhaps as early as 2017—without successful implementation of the PPACA cost containment provisions (Medicare Board of Trustees, 2011). Despite political rhetoric to the contrary, the Medicare program cannot be fundamentally reformed to be more cost efficient in isolation from reforms that affect the health care system as a whole.

The Continued Devolvement of the Employment-Based Health Insurance System

Even if the PPACA's market reforms are fully implemented, they only serve to prop up a failed approach to the sustainable financing of health insurance coverage for millions of Americans, particularly disadvantaged minorities. To the extent that health insurance coverage remains tied to segmented and unstable labor markets, the least advantaged of workers and their families will find themselves without adequate health insurance coverage (Almgren, 2013). An ever-shrinking proportion of Americans will have access to adequate employment-based insurance coverage, and the uninsured will include an ever-larger share of the middle class (aka active voters). Neither major political party can ignore this reality, particularly the GOP.

The Growing Necessity of Universal Health Care Access to Global Competitiveness

The social work profession has embraced the moral arguments for universal health care as a fundamental societal obligation for many decades. Even countries with very dismal human rights records have elected to provide universal health care coverage as a strategy of economic development and global competitiveness. To the extent that the United States fails to make adequate investments in a healthy and productive labor force across all occupational categories, it undermines its prospects for sustaining a high standard of living in the context of a global economy. Findings from the World Economic Forum's *Global Competitiveness Report 2010–2011* underscore this point. The report documents the fact that the United States has been eclipsed in its competeveness ranking in past years by countries (such as Switzerland, Singapore, Finland, and Sweden) that provide universal health insurance coverage while at the same time committing only a fraction of their GDP to health care (World Economic Forum, 2011).

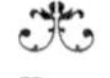

Pearls

- The Patient Protection and Affordable Care Act (P.L. 111–148), signed into law in March 2010, largely accomplishes universal health insurance coverage for all American citizens through a combination of regulatory insurance market reforms, insurance purchase mandates for individuals and employers, and expansions of public entitlement programs, primarily Medicaid.

- The primary policy goals of the PPACA are to (1) expand health insurance enrollment to over 90% of the nation's population, (2) increase health care quality, and (3) "bend the curve" of ever-rising health care costs, while at the same time leaving an extremely complex mixed private/public model of health care financing intact.
- The PPACA both invests in the development of innovative prevention programs and mandates complete health insurance coverage for an array of preventive health care services, including cancer screening. Thus, the PPACA is consistent with the policy goals of the social work profession and the priorities of social workers engaged in oncology practice.
- Although the road to full implementation of the PPACA is long and politically hazardous, there is a growing national consensus across the political spectrum that the PPACA is now the law of the land. The health care industry is rapidly adapting to that reality, with generally positive implications for the role of social workers in health care.

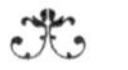

Pitfalls

- Although the PPACA represents the most significant expansion of the nation's health care safety net since the enactment of Medicare and Medicaid in 1965, it falls short of truly universal coverage for the U.S. population because it excludes coverage of undocumented immigrants. This exclusion is certain to negatively impact immigrant families and communities by excluding them from the safety-net hospitals and clinicians serving this population.
- The PPACA is consistent with the policy goals of the social work profession in that it seeks to expand Medicaid coverage to millions of currently uninsured. Because the option of expanded Medicaid is left to the discretion of individual states, however, the PPACA is unlikely to achieve near-universal health insurance coverage in more politically conservative states.
- The PPACA will expand health insurance coverage to millions of the uninsured through the Medicaid program. Unfortunately, the nationwide shortage of health care providers willing to accept Medicaid patients will ensure that health care access for poor and low-income individuals is likely to remain a policy challenge.

The future of the first federal legislation in history to extend health insurance coverage as a universal entitlement of citizenship is uncertain, but comprehensive health care reform that leads toward that end is all but dictated by both domestic and global economic realities. The voice of the social work profession in articulating the moral arguments for a national policy of universal health care that is both adequate and equitable remains more important than ever.

NOTES

1. When fully implemented, the PPACA is expected to achieve health insurance coverage for only 93% of the national population. This shortfall of health insurance coverage is largely due to the exclusion of undocumented immigrant workers and their dependents from health insurance coverage mandates and subsidies. The practice of excluding undocumented immigrants from universal health insurance coverage is a significant injustice but is common among progressive modern democracies that are credited for providing "universal health insurance coverage" to all *citizens*.
2. Interested readers are urged to read sociologist Jill Quadagno's incisive analysis of this paradox (2004).
3. This estimate of the health insurance coverage effects of the PPACA is taken from the Centers for Medicaid and Medicare Service (CMS) actuarial estimates provided to the U.S. Congress on April 22, 2010 (CMS, 2010), combined with U.S. Census projections for the U.S. population as of 2019 (U.S. Census, 2008), the point at which the PPACA will be fully implemented. Absent the PPACA, CMS estimates that by 2019, the number of uninsured would rise to 57 million—leaving 17% of the nation's population without health insurance.
4. Each of the seven health insurance market reforms has several crucial specifics. Readers who desire a more detailed summary of the PPACA are encouraged to consult the Kaiser Family Foundation's "Focus on Health Care Reform: Summary of New Health Reform Law," http://www.kff.org/healthreform/upload/8061.pdf
5. The requirement that insurance coverage be compulsory, through either employer mandates to provide coverage or individual mandates to purchase coverage, is essential to the viability of the elimination of the "preexisting condition" clauses from health insurance policies. Otherwise, many health care consumers would only carry or purchase health insurance when sick or desiring health care; in insurance vernacular, this is known as *moral hazard*. In addition, the compulsory enrollment of healthy persons in health insurance risk pools is essential to the affordability of health insurance to persons at high risk for illness and disability.
6. Accounting for U.S. Census population growth projections, there will be about 23 million uninsured after the PPACA reaches full implementation (CMS, 2010). The 21 million figure cited here holds the U.S. population at its 2010 level to better illustrate the net effects of the PPACA on the size of the uninsured population.
7. A more detailed summary of the PPACA on the coverage expansion specifics is available from the Kaiser Family Foundation's "Focus on Health Care Reform: Summary of New Health Reform Law," http://www.kff.org/healthreform/upload/8061.pdf
8. One crucial component of the PPACA's health care delivery reform provisions is the development of accountable care

organizations—in essence, organizations composed of doctors, hospitals, and other providers representing the full continuum of care for chronic illness that are rewarded financially for integrated and cost-efficient care.

9. The three cases that involved these issues were *National Federation of Independent Business v. Sebelius, No. 11-393, U.S. Department of Health and Human Services v. Florida, No. 11-398,* and *Florida v. Department of Health and Human Services, No. 11-400* (Vincini, 2012).

REFERENCES

Almgren, G. (2013). *Health care politics, policy, and services: A social justice analysis* (2nd rev. ed.). New York, NY: Springer Publishing Company.

Bartolini, E. (2013). Accountable care organizations and innovation: A changing landscape [Web log post]. Health Affairs Blog. Retrieved from http://healthaffairs.org/blog/2013/06/28/accountable-care-organizations-and-innovation-a-changing-landscape

Centers for Medicare & Medicaid Services (CMS). (2010). Estimated financial effects of the Patient Protection and Affordable Care Act. Office of the Actuary. Retrieved from https://www.cms.gov/ActuarialStudies/downloads/PPACA_2010-04-22.pdf

Government Accountability Office. (2013, June 19). Patient Protection and Affordable Care Act: Status of CMS efforts to establish federally facilitated health insurance exchanges. GAO-13-601. Retrieved from http://www.gao.gov/products/GAO-13-601

Institute of Medicine (IOM). (2000). *Crossing the quality chasm: A new health system for the 21st century.* Washington, DC: National Academies Press.

Kaiser Family Foundation. (2013a). Status of state action on the Medicaid expansion decision, as of July 1, 2013. State Health Facts. Retrieved from http://kff.org/medicaid/state-indicator/state-activity-around-expanding-medicaid-under-the-affordable-care-act/

Kaiser Family Foundation. (2013b). ACO "pioneers" feeling skittish about next stage of implementation. Kaiser Health News. Retrieved from http://www.kaiserhealthnews.org/daily-reports/2013/march/08/accountable-care-organizations.aspx

Keehan, S., Cuckler, S., Sisko, A., Madison, A., Smith, S., Lizonitz, J., . . . Wolfe, C. (2012). National health expenditure projections: Modest annual growth until coverage expands and economic growth accelerates. *Health Affairs, 31*(7), 1–13.

Medicare Board of Trustees. (2011). *2011 annual report of the Board of Trustees of the Federal Hospital Insurance and Federal Supplementary Medical Insurance Trust Funds.* Retrieved from https://www.cms.gov/ReportsTrustFunds/downloads/tr2011.pdf

Monegain, B. (2013). Insurance exchanges running late. Healthcare IT News. Retrieved from http://www.healthcareit-news.com/news/insurance-exchanges-run-late

Quadagno, J. (2004). Why the United States has no national health insurance: Stakeholder mobilization against the welfare state, 1945–1996. *Journal of Health and Social Behavior, 45*(Extra Issue), 25–44.

Roberts, J. (2010, June 24). Poll: The politics of health care. CBS News: Opinion. Retrieved from http://www.cbsnews.com/news/poll-the-politics-of-health-care/

Spoerl, B. (2013). 10 considerations for hospitals in the aftermath of Supreme Court's PPACA decision. Becker's Hospital Review. Retrieved from http://www.beckershospitalreview.com/news-analysis/10-considerations-for-hospitals-in-the-aftermath-of-supreme-courts-ppaca-decision.html

U.S. Census. (2008). Projections of the population and components of change for the United States: 2010 to 2050. Retrieved from http://www.census.gov/population/www/projections/summarytables.html

Vincini, J. (2012, March 14). U.S. healthcare legal issues at Supreme Court. Reuters News Service. Retrieved from http://www.reuters.com/article/2012/03/14/us-healthcare-court-idUSBRE82D11N20120314

Wendt, C. (2009). Mapping European healthcare systems: A comparative analysis of financing, service provision, and access to healthcare. *Journal of European Social Policy, 19*(5), 432–445.

World Economic Forum. (2011). *The global competitiveness report 2010–2011.* Retrieved from http://www3.weforum.org/docs/WEF_GCR_Report_2011-12.pdf

85

Gary L. Stein and Jeanne Kerwin

Bioethical Issues in Oncology and the Social Work Response

A bioethics that fails to recognize and respond to the experience of illness will have limited value for patients and their families.

—*Dresser (2011, p. 11)*

Key Concepts

- *The interdisciplinary field of bioethics provides overarching principles for analyzing difficult ethical dilemmas occurring in the care of patients with cancer and other serious medical conditions.*
- *The consensus to empower cancer patients and their surrogates to make important medical decisions is one of the great achievements in health care and bioethics.*
- *Social workers who participate in oncological or palliative care teams or institutional ethics committees bring their expertise in psychosocial concerns and skills in facilitating communication and mediating disagreements among patients, families, and other team members.*
- *Social workers act as liaisons among the patients/families, treating physicians, and cancer patient services.*
- *A central social work role is to communicate patient requests to treating physicians. Such requests involve specific medical questions, including prognosis; expected outcomes of treatment options; expected risks, harms, and benefits of treatments; and informed recommendations.*
- *When difficult ethical issues arise in patient or family care, social workers should be able to identify them and initiate a reasoned process for resolution.*
- *Social workers require formal training on the recognized core competencies of bioethics during their graduate work and ongoing professional education in order to be active participants and leaders on ethics committees.*

Overview of Ethical Principles

Health care and oncology social workers encounter complex ethical issues in their practices. These include assisting in patient and surrogate decision making, contributing psychosocial assessments and capacity determinations, supporting patients and families during disclosure of medical information and bad news, helping with decisions among curative and palliative approaches, clarifying advance directives, respecting diverse cultural and family values, offering financially feasible options, and protecting vulnerable individuals from potential harms. When analyzing and resolving these issues, social workers practice as an integral part of a multidisciplinary team, whether as participants on oncological or palliative care teams, or as members of their institutional ethics committees. Regardless of the setting, social workers bring their expertise in psychosocial concerns and skill in facilitating communication and mediating disagreements among patients, families, and other team members.

There is a professional consensus that four principles support most ethical analyses around clinical practice and research (Beauchamp & Childress, 2009). Foremost is the principle of respecting patient autonomy, which includes providing patients who have decisional capacity with sufficient medical information—that is, their diagnosis, prognosis, and options for care, including their benefits and burdens—to make informed choices if they so desire. Arthur Caplan (2008, p. 1801) reminds us, "Knowledge of one's diagnosis and prognosis are so routine today that it is easy to forget that empowering those patients who wish to know about both represents a major change in the norms of cancer care from the 1950s to the present day." A key component to respecting autonomy is recognizing the patient's legal and ethical right to meaningful informed consent, including the choice to accept or refuse care. The National Association of Social Workers' (NASW, 2008) Code of Ethics reinforces social work's strong commitment to client self-determination and informed consent.

The next two ethical concepts—beneficence and nonmaleficence—require health care professionals to advance their patients' best interests. Beneficence represents a "moral obligation to act for the benefit of others" to further their well-being (Beauchamp & Childress, 2009, p. 197) or, in other words, "to provide the best care for the patient and balance the risks or burdens of care against the benefits" (Post, Blustein, & Dubler, 2007, p. 16). To further protect patients' interests, the concept of nonmaleficence requires professionals to avoid harming their patients, meaning that although most cancer interventions involve some degree of risk, the "benefits of recommended treatments are expected to outweigh the possible harms" (Post et al., 2007, p. 17).

Members of the health care team face competing ethical values, interests, and obligations. Acting to maximize patient benefits and minimize harm underlies the concept of paternalism, in which health professionals override the known or assumed preferences of their patients with the intent of benefiting them or avoiding harm (Beauchamp & Childress, 2009). Ethical perspectives, supported by statutes and case law, support a consumerist model of patient autonomy and self-determination commonly known as shared decision making. Under the new model, "patients would have more control over their treatment. Physicians would continue to apply their special training and experience to determine patients' treatment options, but patients would decide which option they preferred" (Dresser, 2012, p. 60). This tension between paternalism and autonomy underlies many ethical dilemmas in cancer care. For example, physicians who are concerned about causing harm must promote patients' autonomy through informed consent with full disclosure of bad news. They must also deal with requests by family members to withhold information from patients based on cultural and familial practices (Cherny, 2012).

Caplan (2008, p. 1802) argues that the "fight to empower dying cancer patients produced a consensus regarding end-of-life care," which is one of the great achievements in health care and bioethics during the past 60 years. In keeping with the ethical principles of autonomy, the dignity of persons, and legal privacy rights (Cruzan v. Director, Missouri Department of Health, 1990), individuals who have capacity to make decisions, or who once had decisional capacity, have an "absolute right . . . to control their medical care" (Caplan, 2008, p. 1802). Therefore, patients with decisional capacity have the right to consent to or refuse care, including life-sustaining interventions. In addition, they have the right to document their preferences for care should they become incapacitated and to appoint others to make decisions on their behalf if they cannot. Even if patients have not formally documented their wishes, family members can generally be relied upon to make decisions for them using established ethical and legal standards for surrogate decision making (Beauchamp & Childress, 2009; Berlinger, Jennings, & Wolf, 2013).

Dresser (2012) uses her professional and personal experiences with cancer as the basis for revisiting how clinicians implement shared decision making. She states, "Patient autonomy can be a challenging business. Even the most educated and savvy patients facing serious medical decisions may not be very good at applying their values and preferences to this new kind of choice" (p. 66). Brock and Wartman (1990) describe three forms of "irrational" thinking that can influence patient decisions to refuse burdensome care: giving inadequate consideration to future, more serious harms; denial, or refusing to recognize the risks presented by their condition; and overwhelming fear of pain, suffering, or other dreaded medically related experiences. A more refined approach to autonomy calls upon clinicians to describe in greater detail how patients in similar situations coped with alternative interventions. Furthermore, when patients' choices appear irrational and fail to advance their well-being, clinicians should seek to understand these choices, help patients overcome their fears, and press further to change that choice through "frank conversation and strong persuasion to giv[e] shared decision-making real meaning" (Dresser, 2012, p. 68).

The fourth ethical principle supports distributive justice or equity—a fair, equitable, and appropriate distribution of societal benefits and the concomitant responsibilities of its citizens (Beauchamp & Childress, 2009). The justice principle seeks to ensure fairness in access to care and services. In cancer care, distributive justice is most applicable in determinations of who has access to expensive, innovative, and scarce treatments, as well as which communities should assume the burdens and benefits of clinical research.

Critical Role of Communication

As advances in medical technologies and treatments contribute to the complexity of decision making, the role of ongoing and consistent communications with patients and families about diagnosis, prognosis, treatment options, expected outcomes, and individual values and preferences has become an increasingly important. We should elevate the importance of the oncology social worker as the facilitator of good communications among the care team members as we consider the changes in the doctor–patient/family relationship brought about by changes in the health care system, the consensus around ethical principles, the often-fragmented delivery of care, and the increasing attention to religious and cultural beliefs.

The traditional role of the health care social worker is to support the emotional needs of patients and families and facilitate an appropriate care plan that meets their medical and social service needs. What additional ethical issues do social workers face in oncology care? Ethical issues arise when two or more relevant but competing values are in conflict. Thus, patients and their families may introduce issues that conflict with the beliefs or preferences of the care team. Ethical issues that arise in oncology care today include requests for physician-assisted suicide, voluntary cessation of eating and drinking, increased medications to hasten death, discontinuation of life-supporting treatments, withholding of artificial feeding (and accompanying religious concerns), withholding of a cancer diagnosis from a patient (at the family's request), experimental treatments, and many of the ethical issues driven by conflicts among family members and patients (Cherny, 2012; Miller et al., 2004). Because social workers are grappling with the magnitude of contemporary ethical challenges in health care, it is critically important for them to use a reasoned reflective approach to identify these ethical dilemmas (Csikai & Sales, 1998).

Good communication starts with listening to all parties. The communication skills of an oncology social worker enhance the discussions among the care team and also serve to ferret out ethical questions early in the patient's disease trajectory, before the barriers to resolution become more difficult. Social workers trained in the basics of ethical analysis and principled reasoning can help patients and their families sort through an enormous amount of information and their questions (Stein & Kerwin, 2011). Most important, the social worker can act as a liaison between the patient/family and the treating physician, as well as other services that are often available to cancer patients, such as nurse navigators, palliative care teams, support groups, and home care and hospice agencies (Beder, 2006). When difficult ethical issues arise in the care of a cancer patient or with the patient's family, social workers should be able to identify the issue and initiate a reasoned process for resolution. The social worker is aware that emotions can affect professional caregivers, as well as patients and their families, and this knowledge allows the social worker to facilitate a reflective and rational process of working through the issues and developing a resolution that represents the patient's best interests and considers the needs of all parties involved.

Resolving Dilemmas Through Ethics Committees

Most hospitals in the United States actively seek to resolve ethical dilemmas through their ethics committees—interdisciplinary bodies that assume a primary role in reviewing difficult cases, educating staff, and formulating hospital policy (Post et al., 2007). The American Society for Bioethics and Humanities (ASBH, 2011) defines health care ethics consultations as services "in response to questions from patients, families, surrogates, healthcare professionals, or other involved parties who seek to resolve uncertainty or conflict regarding value- laden concerns that emerge in health care" (p. 2). Ethics committees most commonly analyze dilemmas that surface at the bedside of seriously ill and dying patients. These include questions about whether patients have the capacity to make difficult medical decisions, family or physician interpretations of patients' wishes contained in advance directives, disagreement among family members as to the best treatment plan, whether to withhold bad diagnostic or prognostic news from patients, family demands for care that is characterized by the team as futile, and cultural practices and rituals. These situations are publicly illustrated through high-profile legal cases, such as those involving Karen Ann Quinlan, Claire Conroy, Nancy Beth Cruzan, and Terri Schiavo, but most ethics consults are routinely resolved within hospitals and nursing homes, away from the drama and attention of courtrooms, interest groups, and the media.

The ASBH (2011) recommends that ethics committees employ an ethics facilitation approach, in which the ethics consultant "helps to elucidate issues, aid effective communication, and integrate the perspectives of the relevant stakeholders. The consultant helps the relevant decision makers fashion a plan that respects the needs and values of those involved, and that is within the bounds of legal and ethical standards" (p. 7). Effective ethics consultation requires sets of skills and knowledge. The ASBH suggests four categories of beneficial skills in its core competencies for ethics consultation: (1) ethical assessment skills, (2) process skills, (3) interpersonal skills, and (4) the skills needed to run the consultation service. In addition, it suggests nine knowledge areas for ethics consults, including ethical theory; bioethical issues and concepts; the clinical context, beliefs, and perspectives of the patient and staff population; codes of ethics; and health care law (NASW, 2004, 2008). Policy statements also advocate the integration of bioethical principles into professional practice, especially regarding palliative and end-of-life care.

Social workers have great potential to affect the ethics arena. Many social work skills overlap with the ASBH's core competencies, including the abilities to facilitate meetings and discussions, listen empathically, encourage effective and respectful communication among parties, and mediate consensus. However, the little existing research on social worker participation on ethics committees finds that most social workers have had little or no formal training in health care ethics, despite the complex dilemmas they encounter (Csikai, 2004; Csikai & Bass, 2000; Manetta & Wells, 2001). If social workers are to be active participants and leaders on ethics committees, they will require formal training on ASBH core competencies, especially the knowledge components, during their master's programs and ongoing professional education (Stein & Kerwin, 2011).

Larry was a 58-year-old man with an intellectual disability who had lived in a group home for 15 years. The state appointed a legal guardian after Larry's elderly mother could no longer manage his care. Larry's mother and older brother, Hank, remained very involved in Larry's life. Larry was able to verbalize simple things when he wanted something, was displeased, or was frightened. He had friends at the group home and enjoyed watching his favorite TV shows and eating ice cream.

After Larry experienced stomach pain and loss of appetite, he was admitted to the hospital and diagnosed with Stage 4 colon cancer with metastases to his liver. The oncologist informed the guardian and Larry's family that his life expectancy, with or without treatment, was probably less than 6 months, but that he could begin chemotherapy in an attempt to extend his life. Larry did not have the capacity to understand that he had cancer and that he would die. His stomach pain was managed well with pain medications started in the hospital, but Larry was unhappy and wanted to go "home." Larry's mother was vehemently opposed to any chemotherapy or life-prolonging treatment for Larry. She felt that Larry would not understand the need to suffer through treatments and that it would diminish his quality of life significantly. Hank was concerned about Larry's diminished intake of nourishment and felt strongly that his religious teachings dictated that Larry be provided with tube feedings so he would not "starve to death." Larry's legally appointed guardian was uncomfortable denying Larry any treatment that might prolong his life, even by months, because it was his legal responsibility to see that Larry was given "every chance" to extend his life.

The social worker met with Larry, his mother, and his brother every day of the hospitalization. She listened to their differing perspectives and concerns. She also spoke with the guardian on one of his visits and understood his responsibility to act as Larry's advocate and legal decision maker. The doctors were anxious for a decision to be made about Larry's care. The social worker called for an ethics consultation to find a resolution to the conflicting views about the appropriate care plan for Larry.

The meeting was held with all the stakeholders in Larry's care, including Larry, his mother, his brother, the chaplain on the case, the legal guardian, the oncologist, Larry's group home leader, a representative from the state disabilities office, and two ethics consultants. The social worker was also a member of the ethics committee and facilitated the discussions at the meeting.

Everyone had an opportunity to share his or her views and the oncologist summarized Larry's medical situation. Larry's preferences remained at the center of the discussions. Although he was not able to verbally articulate his wishes, he had made his likes and dislikes known over many years. It became clear to all that being in his group home among his friends, watching TV, and eating ice cream were most important to his quality of life. The burdens of chemotherapy far outweighed any medical benefit to Larry and, in fact, would create suffering and unhappiness for him. Hank's religious concerns were appropriately addressed by the chaplain, who was able to assure him that a comfort care plan without tube feeding was in keeping with the doctrine of his church and was in Larry's best interest. Last, the social, financial, and institutional issues impacting Larry's care plan needed to be discussed. The social worker's knowledge and experience in the health care system were critical to the successful outcome of this ethics consultation. Hospice was able to care for Larry in his group home and the state provided extra funding for a home health aide. Hospice provided education for the group home staff. In addition, Larry's family and the guardian were involved in developing a care plan that focused on Larry's comfort and quality of life, as measured by him. The successful resolution of the ethical issues involved in Larry's care was a direct result of the social worker's ability to identify the issues early in the case, and to initiate and participate in the ethics consultation with all involved parties.

Decision Making in Cancer Care

Social workers may be asked to explain medical information or expected prognoses because they address the emotional responses of the patient to a new cancer diagnosis or progression of disease toward the end of life. Decisions about treatment choices may be overwhelming for the patient and family, who need honest and complete information in order to make the best choices in their particular situations. The social worker may also encounter ethical issues surrounding end-of-life care decisions that the patient or family may need to make. These issues often stay beneath the surface until a medical crisis occurs, forcing the patient and family into the stressful situation of making decisions that were not previously discussed.

The preeminent role of autonomy in decision making often places an extraordinary burden on the patient to sort through complex medical information and treatment options while suffering from shock and grief after a new diagnosis, or when facing a worsening condition when the disease progresses despite treatment (Dresser, 2012). The opportunities for the social worker to ask about and listen to the emotional responses from the patient and family during the course of the illness often reveal critical questions—"What should I do?"; "Which treatment is best for me?"; Will I die from this disease?"; "When will I die?"—and other medical, psychosocial, and existential concerns. Patients who are balancing decisions between treatments that may extend life and palliative care plans that will enhance quality of life deserve a response to those questions based upon clinical evidence, medical expertise, ethical principles, and understanding of the individual's values and preferences. The oncology social worker's central role is to communicate with the treating physicians and request that they address the patient's specific medical questions about prognosis, expected outcomes of treatment options, risks and harms of treatments, expected benefits, and recommendations for the patient based upon experience and knowledge.

Another way to assist patients and families with medical choices is to help the patient or family craft questions for the physician in a way that will assist in their decision making. For example, the social worker might help the patient construct a question about prognosis: "Doctor, in your experience with patients who are at a similar disease stage, what might I expect in terms of outcome after treatment X? What might I expect in terms of outcome if I do not take treatment X?" Or "Doctor, how will treatment X affect my quality of life and the things I enjoy, and how will those things be affected if I don't take treatment X?" Patients and their families often do not know how to phrase questions about these important aspects of their decision making. Questions that allow the physicians to speak in general terms about the prognosis of a certain stage of disease or the side effects of a particular treatment make it easier for them to give honest and helpful information to the patient.

Studies have shown that one-fifth of Medicare patients with metastatic cancer started a new chemotherapy regimen within 2 weeks of death, and that hospice and palliative care for patients with cancer are often initiated in the last few days of life (Earle et al., 2004). A patient's hope is often given as the reason to continue treatments in the face of futility. However, unrealistic expectations because of failure to disclose the expected trajectory of the disease robs patients and families of the ability to make realistic choices that better fit their life values (Gwande, 2010). Dr. Neil Wenger of the UCLA Health System Ethics Center states that a "cascade of aggressive care . . . starts when the physician does not discuss a realistic prognosis with the patient or does not anticipate the trajectory of the patient's decline" (Wilson, 2009, p. 573). The result may be aggressive, ineffective care that promotes physical, psychological, and spiritual suffering. Oncology social workers can facilitate discussion of those choices long before the cascade begins. For example, palliative care teams often ask the question, "What is most important to you?" The answer helps illuminate the patient's desire to be at home, surrounded by family, and not in pain. A decision to enter hospice at that point then becomes easier and less fraught with doubt and hopelessness.

Advance Care Planning

Advance care planning for serious and life-limiting illness is an important mechanism for promoting and communicating one's preferences, values, and interests before one lacks capacity for making medical decisions. Planning with formal directives has evolved during the past three-and-a-half decades, primarily in response to medical interventions that allow for artificial respiration, nutrition, and hydration, where it "often became difficult to distinguish saving life from prolonging suffering and death" (Sabatino, 2010, p. 213). Landmark court cases, such as the 1976 New Jersey case involving Karen Ann Quinlan, the 1990 U.S. Supreme Court case of Nancy Beth Cruzan, and the protracted litigation concerning Terri Schiavo, highlight the value of declaring one's preferences regarding life-sustaining care before times of diminished capacity (*Cruzan v. Director, Missouri Department of Health*, 1990; Eisenberg, 2005; *In re Quinlan*, 1976).

In response to the Quinlan case, living wills have been recommended to allow patients to document their wishes regarding life-sustaining interventions in the event of a terminal condition or permanent unconsciousness. Although these documents were intended to permit expression of all choices regarding life-sustaining care, they have most commonly been used to facilitate withholding or withdrawal of care, such as artificial nutrition and hydration, breathing machines, and antibiotics. Because of the limited range of decisions encompassed by living wills, durable powers of attorney for health care (or health care proxy) statutes were developed to allow individuals to appoint a trusted individual, usually a family member or friend, to make decisions on their behalf during times of incapacity. By 1997, every state had laws permitting individuals to designate a health care proxy (Sabatino, 2010). Moreover, in 1990, the federal Patient Self-Determination Act required health care facilities receiving funds, including hospitals and nursing homes, to inform patients of their rights to execute advance directives and obtain assistance in doing so (Patient Self-Determination Act, 1990). Tulsky (2005) promotes the importance of communication among patients, family members, and the health care team as a more critical component of advance care planning than just document completion.

Advance directives have been criticized as being ineffective, primarily because so few Americans execute them. For example, a 2006 survey conducted by the Pew Research Center for the People and the Press found that 29% of respondents had completed living wills (Pew Research Center, 2006). In addition to relatively low completion rates, commentators emphasize people's inability to make thoughtful end-of-life decisions in advance, when the causes of serious illness may be unknown, and the failure of living wills "to increase the accuracy with which surrogates identify patients' preferences" (Fagerlin & Schneider, 2004, p. 38). Therefore, powers of attorney are often supported over living wills as being more simple and direct, because they "probably improve decisions for patients, since surrogates know more at the time of the decision than patients can know in advance" (Fagerlin & Schneider, 2004, p. 39; Lynn, 1991).

Formal directives present important benefits despite the challenges. Supporters of advance care planning maintain that completion rates can be dramatically improved by coordinated and intense outreach. For example, researchers from the Respecting Choices program in La Crosse County, Wisconsin, developed an advance care planning "microsystem" that organized all health care providers in the county to standardize patient education materials and documents, as well as medical records policies (Hammes, Rooney, & Gundrum, 2010). This intensive approach resulted in 90% of patients completing advance directives, an extraordinarily high rate. Other researchers have documented that use of advance directives greatly increased the likelihood that end-of-life preferences were known and followed (Detering, Hancock, Reade, & Silvester, 2010; Silveira, Kim, & Langa,

2010). In addition, most elderly patients who requested comfort care received it (Silveira et al., 2010). End-of-life discussions with physicians decreased costs of care during the last week of life by decreasing ventilator use and intensive care unit admissions and through earlier referrals to hospice (Zhang et al., 2009). This benefit is most important for discussions involving health care reform and cost control.

The Physician Orders for Life-Sustaining Treatment (POLST) paradigm represents an innovative approach to increase advance care planning and ensure that patients' desires are clearly accessible in patient charts across settings of care. These physician orders were initially developed in Oregon in 1991, and incorporate patients' current wishes on life-sustaining treatments and resuscitation. Unlike advance directives, they are designed for present, rather than future, care and are intended for patients who have limited life expectancy. POLST requires active communication between the patient or surrogate and physician to be effective. This communication ensures that the document reflects the patient's current wishes; that these wishes are incorporated into doctors' orders using a unique, brightly colored form that is kept at the front of the medical record; and that the POLST forms travel with the patient to guarantee continuity of care (Sabatino, 2010). Fifteen states have enacted laws or regulations supporting POLST use, and an additional 28 states are developing programs (*New York Times* Editorial Board, 2012). The National POLST Paradigm Task Force provides a range of Internet-based resources for states and coalitions interested in replicating this model (National POLST Paradigm Task Force, 2012).

Religious, Spiritual, and Cultural Issues

Religious, spiritual, and cultural issues are frequent components of difficult decisions for oncology patients and their families (Cherny, 2012; Koenig & Gates-Williams, 1995). Ira Byock (2012, p. 291) states, "Spirituality is rightly considered the province of religion, but it is not an exclusive province. Accompanying people who are dying has taught me that human life is inherently spiritual, whether or not a person practices a religion." However, health care professionals have occasionally avoided the religious aspects of the human response to illness, fears, and existential concerns. These areas of human response to illness often play a key role in decision making and should be acknowledged, supported, and understood as part of clinical practice. Integrating the exploration and understanding of these aspects of belief require the oncology social worker to develop understanding and sensitivity to the spiritual dimension of each patient. "Clients' use of spirituality as a weapon in their coping arsenal is precisely why spirituality must be acknowledged. Strengthening clients' abilities to develop viable strategies to both meet basic needs and maintain mental health is a social work goal" (Sermabeikian, 1994, p. 178).

Whether regarded as religious doctrine, cultural tradition, or a spiritual dimension of patients' beliefs, these perspectives need to be acknowledged and woven into the decision-making process. The increasingly large proportion of U.S. ethnic minorities presents a challenge for oncology social workers to learn how these cultural, religious, and spiritual factors influence patients' responses to illness, suffering, healing, and dying. In addition, professionals need to be aware of their own values and beliefs, which may differ from those of their patients. Reflecting on one's own beliefs and practices prepares us to listen to and understand the beliefs of our patients. Asking patients to talk more about their beliefs so that we might better understand their needs serves two purposes: It enables us to understand and appreciate their beliefs in more depth, and, more important, it offers validation and support to the patient who is relying on his or her beliefs for strength and hope in the face of terminal illness. Building mutual respect and trust with our patients has an enormously positive impact on decision making for oncology patients near the end of life.

Cultural and religious/spiritual beliefs of patients and their families influence medical decision making in some of the following ways (Cherny, 2012; Lapineet al., 2001):

- Families may insist that all diagnostic and prognostic information be given to the family and not to the patient. The adult child of an elderly patient may say, "Do not tell mom that she has cancer." This contrasts with the ethical principle to respect the patient's autonomy and give the patient the opportunity for self-determination.
- Patients and families may believe that the provision of nutrition and hydration, even if given artificially through a tube, is required by their religious doctrine and that "starving the patient" would be considered a sin.
- Patients and families sometimes refuse pain medication in the belief that "suffering" is part of God's plan and that some salvation is achieved through that suffering.
- Patients and families may hold a rigid adherence to the belief that prayer will result in a "miracle" and heal the cancer. This may be difficult for professionals to understand when the medical evidence strongly indicates that the patient's disease will result in an expected death.
- Patients and families may refuse to "hear" anything but positive news, due to beliefs that discussion of poor prognosis or disease progression represents negative thoughts that will influence the patient's outcome.
- Patients and families may hold on to a belief in the power of prayer and wait for that power to heal, despite medical evidence to the contrary.

These and other beliefs bring about ethical conflicts between evidence-based scientific medical information and the psychological and spiritual domains. Social workers can use their communication and conflict resolution skills to facilitate and guide discussions toward a care plan that meets the patient's medical, psychosocial, and spiritual needs.

Pearls

- A clear understanding of ethical principles enables social work staff to clarify and discern issues involving cancer patients and their families.
- To strengthen communication among the care team, patient, and family, elevate the role of the oncology social worker as a facilitator.
- Utilization of hospital ethics committees and ethics consultation services to help resolve value-laden conflicts among patients, families, and caregivers can be an integral part of oncology social work.
- Understanding the emotional and psychological state of the patient and family throughout the illness is critical to social work's ability to support and guide difficult decision making when it is needed.
- Utilize the tools of advance care planning to assist patients in documenting their values, goals, and preferences for medical treatment.
- Awareness and acknowledgment of the spiritual, religious, and cultural values of an individual contribute to the overall success of a care plan that meets the patient's physical, spiritual, and cultural needs.

Pitfalls

- Training in the principles of medical ethics and participation in hospital ethics committees are often lacking for health care social workers, even though they frequently face the ethical issues that challenge patients and families.
- As a "communicator," the oncology social worker needs consistent and constant contact with the medical team in order to understand the medical decisions that need to be made and to appropriately support the patient and family. In today's often fragmented and complex medical environment, this remains a challenge for the social worker.
- Each state has slightly different laws, policies, and procedures for the creation of advance directives, Do-Not-Resuscitate Orders (DNR), and/or Physician Orders for Life-Sustaining Treatments (POLST). Social workers need to have complete information about the laws, policies, and procedures for such documents in order to assist patients and their families with advance care planning.

The interdisciplinary field of bioethics has provided overarching principles for analyzing difficult ethical dilemmas that occur in the care of patients with cancer and other serious medical conditions. Bioethical principles have helped patients, families and surrogates, and health care professionals address the most challenging situations near the end of life, such as how to best discuss bad news, who can make critical decisions and how, and under what conditions the affected parties could forgo life-sustaining treatments. As health care reform advances in the United States, the justice principle will aid providers and policy makers in determining access to costly, innovative, life-extending treatments. The field has used ethics committees and case consultations to develop a process and forums for professional education, conflict resolution for difficult cases, and policy development for institutional change. Social workers, who focus on family systems, effective communication, and problem solving, are an integral part of hospital and hospice ethics deliberations. The social work profession should promote this role through enhanced professional training and education and leadership development for interdisciplinary team practice.

Dresser (2011) suggests:

> *What's too often missing from bioethics is appreciation of the psychological and social context of illness.... Fear, guilt, isolation, fatigue, and despair populate the world of serious illness.... A bioethics that fails to recognize and respond to the experience of illness will have limited value for patients and their families. (p. 18)*

Social workers thoughtfully bring to the bioethics table these very psychosocial perspectives—the experiences of patients, families, and caregivers responding to the challenges of serious illness.

REFERENCES

American Society for Bioethics and Humanities. (2011). *Core competencies for healthcare ethics consultation* (2nd ed.). Glenview, IL: Author.

Beauchamp, T. L., & Childress, J. F. (2009). *Principles of biomedical ethics* (6th ed.). New York, NY: Oxford University Press.

Beder, J. (2006). *Hospital social work: The interface of medicine and caring*. New York, NY: Routledge.

Berlinger, N., Jennings, B., & Wolf, S. M. (2013). *The Hastings Center Guidelines for decisions on life-sustaining treatment and care near the end of life* (2nd ed.). New York, NY: Oxford University Press.

Brock, D. W., & Wartman, S. A. (1990). When competent patients make irrational choices. *New England Journal of Medicine*, 322(22), 1595–1599.

Byock, I. (2012). *The best care possible: A physician's quest to transform care through the end of life*. New York, NY: Avery.

Caplan, A. L. (2008). Cancer and bioethics: Caring and consensus. *Cancer, 113*(7 Suppl.), 1801–1806.

Cherny, N. (2012). Controversies in oncologist-patient communication: A nuanced approach to autonomy, culture, and paternalism. *Oncology, 26*(1), 37–46.

Cruzan v. Director, Missouri Department of Health, 497 U.S. 261 (1990).

Csikai, E., & Sales, E. (1998). The emerging social work role on hospital ethics committees: A comparison of social worker and chair perspectives. *Social Work,43*(3), 233–242.

Csikai, E. L. (2004). Social workers' participation in the resolution of ethical dilemmas in hospice care. *Health and Social Work, 29*(1), 67–76.

Csikai, E. L., & Bass, K. (2000). Health care social workers' views of ethical issues, practice, and policy in end-of-life care. *Social Work and Health Care, 32*(2), 1–22.

Detering, K. M., Hancock, A. D., Reade, M. C., & Silvester, W. (2010). The impact of advance care planning on end of life care in elderly patients: Randomized controlled trial. *British Medical Journal, 340*, c1345.

Dresser, R. (2011). Bioethics and cancer: When the professional becomes personal. *Hastings Center Report,41*(6), 14–18.

Dresser, R. (2012). *Malignant: Medical ethicists confront cancer.* New York, NY: Oxford University Press.

Earle, C. C., Neville, B. A., Landrum, M. B., Ayanian, J. Z., Block, S. D., & Weeks, J. C. (2004). Trends in the aggressiveness of cancer care near the end of life. *Journal of Clinical Oncology,22*(2), 315–321.

Eisenberg, D. (2005, April 4). Lessons of the Schiavo battle: What the bitter fight over a woman's right to live or die tells us about politics, religion, the courts, and life itself. *Time*, 22–30.

Fagerlin, A., & Schneider, C. E. (2004). Enough: The failure of the living will. *Hastings Center Report, 34*(2), 30–42.

Gwande, A. (2010). Letting go. *New Yorker, 86*(22), 36.

Hammes, B. J., Rooney, B. L., & Gundrum, J. D. (2010). A comparative, retrospective, observational study of the prevalence, availability, and specificity of advance care plans in a county that implemented an advance care planning microsystem. *Journal of the American Geriatrics Society, 58*(7), 1249–1255.

In re Quinlan, 355 A.2d 647 (NJ 1976).

Koenig, B., & Gates-Williams, J. (1995). Understanding cultural difference in caring for dying patients. *Western Journal of Medicine, 163*(3), 244–249.

Lapine, A., Wang-Cheng, R., Goldstein, M., Nooney, A., Lamb, G., & Derse, A. R. (2001). When cultures clash: Physician, patient, and family wishes in truth disclosure for dying patients. *Journal of Palliative Medicine, 4*(4), 475–480.

Lynn, J. (1991). Why I don't have a living will. *Medicine and Health Care, 19*(1–2), 101–104.

Manetta, A., & Wells, J. G. (2001). Ethical issues in the social worker's role in physician-assisted suicide. *Health and Social Work, 26*(3), 160–166.

Miller, L. L., Harvath, T. A., Ganzini, L., Goy, E. R., Delorit, M. A., & Jackson, A. (2004). Attitudes and experiences of Oregon hospice nurses and social workers regarding assisted suicide. *Palliative Medicine, 18*(8), 685–691.

National Association of Social Workers (NASW). (2004). *NASW standards for palliative and end of life care.* Washington, DC: NASW Press.

National Association of Social Workers (NASW). (2008). *Code of ethics of the National Association of Social Workers.*Washington, DC: NASW Press.

National POLST Paradigm Task Force. (2012). About the national POLST paradigm. Retrieved from http://www.polst.org/about-the-national-polst-paradigm/

New York Times Editorial Board (2012, November 24). Care at the end of life. Retrieved from http://www.nytimes.com/2012/11/25/opinion/sunday/end-of-life-health-care.html

Patient Self-Determination Act of 1990. 42 U.S.C. §1395cc(a) (1990).

Pew Research Center. (2006). *More Americans discussing—and planning—end of life treatment: Strong public support for right to die.* Washington, DC: Author. Retrieved from http://www.people-press.org/2006/01/05/strong-public-support-for-right-to-die/

Post, L. F., Blustein, J., & Dubler, N. N. (2007). *Handbook for health care ethics committees.* Baltimore, MD: Johns Hopkins University Press.

Sabatino, C. P. (2010). The evolution of health care advance planning law and policy. *Milbank Quarterly, 88*(2), 211–239.

Sermabeikian, P. (1994). Our clients, ourselves: The spiritual perspective and social work practice. *Social Work, 39*(2), 178–183.

Silveira, M. J., Kim, S. Y. H., & Langa, K. M. (2010). Advance directives and outcomes of surrogate decision making before death. *New England Journal of Medicine, 362*(13), 1211–1218.

Stein, G. L., & Kerwin, J. (2011). Social work and bioethics: Enhanced resolution of ethical dilemmas and the challenges along the way. In T. Altilio & S. Otis-Green (Eds.), *Oxford textbook of palliative social work* (pp. 503–507). New York, NY: Oxford University Press.

Tulsky, J. A. (2005). Beyond advance directives: Importance of communication skills at the end of life. *Journal of the American Medical Association, 294*(3), 359–365.

Wilson, J. F. (2009). Cancer care: A microcosm of the problems facing all of health care. *Annals of Internal Medicine, 150*(8), 573–576.

Zhang, B., Wright, A. A., Huskamp, H. A., Nilsson, M. E., Maciejewski, M. L., Earle, C. C., . . . Prigerson, H. G. (2009). Health care costs in the last week of life: Associations with end-of-life conversations. *Archives of Internal Medicine, 169*(5), 480–488.

86

Mary Beth Morrissey

Improving Pain Care Policy: Implications for Social Work Advocacy

Key Concepts

- *As a public health and social problem, pain has underlying social determinants; socioecological, cultural, and relational contexts; and social and economic consequences.*
- *The public health approach to improving pain care and management calls for population-level strategies.*
- *The patient, as the center of moral experience, decision making, and value in care, is the primary beneficiary of laws, policies, and regulations that aim to improve pain care and management.*
- *Improved pain care and management rely on effective national and state policy and its implementation.*
- *The growing incidence and prevalence of cancer and chronic cancer illness require treatment with opioid analgesics, a mainstream therapy for severe pain.*
- *All levels of government and society must address policy gaps in workforce development and professional training in pain management and palliative care.*

Social work advocacy is critical to the advancement of a national policy agenda to improve pain care. Social workers' historical involvement in palliative and end-of-life care, as clinicians, educators, advocates, care managers, navigators, researchers, community organizers, and policy leaders (Bern-Klug, Gessert, & Forbes, 2001), gives them a platform and ripe opportunity for leadership. Adopting a broadly framed socioecological perspective, it is important to acknowledge social work's early recognition of pain and illness as socially determined, its appropriate incorporation of pain assessment into social assessment and social casework, and its deeply rooted commitment to the strengths perspective in social work practice (Gehlert, 2006; Saleeby, 1997). According to Saleeby (1997), the strengths perspective reframes the client's pain through identification of individual strengths and capacities for resilience. An understanding of the client's experience of pain through the "person in environment" perspective and the need for a comprehensive social assessment of pain has long been central to social work practice. Social workers' training and experience in multidimensional assessment—as well as in interventions, pain and symptom management, and collaborative practice—situate social work professionals strategically for understanding the complexities of pain across the continuum of care (NASW, 2004).

Social work participates in a broad consensus that fair resource allocation undergirds the right to health and the constituents of health care justice. This consensus derives from international treaties including the United Nations' *Universal Declaration of Human Rights* (1948), *Single Convention on Narcotic Drugs* (1961, as amended by the 1972 *Protocol Amending the Single Convention on Narcotic Drugs*; see United Nations, 1977), and *International Covenant on Economic, Social, and Cultural Rights* (1966) and the United Nations' Committee on Economic, Social, and Cultural Rights' *General Comment No. 14* (2000), all of which establish the "right to the highest attainable standard of health" and its normative content including rights to palliative care and pain relief (Brennen, 2007; Connor & Sepulveda, 2014; Gilson, 2010; Joranson, Ryan, & Maurer, 2010). The social work profession's code of ethics (NASW, 2008) also informs the development of public policy on pain care. It is timely to issue a call for consensus among all disciplines and professions in recognizing the primacy of the patient in public health. Market-based value goals must be viewed as secondary to providing humanistic, patient-centered pain care (Morrissey, 2011a).

National health reform provides a unique opportunity to strengthen social work policy that improves pain care and reduces inequities in pain treatment. Cancer patients, specifically frail, minority elders with poor cancer prognoses who experience heightened risk for pain vulnerability and undertreatment (Anderson, Green, & Payne, 2009; Institute of Medicine [IOM], 2011), will accrue incremental benefits from health reform. The incorporation of provisions of the National Pain Care Policy Act (2009) into the Affordable Care Act (2010), as described by Meghani et al. (2012), marked a first step in raising awareness about the need for comprehensive, unified public policy to address pain as a public health problem. Pursuant to these provisions, the IOM issued its groundbreaking report *Relieving Pain in America: A Blueprint for Transforming Prevention, Care, Education and Research* (IOM, 2011). In a follow-up to the IOM's Report, the U.S. Department of Health and Human Services created the National Institutes of Health Interagency Pain Research Coordinating Committee to oversee the development of a national strategy to improve pain care. These federal initiatives, together with state-level policies, set the stage for a renewed campaign to change cultural attitudes about pain and to expand access to comprehensive pain and palliative care services.

Four critical stages of the policymaking process will serve to improve pain care: (1) integrating public health strategies for pain management and palliative care into all levels of society, (2) achieving a balance in the legal and regulatory frameworks governing drug availability and control, (3) expanding palliative social services and supports and environmental provision for seriously ill patients living with chronic pain, and (4) fostering more effective social work advocacy for public policy changes.

Epidemiology and Prevalence

Cancer is increasingly becoming a chronic illness that has a long-term symptom burden trajectory, frequently accompanied by chronic pain and psychosocial distress (Kumar et al., 2012; Portenoy, 2011). Pain prevalence rates among cancer patients vary by type and stage, with estimates ranging from over 40% to as high as 90% for patients with advanced or late-stage cancer (IOM, 2011). In studies of cancer patients who smoked (Novy et al., 2012) or had breast cancer surgery (Miaskowski et al., 2012), researchers identified features of high pain intensity, pain persistence, and functional decline. Cases of chronic pain ranged from 15% to 75% in patients with solid tumors (Portenoy, 2011).

Prevalence rates for undertreatment of pain in patients with cancer are universally high, both in the United States and in other countries (IOM, 2011). Study findings of high-intensity, aggressive cancer care at the end of life with poor outcomes, such as low rates of hospice use and high rates of intensive care unit care (Gonsalves et al., 2012; Morden et al., 2012), provide additional evidence of pain undertreatment.

Pain as Public Health and Social Problem: Barriers to Care

Social work policy advocacy must advance understanding of pain as a major worldwide public health and social problem. Both the prevalence of pain and barriers to opioid availability and palliative care illuminate the underlying social dimensions of the problem. According to Meghani et al. (2012, p. 10), "all pain is socially situated." Research suggests that pain has social developmental origins in patients' life histories (Morrissey, 2011b, 2011c) that disclose the social structural dimensions of pain experiences. Factors such as poverty, race and ethnicity, income and occupation, education, English proficiency, health benefits, neighborhood, opioid availability and accessibility, and corporate policies influence the pain experience (Meghani et al., 2012). In particular, minorities experience barriers to pain treatment, with some studies reporting twice the odds of undertreatment among minority cancer patients as non-Hispanic Whites (Fisch et al., 2012). Older adults, women, and cancer patients are also at risk of pain undertreatment (IOM, 2011). Frail elders experience heightened risk for chronic disease and heavy burden of one or more chronic illnesses (IOM, 2011). Overly restrictive drug control policies have also been cited as a barrier to opioid treatment of cancer pain (Gilson, 2010).

The sheer magnitude of the pain problem calls for public health interventions. Leaders in the field have used the World Health Organization (WHO) public health model in palliative care as a foundation to develop four key strategies for integrating pain and palliative care into health care systems at all levels of society: (1) appropriate policy development; (2) adequate drug availability; (3) education of policymakers, health care workers, and the public; and (4) implementation of pain and palliative care services (Stjernswärd, Foley, & Ferris, 2007). Consistent with the classic public health focus on prevention, this approach means both extending the disease-free life span through forestalling the onset of disease and, at the tertiary prevention level, slowing the progression of disease through symptom management and "compression of morbidity" (Fries, 1980, p. 133; Marvasti & Stafford, 2012).

Stjernswärd et al. (2007) describe palliative care as critical for patients with cancer who experience a high pain and suffering burden, as recognized by the WHO (1996). However, barriers to palliative care and pain management persist due to diverse factors including systemic, definitional, and communication issues about the scope of palliative care services (Wentlandt et al., 2012); lack of information and referrals; cultural attitudes and lack of trust in the health care system; fear of addiction to pain medications; social determinants; and personal values and care preferences. Physicians' fear of regulatory scrutiny and prosecution for overprescribing, lack of education and training in pain management, and disciplinary boundaries also hinder access to adequate pain care. In a study of oncology patients' use of services, Kumar et al. (2012) reported that only 8.5% of study participants used pain/palliative care consultations. Researchers have identified associations between graduate education and higher utilization of services, and lack of awareness or lack of physician referral and lower levels of utilization (Kumar et al., 2012).

Of the multiple approaches to management of cancer pain, both pharmacological and nonpharmacological, drug treatment continues to be the mainstay of pain and symptom management (Portenoy, 2011; WHO, 1996). Yet pain interventions introduced for cancer patients are not always successful. In a systematic review of five institutional-based pain interventions reported in the literature between 1966 and 2006, researchers (Goldberg & Morrison, 2007) reported no systematic hospital-wide change in pain severity among cancer patients.

Education is emerging as a prominent social structural factor in equitable access to pain care (Atlas & Skinner, 2010). Specifically, the Atlas and Skinner (2010) data showed a positive association between low educational attainment and higher rates of pain, greater disability, and poorer health outcomes. This research presents a compelling case based on the researchers' findings that education, as well as social norms, alters the experience of pain and pain trajectories over time.

Public Policy Addressing Drug Availability and Control

The previously mentioned data on pain prevalence and undertreatment highlights the importance of public policy governing drug availability. The WHO has identified drug and opioid availability as key components of the public health strategy for palliative care and cancer control (Connor & Sepulveda, 2014; Stjernswärd et al., 2007). However, multiple barriers to opioid availability and accessibility exist, paralleling the barriers to palliative care discussed earlier, such as individual and cultural attitudes about opioids, fears of opioid dependence and addiction and hastened death, inadequate education and training for health care practitioners, practitioners' fears of criminal prosecution, and excessively burdensome and restrictive government regulatory policies (Joranson et al., 2010).

Building on the WHO public health model, Stjernsward and colleagues have mapped out specific recommendations to ensure that patient needs for drugs are met. These steps include conducting a comprehensive situational analysis and needs assessment for patients with cancer; facilitating an adequate and affordable supply of essential medications, including opioid analgesics, in community-based settings and pharmacies and prescribing for appropriate pain management; promoting leadership development, pain policy, and palliative care champions; and evaluating the impact of policy implementation on intermediate and long-term outcomes (2007). Although evidence indicates that opioid-prescribing practices may vary regionally based on factors such as supply of active physicians (McDonald, Carlson, & Izrael, 2012; Zhang, Baicker, & Newhouse, 2010), policymakers and health professionals have an imperative to study the WHO recommendations and organize effectively to implement them. Shortages of anti-cancer drugs for certain populations (Metzger, Billet, & Link, 2012), as well as heightened scrutiny of opioid use by the U.S. Food and Drug Administration and enactment and expansion of prescription drug–monitoring programs by states (Deyo et al., 2013; Perrone & Nelson, 2012), will likely escalate this current public health crisis.

Contextualized Pain in Cancer

Effective government policy on opioid analgesics must be attuned to social and cultural perceptions and meanings of pain, as well as its clinical manifestations. Perceptions of pain may vary widely, as described by Thomas (2013) in his report on an art exhibit at London's Science Museum, *Pain Less*. The exhibit explored and described pain experiences such as the "phantom limb pain" of an amputee, patient responses to pain stimuli during surgery, the lack of sensitivity to pain resulting from a congenital condition, and modulation of sensitivity to pain through emotion (Thomas, 2013). The social work profession has built on contributions of psychology (Wertz et al., 2011), anthropology (Kleinman, 2012), and sociology in the changing paradigm of pain, and it has drawn from its own roots in hospice, medical social work, social casework, and strengths-based practice. The classic definition of pain of the International Association for the Study of Pain, often cited in the social work literature, focuses on both the sensory experience in the body and the emotional dimensions of pain (Cagle & Altilio, 2011; Mersky & Bogduk, 1994; Morrissey, 2011a, 2011b, 2011c). Although pain is well established as subjective, literature and research on empathy suggest a reconceptualization of pain as intersubjectively experienced and socially constituted, encompassing the contexts of interpersonal relationships, communication between patients and caregivers, and both personal and shared meanings (Del Canale et al., 2012; Morrissey, 2011a, 2011b, 2011c).

The various types of pain are manifold. In a comprehensive investigation of pain, Turk and Okifuji (2010) delineated taxonomies for classifying pain based on etiology (cancer or noncancer pain), temporality (acute, chronic), intensity (mild, moderate, severe), physiology, and psychogenic origin. A clinical consensus has also formed around certain types of neural processes that sustain pain. Although neuropathic pain is by convention associated with damage to the nervous system, and nociceptive pain with tissue damage, Portenoy (2011) describes a wide range of chronic cancer pain syndromes that may be related both to the underlying disease process and to the cancer treatment itself.

The emotional, psychological, and contextual dimensions of pain experiences, including pain that may be experienced as trauma (Wertz et al., 2011), and their impact on pain trajectories and quality of life have been closely studied. Research has demonstrated the role of attachment and relational context in the relationship between cancer pain and perceived social support from significant others (Gauthier et al., 2012). Studies of clinical encounters suggest that physicians may experience their patients' pain empathically as evidenced in clinical outcomes (Del Canale et al., 2012) or in neurobiological changes (Jensen et al., 2013).

Reflective Policy Advocacy in Palliative Social Work

To strengthen the role of palliative social work in improving pain care for cancer patients, social work policy advocates must engage in reflection from a stance of empathic attunement and immersion in the cancer patients' worlds. Drawing upon phenomenology, reflective practice in policy advocacy would situate the social work advocate in an authentic life-world encounter with the cancer patient and enable "reflection in action" (Schön, 1983). This type of reflection, embedded in the social contexts in which practice and advocacy occur, would foster the social work advocate's active engagement with the cancer patient in an attitude of mutual dignity, recognition, and vulnerability (Benjamin, 2004), yet with awareness of the strata of the relational pain experience: (1) the first-person experience of the cancer patient, in embodied pain, who is a moral agent and decision maker; (2) the social work advocate who stands in ethical relation to the cancer patient in pain, and in such capacity is called to provide embodied care and improve the conditions of possibility for such care; and (3) the multiple social, developmental, and relational contexts that form the ground of pain experience for the cancer patient and create the care obligation to support the cancer patient as a constituting agent in a movement toward hope and recovery in light of the patient's care needs, intentionalities, and strengths.

Yet reflective activity relevant to social work advocacy has complexity even beyond immediate experience. In reflecting on action (reflecting critically on the encounter with the patient after it has occurred; Schön, 1983) or in meta-reflection (which involves a shift in attitude from the lived experience perspective of the actor or author), the social work advocate opens up worldly engagements and contexts for questioning from a height that may help to inform interprofessional engagement and broad transdisciplinary collaboration in the service of cancer patients.

This multidimensional, layered, and dialectical process of reflection and feedback allows "dwelling upon,... magnification, and amplification" (Wertz et al., 2011, p. 132) of the problem of knowledge in social work presented by experiences of cancer patients in pain. The reflective process further allows the caregiver to identify the essential structures of palliative social work that will be effective in challenging existing pain paradigms, professional practice patterns, and social structures and policies that create barriers to good pain care.

Barriers to effective palliative social work with seriously ill and cancer patients persist. Adherence to a medical model bears some responsibility for the exclusion of social work from full participation in direct practice with seriously ill patients and for regulations limiting the social work scope of practice in palliative care. Although some progressive institutional settings engage social workers in pain assessment and pain management, social workers in many settings remain marginalized in discharge-planning roles by virtue of systems and structures that inadequately meet the needs of seriously ill patients. A first step in addressing this policy gap is strengthening the social work role in patient care processes and conversations in light of social workers' competencies in clinical pain assessments and pain management. The social work perspective takes account of the multidimensional nature of embodied pain and, in particular, its fundamentally social and cultural dimensions.

Social workers are uniquely qualified by virtue of their core training in systems, especially family systems, to advocate for patients in pain, from bedside to system levels, whether presenting a patient's case to team members, ethics committees, or regulators. This role becomes increasingly important in environments where the principle of balance governing drug availability may be threatened. To advocate effectively for adequate pain care, the palliative social worker needs to understand the relationship between policy and direct practice and to articulate that relationship to secure and protect benefits for the patient. Most importantly, social workers need to understand their role from a global perspective, engaging in reflection in action in the local practice context and in meta-reflection on the types of collaborative pain advocacy with other professions and sectors, including regulatory. This interprofessional role depends on social work's professional identity and sense of purpose in service to seriously ill patients, families, and communities.

A paradigm shift is occurring in a movement toward rebalancing medical and social services for cancer patients, their families, caregivers, and health providers and professionals (Lynn, 2005). Palliative social work involves population- and community-level interventions, planning, and management, including advance planning for complex chronic cancers, individual care planning for cancer patients, caregiver assessment and support, crisis care in emergencies and disasters, coordination of basic needs, and decision-making support. The social work policy advocate needs to be a social entrepreneur, building intersectoral relationships, organizing coalitions, and identifying innovative market opportunities for expanding pain management and palliative care.

Pearls

- Balance is the key principle in incorporating a public health approach to the development of comprehensive pain and drug control policies to ensure that both pain care needs and public safety are weighed in policy planning.
- Social work policy advocacy needs to focus on community-level interventions that aim to improve the health and well-being of both the whole community and vulnerable subgroups, such as people living with chronic cancers and chronic pain and at risk for pain undertreatment.
- Successful policy development and policy implementation will require ongoing pain-focused professional education for specialists and generalist-level health care practitioners.
- Education for patients, family caregivers, and surrogate decision makers is an integral component of effective public health strategy to improve pain care.
- Reflective practice will enable more effective social work policy advocacy to improve pain care and outcomes for cancer patients.

Pitfalls

- There may be a systematic failure to recognize and frame the problem of pain as a public health issue that affects population health and well-being, interfering with development of population-level strategies and interventions to improve pain care.
- Issues relating to risks of drug diversion and addiction are not well understood and therefore may not be treated with balance in public health and policy planning.
- Even if policy development is successful, insufficient attention to local planning, workforce development, and organizational and political systems may create implementation problems and contribute to policy implementation failures.
- Lack of funding for training health care workers may compromise the quality of life and quality of dying among cancer patients.
- Social work advocacy that proceeds without informed understanding of diverse pain experiences among cancer patients will be constrained to meet patients' complex social and medical care needs in advanced, life-limiting illness and at the end of life.

The ethical obligation to relieve pain and human suffering transcends the boundaries of international, federal, and state law and policy. Social workers are called on under their professional standards and ethical codes and under core human rights principles to provide pain management and palliative care to persons living through pain because of serious illness, including cancer. Relieving pain is a moral imperative in a just society. The epidemiology and prevalence of pain in cancer illness call for public health interventions and strategies at all levels of society. Development of national and state drug policies that focus on a balanced approach to reducing the risk of drug diversion and abuse and to providing access to affordable drugs is paramount. Such policy making must avoid biological reductionism that would seek to define pain, pain assessment, and treatment solely from a biomedical perspective or to make access to pain relief or medications contingent upon etiology, disease type, or risk group. Rather, pain must be understood as a contextualized, multidimensional experience that calls for deeply empathic care responses. Social work policy advocacy for improved pain care needs to be informed by an understanding of the complexity of living with pain in serious illness. Social work's intimate knowledge of the patient, the patient's milieu, and conditions of human finitude, as well as possibility and resources, will ensure the most effective, strengths-based approach to relieving pain, providing palliative social services, building maternal care environments and supports, and promoting resilience and hope for the cancer patient at all stages of the illness trajectory.

ADDITIONAL RESOURCES

Fishman, S. M., Ballantyne, J. C., & Rathmell, J. P. (Eds.). (2009). *Bonica's management of pain* (4th ed.). New York, NY: Wolters Kluwer, Lippincott Williams & Wilkins.

REFERENCES

Anderson, K. O., Green, C. R., & Payne, R. (2009). Racial and ethnic disparities in pain: Causes and consequences of unequal care. *Journal of Pain, 10*(12), 1187–1204.

Atlas, S. J., & Skinner, J. (2010). Education and the prevalence of pain. In D. A. Wise (Ed.), *Research findings in the economics of aging* (pp. 145–166). Chicago, IL: University of Chicago Press.

Benjamin, J. (2004). Beyond doer and done: To an intersubjective view of thirdness. *Psychoanalytic Quarterly, 73*(1), 5–46.

Bern-Klug, M., Gessert, C., & Forbes, S. (2001). The need to revise assumption about the end of life: Implications for social work practice. *Health and Social Work, 26*(1), 38–47.

Brennen, F. (2007). Palliative care as an international human right. *Journal of Pain and Symptom Management*, *33*(5), 494–499.

Cagle, J. G., & Altilio, T. (2011). The social work role in pain and symptom management. In T. Altilio & S. Otis-Green (Eds.), *Oxford textbook of palliative social work* (pp. 271–286). New York, NY: Oxford University Press.

Connor, S., & Sepulveda, C. M. (Eds.). (2014). *Global atlas of palliative care at the end of life*. Geneva, Switzerland/London, England: World Health Organization and Worldwide Palliative Care Alliance.

Del Canale, S., Louis, D. Z., Maio, V., Wang, X., Rossi, G., Hojat, M., & Gonnella, J. S. (2012). The relationship between physician empathy and disease complications: An empirical study of primary care physicians and their diabetic patients in Parma, Italy. *Academic Medicine*, *87*, 1243–1249.

Deyo, R. A., Irvine, J. M., Millet, L. M., Beran, T., O'Kane, N., Wright, D. A., & McCarty, D. (2013). Measures such as interstate cooperation would improve the efficacy of programs to track controlled drug prescriptions. *Health Affairs*, *32*(3), 1–11.

Fisch, M. J., Lee, J. W., Weiss, M., Wagner, L. I., Chang, V. T., Cella, D., . . . Cleeland, C. S. (2012). Prospective, observational study of pain and analgesic prescribing in medical oncology outpatients with breast, colorectal, lung, or prostate cancer. *Journal of Clinical Oncology*, *30*(16), 1980–1988. doi:10.1200/JCO.2011.39.2381

Fries, J. F. (1980). Aging, natural death, and the compression of morbidity. *New England Journal of Medicine*, *303*, 130–135.

Gauthier, L. R., Rodin, G., Zimmerman, C., Warr, D., Librach, S. L., Moore, M., . . . Gagliese, L. (2012). The communal coping model and cancer pain: The roles of catastrophizing and attachment style. *Journal of Pain*, *13*(12), 1258–1268.

Gehlert, S. (2006). The conceptual underpinnings of social work in health care. In S. Gehlert & T. A. Browne (Eds.), *Handbook of health social work* (pp. 3–22). Hoboken, NJ: John Wiley & Sons.

Gilson, A. M. (2010). Laws and policies involving pain management. In J. C. Ballantyne, J. P. Rathmell, & S. M. Fishman (Eds.), *Bonica's management of pain* (4th ed., pp. 166–182). Philadelphia, PA: Lippincott Williams & Wilkins.

Goldberg, G. R., & Morrison, R. S. (2007). Pain management in hospitalized cancer patients: A systematic review. *Journal of Clinical Oncology*, *25*, 1792–1801.

Gonsalves, W. I., Tashi, T., Krishnamurthy, J., Davies, T., Ortman, S., Thota, R., . . . Subbiah, S. (2012). Effect of palliative care services on the aggressiveness of end of life care in the Veteran's Affairs cancer population. *Journal of Palliative Medicine*, *14*(11), 1231–1235.

Institute of Medicine (IOM). (2011). *Relieving pain in America: A blueprint for transforming prevention, care, education, and research*. Washington, DC: National Academies Press.

Jensen, K. B., Petrovic, P., Kerr, C. E., Kirsch, I., Raicek, J., Cheetham, A., . . . Kaptchuk, T. J. (2013). Sharing pain and relief: Neural correlates of physicians during treatment of patients. *Molecular Psychiatry*, *19*(3), 392–398. doi:10.1038/mp.2012.195

Joranson, D. E., Ryan, K. M., & Maurer, M. A. (2010). Disparities in opioid policy, availability, and access: The way forward. In J. C. Ballantyne, J. P. Rathmell, & S. M. Fishman (Eds.), *Bonica's management of pain* (pp. 194–208). Philadelphia, PA: Lippincott Williams & Wilkins.

Kleinman, A. (2012). The art of medicine: Caregiving as moral experience. *The Lancet*, *380*(9853), 1550–1551.

Kumar, P., Casarett, D., Corcoran, A., Desai, K., Li, Q., Chen, J., . . . Mao, J. J. (2012). Utilization of supportive and palliative care services among oncology outpatients at one academic cancer center: Determinants of use and barriers to access. *Journal of Palliative Medicine*, *15*(8), 923–930.

Lynn, J. (2005). Living long in fragile health: The new demographics shape end of life care. In B. Jennings, G. Kaebnick, & T. Murray (Eds.), Improving end-of-life care: Why has it been so difficult? *Hastings Center Special Report*, *35*(6), S14–S18.

Marvasti, F., & Stafford, R. (2012). From sick care to health care—Reengineering prevention into the U.S. system. *New England Journal of Medicine*, *367*, 889–891.

McDonald, D. C., Carlson, K., & Izrael, D. (2012). Geographic variation in opioid prescribing in the U.S. *Journal of Pain*, *13*(10), 988–996.

Meghani, S. H., Polomano, R. C., Tait, R. C., Vallerand, A. H., Anderson, K. O., & Gallagher, R. M. (2012). Advancing a national agenda to eliminate disparities in pain care: Directions for health policy, education, practice, and research. *Pain Medicine*, *13*(1), 5–28.

Mersky, H., & Bogduk, N. (1994). *Classification of chronic pain* (2nd ed.). Seattle, WA: IASP Press.

Metzger, M., Billet, A., & Link, M. (2012). The impact of drug shortages on children with cancer—The example of mechlorethamine. *New England Journal of Medicine*, *367*, 2461–2463.

Miaskowski, C., Cooper, B., Paul, S. M., West, C., Langford, D., Levine J. D., . . . Aouizerat, B. E. (2012). Identification of patient subgroups and risk factors for persistent breast pain following breast cancer surgery. *Journal of Pain*, *13*(12), 1172–1187.

Morden, N. E., Chang, C.-H., Jacobson, J. O., Berke, E. M., Bynum, J. P. W., Murray, K. M., & Goodman, D. C. (2012). End-of-life care for Medicare beneficiaries with cancer is highly intensive overall and varies widely. *Health Affairs*, *31*(4), 786–796.

Morrissey, M. B. (2011a). Phenomenology of pain and suffering: A humanistic perspective in gerontological health and social work. *Journal of Social Work in End-of-Life and Palliative Care*, *7*(1), 14–38.

Morrissey, M. B. (2011b). Suffering and decision making among seriously ill elderly women. Unpublished dissertation, Fordham University.

Morrissey, M. B. (2011c). Expanding consciousness of suffering at the end of life: An ethical and gerontological response in palliative social work. Schutzian Research, Special Issue: *Phenomenology of the Human Sciences*, *3*, 79–106.

National Association of Social Workers (NASW). (2004). *NASW standards for palliative and end-of-life care*. Washington, DC: Author.

National Association of Social Workers (NASW). (2008). *Code of ethics*. Washington, DC: NASW Press.

Novy, D. M., Lam, C., Gritz, E. R., Hernandez, M., Driver, L. C., & Koyyalagunta, D. (2012). Distinguishing features of cancer patients who smoke. *Journal of Pain*, *13*(11), 1058–1067. doi:10.1016/j.jpain.2012.07.012

Perrone, J., & Nelson, L. (2012). Medication reconciliation for controlled substances—An "ideal" prescription-drug monitoring program. *New England Journal of Medicine, 366*, 2341–2343. doi:10.1056/NEJMp1204493

Portenoy, R. K. (2011). Treatment of cancer pain. *The Lancet, 377*(9784), 2236–2247. doi:10.1016/S0140-6736(11)60236-5

Saleeby, D. (1997). The strengths approach to practice. In D. Saleeby (Ed.), *The strengths perspective in social work practice* (2nd ed.). White Plains, NY: Longman.

Schön, D. (1983). *The reflective practitioner: How professionals think in action*. New York, NY: Basic Books.

Stjernswärd, J., Foley, K. M., & Ferris, F. D. (2007). The public health strategy for palliative care. *Journal of Pain and Symptom Management, 33*(5), 486–493.

Thomas, C. (2013). Perceptions of pain. *The Lancet, 381*(9864), 364.

Turk, D. C., & Okifuji, A. (2010). Pain terms and taxonomies of pain. In S. M. Fishman, J. C. Ballantyne, & J. P. Rathmell (Eds.), *Bonica's management of pain* (pp. 13–23). Philadelphia, PA: Lippincott Williams & Wilkins.

United Nations. (1948, December 10). Universal declaration of human rights, 217 A (III). Retrieved from http://www.un.org/en/documents/udhr/

United Nations. (1977). Single convention on narcotic drugs (1961), as amended by the protocol amending the single convention on narcotic drugs (1972). New York, NY: United Nations; 1977. Retrieved from https://treaties.un.org/Pages/ShowMTDSGDetails.aspx?src=UNTSONLINE&tabid=2&mtdsg_no=VI-17&chapter=6&lang=en#Participants

United Nations. (1966, December 16). International covenant on economic, social, and cultural rights. United Nations, Treaty Series, Vol. 993, p. 3. Retrieved from https://treaties.un.org/Pages/ViewDetails.aspx?mtdsg_no=IV-3&chapter=4&lang=en

United Nations' Committee on Economic, Social, and Cultural Rights. (2000, August 11). *General comment No. 14: The right to the highest attainable standard of health (Art. 12 of the covenant)*. Retrieved from http://www.un.org/documents/ecosoc/docs/2001/e2001-22.pdf

Wentlandt, K., Krzyzanowska, M. K., Swami, K., Rodin, G. M., Le, L. W., & Zimmermann, C. (2012). Referral practices of oncologists to specialized palliative care. *Journal of Clinical Oncology, 30*(35), 4380–4386.

Wertz, F. J., Charmaz, K., McMullen, L. M., Josselson, R., Anderson, R., & McSpadden, E. (2011). *Five ways of doing qualitative analysis: Phenomenological psychology, grounded theory, discourse analysis, narrative research and intuitive inquire*. New York, NY: Guilford Press.

World Health Organization (WHO). (1996). *Cancer pain relief: With a guide to opioid availability* (2nd ed.). Geneva, Switzerland: World Health Organization. Retrieved from http://whqlibdoc.who.int/publications/9241544821.pdf

Zhang, Y., Baicker, K., & Newhouse, J. (2010). Geographic variation in the quality of prescribing. *New England Journal of Medicine, 363*, 1985–1988.

XVI

Care Coordination, Managing Transitions, and Providing Resources

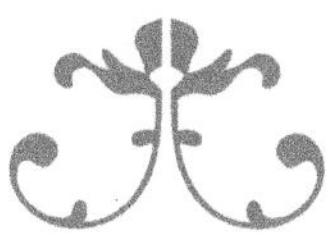

Carol P. Marcusen

Care coordination is a collaborative process between the medical team, the patient, the family, and the community. It includes assessment of, planning for, and facilitation of options and services to meet an individual's complex needs across the continuum of care. This includes the tasks of arranging, coordinating, monitoring, evaluating, and advocating for the multiple services and interventions needed for the client. Care coordination not only is about the client's biopsychosocial and spiritual state but also includes the environment and social systems in which the client lives. This section of the *Handbook* addresses the oncology social worker's role as care coordinator and navigator and defines it as distinct from other support disciplines. This section highlights crucial information about legal issues, financial assistance, and education with a spotlight on the increasing gaps in service in today's health environment. Oncology social workers have been change agents for society in health care from the beginning. With this knowledge, oncology social workers will continue to lead the policy change and implementation necessary to create improved access to quality health care across the continuum in our society.

In "Transitions During Cancer Care," Carol P. Marcusen introduces the oncology social worker to the role of case manager. A definition of social work case management has been endorsed and a multidisciplinary collaborative case management model is provided with a training paradigm for the new oncology social worker.

In "Patient Navigation in Oncology," Melissa Sileo Stewart and Rian Rodriguez increase the understanding of how oncology social workers work with other support disciplines in the emerging field of navigation. The authors identify the needs of a community to whom an oncology social work navigator will provide support and discuss the need for clear evaluation strategies and outcome measures to show the impact of oncology social worker navigators.

In "Bridging Increasing Financial Gaps and Challenges in Service Delivery," Jane Levy and Michele McCourt explore the financial challenges that can affect the patient's and family's ability to cope with a cancer diagnosis and can result in psychosocial stress. The authors point out evidence that financial hardship can complicate adherence to prescribed treatment protocols and that many patients are reluctant or embarrassed to discuss costs with the oncology treatment team. The oncology social worker can facilitate difficult conversations about financial barriers, open communication with the treatment team, and link patients to financial and community resources.

In "The Importance of Patient Education," Julie Keany Hodorowski, Carolyn Messner, and Caroline Kornhauser describe how the changing landscape of cancer treatments has impacted the delivery of patient and caregiver education programs. They identify the nuts and bolts of providing psychosocially sensitive programs using innovative technology, including teleconferences, live streaming, webcasts, and webinars, to increase access to state-of-the-art information about biopsychosocial care and treatment.

In "Legal Issues That Affect Quality of Life for Oncology Patients and Their Caregivers," Kathryn M. Smolinski and Debra Wolf propose that social workers can play a key role in obtaining and facilitating legal services and information for oncology patients and the health care team. The authors suggest the idea of including an attorney as part of the treatment team and using his or her expertise to learn about the latest laws, regulations, and policies that affect cancer care.

87 Transitions During Cancer Care

Carol P. Marcusen

Key Concepts

- *A multidisciplinary collaborative model for case management is endorsed and a conceptual model of this approach is provided.*
- *The training paradigm provides a disease management approach and focuses on major events in the disease process.*
- *Each event in the training paradigm highlights the mastery of a primary challenge for that event.*
- *Interventions are suggested from a "person in environment" perspective, community interventions, medical system interventions, and interventions specific for the individual/family.*
- *Successful oncology social workers have embraced their role in case management and have highlighted the effectiveness of social work interventions in achieving the overall goals of case management.*

The social work profession has at its roots the practice of case management. Case management has been an important concept in social work from the time of Jane Addams and the settlement houses, notably Chicago's Hull House in the late 1800s, which were built around programs designed to coordinate services and resources. Another event that affected case management in the United States was the deinstitutionalization of the mentally ill in the 1960s and 1970s. Social factors leading to deinstitutionalization included criticism of public mental hospitals, a desire to shift to community-based care, better treatments for mental illness, and interest in reducing the high costs of hospitalization. Support from President John F. Kennedy's Presidential Panel of Mental Retardation and two important pieces of legislation passed in 1963—the Maternal and Child Health and Mental Retardation Planning Amendments and the Mental Retardation Facilities and Community Mental Health Centers Construction Act—furthered this process (Stroman, 2003).

In the 1970s, the country saw the creation of the Department of Health, Education, and Welfare. This continued to further the concept of coordination of services and resources to increase the quality of care while at the same time decreasing costs by reducing waste (Stefanacci, 2013). In the 1990s, these principles and concepts began to be integrated across the health care industry as better treatments became available, public desire for access to health care and resources increased, and costs of health care rose, most notably in acute hospitalizations (Dzyacky, 1998).

The country now has three major case management organizations, several professional journals specifically dedicated to case management, and a host of various types and models of case management and/or care coordination being used. This chapter describes the efficacy of a multidisciplinary collaborative model for case management utilized by oncology social workers.

Definition

Social work case management standards describe the functions of the social worker as the primary provider of social work case management:

> *A professional social worker assesses the needs of the client and the client's family, when appropriate,*

> *and arranges, coordinates, monitors, evaluates, and advocates for a package of multiple services to meet the specific client's complex needs... Distinct from other forms of case management, social work case management addresses both the individual client's bio psychosocial status as well as the state of the social system in which case management operates. Social work case management is both micro and macro in nature: intervention occurs at both the client and system levels. It requires the social worker to develop and maintain a therapeutic relationship with the client, which may include linking the client with systems that provide him or her with needed services, resources, and opportunities. Services provided under the rubric of social work case management practice may be located in a single agency or may be spread across numerous agencies or organizations.*
>
> —*National Association of Social Workers (NASW), 1992*

An updated version emphasizes the collaborative functions as well, noting that "case management limits problems arising from fragmentation of services... and inadequate coordination among providers. Case management can occur within a single, large organization or within a community program that coordinates services among settings" (NASW, 2013, p. 13).

Current changes in health care brought on by rising costs, advances in technology, and the movement from inpatient to ambulatory care have accelerated the traditional American health care system to evolve into a more fluid and holistic approach to patient care. No longer can we afford to treat episodically, as patients are presenting in ever-increasing numbers with multiple, chronic health problems. Specifically, cancer is no longer an acute illness but a chronic condition to be treated and monitored over a lifetime (Berkman, 1996). Oncology social work case management has the skill sets needed to optimize client functioning by providing quality services in the most efficient and effective manner to individuals with multiple complex needs over a person's life span (Cesta, 2012).

Terminology

Important terms related to social work case management in the oncology setting include *managed care, utilization/financial management, transitions, advocacy, education*, and *resource availability*.

Managed care is often used interchangeably with case management and denotes the limiting of unnecessary health services through budget restrictions, case management review of treatment plans against preestablished criteria, the use of primary care providers as gatekeepers, and financial incentives for providers to limit services (McGeehan, 2007).

Utilization/financial management uses preestablished criteria to review treatment plans and provide resources. *Transitions* refer to the continuum of care that is now the standard for most clients with chronic illnesses such as cancer (see Chapter 6). Health care involves not only inpatient care but also outpatient treatments, such as chemotherapy, rehabilitation, monitoring, and end-of-life care, which includes hospice services or skilled nursing for other functional care needs dependent upon the client's ability to function independently (Dzyacky, 1998).

Advocacy refers to the need for the client to have interventions occur not only at the individual level but also at the system level. Advocacy implies the need for someone with training and skills to intervene for the client and family to ensure appropriate health care is received. Collaboration with community agencies, local community programs, hospices, and support groups to secure services needed by the client is an advocacy skill used by the social work case manager (NCCS, 2011).

Interventions require education by the social work case manager to provide the needed resources for the client. The social work case manager is able to improve a patient's condition through effective early interventions (Robbins & Birmingham, 2005).

Oncology Social Worker as Case Manager

An oncology social work model for case management uses a multidisciplinary approach. The oncology social worker collaborates with other professionals and engages the patient and family in decision making about care planning. A basic social work premise of "person in environment" focuses the oncology social work case manager on addressing both the individual client's biopsychosocial status and the social system in which he or she operates. The social work case manager screens and assesses the needs of the client and advocates for a package of services to meet the client's needs (NASW, 1992). The scope of practice for social work case management includes screening/assessment, planning, facilitation, coordination, advocacy, education, communication, and evaluation, which are addressed in more detail in the following sections.

Case management also includes direct clinical assessment and management; fiscal and clinical coordination; utilization and variance management; benefits and reimbursement management; concurrent coding, measurement, and evaluation; and pathway and guideline development. Because not any one discipline can encompass all these functions (Cowles, 1992), it has been necessary (and successful) to use a multidisciplinary case management model throughout the country (Robbins & Birmingham, 2005).

Screening

Screening criteria are selected based on the type of case management services offered. Screening identifies those at risk, such as stage of cancer, cost of treatment, no adherence, terminal phase, and other risk factors for discharge complications and psychosocial problems. A key rationale for screening is to identify and provide early intervention for patients at high risk for discharge complications (Auerbach, Mason, & Laporte. 2007).

Assessment

A psychosocial assessment constitutes the foundation of a good plan. Planning will incorporate a medical assessment. Other plans depend on the needs and stage of illness. The psychosocial assessment includes cognitive functioning, emotional, spiritual/cultural, financial, support system, vocational, and end-of-life planning. The assessment also includes the identification and referral of patients and families to appropriate practical, psychiatric, psychological, or spiritual services.

Planning

A comprehensive case management plan requires social workers to consider education, coordination, facilitation, advocacy, and communication. A plan could fail at any time if a step is missed in planning. All members of the team, including the client/family, must communicate. At times, all members will require some education. The social work case manager facilitates education and communication, coordinates many of the details of the plan, and advocates for services for the client/family to ensure quality services and a reduction in fragmentation (Ellis, 2012).

Crisis Intervention

The oncology social worker provides clinical interventions to stabilize an individual or family during a traumatic event or experience. Over the trajectory of the different experiences that can occur at diagnosis, during changes in therapy, at recurrence, and through the disease progression when the individual or family experiences a loss of stability, the oncology social worker seeks to assist

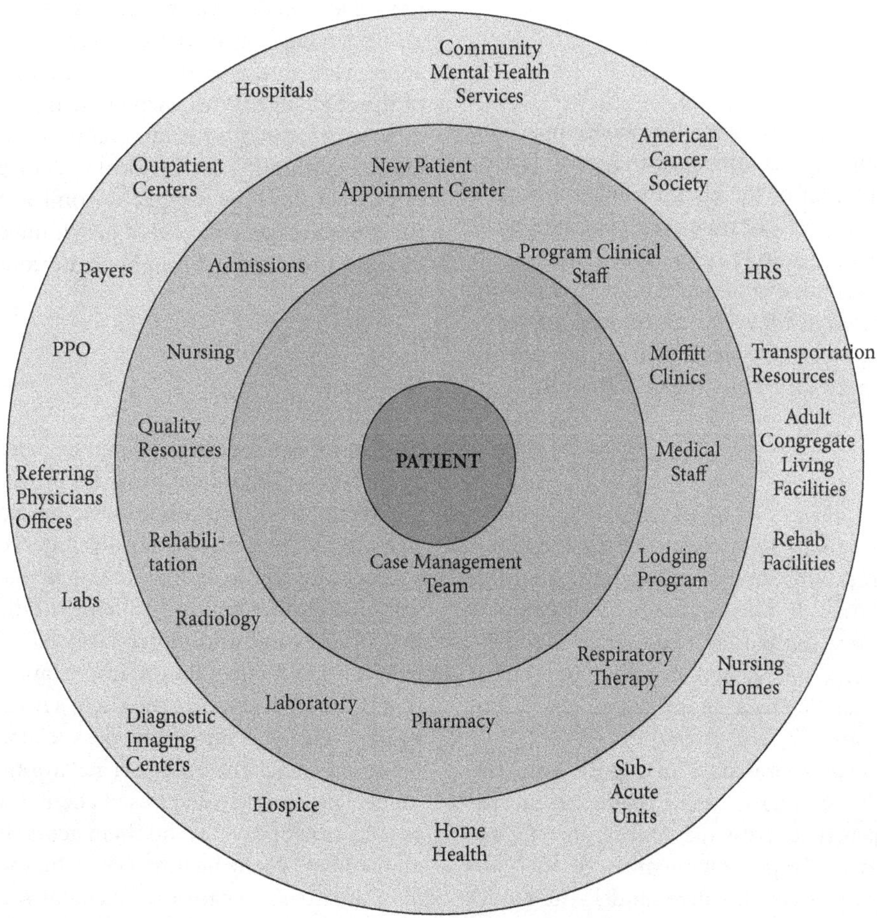

Figure 87.1. Patient-centered, collaborative community approach to case management.
Source: Mizrahi & Davis (2008).

in rebalancing the situation. Interventions may include assessment of the current situation and education about the current condition, including identification of options for solving problems and recognition of the feelings being experienced. Further exploration and clarification of these feelings along with the common emotional responses that are expressed is valuable for regaining equilibrium. The oncology social worker assists with managing these feelings by encouraging familiar coping mechanisms and teaching new ways of coping. Providing resources and support is critical.

Coordination of Discharge Planning

The social worker identifies and coordinates community support systems and resources that enable the client to return home or to a safer level of care to continue the treatment plan. Discharge planning begins immediately upon admission to the hospital, treatment center, or ambulatory setting and extends throughout the period of treatment. Discharge planning is the culmination of a proper assessment combined with specific interventions and the use of patient, family, and community resources.

Evaluation

A crucial step for the team is evaluation. Evaluation is done throughout the development, at initiation, and, periodically, during the implementation of the plan. Evaluation during the process allows the team to activate corrective actions to improve upon quality of care and to prevent or minimize an adverse occurrence. Periodic evaluation at diagnosis, during treatment, and at discharge allows for continuous improvement and the development of systems that ensure quality and safety and maximize success for the client/family.

Outcome Measures

Outcome measures evaluate previously agreed-upon goals, use of resources, and client satisfaction. The discharge plan should include measurable goals. Examples of goals are to improve the patient experience; decrease costs; optimize patient, payer, and provider outcomes; and ensure appropriate utilization of resources at the appropriate level of care.

A conceptual model is presented in Figure 87.1. The model illustrates the emphasis on a patient-centered, cost-effective approach that spans the continuum of care. The social worker is an important member of the case management team for this collaborative model. The model further conceptualizes the full continuum of care and the many community partners and resources needed to ensure the optimal patient experience.

Training

Much of a model's success can be attributed to the training of the personnel involved with the social worker and the multidisciplinary team. The proposed training model (Table 87.1) has been introduced specifically for the oncology social worker. The model provides the social worker with a conceptual framework using a disease management approach. This model was originally introduced in a poster session at the 1991 Association of Oncology Social Work national conference (Morrison & Marcusen, 1991). It has been well received and used over the years with some modifications.

The model uses a disease stage approach similar in some ways to Erikson's developmental stages (Erikson, 1959). The client advances from one stage to the next. Not all individuals will necessarily need to advance through each stage. The stages for the oncology client focus on major events in the disease process: diagnosis, treatment, remission, recurrence, end of life, and survivorship. In this framework, each stage highlights the mastery of a primary challenge for that stage. Each mastery builds upon the ones previously learned. Those not mastered at one stage may reappear and need additional work in another stage. The framework is an understanding of the challenges with an emphasis on appropriate interventions that facilitate the client's mastery of the challenge. With each challenge, the social work student is presented with interventions from the standpoint of the community, the medical system, and the individual/family. This unique perspective on learning coincides with the case management goal of providing coordination of services and resources throughout the continuum of care (see Section 2).

Diagnosis

At diagnosis, the patient faces the challenge of crisis versus equilibrium. The model provides primary interventions in the areas of the community, the medical system, and the individual client and/or family. Interventions are used to successfully reconcile these challenges. The primary intervention for the community during the diagnosis is education that is accessible and understandable. The medical system intervention focuses on the importance of communication that is timely and meets the client's needs. The patient/family intervention is support by the social worker, the staff, and others in the client's support network. Working with this model with a newly diagnosed client, the case management social worker provides the client access to information from all members of the health care team, including the medical plan of care. The case management social worker ensures a support network for the client. The skill of learning how to use and find information is very useful to cope with the diagnosis of cancer.

Table 87.1.
Social Work Training Model

Stage	Primary Challenge	Community Interventions	Medical System Interventions	Patient/Family Interventions	Focused Skill Mastery
Diagnosis	Crisis vs. equilibrium	Education	Communication	Support	Finding information
Treatment	Acute stress vs. effective learning	Resource development	Bioethics communication	Decision making	Decision making
Remission	Chronic stress vs. adaptability	Advocacy	Continuity of care	Family therapy	Problem solving
Recurrence	Posttraumatic stress reaction vs. reframing	Socioeconomic support	Team approach	Cognitive restructuring	Negotiation
End of Life	Despair vs. integration	Legal aid	Hospice	Bereavement	Effective communication
Survivorship	Victimization vs. empowerment	Political action	Separation	Goal setting	Advocacy

Source: Morrison and Marcusen (1991).

Treatment

During the treatment phase of cancer, the client faces a psychosocial crisis of acute stress versus effective learning. The community interventions in the treatment phase focus on resource development, the medical system interventions center on bioethics, and the individual/family intervention is decision making. Working with this model, the social worker offers the client resources needed to access the preferred treatment. He or she might ask: Is the treatment available, accessible, and affordable? The medical system addresses the ethical considerations and their consistency with the client's wishes and the standard of care. The social worker works with the client to use optimal decision-making tools to improve disease management (Miller et al., 2007).

Remission

During this phase, the client faces the possibility of chronic stress versus the adaptability to cope and deal with change. Mastery in this phase means that the client feels that he or she has been able to adapt to the changes brought on by the cancer and/or the treatment. The client typically achieves some level of comfort with treatment and the ongoing physical support of the medical system, but when the client goes into remission, he or she may experience long-term effects. Acknowledgment of the new psychological and physical challenges is important. The client is expected to return to normal functioning, but much has changed and he or she has not yet fully integrated the reality of his or her medical condition into sense of self and social functioning. In addition, the client may have new physical challenges related to the effects of treatment. The community interventions focus on advocacy for continued support and assimilating back into the society. Legislation, job protections, and legal rights are important for the community to establish and for the social worker to assist the client to access. The medical system interventions focus on continuity of care and then follow-up. The client understands follow-up, whom they call for support, what to pay attention to, and what not to worry about. The individual and family may need family therapy as they assume new roles or give up roles that were taken on during treatment. Inventive problem solving is an important skill to master during this phase.

Recurrence

During recurrence, the client faces the challenge of posttraumatic stress reactions versus reframing. In this phase, social workers can help clients reframe recurrence as another challenge to be mastered, make decisions about new treatments, and develop a new plan of care. Community interventions may focus on financial assistance, resources, and clinical trials. The medical system offers a team approach for the management of the patient and treatment plan. The patient and family are focused on the work of cognitive restructuring. Negotiation becomes a skill that is integral to this phase, and effective negotiation can help the individual better manage job and family responsibilities while receiving treatment and experiencing the effects or challenges brought on by the disease or the treatment.

End of Life

End-of-life themes range from despair to integration. Community interventions include legal resources for estate planning, care at end of life, health care proxy, and decision-making capacity. The medical system offers hospice services, palliative care, and symptom management to ensure comfort, but the individual and family need to grieve. The social worker offers support groups and individual counseling and creates an environment in which to share memories. Effective communication is essential to this phase. Communication that introduces sad news, encourages final conversations, and shows respect is part of this sensitive and difficult time.

Survivorship

During survivorship, the client has the opportunity for empowerment. Using the National Coalition for Cancer Survivorship definition of survivorship, the cancer patient becomes a survivor at diagnosis. To master empowerment, the survivor incorporates self-advocacy skills. The community intervenes for the cancer survivors with political action. The medical team's focus is on survivorship care planning and providing the information needed to ensure the client's continued health-promoting behaviors. The individual and family are focused on goal setting. The client and family may be forever changed by this experience. The social worker's interventions are to focus on ensuring the client is able to progress in his or her community. Self-advocacy is a primary skill in this phase.

As discussed earlier, each phase of this model focuses on specific skills primary to that phase. However, the five basic skills are needed throughout the process and, when learned early and understood, allow the client empowerment. Empowerment felt by the client is the ultimate goal for the social worker and the client. Management of the client's case throughout the process is about empowerment and the individual's ability to move forward. These skills have been defined and explored in the "Cancer Survival Toolbox" (Walsh-Burke & Marcusen, 1999). The model embraces and builds upon the toolbox premise.

Pearls

- Many of the interventions and skills introduced in the training paradigm will be used during multiple stages of the cancer disease process.
- Staff engagement and leadership support are key to the implementation of a multidisciplinary collaborative case management model.
- Client empowerment and the individual's ability to move forward are the measures of success for social work case management.

Pitfalls

- The tendency to want defined roles for each provider and lack of flexibility can limit the social worker's ability to focus on the needs and care of the patient.
- Insufficient attention to communication by the collaborative multidisciplinary team can lead to distrust, territoriality, and poor outcomes.
- Fears about increasing workload are obstacles to implementation of a collaborative model.

This chapter has introduced the oncology social worker to the role of social worker as case manager. A definition of social work case management has been endorsed and a multidisciplinary collaborative case management model introduced. Finally, a training paradigm has been provided for the new social worker.

REFERENCES

Auerbach, C., Mason, S. E., & Laporte, H. H. (2007). Evidence that supports the value of social work in hospitals. *Social Work in Health Care, 44*(4), 17–32.

Berkman, B. (1996). The emerging health care world: Implications for social work practice and education. *Social Work, 41*(5), 541–551.

Cesta, T. (2012). The role of the social worker on the case management team. *Hospital Case Management, 6*, 87–88.

Cowles, L. (1992). Interdisciplinary expectations of the medical social worker in the hospital setting. *Health and Social Work, 17*(1), 57–65.

Dzyacky, S. (1998). An acute care case management model for nurses and social workers. *Nursing Case Management, 3*(5), 208–215.

Ellis, P. M. (2012). The importance of multidisciplinary team management of patient with non-small-cell lung cancer. *Current Oncology, 19*(1), S7–S15.

Erikson, E. H. (1959). *Identity and the life cycle*. New York, NY: International Universities Press.

McGeehan, R. (2007). Best practice in record-keeping. *Nursing Standard, 21*(17), 51–55.

Miller, J. J., Frost, M. H., Rummans, T. A., Huschka, M., Atherton, P., Brown, P., . . . Clark, M. M. (2007). Role of a medical social worker in improving quality of life for patients with advanced cancer with a structured multidisciplinary intervention. *Journal of Psychosocial Oncology, 25*(4), 105–119.

Mizrahi, T., & Davis, L. E. (Eds.). (2008). *Encyclopedia of social work* (20th ed.). Oxford, England: Oxford University Press.

Morrison, D., & Marcusen, C. (1991, April–May). *A new training program for oncology social workers. NAOSW's Navigating the Course Thru Creative Interventions.* Poster presented at the meeting of the Association of Oncology Social Work, Monterey, CA.

National Association of Social Workers. (1992). NASW standards for social work case management. Retrieved from http://www

.courts.state.ny.us/reporter/webdocs/nasw_standards_social-work_casemgt.htm

National Association of Social Workers. (2013). *NASW standards for social work case management*. Washington, DC: Author. Retrieved from http://www.socialworkers.org/practice/nasw-standards/casemanagementstandards2013.pdf

National Coalition for Cancer Survivorship (NCCS). (2011). *Cancer survivor toolbox and resource booklet*. Silver Spring, MD: Author.

Robbins, C. L., & Birmingham, J. (2005). The social worker and nurse roles in case management: Applying the three R's. *Lippincott's Case Management, 10*(3), 120–127. PubMed PMID: 15931043

Stefanacci, R. (2013). Care coordination today: What, why, who, where, and how? *Annals of Long-Term Care: Clinical Care and Aging, 21*(3), 38–42.

Stroman, R. (2003). *The disability rights movements: From deinstitutionalization to self-determination*. Lanham, MD: University Press of America.

Walsh-Burke, K., & Marcusen, C. (1999). The cancer survival toolbox. *Self-Advocacy Training for Cancer Survivors, 7*(6), 297–301.

88

Melissa Sileo Stewart and Rian Rodriguez

Patient Navigation in Oncology

Key Concepts

- *Patient navigation is a method to improve patient access to cancer prevention and treatment and reduce health disparities.*
- *Oncology social workers are trained to assess barriers, identify options to overcome them, and work within the patient's existing social system. This knowledge, skill, and value base is closely aligned with the goals of patient navigation.*
- *There is an emerging consensus on the principles and programs of patient navigation.*
- *Patient navigation encompasses a broad range of models, interventions, and service roles.*
- *Programs are increasingly focused on defining outcomes and metrics for patient navigation services and programs that will demonstrate their effectiveness.*

In 2012, the American College of Surgeons' Commission on Cancer (COC) announced patient navigation as a new accreditation standard for cancer programs in hospitals. Recognizing that patients and loved ones have needs that extend beyond clinical treatment, the standard emphasizes a multidisciplinary approach to cancer care. The standard requires that all COC-accredited programs have a patient navigation program to address patients' barriers to care and to provide psychosocial support and posttreatment survivorship care services (COC, 2012). The standard is projected to go into effect in 2015.

Navigation processes are acknowledged to be fundamental in social work. In 2010, patient navigation in the cancer care setting was addressed in a position paper by a work group of the Oncology Nursing Society (ONS), Association of Oncology Social Work (AOSW), and National Association of Social Workers (NASW). It was defined as "individualized assistance offered to patients, families, and caregivers to help overcome healthcare system barriers and facilitate timely access to quality health and psychosocial care from pre diagnosis through all phases of the cancer experience" (ONS, AOSW, & NASW, 2010). Navigation programs were expected to incorporate collaboration with community-based resources, reflecting the strengths and the challenges of the community, system, and facility in which the programs reside. Programs were described as either barrier focused, addressing the specific challenges of access to care, or service focused, addressing the provision of services such as coordinating patient care and education (Dohan & Schrag, 2005). This work group further clarified the scope of education for navigation "to include the ability to conduct community assessments and the identification and crafting of interventions to resolve systems barriers that interfere with timely access to treatment and care" (NASW, 2010).

Overview and Historical Perspective of the Patient Navigation Model

Patient navigation has evolved as a strategy to improve outcomes in vulnerable populations by eliminating barriers to timely diagnosis, treatment, and survivorship care for people with cancer. Some Americans in particular—the poor, the uninsured, and the underinsured—have not fully

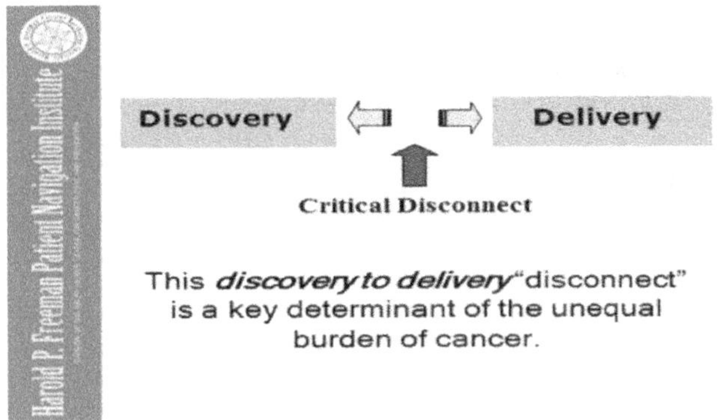

Figure 88.1. The Discovery–Delivery Disconnect
Source: Freeman (2002).

benefited from medical advances in cancer treatment as measured by their higher cancer mortality and lower cancer survival. Poor and uninsured Americans meet barriers to obtaining timely diagnosis and treatment of cancer and other life-threatening diseases, which leads to late diagnosis and treatment and increased mortality (Freeman, Muth, & Kerner, 1995). These findings suggest a disconnect between the nation's discovery and delivery enterprises—a disconnect between what we know and what we do—believed to be a principal determinant of the unequal burden of cancer and resultant cancer health disparities (Figure 88.1).

By 1985, Dr. Harold Freeman was serving as chief of surgery for Harlem Hospital, a position that allowed him to further his research on the particular issues driving the poor survival rates (39% and 27% at 5 and 10 years, respectively) of Black women diagnosed with breast cancer at Harlem Hospital (Freeman & Wasfie, 1989). Dr. Freeman was among the early researchers realizing the correlations between socioeconomic inequality and health outcomes (Freeman, 1991). Based on much of Dr. Freeman's work, the American Cancer Society issued its 1989 "Report to the Nation: Cancer in the Poor," which concluded that the following were the most critical issues confronting poor people with cancer:

- Poor people face substantial barriers to obtaining cancer care and often do not seek care if they cannot pay for it.
- Poor people and their families often make extreme personal sacrifices to obtain and pay for care.
- Fatalism about cancer is prevalent among the poor and may prevent them from seeking care.
- Cancer education programs are often culturally insensitive and irrelevant to many poor people.
- Poor people endure greater pain and suffering from cancer than other Americans.

These findings, combined with the community clinical experience, led to the concept of patient navigation. The nation's first patient navigation program (Figure 88.2) was initiated by Dr. Freeman in 1990 at Harlem Hospital, a public health care delivery facility in New York. The original program, funded with a grant from the American Cancer Society, focused on the critical window of opportunity to save lives from cancer by eliminating barriers to timely care between the point of suspicious finding and the resolution of the finding by diagnosis and treatment.

The programmatic aim of the original program was to diminish the extremely high breast cancer death rate in a population of poor Black women. Retrospective studies of the Harlem Hospital breast cancer experience provided evidence that the combined interventions of patient navigation and free or low-cost breast cancer screening resulted in an increase in early-stage cancer diagnosis and treatment and a marked increase in 5-year survival (39% to 70%) in a population of poor Black women, half of whom were uninsured (Oluwole et al., 2003). Subsequently, the scope of patient navigation was expanded to be applied across the entire health care continuum, including prevention, detection,

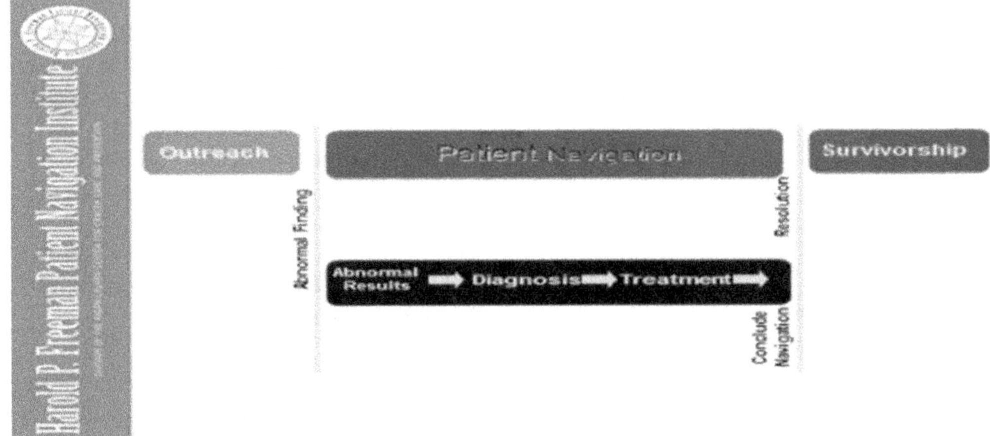

Figure 88.2. Original Patient Navigation Model
Source: Freeman, Muth, and Kerner (1995).

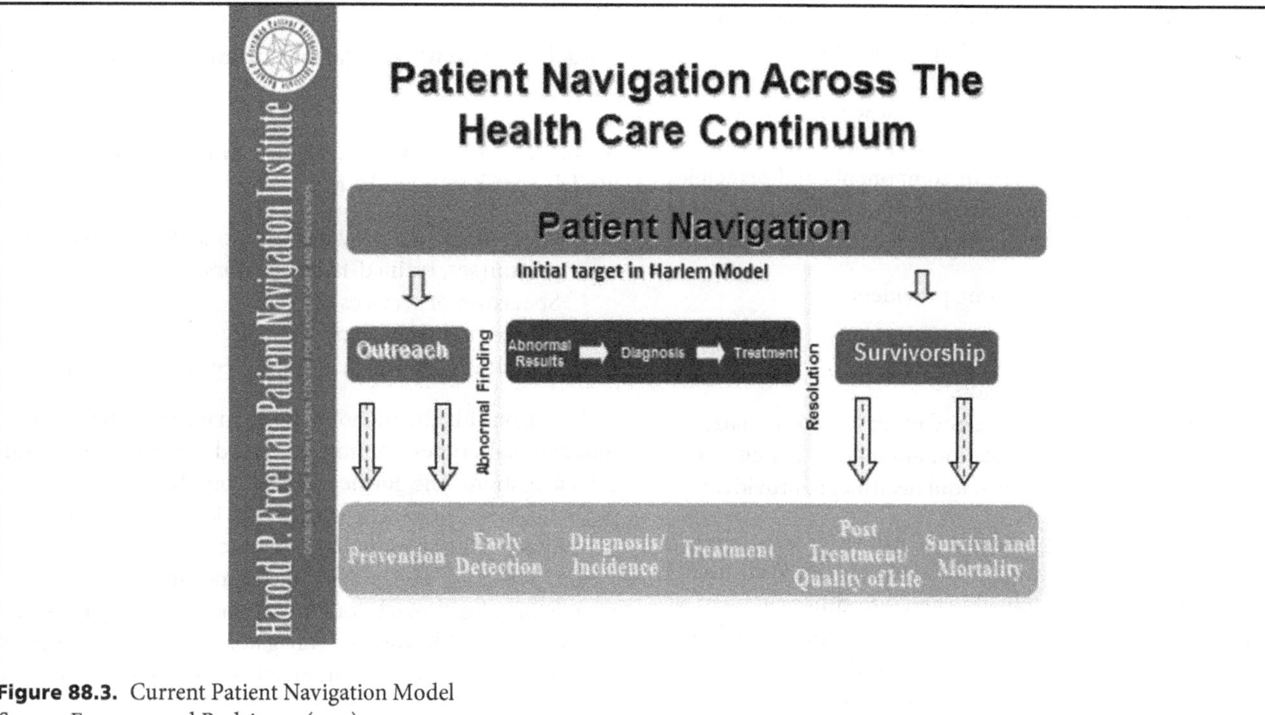

Figure 88.3. Current Patient Navigation Model
Source: Freeman and Rodriguez (2011).

diagnosis, treatment, and survivorship to the end of life (Figure 88.3).

Oncology social workers are trained to assess barriers, identify options to overcome them, and work within the patient's existing social system. This knowledge and skill base is closely aligned with the goals of patient navigation. Within the social work discipline, patient navigation and its basic tenets and related skills are an ideal match with the extensive education, training, and licensure oversight that is already a rigorous part of the profession.

Principles of Patient Navigation

Freeman and Rodriguez (2011) explain the following principles of patient navigation:

- Patient navigation is a patient-centered health care service delivery model. The focus of navigation is to promote the timely movement of an individual patient through an often complex health care continuum.
- Patient navigation serves to virtually integrate a fragmented health care system for the individual patient.
- The core function of patient navigation is the elimination of individual and systemic barriers to timely care across all phases of the health care continuum.
- Patient navigation should be defined with a clear scope of practice that distinguishes the role and responsibilities of the navigator from those of all other providers.
- Delivery of patient navigation services should be cost-effective and commensurate with the training and skill necessary to navigate an individual through a particular phase of the care continuum.
- The determination of who should navigate should be based on the level of skill required at a given phase of navigation. There is a spectrum of navigation extending from services that may be provided by trained lay navigators to services that require navigators who are professionals, such as nurses and social workers.
- In a given system of care, there is the need to define the points at which navigation begins and ends.
- There is a need to navigate patients across disconnected systems of care, such as primary care sites and tertiary care sites. Patient navigation can serve as the process that connects disconnected health care systems.
- Patient navigation systems require coordination. In larger systems of patient care, this coordination is best carried out by assigning a navigation coordinator or champion who is responsible for overseeing all phases of navigation activity within a given health care site or system.

Patient Navigators and Roles: Oncology Social Work and Other Allied Health Professionals

Though patient navigation programs are spreading rapidly across the country in underserved communities and medical institutions, there is little consensus about what programs should include and what outcome measures should be used (Wells et al., 2008). The lack of a universal definition of patient navigation has resulted in confusion regarding a patient navigator's role and the direction of navigation as a field. Currently, patient navigation programs are customized depending on the needs of the community, and much of the literature agrees on certain components and principles of patient navigation. Commonly found services provided by patient navigation in the literature include the following:

- Coordinating care among providers.
- Educating patients.
- Offering therapeutic support.
- Arranging transportation.
- Coordinating child care and other logistical matters.
- Facilitating communication among the patient, family members, caregivers, and health care providers.

The role of a patient navigator is also to identify barriers to timely care and determine the best strategies to eliminate those barriers for each client. There are different types of patient navigators, but due to the aforementioned lack of a clear universal definition of navigation, the responsibilities associated with each of these roles is often blurred (Center for Health Affairs, 2012). According to Pratt-Chapman and Willis (2013), there are five different types of navigators:

- Nurse navigators: Also known as clinical navigators, nurse navigators assist patients and their families in understanding a diagnosis and educating them about the disease. They also connect clients to community resources.
- Social workers: Also known as psychosocial or professional navigators, oncology social workers often provide emotional support services to patients and their families. Like nurse navigators, oncology social workers provide clients with appropriate community resources.
- Lay, trained navigators: Also known as resource locators or care coordinators, lay navigators help coordinate patients' schedules and connect them to local resources.
- Peer navigators: Peer navigators are cancer survivors or caregivers who inform patients and their families about what to expect during treatment and posttreatment.
- Community health workers: Community health workers are responsible for the outreach element of the navigation process.

As the goal of navigation is to offer comprehensive cancer care services, the roles of navigators often overlap to ensure a smooth transition between services and that each service is complementary (Center for Health Affairs, 2012). Required qualifications for navigators vary based on the type of position (nurse, social worker, peer, etc.) and include individuals with undergraduate degrees or master's degrees, research assistants, and more (Wells et al., 2008).

Models of Patient Navigation: Community Based and Clinical

According to Varner and Murph (2010), patient navigation models vary based on the following:

- Type of service provider (e.g., oncology social workers, nurses, trained/lay navigators).
- Spectrum of services offered.
- Client qualification or eligibility requirements.
- Timeframe for when services begin and conclude.

Based on this distinction, patient navigation has evolved into two main types: community-based navigation and clinical navigation. The former focuses on the emotional and practical effects of cancer, whereas the latter focuses more on the physical effects and medical care coordination and education. Typically, navigators in a community-based program include oncology social workers, lay and peer navigators, and community health workers. Navigators in a clinical program usually include oncology nurse navigators and social workers.

Navigation Programs

The scope of services offered through a patient navigation program varies depending on the type and model of the program and the needs of the communities it serves. Wells et al. (2008) identified common characteristics of navigation programs:

- They are provided only to individuals for a "defined episode of cancer-related care."
- They target a "defined set of health services that are required to complete an episode of cancer-related care."
- Tracking clients over time is encouraged, but navigation programs have a specific end point when the services are considered complete.
- They focus primarily on identifying individual-level barriers to accessing care along the cancer care continuum.
- They aim to decrease delays in accessing care services in a timely manner and to reduce the number of clients who get lost in the follow-up process.

In most cases, licensed oncology social workers and psychologists in the organization are not part of the navigation team. However, clients who need emotional support or counseling services are often referred to social workers and psychologists as needed. Almost all existing navigation programs do, however, include the following services:

- Coordination of care: Scheduling cancer-related appointments and sending reminders.

- Connecting resources: Identifying relevant and helpful community resources for clients and facilitating the connection.
- Financial management: Assisting clients in managing finances related to medical care.

Coordination of care is the most common characteristic of clinical patient navigation programs. However, the following services were rarely offered as part of a navigation programs:

- Transportation: Providing or locating transportation services for all cancer-related appointments.
- Emotional/psychosocial support services: Licensed social workers or psychologists providing emotional and/or psychosocial support to survivors and their loved ones.

A woman is newly diagnosed with breast cancer during a routine mammogram. She does not have adequate insurance coverage and, therefore, has delayed treatment of her cancer and is now experiencing physical symptoms and comes to the emergency room. An oncology social worker navigator would assess the woman's options to gain adequate insurance coverage and/or access to treatment options through other means, such as compassionate care programs. Additionally, through a formal assessment of the woman's current environmental status, the oncology social worker navigator would determine if there were other barriers to care, such as lack of transportation to treatment, child care or employment concerns, and lack of access to adequate support systems.

Through appropriate assessment and interventions, the oncology social worker navigator would determine a course of action to identify the access to care issues and put a plan in place to address these issues during the woman's cancer diagnosis, treatment, and survivorship.

Outcome Measures and Metrics for Patient Navigation

Despite the rapid expansion of navigation programs across the United States, a review of the literature reveals an inconsistency in the outcome measures and metrics (Fiscella et al., 2011; Wells et al., 2008). Outcome measures are more commonly recorded for the clinical model of patient navigation but are not as frequently documented for community-based patient navigation programs. Currently, clinical navigation programs, which tend to focus on screening, diagnosis, and outreach, such as Freeman's original program, have had the most demonstrable success (Varner & Murph, 2010). To establish patient navigation as a standards- and evidence-based approach to providing cancer care, and to allow it to grow as a sustainable field within health care, it is imperative that tasks, target populations, and related intended outcomes be standardized (Crane-Okada, 2013; Wells et al., 2008). Without established core outcome measures and metrics, replication of navigation programs with successful outcomes will not be possible (Battaglia, Burhansstipanov, Murrell, Dwyer, & Caron, 2011).

However, Battaglia and colleagues also state that many of the differences observed in the study of prevention and early detection programs are "either in the nomenclature used to describe them or the analyses used to report them" (2011, p. 3559) and not in the data elements collected. Key data elements can also be called key performance indicators (KPIs). Based on this finding, Battaglia and colleagues (2011) suggest defining common KPIs as an alternative to developing rigid outcome metrics because this will allow for variability in navigation programs. Suggested methods to collect KPIs include self-reports by patients, navigator logs, clinical data sources, and observation.

Although the literature on community-based navigation is limited in comparison to clinical navigation, some outcome measures identified for clinical navigation programs can be adapted for use in community-based programs as well. For example, Crane-Okada (2013) identified KPIs that could be measured and used to assess the degree to which an oncology nurse navigation program was achieving its intended goal:

- Number of patients seen.
- Average caseload.
- Demographic characteristics of patients seen (e.g., age, gender, diagnosis, stage, treatment complexity, acuity).
- Number of contacts with patients.
- Types of barriers identified (individual or system).
- Barriers resolved.
- Duration of contacts (e.g., minutes of contact and/or duration of follow-up).
- Use of translation services.
- Documentation completion.
- Number of requests from professional colleagues for assistance with patients or families.
- Committee or task force involvement.
- Costs (e.g., fixed expenditures for salary and benefits, as well as grants or donations generated as a result of activities).
- Types of services delivered to patients and families (e.g., education, referrals to specific resource, validation, coaching).

Additionally, Freund and colleagues (2008) developed a navigator tracking log, which includes the following:

- Date of appointment (including walk-ins).
- Length of actual time spent with the client.
- Type of encounter.
- Barriers to care.
- Navigator's actions.

This tracking log complements the list of KPIs Crane-Okada (2013) identified. The purpose of this log is to have a tool that can be used to compare core variables across all sites.

In addition to identifying KPIs, Battaglia and colleagues (2011) state the need for consistent modifiable and nonmodifiable navigation program characteristics, explaining that these characteristics "will facilitate meaningful program comparisons even in the absence of common outcome metrics." Although the amount and type of information gathered can be extensive, each program should collect data that is valuable in evaluating and growing the program. Wells et al. (2008) emphasize being aware of the type of organization collecting the data and its capability to analyze it. The results of the little available literature on the evaluation of navigation programs are not comparable because the studies did not use similar outcome measures. The studies also had limitations, including small sample sizes and lack of control groups, which prevented generalization of results (Wells et al., 2008). The literature is lacking in its review of community-based navigation programs and the associated outcome measures and metrics.

Evaluation Tools and Policy Implications

Because standard program evaluation procedures have not yet been developed, navigation programs have thus far been evaluated through individual studies. Based on the limited information currently available on evaluation of navigation programs, it seems that the most common evaluation tools are patient satisfaction surveys and navigator logs (Crane-Okada, 2013; Freund et al., 2008).

As hospitals with cancer programs across the country begin the development and implementation of their patient navigation programs, the need for qualified navigators is increasing. Through the review of navigation programs in the United States and a review of news articles from reputed sources in 2013, there appears to be a noticeable trend toward navigators seeking professional education. Although 10 of the programs reviewed indicated that they had not sought professional certification, all programs reviewed indicated that their navigators attended professional development courses or conferences throughout the year. The 2013 review also revealed that only 12 out of the 26 programs reviewed provided psychosocial or emotional support as part of navigation services. Other programs referred the patient to another source for psychosocial support. The psychosocial support was often provided by oncology nurse navigators, and not by licensed social workers or psychologists.

Because the COC standard is directed toward hospital-based cancer programs, clinical programs continue to be the primary focus in navigation growth, evaluation, and analysis. Although the number of community-based navigation programs is growing, the expansion of this type of program is slower than clinical programs. In addition, federal policies related to patient navigation and survivorship is limited. In 2005, President George W. Bush signed the Patient Navigator Outreach and Chronic Disease Prevention Act (PNOCDP), which allotted $25 million to be distributed via grants to eligible organizations providing patient navigation services. The purpose of the bill was to determine whether navigators play a role in reducing barriers to care and improving health care outcomes. The bill required that applying organizations demonstrate a plan to establish baseline measures to evaluate the program's outcomes and impact.

The funding cycle concluded in 2010 but was extended for an additional 5 years (2010–2015) through the 2010 Affordable Care Act, which added an additional eligibility criterion that requires patient navigators to meet core proficiencies defined by the applying organization.

Pearls

- It is important to understand ways oncology social workers can best work with and alongside other support disciplines.
- The social work navigator begins by identifying the needs of the community/population assigned to receive navigational services.
- Ensure clear evaluation strategies and outcome measures to show the impact of oncology social work navigators.
- Learn the policy implications and grant opportunities available to support a patient navigation program.

Pitfalls

- Insufficient attention to evaluation and outcome measures will result in a lack of evidence and understanding about the impact of oncology social work navigators.
- Unclear role delineation of oncology social work navigators and other types of navigators may lead to difficult work environments and confusion for patients and families.
- Lack of clearly stated competencies and ongoing assessment of training opportunities may affect the ability of oncology social work navigators to be successful in their settings.

Navigation services have been fundamental to social work since its earliest development as a profession. It is in the profession's best interest to find ways to work with patient navigators from allied health professions while also defining a clear and distinct role for oncology social work navigators. Social workers can be instrumental in defining these varied competencies. The 2010 joint position paper by the Oncology Nursing Society, Association of Oncology Social Work, and National Association of Social Workers, cited at the beginning of this chapter, is an example of how professional groups can align on these issues and be seen as championing a movement rather than challenging it.

REFERENCES

American Cancer Society. (1989). A summary of the American Cancer Society report to the nation: Cancer in the poor. *CA: A Cancer Journal for Clinicians*, *39*(5), 263–265.

American College of Surgeons' Commission on Cancer. (2012). Cancer program standards 2012: Ensuring patient-centered care. Retrieved from https://www.facs.org/~/media/files/quality%20programs/cancer/coc/programstandards2012.ashx

Battaglia, T., Burhansstipanov, L., Murrell, S. S., Dwyer, A. J., & Caron, S. E. (2011). Assessing the impact of patient navigation. *Cancer*, *117*(15), 3553–3564. Retrieved from http://onlinelibrary.wiley.com/doi/10.1002/cncr.26267/full

Crane-Okada, R. (2013). Evaluation and outcome measures in patient navigation. *Seminars in Oncology Nursing*, *29*(2), 128–140.

Center for Health Affairs. (2012). *The emerging field of patient navigation: A golden opportunity to improve healthcare*. Retrieved from http://www.chanet.org/TheCenterForHealthAffairs/MediaCenter/NewsReleases/~/media/A92355F0A6E140F1A13493BC3C349CAB.ashx

Dohan, D., & Schrag, D. (2005). Using navigators to improve care of underserved patients: Current practices and approaches. *Cancer*, *104*(4), 848–855.

Fiscella, K., Ransom, S., Jean-Pierre, P., Cella, D., Stein, K., Bauer, J. E., . . . Walsh, K. (2011). Patient-reported outcome measures suitable to assessment of patient navigation. *Cancer*, *117*(15), 3603–3617.

Freeman, H. P. (2002). *Voices of a broken system: Real people, real problems*. Bethesda, MD: National Cancer Institute.

Freeman, H. P., Muth, B. J., & Kerner, J. F. (1995). Expanding access to cancer screening and clinical follow up among the medically underserved. *Cancer Practice*, *3*, 19–30.

Freeman, H. P., & Wasfie, T. J. (1989). Cancer of the breast in poor black women. *Cancer*, *63*(12), 2562–2569.

Freeman, H. P. (1991). Race, poverty, and cancer. *Journal of the National Cancer Institute*, *83*, 526–527.

Freeman, H. P., & Rodriguez, R. L. (2011). Principles of patient navigation. *Cancer*, *117*(15 Suppl.), 3539–3542.

Freund, K., Battaglia, T. A., Calhoun, E., Dudley, D. J., Fiscella, K., Paskett, E., . . . Roetzheim, R. G. (2008). National Cancer Institute Patient Navigation Research Program: Methods, protocol, and measures. *Cancer*, *113*(12), 3391–3399.

National Association of Social Workers (NASW). (2010, April 19). Oncology nursing and social work professional associations release position on patient navigation. Retrieved from http://www.naswdc.org/pressroom/2010/041910.asp

Oluwole, S. F., Ali, A. O., Adu, A., Blane, B. P., Barlow, B., Oropeza, R., & Freeman, H. P. (2003). Impact of cancer screening program on breast cancer stage at diagnosis in a medically underserved urban community. *Journal of the American College of Surgeons*, *196*(2), 180–188.

Oncology Nursing Society (ONS), Association of Oncology Social Work (AOSW), & National Association of Social Workers (NASW). (2010, March). *Joint position paper on the role of oncology nursing and oncology social work in patient navigation*. Retrieved from http://www.socialworkers.org/pressroom/2010/Position%20on%20Patient%20Navigation%20BW.pdf

Pratt-Chapman, M., & Willis, A. (2013). Community cancer center administration and support for navigation services. *Seminars in Oncology Nursing*, *29*(2), 141–148.

Varner, A., & Murph, P. (2010). Cancer patient navigation: Where do we go from here? *Oncology Issues* (May/June), 50–53.

Wells, K., Battaglia, T. A., Dudley, D. J., Garcia, R., Greene, A., Calhoun, E., . . . Raich, P. C. (2008). Patient navigation: State of the art or is it science? *Cancer*, *113*(8), 1999–2010. doi:10.1002/cncr.23815

89

Jane Levy and Michele McCourt

Bridging Increasing Financial Gaps and Challenges in Service Delivery

Cancer can be a big financial burden on families, particularly those with lower incomes and those facing cancer without health insurance. Many have to dip into or deplete their savings . . . and some have trouble paying for basic necessities like food and housing.

—*Kaiser Family Foundation, USA Today, and Harvard School of Public Health (2006)*

Key Concepts

- *Financial challenges can affect the patient's and family's ability to cope with a cancer diagnosis and is a major source of psychosocial stress.*
- *Financial hardship can complicate adherence to prescribed treatment.*
- *Patients may be reluctant or embarrassed to discuss costs with the oncology treatment team.*
- *Oncology social workers can facilitate difficult conversations about financial barriers, open up communications with and among the treatment team, and link patients to financial and community resources.*

Cancer is an expensive illness. Its costs include the direct and related expenses of diagnosis and treatment, as well as the societal costs related to loss of earnings, earning power, and productivity. The costs to patients and their families can be particularly devastating on the unemployed, people without adequate or any health insurance, and people without savings or other resources. Even the most fiscally astute family can find itself overwhelmed and unprepared for the out-of-pocket expenses associated with a cancer diagnosis (Didem, Bernard, Farr, & Fang, 2011).

The three types of expenses associated with cancer are those of direct medical costs, related nonmedical expenses, and expenses of daily living. First, direct medical costs include physicians' fees, hospital charges, and medications. Basic health insurance may cover such expenses with the extent or terms of coverage dictating the cost to the patient, but millions who have health insurance may still have inadequate coverage for outpatient care or prescription costs (Arozullah et al., 2004). Additionally, an estimated 49 million persons are not covered by any type of insurance (Martinez & Cohen, 2012). Second, health insurance does not cover most of the nonmedical costs of cancer. These costs include such services as transportation to treatment, child care, home care, products like wigs and prostheses, over-the-counter medications, and other devices and medical aids. Third, expenses related to daily living such as food, shelter, utilities, and insurance premiums often become hardships due to lack or loss of income after receiving a cancer diagnosis. The options for assistance are few and often have to be pieced together from several sources (Kaiser Family Foundation, *USA Today*, & Harvard School of Public Health 2006).

Financial concerns affect patients' and families' abilities to marshal their emotional resources to cope with cancer. A 2010 *Cancer* journal article reported, for example, that financial pressure put low- and middle-income women at higher risk for anxiety and depression following a diagnosis of ductal carcinoma in situ. Neither higher educational level nor strong social support eased the negative impact of financial problems, leaving women to manage the competing stressors of both "financial hardship and the stress of a major health event" (DeMoor, Partridge, Winer, Ligibel, & Emmons, 2010).

Financial stress may also interfere with treatment compliance or access to clinical trials when patients cannot afford transportation to treatment or prescribed medications (Shankaran, Jolly, Blough, & Ramsey, 2012). The topic of money, often taboo under normal circumstances, may be even more so under the strained circumstances of illness, with families finding it difficult to face the problem and ask for help before a crisis begins (Weissman, 1979).

In a study of three low-income communities that evaluated the consequences of medical debt on those with chronic illnesses, including cancer, the authors reported that the accumulation of medical debt caused feelings of stress, anxiety, and hopelessness, with patients and families feeling financially punished for medical events that were out of their control (Total Access Project, 2003).

Similarly, a 2009 survey by the Association of Oncology Social Work (AOSW) demonstrated the extraordinary financial hardships that complicate or compromise cancer treatment. The survey, which included data from oncology social workers, patients, and caregivers, underscored financial stress as a factor in reducing patient compliance with treatment, creating difficulty in affording treatment, and rapidly depleting savings and resources. Two thirds of patients and caregivers experienced financial hardship due to medical bills, and 55% of all patients surveyed said that the stress of dealing with costs negatively affected their ability to focus on their recovery. That number increased to 87% for those patients with major financial burdens. Despite this overwhelming stress, only one third of patients reported discussing costs with their oncologists and, although the data showed that social workers were well trained at helping patients with financial concerns, only 34% of patients utilized a social worker as a resource. It was noted that many oncology settings do not employ social workers and those that do may have insufficient numbers to provide the full range of supportive services that patients need (Eicholz, Pevar, & Bernthal, 2010).

Bridging the Increasing Gaps in Services

The Institute of Medicine (IOM) report *Cancer Care for the Whole Patient: Meeting Psychosocial Health Needs* identified six areas of psychosocial concern associated with cancer that, when unaddressed, cause additional suffering, weaken adherence to prescribed treatments, and threaten a return to health. Chief among these concerns was the need for financial advice, planning, and assistance, as well as logistical support, such as transportation and lodging resources. The IOM report established a standard of care that calls for facilitating effective communication between patients and care providers, identifying psychosocial needs, and designing plans that link patients to services, coordinate biomedical and psychosocial care, engage and support patients in managing their care, provide follow-up, and allow for re-evaluation to monitor effectiveness. The committee found that although the supply of services was not sufficient to resolve all psychosocial problems, there were untapped services available often at no cost to patients, who were unaware that they existed or knew how to access them (IOM, 2007).

Role of Oncology Social Work

Oncology social workers, with their focus on the needs of the whole person, can assist cancer patients by engaging them in discussions of the financial challenges they face and helping them develop strategies to address these concerns. Such discussions include but are not limited to facilitating communication among family members and the health care team; helping patients manage their finances and understand, maintain, or obtain health insurance and prescription coverage; providing access to and information about available public and private resources and sources of financial support by linking patients to resources in the community; and helping patients understand their rights in the workplace and other protections from existing legislation (Kennedy, Smolinski, & Colon, 2010).

Oncology social workers are no strangers to sensitive subjects and can help initiate delicate conversations among family members about financial stress and its impact on family roles and relationships. They can encourage a dialogue among members to explore sources of support among each other, friends, neighbors, and trusted members of the community who may be willing to assist financially by helping patients pay bills, making phone calls, organizing paperwork, or spearheading a fund-raising campaign.

Oncology social workers can also encourage frank conversation with the health care team about issues of cost. Patients are often embarrassed or reluctant to discuss the costs of care, but many providers understand that patients have concerns (Zafar & Abernathy, 2013). In many respects, the time has never been riper for this discussion, because we are in the midst of a larger national health care debate (in the United States) concerning, in part, greater cost shares for patients and the rise of expensive therapies. As such, discussions on limiting treatment because of the cost of care are no longer taboo. In its 2009 guidance statement "The Cost of Cancer Care," the American Society for Clinical Oncology concluded that frank talk about costs had positive outcomes in improving communication that led to referrals to resources and discussions of comparable treatment alternatives (Merepol et al., 2009).

Social workers can facilitate these discussions and identify and direct patients to key persons who can also help, such as financial counselors, case managers, patient navigators and advocates, and reimbursement and claims specialists. Uninsured patients can be helped to obtain charity care or assistance in accessing health insurance and prescription medications.

Social workers can help patients manage their financial concerns by assisting them in organizing their personal finances. Simple directives, such as tracking income and expenses, completing a budget worksheet, exploring opportunities to lower costs, and consolidating debt, can help patients feel more in control and possibly avert a financial crisis. Helping patients review their health insurance policies to determine deductibles, co-payments, and covered services can allow them to better estimate their medical expenses. Patients can be advised on filing for appeals in the case of denials and may also be surprised that their plan will provide them with a case manager. Dealing with insurance concerns can be time-consuming and daunting, and social workers can link patients to organizations that will advocate for patients and their insurers, as well as fee-for-service claims specialists. Finally, in this age of expensive therapies, social workers can direct patients to both pharmaceutical and co-pay assistance described in detail in the next section (Cancer Support Community, 2013).

Tips for Helping Patients Manage the Cost of Care

- *Review income and expenses.*
- *Complete a budget worksheet.*
- *Communicate with health care team about costs.*
- *Understand health care insurance and covered costs.*
- *Save on medications.*
- *Link up with advocacy and nonprofit organizations.*
- *Know rights and protections under the law.*

Closing the Gaps Through Pharmaceutical Assistance Programs

Although new biologics and targeted treatment cancer medications are on the horizon, the cost for these innovative treatments are expensive, with some costing over $100,000 a year (Mustaqeem & Rajkumar, 2012). As pharmaceutical companies prepare for U.S. Food and Drug Administration approval of these treatments, they will also prepare to provide "safety net" programs designed to provide access to therapy for patients who would not be able to afford the medication without assistance.

If a patient has no insurance or does not have a prescription plan through an insurance policy, he or she may be eligible to receive the medication for free from the drug company. To be eligible for a free drug program, the patient must meet certain financial and medical criteria established by the program.

A good way to access information about these safety-net programs is through an Internet search. Type in the name of the prescribed medication and the search results should bring you to the product-specific website and/or the drug manufacturer's website. There you should find all the resources available through the drug company about reimbursement and patient assistance programs. Some services will include benefits investigation or assistance with prior authorizations and coverage appeals. For uninsured or underinsured individuals, the site will provide information on the types of assistance available to them directly through the drug manufacturer or provide resources to other types of assistance programs.

For people who do not have access to the Internet, another way to find out about these programs is by calling the reimbursement hotline or toll-free number associated with the drug. Typically, with more expensive medications, the prescribing health care provider will provide the patient with information on accessing these services. Health care providers may also have a financial counselor on staff available to help patients navigate and enroll in the different types of programs available.

To be eligible for a drug company's patient assistance program (PAP), the patient must meet certain financial and medical criteria. Typically, these programs are for individuals who do not qualify for Medicare or Medicaid and have no other insurance. In some cases, patients who do have Medicare with a Part D prescription drug plan may also be eligible for these programs. However, if a patient qualifies and chooses to participate in such a program, the medication received through a free drug program cannot be submitted through the person's Part D prescription drug plan and will not count toward the patient's true out-of-pocket costs, to get him or her through the Medicare coverage gap and into the catastrophic phase of coverage. Another caveat, once the drug manufacturer assists a Medicare Part D patient with a free drug, it must continue that assistance for the remainder of the calendar year (Federal Register, 2005).

Drug Manufacturer Co-Pay Card Programs for Privately Insured Patient

Many cancer patients with insurance coverage still face high out-of-pocket costs for oral prescription medications. Drug manufacturers offer co-pay cards for their branded products, but they are only available to privately insured individuals, not those with Medicare, Medicaid, or other federally funded insurance plans. As with all of these programs, patients must meet certain medical and financial criteria. For infused therapies, for example, drug companies have programs that work directly with treating physicians to replace medications used for patients who cannot afford out-of-pocket treatment costs.

Drug Co-Payment Assistance Programs for Privately Insured Patients

Also available through some drug companies are product-specific co-payment assistance programs. Similar to the co-pay card programs, only patients with non-federally funded insurance are eligible to apply to these programs.

Disease-Specific Co-Payment Assistance Programs Through Independent Not-for-Profit Organizations

While the drug companies provide many safety-net options for patients taking their medications, they are limited in how they can assist a patient with Medicare and other federally funded insurance plans. To assist this patient population, pharmaceutical companies will look to donate funds to an independent not-for-profit organization that offers financial assistance through a co-payment assistance foundation for a specific disease. If the pharmaceutical company manufactures a medication that would be covered through the foundation, it can make a donation to the foundation but cannot dictate or influence how the program is administered or what medications are covered (Federal Register, 2005).

There are approximately nine co-payment assistance foundations throughout the United States. Some foundations provide assistance with co-payments and coinsurance for prescription medications, whereas others also offer assistance with insurance premiums. Each foundation has its own criteria and application review process. However, for the most part, all foundations require that applications include supporting medical and financial documentation. Because most donations to support these foundations are provided by the pharmaceutical industry, the foundations must adhere to the guidance set forth by the Department of Health and Human Services' Office of Inspector General (OIG). Most foundations have received their own individual opinions from the OIG to ensure that they are in compliance with the regulations to be able to assist patients who may have Medicare or other federally funded insurance plans.

Federal Laws and Protections

Oncology social workers can help patients understand protections and benefits that affect people with cancer regarding legal rights, access to care, insurance protection, antidiscrimination laws, and federal benefits. Most prominent among these laws is the Patient Protection and Affordable Care Act (PPACA) with key components regarding preexisting conditions, lifetime caps, and quality-of-care guidelines. The Consolidated Omnibus Budget and Reconciliations Act (COBRA) is designed to help people have access to insurance if they lose their jobs, and the Health Insurance Portability and Accountability Act (HIPAA) is related to privacy of medical information and "portability of insurance." The Family and Medical Leave Act (FMLA) requires unpaid leave under certain circumstances for family and medical reasons, and the Women's Health and Cancer Rights Act requires insurance coverage for mastectomies and breast reconstruction. The Americans With Disabilities Act (ADA), which prevents workplace discrimination and provides federal benefits from Social Security Disability, Supplemental Security Income, and the U.S. Department of Veterans Affairs (VA), as well as insurance coverage under Medicare and Medicaid, is of vital interest to cancer patients looking to preserve income and insurance coverage.

Because federal health care laws are so complex, it is essential for oncology social workers to discuss them with patients and direct patients to free sources of expert knowledge maintained by law centers, nonprofit organizations, and government agencies through websites and toll-free phone lines.

Linking Patients to Resources in the Community

Oncology social workers can also link patients to an array of community resources that they may not be aware of or may have difficulty accessing. Social workers can educate patients about these resources, help patients frame questions, and complete forms and applications. These resources include government and public programs and national nonprofit organizations, as well as local and community-based programs that assist with some of the related uncovered expenses, such as transportation, and programs that provide direct assistance with housing, food, rent, and utilities; eviction protection; and credit counseling. Organizations such as the American Cancer Society, Cancer*Care*, and the Patient Advocate Foundation maintain resource databases both cancer specific and general that can be searched by ZIP code. The United Way 211 Collaborative can link patients to information specialists for help with local community resources that can help, for example, with daily living expenses (Levy, 2002).

Pearls

- Initiate a discussion on financial challenges early in the assessment process. For some, financial concerns may be on the back burner when faced with a diagnosis of cancer, but a frank discussion on the costs of care and other financial obligations may prevent problems later on.
- Sorting through bills and applying for benefits can be time-consuming and the paperwork daunting.

Helping patients identify key players in their personal and professional support networks is central to helping them gain a sense of control.

- Ignoring medical and other debts can lead to severe consequences. Encouraging patients to speak promptly with their medical team and other creditors may help avert a financial crisis. Assist patients in applying promptly for all benefits because the waiting period for government entitlements is often lengthy.
- Link patients with advocacy and case management resources within their communities especially if one will not be available for ongoing follow-up.
- Make photocopies of all financial assistance applications and supporting documentation before submitting them to an organization. Be sure to follow up with referral organizations to confirm that all paperwork has been received and is being processed.

Pitfalls

- Some patients may be reluctant or inexperienced when asking for help or accessing resources. Without a sufficient discussion on the process, many will feel overwhelmed and confused with just a list of organizations and phone numbers to call. Outdated resource information will compound this problem.
- Despite social workers' best intentions, not all financial challenges can be addressed or ameliorated, and clients can easily become demoralized by the lack of resources. Stay focused on what can be accomplished to assist patients in meeting some of their financial concerns, even if the goals seem relatively small in comparison to the need.
- Funding for financial assistance is limited and awards are granted on a first-come, first-served basis. Patients may need to apply to more than one foundation before receiving assistance, and they may be placed on a wait-list until funding becomes available.

Although there has been some thrust on the policy front to decrease gaps in service, many cancer patients continue to struggle with rising expenses, diminished income, and difficult economic circumstances. The challenge for oncology social workers is to stay focused on their ability to assist patients in areas of financial concern and not to feel overwhelmed or discouraged by what often feels to be too few or piecemeal resources and too little time to assist so many in need. Social work skills such as engagement, education, and advocacy can help patients and families manage the stress related to financial concerns. Helping remove, or at least diminish, barriers to care is important. Although the advent of health care reform and the prospect for expanded coverage and access is welcome, one can expect some confusion and a steep learning curve for patients and professionals as they acclimate to new regulations and guidelines. Oncology social workers will need to stay current and versed on all ramifications of new laws and their impacts on care to guide patients through the ever-changing landscape of health care funding reform.

Oncology social workers, who are acutely aware of the stress of financial concerns and gaps in services, can provide a voice for patients. They can raise awareness by forming coalitions to identify gaps, strategizing ways to work collaboratively, and organizing advocacy efforts to educate patients and other professionals. By sharing client stories with the media and legislative bodies examining issues such as access to care, health insurance, legal protections, privacy, and other aspects of psychosocial care, oncology social workers can implement and lead, in the words of the IOM report, cancer care for the whole person.

ADDITIONAL RESOURCES

American Cancer Society: http://www.cancer.org
American Society of Clinical Oncology: http://www.cancer.net (patient website)
Cancer Financial Assistance Coalition: http://www.cancerfac.org
Cancer Legal Resource Center: http://www.cancerlegalresource-center.org
Cancer*Care*: http://www.cancercare.org
Cancer*Care* Co-Payment Assistance Foundation: http://www.cancercarecopay.org
Centers for Medicare and Medicaid: http://www.cms.gov
Chronic Disease Fund: http://www.cdfund.org
HealthCare.gov: http://www.healthcare.gov
Healthwell Foundation: http://www.healthwellfoundation.org
The Leukemia & Lymphoma Society's Co-Pay Assistance Program: http://www.lls.org/copay
National 211Collaborative: http://www.211.org
National Organization for Rare Disorders: http://www.raredis-eases.org
Needy Meds: http://www.needymeds.org
Partnership for Prescription Assistance: http://www.pparx.org
Patient Access Network Foundation: http://www.panfounda-tion.org
Patient Advocate Foundation: http://www.patientadvocate.org
Patient Advocate Foundation, Co-Pay Relief Program: http://www.copays.org
Patient Assistance Link: http://www.patientassistancelink.org
Patient Services Inc.: http://www.patientservicesinc.org
Survivorship A to Z: http://www.survivorshipatoz.org

REFERENCES

Arozullah, A. M., Calhoun, E. A., Wolf, M., Finley, D. K., Fitzner, K. A., Heckinger, E. A., . . . Bennett, C. L. (2004). The financial burden of cancer: Estimates from a study of insured women with breast cancer. *Journal of Supportive Oncology*, 2, 271–278.

Cancer Support Community. (2013). *Frankly speaking about cancer: Coping with the cost of care*. Washington, DC: Author.

DeMoor, J. S., Partridge, A. H., Winer, E. P., Ligibel, J., & Emmons, K. (2010). The role of socioeconomic status in adjustment following ductal carcinoma in situ. *Cancer, 116*, 1218–1225.

Didem, S. M., Bernard, S., Farr, L., & Fang. (2011). National estimates of out-of-pocket health care expenditure with cancer: 2001–2008. *Journal of Clinical Oncology, 29*(20), 2821–2826.

Eicholz, M., Pevar, J., & Bernthal, T. (2010). Perspectives on the financial burden of cancer care: Concurrent surveys of patients (Pts), caregivers (CGs), and oncology social workers (OSWs). *Journal of Clinical Oncology*, 2012 ASCO Annual Meeting abstracts, *28*(15 Suppl.), 9111.

Federal Register. (2005). Vol. 70, No. 224/Tuesday, November 22, 2005/Notices pg. 70624–70627.

Institute of Medicine. (2007). *Cancer care for the whole patient: Meeting psychosocial health needs*. Washington, DC: National Academies Press.

Kaiser Family Foundation, USA Today, Harvard School of Public Health. (2006, November 1). Summary and chartpack: National survey of households affected by cancer. Retrieved from http://kff.org/health-costs/poll-finding/summary-and-chartpack-national-survey-of-households/

Kennedy, V., Smolinski, K., & Colon, Y. (2010). Training professional social workers in psycho-oncology. In J. Holland (Ed.), *Psycho-oncology* (pp. 588–593). New York, NY: Oxford.

Levy, J. (2002). Financial assistance from national organizations for cancer survivors. *Cancer Practice, 10*, 48–52.

Martinez, M., & Cohen, R. (2012, Jan.–Sep.). *Health insurance coverage: Early release of estimates from the National Health Interview Survey*. Retrieved from http://www.cdc.gov/nchs/data/nhis/earlyrelease/Insur201303.pdf

Merepol, N., Schrag, D., Smith, T., Mulvey, T., Langdon, R., Jr., Blum, D., . . . Schnipper, P. (2009). American Society for Clinical Oncology guidance statement: The cost of cancer care. *Journal of Clinical Oncology, 27*, 3868–3874.

Mustaqeem, S., & Rajkumar, S. V. (2012). The high cost of cancer drugs and what we can do about it. *Mayo Clinic Proceedings, 87*(10), 935–943.

Shankaran, V., Jolly, S., Blough, D., & Ramsey, R. D. (2012). Risk factors for financial hardship in patients receiving adjuvant chemotherapy for colon cancer. *Journal of Clinical Oncology, 30*, 1608–1614.

The Access Project. (2003). *Consequences of medical debt: Evidence from three communities*. Boston, MA: The Access Project. http://www.accessproject.org/downloads/med_consequences.pdf

Weissman, A. (1979). *Coping with cancer*. New York, NY: McGraw-Hill.

Zafar, S. Y., & Abernathy, A. P. (2013). Financial toxicity, Part 1: A new name for a growing problem. *Oncology, 27*(2), 1–5.

90

Julie Keany Hodorowski, Carolyn Messner, and Caroline Kornhauser

The Importance of Patient Education

The single biggest problem in communication is the illusion that it has taken place.
—George Bernard Shaw (Caroselli, 2000, p. 71)

Key Concepts

- *Cognitive mastery of cancer and its treatments, side effects, and management enhances coping.*
- *Patient education initiatives are well-respected psychosocial interventions for cancer patients and their caregivers.*
- *The challenge for oncology social workers is to make patient education programs as accessible as possible to maximize patient participation.*

Scientific advances in oncology have revolutionized cancer treatment. The need for patient education is increasing regarding improved treatment options due to advances in personalized care, targeted therapies, and palliative care. Communication with the health care team is essential in the successful implementation of patient education. It focuses on enhancing cognitive mastery of medical terms, treatment, clinical trials, and pain and symptom management with expertise, art, and compassion. Effective delivery of information not only relieves anxiety but also facilitates more informed decision making in coping with cancer (Adler, 2008).

Patients and caregivers are faced with profound challenges throughout their cancer trajectory, including the comprehension of complex medical information and its application to their unique condition (Jacobsen, Holland, & Steensma, 2012). Knowledge may lead to adherence, decreased anxiety, and more satisfaction with care (Fleishman, 2011).

Since the establishment of the Health Information Technology for Economic and Clinical Health (HITECH) Act in 2009, which was created to stimulate the adoption of electronic health records and supporting technology to improve health care quality, safety, and efficiency, health care providers have had to anticipate more questions and plan for accessible educational programs to help patients understand their electronic health records. Shifts in consumerism now place patients in greater charge of their health care and require greater attention to issues of health literacy and communication barriers.

The Role of Patient Education

Patients and families have a right to understand the cancer diagnosis. Most patients wish to be considered equal partners with their providers when making informed decisions regarding cancer screening, diagnosis, treatment, and follow-up care. Because it is a patient's right to be informed, the health care team has a professional and legal responsibility to meet this need. With the focus on patient-centered care, shorter hospital stays, increasing complexity of caregiver responsibilities, and shorter patient/physician appointments, it is essential that the treating health care team play a key role in patient education.

Oncology social workers are relied on to attend to psychosocial concerns. Many providers already use lay language and adapt materials to fit their patients' needs, but this may be difficult and time-consuming when communicating intricate medical information. Building in time to find an interpreter, produce images, or find multimedia teaching materials for a diverse patient population is challenging for busy practitioners. Because time is short, it is important to refer patients to trustworthy websites, cancer information services, and other forms of support to complement providers' efforts in patient education.

Providers are expected to help filter the information their patients collect by answering questions, addressing immediate issues, and giving small amounts of meaningful information. It is important to view every interaction as a teachable moment and an opportunity to fine-tune communication skills in patient education, even when that means simply listening. Because of the chronic nature of cancer, however, the need for information and patients' ability to absorb information change over time. Data from the 2008 Health Information National Trends Survey (HINTS), sponsored by the National Cancer Institute, found that 55.3% of patients and caregivers most frequently seek cancer information on the Internet, compared to 24.9% seeking information from their health care providers (NCI, 2010). Patients initially sought information on the Internet and subsequently sought approval or assessment by their physicians about their findings. Though the Internet is often the source of information for over 50% of the U.S. population, Hesse, Moser, and Rutten (2010) found that between 2002 and 2008, trust in information from health care professionals increased compared to health information obtained from the Internet. Health care team members must ensure that any information gathered on the Internet is relevant and accurate. Asking patients if they have collected information on their own is necessary in maintaining open lines of communication and correcting any false or incomplete data they may have found.

Patient education must be planned with a patient-centered approach to have the desired impact. Patient-centered communication encompasses several core functions, including fostering healing relationships, exchanging information, responding to emotions, managing uncertainty, making decisions, and enabling patient self-management (Epstein & Street, 2007). The patient-centered approach empowers the patient to ask questions and to get clear information regarding his or her diagnosis and treatment options. As medical care becomes more transparent and access to personal medical information becomes increasingly commonplace, patients will be encouraged to become informed, active participants in their care.

Issues of Health Literacy in Patient Education

Many health care providers are unaware that poor health literacy is a stronger predictor of a person's overall health than age, income, employment status, education level, or race (Weiss, 2007). Only 12% of American adults are considered to have proficient health literacy skills, whereas most Americans struggle to understand consent forms, medication instructions, directions for tests and procedures, or discharge plan instructions (White, 2008). Because many patients develop methods to disguise their lack of understanding, providers often have blinders on to the issues of health literacy. Asking a patient "Was that clear to you?" or "Do you understand when you have to take your medication?" will often yield dishonest answers because many patients don't like to trouble authority figures, want to be considered a "good patient," or are embarrassed to admit they don't understand. However, doctors are not mind readers. Encouraging patients to organize their thoughts and prepare for each doctor visit will enable them to articulate their concerns and ask educated questions, instead of concealing worries and anxieties. Limited health literacy truly affects everyone. Even those with strong literacy skills have trouble understanding complex health information, especially under demanding and stressful circumstances. Strong consideration needs to be given to the choice of educational materials health care providers present their patients. Print or verbal communication is the preferred method for receiving health information for older adults. This is important because the average age of patients receiving a cancer diagnosis is 68 years (ACS, 2013). An aging patient population coupled with increasing numbers of cancer survivors and long-term effects calls for information to be available in print and multiple media formats.

Basics of Patient Teaching Encounter

In patient-centered care, the onus is on the provider to ensure that patients can make informed decisions and safely follow through with medical instructions for their care. If patients cannot explain their illness or demonstrate steps they need to take to maintain their safety or well-being, the provider must try a different approach.

When educating patients, it is crucial for the oncology social worker to ensure open lines of communication. At the start, ask patients what they wish to learn in each session. If the medical information is unfamiliar, present patients with an outline of information you hope to convey and ask them to agree on end goals. Write down three goals to prevent patients from feeling overwhelmed with overambitious objectives. Research shows that people cannot absorb a large quantity of information during one session. Allow enough time so patients are able to relay the information presented to demonstrate their comprehension. If all was not understood during the first session or if you run out of time, allocate enough time to repeat information during a follow-up meeting. As part of the health care team, social workers must communicate and document patient teaching encounters to help identify gaps in learning for team follow-up on patient education needs.

If you are planning larger group trainings, the pattern of attendance, such as high or low enrollment or participant dropout rate, will be a good indicator of which sessions are worthy of repeating and which need to be restructured to fulfill attendees' needs. Audience evaluations of speakers, such as their ability to engage the audience by presenting relevant material, will help guide future speaker selection. Asking a question about whether attendees would recommend the training to a friend or family member can speak volumes about the efficacy of the workshop training.

The type of evaluation required depends on the audience and the desired information needed, including informal observations (e.g., for speaker feedback and internal planning) or evaluation data to fulfill grant-funded program requirements. Formal research studies follow much more stringent rules and regulations. If a formal evaluation is required and it is not a skill you possess, consider including the cost of an evaluator in the budget. Alternatively, solicit a pro bono or student evaluation specialist, epidemiologist, or statistician upfront to design pre- and postassessment tools, create measurable goals and objectives, plan analysis and interpretation of data to determine if you meet your measurable goals, and write the evaluation section for funders or publications. Remember, evaluation loops back to your goal and is key to planning future educational sessions (NCI, 2005).

Patient Education: From Bench to Bedside

Innovations in treating cancer are unfamiliar to many patients. Oncology social workers, as well as other member of the health care team, are tasked with relaying updated scientific findings to their patients. Organizing educational workshops and seminars aimed at decoding new scientific research can be very difficult because there are barriers that preclude patient participation in these initiatives. Major barriers in attending on-site workshops include cost, travel logistics, fatigue, rural isolation, geography, language, low literacy, dependent care (children, parents, and other family members), work, time, and busy lifestyles.

Core sources from which patients may receive information about their cancer and its treatment are the oncologist and oncology nurse during and between appointments; materials and booklets provided by the cancer treatment team, American Cancer Society, National Cancer Institute, and site-specific cancer organizations (Hornyak, Zahora, & Matarese, 2013); Internet searches; on-site patient or caregiver education workshops; support groups and informal exchanges with other patients; and virtual workshops via teleconferences, webcasts, and podcasts.

Virtual Workshops

I really appreciate the quality of the speakers and the information given on cutting-edge therapies. We have many treatment options and new therapies that are coming along that I may need. I always learn something new. We NEED this quality information to make informed decisions and to discuss options intelligently with our local physicians, many of whom don't share or don't know.

—Patient feedback, December 2013

This patient poignantly describes the need for patient education workshops, which help patients make more informed decisions and ask more thoughtful and knowledgeable questions of the health care team. The need for more candid conversations between patients and their doctors is essential for improved medical outcomes and increased patient satisfaction (Gilligan, 2012). Because patients and their caregivers often feel anxious in meetings with their health care team and retain little of the information discussed, they benefit from repetition of their treatment options, potential side effects and their management, and tips on how to prepare for upcoming doctor visits. Many oncology social workers, nurses, and cancer organizations offer workshops on different types of cancer, their treatments, and management of side effects and pain.

Cancer*Care*'s Connect Education Workshops, established in 1988, are one such example. An oncology social worker teamed up with a teleconference vendor to host Cancer*Care*'s first workshop over the telephone. Twenty-five years later, this modest program has blossomed into an extensive educational tool for patients, their families and friends, and health care professionals. Currently, Cancer*Care* offers over 65 workshops each year, reaching over 54,000 participants worldwide. The workshops grew from basic telephone technology to webcasts and podcasts. Speakers are carefully selected as leading experts in oncology with outstanding communication skills, compassion, and psychosocial sensitivity. These workshops combine a talented interdisciplinary team on each program, including medical oncologists, radiation and surgical oncologists, dentists, nutritionists, oncology social workers and nurses, and physical therapists. Each workshop begins with a 30-minute didactic presentation, followed by a question-and-answer session with participants. Each workshop is moderated by an oncology social worker, and questions not answered during the live workshop due to time constraints are immediately followed up after each workshop by oncology social workers.

These workshops are free and provide a way for people to learn about cancer-related issues from the convenience of their home or office. Some geographic, socioeconomic, and physical barriers that may limit participation in on-site programs can be obviated through these virtual teleconference programs (Adler, 2008).

Many other cancer organizations offer comparable free virtual workshops. Their goal is to bring cutting-edge advances in cancer treatments to the public by reliable experts from academic cancer centers, community cancer centers, and National Cancer Institute–designated cancer centers. Because many people living with cancer struggle with health literacy, physical and financial challenges, and geographic isolation, these workshops allow clinicians to offer patients quality information in an easily accessible manner. Because the workshops take place on the telephone and online, replay versions are also available for anyone wishing for repeated information. Teleconference and webcast workshops are wonderful tools to empower and encourage patients throughout their learning process and to increase their cognitive understanding of their diagnosis, treatment, and overall health outcome.

Pearls

- Before any presentation, it is wise to prepare speakers about the type of audience they are addressing, especially if it is a patient audience. Experience has shown that many patients do not want to hear grim statistics and prognostic information. Patients and caregivers should not come away from the presentation upset by something the speaker said.
- Resourcefulness is a talent that helps in program planning. Keep in mind that medical librarians are excellent resource people. They can help you find multilingual, plain language, audio, and Braille resources tailored to patient needs.
- Practice self-reflection after patient interactions to raise awareness of communication barriers you want to work on. During self-reflection, you may discover that assumptions based on preconceived notions and biases are affecting your cultural sensitivity.
- Learn culturally appropriate terminology and use it consistently to ensure an open and welcoming environment that is respectful of diversity.
- Patient education is a joint enterprise between the treating health care team and the patient and caregiver.

Pitfalls

- Assuming one size fits all in patient education planning.
- Thinking that relaying information once to patients or caregivers is sufficient; believing that repetition will bore or alienate patients.
- Not paying attention to how difficult it is for patients and caregivers to attend on-site workshops; thinking there is no other way to provide patient education workshops except face to face.
- Forgetting that some of your patients may be technologically challenged whether due to the cost of cell phone or Internet access or lack of transportation or a computer.

This chapter explored how access to understandable health information empowers patients to participate in self-care. Providers, patients, and caregivers must ensure that information for self-care is accessible, reliable, and patient centered. This is particularly challenging given low health literacy rates and a multitude of barriers that preclude patients from receiving state-of-the-art care. The information discussed regarding how to conduct educational workshops will start the process of learning the best practices to incorporate when planning educational sessions. Oncology social workers need to stay abreast of the latest research, technologies, and health sites to best guide their patients to supportive resources. As technology continues to expand at a rapid rate, remember that many patients cannot or will not adopt the use of the most current technology. Simplicity, coupled with the involvement of a trusted and effective oncology social worker, will make a difference in patient and family learning. Open lines of communication will increase positive patient outcomes and adherence to treatment protocols.

SELECTED FREE CANCER-RELATED WEBCASTS, PODCASTS, AND TELECONFERENCES

American Cancer Society: http://www.cancer.org
Cancer and Careers: http://www.cancerandcareers.org
Cancer Support Community: http://www.cancersupportcommunity.org
Cancer*Care*: http://www.cancercare.org
Leukemia Lymphoma Society: http://www.lls.org
LIVE**STRONG** Foundation: http://www.livestrong.org
Living Beyond Breast Cancer: http://www.lbbc.org
Lymphoma Research Foundation: http://www.lymphoma.org
Multiple Myeloma Research Foundation: http://www.mmrf.org
Stupidcancer: http://www.stupidcancer.org
Vital Options International & the Group Room: http://www.vitaloptions.org

ADDITIONAL RESOURCES

Agency for Healthcare Research and Quality: *Patient Education Materials Assessment Tool (PEMAT) and User's Guide: An*

Instrument to Assess the Understandability and Actionability of Print and Audiovisual Patient Education Materials: http://www.ahrq.gov/professionals/prevention-chronic-care/improve/self-mgmt/pemat/index.html

Centers for Disease Control and Prevention Social Media Tools, Guidelines & Best Practices: http://www.cdc.gov/socialmedia/tools/guidelines/index.html

Health Information Technology for Economic and Clinical Health (HITECH) Act of 2009: http://www.cdc.gov/ehrmeaningfuluse/introduction.html

Health Literacy Consulting: http://www.healthliteracy.com/

Health Resources and Services Administration (HRSA): Health Literacy: http://www.hrsa.gov/healthliteracy/

International Assessment of Adult Competencies 2012: First Look: http://nces.ed.gov/surveys/piaac/

REFERENCES

Adler, N. E. (2008). *Cancer care for the whole patient: Meeting psychosocial health needs*. Washington, DC: Institute of Medicine of the National Academies Press.

American Cancer Society. (2013). *Cancer treatment and survivorship facts and figures 2012–2013*. Atlanta, GA: Author.

Caroselli, M. (2000). *Leadership skills for managers*. New York, NY: McGraw-Hill.

Epstein, R. M., & Street, R. L., Jr. (2007). *Patient-centered communication in cancer care: Promoting healing and reducing suffering*. Bethesda, MD: National Cancer Institute.

Fleishman, S. B. (2011). *Learn to live through cancer: What you need to know and do*. New York, NY: Demos Medical Publishing.

Gilligan, T. (2012). If I paint a rosy picture, will you promise not to cry? *Journal of Clinical Oncology, 30*(27), 3421–3422.

Hesse, B. W., Moser, R. P., & Rutten, L. J. (2010). Surveys of physicians and electronic health information. *New England Journal of Medicine, 362*(9), 859–860.

Hornyak, K. A., Zahora, J., & Matarese, M. (2013). *A helping hand: The resource guide for people with cancer*. New York, NY: Cancer*Care*.

Jacobsen, P. B., Holland, J. C., & Steensma, D. P. (2012). Caring for the whole patient: The science of psychosocial care. *Journal of Clinical Oncology, 30*(11), 1151–1153.

National Cancer Institute. (2005). *Theory at a glance: A guide for health promotion practice*. Bethesda. MD: U.S. Department of Health and Human Services, Public Health Service, National Institutes of Health.

National Cancer Institute. (2010). *Health information national trends survey (HINTS). Brief 16: Trends in cancer information seeking*. Bethesda, MD: U.S. Department of Health and Human Services, Public Health Service, National Institutes of Health.

Weiss, B. D. (2007). *Health literacy and patient safety: Help patients understand* (2nd ed.). Chicago, IL: American Association Foundation and American Medical Association.

White, S. (2008). *Assessing the nation's health literacy: Key concepts and findings of the national assessment of adult literacy (NAAL)*. Chicago, IL: American Medical Association Foundation.

91

Kathryn M. Smolinski and Debra Wolf

Legal Issues That Affect Quality of Life for Oncology Patients and Their Caregivers

Key Concepts

- *Unmet legal needs produce stress in cancer patients and their families and can affect access and delivery of services during cancer treatment.*
- *Legal issues for cancer patients can vary, but problems attaining health care insurance and public benefits, fear of loss of employment or housing concerns, and a desire to draft estate-planning and advance-directive documents are the most common concerns.*
- *Social workers can play a key role in obtaining and facilitating legal services and information for both oncology patients and the health care team.*

Oncology social workers often focus their interventions on the social determinants of health affecting oncology patients. Social determinants of health are "the conditions in which people are born, grow, live, work and age" (World Health Organization, cited in Tyler & Lawton, 2011, p. 4). Typical social determinants of health are nonmedical factors, such as finances, education level, nutrition, and housing, that influence health outcomes. Although social workers minimize the stress that such determinants can cause, they are limited in their scope and reach. In fact, social determinants, by definition, are environmental stressors *outside* the hospital but *within* the daily life of the patient and caregivers (McCabe & Kinney, 2010).

Oncology social workers know a cancer diagnosis often requires immediate treatment decisions that are often complicated by the emotional impact of the diagnosis. Additionally, the physical and financial tolls of treatment often require patients to face a variety of legal issues, though "the legal needs of cancer patients often go unaddressed" (Retkin, Rodabaugh, & Mochizuki, 2011, p. 399). Several studies have explored these needs among cancer patients, including a 2007 study that included a survey of cancer patients who identified and prioritized their legal needs into four categories: health care, employment, financial, and estate planning. The authors noted that cancer patients' legal needs "have a substantial impact on their quality of life," yet these needs are often overlooked by supportive care staff (Zevon, Schwabish, Donnelly, & Rodabaugh, 2007). Other studies have identified the following:

- The range of common legal needs of cancer patients and their families, including the impact of employment-related needs (Francoeur, 2005)
- The barriers to care created for oncology patients by unmet nonmedical cancer needs including benefit and legal issues (Wolff et al., 2005)
- The burden of financial and legal issues can be decreased with intervention (Miller et al., 2007)
- That providing legal services to people with cancer reduces stress (Retkin, Brandfield, & Bacich, 2007)

The fact that cancer patients report stress reduction when legal problems are solved indicates why oncology social workers need to incorporate access to and facilitate referrals to affordable legal services. As Fleishman, Retkin, Brandfield, and Braun (2006, p. 2124) note, "expanding the spectrum of services available to a cancer patient to include legal assistance has the potential to substantially improve patient health and family stability over time." As Colvin, Nelson, and Cronin (2012, p. 335) recognize, "When the legal issue is framed by a social worker, the legal strategy is pursued by means of a more holistic and longitudinal approach." A social worker empowering a patient to know and exercise his or her legal rights and access to benefits is a social worker focused on helping a client find solutions. Similar to social workers advocating for early detection of mental health issues, financial stress, and adjustment problems in cancer patients, legal advocates within health care "strive to identify and address legal problems early, before legal needs become crises requiring litigation" (Cohen et al., 2010, p. S136). Although there is no limit to the legal issues in oncology, the most prevalent are many of the same issues oncology social workers already address daily.

Legal Issues Oncology Patients Face

Most legal issues in the oncology setting focus on employment, public benefits, housing, and estate planning. Both federal and local laws govern each of these areas and provide rights, access, and benefits to cancer patients and their families. When oncology social workers have a fundamental understanding of these legal areas, they can advocate for patients to access legal assistance to improve coping and expand available patient services and resources.

Maria S., 39, is the single mother of John, 8. She was never married to John's father, who has not been a part of their lives. Maria has been working as a full-time clerk in a large department store for 8 years. She was diagnosed with colon cancer and needs surgery and chemotherapy. Maria's doctor told her that she should be able to return to work after 6 weeks with some physical restrictions.

Many legal issues stem from the impact a diagnosis has on a cancer patient's ability to work and thereby provide financially for the family. Whether facing a temporary disability period, increased time off for treatment, or a permanent disability leave, a patient will often experience some financial hardship. Without income, a cancer patient cannot pay rent or a mortgage, health insurance premiums or co-pays, or credit card and automobile loan debts. Despite income loss, patients often are unable to access benefits like state health insurance programs or food stamps because their assets (such as work-based retirement savings) make them ineligible. Workplace legal protections often require the employee to request the benefit, so patients need to understand these laws. Once patients are educated about their rights and their employer's responsibilities, many legal issues might be avoided.

The two central laws offering job protection to employees are the 1990 Americans With Disabilities Act (ADA, amended in 2009) and the Family Medical Leave Act of 1993 (FMLA). The ADA applies to employers with 15 or more employees and prohibits employment discrimination based on disability. It also requires that employers provide reasonable accommodations to employees, which can be anything from an alteration in work hours, additional break time, ergonomically correct furniture, or even working from home in some circumstances.

FMLA applies to employers with 50 or more employees, and employees must have worked at their job for a minimum of 1 year. Eligible employees receive 12 weeks of job-protected leave per 12-month period with the continuation of employee benefits. FMLA also requires protected intermittent leave for medical appointments and treatment (see http://www.dol.gov/compliance/laws/comp-fmla.htm).

Maria is cleared to return to work. Her doctor advises her to take frequent breaks and not to lift, push, or pull for another 4 weeks. Maria may request these as reasonable accommodations. She needs to begin her chemotherapy and is concerned that the side effects may affect her ability to work. Maria might schedule chemotherapy for every other Friday at 1 p.m., take these afternoons off with FMLA intermittent protection, and have the weekend to recover.

Some state laws offer broader protection than the ADA or apply to employers with fewer than 15 employees. The Job Accommodation Network has information on reasonable accommodation requests including sample letters (see http://www.askjan.org).

Maria has found that she is unable to continue working. She is very concerned about her ability to pay her monthly expenses. She has applied for Social Security Disability but has to wait for 26 weeks until benefits begin. She has been advised to contact her local benefits office to see if she is eligible for public assistance.

Although many cancer patients use the protections under FMLA and the ADA to continue working, this may not always be an option. Unemployment insurance may only be an option if the patient is able to work part time or in a more sedentary capacity but is unable to find a job.

For those patients who cannot work, filing a disability claim may be the appropriate action to help them receive an income. Short-term solutions include using sick pay, accrued vacation time, or short-term disability if available. The benefits that states and employers offer vary and are usually a percentage of wages with a certain maximum payment. The Social Security Administration (SSA) provides two forms of disability benefits for patients that meet the strict SSA requirements: Social Security Disability (SSD) and Supplemental Security Income (SSI). Although the determination of disability is the same for both benefits, eligibility criteria and the amount paid vary greatly.

Social Security Disability Characteristics

- *Entitlement program based on a person's work history*
- *Paid as a monthly benefit that has no upper limit*
- *Does not consider an applicant's assets or family income*
- *A 26-week waiting period from onset of disability before any benefits payable*
- *Minor children and other dependents may be eligible for benefits*
- *Recipients eligible for Medicare after receiving SSD for 24 months*

Supplemental Security Income Characteristics

- *A cash benefit program for low-income individuals without sufficient work history to qualify for SSD*
- *Maximum monthly benefit of $721*
- *Limits assets and other family resources to $2,000 for an individual*
- *No waiting period for benefits once eligibility has been determined by the SSA*
- *No benefits available to dependents*

In determining eligibility, the SSA rules are complicated and factor in the applicant's age, work history, and medical conditions (http://www.ssa.gov). The SSA also has two programs that benefit cancer patients and provide for expedited application reviews:

- Terminally ill (TERI) patients are entitled to expedited action on their application.
- Compassionate Allowances expedite approval for several specific medical conditions and diagnoses.

A high percentage of SSI and SSD applications are initially denied and a request for a hearing may be required. Social workers can also assist in preventing denials by gathering the required documents and requesting supporting letters from the medical team to provide the most comprehensive application for the patient.

In addition to the federal programs that can assist oncology patients, there are many state programs. Patients often struggle with the stigma associated with applying for public assistance benefits, including cash assistance and food stamps. Many of the public assistance centers require long, tiresome waits and eligibility for public benefits varies state to state. Important benefits include the following:

- Temporary Assistance for Needy Families provides temporary financial assistance including cash benefits, rental assistance, job training, and child care (http://www.acf.hhs.gov/programs/ofa/programs/tanf).
- The Supplemental Nutrition Assistance Program (SNAP), which was formerly known as food stamps (http://www.fns.usda.gov/snap/outreach/map.htm).
- Subsidies for housing are difficult to find. Low-income housing projects have long waits and Section 8 subsidy applications have been closed in many areas.

Maria is now collecting SSD of $1,550 per month and food stamps. After paying her rent and utilities, Maria cannot afford the $600 monthly insurance payment for herself and John.

The Consolidated Omnibus Budget Reconciliation Act (COBRA) is a federal law that allows employees to maintain their employer group health insurance coverage after a qualifying event results in loss of insurance. COBRA requires 18 months of health insurance continuation after job loss at the reduced group rate and can be extended to 29 months if the patient is approved for SSD.

States sponsor various health insurance plans including Medicaid, which is often the most comprehensive for people who have little income. Medicaid eligibility varies by state because it is based on income and assets, and elderly or disabled persons may be approved even if they are over the income limits.

Medicare is another government-sponsored health insurance that is available only to individuals over age 65 or who have been collecting SSD or SSI for 24 months or who have been diagnosed with end-stage renal disease (http://www.medicare.gov). Medicare alone is generally inadequate to meet the needs of most patients and gap coverage is generally required, which is usually provided through a supplemental policy or, for lower income patients, Medicaid. Affordable health insurance policies are also offered (as of January 2014) through the state marketplaces under the Patient Protection and Affordable Care Act (PPACA), which was signed into law in 2010.

Many legal issues involving housing may arise for cancer patients. These can include requiring accommodations in their apartment, such as widening a door to allow for a wheelchair. Patients who reside in walk-up apartments may need relocation to a lower floor or a building with an elevator. Patients unable to pay rent may also face eviction. An attorney can assist in negotiating reasonable accommodations and rent repayment terms and help the patient access programs to help him or her pay for rent arrears. Finally, many cancer patients may face foreclosure. Fortunately, the government has established several loan modification programs to help homeowners who are unable to pay at their current rate due to a reduction in their income. Cancer patients also often require legal help in accessing estate-planning tools.

Common Estate-Planning Needs of Cancer Patients

- *Wills: provide for the distribution of assets after death and allow for the naming of a guardian or setting up a trust for minor children.*
- *Health care proxy: allows a person to name an agent to make health care decisions should he or she become incapacitated and unable to communicate with health care providers.*
- *Living will: allows a person to express end-of-life wishes regarding medical treatment.*
- *Financial power of attorney: allows a person to choose an agent to assist him or her with conducting his or her daily business needs including banking.*
- *Guardianship for minor children: guardianship wishes can be expressed in a will, but some states allow someone who is facing serious illness to appoint a stand-by guardian in advance. This allows the named guardian to take custody of minor children upon the incapacity or death of the parent.*

The Role for Oncology Social Workers and Legal Services

Facing legal issues can be overwhelming, and "seeking free legal help outside of the treatment setting is often fraught with bureaucratic obstacles even if one can access the services" (Fleishman et al., 2006, p. 2125). Legal services provided *within* health care, while newer to the oncology setting, have been embraced within geriatric settings for years (Fleishman et al., 2006). Legal services in oncology are gaining momentum, including the development of the National Cancer Legal Services Network and the long-standing Cancer Legal Resource Center.

At the direct care level, oncology social workers can lead the integration of legal services in several ways. Given the need for client trust, timely action, and client empowerment in solving many legal issues, oncology social workers are positioned as excellent collaborators with legal advocates (Colvin et al., 2012; Fleishman et al, 2006; Miller et al., 2007). The first step is an awareness of the legal issues that affect cancer patients and providing comprehensive assessments to elicit them. Beyond the simple provision of a list of local attorneys, oncology social workers can advocate with administration to bring legal services on-site, allowing for easier access, faster response, and less stigmatization for patients and families. Social workers can create a partnership with community legal aid providers or develop a panel of local pro bono attorneys who will come to the hospital or clinic, complete intakes, and answer questions.

One of the most comprehensive ways to address the legal issues affecting cancer patients is the integration of a medical–legal partnership (MLP) into the direct services provided to cancer patients (Colvin et al., 2012; Rosenthal, 2010; Weintraub et al., 2010). An MLP is a legal services delivery model where attorneys are members of the interdisciplinary team, providing legal solutions alongside the health care team. Those MLPs that work closely with social work staff report that the social worker's abilities to build trust with clients, introduce the legal staff, and facilitate the referrals are integral to the success of the MLPs (Colvin et al., 2012; Yacobucci & Sprecher, 2009). Social workers historically have been shown to help "cancer patients maintain a sense of control over their . . . legal matters . . . [which allows] them to focus their energies on their treatment and recovery" (Snow, Warner, & Zilberfein, 2008, p. 379).

Because much of our current health care relies on shortened hospital stays and a quick return to a safe and adequate home environment (McCabe & Kinney, 2010), social workers constantly assess the patient's world beyond the clinic doors. Legal partners can help provide additional support by taking on patients as clients and resolving issues outside the hospital, such as challenging evictions, fighting employer discrimination, and attending hearings for public benefits denials.

Oncology social workers can integrate legal assistance into oncology care at the institutional and policy level. Palliative care programming and ethics services can benefit from MLP collaboration (Campbell, Sicklick, Galowitz, Retkin, & Fleishman, 2010; Rodabaugh, Hammond, Myszka, & Sandel, 2010). Legal advocacy could become a central component for oncology social workers positioned on those services. "MLPs effectively combine and deploy increasingly limited legal aid and hospital resources and therefore offer a key strategy to abate some of the worst consequences of the recession" (Retkin, Brandfield, & Hoppin, 2009, p. 29). Oncology social workers are invaluable when they maximize services to patients without increasing costs. Helping establish an MLP is definitely one way social workers can bring in services that can ultimately impact the institution's bottom line by assisting patients in collecting income and insurance benefits that help them pursue, continue, and finish treatment plans with decreased stress. Additionally, social workers can raise patient awareness by coordinating legal educational presentations and facilitate legal seminars for staff and health care professionals to increase awareness of and referrals for legal services.

Social workers and lawyers share many professional values, such as trust, advocacy, problem solving, and client decision making. However, the two professions need to be aware of and respect the differences in their approach to client and patient interactions. Whereas social workers may work to keep family harmony and challenge patients to consider all angles of a particular action, lawyers are bound to advocate tirelessly for their one identified client, regardless of the impact that may befall the caregivers involved (Boumil, Freitas, & Freitas, 2010). Practical solutions can be implemented to help resolve the differing legal and ethical obligations of social workers and lawyers, and most MLPs find the collaboration very beneficial to everyone involved (Colvin et al., 2012).

Pearls

- Legal concerns are often intertwined within the bramble of psychosocial issues that oncology social workers already are addressing in their work. Keenly assessing for such concerns allows for timely referrals.
- Social workers and lawyers bring different yet essential and often complementary problem-solving tools when working with cancer patients and their families.
- By incorporating an attorney as part of treatment, the team can leverage his or her expertise on the latest laws, regulations, and policies that affect cancer care.

Pitfalls

- Social workers and lawyers may problem solve with cancer clients in very different ways based on their professional relationship and approach. Lawyers may focus on the client's best interest, at all costs, whereas social workers may look to resolve an issue to promote family and caregiver harmony.
- The medical team may be wary of sharing information with lawyers or suspect their role on the health care team. There is a history of adversity between the health care and legal professions that must be acknowledged and overcome.
- Legal needs may be identified too late in a patient's treatment plan, foregoing the timely opportunity to seize access to legal solutions that may be governed by statutes of limitations or other deadlines.

The law and social work professions both share core values of social justice and advocacy embedded in service. Clinicians "are often in the best position to identify legal issues impacting their patients" (Fleishman et al., 2006, p. 2124). As with other resources available to patients, oncology social workers can facilitate legal referrals, help clients normalize the need for a lawyer, and provide support and understanding for the trepidation an already vulnerable client may feel in talking with a lawyer. That is precisely why having a legal advocate as part of the cancer care team can work to assimilate this service as necessary and vital to recovery and minimize the stigma and burden of seeking legal assistance (Fleishman et al., 2006).

ADDITIONAL RESOURCES

Cancer Legal Resource Center: http://www.disabilityrightslegalcenter.org/cancer-legal-resource-center
Federal Trade Commission: Garnishing Federal Benefits: http://www.ftc.gov/bcp/edu/pubs/consumer/alerts/alt135.shtm
Job Accommodation Network: http://askjan.org
Making Home Affordable: http://www.makinghomeaffordable.gov/pages/default.aspx
Medicare Eligibility: http://www.medicare.gov/MedicareEligibility/Home.asp?dest=NAV|Home|GeneralEnrollment#TabTop
National Cancer Legal Services Network: http://www.nclsn.org
National Center for Medical-Legal Partnership: http://www.medical-legalpartnership.org
Social Security Administration: Compassionate Allowances: http://www.ssa.gov/compassionateallowances/
Social Security Administration: Outcome of Applications For Disability Benefits: http://www.ssa.gov/policy/docs/statcomps/di_asr/2010/sect04.html
Social Security Administration: Supplemental Security Income: http://www.socialsecurity.gov/policy/docs/quickfacts/prog_highlights/
Social Security Listing for Malignant Neoplastic Diseases: http://www.ssa.gov/disability/professionals/bluebook/13.00-NeoplasticDiseases-Malignant-Adult.htm
SSI Federal Payment Amounts for 2013: http://www.socialsecurity.gov/OACT/COLA/SSI.html
U.S. Department of Labor, Family Medical Leave Act: http://www.dol.gov/compliance/laws/comp-fmla.htm
USDA Food and Nutrition Service, Supplemental Nutrition Assistance Program: http://www.fns.usda.gov/snap/outreach/map.htm

REFERENCES

Boumil, M., Freitas, D., & Freitas, C. (2010). Multidisciplinary representation of patients: The potential for ethical issues and professional duty conflicts in the medical-legal partnership model. *Journal of Health Care Law and Policy*, *13*(1), 107–138.

Campbell, A., Sicklick, J., Galowitz, P., Retkin, R., & Fleishman, S. (2010). How bioethics can enrich medical-legal collaborations. *Journal of Law, Medicine & Ethics*, *38*(4), 847–862.

Cohen, E., Fullerton, D., Retkin, R., Weintraub, D., Tames, P., Brandfield, J., & Sandel, M. (2010). Medical-legal partnership: Collaborating with lawyers to identify and address health disparities. *Journal of General Internal Medicine*, *25*(Suppl. 2), S136–S139.

Colvin, J., Nelson, B., & Cronin, K. (2012). Integrating social workers into medical–legal partnerships: Comprehensive problem solving for patients. *Social Work*, *57*(4), 333–341.

Fleishman, S., Retkin, R., Brandfield, J., & Braun, V. (2006). The attorney as the newest member of the cancer treatment team. *Journal of Clinical Oncology*, *24*(13), 2123–2126.

Francoeur, R. B. (2005). Cumulative financial stress and strain in palliative radiation outpatients: The role of age and disability. *Acta Oncologica*, *44*(4), 369–381.

McCabe, H., & Kinney, E. (2010). Medical legal partnerships: A key strategy for addressing social determinants of health. *Journal of General Internal Medicine*, *25*(Suppl. 2), S200–S201.

Miller, J., Frost, M., Rummans, T., Huschka, M., Atherton, P., Brown, P., . . . Clark, M. (2007). Role of a medical social worker in improving quality of life for patients with advance cancer with a structured multidisciplinary intervention. *Journal of Psychosocial Oncology*, *25*(4), 105–119.

Retkin, R., Brandfield, J., & Bacich, C. (2007). *Impact of legal interventions on cancer survivors*. New York, NY: LegalHealth—A Division of the New York Legal Assistance Group.

Retkin, R., Brandfield, J., & Hoppin, M. (2009). Medical legal partnerships: A key strategy for mitigating the negative health impacts of the recession. *The Health Lawyer, 22*(1), 29–34.

Retkin, R., Rodabaugh, K., & Mochizuki, T. (2011). Cancer patients, survivors and their families. In E. Tyler & E. Lawton (Eds.), *Cancer patients, survivors, and their families. Poverty, health and law: Readings and cases for medical-legal partnership* (pp. 395–429). Durham, NC: Carolina Academic Press.

Rodabaugh, K., Hammond, M., Myszka, D., & Sandel, M. (2010). A medical-legal partnership as a component of a palliative care model. *Journal of Palliative Medicine, 13*(1), 15–18.

Rosenthal, E. (2010). How legal services are supplementing the work of the cancer care team for certain psychosocial issues. *Oncology Times, 32*(8), 24–27.

Snow, A., Warner, J., & Zilberfein, F. (2008). The increase of treatment options at the end of life: Impact on the social work role in an inpatient hospital setting. *Social Work in Health Care, 47*(4), 376–391.

Tyler, E., & Lawton, E. (Eds.). (2011). *Poverty, health, and law: Readings and cases for medical-legal partnership*. Durham, NC: Carolina Academic Press.

Weintraub, D., Rodgers, M. A., Botcheva, L., Loeb, A., Knight, R., Ortega, K., . . . Huffman, L. (2010). Pilot study of medical-legal partnership to address social and legal needs of patients. *Journal of Health Care for the Poor and Underserved, 21*(2), 157–168.

Wolff, S. N., Nichols, C., Ulman, D., Miller, A., Kho, S., Lofye, D., . . . Armstrong, L. (2005). Survivorship: An unmet need of the patient with cancer—implications of a survey of the Lance Armstrong Foundation (LAF). *Journal of Clinical Oncology (Meeting Abstracts), 23*(Suppl. 16), 6032. Retrieved from http://meeting.ascopubs.org/cgi/content/abstract/23/16_suppl/6032

Yacobucci, J., & Sprecher, M. (2009). Beacon of hope for immigrants: The medical-legal partnership. *Social Work Today, 9*(4), 38–39.

Zevon, M., Schwabish, S., Donnelly, J., & Rodabaugh, K. (2007). Medically related legal needs and quality of life in cancer care. Retrieved from http://onlinelibrary.wiley.com/doi/10.1002/cncr.22682/pdf

XVII

Practice Settings: Where Oncology Social Workers Work

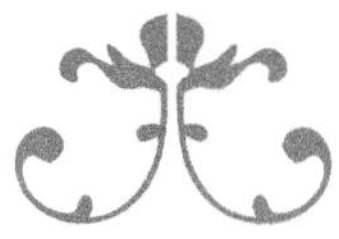

Victoria Kennedy

Oncology social workers are making a difference in the lives of people touched by cancer in a variety of settings. This section of the *Handbook* highlights diverse work environments in which oncology social workers ensure the integration of psychosocial care into quality cancer care.

Oncology social workers provide services in many community settings, from nonprofit organizations and agencies to hospice and palliative care to private practice and consulting businesses. In "Oncology Social Work Across Sites of Care," Victoria Kennedy outlines the opportunities that exist for oncology social workers outside of the traditional medical setting. These include honing skills and expertise in direct service, program planning and development, research and training, administration, and even self-employed enterprise.

With medical social work at the very foundation of our profession, oncology social workers serve as the pivotal psychosocial oncology experts in hospitals and cancer centers across the globe. In "Oncology Social Work Practice in Hospitals and Cancer Centers," Louise Knight shares how individual oncology social workers and oncology social work departments have unique opportunities to distinguish the role of social workers on a multidisciplinary team as change agents affecting individual patients, family members, and the system as a whole.

In "Veterans and Cancer," Louisa Daratsos highlights the ever-growing role of oncology social workers with veterans and unveils the unique nature of the U.S. Department of Veterans Affairs' health care system and the impact of military service on the lives of veterans with cancer and their loved ones. This chapter also reminds us that veterans are treated for cancer in many different settings, and that a thorough oncology social assessment will include determining if the patient is a veteran, the significance of that experience in the patient's life, and the potential for added benefits and access to quality care.

Finally, oncology social workers play a highly valued role in industry. In "The Evolving Role for Oncology Social Workers in Business," Jennifer Mills provides readers with insight into the intersection of business and social work as it relates to ameliorating barriers that affect patient access to quality cancer care. A robust understanding of the cancer patient experience, astute problem-solving skills, and a keen eye for patient-centered solutions can create a successful career in for-profit business for oncology social workers.

Whatever the preferred setting of choice, oncology social workers provide the highest standard of psychosocial care for patients and families. Oncology social workers are challenged to be conversant with the changing landscape in health care. As Mills so aptly states, "It is not the training that limits the applicability of social work skills to almost any sector of health care, but rather social workers' beliefs in the utility of their skills" (p. 709). By being open to examining a variety of practice settings, social workers can find meaningful, life-affirming work that makes a difference in the lives of people touched by cancer.

92 Oncology Social Work Across Sites of Care

Victoria Kennedy

Key Concepts

- *Oncology social work is not confined to the hospital or cancer center setting.*
- *The practice of oncology social work in community settings is well defined, evidence based, and profoundly meaningful.*
- *Oncology social workers can serve as clinicians, educators, administrators, researchers, and policymakers in a variety of settings.*
- *Innovative partnerships between health care providers and community organizations can create a seamless network of support services.*

Oncology social work practice is not confined to the hospital or cancer center setting; there are many community settings where oncology social workers find meaningful work outside of the traditional hospital environment. For decades, oncology social workers have provided valuable contributions to the care of cancer patients and their families through local, regional, and national nonprofit community service organizations. Professionals who identify themselves as oncology social workers also work in hospice and home health agencies, where a preponderance of their caseload is oncology patients. Social workers may work in private practice with a specific emphasis in oncology or may own or work for a consulting business providing oncology social work expertise to industry or nonprofit organizations. Across all these settings, oncology social workers demonstrate the highest professional standards in the development and delivery of psychosocial programs and services aimed at improving quality of life and the health and well-being of the patients and families they serve.

Across community settings, oncology social workers provide similar services as their hospital counterparts—screening, assessment, therapeutic interventions, education, and referral across the cancer continuum—from primary prevention, diagnosis, and treatment through survivorship, palliative care, and end of life. Through these organizations, oncology social workers provide direct psychosocial services, develop and manage evidence-based programs, conduct research or promote health policy, and manage or even run the organization as a high-level executive.

This chapter examines the scope and depth of oncology social work practice in these settings and the opportunities and challenges that working outside the hospital environment may bring. Finally, I propose a call to action to forge strong collaborative partnerships between health care providers and community based organizations to create a seamless network of support for patients and families as they move from the cancer center into the community, workplace, and home. Oncology social workers provide leadership in mobilizing community alliances to ensure that cancer patients and their families remain engaged, empowered, and supported throughout the cancer experience and beyond.

Oncology Advocacy Organizations

There are over 13 million cancer survivors alive in the United States today, and the National Cancer Institute (NCI) estimates that because of the aging baby-boomer population, the number of Americans diagnosed will double in the next 50 years, from 1.3 million to 2.6 million. With 5-year survival rates increasing, most of those diagnosed (approximately 70%) can expect to be alive in 5 years, and many of them, and their caregivers, will be over age 65 (NCI, 2012).

Cancer and its treatment have changed dramatically over the past 20 years, with greater emphasis on outpatient care, chronic disease management, and survivorship. People with cancer spend less time in traditional medical settings than a decade ago. More often, many patients continue to work through treatment or manage the physical, emotional, and practical concerns out in the community where they work and live.

Community-based support services and interventions have become increasingly important in total cancer care, rehabilitation, and survivorship for the whole family. There are numerous cancer-related community support organizations, often called "advocacy" organizations, that provide psychosocial services—many of them at no cost to the patient. Hospitals and cancer centers are increasingly challenged to sustain psychosocial oncology programs that are, in general, non-revenue producing. Yet there is a growing volume of patients with unmet needs over an extended cancer trajectory. Although professional community-based support services are available in many communities, on a national scale, some evidence suggests that health care providers are not providing information or referring patients (Guidry, Aday, & Zhang, 1997; Matthews, Baker, & Spillers, 2002).

Cancer-specific nonprofit organizations in the United States have been in existence for over 100 years. Some global organizations, like the American Cancer Society and the Leukemia and Lymphoma Society, have a broad focus of raising vital funds for research and cancer prevention in addition to providing patient education and support programs. Others, like the Cancer Support Community, Cancer*Care*, and the LIVE**STRONG** Foundation, are service delivery organizations that develop and provide comprehensive psychosocial, educational, and navigational services to patients and families through local offices, chapters, or affiliates, as well as by telephone and online. Several organizations also conduct research and/or advocate for patients and families through public policy and legislative efforts at the state and national level. An array of independent, local cancer organizations such as The Gathering Place and Cancer Family Care also provide valuable psychosocial support services facilitated by licensed mental health professionals.

Examples of Organizations That Employ Oncology Social Workers

- *American Cancer Society*
- *Bear Necessities Children Cancer Foundation*
- *Cancer*Care
- *Cancer Family Care*
- *Cancer Legal Resource Center*
- *Cancer Support Community*
- *The Gathering Place*
- *Leukemia and Lymphoma Society*
- *Life With Cancer*
- *LIVESTRONG Foundation*
- *Lung Cancer Alliance*
- *Patient Advocate Foundation*

There are hundreds, if not thousands, of cancer-specific nonprofit organizations in the United States. Some are well-known global or national organizations focused on raising funds for cancer research and/or providing direct service, research, and policy programs. Some may focus on cancer education or provide a peer support network, whereas others may provide support groups or social services or assist patients in navigating survivorship. Nonprofit cancer organizations are generally philanthropically supported by individuals, corporations, and foundations; possibly state or federal funding; or fee-for-service models. Regardless of the size, mission, or budget, oncology social workers find meaningful careers fulfilling many roles in community cancer organizations.

Roles for Oncology Social Workers in Community Cancer Organizations

The primary emphasis in community cancer organizations is on helping patients and families navigate the complex emotional, social, and practical aspects of cancer across the continuum. Oncology social workers assist patients in decision making and problem solving issues related to disease management and coping with the stressors on work, family, and home life. Brief and long-term therapeutic relationships are formed as patients and family members engage in various programs and services. Depending on the assigned position, mission, and services of the organization, oncology social workers use their expertise in patient engagement, problem solving, cognitive behavioral intervention, and support service to deliver professional community-based services.

Patient advocacy is educating, supporting, and empowering patients to make informed decisions, navigate the system to get the health care they need, and build strong partnerships with providers while working toward system improvement to support patient-centered care. Patient advocates are dedicated foremost to the well-being of the patients they serve (Gilkey & Earp, 2009).

Direct Clinical Practice

Oncology social workers in community organizations may provide distress screening and biopsychosocial assessment; individual, group, or family counseling; problem-solving interventions; crisis management; complementary therapies; and resource information and referral services across the disease trajectory. Services and programs in community organizations are generally available at a stand-alone center, by telephone, and, increasingly, online. Patients and family members may be referred by a health care provider or other patients and families, or they may just become aware of the available services on their own. Generally, a referral from a health care provider is not required. Services may be free of charge or provided on a fee-for-service or sliding-scale basis.

One example, the Cancer Support Community, formed from a merger between the Wellness Community and Gilda's Club in 2011 and employs over 400 social workers who work full time, part time, or contractually to develop and deliver its evidence-based psychosocial oncology program rooted in a patient-powered, social-cognitive model (Golant & Thiboldeaux, 2010). Life With Cancer, a cancer support organization part of northern Virginia's Inova Health System, employs oncology social workers and oncology nurse educators who actively provide direct clinical services in person, by telephone, and online. Oncology social workers manage clinical programs, conduct intake screenings and assessments, facilitate a multitude of individual and support group interventions, and administratively manage and raise funds for the organization.

Patient/Family Education and Outreach

Like their hospital counterparts, community-based oncology social workers participate in the development and delivery of high-quality educational programs targeted at creating an informed, activated patient and/or caregiver. This helps to better inform the patient and caregiver about cancer and its treatment, as well as to improve communication with the health care team. Cancer*Care*, a national nonprofit organization, offers free counseling and support groups, education, financial assistance, and practical help by professional oncology social workers. Cancer*Care* also provides 1-hour Connect Education Workshops led by leading cancer experts on a variety of topics including disease and symptom management, psychosocial coping, including cancer in the workplace, and helping children and teens understand cancer in the family (Cancer*Care*, 2014). These popular workshops, organized and facilitated by oncology social workers, attract patients, family members, and health care professionals across the United States and internationally and are available free of charge by phone and online.

Material and Logistical Resources

Several community organizations provide assistance in securing transportation, co-pay assistance, referrals for medical equipment, at-home care, wigs and other self-care products and activities, and basic needs such as housing and legal services. Social workers in the community are experts at mobilizing resources and/or networking to help patients and families locate valuable assistance from local, regional, and national resources. The frustrating reality is that often there are limited resources available to assist families in need, so social workers must be creative in helping the family to prioritize and problem solve unmet needs.

Program Development and Evaluation

Oncology social workers bring skilled knowledge and expertise in the development and evaluation of innovative survivorship programs for patients and families. Community organizations deliver many services and programs based on assessed needs of the clients being served, available resources, and the overall mission of the organizations. Oncology social workers develop and/or implement innovative, evidence-based services for patients and caregivers such as psychoeducational, cognitive behavioral programs. Frequently in this setting, the oncology social worker has autonomy in creating psychosocial programs from start to finish including conducting a needs assessment, program design and implementation, marketing and outreach, and evaluation. Highly effective community organizations implement continuous quality improvement of their programs, services, and staff. The oncology social work program manager must be proficient in measuring both the output and the outcomes of service delivery. For example, although a successful community organization tracks the number of programs it provides and the number of people it serves (outputs), it must also measure the impact of programs on quality of life, behavior change, and/or satisfaction of its participants (outcomes).

Fund and Resource Development

Most social workers who work in community support organizations know all too well the challenge of securing adequate funds to develop and deliver quality programs. Oncology social workers acquire skills in fund-raising, including grant writing, major donor cultivation, and special event planning. Depending on the size and structure of the organization, social workers can play a small or large role in fund development. Oncology social workers who develop special expertise in fund-raising are a valuable asset to community service organizations. Fund-raising courses such as those at Indiana University's The Fund Raising School are accessible across the country to interested professionals. Many community organization jobs require this expertise, whereas others provide on-the-job training or expect the clinical staff person to work closely with development professionals in the organization.

Administration and Management

Community organizations provide many opportunities for career advancement in oncology social work. Social workers provide clinical supervision, program planning and management, board development, and outreach and marketing. Oncology social workers have founded nonprofit community organizations and been instrumental in leading key movements in areas such a pain, legal advocacy, and palliative care. With additional skills and training, oncology social workers function as executive directors, chief executive officers, and board members of nonprofit organizations.

Research and Training

Some community advocacy organizations conduct research and/or provide training on psychosocial interventions and program delivery. At the Cancer Support Community Research and Training Institute, clinical social workers collaborate on a multidisciplinary research team in developing and evaluating innovative programs in distress screening, treatment decision support, and online support groups. Life With Cancer also conducts many research projects and training programs for professionals. Oncology social workers in community settings publish in peer-reviewed journals and present at major professional meetings such as those of the Association of Oncology Social Work, American Psychosocial Oncology Society, and American Society of Clinical Oncology (Kennedy, Smolinski, & Colón, 2010).

Policy and Advocacy

Advocacy can occur at the individual, institutional, or professional level. Community cancer organizations may have oncology social workers who are educating and empowering patients and families to advocate for themselves, advocating for standards of care or system changes such as with the American College of Surgeons' Commission on Cancer, or influencing policy and legislation at the state or federal level.

Palliative Care, Home Health, and Hospice

People with cancer, and their family members, should receive care that reflects the principles of excellent palliative care across various settings (home, hospice, hospital, or residential facility) from the time of diagnosis through the end of life (National Consensus Project for Quality Palliative Care, 2004). Many social workers, who also identify themselves as oncology social workers, are embedded in community-based hospice, home health agencies, or community palliative care programs. In 2007, there were over 4,700 unique hospital programs operated by 3,700 different organizations or companies focused on hospice and/or palliative care (National Hospice and Palliative Care Organization [NHPCO], 2008). Hospice and palliative care services are delivered in a host of settings—acute care, assisted-living facilities, group homes, nursing facilities, and inpatient hospice. Home-based professionals are the primary providers of palliative care. In fact, over 70% of hospice patients died in personal residences, nursing homes, or assisted-living facilities (NHPCO, 2008).

Oncology social workers play a key role in palliative—also called supportive—care across the cancer continuum. Supportive care planning from diagnosis across the continuum of the disease is increasingly accepted as a standard of care. As advanced stages of cancer now span months or even years, patients and families are challenged to maintain quality of life and emotional, social, and practical resources. With the depth and breadth of research that has emerged about the importance of supportive care across the cancer continuum, oncology social workers are essential in the delivery of evidence-based interventions for patients, family, and staff working in community settings (National Association of Social Workers, 2014).

Although the caseload in hospice or palliative care programs may not be exclusively oncology, oncology social workers are finding that their skills are vital in alleviating physical, psychological, social, and spiritual pain and suffering. Post-master's certificate programs in palliative and end-of-life care such as at the NYU School of Social Work (2013) provide advanced training for oncology social workers seeking to specialize in this area. Professional associations such as the Social Work in Hospital and Palliative Care Network provide professional education, leadership, and quality standards for the social work role. Much like their colleagues in community cancer organizations, hospice and palliative care social workers engage across the domains of social work practice, research, education, and policy (Altilio & Otis-Green, 2011).

Oncology social workers who specialize in end-of-life care focus on assisting patients and families with the tasks of terminal illness. Oncology social workers provide distress screening and psychosocial assessment; individual, family, and group counseling; information and referral; advance care planning; and bereavement services to assist the patient and family in the tasks of coping with terminal illness (Christ & Blacker, 2005).

Tasks of Terminal Illness *(Moynihan, Christ, & Gallo-Silver, 1988)*
• *Maintaining acceptable quality of life during advanced stages* • *Coping with a deteriorating physical condition* • *Confronting existential, spiritual, or religious issues* • *Planning for remaining family and friends*

Of critical importance is the need for effective communication among the patient, his or her family members, and the health care team. Oncology social workers are adept at providing support and education to patients, families, and health care professionals, as well as assisting health care providers in navigating cultural, ethnic, and religious issues that may affect optimal communication and informed decision making.

In summary, oncology social workers who have traditionally worked in an acute care or outpatient medical setting may find specializing in community-based hospice and palliative organizations to be profoundly rewarding.

Private Practice and Consulting

Oncology social workers also work in private group and solo practices (NASW, 2011). Mental health practitioners with specific expertise in psychosocial services and cancer survivorship are a valuable resource in any community. Although reimbursement and fee-for-service practice can be challenging in the current health care environment, the need for community mental health services for cancer patients and families continues to grow, particularly with the reduction in hospital-based services and programs in some institutions.

Oncology social workers have unique skill sets that include problem solving, individual and group dynamics, health education, and health care communication. This set of skills provides an opportunity for oncology social workers to branch out of their current practice area and engage in health care consulting. Current workforce trends allow for working remotely and contracting with consultants on specific projects or as subject matter experts. Oncology social work clients in this field may include nonprofit institutions, industry, professional societies, the National Institutes of Health, and various community partners. Getting started in the consulting field may be a matter of joining an existing firm or starting an independent, entrepreneurial consulting practice. As with oncology social work, the key to successful consulting is networking. Oncology social workers are poised to utilize their vast array of resources, contacts, and experiences to create a new and meaningful way to practice in unique setting.

Call to Action: Community Partnerships for Quality Care

Oncology social workers are employed by large academic, comprehensive cancer centers or, where over 70% of cancer care is delivered, smaller local or regional cancer centers and hospitals. With some institutions facing reduction in the number of staff oncology social workers, psychologists, or other allied professionals, there is an ever-present need to better engage community organizations to assist in the delivery of professional psychosocial services. Hospital-based psychosocial services, particularly those not covered by insurance (support groups, wellness programs, and education programs) may not be sustainable and are nonexistent in some institutions. Ironically, community cancer organizations are often underutilized and undervalued as part of the cancer care paradigm (Institute of Medicine, 2008). The time is now to unite medical care with community support programs and services. Health care institutions are charged with developing innovative models for the delivery of high-quality care. Community partnerships provide innovative solutions for meeting the growing unmet needs of cancer patients and their families.

Oncology social work plays a pivotal role in mobilizing alliances across the community to ensure that patients and families can obtain timely access to appropriate services. Whether employed by a hospital or community organization, social workers can lead the charge to forge formal partnerships and written referral agreements between community organizations and health care providers. As the number of cancer survivors and their families explodes amid a diminishing health care workforce, providers and community organizations must take action and think outside the proverbial box. The increasing demand for high-quality, value-based cancer care integrates cost containment and quality standards. Community partnerships will strengthen the quality of and reduce gaps in care. Oncology social workers are the ideal health care professionals to broker and navigate key partnerships across the community.

Pearls

- Working in a community setting where the primary mission is the provision of psychosocial care and/or social services can create an ideal oncology social work environment with fewer turf conflicts and less role confusion that can exist in a medical setting.
- Be open to taking that "leap" out of direct practice and applying skills and expertise in a new and unique environment such as nonprofit management, fund development, or consulting.

- Successful social workers in this setting are creative, self-directed professionals who stay well versed on the latest research and practice trends in psychosocial oncology.
- Community-based oncology social workers must have knowledge and understanding of the business of the nonprofit organization. Skills in strategic planning, program management and evaluation, and coalition building are essential building blocks for a successful career in community organizations.

Pitfalls

- Nonprofit sustainability and growth are contingent upon economic factors and the organizational capacity for successful fund-raising. This means that fiscal instability can create stress and threaten job security.
- Oncology social workers in the community setting risk becoming disconnected from the hospital or cancer center milieu, thereby losing touch with the patient's medical experience or trends in treatment and issues in modern health care.
- Recruiting patients and families to utilize psychosocial services, even free services, can be a challenge. Services need to be accessible to patients and families (including by telephone and online) and aligned with their primary concerns, needs, and capacities.

Oncology social workers find truly meaningful work in community cancer organizations, in private enterprise as mental health practitioners or psychosocial oncology consultants, in hospice and home health agencies, as community organizers, as nonprofit administrators, and as patient/family advocates. With the impending explosion of new cancer diagnoses combined with growing numbers of long-term survivors and the declining workforce in oncology, community cancer organizations and health care agencies will play an even more critical role in the integration of psychosocial care into the patient, family, and survivor experience. Oncology social workers are leaders in the provision of direct services, program planning and management, research, and policy across a multitude of community settings. By bringing professional values, skills, and passion for attending to the *whole* needs of the patient and family, oncology social workers in the community ensure that patients and families have access to quality psychosocial care. Community-based oncology social workers are at the center of a movement that improves quality of life and affects the health and wellness of all people touched by cancer.

ADDITIONAL RESOURCES

Cancer Family Care: http://cancerfamilycare.org
Cancer Support Community: http://www.cancersupportcommunity.org
The Fund Raising School, Indiana University: http://www.philanthropy.iupui.edu/about-the-fund-raising-school
The Gathering Place: http://www.touchedbycancer.org/
Life With Cancer: http://www.lifewithcancer.org
Social Work in Hospital and Palliative Care Network: http://www.swhpn.org

REFERENCES

Altilio, T., & Otis-Green, S. (2011). *Oxford textbook of palliative social work*. New York, NY: Oxford University Press.

Cancer*Care*. (2014). Connect Education Workshops™. Retrieved from http://www.cancercare.org/connect

Christ, G., & Blacker, S. (2005). Setting an agenda for social work in end-of-life and palliative care: Overview of leadership and organizational initiative. *Social Work in End-of-Life and Palliative Care*, *1*(1), 9–22.

Gilkey, M., & Earp, J. (2009). Defining patient advocacy in the post-quality chasm era. *North Carolina Medial Journal*, *70*(2), 120–124.

Golant, M., & Thiboldeaux, K. (2010). The wellness community's integrative model of evidence-based psychosocial programs, services, and interventions. In J. Holland, W. Breitbart, P. Jacobsen, M. Lederberg, M. Loscalzo, & R. McCorkle (Eds.), *Psycho-oncology* (2nd ed., pp. 473–478). New York, NY: Oxford University Press.

Guidry, J. J., Aday, L. A., & Zhang, D. (1997). The role of formal and informal social support networks for patients with cancer. *Cancer Practice*, *5*(4), 241–246.

Institute of Medicine. (2008). *Cancer care for the whole patient: Meeting psychosocial health needs*. Washington, DC: National Academies Press.

Kennedy, V., Smolinski, K., & Colón, Y. (2010). Training professional social workers in psycho-oncology. In J. Holland, W. Breitbart, P. Jacobsen, M. Lederberg, M. Loscalzo, & R. McCorkle (Eds.), *Psycho-oncology* (2nd ed., pp. 588–593). New York, NY: Oxford University Press.

Matthews, B. A., Baker, F., & Spillers, R. L. (2002). Healthcare professionals' awareness of cancer support services. *Cancer Practice*, *10*(1), 36–44.

Moynihan, R., Christ, G., & Gallo-Silver, L. (1988). AIDS and terminal illness. *Social Casework*, *68*, 380–387.

National Association of Social Workers. (2011). *Social workers in private practice. NASW Center for Workforce Studies and Social Work Practice*. Washington, DC: Author.

National Association of Social Workers. (2014). *Standards for social work practice in palliative and end-of-life care*. Washington, DC: Author. Retrieved from http://www.socialworkers.org/practice/bereavement/standards/standards0504New.pdf

National Cancer Institute. (2012). *Cancer trends progress report: 2011/2012 update*. Bethesda, MD: Author. Retrieved from http://progressreport.cancer.gov

National Consensus Project for Quality Palliative Care. (2004). Clinical practice guidelines for quality palliative care, executive summary. *Journal of Palliative Medicine*, *7*, 611–627.

National Hospice and Palliative Care Organization. (2008). NHPCO facts and figures: Hospice care in America. Retrieved from www.nhpco.org/research

NYU School of Social Work. (2013). Post-master's certificate program: Palliative and end-of-life care. Retrieved from http://socialwork.nyu.edu/alumni/continuing-education/post-masters/palliative-care.html

93 Oncology Social Work Practice in Hospitals and Cancer Centers

Louise Knight

Key Concepts

- *The importance of oncology social work in hospitals and cancer centers is increasing due to treatment advances that result in more cancer survivors and to the greater focus by regulatory agencies on the psychosocial aspects of care of patients and families.*
- *Social workers need to be intentional in defining their team and institutional roles as they comply with mandates for integrating effective psychosocial services while maximizing efficiency in patient- and family-centered care.*
- *Development and use of a psychosocial acuity scale helps to document the complexity of social work tasks and provides important data for use in resource advocacy.*
- *Defining relevant demographic and health care barriers of the surrounding hospital community, oncology social workers can provide the workplace with public health data essential to directly impact health outcomes.*
- *Social workers are challenged to demonstrate measurable outcomes for patient satisfaction, patient safety, cost reductions, and quality of care.*

Early hospital social work leaders at both Massachusetts General Hospital (1905) and Johns Hopkins Hospital (1907) helped establish the role and functions of social work within the medical setting. These founders recognized that patients were more than their illness, which was impacted by their coping, living conditions, family structure, and finances (Johns Hopkins Medicine, 2014; Rehr & Rosenberg, 2006). Since the 1970s, oncology social work has become a well-established profession whose practitioners provide comprehensive psychosocial care in hospital settings around the world, following a set of core values, implementing standards of practice, achieving professional certification, and participating in a national organization at the forefront of legislative and clinical practice discussions. Across cancer care settings, oncology social workers are found to provide most mental health and social services, yet securing sustainable departmental funding continues to be a challenge (Fobair et al., 2009). For oncology social work to continue playing a key role in cancer care, it is incumbent upon the profession to understand and mobilize economic and political forces within the health care system.

This chapter examines oncology social work practice in hospital and cancer centers by clarifying the traditional and unique clinical and administrative leadership opportunities and challenges facing social work practice.

Unifying Expectations Within the Institution

It is important to understand the expectations of hospital administration, the health care team, and patients of oncology social work. What role does the hospital, physician, or administration expect social work to fulfill? How do patients and their families perceive the role of social work? These are questions that guide the oncology social work department/program to have a clear operational and clinical agenda. Administrative expectations and the social work department's mission and goals work best when aligned, although there may be shifts over time. For example, hospital and physician leadership may be versed in more practical aspects of social work practice but not fully recognize its operational and clinical contributions (Davies & Connolly, 1995).

Oncology social workers and their departments and programs often need to advocate for their own role definition. It is essential that the social work program satisfy the core hospital operational functions and accreditation standards, combined with clinical expertise, innovative programming, disease-specific resources, and enhanced patient- and family-centered care. Merging these sometimes competing agendas requires clinical and leadership skills on the part of the individual social worker and the department. The social worker makes a difference one patient at a time and changes a hospital's expectations of not only social work but also what quality care is for oncology patients and their families.

Changing the Culture: Hospital Expectations Intersect With Clinical Care

The hospital has one social worker for an 18-bed inpatient unit, radiation oncology, and a 10-chair infusion center. The primary hospital expectation is for social work to address the discharge planning needs on the inpatient unit. The oncology social worker recognizes that preventative psychosocial interventions in ambulatory care will improve the overall patient care experience. Case by case, the value of early intervention and increased support is demonstrated. The hospital expectations and the clinical care provided by social work intersect, allowing for the practical, social, financial, and psychological needs of patients and caregivers to be addressed as one. Ambulatory interventions reduce readmissions caused by social factors, improve compliance with the oncology plan of care, and support the patient and caregiver through the trajectory of the illness. In the provision of excellent patient care, the social worker can raise the expectations of the hospital from bed flow and volume to quality patient- and family-focused care.

Promoting Understanding of Unique Oncology Social Work Contributions

Social work stands alone among the various disciplines, specialties, and subspecialties that consider not only the impact of a cancer diagnosis and treatment on the patient and family but also the influence of such factors as mental health history, financial stability, social engagement, living environment, spirituality, and cultural influences. In an urban hospital setting, social issues present within the community can and do surface in the cancer patient population. Social workers may find themselves working with patients and families impacted by limited or no income, foreclosure, homelessness, alcohol abuse, prescription and other substance abuse, incarceration, violence, domestic violence, divorce, and child custody issues, as well as language and cultural differences, all of which can present challenging barriers to cancer treatment.

The health care team looks to the social worker to resolve these obstacles to care. He or she may identify a resource, advocate for the patient, and empower and guide the patient/family, but in the end, the social problems often follow the patient throughout his or her cancer experience. How the social work department develops, provides, and documents services and resources that help patients with the greatest needs for psychosocial support clarifies the social work contribution to the health care team. Strategic use of this outcome data can help the hospital understand the importance of integrating social work within the hospital framework (Ezell, Menefee, & Patti, 1997).

Using a Psychosocial Acuity Scale to Document Case Complexity

Hospital administrators regularly ask social work directors to describe cases and volumes in an attempt to establish a staffing formula (Guo & Company, 2007). Because the field lacks a national staffing standard, many hospital social work programs have developed tools designed to numerically represent their patient profiles. For hospital leadership to utilize the results of an acuity tool for prospective fiscal and personnel planning, the tool will need to be tested for reliability and validity. In 2006, The Johns Hopkins Hospital Social Work Department developed the *Johns Hopkins Hospital Inpatient Psychosocial Acuity Scale* (Figure 93.1; Knight, Stansbury, Withrow, & Heneberry, 2006). The tool has established reliability and is working to establish validity.

The *Johns Hopkins Hospital Inpatient Psychosocial Acuity Scale* allows a social worker to code a discharged inpatient case using a 1 to 4 numeric value that corresponds to the psychosocial case complexity. A rating of 1 represents a case with no psychosocial barriers/issues. A rating of 2 represents a case with minimal psychosocial barriers/issues. A rating of 3 represents a case with complex psychosocial barriers/issues. A rating of 4 represents a case with extreme psychosocial barriers/issues. The scale offers the first step in describing clinical cases using language similar to Eastern Cooperative Oncology Group (ECOG) and Karnofsky scales in oncology (Oken et al., 1982). Tracking psychosocial acuity trends over time will allow social work departments to describe patient profiles to administrators and develop methods to map psychosocial acuity to other staffing variables (Knight et al., 2006).

Using Social Work Department Data to Further Define Role

Departmental and individual social work case data is one of the most powerful tools available to an oncology social work program. Case volumes, identified problems, barriers to

The Johns Hopkins Hospital
Inpatient Psychosocial Acuity Scale©

Instructions: The inpatient acuity rating is determined at the time of transfer or discharge. The rating is based on the professional judgment of the clinician. Determine which acuity level **BEST** describes a patient and family/caregiver dyad. In the event that a case seems split between two levels, your clinical judgment should be used to guide your decision. The examples following the general level description may provide assistance in determining the acuity score.

Level 1 General Description
Patient – Cooperative, no barriers to assessment and services, self-mobility (either ambulatory or assistive device), general self-care, minimal identified needs or problems, safe alone for long periods of time, good social supports, coping well, effective coping skills, coping and adapting to illness/medical/psychiatry condition, supportive intervention, simple information/referral. **Family/Caregiver** – Able to manage patient care needs, no identified needs.

Examples of a Level 1 patient profile:

- Basic Needs – Able to perform ADL independently or with simple assistance
- Living Situation – Stable housing without concern for cost or cleanliness
- Mental Health – No history of mental illness or current mental health concerns
- Health Insurance Coverage – Active health insurance
- Substance Use – No history or current use/abuse of substances: alcohol, drugs, other
- Transportation – Transportation is not a barrier to care
- Culture/Language – Language/culture are not a barrier to care
- Violence – No history of violence/abuse
- Developmental/Cognitive Impairment – Able to function independently
- Legal – Simple request for Advance Directives or other information
- Financial – Stable income
- Support System – Identifiable support system
- Treatment – Engages in treatment planning and is compliant with plan

Level 2 General Description
Patient – Needs assistance with ADLs, safe alone for limited time period, expresses emotional upset/distress effectively, and utilizes established coping skills. **Family/Caregiver** – Able to manage most needs with support of community agency or friends/extended family.

Examples of a Level 2 patient profile:

- Basic Needs – Needs assistance with some ADLs
- Living Situation – Stable housing, needs assistance for payment of rent/utilities and assistance with general maintenance
- Mental Health – High level of stress/distress, needs counseling
- Health Insurance Coverage – Need to contact insurance case manager to address coverage/needs
- Substance Use – Remote history of substance use, uses recovery program
- Transportation – Occasional difficulty with transportation and/or cost
- Culture/Language – Need interpreter services, some cultural barriers present
- Violence – History of violence/abuse
- Developmental/Cognitive Impairment – Signs of impairment present
- Legal – Needs assistance understanding and completing Advance Directives or other information
- Financial – Stable income in jeopardy, applications pending
- Support System – Support system not always responsible or responsive
- Treatment – Engages in treatment planning, but is not always compliant with plan

Level 3 General Description
Patient – Needs significant amount of assistance, unable to be left alone, limited activity level, overwhelmed by the illness/diagnosis/condition, past coping skills ineffective, needs support/counseling to re-establish daily coping. **Family/Caregiver** – needs emotional support, instruction and problem solving assistance.

Examples of a Level 3 patient profile:

- Basic Needs – Needs assistance with all ADLs, cannot be left alone
- Living Situation – Lives alone, no home supports in place
- Mental Health – Crisis intervention, needs ongoing counseling
- Health Insurance Coverage – Limitation on health care coverage requires need for SNV or other financial support for medications, pharmacy assistance, community referral
- Substance Use – Active use of substance, requests assistance/treatment
- Transportation – Needs regular assistance with transportation/cost
- Culture/Language – Need interpreter services, patient/family lack understanding due to cultural barriers
- Violence – Open referral to protective agency/police
- Developmental/Cognitive Impairment – Diagnosis of developmental disability/cognitive impairment
- Legal – Presents with significant legal concerns
- Financial – No income, applications denied
- Support System – No family or supports identified
- Treatment – Medical/mental health negatively impacting all aspects of patient's life

Level 4 General Description
Patient – Unable to ambulate or independently use a wheelchair, unable to perform ADLs independently, needs 24/7 supervision, immobilized by negative thoughts/fears/anxiety related to the illness/diagnosis/condition. **Family/Caregiver** – Unable to problem solve to a solution, obstructing care delivery, argumentative.

Examples of a Level 4 patient profile:

- Basic Needs – Homeless, living at a shelter, no consistent source of food and shelter
- Living Situation – Unable to return to home setting, needs placement in a community facility (boarding home, SNF, rehabilitation, chronic care, hospice)
- Mental Health – Danger to self/others, needs immediate psychiatric care, psychiatry disorder – unmanaged
- Health Insurance Coverage – No insurance
- Substance Use – Active use of alcohol/drugs which impacts current health/mental health condition/care plan, not willing to engage in substance abuse treatment
- Transportation – Transportation is a barrier to care with no viable solution
- Culture/Language – Culture significantly impacts the care plan
- Violence – Violence/abuse has been/is being reported
- Developmental/Cognitive Impairment – Cognitive/developmental disability significantly impact judgment and care, dementia with behavior problems
- Legal – Legal authorities involved in current admission or ambulatory care, guardianship required
- Financial – No income, urgent financial assistance needed
- Support System – No identifiable support system
- Treatment – Unable to engage in treatment planning, non-compliant with plan of care, violence/trauma primary cause of admission, end-of-life care planning, terminal illness/death

Figure 93.1. *Johns Hopkins Hospital Inpatient Psychosocial Acuity Scale*

resolution, interventions, and outcomes/dispositions allow program administrators an objective overview of the clinical work. Elements such as time spent on a case and acuity level offer a deeper understanding of the case, because not all patients with the same identified problem will require the same amount of social work resources. Although many hospitals engage in national benchmarking efforts, until there is a nationally accepted social work staffing standard, trying to do the same regarding staffing, case volume, and budgets among hospitals offers little reliable insight.

Social work department case data can be extremely useful in highlighting changes in clinical practice patterns, patient profiles, psychosocial acuity, and resource availability. The data may provide insight into clinical oncology trends and practice behaviors. Data analysis may also document improved quality of service delivery and higher levels of patient satisfaction.

New Standards of Care: Defining the Social Work Role on the Health Care Team

Although oncology social work has had a long-standing role in addressing psychosocial variables in patient care, the awareness of the importance of this role has been increased by the advent of new patient- and family-centered standards by accrediting bodies such as the American College of Surgeons' Commission on Cancer. These standards have created opportunities to demonstrate to the larger health care team social work's unique knowledge, skills, and access to helpful resources (ACOS, 2014). Oncology social workers are experts in distress screening, assessment and care planning, resource mobilization, patient navigation, and survivorship programs (Ganz, 2014). Oncology social workers and departments can also demonstrate leadership in helping meet new accreditation standards by enhancing patient satisfaction, another critical measure of quality cancer care (Adler & Page, 2008).

Social workers demonstrate competence and professional expertise in their work as oncology team members. They utilize advanced communication and problem-solving skills to respond quickly to requests for assistance and identify key options for addressing complex social and psychological problems of patients and families, as well as helping improve team communication. Social workers are not only reactive to an immediate concern but also proactive in using their expertise to find novel systemic approaches to troubling service problems (Zabora, 2009).

The oncology social work role can be enhanced or circumscribed by the availability of key resources. Staffing patterns, recruitment and retention of satisfied staff, and delivery of innovative programs and services that are cost-efficient and highly effective are all dependent on the cultivation of revenue streams and philanthropic dollars. Therefore, oncology social workers must be increasingly trained to raise funds for programs from internal and external sources and to use evidence-based metrics to ensure that services developed are supported by the institution, patients, medical staff, and community (Benson & Messner, 2011).

Helping Hospital Compliance With New Psychosocial Regulations

Employees of hospitals are familiar with the various regulatory, accrediting, and compliance organizations that oversee the provision of hospital services. In addition, the oncology field has specific review committees that set cancer program standards. Over the years, the presence of psychosocial language within the standards has increased dramatically, with specific stand-alone standards solely addressing screening, survivorship, depression, and distress. During on-site reviews, social work leadership is called upon to speak to compliance, present relevant data, and outline plans for compliance with proposed regulations. Theoretically, cancer program standards addressing psychosocial issues are a positive development; however, compliance with the standards presents challenges. These quality-based organizations have recognized the importance of overall patient safety, quality-of-life domains, and a comprehensive patient/family perspective that may require resources and personnel to address these issues in more systematic ways.

Maximizing Efficiency in Patient- and Family-Centered Care

As hospitals consider ways to maximize efficiency, social work departments are asked to document and outline the tasks and functions provided by the licensed clinical social worker and determine the amount of time required to complete them. These self-reviews offer an opportunity for the social work department to examine each task and function and determine whether it requires a trained oncology social work skill set. Isolating the tasks that do not require social work skills allows a department to consider alternate staffing specific to these functions. For example, locating an appropriate nursing care facility to facilitate a safe discharge may be enormously time-consuming. Countless phone calls in search of an available bed, extended wait times on hold with insurance companies, and photocopying and faxing are examples of the tasks that could easily be assigned to a person who is not a social worker. By realigning these tasks, the social worker can focus on providing counseling and support to the patient, facilitating the discharge, and working to the top of his or her license and professional competence. Para-professional staff can be highly cost-effective, allowing the licensed social worker to increase the amount of direct patient contact hours and program planning and consultation to other health care professionals.

Efficiency Is Often a Team Approach

A 68-year-old patient has undergone extensive abdominal surgery. His postoperative recovery has been slow with serious complications. Upon discharge, he will require extensive rehabilitation and antibiotic therapy. The social worker provides the medical information required to initiate a referral to a community facility to the department's resource coordinator. The social worker returns to work on the unit focusing on the overall psychosocial needs of patients and families.

The resource coordinator contacts the insurance case manager, refers the case to the appropriate facilities, and photocopies and faxes the chart notes. This process takes the better part of a day considering the number of phone calls, return calls, and time on hold. A skilled social work resource coordinator can be a highly effective and efficient way to maximize direct patient care time for the social work staff.

Work Assignment Models That Promote Effectiveness, Efficiency, and Work Satisfaction

There are various models to consider when deploying social workers within a hospital or cancer center—for example, geographically assigned to a location, team assigned with various work sites, and diagnostically assigned by cancer diagnosis. Arguments can be made for each of these models, but leadership must determine the model that will offer the most effective, innovative, satisfying, and efficient social work utilization.

The greatest assets of the department are dedicated and skilled social workers. Each oncology social worker, balancing the needs of patients, payer constraints, and regulatory mandates, benefits from the support and guidance of a skilled supervisor and department leader. Social work leadership must consider patient needs, hospital initiatives and accreditation requirements, and staff when considering competing priorities, budgets, agendas, work assignments, and department operations (Turning Point Resources on Leadership Development, 2001).

Educating the Hospital About the Community

Whether clinical practitioners, supervisors, field instructors, or administrators, oncology social workers help provide an understanding of the local community so that the hospital can address local, state, and national issues and trends. Social work department/program data can be a source to identify early demographic shifts and trends that may impact the need to develop novel cancer programs for the provision of optimal patient care. For example, a gradual rise of homeless patients seeking cancer care can be an isolated problem for the social worker to manage or an alert to a hospital of a community in crisis. Social work data presents the hospital with a unique understanding of the community it serves and its client base and with an appreciation of its patients' perspective and behaviors from a macro-level view. Social work leadership using social work case data and state and local demographics can educate hospital leadership about the economic health of the community, ethnic and cultural patient trends (e.g., the volume of immigrants in the community), uninsured patient profiles, and proposed state regulations. Early identification of social trends combined with program planning may help build new outreach and screening interventions (e.g., for emerging vulnerable populations the social work department identifies).

Giving Voice to the Vulnerable Cancer Patient

In reviewing the monthly case data, there is a noted rise in homeless women with cancer. Historically, homelessness would account for less than 1% of the annual cases and be confined to male patients. In this past month, there has been a dramatic increase in homeless women with cancer. The women range in age from 52 to 65 and report to have been homeless for 2 to 8 months. The women know each other, because they are part of the only all-women's shelter in the city. They share that they have had symptoms (weight loss, fatigue, night sweats, fever, cough, and rectal bleeding) for over a year but did not seek medical attention. They also tell you that many women on the street have similar symptoms. You recognize that with early diagnosis and treatment, these women would have had a treatable cancer. You bring this data to the attention of your social work director and the cancer center clinical director. This data drives the cancer center to reach out to the women's shelter to offer a free cancer screening. You have not only offered a voice to the homeless women but also offered a voice to the social work profession in the area of public health.

Taking Leadership in Program and Hospital Culture Change

The principles of social change, recognition of power dynamics within an organization or community, and steps to effect change are just a few of the topics covered in social work undergraduate and graduate programs (Jason, 2013). The social work discipline often steps into leadership when change is needed. Clear and thoughtful planning is essential for success (Kouzes & Posner, 1997). The framework described here guides the process when considering a culture or program change, such as integrating distress screening, developing a formal recognition of bereaved family members within the hospital setting, or making operational changes within a social work department (Knight, Cooper, & Hypki, 2012):

- Understand the decision-making structure and hierarchy.
- Clearly outline and analyze the subject.
- Identify hospital culture and barriers.
- Engage and establish partnerships with key stakeholders invested in the project. Partners may be hospital colleagues/leadership, community program leaders, national professional organizations, or local/state/national political leaders.
- Outline each step.
- Design a method for evaluation.
- Present the written proposal to key decision makers and address/edit for concerns.

Staffing Standards and Department Funding

Without a national staffing standard, staffing patterns are driven by budgetary constraints. For most hospitals, social work departments will operate through a flat budget where the number of full-time equivalents remains constant. These budgets are not patient-volume adjusted (projected patient volumes for the fiscal year) with staffing dollars matched. With flat budgets and hospital operating cuts, philanthropic support becomes pivotal for programs interested in offering innovative patient- and family-focused educational programs and cutting-edge services. Grateful patients and families are often interested in providing ongoing support or donating to a program that cares for the emotional, social, and practical needs of patients/families. Fostering relationships with and among potential donors and development staff can lead to very positive outcomes for the facility. Identified donors can be named to support specific events, services, or overall programs. Donor relationships are often the catalyst to moving an oncology social work program beyond providing basic services to providing comprehensive services in a sustainable environment.

Grateful Families

After months of chemotherapy, a young woman is referred to hospice care. You are supporting her decision, and her husband thanks you for your compassionate and skilled care. A few weeks later, you receive a call from the husband sharing that his wife has died. He wants to have memorials donated in his wife's name come to the hospital to support other patients. You offer to contact your development officer. A few weeks later, the development officer and the husband meet with social work to consider ways to honor his wife's name. A program is named for her that will provide free parking to patients during chemotherapy treatments. You realize that you made a difference in the lives of this couple, and as a result they will make a difference in the lives of many more.

Pearls

- Social workers should be a resource to problem solve highly complex medical and psychosocial care plans and meet new regulatory requirements for patient- and family-centered care and psychosocial screening.
- Oncology social workers encounter grateful patients and families interested in philanthropy. Partnering with the development office, donors can support new psychosocial programs and services.
- Oncology social work is defined by its ability to demonstrate confidence, competence, and professional acumen within the oncology team.

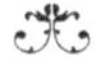

Pitfalls

- Within the hospital budget structure, oncology social workers must establish fiscal viability through data supported readmission reductions, expedient discharges, preventative social admissions, and increased patient satisfaction.
- Without a social work staffing benchmark, departments are vulnerable to budget-driven staffing, which fails to account for patient profiles and psychosocial acuity.
- Without thoughtful planning, staff engagement, and appreciation of potential barriers, new program ideas and services can fail.

There is evidence that supports the integration of psychosocial care as essential to the health outcomes for those with cancer (Adler & Page, 2008). Oncology social work must continue to support and counsel the distressed, educate survivors, and be prepared to respond appropriately to changing populations of cancer patients and their families. Oncology patients of the baby boomer generation, who have unique needs simply due to their age, will soon become the predominant cancer patient profile. Future oncology social workers will require health-finance knowledge and donor cultivation expertise to identify ways to generate sustainable revenue. They will need to be politically vocal at the institution, state, and national levels about the importance of mitigating psychosocial needs to ensure optimal health care utilization. They will need to partner with other disciplines in developing new community resources to care for patients at home, and they will need to consider their training in social policy and seek solutions at a macro level. Finally, oncology social workers can serve as the natural leaders and facilitators of integrated programs of psychosocial care across professional silos.

Oncology social work in a hospital or cancer center is far more than the work within the walls of the facility itself. Oncology social workers are change agents with the power to organize people to problem solve their personal challenges and to help institutions design and deliver the highest quality cancer care across the cancer continuum.

REFERENCES

Adler, N. E., & Page, A. E. K. (Eds.). (2008). *Cancer care for the whole patient: Meeting psychosocial health needs*. Washington, DC: National Academies Press. Retrieved from http://www.ncbi.nlm.nih.gov/books/NBK4011/

American College of Surgeons (ACOS). (2014). *Cancer program standards 2012, Version 1.2.1: Ensuring patient-centered care*. Revised January 21, 2014. Retrieved from http://www.facs.org/cancer/coc/programstandards2012.html

Benson, L., & Messner, C. (2011). *Oxford textbook of palliative social work*. New York, NY: Oxford University Press.

Davies, M., & Connolly, J. (1995). The social worker's role in the hospital: Seen through the eyes of other healthcare professionals. *Health and Social Care in the Community*, 3, 301–310.

Ezell, M., Menefee, D., & Patti, R. J. (1997). Factors influencing priorities in hospital social work departments: A director's perspective. *Social Work Health Care*, *26*(1), 25–40. Retrieved from http://www.ncbi.nlm.nih.gov/pubmed/9406337

Fobair, P., Stearns, N. N., Christ, G., Dozier-Hall, D., Newman, N. W., Zabora, J., & Desonier, M. (2009). Historical threads in the development of oncology social work. *Journal of Psychosocial Oncology*, *27*(2), 155–215.

Ganz, P. (2014). *Delivering high-quality cancer care: Charting a new course for a system in crisis*. Washington, DC: Institute of Medicine.

Guo, K. L., & Company, J. D. (2007). Leaders in hospital-based social work: The roles and functions of directors of social work in the case management model. *Leadership Health Service*, *20*(2), 124–133.

Jason, L. A. (2013). *Principles of social change*. New York, NY: Oxford University Press.

Johns Hopkins Medicine. (2014). Social work history at Johns Hopkins Hospital. Retrieved from http://hopkinsmedicine.org/socialwork/medsurg/about/

Knight, L., Cooper, R., & Hypki, C. (2012). Service of remembrance: A comprehensive cancer center's response to bereaved family members. *Journal of Social Work in End-of-Life and Palliative Care*, *8*(2), 182–198.

Knight, L., Stansbury, C., Withrow, G., & Heneberry, P. (2006). *Johns Hopkins Hospital Inpatient Psychosocial Acuity Scale©*. Baltimore, MD: Johns Hopkins Health System Corporation.

Kouzes, J., & Posner, B. (1997). *The leadership challenge*. San Francisco, CA: Wiley.

Oken, M. M., Creech, R. H., Tormey, D. C., Horton, J., Davis, T. E., McFadden, E. T., & Carbone, P. P. (1982). Toxicity and response criteria of the Eastern Cooperative Oncology Group. *American Journal of Clinical Oncology*, *5*(6), 649–655.

Rehr, H., & Rosenberg, G. (2006). *The social work-medicine relationship*. New York, NY: Haworth Press.

Turning Point Resources on Leadership Development. (2001). *Collaborative leadership and health: A review of the literature*. Leadership Development National Excellence Collaborative. Retrieved from http://www.turningpointprogram.org/toolkit/content/cllitreview.htm

Zabora, J. (2009). The oncology social worker in a medical setting. In A. E. Roberts (Ed.), *Social workers' desk reference* (pp. 77–85). New York, NY: Oxford University Press.

94 Veterans and Cancer

Louisa Daratsos

Key Concepts

- *The U.S. Department of Veterans Affairs (VA) is a source of various benefits for eligible veterans and their families.*
- *Most veterans receive their oncology care in non-VA facilities.*
- *For oncology social workers, conducting a military assessment on every patient who served in the military will facilitate an understanding of a veteran's connection to his or her military service.*

This chapter discusses veterans of the U.S. military as a unique population within any oncology social worker's caseload. Many think that veterans get their medical treatment at any of the nearly 1,000 national Veterans Health Administration (VHA) medical centers, community living centers, and community-based outpatient clinics. In fact, a large proportion of veterans receive care in non-VHA facilities.

Veterans and psychosocial oncology is a growing area of research, and although there is little published research specifically about veterans and psychosocial oncology, oncology social workers should be familiar with the demographic characteristics of veteran cohorts, the historical contexts of how they came of age, and the degree to which a veteran does or does not self-identify as a veteran. Understanding the veteran population can deepen a clinician's concept of patient-centered care. In addition, because the U.S. Department of Veterans Affairs (VA) offers an array of services and benefits to qualified veterans and their families, from housing to palliative care to burial benefits, the oncology social worker must be familiar with these benefits and be able to facilitate a veteran's ability to apply for these services.

The word *veteran* comes from the Latin *vetus*, meaning "old." When a person is experienced in an activity, he or she is called a veteran of that endeavor. Used in this sense of the word, veteran implies that the person has experience, maturity, and resiliency—all strength-based qualities that can help social workers conceptualize the character attributes of their patients who are veterans of the U.S. military.

The Department of Veterans Affairs and Its History

According to the VA's website, the agency's origins pre-date the formation of the nation.[1] In 1776, the Continental Congress offered pensions to men if they became disabled as an inducement to fight the British. Table 94.1 highlights some history of the VA and, most important, shows the expansion of benefits to veterans and their families. In 1989, President Reagan elevated the VA to a cabinet-level agency, which signified an elevation of the status of veterans and put their issues on par with other national interests (Kizer & Dudley, 2009).

Table 94.1.
Timeline of Veterans Benefits

Year	Benefit
1789	The first of many pension laws for veterans was passed, which also provided financial support to widows.
1812	The first home for disabled veterans, The Naval Home, opened in Philadelphia.
1818	The 1818 Service Pension Law provided that veterans who served in the War for Independence and needed assistance would receive a lifetime pension.
1873	Congress passed a law allowing any honorably discharged veteran to be buried in a veterans cemetery.
1922	22 Public Health Hospitals were transferred to the U.S. Veterans Bureau (Kizer & Dudley, 2009).
1930	President Herbert Hoover consolidated several federal organizations serving veterans into the Veterans Administration.
1941–1946	More than 12 million people entered the military in World War II. During the war, the federal government planned the reintegration of the military into American society at the war's conclusion and developed plans to address the needs of aging veterans (Siegel & Taylor, 1948).

The VA's motto, "To care for him who has borne the battle, his widow and his orphan," is taken from President Abraham Lincoln's second inaugural address and underscores a continuum of care that includes the veteran and his or her family. The Veterans Benefits Administration has responsibility for financial benefits, whereas the Veterans Health Administration facilitates medical and mental health care in its hospitals and community-based outpatient clinics, sponsors medical research, and provides training in medical and health related professions through its academic affiliation program. The National Cemetery Administration manages the 131 national veterans' cemeteries.

How Veteran Identity Develops

Spiro, Shnurr, and Aldwin (1997) wrote that military service is the "hidden variable in the lives of men." The U.S. Census (2011) indicates that in 2010, there were approximately 21.8 million veterans, or 7% of the population. In contrast, about 22% of the population over age 65, or 9 million people, are veterans. Social workers might not always be aware of which individuals on their caseloads are veterans except when they see someone wearing an article of clothing, such as cap with a U.S. Navy vessel's name on it, or when they hear patients who might be of the same approximate age ask one another, "Where were you stationed? What did you do?"

To understand the term *veteran identity*, an oncology social worker must first understand the military experience. In all military branches, basic training is the introduction to military values and warrior skills. Entry into the military happens during young adulthood and can often be the first time an individual has been away from home for an extended period. According to Daley (1999, p. 292), the secured gate that one passes through when first entering a base signifies a literal and figurative demarcation between the "outside world" and the military community inside the installation boundaries. Every base has similarities to other military bases and all constitute self-contained communities, but the military community as a whole can be quite different from the world just outside the gates.

There are differences specific to each of the five branches of service, but they all share the core values of cohesion, physical fitness, respect for authority, and stoicism. Every activity is immersed in ritual, tradition, and history. People are addressed by rank as a sign that they are part of a larger hierarchy with a specific mission, and when one person leaves a position, the next person with that title will seamlessly assume the role. Listening to conversations among patients in oncology offices, one will hear veterans talk about learning how to make a perfect bed and how not to show emotions during those first weeks of basic training. Such stories are ubiquitous regardless of when or where patients served or in which branch they served. Just as some people can feel strong associations to their alma maters long after graduation, many veterans feel strong associations with the military. A veteran once told me, "My time in the Army was my Harvard." Conversely, some veterans barely acknowledge their service and may want to limit discussion of that time of their lives.

Demographics of Veterans

Knowledge of the various groups, or cohorts, of veterans is essential to understanding their unique experiences. In addition, as explained in a later section, some veterans may be eligible for additional services based on when they were in the military and where they served. According to the 2013 *Federal Benefits for Veterans, Dependents, and Survivors* (the so-called VA benefits book), the following list indicates federally recognized wartime periods:

- World War II: December 7, 1941–December 31, 1946
- Korean Conflict: June 27, 1950–January 31, 1955
- Vietnam War: August 5, 1964 (February 28, 1961, for veterans who served "in country" before August 5, 1964)–May 7, 1975
- Gulf War: August 2, 1990–date yet to be prescribed

Table 94.2. Number (in Millions) of Veterans by Cohort	
World War II	2
Korean Conflict	2.4
Vietnam Era	7.5
Gulf War	5.7
Peacetime	5.8

Although the current military activity in Afghanistan and Iraq are not specifically outlined as wartime periods, Chapter 1 of the VA benefits book describes the scope of mental health and medical care and other services available to eligible veterans of these conflicts in detail. Oncology social workers meeting veterans who were in Southwest Asia during the Gulf War should refer veterans to the Gulf War Registry, which gives veterans access to special health evaluations and health-related information. The benefits book is updated annually and is available for download from the VA's website.

As of this writing, there are approximately 21.8 million U.S. veterans living in the United States (see Table 94.2). Nearly 34% were in combat. According to the 2010 National Survey of Veterans, the states with the highest concentration of veterans are California, Texas, Florida, New York, and Pennsylvania, with between 950,000 and 1,970,000 veterans combined in these states. California, Texas, and Florida have the highest number of veterans over age 65, with between 500,000 and 800,000 older veterans in these states. Oncology social workers working in these states, therefore, are quite likely to encounter many veterans receiving cancer care in their treatment sites. A working knowledge of veterans' demographics and some of the contexts of their time in the military will help social workers engage in, assess, assist with, and design programs for their veteran patients.

Individual demographic characteristics pertaining to veterans (see Table 94.3) change when specific cohorts are examined or the demographics of the current military with veterans are compared. For example, Patten and Parker (2011) report that approximately 15% of the current active duty forces are women and that women represent 19% of the 2.2 million post 9/11 veterans. The VA projects that women will represent 18% of the veteran population by 2040.

Table 94.3. Veteran Demographics by Percent	
Male	92
Age > 55	64
Married	70
No dependent children	70
Caucasian	85

Research shows veterans are better educated, have higher incomes, and have more social and financial stability than nonveterans. According to Edwards and McLean (2010), veterans surpass nonveterans in rates of high school completion (85% vs. 71%). The National Survey of Veterans indicates that veterans have lower rates of poverty (8% vs. 10%) and higher median incomes than the general population ($36,000 vs. $33,500).

When working with veterans, oncology social workers should consider some differences among the oldest cohorts (World War II, Korean Conflict, and Vietnam era). On the one hand, World War II veterans participated in a war supported by society through expressions of patriotism and mutual sacrifice, such as rationing. Their return to civilian life was supported though programs such as the GI Bill (Bennett, 1996). On the other hand, Vietnam veterans fought in an undeclared and unpopular war (Grassman, 2009). One study finds that Vietnam veterans report greater difficulties with daily activities than do World War II and Korean Conflict veterans; they were twice as likely to self-rate their health as poor compared to the two older war cohorts and reported more mental health issues than their older counterparts (Villa, Harada, Washington, & Damron-Rodriguez, 2002).

Service-Connected Compensation

Oncology social workers are encouraged to review the benefits book for a complete discussion on available benefits for their veteran patients. The 2010 National Survey of Veterans underscored the need for professionals not to assume that veterans know the benefits to which they may be entitled (see, for example, Table 94.4, which shows how Vietnam-era veterans understand the benefits to which they may be entitled).

When oncology social workers assess veteran patients, they are performing a critical task. Oncology social workers have the ability to educate veterans about and connect

Table 94.4. Vietnam-Era Veterans' Understanding of Benefits by Percent	
Understand VA benefits[a]	44
Understand VA health care benefits[a]	37
Understand VA burial benefits[b]	31
Understand VA education and training benefits[b]	43

[a] Similar understanding as World War II and Korean Conflict veterans.

[b] Poorer understanding than World War II and Korean Conflict veterans.

veterans to health care, financial, and other VA benefits at a point when veterans and their families might be most in need of these services.

According to the VA benefits book, "Disability compensation is a monetary benefit paid to Veterans who are disabled by an injury or illness that was incurred or aggravated during active military service. These disabilities are considered to be service-connected" (p. 28). Service-connected compensation is a fulfillment of the nation's promise to care for its veterans who were harmed during military service.

Military Service and Cancer

The VA's public health website contains information about chemical, physical, and environmental hazards that one may have encountered during military service. The oncology social worker should check this site frequently to keep abreast of expansions of VA benefits in this area. Exposures are not limited to one war or one location. For example, marines and their families who were stationed at Camp Lejeune from 1957 to 1987 may have been exposed to contaminated drinking water, leading to several diseases, including cancers. People who can prove exposure and have one of the listed diseases may be entitled to health care from the VA.

Agent Orange was a chemical defoliant used in Vietnam and elsewhere in Southeast Asia and is connected with numerous cancers and other diseases. Because it was stored on bases worldwide, members of all branches of service might have been stationed at locations where these chemicals were present. Veterans who can prove they were exposed and who have any of the listed diseases may apply for service-connected compensation in addition to having access to cancer treatment from VA medical centers.

A veteran may apply for a service-connected claim or apply for VA health benefits through the VA's eBenefits portal. Veterans who need assistance with the benefits application process may receive guidance from a variety of trained public and volunteer agencies, including state and local governments and elected representatives who have staff who specialize in obtaining veterans' benefits. Veterans service organizations, such as the American Legion and Disabled American Veterans, also have members who help veterans to obtain benefits. Through the resources discussed previously and their associated websites listed in the Additional Resources, oncology social workers can locate the personnel who can help a veteran in filing a claim. In addition, the oncology social worker can offer emotional support as the veteran pursues applying for service-connected compensation and can provide counseling to help the veteran with cancer, particularly an Agent Orange–related cancer, make meaning of his or her cancer experience.

R. is a 69-year-old with suspected metastatic lung cancer who resides between the homes of relatives and friends and now needs a workup and treatment for his symptoms. By taking a military history during your assessment, you learn that R. is a Vietnam veteran. He describes his work history after serving in the military as "just got by." By consulting the VA website, you confirm that his lung cancer diagnosis makes him eligible for Agent Orange service-connected compensation. R.'s veteran status qualifies him for housing assistance, medical and mental health care, and palliative care from the VA. Your cancer center can collaborate with the local VA to share or transfer care as appropriate to this veteran's preferences and needs.

Military Assessment

When doing a military assessment of a veteran, the oncology social worker has certain important goals in mind. First, the military assessment prompts the social worker to determine if a patient served in the military and allows for a deeper exploration of patient-centered care specific to veterans that can then be useful to other members of the treatment team and improve the quality of care. It also links the veteran to necessary services and, potentially, compensation. One useful tool for doing military assessments is the VA's Military Health History Pocket Card for Clinicians (see the list of VA-related websites in the Additional Resources).

As stated earlier, there is little research about veterans and psychosocial oncology. I performed my doctoral research at the VA on Vietnam-era combat and noncombat veterans with advanced cancer. In the qualitative portion of my study, 35% ($n = 12$) of combat veterans indicated that their military experience is a source of strength for them compared with 23% ($n = 11$) of noncombat veterans. Twenty percent ($n = 7$) of the combat veterans stated that Agent Orange was somehow related to their cancer. Noncombat veterans reported more concerns about their declining health (31%, $n = 15$) compared to combat veterans (2%, $n = 8$; Daratsos, 2011).

Call for Future Research

The results of my research suggest that future studies should distinguish when and where people served to better approach the meaning of "patient centered" or "veteran centered" care (Daratsos, 2011). Furthermore, research is needed to study relationships among issues commonly associated with veteran status, such as posttraumatic stress, substance abuse, and pain management, and issues of importance in cancer care, such as survivorship. Oncology social workers unable to engage in research can still contribute to developing a larger awareness of veteran issues among treatment teams. Psychosocial assessments can be revised to include taking a military history, and information regarding the availability of veteran-specific resources should be presented to veteran patients and discussed in clinical conferences. With the engagement of committed community partners, the VA can fulfill its promise to care for our nation's heroes.

A. is a 92-year-old veteran with multiple medical problems including breast cancer and melanoma. She is not on treatment but remains well known in the clinic and is a longtime volunteer in your hospital. Her frailty is evident and yet she refuses to accept home care and she is reluctant to take opioids for pain management. Noticing an American flag lapel pin, you ask her if she is a veteran. A. smiles and says she was in the Army during World War II. She shares that she worked in a military hospital as a clerk and when the war ended, she continued to work in hospitals. After retirement, she decided to volunteer in this hospital to keep busy and "do service."

You ask A. to tell you more about her experience in World War II. She recalls joining the Army because she needed a job. She was unprepared for her assignment to a hospital and deeply affected by the sight of so many young injured men in pain. She remembers morphine was used liberally and that most patients died. Over several sessions with A., you are able to help A. with life review, to make meaning of her military experience and her continued life of service to others through her volunteer work. Along with the medical team, you educate her about pain management to alter her belief that opioids are for dying patients. You facilitate her acceptance of home care as a way to allow others to give back to her in exchange for a lifetime of service to others.

Pearls

- The only way to determine whether someone is a veteran is to ask.
- Knowledge of the VA and its services will facilitate social workers' ability to assist patients who are veterans in finding needed services.

Pitfalls

- The degree to which anyone identifies as a veteran is unique. Not everyone who served will want his or her service recognized, nor will every veteran wish to pursue VA services.
- Most veterans have served during "peacetime." Nevertheless, they may also have been exposed to hazardous conditions that continue to have an impact on their physical or mental health.

NOTE

1. For a list of VA-specific websites referred to in this chapter, see the Additional Resources.

ADDITIONAL RESOURCES

For further information on the VA programs referred to in this chapter, see the following U.S. VA Websites:

eBenefits: https://www.ebenefits.va.gov/ebenefits-portal/ebenefits.portal
Gulf War Veterans' Illnesses: http://www.publichealth.va.gov/exposures/gulfwar/index.asp
National Center for Veterans Data and Statistics: *Health Insurance Coverage, Poverty, and Income of Veterans, 2000 to 2009*: http://www.va.gov/vetdata/docs/SpecialReports/HealthIns_FINAL.pdf
National Center for Veterans Data and Statistics: Veteran Population: http://www.va.gov/vetdata/Veteran_Population.asp
National Center for Veterans Data and Statistics: Veteran Population 65 Years and Older by State: Fiscal Year 2010: http://www.va.gov/vetdata/docs/Maps/VetPop_Age65Plus.pdf
National Center for Veterans Data and Statistics: Veteran Population by State: Fiscal Year 2012: http://www.va.gov/vetdata/docs/Maps/VetPop_State.pdf
Office of Academic Affiliation: Military Health History Pocket Card for Clinicians: http://www.va.gov/oaa/pocketcard/
Office of Academic Affiliation: Mission: http://www.va.gov/OAA/OAA_Mission.asp
Office of the Actuary: *Veteran Population Projections: FY2010 to FY2040*: http://www.va.gov/vetdata/docs/quickfacts/Population_slideshow.pdf
Public Health: http://www.publichealth.va.gov/index.asp
Public Health: Agent Orange: http://www.publichealth.va.gov/exposures/agentorange/index.asp
Public Health: Camp Lejeune: Past Water Contamination: http://www.publichealth.va.gov/exposures/camp-lejeune/index.asp
VA History in Brief: http://www.va.gov/opa/publications/archives/docs/history_in_brief.pdf
VA History: http://www.va.gov/about_va/vahistory.asp

REFERENCES

Bennett, W. (1996). *When dreams came true*. Washington, DC: Brassey's.
Daley, J. (1999). Understanding the military as an ethnic identity. In J. Daley (Ed.), *Social work practice in the military* (pp. 291–306). New York, NY: Haworth Press.
Daratsos, L. (2011). *The end of life preferences of Veterans Health Administration using Vietnam-era veterans with terminal cancer* (Doctoral dissertation). Retrieved from http://gradworks.umi.com (3437242)
Edwards, R., & MacLean, A. (2010). Military service, combat exposure, and health in retirement. Retrieved from http://paa2011.princeton.edu/papers/111911
Grassman, D. (2009). *Peace at last: Stories of hope and healing for veterans and their families*. St. Petersburg, FL: Vandamere Press.

Kizer, K., & Dudley, R. (2009). Extreme makeover: Transformation of the veterans' healthcare system. *Annual Review of Public Health*, 30, 313–339.

Patten, E., & Parker, K. (2011). *Women in the U.S. military: Growing share, distinctive profile*. Washington, DC: Pew Research Center. Retrieved from http://www.pewsocialtrends.org/files/2011/12/women-in-the-military.pdf

Siegel, I., & Taylor, M. (1948). Public expenditures for veterans' assistance. *Journal of Political Economy*, 56(6), 527–532.

Spiro, A., Schnurr, P., & Aldwin, C. (1997). A life-span perspective on the effects of military service. *Journal of Geriatric Psychiatry*, 30, 91–128.

U.S. Census Bureau. (2011, November 1). Profile America facts for features: Veterans Day 2011. Retrieved from http://www.census.gov/newsroom/releases/archives/facts_for_features_special_editions/cb11-ff23.html

U.S. Department of Veteran's Affairs. (2013). Federal benefits for veterans, dependents, and survivors. Retrieved from http://www.va.gov/opa/publications/benefits_book.asp

Villa, V., Harada, N., Washington, D., & Damron-Rodriguez, J. (2002). Health and functioning among four war eras of U.S. veterans examining the impact of war cohort membership, socioeconomic status, mental health, and disease prevalence. *Military Medicine*, 167(9), 783–789.

95

Jennifer Mills

The Evolving Role for Oncology Social Workers in Business

Key Concepts

- *Cancer care in our evolving health care system yields new business opportunities for oncology social workers.*
- *Oncology social workers possess unique skills that businesses find valuable.*
- *Considering nontraditional positions requires broadly defining contributions to oncology challenges, as well as adapting skills.*

Today, individuals' careers evolve rapidly, sometimes leading them to positions they never considered during their formal education. The evolving health care system and the dynamic needs of individuals affected by cancer continually produce new opportunities for oncology social workers to explore. Successfully addressing today's health care challenges requires both nonprofits and for-profits to adopt an agile, committed approach to finding the most appropriate people to contribute the most meaningful solutions.

Social work evolved from a long line of innovators aiming to find better solutions to complex situations. The approach of identifying a problem, assessing the environment, and mobilizing resources necessary for change set forth by early leaders still benefits social workers facing today's complex health care challenges. However, the applications of these skills differ and now include integration into areas of the workforce traditionally held by other professions. Very few professions train their students to apply their skills to complex socioeconomic, physical, psychosocial, and geographic challenges with the same tenacity as the social work profession. These skills hold value for nearly all areas of the health care field, including for-profit businesses.

An appreciation for the unique perspective social workers bring to a problem may not be immediately recognized until business leaders see it in action. Social work remains an enigma outside professions focused on human service. If 10 people on the street were asked what social workers do, 10 different answers would result. This is not negative; it offers a unique opportunity for social workers to define themselves and demonstrate value based on the merit of their training and perspective. Patient-focused teams in health care recognize the value of having oncology social workers as active team members. The trend in business is just now burgeoning.

Advances in modern medicine have changed the way individuals affected by cancer are treated and cared for across the continuum, from diagnosis through long-term survivorship. Each advance yields new, unexpected needs; complex challenges; and disparities across demographic subgroups. Until all individuals diagnosed with cancer have equal access to quality care, oncology social workers must continue exploring new ways to infuse their skills into the health care system. Companies who derive profit from their work (herein called businesses) represent one sector in the global health care system where oncology social work skills positively impact patients' lives.

My professional career began with community mobilization around infectious disease in rural Alabama and transitioned to leadership at a national nonprofit cancer organization for nearly a decade. While earning bachelor, master's, and doctoral degrees in social work, as well as a master's degree in public health, I never realized the transferability of social work skills to other areas of health care, nor did I recognize how and why businesses needed social workers. The result of a transition to a for-profit health care company served as the catalyst for this chapter.

Integration of the concepts in this chapter requires readers to open their minds to the needs of the oncology community and the definition of business. The chapter will provide a summary of the changing oncology health care landscape and explain why employment opportunities for social workers are expanding within businesses. A description of how and why social work skills bring value to nontraditional employment opportunities (e.g., consulting, pharmaceutical/biotechnology/device industries, PR/marketing companies) will be discussed. Strategies to prepare social workers for a transition will also be presented.

How Social Workers Define Their Commitment to Change Must Evolve

At the heart of the social work profession lies the desire to problem solve and effect change (Hare, 2004). Social workers must, therefore, identify the problem and be open and creative about the opportunities to promote positive change. Today's health care system supports the need to cross-fertilize professions for the welfare of patients globally. The cumulative burden of cancer around the world, coupled with the dynamic needs of people affected by the disease from diagnosis through long-term survivorship and end-of-life care, support the rationale for why oncology social workers are needed in business more now than ever before. More people around the globe die from noncommunicable disease (NCD) than communicable disease (e.g., HIV/AIDS, tuberculosis). The four most common diseases, accounting for 80% of NCD-related deaths, include cancer, diabetes, cardiovascular disease, and chronic respiratory diseases. Estimates suggest that, in 2008, 36 million deaths around the world resulted from NCDs, and this number is expected to grow to 52 million in 2030 (United Nations, 2011).

Thus, global health efforts now include an increased emphasis on NCDs, including cancer. This is evidenced by the United Nations summit on prevention and control of noncommunicable diseases in 2011, the results of which formed a report that describes the burden of NCDs on all countries, especially low-income countries (Marrero, Bloom, & Adashi, 2012). The report calls for system-wide strategies to prevent NCDs, such as screening, counseling, nutrition changes, and tobacco control. It also highlights the need for care for those already impacted by NCDs. Close examination of these needs, and the collaborators required to positively impact change, reveal many opportunities for oncology social workers. The following case study offers a practical example of how social workers may contribute to innovative efforts around the globe.

Examining the development of cancer care in low-income countries reveals many opportunities for social workers. Shulman (2012) describes the collaborative effort required to care for patients in these countries by illustrating one example in Rwanda. Collaborators include medical institutions, global nonprofits, local government leaders, and industry. The continuum of cancer care and access to not only medicines but also the infrastructure necessary to care for individuals diagnosed with cancer differs across the globe. Thus, the experiences of Shulman and team set forth several principles of care for low-income countries. Examples include prioritizing where resources should be allocated, defining value-based care, and creating a research agenda. Shulman purports that an integrated approach is required. The possibilities for social work involvement in global projects such as this are endless. Social workers could contribute meaningfully to companies' efforts to provide access to medicines and services, consulting companies' assessment of needs and resources, economic institutions' ability to understand the social impact of proposed strategies, and more. Consider how the "person in environment" perspective might help this team identify ways that resources should be allocated considering needs on an individual, family, and community level.

Existing and New Barriers

The barriers to providing optimal oncology care can be characterized by two concentric forces: (1) needs and challenges well documented in the literature and agreed upon by experts (see consensus reports from the Institute of Medicine [2008] for further reading) and (2) emerging aspects of medical care where the impact on patients has yet to be defined. New advances in oncology care create additional opportunities and challenges for the system and patients. Identifying and implementing solutions to address well-documented challenges and emerging barriers require collaboration across government, academia, the private sector, and the public sector. For example, the disparate rates of participation in clinical trials across demographic populations remain a challenge (Murthy, Krumholz, & Gross, 2004). Innovative solutions might involve nonprofit organizations identifying a social media campaign to change knowledge, attitudes, and behaviors; contracting with a public relations firm to develop a message; requesting that government and businesses financially support the effort; and having academics evaluate the impact. The social work perspective could add to all phases, including needs assessment, program development and implementation, and process and outcome evaluation.

Emerging Issues in Oncology Care

- *Oral oncolytics*
- *Cancer as a chronic disease and the financial burden of long-term treatment and care*
- *Long-term survivorship*
- *Health information technology*
- *Electronic medical records*
- *Increased focus on global noncommunicable diseases*
- *Employment issues in the context of new modalities of treatment*
- *Survivors of pediatric cancers*
- *Impact of secondary malignancies and long-term toxicity on survivors' lives*

Where Business and Social Work Intersect

The ultimate goal of all involved in oncology care is to improve the lives of patients. Close examination of the missions and values of for-profit oncology companies, nonprofit health organizations, and government entities reveal a primary focus on patients. Nonprofit companies make decisions based on how to support activities to achieve their mission, whereas for-profit companies do the same while also intending to generate profit.

Exercise: Mission Comparison

Nonprofit health care organizations may share more in common with for-profit health care companies than one would assume. To identify commonalities, explore the websites of two nonprofit organizations that focus on patient education and research and two health care companies. Examine each entity's:

- *Mission*
- *Focus*
- *Program and activities*

What commonalities can you identify? What differences? Compare their budgets and approaches to challenges in oncology.

The three most common reasons social workers cite for not considering roles outside of those most defined as "traditional social work" (e.g., direct clinical practice with individuals, families, and communities) are as follows:

- "I want to help people. Going to the dark side of for-profit industries will not allow me to do this."
- "I trained as a social worker. That is all I know how to do."
- "Why would anyone in business want to hire me?"

A narrow definition of how people are helped may be a contributing factor to this rationale. As described in the previous section, patients' needs are dynamic, and thus, social workers must adapt and find new ways to help. The second contributing factor may stem from the way social workers *perceive* their training. It is not the training that limits the applicability of social work skills to almost any sector of health care, but rather social workers' beliefs in the utility of their skills. Expanding the scope of social work roles, therefore, requires a shift in perception about the value social work skills bring to other areas.

Social workers have long been embarking on new areas. These areas did not evolve without awareness of the market for social work skills and the desire to learn new skills. Opening up a private practice, for example, requires financial and marketing skills beyond what students learn in school. The same transition can be applied to considering opportunities within businesses. Statistics illustrate social workers' ability to pursue additional areas. The majority (53%) of social workers over age 65 are employed in a private practice, thus suggesting the ability to blend business skills (e.g., marketing services, budgets, billing systems) with social work. Sixty-nine percent of surveyed social workers report spending some of their time on administration. More social workers specializing in the areas of aging, health, and mental health are employed by private, for-profit companies than any other area of practice (Center for Health Workforce Studies and National Association of Social Work, 2004).

How Social Work Skills Bolster Business Approaches and Ultimately Benefit Oncology Care

Just as social work practice grounds itself in theoretical frameworks, so too does business practice. Business frameworks serve as a foundation upon which one can propose strategic positioning recommendations (Porter, 1996). As described by Porter, a business's competitive advantage is gained by performing different activities than its competitors; frameworks serve as a tool for analyzing which activities a business should be engaged in to maximize success. Social workers can turn to common frameworks, such as SWOT analyses (strengths, weaknesses, opportunities, and threats; Kotler, Berger, & Bickhoff, 2010) or Porter's Five Forces (Porter, 1980), as they assess any situation and prepare for action. Critical examination of the scientific method, as described by Friga and Chapas (2008), in business reveals countless opportunities for social workers to lend unique insight and skills. These are illustrated through the following case study.

Case Study

Challenge: *Limited Awareness of Personalized Medicine Among Patients*

Illustration: *How Social Work Skills Integrate into the Scientific Method Applied by Businesses*

Personalized medicine refers to a physician's ability to tailor treatment for each person, based on his or her tumor (Schilsky, 2010; Yeatman, Mule, Dalton, & Sullivan, 2008). Translating the concept of personalized medicine into practice requires the coordination of numerous stakeholders from all sectors. Pharmaceutical/biotechnology companies aim to develop treatments for specific molecular targets expressed on a cancer cell. Diagnostic testing companies refine the way these targets are tested and characterized. Laboratories conduct the tests. Insurance companies are needed to reimburse for the testing and treatment. Researchers at academic medical centers dedicate their careers to the detection and treatment of one subgroup of one type of cancer. Government authorities contribute to the approval, monitoring, and reimbursement of testing. Patient advocacy groups provide support to patients and families while also educating people affected by cancer about the various biomarkers and tests available to them and how they seek testing. I realized in my career that my early social work experience mobilizing communities around health issues in rural Alabama translated seamlessly into organizing key stakeholders within the context of a business and beyond.

Hypothetically, limited awareness among patients with certain types of cancer about personalized medicine and what it means for their cancer treatment represents a problem businesses may want to analyze more deeply and develop a plan to address. Using the scientific method (Friga & Chapas, 2008) as a strategy to assess this hypothetical scenario provides the opportunity to illustrate how the social work perspective adds value to the analysis.

The first phase of the scientific method requires a clear definition of the problem and exploration of existing data (Friga & Chapas, 2008). I have found that social workers are skilled at examining not only the manifested problem but also the underlying root of the problem. The application of the person-in-environment approach enables you to define for whom the problem exists, under what conditions, and others that might be impacted. Friga and Chapas (2008) identify the role of intuition, as well as data, in the creation of hypotheses regarding why patients might not possess high awareness and knowledge of personalized medicine. As a social worker, I realize that I have more robust experience than my colleagues trained in business at understanding knowledge, attitudes, and behaviors among patients diagnosed with cancer, their loved ones, and health care professionals. Thus, social workers' contribution to this phase may be based on their assessment of how patients assimilate knowledge under the duress of illness, as well as where barriers in the health care system may be influencing patients' understanding of information about personalized medicine.

When the scientific model requires data collection, social workers' approach to creating appropriate questions and testing these with sensitivity to various patient factors (e.g., socioeconomic and cultural) may add to the effort. For example, social workers may pinpoint exactly when to query patients following a diagnosis. They may make such recommendations to a team, based on their experience administering surveys and forms to patients during or after treatment and understanding how patients' anxiety levels may influence surveys.

Interpreting the results once again blends evidence with intuition, according to Friga and Chapas (2008), thus requiring the user to ask if the results are reasonable. I quickly realized that my social work skills allowed me to compare the results to my experience working with people diagnosed with cancer. This often results in me asking additional questions, such as "Could these results vary across populations?" or "What other factors might be influencing patients' knowledge and attitudes toward personalized medicine?" The latter may lead to further investigation of variances in how people diagnosed with cancer seek or interpret information about their disease and treatment options.

Finally, making a decision and moving to a business plan are areas where social workers lend perspectives on the practicability and feasibility of implementing efforts to address the problem. Their understanding of human behavior and the interaction of systems related to patient care (e.g., patient–physician dynamic, the role of the caregivers' knowledge-seeking patterns in oncology care) can lend additional perspective to these steps.

Making the Transition

Strategies for Social Workers Considering Business Opportunities

Social workers interested in contributing to the for-profit sector must assess the transferability of their skills and recognize areas where they may require additional training. Finding the right fit and appropriate marketing of social work skills are also imperative for success.

Identification of Applicable Skills

Identifying what innate and learned skills an individual social worker possesses can be accomplished through the following steps:

1. Conduct a 360-degree assessment of strengths and skills. This should be based not only on the individual's perspective but also on the summation of others' observations, proven success in certain areas of his or her career, and a ranked order of the most developed strengths. Social workers should try to create a list with these strengths alongside a column of evidence to support the identified strength.

2. Align strengths and skills with categories of employment opportunities. This involves identifying a type of business and position. Dissecting the requirements of the job should be done alongside conversations with individuals who have experience either in that role or in the industry. This will create the most robust picture of the expectations for success, which may vary dramatically, as well as the daily skills needed.

Minding the Gap: Additional Training

The assessment of skills may uncover areas where additional training is needed. The 2010 Social Work Congress Imperatives for the Next Decade reference the integration of business into social work training and practice (National Association of Social Work, 2010). This will no doubt increase social workers' preparedness to explore various career paths to meet the needs of the populations they serve. Social workers considering roles in business might benefit from additional training in finance, marketing, strategic planning, and project management.

Finding an Appropriate Fit

Not all businesses are created equal. Guiding principles, culture, and approach may vary. Thus, finding a position to consider and a company whose values match those of social work and the individual can be equally as challenging as finding the "perfect" fit in the nonprofit sector. Start by observing the company in action. Joining a health care professional society may also stimulate new connections and insight.

Marketing Social Work Skills and What You Have to Offer

Transitioning from a traditional social work role to one in business requires the development of a revised resume. Because social work is somewhat of an enigma, business leaders will not immediately recognize how social workers can benefit their efforts. Thus, interested social workers must assume the responsibility for making the link; businesses will not yet automatically identify social workers as a good fit for a position within their company without the candidate making the linkage.

Exercise: How Might Social Workers Improve Health Information Technology for Patients?

Background: *The utility and impact of health information technology (IT) in cancer care spark great debate. Defined as anything (e.g., software, hardware, solutions) that could be used for the exchange of information (Health Information Technology for Economic and Clinical Health Act of 2009), health IT holds the potential to empower patients to take control of their medical records and engage in more informed conversations with their health care team. However, this may not be the panacea for a disjointed health care system. Hesse, Hana, Massett, and Hesse (2010) advocate a user-centered approach that focuses on how individuals with cancer might utilize health IT and the systems needed to support meaningful use.*

Exercise: *Imagine you have been employed by one of the most reputable health IT companies in the United States. Your job is to assess patients' understanding of their health history and what their options are to access their personal information after they have been diagnosed with cancer.*

- *List three major questions you would want to answer in your assessment.*
- *What demographics might you identify to examine more closely?*
- *How would you assess patients' perspectives on privacy?*
- *What do you hypothesize patients' needs are regarding their health information following a cancer diagnosis?*

Pearls

- As the medicine of treating people with cancer evolves, the for-profit sector could benefit now, more than ever, from social workers' unique skills.
- Businesses are not as different from nonprofits as you may think.
- Oncology social workers' possess the innovative thinking needed to transfer their skills to areas of health care and business.

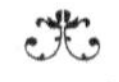

Pitfalls

- Businesses may not instantly recognize the transferability of oncology social work skills. Thus, the responsibility lies with social workers to illustrate how their previous experience would enhance businesses' efforts.
- Social workers interested in the for-profit sector must conduct an honest assessment of their skills and identify the areas where additional training might be needed.
- Social workers often do not acknowledge their value. This must change for the social worker to embark on new roles in business.

As the needs of patients and the success of modern medicine evolve, unanticipated barriers to quality health care continue to arise. Nonprofits, academia, hospitals, and government will need to collaborate with for-profit businesses to ameliorate barriers for people affected by cancer. Therefore, it is incumbent upon oncology social workers, both novice and seasoned, to erase traditional boundaries and demonstrate how they can contribute to integrated teams across many sectors in meaningful ways to improve outcomes in oncology. People diagnosed with cancer today and tomorrow depend on this innovative thinking.

ADDITIONAL RESOURCES

The MIT Sloan School of Management offers free online business courses: http://mitsloan.mit.edu/

The Oncology Business Review (OBR) provides free updates on the latest business news in oncology and is free of charge to registrants. This is a great way to identify trends in the industry and new opportunities for social workers: http://obroncology.com/

REFERENCES

Center for Health Workforce Studies and National Association of Social Work. (2004). *Licensed social workers in the United States*. Retrieved from http://workforce.socialworkers.org/studies/fullStudy0806.pdf

Friga, P. N., & Chapas, R. B. (2008). Make better business decisions. *Research Technology Management*, *51*(4), 8–16.

Hare, I. (2004). Defining social work for the 21st century: The International Federation of Social Workers' revised definition of social work. *International Social Work*, *47*(3), 407–424.

Hesse, B. W., Hana, C., Massett, H. A., & Hesse, N. K. (2010). Outside the box: Will information technology be a viable intervention to improve the quality of cancer care? *Journal of the National Cancer Institute Monographs*, *40*, 81–88.

Institute of Medicine (IOM). (2008). *Cancer care for the whole patient: Meeting psychosocial health needs*. Washington, DC: National Academies Press.

Kotler, P., Berger, R., & Bickhoff, N. (2010). *The quintessence of strategic management: What you really need to know to survive in business*. New York, NY: Springer.

Marrero, S. L., Bloom, D. E., & Adashi, E. Y (2012). Noncommunicable diseases: A global health crisis in a new world order. *Journal of the America Medical Association*, *307*(19), 2037–2038.

Murthy, V. H., Krumholz, H. M., & Gross, P. (2004). Participation in cancer clinical trials: Race-, sex-, and age-based disparities. *Journal of the American Medical Association*, *291*(22), 2720–2726.

National Association of Social Work. (2010). The 2010 Social Work Congress imperatives. Retrieved from http://www.socialworkers.org/2010congress/documents/2010Imperatives.pdf

Porter, M. (1980). *Competitive strategy*. New York, NY: Free Press.

Porter, M. (1996). What is strategy? *Harvard Business Review*, 61–78. Retrieved from http://maaw.info/ArticleSummaries/ArtSumPorter96.htm

Schilsky, R. L. (2010). Personalized medicine in oncology: The future is now. *Nature Reviews Drug Discovery*, *9*, 363–366.

Shulman, L. N. (2012). *Building a cancer care infrastructure in low-income countries: The Rwanda experience*. Chicago, IL: American Society of Clinical Oncology.

United Nations. (2011). Prevention and control of non-communicable diseases: Report to the Surgeon General. Retrieved from www.un.org/ga/search/view_doc.asp?symbol=A/66/83&Lang=E

Yeatman, T. J., Mule, J., Dalton, W. S., & Sullivan, D. (2008). On the eve of personalized medicine in oncology. *Cancer Research*, *68*, 7250–7252.

XVIII

Professional Development and Education

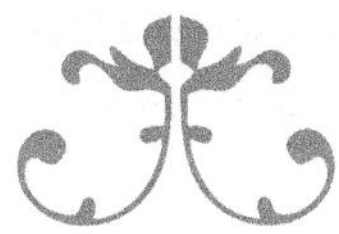

Katherine Walsh

Throughout this *Handbook*, the reader has had the opportunity to learn about the knowledge base, skills, and contributions of the profession of oncology social work. This section informs both the individual social worker and other readers about the many educational programs and organizations created to develop and sustain careers in this field. The chapters are written by leaders in the profession who have established longevity in their own careers and, in turn, have created supervisory, training, and credentialing programs to support the professional development of others.

In "Supervision and Professional Development," Annamma Abraham Kaba and Penny Damaskos discuss the importance of relationship building within the supervision dyad, within the interdisciplinary cancer program, and within the larger institutional work setting. Other specific clinical competencies are taught as well. Their model of staff education, development, and resilience-based supervision includes peer supervision, informal debriefing, mentoring by senior social workers with an open-door policy, case conferences, management meetings, external resources, and professional conferences. Additionally, they describe skill building along the trajectory from the beginning of a career throughout midcareer to the senior staff professional level.

Creating a strategic plan for a career in the evolving health care arena that incorporates academic teaching is important. In "Life as an Oncology Social Worker: Career Planning and Professional Development," Katherine Walsh uses a developmental framework to identify and promote the multiple paths open to oncology social workers in education, research, policy, and practice throughout the continuum of oncology care. This chapter offers guidelines for decision making and identifies programs that support professional development options such as post-master's and doctoral training and leadership roles.

In "Grant-Funded Educational Programs in Psychosocial Oncology," Shirley Otis-Greene and Sheila L. Hammer describe the collaboration and research required to construct the ExCEL program, a National Cancer Institute–funded training program provided to Association of Oncology Social Work (AOSW) members. They provide a step-by-step guide on ways to develop grants to support such educational initiatives.

Debra Mattison, an early oncology social work advocate and author, has diligently promoted self-care over the many years of her own career. Her chapter, "Vicarious Resilience: Sustaining a Career Over the Long Haul," gives personal examples and integrates spirituality and social work knowledge. This chapter provides a theoretical and practical guide to sustaining a career that includes identification with and learning from the coping and resilience of the individuals affected by cancer whom we serve.

Virginia Krawiec and Greta Greer coauthored "The American Cancer Society's Contributions to Oncology Social Work," describing the countless ways in which the American Cancer Society (ACS) has worked to develop and support the field of oncology social work, beginning with its assistance to the founders of the Association of Pediatric Oncology Social Workers (APOSW) and the National Association of Oncology Social Work (now the AOSW). The ACS continues to employ oncology social workers in its national and local organizations in many different roles. It also provides a broad range of education and direct services to professionals, patients, and family members. The ACS's funding of master's and doctoral students is invaluable, and social workers are urged to apply for these training and research grants.

The AOSW and APOSW have been crucial to establishing professional standards and providing a means to achieve professional competence and interdisciplinary recognition in the specialized field of oncology. In "APOSW and AOSW: Education and Development of Professional Networks," Ann Fairchild, Christa G. Burke, Paula

G. McCarthy, Stacy Stickney Ferguson, and Katherine Walsh describe the ways in which these organizations support competence through annual conferences, listservs, continuing education programs, publications, special interest groups, partnerships, and advocacy.

Virginia Vaitones, Johanna Schutte, and Debra Mattison describe the content and development of the current oncology social work specialty credential in "OSW-C: The Importance of Certification for Oncology Social Workers." These authors helped spearhead the development and implementation of this important credential to ensure the highest level of competent psychosocial care to those affected by cancer. They provide an understanding of the requirements and process for obtaining this certification based on the AOSW Standards of Practice and the National Association of Social Workers (NASW) Code of Ethics.

Elizabeth J. Clark and Stacy Collins describe the significant role the NASW has played through its commitment to social work in health care and oncology in "NASW and Oncology Social Work." They remind us that the NASW Code of Ethics remains the most comprehensive guide addressing the values, principles, and standards for all social work practitioners. The NASW's support is often provided through its partnerships with other professional and cancer service organizations, as well as its continuous advocacy activities.

96

Annamma Abraham Kaba and Penny Damaskos

Supervision and Professional Development

Key Concepts

- *This chapter discusses the role of recruitment, supervision, and training in oncology social work.*
- *Individual supervision involves building relationships, learning core competencies, developing clinical judgment, managing emotions and reactions to highly distressed patients and families, and developing specialty social work interests.*
- *Using peer supervision, informal debriefing, mentoring by senior social workers with an open-door policy, case conferences, external resources, and professional conferences are methods to prepare social workers for the growing demand for their services.*
- *It is necessary for oncology social workers to build skills throughout the professional trajectory.*

Studies indicate that oncology care represents a growth area, and as demand grows, so does the need for well-trained, clinically experienced staff (Adler & Page, 2008; Levit, Smith, Benz, & Ferrell, 2010). As experienced social workers retire, leaders and supervisors require preparation to train and mentor the field's new and midcareer oncology social workers (Messner, 2010). Helping patients and families navigate the current system—the economics of managed care and cost-effectiveness, technological advances, and more patients moving faster through the hospital system than in the past—requires social workers to have specific skills and expertise to deliver quality care in an increasingly pressured environment. Because of these realities, concentrated and innovative training for qualified oncology social workers should begin well before they're hired into an oncology setting or in the first years of employment (Adler & Page, 2008; Levit et al., 2010).

The Growing Need for Well-Trained Oncology Social Workers

There is a growing demand for social workers throughout the health care system due to the increasing population of older adults with complex medical needs, medical advances that make it increasingly possible to manage previously terminal conditions as chronic illnesses, and shifts in locus of care to families and communities, which requires management of care transitions. In 2006, social workers accounted for over half-a-million jobs in the United States, with a quarter of those in medical and public health settings. Over the next 10 years, the projected need for social workers in health care will increase by 22% (Bureau of Labor Statistics, 2008–2009). As such, a renewed focus on adequate training and preparation for oncology social work is consistent with the Institute of Medicine's report *Cancer Care for the Whole Patient: Meeting Psychosocial Needs,* where recommendations for a well-trained oncology workforce is a primary concern (Adler & Page, 2008).

This chapter examines the role of supervision and training for oncology social workers and suggests methods to prepare them for the growing demand for their services. Supervision and innovative training, as well as focus on the impact of the work of oncology social workers, will be described.

Stress in Work Settings for All Oncology Staff

Working in oncology has long been recognized as complex and challenging, with high rates of burnout and turnover (Ablett & Jones, 2007; Graham & Ramirez, 2002; Levit et al., 2010, Peteet et al., 1989; Pockett, 2003; Rohan & Bausch, 2009; Zander, Hutton, & King, 2009). Studies of job satisfaction in all oncology staff found that high stress and dissatisfaction were correlated to job changes, reduction in work hours, or leaving the field altogether (Grunfeld et al., 2000). In their study, Supple-Diaz and Mattison (1992) suggested that complex clinical issues and lack of organizational support were common complaints among oncology social workers.

However, a study by Rohan and Bausch (2009) examined oncology social workers' professional influence and function within the medical team and illuminated the positive value of an interprofessional team approach and each team member's unique contribution to patient care. Interestingly, a major part of the oncology social worker's function and value to other team members included team maintenance with attention to emotional needs of their colleagues (Rohan & Bausch, 2009). Attention to the role of the oncology social worker within the team and larger organization as an essential component of supervision will be discussed later.

Recruitment, Supervision, and Training in Oncology Social Work

Relationship Building With Interns

Supervision and professional development can begin during a master's level internship in an oncology setting, because many have specialized educational programs in oncology social work on-site as a curriculum supplement. In addition, schools of social work are creating pathways to develop and recruit oncology social workers, including fellowships for end-of-life and palliative care. Likewise, hospital social work departments have an opportunity to cultivate potential staff through their internships.

As students practice in an oncology setting, they increase self-awareness and insight for working with an oncology population (Cohen & Gagin, 2005). During the internship, the department can determine if a student demonstrates maturity, self-awareness, autonomy, and clinical acumen to work with such a clinically complex population (Sormanti, 1994). Both self-awareness and the ability to articulate clinical interventions and the rationale for their use continue to evolve after students complete their training.

Relationship Building Within the Setting

Supervision is an essential part of clinical social work practice and foundational for developing and assessing clinical skills, competencies, and implementation of social work values (Joubert, Hocking, & Hampson, 2013; Tsui & Ho, 1997). In a medical setting, supervision does not simply involve the supervisor and supervisee but includes the organization, medical team, colleagues, and patients.

Understanding institutional culture is an important aspect of supervision, as is internalizing the value of the oncology social work role and function within each service and team. This can include how the medical team addresses end-of-life care and the role social workers have within those discussions (Christ & Sormanti, 1999; Kadushin & Harkness, 2002).

Relationship Building Within the Supervisory Dyad

Developing a supervisory relationship that promotes self-reflection and understanding will provide a basis from which the supervisee can grow as both a clinician and a professional (Kadushin & Harkness, 2002). Supervision between the oncology social worker and the supervisor should foster candid discussion of complex cases, vulnerabilities, challenges, and successes. Throughout the supervisory process, the supervisor is a liaison between the organization and the oncology social work supervisee, as well as a mentor, helping him or her develop competency in psychosocial interventions and clinical knowledge.

Learning about the institutional culture and the psychological impact of the clinical work is essential content of the supervision. It is important for the supervisor to engage in ongoing reflection with the supervisee about the content of the clinical work to support and empower the supervisee. Modeling self-awareness also helps the supervisee understand the psychological strengths, realities, and limitations of working in an oncology setting.

However, the roles of supervisor and supervisee can be complicated by the power imbalance inherent to this learning structure, and therefore, open dialogue is an important aspect of the supervisory process. The supervisor should be transparent about the various roles he or she may need to play—such as administrator, supervisor, and clinician—and should model relationship building with social work colleagues and with other medical staff. This can happen through examination of clinical cases, discussions around cofacilitation of groups, conjoint participation, or observation of multidisciplinary team meetings or other collaborations such as research.

The oncology social worker brought to supervision her frustration with the team's inability to address end-of-life transitions in care with cases on the unit. The oncology social worker discussed how distraught she felt about the ethical lapses that she perceived occurring when certain physicians avoided end-of-life decisions and discussions. She felt that both the patients and their loved ones were suffering unnecessarily because the physicians did not have "the decency" to talk with patients. She further explained how it went against the social work value of patient autonomy, but she did not know how to negotiate this "ethical lapse" to help alleviate suffering in the patient. In supervision, the social worker was encouraged to explore her own reactions to the case and consider alternative explanations for the physician's reactions, such as being upset at the failure of treatment and needing help to communicate with patients about their terminal condition. Discussion included ways the oncology social worker might encourage patient and family autonomy in end-of-life decision making. The oncology social worker felt more equipped to address the complexities of this case after the importance of end-of-life advocacy was underscored in supervision. With the use of role-modeling, the supervisee felt more empowered and less conflicted.

Elements of Supervision

Understanding Use of Self

Highly stressed patients and families can elicit strong emotional responses in oncology social workers. Understanding and identifying how a clinician feels when working with patients and families are necessary to preventing burnout and remaining clinically innovative. When such responses are discussed in supervision, they provide valuable information about how to intervene and foster a sense of self-efficacy in the social worker's practice (Cohen & Gagin, 2005). Supervision offers the opportunity to discuss case content on multiple levels. However, as supervisors are in a power differential with the supervisee, supervisors need to be aware of the vulnerability that can emerge if the supervisees report their true reactions about a case (Munson, 2002). Supervisees need to feel that they won't be judged for their reactions to a patient but that, rather, this information will be used to develop self-awareness necessary for clinical development.

Teaching Clinical Judgment

Clinical judgment is a difficult-to-measure yet essential part of professional development and includes autonomy in decision making, connection to social work values and ethics, maturity in clinical practice, and an understanding of the oncology social work role within the larger organizational setting (Kadushin & Harkness, 2002; Mattison, 2000). Clinical judgment is developed through direct, in-depth case review that incorporates social work values, use of self, and knowledge of patient and family coping processes. Because of its crucial nature, clinical judgment is studied with respect to social work values and its impact on interventions in ethically complex cases (Mattison, 2000), with decision-making models providing the teaching framework (Kadushin & Harkness, 2002; Mattison, 2000; Taylor & White, 2001).

When achieved, clinical judgment represents the maturation of the clinician as the direct result of supervisory discussion that freely examines both mistakes and successes. It is not uncommon for supervisors to leap into a solution and discuss how they would handle a case. However, to do so prematurely not only shuts down fruitful dialogue but also inhibits the supervisee's thinking process essential to the development of clinical judgment. Before the oncology social worker can develop professional autonomy, the professional boundaries within the organization need to be explicit. Use of open discussions regarding decision making cultivates clinical judgment within a supervisory context (Kadushin & Harkness, 2002).

Clinical Competencies Within Areas of Specialization

Supervision is a process in which social workers can hone their clinical competencies and examine mastery of them. Within the field of oncology, there are many areas of specialization, such as pain and palliative care, young adults, geriatrics, survivorship, ethics, bereavement, group work, couple and family work, pediatrics, sexual health, and disease-specific practices, that provide opportunities for a social worker to develop specific areas of expertise.

When clinicians specialize, a level of proficiency develops to support patients and educate the interdisciplinary team. This fosters a sense of mastery within the worker and highlights his or her knowledge and skill, which leads to more gratification in his or her work. Development of recognized competencies and expertise is beneficial in oncology where caseload acuity can also cause compassion fatigue and burnout.

Learning Multiple Theoretical Approaches to Assessment and Intervention

Oncology social workers use multiple theoretical approaches to assess patient functioning, such as cognitive behavioral and crisis intervention theory. Mastery of individual, couple, family, and group counseling can be employed in any clinical setting. In addition, oncology social workers employ assessment approaches that include meaning-centered, existential and spiritual domains for a complete understanding of the patient's functioning. As a result, oncology social workers learn to integrate these perspectives, utilizing them in clinical interventions, and consequently developing expertise in multiple modalities and approaches.

For many patients, cancer represents a disruption to roles and functions within their family or community. The clinician is responsible for helping patients make optimal adjustments to diagnosis and treatment by grieving losses and negotiating challenges to self-concept. The clinician's competency is based in his or her ability to support the patient and family through the treatment continuum, assessing the patient's strengths and those of his or her support system and providing resources and counseling.

Thoughtful, multifaceted supervision is essential to develop the skills to complete psychosocial assessments and provide interventions—even more so in the context of brief hospital stays, busy clinics, and rapid discharges.

Multiple Modalities for Professional Development

Utilizing multiple modalities to facilitate professional and clinical oncology social work development can be beneficial to overall clinical skill development. The following can all be utilized.

Peer Supervision in Case Conference

There are many forms of peer supervision. The individual case conference uses a model to stimulate in-depth clinical discussions where case presentations are facilitated by a senior staff member without direct supervisory duties. Discussions are initiated by introducing a concept or a topic to generate a dialogue about a challenging clinical situation, such as how to approach patients and families with personality disorders, managing ethical issues, or examining the social work role within the medical team.

In these, a variety of topics are chosen to generate discussions that support and expand the oncology social worker's understanding of her or his work. Colleagues provide educational feedback, drawing on their own expertise. In these types of supervision groups, peers are not critiquing one another but rather exchanging ideas, experiences, and approaches as part of a discussion emphasizing growth and reflection.

This model has the ability to enhance morale and confidence without staff feeling evaluated by the other clinicians. In addition, leadership of the peer-run case conference format can shift from meeting to meeting, allowing members of the group to facilitate, lead, and provide input from multiple perspectives and roles within the organization.

Case conference example: *An oncology social worker presented a case about a patient she had been seeing for over 2 years. The patient was a 45-year-old African American man, now with progressing metastatic disease. Over the last few weeks, he had multiple admissions to the hospital to address pain issues. The patient was isolated from his family with few friends, and the oncology social worker provided consistent support to him over the years he received treatment. In a meeting, the patient said to the oncology social worker that he felt her respect for him and that he felt understood for the first time in his life. He acknowledged to her that their talks were a "healing bond that kept me going." When she recognized the depth with which they connected, she found herself struggling with tears in the session. The oncology social worker asked the group for help about whether it was appropriate to cry with the patient. The group responded with many points of view: While some related similar instances, others felt conflicted about showing emotion to patients and family members. The role of social work was discussed in depth and the format of the group facilitated understating of various ways one can manage intimacy in the professional role, acknowledging the power of the therapeutic relationship.*

Informal Peer Supervision

Informal supervision/consultation can take place in person or through online forums like the Social Work Oncology Network (SWON) of the Association of Oncology Social Work (AOSW). Members sign on to the list and discuss clinical cases, ethical issues, research projects, and community resources; others offer thoughtful reflection and insights to assist colleagues with troubling issues or stress in their workplace. This format allows for group cohesion throughout a network of oncology social workers; for many sole practitioners, SWON serves as a community of expert peers.

Practice Group Led by Senior Managers

In some settings, such as Memorial Sloan Kettering Cancer Center, "practice group" is a group supervisory model that addresses the administrative functions within the organization. Practice group members are oncology social workers from all areas of the organization and provide expertise to the group from diverse perspectives.

Led by a social work senior manager, the group is oriented to organizational procedures and gains understanding of shared issues, including consistency in documentation, privacy policies, palliative care updates, abuse and neglect issues, and community resources. This supervisory group complements the individual supervisor and peer-led clinically focused formats while emphasizing the role social workers have within the larger organization.

Group Case Conference Led by Senior Workers and Supervisors

For most social workers, group training commonly occurs during internships or on-the-job training. Support groups are offered to patients and/or caregivers to help with adjustment to illness by providing education about the diagnosis and normalizing common reactions, concerns, and experiences. A group case conference lets oncology social workers discuss group development and design, outreach strategies, complex group dynamics, and problems associated with cofacilitation. Topics such as how to handle the death of a group member and recruitment to a group that focuses on living with advanced cancer are also addressed.

Supervisors with group work expertise can present their group work and/or facilitate group case examination and discussion, which is both didactic and experiential. Peer feedback is encouraged for optimal discussion and group skill development.

Within the case conference format, oncology social workers develop leadership skills and a sense of competency as they explore the mechanics of group process. These skills can be utilized in multiple settings, either in hospital-based practice or through collaborations with community organizations.

External Resources for Supervision and Guidance

Because some social work settings lack the resources or specialized expertise to provide adequate supervision, workers may elect to seek additional training through peer or individual supervision outside of their primary place of employment. In addition, some receive additional training through advanced training programs such as institutes or certificate programs that specialize in end-of-life and palliative care.

Such programs offer in-depth training with feedback on clinical cases through direct supervision. When a social worker is the sole practitioner in an organization or lacks direct supervision opportunities, supervision can take place through telephone or other remote access modalities such as Skype (with attention to preserving confidentiality and privacy).

Professional Conferences

Professional conferences can also provide oncology social workers with topic-specific information, cutting-edge research, clinical approaches, collegial networking, and general rejuvenation. Although they do not provide direct supervisory experiences, conferences do provide the opportunity for networking, advancement in clinical understanding, and a forum that inspires connection to one's clinical practice with a fresh approach. Organizations such as the AOSW, Association of Pediatric Oncology Social Workers, and Social Work Hospice and Palliative Care Network offer conferences with oncology- and social work–specific focuses.

Skill Building Throughout a Professional Trajectory

Development of Staff in the Beginning of Their Career

The inexperienced social worker navigates her or his professional role on multiple levels: within the organization, within the medical team, with social work colleagues, and with the patient and family (Smith, Walsh-Burke, & Cruzan, 1998). A key role of the supervisor is to recognize the stresses the worker is experiencing and normalize the helplessness and sadness the worker may be feeling as parallel processes (Ben-Zur & Michael, 2007).

Support, education, and administrative assistance are necessary to help new professionals divide and manage their responsibilities, including mastering psychosocial screening and assessment, pertinent medical information, and multiple clinical modalities such as individual, family, and group interventions as they meet a daily patient quota. Nurturing self-confidence and trust in clinical judgment and recognizing the supervisee's value as a team member are important aspects of supervision for the beginning social worker (Smith et al., 1998). Individual learning styles are acknowledged and utilized to facilitate absorption of new information (Cohen & Gagin, 2005), but fostering interdisciplinary approaches to clinical care when working in a medical setting is essential.

The supervisor's goal for an oncology social worker is to help him or her develop professional autonomy and the ability for quick decision making while working within a crisis model (Simon, Pryce, Roff, & Klemmack, 2005). Discharge planning duties, as well as in-depth counseling with acute cancer patients, can lead to burnout (Pockett, 2003). Oncology social workers must learn administrative tasks such as discharge planning, but professional development should also include a wider application of the role of social work as it intersects with the medical model (Berger & Mizrahi, 2001; Werner-Lin & Biank, 2006).

Development of Midcareer and Senior Staff

The midcareer oncology social worker has likely developed areas of expertise that are utilized within his or her practice. However, long-term exposure to suffering increases the risk for burnout or compassion fatigue. The supervisor's task is to help midcareer social workers recognize ways to remain engaged or to re-engage with their work through educational training, new clinical programs, and/or opportunities to use leadership skills. At this point, oncology social workers are often supervisors themselves, so the developmental process shifts to expanding and achieving supervisory skills and self-awareness as a teacher and mentor. However, some supervisors can experience the separation from clinical work as loss and feel dissatisfied as a result (Blum & Euster-Fisher, 1983).

It is important to recognize frustration, boredom, or disconnectedness in a supervisee and help him or her identify ways to reconnect to his or her practice. The mid- and advanced career oncology social worker should have new responsibilities and clinical projects to apply his or her expertise and have opportunities for growth. Promotions and additional responsibility can contribute to a sense of mastery and provide opportunities to make contributions within a larger context. The experienced oncology social worker may consider further specialization through institute or certificate training; some oncology social workers may attend doctoral or additional master's programs to further their administrative or research skills.

Building Resilience Among Oncology Social Workers

In answer to the Institute of Medicine and other organizational recommendations for innovative staff education and training programs, some programs are developing a resilience-based perspective within supervision (Levit et al., 2010).

Rather than examining burnout and compassion fatigue, resilience-based supervision attempts to manage the toll of human grief and trauma through insight and reflection about the quality of the patient interactions rather than the shortcomings of the work environment. By raising staff awareness about patient interactions and their meaning and encouraging identification of the power and strength of patients rather than their helplessness, the quality of the journey becomes important, not the outcome.

However, incorporating resilience-based trainings into staff orientations and ongoing supervision structures represents a culture change for most organizations and, in some cases, a reconfiguration of resource allocation to training and development (see Chapter 104). However, resilience awareness can result in higher retention rates and more overall engagement in the meaning of their work (Jackson, Firtko, & Edenborough, 2007).

Developing educational modules for both staff and supervisors can encourage professional networks, foster emotional insight and positivity, help staff develop work–life balance, and cultivate reflection about the content of one's clinical practice (Jackson et al., 2007). Such training can also utilize a coaching/supervision hybrid that again focuses on a strengths-based model. In this type of supervision, the goal is to empower the midlevel employee and facilitate professional growth that enhances engagement with his or her clinical work. This model incorporates leadership workshops to not only increase productivity but also assess when to coach and when to manage the supervisee. With these approaches, clinicians are encouraged to attend seminars and advanced clinical training programs.

Pearls

- There are multiple models of supervision that enhance competencies, help avoid burnout, and reinforce social work values.
- There are different goals for supervision across the oncology social work career trajectory that foster increasing leadership skills.
- Newer models include resilience-based and reflective supervision.

Pitfalls

- The constraints of managed care with high patient acuity levels and turnover create barriers to the development of effective oncology social work interventions.
- Replacing leadership of retiring experienced social work staff is needed to train new staff.
- There may be a lack of organizational understanding and support for continuing education and training of professional staff working with complex and highly stressed patients and families.

Social work departments can add resilience-based components to new staff orientations to raise awareness of burnout, compassion fatigue, and resilience at the beginning of an oncology social worker's career. An introduction to the realities of the oncology social worker normalizes these concepts as an expected facet of the work. Recognizing the impact the work can have over a professional career serves as a foundation for sustainability and self-care for all oncology social workers. Supervisors with a resilience-based orientation can effectively shepherd oncology social workers through complex cases with self-reflection, emotional insight, and mindful self-care.

As oncology social workers build a deepening trust in their own judgment and increased awareness of the important impact of their work on patients, they will cultivate an increased sense of personal control and competence, as well as recognition of the viability of their role within the team (Gillespie, Chaboyer, & Wallis, 2007). A resilience-based supervisory model is grounded in self-reflection as a way to illuminate the significance of the work. Finally, resilience-based supervision in oncology social work promotes self-care and work–life balance that fosters longevity in the field. These activities encourage oncology social workers to remain connected with their work from multiple perspectives over time. They foster interest, engagement, and sustainability in the face of an intense and often emotionally demanding clinical practice.

Supervision is multifaceted and fosters building relationships and core competencies, developing clinical judgment, and managing highly distressed patients and families throughout the disease continuum. Supervision can utilize multiple modalities such as informal debriefing, mentoring, group format, peer supervision, and individual guidance to develop oncology social workers over their careers. Supervision provides an opportunity for innovative approaches that include building resilience and recognizing risk factors such as compassion fatigue and burnout. With projected shortages and difficulties with staff retention, the need to cultivate creative approaches to supervision is necessary in this complex field.

REFERENCES

Ablett, J. R., & Jones, R. S. (2007). Resilience and well-being in palliative care staff: A qualitative study of hospice nurses' experience of work. *Psycho-Oncology, 16*(8), 733–740.

Adler, N. E., & Page, A. E. K. (Eds.). (2008). *Cancer care for the whole patient: Meeting psychosocial health needs.* Washington, DC: National Academies Press.

Ben-Zur, H., & Michael, K. (2007). Burnout, social support, and coping at work among social workers, psychologist, and nurses: The role of challenges/control appraisals. *Social Work in Health Care, 45*(4), 63–82.

Berger, C., & Mizrahi, T. (2001). An evolving paradigm of supervision within a changing health care environment. *Social Work in Health Care, 32*(4), 1–18.

Blum, D., & Euster-Fisher, S. (1983). Clinical supervisory practice in oncology settings. *Clinical Supervisor, 1*(1), 17–27.

Bureau of Labor Statistics. (2008–2009). *Occupational outlook handbook.* Retrieved from http://www.bls.gov/ooh/

Christ. G., & Sormanti, M. (1999). The social work role in end-of-life care: A survey of practitioners and academicians. *Social Work in Health Care, 30*(9), 81–99.

Cohen, M., & Gagin, R. (2005). Can skill-development training alleviate burnout in hospital social workers? *Social Work in Health Care, 40*(4), 83–97.

Gillespie, B. M., Chaboyer, W., & Wallis, M. (2007). Development of a theoretically derived model of resilience through concept analysis. *Contemporary Nurse, 25*(1/2), 124.

Graham, J., & Ramirez, A. (2002). Improving the working lives of cancer clinicians. *European Journal of Cancer Care, 11*, 188.

Grunfeld, E., Whelan, T. J., Zitzelsberger, L., Willan, A. R., Montesanto, B., & Evans, W. K. (2000). Cancer care workers in Ontario: Prevalence of burnout, job stress, and job satisfaction. *Canadian Medical Association Journal, 163*(2), 166–169.

Jackson, D., Firtko, A., & Edenborough, M. (2007). Personal resilience as a strategy for surviving and thriving in the face of workplace adversity: A literature review. *Journal of Advanced Nursing, 60*(1), 1.

Joubert, D. L., Hocking, A., & Hampson, R. (2013). Social work in oncology—managing vicarious trauma—the positive impact of professional supervision. *Social Work in Health Care, 52*, 296–310.

Kadushin, A., & Harkness, D. (2002). *Supervision in social work.* New York, NY: Columbia University Press.

Levit, L., Smith, A. P., Benz, E. J., & Ferrell, B. (2010). Ensuring quality cancer care through the oncology workforce. *Journal of Oncology Practice, 6*(1), 7–11.

Mattison, M. (2000). Ethical decision making: The person in the process. *Social Work, 45*(3), 201–212.

Messner, C. (2010). Impending oncology social work shortage? Brain drain, retention, and recruitment. *Oncology Issues*, (Sept./Oct.), 46–47.

Munson, E. C. (2002). *Handbook of clinical social work supervision.* New York, NY: Haworth Social Work Practice Press.

Peteet, J. R., Murray-Ross, D., Medeiros, C., Walsh-Burke, K., Rieker, P., & Finkelstein, D. (1989). Job satisfaction and satisfaction among the staff members at a cancer center. *Cancer, 64*, 975–982.

Pockett, R. (2003). Staying in hospital social work. *Social Work in Health Care, 36*(3), 1.

Rohan, E., & Bausch, J. (2009). Climbing Everest: Oncology work as and expedition in caring. *Journal of Psychosocial Oncology, 27*(1), 84–118.

Simon, E. C., Pryce, G. J., Roff, L. L., & Klemmack, D. (2005). Secondary traumatic stress and oncology social work: Protecting compassion from fatigue and compromising the worker's worldview. *Journal of Psychosocial Oncology, 23*(4), 1–14.

Smith, E., Walsh-Burke, K., & Cruzan, C. (1998). Principles of training social workers in oncology. In J. C. Holland & W. Breitbart (Eds.), *Psycho-oncology* (pp. 1061–1068). New York, NY: Oxford University Press.

Sormanti, M. (1994). Field work instruction in oncology social work. *Journal of Psychosocial Oncology, 12*(3), 73–87.

Supple-Diaz, L., & Mattison, D. (1992). Factors affecting survival and satisfaction: Navigating a career in oncology social work. *Journal of Psychosocial Oncology, 10*(1), 111–131.

Taylor, C., & White, S. (2001). Knowledge, truth, and reflexivity: The problem of judgment in social work. *Journal of Social Work, 1*(1), 37–59.

Tsui, M., & Ho, W. (1997). In search of a comprehensive model of social work supervision. *Clinical Supervisor, 16*(2), 181–205.

Werner-Lin, A., & Biank, N. M. (2006). Oncology social work. In S. Gehlert & T. A. Browne (Eds.), *Handbook for health social work* (2nd ed., pp. 498–525). Hoboken, NJ: Wiley.

Zander, M., Hutton, A., & King, L. (2009). Coping and resilience factors in pediatric oncology nurses. *Journal of Pediatric Oncology Nursing, 20*(10), 1–15.

97

Katherine Walsh

Life as an Oncology Social Worker: Career Planning and Professional Development

Key Concepts

- *Oncology social work connects you to a network of highly skilled and dedicated professionals who can serve as mentors and role models at every level and stage of your career.*
- *There has been a burgeoning of career choices in oncology social work, including direct practice, program development, administration, education and teaching, research, and policy development.*
- *New direct-practice roles include facilitating better integration of care services through interventions such as patient navigation, improving transitions in the continuum of care, and developing community practice programs.*

If you are an oncology social worker, you already know that this is one of the most rewarding career choices in the social work profession. If you are considering entering this field, this *Handbook* will expand your understanding of the complex satisfactions, sophisticated skills, and unique opportunities that working closely with those affected by cancer involves. Oncology social work is a career choice that not only comes with challenges and demands but also provides many options including direct service, program planning, administration, supervision, research, teaching, and advocacy. Opportunities for leadership are available in each of these arenas due to the wide range of organizations and activities that require the knowledge and skills of oncology social workers. In fact, some of the most prominent leaders in the social work profession are those who have worked in, and identify with, this specialized area of practice (Fobair et al., 2009). The field of oncology social work connects you to a network of highly skilled and dedicated professionals who can serve as mentors and role models at every level and stage of your career.

Formulating a career plan is not always a task oncology social workers undertake in the formative stages of their professional development. This chapter provides a rationale for doing so, as well as an overview of the professional requirements and training options oncology social workers are likely to need to practice, teach, and carry out administrative roles or conduct research. Subsequent chapters in this section expand on these topics and provide a foundation for career planning that heretofore has not been available in one publication.

Historical Perspective

For those new to the profession or planning a career in this field, some history is important. Medical social work was first established in the United States in 1905 in Boston, Massachusetts, at Massachusetts General Hospital, where Dr. Richard Cabot had advocated for and established a social work department, recognizing that many medically ill patients' access to care and treatment was hindered by psychosocial problems that could be most effectively addressed by a social worker. Ida Maud Cannon, a graduate of the Boston School for Social Workers, was hired in 1907 as one of four social workers in the department.

> *As a hospital social worker, ... [s]he began each case with a thorough investigation of the patient's health, family life, financial situation, living conditions, and capacity for work. She then offered patients a variety of services provided by collaborating agencies, such as lessons about hygiene and self-care, post-discharge transfers to other institutions, financial help, and "friendly and understanding counsel."*
>
> (Chu, 2013)

In addition to carrying out these activities, Cannon was a passionate advocate for patients, serving on special commissions and as a trustee of the Massachusetts State Infirmary, and testifying before the Massachusetts legislature. She was awarded three honorary doctoral degrees and authored *On the Social Frontier of Medicine: Pioneering in Medical Social Service* (1952). Her career continues to serve as a model for what is possible in the profession.

The first social workers specializing in oncology also began their careers in Boston approximately 50 years later when Antoinette Pieroni, a Simmons master's of social work graduate, worked alongside researcher Dr. Sidney Farber at Boston Children's Hospital (Pieroni, 1967). In the mid-20th century, while Pieroni addressed the psychosocial issues presented by children with cancer and their families, Ruth Abrams worked at Massachusetts General Hospital with adult cancer patients (Abrams, 1971).

Pioneers like Cannon, Pieroni, and Abrams helped increase awareness of the psychosocial needs of those affected by cancer among their interdisciplinary professional colleagues and in professional training programs. This contributed to the increasing numbers of social workers entering the profession following the signing of the National Cancer Act in 1971, which fueled both cancer research and the training of oncology physicians, nurses, and social workers. Parallel developments of the social work profession occurred in other major cancer hospitals such as Memorial Sloan-Kettering Hospital Cancer Center in New York City; MD Anderson Cancer Hospital in Houston, Texas; Fox Chase Cancer Center in Philadelphia, Pennsylvania; H. Lee Moffitt Cancer Center in Tampa, Florida; and the Fred Hutchison Cancer Research Center in Seattle, Washington.

In the first decades of the profession, before the establishment of the Association of Pediatric Oncology Social Workers (APOSW) and the Association of Oncology Social Work (AOSW), many contemporary leaders in the field were just beginning their careers. The territory was uncharted, with most oncology social workers providing direct service to patients and families even if they were the directors of their departments, and career paths to mezzo- and macro-level roles and functions were not yet formally identified. In the early years, before passage of the National Cancer Act, cancer mortality rates were high. At the same time, many cancer treatments were investigational with limited evidence of their effectiveness in controlling or curing cancer. Perhaps tellingly, the term *cancer survivor* had not yet come into use. The associated realm of cancer survivorship and the social work roles and functions related to managing life after cancer were more of a dream than a reality.

Oncology Social Work: Expanded Roles and Functions

Since the inception of the APOSW in 1976 and the AOSW in 1984, the number of career choices for those in the oncology social work field has been growing. With advances in cancer treatment, genetics, and technology, as well as funding for community cancer care, specialized positions in academia, and advocacy organizations, the options and range of social work roles and functions were expanded. In addition, development of the hospice, palliative care, and survivorship fields, as well as the establishment of licensure for independent social work practitioners, has increased the types and nature of the settings in which oncology social workers practice and the varied roles and functions they fulfill.

Figure 97.1 provides a graphic view of the variety of oncology social work roles and functions possible across the continuum of oncology care.

Concurrent with changes in the field of oncology and survivorship, cultural diversity and globalization have expanded career choices. Personal interests, preferences, time availability, values, and beliefs have also influenced, and will continue to influence, career decision making.

The Importance of Career Planning

With all of the choices of roles and functions available in oncology social work settings, planning and preparing for a career can be seen as an important step. Each individual must consider multiple factors, from both oncology social work and personal development perspectives. Decisions include undertaking master's-level or doctoral training in social work or related areas that might lead to a career in research, teaching, and administration; applying for oncology social work certification or other specialized social work or health-related credentials; pursuing courses or degrees in management and administration; or becoming a participant in a mentoring relationship to pursue specialized areas of interest. For each decision, one must assess how much time, money, and effort are necessary to allocate. It is also important to be aware of what resources, both internal (intellectual interests and capacities) and external (fellowships or educational leaves), are available to support career choices.

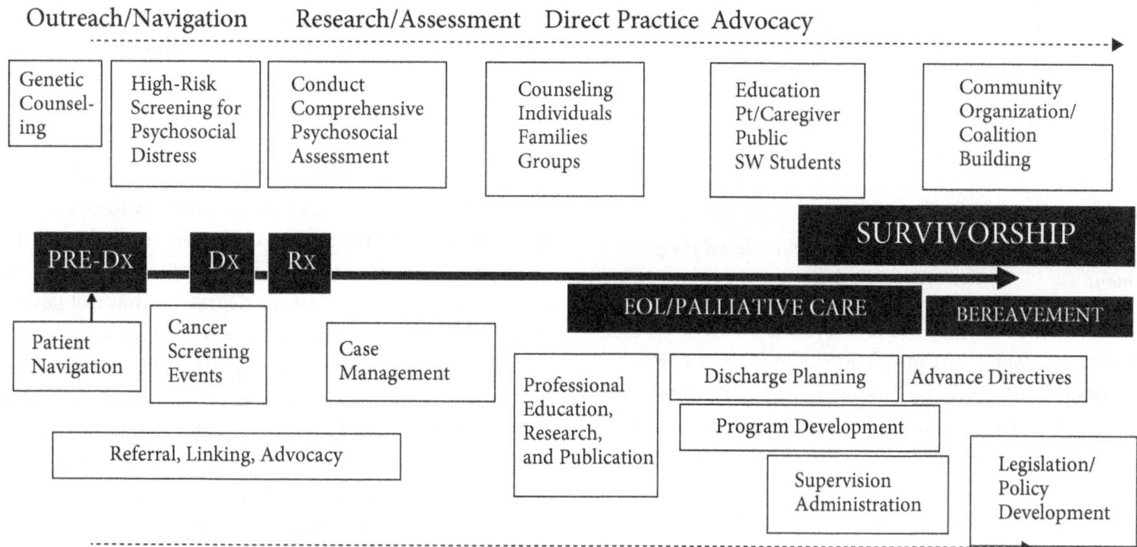

Figure 97.1. Oncology Social Work Services Through the Continuum of Care

Many of our seasoned colleagues in the field began without a road map and took advantage of opportunities either that they identified through their practice or that were presented to them by others who recognized their capabilities. These social workers also found the paths traveled to be both rich and frustrating, rewarding and challenging in the deepest ways. Although the complexity and variety of choices preclude a single road map for any individual social worker, taken together, they can serve as a useful guide to assist aspiring oncology social workers to plan for a rewarding career.

Self-Assessment and Readiness for Practice

To develop a career plan, assessing one's interests, skills, strengths, and limitations is essential. The assessment should be ongoing to integrate the acquisition of new skills, the changes that influence one's personal life, and the new challenges and opportunities that will inevitably arise in the field as cancer treatment continues to evolve.

Psychological Preparedness

The field of oncology requires the ability to manage one's own emotions, particularly related to attachment and loss. Loss can come at any time from childhood through advanced age. The ability to confront one's own losses in life and at the same time stay connected with clients' and colleagues' feelings related to loss is imperative in oncology. It is important to review one's own experiences, not only to understand and respond effectively to the grief of others, but also to ensure that one is adequately aware of, and attending to, his or her own grief (Walsh, 2012). This assessment will help both in decision making about entering the field and when making choices as one's career evolves. Unresolved issues regarding early loss should be addressed before beginning work with clients. Many schools of social work now offer courses on grief and loss, as well as oncology social work internships, that require students to examine their own loss experiences and learn how these experiences are likely to impact one's practice. As personal and professional losses accumulate throughout a career, they can be integrated into one's professional practice through supervision, personal therapy, consultation, and resilience-building practices.

Two roads diverged in a wood, and I—
I took the one less traveled by,
And that has made all the difference.
—*Robert Frost*

I was fortunate to discover within the first 5 years of my oncology social work career that I loved direct practice and also enjoyed teaching. After 30 years of practice and 20 years of teaching, I continue to find both richly rewarding. I often say that my teaching informs my practice and my practice informs my teaching. I believe that doing both is, in part, what has provided the professional rewards to sustain a career in an intellectually and emotionally demanding field.

Many other colleagues, including the authors of chapters in this and other sections of this book, have combined interests in

administration, supervision, research, and advocacy in their careers, whereas some have been very clear that they are most interested in one of these arenas and have concentrated their professional development pursuits in that area. For many, conducting research, publishing their results, and attending research-focused, as well as clinical practice–focused, conferences has been their passion. Others may have preferred to concentrate their efforts in direct practice and related program development.

The annual conferences of the AOSW, APOSW, and Social Work Hospice and Palliative Care Network (SWPHN), as well as interdisciplinary conferences such as the American Psychosocial Oncology Society (APOS) and International Psychosocial Oncology Society (IPOS), provide a forum for learning about social work and oncology and for networking with others who share similar interests. Although areas of interest may change over time, it is important to work with populations and problems you love whenever possible. Finding one's area of greatest interest may only come with exploration and experience. Fortunately, in health social work, basic professional knowledge and skills transfer readily to different specialty areas where the skill set is then expanded.

Professional Skills

In every area of oncology practice, expertise on the levels of individual, family, and group systems is essential to working effectively with clients, other professionals, and policymakers. Research, instructional, and advocacy skills are also important because these arenas of social work practice may ultimately better match one's talents and interests. However, before one can fully be prepared to manage others through supervisory or administrative roles, design and conduct relevant studies, advocate effectively, and fully appreciate the impact of policies on individuals and families experiencing cancer, some direct practice experience is an important, if not mandatory, preparatory experience.

Direct oncology social work practice requires mastery of a wide spectrum of knowledge and skills to carry out the primary tasks of comprehensive biopsychosocial assessments, adjustment to illness counseling, case management, discharge planning, mental health risk assessment, symptom management, psychosocial care at the end of life, and bereavement counseling (Smith, Walsh-Burke, & Cruzan, 1998; Taylor-Brown, Altilio, Blacker, Christ, & Walsh-Burke, 2001; Walsh & Hedlund, 2011).

Education and Training Options

While some bachelor-level social workers are employed in case management roles serving oncology populations, most oncology social workers have a master's degree and clinical licenses in the states and countries that require them. At a minimum, choosing a master's of social work program that has field internship affiliations with oncology settings, and preferably faculty with oncology experience, is important to enter the field. Some master's programs and affiliated agencies have obtained master's of social work training grants from the American Cancer Society (ACS) that provide financial support to students and field instructors in oncology settings. If one has obtained a master's degree but has not gained experience in oncology-related settings, there are post-master's training opportunities such as pain and palliative care fellowships and mentoring programs that provide or supplement on-the-job training. Continuing education options including certificate programs and new oncology social work training workshops can enhance one's preparedness.

Doctoral preparation is essential for primary careers in research and academia, although many social workers with master's degrees engage in research and adjunct teaching activities. Although not a prerequisite, engaging in direct practice for some years after completing a master's degree to gain valuable knowledge and skills before pursuing a doctorate can be an asset. A doctoral program that has funding to support doctoral students and with faculty who are conducting oncology-related research or who are also practicing in oncology-related settings is advantageous because these faculty can assist with mentoring, networking, and grant funding. The Kent School of Social Work at the University of Kentucky is the first school of social work to establish an endowed faculty chair in oncology, thereby demonstrating a commitment to training researchers and practitioners in this field and providing specialized opportunities for both doctoral and master's students. The ACS also provides funding to selected doctoral candidates in oncology social work to support completion of their doctoral research, in addition to providing stipends to students in selected master's programs who apply for funding. (See Chapter 100 regarding ACS funding.)

Post-Master's and Continuing Education

Professional licensing, as well as the ongoing evolution of knowledge, requires that social workers continuously engage in professional development and continuing education. This is also required for specialized credentialing in oncology and the related fields of hospice and palliative care (the AOSW offers the oncology social work certification [OSW-C] and the National Association of Social Work [NASW] with the National Hospice and Palliative Care Organization (NHPCO) offers the Advanced Certified Hospice and Palliative Care Social Worker credential [ACHP-SW]). The AOSW, APOSW, NHPCO, NASW, APOS, and SWPHN offer a wide variety of excellent learning options from free online courses and webinars to annual conferences and training intensives.

Oncology Settings

Oncology social workers are employed in many settings, from independent private practice offices (micro systems) to large multihospital organizations (mezzo systems) to major government and advocacy organizations (macro systems). Many oncology social workers find themselves working in different settings and carrying out different roles over a career. To follow is a list of some, but not all, of the oncology-specific settings from which one might choose:

- Private practice and physician practices
- VNA, hospice, and home-care agencies
- Community hospitals and health clinics
- Teaching- and university-affiliated medical centers
- Community cancer programs
- National cancer service organizations
- Cancer advocacy organizations
- Industry/corporations
- Professional organizations

Additional settings for cancer-informed practice in the following:

- Schools
- Mental health organizations
- Pharmaceutical companies

In addition to employment opportunities, there are many volunteer and funded opportunities for leadership within professional, community, and government organizations that can contribute to one's own and others' career advancement. These include serving on boards of directors of international professional organizations, such as the AOSW and APOSW, and service organizations, such as the ACS. To follow is a description of one career trajectory in oncology social work. This is followed by a depiction in Figure 97.2 of the related career timelines with affiliated organizations that were engaged.

Early Years Mid-Career Advanced Retirement

BSW/MSW Training Yrs 1 Yrs 2–7 Yrs 8–15 Yrs 15–20 Yrs 21–?

direct practice
education
research, publication
advocacy
supervision
program development
administration

Figure 97.2. Planning a Social Work Career Over Time

Although I started my career in 1977 in a small rehabilitation hospital, following internships in a school and on a neurological unit of a Veterans Administration hospital, I spent my first 5 years in one of 12 National Cancer Institute (NCI)–designated comprehensive cancer centers as a clinical social worker and field supervisor. I then began my family and my doctoral study and moved from metropolitan Boston to semirural western Massachusetts, altering my career path in ways I could not have anticipated when obtaining my master's degree. While completing a doctorate on a part-time basis, I also worked part time for a small community hospital and a local chapter of the Visiting Nurse Associations of America (VNAA) before taking a position as director of psychosocial services for a hospice. In this position, I supervised four social workers, two volunteer coordinators, a bereavement counselor, and a spiritual counselor and worked closely with the nursing, medical, and admissions directors. When I completed the doctorate (it took 7 years), I taught as an adjunct professor for a year before taking a full-time faculty position. I continued the private practice I had initiated while working for the VNAA. While teaching and practicing I have also held several leadership positions with the AOSW, NASW, and SWHPHN that have allowed me to lead professional exchanges in China, Cambodia, and Hungary and to present at international conferences, experiences that have been invaluable in expanding my own expertise and led to a rich professional support network of experts in the profession. Finally, professional writing is an aspect of an oncology social work career that the authors of each chapter of this handbook have found rewarding.

Mezzo and Macro Systems Roles and Functions

If one aspires to a career that includes having an impact on larger systems, there are many roles and functions that social workers carry out and are described in chapters in this handbook. A master's (and sometimes a doctoral) degree is required for most of these roles. For some roles, additional degrees or training, such as business or management, will be useful. Some schools offer dual-degree programs, but professional development opportunities can be pursued after a master's degree as well. Doctoral education prepares researchers and educators; supervising, managing, and leading small organizations can serve as excellent preparation for leadership positions in larger organizations. Many social workers are administrators of hospital oncology programs, directors of interdisciplinary psychosocial and palliative care programs, and administrators of patient support services, as well as administrators in social work departments. Finding a mentor and role models who can guide, instruct, and demonstrate collaboration, mediation, advocacy, and leadership skills is perhaps the best preparation for these mezzo and macro systems roles and functions.

Mezzo systems:

- *Program development for particular populations or problems*
- *Supervision and consultation*
- *Administration and management in both social work and interdisciplinary programs*
- *Dean and executive director positions*
- *Pharmaceutical and product marketing and distribution*

Macro systems:

- *Education*
- *Research*
- *Leading advocacy and professional organizations*
- *Government and policy organizations*

Capitalizing on Opportunities

Even if one's career plan anticipates a trajectory, for example, from master's degree to practitioner to manager, it is important to be alert to the inevitable opportunities that might arise even outside the planned arenas. Because of the rapidly changing world of oncology, innovations are likely to open possibilities that may appeal and enhance one's professional development. An example is patient navigation. Although social workers have always assisted patients and families in navigating the health care system, the identified role of patient navigator gained widespread recognition in the first decade of the 21st century. With funded patient navigator programs like the one the ACS sponsors, social workers have had the opportunity to both occupy these roles and train and supervise others, augmenting their resumes and adding to their skill sets.

Another example is the many cancer advocacy organizations that have evolved over the past four decades. Organizations like the Lymphoma Research Foundation and the National Marrow Donor Program have offered social workers many new opportunities for leadership that could not have been predicted 30 years ago when many were beginning their careers. Other organizations like Cancer*Care* and the Cancer Support Community have grown from local to national organizations, and oncology social workers have not only served in leadership positions in these organizations but also led the development and implementation of technology-based programs, publications, and networking. These roles and functions can provide social workers with the opportunity to travel and deliver education, training, and support programs to many professionals and supervise more social workers than would be possible in many medical settings. Due to medical advances and an increasing geriatric population, palliative care has provided new social work positions in gerontology and oncology at micro, mezzo, and macro levels (Altilio & Otis-Green, 2011).

Finally, the changes in the health care system brought about by health reform have created new opportunities for the use of social work skills in areas such as developing better integrated systems of care, managing transitions across the continuum of care, developing and implementing care evaluation, and using technology to access patient populations and fully implement person-centered care. These are discussed more fully in Section 14.

Pearls

- Connecting with a network of skilled oncology social work professionals provides continuous mentoring and training throughout a career.
- Oncology social work knowledge and skill base provides exceptional preparation for contributing to the new health care mandates of creating more accessible and integrated systems of care.

Pitfalls

- Failing to engage with established oncology social work networks of support, education, and training.
- Devoting insufficient attention to building personal and professional resilience.

Oncology social work now has an established history, and members of our profession have been, in many cases, practicing for more than 30 years. These seasoned professionals often report that mentoring others has become a most satisfying part of their career. A mentoring relationship can meet the generative needs most midcareer professionals experience in their personal and professional lives and may be a rewarding component of a comprehensive career plan. Finding a mentor in the earlier years of one's career can be a very important strategy for modeling, networking, and securing informed support in decision making. A seasoned oncology social worker who has experienced the highs and lows of this challenging and rewarding work, and accumulated years of expertise, can be an invaluable adviser to those newer to the field. The energy and interest brought to a mentoring relationship by a newer worker can be a refreshing addition to a seasoned worker after the establishment of one's own career, and mentoring can be a most satisfying way to contribute to the continuity of an important profession.

REFERENCES

Abrams, R. (1971). Denial and depression in the terminal cancer patient—a clue for management. *Psychiatric Quarterly*, *45*(3), 394–404.

Altilio, T., & Otis-Green, S. (Eds.). (2011). *Oxford textbook of palliative social work*. New York, NY: Oxford University Press.

Cannon, Ida M. (1952). *On the social frontier of medicine: Pioneering in the medical social service*. Cambridge, MA: Harvard University Press.

Chu, A. (2013). *Ida Maud Cannon*. Unitarian Universalist History and Heritage Society. Retrieved from http://uudb.org/articles/idamaudcannon.html

Fobair, P., Stearns, N., Christ, G., Dozier-Hall, D., Newman, N., Zabora, J., … Desoneir, M. (2009). Historical threads in the development of oncology social work. *Journal of Psychosocial Oncology*, *27*(2), 155–215.

Pieroni, A. (1967). The role of the social worker in a children's cancer clinic. *Pediatrics*, *40*(3), 534–536.

Smith, E., Walsh-Burke, K., & Cruzan, C. (1998). Education and training needs of oncology social workers. In J. Holland & W. Brietbart (Eds.), *Psycho-oncology*. New York, NY: Oxford University Press.

Taylor-Brown, S., Altilio, T., Blacker, S., Christ, G., & Walsh-Burke, K. (2001). *Best practices in end of life care*. Philadelphia, PA: Society for Leadership in Social Work and Health Care.

Walsh, K. (2012). *Grief and loss: Theories and skills for the helping professions*. Boston, MA: Pearson.

Walsh, K., & Hedlund, S. (2011). Assessment of mental health risk in palliative care: The social work role. In T. Altilio & S. Otis-Green (Eds.), *Oxford textbook of palliative social work*. New York, NY: Oxford University Press.

98

Shirley Otis-Green and Sheila L. Hammer

Grant-Funded Educational Programs in Psychosocial Oncology

Key Concepts

- *Innovative educational programs are urgently needed to provide oncology professionals with the skills to more efficiently and effectively provide quality, evidence-informed care.*
- *Oncology social workers are well positioned to develop grant-funded educational programs to meet these needs.*

Although oncology social workers are well positioned to identify unmet educational needs, most have received little formal preparation as educators or grant writers and need to deliberately seek opportunities to add these skills. This chapter explores strategies to support the development of educational initiatives for psychosocial oncology professionals and highlights lessons learned while writing grants to support professional education. Suggestions for further readings and a learning exercise at the end of the chapter aid readers in applying the concepts.

The Need for Grant-Supported Education in Oncology Social Work

Health care is in transition in the United States. Workforce shortages, the demands of an aging population, complexities of evolving legislative guidelines, and uncertainties in reimbursements are colliding to create a perfect storm. A robust and dynamic system of professional education is urgently needed to provide clinicians with the leadership and advocacy skills necessary to nimbly adapt to these complex changes in health care delivery (Grand Challenges Executive Committee, 2013).

Oncology social workers are well positioned to recognize gaps in service and, with sufficient resources and support, to lead efforts to develop programs to address these needs. The Patient Protection and Affordable Care Act (PPACA, 2010) and Institute of Medicine (IOM) reports (IOM, 2008, 2010, 2013a, 2013b) all call for health care professionals to have the appropriate training in evidence-informed practice to provide efficient, quality care that incorporates patients' and families' culture and values. Oncology social workers are urgently needed to develop externally supported continuing education programs that enhance clinical care and prepare learners for leadership roles in collaborative practice (Raymer & Gardia, 2011).

Unfortunately, few master's-prepared social workers have formal training as educators or grant writers. And although oncology social workers routinely provide education to patients, families, communities, and colleagues, they are seldom explicitly taught the principles of andragogy (teaching adult learners), which limits their effectiveness as both educators and change agents.

Knowledge of adult learning principles is necessary if oncology social workers are to effectively develop the sophisticated educational programs necessary to enhance practice and secure extramural funding. The field of andragogy has identified six key adult learning principles (Knowles, Holton, & Swanson, 2012):

1. Learners need to understand the reason for learning.
2. Learners want to be responsible for decisions related to their learning.
3. Prior experiences provide the foundation for learning.
4. Learners are most motivated to learn information that has immediate relevance to their personal and professional lives.
5. Learners focus on development of competencies to fulfill their potential.
6. Learners' primary motivation is internal rather than external.

Many social work projects and programs, including professional development, rely on supplemental funding to survive. Success in grant writing depends on mastering several core skills and understanding the needs and goals of the potential funding source. Funding may come from the government or private foundations and can range from a few hundred dollars to several million. Funders want their resources to go to a program that will be successful and leverage their funds to achieve maximum impact. The task for the grant writer is to accurately interpret the "call for proposals" and to create a convincing argument that his or her team will successfully accomplish the proposal's goal, measure results, and widely disseminate findings.

As with most skills, it is wise to think of educational grant writing in stages, then master each skill needed to successfully realize the larger project. Collaborating with colleagues is a helpful way to maximize your learning. Seek mentorship from those in your institution who provide professional or patient education and from those who have successfully secured extramural funding for their work. Grant writing and education are team sports, so generously share what you learn with others.

Identifying a topic for a departmental in-service program is a useful first step toward a larger, multiyear educational program. Select a topic that emerges from your clinical experience. Your passion for the project will be contagious and will help with seeking funding for even relatively modest educational activities.

Each institution has rules regarding extramural solicitation, so identify these guidelines early to ensure that you are not in violation of your organization's formal policies or informal codes of conduct (for instance, pharmaceutical contributions may not be sanctioned). Your institution may have discretionary educational funds in support of honoraria for grand rounds or other targeted in-service activities that may be set aside in a "grateful patient" fund that can provide additional support for your program. Explore the mechanisms to access these funds and determine if your organization has a development department that can provide you with information regarding community resources. Institutions may have very specific restrictions regarding who can request donations from potential sources. Nonetheless, many social workers have successfully collaborated with their colleagues in donor departments to raise monies to supplement clinical services or for specific patient support programs. Although it may seem more daunting to request resources in support of clinical education, many social workers have found internal and external funding to support educational programs.

A Journey From Clinician to Educational Grant Writer

At City of Hope, a National Cancer Institute (NCI)–designated comprehensive cancer center in Southern California, we recognized that patients were eager for reliable information and created a series of psychoeducational support services within our expanding Transitions Program (Otis-Green, 2006). At that time, there were limited services to support those facing end of life, the bereaved, and those who cared for them. The Transitions Program was developed to address these needs. The program was initially supported by the institution and community grants and later supplemented with donations from grateful patients. Early community grants were written to establish a musical program called Hands on Harps that provided the seed money for the first City of Hope musician in residence (Otis-Green, Yang, & Lynne, 2013).

In an attempt to address the educational needs of staff caring for patients nearing the end of life, we developed a dynamic monthly Psycho-Oncology Grand Rounds program. Supported with discretionary educational funds from the institution, volunteer speakers, and limited pharmaceutical support, this targeted educational program focused on the psychosocial-spiritual concerns of patients and families, highlighting the social work perspective for an interprofessional audience.

As the Transitions Program flourished, we recognized the need to offer the same level of education and support services to Spanish-speaking patients and their families. We received funding from the Open Society Institute's Project on Death in America for the creation of a parallel Spanish support program (Proyecto de Transiciones: Enhancing End-of-Life and Bereavement Support Services for Latinos Within a Cancer Care Setting).

During this time, the need for targeted transdisciplinary palliative care education for social workers, psychologists, and chaplains became more evident because there were few opportunities for psychooncology professionals to obtain skills for palliative care specialization. Our institution had a robust nursing research and education program with a history of success in obtaining funding through the NCI's R25 educational funding mechanism. Transitioning from clinical work to partner full time with these nursing leaders offered the opportunity to develop an

NCI R25 educational grant proposal. The process of developing an NCI-funded grant is daunting and time-consuming, typically requiring many revisions and resubmissions.

During the lengthy NCI grant application process, we sought community support for a 5-year educational program—Promoting Excellence in Pain Management and Palliative Care for Social Workers—which provided practical palliative care education to over 500 health social workers (Otis-Green, Lucas, Spolum, Ferrell, & Grant, 2008). This program was supported through a collection of small grants from the community and several foundations. In 2008, the course was recognized by the American Society on Aging with their Healthcare and Aging Network Award for "innovation and quality in health care and aging."

Success in receiving an NCI grant requires demonstration of need and proof of concept, which these earlier educational activities provided. The ACE Project—Advocating for Clinical Excellence: Transdisciplinary Palliative Care Education grant was a 5-year NCI R25-funded program (Otis-Green et al., 2009; Otis-Green & Ferrell, 2010). Three hundred social workers, psychologists, and chaplains were educated through the ACE Project, which was selected by the Association of American Medical Colleges (AAMC) for an Interprofessional Education and Collaborative Practice Resources Award. An unexpected outcome from this project was a special double issue of OMEGA Journal of Death and Dying, which published information on the change projects of 28 ACE Project participants (Otis-Green, 2013).

Work on these two projects confirmed the continuing need for leadership skill building tailored for oncology social workers and led to a subsequent NCI-funded grant in partnership with the Association of Oncology Social Work (AOSW) and the Association of Pediatric Oncology Social Workers (APOSW). Cancer Care for the Whole Patient (IOM, 2008): An Oncology Social Work Response (ExCEL in Social Work: Excellence in Cancer Education and Leadership) sought to enhance the leadership skills of 400 oncology social workers (Jones et al., under review; Otis-Green et al., under review; and Otis-Green, Jones, et al., 2014).

Competitively selected participants for these two NCI-funded projects were asked to identify an institutional-change goal and were held accountable to provide periodic progress reports toward achieving their goals. Evaluation metrics included application data, precourse surveys, educational evaluations at the close of each day's training, and 6- and 12-month follow-up surveys, including retrospective self-reports on pre- and postcourse confidence levels on designated key competencies. Dissemination of lessons learned through these projects has included abstracts and presentations at professional conferences and publications in newsletters, peer-reviewed journals, and book chapters. ExCEL in Social Work was honored in 2014 by the American Psychosocial Oncology Society (APOS) with an Outstanding Education and Training Award.

Making Metrics Matter

These grants serve as examples of successful grant writing to fund professional education projects. A key task of the grant writer is to understand what "success" looks like for each funder and to be sure that the submission clearly communicates how the project fits within his or her framework. Funders require evidence of impact through carefully reported evaluation metrics, and proposals need to clearly state how the program will be measured.

Program progress reports typically require more information than a listing of the demographics of who attended and how satisfied they were with the speakers. Fortunately, both process and outcome measures can be useful in measuring progress toward program goals. Process measures tend to focus on the narrative of your project, and outcome measures look at the impact of the project. Ideally, educational impact could be measured by evaluating clinical change, but the world is seldom ideal. Therefore, indirect measures are more typically used. Educational program assessments can be thought of in the following levels:

- Level 1: Learner satisfaction survey. Were the presenters effective in meeting the learning objectives and knowledgeable of their topic?
- Level 2: Learning occurs, as demonstrated by change in attitude, knowledge, or skill development. This may be measured by pre- and postcourse surveys.
- Level 3: Change in practice/behavior. This is measured through chart reviews, patient/staff surveys, audits, and so on.
- Level 4: System change. This is measured by patient satisfaction scores, staff surveys, institutional audits, and so on.

Requests for larger grants or from governmental agencies will typically require more sophisticated evaluation efforts to demonstrate program effectiveness.

Principles of Instructional Design

Developing the curriculum for your program requires knowledge of instructional design (Ambrose, Bridges, Lovett, DiPietro, & Norman, 2010). To actively engage professionals, the educator's task is to create an environment for interactive learning such that the learner is free to "discover" the material and can safely practice application of the concepts/skills being explored. Allow time to carefully review the literature to ensure that your educational offerings are evidence informed. Successful educators know their audience's interests and educational needs and create educational tension (what would learners say if asked: "What do you find most challenging about this topic?") to motivate the learner and develop a lesson plan with clear objectives (attitude, knowledge, and skill objectives are the most common) matched to the appropriate teaching format.

A variety of teaching formats should be selected to maintain learner interest and match compatibility with the desired objectives (Caffarella & Daffron, 2013). Lectures, dyadic discussions, facilitated small group meetings, self-study, role-play, homework assignments, video presentations, modeling desirable behaviors, and pop quizzes can all be used to stimulate adult learning. A detailed lesson plan with clearly outlined objectives, paired with an appropriate teaching format, includes who will be presenting the information and the approximate time allotted for each training segment. Needs assessments and retrospective pre- and posttest surveys can be useful tools in evaluating program impact.

Interprofessional Education

Quality health care is most effectively delivered in a collaborative environment with integrated teams working closely together in the delivery of person-centered, family-focused, culturally congruent care (Fletcher & Panke, 2012). Palliative care offers a model for collaborative practice that can be successfully applied to the oncology environment (Stark, 2011). The rapidly evolving U.S. health care system demands increasing efficiencies and heightened accountability. Supporting colleagues in developing the shared competencies necessary to maximize collaborative practice is urgently needed. Most professionals have received most of their training within their own discipline and lack understanding of what other disciplines offer. Transdisciplinary educational curricula provide explicit attention to team dynamics in addition to the core content being taught so that learners have sufficient knowledge of what differing disciplines have to offer and what are shared areas of overlapping competencies with the goal of discovering how they might work most effectively to meet the multidimensional needs of those facing cancer. Social work's systems perspective and emphasis on social dynamics and cultural context serves us well in developing innovative transdisciplinary educational curricula to meet this growing need.

Pearls

- Have confidence in your competence and share what you know. Too often, social workers have been ignored and are then surprised when others "discover" what they had always known.
- Seek a mentor and be a mentor. There are folks who know what you need to learn and you know what others seek to learn.
- Be a role model. Demonstrate your commitment to continual education and professional development.
- Build from a strong foundation. Think in terms of "stages" and "phases."

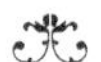

Pitfalls

- It has been said that "If you are not at the table, you will be on the menu." Your voice represents the needs of patients and families and deserves to be heard. Do not wait for an invitation.
- Grant writing requires perseverance. "Rejections" are the norm. Revise and resubmit. Consider alternative funding strategies. Collaborate with others who share your commitment.

As health care faces reform with a heightened drive toward efficiency, it is imperative that oncology social workers demonstrate leadership in providing ongoing education in evidence-informed interventions. Oncology social workers can identify educational gaps and develop targeted grant-funded programs to address these areas of need.

Steps in the Grant-Writing Process

Identify an innovative solution to a real problem. Needs assessments, institutional surveys, and focus groups are good ways to confirm your intuitive feeling about what needs to be better. What can you do to improve the delivery of patient care? Determine what needs doing and how you can be part of making your setting and services better. Obtaining a grant is difficult, so you want to tackle something that you are passionate about and confident will be worth the effort. Remember, if successful, you are crafting your own job description for the time period of the project.

- *Identify "champions" within your area or program with the skills to assist you in the project. Surround yourself with those with the skills to make this happen (e.g., people who know and understand grant writing, budgets, and the ethics process at your institution). You are asking a funder to "bet" on your team being successfully able to carry out this project. You need to demonstrate that your team has the expertise, talent, and skills necessary to do the work requested within the timeframe and with the resources you receive. Prepare well.*
- *Volunteer to be part of other people's grants to learn what works and what does not. Attend grant-writing workshops, seminars, and classes. Review what is available online (the National Institutes of Health has excellent resources available that offer guidance and advice).*
- *Review funding options in your area. Are there institutional funds? Community foundations? Are you eligible for government funding? Can you pull together a partnership with funding from several different sources?*

- *Once you have identified a potential funding source, carefully review its grant process and explore its previously awarded grants. What is the mission of the funding source? When does it accept applications? Is a letter of intent necessary? Does the funding source accept unsolicited applications? Talk with others who have been successfully funded by the funding source. Identify a funder's program officer who can provide personal guidance regarding the application process. You need to know what the funding source is looking for so you can tailor your application to meet its specific goals.*
- *Carefully read and follow grant instructions, rereading and editing accordingly. Many grant applications are denied because the applicants ignored the guidance provided by the funders. Allow sufficient time for others to read your work and for you to edit accordingly. Review the guidelines again before submission to ensure that formatting and length are within recommendations.*
- *Know who you are writing for and what they need from you and make it clear that you are offering exactly what they want to fund. You need excellent grantsmanship skills to do this well. Write your first draft far in advance of the due date to allow time for several people to read the proposal and for you to revise (and re-revise) as needed. There are numerous people asking for money, so your proposal needs to be compelling, innovative, clear, and concise. Check for content and grammar and recheck that you have followed the guidelines. Then check again.*
- *Think in terms of phases. Start with a pilot project and gather preliminary data on feasibility and effectiveness before expanding to a larger project. Consider how each step builds on the previous one. Your goal might be to develop an educational program on self-care for nurses caring for dying patients. Your first step might be to conduct a mini in-service training on one unit of the hospital (perhaps the critical care floor), collecting data demonstrating the feasibility and interest in this topic, as well as evaluating data about its impact. That data can then be used as "pilot data" in support of a request for funding from your institution to broaden this training to a larger population (e.g., offer self-care education to all the nurses who engage with patients who may die within the hospital). The findings from that project provide data that support a larger community grant so that you can offer this program on a wider basis (all clinical care providers). Grants beget grants. Grant-funded projects are best thought of in terms of years, not months. Patience and perseverance are necessary virtues of successful grant writers.*
- *When funded, commit to excellence in completion of the grant-funded work. Evaluate your work so that you can demonstrate your success.*
- *You have a responsibility to be accountable to the funding organization and an obligation to disseminate your findings. Submit abstracts, do in-services, and publish your findings. Many funders measure success through publications produced.*
- *Collaborate with others to leverage the impact of your project. What is the next logical step? Consider next steps, subsequent phases, and additional ways to expand your program. Revise and improve your project based on what you have learned. Think in terms of quality improvement cycles (such as Plan, Do, Study, Act). Identify compelling narratives, selecting examples that will be meaningful to your constituents. Build organically from your success and mentor others as you go. Few oncology social workers have grant-writing skills; share what you have learned.*
- *Successfully writing a grant, completing a project, and disseminating the results of that work are skills that reassure others that you are a good "bet" to successfully complete future work. These competencies set your curriculum vitae apart from others. More importantly, the knowledge that you have contributed to the skill development of your colleagues and has led to improved care for those facing cancer is of tremendous significance.*

ADDITIONAL RESOURCES

Anastas, J. W. (2010). *Teaching in social work: An educators' guide to theory and practice.* New York, NY: Columbia University Press.

Csikai, E. L., & Jones, B. (2007). *Teaching resources for end of life and palliative care courses.* Chicago, IL: Lyceum.

Friedman, B. D. (2008). *How to teach effectively: A brief guide.* Chicago, IL: Lyceum.

Huff, M. B., Murphy, M., & Wiesenfluh, S. (2008). *End-of-life care: A manual for social work students and practitioners.* Alexandria, VA: National Hospice and Palliative Care Organization.

Kennedy, V., Smolinski, K. M., & Colon, Y. (2010). Training professional social workers in psycho-oncology. In J. Holland, W. S. Breitbart, P. B. Jacobsen, M. S. Lederberg, M. J. Loscalzo, & R. McCorkle (Eds.), *Psycho-oncology* (2nd ed., pp. 588–593). New York, NY: Oxford.

National Hospice and Palliative Care Organization. (2008). *Social work guidelines* (2nd ed.). Alexandria, VA: Author.

Raymer, M., & Gardia, G. (2007). *What social workers do: A guide to social work in hospice and palliative care.* Alexandria, VA: National Hospice and Palliative Care Organization.

Reith, M., & Payne, M. (2009). *Social work: In end-of-life palliative care.* Chicago, IL: Lyceum.

Wolfer, T. A., & Runnion, V. M. (2008). *Dying, death and bereavement in social work practice: Decision cases for advanced practice.* New York, NY: Columbia University Press.

REFERENCES

Ambrose, S. A., Bridges, M. W., Lovett, M. C., DiPietro, M., & Norman, M. K. (2010). *How learning works: 7 research-based principles for smart teaching.* San Francisco, CA: Jossey Bass.

Caffarella, R. S., & Daffron, S. R. (2013). *Planning programs for adult learners: A practical guide* (3rd ed.). San Francisco, CA: Jossey Bass.

Fletcher, D. S., & Panke, J. T. (2012). Improving value in health care: Opportunities and challenges for palliative care professionals in the age of health reform. *Journal of Hospice and Palliative Nursing, 14*(7), 452–459.

Grand Challenges Executive Committee. (2013). Grand challenges for social work. *Journal of the Society for Social Work and Research, 4*(3), 165–170.

Institute of Medicine (IOM). (2008). *Cancer care for the whole patient: Meeting psychosocial health needs.* Washington, DC: National Academies Press.

Institute of Medicine (IOM). (2010). *Redesigning continuing education in health professions.* Washington, DC: National Academies Press.

Institute of Medicine (IOM). (2013a). *Interprofessional education for collaboration: Learning how to improve health from interprofessional models across the continuum of education to practice: Workshop summary.* Washington, DC: National Academies Press.

Institute of Medicine (IOM). (2013b). *Establishing transdisciplinary professionalism for health: Workshop summary.* Washington, DC: National Academies Press.

Jones, B., Phillips, F., Head, B., Hedlund, S., Kalisiak, A., Zebrack, B., ... Otis-Green, S. (In Press). Enhancing collaborative leadership in palliative social work in oncology. *Journal of Social Work in End-of-Life and Palliative Care.*

Knowles, M. S., Holton, E. F., & Swanson, R. A. (2012). *The adult learner: The definitive classic in adult education and human resource development* (7th ed.). New York, NY: Routledge.

Otis-Green, S. (2006). The Transitions Program: Existential care in action. *Journal of Cancer Education, 21*(1), 23–25.

Otis-Green, S. (2013). Editorial: Changing the change agents through palliative care education for psycho-oncology professionals. *OMEGA—Journal of Death and Dying, 67*(1–2), 1–4.

Otis-Green, S., & Ferrell, B. R. (2010). Professional education in psychosocial oncology. In J. C. Holland, W. S. Breitbart, P. B. Jacobsen, M. S. Lederberg, M. J. Loscalzo, & R. McCorkle (Eds.), *Psycho-oncology* (2nd ed., pp. 610–616). New York, NY: Oxford University Press.

Otis-Green, S., Ferrell, B., Spolum, M., Uman, G., Mullan, P., Baird, P., & Grant, M. (2009). An overview of the ACE Project—Advocating for Clinical Excellence: Transdisciplinary palliative care education. *Journal of Cancer Education, 24*(2), 120–126.

Otis-Green, S., Ferrell, B., Jones, B., Zebrack, B., Uman, G. C., Kilburn, L., & Grant, M. M. (In Progress). Evaluating programmatic effectiveness: ExCEL in social work: Strategies to enhance leadership skills of oncology social work professionals. *Research on Social Work Practice.*

Otis-Green, S., Jones, B., Zebrack, B., Kilburn, L., Altilio, T., & Ferrell, B. (2014). ExCEL in social work: Excellence in cancer education and leadership, an oncology social work response to the 2008 Institute of Medicine report. *Journal of Cancer Education.* PMID:25146345, DOI:10.1007/s13187-014-0717-8

Otis-Green, S., Lucas, S., Spolum, M., Ferrell, B., & Grant, M. (2008). Promoting excellence in pain management and palliative care for social workers. *Journal of Social Work in End-of-Life and Palliative Care, 4*(2), 120–134.

Otis-Green, S., Yang, E., & Lynne, L. (2013). ACE Project—Advocating for Clinical Excellence: Creating change in the delivery of palliative care. *OMEGA—Journal of Death and Dying, 67*(1–2), 5–19.

Patient Protection and Affordable Care Act (PPACA). (2010). Pub. L. No. 111-148, §2702, 124 Stat. 119, 318–319.

Raymer, M., & Gardia, G. (2011). Enhancing professionalism, leadership, and advocacy: A call to arms. In T. Altilio & S. Otis-Green (Eds.), *Oxford textbook of palliative social work* (pp. 683–687). New York, NY: Oxford University Press.

Stark, D. (2011). Teamwork in palliative care: An integrative approach. In T. Altilio & S. Otis-Green (Eds.), *Oxford textbook of palliative social work* (pp. 415–424). New York, NY: Oxford University Press.

99

Debra Mattison

Vicarious Resilience: Sustaining a Career Over the Long Haul

Key Concepts

- *We can only promote and provide best clinical practices for our clients over time in the context of professional resilience.*
- *Just as vicarious trauma over time can have a negative impact on social workers, witnessing how clients cope with trauma can result in a vicarious resilience that can increase one's ability to find meaning, hope, and sustainability throughout the duration of a career.*
- *Resilience results from thoughtfully making choices based in values and professional guidelines.*

This chapter offers social workers the opportunity to reflect on their practice—where they have been, where they are, and where they desire to be. First, the chapter briefly reviews the resiliency literature and looks at self-reflection on one's personal level of burnout and compassion fatigue. Second, it explores the foundations of resilience in oncology social work. Last, it considers the resilience choices one can make to foster a long and meaningful career. Some social workers may be at a point professionally where they are experiencing unrest, dissatisfaction, or a longing to be in a different place internally or externally. Others may find themselves making choices that keep them "stuck" in a prison of self-doubt or negative patterns that rob them of the energy, passion, and purpose once felt in their work. This is an invitation to not only examine the personal toll, cumulative impact, and collective weariness of ongoing exposure to pain, trauma, and loss in our work but also strategize about how to sustain ourselves through actively making resilience choices to stay connected to the meaning of our work.

The Emotional Costs of Caring

There is debate over terminology and overlapping definitions, but *burnout, compassion fatigue, secondary traumatic stress*, and *vicarious trauma* are all used to characterize the toll on social workers and others in helping professions who work with clients who experience trauma including life-threatening and chronic illness such as cancer (Adams, Boscarino, & Figley, 2006; Figley, 2002; Maslach, Schaufeli, & Leiter, 2001; Mathieu, 2012; Saakvitne, Pearlman, & Staff of the Traumatic Stress Institute, 1996). Extensively explored, vicarious trauma is seen as a natural rather than pathological process that occurs during ongoing empathic, caring engagement with traumatized clients, resulting in the clinician developing symptoms similar to posttraumatic stress disorder (Figley, 1995; McCann & Pearlman, 1990; Pearlman & MacIan, 1995). Mathieu (2012) reviews studies that reported that an estimated 40% to 85% of helping professionals who work closely with clients experiencing trauma have experienced compassion fatigue and/or high rates of traumatic stress symptoms.

Stress and burnout among social workers are well documented in the literature (Acker, 1999; Adams et al., 2006; Gilbar, 1998; Lloyd, King, & Chenoweth, 2002; Um & Harrison, 1998). Kim, Ji, and Kao (2011) further document the positive correlation between high burnout levels and increased physical health concerns. Identified sources include severity and breadth of client problems, heavy workloads, staffing levels, role ambiguity and overlap, perceived lack of power and status, decreased sense of job security, shrinking resources, delivery models that conflict with professional values, reduced work autonomy, and incongruence between what one desires to do in his or her social work practice and what one actually does (Lloyd et al., 2002; NASW Center for Workforce Studies, 2006; Supple-Diaz & Mattison, 1992). Thus, to prevent adverse reactions and sustain effective practice, self-awareness and attention to one's level of work-related stress are essential throughout the duration of one's career.

Resilience and Vicarious Resilience

Resilience is often defined as an ability to adapt to adversity and bounce back after a challenge (Neenan, 2009). Although several scales measure resilience, including the Resilience Scale for Adults (Friborg, Hjemdal, Rosenvinge, & Martinussen, 2003) and the Professional Quality of Life Scale (ProQol; Stamm, 2010), the concept is far more complex. Resilience requires a pattern of positive adaptation to challenges; the capacity for growth through the experience of stress, hardship, loss, and trauma; and the ability to move forward in pursuit of what is important in one's life even in the face of difficulties (Davydov, Stewart, Ritchie, & Chaddieu, 2010; Frankl, 1959; Masten & Coatsworth, 1998; Neenan, 2009; Reich, Zautra, & Hall, 2010).

Research on professionals working with clients who experience trauma and adversity suggest that an exclusive focus on the professional's vicarious trauma does not appropriately acknowledge the potential positive impact of working with clients who experience adversity (Hernandez, Gangsei, & Engstrom, 2007). This relatively new concept of *vicarious resilience* provides a counterbalance focusing on the potentially positive impact on the clinician of witnessing and learning from clients' capacity to survive adversity. Vicarious resilience results from seeing how clients cope with, survive, face, and transcend the challenges of their illness and treatment. Such positive effects develop resilience characteristics in the professional, such as reassessing the significance of one's own problems, developing tolerance for frustration, and increasing confidence and hope in one's work.

> *I have learned about possibility and hope from a woman diagnosed with Stage 4 metastatic lung cancer with a life expectancy of 6 months who, with a somewhat mischievous smile, often proclaims, "I am 18 months past my expiration date!" I believe transformation is always possible, and I remember a woman who began her cancer journey extremely angry and with no tolerance or space in her life for others' stories of their cancers. She endured pain, multiple surgeries, and the loss of much that she valued and yet blossomed into a loving, sensitive, spiritually grounded person. She will be forever remembered for the joy and love she brought to her cancer support group members. We witness our clients' immense capacity to face unknowns, tolerate and bear pain and loss, die with courage, or survive, heal, and reassess goals and priorities, often showing deep compassion for others and great generosity—and we are changed. We begin to believe in things we never thought possible because our clients show us that they are indeed possible. Witnessing the resilience of the human spirit of our clients empowers us to continue our work with hope despite adversity and challenge.*

Foundations of Resilience in Oncology Social Work

A key concept in sustaining resilience lies in the ability to tap into a "reserve capacity" to help manage the daily challenges of life while fueling the potential for ongoing personal and professional growth (Brooks & Goldstein, 2004). Oncology social workers can draw upon the following three primary sources of "resilience reserve" for sustenance and renewal.

Social Work Values and Convictions

Neenan (2009) advocates for conscious and continual grounding in one's values—recognizing which values are most important to oneself and determining when one has strayed from them and how to return to one's core values if that has occurred—as the first source of a resilience reserve.

In addition to personal values, the social work profession's core values regarding what we believe and hold true about clients are vitally important. Social workers have long led the way in valuing diversity and honoring each client's inherent dignity and worth. Each person is unique. All women are not the same, nor do all elderly feel a certain way. All members of a particular religion do not practice their faith in the same manner, nor do all homeless people share a predetermined set of personal traits. Likewise, the cancer patient in front of you is like no other, no matter how many similar patients you may have seen. Social work is grounded in a central belief of self-determination, validating that clients can make choices with which others do not agree, including treatment choices. Oncology social workers seek justice for those who often have no voice and work to increase access to care. They turn the picture upside down and inside out, inviting others to see things from the client's worldview or life experience perspective.

Oncology social workers are advocates for the client's well-being and may take positions that have costs and risk personal gain. In a world often driven by profit and productivity models that promote counting over caring and deemphasize individual therapeutic relationships, social workers continue to assert that the most effective practice occurs in the context of relationship.

Skills and Training

Professional academic training, ongoing continuing education, specialty certification, and a commitment to learning form a second key source for building resilience (Joubert, Hocking, & Hampson, 2013). Keeping abreast of relevant literature and ongoing skill building are essential to maintaining an oncology social work career that requires a breadth and depth of knowledge ranging from direct clinical practice skills to budget creation and boardroom leadership, from conducting research to identifying and accessing community resources, from political advocacy to academic teaching, and from interpreting policies to drafting legislation proposals. Damaskos (2011) found that social workers who reported advanced training evidenced higher levels of resilience. Training and certification options are plentiful and are described in other chapters in this section.

Collaboration and Teamwork

Clients have complex needs that cannot be met by any one discipline and often require simultaneous or sequential help from multiple individuals and services. Collaboration and teamwork are increasingly necessary to meet client needs. Trusting relationships must be built and fostered to sustain an effective and meaningful social work career and serve as a third building block of resilience.

Oncology social workers should be actively curious about collaborations such as educational opportunities or connections with seemingly unlikely partners or departments. For example, social work might connect with a local business school to learn more about budgeting and marketing strategies or with hospital morgue staff to develop program initiatives for grieving families. There are many creative solutions and service delivery innovations that could not be imagined, much less accomplished, without collaboration and assistance.

It is regretful that in our competitive world, often only the visible "designated" individual or discipline leader is acknowledged and other team members are seen as "support" or "ancillary" and thereby less important. The sport of hockey illustrates a useful team approach of acknowledging not only the goal scorer but also the player who assists in making the goal possible. Sometimes social work is the scorer, and other times another discipline may fill this role. Never count it as a diminishment to be the person with a high number of "assists." Strongly promoting our profession never requires disparaging others. We only achieve our full potential in the power of effective teamwork.

Oncology social workers also need to develop skills to assess and address health care trends. How can social work contribute ideas about innovation and skills that match emerging best practice models? How can we use our knowledge of the community and resources, our commitment to ensuring access to services, and our skills in assessment and crisis intervention to address the current needs and to be at the table when future innovations are being developed?

Involvement on committees regarding core issues—for example, disaster planning, quality assurance and improvement, patient- and family-centered care, safety and quality initiatives, clinical trials, and even such common organizational issues as parking—offer opportunities to demonstrate social work values, knowledge base, and problem-solving skills. Providing annual reports of social work's accomplishments and outcomes that support the organization's mission to executive leadership, even when not required or requested, illustrates social work's value in system-wide collaborations.

Choices That Make a Difference in Maintaining Resilience

Resilience is an ongoing, dynamic process that, at its core, is about taking ownership of the choices one makes. The choices we make in our careers often matter as much as our capabilities, often defining and exemplifying who we are and what we stand for. We make many seemingly small choices in a career, but ultimately they accumulate to define our work's meaning. The following six personal resilience-promoting choices can help sustain oncology social workers' careers over time.

Choose the Road You Travel

Maintaining resilience requires continual questioning of one's core values (Neenan, 2009). "What is really important to me?" "Does this road take me toward my values or away from them?" Exploration of inner thoughts and feelings is needed to determine the "right" road to be traveling. We need to listen to the "still, small voice" inside. Sometimes we may hear challenging questions such as "This would be good for my career, but would it be good for my health and integrity?" and "This approach may be faster, but does it result in higher quality?" When considering opportunities, think carefully about where a particular road may lead.

Choose to Work Using a "Principles and Values Compass"

Using a "principles and values compass" can help determine whether we are on the desired path or have strayed from our "true north" in times of challenge and controversy. It would be nice to have a professional navigation system that announces the distance to the next turn you need to make and how to "re-route" if you get lost. Although this professional GPS doesn't exist, social workers have a compass of professional principles and values available for guidance. The National Association of Social Work's *Code of Ethics* (NASW, 2008) and Association of Oncology Social Work's *Standards of Practice for Oncology Social Work* (AOSW, 2012) represent professional navigation systems that focus on value-based decisions and lessen the risks of professionally losing our way.

Making choices and "correct turns" in a career—when to hold fast to a particular direction and when to compromise—can be difficult even with principles and values to guide us. Compromise is an essential collaboration skill and is effectively used when considering such things as approaches and solutions to problems, preferences regarding program planning, strategies for service delivery, and priority goal setting. However, compromise has less utility when it impinges upon professional values and integrity. When faced with choices regarding ignoring or abandoning core professional values, we may find ourselves going alone down a "road less traveled" by taking a stand that is unpopular, being the "odd one out," or even being perceived as a "problem." We remind ourselves that doing the right thing is not always easy.

Choose to Value Self

We all live in a world of evaluation and judgment, which may prompt us to ask, "Am I good enough?" Sometimes, we have to remember that no matter how we are judged, the goal is to leave no doubt about our passion to help patients overcome the adversities they confront.

There will be times when we may doubt our knowledge, skills, and capabilities. There will be times when we fail, do not reach desired outcomes, and are rejected or even fired. We can learn from failures and from our limitations without getting stuck living in "if only" and thinking about the past. We can resist the temptation to establish our personal worth through comparisons to others or based on others' evaluations of us. We are more than our efforts, more than our failures and successes. Our value and worth includes our lived experiences, connections made, and lessons learned that often abound in oncology social work. James (1983) reminds us that in life, success is not a destination, but the process of living and noticing the moments of meaning along the way. Success is the quality of the journey.

When conducting workshops on understanding the value of our work as social workers, I often ask people to identify the names of the three wealthiest people in the world or the last few Heisman Trophy winners or past best actor/actress awardees. The response often results in participants only being able to identify a few answers in each category. However, when I ask people to identify three people who gave them comfort in a time of need, a few people in their lives who stood up and advocated for them, or an experience of having someone impact their lives by believing they had worth and value when others doubted that, the result is completely different. Virtually everyone can identify these people in their lives. They may not be wealthy or famous or well known to others, but they are people who had a tremendous impact on them. Oncology social workers are these people to their clients and their families.

Choose to Let Go of Fixing and Embrace Companioning

Referrals often come to oncology social workers with the heavy expectation that the change others desire in a client will somehow be brought about by social work interventions. Despite the lack of evidence to support the effectiveness of determining goals for clients and cajoling them to make "our change," this approach remains common in health care delivery. As a powerful alternative to the approach of attempting to "fix" or "do to" a client, Wolfelt (2009) introduces 11 tenets of an approach he calls "companioning" with clients. His first tenet defines companioning as the process of being with another person and his or her pain rather than trying to take away the pain. Through his remaining 10 tenets, Wolfelt suggests a model that offers clinicians freedom from the expectation and responsibility of changing or fixing the client. Companioning is about sharing the journey with clients rather than leading them or feeling responsible for where their journey goes. The worker takes on the role of witness rather than expert and seeks to discover options with the client rather than prescribe solutions. There is no responsibility to change or fix. Rather, we "companion" with the client as we bear witness to, advocate for, support, invite change from, talk "with" rather than "to," and offer presence in the moment to them.

Choose to Make Self-Care a Priority Practice

Resilience is not simply reactive but requires a choice to consider proactive approaches to maintain a balanced life that reaches out to the possibilities and pursuit of what is valued and important to us (Neenan, 2009; Reivich & Shatté, 2002). We need to balance "head living" with "heart feeling," inner life with outer life, running away from stress with running toward goals, and life at work with life outside of work. Renzenbrink (2004) suggests that social workers be proactive by engaging in "relentless self-care," especially when working with patients with advanced and terminal illnesses.

Rather than a call to self-care, some may view resilience as an ability to "suck it up" or "grin and bear it" by suppressing emotions and vowing to be less vulnerable. However, this is a recipe for burnout and can lead to a disconnection from the very emotional connections that make work with clients meaningful and effective. Resilience is about both feeling and managing our feelings rather than suppressing them (Neenan, 2009).

Mathieu (2012) suggests consideration of self-care at three levels—professional, organizational, and personal—and provides a variety of strategies that have been found useful in reducing compassion fatigue. In this schema, supervision is identified as a professional self-care strategy. Clinical supervision is based on a belief that social workers learn through the opportunity to have themselves and their work experiences be seen, heard, and understood in a context that focuses on support and exploration of options and strategies to manage and cope (Simon, Pryce, Roff, & Klemmack, 2005). Thus, clinical supervision is very similar and a parallel process to our work with clients, who also desire to be seen, heard, and understood. Creative strategies to obtain clinical supervision or consultation include peer supervision and consultation, mentoring from senior colleagues, connecting through online groups and training opportunities, and purchasing supervision.

Resilience building is not done in isolation or as an exclusively internal process. Social connections and support from others are critical components of self-care and increase our reservoir of resilience (Neenan, 2009). Spiritually, resilience is fed by a connection to our personal sense of our calling or mission, as well as our connection to self, others, ideas, causes, faith, and hope. Canda and Furman (2010) state, "Our professional roles, theories, and skills become rote, empty, tiresome, and finally lifeless without a connection to our spirituality, however we define it" (p. 3).

Choose to Make Changes When They Need to Be Made

Resilience is not exclusively an internal trait but is clearly interactive with the environment in which we live and work (Neenan, 2009). Organizational culture and working conditions impact how employees manage exposure to trauma. Resilience building is dependent upon the resources and conditions an employer does or does not provide, which either support or impede workers' efforts to fulfill their goals and missions (Lipsky & Burk, 2009). Thus, choices about work environment that are congruent with our sense of purpose, passion, and inner truths need to be examined. Sometimes career changes are possible and are helpful to pursue environments or roles that are more in line with one's professional and personal goals and values. The choice may be to make a position change, an institutional change, or perhaps even a career change. Alternatively, oncology social workers may advocate for developing structures that foster the capacity of all staff to be more supportive and facilitative of professional practice that focuses on treating the whole person and on patient- and family-centered care.

Pearls

- Continue to take the risk to ask the hard questions—there is no questing without questions.
- Everything that counts can't always be counted.
- Will what is stressing you today really matter next week?
- Life is about the people you meet, the lives you touch, and the differences you make.
- Ordinary work can lead to extraordinary connections, meanings, and outcomes.
- Tell yourself, "Just here and just now, I can be present."
- Tell yourself, "I have enough. I do enough. I am enough."

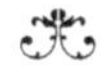

Pitfalls

- Activity alone neither equates with accomplishment nor guarantees a good outcome or rewarding career.
- Counting does not always equal caring.
- We can be very busy and meet productivity standards but not be making a difference.

As oncology social workers, our work will always involve struggle and sacrifice. Rachel Naomi Remen (1996) eloquently described the realities of our work, stating, "The expectation that we can be immersed in suffering and loss daily and not be touched by it is as unrealistic as expecting to be able to walk through water without getting wet" (p. 52). We will get wet! Yet we can remain resilient.

Thomas Moore (2004) describes the "dark nights of the soul" as those times in life that shake us to the core—times involving challenge, failure, loss, illness, and sadness. He offers encouragement to use these times as opportunities to "sift for the gold" that resides in these experiences, stating, "We are not out to solve the dark night, but to be enriched by it" (p. xvi). As we mine for gold in our oncology social work careers, some of our best teachers about resilience are the many clients in our lives who have displayed rich examples of resilience. We have witnessed our clients take the challenges, loss, adversity, suffering, and limitations of a cancer diagnosis and use them in transforming ways to endure suffering, let go of toxic relationships, reach out to others, seek new adventures and opportunities, take risks, face mortality, and find meaning. We are honored to have them as resilience teachers. May their inspiration join with your purpose and passion to lead you toward resiliency and meaning.

ADDITIONAL RESOURCES

Mathieu, F. (2012). *The compassion fatigue workbook*. New York, NY: Routledge/Taylor & Francis. This book contains "making it personal" homework, which helps users relate to the material in the book.

Professional Quality of Life Scale (ProQoL): A tool used to measure negative and positive effects of helping others who experience suffering and trauma with subscales for compassion satisfaction, burnout, and compassion fatigue: http://proqol.org/ProQol_Test.html

Resilience Quotient: 56-item tool to measure seven abilities related to resilience (in Reivich & Shatté, 2002)

REFERENCES

Acker, G. (1999). The impact of clients' mental illness on social workers' job satisfaction and burnout. *Health and Social Work, 24*, 112–119.

Adams, R. E., Boscarino, J. A., & Figley, C. R. (2006). Compassion fatigue and psychological distress among social workers: A validation study. *American Journal of Orthopsychiatry, 76*(1), 103–108.

Association of Oncology Social Work (AOSW). (2012). *Standards of practice in oncology social work*. Retrieved from http://www.aosw.org/iMIS201/AOSWMain/professionals/standards-of-practice/AOSWMain/Professional-Development/standards-of-practice.aspx?hkey=51fda308-28bd-48b0-8a75-a17d01251b5e

Brooks, R., & Goldstein, S. (2004). *The power of resilience: Achieving balance, confidence, and personal strength in your life*. New York, NY: McGraw Hill.

Canda, E. R., & Furman, L. D. (2010). *Spiritual diversity in social work practice: The heart of helping*. New York, NY: Oxford University Press.

Damaskos, P. (2011). *The presence of resilience in oncology social workers*. ProQuest Dissertations and Theses. Retrieved from http://www.library.nhs.uk/booksandjournals/details.aspx?t=Social+Workers&stfo=True&sc=bnj.ebs.cinahl,bnj.pub.MED,bnj.ovi.psyh&p=1&sf=srt.unspecified&sfld=fld.title&sr=bnj.ovi&did=ovid.com:/bib/psycdb/2012-99150-454&pc=100&id=18

Davydov, F., Stewart, R., Ritchie, R., & Chaddieu, R. (2010). Resilience and mental health. *Clinical Psychology Review, 30*(5), 479–495.

Figley, C. R. (Ed.). (1995). *Compassion fatigue: Coping with secondary traumatic stress disorder in those who treat the traumatized*. New York, NY: Brunner/Mazel.

Figley, C. R. (2002). Compassion fatigue: Psychotherapists' chronic lack of self-care. JCLP/In Session: *Psychotherapy in Practice, 58*(11), 1433–1441.

Frankl, V. (1959). *Man's search for meaning*. New York, NY: Simon & Schuster.

Friborg, O., Hjemdal, O., Rosenvinge, J., & Martinussen, M. (2003). A new rating scale for adult resilience: What are the central protective resources behind health adjustment? *International Journal of Methods in Psychiatric Research, 12*(2), 65–76.

Gilbar, O. (1998). Relationship between burnout and sense of coherence in health social workers. *Social Work in Health Care, 26*, 39–49.

Hernandez, P., Gangsei, D., & Engstrom, D. (2007). Vicarious resilience: A new concept in work with those who survive trauma. *Family Process, 46*(2), 229–241.

James, J. (1983). *Success is the quality of your journey*. New York, NY: Newmarket Press.

Joubert, L., Hocking, A., & Hampson, R. (2013). Social work in oncology—Managing vicarious trauma—The positive impact of professional supervision. *Social Work in Health Care, 52*(2–3), 296–310.

Kim, H., Ji, J., & Kao, D. (2011). Burnout and physical health among social workers: A three-year longitudinal study. *Social Work, 56*(3), 258–268.

Lipsky, L., & Burk, C. (2009). *Trauma stewardship: An everyday guide to caring for self while caring for others*. San Francisco, CA: Berrett-Koehler Publishers.

Lloyd, C., King, R., & Chenoweth, L. (2002). Social work, stress and burnout: A review. *Journal of Mental Health, 11*, 255–265.

Maslach, C., Schaufeli, W. B., & Leiter, M. P. (2001). Job burnout. *Annual Review of Psychology, 52*, 397–422.

Masten, A., & Coatsworth, J. (1998). The development of competence in favorable and unfavorable environments: Lessons from successful children. *American Psychologist, 53*, 205–220.

Mathieu, F. (2012). *The compassion fatigue workbook*. New York, NY: Routledge/Taylor & Francis Group.

McCann, I. L., & Pearlman, L. A. (1990). Vicarious traumatization: A framework for understanding the psychological effects of working with victims. *Journal of Traumatic Stress, 3*(1), 131–149.

Moore, T. (2004). *Dark nights of the soul: A guide to finding your way through life's ordeals*. New York, NY: Penguin Group.

National Association of Social Workers (NASW). (2008). *Code of ethics: Approved by the 1996 NASW delegate assembly and revised by the 2008 NASW delegate assembly*. Washington, DC: NASW Press.

National Association of Social Workers (NASW) Center for Workforce Studies. (2006). *Assuring the sufficiency of a frontline workforce: A national study of licensed social workers: Executive summary*. Washington, DC: NASW.

Neenan, M. (2009). *Developing resilience: A cognitive behavioral approach*. New York, NY: Routledge.

Pearlman, L. A., & Mac Ian, P. S. (1995). Vicarious traumatization: An empirical study of the effects of trauma work on trauma therapists. *Professional Psychology: Research and Practice, 26*, 558–565.

Reich, J., Zautra, A., & Hall, J. (Eds.) (2010). *Handbook of adult resilience*. New York, NY: Guildford Press.

Reivich, K., & Shatté, A. (2002). *The resilience factor: 7 keys to finding your inner strength and overcoming life's hurdles*. New York, NY: Three Rivers Press.

Remen, R. N. (1996). *Kitchen table wisdom*. New York, NY: Riverhead Books.

Renzenbrink, I. (2004). Relentless self care. In P. Silverman & J. Berzoff (Eds.), *Living with dying: A handbook for end of life care practitioners*. New York, NY: Columbia University Press.

Saakvitne, K. W., Pearlman, L. A., & Staff of the Traumatic Stress Institute. (1996). *Transforming the pain: A workbook on vicarious traumatization*. New York, NY: W. W. Norton.

Simon, C. E., Pryce, J. G., Roff, L. L., & Klemmack, D. (2005). Secondary traumatic stress and oncology social work: Protecting compassion from fatigue and compromising the worker's world view. *Journal of Psychosocial Oncology*, 23(4), 1–14.

Stamm, B. H. (2010). *The concise ProQol Manual* (2nd ed.) Pocatello, ID: ProQOL.org.

Supple-Diaz, L., & Mattison, D. (1992). Factors affecting survival and satisfaction: Navigating a career in oncology social work. *Journal of Psychosocial Oncology*, *10*(1), 111–131.

Um, M. Y., & Harrison, D. F. (1998). Role stressors, burnout, mediators, and job satisfaction: A stress-strain-outcome model and an empirical test. *Social Work Research*, *22*, 100–115.

Wolfelt, A. (2009). *The handbook for companioning the mourner: Eleven essential principles*. Fort Collins, CO: Companion Books.

100

Virginia Krawiec and Greta Greer

The American Cancer Society's Contributions to Oncology Social Work

Key Concepts

- *The American Cancer Society (ACS) is a voluntary health care organization that relies on volunteers to provide a broad range of education, information, referral, and support services for cancer patients and their families.*
- *The ACS provides practice, research, and training opportunities for oncology social workers and other health care disciplines around all aspects of oncology.*
- *The ACS was instrumental in the development of oncology social work and the Association of Oncology Social Work (AOSW).*
- *The ACS is a key stakeholder and collaborator with the AOSW on providing access and services to marginalized populations and a broad range of psychosocial services, education, and research.*

The founders of the American Cancer Society (ACS) understood that cancer presents a complex set of problems addressable only by the concerted effort of individuals from many different health disciplines. When the organization was founded in 1913 as the American Society for the Control of Cancer (ASCC), its initial purpose was "to collect, collate, and disseminate information concerning the symptoms, diagnosis, treatment, and prevention of cancer; to investigate the conditions under which cancer is found and to compile statistics in regard thereto" (ACCS, 1913). The society's initial focus was "dissemination of information provided by the multitude of present workers in the field" through "an active campaign of publicity and education" (Survey Press Bureau, 1913). Social workers involved with the ACS can be traced back 90 years, almost to the beginning of the society in 1913 and the birth of medical social work in 1905.

This chapter focuses on some of the notable professional contributions of oncology social workers to major ACS initiatives, the ACS's support of social work professional development, and current ACS services, training, and research support opportunities. Countless social workers have generously served in influential volunteer roles at all levels of the ACS in local offices, regional divisions, and the corporate center on advisory committees, workgroups, boards, and the ACS National Assembly. Social workers have helped shape many aspects of the ACS's mission in the areas of psychosocial services, resource development, information distribution, education, and research. Social workers have also helped organize and conduct ACS conferences, workgroups, committee meetings, workshops, and trainings. They have played major roles in the development and delivery of patient support programs, facilitated support groups, and designed new psychosocial interventions. They have researched patient and caregiver needs, reported gaps in needed services and related trends, and recommended ways the ACS could improve its support services and reduce the barriers to care. Social workers have given expert testimony; served in advocacy roles to raise awareness of cancer's effect on families and society; and fought for legislation to prevent cancer, ensure access to quality cancer care, and reduce the effects of cancer on all. They have written publications, white papers, and content for the ACS website and have contributed to materials for which the ACS is well known. Social workers have helped plan and have participated in ACS fundraisers. The ACS's employment of social workers has increased over time. New positions requiring credentialed social workers or social work knowledge and skills include patient navigators, patient advocates, smoking cessation counselors, cancer information specialists, program managers, program directors, and various planning and administration positions. Finally, oncology social workers are the leading professional source of patient/family referrals to the society (AOSW, 2006).

Current ACS Programs for Patient and Family Education, Referral, and Support

One hundred years ago, cancer patients and caregivers were on their own when it came to information and support. Today, the ACS helps cancer patients and caregivers everywhere with a variety of free services and programs. Last year alone, the ACS assisted more than 1 million people. What follows are some of the services the ACS provides:

- **National Cancer Information Center:** Available 24 hours a day, 7 days a week, cancer information specialists answer questions about cancer, link people to resources and events, and more: 1-800-227-2345.
    - **Website:** Comprehensive cancer information, current news, resources, and much more: http://www.cancer.org
- **Cancer Facts and Figures:** An annual publication with estimates of new cancer cases and deaths; current cancer incidence, mortality, and survival statistics; and information on cancer symptoms, risk factors, early detection, and treatment; available electronically (http://www.cancer.org) and on hard copy
- **Cancer Survivors Network:** Online peer support community for cancer survivors and caregivers: http://csn.cancer.org
- **I Can Cope online:** Free self-administered online cancer education classes for people dealing with cancer and their families: http://www.cancer.org/icancope
- **Look Good, Feel Better:** Program to help women, men, and teens cope with appearance-related side effects of cancer treatments
- **Reach to Recovery:** Program to help women and men cope with their breast cancer experience by linking them to a specially trained volunteer who is a cancer survivor
- **Road to Recovery:** Free, volunteer-provided transportation to get patients to treatment
- **Patient Navigation:** Patient navigators guide newly diagnosed cancer patients through the complex treatment maze at more than 100 U.S. hospitals
- **ACS Hope Lodges:** Provide free, supportive places to stay for cancer patients who must travel for treatment at 31 locations nationwide. In addition, the ACS has a cooperative arrangement with hotels across the country to offer free or reduced-rate lodging.

ACS Support for the Oncology Social Work Profession

In 1979, social worker Virginia Conkling joined the ACS, setting the stage for an increased, systematic, and more visible role for oncology social work in the ACS. Conkling put plans in motion that resulted in the formation of the Association of Oncology Social Work (AOSW) and supported the fledgling Association of Pediatric Oncology Social Workers. By 1980, she created the ACS's first social work advisory committee whose members documented the increase in medical social workers with a full or partial oncology caseload and the lack of specialized training for these roles. In response, the ACS established a grant to fund a postgraduate course that ultimately has trained hundreds of oncology social workers and other mental health professionals (Fobair et al., 2009, p. 174).

In 1982, the ACS sponsored a workshop on then-state-of-the-art oncology social work practice, education, and research with a panel of social work experts. Their discussions yielded the recommendation to "convene a national educational workshop for oncology social workers that would have as a secondary purpose, the creation of a national organization" (Fobair et al., 2009, p. 167). In 1983, the ACS held the National Conference on Practice, Education, and Research in Social Work in New York City, where committees met that would guide the formation of the National Association of Oncology Social Workers (NAOSW), which subsequently became the AOSW.

The ACS sought to maintain close ties with the AOSW by creating a liaison position to be filled by then AOSW president Naomi Stearns, who chaired the National Advisory Committee on Oncology Social Work (Fobair et al., 2009). The committee recommended to the ACS board of directors that grants be created to support the training of oncology social workers.

Current Training and Research Opportunities

The ACS Health Professional Training Grants in Cancer Control program provides grants for graduate students through an annual competitive application process. Grants include:

- **Master's Training Grants in Clinical Oncology Social Work:** Awarded to institutions to support the training of second-year master's degree students to provide psychosocial services to persons with cancer and their families.

- **Doctoral Training Grants in Oncology Social Work:** Awarded to qualifying doctoral students at schools of social work that train individuals to conduct research relevant to oncology social work.

Social work researchers also have access to ACS postdoctoral fellowship, career development, and research project grants.

Almost concurrent with the start of the ACS Research Program in 1946, the National Clinical Fellowships Program was created to train oncologists and expanded over the next few decades to become the National Clinical Awards Program, now the Health Professional Training Grants Program (Krawiec, 1995). In 1989, the first oncology social work training grants were funded to increase the number of oncology social workers in clinical practice and to support psychosocial research in oncology. Since then, 369 master's-level traineeships and 84 post-master's-level traineeships have been awarded. The master's-level clinical oncology social work traineeships now award $12,000 per year with up to $10,000 as a student stipend and the remaining $2,000 for field instructor and program faculty professional development. The grant term is now 2 years to lessen the administrative burden on field instructor applicants.

Following a 1998 evaluation of the post-master's clinical oncology social work training grants, the program was changed to the doctoral training grants in oncology social work to produce individuals capable of doing clinically relevant research and the award amounts were increased to $20,000 per year. In 2004, eligibility was extended to doctoral students in any phase of their studies. Sponsoring institutions are limited to schools of social work, and grantees are required to attend an ACS-sponsored student institute at the Society for Social Work and Research annual conference.

Doctoral Training Grants Sponsored by the ACS	
Joyce Grater, PhD, MSW	Impact of Health Care Provider-Caregiver Interaction on Caregiver Burden in Elderly Female Caregivers of Oncology Patients
Daniel S. Gardner, MSW	Family Functioning and Individual Adaption to Cancer
Robert W. Butler, PhD	Adolescents' Experience of Cancer
Elizabeth A. Rohan, PhD	Vicarious Traumatization in Oncology Health Professionals
Carol L. Decker, DSW	Resilience and Quality of Life in Adolescents with Cancer
Sophia K. Smith, MSW	Quality of Life of Aging and Elderly Lymphoma Survivors
Denis P. Cronin, MSW, MPH, MPhil, PhD	Spousal Loss From Terminal Cancer—Helping the Elderly Survivor Cope
Sophia K. Smith, MSW	Quality of Life of Older Long-Term Lymphoma Survivors
Louisa Daratsos, MSW	Serving Veterans With Advanced Cancer and Their Families
Jennifer M. Mills, MSSW, MPH	The Experience of Long-Term Lymphoma Survivorship
Annemarie C. Redelmeier, MSW, MBA, LCSW	Impact of Stigma on Behavior and Psychosocial Needs of Lung Cancer Patients
Anjanette A. Wells, MSW, LCSW	Low-Income Depressed Ethnic Minority Patients With Cancer
John Linder, MSW, LCSW	Advance Medical Directives: Resolving Racial/Ethnic Utilization Disparities
Frances Nedjat-Haiem, PhD, MSW, LCSW	Cultural Beliefs and Attitudes of Latinos With Terminal Cancer
Philip M. Domingue, MSW	Clinical Trial of Adapted Emotionally Focused Therapy for Bereaved Parents
Kelly Turner, BA, MSW	Spontaneous Remission of Cancer: Theories From Doctors, Healers, and Cancer Survivors
Michele L. Day, MSW	Team Communication and Collaboration in Hospice Pain Management
Karen L. Parker, MSW	Social Workers and Smoking Cessation Counseling
Louisa Daratsos, MSW	Serving Veterans With Advanced Cancer and Their Families
Annemarie C. Redelmeier, MSW, MBA, LCSW	Impact of Stigma on Behavior and Psychosocial Needs of Lung Cancer Patients
Tara J. Schapmire, MSSW	Distress in Older Adults With Cancer: A Multilevel Longitudinal Study
Sage Bolte, MSW	The Impact of Cancer and Its Treatment on a Young Adult's Sexual Self

Christine C. Callahan, MSW	Cancer and Financial Vulnerabilities in Three Underserved Populations
Penelope Damaskos, MSW	Resiliency in Oncology Social Work
Gail Adorno, MSW	Quality-of-Life and Chemotherapy Use in Older Adults With Late-Stage Cancer
Frances Nedjat-Haiem, PhD, MSW, LCSW	Improving End-of-Life Communication With Low-Income Latino Cancer Patients
Tara J. Schapmire, MSSW	Distress in Older Adults With Cancer: A Multilevel Longitudinal Analysis
Philip Higgins, MSW	A Community-Based Palliative Care Social Work Intervention
Alison Snow, MSW	Hypnosis for Treatment of Pain and Anxiety in Patients Receiving BMBX
Sarah Bollinger, MSW	Psychosocial Disparities in Breast Cancer and the Triple-Negative Diagnosis
Daniela Wittmann, MSW	Promoting Sexual Health in Prostate Cancer
Melissa A. Lundquist, MSW	Doctoral Training in Oncology Social Work
Christine C. Callahan, MSW	Cancer, Vulnerability, and Financial Quality of Life: A Mixed Methods Study
Danetta E. Hendricks, MA, MSW	The Impact of Medicaid State Waiver Programs in Advanced Cancer
Connie F. Rust, MS	Health Literacy and Medication Adherence in Breast Cancer Survivors
Meredith J. Barnhart, MS, LMSW	Enhancing Concurrent Child and Caregiver Oncology Treatment
Edith Crumb Gunter, MSW	Examining the Psychosocial Needs of Siblings of Childhood Cancer Patients
Crystal S. Broussard, MSW	Exploring Transitions From Curative Treatment to Hospice Care
Philip Higgins, MSW	The Waiting: The Hardest Part? Surrogate Decision-Makers at the End of Life
Marcela Blinka, MSW	Participant Centered Informed Consent
Daniela Wittmann, MSW	Couples' Sexual Recovery After Prostatectomy and the Role of the Partner
Kristen Admiraal, MSW	Quality of Life Outcomes Among Older Adults With Colorectal Cancer
Sarah Bollinger, MSW	Young, African American Women With Triple-Negative Breast Cancer
Alison Snow, MSW	Hypnosis for Treatment of Pain and Anxiety in Patients Receiving BMBX
Ashley Varner, MSW, MBA	Decreasing Distress and Increasing Quality of Life for Brain Tumor Caregivers
Melissa A. Lundquist, MSW	Parenting Through Advanced Cancer: Exploring the Father's Experience
Chiara Acquati, MSW	Psychosocial Distress Screening for Cancer Patients and Their Caregivers
Denalee O'Malley, MSW	Enhancing Survivorship Care: A Focus on the Patient-Centered Medical Home
Crystal S. Broussard, MSW	Exploring Transitions From Curative Treatments to Hospice Care

Awards and Honors

Oncology social workers are recognized by the ACS through the presentation of several different awards. The ACS Lane Adams Quality of Life Award was originally created in 1989 "to provide special recognition to nurses who provided extraordinary and compassionate care to their patients" (ACS, 2013b). In 1991, oncology social workers became eligible for the award in recognition of their service to the psychosocial needs of cancer patients and their families. Over the past 21 years, 40 social workers have received this award.

A second ACS award also recognizes individuals devoted to enhancing the quality of life for those affected by cancer: the Trish Greene Quality of Life Award. The award was conceived to honor the memory of Patricia (Trish) Greene, former ACS vice president for nursing, and was originally "presented for the best quality of life manuscript published in the *Cancer Practice* journal" (ACS, 2013a). The first recipients of this award were oncology social workers Katherine Walsh and Carol Marcusen for their article "Self Advocacy Training for Cancer Survivors: The Cancer Toolbox," published in the November–December 1999 issue of *Cancer Practice*.

Each November, the ACS board of directors honors recipients of its Distinguished Service Award, which is presented "to individuals in recognition of major achievements in the field of cancer." Three oncology social workers have received this award: Joan Hermann, Grace Christ, and Barbara Berkman.

Annually, the ACS sponsors two AOSW awards. The Leadership in Oncology Social Work Award recognizes an exceptional member of the AOSW who has significantly contributed to the field of oncology social work and demonstrated leadership through administration, education, clinical practice, or research. The AOSW also offers the ACS Quality of Life Lectureship Award annually at the AOSW conference. The AOSW describes the lectureship award as a presentation that seeks to encourage oncology social workers to pursue excellence in the provision of care to cancer patients and their families. Excellence can only be attained if programs and services are based on theory, principles of evidence-based practice, and effective leadership.

Social Workers and ACS Publications

With the support of the ACS, volunteer and staff oncology social workers have contributed several seminal works, published by the ACS, to the oncology social work literature. In 2001, the ACS published *Cancer Support Groups: A Guide for Facilitators* (Hermann, 2005) to assist both professional and laypersons facilitating support groups for people with cancer and their families. Now available as an e-book at http://www.cancer.org/bookstores, this resource drew heavily on previous internal ACS guidebooks written by numerous social workers and other oncology experts.

The first edition of the *American Cancer Society Textbook of Clinical Oncology* (Holleb, Fink, & Murphy, 1991) included two chapters authored by social workers. Grace Christ outlined the primary functions of clinical social work, described the oncology social work practice model based on identified cancer stages, and discussed the treatment modalities used by social workers in each stage (Christ, 1991). "Sexuality and Cancer" provided an overview of sexual function and dysfunction related to cancer types and included a brief sexual function assessment model (Anderson & Schmuch, 1991).

The ACS has published two oncology social work texts. *Oncology Social Work: A Clinician's Guide* (Stearns, Lauria, Hermann, & Fogelberg, 1993) provided comprehensive information about social work practice in the field of clinical oncology. *Social Work in Oncology: Supporting Survivors, Families, and Caregivers* (Lauria, Clark, Hermann, & Stearns, 2001), the second text in less than a decade, was a response to sweeping changes in every facet of oncology care that made a dramatic impact on the practice of oncology social work. Major strides were made in assessing cancer risks, diagnostics, earlier detection, and increased treatment options that considered quality-of-life measures along with other clinical side effects. Advances in technology, use of computers, and the advent of the Internet had a big impact. Health care system changes affected how care was delivered and paid for. As costs of care spiraled upward, so did the number of people unable to access quality cancer care. These conditions increased the number and severity of psychosocial problems experienced by patients with cancer and their families. Both texts aimed to build or enhance the practice of all oncology social work practitioners.

ACS and Social Work Collaborate on Accessing Marginalized Populations

A field study was conducted in 1996–1997 of the ACS's work with poor and underserved populations. The findings were important in helping the ACS develop key strategies and tactics to continue to improve prevention, early detection, support program outreach, and services to vulnerable and at-risk populations. Social workers also participated in the Joint Workgroup on Family Caregiving and Cancer in 1996 to research a relatively new psychosocial concern that emerged in the 1990s as a result of changes in health care delivery. Shorter hospital stays, earlier discharges, and more outpatient treatment forced family members to assume greater responsibility for the physical and other needs of the person with cancer. Social workers were expert in helping family members address the details of these responsibilities and facilitate their ability to carry them out.

The workgroup delivered its report in 1997, "Family Caregiving and Cancer," outlining specific recommendations for the ACS designed to address caregivers' most pressing needs and to help position the ACS as a leader in the caregiver arena. It represented the earliest concerted effort by social workers to bring attention to the unmet needs of cancer caregivers and describe the kind of psychosocial interventions that could help address them.

Pearls

- The growth of oncology social work was supported by a champion national organization, the American Cancer Society. Recognition of the synergy of the ACS and the oncology social work mission, goals, and values formed the basis of their joint efforts.
- The ACS has maintained a unique relationship with oncology social workers in funding support for the creation of a professional organization and by funding training grants, sponsoring awards for AOSW members in recognition of their outstanding contributions to the field, and engaging social workers in the development of ACS publications and new initiatives.

Pitfalls

- Oncology social workers need to expand their participation in the education, training, and especially research opportunities provided by the ACS.
- Continuing collaboration and development of partnerships with key stakeholders such as the ACS is vital to oncology social workers' professional development and leadership in patient- and family-centered care.

The long association between the oncology social work profession and the ACS has championed whole-person care in cancer treatment, as well as effective interprofessional practice. Historically, it was a critical developmental precursor of the current psychosocial and patient- and family-centered initiatives that dominate current health care directions. Despite incredible changes over the past 100 years, these principles remain paramount and continue to unite our visions.

REFERENCES

American Cancer Society (ACS). (2013a). *About the Trish Greene Quality of Life Award*. Retrieved from http://www.cancer.org/aboutus/honoringpeoplewhoaremakingadifference/about-trish-greene-quality-of-life-award

American Cancer Society. (2013b). *Lane Adams Award*. Retrieved from http://www.cancer.org/aboutus/honoringpeoplewhoaremakingadifference/laneadamsaward/index

American Society for the Control of Cancer. (1913, May 22). *Certificate of incorporation*. ACSS Archives. New York, NY: Author.

Anderson, B. L., & Schmuch, G. (1991). Sexuality and cancer. In A. Holleb, D. Fink, & G. Murphy (Eds.), *American Cancer Society textbook of clinical oncology* (pp. 606–616). Atlanta, GA: American Cancer Society.

Association of Oncology Social Work. (2006). *The AOSW member survey report*. Philadelphia, PA: Author.

Christ, G. (1991). Principles of oncology social work. In A. Holleb, D. Fink, & G. Murphy (Eds.), *American Cancer Society textbook of clinical oncology* (pp. 594–605). Atlanta, GA: American Cancer Society.

Fobair, P., Stearns, N. N., Christ, G., Dozier-Hall, D., Newman, N. W., Zabora, J., ... Desonier, M. J. (2009). Historical threads in the development of oncology social work. *Journal of Psychosocial Oncology, 27*(2), 155–215. doi:10.1080/07347330902775301

Hermann, J. (2005). *Cancer support groups: A guide for facilitators*. Atlanta, GA: American Cancer Society.

Holleb, A., Fink, D., & Murphy, G. (Eds.). (1991). *American Cancer Society textbook of clinical oncology*. Atlanta, GA: American Cancer Society.

Krawiec, V. (1995). *Background and history of the National Clinical Awards Program*. Atlanta, GA: American Cancer Society.

Lauria, M. M., Clark, E. J., Hermann, J. F., & Stearns, N. M. (Eds.). (2001). *Social work in oncology: Supporting survivors, families, and caregivers*. Atlanta, GA: American Cancer Society.

Stearns, N. M., Lauria, M. M., Hermann, J. F., & Fogelberg, P. R. (Eds.). (1993). *Oncology social work: A clinician's guide*. Atlanta, GA: American Cancer Society.

Survey Press Bureau. (1913, November 29). *Press bulletin No. 4. National fight against cancer. Campaign of education to check its spread. Hope in early treatment*. New York, NY: The Survey. Copy on file at ACSS Archives, New York, NY.

Walsh, K., & Marcusen, C. (1999). Self advocacy training for cancer survivors: The cancer toolbox. *Cancer Practice, 7*(6), 297–301.

101

Ann Fairchild, Christa G. Burke, Paula G. McCarthy, Stacy Stickney Ferguson, and Katherine Walsh

APOSW and AOSW: Education and Development of Professional Networks

Key Concepts

- *The Association of Pediatric Oncology Social Workers (APOSW) and the Association of Oncology Social Work (AOSW) are professional oncology social work organizations that provide professional development, education, tools, and resources.*
- *The APOSW and AOSW are guided by their organizational missions and goals.*
- *The APOSW and AOSW are volunteer-led, nonprofit professional organizations.*

Professional organizations have played a major role in developing the field of oncology social work and provided professional development and training opportunities for thousands of social workers practicing in adult and pediatric oncology and the related fields of hospice and palliative care. The first pediatric oncology social workers began practicing in the late 1950s and early 1960s, hired by research centers to assist children diagnosed with cancer and their families with psychosocial problems related to cancer and its treatments. The Association of Pediatric Oncology Social Workers (APOSW) was formed by these pioneering oncology social workers to provide a network for training and support for the field (APOSW, 2006). With increased federal funding for cancer control in the 1970s, more centers began hiring social workers to assist adults diagnosed with cancer and their families, leading to the formation of the National Association of Oncology Social Workers, later renamed the Association of Oncology Social Work (AOSW; Fobair et al., 2009). This chapter reviews the training and development activities provided by these vital professional organizations.

The Association of Pediatric Oncology Social Workers

The APOSW is a volunteer-led organization whose primary role is to advance pediatric psychosocial oncology care and promote the interests of social work within pediatric oncology. Within the larger world of childhood cancer, it is the voice of the social work profession designed to educate professionals, the general public, and cancer patients and their families and friends.

The APOSW was founded in 1976 when six pediatric oncology social workers met to discuss common issues and provide mutual support. It was during a time of continued improvement in treatment outcomes for children with acute lymphoblastic leukemia when survival outcomes were approaching 60% for children 10 years off treatment (Rivera, Pinkel, Simone, Hancock, & Crist, 1993). However, for other pediatric cancer diagnoses, the prognosis remained poor. To best respond to the psychosocial health needs of pediatric cancer patients and their families, these innovative social workers knew there was a need to share their specific clinical experience. They recognized the value of formally supporting and promoting resilience among psychosocial professionals in this specialty field and had the foresight to understand the benefit it would provide children and families coping with the psychological and psychosocial sequelae from cancer treatment. In 1978, the first APOSW national meeting was held in Bethesda, Maryland, focused on "Issues for Survival and the Needs of the Family" (APOSW, 2013).

Since the late 1970s, APOSW has evolved into a diverse, international organization. APOSW members include pediatric hematology, oncology, and bone marrow transplant social workers and allied health professionals who work in hospitals, clinics, educational institutions, private practice, and community-based organizations, providing support and treatment to children, young adults, and their families living with cancer. The APOSW promotes knowledge and skill competency in part through its continuing education programs (Institute of Medicine, 2008).

Scope and Standards of Practice

APOSW members share common goals focused on enhancing the psychosocial well-being of pediatric, adolescent, and young adult patients and their family members by advancing pediatric psychosocial care through clinical social work practice, research, advocacy, education, and evidence-informed program development. The APOSW endorses standards of practice for pediatric social workers in five areas: (1) qualifications, (2) scope of knowledge, (3) scope of skills, (4) competencies, and (5) professional development (APOSW, 2009).

APOSW Organizational Goals

APOSW membership gives social work members, including associate and student members, an opportunity to further their clinical skills and professional development and increase their awareness of psychosocial issues and support for collective actions among members. Educational, personal, and professional development are enhanced through the organization's network, conferences, committees, special interest working groups, and scholarship opportunities. The APOSW also affords members opportunities for visibility, support, and access to leaders and partners who share an interest in advancing pediatric psychosocial oncology care through clinical social work practice, research, advocacy, education, and program development.

Pediatric oncology social workers are encouraged to join the APOSW to:

- *Increase awareness of psychosocial issues facing patients and families/caregivers*
- *Develop and support advocacy interventions and practice skills among members*
- *Further educational, personal, and professional development*
- *Embrace opportunities to pair with leaders and partners who share an investment in improving childhood cancer health outcomes*
- *Broaden the professional networking community*

APOSW Listserv and Newsletter

The APOSW maintains a members-only listserv that allows access to the collective knowledge base and provides an online forum to discuss challenging cases and ethical dilemmas and to share ideas for intervention and resources. The APOSW publishes a quarterly online newsletter to keep members current with its conference announcements and activities, report on accomplishments of APOSW members, and highlight new resources, innovative programs, and relevant legislative action.

APOSW Website

The APOSW website (http://www.aposw.org) provides a benefit to both APOSW members and the public. The public section offers resources and information for patients and their families who are coping with childhood cancer, provides career postings announcing open pediatric oncology social work positions, and offers extensive information about the organization itself. The members-only section provides a searchable online membership directory and a clinical tool kit that addresses specific clinical topics such as assessment, psychosocial needs throughout the continuum of care, bereavement, school re-entry, sibling needs, survivorship, professional boundaries, ethics, and self-care. Specific assessment tools designed by APOSW members include psychosocial assessment guides for general assessment, bone marrow transplant, and survivorship. Other pages offer listings of educational, financial, and legal resources for patients and their families and suggested standards of practice and position papers for professionals.

APOSW Annual Conference

As a major APOSW educational initiative, the annual conference offers plenary sessions, specialty sessions, and poster presentations relevant to clinical social work practice. Topics include clinical practice skill building, program development and evaluation, ethics, survivorship, unique needs of special populations, and research. A seminar for new social workers is presented annually, and sponsors and exhibitors provide information and resources of interest to pediatric hematology oncology social workers.

APOSW Collaborative Relationships

The APOSW welcomes the involvement of community and national organizations representing a range of community advocacy and resource organizations, all dedicated to addressing the needs of pediatric cancer patients and families.

The work of the APOSW and its members contributes to the body of oncology social work knowledge through publications in peer-reviewed journals and collaboration with other professional associations to disseminate position papers. The APOSW jointly prepared a position paper with the Association of Oncology Social Work on family-centered care (AOSW & APOSW, 2007) and contributed to the development of *Standards for Social Work Care and Staffing in Pediatric Health Care Settings* (APOSW, 2011).

Advocacy

The APOSW is a member of patient and community advocacy organizations such as the Alliance for Childhood Cancer, Children's Oncology Group Behavioral Sciences Committee, and Alliance for Quality Psychosocial Cancer Care, with many APOSW members serving in leadership roles within these organizations. Their aim is to advocate and contribute to the development of national and international policies and initiatives to improve health outcomes and enhance the quality of life for children with cancer and their families.

The Association of Oncology Social Work

The AOSW is a nonprofit, international, 501(c)3 organization dedicated to the enhancement of psychosocial services for people with cancer and their families. Created in 1984 by social workers interested in oncology, the AOSW has over 1,300 current members who embrace the AOSW mission statement: "to advance excellence in the psychosocial care of persons with cancer, their families and caregivers through networking, education, advocacy, research and resource development" (AOSW, 2001). The AOSW envisions a global society in which oncology care meets the physical, emotional, social, and spiritual needs of all people affected by cancer, demonstrated by its commitment to the training and development of oncology social workers.

AOSW Organizational Goals

The organizational goals of AOSW are to:

- Increase awareness of the psychosocial effects of cancer.
- Advance the practice of psychosocial interventions that enhance quality of life and recovery of persons with cancer and their families.
- Foster communication and support among psychosocial oncology caregivers.
- Further the study of psychological and social effects of cancer through research and continuing education.
- Advocate for programs and policies to meet the psychosocial needs of oncology patients and their families.
- Promote liaison activities with other psychosocial oncology groups and professional oncology organizations.
- Promote the highest professional standards and ethics in the practice of oncology social work.

Scope and Standards of Practice

The AOSW *Standards of Practice* state that "oncology social work is the primary professional discipline that provides psychosocial services to patients, families, and significant others facing the impact of a potential or actual diagnosis of cancer" (AOSW, 2012). The scope of practice identified in the standards includes the following:

- Services to cancer survivors, families, and caregivers through clinical practice providing comprehensive psychosocial services and programs through all phases of the cancer experience.
- Services to institutions and agencies to increase their knowledge of the psychosocial, social, cultural, and spiritual factors that affect coping with cancer and its effects, and to ensure provision of quality psychosocial programs and care.
- Services to the community through education, consultation, research, and volunteering to use, promote, or strengthen the community services, programs, and resources available to meet the needs of cancer survivors.
- Services to the profession to support the appropriate orientation, supervision, and evaluation of clinical social workers in oncology; participation in and promotion of student training and education in oncology social work; and advancement of knowledge through clinical and other research.

AOSW Website

The AOSW's website (http://www.AOSW.org) offers a wealth of information and resources to members, including access to a members-only blog, committee and conference information, oncology social work credentialing (OSW-C), projects and partnerships, annual award recipients, regional news, a member directory, mission and vision statements, information about the board of directors, and special interest groups' pages. In addition, members can download a brochure describing the role and functions of oncology social workers and other tools to enhance practice and educate interdisciplinary colleagues, as well as access frequently requested resources.

AOSW Newsletter Blog

AOSW produces a blog featuring articles, resources, information about continuing education programs, special interest group reports, introduction to leaders of the organization, book reviews, and member-written clinical articles. The online format provides a platform for ongoing member interaction about timely issues influencing practice and is accessible to the public in hopes of increasing the visibility and awareness of the functions of oncology social workers. It is moderated by volunteer communication team members and underwritten by AOSW industry partners.

Social Work Oncology Network Listserv

The Social Work Oncology Network (SWON), founded by AOSW, provides a 24/7 members-only information platform for dissemination and sharing of oncology-related resources and problem-solving tools for professionals working with people with cancer. SWON also offers the exchange of the most current information related to assisting patients and families, educational opportunities for professional providers and consumers of oncology care, and a sounding board/peer consultation venue for professional concerns. Ninety-five percent of AOSW members subscribe to SWON. These members are oncology social workers and cancer patient navigators from all over the United States and seven countries around the world. The average number of SWON postings is approximately 250 per month. SWON topics are archived to provide a continuously accessible resource for new and seasoned oncology social workers. AOSW members report that SWON is one of the most highly valued member benefits.

Journal of Psychosocial Oncology

The *Journal of Psychosocial Oncology* (*JPO*), the official journal of the AOSW, was started in 1983 and has been edited by oncology social workers for three decades (Fobair et al., 2009). All active AOSW members receive a subscription. This peer-reviewed publication is an essential source of clinical and research material for health professionals who provide psychosocial services to cancer patients, their families, and their caregivers. The first interdisciplinary resource of its kind, *JPO* disseminates exploratory, hypothesis testing, and program evaluation research data in critical areas including clinical practice, patient and family education, and psychosocial distress associated with cancer.

AOSW Annual Conference

AOSW's annual conference is the organization's largest educational and professional development offering, typically drawing 350 to 450 attendees or over one third of its membership. The themed annual conference offers paper presentations, workshops and posters, and preconference institutes and specialty tracks on subjects such as leadership, end-of-life and palliative care, ethics, legal issues, and the rights of cancer patients. A strategic priority of the AOSW is to increase the availability of online educational resources, provide live-streamed and video presentations from the conference, and provide daily updates for those members unable to attend the annual conference.

AOSW's Role in Supporting Practicing Oncology Social Workers

The AOSW provides a rich variety of tools and documents to support oncology social workers in practice and the profession at large. Because many members are sole practitioners in their institutions, the AOSW provides a virtual community of collegial support through SWON, the member directory, and online resources, culminating in the annual conference. The AOSW's mission includes the development of resources that can be accessed by members such as the oncology social work brochure, sample job descriptions, sample performance evaluations, and distress screening and assessment tools. The AOSW provides abstract mentoring before each conference to encourage member presentations. The AOSW also provides tools for master's-level field instructors, such as student interview questions, a student orientation manual, and suggestions for student assignments. AOSW members collaborate to create position papers independently and in partnership with other organizations. These papers may be used as advocacy tools on a national scale and also provide members with a resource to help them articulate as patient advocates in their practices.

AOSW Collaborative Relationships With Other Organizations

As part of its mission to advance excellence in the psychosocial care of persons with and affected by cancer, the AOSW maintains strong partnerships with key organizations such as the Commission on Cancer, C-Change, American Psychosocial Oncology Society, APOSW, Oncology Nursing Society, American College of Surgeons, Association of Community Cancer Centers, American Cancer Society,

Leukemia and Lymphoma Society, LIVE**STRONG**, and others. The AOSW has member liaisons in many of these organizations and also collaborates to develop organizational position statements on topics such as psychosocial distress screening, end-of-life care, and patient navigation. A key partner of the AOSW is the Board of Oncology Social Work, an organization founded to create oncology social work credentialing (OSW-C) (see Chapter 102).

AOSW Special Interest Groups

The AOSW offers 11 special interest groups (SIGs), providing members an opportunity to develop and refine skills and exchange ideas in specific areas of practice. SIGs form an integral part of the AOSW, drawing their individual membership from the larger association. Each SIG maintains a space on the AOSW website to share materials and resources and meets in person at the annual conference.

Special Interest Groups
• *Ambulatory Care/Fee-for-Service*
• *Adolescents and Young Adults*
• *Blood Cancers*
• *Brain Tumor*
• *Children and Cancer*
• *Complementary/Alternative Medicine*
• *Ethics*
• *Pain and Palliative Care and End of Life*
• *Patient Navigation*
• *Radiation Therapy*
• *Spirituality*

Social Work Oncology Research Group

The Social Work Oncology Research Group (SWORG) is a committee within the AOSW that provides opportunities for networking, as well as information and consultation, for conducting psychosocial oncology research. SWORG members are academic researchers and clinicians involved in, or interested in, clinical research. A primary goal of SWORG is to ensure that social work research in oncology serves the interests of patients and families dealing with cancer and remains relevant to the field. SWORG meetings are venues for research to inform practice and for practitioners to inform and direct research.

AOSW Cancer Survivors Network

The AOSW Cancer Survivors Network is open to AOSW members who have or have had cancer. This network provides an opportunity for sharing resources, talking about experiences, and discussing the challenges of being oncology social workers and cancer survivors.

Pearls

- The APOSW and AOSW are member organizations formed by and for oncology social work professionals who are solely responsible for their missions, educational and research activities, and advocacy efforts.
- Active participation in the APOSW and AOSW offers wonderful leadership opportunities for all members.
- The AOSW and APOSW provide a unique voice, or advocacy agent, devoted to the concerns of oncology social workers.
- Oncology social work is intensely challenging. It is essential for practitioners to develop strategies to foster self-care and professional growth.
- Membership in a professional association can help to sustain you, broaden your practice, and provide a forum for support within your specific specialty.

Pitfalls

- The demanding tasks of the boards of directors are carried out by busy professionals who volunteer their time and talent beyond the paid workplace.
- It is an ongoing challenge for the volunteer leadership of these organizations to focus on developing outside funding sources to underwrite new initiatives.
- Oncology social workers are at risk for compassion fatigue and burnout in spite of improved survival rates for patients.

The APOSW and AOSW are professional organizations dedicated to enhancing the psychosocial well-being of children, adolescents, and adults with cancer through the support and education of its members. Both are member-driven nonprofits that strive to promote professional excellence in oncology social work practice. These organizations endeavor to grow and expand member resources and also produce products and programs to equip social workers whose practice and research focus directly on persons affected by cancer.

Presidents of the APOSW and AOSW have seats at important oncology forums such as C-Change and the President's Cancer Panel. Reviewers from these organizations are often sought by offices of the National Cancer Institute for input on patient education materials. Service organizations such as the Leukemia and Lymphoma Society and the American Cancer Society seek expertise on psychosocial issues and cancer from within their memberships.

Additions to require psychosocial distress screening in institutions credentialed through the Commission on Cancer (COC, 2012) have provided a whirlwind of opportunity for the advancement of oncology social work in clinical practice. The APOSW and AOSW strive to arm their members with the knowledge and tools they need to be the experts in their practices on this important initiative backed by clinical research regarding best practices and implementation.

The changes in the need for more credentialing and continuing education units bring more value to membership, mentorship, and attending annual conferences. The APOSW and AOSW are also becoming vibrant virtual communities through their websites, blogs, and listservs.

The APOSW and AOSW grapple with the financial limitations faced by many nonprofits, but the boards of directors are continuously fostering partnerships and developing programs to expand the breadth and depth of member resources and offerings for public education. The AOSW, like the APOSW, recognizes that its primary resource is its membership and continuously strives to provide members with valuable, useful, and timely professional development tools and resources that will enhance practice.

REFERENCES

Association of Oncology Social Work. (2001). *AOSW mission statement*. Retrieved from http://www.aosw.org/iMIS201/AOSWMain/About-AOSW/Mission-and-Goals/AOSWMain/About-AOSW/mission-and-goals.aspx?hkey=782e2be0-de81-4c24-af6d-36c11e7bca43

Association of Oncology Social Work. (2012). *AOSW oncology social work standards of practice*. Retrieved from http://www.aosw.org/iMIS201/AOSWMain/professionals/standards-of-practice/AOSWMain/Professional-Development/standards-of-practice.aspx?hkey=51fda308-28bd-48b0-8a75-a17d01251b5e

Association of Oncology Social Work & Association of Pediatric Oncology Social Workers. (2007). *Association of Oncology Social Work and Association of Pediatric Oncology Social Work joint position on family centered care*. Retrieved from http://www.aosw.org/imis201/AOSWMain/pdfs/aosw-public-docs/pos-family.pdf

Association of Pediatric Oncology Social Workers. (2006). *APOSW history*. Retrieved from http://www.aposw.org/html/history.php

Association of Pediatric Oncology Social Workers. (2009). *Association of Oncology Social Work standards of practice*. Retrieved from http://www.aposw.org/html/standards.php

Association of Pediatric Oncology Social Workers. (2011). *Standards for social work care and staffing in pediatric health care settings*. Retrieved from http://www.aposw.org/docs/StandardsCareAndStaffing.pdf

Association of Pediatric Oncology Social Workers. (2013). *APOSW annual conferences from 1976 to 1999*. Retrieved from http://www.aposw.org/html/past-confs.php

Commission on Cancer. (2012). *Commission on Cancer: Cancer program standards version 1.2*. Retrieved from http://www.facs.org

Fobair, P., Stearns, N. N., Christ, G., Dozier-Hall, D., Newman, N. W., Zabora, J., ... Desonier, M. J. (2009). Historical threads in the development of oncology social work. *Journal of Psychosocial Oncology*, *27*(2), 155–215. doi:10.1080/07347330902775301

Institute of Medicine. 2008. *Cancer care for the whole patient: Meeting psychosocial health needs*. Washington, DC: National Academies Press.

Rivera, G. K., Pinkel, D., Simone, J. V., Hancock, M. L., & Crist, W. M. (1993). Treatment of acute lymphoblastic leukemia. 30 years' experience at St. Jude Children's Research Hospital. *New England Journal of Medicine*, *329*(18), 1289–1295.

102

Virginia Vaitones, Johanna Schutte, and Debra Mattison

OSW-C: The Importance of Certification for Oncology Social Workers

Key Concepts

- *OSW-C validates that oncology social workers meet rigorous standards of knowledge and experience and fulfill stringent requirements for continuing education in oncology social work.*
- *Criteria for evaluation of applicants for OSW-C use the Association of Oncology Social Work* Standards of Practice *and the National Association of Social Workers* Code of Ethics.
- *Continuous updating of standards, raising the bar on specific knowledge and skill competencies, will provide a strong foundation for psychosocial care and support new roles for oncology social workers such as patient care coordinators, patient navigators, and patient advocates.*

Psychosocial care for patients with a cancer diagnosis is highly complex and requires social workers with specialized experience and defined skill sets. As articulated by Smith, Walsh-Burke, and Cruzan (1998) in *Psycho-Oncology*:

> *Oncology social workers are primary providers of psychosocial services in major oncology treatment centers and community health care settings throughout the world, both because of their knowledge about cancer and its psychosocial impact, and because of their practice versatility. Oncology social workers are trained in prevention, education, advocacy, research, and counseling (p. 1061).*

A 1995 national survey found that 75% of supportive counseling for all cancer patients at National Cancer Institute (NCI)–designated cancer centers was provided by social workers (Coluzzi et al., 1995). A survey of 786 pediatric psychooncology professionals from 63 countries reported that social workers were the most frequent providers of psychosocial services to both children and families (Wiener et al., 2012). Similar to other professions, such as nursing and teaching, certification validates that oncology social workers meet rigorous standards of knowledge and experience, as well as more stringent requirements for continuing education in oncology social work. This not only benefits cancer patients, their families, and caregivers but also the employers of oncology social workers and society in general. Employers who support and hire certified oncology social workers convey their dedication to the highest quality of patient care. Oncology social work certification can be used to demonstrate to surveyors and accrediting bodies that the social workers in their program have attained an exceptional level of experience and competency. In short, having certified oncology social workers can be a strong marketing tool for the oncology program.

To attain oncology social work certification, social workers are required to demonstrate experience in multiple arenas including psychosocial care, education, research, cancer support group facilitation, program development, and community involvement. These expectations confirm the profession's commitment to at-risk populations by promoting professional excellence and encouraging involvement in community agencies and activities that serve cancer patients. In summary, certification affirms to patients and their families, employers, social work colleagues, and other interdisciplinary team members that certified oncology social workers have met oncology-specific criteria of education, work experience, and service at the highest level to provide quality psychosocial care throughout the continuum of diagnosis, treatment, survivorship, remission, recurrence, and end-of-life care.

Initial Survey of the Association of Oncology Social Work Membership

In 2000, a small working group of oncology social work leaders discussed the need for oncology social work certification similar to that available to oncology nurses, where, in many hospitals, clinical ladders were established to encourage and compensate nurses who go beyond their expected duties. As a result, the group identified the need to recognize oncology social work as a specialty and to reward field expertise and experience.

This working group developed a survey and mailed it to 200 Association of Oncology Social Work (AOSW) members in the United States in 2001. Forty-three percent of the surveys were returned, and of these respondents, an overwhelming 83% supported the formation of a specialty accreditation for oncology social workers, with 93% of respondents reporting that they believed the practice of oncology social work required specialized skills. In May 2001, the survey results were presented to the AOSW board and general membership at the well-attended annual conference in Cleveland, Ohio (Schutte, LaGrange, & Priestly, 2001), resulting in clear support for specialty accreditation. The findings of this survey were also presented in a letter to the AOSW president to formally inform the board of the strong support for oncology social work certification and to encourage further action by the AOSW.

Development of Oncology Social Work Certification

In early spring 2002, the AOSW board of directors established a committee to explore the feasibility of a certification program, requesting investigation of the economics, logistics, and organizational support for such a certification. Discussion included the potential of developing the certification independently within the organization of the AOSW versus partnering with other related organizations, such as the National Association of Social Workers (NASW), the Association of Pediatric Oncology Social Workers (APOSW), or the American Board of Examiners.

The work of the feasibility committee ultimately led to a decision to offer an oncology social work certification through the AOSW. On June 15, 2003, the AOSW board of directors voted to provide an oncology social work certification and announced this to its membership. A separate 501(c)6 entity (a classification of business/professional trade organizations, vs. a 501(c)3, which is classified for charitable donations and allows an open membership) was required to oversee the certification program. The board submitted the criteria for certification, policies and procedures, and bylaws, and the Internal Revenue Service approved program on July 9, 2003, as a 501(c)6.

By September 2003, application packets had been mailed to all AOSW members (with the exception of international members, who were not eligible due to differing education and licensing). Letters sent to oncology-related organizations, including the Association of Community Cancer Center (ACCC), the NASW, and the Society for Social Work Leadership in Health Care, announced the creation of the certification program and encouraged application. By October 2003, the first applications had been received. By 2004, the number of certified oncology social workers had begun to grow as members of the APOSW were also invited to apply for certification. Canadian AOSW members were then invited to apply for certification because it was determined that they also met relevant U.S. education and licensing requirements. The Board of Oncology Social Work Certification (BOSWC) logo and name (OSW-C) received its official trademark on May 20, 2005, and in 2006, the BOSW-C became an independent organization with the support of the AOSW board of directors. The program is now financially self-sustaining based on initial and renewal fees.

Oncology Social Work Certification

The mission of the BOSWC is to promote and ensure excellence in psychosocial care to oncology patients, families, caregivers, and their communities. Oncology social work certification was developed to ensure the highest level of competency and experience in the field of oncology social work and to reflect a knowledge base, skill set, and set of ethical standards specific to psychosocial oncology. Thus, the criteria for the certification reflect this core mission and desired outcomes. Rather than selecting an examination, a different process was developed to determine an individual practitioner's level of training, knowledge, and skill. Other professional certifications have followed a similar certification path, including the Advanced Certified Hospice and Palliative Care social Worker (ACHP-SW). The certification is open to members of both the AOSW and APOSW.

Certification criteria require demonstration of the following:

- A master's degree from a school of social work accredited by the Council on Social Work Education.

- A minimum of 3 years of post-master's program employment in the field of social work with greater than 50% of one's workload specifically in oncology social work.
- A current social work license in good standing.
- Current membership in the AOSW or APOSW.
- Two written recommendations from professional coworkers and a written recommendation from one's current immediate supervisor.
- Demonstration of community involvement in one of the following oncology-specific activities: program planning, support groups, educational presentations, research and publication, leadership roles, and professional teaching.

Applicants must also agree and attest to uphold the *AOSW Standards of Practice for Oncology Social Work* (AOSW, 2012) and the NASW *Code of Ethics* (NASW, 2008) and to notify the BOSWC if their license to practice social work is suspended or revoked.

References for the applicant are asked to rate the individual on his or her competencies in each of the areas of the *AOSW Standards of Practice* that are provided in the following box.

AOSW *Standards of Practice in Oncology Social Work* ©2012

Oncology social work is the primary professional discipline that provides psychosocial services to patients, families, and significant others facing the impact of a potential or actual diagnosis of cancer. The scope of oncology social work includes clinical practice, education, advocacy, administration, policy, and research. The standards of practice provided in this document are intended for clinical social workers practicing in the specialty of oncology social work.

The master's in social work degree provides oncology social workers with theoretical knowledge, clinical expertise, and practical experience with patients, their families, and their significant others. In addition, oncology social workers often receive specialized training in cancer care through clinical supervision, continuing education, in-service training, and on-the-job experience.

Psychosocial services provided by oncology social workers include individual, family, and group counseling; education; advocacy; discharge planning; case management; patient navigation; and program development. These services are designed to maximize the patient's utilization of the health care system, foster coping, mobilize community resources to support optimal functioning, and empower the patient and family to be active participants in health care decisions and management.

Oncology social work services are available to patients and families throughout all phases of the cancer continuum, including prevention, diagnosis, treatment, survivorship, palliative care, end-of-life care, and bereavement. Services are delivered in a wide variety of settings including specialty cancer centers, community hospitals and health systems, ambulatory centers, home health and hospice programs, community-based agencies, and private practice settings.

Oncology social workers are an integral part of the health care team and contribute to the development and coordination of the overall treatment plan. In collaboration with the patient and family and other health care disciplines, oncology social workers provide counseling, education, discharge planning, case management, and navigation, linking patients with a variety of services necessary to meet the person's multiple needs.

In addition to services to patients and families, oncology social workers address organizational and community needs through professional practice. Services are provided to institutions, voluntary health organizations, and community agencies with the overall aim of promoting health and safety and improving the delivery of care to individuals at risk for or affected by cancer.

Oncology social workers embrace patient- and family-centered care at all levels of practice. Social work training and professional values are congruent with this approach at the clinical level and position oncology social workers to substantially contribute to the development of a health care environment that embodies the core concepts of patient- and family-centered care organizationally. This approach includes respect for patients' values, preferences, and expressed needs; coordinated and integrated culturally competent care; timely, affirming, and useful information, communication, and education; individualized care; physical comfort; emotional support; involvement of family and friends; shared decision making; and collaboration with patients and families in the evaluation, planning, and delivery of care.

AOSW Standards of Practice

Standard I. Qualifications

Oncology social workers shall be knowledgeable about oncologic diseases and their treatments, psychosocial implications for individuals and families, appropriate interventions, and available community and governmental resources. Oncology social workers must have knowledge of the usual course of cancer and its treatment, including genetics, so that patients and families can be helped to anticipate and deal with changes in individual and family life.

The oncology social worker shall be master's prepared from a graduate program accredited by the Council on Social Work Education. It is preferred that the graduate have had prior employment or field placement experience in a health care setting.

Standard II. Services to Patients and Families

Oncology social work programs shall provide the following clinical and programmatic services:

A. Screening for psychosocial distress
B. Completion of a psychosocial assessment of the patient and family's response to the cancer diagnosis and treatment to include:
  1. Age and stage of human development

2. *Knowledge about cancer and its treatment including level of understanding, reactions, goals for care, and expectations*
3. *Characteristics of the patient's support system, including family, related biologically, legally, or emotionally*
4. *Patient and family psychosocial functioning including strengths, limitations, and coping skills*
5. *Race, ethnicity, religion, culture, language, physical or mental disability, socioeconomic status, sexual orientation, and gender identity or expression*
6. *Identification of barriers to care*
7. *The source, availability, and adequacy of community resources*
8. *Patient and family level of interest in participation in care and decision making*
9. *Development of a case plan with patient and family based on mutually agreed upon goals to enhance, maintain, and promote optimal psychosocial functioning throughout cancer treatment and its outcome*

C. *Utilization of a wide range of clinical interventions designed to address current and/or future problems as the patient's medical and psychosocial needs evolve*
D. *Outreach activities to vulnerable populations*
E. *Maintenance of knowledge of community resources and governmental programs available from local, state, and national health and social service agencies including expertise in accessing these for patients and families*
F. *Organization and facilitation of patient and family education*
G. *Utilization of knowledge and clinical skills in assisting the patient and family with advance care planning and advance directives*
H. *Proactive provision of services to at-risk populations, including assistance with negotiating barriers to cancer information, screening, treatment, and resources within the institution and in the community*
I. *Collaboration with patients and family members who serve as advisers in policy and program development, implementation, and evaluation; health care facility design; professional education, and the delivery of care*
J. *Collaboration with other professional disciplines in the planning and provision of timely and efficient clinical services to cancer patients and their families*
K. *Advocacy for and protection of patients' dignity, confidentiality, rights, and access to care*
L. *Development and utilization of research to improve clinical practice and implement evidence-based psychosocial support programs, services, and interventions*

Standard III. Services to Institutions and Agencies

Oncology social work programs shall address institutional and agency needs including the following:

A. *Provision of education and consultation to other disciplines and staff regarding biopsychosocial, environmental, spiritual, and cultural factors that affect oncology care*
B. *Collaboration with other disciplines and staff in the areas of psychosocial clinical services, patient- and family-centered care, research, and education*
C. *Provision of services to professional caregivers that are designed to assist staff in the management of stresses inherent in clinical practice*
D. *Utilization of clinical documentation, statistical reporting, and evaluation to improve services, ensure quality, and develop programs*
E. *The advancement of the practice of patient- and family-centered care at the clinical and organizational levels*
F. *Representation on CancerCare and other related hospital committees*

Standard IV. Services to the Community

Oncology social work programs shall address community needs including the following:

A. *Identification of barriers to effective service delivery and participation in institutional and community responses to these problems*
B. *Provision of services to at-risk populations, including navigation assistance with access to cancer information, screening, treatment, and resources*
C. *Provision of consultation and volunteer services to institutions, voluntary health organizations, and community agencies to promote health, provide education, and develop programs to better serve the community*

Standard V. Services to the Profession

Oncology social work programs shall address the following needs of the profession and its practitioners:

A. *Provision of the appropriate orientation, supervision, and evaluation of practitioners by clinical social workers, preferably with experience in oncology*
B. *Commitment to continuing professional education*
C. *Promotion of professional practice in accord with the NASW Code of Ethics*
D. *Participation in student and professional training and education in the area of oncology social work*
E. *Contribution to oncology social work through participation in professional associations*
F. *Contribution to oncology social work knowledge base through psychosocial research, publications, presentations, and evidence-based practice*
G. *Proactive provision of patient navigation services to at-risk populations, including assistance*
H. *Collaboration with other professional disciplines in the planning and provision of timely and efficient clinical services to cancer patients and their families*
I. *Development of research-based knowledge that relates to clinical issues, interventions, and outcomes*

The certification requires renewal every 2 years with submission of proof of at least 30 continuing education units, of which 15 units must be primarily and specifically related to oncology, palliative care, or end-of-life care. There is an initial cost for the certification and a fee for renewal. Payment of the coordinator to manage monthly organizational business, accountant fees for yearly financial audits, and mailing costs are the primary ongoing expenses.

As of 2014, there are 530 social workers with the BOSWC certification, which is approximately one half of the entire current AOSW membership. In a 2009 survey of the BOSWC members, responses showed that the membership tended to be a very experienced group of practitioners, with nearly 79% having 10 or more years experience and over 57% with 16 or more years of experience in social work. When looking at oncology-specific social work experience, 57% had 11 or more years of specific oncology experience and 35% had over 15 years of oncology social work experience. Most members, approximately 80% in this survey, worked in direct clinical practice, with two thirds working in a community or teaching hospital. When asked to identify the top reasons for choosing to apply for OSW-C, members most often cited a personal sense of accomplishment and professionalism and to be on par with other interdisciplinary team members who were also certified professionals.

New applications for oncology social work certification have continued to increase over the last 3 years, with 47 new applications in 2009, 53 new applications in 2010, 96 new applications in 2011, 109 new applications in 2012, and 122 new applications in 2013. This increase may in part be related to the American College of Surgeon's Commission on Cancer's (ACOS COC, 2012) new mandate that its certified institutions provide psychosocial care across the continuum of diagnosis, treatment, and survivorship. Employers also started to support and encourage oncology social work certification.

An oncology certified social worker reported: "Having my OSW-C allowed me to present myself as an advanced practice oncology professional, which my administration took very seriously and which I am sure was one of the many reasons the position of Community Outreach & Cancer Support Services, Director was approved."

Pearls

- OSW-C distinguishes specifically trained and skilled social workers capable of providing quality psychosocial care and meeting the specialized needs of oncology patients, families, and others impacted by cancer.
- OSW-C demonstrates to clients and colleagues that oncology social workers have a defined and specialized skill set and opens the door for conversations about the knowledge, experience, and commitment needed to attain this designation.
- OSW-C promotes positive employment opportunities for oncology social workers, sometimes providing financial rewards and incentives.
- Hospitals can use the OSW-C to demonstrate to surveyors and accrediting bodies that the social workers on staff have attained an exceptional level of experience and competency. This is a strong marketing tool.

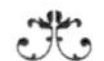

Pitfalls

- Need for continuous updating of standards and competencies to provide a strong foundation for social workers to be involved in the growing opportunities of oncology psychosocial care, as well as in new roles such as psychosocial coordinators, patient navigators, and patient advocates.
- Organizational and financial challenges specifically related to continuing education and certification fees.

The establishment of a professional certification proved to be a complex undertaking requiring professional, legal, accounting, and organizational consultations. An organizational structure to support the ongoing maintenance of a certification organization is essential. The BOSWC has been successful due to a committed board and coordinator who volunteer time to review new applications, renew applications, and attend annual board meetings.

Active collaboration and marketing with other social work organizations have been very useful. Increased awareness of the certification with these groups should be an ongoing focus in the future. Retention of BOSWC members is an area for continued exploration and attention. Assessment of nonrenewing members is necessary to ensure that the certification remains meaningful and relevant to its members and the current status of oncology social work. In our 2009 survey of the members who stated that they did not plan to renew their membership, the reasons indicated for this choice were "no longer working in an oncology social work position," "no longer meeting guidelines," and "the cost." The reasons suggest a shifting health care environment in hospital-based oncology social work positions and the economic challenges of maintaining continuing education requirements and certification fees.

The establishment of an oncology social work certification has been a very successful and timely undertaking. The OSW-C is now part of the ACCC's best practice guidelines and the National Accreditation Program for Breast Centers' preferred standards. In January 2012, OSW-C became part of the ACOS COC's new psychosocial standards and is a preferred certification for its role description of psychosocial coordinator.

REFERENCES

American College of Surgeons' Commission on Cancer (ACOS COC). (2012). Cancer program standards. Ensuring patient-centered care. Retrieved from www.facs.org/cancer.

Association of Oncology Social Work (AOSW). (2012). *AOSW standards of practice in oncology social work*. Retrieved from http://www.aosw.org/iMIS201/AOSWMain/professionals/standards-of-practice/AOSWMain/Professional-Development/standards-of-practice.aspx?hkey=51fda308-28bd-48b0-8a75-a17d01251b5e

Coluzzi, P. H., Grant, M., Doroshow, J. H., Rhiner, M., Ferrell, B., & Rivera, L. (1995). Survey of the provision of supportive care services at National Cancer Institute—Designated cancer centers. *Journal of Clinical Oncology*, *13*(3), 756–764.

National Association of Social Workers (NASW). (2008). *Code of ethics: Approved by the 1996 NASW Delegate Assembly and revised by the 2008 NASW Delegate Assembly*. Washington, DC: Author.

Schutte, J., Lagrange, A., & Priestley, A. (2001, May). *Is oncology social work certification needed? A pilot study of AOSW members*. Presentation at the Association of Oncology Social Work Conference, Cleveland, OH.

Smith, E., Walsh-Burke, K., & Cruzan, C. (1998). Principles of training social workers in oncology. In J. C. Holland & W. Breitbart (Eds.), *Psycho-oncology* (pp. 1061–1068). New York, NY: Oxford University Press.

Wiener, L., Oppenheim, D., Breyer, J., Battles, H., Zadeh, S., & Patenaude, A. F. (2012). A worldview of the professional experiences and training needs of pediatric psycho-oncologists. *Psycho-Oncology*, *21*, 944–953. doi:10.1002/pon.3064

103 NASW and Oncology Social Work

Elizabeth J. Clark and Stacy Collins

Key Concepts

- *The National Association of Social Workers believes that collaboration among social work groups is an essential element in furthering comprehensive psychosocial oncology and advancing quality cancer care.*
- *Since first adopted, the social workers' professional code of ethics has mandated advocacy for fairness and social justice including providing services and care to patients who are underserved and marginalized.*
- *Learning how to self-advocate is essential for persons living with cancer because they must learn to navigate a complex health care system and stand up for their rights.*

Formed in 1955, the National Association of Social Workers (NASW) began when seven existing social work associations merged to form one overarching association, the oldest group being the American Association of Medical Social Workers, in operation since 1918 (Clark, 2008). Since its founding, many social work pioneers and leaders—including Eleanor Cockerill (oncology and rehabilitation), Ruth Abrams (oncology and chronic illness), and Bernice Catherine Harper (oncology, hospice, and end-of-life care)—have ensured the NASW's long-standing commitment to medical social work.

Cockerill led social work in the post–World War II era, working with cancer patients in Texas. In 1950, in an effort to bring attention to and enrich medical social work across the country, she assembled directors of medical social work agencies and departments to find ways to improve practices, being especially attuned to multidisciplinary collaboration to help infuse social work values into medical education (Curran & Cockerill, 1948).

In 1966, Abrams, one of the first social workers to specialize in oncology, published a groundbreaking paper in the *New England Journal of Medicine* entitled "The Patient With Cancer: His Changing Pattern of Communication." The paper focused on a qualitative study of 30 cancer patients in various stages of the disease, drawn from her caseload at Massachusetts General Hospital. Abrams further developed her premise and published an important book for social workers in oncology, *Not Alone With Cancer: A Guide for Those Who Care*. In its preface, Abrams notes that it was her intent "to break through the wall of silence" about cancer (Abrams, 1974).

In California, Harper was directing social work at the City of Hope National Medical Center, where she worked with both pediatric and adult leukemia patients. In 1967, she was asked to write and present a paper on professional anxieties in terminal illness, which formed the basis for her later book, *Death: The Coping Mechanisms of the Health Professional* (Harper, 1977/1994). Harper also published an early article in the journal *Cancer* entitled "Social Aspects of Cancer Recovery" (1975). In the 1980s, Harper began working with the Health Care Financing Administration in Washington, DC, and her focus shifted to hospice. She is especially well known for preparing the initial briefing material on hospice for the Secretary of Health, Education, and Welfare in 1978.

These three women helped lay the groundwork for oncology social work during the 1940s, 1950s, and 1960s, realizing the importance of both documenting their experiences and educating colleagues and students while continuing to learn, stay current, and maintain competency in their areas of practice. Likewise, the NASW has endorsed and expanded the work of these three remarkable social workers. Like Cockerill, the association believes that a strong professional identity is essential, as is multidisciplinary practice. Like Abrams, the NASW recognizes the importance of research and evidence-based practice. And like Harper, the NASW understands that linking practice to policy is critical.

Most of the NASW's activities related to oncology social work have been done in partnership with other groups and organizations, drawing on their specialized expertise and willingness to collaborate with the organization's members. As we now live in a global society, our profession has also become global, and NASW leaders take seriously their commitment to support like-minded groups of practitioners to work toward capacity building for the social work profession around the world.

Partnerships in Patient Education and Professional Development

The NASW engages in many coalitions and partnerships serving countless purposes, including patient education, professional education, capacity building, policy advocacy, and special projects such as standard setting and credentialing. The following are specifically related to oncology social work.

Patient Education Efforts

Cancer Survival Toolbox in Partnership With the National Coalition for Cancer Survivorship

One of the NASW's longest standing partnerships has involved the development and promotion of the Cancer Survival Toolbox, a self-advocacy training program for persons living with cancer. The toolbox program, launched in 1998, originally was a collaborative effort between the National Coalition for Cancer Survivorship (NCCS), Oncology Nursing Society (ONS), and Association of Oncology Social Work (AOSW). The NCCS received a grant to plan a program to benefit cancer survivors. Recognizing the importance of self-advocacy (Clark & Stovall, 1996), the NCCS deemed a training toolbox an appropriate goal. However, to be certain of its accuracy and applicability, it decided that the toolbox needed to be developed by those on the front line—cancer survivors, oncology nurses, and oncology social workers. Therefore, the NCCS invited both the ONS and the AOSW to partner in the project. In 2000, the NASW became the toolbox initiative's newest partner.

The toolbox provides audio programs (compact discs or audio tapes) of training modules that teach basic skills needed to navigate the cancer care maze, including finding information, communicating, decision making, problem solving, negotiating, and advocating for one's rights. The data-driven content also includes case examples, practice exercises, and resources, with attention paid to reading level, vocabulary, currency of material, and diversity. Nurses and social workers can order the free discs or tapes in bulk for their hospitals and clinics, and, to date, over 600,000 Cancer Survival Toolboxes have been distributed. They can also be read online on the NCCS website (http://www.canceradvocacy.org), downloaded as MP3 files (http://www.cancersurvivaltoolbox.org), or downloaded free through iTunes or Amazon. Since 2000, many other modules have been developed, including five on blood cancers funded by the Centers for Disease Control and Prevention (NCCS, 2007).

Toolbox Modules
Basic Modules
Communicating
Finding Information
Making Decisions
Negotiating
Standing Up for Your Rights
Special Topics
First Steps for the Newly Diagnosed
Topics for Older Persons
Finding Ways to Pay for Care
Caring for the Caregiver
Living Beyond Cancer
Dying Well—The Final Stage of Survivorship
Blood Cancer Modules
Living With Chronic Myelogenous Leukemia
Living With Chronic Lymphocytic Leukemia
Living With Non-Hodgkin Lymphoma
Living With Multiple Myeloma
Living With Bone and Marrow Transplant

Professional Education Efforts

Partnership With Cancer*Care*

Cancer is rapidly becoming the leading cause of death in the United States (World Health Organization, 2008), and with the aging of the baby-boomer generation, the incidence of cancer will continue rising. Social workers in all practice areas will inevitably encounter clients diagnosed with cancer or who have a family member with cancer. Whether working in a health care setting, a school, a community agency, or private practice, a basic competency about cancer is essential for social workers.

For several years, the NASW has partnered with Cancer*Care*, a national leader in education for cancer survivors and health professionals, to develop educational opportunities for social workers. Founded in 1944, Cancer*Care* was established to provide social work counseling for residents of New York City. The organization expanded its services in the 1990s to telephone counseling and made its HOPE line available to all persons living with cancer (800-813-HOPE). The approximately 50 social work staff members conduct a variety of counseling services and web-based trainings for patients and professionals. In 2004, with support from the Bristol Myers Squibb Foundation, the NASW and Cancer*Care* launched an online course, Understanding Cancer: The Social Worker's Role. Available to all social workers and offering two continuing education credits upon completion, the course reviews basic aspects of cancer, including the different types, treatments, treatment effects, pain management and palliative care, pediatric and adult cancers, survivorship, and end-of-life care. In 2007, the NASW and Cancer*Care* created a second online course, Understanding Cancer Caregiving: The Social Worker's Role, for social workers and other professionals who work with cancer caregivers. Almost 12,000 social workers in 80 countries have taken the two courses.

Realizing the need for more comprehensive training on counseling and psychosocial services for individuals affected by cancer, the NASW, Cancer*Care*, and the American Psychosocial Oncology Society (APOS) partnered in 2005 to create a face-to-face training for social workers using a psychosocial oncology curriculum entitled Counseling Individuals and Their Loved Ones Affected by Cancer: A Strengths-Based Perspective.

HelpStartsHere

The NASW's consumer website (http://www.HelpStartsHere.org) provides visitors with information on four key areas of social work practice: aging, children and family services, mental health, and health. The website provides individuals and families with timely and useful information and offers coping resources. Social workers in multiple disciplines—including oncology—contribute materials to the site. In addition to cancer-related articles for survivors and family members, the site contains a patient education version of the Understanding Cancer course, geared to persons living with cancer and their caregivers.

Partnership With the NCCS and ONS: Oncology-Focused Train-the-Trainer Workshops

First used in the NASW's Spectrum Project for social work HIV/AIDS education, "train the trainer" develops a cadre of local and regional practitioners equipped to train their colleagues in a particular intervention and has become a reliable and cost-effective skills-building vehicle for expanding the reach of social work continuing education in many subject areas (NASW, 2009). The NASW employed this model in a partnership with the NCCS and the ONS, and in 2010, the three organizations hosted a train-the-trainer workshop on promoting use of the Cancer Survival Toolbox with cancer survivors and their families. Through a competitive application process, the organizations selected 10 nurses and 10 social workers, representing 20 states, to attend a training led by experts from each discipline. Each trainee made a commitment to training 20 colleagues in the following year, during which they received ongoing follow-up and support from the trainers and organizational staff.

In response to national concerns about low adherence rates for oral cancer agents, the NASW, NCCS, ONS, and an additional partner—the AOSW—collaborated in a train-the-trainer workshop devoted to promoting oral chemotherapy adherence. This workshop was open to three-person teams composed of a social worker, nurse, and pharmacist. Twenty teams representing hospitals, cancer centers, and rural health clinics attended the 1½-day workshop, which featured scientific information on oral agents and discussion and role-playing on multidisciplinary approaches to promoting adherence and motivational interviewing techniques.

C-Change—Partnership to Advance Cancer Patient Navigation

The concept of patient navigation was developed over 25 years ago by Harold Freeman, then a surgical oncologist at Harlem Hospital in New York City. Freeman found that many patients were presenting with late-stage disease because they were unable to overcome access barriers to cancer care. Patient navigation services, provided by trained lay navigators, were introduced in the early 1990s to ensure access to cancer screening and to reduce delays in cancer diagnoses, which particularly affect poor and underserved populations (Newman-Horm, 2005).

In an effort to increase the availability of community-based patient navigation programs, a Washington-based cancer coalition, C-Change: Collaborating to Conquer Cancer, contracted with the NASW to develop a cancer patient navigation promotional toolkit. The project contains a professionally developed training video plus an online resource kit with curricular materials.

With cancer patient navigation programs opening around the country, the NASW's involvement in the toolkit project helped ensure that the information, training, and supervision provided to trainees was skill based and grounded in social work theory. Under the NASW's direction, the toolkit also illuminated the difference between peer navigation, usually offered by peer volunteers drawn from the community, and professional navigation offered by oncology social workers, oncology nurses, and case managers. The Cancer Patient Navigation Toolkit: A Guide to Community Navigation was released in 2008 and is available on the C-Change website (http://www.cancerpatientnavigation.org).

Children's Cause—Partnership to Advance Pediatric Cancer Education

In 2004, the NASW and the Children's Cause for Cancer Advocacy created an educational tool, Childhood Cancer Survivorship: An Overview for Social Workers. This tool teaches social workers about the unique needs of these medically vulnerable children and adolescents and offers concrete strategies for assisting childhood cancer survivors in managing the long-term effects of survivorship. The tool is available free of change on the NASW website (http://www.socialworkers.org/practice/health/cancerflyer0206.pdf).

Social Workers Across Nations—Capacity Building in Oncology and Palliative Care Social Work

The NASW Foundation sponsors an international initiative to foster capacity building for the social work profession. Social Workers Across Nations (SWAN) is the NASW vehicle for promoting and expanding social work internationally. In 2008, Hungary was identified as an initial site for an oncology social work education project.

Hungary has one of the highest cancer mortality rates in the world, yet the country has very few oncology social workers (Berrino et al., 2007). Having identified a funder with particular interest in cancer in Eastern Europe, Cancer*Care* and the NASW wrote a joint proposal and were awarded funds to conduct an educational project for an exchange of best practices in psychosocial oncology between the United States and Hungary. A multidisciplinary summit was the cornerstone of the project, which would also serve as an opportunity for capacity building under the SWAN international initiative.

NASW staff began by working with U.S. social work practitioner and Fulbright Award recipient Ellen Csikai, who was teaching in Budapest for a year. She had a contact at the University of Debrecen in Nyiregyhaza, which was just beginning a program in health social work. The university expressed great interest in the project and in hosting the summit.

A summit planning committee was formed, including six U.S. social workers with expertise in oncology and a team of Hungarian oncology social workers and other psychosocial oncology professionals. Together they planned a 2-day international summit and identified the participant list. Crucial grant funding was included for participant travel expenses; without such funding, most individuals would have been unable to attend.

The goals of the 2008 summit were to exchange best practice information and identify strategies to improve psychosocial oncology care throughout Hungary, as well as for Hungarian immigrants in the United States. Supported by keynote presentations, workshops, and consensus development activities, summit participants selected 10 imperatives, based on greatest need, to improve psychosocial oncology care. The summit was webcast and archived in both English and Hungarian (http://www.socialworkers.org/practice/intl/hungary2008/default.asp). In addition, the original grant funding included seed grants for helping social workers in Hungary achieve the imperatives. This partnership with Hungarian social workers was an important and successful initiative in capacity building, cultural awareness, and advocacy.

Sub-Saharan Africa

Established in 1999, the Foundation for Hospices in Sub-Saharan Africa (FHSSA) was created to build capacity for comprehensive, compassionate palliative and hospice care by connecting organizations in the United States and Sub-Saharan Africa through a partnership program. Hospice programs from the United States provide resources for hospices in 15 African countries. In 2014, based on this proven model of partnership, the program was renamed Global Partners in Care and expanded to countries outside of Africa (Global Partners in Care, 2014a).

Bernice Harper, the pioneering social worker in health and end-of-life care previously mentioned, was one of the founders of FHSSA. Selected as its first president, Harper remains on the board of directors for Global Partners in Care. In 2011, the nursing community developed an endowment to train palliative care nurses within the African Palliative Care Association. Since palliative care social workers are also in short supply in most parts of Africa, a similar fund for social work training seemed appropriate (African Palliative Care Association, 2012).

The NASW Foundation and its SWAN program established such an endowment and named it in honor of Harper. To achieve this goal, NASW partnered with Global Partners in Care, which is housed within the National Hospice Foundation. With generous financial support from social workers, the two foundations were able to raise sufficient funds to make the endowment a reality and to honor Harper's lifetime work (Global Partners in Care, 2014b).

Code of Ethics and Credentials: NASW Hallmarks That Support Oncology Social Work Practice

NASW Code of Ethics

The values of the social work profession are clearly articulated in the mission of the *Code of Ethics of the National Association of Social Workers* (2008). In recent years, ethics has emerged as an area of increased attention and significance in the social work profession. Contemporary social, professional, technological, and other developments have introduced new ethical considerations. Today's social realities have complicated and, in some instances, changed the delivery of social work services in virtually all practice settings, including oncology. The NASW *Code of Ethics* remains the most comprehensive guide addressing the values, principles, and standards that direct the professional conduct of all social work practitioners. Indeed, the updated

AOSW *Standards of Practice in Oncology Social Work* (2012) indicate that all oncology social workers will promote professional practice in accordance with the NASW *Code of Ethics.*

NASW Credentials

The NASW Specialty Certification Program helps social workers attain enhanced professional and public recognition and increased visibility. Possessing a social work credential signals to employers and the public that a social worker has met high national standards for practice and has demonstrated knowledge and experience beyond the entry level of the profession. Three credentials in particular support social workers who work with oncology patients and their families: Certified Social Worker in Health Care (C-SWHC) certification, Advanced Certified Hospice and Palliative Social Worker (ACHP-SW), and Certified Hospice and Palliative Care Social Worker (CHP-SW; http://socialworkers.org/credentials/list.asp).

Advocacy in Support of Oncology Social Work Practice and Quality Cancer Care

The NASW's advocacy in support of oncology social work practice and quality cancer care seeks to reduce cancer health disparities; improve quality of care and increase access to psychosocial services; support cancer prevention measures; fund psychosocial research; and support education and training of social workers, including those practicing in oncology settings. The NASW also works to ensure that the role of professional social workers is acknowledged, protected, and supported in federal legislation.

Coalition activity is important in the NASW's advocacy activities. Recognizing the growing importance of patient navigation in cancer care, the NASW partnered in 2010 with the AOSW and ONS in developing a joint position paper on the role of oncology nursing and oncology social work in patient navigation. The paper offers policy guidance in the emerging field of patient navigation and clearly delineates the role of nurses and professional social workers in this care model (ONS, AOSW, & NASW, 2010).

The NASW has championed federal advocacy in support of oncology social work practice and quality cancer care, including the Comprehensive Cancer Care Improvement bill (H.R.3705; S.2097) and the Conquer Childhood Cancer bill (H.R.4927; S.2393). The NASW was an early and consistent supporter of the Patient Protection and Affordable Care Act (PPACA) of 2010. The PPACA represents the most significant national advancement in health policy since the 1965 establishment of Medicaid and Medicare and is also a victory for cancer survivors and oncology social workers. The legislation eliminates barriers often faced by cancer survivors, including annual and lifetime limits on health insurance expenditures and preexisting condition exclusions. Through the PPACA, 30 million previously uninsured people—including many with cancer—will receive coverage through the development of state health insurance exchanges and a national expansion of the Medicaid program. The PPACA also established the Prevention and Public Health Fund to pay for obesity prevention, tobacco cessation, cancer screenings, and other critical cancer prevention programs (PPACA, 2010).

Pearls

- The need for oncology social workers has never been greater.
- Social workers are excellent advocates at all levels from client advocacy to national policy.

Pitfalls

- Oncology social workers must be adaptable to new roles and practice settings.
- Staying current with the rapid transformation of cancer treatment and care is essential.

When the NASW was formed by a merger of seven predecessor social work organizations in 1955 (Clark, 2008), the new organization agreed to carry out three major responsibilities:

- Strengthen and unify the profession.
- Promote the development of social work practice.
- Advance sound social policies.

The importance of these responsibilities has never changed, and they remain in today's mission statement of the NASW *Code of Ethics* (2008). As such, social work practice is broadly interpreted. It spans all practice settings, all social work methodologies and interventions, and all levels of practice from micro to macro, and it continues to address emerging areas.

Since its inception, the NASW has consistently supported the practice area of health social work. It has established standards and advanced practice credentials in health, palliative, and end-of-life care; maintained a specialty practice section in health and a health-focused journal; and advocated for health issues of importance to our profession and the client populations.

Over the past decade, the association has placed particular focus and emphasis on several health care areas: HIV/AIDS, genetics, hospice and palliative care, aging, and oncology. Numerous initiatives have been undertaken, and almost all of them have been done in collaboration with groups such as the Genetics Alliance, National Coalition for Cancer Survivorship, National Hospice and Palliative Care Organization, Case Management Society of America, and Association of Oncology Social Work. The NASW has been pleased to work with groups like these to expand social work practice in important areas.

As noted in the *NASW Standards for Continuing Professional Education* (NASW, 2003, p. 1): "By consistent participation in educational opportunities beyond the basic, entry-level professional degree, social workers are able to maintain and increase their proficiency in service delivery. New knowledge is acquired, skills are refined, professional attitudes are reinforced, and individual lives are changed."

REFERENCES

Abrams, R. D. (1966). The patient with cancer: His changing pattern of communication. *New England Journal of Medicine, 272*, 317–322.

Abrams, R. D. (1974). *Not alone with cancer: A guide for those who care.* Springfield, IL: C. C. Thomas.

African Palliative Care Association. (2012). *African palliative care scholarship fund for social workers involved in palliative care: An APCA/FHSSA partnership2012.* Retrieved from http://africanpalliativecare.org/index.php?option=com_content&view=article&id=167:apcafhssa-social-work-scholarship-scheme&catid=8:frank&Itemid=221

Association of Oncology Social Work. (2012). *AOSW standards of practice in oncology social work.* Retrieved from http://www.aosw.org/iMIS201/AOSWMain/professionals/standards-of-practice/AOSWMain/Professional-Development/standards-of-practice.aspx?hkey=51fda308-28bd-48b0-8a75-a17d01251b5e

Berrino, F., De Angelis, R., Sant, M., Rosso, S., Lasota, M. B., Coebergh, J. W., ... EUROCARE Working Group. (2007). Survival for eight major cancers and all cancers combined for European adults diagnosed in 1995–99; results of the EUROCARE-4 study. *The Lancet Oncology, 8*(9), 773–783.

Clark, E. J., (2008). National Association of Social Workers. In T. Mizrahi & L. E. Davis (Eds.), *Encyclopedia of social work* (20th ed., Vol. 3, pp. 292–295). New York, NY: Oxford University Press and NASW Press.

Clark, E. J., & Stovall, E. S. (1996). Advocacy: The cornerstone of cancer survivorship. *Cancer Practice, 4*(5), 239–244.

Curran, J. A., & Cockerill, E. (1948). *Widening horizons in medical education: A study of the teaching of social and environmental factors in medicine. 1945–1946.* New York, NY: The Commonwealth Fund.

Global Partners in Care. (2014a). About us. Retrieved from http://www.globalpartnersincare.org/about-us

Global Partners in Care. (2014b). African Palliative Care Social Work Scholarship Fund—in honor of Bernice Catherine Harper. Retrieved from http://www.globalpartnersincare.org/education-0/scholarships

Harper, B. C. (1975). Social aspects of cancer recovery. *Cancer, 3*(1), 1–2.

Harper, B. C. (1977/1994). *Death: The coping mechanisms of the health professional.* Greenville, SC: Southeastern University Press and Swiger Associates.

National Association of Social Workers. (2003). *NASW standards for continuing professional education.* Washington, DC: Author.

National Association of Social Workers. (2008). *Code of ethics of the National Association of Social Workers.* Washington, DC: Author.

National Association of Social Workers. (2009). HIV/AIDS spectrum: Mental health training and education of social workers project overview. Retrieved from http://www.naswdc.org/practice/hiv_aids/siteInfo/overview.asp

National Coalition for Cancer Survivorship. (2007). Hematologic cancers strategies for education and outreach—2007. Retrieved from http://www.canceradvocacy.org/about-us/what-weve-done/

Newman-Horm, P. A. (2005). *Cancer patient navigation.* Washington, DC: C-Change: Coming Together to Conquer Cancer.

Oncology Nursing Society (ONS), Association of Oncology Social Work (AOSW), & National Association of Social Workers (NASW). (2010). Joint position on the role of oncology nursing and oncology social work in patient navigation. Retrieved from http://www.socialworkers.org/pressroom/2010/Position%20on%20Patient%20Navigation%20BW.pdf

Patient Protection and Affordable Care Act, Pub. L. No. 111-148 §2702, 124 Stat. 119, 318–319 (2010).

World Health Organization. (2008, December 9). Cancer to be top killer by 2010: WHO. Retrieved from http://usatoday30.usatoday.com/news/health/2008-12-09-cancer_N.htm

XIX

Building Resilience in Interprofessional Practice

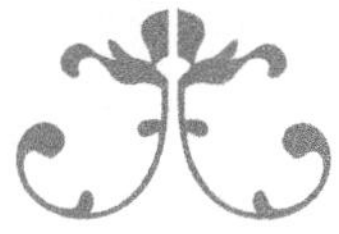

Penny Damaskos

Over the years, much research has examined the risk factors inherent in oncology care that contribute to staff burnout and compassion fatigue. Although each section in this textbook provides evidence of the extensive contributions oncology social workers make to patient care, "Building Resilience in Interprofessional Practice" is the only section specifically dedicated to the emotional well-being of oncology social workers and their colleagues. Every chapter within it provides innovative perspectives and programs to address relief for burnout and compassion fatigue ultimately aimed to enhance professional and team competence. Recommendations for system-wide education and support initiatives, strengthening interprofessional collaboration, increasing communication among team members, work–life balance, and respite opportunities that allow for time away from the intensity of the work make up the chapters' themes. Early efforts to identify the efficacy of interdisciplinary programs, such as numbers of staff attending, participant comments, and levels of compassion fatigue and burnout, are addressed in each chapter.

In "Building Resilience: A Multifaceted Support Program for Professional and Support Staff in a Cancer Center," Jane Bowling and Penny Damaskos outline a multifaceted program to address compassion fatigue and burnout in staff at a large cancer center. This social work–led program combines an arts-based, general lecture series designed to provide respite using smaller, targeted support groups for specific staff needs. Through the process of interviewing staff members for these programs, the social work leaders describe their growing awareness of the need to focus on positive coping strategies and building resilience, in addition to becoming aware of compassion fatigue and burnout. This chapter illustrates several approaches to address burnout across a large, eclectic staff, including support and allied health services personnel, whose exposure to ongoing stressors is rarely acknowledged.

In "How Oncology Professionals Manage the Emotional Intensity of Their Work," Elizabeth A. Rohan provides a series of coping strategies to better manage the intensity of working in oncology. Examples of individual stress management, such as journaling or changing a work schedule, can create room for work–life balance and new points of engagement with clinical work. This chapter emphasizes the rewards that come from working in this field, such as making meaning and the profound intimacy that contributes to a broader perspective on life for the clinician.

In "Developing Core Competencies for Interprofessional Teams: A Script-Reading Approach," Patricia McGillicuddy, Karen Gold, and Mandy Lowe describe innovative, educational programs that promote interprofessional collaboration while developing core competencies. With scripted patient narratives, staff reflect on their content to better understand the patient's experiences and their own reactions. This approach promotes the expression of shared team values using a framework that strengthens the core competencies while building a foundation to create a significant relational approach not only to one another and the team but also to patients.

In "Schwartz Center Rounds®: Process, Outcomes, and Opportunities for Improving Interprofessional Practice," Margaret S. Wool provides an overview of the structure and impact that the Rounds can provide to an interdisciplinary oncology staff. Schwartz Center Rounds provide a public forum in which all staff can discuss the complexities of a case from multiple perspectives but, unlike the traditional case conference, in a nondidactic approach. The emphasis is on the impact and meaning of the case through emotional expression by all staff. This chapter emphasizes the valuable contributions social workers provide to enhance self-reflection and self-awareness while connecting team members to the patient experience.

In "Maintaining Competent Teams in Pediatric Oncology," Sima Zadeh, Jayne Phillips, Jeasmine E. Aizvera, and Lori Wiener focus on the unique characteristics that contribute to social work in pediatric oncology. This chapter provides a comprehensive series of approaches to building competent interdisciplinary teams that can support the highest quality of empathic and connected care to patients and families while reducing compassion fatigue and burnout among individual team members. They emphasize team flexibility in understanding and problem solving around the psychological, social, and familial challenges confronted in pediatric oncology. However, leaders are cautioned to be vigilant to maintain an environment of open communication that requires ongoing assessment of appropriate boundaries and considers new ideas and resources from outside the team, as well as from its own members. Oncology social workers have the substantive psychological, communication, and relational skills to take leadership in implementing suggested interventions that can maintain competent team functioning in this most intense work environment.

104

Jane Bowling and Penny Damaskos

Building Resilience: A Multifaceted Support Program for Professional and Support Staff in a Cancer Center

When individuals bring their traumatic stories to a caregiver a "radiating distress" can pass over onto another human being and may impact them through a process of secondary traumatization. When this occurs, the caregiver is no longer able to function effectively due to the overwhelming nature of compassion fatigue.

—Gentry, Baranowsky, and Dunning (2002, p. 124)

Key Concepts

- *Developing a hospital-wide staff support program should include tailored programming to manage stress for all oncology staff professionals, including administrative, unit-specific, service, and allied health professional staff.*
- *Moving to a focus on building resilience skills and capacities, rather than only addressing compassion fatigue and stress, more accurately characterizes staff experiences in the oncology environment.*
- *Developing an arts-based respite program for all staff is widely supported.*
- *Using opportunities for collaboration with other disciplines and existing resources is essential to sustain support programs.*
- *Identifying opportunities for community resources when developing a staff support program is important.*

It is well known that oncology settings are stressful and that staff are at risk for compassion fatigue and burnout. Therefore, staff support is essential to maintaining high-quality patient care. There is also a need to concentrate on the growing importance of recruitment and retention of all oncology staff, and thus, closer attention to staff resilience is essential (Graham & Ramirez, 2002; Peteet et al., 1989; Rohan & Bausch, 2009). This chapter describes the development of an institution-wide program designed to address this aspect of staff support and training.

Compassion Fatigue and Burnout

Often used interchangeably, the terms *compassion fatigue* and *burnout* have different qualities. Compassion fatigue is defined as an overexposure to suffering and pain that can cause personal stress and a reduced ability to be empathic. For professional caregivers, this stress occurs from a wish to relieve another person's suffering (Figley, 1995), but when work or personal stressors exceed the ability to cope, it results in psychological or physical symptoms such as frustration, irritability, tension, sad feelings, anger, withdrawal, numbness, and emotional detachment. In addition, there are physical manifestations of compassion fatigue, including fatigue, insomnia, headaches, backaches, appetite changes, and gastrointestinal disturbances, that can disrupt an individual's ability to function at work and in his or her personal life.

Burnout is defined as job-related stress with individuals feeling overworked and underpaid and dealing with workloads that exceed available resources. Inadequate staffing and conflicts between administrative and clinical responsibilities, along with conflicting time demands, also contribute to burnout (Gentry et al., 2002). Characterized by persistent exhaustion, increased absences and sickness, a sense of inability to accomplish tasks, a loss of interest in or motivation to work, reduced sense of personal accomplishment, and a general feeling of being overwhelmed (Maslach, Schaufeli, & Leiter, 2001; Simon, Pryce, Roff, & Klemmack, 2005), burnout refers to our reaction to our work environment. Conversely, compassion fatigue is grounded in the reaction to our clinical experiences (Figley, 1995; Maslach et al., 2001; Simon et al., 2005).

Presenting Problem

Social work administrative staff at Memorial Sloan-Kettering Cancer Center (MSKCC) observed increasing compassion fatigue and burnout in the social work department staff, as evidenced at the end of the workday when staff would stop by the central social work office appearing to be emotionally drained. When questioned about their day, the social workers' responses were usually about a patient or family situation that caused them to feel lingering distress. The social work supervisory staff thought some of the stress may have also been related to work conditions, specifically during significant patient and family transitions. Social workers were no longer expected to plan and implement patient discharges, but instead, solely to provide counseling and psychological support. It was anticipated that this transition might increase staff stress because social workers would now be intensely involved with the "radiating distress" of patients and families. Paradoxically, with the increased focus on the clinical counseling function, the staff no longer had relief through the structure of concrete services involved in discharge planning. Though social workers reported personal stress with this transition, they were also able to focus more on programmatic approaches to patient, family, and staff support that evolved over time.

Forming a Work Group

In 2006, five social workers demonstrating an interest in the issue of compassion fatigue for themselves and their colleagues formed a work group to address these issues. An outside consultant—a retired leader who had been a member of the department—was brought in to lead the group, which was charged with developing a proposal for an institution-wide program on compassion fatigue and burnout by the director and hospital administration. They met on a biweekly basis over lunch, reviewing literature and institutional resources. The group soon evolved into a forum for discussion about compassion fatigue related to the provision of psychosocial care. Charged with providing recommendations for an institutional program, the group in the beginning phase focused on existing concepts and programs that might inform their thinking. As the group continued to work together, they noticed that they became more comfortable revealing their own compassion fatigue experiences, including its negative effects on their functioning. They experienced relief in recognizing compassion fatigue as a shared experience.

Identifying Existing Institutional Resources

The group realized that within the institution, an informal structure already existed to address staff stress. For many years, clinical social work staff were asked to facilitate nursing and house staff support groups and provide impromptu individual sessions with interdisciplinary staff. The group identified less familiar support resources, including employee assistance program (EAP) workshops and other employee wellness activities. However, there was no formal institution-wide program designed to address staff stress.

Literature Review

In reviewing the literature, the group found that many medical settings reported that staff had a loss of interest in job responsibilities and an increase in sick leave, early termination, retention issues, low morale, and key people leaving institutions (Keidel, 2002; Schwarm, 1998). The group also found articles reporting staff having intrusive thoughts and images of another's traumatic experience, difficulty separating work from personal life, lowered frustration tolerance, and increased outbursts of anger and rage. In addition, there were reports of dread of working with certain individuals who had difficult responses or with whom staff had marked transference/countertransferential experiences. Difficult patient responses included depression, perceptive disturbances (seeing the world in terms of victims and perpetrators), ineffective and self-destructive behaviors, hypervigilance, diminished sense of purpose, and loss of hope (Gentry et al., 2002).

Work Group Recommendations

The work group made several recommendations:

- Create an institution-wide compassion fatigue program. Components of this program would include a consistent format to educate nursing staff on issues, such as the impact of working with patients with serious and potentially life-threatening illness, gaining insights into one's own responses and reactions and those of coworkers, and practicing ways of coping and managing a range of emotions.
- Develop an interdisciplinary planning committee. This committee would be composed of staff from all major clinical areas: nursing, psychiatry, social work, employee health and wellness, integrative medicine, chaplaincy, EAP, and human resources. This larger

institution-planning committee was charged with defining the rationale for this program utilizing a strengths-based perspective.

- Define goals and objectives for an institution-wide program, initially called the Compassion Fatigue Initiative, and evaluate the benefits of integrating this proposal into a quality assurance activity, partnering with an established employee health and wellness program. This program had a shared goal of staff well-being and a mission compatible with the Compassion Fatigue Initiative.

The Compassion Fatigue Initiative

With the goal of spreading the word about the Compassion Fatigue Initiative, an inaugural panel presentation included speakers from psychiatry, social work, nursing, and psychology. The presentations defined compassion fatigue and burnout and offered personal reflections by the presenters that gave a comprehensive overview of the issues facing staff. The more than 100 attendees provided evidence of how the topic resonated with staff, and evaluation feedback was overwhelmingly positive. The panel presentations were then placed on the institution's Quality of Care website and intranet for future viewing in an effort to disseminate the information to the entire institution.

The interdisciplinary planning committee recommended use of a professional quality-of-life scale, the Professional Quality of Life Scale, Revision 5 (ProQol R-5), to measure compassion fatigue and burnout among staff and to inquire about compassion satisfaction. The ProQol R-5 consists of 30 items with both reliability and validity for health workers of all disciplines and administrators. It is widely applicable to all staff populations (Stamm, 2002). Reviewing some sample statements from the ProQol R-5 illustrates its wide application (accessible for download at http://www.proqol.org/uploads/ProQOL_5_English.pdf):

> I get satisfaction from being able to help people.
> I am losing sleep over traumatic experiences of a person I helped.
> I feel overwhelmed by the size of my caseload and amount of work.
> I am preoccupied by more than one person I help. (Stamm, 2002)

Compassion Fatigue and Burnout Assessment of Staff of All Areas

Following the inaugural panel, the ProQol R-5 was shared at a staff health fair attended by a cross-section of employees. The self-scored ProQol R-5 was distributed to 167 staff spanning all areas of the institution; participation was entirely voluntary. The finding revealed that 44% of staff reported above-average scores for compassion fatigue and 62% reported high levels of compassion satisfaction. This illustrated that, although staff were experiencing compassion fatigue, they also had high levels of compassion satisfaction, which related to their ability to be effective caregivers. Approximately 10% of staff experienced low compassion satisfaction and high rates of compassion fatigue. These findings suggested that the work environment contains factors that create both high levels of stress and satisfaction from the work but there was a small percentage of staff potentially at risk for compassion fatigue (1.6%) and in need of support. Following an on-site review of results at the health fair, respondents were not only provided with their scores but also given resources and referrals to the EAP for counseling and to employee health and wellness for other stress reduction modalities.

Implementation of a Unit-Based Staff Support Project

Following the assessments, members of the Compassion Fatigue Initiative implemented a unit-based support project for nurses to be co-led by social workers and nurses. The goal was to determine levels of compassion fatigue in a smaller, more focused population and provide education and support. The program consisted of six weekly group sessions on topics such as coping with critical events and traumatic stress, death and dying, work–life balance, managing the challenging patient, self-care, and compassion satisfaction. In the topic-driven groups, candid discussion focused on feelings related to both clinical work and administrative issues. Comments exemplified the complex stressors that participants experienced in their work, including "unrealistic expectations on the part of the physicians," "constant exposure to the suffering of fellow human beings," systems shortcomings (such as patients having to wait for a procedure and staff not being able to do anything about it), and feelings of helplessness when talking to patients. The ProQol R-5 was given to the participants both before and after the 6-week group. Eight nurses participated and 65 unit staff completed the survey. Results suggested that although the unit staff experienced high levels of compassion fatigue and compassion satisfaction, there was also high exposure to stressful events. Group participants indicated that they experienced meaningful reward by providing care to people at such a critical time in their lives. Similar to the results from the employee health fair, which was a random sample from many disciplines, this group of nursing staff seemed to cope well as they discussed the effects of compassion fatigue and burnout.

From Compassion Fatigue to Building Resilience

Given these findings, the program's emphasis began to shift from burnout and compassion fatigue to including a more strengths-based concept of "resilience." This change in approach to staff wellness and support was introduced through the literature review and encouraged by research, which suggested that despite loss and trauma, there is greater human resilience than previously understood (Bonanno, 2004). Individuals develop resilience by experiencing and processing stress rather than through avoidance. Resilience as a program model requires an openness to examine those issues that cause individuals to grow, expand, and refocus. A resilient response to stress is not static but fluid (Connor & Davidson, 2003; Wagnild & Young, 1993) and is cultivated when individuals make meaning out of life stressors and incorporate lessons learned about how to live their lives. Resilience occurs through mind, body, and spirit and the development of personal strengths, which reduce vulnerability (Connor & Davidson, 2003; Jackson, Firtko, & Edenborough 2007; Wagnild & Young, 1993).

The Compassion Fatigue Initiative was then integrated into a newly evolving, institution-wide employee health and wellness program named Building Resilience. The Building Resilience Program incorporated all of the compassion fatigue initiative goals and objectives, as well as programmatic efforts to foster resilience. At the same time, a series of hospital-wide events were held, including an introductory lecture on resilience, lectures on sleep and nutrition, a film of staff recollections on their own resilience, and a writing program for staff to express themselves about their work.

Building Resilience Through the Arts: Respite Model

Building Resilience Through the Arts (BRTA) was part of the larger institution-wide Building Resilience Program to provide staff respite from their day-to-day stress through the arts. Conducted at noon and including lunch, the lectures and performances included presentations by museum docents and art historians, dance performances, humor, film, classical and jazz music, and poetry. In addition, some staff, including physicians and administrators, performed and lectured in these programs. The programs averaged 250 attendees per event and were composed of staff from all areas of the hospital. In a period of 2 years, over 1,500 staff attended the various arts programs. Evaluations have yielded consistently high levels of satisfaction and enthusiasm. Participants invited from the community were more than willing to present without fees as an acknowledgment to staff. Because of its popularity, outreach and advertising for these programs was minimal and consequently cost-effective. Staff was notified thorough e-mail, intranet and Internet postings, and word of mouth.

The program's popularity and success was largely due to the "sanctioned" time away from work assignments and allowed attendees to be nourished by something other than their daily work. It was expected that they would return to their assignments refreshed and able to provide better patient care. A few representative comments on evaluations are found later.

Many of the more than 1,500 participants of the BRTA program commented on the aspect of respite and refreshment they experienced from the programs. Over 98% of attendees consistently reported that they experienced respite by attending the programs:

"It really helped me. My stress level dropped completely. Please continue your wonderful work. Thank you so much for doing it."

"This was wonderful. The photography took me away in time and space."

"Thank you so much for doing this. Every time I attend one of your events, I feel so much better after it. Please continue your wonderful work."

Through the smaller unit-based groups described previously, staff reported making changes in their workday to incorporate moments of relaxation and self-care activities. One nurse reported that she changed her commuting routine to incorporate exercise, and another said he made a point of having lunch with colleagues once a week. These small changes represent the positive effects of the group discussion program in raising the level of awareness and self-care. The fact that it is sanctioned by the hospital administration only adds to its impact.

Extending Building Resilience to Support and Allied Health Services

As an adjunct to the institution-wide program, another smaller group-meeting model was implemented targeting support and allied health services departments throughout the institution. The rationale for providing these support services across the institution was that support for nonprofessional and/or allied health professional staff is often overlooked, even though they also experience compassion fatigue and job stressors (Cashavelly et al., 2008).

These groups convened at the request of department or service managers. Two social workers from the building resilience committee met with staff to learn about their unique stressors, complex reactions to patients, and feelings of pride and vulnerability. After this preliminary discussion, the cofacilitators formed a group to address their particular needs. Issues addressed in these groups included managing complicated patient situations, disenfranchised grief and mourning, compassion fatigue, burnout, resilience, difficult conversations with patients, death and dying, self-care and work–life balance, and meaning in work life and life outside of work. In some cases, a series of groups were provided to cover these topics in greater depth, usually conducted jointly with nurses who were working in the inpatient and outpatient settings.

The groups were typically one session in an information and discussion format. In some instances, a film was shown, *In Our Own Words*, containing thoughts and comments from a wide cross-section of staff. The discussion of this film, which was produced by members of the planning committee, centered on impact of the work and the ways in which they manage it daily. After the film, the group facilitator generated a lively discussion between the staff members, followed by a review of some basic self-care concepts. The groups also provided space where members could speak freely about the difficulties and the rewards of their work. In addition, because the groups were held during work hours, the message was clear to group members: this was an important issue supported by the administration.

The departments and services who requested these meetings represented staff from many areas. Most had direct contact with patients and family members. These included housekeeping, security, parking garage attendants, food service workers, research assistants, physician referral service staff, patient representatives, session assistants, physician's office assistants, imaging techs, physical therapists, new nursing trainers, and patient escorts. Through these workshops, it was discovered that there were unique stressors to each area and department. For example, many of the staff developed connections to patients during their tasks. Patient escorts told how they had long-standing relationships with patients and family members only to find that they had progressed or died without notification or follow-up. The importance of allowing the expression of the unique and particular stressors staff encountered was twofold: They felt acknowledged and valued while program facilitators were able to learn more about their exact experiences and therefore better support them.

Through the Building Resilience groups, institution-wide programs (EAP and employee health and wellness) were offered to all staff as additional resources to be utilized after the group or meeting. In 1 year, over 1,000 staff attended stress-reduction programs. However, the primary benefit was the provision of a confidential arena in which attendees could discuss their honest reactions to the experience of their work with staff and facilitators who understood. Many staff said they did not talk with family members and loved ones about their day in an effort to shield them from the evocative nature of their work (Larson, 1993). Through these groups, staff were able to reconnect with their own meanings associated with patient care and with the mission of the hospital.

Lectures Open to All Staff

Lunchtime Lectures

Provide lectures on art, music, and poetry
Respite focused

General Information

Didactic focus
Topics including burnout, compassion fatigue, resilience, stress management, nutrition, weight, exercise

Groups

One-Time Group
Targeted groups taking place once or twice
Staff support response team to respond to staff emergencies throughout institution
Service/area specific: for example, breast service, urgent care center
Staff specific: focus on a specific group of staff such as nurses, physical therapists, nutritionists, patient escorts, security, and so forth

Ongoing Groups

Specific floors/units/areas facilitated by social work
Nurses only
All staff
Closed, time-limited groups for cohesive populations: nurses, nursing assistants, facilities management, housekeeping

Pearls

- Staff support programs provide positive branding of social work skills to the hospital at large.
- To develop a hospital-wide resilience-building program, the planning needs to be hospital wide and interdisciplinary.
- Developing data about the reality of exposure to stress, its impact on staff, and the helpfulness of interventions increases administrative support for programs.
- Integration of the new program into existing departments and related programs such as employee health and wellness establishes program credibility and increases possibility of continuance.
- Engaging hospital administration from the beginning is essential.

Pitfalls

- Failure to engage hospital administration and medical staff for support and inclusion limits the possibility of effectively engaging staff.
- Focusing only on the stresses (compassion fatigue and burnout) without also exploring strategies for positive coping and self-care (resilience) fails to accurately address the experience of caregiving in oncology.
- Keeping the program only within the social work department limits the possibility of important interdisciplinary collaborations.

The initial development of the staff support program was driven by the social work line staff. Daily contact with patients and the subsequent radiating distress had an impact on them and others. Their recommendations to include all hospital-wide departments in the planning committee and subsequent support programs engaged key support from hospital leadership, including the physician-in-chief and medical and administrative department heads. The interest shown by the number of staff who attended the programs underscored the need and interest of all employees.

The first lesson learned was to secure administrative support for the program. Second, the Building Resilience committee members collected statistics about program satisfaction, evaluated the program, and kept records of activities. This data helped obtain additional funding. The third lesson was that the program was perfectly poised to partner with employee health and wellness and grew into a two-pronged program of local and institution-wide interventions. This model can be replicated in other organizations using existing resources and interdisciplinary collaboration at all levels from line staff to administration. Maintaining high-quality oncology care requires programmatic support to address compassion fatigue and burnout experienced by staff confronted with life-threatening conditions and facilitating resilience-building approaches and activities. Social work knowledge, values, and skills are ideally suited to lead the development of staff support programs, which in turn provide positive branding of the social work role capacities in this critical area.

REFERENCES

Bonanno, G. A. (2004). Loss, trauma, and human resilience: Have we underestimated the human capacity to thrive after extremely adverse events? *American Psychologist*, *59*, 20–28.

Cashavelly, B. J., Donelan, K., Binda, K. D., Mailhot, J. R., Clair-Hayes, K. A., & Maramaldi, P. (2008). The forgotten team member: Meeting the needs of the oncology support staff. *The Oncologist*, *13*, 530–538.

Connor, K. M., & Davidson, J. R. (2003). Development of a new resilience scale: The Connor-Davidson resilience scale (CD-RISC). *Depression and Anxiety*, *18*(2), 76–82.

Figley, C. R. (1995). Compassion fatigue as secondary traumatic stress disorder: An overview. In C. Figley (Ed.), *Compassion fatigue: Coping with secondary traumatic stress disorder in those who treat the traumatized* (pp. 1–20). New York, NY: Brunner-Routledge.

Gentry, J. E., Baranowsky, A. B., & Dunning, K. (2002). ARP: The accelerated recovery program (ARP) for compassion fatigue. In C. R. Figley (Ed.), *Treating compassion fatigue* (pp. 123–137). New York, NY: Brunner-Routledge.

Graham, J., & Ramirez, A. (2002). Improving the working lives of cancer clinicians. *European Journal of Cancer Care*, *11*, 188.

Jackson, D., Firtko, A., & Edenborough, M. (2007). Personal resilience as a strategy for surviving and thriving in the face of workplace adversity: A literature review. *Journal of Advanced Nursing*, *60*(1), 1.

Keidel, G. C. (2002). Burnout and compassion fatigue among hospice caregivers. *American Journal of Hospice and Palliative Medicine*, *19*(3), 200.

Larson, D. G. (1993). Self-concealment: Implications for stress and empathy in oncology care. *Journal of Psychosocial Oncology*, *11*(4), 1–16.

Maslach, C., Schaufeli, W. B., & Leiter, M. P. (2001). Job burnout. *Annual Review of Psychology*, *52*, 379–422.

Peteet, J. R., Murray-Ross, D., Medeiros, C., Walsh-Burke, K., Rieker, P., & Finkelstein, D. (1989). Job satisfaction and satisfaction among the staff members at a cancer center. *Cancer*, *64*, 975–982.

Rohan, E., & Bausch, J. (2009). Climbing Everest: Oncology work as an expedition in caring. *Journal of Psychosocial Oncology*, *27*(1), 84–118.

Schwarm, K. (1998). The phenomenon of compassion fatigue in perioperative nursing. *AORN Journal*, *68*(4), 642.

Simon, C., Pryce, J., Roff, L., & Klemmack, D. (2005). Secondary traumatic stress and oncology social work: Protecting compassion from fatigue and compromising the worker's worldview. *Journal of Psychosocial Oncology*, *23*(4), 1–14.

Stamm, B. H. (2002). Measuring compassion satisfaction as well as fatigue: Developmental history of the compassion satisfaction and fatigue test. In C. Figley (Ed.), *Treating compassion fatigue* (pp. 107–119). New York, NY: Brunner-Routledge.

Wagnild, G. M., & Young, H. M. (1993). Development and psychometric evaluation of the resilience scale. *Journal of Nursing Measurement*, *1*(2), 165.

105 Elizabeth A. Rohan

How Oncology Professionals Manage the Emotional Intensity of Their Work

Key Concepts

- *Although literature posits that oncology health care clinicians are at risk for compassion fatigue, empirical studies have not necessarily supported this assertion.*
- *Many oncology clinicians have had transient traumatic responses to their work; this is a potential deleterious effect of the emotional intensity involved.*
- *Oncology clinicians use a variety of coping strategies, both individually and with the support of other team members, to manage the emotional intensity of their work.*
- *Many oncology clinicians experience a high degree of satisfaction with their work, particularly through patient relationships.*
- *Oncology clinicians often vicariously gain the wisdom and perspective their patients have learned through their experiences facing a life-threatening illness.*

Working in oncology is inherently emotionally intense. Oncology clinicians, to a degree commensurate with their professional role and the population they serve, may repeatedly witness loss, dying, and death; see physical disfigurement and deterioration; tolerate another's physical and emotional pain; negotiate intense emotional relationships with cancer patients and their families; contend with their own feelings of helplessness; and confront their own mortality and that of loved ones (Rohan, 2009; Rohan & Bausch, 2009; Stearns, 2001). Indeed, oncology professionals have described their work as laborious, heavy, intense, time-consuming, hard, and exhausting (Rohan, 2009; Rohan & Bausch, 2009).

Emotional Intensity of Oncology Work

"It's very time-consuming to do this work. I look at friends who did other things; they don't work this hard. . . . It's very time-consuming. . . . It's relentless, right? . . . I think this is intense, laborious, lengthy work. You know, it's hard."

—Oncology physician

"I know in my group that eighty-plus percent of these people are going to die, and that's an incredible number of patients."

—Oncology nurse

"You're a little further in emotionally than you would be doing other types of work because it's so intense for the family. You're in an intense time and you're drawn in and let in [to their lives] in a way that maybe you wouldn't be [otherwise]."

—Oncology social worker

Excerpted with permission from Rohan (2009, p. 89).

Oncology social workers are the primary professionals in the health care setting who have provided psychosocial support and services to cancer patients and their significant others for decades (Abrams, 1974; Association of Oncology Social Work, 2012; Fobair, 2007; Holland, 2002; Institute of Medicine, 2008; Rohan & Bausch, 2009; Stearns, 2001). As such, accrediting bodies have recognized oncology social workers as essential members of the interdisciplinary oncology health care team necessary for comprehensive cancer care (Association of Community Cancer Centers, 2009; Commission on Cancer, 2012). Given the necessity of an oncology team to provide quality cancer care, this chapter will address how members of the oncology team, with a particular focus on social workers, nurses, and physicians, manage the emotional demands of their work so they can continue to help others—in other words, how to help them put on their "own oxygen masks before helping others."

Potential Deleterious Effects of Working in Oncology

Oncology social workers, nurses, and physicians each play a different but important role in helping cancer patients and their families bear the burden of living with this often life-threatening illness. Given the intensity of oncology work, many authors have suggested that oncology social workers, nurses, and physicians are at risk for experiencing burnout and/or compassion fatigue (Kearney, Weininger, Vachon, Harrison, & Mount, 2009; Lyckholm, 2001; Penson, Dignan, Canellos, Picard, & Lynch, 2000; Shanafelt & Dyrbye, 2012). Although some authors use the terms *burnout* and *compassion fatigue* synonymously, there is an important distinction between the two phenomena. On the one hand, burnout is defined as feelings of emotional exhaustion, emotional detachment, and reduced personal efficacy that can result from working in a stressful working environment over time (Graham & Ramirez, 2002; Maslach, Schaufeli, & Leiter, 2001; Rohan, 2009). On the other hand, compassion fatigue relates directly to the emotional content of the work and to the relationship between the clinician and the patient. Compassion fatigue, also known as secondary traumatic stress or vicarious traumatization, is seen as "the cost of caring"—in other words, the predictable consequence of working with people who are suffering, resulting from empathic connection with patients (Figley, 2002; Kearney et al., 2009; Pearlman & Saakvitne, 1999; Stamm, 2002).

Empirical Findings on Compassion Fatigue in Oncology Professionals

Despite the assertions in the literature that oncology clinicians experience compassion fatigue, most empirical studies of compassion fatigue in oncology social workers, nurses, and physicians and the hospice/palliative care workforce have reported that oncology clinicians did not score at or above threshold levels on measures of compassion fatigue or vicarious traumatization (Cunningham, 2003; Dane & Chachkes, 2001; Rohan, 2009; Slocum-Gori, Hemsworth, Chan, Carson, & Kazanjian, 2013).

Aiming to understand a more complete picture of clinicians' experiences of emotionally laden work, Stamm (2002) developed the Professional Quality of Life Scale (ProQoL) that measures compassion fatigue and compassion satisfaction (the positive aspects of working in a helping profession). Using this scale, researchers have found that oncology and hospice/palliative care clinicians were protected from compassion fatigue by their experiences of compassion satisfaction (Rohan, 2009; Slocum-Gori et al., 2013).

Traumatic Responses to Oncology Work

Although oncology clinicians have not been found to experience compassion fatigue or vicarious traumatization in higher numbers than other clinicians, oncology clinicians do sometimes struggle with the emotional demands of their work. Mixed-methods research has found that clinicians who did not score at threshold levels on compassion fatigue or vicarious traumatization scales did describe "traumatic responses" to their work at different points throughout their careers (Rohan, 2009). An oncology nurse described how strain in her marriage had resulted from her reaction to her work: "I used to come [home] every night and just cry about a patient, and my husband couldn't deal with it" (Rohan, 2009, p. 56). Working in oncology can engender worry about one's health or the health of loved ones, but some clinicians have described worry to the point of impaired functioning. One physician explained, "It was during fellowship, and I was working with breast cancer patients. It really interfered with my intimacy with my wife. I was afraid to touch her breasts, fearful that I'd palpate a tumor" (Rohan, 2009, p. 57). Other clinicians recounted having had dreams of dead patients or having dreamed of themselves dying, as this social worker described: "I have dreamed that I've said goodbye to my family as I'm on my deathbed" (Rohan, 2009, p. 57).

Oncology social workers often experience additional emotional demands because of their role in specifically dealing with the emotional aspects of illness. All oncology professionals witness pain, suffering, and death regularly, but it is the primary job of the social worker to help patients and families acknowledge their reactions to illness, incapacity, death, and dying; establish or sustain open communication; and access necessary external resources (Rohan, 2009; Rohan & Bausch, 2009; Stearns, 2001).

Managing the Emotional Intensity of Oncology Work

Given the intense emotional demands of, and potential for, traumatic responses to oncology work, why are these clinicians not found particularly susceptible to compassion fatigue? Part of the answer to this question is adaptive coping. To continue working in oncology over one's career, clinicians find adaptive ways to manage the emotional intensity of their work. Here, it is important to highlight professional differences, because a clinician's training and the culture of his or her profession may influence how he or she manages the emotional demands of oncology work.

Coping Strategies Oncology Professionals Use With Other Team Members	
Strategy	**Quote From Oncology Clinician**
Informal discussions with colleagues	*"[It's helpful] having co-workers being able to listen to what I'm talking about or for them to share with me something.... I don't think that we have that well-structured into our work life here. It's sort of hallway and in-the-doorway stuff more often than not."* *—Oncology social worker*
Interdisciplinary rounds	*"We have Schwartz [Center] Rounds®, which [are] really about helping the caregivers take care of themselves and recognize their own issues to improve the patient's care."* *—Oncology social worker*
Supervision groups	*"I have group supervision ... where we talk about the particular cases, and that's a place to bring some of the [emotional] stuff."* *—Oncology social worker*
Off-color or gallows humor	*"You know with my colleagues ... we have a sick sense of humor. But I think we use humor a lot [to cope]."* *—Oncology nurse*
	"We sort of deal with it ... informally and actually with humor in making what would probably be considered really bad taste jokes ... callous jokes about things ... but it works." *—Oncology physician*
Acknowledging deaths together	*"We have a yearly memorial service for all our patients who've died. All the different staff ... come, and we all read the names of the patients [who have died]."* *—Oncology nurse*
Quotes excerpted with permission from Rohan (2009, pp. 63–66).	

Using Deliberate Coping Strategies

Coping With Team Members

Oncology clinicians use coping strategies both individually and with other team members. Professional differences are particularly evident regarding the use of individual supervision or supervision groups. Specifically, social work training requires, and the culture of the profession encourages, social workers to engage in ongoing clinical supervision where they discuss not only patient care but also the emotional aspects of their work (see Chapter 96). Neither medical training nor the culture of the profession encourages oncology physicians to do the same (Graham & Ramirez, 2002). The experiences of nurses lie somewhere in between: Nurses are mentored early in their careers, but formal clinical supervision is haphazard subsequently (Rohan, 2009). Another professional difference in how oncology professionals cope is that oncology social workers often provide informal support to other members of the health care team who are having difficulty managing their feelings about their work (Rohan, 2009; Rohan & Bausch, 2009; Stearns, 2001). Recognizing the importance of processing the emotional and relational content of oncology work, oncology social workers have helped to institute Schwartz Center Rounds® and initiated other programs (Lynch, 2002; see Chapter 107 in this section) to provide outlets for clinicians to discuss their relationships with patients and explore the emotional, psychological, and existential impacts of the work.

Among many oncology clinicians, there is a sense that people engaged in other professions cannot tolerate hearing the details of their work (Rohan, 2009; Rohan & Bausch, 2009). This notion has two important implications. On the one hand, it may indicate that oncology professionals consider their work special, which may contribute to job satisfaction. On the other hand, oncology clinicians may feel isolated, unable to find others outside of the work environment willing to engage in discussions about what they do. This isolation highlights the opportunity oncology team members have to help each other cope with the emotional demands of the work. The importance of acknowledging the emotional aspects of oncology work with trusted team members cannot be overestimated.

Coping Individually

Clinicians engage in numerous coping strategies, several of which can be characterized as self-care activities aimed at achieving work–life balance. Other approaches clinicians use to manage the emotional intensity of the work are mindful meditation, journaling (see Gallo-Silver & Damaskos, 2004), and developing self-awareness (Kearney et al., 2009; Slocum-Gori et al., 2011).

Coping Strategies Oncology Professionals Use Individually	
Strategy	*Quote From Oncology Clinician*
Exercise and hobbies	*"I exercise regularly, without which I would probably go nuts ... and I like gardening as a hobby.... I enjoy mowing the lawn and pruning and planting and all that stuff."* *—Oncology physician*
Seeking refuge	*"I try to deliberately not [talk about my work at home] because I like being able to separate it and having [my home be] sort of a refuge."* *—Oncology physician*

Spiritual practices and other rituals	*"I light candles for my patients [at my place of worship], and that actually helps quite a bit.... It's not just when they die, but it's a good way of thinking of them, and a way of remembering them."* *—Oncology social worker* *"This is a tradition I have: I ask [family] for a picture. ... Because you have this mental picture [of a sick person near the end of life]. Who wants to remember that? I usually want a picture of them when they were really healthy."* *—Oncology physician*
Adjusting expectations of success	*"I think many people consider success as curing the patient, which is just not feasible, so you have to adjust that .... I consider a success is someone having a dignified death with no pain, family dynamics are working ... sometimes that can actually be a wonderful experience."*[a] *—Oncology physician* *"I do have an awareness that the disease isn't my fault. And the disease runs a particular course, and we may not be able to change that course. If we can to anything to help people, you know, guide them through that course—that can be a good thing.* *—Oncology physician*
Perceiving work differently over time	*"As I've gotten more mature and more solid and a little older, I think I certainly am able to handle [the sadness of my work] more. I remember early on ... like every year or two ... all of a sudden I would be crying ... [about a particular patient] ... and over the years I've realized that I sometimes cry collectively for people ... and then [I am] fine."* *—Oncology social worker* *"I've learned better coping skills over the years, and I think of the people that I've worked with who also had longevity at this institution—you get a good network of support at all levels, as in people who feel similar in their ... stresses and emotional [responses], you know, the downside of this job."* *—Oncology nurse*
	Quotes excerpted with permission from Rohan (2009, pp. 65–70).

Reorganizing Career and Work

Changing Work Setting or Schedule

Some oncology clinicians have shifted to a less intense position, for example, from inpatient to outpatient work or from a clinical to an administrative position, to manage the emotional intensity of their work and to create more work–life balance (Rohan, 2009; Rohan & Bausch, 2009). Others found that reducing their hours to part time helped them manage the intense emotions associated with oncology work. Having the self-awareness to realize when it is time to put some distance between themselves and clinical oncology work, even if temporarily, can help clinicians achieve longevity in oncology.

Engaging in Research

Oncology physicians, more often than oncology nurses or social workers, are afforded time (or are required) to engage in academic research, which can help clinicians manage the emotional intensity of oncology work (Kearney et al., 2009; Rohan, 2009). A medical oncologist explained that

> *one of the exciting things ... is trying to find new treatments and better treatments, and that's a great mission and a great project to have because you think that you are at least working toward really making a big difference. You can recharge because the patient interactions are very intense and—even though one of the most positive parts of the work—very draining emotionally.*
>
> *—Rohan, 2009, p. 71*

Oncology social workers can also feel they are making a big difference when they discover new ways to understand and support patients and families through the more difficult aspects of the cancer experience (Christ, 2001).

Making Meaning

Another strategy oncology clinicians use to manage the emotional intensity of their work is through actively making meaning of their work (Fillon et al., 2009; Kearney et al., 2009). There are many ways to assign meaning to one's work, but the essential task is to find purpose in the work—in other words, to justify the "cost of caring." One powerful way to make meaning is through using a metaphor to conceptualize their work (Rohan & Bausch, 2009). Through the metaphor, a clinician may gain a deeper understanding of what sustains him or her in the work and how this work fits into a larger worldview. However accomplished, assigning meaning to one's work is an essential component to longevity in oncology work.

Rewards of Oncology Work

Despite the difficulties of working in oncology, there are abundant rewards for all professionals. Oncology clinicians derive satisfaction from easing the suffering of others, receiving gratitude from patients, forming close emotional connections with patients, being inspired by the human spirit, gaining wisdom or perspective, and deriving meaning from their work (Christ, 1993; Kearney et al., 2009;

Rohan, 2009; Rohan & Bausch, 2009). Like adaptive coping, compassion satisfaction is protective against compassion fatigue.

Easing Pain and Suffering

Oncology clinicians find it professionally rewarding to ease the pain and suffering of their patients. This is notable in oncology work, because sometimes relieving the physical pain or easing the existential suffering of another is the most a clinician can offer. Often this is no small feat.

Receiving Gratitude

Another reward related to easing pain and suffering is the gratitude of patients and families. An oncology clinician's comments are representative of the statements of other clinicians. He said, "Helping people out who are in tremendously dire straits . . . can be hugely appreciated. I think patients and family members are incredibly grateful sometimes" (Rohan, 2009, p. 85).

Forming Close Connections

Oncology clinicians and their patients often form close bonds. This may be partly due to the bond that often forms between individuals who have experienced or witnessed suffering or trauma together. Clinicians often view this intimacy as a "privilege" or a "gift" afforded to them by patients and their families (Rohan, 2009; Rohan & Bausch, 2009).

Deriving Inspiration

Oncology clinicians report they derive inspiration from witnessing the strength and resilience of their patients and families throughout the illness trajectory. They are amazed at the strength of the human spirit and what people can endure in the face of life-threatening illness and often harsh or disfiguring treatment (Rohan, 2009; Rohan & Bausch, 2009).

Gaining Wisdom or Perspective

Not all oncology clinicians necessarily gain wisdom or perspective from their work, but those who do find it a rewarding by-product. Working in oncology inevitably brings one's own mortality into stark relief. The continual reminder that life is finite sometimes engenders behavioral changes for clinicians hoping to minimize regrets at the end of life. The wisdom and perspective oncology clinicians gain from their patients on their deathbeds is to nurture relationships with loved ones; the rest (money, job status, prestige) doesn't matter (Rohan, 2009).

Implications for Future Research, Training, and Practice

There are several implications for future research, training, and practice that can be gleaned from this chapter. First, it is important for research, training, and practice to focus on helping oncology clinicians make meaning of their work and foster resilience (see chapters in Section 19). Much attention in quantitative research has been paid to the potential deleterious effects of oncology work, but research that seeks a deep understanding of the complex ways in which professionals manage this work is often qualitative. Despite its acceptance in the social sciences for decades, qualitative research has been slow in gaining acceptance in the medical literature. Additional resources dedicated to qualitative analyses would assist in recognizing this very valuable method of inquiry. Additionally, professional training and ongoing programs dedicated to helping oncology clinicians manage the emotional intensity of their work can help mitigate the potential deleterious effects of their work and should be supported by the institutions in which oncology clinicians work.

Pearls

- Even across disciplines, oncology clinicians cope with the emotional intensity of their work in surprisingly similar ways.
- For oncology clinicians, compassion satisfaction is protective against compassion fatigue.
- Interdisciplinary collaboration promotes recognition and value of individual roles.

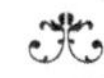

Pitfalls

- Lack of institutional support for staff to process emotional aspects of work contributes to compassion fatigue.
- Oncology social workers may be at risk for placing the care of team members before their own self-care.
- Professionals with little or no ability to balance clinical work with other activities (e.g., research, teaching, developing specialty areas of interest) are more susceptible to experiencing compassion fatigue.

Oncology social workers, nurses, and physicians each play a different but important role in helping cancer patients and their families bear the burden of living with this often life-threatening illness. Oncology work is emotionally intense and fraught with difficulties, sadness, and traumatizing aspects that clinicians navigate on a daily basis. Oncology clinicians continually bear witness to the pain, suffering, and death of others. They repeatedly experience loss and grief. But they also witness resilience in those who are suffering, establish meaningful relationships with their patients and families, and often develop coping skills and self-awareness as a result of this work. Christ (1993), speaking about oncology social work specifically, summarized: "[Although] the tasks are difficult, the work load is heavy, and the hours [are long] . . . few areas bring as much personal satisfaction to the social worker as work with cancer patients and their families" (p. 98). So, as oncology clinicians engage in the self-care and meaning-making essential to career longevity—that is, as they "put on their oxygen masks before helping others"—they may realize that the rewards of the work are akin to the oxygen that flows through that mask.

Exercise

As noted previously, one way clinicians manage the emotional intensity of oncology work and remain effective to their patient for the long haul is through the meaning they assign to their work. This exercise is designed to help the clinician think through the process for developing an effective metaphor. Because this is an iterative process, it is unlikely that you will complete this exercise to your satisfaction in one session. Be sure to record your work so you can return to it. This exercise can be done individually, in small groups, or in a larger classroom setting.

1. Brainstorm to arrive at several metaphors (concrete representation of a more complex idea) that may be applicable to your work in oncology. One published example is climbing Mount Everest (see Rohan & Bausch, 2009), but other examples might be embarking upon a journey or paying the cost of caring. The brainstorm session should last several minutes. In general, do not proceed with the first metaphor you think of unless you've already ruled out others in the past (or have used this metaphor for your work for years but have not gone through this process formally).
2. Choose among the metaphors and work with one (or if in a group setting, you may have different groups work on different metaphors to determine a good fit). Keep in mind that metaphors necessarily highlight some aspects of the phenomenon in question and deemphasize others. The best fit highlights the aspects that are most important to you or make the most sense overall. By definition, no metaphor will correspond 100% with the phenomenon. You may work with one idea and then rule it out because it doesn't resonate with you. Follow steps 3–5 to determine fit.
3. "Unpack" the experience. Be concrete. Using a journey and the cost of caring as examples, to follow are suggestions for the types of questions that help you unpack each experience. They are not exhaustive.
   a. Journey example: Where are you going? Who is going with you? How are you getting there? What kind of preparation is required? What do you hope to see or do once you're there? How long will it take to complete the journey? How will you know when you've arrived? What are the obstacles you might face along the way? How might you overcome them? What satisfaction will you derive from this journey?
   b. Cost of caring example: When you purchase something, when do you look at the cost? Before you touch it? After you like it? How much will you pay for the item? What is the highest price you will pay for this item? Is there a price cap, or will you pay any amount? What sacrifices will you make (i.e., what will you not be able to buy) because you purchased this item? How do you determine whether the item is worth the price? In other words, how do you weigh the cost with the benefit you will receive from the item?
4. Once you have "unpacked" the concrete experience, draw parallels to your oncology work. For each question you've asked and answered (in step 3), ask and answer for oncology work. As you proceed with this, the fit will become more apparent. If the metaphor doesn't resonate or hold up, try a different one.
5. If you have done this exercise alone, you might find it useful to share with a friend or colleague. Discuss the strengths and limitations of the metaphor.
6. Once you've arrived at a metaphor that resonates with your experience, use it to help make meaning of the work and to manage the emotional intensity of your professional oncology practice.

REFERENCES

Abrams, R. (1974). *Not alone with cancer: A guide for those who care, what to expect, what to do.* Springfield, IL: Charles C. Thomas.

Association of Community Cancer Centers. (2009). *Cancer program guidelines.* Retrieved from http://www.accc-cancer.org/publications/CancerProgramGuidelines-4.asp#section 6

Association of Oncology Social Work (AOSW). (2012). *Standards of practice in oncology social work.* Retrieved from http://www.aosw.org/iMIS201/AOSWMain/professionals/standards-of-practice/AOSWMain/Professional-Development/standards-of-practice.aspx?hkey=51fda308-28bd- 48b0-8a75-a17d01251b5e

Christ, G. (1993). Psychosocial tasks throughout the cancer experience. In M. Lauria, P. J. Clarke, J. Hermann, & N. Stearns (Eds.), *Social work in oncology: Supporting survivors, familes, and caregivers* (pp. 79–99). Atlanta, GA: American Cancer Society.

Christ, G. (2001). *Healing children's grief.* New York, NY: Oxford University Press.

Commission on Cancer. (2012). *Cancer program standards 2012: Ensuring patient-centered care, V1.0.* Chicago, IL: American College of Surgeons. Retrieved from http://www.facs.org/cancer/coc/programstandards2012.html

Cunningham, M. (2003). Impact of trauma work on social work clinicians: Empirical findings. *Social Work, 48*(4), 451–459.

Dane, B., & Chachkes, E. (2001). The cost of caring for patients with an illness: Contagion to the social worker. *Social Work in Health Care, 33*(2), 31–51.

Figley, C. R. (Ed.). (2002). *Treating compassion fatigue.* New York, NY: Brunner-Routledge.

Fillon, L., Duval, S., Dumont, S., Gagnon, P., Tremblay, I., Bairati, I., & Breitbart, W. S. (2009). Impact of a meaning-centered intervention on job satisfaction and on quality of life among palliative care nurses. *Psycho-Oncology, 18*(12), 1300–1310.

Fobair, P. (2007). Oncology social work for survivorship. In P. Ganz (Ed.), *Cancer survivorship today and tomorrow* (pp. 14–27). New York, NY: Springer.

Gallo-Silver, L., & Damaskos, P. (2012). September 11: Reflecting on living with dying in disaster relief. In J. Berzoff & P. Silverman (Eds.), *Living with dying: A handbook for end-of-life healthcare practitioners* (pp. 72–93). New York, NY: Columbia University Press.

Graham, J., & Ramirez, A. (2002). Improving the lives of cancer clinicians. *European Journal of Cancer Care, 11*, 188–192.

Holland, J. C. (2002). History of psycho-oncology: Overcoming attitudinal and conceptual barriers. *Psychosomatic Medicine, 64*(2), 206–221.

Institute of Medicine (IOM). (2008). *Cancer care for the whole patient: Meeting psychosocial health needs.* Washington, DC: National Academies Press.

Kearney, M. K., Weininger, R. B., Vachon, M. L., Harrison, R. L., & Mount, B. M. (2009). Self-care of phsycisians caring for patients at the end of life. *Journal of the American Medical Association, 301*(11), 1155–1164.

Lyckholm, L. (2001). Dealing with stress, burnout, and grief in the practice of oncology. *The Lancet Oncology*, 2(December), 750–755.

Lynch, T. J. (2002). Introduction. *Oncologist* 7(Suppl. 2), 3–4.

Maslach, C., Schaufeli, W. B., & Leiter, M. P. (2001). Job burnout. *Annual Review of Psychology, 52*, 397–422.

Pearlman, L. A., & Saakvitne, K. W. (1999). Self-care for trauma therapists: Ameliorating vicarous traumatization. In B. H. Stamm (Ed.), *Secondary traumatic stress: Self-care issues for clinicians, researcher, and educators* (2nd ed., pp. 51–64). Lutherville, MD: Sidran Press.

Penson, R. T., Dignan, F. L., Canellos, G. P., Picard, C. L., & Lynch, T. J. (2000). Burnout: Caring for the caregivers. *Oncologist, 5*, 425–434.

Rohan, E. A. (2009). *Laboring at the edge: Effects of repeated exposure to death and dying on oncology doctors, nurses, and social workers.* Saarbrücken, Germany: VDM Publishing House.

Rohan, E. A., & Bausch, J. (2009). Climbing Everest: Oncology work as an expedition in caring. *Journal of Psychosocial Oncology, 27*(1), 84–118.

Shanafelt, T., & Dyrbye, L. (2012). Oncologist burnout: Causes, consequences, and responses. *Journal of Clinical Oncology, 30*(11), 1235–1241.

Slocum-Gori, S., Hemsworth, D., Chan, W. W. Y., Carson, A., & Kazanjian, A. (2013). Understanding compassion satisfaction, compassion fatigue, and burnout: A survey of the hospice palliative care workforce. *Palliative Medicine, 27*(2), 172–178.

Stamm, B. H. (2002). Measuring compassion satisfaction as well as fatigue: Developmental history of the compassion satisfaction and fatigue test. In C. Figley (Ed.), *Treating compassion fatigue* (pp. 107–122). New York, NY: Brunner-Routledge.

Stearns, N. (2001). Professional issues in oncology social work. In M. Lauria, P. J. Clarke, J. Hermann, & N. Stearns (Eds.), *Social work in oncology: Supporting survivors, familes, and caregivers* (pp. 213–232). Atlanta, GA: American Cancer Society.

106

Patricia McGillicuddy, Karen Gold, and Mandy Lowe

Developing Core Competencies for Interprofessional Teams: A Script-Reading Approach

Key Concepts

- *The interprofessional competency framework, including interprofessional education (IPE), interprofessional care (IPC)—together referred to here as IPEC—and collaborative practice, is reviewed.*
- *Teaching more complex relationally and ethically based competencies (e.g., the ability to accept, respect, and value others and their contributions in relational-centered care) challenges educators to develop meaningful learning experiences that address the development of values, empathy, and respect integral to interprofessional team-based practice.*
- *Three educators describe their use of patient-focused narratives as a tool for promoting interprofessional collaboration, specifically the use of reader's theater approaches using prepared scripts as tools for enhancing the understanding of patients' and colleagues' experiences with patients with advanced breast cancer.*

In striving to address the often unmet psychosocial needs of cancer patients and their families, this chapter explores the role of education in building interprofessional care competencies and sensitivities, drawing on the experiences of the three authors, two social workers and an occupational therapist who work as point-of-care educators. They describe their use of patient-focused narratives as a tool for promoting interprofessional collaboration, specifically the use of reader's theater approaches as tools for enhancing the understanding of patients' and colleagues' experiences.

Interprofessional Competency Framework

Research demonstrates that good communication and collaborative care plans among clinicians and their patients improve patient satisfaction and enhance patient safety and clinical outcomes. To address shortfalls in the health care system, Canadian governmental and academic institutions have encouraged the development of collaborative and patient-centered learning initiatives and have recommended that practices be built around good communication, collaboration across different disciplines, and empathic recognition of the impact of illness on people's lives (Konrad & Browning, 2012).

To facilitate the development of competence across various levels of learning and experience, some competency frameworks also include graded competencies to enable tailored approaches to learning across a continuum. For example, the University of Toronto, Centre for Interprofessional Education (2008) and Nelson, Tassone, and Hodges (2014) created an IPE competency framework spanning exposure, immersion, and competence levels of learning. These competencies build on each other developmentally as in the following example. In *exposure* or initial learning stages, competencies may be related to understanding one's own role. In *immersion*, this competence is further developed as the ability to describe the roles, responsibilities, and scopes of practice of other professions. *Competence* connotes the level of practice required by a professional moving in to a health care position.

> *In the 21st century, creating a therapeutic context in which healing can occur relies not only on the caring dispositions of individual clinicians but also on the collective relational capacities of interprofessional health care teams (Konrad & Browning, 2012).*

In addition to this focus on role understanding, the other domains often cited in interprofessional care approaches include appreciation of team processes, interprofessional communication, and values/ethics for interprofessional practice (Interprofessional Education Collaborative Expert Panel, 2011). Many interprofessional learning activities focus on the early-exposure stages of learning in which students are exposed to learners from other professions. However, some competencies are more complex to address. The professional development of these more complex relationally and ethically based competencies—for example, the ability to "accept, through respect and value, others and their contributions in relational-centred care" (University of Toronto, Centre for Interprofessional Education, 2008)—can benefit from an intentional, reflective, shared-learning approach using narrative or nondeliberative teaching and learning opportunities. As educators and leaders seek to build meaningful learning experiences that address the development of *values, empathy,* and *respect* integral to interprofessional team-based practice, new approaches to curricula, such as those embracing the use of patient narratives, hold promise.

Layered learning is an important concept because staff members often have different roles on a team that require unique knowledge and skills but, at the same time, need to move beyond a notion of rigid professional boundaries to enable a more flexible approach where one shares skills, expertise, and resources to enhance the capacity of the whole team. A speech language therapist, for example, might teach the rest of the team how to do an assessment or intervention so that the whole team builds their capabilities and skills to help patients. This can improve the quality of patient outcomes and the quality of relational care. Respect for the unique expertise and professional identity that different practitioners bring to patient care can be enhanced while encouraging flexible use of knowledge and skills and increasing relevant, timely referral to experts and effective collaboration.

Flexibility, responsiveness, professional humility, attention to clear communication, delineation of roles, and identification of shared goals are the basis for collaborative care. Collaborative care characterizes a model of psychosocial oncology consistent with a more holistic approach to care that meets the complex needs of patients.

Collaborative Cancer Care and Social Work Practices

Different people can be the "experts" at different times depending on what the patient goals and needs are and what practitioners can offer. Various team members can lead the care at different times in different circumstances. Values both shared and unique to person and profession, to context and team, are important to articulate, examine, teach, reaffirm, and, at times in a productive team, constructively challenge.

Social workers are a key part of interprofessional care planning processes. They function as collaborative clinical and academic professionals, frontline clinicians, team members, educators, care leaders, and point-of-care researchers on psychosocial oncology teams, operating in acute care inpatient units, outpatient care settings, primary care, survivorship programs, and rehabilitation programs. The contributions of social workers to theory and practice in cancer care reflect a shared professional ideology with an emphasis on attending to transitions in care, negotiating equity, reflecting on practice, facilitating client voice, paying attention to the impact of illness on family and informal caregivers, and attending to the vicarious nature of care and caregiving (Barlow & Reading, 2008; Hair & Learn, 2007; McGillicuddy, Johnson, Jensen, Fitch, & Jacobs, 2011; Sinding, Gray, Fitch, & Greenberg, 2002).

When addressing the complexity of these issues, we need to recognize that teams shift and change to respond to different patients' needs and the needs of patients at different points of care. As patients' and families' journeys evolve, there also needs to be a change in terms of who the "team" is at different touch points throughout. Some members will be with a person throughout an entire journey, like a primary community care provider, and some will be with the patient and family at specific points. Collaboration is critical from this perspective to ensure that we are collaborating effectively not only with patients and families but also with our colleagues and those who might have more specific or time-limited roles with patients. Gaps and insurmountable barriers to care are places where inequities and unaddressed relapses occur, negatively affecting patient safety and successful outcomes (Gould, Sinding, Mitchell, & Fitch, 2009; Miller et al., 2014; Sinding, Barnoff, Grassau, Odette, & McGillicuddy, 2009).

Patient Stories and Reader's Theater: IPEC-Facilitated Learning

Communication theorist Kenneth Burke (1973) described literature as equipment for living, implying that stories are powerful resources for assisting people to navigate life problems. Interest is growing in the use of narrative in health professional education to promote empathy, improve listening skills, and enhance understanding of patients' and clients' experiences. According to narrative medicine scholar and physician Rita Charon (2001), narrative approaches are part of an emerging framework for practice emphasizing the relational capacities of *attention, reflection,* and *affiliation* and are thus in close alignment with many of the aims of interprofessional and patient-centered care approaches.

Drama and theater are powerful narrative-based education tools to raise awareness on many critical practice issues including communication, ethics and end-of-life care (Case & Guy, 2006), cultural sensitivity (Kumagai et al., 2007), HIV and ovarian cancer (Shapiro & Hunt, 2003), interdisciplinary geriatric care (MacRae & Pardue, 2007), other cancer-related issues (Saldaña, 2010), and reflective practice in pediatric oncology (Charon, 2008).

Commenting on the unique role of theater in enhancing students' understanding of patient experiences and promoting empathy, Smith, Gair, McGee, Valdez, and Kirk (2014) point out that dramatic performance allows us to identify with imagined roles and situations from the perspectives of viewer and/or participant.

> *Reader's theater is a scripted dramatic reading. It is a simple theatrical method in which texts are read aloud with a focus on verbal expression (readers) and listening (audience). It has been called "theater of the mind" because it focuses on our imagination much like listening to a radio show. "Medical reader's theater" is the use of scripted readings to raise awareness of health issues for academic, professional, or community audiences.*

Farrell, Towle, and Godolphin note, "Students remember what they hear from patients. The authentic and autonomous patient's voice promotes the learning of patient-centred care" (2006, p. 14). Strategies for incorporating the patient voice in training and practice include using standardized patients, involving patients in health research, and incorporating patient stories into education so that students and practitioners learn directly about the "illness experience" from the perspective of patients.

Using content that resonates with both patients' and practitioners' lived experiences provides multiple entry points for engagement. Deepening the narrative through interprofessional discussion makes this approach very congruent with the stated competencies and goals of collaborative care. In the next section, we turn to our use of patient stories to promote interprofessional dialogue on breast cancer.

The Educational Sessions: "Handle With Care: Do You Know How?"

> *A doctor has to keep her wits about her—things can be taken the wrong way. Words are a minefield.*
>
> —*Ivonoffski and Gray (1999)*

Inspired by the power of theater to "dramatize data" (Saldaña, 2010), we developed and ran sessions of "Handle With Care" (Ivonoffski & Gray, 1999) as part of the interprofessional education curriculum at the University of Toronto and its teaching hospitals. In sharing this approach with others, we have also successfully used other scripts. The primary purpose of these sessions is to improve understanding of the issues facing women with metastatic breast cancer and highlight the importance of and skills relevant to interprofessional care. The development of these sessions was guided by "Handle With Care: Do You Know How? Using Reader's Theatre to Build Interprofessional Values and Ethics" (written by Vrenia Ivonoffski and Ross Gray in 1999), and their stated purpose is to "explore patients' stories of care, professional roles, values and ethics and ways we can work best with patient partners in interprofessional collaborative teams."

"Handle With Care" documents the experiences of women living with breast cancer. The dramatic script was a collaborative effort by a health care research team, a theater troupe, and women with breast cancer (Sinding et al., 2002). The script unfolds as a series of dramatic narrative vignettes dealing with issues such as the impact of diagnosis, dealing with treatments, the impact of illness on the patient and family, and communication with health care providers. The script also highlights some of the dilemmas practitioners face. It raises complex and often unspoken challenges facing patients as they navigate and cope with illness and treatment and deal with the intertwined feelings of fear, shame, self-blame, and hope.

Using patients' stories as a jumping-off point, we wanted to highlight and explore how our own professional lens informs our responses to patient scenarios and thus encourage participants to consider the many perspectives circulating in cancer care. Information overload, for example, was a common phenomenon that patients identified when provided this opportunity.

> **Information Overload**
>
> *Patient 1: I'm a nurse and yet, what the doctor told me was gone. I didn't take anything in for the first two or three months.*
>
> *Patient 2: For two days I couldn't think. I just kept crying. If I would have had information, I couldn't have processed it. I couldn't think (Ivonoffski & Gray, 1999).*

The patients' stated experiences of information overload resonated for staff and students as they heard about the effects of taking in news, trying to absorb information, *and* making decisions in a state of crisis—and they themselves experienced some overload just from being part of the reading. This lived experience contributed to increased empathy with the storytellers. Staff and students were able to share their experiences of burden, or load and overload. Particular professionals were able to share their perspectives, clinical knowledge, and ideas about ways to talk with patients, mobilize supports, organize visits, share responsibilities, and pace accessible information. Occupational therapists share concepts about the *job of the patient* and the impact of changes in occupation. Social workers share their perspectives on the challenges of gaps and transitions in care. Spiritual care providers talk about struggles around meaning, grief, and loss. Physiotherapists share the ways in which resilience can be maintained in palliative care. A medical student shares his experiences working with community theater in international health care. A nursing student talks about script reading in a woman's voice about breast cancer. Another reader shares the story of his male high school friend who has breast cancer and is going out for a night with the boys. The stories go on: People say "I did not know," "I do know," "In my profession we . . .," "On my team we . . .," "I didn't know you were doing that with patients . . . that you assessed their distress when they went there . . . that diagnosis was in your scope of practice." As illustrated, this approach is about creating and holding space that is flexible and expansive, allows divergent and diverse voices, is cofacilitated and models interprofessional values, with a chance to hear from readers in small-group break-out times, large-group time, and appreciations. This workshop has worked with from 15 to over 50 people in attendance.

Often spontaneously and always with cofacilitation, the group begins to share in this way and often a list is formed, an example of which follows here, that acts as information, confirmation, and a symbol of working together. Many similar statements to those generated in the group reoccur in the evaluations as positive learning points.

Practical Strategies for Interprofessional Relational Care

- *Pace information; offer to repeat it and/or write it down.*
- *Call clients/patients by their preferred name.*
- *Understand who is part of the patient's family as they define it.*
- *Check in with patients on how they are coping throughout.*
- *Offer support to patients and families to deal with the emotional impact of diagnosis and treatment (cancer is a "family" illness).*
- *Be sensitive to the impact of the experience of hearing advice from well-meaning, but sometimes conflicting, sources.*
- *Let the patient and family know you are part of a team focused on their care; share team members' names and information.*
- *Remember that the patient's care "team" includes all the providers the patient is in contact with throughout the cancer journey; get to know each other.*
- *Understand the challenges of transitions in care; act as a bridge.*
- *Pay attention to your own reactions to patients; seek and offer individual, professional, and team support.*
- *Understand that every profession and person is impacted by his or her work in cancer care.*
- *Share your profession expertise generously, humbly, and with curiosity.*
- *Every story matters, stories change, and there is always more than one.*

Navigating Fear and Hope

Emphasizing the theme of fear and hope provides another opportunity to use the reflective power of this approach in opening up rich discussion.

> *Patient 1: One doctor told me I wouldn't be around very long—a couple of years or something. I mean that's very debilitating. They shouldn't tell you that. Patient 2: Don't dash my hope. Don't say "when this treatment fails"—say "if." You've been through this a hundred times but this is my first time and I'm hanging on day-to-day to the hope that this will work . . . . It's a small thing for you, but for me it makes a big difference (Ivonoffski & Gray, 1999).*

The patients' navigation of fear and hope as narrated here provides the reflecting staff and students the opportunity to discuss ways in which they cope with the telling of "bad news"; surfaces an understanding that they have similar reactions, stresses, and worries; and allows them to articulate individual needs regarding finding support and building resilience. Also, the importance of enhancing mutual support through team engagement is emphasized. There is a discussion of empathy and appreciations across professions followed by, for example, radiation therapists talking about the kinds of conversations they have with patients in the isolated rooms of radiation therapy and the challenges of shaping hope when the treatment is palliative. An invitation to attend palliative radiation rounds is extended and accepted. A speech language pathology student asks if it is possible to spend some time shadowing in radiology. A lab technology student talks about her sense of responsibility and need for precision regarding diagnoses and the importance of knowing about the patient's journey. A dietitian and the speech language student discuss swallowing and the hope a partner has when his loved one can eat. Everyone listens and reflects, and the facilitators go back and forth to the IPEC themes through the stories.

Informed by the idea that discussion is at the heart of the session, we developed questions to elicit participants' responses to the script and to encourage participants to think about implications for team-based care: What are your initial responses to the reading? What did you learn about patients' experiences and needs? Did anything surprise you—or resonate with you? How does this relate to your own profession's values, scope, and roles? What does this have to do with collaboration and teamwork? What is mutual care? How do we talk similarly and differently about care? What works? What reminds you of your work? How does our academic work link to point of care? Is there education, research, evaluation, or care innovation we could be doing together?

Many issues and practical strategies related to patient care and teamwork grew out of these discussions, including a greater understanding that the way we respond to patients' stories are shaped by our personal experiences and by our professional training and roles. The importance of mutual support among team members in managing the day-to-day demands of clinical practice (e.g., sharing stories about difficult days, debriefing, and dealing with the impact of loss) gives us a greater understanding of the patient journey and the critical role of the "team" in recognizing the ongoing needs of family and friends. Perhaps most important, our discussions reinforced that relational care involves honoring the value of connections between patients and practitioners—as well as those between colleagues and health care teams.

Pearls

- Teaching interprofessional values using narrative approaches and incorporating the patient's voice can elicit reflection and advance learning about shared values, empathy, and respect, which can also enhance engaged teamwork.
- Improvements in interprofessional understanding and respect for the role and relationship of other professions can lead to improved patient care and timely referrals for service.

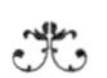

Pitfalls

- Underestimating the stress levels on patients being diagnosed and treated for cancer and their need for staff to provide clarity, coherence, consistency, repetition, and connection with their personal tragedy and challenge.
- Failing to honor the patient's connection with many current staff and with previous staff they have engaged with and may feel abandoned by.

When participants hear that these words are actually the voices of patients and health care providers, they come from and to a more engaged and respectful place. Reading or attending a performance of a health-related script has multiple benefits. Health care providers may learn more about the experience of illness from a patient's perspective; patients may find resonance in someone else's story and have diminished feelings of isolation. If we are neither patient nor provider, we may come to a greater understanding of those affected by illness (Saldaña, 2010). All of these are powerful reasons to engage in learning through narrative and reader's theater, but we invite you to consider another purpose—to promote reflection and dialogue on engaged teamwork in cancer care.

Finding Scripts and Developing Reader's Theater for Interprofessional Learning

- *Understand and articulate clearly the purpose and goals, including interprofessional learning objectives (which can be linked to competencies) of your session.*
- *Use (and incorporate) an evaluation tool linked to goals and purpose.*
- *As educators, use cofacilitation to role model interprofessional collaboration and share tasks.*
- *Focus on roles, scopes, communication strategies, and shared goals (e.g., equity, excellence in care) when selecting questions to facilitate discussion.*
- *Find scripts, research, plays, or stories that resonate, can be easily read by four to six people, can be adapted for length and audience, and are applicable and adaptable to your practice setting.*
- *Check the articles, materials, and stories created in Shapiro and Hunt (2003), Saldaña (2010), and Savitt (2002) for health-related scripts. The best reference for related videos and plays like "Handle With Care" is Gray and Sinding (2002).*
- *Include multiple voices and perspectives and different professions, health care roles, and patients and families to understand relational care and highlight differences.*
- *Articulate and physically post clear simple listening and reading tips for the session.*
- *Use appreciative inquiry approaches, for example, asking, "What has energy?" "What moves us forward?" "Where does IPE and IPC live in our own work?" "What words inspired reflective dialogue?"*
- *Keep it simple to create room for stories/reflections/surprises. Don't overcomplicate with theory or interpretation. Recognize emotional impact. Honor links to academic/professional knowledge.*

Social Workers, Colleagues, and Oncology Care Teams: Strategies for Collaborative Practice

- *Find allies with shared competencies that promote IPE and IPC. Look for and build opportunities for interprofessional cooperation with colleagues.*
- *Research and adopt a competency framework and evaluate and build skills together.*
- *Build your interprofessional skills in group, team, and individual modalities, as well as in patient education, professional development, and research.*
- *Be flexible. Consider both meaning and function in relational care processes, systems, and outcomes. There are many roles necessary to ensure dynamic interprofessional care.*
- *Recognize that building collaborative relationships takes time. This is about lifelong learning and teaching as we reflect and work with colleagues, students, clients, patients, families, and communities.*

- *Balance professional pride and autonomy with humility, cooperation, and curiosity.*
- *Use and develop your professional skills as group facilitators and applied social scientists.*
- *Consider opening up profession-specific training and development to other professions, other health care employees, students, patients, and communities.*
- *Attend to building your own resilience and to actively engaging in team resilience.*
- *Evaluate and research with colleagues and patients and across boundaries of care.*

ADDITIONAL RESOURCES

Websites

American Interprofessional Health Collaborative: http://www.aihc-us.org/what-is-aihc/

Canadian Interprofessional Health Collaborative: http://www.cihc.ca

Books and Reports

Frodeman, R., Kline, J. T., & Micham, C. (Eds.). (2010). *Oxford handbook of interdisciplinarity.* London, England: Oxford University Press.

Interprofessional Education Collaborative Expert Panel. (2011). *Core competencies for interprofessional collaborative practice: Report of an expert panel.* Washington, DC: Author. Retrieved from http://www.aacn.nche.edu/education-resources/ipecreport.pdf

Turnbull, G., Baldassarre, F., Brown, P., Hattan-Bauer, J., Li, M., Lebel S., … Psychosocial Oncology Expert Panel. (2010). *Psychosocial health care for cancer patients and their families.* Evidence Based Series 19-3, Section 1. Toronto, ON, Canada: Cancer Care Ontario. Retrieved from http://www.cancercare.on.ca/common/pages/UserFile.aspx?fileId=43602

REFERENCES

Barlow, K., & Reading, C. (2008). *Relational care: A guide to health care and support for aboriginal people living with AIDS.* Ottawa, ON, Canada: Canadian Aboriginal AIDS Network.

Burke, K. (1973). Literature as equipment for living. In Burke (Ed.), *Philosophy of the literary form: Studies in symbolic action* (3rd ed.). Berkeley, CA: University of California Press.

Case, G., & Guy, M. (2006). Moral imagination takes the stage: Readers' theater in a medical context. *Journal for Learning Through the Arts, 2*(1). Retrieved from http://escholarship.org/uc/item/7380r49s

Charon, R. (2001). Narrative medicine: A model for empathy, reflection, profession, and trust. *Journal of the American Medical Association, 286*(15), 1897–1902.

Charon, R. (2008). *Narrative medicine: Honoring the stories of illness.* London, England: Oxford University Press.

Farrell, C., Towle, A., & Godolphin, W. (2006). *Where's the patient's voice in health professional education?* Vancouver, BC, Canada: Division of Health Care Communication, College of Health Disciplines, University of British Columbia. Retrieved from http://www.health-disciplines.ubc.ca/DHCC/

Gould, J., Sinding, C., Mitchell, T., & Fitch, M. (2009). Listening for echoes: How social location matters in women's experiences of cancer care. In J. Nelson, J. Gould, & S. Keller-Olaman (Eds.), *Cancer on the margins: Method and meaning in participatory research.* Toronto, ON, Canada: University of Toronto Press.

Gray, R. E., & Sinding, C. (2002). *Standing ovation: Performing social science research about cancer.* Walnut Creek, CA: Altamira Press.

Hair, H., & Learn, L. (2007). Identity challenges and supportive care needs: A response from a social work perspective. In L. Elit (Ed.), *Women and cancer* (pp. 203–226). Toronto, ON, Canada: Nova Science Publishers.

Interprofessional Education Collaborative Expert Panel. (2011). *Core competencies for interprofessional collaborative practice: Report of an expert panel.* Washington, DC: Interprofessional Education Collaborative.

Ivonoffski, V., & Gray, R. (1999). Handle with care: Do you know how? Using reader's theatre to build interprofessional values and ethics. An unpublished script developed through the Psychosocial and Behavioural Research Unit, Odette Cancer Centre, Sunnybrook Health Sciences Centre, Toronto, Canada, with ACT II Studio, Ryerson University, Toronto, Canada. This play was performed and recorded as cited in Gray, R. E., & Sinding, C. (2002). *Standing ovation: Performing social science research about cancer.* Walnut Creek, CA: AltaMira Press.

Konrad, S., & Browning, D. (2012). Relational learning and interprofessional practice: Transforming health education for the 21st century. *Work, 41*(3), 247–251.

Kumagai, A. K., White, C. B., Ross, P. T., Purkiss, J. A., O'Neal, C. M., & Steiger, J. A. (2007). Use of interactive theatre for faculty development in multicultural medical education. *Medical Teacher, 29*(4), 335–340.

MacRae, N., & Pardue, K. T. (2007). Use of readers theater to enhance interdisciplinary geriatric education. *Educational Gerontology, 33*, 529–536.

McGillicuddy, P., Johnson, T., Jensen, P., Fitch, M., & Jacobs, M. (2011). The stories we hold: Vicarious traumatization in health care providers. *Canadian Social Work, 18*(3), 41–55.

Miller, P., Sinding, C., McGillicuddy, P., Gould, J., Fitzpatrick-Lewis, D., Learn, L., & Fitch, M. (2014). Disparaties in cancer care: Perspectives from the front line. *Palliative and Supportive Care, 12*(3), 175–181.

Nelson, S., Tassone, M., & Hodges, B. (2014). *Creating the heath care team of the future.* Ithaca, NY: Cornell University Press.

Saldaña, J. (2010). Ethnodramas about health and illness, staging human vulnerability, fragility and resiliency. In C. L. Mclean & R. Kelly (Eds.), *Creative arts in interdisciplinary practice: Inquiries for hope and change.* Calgary, AL, Canada: Detselig Temeron Press.

Savitt, T. (Ed.). (2002). *Medical readers' theater: A guide and scripts.* Iowa City, IA: University of Iowa Press.

Shapiro, J., & Hunt, L. (2003). All the world's a stage: The use of theatrical performance in medical education. *Medical Education, 37*, 922–927.

Sinding, C., Barnoff, L., Grassau, P., Odette, F., & McGillicuddy, P. (2009). The stories we tell: Processes and politics of representation. In J. Nelson, J. Gould, & S. Keller-Olaman (Eds.), *Cancer on the margins: Method and meaning in participatory research*. Toronto, ON, Canada: University of Toronto Press.

Sinding, C., Gray, R., Fitch, M., & Greenberg, M. (2002). Staging breast cancer, rehearsing metastatic disease. *Qualitative Health Research*, *12*(1), 61–73.

Smith, A., Gair, J., McGee, P., Valdez, P., & Kirk, P. (2014). Teaching empathy through role-play and fabric art: An innovative pedagogical approach for end-of-life health care providers. *International Journal of Creative Arts in Interdisciplinary Practice*, *10*. Retrieved from http://www.ijcaip.com/archives/IJCAIP-10-Smith.html

University of Toronto, Centre for Interprofessional Education Curriculum. (2008) Advancing the interprofessional education curriculum, curriculum overview. Toronto, ON, Canada: University of Toronto, Office of Interprofessional Education Competency Framework. Retrieved from http://www.ipe.utoronto.ca

107

Margaret S. Wool

Schwartz Center Rounds®: Process, Outcomes, and Opportunities for Improving Interprofessional Practice

Key Concepts

- *Schwartz Center Rounds® is a unique model for preventing burnout and enhancing staff support and capacity for compassion.*
- *There are important contributions and varied roles for clinical social workers in Schwartz Center Rounds.*
- *Descriptions and illustrations of the Schwartz Center Rounds experience illustrate its process and contribution.*

Caregiving, Collegial Support, and Schwartz Center Rounds

Helping patients and their families with life-threatening illness and treatment is challenging and can pose stress, burnout, and compassion fatigue risks that most of us know about and hope to avoid. Although the tasks of self-care and supporting one another add sustenance, finding time and space for these is often difficult.

Schwartz Center Rounds is a multidisciplinary case conference whose mission is mindful of the complex interdependency of patient and caregiver as well as the bonds between caregivers. Through case presentations and discussions, Rounds aims to cultivate and enhance compassion in these fundamental caregiving relationships, thereby supporting hope and healing. This unique facilitated program engages panelists and audiences from a range of health care disciplines to discuss the challenges of patient care with, an emphasis on the *experience of caregiving* rather than medical diagnosis and treatment. In this respect, Schwartz Center Rounds is unlike virtually all other medical case conferences.

The panel, along with the audience, shares support and has the opportunity to debrief—even grieve—the complex situations faced in daily practice. The discussion can have healing benefits and at times emotional catharsis takes place in this supportive environment. The extent to which a large group (up to 100 or more) can become a safe and beneficial holding environment for strong emotion is remarkable.

This chapter describes the process and strategies used in developing a successful Schwartz Center Rounds program and gives examples of our teams' experiences.[1] It cites nationally observed outcomes of the Rounds experience for staff (Lown & Manning, 2010) and suggests opportunities specifically for oncology social workers to contribute to, and benefit from, Schwartz Center Rounds.

Clinical Social Workers in Health Care: "Resident Experts" in Interpersonal and Communication Skills

The need to address qualitative aspects of caregiving has received increased attention in the past decade (Joint

Commission 2010; Wen, Huang, Mosley, & Afsar-Manesh, 2012; Youngson, 2011). The American College of Graduate Medical Education introduced six core competencies for training and assessing intern and resident performance, including integrating interpersonal and communication skills into training experiences (Browning, Meyer, Truog, & Solomon, 2007; Cubic & Gatewood, 2008; Karnieli-Miller, Vu, Holtman, Clyman, & Inui, 2010; Mainiero & Lourenco, 2011; Porcel et al., 2012; Short, Jorgensen, Edwards, Blankenship, & Roth, 2009). Clinical social workers can make meaningful contributions to medical education by reinforcing improved interpersonal skills and attunement to the interrelated biopsychosocial issues in patient care. Schwartz Center Rounds is one opportunity for highlighting these essential dimensions and is a successful and growing program being widely disseminated in U.S. hospitals (The Joint Commission, 2010; Schwartz, 1995).

About the Schwartz Center

The Schwartz Center for Compassionate Healthcare, founded in 1995 by Kenneth B. Schwartz, has developed several programs to support caregiving and counter the stressful challenges to optimal and well-rounded patient care (Schwartz, 1995).[2] As of 2013, Schwartz Center Rounds is being offered in more than 300 facilities in 40 American states, as well as more than 30 sites in the United Kingdom. In some settings, the forum and participants draw from an entire general adult or pediatric hospital, whereas in others, the oncology department hosts Rounds. Still others are based in hospice facilities.

The Schwartz Center Rounds Program

The program is distinctive in its emphasis on interdisciplinary dialogue in the context of a level playing field. The full array of disciplines is welcome to attend Rounds as caregivers and the panel strives to represent caregivers from different professions. Brief presentations by each panelist are followed by audience members sharing their views on the case as well as broader related concerns. A planning committee, customarily led by a physician with representatives of varied institutional disciplines and the Rounds facilitator, identifies appropriate cases for presentation. In some instances, a uniquely painful case will be presented, offering staff the time they need to process their feelings and clinical experiences. In general, though, the cases are not so current as to be too raw but rather tend to be those that linger with staff, having triggered stress and intense emotions. The cases typically include elements that challenge caregiving, making it difficult to maintain a professional and balanced expression of empathy and compassion. They may involve highly charged feelings, such as friction between professionals about patient care or emotional reactions to the patient—positive or negative—in which perspective and neutrality may be lost. The multidisciplinary panel briefly presents their respective roles in the case and their experiences of the caregiving. After each case is presented, the facilitator invites discussion and the audience can respond, ask questions, relate their own experiences, and generally process raised feelings and challenges.

This type of exchange is rare in the health care environment. Most facilities have a regular schedule of clinical case conferences and medical grand Rounds, as well as Rounds in various specialties, ethics committee meetings, and M&M (morbidity and mortality) Rounds. None of these forums places the experience, feelings, and needs of the caregiver at the forefront; instead, they focus on empathy, support, and compassion. Some forums may, in fact, frown upon personal expression. As one participant stated, "[Schwartz Center] Rounds are a place where people who don't usually talk about the heart of the work are willing to share their vulnerability, to question themselves. *Rounds are an opportunity for dialogue that doesn't happen anywhere else in the hospital.*"

Schwartz Center Rounds serves multiple functions for multidisciplinary caregiving. Schwartz Rounds gives staff a chance to debrief, foster trusting collaboration between professionals, better acquaint caregivers with the unique and specialized skills of their colleagues in different disciplines, and encourage enhanced compassion in the activities of patient care. Discussions in Rounds help caregivers examine and model ethical behavior and professionalism.

Social Work and Schwartz Rounds: A Mutually Beneficial Effort

Schwartz Center Rounds has a strong concurrence with the role of clinical social workers in health care settings, reinforcing a broad view of the patient and professional reflection and self-awareness. Hospital-based oncology social workers are members of a multidisciplinary team (Sorensen & Liu, 1995), and although their principal function involves providing direct services to and coordinating services for patients and their families, social workers also serve a vital role in relation to team members, serving as liaisons for patients and families and facilitating and assisting communication with physicians, nurses, and other medical professionals providing care. Beyond this, social workers frequently offer the grounding function of staff support, interacting with colleagues, together or individually, to discuss and process personal reactions, countertransference, secondary trauma, and compassion fatigue. At case conferences and team meetings, social workers bring "the person in the patient" into the room, integrating interpersonal, psychosocial, and spiritual concerns into the discussion and keeping the thread of caring and emotional commitment in the fabric of the conversations about patients (Goodrich, 2008; Jones, 2005; Snow & Gilbertson, 2011).

Potential Roles for Social Workers in the Schwartz Center Rounds Program

Clinical social work is among the multiple disciplines in the hospital setting intended to be part of every planning committee for Schwartz Center Rounds. The committee usually has eight to 10 members, representing medicine, nursing, social work, case management, and a range of other disciplines and/or specialties such as occupational and physical therapy, as well as, ideally, a support staff member for administrative help. Social workers often hear about high-impact cases in units where they work and can play a role in case finding for Rounds. This case-finding activity is often part of every committee member's charge.

Each Rounds site committee has a facilitator to moderate the panel, field and pose questions, and offer thematic summaries for the audience. The role of the facilitator can be a natural fit for clinical social workers, who have skills in active listening, cultivating a therapeutic alliance, and understanding how interpersonal and group dynamics align with the goals and function of Schwartz Center Rounds. Most facilitators work at the organization and perform the role of facilitator as part of their job. A caveat here is that in the interest of the facilitator's independence from the host agency hierarchy and internal politics. Sometimes, an outside consultant who is not employed at the host site can fill this role. Exceptions may be made, however, and this may be the right fit for a clinical social worker from within the institution. This question is best negotiated directly with the Schwartz Center for Compassionate Healthcare to tailor the team and committee to the needs and characteristics of the institution.

Process of Schwartz Center Rounds

The Schwartz Center for Compassionate Healthcare has staff dedicated to guiding and supporting new sites in the process of preparing and offering Rounds. Rounds are organized at each site beginning with the endorsement of institution administration and then by convening the planning multidisciplinary committee with an identified physician leader. Any member of the health care team can initiate the inquiry process about launching a Rounds program by contacting the Schwartz Center.

Before a site initiates Schwartz Center Rounds, proposed team members attend. Rounds at another facility accompanied by a Schwartz Center staff member. They then debrief with the staff member and the leaders at the host site. It is important to experience firsthand this style of unique educational exchange that integrates recounting clinical transactions with personal responses.

Institutional Endorsement

Support from an institution's senior management is essential, and the Schwartz Center provides materials and strategies for educating and enlisting key administrators. Once begun, Rounds usually take place every 1 or 2 months. In partnership with the site, staff from the Schwartz Center provide consultation, ongoing support, and periodic site visits. Before starting Rounds, sites must become a member of the Schwartz Center. In addition, expenses, which include the facilitator's stipend (if that person does not work at the site), equipment or room charges, and the cost of meals or refreshments, are borne by the institution.

Because health care environments operate in an atmosphere of considerable pressure and limited discretionary time, a couple of inducements are included to encourage robust attendance. In the spirit of nurturing, Rounds hosts are encouraged to provide breakfast or lunch, a tangible expression of support and appreciation. Another form of inducement is the opportunity to attain continuing education credits, which include general CME/CEU credits and often risk management, universal precautions, and ethics or cultural diversity categories depending on the case.

In addition to providing professional support, the Schwartz Center maintains a website for the *Rounds Community* that contains resources and materials. There are documents and slide shows for educating administration and colleagues about Rounds and building support for the program, along with features of a good case for Rounds and common topics for presentation. There is also a discussion board for interaction between sites for committee members and facilitators. Participants can share their problems and successful strategies for dealing with such issues as increasing attendance, managing disruptive participants, or long silences.

When working in health care's province of life and death and life-altering decision making, an outlet and platform for emotional responses provides a place for healthy self-care, increasing insight and esteem and decreasing risk of secondary trauma, compassion fatigue, and burnout (Lown & Manning, 2010). Caring for very ill patients, particularly at the end of life, is a deeply personal job for health care professionals. Many find that they sense true understanding and empathy only with colleagues, enabling them to process the grief and stress of the work.

> *I don't [know] about anyone else's family, but I talk to my husband and he has no idea what I am talking about.*
>
> *They'll say, "I don't understand why you do it." They'll say that, and I hate that.... They'll say, "I can't believe you do it. I could never do that." And you really don't want to hear that, either. (Wenzel, Shaha, Klimmek, & Krumm, 2011, p. E276)*

Barriers of Culture and Geography

A Syrian man in his 50s was living in the United States while his wife had remained in Syria for the past 11 years. A medical crisis during his illness left him intubated and in the hospital intensive care unit. The brain death protocol was administered and the patient met criteria. With considerable difficulty involving both language barrier and access to active phone lines in Damascus, staff was able to speak (with the aid of a bilingual staff social worker) with the wife. The doctor explained the circumstances and the husband's irreversible condition and asked the wife for guidance on how she wanted him to proceed. Her response was, "I don't disagree with the doctors but I'm not going to say it." The cultural elements of her stance were discussed at Rounds: did her concurrence with the doctors represent consent, or was an affirmative statement necessary? There were varied responses to this dilemma.

In cases when family cannot or will not participate in decision making, there is a process through which the hospital ethics committee employs a policy for medical futility (AMA, 1997). In some circumstances, the policy permits a physician to act as a surrogate decision maker for the patient. The physician may institute what would be deemed a reasonable and expected decision of an ordinary person that may include initiating or terminating a treatment or intervention. The aforementioned case would have permitted the doctor to proceed with extubation after the discussion with the wife, but he did not feel that there was unanimous support of the team and would not proceed.

Some of the questions that emerged at Rounds regarding this case involved the caregivers' experiences of their feelings and of the challenges in decision making. They were asked: How were you feeling during the time the patient was deteriorating and you sought family directives? What were your emotions and thoughts? What would you have done if the family was here? What if the family had been here and said no to extubation? Was the medical futility policy helpful to you? Did it provide the needed support to make a decision? How can the caregiver group best be supportive in situations like this? The discussion that ensued offered empathy and support to the caregivers, and hospital leaders underscored their commitment to supporting the caregivers' taking actions consistent with their conscience and sense of ethics.

After some time, a brother was contacted and came from New York to the patient's bedside. He phoned family in Syria from the hospital and spoke with the wife and other male relatives. When he gave consent to the physician, the extubation was conducted. The patient died 30 minutes later.

Grief Touches Grief

One of our Rounds sessions at Women and Infants Hospital, entitled "Grief Touches Grief," addressed the impact of patient losses on health care professionals' personal loss experiences. The ways in which work is affected were key elements of the exchange. A hospital chaplain spoke of sitting with a woman who was being comforted by her sister following perinatal loss. The chaplain was recently bereaved, her sister having died. She spoke about how difficult it was to stay focused on the patient as thoughts of missing the love and closeness with her own sister intruded into her mind. A physician on the panel talked about his experience being treated for cancer and, while interjecting humorous moments from his encounters, discussed his feelings of occupying the dual perspective of doctor and patient. Members of the audience also shared.

Staff sharing loss and also the vicarious comfort they sometimes derive from caregiving provided a powerful experience. Among the comments shared following the presentations was this one by a social worker: "I am so appreciative to everyone: sharing their own grief and loss experiences. It is so very difficult to do. I also appreciated Dr. L's willingness to be vulnerable and share his own experiences working with physicians every day, this means so much."

When Birth and Death Collide

Another case inspired an unusually high degree of compassion when a young, homeless woman was admitted to deliver her baby only to learn that what she thought was the baby's foot emerging from the birth canal was a cervical tumor. The baby was delivered by cesarean section and the woman was treated for cancer. This tragic collision of birth and approaching death in this case led staff to be supportive and attentive to a degree they rarely feel compelled to exhibit. They fulfilled one of the patient's wishes by taking her from the hospital to go shopping at a local discount store and out for a meal. This patient received her hospice care in the same oncology unit that treated her, and the staff, in a very real sense, became her family. The patient's actual family, who lived several hours away, arrived only after death to collect her belongings. When the patient's mother began to look for the patient's checkbook and her disability checks, one of the nurses took the checkbook with the promise to "take care of it." This fiercely protective instinct toward the patient, as well as negative affect toward the neglectful and exploitative family, was powerful.

In some instances, staff members experience their role of providing care and safe passage to dying patients as a spiritual function: "There is a presence of God, and for me that presence manifests itself during the day-to-day acts of kindness, the acts of love, the acts of caring and understanding even if we are struggling as a team and label a patient as 'difficult'" (Sinclair, Raffin, Pereira, & Guebert, 2006).

Outcomes

In 2006–2007, the Schwartz Center for Compassionate Caregiving commissioned the Goodman Research Group to evaluate the outcomes of Schwartz Center Rounds. Investigators gathered self-reported changes in health care providers who had attended Rounds, including emotional and psychosocial dimensions of patient care interactions, teamwork, and support for the providers. Goodman made an effort to see how sites who offered Rounds differed, comparing experienced and new sites, and revisiting new sites after the Rounds had been presented seven or more times to examine changes over time. There were six "experienced" sites and 10 "new" sites in the study. Most of the hospitals were located in the Northeast, but several of them were located in the Midwest, and one each in the South and in the West.

Respondents were characterized by demographic characteristics, discipline, and years of practice. In addition, respondents were asked about the frequency of attending Rounds, allowing for the examination of any "dose response"—the impact of ongoing exposure to and participation in Rounds on patient care, teamwork, and staff support.

A positive relationship emerged between attending Rounds and respondents reporting more attunement to patients' nonverbal cues, feeling more compassion and comfortable working with patients and families, and experiencing greater energy and a wider range of strategies for handling difficult situations. Frequency of attendance was statistically significantly correlated with more positive responses in these areas. Positive correlations were also seen between Rounds attendance and respondents' ratings of their appreciation of the roles of team members, as well as the level of their own participation on the team.

Overall, medical caregivers who attended Schwartz Center Rounds reported an improved capacity to cope with the emotional demands of caregiving and a reduction in overall stress. Respondents described improvements in the culture of their institutions and that they became more patient centered. In addition, clinicians noted enhanced insight regarding patients' psychosocial needs and concerns through regular Schwartz Center Rounds participation (Lown & Manning, 2010).

Pearls

- **Shared support:** Schwartz Center Rounds establishes a level playing field—not a given in the general medical environment. Colleagues' compassion and empathy are enhanced.
- **Reduced risk of burnout and compassion fatigue**: The communal sharing and support of the Schwartz Center Rounds relieve stress and bolster collegial relationships. Participants have described the Rounds experience as offering moments of clarity. The validation of the emotions invested in caregiving, recognition of the ways in which those emotions are triggered and expressed, are supportive to staff. This experience provides a needed outlet, plus models and reinforces the value of compassionate caregiving at all levels. Nowhere else amidst the more typical clinical discussions, focused as they are on the technical dimension of healthcare, are the emotional needs of staff confronted in an affirmative group context. While most medical case conferences engage the mind, Schwartz Center Rounds deliberately engages also the heart and the soul.
- **Validation from senior leaders:** It is good practice to invite senior administrators to attend Schwartz Center Rounds. Impressive examples of compassion and teamwork are described. Having executives and professionals, who do not spend their days at the bedside, show their interest in and admiration for the clinicians' work is mutually beneficial.

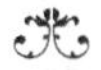

Pitfalls

- **Knowing the audience members:** Sometimes comments are made that can feel critical. It is the facilitator's job to intervene to support everyone and create a secure environment. Rounds are not intended to be self-congratulatory sessions, but it is essential that they be a climate of respect and safety. The author had one experience in which visitors from a neighboring hospital commented in a way that felt critical and like grandstanding to some members of the panel and in-house audience. The facilitator, not an employee of either institution, did not recognize the dynamic as it was unfolding. The fallout was significant in the uptick of negative evaluations. Subsequent cases were chosen very carefully to be noncontroversial. In addition, all members of the audience were asked to offer their name and job/institution before adding to the discussion. Finally, the planning committee "deputized" all of its members to jump in directly or signal to the facilitator in the interest of protecting the participants and climate of Rounds. This hospital has continued to have many successful and well-attended Rounds.
- **Planning committee management:** Planning committees, like any working group, will experience varied group dynamics. Cultivating open reflection and feedback are important for the working relationships and success of the program. In fact, conflicts in the committee can contaminate the process, the ability to find and agree upon cases, and the stability of group membership. It is important to seek consultation from the professional staff at the Schwartz Center for guidance and support.

In the broadest terms, the enhancement of quality of life for patients *and* their medical caregivers by improving communication, compassion, empathy, and stress reduction is a positive legacy of Kenneth Schwartz's vision that resonates with the role and mission of clinical social work in the oncology setting. As caregivers, we do well to remember the powerful impact of the compassion we offer to those facing life-altering illnesses: As caregivers, we do well to remember the powerful impact of the compassion we offer to those facing life-altering illnesses; even simple acts of compassion make "the unbearable bearable" (Abbasi, 2012, p. 93).

Revisiting the opening theme of "quality of life," the staff support function of oncology social work and the contribution of Schwartz Center Rounds in the oncology setting both aim to nurture the quality of the lives of caregivers providing care for cancer patients and their families. Caring for the caregivers is a vital pillar in the structure of compassionate, quality health care.

Because clinical social work in the medical environment is an ancillary profession, a secondary benefit of Schwartz Center Rounds is the opportunity to demonstrate and underscore the contribution of social workers to the multidisciplinary team, as well as to patient care. The fundamental philosophy of Rounds is that dialogue takes place on a level playing field where caregivers share the burdens and joys of investing fully in the care of patients and the partnership with colleagues. It is a positive opportunity for all involved to have open and candid communication about their work.

As caregivers in the medical environment, we need a place where can we share on a personal level about our cases and bear witness to *our* pain, as well as our patients'. Schwartz Center Rounds is a sheltered and confidential place to mutually recognize and sustain our efforts in the often-arduous circumstances that accompany caring for those facing challenging illnesses. The quality of the caregiving itself—beyond the medical orders and details of nursing ministrations—is acknowledged and honored. Schwartz Center Rounds is a process that allows emotional wisdom and intelligence to occupy its rightful place alongside intellect, conceptual mastery, and technical expertise. Compassionate caregiving protects health care professionals from burnout and the erosion of morale that accompany stressful work. This unique forum supports and sustains both compassionate caregiving and ethical practice. Though Emerson's statement, "It is one of the most beautiful compensations of this life that no man can sincerely try to help another without helping himself," may be true, I would argue that the reverse is true as well. In its capacity to benefit both staff and patients, it is "twice blest."

NOTES

1. Miriam Hospital, Providence, Rhode Island, and Women and Infants Hospital, Providence, Rhode Island, each have Rounds six times per year. Each of these hospitals offers Rounds to the entire institution, featuring cases from a wide representation of departments. The author facilitates Rounds at both sites.
2. The poignant history of Schwartz's inspiration to create the program is beyond the scope of this chapter, but very much worth reading about.

REFERENCES

Abbasi, K. (2012). Making the unbearable bearable. *Journal of the Royal Society of Medicine*, *105*(3), 93.

American Medical Association (AMA). (1997, June). Physician resources, medical ethics, opinion. Retrieved from http://www.ama-assn.org//ama/pub/physician-resources/medical-ethics/code-medical-ethics/opinion2037.page

Browning, D. M., Meyer, E. C., Truog, R. D., & Solomon, M. Z. (2007). Difficult conversations in health care: Cultivating relational learning to address the hidden curriculum. *Academic Medicine: Journal of the Association of American Medical Colleges*, *82*(9), 905–913. doi:10.1097/ACM.0b013e31812f77b9

Cubic, B. A., & Gatewood, E. E. (2008). ACGME core competencies: Helpful information for psychologists [Congresses]. *Journal of Clinical Psychology in Medical Settings*, *15*(1), 28–39. doi:10.1007/s10880-008-9101-3

Goodrich, J. C. J. (2008). Seeing the person in the patient: The point of care review. In E. Rowling (Ed.), *The king's fund*. London, England: The King's Fund.

The Joint Commission. (2010). *Roadmap for hospitals*. Oakbrook Terrace, IL: Author.

Jones, B. L. (2005). Pediatric palliative and end-of-life care: The role of social work in pediatric oncology. *Journal of Social Work in End-of-Life and Palliative Care*, *1*(4), 35–61.

Karnieli-Miller, O., Vu, T. R., Holtman, M. C., Clyman, S. G., & Inui, T. S. (2010). Medical students' professionalism narratives: A window on the informal and hidden curriculum. *Academic Medicine: Journal of the Association of American Medical Colleges*, *85*(1), 124–133. doi:10.1097/ACM.0b013e3181c42896

Lown, B. A., & Manning, C. F. (2010). The Schwartz Center Rounds: Evaluation of an interdisciplinary approach to enhancing patient-centered communication, teamwork, and provider support. *Academic Medicine: Journal of the Association of American Medical Colleges*, *85*(6), 1073–1081. doi:10.1097/ACM.0b013e3181dbf741

Mainiero, M. B., & Lourenco, A. P. (2011). The ACGME core competencies: Changing the way we educate and evaluate residents. *Medicine and Health, Rhode Island*, *94*(6), 164–166.

Porcel, J. M., Casademont, J., Conthe, P., Pinilla, B., Pujol, R., & Garcia-Alegria, J. (2012). Core competencies in internal medicine. *European Journal of Internal Medicine*, *23*(4), 338–341. doi:10.1016/j.ejim.2012.03.003

Short, M. W., Jorgensen, J. E., Edwards, J. A., Blankenship, R. B., & Roth, B. J. (2009). Assessing intern core competencies with an objective structured clinical examination. *Journal of Graduate Medical Education*, *1*(1), 30–36. doi:10.4300/01.01.0006

Sinclair, S., Raffin, S., Pereira, J., & Guebert, N. (2006). Collective soul: The spirituality of an interdisciplinary palliative care team. *Palliative and Supportive Care*, *4*, 13–24.

Snow, A., & Gilbertson, K. (2011). The complexity of cancer in multiple family members: Dynamics of social work collaboration. *Social Work in Health Care*, *50*(6), 411–423. doi:10.1080/00981389.2011.579693

Sorensen, M., & Liu, E. T. (1995). With a different voice: Integrating the psychosocial perspective into routine oncology care. *Breast Cancer Research and Treatment*, *35*(1), 39–42.

Wen, T., Huang, B., Mosley, V., & Afsar-Manesh, N. (2012). Promoting patient-centred care through trainee feedback: Assessing residents' C-I-CARE (ARC) program. *BMJ Quality and Safety*, *21*(3), 225–233. doi:10.1136/bmjqs-2011-000332

Wenzel, J., Shaha, M., Klimmek, R., & Krumm, S. (2011, July). Working through grief and loss: Oncology nurses' perspectives on professional bereavement. *Oncology Nursing Forum*, *38*(4), E272–E282.

Youngson, G. G. (2011). Teaching and assessing non-technical skills. The surgeon: *Journal of the Royal Colleges of Surgeons of Edinburgh and Ireland*, *9*(Suppl. 1), S35–S37. doi:10.1016/j.surge.2010.11.004

108

Sima Zadeh, Jayne Phillips, Jeasmine E. Aizvera, and Lori Wiener

Maintaining Competent Teams in Pediatric Oncology

Key Concepts

- *Oncology social workers have substantive relational, psychological, communication, and interpersonal skills to lead interventions and develop and maintain competent team functioning in this intense work environment.*
- *Competent interdisciplinary pediatric oncology teams can offer the highest quality of care to patients and families while reducing compassion fatigue and burnout among team members.*
- *Conceptual models that include four domains of stress and the process of worker engagement help to understand ways to improve team functioning.*
- *However, there are specific challenges to maintaining competent teams in pediatric oncology, such as providing continuous improvement in timely and empathic communication and support of patients and families.*
- *A broad range of interventions and their benefits and considerations are suggested.*

Working in the field of pediatric oncology can be both exceptionally rewarding and emotionally exhausting. When health care providers are highly stressed, their work performance and personal health can be affected. Staff support and wellness interventions not only benefit the individual provider and the interdisciplinary team but also are necessary to the delivery of high-quality care. This chapter addresses the unique stresses that pediatric oncology social workers face; reviews research in occupational stress, burnout, and compassion fatigue; and describes risk factors along with health-promoting behaviors. Programs of intervention that encourage health care systems to pay attention to staff wellness and foster healthy team functioning are discussed.

Pediatric Care and Stress

Having a child diagnosed with cancer is always a devastating experience. It is also profoundly challenging for the pediatric health care provider. From a global survey of over 700 professionals working in pediatric oncology, social work was reported to be the discipline providing services most frequently to parents and children in oncology settings (Wiener et al., 2012). Social workers support parents and children at a time when their family's future is threatened and complex medical decisions need to be made. Social workers bring essential and unique skills to the interdisciplinary team to assist in the provision of optional psychosocial care (Jones, 2006) throughout the treatment trajectory, in preparation for survivorship, or when end-of-life care is needed. The Society of International Pediatric Oncology published guidelines for the recognition, prevention, and remediation of burnout in health care professionals participating in the care of children with cancer (Spinetta et al., 2000). Although these guidelines were written many years ago, the causes of burnout have not changed. These include

> *dealing on a daily basis with life-threatening illness, seeing many young children with compromised health, being in frequent contact with children having difficult treatment and recovery trajectories, having to*

> *assume the emotional burdens of the patients and their families, seeing children die, living within a professional culture of never being allowed to complain, always having to be "up" for all patients and families, and being drained by the most highly distraught families with little or no time left over for the rest of the families.*
>
> —*Spinetta et al., 2000, p. 123*

Wanting to "make things better" is a natural response but also can risk exposing professional boundaries and insufficient competence.

Impact of Burnout and Compassion Fatigue

Overall, work-related stressors in the health care field have increasingly become an area of concern (Reaves & Groninger, 2013). Research has sought to clarify particular stressors and develop appropriate preventative interventions. There are several factors associated with work-related stressors including limited resources, staffing difficulties, and insurance reimbursement changes. In addition, health care professionals are working more hours per week than ever (Medland, Howard-Ruben, & Whitaker, 2004). Although the terms *burnout* and *compassion fatigue* are related to cumulative stressors and are often used interchangeably, there are distinct differences. Reaves and Groninger (2013) describe the concepts as different entities on a spectrum of job satisfaction.

Burnout

Burnout results from stressors that arise from the clinician's interaction with the work environment (Maslach, Schaufeli, & Leiter, 2001), whereas compassion fatigue evolves from the relationship between the clinician and the patient (Bush, 2009). Burnout is a prolonged stress reaction experienced as emotional exhaustion. This depletion of one's emotional resources coupled with decreased energy is the core element of burnout (Maslach et al., 2001). This sense of "running on empty" fuels the need to detach from one's work. This detachment, known as depersonalization, further detracts from a feeling of reward and personal accomplishment that previously was so gratifying.

Compassion Fatigue

Compassion fatigue has been described as a gradual process that moves from compassion discomfort to compassion stress to compassion fatigue (Bush, 2009). When examining causes or predictors of compassion fatigue, one must consider the variability of individual responses to stress. For example, providers who are highly motivated, idealistic, and self-giving may be at increased risk

Table 108.1.
Red Flags for Symptoms of Burnout

At Work
• I find myself less engaged in my work with patients, work projects, or colleagues.
• I feel irritable with colleagues who invest so much (or so little) time with our patients.
• I feel unable to concentrate at work or get through my daily work tasks.
• I feel unsupported by or unappreciated by my coworkers or supervisors.
• I feel my paycheck is too low for the work I do.
• I have difficulty feeling satisfied that I have done a good job for my patients.
Outside of Work
• I have had work-related bad dreams/nightmares.
• I have been unable to get something specific to work out of my head.
• I have thought a lot about quitting my job.
• I worry about my own child/family member getting the same disease as my patients.
• I have unwanted thoughts or memories of children I have worked with pop up in my head.
• I have been questioning my competency in doing the work I have been doing.
• I have been feeling dread about going to work.

Note: Endorsing two or more statements in any category suggests a need for assessment of compassion fatigue.

of compassion fatigue if they do not perceive they are moving toward their care goals and/or are powerless to change their environment to do so (Bush, 2009). Team members may struggle with countertransference and boundary issues, with trying to meet personal needs through the patient, with an overwhelming sense of responsibility, with unrealistic expectations and feelings of personal and/or professional inadequacy, with unresolved grief from previous deaths in their personal or professional lives, and with a lack of sufficient knowledge (Bush, 2009; Keidel, 2002; Medland et al., 2004).

Consequences of Burnout and Compassion Fatigue

Burnout and compassion fatigue have been shown to have an impact on the individual in multiple domains of functioning. Specifically, burnout has been linked to poorer quality of work performance and decreased ability to express empathy. Burnout has also been associated with health consequences, from headaches to cardiovascular mortality, and psychological consequences, such as depression (Showalter, 2010; Wallace, Lemaire, & Ghali, 2009).

Stress-Reducing Factors

The concept of Total Stress structures a way to consider multiple domains impacting adaptation simultaneously: physical, psychological, social, and spiritual factors (Figure 108.1; Reaves & Groninger, 2013). The value of considering the concept of Total Stress lies in the ability of the health care provider to think globally about the impact of these four factors in terms of his or her own situation. Compassion fatigue and burnout are fluid concepts that wax and wane in intensity and influence as each provider confronts his or her own level of stress. Therefore, when we consider interventions to reduce stress, it is helpful to picture how each domain plays a critical role in our well-being. It is within this framework that we describe factors known to reduce stress, compassion fatigue, and burnout.

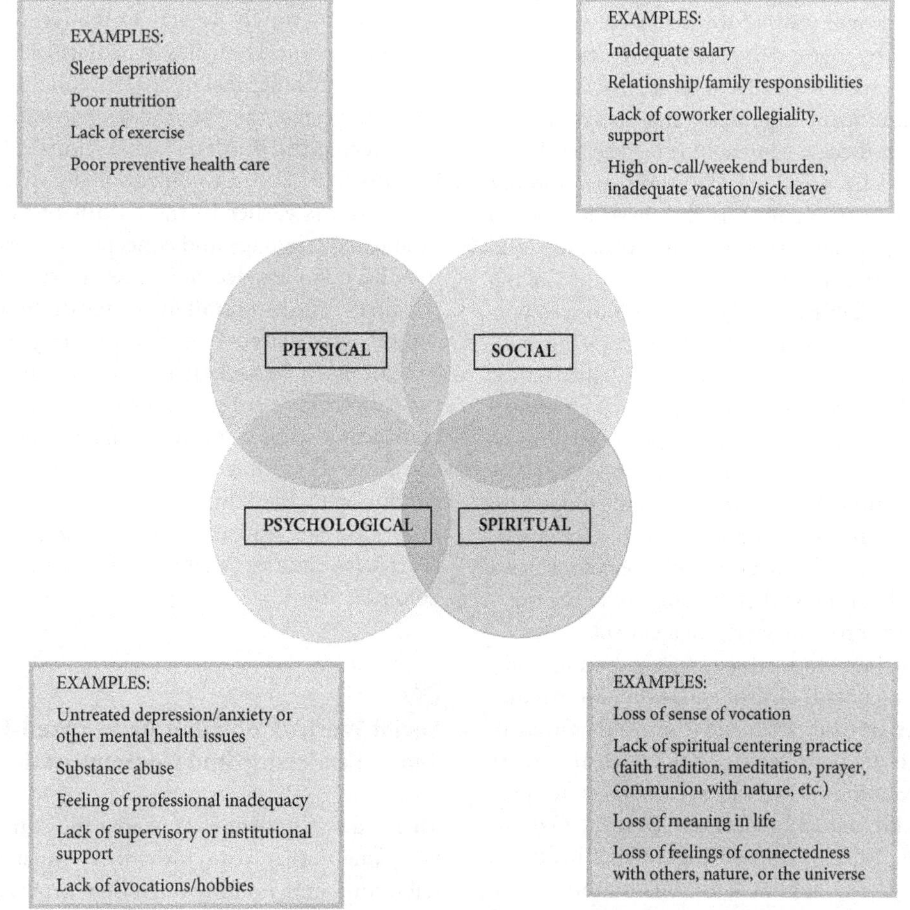

Figure 108.1. Venn Diagram of Total Stress
From Reaves and Groninger (2013).

Reducing Burnout Through Work Engagement

The idea that burnout and compassion fatigue can reduce the quality of an individual's work and well-being implies that ensuring provider wellness not only protects the provider's well-being but also the quality of the care provided. The term *wellness* is used to describe the care provider's physical, mental, and emotional health and well-being. Wellness extends beyond the absence of distress to infer that the provider is challenged, thriving, and achieving professional and personal success (Wallace et al., 2009). Appropriate work–life balance, personal healing activities, spiritual self-care, realistic tolerance of failure, awareness of personal and professional goals, thriving professional networks, a workplace culture of support and respect, and resilience are critical characteristics and strategies that can improve the wellness of providers. A combination of personal, professional, and organizational strategies have consistently been found to reduce compassion fatigue among cancer care providers (Najjar, Davis, Beck-Coon, & Doebbeling, 2009; Medland et al., 2004). Success, however, often depends on culture change within the health care environment.

Bakker, Schaufeli, Leiter, and Taris (2008, p. 187) introduced the concept of *work engagement* as a "positive, fulfilling, affective-motivational state of work-related well-being that is characterized by vigor, dedication, and absorption." Work engagement is characterized as a protective factor and one of the most significant organizational approaches to dealing with burnout. Because burnout is largely predicted by job demands and by a lack of job resources, another approach to dealing with burnout is the provision of job resources, including social support from colleagues and supervisors, performance feedback, and autonomy. Having such job resources available to staff has been found to buffer the impact of high job demands (Bakker, Demorouti, & Euwema, 2005) and reduce turnover (Schaufeli & Baker, 2004). In fact, studies have shown how the lack of critical job resources—autonomy and social support—are linked with turnover intention. Supervisory support, specifically task-centered communication and informal, supportive interactions, reduces burnout among health care social workers (Kim & Lee, 2009). Social work supervision, as a job resource, can help build worker attachment to the organization and may also promote work engagement.

Factors that contribute to work engagement on an individual level can have a positive impact on team performance as engaged workers transfer their vigor and dedication in collaborative efforts to their teams (Bakker et al., 2008). Team-based interventions have shown promise in promoting wellness and reducing burnout (Zadeh, Gamba, Hudson, & Wiener, 2012). Common ingredients include a team-based, particpatory approach in which work group members have a shared responsibility in developing educational topics, supporting peers, identifying and planning ways to address areas of work-related stress, or implementing best practices.

Benefits and Challenges of the Pediatric Team

Integrating multiple disciplines into a unified psychosocial team creates many opportunities while also presenting several unique challenges. Caring for children with cancer presents team members with dire circumstances in which pediatric team members must function without being overwhelmed by the family's grief, confusion, disorganization, despair, or suffering. Furthermore, the pediatric team works with the patient and with his or her parents/caregivers who are often trying to maintain an active and central role in their child's care (Papadatou, Bluebond-Langner, & Goldman, 2011).

In the process of providing care, the bonds that develop among pediatric team members may appear to exclude or imply that those outside the pediatric care setting would not understand. This can indicate the development of a closed system among pediatric staff in which new or different approaches to the extreme stress of the situation may not be considered. For example, the difficulty of staff communicating in a timely way about the terminal illness process with patients and families in pediatrics has been well documented (Durall, Zurakowski, & Wolfe, 2012). Some authors have suggested that physicians introduce the concept of considering the burdens (e.g., serious side effects) and the benefits (e.g., cure or control of the disease) of treatment with parents earlier in the treatment process. This might establish a language and concept for more readily addressing the complex decision making required if the illness advances. Training staff to engage in these difficult conversations with patients and families in pediatrics is another educational approach that has shown effectiveness in building team competence. The bonds among a well-functioning team can also be a means to sustain, nourish, and replenish the staff so they can have a continued empathic connection with the family's unique tragedy while remaining grounded in a realistic understanding of the boundaries of their roles and responsibilities (Browning, Meyer, Truog, & Solomon 2007).

Social Work's Contribution to a Well-Functioning Team: Leadership and Communication

There are challenges to creating and maintaining a well-functioning team. Members must respect the contributions and opinions of other professional disciplines. They must acclimate to a field of work with high emotional burden and be able to tolerate the uncertainty of providing

Table 108.2.
Intervention Strategies for Enhancing Team Performance and Reducing Burnout

Intervention	Benefits	Considerations
Staff Support		
Peer support groups	Support and consultation; connection to others; sense of mutual aid	Staff required to organize and lead sessions
Support in dealing with appropriate engagement and team complaints	Help staff feel heard; help problem solve; opportunity to process or debrief for a defined purpose	Staffing required; difficult to have staff feel safe sharing; may pit staff against managers; unclear outcomes
Educational		
Staff-designed lecture or wellness series	Staff ownership of topics raises autonomy and problem-solving skills	Investment of time and resources to plan and implement a meaningful curriculum
Coping strategies	Increases ability to manage stressful situations and maintain high-quality self-care and work	Tremendous variability must be respected
Self-Care		
Physical activity; exercise	Helps maintain stress relief and keep body healthy	Time required; availability of exercise modalities at work is based on facility resources
Meditation/relaxation	Provides individual the ability to release stress	A quiet space for meditation/relaxation needed
Proper eating/healthy sleep habits, personal recreation	Supports physical and emotional well-being	Offering nutritious options at work can be a cost issue; personal sleep/recreation habits are up to individual to harness
Finding a balance between professional obligations and personal time	Maintains healthy work–life balance	Flexible work scheduling may be needed
Shared decision making when tackling new issues or problems	Raises autonomy, encourages active problem solving and promotes investment in outcomes	Coordination and identified team leadership required
Team Based		
Relationship building	Allows individuals to feel comfortable with their peers and increases support from others	Staff reluctance to engage with their peers based on fear of breaches in confidentiality
Communication skills	Helps individuals communicate needs	Communication styles will vary based on individual and cultural variants
Work/Organizational		
Sustainable workload	Allows staff to have personal time without feeling overwhelmed; provides opportunity to maintain quality care when not spread thin	Limited resources; staffing turnover may inhibit
Recognition, rewards, and opportunity for career advancement	Provides staff a sense of accomplishment and motivation to maintain work responsibilities	Creativity, flexibility, and strong leadership required
Agency-based programs that promote healthy lifestyles—e.g., on-site exercise facilities, meditation, yoga; proper eating/sleeping habits; work–life balance	Staff can integrate healthy practices as part of their work life; conveys a sense of organizational concern and caring for individual wellness	Limited time to access resources, if available
Mentoring	Encourages reframing of clinical experience and clinical role	Nonjudgmental, timely
Professional skill building/development considerations	Enhances sense of mastery and self-confidence	Requires flexibility to be tailored to individual learning style and level of education
Bereavement activities	Provides opportunity for closure, loss recognition, and building resiliency skills	Coordination of multiple interventions on a regular basis, allow for self-selection of activities

services when well-defined psychosocial standards of care are absent. Disease acuity and team size play an important role because the sicker the child is, the more complex the care becomes. The more complex the care is, the more disciplines are involved, and the more time the team needs to work to sustain functionality and growth (Jünger, Pestinger, Elsner, Krumm, & Radbruch, 2007). Caring for a child with cancer is almost always complex, and hence, healthy teamwork is essential.

Leadership

Strong and visionary leadership is necessary for any team to succeed. This calls for oncology social work leaders who are proactive, inspire teamwork and mutual support, provide time and space for collaborative projects, recognize that conflict is inevitable, and mediate conflict before it becomes destructive (Bronstein, 2003; Wittenberg-Lyles, Oliver, Demiris, & Courtney, 2007). Although each setting is dependent on available resources, the skilled social work leader in pediatric oncology works to sustain manageable caseloads, professional autonomy, and flexible work hours and offers training that includes self-care to support a healthy work–life balance. The strong leader also formally evaluates team health, is not afraid to recognize when the team is not dynamic or functioning at its highest, and is willing to bring in outside help for team maintenance, new ideas, or enhancing or rebuilding communication processes (O'Connor, Fisher, & Guilfoyle, 2006).

Communication

Regularly scheduled interdisciplinary team meetings where patient and/or family care are discussed are essential. Within these meetings, communication patterns must be established, respected, and honored so that each member is invited to share his or her insights and concerns and care plans are collaboratively established.

Steps to Avoid Dysfunctional Teams

The field of pediatric oncology is ripe for the easy blurring of professional boundaries with patients and families. Social workers spend considerable time with family members, learning family history and values and addressing day-to-day challenges. This can lead to relationships that resemble "pseudo" families (Smith, 1997). Such closeness can be comforting for patients and family members but can also put pressure on professional limits or boundaries. This requires vigilance to ensure objectivity in professional judgments. Increased usage of different forms of social media, such as blogging, social networks (e.g., Facebook, Twitter, and LinkedIn), being invited to private websites where families update their child's health status (e.g., CaringBridge), or multimedia sharing (e.g., YouTube), is making it progressively more difficult to maintain clear professional boundaries (Wiener, Crum, Grady, & Merchant, 2011).

Clearly defined roles are critical both within the pediatric oncology team and for those who refer patients for care from outside the team. Leadership must respect the culture of each discipline and support the role social work plays. This is particularly important for the physician(s) in charge of a pediatric oncology program. Many disciplines feel a sense of ownership over "psychosocial support." Poor role clarity, role conflict, turf issues, and perceptions of lack of professional respect can cause frustration and work dissatisfaction for pediatric psychosocial oncology providers (Wiener et al., 2012). Table 108.2 lists interventions currently used to improve team functioning in pediatrics and reduce burnout, as well as the benefits and possible limitations of each.

Pearls

- Social work has substantive relational, psychological, communication, and interpersonal skills to take leadership in implementing interventions that will develop and maintain competent team functioning in this most intense work environment of pediatric oncology.
- There are multiple interventions that can help staff manage the challenges of working with pediatric patients and their families.
- The bonds with team members in pediatric oncology can nourish and replenish staff, but leaders must be vigilant to maintain an environment of open communication that requires ongoing assessment of appropriate boundaries, encourages empathic engagement and communication with patients and families, and considers new ideas and resources from outside the team, as well as from its own members.
- All staff require ongoing training in communication and relational skills to engage in the difficult conversations and empathic connection required, especially when the illness advances.

Pitfalls

- The emotional intensity of caring for highly distressed pediatric patients and their families can result in burnout, avoidance, and lack of empathy in professional interactions with this population.

- Failure to have ongoing training and support of all staff to engage in difficult conversations and empathic connections can decrease team functioning and morale.

Social workers are accustomed to caring for others, including patients and their family members and the staff who care for them. Social workers offer a unique voice to the care provided to children with cancer and their families (Jones, 2006), but a lack of recognition of one's own limitations or professional fatigue can lead to denial, shame, fear, and problematic countertransference responses. Awareness of the need to refresh, and proactive steps to refuel, as individual and teams, mitigates the severity of stress and compassion fatigue. Attending to how similarities or differences between oneself and the patient/family in terms of culture, race, sex, sexual orientation, age, illness trajectory, spiritual beliefs, education, and economic situation may influence the level of worker involvement can provide important insight into the risk of developing burnout (Keidel, 2002). As leaders and integral members of the interdisciplinary team, oncology social workers have the potential to serve as role models in self-awareness and self-care and can promote programs that sustain resilience and work engagement among the various teams with which they work, ultimately yielding excellence in pediatric psychosocial care. There is no doubt that working in the field of pediatric oncology harbors tremendous stresses, but this goes hand in hand with many extraordinarily beautiful human moments. As Jones and Weisenfluh (2003, p. 443) so eloquently expressed:

> *One must bring to the challenge a willingness to bear witness to suffering, an ability to hold hope and despair in the same moment, a sense of personal balance to the work, a tremendous amount of personal insight, and a way to make meaning out of the loss. Some say this is impossible work, but it is not only possible but also powerful and life affirming.*

REFERENCES

Bakker, A. B., Demerouti, E., & Euwema, M. (2005). Job resources buffer the impact of job demands on burnout. *Journal of Occupational Health Psychology, 10*(2), 170–180.

Bakker, A. B., Schaufeli, W. B., Leiter, M. P., & Taris, T. W. (2008). Work engagement: An emerging concept in occupational health psychology. *Work and Stress, 22*(3), 187–200.

Bronstein, L. R. (2003). A model for interdisciplinary collaboration. *Social Work, 48*(3), 297–306.

Browning, D. M., Meyer, E. C., Truog, R. D., & Solomon, M. Z. (2007). Difficult conversations in health care: Cultivating relational learning to address the hidden curriculum. *Academic Medicine, 82*(9), 905–913.

Bush, N. J. (2009). Compassion fatigue: Are you at risk? *Oncology Nursing Forum, 36*, 24–28.

Durall, A., Zurakowski, D., & Wolfe, J. (2012). Barriers to conducting advance care discussions for children with life-threatening conditions. *Pediatrics, 129*(4), 975–982.

Jones, B. L. (2006). Companionship, control, and compassion: A social work perspective on the needs of children with cancer and their families at the end of life. *Journal of Palliative Medicine, 9*(3), 774–788.

Jones, B. L., & Weisenfluh, S. (2003). Pediatric palliative and end-of-life care: Developmental and spiritual issues of dying children. *Smith College Studies in Social Work, 73*(3), 423–443.

Jünger, S., Pestinger, M., Elsner, F., Krumm, N., & Radbruch, L. (2007). Criteria for successful multiprofessional cooperation in palliative care teams. *Palliative Medicine, 21*, 347–354.

Keidel, G. C. (2002). Burnout and compassion fatigue among hospice caregivers. *American Journal of Hospital Palliative Care, 19*(3), 200–205.

Kim, H., & Lee, S. Y. (2009). Supervisory communication, burnout, and turnover intention among social workers in health care settings. *Social Work in Health Care, 48*(4), 364–385.

Maslach, C., Schaufeli, W. B., & Leiter, M. P. (2001). Job burnout. *Annual Reviews Psychology*, 52, 397–422.

Medland, J., Howard-Ruben, J., & Whitaker, E. (2004). Fostering psychosocial wellness in oncology nurses: Addressing burnout and social support in the workplace. *Oncology Nursing Forum, 31*(1), 47–54.

Najjar, N., Davis, L. W., Beck-Coon, K., & Doebbeling, C. C. (2009). Compassion fatigue: A review of the research to date and relevance to cancer-care providers. *Journal of Health Psychology, 14*, 267–277.

O'Connor, M., Fisher, C., & Guilfoyle, A. (2006). Interdisciplinary teams in palliative care: A critical reflection. *International Journal of Palliative Nursing, 12*(3), 132–137.

Papadatou, D., BluebondLangner, M., & Goldman, A. (2011). The team in pediatric palliative care: Development, organization, functionality, and effectiveness. In J. Wolfe, P. Hinds, & B. Sourkes (Eds.), *Textbook of interdisciplinary pediatric palliative care* (pp. 55–63). Philadelphia, PA: Elsevier Publishers.

Reaves, A. L., & Groninger, H. (2013). Staff stress and burnout. In A. M. Berger, J. L. Shuster, & J. H. Von Roehnn (Eds.), *Principles and practice of palliative care and supportive oncology* (4th ed., pp. 730–738). Philadelphia, PA: Williams and Wilkins.

Schaufeli, W. B., & Bakker, A. B. (2004). Job demands, job resources, and their relationship with burnout and engagement: A multi-sample study. *Journal of Organizational Behavior, 25*, 293–315.

Showalter, S. E. (2010). Compassion fatigue: What is it? Why does it matter? Recognizing the symptoms, acknowledging the impact, developing the tools to prevent compassion fatigue, and strengthen the professional already suffering from the effects. *American Journal of Hospital Palliative Care, 27*, 239–242.

Smith, J. B. (1997). Can you handle home care? *RN Journal, 60*, 51–53.

Spinetta, J. J., Jankovic, M., Ben Arush, M. W., Eden, T., Epelman, C., Greenberg, M. L., . . . Masera, G. (2000). Guidelines for the recognition, prevention, and remediation of burnout in health care professionals participating in the care of children with cancer: Report of the SIOP working committee on psychosocial issues in pediatric oncology. *Medical and Pediatric Oncology*, *35*, 122–125.

Wallace, J. E., Lemaire, J. B., & Ghali, W. A. (2009). Physician wellness: A missing quality indicator. *Lancet*, *374*(9702), 1714–1721.

Wiener, L., Crum, C., Grady, C., & Merchant, M. (2011). To friend or not to friend: The use of social media in clinical oncology. *Journal of Oncology Practice*, *8*, 103–106.

Wiener, L., Oppenheim, D., Breyer, J., Battles, H., Zadeh, S., & Farkas-Patenaude, A. (2012). A worldview of the professional experiences and training needs of pediatric psycho-oncologists. *Psycho-Oncology*, *21*(9), 944–953.

Wittenberg-Lyles, E. M., Oliver, D. P., Demiris, G., & Courtney, K. L. (2007). Assessing the nature and process of hospice interdisciplinary team meetings. *Journal of Hospice and Palliative Nursing*, *9*(1), 17–21.

Zadeh, S., Gamba, N., Hudson, C., & Wiener, L. (2012). Taking care of care providers: A wellness program for pediatric nurses. *Journal of Pediatric Oncology Nursing*, *29*(5), 294–299.

Epilogue: Oncology Social Work Leadership: Innovators in a Changing World

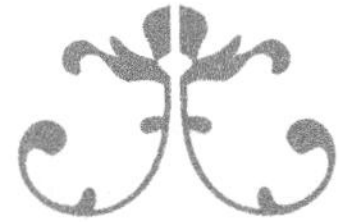

Grace Christ, Carolyn Messner, and Lynn Behar

The development of this inaugural *Handbook of Oncology Social Work: Psychosocial Care for Persons with Cancer* affords an opportunity to create a repository of the state of the art of this specialty, to consider what has been achieved, and to explore directions for the future. Special thanks are due to those who have contributed directly as authors and to the many oncology social workers and other practitioners who have contributed indirectly through their extraordinary practice competence, professional presentations and publications, and passionate and persistent commitment to helping patients and families affected by cancer in the best possible evidence-based ways.

The authors document a growing capacity to lead in critical areas of scientific and system change and to engage in the development of psychosocial science and practice-relevant research. They have become effective leaders and innovators in ways not previously imagined. The *Handbook* includes contributions from a broad range of social work scholars, practitioners, academics, researchers, and administrators. The breadth of roles played by oncology social workers in cancer centers, community cancer programs, major cancer education initiatives, private therapy and consultative practices, academic institutions, pharmaceutical and medical businesses, and governmental research and policy agencies documents the widening recognition of the importance of social work knowledge, skills, and values in the psychosocial care of cancer patients and their families.

Two areas of change have also affected the professional role of the oncology social worker (see Chapters 1 and 79):

1. Changes in the science of cancer treatment have led to cancer patients' greater longevity, more survivors, greater complexity of diagnostic and treatment processes, and additional psychosocial, economic, and other resource and support needs.
2. Major changes in the health care system have also presented new challenges and opportunities for the oncology social worker.

Bridging the Gap Between Scientific Advances and the Human Experience

The science of cancer has always exceeded patients' and families' human experiences of the disease, its treatment, and their capacity to cope with its impact on their lives. Oncology social workers are charged with implementing myriad ways to bridge the gap between scientific advances and the challenges they pose for patients' abilities to maintain a meaningful quality of life.

Scientific advances in cancer treatment have succeeded in lengthening people's lives; providing hope for extended, quality survival time; and even curing what was previously considered a uniformly fatal disease. These advances have resulted in extended diagnostic processes and treatments in which the cancer can be managed as a chronic illness. It is no longer a "one size fits all" approach to medical treatment, but requires complex decision making that takes into account the increasing variety and accessibility of targeted treatments. It also requires patients and physicians to weigh the benefits and burdens of treatments while confronting the uncertainties of treatment outcomes. The diagnostic process may be extended as physicians determine the optimal type and time of treatment. Patients may need to endure longer periods of treatment under constant medical surveillance. Newer treatment approaches, such as "watchful waiting," may be difficult for patients to accept because they have come to expect immediate treatment or the removal or containment of the cancer.

The high costs of specialized treatments can add to the stress of decision making; some have referred to this as "financial toxicity." Patient-reported outcome measures are being developed to account for the impact of the costs of treatment on patients' lives (Souza et al., 2014).

All treatments have side effects. Some of these side effects, or toxicities, can now be anticipated, prevented, and proactively treated when they occur. The technological advances have, in many instances, made such toxicities tolerable or even avoidable and have saved countless lives and minimized emergency hospitalizations. Pain, nausea, and fatigue are much more treatable, and social workers are now required to develop skills in supporting pain and symptom management. This ability to anticipate the effects of treatment has had a positive impact on the patient's quality of life and has reduced traumatic treatment experiences and improved functioning.

The chapters in this *Handbook* document the many ways in which social work has effectively bridged the worlds of scientific advances, medical treatment, and the human experience of the treatment and recovery processes.

Social Work Leaders: Innovators in a Changing Care Delivery System

A broad range of patient- and family-centered care initiatives and regulatory mandates are now requiring what has been advocated by social work for decades—that is, the integration of psychosocial care into the cancer treatment system (ACOS, 2014; IOM, 2006, 2007; IOM, Committee on Improving the Quality of Cancer Care, 2013). This initiative includes the promotion of a new paradigm that emphasizes that health care is not something that is "done to" patients; rather, it is a team effort with the patient at the center. Related research is aimed at finding ways to empower patients, thereby strengthening provider–patient communication and improving health outcomes. Social work leadership and innovation aim to advance these transformations in the health care system in at least four areas: care management, shared decision making, innovative use of technology, and partner engagement.

Improving Care Management

Identifying psychosocial risks earlier in patients' cancer experiences is critical to proactive rather than reactive interventions. Oncology social workers have been leaders in developing both distress and problem screening measures (see Section 4) and psychosocial acuity measures (see Section 16) that identify economic, social, cultural, familial, language, and other characteristics of individuals and groups that often require additional support to cope effectively with the rigors of cancer treatment. In addition to distress screening and psychosocial acuity measures, oncology social workers use their expertise and skill to champion the following patient- and family-centered programs (see Section 14):

- Effective health system and community resource referrals
- Programs that ensure patient and family participation in institutional programming and policy development
- Counseling to overcome educational, emotional, social, psychological, and financial barriers to treatment adherence and compliance
- Self-management and wellness approaches for common symptoms following cancer treatment. These approaches have been remarkably effective in helping patients manage other chronic diseases such as diabetes.

Promoting Shared Decision Making

Shared decision making in oncology has been linked to improved patient outcomes in areas such as patient satisfaction, anxiety, and quality of life. In response to these findings, the Patient Protection and Affordable Care Act (2010) mandates the establishment of programs to support shared decision making. Oncology social workers' communication and team management skills prepare them to develop patient education approaches that will ensure that the treatment and care reflect the patient's values and goals and that both the patient and family are engaged in effective self-care and communication with the health care team. Social workers have also led in the development of a broad range of interdisciplinary training and support programs that promote open communication with patients (see Section 19).

Toward this end, patients are encouraged to do the following:

- Understand their role in decision making
- Clarify their values and goals
- Weigh benefits and burdens of different treatment options—for example, aggressive treatment palliative care and hospice
- Engage in advance care planning earlier in the illness process

Innovative Use of Technology to Increase Patient and Family Access to Services

Considerable evidence suggests that the use of frequent reminders and monitoring can be effective in improving health outcomes in chronic illnesses. Social work will need to continue to develop innovative uses of telemonitoring, teleconferencing, webcasts, podcasts, and other technologies, such as text messaging, to improve the patient's understanding of his or her care and outcomes and to reduce costs.

Engaging Effective Community Partners to Share Services and Costs

Social work has a well-documented ability to partner with families, services, and community agencies to foster collaboration, improve referral mechanisms, and extend services (see Sections 16 and 17). Multiple chapters in this *Handbook* demonstrate the effectiveness of such partnerships. Oncology social workers need to continue to take the lead in developing network contacts, contracts, and implementation plans that draw on the capacities of other care providers to reduce costs and improve care coordination.

Expansion of Oncology Social Work

The chapters in this *Handbook* reflect the remarkable number of new areas social work has engaged in since its inception 30 years ago, including (1) expanding the depth and breadth of knowledge and skill through specialization, (2) increasing engagement with research and psychosocial science, and (3) leading in the development of innovation in psychosocial interventions and programs for cancer patients and their families.

Expanding Knowledge and Skills Through Specialization

Oncology social workers are developing greater expertise in particular areas that can be integrated into the breadth of psychosocial practice knowledge. With more cancer survivors living with cancer as a chronic illness, patients face a broad range of adaptive challenges that require diverse skills and interventions. Assessments now routinely include areas such as cultural, sexual, and economic diversity; mental health; and substance abuse. Oncology social workers may develop expertise in life span issues, spirituality, sexuality, children of adult cancer patients, mental health, substance abuse, pain management, genetics, cognitive behavioral interventions, meaning-making interventions, group or couples interventions, interventions with advanced cancer patients, interdisciplinary staff support, patient education, and/or working with volunteers. Trauma-informed assessments and interventions have also been developed to recognize and treat acute stress reactions that occur during the cancer trajectory (Abbey, Thompson, Heathcote, & Hickish, 2014).

Oncology social workers see patients and families through a wide-angle lens that reflects breadth, depth, complexity, and a time perspective that extends beyond the hospital experience or medical appointment. Oncology social workers have always championed, recognized, and supported the needs of families of cancer patients and will continue to do so as care moves toward outpatient and community locations. Assessment and intervention skills are developed in relation to that vision, which includes understanding family and community contexts, cultures, connections, communication, and strengths, and a broad range of related issues are becoming increasingly important in the quality of care.

The ability to adapt and innovate based on the perceived needs of the patient, family, staff member, research questions, or programmatic needs remains a signature social work skill. For example, one institutional, multifaceted staff program moved from an exclusive focus on compassion fatigue to a shared focus on building resilience (see Chapter 104). This change was based on staff reports about the helpfulness of sharing strategies that support and sustain their ability to function in working with serious illnesses and of acknowledging the stresses of this work that challenge their capacity to cope. These skills also align well with developing innovative programs to promote shared decision making with patients and families.

Explosion in Research and Psychosocial Science

Oncology social workers have expanded their use of research findings, including meta-analyses and research reviews, to inform their practice. More social workers are involved in conducting research through quality improvement initiatives within their organizations, collaborations with academic and practice institutions, and interdisciplinary research. Research has included both quantitative and qualitative methods. A current challenge in intervention research in oncology is that although interventions may be found to be effective, they are often unable to be applied in current practice settings. Practitioners need research that is relevant to their daily needs, and researchers need knowledge of the practice environment and its challenges and opportunities to be able to implement practice-relevant interventions (Northouse, Williams, Given, & McCorkle, 2012). Social work practitioners are uniquely positioned to be effective users of knowledge because they integrate evidence-based practice into their work. Many are now generating new knowledge through practice-based research (see Section 4).

Perhaps the most significant new practice-based opportunity for oncology social workers has been created by the mandate for distress and psychosocial screening (Clark et al., 2012; IOM, Committee on Improving the Quality of Cancer Care, 2013; Kayser, Acquati, & Tran, 2012; Parry, Padgett, & Zebrack, 2012; Zabora & MacMurray, 2012; Zebrack, Burg, & Vaitones, 2012) and the development of acuity measures. This mandate enables the documentation of social work screening knowledge and skills, identification of relevant problems for patients and families, and support for the creation of practice-relevant interventions for problems identified through the screening process. Social work visibility and opportunities for practice-based research have been vastly increased by these mandates that all cancer treatment programs have distress screening procedures in place by 2015 (ACOS, 2014). The use of touch-screen technology for screening and interfacing with the electronic medical record is one example of social work innovation in this area (see Chapter 19).

Oncology Social Workers as Leaders and Inventors

The initial outline for this *Handbook* included a section on leadership. However, we realized early on that the descriptions of the accomplishments, processes, and visions of these oncology social work authors/leaders provided much better exemplars of important leadership qualities than could be accomplished through a series of conceptual discussions. Oncology social workers have described leadership in developing complex, multilevel, and multidisciplinary programs of group and individual support not just for patients, but also for families and caregivers, for whom social workers have always been champions. Many of the chapters contained herein describe programs that social workers have developed for interdisciplinary staff support. Some describe complex patient service programs, programs of distress screening and developing psychosocial acuity measures, large interdisciplinary psychosocial support programs, stand-alone social work departments, complex care coordination initiatives, and survivorship programs. Many authors are teaching and developing ongoing education for multiple disciplines, patients and their caregivers, and large populations. Some are hired into research and policy positions. These initiatives are often developed in conjunction with their ongoing individual and group counseling programs.

Oncology social workers have become more innovative in implementing interventions. They were among the first to implement cognitive behavioral interventions, life review and meaning-making interventions, survivorship interventions, caregiver interventions, and interventions with children and families. They were early champions—and in some ways, the inventors—of screening and psychosocial acuity measures, being among the first to identify the special needs of different populations based on disease; treatment; life span issues, such as those of children and adolescents or young adults and older adults; social support challenges; cultural or religious complications; mental health complications; financial toxicity; and resource deficits. They engaged patients early in online groups, telephone counseling, telemedicine, and teleconferencing/webcasts by using technology to make services more accessible to patients and families.

Proactive and Preventive Psychosocial Care

Oncology social workers will continue to lead in developing psychosocial interventions that anticipate and prevent distress, to effectively treat problems that arise in a timely way, to report on findings from practice and research, and to publish their findings. Health social work professionals have always been excellent "psychosocial" first responders—that is, answering the page in a timely way, conducting a quick and informed assessment of the situation, and proceeding to address the problems on multiple levels. Now they are developing and implementing more interventions that anticipate reactions to diagnosis, treatment, and survivorship. They have become increasingly proactive in their advocacy for creating systems of care that support patients' and families' needs, anticipate and prevent adverse consequences, and reduce unnecessary psychological and physical pain. Oncology social workers understand that patients' problems do not end when they walk out of the hospital. They are committed to providing the resources and structures patients will need in their communities.

Increased specialist knowledge has been added to generalist capacities. Distress screening and acuity measures have become powerful approaches to show what social workers do and enable active engagement in practice-based research. A Hopi Indian proverb notes that "those who tell the stories rule the world." Social workers have always "told the stories" of those in great need, given voice to the more vulnerable, and in so doing, transformed the profession and provided outstanding leadership in psychosocial oncology.

Current and Future Challenges

Current and future challenges include increasing numbers of cancer patients for whom there is no safety net and large numbers of cancer patients seeking asylum or a safe place to live. Oncology social work's signature efforts are for the many who are denied access to care, culturally diverse populations, and people who live below the poverty level and have limited resources. How do we help them find their voice at the table and express their needs and stories?

Now that the field has established benchmark practice and research, the question becomes how to foster the next generation of leaders to innovate and create novel interventions and practices, access foundation grants, and conduct community-based research to provide help to the increasing numbers of people falling into the great fiscal divide—with their cancer being the touch point for access to oncology social work services.

We write this book during a time when the world is experiencing great social and political problems in the midst of environmental upheaval. We stand on the shoulders of giants, poised to make a difference for the many patients we serve. The road ahead will not be easy. It will take collaboration, work with new partners and funding streams, and outreach to populations with greater need than any previous generations have witnessed. Many of the advances in cancer treatment are costly and not financially viable for our patients with limited resources. How do we build a firm foundation of fiscal help to those whose lives could be transformed by the scientific innovations in cancer treatment but who cannot afford care?

Our charge to you as you conclude reading this book—this repository of the exemplary work of this 30-year-old profession—is for you to not only grow in your knowledge from reading this book but also to identify new areas where you will leave your mark. Our strength is defined by our courage, our courage by our fortitude, our fortitude by our willingness to stretch beyond the possible to find new ways to make a difference for those in great need.

These will not be easy times. But as our history shows, oncology social workers will never shy from challenges.

Ours is a profession that takes on the complex and makes it understandable, takes on the impossible and makes a difference, teaches the next generation to find their voice, and continues to provide innovative psychosocial services to cancer patients and their loved ones.

REFERENCES

Abbey, G., Thompson, S., Heathcote, D., & Hickish, T. (2014). A meta-analysis of prevalence rates and moderating factors for cancer-related post-traumatic stress disorder. *Psycho-Oncology*, 23, 7-7.

American College of Surgeons (ACOS). (2014). *Cancer program standards 2012: Ensuring patient-centered care*. Retrieved from http://www.facs.org/cancer/coc/programstandards2012.html

Clark, P., Bolte, S., Buzaglo, J., Golant, M., Daratsos, L., & Loscalzo, M. (2012). From distress guidelines to developing models of psychosocial care: Current best practices. *Journal of Psychosocial Oncology*, 30(6), 694–714.

Institute of Medicine (IOM). (2006). *From cancer patient to cancer survivor: Lost in transition*. Washington, DC: National Academies Press.

Institute of Medicine (IOM). (2007). *Cancer care for the whole patient: Meeting psychosocial health needs*. Washington, DC: National Academies Press.

Institute of Medicine (IOM), Committee on Improving the Quality of Cancer Care. (2013). *Delivering high-quality cancer care: Charting a new course for a system in crisis*. Washington, DC: National Academies Press.

Kayser, K., Acquati, C., & Tran, T. (2012). No patients left behind: A systematic review of the cultural equivalence of distress screening instruments. *Journal of Psychosocial Oncology*, 30(6), 679–693.

Northouse, L., Williams, A., Given, B., & McCorkle, R. (2012). Psychosocial care for family caregivers of patients with cancer. *Journal of Clinical Oncology*, 30(11), 1227–1234.

Parry, C., Padgett, L., & Zebrack, B. (2012). Now what? Toward an integrated research and practice agenda in distress screening. *Journal of Psychosocial Oncology*, 30(6), 715–727.

Patient Protection and Affordable Care Act. (2010). Retrieved from http://www.hhs.gov/healthcare/rights/

Souza, J., Yap, B. J., Hlubocky, F. J., Wroblewski, K., Ratain, M. J., Cella, D., & Daugherty, C. K. (2014). The development of a financial toxicity patient-reported outcome in cancer. *Cancer*. doi:10.1002/cncr.28814

Zabora, J., & MacMurray, L. (2012). The history of psychosocial screening among cancer patients. *Journal of Psychosocial Oncology*, 30(6), 625–635.

Zebrack, B., Burg, M., & Vaitones, V. (2012). Distress screening: An opportunity for enhancing quality cancer care and promoting the oncology social work profession. *Journal of Psychosocial Oncology*, 30(6), 615–624.

INDEX

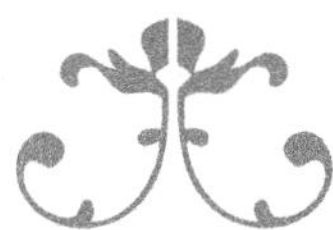